McGraw-Hill
Encyclopedia of World Drama
VOLUME
A-D 1

McGraw-Hill Encyclopedia

an international reference
work in four volumes

# of World Drama

VOLUME
A-D **1**

McGraw-Hill Book Company

NEW YORK	DÜSSELDORF	NEW DELHI
ST. LOUIS	JOHANNESBURG	PANAMA
SAN FRANCISCO	KUALA LUMPUR	RIO DE JANEIRO
	LONDON	SINGAPORE
	MEXICO	SYDNEY
	MONTREAL	TORONTO

McGraw-Hill Encyclopedia of World Drama

Library of Congress Cataloging in Publication Data
Main entry under title:

McGraw-Hill Encyclopedia of World Drama.

    1. Drama—Biography—Dictionaries. 2. Drama—
Bibliography. I. Title: Encyclopedia of world
drama.
PN1625.M3   809.2   70-37382
ISBN 0-07-079567-3

McGraw-Hill Editorial Staff

David I. Eggenberger	*Executive Editor*
Leonard Josephson	*Editor-in-Chief*
Robert O'Brien	*Editor-in-Chief*
Lila Sherman	*Senior Editor/ Photo Editor*
Stanley Hochman	*Senior Editor*
Eva Schmergel	*Associate Editor*
Tobia L. Worth	*Editing Manager*
Beatrice E. Eckes	*Copy Editor*
Rita Vesce	*Assistant to the Editors*

Assistant Editors

Claudette Asselin
Beth Atkins
Erdmut Brown
Faith Hanson
Eveline Hunt
Deborah Lipton
Perry Morley
Izola Porter
Ennio I. Rao
Marie E. Weber

Editorial Assistants

Patsey Bettridge
Mark Blandford
Staphanie Brill
Jonnie Carter
Mary Ceppaglia
Mary Clemmons
Frances A. De Masi
Ann Dickter
Bonnie B. Finkelstein

Woodman B. Franklin
Irene Gavigan
Eleanor C. Kramer
Roberta D. Levine
Merrill K. Lindsay, III
Susan Mescall
Ellen Popofsky
Cathy Rockfol
Adriene Rosenberg

Renee Rosenberg
Victoria Schultz
Janet Shepard
Paula Silberberg
Patrick B. Silva
Maria Aurilia Vesce
Sophia E. Walters
Gail S. Werblood

McGraw-Hill Production Staff

Gerard G. Mayer	*Director of Production*
Rosemary DeMaria	*Production Assistant*
Edward J. Fox	*Art Director/Designer*
Ann Bonardi	*Art Assistant*
Donna Zloty	*Art Traffic*

Contributing Editors

Dolores Bagley	Laurel H. Grell	Brian McKenna
Harry Bakalar	Geneve Hard	Thomas B. Markus
Roslyn Brauer	Joyce Harper	Adele Milch
Elias Budman	G. Eric Hauck	J. William Miller
Nan Buranelli	Lee Healey	Karen Molishever
Vincent Buranelli	Andrew Herz	Madeline M. Muecke
Eileen Coblens	Thomas L. Hester	Ruth Mueller
Ruby Cohn	Arlin Hiken	Marie Nersoyan
Margaret Cooper	Leonard Jenkin	Albert Orbann
Xenia Dargahi	Deborah Jowitt	Elena Paz
Zita Z. Dressner	George Kalbouss	Jo C. Petratos
Lily Feiler	George Kisban	Judith Raskin
Gordon Finley	Lawrence H. Klibbe	Judith Ressencourt
Rolf Fjelde	Barbara Knowlton	Alfonso Rosati
Lea G. Forsman	Jacques Koppel	Lee Rosenthal
Thomas Froncek	Algirdas Landsbergis	Zara Shakow
Richard Gallup	Izaak A. Langnas	Matila Simon
Marion P. Geisinger	Elsa Lattey	Judith Steinberg
Robert Geisinger	Joan J. Levy	Max M. Tamir
Yvette Gindine	Robert Lima	Vicki Tamir
William Giuliano	Ann Lindsay	Gerald Weales
Carol Gold	Gretchen Lingg	Clara Weinberg
Joan Goldstein	Larry Lyall	

Introduction

The *McGraw-Hill Encyclopedia of World Drama* is a reference work which brings into focus the accomplishments of the world's major dramatists. It also touches on many of the lesser figures in the history of drama, playwrights whose body of work, although perhaps small or transitory, has had some observable impact on the movement of drama toward modern-day forms. The book ranges from the ancient writings of the Greeks and Romans, through the earliest stirrings of dramatic modes in the churches of Western Europe, to the symbolic and sometimes amorphous theatre of the twentieth century. The emphasis tends toward dramatists of the English-speaking nations and those of Western and Eastern Europe, since one of the criteria for inclusion was the existence of a reasonably long history of national drama that permitted evaluation from the perspective of time.

The purpose of the book is to present, in the clearest possible format, factual information and critical evaluations of each dramatist's work and stature. These critical evaluations have been arrived at under the aegis of an eminent board of advisers and in the case of major dramatists are accompanied by a factual discussion of the author's life, short synopses of several if not all of his plays, comprehensive listings of his entire body of work, and bibliographical information. Brought together, they provide an invaluable source for study and reference.

In general, the two types of dramatists covered in this work can be roughly classified as *major* and *lesser*. Each article about a *major* dramatist is divided into several sections as described above: a complete biography; a critical section on his work; a group of selected synopses; a play list; and two bibliographical sections, one listing editions and the other, critical material. The first part of the article outlines the historical highlights of the dramatist's life, while the second, dealing with his creative achievements, constitutes a critique of his work both as a unique entity and in historical context. As such, it takes into account the spectrum of criticism that already exists in the literature of the theatre.

The third section is devoted to a selection of short synopses of the author's plays (in the case of the few master dramatists of the world, almost all their plays are synopsized). A number of factors figured in the decisions about the plays to be dealt with in this way: (1) How do they rank within the author's own body of work? (2) What is their place in the development of drama and the theatre? (3) Are they representative of the author's work? (4) Have they been published and are they available for study? It should be noted that critics and sources sometimes differ widely in evaluating the works of individual writers; in this book, the editors, having attempted to present consensus information, make no claim to be a final authority on the ranking of plays within the *oeuvre* of a particular dramatist.

The fourth section, perhaps one of the most important to students and scholars, is a play list—in the case of most major dramatists, a list of their entire body of dramatic writings—wherein the titles commonly appear in the original language of the text, accompanied where necessary by an English translation. (The titles of published translations have been used wherever possible and are indicated by an asterisk following the foreign title; otherwise a literal translation has generally been provided.) The listing is chronological (ordered by the earliest available dating, regardless of category) except in a few cases where, because exact or even approximate dating was impossible, an alternative principle of organization is indicated. The other information provided in the play lists concerns the type of play, usually following the author's own designation but sometimes the editors' where the author has not specifically described his play; the number of acts; the publication date; and the place and date of the premiere production. Coauthors are listed, and so are the sources of plays that are adaptations or are based on another literary form.

In considering the datings in these play lists, it should be understood that the process of placing the creation of a work of literature in time is at best exceedingly difficult. The variance of dating within the discipline itself is wide. This book uses primary sources for dating whenever possible. When that has been impossible, the editors have depended on the scholarship of existing sources including the most up-to-date research material available. All literatures, however, do not present problems of equal difficulty. Spanish drama of the seventeenth century, for example, probably one of the most difficult bibliographical fields in existence, is treated here in as much depth as a large work treating many other areas permits.

The last two sections of the articles deal with bibliographical material. The first is a selective bibliography that covers collected editions of the dramatist's plays, plays in anthologies, and editions of individual plays. The second section is a short and selective bibliography of books about the dramatist—those supplying the facts of his personal history and personality and those analyzing his work.

Entries on *lesser* dramatists, those considered noteworthy but not necessarily moving forces in the field—and a few of those popular modern dramatists who have been commercially successful—have been dealt with in the conventional encyclopedic way. Each of these articles traces the dramatist's span of life, touches on significant activities that relate to his dramatic writing, and briefly discusses some of his more prominent plays.

The articles devoted to dramatists comprise an enormous amount of concentrated information supplied from the most current of historical studies and research. Even relatively short entries offer a large quantity of factual data and criticism. The coverage of contemporary events in drama, however, is as up-to-date as editorial practicability allowed. For an encyclopedia of this complexity and scope, a cut-off date that would allow for careful editing and a lengthy production schedule had to be established. Some very recent plays, therefore, and new dramatists who have only begun to attract critical attention have not been included.

The editors have taken particular pains to provide a comprehensive index of plays so that readers knowing only a title, whether in English or the original language, would be able to locate it in the book. A play is included in the index even if the only piece of information about it in the text is a date or a listing in the play list. The index may also be thought of as an independent reference source, since it provides the reader with a simple device for determining the authorship of any play.

Scattered among the biographical entries in the text are some hundred abbreviated nonbiographical entries—dramatic terms, theatre movements and styles, anonymous plays—serving as useful collateral material. The editors eschewed lengthy discussions of these topics, or of the history of drama in specific areas or countries, in the knowledge that other sources readily available to any reader provide this material. The choice was made to create an overview of the progression of world drama by concentrating on *individual dramatists* and their work rather than on truncated descriptions of large national movements.

One nonbiographical article is unusual in both length and content; it deals with perhaps the only indigenous American contribution of the world of theatre, musical comedy. Because the editors felt that this dramatic form supersedes its individual practitioners, all musical comedies are treated in the one comprehensive article: following a discussion of the origins of musical comedy and its development is a series of abbreviated descriptions of significant musical comedies, arranged alphabetically for easy research.

Beyond the presentation of material in verbal form, the *McGraw-Hill Encyclopedia of World Drama* seeks to inform visually. The selection of illustrations was circumscribed by a series of conscious choices on the part of the editors and also by practical limiting factors. Primarily, the effort was made to add to the understanding of each article by providing a supplementary illustration. Sometimes rare photographs of lesser-known plays were used in preference to the better-known works of a particular dramatist. When the reproduction quality of a rare or unusual photograph was brought into question, the editors sometimes chose to use an imperfect photograph rather than none at all. In addition, when an illustration of a scene from a production of a play seemed helpful to the article in depicting visually the performance of a play but certain information was lacking about the performers, the date, or the theatre of production, often the editors decided to use it. To indicate the universality of the dramatic art form, photographs of foreign productions of as many plays as possible were enthusiastically included. As often as possible the attempt was made to choose pictures which tell something significant about the play rather than only about the performers. It must be admitted, however, that the editors have succumbed, in certain few instances, to purely personal, subjective choices of plays, scenes, actors, and actresses—and the results, we believe, are not at all unhappy. Special problems of this order were posed by a famous and excellent collection of photographs taken by Florence Vandamm and housed at the New York Public Library at Lincoln Center. Most of the pictures in this collection are superior in quality and substance, and it became a sore test to limit selection to only some two hundred of them.

To produce a book of this scope and magnitude, the editors relied heavily on its board of advisers who read, reviewed, and commented on the entire manuscript. However, in the case of the illustrations, the editors made the final selections and assume sole responsibility for what has been included. Much of the picture research was done at the Theatre Collection in the Library of the Performing Arts at Lincoln Center; there, the entire staff was enormously helpful by dispensing their boundless knowledge with generosity and good humor. Our gratitude and good wishes can be but small compensation for their collective patience: Mr. Paul Myers, Curator; Miss Dorothy Swerdlove, Assistant to Mr. Myers; Mr. Donald Fowle; Dr. Roderick Bladel; Mr. Maxwell Silverman; Mrs. John Wharton; Mr. Monty Arnold; and Mr. Donald Madison of Photoservice.

The task of photo research was also aided immeasurably by the open-hearted interest of many of the offices of foreign governments in this country: the Austrian Cultural Affairs Institute, Consulate General of Belgium, Czechoslovak Society, Danish Information Office, French Cultural Services, German Information Center, Goethe House, Greek National Tourist Office, Information Service of India, Irish Tourist Board, Italian Cultural Institute, Japanese Consulate General, Netherlands Information Service, Royal Norwegian Embassy Information Service, Spanish Embassy, Swedish Information Service, and Swiss National Tourist Office. Other foreign governments as well as many individuals, authors' representatives, photographers, and photo agencies also made valuable contributions. In addition, innumerable theatre companies throughout the world generously supplied photographs of their productions for consideration and use in this book.

The Editors

Explanatory Notes

Alphabetization

1. *General scheme.* The *McGraw-Hill Encyclopedia of World Drama* uses the letter-by-letter principle of alphabetization rather than that of word-by-word.

2. *Index.* English titles beginning with articles of speech are alphabetized according to the first significant word (e.g., *A View from the Bridge* is alphabetized under "V"). Although the articles of certain foreign languages are familiar to most readers ("le" or "la" in French; "der," "die," or "das" in German), many are not; therefore, in the interest of consistency in the alphabetization of foreign titles, the editors decided to present these entries in normal order (e.g., *Le malade imaginaire* is alphabetized under "L").

Cross-references

1. *The "see" reference.* A conventional *see* or *see also* form has been used for cross-references, which appear at the first mention only of the related article title within the text. They have been used to indicate collateral information, not merely the existence of an article in this encyclopedia.

2. *The main reference.* The main reference, or reference entry, has also been used, for pseudonyms, variant spellings, alternate genre names, changes of name, and so on.

Translation of Foreign Titles

1. *General scheme.* At first mention in text, the English translation of a foreign title is followed parenthetically by the original title and its date of premiere performance (see below). Further reference to this work, both in running text and in other articles, is by the English title only. The synopsis recapitulates this information in the described order.

2. *Play lists.* In the play list the order is reversed: the original title is followed parenthetically by the English translation. An asterisk following the title of a foreign play indicates that that play has been translated into English; the English title supplied is that of an actual published or produced version of the play. The absence of an asterisk indicates that the editors have supplied an approximate or literal translation of the foreign title.

Dates

In the running text, the parenthetical date following a play title refers to the premiere performance of that play. When the original production postdates the writing of a play by three or more years, the writing date is given in conjunction with the production date (wr. 1834, prod. 1847). In cases where no production date is known, only the date of writing is given; when neither of these is known, only the publication date is supplied. Titles of critical works, novels, biographies, and so on are followed by the date of publication.

Indeterminate dates are expressed in several ways:

1. ca. 1635 when a range of indeterminate dates is very small

2. 1635/42 to indicate two terminal points: no earlier than 1635, no later than 1642

3. 1635? where there is uncertainty as to the exact date

4. 1635–1642 to refer to a definite period of activity starting in 1635 and ending in 1642

McGraw-Hill
Encyclopedia of World Drama

VOLUME A-D 1

ABAG. *See* GOTTLOBER, ABRAHAM DOV BER.

ABBOTT, George (1887–   ). American actor, director, producer, screenwriter, and playwright, one of the most successful and versatile theatre craftsmen of the modern American stage. His *Three Men on a Horse* (with John Cecil Holm, 1935) is based on a short story by Damon Runyon, in which a trio of horseplayers abduct a mild-mannered writer of greeting-card verses in order to profit by his uncanny knack for picking winning horses. *Broadway* (with Philip Dunning, 1926) is considered the best play about prohibition and racketeering written during the 1920s (*see* DUNNING, PHILIP). Later, Abbott became noted for a series of highly successful musical comedies such as *On Your Toes* (with Rodgers and Hart, 1934), *The Boys from Syracuse* (1938), *Where's Charley?* (1948), *The Pajama Game* (1954), *Damn Yankees* (1955), and *New Girl in Town* (1957). *See* MUSICAL COMEDY.

George Abbott. [Theatre Collection, The New York Public Library at Lincoln Center, Astor, Lenox and Tilden Foundations]

Kjeld Abell
(1901 – 1961)

Kjeld Abell, Danish dramatist, stage designer, and theatre and film director, was born in Ribe, southern Jutland, on August 25, 1901. After studying at the Academy of Fine Arts of Copenhagen University, he traveled abroad, in particular to London and Paris, where he studied stage design under Picasso and was influenced by the plays of Giraudoux (*see* GIRAUDOUX, JEAN).

Upon his return to Copenhagen, Abell was employed by the Royal Theatre, where he collaborated with George Balanchine. His first original creation for the stage was the text of a ballet performed in 1934, *The Widow in the Mirror* (*Enken i Spejlet*). His first play, *The Melody That Got Lost* (*Melodien, der blev vaek*), was produced in 1935, followed by *Eve Serves Her Tour of Duty as a Child* (*Eva aftjener sin Barnepligt*, 1936).

Abell became increasingly preoccupied with the rising power of Nazism, and he recorded his reactions in *Anna Sophie Hedvig* (1939), about a schoolteacher who becomes a symbol of resistance to tyranny; and *Judith* (pub. 1940), a reworking of the Old Testament story. In *The Queen on Tour* (*Dronning gaar igen*, 1943), his thinly concealed references to

The Melody That Got Lost. Copenhagen, Riddersalen Theatre, 1935. [Danish Information Office]

the German occupation of Denmark resulted in his imprisonment. Following his release, upon hearing of the Nazis' murder of the Danish playwright Kaj Munk (January, 1944), Abel stopped a performance at the Royal Theatre in protest; he was then obliged to go into hiding until the liberation of Denmark. *See* MUNK, KAJ.

His play of 1946 about the German occupation, *Silkeborg*, was among the most popular of the many accounts appearing after the liberation of Denmark. It was followed in 1947 by his brooding reaction to the atomic bomb, *Days on a Cloud* (*Dage paa en Sky*). In 1948 Abell was asked to write the play commemorating the two-hundredth anniversary of the Royal Theatre in Copenhagen; the result was *Lot No. 267, Eastern Quarter* (*Ejendommen Matr. NR 267, Østre Kvarter*).

The Blue Pekingese (*Den blå Pekingeser*, 1954) reflects his travels in China in 1952. Abell had barely finished writing *The Scream* (*Skriget*, 1961) at the time of his death, on March 5, 1961.

WORK

Abell's early plays are concerned with the constricting and stultifying effects of bourgeois conformism. *The Melody That Got Lost* (1935), for example, portrays an average Dane who suddenly awakes to discover the barrenness of his life. *Eve Serves Her Tour of Duty as a Child* (1936) bitterly attacks the stranglehold of a bourgeois parent who is anxious to suppress his child's creativity.

At the turn of the decade, with *Anna So-*

Kjeld Abell.
[Danish
Information Office]

phie Hedvig (1939) and *Judith* (1940), Abell began to articulate his struggle to determine his feelings in the face of fascism. In the first play he appears to condone the assassination of a tyrant, while in the second such a murder is shown to be irrelevant—it fails to stem the growth of tyranny. Tyranny, he says, exists because we not only tolerate it but have helped cause it.

Denmark's liberation created no sudden illusions for Abell. *Silkeborg* (1946), unlike many contemporary plays rejoicing in victory and optimistically looking to the future, reminds its audiences that true freedom is more difficult to achieve and maintain than the mere military defeat of an enemy. In *Days on a Cloud* (1947), Abell analyzed a scientist's responsibility to society to control his lethal creation, the atomic bomb.

The Blue Pekingese (1954), an expressionistic fantasy, and *Andersen* (1955), in which Abell declared his indebtedness to Hans Christian Andersen, preceded his last play, *The Scream* (1961), which deals in expressionistic terms with a theme recurrent throughout his work: the ease with which one slips into a state of emotional and intellectual stagnation despite the need for constant human growth. In it Abell explored the meaning of life on several levels of awareness and the search for liberation from conformity.

An imaginative experimenter and a man of conscience, Abell as a playwright was primarily interested in ideas rather than character. Along with Munk, he will be remembered as one of the important Danish playwrights of the twentieth century.

The Melody That Got Lost (*Melodien, der blev vaek,* 1935). Allegorical satire in which Mr. Johnson, the average man, struggles to choose between security and freedom; he reluctantly rejects the Melody of Life for a respectable but dreary office position. Caught in the monotony of his existence, he becomes increasingly resigned and dull until his wife realizes that they have made a mistake in abandoning the Melody, which they can no longer hear. When she asks Religion, Death, and Nature about the Melody, she is told that it is all around her; it must simply be recognized. Finally she finds it: a little girl, the child Mrs. Johnson once was, possesses it.

Mr. Johnson, tired of conforming to the expectations of others, interrupts a radio broadcast and is carried away by the police. When he leaves the police station, he leaves behind his former self, symbolized by his old clothes. Meanwhile, Mrs. Johnson brings the Melody of Life home in her purse, and husband and wife have a joyous reunion, determined to begin a new life under the spell of the Melody.

Anna Sophie Hedvig (1939). Symbolic

Scene from *Anna Sophie Hedvig.* Copenhagen, Royal Theatre, 1939. [Teatermuseet, Christiansborg Palace, Copenhagen]

play that takes place before World War II. Anna Sophie Hedvig, a schoolteacher in the provinces, visits the city, where her cousin is giving a dinner party. She interrupts the gathering with the story of how she dispatched the evil woman who was to become headmistress of her school. Most of the guests are horrified, taking the view that bold action against evil falls outside the purview of ordinary people. Only her cousin's son agrees with her. Finally, Anna, having acted contrary to convention, is executed in a symbolic sacrifice to conformity and passivity.

PLAYS

Unless otherwise noted, the plays were first performed in Copenhagen.

1. *Melodien, der blev vaek** (*The Melody That Got*

Stage design by Helge Refn for *Days on a Cloud.* Copenhagen, Royal Theatre, 1947. [Teatermuseet, Christiansborg Palace, Copenhagen]

Marcel Achard.
[French Cultural
Services]

ACHARD, Marcel, pseudonym of Marcel-Auguste Ferréol (1899–   ). French screenwriter and dramatist who first attracted attention after Charles Dullin's production of his play *Do You Want to Play with Me?* (*Voulez-vous jouer avec moâ?*, 1923), a poetic comedy about circus clowns. In this play and the majority of those that followed, the characters are essentially modern versions of the traditional *commedia dell'arte* figures Pierrot and Columbine, and the basically sentimental love story is seasoned with a dash of fashionably bittersweet melancholy. In *The Dreamer* (*Jean de la lune*, 1929), the credulous Pierrot-like hero Jef is so firmly convinced of the virtue of his flagrantly unfaithful wife that she ends by conforming to his conception of her. In *Domino* (1932), a woman who hires a scoundrel to pay her court—and so disguise from her jealous husband the existence of her real lover—ends by truly falling in love with the character he creates for her. The atmosphere of Achard's plays is always vaguely suggestive of an enchanted never-never land, a factor emphasized by the very titles themselves, often the names of traditional songs: *Malborough s'en va-t-en guerre* (1924), *Noix de coco* (1935), *Auprès de ma blonde* (1946), *Savez-vous planter les choux?* (1946), and *Nous irons à Valparaiso* (1948). *See* COMMEDIA DELL'ARTE.

Achard's plays were extremely fashionable before World War II, and he was often glowingly represented as working in the tradition of Marivaux and Musset. Later critics reproached him for his limited range (he

Lost). Allegorical drama. Published 1935. Produced Riddersalen Theatre, Sept. 6, 1935.

2. *Eva aftjener sin Barnepligt* (*Eve Serves Her Tour of Duty as a Child*). Comedy, 11 scenes. Published 1936. Produced Royal Theatre, Dec. 8, 1936.

3. *Oliver Twist*. Play, 19 scenes. Produced Skolescenen, Det Ny Theatre, Apr. 25, 1938. Adapted from Charles Dickens's novel (1837–1839).

4. *Anna Sophie Hedvig**. Play, 3 acts. Published 1938. Produced Royal Theatre, Jan. 1, 1939.

5. *Judith*. Play, 6 scenes. Published 1940. Produced Apollo Theatre.

6. *Dronning gaar igen** (*The Queen on Tour*). Play, 3 acts. Published 1955. Produced Royal Theatre, Mar. 5, 1943.

7. *Silkeborg*. Play, 6 scenes. Published 1946. Produced Det Ny Theatre, Mar. 1, 1946.

8. *Dage paa en Sky** (*Days on a Cloud*). Play, 3 acts. Published 1947. Produced Royal Theatre, Dec. 11, 1947.

9. *Ejendommen Matr. NR 267, Østre Kvarter* (*Lot No. 267, Eastern Quarter*). Play, 1 act. Published 1948. Produced Royal Theatre, Dec. 18, 1948.

10. *Miss Plinckeys Kabale, eller en Juinatt* (*Miss Plinckey's Solitaire, or A Night in June*). Comedy, 3 acts. Published 1949. Produced Royal Theatre, Feb. 13, 1949.

11. *Vetsera blomstrer ikke for enhver* (*Vetsera Does Not Come Out for Everyone*). Play, 3 acts. Published 1950. Produced Frederiksberg Theatre, Nov. 12, 1950.

12. *Den blå Pekingeser* (*The Blue Pekingese*). Play. Published 1954. Produced Royal Theatre, Dec. 16, 1954.

13. *Andersen, eller Hans livs eventyr* (*Andersen, or The Fairy Tale of His Life*). Play. Published 1955. Produced Royal Theatre, Apr. 3, 1955.

14. *Kameliadamen* (*The Lady of the Camellias*). Play, 3 acts. Published 1959. Produced Det Ny Theatre, Mar. 17, 1959.

15. *Skriget* (*The Scream*). Play. Published 1961. Produced Royal Theatre.

EDITIONS

Anna Sophie Hedvig. Published in *Scandinavian Plays of the Twentieth Century*, tr. by H. Larsen, vol. 2, Princeton, N.J., 1944–1951; *Masterpieces of the Modern Scandinavian Theatre*, ed. by R. W. Corrigan, New York, 1967.

Days on a Cloud. Published in *The Genius of the Scandinavian Theatre*, ed. by E. Sprinchorn, New York, 1964.

The Queen on Tour. Published in *Contemporary Danish Plays*, tr. by J. Pearce, London, 1955.

CRITICISM

F. Schyberg, *Kjeld Abell*, Copenhagen, 1947.

Le mal d'amour, with (l. to r.) Dominique Blanchar, Jacqueline Monsigny, and François Périer. Paris, Théâtre de la Michodière, 1955. [French Cultural Services]

Auprès de ma blonde, with Pierre Fresnay and Yvonne Printemps (top left). *Les compagnons de la Marjolaine,* with Arletty (top right). *Savez-vous planter les choux?* (bottom left). [French Cultural Services]

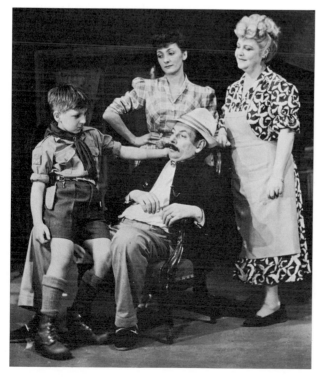

A revival of *Noix de coco,* with Françoise Dorléac and Madeleine Robinson (below), Théâtre du Palais-Royal, Paris. [French Cultural Services]

became somewhat mockingly known as a *spécialiste de l'amour*) and for the often-saccharine quality of his poetic fantasy. Nevertheless, some of his plays show interesting thematic and technical innovations. *The Beautiful Bargewoman* (*La belle marinière*, 1929) is a play with realistic overtones (somewhat marred by the often fanciful nature of the dialogue) that examines the conflict caused when the wife of a bargeman falls in love with his mate and best friend. *The Woman in White* (*La femme en blanc*, 1933) uses a technique similar to cinematic flashback, and events related by the protagonist are simultaneously reenacted onstage. A Pirandellian play-within-a-play is the basis for *The Corsair* (*Le corsaire*, 1938), in which actors preparing to film the story of a long-dead pirate find strange parallels between their lives and his. *Adam* (1938) relates the story of a homosexual and caused a scandal that now seems disproportionate to its theatrical worth.

Achard's postwar plays include *Les compagnons de la Marjolaine* (1952) and *Le mal d'amour* (1955). He has achieved considerable success with a comedy about an irascible fellow known as *Patate* (1957) and a comedy-mystery entitled *A Shot in the Dark* (*L'idiote*, 1962). He has also written for the screen, his best-known scripts being *Mayerling* (1936), *Orage* (1938), and *Félicie Nanteuil* (1942). In 1959 he was elected to the Académie Française.

ADAM DE LA HALLE (b. Arras, France, ca. 1240; d. Naples?, ca. 1288). French musician, poet, and dramatist who was also variously known as Adam Le Bossu and Adam d'Arras. He was the major talent of the Puy d'Arras, one of several medieval societies of poets formed to encourage competitions in lyric poetry and the drama. Adam is sometimes credited with having initiated secular drama with the two works for which he is best known, *The Play of the Greenwood* (*Le jeu de la feuillée*, ca. 1276) and *The Play of Robin and Marion* (*Le jeu de Robin et Marion*, ca. 1285). In addition to these dramatic works, he wrote a variety of poetic and musical compositions, including a satirical *congé*, or farewell poem, about 1262, when he left Arras for a time, presumably to study in Paris. About 1283 he accompanied his patron, Robert II, Count of Artois, to Italy and there joined the entourage of Charles of Anjou, King of the Two Sicilies. He remained in Italy until his death some five years later.

The Play of the Greenwood (*Le jeu de la feuillée*, ca. 1276). Possibly the oldest French comedy, it is unique in the literature of the Middle Ages in that it makes use of a profane subject which is developed at some length. The *feuillée* of the title has been variously explained as a reference to the leafy bower or canopy under which the play may have been enacted or as an indication that the play was meant to be performed on the spring night when fairies were believed to meet under a special leaf where a meal had been prepared for them. The author is himself the hero of the play and follows the traditional scheme of satirizing his family and his misfortunes. As in his *congé*, the poet speaks of his intention of going to study in Paris. His friends try to dissuade him from leaving his wife, and his father claims to be sick (an itinerant doctor identifies the father's illness as "chronic avarice"). Various local types animate the scene. Eventually the fairies of this spring festival appear and distribute good and bad fortune. All retire to a tavern, and as dawn approaches, they decide to go and offer a candle to the Virgin. The occasional incoherence of the plot is redeemed by the lively scenes from daily life.

The Play of Robin and Marion (*Le jeu de Robin et Marion*, ca. 1285). The origins of the French *opéra comique* are often traced to this dramatized pastoral, which uses dialogue and song to present the love story of a shepherd and shepherdess against a vivid background of thirteenth-century peasant life. Robin and Marion have sworn to be true to one another, but the future is temporarily threatened by the appearance of a dashing knight who tries to win Marion. The shepherdess, however, successfully resists the blandishments of the knight and remains faithful to Robin. The play concludes with singing and dancing at a rustic feast in celebration of the couple's approaching marriage. The play was probably preceded by a prologue, *The Play of the Pilgrim* (*Le jeu de pèlerin*), written by disciples of Adam de la Halle, in which a traveler returning from the kingdom of the Two Sicilies explains the origins of the comedy about to be presented.

Arthur Adamov
(1908 — 1970)

Arthur Adamov, French dramatist, was born in Kislovodsk, in the Russian Caucasus, on August 23, 1908. He was taken from Russia in 1912, and the early years of his education were spent first in Geneva and then in Mainz. In 1924 he moved to Paris and there completed his studies. As a young man he was strongly influenced by the French surrealist movement, which was at its peak during the 1930s.

After the fall of France in 1940, Adamov was arrested by the Vichy government and held at Argèles as an enemy alien. He did not begin his career as a dramatist until the late 1940s. In 1949, inspired by Strindberg, he wrote *The Invasion* (*L'invasion*). His Russian background played a major role in his career, and he both translated and adapted works by Gogol, Chekhov, and Gorky. His interest in psychoanalysis led him to translate some of the works of Carl Jung. *See* CHEKHOV, ANTON PAVLOVICH; GOGOL, NIKOLAY; GORKY, MAXIM; STRINDBERG, AUGUST.

Though with the exception of *Ping-Pong* (*Le ping-pong,* 1955), none of his plays have been professionally produced in the United States, Adamov earned a successful reputation in France and was commissioned by the British Broadcasting Corporation for one-acters that were translated into English. He died in Paris on March 16, 1970.

WORK

Isolation, alienation, and failure in the face of formless opposition—these are the areas Adamov explored in his rather terrifying dramas, whose characteristic atmosphere is anxiety and futility. Some of these works, because of the antilogical situations around which they are built, are related to the theatre of the absurd, but Adamov wrote more conventionally than the absurdist dramatists and did not rely on wordplay or the cumulative effect of pure nonsense to render the absurd. Rather, he guided his audience through a nightmare experience, playing on its nerves and giving substance to its horrible imaginings. *See* THEATRE OF THE ABSURD.

Some critics have noted two phases in Adamov's drama: the earlier, phantasmagoric plays; and, beginning with *Ping-Pong* (1955), plays that focus, and comment more explicitly, on society's evils. However, this distinction is not clear-cut, for social comment is implied even in the most dreamlike plays. Nevertheless, Adamov's conversion to Marxism is reflected in the very form of his later plays, underlining the fact that his mentor was no longer Artaud but Brecht. *See* ARTAUD, ANTONIN; BRECHT, BERTOLT.

Adamov's three most notable plays are *The Invasion* (1950), which depicts a hopeless quest for meaning; *Ping-Pong,* a commentary on mechanized society; and *Paolo Paoli* (1957), which satirizes French life at the close of *la belle époque* before World War I.

Among other outstanding dramas are *The Parody* (*La parodie;* wr. 1947, prod. 1952), his first play, which demonstrates that both ac-

Paolo Paoli, with Malka Ribowska, Armand Meffre, and Alain Mottet, Théâtre du Vieux-Colombier, Paris. [French Cultural Services]

ceptance and refusal of life end in failure; *The Large and the Small Maneuver* (*La grande et la petite manoeuvre,* 1950), in which both the Mutilated One, a passive figure who gradually loses all his limbs, and the Militant, a revolutionary leader who fights the police state, are victims of an enigmatic fatality; *The Direction of the March* (*Le sens de la marche,* 1953), in which Henri, dominated by a father figure embodied in various characters—an officer, a pastor, a headmaster—murders his dead father's friend, who threatens to become another tyrant, but rebels too late to free himself; *Professor Taranne* (*Le professeur Taranne,* 1953), a play derived from a dream, in which a man accused of indecent exposure tries to clear his reputation but in protesting his innocence ironically becomes more and more suspect; *All Against All* (*Tous contre tous,* 1953), about the plight of official scapegoats in a police state whose policy is constantly shifting; *The Recoveries* (*Les retrouvailles,* wr. 1952), an attack on the domineering mother who prevents her son from establishing an adult relationship with another woman; and *As We Were* (*Comme nous avons été,* pub. 1953), which describes an adult man's regression to childhood.

Other plays by Adamov include three short pieces forming topical attacks on Gaullist policies and on the French war in Algeria; *In a Fiacre* (*En fiacre,* 1959), a radio play about three old ladies based on a psychiatrist's casebook; *Spring 71* (*Le printemps 71,* 1962), a Brechtian epic about the suppression of the Paris Commune in 1871, whose end, however, heralds the worldwide victory of the Communist revolution; and *The Scavengers* (*La politique des restes,* 1963), in which Adamov combined the nightmare visions of his earlier plays with the more direct social criticism of his later works. *See* EPIC THEATRE.

Among Adamov's nontheatrical publications are *The Confession* (*L'aveu,* 1946), a psychoanalytical autobiography; and *Here and Now* (*Ici et maintenant,* 1964), a collection of texts, prefaces, and discussions. Both works throw considerable light on the themes and aims of his theatre.

The Invasion (*L'invasion,* 1950). Drama in which Pierre attempts to decipher and put together the illegible manuscript left by Jean, his deceased brother-in-law. His friend Tradel tries to help but seems to invent rather than decipher the text. Pierre's wife Agnès, impatient with his dedication to this task, deserts him. Finally, Pierre withdraws from the world and retires to the attic, ordering his mother, who brings him food, never to speak to him for fear of disturbing his search. He dies without having discovered the meaning of the manuscript, his life "invaded" by another's work.

Ping-Pong (*Le ping-pong,* 1955). Drama presenting a sardonic commentary on contemporary industrial society. Victor and his friend Arthur meet daily at Mme. Duranty's café, where they are addicted to playing the pinball machine. There they meet Sutter, an opportunist, who wields his alledged influence on the pinball corporation to manipulate Annette, a young girl, and M. Roger, a young dandy. Intrigued by the business possibilities of the machine, Arthur and Victor present a scheme for its perfection to the worried head of the financially endangered corporation, the Old Man; the scheme is rejected. Victor becomes disillusioned with the machine, but Arthur's life becomes progressively more involved with it.

Meanwhile, the corporation is steadily losing ground, and Annette and Roger attend the failing Old Man in his sickroom. Arthur arrives with a new scheme for introducing a more complex element of chance into the machine, and in a fit of excitement the Old Man dies. Later Annette is found dead in front of a pinball machine. The last scene shows Arthur and Victor, now old men, engaged in a game of Ping-Pong that they have depersonalized and mechanized with complex rules. Prodded by each other's irritation, they abandon themselves to playing wildly, using their hands instead of paddles, until Victor falls dead.

Paolo Paoli (1957). Drama in the style of Brecht that virulently satirizes the 1900–1914 period in terms of social, political, national, and religious forces. Frequent projections of newspaper photographs and the like provide the necessary historical background. Paolo Paoli is a dealer in rare butterflies who exploits the prisoners of Devil's Island as ill-paid butterfly hunters. One of them, Robert Marpeaux, manages to escape and returns to France, where he works in the ostrich-feather and button factory of Halot-Vasseur, a friend and customer of Paolo Paoli. He joins the Socialists and is imprisoned when he opposes the employer-oriented Catholic unions directed by Abbé Saulinier, also a friend of Paoli. This last incident provokes a change of heart in Paoli, who vows to reform his ways and help the needy peoples of the world.

PLAYS

Unless otherwise noted, the plays were first performed in Paris.

1. *La parodie* (*The Parody*). Play, prologue and 2 acts. Written 1947. Published 1950. Produced Théâtre Lancry, June 5, 1952.

2. *L'invasion** (*The Invasion*). Play, 4 acts. Written 1949. Published 1950. Produced Studio des Champs-Élysées, Nov. 14, 1950.

3. *La grande et la petite manoeuvre* (*The Great and the Small Maneuver*). Play, 2 parts. Published 1951. Produced Théâtre des Noctambules, Nov. 11, 1950. Music: Pierre May.

4. *Le professeur Taranne** (*Professor Taranne*). Play, 2 tableaux. Written 1951. Published 1953. Produced Lyon, Théâtre de la Comédie, Mar. 18, 1953.

5. *Les retrouvailles* (*The Recoveries*). Play, 1 act. Written 1952. Published 1955.

6. *Le sens de la marche* (*The Direction of the March*). Play, 4 acts. Published 1955. Produced Lyon, Théâtre de la Comédie, Mar. 18, 1953.

7. *Tous contre tous* (*All Against All*). Play, 2 parts. Published 1953. Produced Théâtre de l'Oeuvre, Apr. 14, 1953. Music: Georges Delerue.

8. *Comme nous avons été** (*As We Were*). Published 1953.

9. *Le ping-pong** (*Ping-Pong*). Play, 2 parts. Published 1955. Produced Théâtre des Noctambules, Mar. 2, 1955.

10. (Adaptation). *Le pélican* (*The Pelican*). Play, 3 acts. Published 1956. Based on August Strindberg's *Pelicanen.*

11. *Paolo Paoli**. Play, 2 parts. Published 1957. Produced Lyon, Théâtre de la Comédie, May 24, 1957.

12. (Adaptation). *Les âmes mortes** (*Dead Souls*). Play, 15 scenes. Published 1958. Produced Villeurbanne, Théâtre de la Cité, Feb. 12, 1960. Based on Nikolay Gogol's novel (1842).

13. *Intimité* (*Intimacy*). Play, 1 act. Published 1958.

14. *La complainte du ridicule* (*The Lament of the Ridiculous*). Play, 1 act. Published 1958.

15. *Je ne suis pas français* (*I Am Not French*). Play, 1 act. Published 1958.

16. (Adaptation). *Les petits bourgeois* (*The Petty Bourgeois*). Play, 4 acts. Published 1959. Produced Théâtre de l'Oeuvre, Sept. 29, 1959. Based on Maxim Gorky's *Meshchanye.*

17. *Le printemps 71* (*Spring 71*). Play, 3 acts. Published 1960. Produced London, Unity Theatre Club, July, 1962; Paris, Théâtre Gérard-Philipe, Apr. 26, 1963.

18. *La politique des restes** (*The Scavengers*). Play, 2 parts. Published 1962. Produced London, Unity Theatre Club, May 31, 1963.

19. *Sainte Europe*. Play, prologue and 2 parts. Published 1966.

20. *Off Limits.* Play. Produced Théâtre d'Aubervillers, 1968.

21. *M. Le Modéré* (*Mister Moderate*). Play.

EDITIONS

Collections.
Two Plays, New York, 1962; *Théâtre,* 3 vols., Paris, 1953–1966.

Individual Plays.
Paolo Paoli. G. Brereton, tr., New York, 1959.
Professor Taranne. Published in *Four Modern French Comedies,* ed. by W. Fowlie and tr. by A. Bermel, New York, 1960.

CRITICISM

M. Esslin, "Arthur Adamov: The Curable and the Incurable," in *The Theatre of the Absurd,* Garden City, N.Y., 1961; G. E. Wellwarth, *The Theater of Protest and Paradox,* New York, 1967.

Joseph Addison
(1672 – 1719)

Joseph Addison, English essayist, poet, and statesman, was born on May 1, 1672, near Amesbury, Wiltshire. He was the son of Lancelot Addison, who later became dean of Lichfield, and his first wife. Addison was educated at various schools, including Charterhouse, and at Queens College, Oxford, where he took his master's degree in 1693. In 1696 he gained a demyship at Magdalen College, and the following year a fellowship, which he held until 1711. His reputation for classical scholarship grew, and he was praised highly for his knowledge of Latin poetry.

In 1699, having received a stipend for the purpose of training himself for foreign service, Addison left England and traveled through Europe, meeting diplomats and men of high rank along the way. In 1701 he wrote *Letter from Italy,* one of his best poems. Upon his return to England in 1703, he entered upon a political career, becoming a member of the well-known Kit-cat Club, which had been formed by prominent Whigs. In 1705 he became an Undersecretary of State, and in 1708 he entered Parliament, where he remained until his death. In the same year he was made secretary and keeper of the records to the Lord Lieutenant of Ireland.

With the accession of the Tories to power in 1710, Addison was released from government service. Able to devote himself entirely to writing, he produced in the next four years many of his essays. Working with his friend Steele (*see* STEELE, RICHARD), whom he had known at Charterhouse, he contributed to the *Tatler,* a periodical that Steele directed, and later to the *Spectator,* a publication they launched together. It was in the *Spectator* that the *Sir Roger de Coverley Papers* first appeared. In 1713 Addison's tragedy *Cato,* a political drama replete with noble sentiments, was presented to the acclaim of Whigs and Tories alike. The Whigs wholeheartedly approved of the play, while the Tories did not dare oppose it.

Soon after the death of Queen Anne, in 1714, Addison's literary career seems to have ended. In 1716 he returned briefly to his former office under the Lord Lieutenant of Ireland, and later he was made one of the Lord Commissioners of Trade. A much-discussed feud with Alexander Pope, in which Pope berated Addison for his less than enthusiastic reaction to Pope's translation of the *Iliad,* developed at this time. The appearance in 1716 of *The Drummer* contributed nothing to Addison's literary reputation. The same year, Addison married Charlotte, Countess Dowager of Warwick, and two years later, with another change in government, he was appointed one of the two principal Secretaries of State. Just as in Parliament he was unable to speak because of an inherent shyness, so it was in this new office, and Addison failed miserably. He soon retired on an ample pension. In poor health, his asthma now accompanied by dropsy, he died in Kensington on June 17, 1719. He was buried in the Poets' Corner in Westminster Abbey.

WORK

Addison, known principally as an essayist and poet, wrote two plays and an opera. Of these, the neoclassical drama *Cato* (1713), based on Plutarch's version of the life of Cato the Younger, is the best known. Although the language now seems stilted and dull, the play has interest for its adherence to the principles of neoclassicism. Unlike his contemporaries, who tried to deal with the theme of

Joseph Addison. [Theatre Collection, The New York Public Library at Lincoln Center, Astor, Lenox and Tilden Foundations]

John Kemble in title role of *Cato*. Liverpool, Theatre Royal, 1812. [Theatre Collection, The New York Public Library at Lincoln Center, Astor, Lenox and Tilden Foundations]

love within a classical mold, Addison chose as his central character a philosopher and concentrated on thought rather than passion. He thus succeeded with the neoclassical form where most of his contemporaries failed. His choice proved ideally suited to the restrictions of the classical unities. *See* NEOCLASSICISM; UNITIES.

His other two ventures in the theatre were less successful: the opera *Rosamund* (1707) is an attempt to counter the kind of part-Italian, part-English opera that Addison was to ridicule in the *Spectator,* and *The Drummer* (1716) is a comedy of a husband and father who pretends to have died in order to test his family.

Cato (1713). Tragedy in which Cato and his followers, having unsuccessfully opposed Caesar, have been given refuge in Numidia, where a conspiracy is afoot to betray Cato. The conspirators, led by Sempronius, a senator, and Syphax, a Numidian, try to win over Juba, Prince of Numidia, but Juba not only is a disciple of Cato but also is in love with Cato's daughter Marcia, and he remains loyal. The conspiracy is launched, but Cato sup-

presses it by his brilliant oratory. Caesar's troops now approach the city, and Sempronius and Syphax desert to the Romans. Cato's son Marcus is slain in the ensuing battle, and rather than be captured Cato takes his own life. His friend Lucius, in an oration over Cato's body, declaims the famous lines:

From hence, let fierce contending nations know
What dire effects from civil discord flow.

PLAYS

All were first performed in London.
1. *Rosamund.* Opera, 3 acts; verse. Published 1707. Produced Drury Lane Theatre, March, 1707.
2. *Cato.* Tragedy, 5 acts; verse. Published 1713. Produced Drury Lane Theatre, Apr. 14, 1713.
3. *The Drummer, or The Haunted House.* Comedy, 5 acts; prose. Published 1716. Produced Drury Lane Theatre, Mar 10, 1716.

EDITIONS

Collections.
Works, 6 vols., London, 1811, 1854–56; New York, 1811, 1854; Philadelphia, 1883 (plays in vol. I).
Individual Plays.
Cato. Published in *Plays of the Restoration and Eighteenth Century,* ed. by D. MacMillan and H. M. Jones, Holt, New York, 1938; *Representative English Plays,* ed. by J. S. P. Tatlock and R. G. Martin, 2d ed., rev. and enl., Appleton-Century, New York, 1938; *British Dramatists from Dryden to Sheridan,* ed. by G. H. Nettleton and A. E. Case, Houghton Mifflin, Boston, 1939; *Eighteenth Century Plays,* ed. by R. Quintana, Modern Library, New York, 1952.

CRITICISM

L. Aikin, *The Life of Joseph Addison,* 2 vols., London, 1843; 1 vol., Philadelphia, 1846; W. J. Courthope, *Addison,* London, 1884; New York, 1894, 1902; T. B. Macaulay, *The Life and Writings of Addison,* Boston, 1906; P. Smithers, *Life of Joseph Addison,* Oxford, 1954; L. A. Elioseff, *The Cultural Milieu of Addison's Literary Criticism,* Austin, Tex., 1963.

ADE, George (1866–1944). American short-story writer and dramatist. Born in Kentland, Ind., he attended Purdue University, graduating in 1887. Thereupon he embarked on a career in journalism, writing for newspa-

George Ade. [Theatre Collection, The New York Public Library at Lincoln Center, Astor, Lenox and Tilden Foundations]

pers in Indiana and Chicago. He became famous with a collection of short stories, *Fables in Slang* (1900), in which rural characters speak their own patois. Having been "absurdly in love with the theatre," he then turned to writing plays. Among them are *The Sultan of Sulu* (1902), an operetta; *The County Chairman* (1903); *The College Widow* (1904); *Just Out of College* (1905); *The Bad Samaritan* (1905); *Marse Covington* (1906); *Mrs. Peckham's Carouse* (1906); *Father and the Boys* (1907); *The Fair Co-Ed* (1908); *The Old Town* (1909); and *Nettie* (1914). He also wrote scripts for several motion pictures, including *Our Leading Citizen* and *Woman Proof.*

A.E. *See* RUSSELL, GEORGE WILLIAM.

Aeschylus
(ca. 525 — 456 B.C.)

Aeschylus, the earliest of the three major Greek tragedians, was born about 525 B.C. in Eleusis, a small community near Athens where the goddess Demeter was worshiped in the ritual Eleusinian mysteries. Aeschylus was the son of Euphorion, a member of the old nobility (eupatridae) of Athens. According to the short *Life* given in the Medicean manuscript of his plays, he fought in the Persian Wars at Marathon (490 B.C.) and probably at Salamis (480 B.C.); some accounts state that he was present at the battles of Artemisium and Plataea as well, but this information is uncertain.

His career as a dramatist spanned more than forty years, from the beginning of the fifth century B.C., when he first competed for the dramatic prize at Athens, to 458 B.C., when the *Oresteia* trilogy was presented. The lexicographer Suidas states that Aeschylus wrote a total of ninety plays, but this figure has not been verified. Seven tragedies are extant in their entirety, and the titles or fragments of seventy-two others have survived. Aeschylus's first victory in the dramatic festival at Athens was recorded in 484 B.C., and he won thirteen times in all. His status among the tragedians of his generation is also indicated by the decree passed shortly after his death, that anyone wishing to produce a play by Aeschylus at the Dionysia should be granted a chorus by the archon.

Aeschylus is known to have made at least two visits to Sicily. During his first visit he stopped at the court of Hiero I (ruler of Syracuse from about 478 to 467 B.C.), who had also invited such poets as Pindar, Bacchylides,

Bust of Aeschylus in the Capitoline Museum, Rome. [Alinari]

and Simonides. At his request, Aeschylus wrote a play called *The Women of Aetna,* to celebrate Hiero's founding of the new city of Aetna in 476 B.C., on the site of the captured city of Catina (now Catania). Perhaps during the same visit, Aeschylus produced *The Persians (Persai)*, part of a trilogy that won him the first prize when first produced at Athens in 472 B.C. After 458 Aeschylus returned to Sicily, and he died in Gela in 456 B.C. On his tomb was placed this epitaph: "Beneath this stone lies Aeschylus, son of Euphorion, the Athenian, who perished in the wheat-bearing land of Gela; of his noble prowess Marathon can speak, or the long-haired Persian, who knows it well." The authorship of this epitaph is variously ascribed to the people of Gela (the *Life*) and to Aeschylus himself (Athenaeus, Pausanias). It seems unlikely, however, that anyone but the poet himself could have neglected to mention his poetry.

The tragedian's fame during and after his lifetime gave rise to many popular anecdotes connected with his name. One concerns the charge that he revealed the "secrets of Demeter." While acting in one of his own plays, Aeschylus is said to have referred to Demeter in a manner that led the audience to believe he was exposing secrets of the Eleusinian mysteries, which should have been inviolable, whereupon the audience rose in fury. Aeschylus ran for sanctuary to the altar of Dionysus in the orchestra and thus escaped injury or death at the hands of the angry crowd. He was later acquitted after he proved that he had never been initiated into the mysteries. In another famous legend, recounted in the *Life,* an eagle, mistaking the poet's bald head for a stone, let a tortoise fall upon it to break the shell and so fulfilled a prophecy according to which Aeschylus was fated to die as the result of a blow from heaven.

Contemporary appraisal of Aeschylus is thought to be contained, by way of oral tradition, in Aristophanes's statement (quoted at the head of the *Life*) that Aeschylus was the "first of the Greeks to build up a towering fabric of majestic phrases." After his death, his tomb was worshiped. *See* ARISTOPHANES.

WORK

Aeschylus, the first dramatist whose works have, at least in part, come down to us, inherited a genre that had already undergone considerable development from its initially choral, dithyrambic origins. We know of some of his predecessors and of their contributions to the drama: Pratinas, who, according to Suidas, was the first to compose satyr plays;

Phrynichus, the first to put women in the chorus; and Choerilus, the first to employ the mask and majestic costume. But the major innovation leading up to the drama of Aeschylus was the introduction by Thespis of the first actor, separate from the chorus, who spoke a prologue and set speeches. With the presence of this first actor, dialogue became possible, and with dialogue there came the dramatic representation of events rather than their simple narrative recitation. *See* SATYR PLAY.

Aeschylus, whom Gilbert Murray called "the creator of tragedy," created new forms, both external (costume, dance, mechanical devices) and internal (his characters, although not detailed, nevertheless possess the ability, in the form of free will, to work out their own destiny in the face of divine will). Having increased the number of actors to two, he allowed for heightened dramatic conflict by way of increased complexity of plot and action. Moreover, this innovation made the dialogue predominant, giving the chorus a subordinate role. Because of Aeschylus's interest in cosmic themes such as justice, in-

Prometheus Bound in a production at Epidaurus. [Royal Consulate General of Greece]

herited guilt, and the transmittal of evil from generation to generation, Aeschylus preferred the grand scale of the trilogy, in which he was able to review the entire history of a house or of a whole race. Flowing from this epic subject matter was a grandeur of language that left an indelible mark on tragedy. In fact, it was Aeschylus who opened tragedy to the epic domain by using as his chief source the mass of heroic poetry to which the *Iliad* and the *Odyssey* belonged. So indebted was he to the epic that he declared that his dramas were morsels from the great banquet of Homer. He delighted in violent metaphors, compound adjectives, neologisms, repetitions (especially in the choral passages), and long lists of epithets. Aristophanes in *The Frogs* criticized Aeschylus for occasionally using words for their sound value rather than for their meaning. Indeed, Aeschylus utilized even foreign words by introducing foreigners on the stage, as in *The Persians*. It is probable, furthermore, that he invented the dress of tragic actors which was to become traditional: the rich robes of brilliant colors; the *cothurnus,* or buskin; the *onkos,* or projection of the mask above the forehead; and the mask adapted to the personality of the character.

But the full scope of Aeschylus's genius is revealed in his choice of tragic themes and their dramatic treatment in his works. His earliest surviving play is *The Persians,* the only extant Greek tragedy to deal explicitly with contemporary events and part of the tetralogy that won the first prize in 472 B.C. The play concerns the period following the Greek defeat at Salamis of the Persians, who had been led in battle by their rash and proud king, Xerxes. Never succumbing to crass exultation over the fall of Greece's enemy, Aeschylus is able to infuse that historical event with the aura of divine justice. Already the characteristic themes of his mature tragedy are obvious, as well as his extraordinary ability to create effective and powerful theatre. The ghost of Xerxes's father Darius, summoned up by the chorus in a spellbinding invocation, appears above his funeral mound and explains the significance of the event at Salamis: Zeus is punishing Xerxes's hubris, which had threatened to destroy the order of the universe. Xerxes is ultimately the victim of Ate, the moral blindness and self-infatuation that Zeus employs to lead arrogant men along the path of their own destruction. *See* HUBRIS.

The next surviving play, *The Seven Against Thebes* (*Hepta epi Thēbas,* 467 B.C.), is the last of a trilogy recounting the story of the royal house of Thebes. Written when the capture of Athens by the Persians was still fresh in its

Agamemnon. Epidaurus, National Theatre of Greece, 1959. [Greek National Tourist Office]

citizens' memory, the play depicts the terror of a city under siege. Although criticized by some for its static quality and by others as a primitive conception of drama, nevertheless it displays the sure hand of dramatic genius at grips with the problem of human freedom and divine compulsion. Eteocles, who sees himself as the benevolent king responsible for the defense of his city, feels that to fulfill this role he must take immediate personal action, although he is aware that by doing so he will fulfill Oedipus's prophecy that he and his brother Polynices would divide their kingdom by the sword. Eteocles's doom can be averted only by the stubborn opposition of his will to act. But he sees in action the fulfillment of what he considers his destiny, and he finally surrenders to it, rejecting the chorus's invitation to pray.

The first play of a trilogy that concluded with *The Egyptians* and *The Daughters of Danaus* (*Danaides*), both lost, *The Suppliants* (*Hiketides,* 463? B.C.) presents the theologically advanced notion of Zeus as enforcer of justice in the universe and special protector of the oppressed. From the closing lines of this play and from the fragments of the following two, we can deduce that the trilogy set forth the theme of harmony with nature, showing the tragic consequences of the brutal lust of the Egyptians coupled with the Danaides' irrational refusal to recognize the power of the cosmic Aphrodite, who brings men and women together. It is possible that the trilogy ended in a trial scene like that of *The Eumenides* and that the Danaides, who demonstrated excessive devotion to the virgin Artemis, conquered their aversion to marriage and were reconciled with Aphrodite.

Prometheus Bound (*Promētheus desmōtēs,* 466/459? B.C.), a brilliant drama for all its static quality, maintains interest by a parade of colorfully conceived characters who visit Prometheus on the rock to which he is chained. They make it possible for Prometheus gradually to reveal his state of mind: his fierce hatred for the tyrant Zeus, his sympathy for Io and the plight of mankind, and his faith in the righteousness of his cause and in the ultimate triumph of wisdom.

Scholars have found it difficult to reconcile the representation of Zeus in *Prometheus Bound* as the arrogant, ruthless tyrant with the just ruler of the universe depicted in *The Suppliants* and *Agamemnon.* It has been suggested that Zeus is here depicted as the youthful king of heaven who still rules by might and that, by suffering from Prometheus's refusal to reveal his secret, he eventually acquires wisdom and learns the virtue of moderation. But evidence fails to justify this view of an evolving Zeus, while there is, in fact, good reason to see in the *Prometheus* trilogy the reconciliation of originally opposing forces, as in *The Eumenides,* where the Furies do not evolve but realize the benign side of their character.

Two other tragedies are associated with *Prometheus Bound: Prometheus the Fire Bringer* and *Prometheus Unbound.* It is certain that the latter play followed *Prometheus Bound,* but the position of *Prometheus the Fire Bringer* is doubtful. If it opened the trilogy, it may have dealt with Prometheus's theft of fire from heaven, leading to the punishment portrayed in the extant play; but it may well have belonged to a different trilogy from the other two tragedies.

Finally, utilizing the latest theatrical techniques and devices, such as the third actor introduced by Sophocles, the scene building (*skene*), which represents the royal palace, and various machines to provide striking stage effects, Aeschylus wrote the *Oresteia,* his masterpiece and one of the world's greatest achievements. It is the only trilogy to survive intact, although the accompanying satyr play, *Proteus,* is now lost. The trilogy, which won the first prize at its presentation in Athens in 458 B.C., consists of *Agamemnon, The Libation Bearers* (*Choēphoroi*), and *The Eumenides. See* SOPHOCLES.

Agamemnon, the longest of the three plays, sets the theme for the trilogy. Even before the climactic murder of Agamemnon, the reader is overwhelmed by the mounting tension that Aeschylus creates as the past crimes of the house of Atreus and their punishments are reviewed and as fears that more recent acts might extend the blood chain to the present generation are confirmed.

Because of his awesome power and the concomitant responsibility to all Greeks, Agamemnon, putting on "the yoke of necessity," has chosen to sacrifice his daughter Iphigenia and to engage in a retributory war that itself has become cursed because of the excesses perpetrated in the name of justice. Agamemnon has been forced to act, to become a doer, but as Zeus has decreed, "the doer must be the sufferer." By the time the King reluctantly commits his final incriminating act of walking on a purple carpet into the palace, his downfall is inevitable, and the cycle of guilt begins with his death, since Clytemnestra's avenging of Agamemnon's crime itself constitutes a new crime that must be expiated. The question is raised: how can the vicious circle of crime that breeds further crime be ended?

In *The Libation Bearers,* Orestes becomes the unwilling victim of the family's evil genius. He is lured into action by Apollo, who promises him protection. But as soon as he kills Clytemnestra, the Furies (Erinyes), the ancient chthonic deities who belong to a matriarchal generation antedating that of Zeus and the Olympians and whose office it is to punish wrongs done to kindred, begin to pursue him, and he seeks shelter at Apollo's shrine in Delphi.

In *The Eumenides,* the human conflict becomes a cosmic struggle involving three generations of deities, each trying to assert its own theory of justice. The primitive, brutal, animalistic Furies, roused by the cries of vengeance of Clytemnestra's ghost, press the hunt. Apollo cleanses Orestes of his sin with rites of purification, but the Furies continue their relentless pursuit until Apollo sends Orestes to Athens, to be tried before the court of the Areopagus, composed of Athenian citizens and presided over by Athena, protectress of the polis (city-state). The play is thus dramatically and unexpectedly brought into the very city where it was being performed. The Furies, whose realistic portrayal by the

actors caused panic and (according to legend) some miscarriages among the women in the audience, begin a ritualistic dance and sing a "binding song." Before Athena they assert their concept of justice as simple retaliation. Apollo claims that Orestes cannot be held accountable for murder of kin, because the mother is not a true parent but only a nurse. Furthermore, he says that Zeus himself had willed the murder of Clytemnestra. When the human vote is deadlocked, Athena votes for Orestes' acquittal, signifying the rejection of both the Furies' and Apollo's concept of justice. Neither of them is adequate: they are both too narrow and inhuman. Athena, goddess of wisdom, heralds a new concept of justice tempered with mercy, guaranteed and defended by Zeus and enshrined in the democratic processes of the polis. This concept reconciles opposing forces and holds a place even for the Furies, who are to be worshiped as the Eumenides, or Kindly Ones, for their power to promote fertility and ward off conflicts among fellow citizens.

Thus Aeschylus shows a happy resolution of the conflict among the gods as well as of the conflict among men. In the final words of the chorus, "Zeus, the all-seeing, and Fate have together reached their goal." The poet's religious philosophy arrives at the reconciliation between impersonal, irrational fate and a personal, rational world ruler, a reconciliation embodied in the loftiest creation of Aeschylus's mind: the person of Zeus.

The Persians (*Persai; Persae;* 472 B.C.). The only extant Greek tragedy based on actual historical events, specifically, the continuing efforts of the Persians to extend their empire across the Aegean Sea into Greece. The first Persian expedition, dispatched by Darius the Great (r. 522–486 B.C.), was defeated at the Battle of Marathon in 490 B.C. Ten years later Darius's son Xerxes (r. 486–465 B.C.) led a second expedition, a tremendous undertaking involving the construction of bridges across the Hellespont and the cutting of a channel through the isthmus of Mount Athos. Having overcome a valiant force of Spartans at Thermopylae, Xerxes penetrated deep into Greece by sea and land. But in 480

B.C. the Persian Fleet was decisively defeated in the Bay of Salamis, and in the following year the Persian Army was all but annihilated at Plataea, in Boeotia. These two battles, from which the Persian Empire never recovered, ensured the continued independence of the Greek states.

The play takes place before Xerxes's palace at Susa, in Persia. There has been no word from the mighty Persian forces, and the chorus of Persians shares the apprehension of Queen Atossa, Xerxes's mother. When a messenger arrives with news of the disaster at Salamis, the people mourn their losses and invoke the ghost of Darius. His ghost arises to confirm their worst fears: Zeus is punishing Xerxes for his pride and the excesses into which it has led him. He explains that by uniting the continents of Europe and Asia and by making sea of what once was land the rash, youthful Xerxes has upset the balance of nature and disturbed the order of the universe. Darius predicts a further defeat (Plataea) the following year. Finally, the humbled Xerxes returns, and the play ends in a long scene of mourning and lament, as the grieving chorus follows him into the palace.

The Seven Against Thebes (*Hepta epi Thēbas; Septem contra Thebas,* 467 B.C.). Third play in a Theban tetralogy that included the lost tragedies *Laius* and *Oedipus* and a satyr play, *The Sphinx.* The subject of the tetralogy was the destruction of the house of Laius as the result of a hereditary curse. *The Seven Against Thebes* shows the fulfillment of Oedipus's curse on his two sons, Eteocles and Polynices, that they would "di-

The Eumenides, in a production at Epidaurus. [Royal Consulate General of Greece]

vide their inheritance with the sword in such manner as to obtain equal shares." Though the curse was interpreted to mean that they were to rule for equal durations of time, the equal shares, in fact, are their graves.

The play opens on the morning of the final attack by Polynices and his allies (six Argive heroes) against the city of Thebes, which is ruled by his brother Eteocles, a man heavily burdened both by public responsibility and by his consciousness of impending doom. There is little action in the play. The first part shows Eteocles trying to calm the chorus of Theban women terrified by the thought of defeat. Then, in a long static scene reminiscent of epic poetry for its descriptions of warriors' armor, Eteocles is told by a scout of the preparations of each of the seven chieftains to attack a city gate, and he names seven Thebans to oppose them. The last of these is Eteocles himself, and his opponent is to be his brother Polynices.

Shortly after Eteocles's exit, a messenger reports the death of the two brothers, each by the other's hand, and the bodies are brought in. The Senate decides that Eteocles should be buried in the royal tomb but that the body of Polynices should be thrown to the dogs outside the city gate. However, Antigone, the sister of the two dead warriors, in a short scene usually considered spurious, states her intention to give Polynices burial. The play ends with the chorus's lamentations over Polynices and Eteocles and the fate of their house.

The Suppliants (*Hiketides; Supplices,* 463? B.C.). This play was the first part of a tetralogy that might have included the lost tragedies *The Egyptians* and *The Daughters of Danaus* and a satyr play, *Amymone.* According to the legend, Danaus, the son of Belus, has fifty daughters; his twin brother Aegyptus has fifty sons, who wish to marry their cousins. Objecting to this proposal, Danaus flees with his daughters to Argos, where King Pelasgus gives them asylum. Aegyptus and his sons arrive in due course to press their suit. After many threats, Danaus seemingly grants his consent to the multiple wedding but gives his daughters daggers with which they are to slay their husbands on the bridal night. All the sons of Aegyptus are thus murdered except Lynceus, who is spared by Hypermnestra; and he afterward avenges his brothers by killing Danaus. Put on trial for having spared her husband, Hypermnestra is defended by Aphrodite in a speech that stresses the all-pervasive power of love.

The Suppliants begins when the fifty daughters of Danaus have just arrived in Argos. Crouching around an altar in supplication, with passionate entreaties they persuade King Pelasgus to grant them refuge and to protect them from their cousins' violence. They claim this protection as descendants of the Argive Io. When Pelasgus hesitates, they threaten mass suicide, which according to Greek religious feeling would stain his city forever with their blood. Later the herald of the suitors arrives and commands the maidens to come with him, threatening to take them by force if they refuse. After a violent debate with Pelasgus, he departs without the women. The play ends as Danaus, with the consent of Pelasgus and the Assembly of the people of Argos, conducts his daughters to the city for greater security.

Prometheus Bound (*Promētheus desmōtēs; Prometheus vinctus*, 466/459? B.C.). Probably the second play in a trilogy, now lost, of which the other plays were *Prometheus the Fire Bringer* and *Prometheus Unbound*. The satyr play produced with the trilogy is unknown. *Prometheus Bound* deals with the conflict between brute force and rational intelligence.

Because Prometheus, a Titan, has stolen fire from heaven for the benefit of the infant human race, Zeus has had him chained to a rock in the Caucasus and later plunged him into the depths of Tartarus. Prometheus has subsequently been restored to the light of day, with the added punishment of a vulture that comes every day to devour his heart, which grows back at night. He has eventually won his freedom by revealing to Zeus that Thetis, whom Zeus had intended to wed, would bear a child mightier than his father. The actual liberation has been effected by Heracles, a descendant of Io and son of Zeus.

The plot of *Prometheus Bound* is simple in the extreme. It opens with the fastening of Prometheus to a lonely rock by Hephaestus, under the direction of the personifications of Strength and Might, the attendants of Zeus. The chorus of ocean nymphs (Oceanides) enters, and Prometheus tells them how by his counsel Zeus had been able to defeat the Titans. Then, to consolidate his newly won empire, Zeus had decided to destroy mankind, but Prometheus had saved humanity by the gift of fire from heaven. Oceanus enters, professing sympathy and urging Prometheus to submit to the greater power of Zeus. Prometheus rejects this advice. After the chorus sings a short ode, Prometheus speaks of his services to mankind, for whose sake he is suffering great tortures, until Io enters. Her beauty had attracted the love of Zeus and aroused the jealousy of Hera, who had turned her into a heifer eternally plagued by a gadfly. Arriving in the course of her wanderings, she tells Prometheus of her past adventures. In turn, Prometheus prophesies that

An adaptation of the *Oresteia* entitled *The House of Atreus*, in a Minnesota Theatre Company production presented by the Center Theatre Group. [Center Theatre Group, Mark Taper Forum, Los Angeles, Calif.]

she will soon find peace, when, upon reaching Egypt, Zeus will free her from her plight by his magic touch, and that his own deliverer, Heracles, will be the thirteenth in descent from her. He further tells her that Zeus will be overthrown, by a marriage against which Prometheus alone can warn him. The chorus sings of the dangers involved in union with the gods. Prometheus again foretells the downfall of Zeus at the hands of his own son. Now Hermes enters, sent by Zeus to learn Prometheus's secret. The defiant Titan refuses and mocks him. Hermes warns him of still greater tortures, and the chorus urges him to submit to the will of the stronger Zeus, but Prometheus, still defiant, is hurled into the depths of Tartarus with the Oceanides, who loyally refuse to leave him, amid an upheaval of all natural phenomena.

Agamemnon (*Agamemnōn*, 458 B.C.). First play in the *Oresteia* trilogy, dealing with the murder of Agamemnon by his wife Clytemnestra. Queen Clytemnestra, plotting with her lover Aegisthus to take her husband's life, has ordered that watch be kept upon the roof of the palace at Argos, because a succession of beacon fires is to bring the news from Troy when the city is captured by Agamemnon. For a whole year a watchman has been on the lookout.

The play opens as the watchman waits in the dead of night. Suddenly he sends out a cry of joy as the signal blazes forth, announcing the imminent return of Agamemnon. But his joy is of short duration: he strikes the first note of approaching calamity by guarded hints and allusions to Clytemnestra's adulterous relation with Aegisthus, Agamemnon's mortal enemy. The chorus of old men enters, reviewing the history of the house of Atreus in a long choral passage. They chant the tale of how the Greeks, led by Agamemnon and Menelaus, sought to take revenge on Paris for having outraged Zeus, the guardian of the rights of hospitality, by his abduction of Helen. Thus, when the Greeks were planning to set out for Troy, a portent appeared before the palace of Argos: two eagles were seen tearing a pregnant hare apart with their talons. The eagles were interpreted to represent Agamemnon and Menelaus; the pregnant hare, the city of Troy teeming with innocent people. Furthermore, Artemis, the goddess of nature, was angry with the kings and sent adverse winds to blow at Aulis, where the Greek Fleet had gathered for the expedition against Troy. The seer Calchas declared that Artemis demanded as appeasement for the destruction of Troy the sacrifice of Agamemnon's daughter Iphigenia. To realize the just expedition against Troy in the name of Zeus, Agamemnon consented, incurring the rage of Clytemnestra, who thereupon vowed vengeance. The chorus concludes by calling upon Zeus to lead man to the path of knowledge.

Clytemnestra enters, sacrificing to the gods. When the chorus asks why she sacrifices, she answers that she is thankful for the fall of Troy. She pictures the state of the captured city and pretends to hope that the victorious Greeks have not sinned against the gods, who are quick to punish. The chorus gives thanks to Zeus and moralizes on the downfall of human pride. A herald appears, announcing that Agamemnon will soon arrive in Argos. While he describes the fall of Troy, he tells of the acts of sacrilege committed by the Greeks against the very temples of the gods. Thus the fears that Clytemnestra has voiced are confirmed. She sends the herald away with her welcome for Agamemnon and speaks of her love for him. The chorus leader hints at the hypocrisy of her words, and the chorus sings of Helen and the fatal power of her beauty.

Agamemnon enters, followed by the prophetess Cassandra, priestess of Apollo, who has become his unwilling mistress. He speaks proudly of his victory, as Clytemnestra greets him with effusiveness and hypocritically reaffirms her conjugal love. Then she persuades him to walk into the palace over a rich purple carpet. He does so unwillingly, knowing that it constitutes an act of hubris. Clytemnestra accompanies him indoors, while the chorus sings of its fears.

Clytemnestra comes out of the palace and commands Cassandra to follow her within, but the prophetess does not answer and Clytemnestra goes in alone. Cassandra, left with the chorus, voices incoherent cries of horror. She recalls the bloody history of the house of Atreus and predicts the death of Agamemnon, as well as her own, and the coming of an avenger. She goes into the palace. After the chorus sings of wicked prosperity, Agamemnon's voice is heard from within, crying that he is being murdered. Another shriek follows, and then silence.

The old men debate on the manner in which they should intervene, but the palace doors are flung open, revealing Clytemnestra standing over the corpses of Agamemnon and Cassandra with a bloody ax in her hands. She describes how she has killed her husband with the ax, after ensnaring him in the folds of a robe while in his bath. She reveals that all her previous professions of love for her husband were a sham to facilitate his murder. She glories in her deed. When the chorus reproaches her, she answers that she is the personification of the ancestral curse, the family daemon that is now exacting vengeance on Agamemnon for the murder of Thyestes' children by Atreus. She reminds the chorus of Agamemnon's murder of young Iphigenia and the reproach she was made to suffer when Agamemnon took his foreign concubine to live under the same roof with his wedded wife. She further declares her intention to make a pact with the daemon so that it will stop plaguing the family with murder of kin and be satisfied with the blood already shed.

The chorus sees in Agamemnon's death the work of Ate, but it refuses to free Clytemnestra from guilt and predicts her own future punishment. It affirms Zeus's law that the doer must suffer. Aegisthus enters, exulting in Agememnon's murder as proper vengeance for the murder of Thyestes' children. The chorus warns him and Clytemnestra that Orestes is alive and will soon return to Argos to avenge his father.

The Libation Bearers (Choēphoroi; Choephoroe, 458 B.C.). Second play in the *Oresteia*, dealing with Orestes' revenge on Clytemnestra and Aegisthus for their slaying of his father, Agamemnon. Accompanied by his friend Pylades, Orestes arrives in Argos and salutes his father's grave, laying on it a lock of his hair as a sign of mourning; he and Pylades then withdraw. The chorus, led by

Scene from a performance of the *Oresteia* trilogy at Epidaurus. [Greek National Tourist Office]

Orestes' sister Electra, enters carrying libations, having been sent by Clytemnestra, who has been terrified by a dream in which she suckles a snake that draws blood from her. Electra pours the libations over the grave and calls upon the gods and Agamemnon's spirit to bring Orestes home to punish the murderess. Discovering the lock of hair, she recognizes it as Orestes'; he then reveals himself to her and shows her a piece of embroidery in further proof of his identity. Orestes explains that Apollo has sent him home as an avenger and that Clytemnestra's dream has foretold her death at his hands. Posing as a traveler, he tells Clytemnestra that Orestes is dead.

After Orestes enters the palace, his aged nurse comes forth, lamenting the loss of her foster son, to summon Aegisthus and his bodyguards to the palace. The chorus persuades her to alter the message so that Aegisthus will come unattended, and shortly after his arrival his screams are heard from within. Clytemnestra appears, followed by Orestes, of whom she begs mercy. Unnerved, Orestes asks the counsel of Pylades, who reminds him of his oath of revenge and of the command of Apollo. After justifying in vain

her murder of Agamemnon and menacing Orestes with her curse, Clytemnestra is driven inside to be slain beside her lover. Orestes displays the two corpses and the bloody robe in which Agamemnon had been snared. But the sight then brings upon him the beginnings of madness. He sees the Furies (Erinyes) sent by his mother's spirit and rushes away in torment to seek at Delphi the protection Apollo has promised.

The Eumenides (*Eumenides*, 458 B.C.). Third and last play in the *Oresteia*, dealing with the absolving of Orestes' guilt and the placating of the Furies (Erinyes). As the play opens in Delphi, the Pythian priestess is terrified by the sight of the bloodstained Orestes seated on the altar of Apollo's temple with the Furies sleeping around him. Apollo purifies him and sends him forth on his wanderings, which he predicts will end in Athens. But Clytemnestra's ghost awakens the Furies, who burst from the temple in a frenzy at the escape of their victim. The scene now changes to Athens, where Orestes seeks the protection of Athena. Entering in pursuit, the Furies chant their fearful binding song. When Athena rules that the suit shall be tried by a court of her own citizens (Athenians), a court of justice is assembled on the Areopagus, presided over by the goddess.

The trial begins with a cross-examination of Orestes by the Furies. Apollo then gives the justification for the matricide: it was the command of Zeus, Agamemnon was a great king, and the real blood parent of the child is the father. He ends by promising that Orestes, if acquitted, will be a firm and useful ally to Athens. Before the votes are counted, Athena gives her ruling that if an equal number are cast on both sides Orestes shall be acquitted, for she will vote in his favor. The votes are counted and found equal, and Orestes departs. Athena proclaims the establishment of the Court of Areopagus, which shall forever try all cases involving the shedding of blood. The goddess is then faced with the irate Furies, who feel dishonored by the younger gods and threaten to blight Athens. She eventually persuades them to take up residence in the city, where they will be worshiped as the Eumenides (Kindly Ones) for their power to promote fertility and ward off plagues. The play ends as the Athenians escort the Eumenides to their new home in a cave beneath the Acropolis.

PLAYS

The chronology (with the exception of No. 4) and the dating of Nos. 1, 2, 5, 6, and 7 are precise. Until recently, the usual date for No. 3 was ca. 490 B.C., but new evidence makes a much later dating possible. Some critics have suggested the possibility that No. 4 was Aeschylus's last extant play. In each case the first title given is a transliteration from the Greek; the first in parentheses is the Latin designation.

1. *Persai** (*Persae; The Persians*). 472 B.C.
2. *Hepta epi Thēbas** (*Septem contra Thebas; The Seven Against Thebes*). 467 B.C.
3. *Hiketides** (*Supplices; The Suppliants*). 463? B.C. Until recently there was general agreement among scholars that *The Suppliants* was the earliest surviving play of Aeschylus, possibly antedating the Battle of Marathon (490 B.C.). Their arguments were based on the play's archaic qualities, such as the assignment to the chorus of the role of protagonist in comparison to the seeming advances in dramatic technique that took place between its composition and that of the *Oresteia*. However, a newly discovered papyrus, first published in 1952, contains the remains of a didascaly (catalogue of dramas) that informs us that Aeschylus won the annual Athenian competition with the trilogy containing *The Suppliants;* in the same competition Sophocles received the second prize. Since we know that Sophocles presented his first play in Athens in 468 B.C., on which occasion he won first prize, and that in 467 B.C. Aeschylus won with the trilogy to which *The Seven Against Thebes* belonged, *The Suppliants* cannot have been written before 466 B.C. Nor can it have been written in or after 458 B.C., the year of the production of the *Oresteia*, Aeschylus's last known work. The name that the papyrus gives has been deciphered as Archedemides, archon of Athens in 463 B.C., and this date has been generally accepted as the date of production of *The Suppliants*.
4. *Promētheus desmōtēs** (*Prometheus vinctus; Prometheus Bound*). 466/459? B.C. Although the simple language of this play has caused some scholars to doubt Aeschylus's authorship and to point to obvious signs of

the influence of the Sophist rhetorical school, the elements that are characteristically Aeschylean far outweigh these considerations. Attempts to date the play accurately have been problematical. The scholars who link *Prometheus Bound* directly to Aeschylus's visits to Sicily because of similarities of language to some Sicilian poets and of a passage in the play (lines 363–372) describing an eruption of Mount Etna, have failed to gain general agreement. Others see evidence of a Sicilian production in the brevity of the choral passages, arguing that Aeschylus was forced to limit their length because of the difficulties involved in training a local Sicilian chorus totally lacking in experience. Whatever their virtue, none of these arguments helps pinpoint the date of the play, since Aeschylus is known to have traveled to Sicily at least twice. Perhaps more telling is the probable use of a third actor, an innovation introduced by Sophocles. This might provide a *terminus post quem* of 468 B.C. The prevailing view is that the play was composed not far in time from the *Oresteia*.

5. *Agamemnōn** (*Agamemnon*). 458 B.C.
6. *Choēphoroi** (*Choephoroe; The Libation Bearers*). 458 B.C.
7. *Eumenides** (*Eumenides; The Eumenides*). 458 B.C.

EDITIONS

Collections.

Tragedies, 2 vols., Loeb Classical Library, New York, 1923–1926; *The Complete Greek Drama,* ed. by W. J. Oates and E. J. O'Neill and tr. by E. Morshead, R. Potter, and P. More, vol. 1, New York, 1938; *Complete Plays,* tr. by G. Murray, New York, 1952; *Great Books of the Western World,* ed. by R. M. Hutchins and tr. by G. Cookson, vol. 5, Chicago, 1952; *Aeschylus,* ed. by H. W. Smyth, 2d ed., 2 vols., London, 1953; *The Complete Greek Tragedies,* ed. and tr. by D. Grene and R. Lattimore, vol. 1, Chicago, 1959.

Also published in *Greek Dramas,* ed. by B. Perrin and tr. by R. Potter and E. Browning, New York, 1900; *Harvard Classics,* ed. by C. W. Eliot and tr. by E. Morshead and E. Plumptre, vol. 8, New York, 1909–1910; *Ten Greek Plays Translated into English,* tr. by G. Murray, New York, 1930; *Three Greek Plays,* tr. by E. Hamilton, New York, 1937; *Fifteen Greek Plays Translated into English,* tr. by G. Murray, New York, 1943; *Greek Literature in Translation,* ed. by W. J. Oates and C. T. Murphy and tr. by E. Morshead and P. More, New York, 1944; *Plays of the Greek Dramatists,* tr. by A. Way, New York, 1946; *Greek Plays in Modern Translation,* ed. by D. Fitts and tr. by R. Lattimore et al., New York, 1947; *The Portable Greek Reader,* ed. by W. H. Auden and tr. by G. Thomson, New York, 1948; *Seven Famous Greek Plays,* ed. by W. J. Oates and E. J. O'Neill and tr. by E. Morshead and P. More, New York, 1950; *An Anthology of World Literature,* ed. by P. M. Buck, Jr., and H. S. Alberson and tr. by J. Blackie, Jr., 3d ed., New York, 1951; *An Anthology of Greek Drama,* ed. by C. A. Robinson, Jr., and tr. by G. Thomson, 2d ser., New York, 1954; *Greek Drama for Everyman,* ed. and tr. by F. L. Lucas, London, 1954; *Six Greek Plays in Modern Translation,* ed. by D. Fitts and tr. by G. Thomson, New York, 1955; *Ten Greek Plays in Contemporary Translations,* ed. by L. R. Lind and tr. by L. MacNeice and R. Warner, Boston, 1957; *Greek Tragedies,* ed. and tr. by D. Grene and R. Lattimore, 3 vols., Chicago, 1960.

Individual Plays.

Agamemnon. A. C. Person, ed., and W. Headlam, tr., Cambridge, England, 1910; E. Fraenkel, ed., 3 vols., Oxford, 1950; J. D. Denniston and D. Page, eds., New York, 1957; also published in *The Genius of the Greek Drama,* ed. and tr. by C. E. Robinson, Oxford, 1921; *Four Famous Greek Plays,* ed. by P. N. Landis and tr. by L. Campbell, New York, 1929; *Poetic Drama,* ed. by A. Kreymborg and tr. by E. Hamilton, New York, 1941; *Greek Literature in Translation,* ed. by G. Howe and G. A. Harrer and tr. by

E. Morshead, rev. ed., New York, 1948; *An Anthology of Greek Drama,* ed. by C. A. Robinson, Jr., and tr. by G. Thomson, 1st ser., New York, 1949; *A Book of Dramas,* ed. by B. Carpenter and tr. by G. Murray, rev. ed., New York, 1949; *Classics in Translation,* ed. by P. MacKendrick and H. M. Howe and tr. by L. MacNeice, vol. 1, Madison, Wis., 1952; *Writers of the Western World,* ed. by C. A. Hibbard and H. Frenz and tr. by E. Plumptre, 2d ed., Boston, 1954; *Masterworks of World Literature,* ed. by E. M. Everett et al., vol. 1, New York, 1955; *Nine Great Plays, from Aeschylus to Eliot,* ed. by L F. Dean and tr. by L. MacNeice, rev. ed., New York, 1956; *Four Greek Plays,* ed. by D. Fitts and tr. by L. MacNeice, New York, 1960; *The Continental Edition of World Masterpieces,* ed. by M. Mack et al. and tr. by L. MacNeice, New York, 1962.

The Libation Bearers. A. Sidgwick, ed., rev. ed., New York, 1900.

Oresteia. G. Thomson, ed., 2 vols., Cambridge, England, 1938; G. Murray, tr., 2d ed., London, 1946.

The Persians. A. Sidgwick, ed., New York, 1903; H. D. Broadhead, ed., Cambridge, England, 1960.

Prometheus Bound. Published in *Attic Tragedies,* vol. 3, Boston, 1927; *Heath Readings in the Literature of Europe,* ed. by T. P. Cross and C. H. Slover and tr. by E. Plumptre, Boston, 1933; *World Drama,* ed. by B. H. Clark and tr. by J. Blackie, Jr., New York, 1933; *World Literature,* ed. by E. A. Cross and tr. by E. Browning, New York, 1935; *Three Greek Tragedies in Translation,* tr. by D. Grene, Chicago, 1942; *Chief Patterns of World Drama,* ed. by W. S. Clark II and tr. by C. Mendell, Boston, 1946; *Greek and Roman Classics in Translation,* ed. by C. T. Murphy, K. Guinagh, and W. J. Oates and tr. by P. More, New York, 1947; *The Art of the Play,* ed. by A. S. Downer and tr. by E. Hamilton, New York, 1955; *Eight Great Tragedies,* ed. by S. Barnet et al. and tr. by E. Havelock, New York, 1957.

CRITICISM

L. Campbell, *Tragic Drama in Aeschylus, Sophocles, and Shakespeare,* New York, 1904; H. W. Smyth, *Aeschylean Tragedy,* Berkeley, Calif., 1924; G. Murray, *Aeschylus, the Creator of Tragedy,* Oxford, 1940; G. Thomson, *Aeschylus and Athens,* London, 1941; W. B. Stanford, *Aeschylus in His Style,* Dublin, 1942; A. Turyn, *The Manuscript Tradition in the Tragedies of Aeschylus,* New York, 1943; F. R. Earp, *The Style of Aeschylus,* Cambridge, England, 1948; F. Solmsen, *Hesiod and Aeschylus,* Ithaca, N.Y.,1949; E.T.Owen,*The Harmony of Aeschylus,* Toronto, 1952; H. J. Finley, *Pindar and Aeschylus,* Cambridge, Mass., 1955; H. J. Rose, *A Commentary on the Surviving Plays of Aeschylus,* 2 vols., Amsterdam, 1957–1958; R. Kuhns, *The House, the City, and the Judge: The Growth of Moral Awareness in the "Oresteia,"* Indianapolis, 1962; J. T. Sheppard, *Aeschylus and Sophocles: Their Work and Influence,* reprint, New York, 1963; R. D. Dawe, *Collation and Investigation of Manuscripts of Aeschylus,* Cambridge, England, 1964; G. Italie, *Index Aeschylus,* Leiden, 1964; R. D. Dawe, *Repertory of Conjectures on Aeschylus,* New York, 1965; W. H. Matheson, *Claudel and Aeschylus,* Ann Arbor, Mich., 1965; A. J. Podlecki, *Political Background of Aeschylean Tragedy,* Ann Arbor, Mich., 1966.

Aleksandr Nikolayevich Afinogenov
(1904 – 1941)

Aleksandr Nikolayevich Afinogenov, Soviet Russian dramatist, was born in Skopin on March 22, 1904 (O.S.), the son of a self-educated peasant writer and a schoolteacher, both active revolutionaries. Afinogenov joined the Young Communist League and became active in party work, and in 1922 he entered the Institute of Journalism in Moscow. His first play, *Robert Tim* (1923), was presented at the Proletkult Theatre in 1923. Before deciding to write exclusively for the theatre, Afinogenov worked on the Yaroslavl newspaper *Severny Rabochy,* but in 1926 his career as a dramatist began with the staging of *The Other Side of the Slot (Po tu storonu shcheli).* From 1926 to 1928 his plays were staged at the Proletkult Theatre, of which he became one of the earliest leaders and proponents. These early plays dealt with instructive themes for the enlightenment of Communist youth and the proletariat, and all were directed toward the creation of a proletarian culture. Afinogenov's later plays were more creative and individualistic. With *The Eccentric (Chudak,* 1929) and *Fear (Strakh,* 1930) he exhibited his best work.

In 1928 Afinogenov broke ideologically with the Proletkult Theatre when he wrote *The Eccentric* and became a member of the Russian Association of Proletarian Writers (RAPP), an orthodox organization many of whose members, like Afinogenov, sincerely believed in its purpose of producing "Communist" art. Afinogenov was perhaps the best dramatist in RAPP at the time, but his best play, *Fear,* won renown because of its production by Konstantin Stanislavski and the Moscow Art Theatre, two class enemies. RAPP did not approve of *Fear* or of Afinogenov's theoretical work on dramatic art, *The Creative Method of the Theatre (Tvor-*

Aleksandr Afinogenov. [Theatre Collection, The New York Public Library at Lincoln Center, Astor, Lenox and Tilden Foundations]

chesky metod teatra, 1931). Eventually the organization became so vigorous in its persecution of "nonproletarian" writing that comparatively faithful proletarian writers such as Afinogenov became disenchanted. Finally, in 1932, recognizing the harm in this policy, Stalin dissolved RAPP and instituted the Union of Soviet Writers. Soon, because of his insistence on the psychological portrayal of real characters, Afinogenov was attacked by Nikolay Pogodin, who was supported by the major critics. But by 1934 the principles of socialist realism were firmly set down, and Afinogenov slowly accommodated himself to them, as is shown in his plays after that date. *See* POGODIN, NIKOLAY.

In 1937, during the period of the Moscow trials, Afinogenov was among the writers arrested and expelled from the Communist party. But eventually, after the purge had run its course, his party membership was restored. When the U.S.S.R. entered World War II, Afinogenov became the head of the Literary Department of the Sovinformbyuro (Soviet Information Bureau). On October 29, 1941, he was killed during an air raid on Moscow.

WORK

Initially a theorist who tried to apply the methods of dialectical materialism to the stage, Afinogenov began by creating a number of mediocre, artificial plays: Communist melodramas and undistinguished dramas about workers' movements in other countries. His early Proletkult Theatre plays represent the two central themes then popular with proponents of proletarian culture. One theme, the early labor struggles in other countries, was represented in *Robert Tim* (1923), about the weavers' revolt in England early in the nineteenth century; *The Other Side of the Slot* (1926), based on a Jack London story about an early-twentieth-century strike in San Francisco; and *At the Turning Point (Na perelome,* 1926), which deals with socioeconomic unrest in Germany during World War I. The second theme, the constant vigilance and alertness needed to be a good Communist, is represented in *Keep Your Eyes Open (Glyadi v oba,* 1927), describing student life and the hero's encounter with forces inimical to the U.S.S.R.; *Raspberry Jam (Malinovoye varenye,* 1928), about the danger resulting from a Red Army officer's neglect of duty; and *The Trail of the Wolf (Volchya tropa,* 1928), in which an old engineer vainly tries to conceal his non-proletarian past.

As Afinogenov matured, his individualism asserted itself. To a greater degree than the works of his more orthodox contemporaries, his plays written between 1928 and 1933 are psychological, analytical, and profound. The first of these was *The Eccentric* (1929), the young hero of which is not only a non-Communist but a romantic, an idealist, and something of an intellectual. Although naïve, he is basically good, whereas the Communists in the piece can be considered villainous. *The Eccentric* initiated a break in the relationship between Afinogenov and the Proletkult Theatre for reasons best described by the *Great Soviet Encyclopedia:*

In this play, Afinogenov combined a sharp political theme—the call to intellectuals to join in the building of socialism—with a profound portrayal of the psychology of the dramatis personae. However, Afinogenov incorrectly portrayed the character of the Communists and did not succeed in showing the organizational role of the party in the building of socialism.

Afinogenov's best play, *Fear* (1930), portrays the ideological and psychological con-

Listen, Professor! with (l. to r.) Susan Robinson, Frances Reid, and Dudley Digges. New York, Forrest Theatre, 1943. [Photograph by Vandamm. Theatre Collection, The New York Public Library at Lincoln Center, Astor, Lenox and Tilden Foundations]

flict between the ideals of Professor Borodin, a scientist and a member of the old intelligentsia, and the realities of the new Communist order. Borodin finally sees the error of his bourgeois philosophy and repents, but not before he reveals his theory that fear motivates people and that science should be free from political ideology. *The Lie* (*Lozh*, 1933), a psychological analysis in which Afinogenov tries to reconcile personal conflicts with Communist bias and socially pragmatic purposes, had only two performances.

In 1934 Afinogenov accommodated his work to the literary dictates of socialist realism and became one of its better dramatists. His psychological style, now very much modified, helped him portray ordinary human beings realistically. His best plays of this period are *Distant Point* (*Dalyokoye*, 1935), describing the need for recognition in people who live in a remote, forgotten whistle-stop; and *Mashenka* (1941), about a Soviet Heidi who gives new meaning to her grandfather's life. Afinogenov's last play, *On the Eve* (*Nakanune*, 1942), takes place on the eve of the Nazi invasion and describes the effect it has on a Russian family.

The Eccentric (*Chudak*, 1929). Psychological drama depicting the struggles of Boris Volgin, a non-Communist worker in a paper factory. Bold in concept and novel in style, the play unfolds Volgin's personal drama against a background of the mass enthusiasm in the early days of socialist industrialization. Struggling against indifference, bureaucracy, favoritism, and anti-Semitism, the young, idealistic Volgin confronts such external difficulties as slander, betrayal, and his wife's infidelity as well as internal, psychological problems, such as his inability to fight for personal causes. Courageous in implementing socialist goals, he is too softhearted, too proud, and not sufficiently self-centered to stand up for his rights. A romantic in love, he loses his wife to a cunning friend; an honest worker, he is framed, unjustly accused, and dismissed. Yet he is triumphant, not so much because he is eventually reinstated, for the villains are not really punished, as because he continues to carry a dream in his heart.

Fear (*Strakh*, 1930). Professor Borodin, director of the Institute of Physiological Stimuli, is a prerevolutionary intellectual who refuses to accept the dictatorship of the proletariat in his laboratory and deplores the proletariat's lack of scientific objectivity. With Kastalsky, his favorite pupil, Borodin has been working on extensive experiments that have led him to believe that fear determines man's conduct even more than the basic stimuli of hunger, love, and hate. Borodin presents this theory, based on his research, in

a paper that he reads at a scientific meeting. He recommends that to make the proletariat more efficient the Soviet government must eliminate methods based on fear, reorganize its system of administration according to Borodin's scientific findings, and direct the masses through science. As a scientist, he is completely confused by the resulting uproar. Klara, the old Bolshevik, denounces him and "shows" him the faultiness of his thinking, after which he is arrested by the secret police. Kastalsky, caught while attempting to escape across the border, turns out to be a counterrevolutionary and a scoundrel; he renounces Borodin at the GPU headquarters. The proletariat has crushed its opposition, and Borodin sees the error in his thought. Once liberated from prison, he submits to the new order and starts anew as a scientist "devoted to the party and government."

Distant Point (*Dalykoye*, 1935). Matthew, a Red Army commander, finds himself in a tiny, isolated collective near a railroad siding in the Siberian forest when his train is forced to stop there for repairs. The event is an exciting one for the inhabitants of the community, who turn out with patriotic zeal to welcome the hero. Most of the inhabitants are warmhearted, dedicated Communists. Only Vlas is arrogant, and Lavrenty is dissatisfied, for he wants to desert his wife and go to the city. During Matthew's stay the little community learns that he is dying of an incurable disease. Moved by his heroism, the citizens begin to lay plans for their own self-improvement. One decides to establish a sable farm; another, to prospect for gold. Even the faithless Vlas is humbled before the commander's courage, and Lavrenty is shamed into staying home with his wife.

PLAYS

1. *Robert Tim*. Drama, 4 acts. Published 1924. Produced Moscow, Proletkult Theatre, 1923.
2. *Po tu storonu shcheli** (*The Other Side of the Slot*). Play. Published 1926. Produced Moscow, Proletkult Theatre, 1926. Based on a story by Jack London.
3. *Na perelome* (*At the Turning Point*). Drama, 4 acts. Published 1926. Produced Moscow, Proletkult Theatre, 1927.
4. *Glyadi v oba* (*Keep Your Eyes Open*). Play. Published 1927. Produced Moscow, Proletkult Theatre, 1927.
5. *Malinovoye varenye* (*Raspberry Jam*). Play, 4 acts. Published 1927. Produced Moscow, Proletkult Theatre, 1928.
6. *Tovarishch Yanshin* (*Comrade Yanshin*). Play. Published 1927.
7. *Volchya tropa* (*The Trail of the Wolf*). Drama. Published 1928. Produced Leningrad, Krasny Theatre, 1928.
8. (Adaptation). *Chyorny yar* (*The Black Ravine*). Play. Produced First Pedagogichesky Theatre, 1928. Based on a novel by Lev Gumilyovsky.
9. *Chudak* (*The Eccentric*). Drama, 4 acts. Published 1929. Produced Moscow, Second Moscow Art Theatre, 1929.

10. *Strakh** (*Fear*). Drama, 4 acts. Published 1930. Produced Leningrad, Leningrad Academic Dramatic Theatre, and Moscow, Moscow Art Theatre, 1930.

11. *Lozh* (*The Lie*). Drama. Written 1933. Produced Kharkov, Theatre of the Russian Drama (two performances), 1933.

12. *Portret* (*The Portrait*). Drama, 3 acts. Published 1934. Produced Leningrad, State Theatre of Drama, 1934.

13. *Dalyokoye** (*Distant Point; also translated as Far Taiga*). Drama, 3 acts. Published 1935. Produced Moscow, Vakhtangov Theatre, 1935.

14. *Salyut, Ispaniya!* (*Greetings, Spain!*). Drama, 2 parts and epilogue. Published 1936. Produced Moscow, Theatre of the Moscow Soviet, 1936.

15. *Eyo igra* (*Her Game*). Comedy. Written 1938.

16. *Vtorye puti* (*Second Roads*). Play, 3 acts. Published 1939. Produced Moscow, Theatre of Transportation, 1939.

17. *Mat svoikh detey* (*The Mother of Her Children*). Play, 3 acts. Published 1939. Produced in all parts of the Soviet Union, 1954–1955.

18. *Otel Lyuks* (*Deluxe Hotel*). Tragicomedy, 3 acts. Written 1940.

19. *Mashenka** (*Mashenka; also translated as Listen, Professor!*). Comedy, 3 acts. Published 1940. Produced Moscow, Theatre of the Moscow Soviet, 1941.

20. *Nakanune* (*On the Eve*). Drama, 3 acts. Written 1940/41. Published 1942. Produced Moscow, Theatre of the Moscow Soviet, 1942.

EDITIONS

Collections.
Izbrannoye, Moscow, 1951; *Pyesy*, Moscow and Leningrad, 1947, Moscow, 1956; *Statyi, dnevniki, pisma*, ed. by A. O. Boguslavsky, Moscow, 1957.

Individual Plays.
Distant Point (*Far Taiga*). Published in *Soviet Scene: Six Plays of Russian Life,* ed. by A. Bakshy, Yale, New Haven, Conn., 1946.

Fear. Published in *Six Soviet Plays,* ed. by E. Lyons and tr. by C. Malamuth, Houghton Mifflin, Boston, 1934.

On the Eve. Published in *Seven Soviet Plays,* ed. by H. W. L. Dana and tr. by E. Afinogenova, Macmillan, New York, 1946.

CRITICISM

A. O. Boguslavsky, *A. N. Afinogenov: Ocherk zhizn i tvorchestva,* Moscow, 1952; A. V. Karaganov, *Aleksandr Afinogenov: Kritico-biografichesky ocherk,* Moscow, 1957.

AHERN, JAMES. *See* HERNE, JAMES A.

AHLSEN, Leopold (1927–   ). German dramatist. He studied Germanic philology, psychology, and theatre at the University of Munich, receiving scholarships from the Deutsche Schauspielschule (German Drama School). An actor and director at southern German theatres between 1947 and 1949, he later lectured over the Bavarian Radio on the subject of radio drama.

Ahlsen's plays, simple and unpretentious, express the antimilitarism of his generation, as in *Philemon and Baucis* (*Philemon und Baukis,* 1956), also known as *The Trees Are Standing Outside* (*Die Bäume stehen draussen*), a commentary on a people's involvement in war, set in Greece in 1944. The hero and heroine, having aided partisan fighters hiding in the woods, also help a wounded German soldier. For this they are condemned by their countrymen, and they go to their death drunk and hand in hand. Anti-Communism is the theme of *Time of the Wolf* (*Wolfszeit,* 1954), a series of pictures dramatizing, in a style reminiscent of Hauptmann's *The Weavers,* the Bolshevik Revolution of November, 1917. Ahlsen deals in serious comedy with *You Will Die, Sire* (*Sie werden sterben, Sire,* 1963), in which a king is isolated from society in the solitude of impending death, in much the same way as the characters of Ionesco, although Ahlsen puts him in a specific historical setting. Other dramas are *Poor Luther* (*Der arme Mann Luther,* 1965), *Duty to Sin* (*Pflicht zur Sünde*), and *Raskolnikoff. See* HAUPTMANN, GERHART; IONESCO, EUGÈNE.

Ahlsen has written *All Power on Earth* (*Alle Macht der Erde*) for television; and his radio plays—which include *Philemon and Baucis, Time and Mr. Adolar Lehmann* (*Die Zeit und Herr Adolar Lehmann*), *Niki and the Yellow Paradise* (*Niki und das Paradies in Gelb*), and *Ballad of the Half Century* (*Die Ballade vom halben Jahrhundert*)—earned him the Radio Drama Award of the War Blind in 1955. He also received the Gerhart Hauptmann Award in 1955 and the Schiller Incentive Award in 1957.

AIKEN, George (1830–1876). American actor and dramatist, remembered for his dramatization in 1852 of Harriet Beecher Stowe's novel *Uncle Tom's Cabin* (1852).

George Aiken.
[Brander Matthews Dramatic Museum, Columbia University]

AKINS, Zoë (1886–1958). American poet, screenwriter, and dramatist whose observations of the American scene were made droll by her graceful humor and wit. Her drama *Déclassée* (1919) was typical of her early, more serious plays. A great success, it describes the decline of an English noblewoman because of her love for a man other than her husband. Soon after, Miss Akins turned to light romantic comedies such as *Daddy's Gone a-Hunting* (1921), based on the conflict between love and art; *The Varying Shore* (1921); *The Texas Nightingale* (1922); *A Royal Fandango* (1923); *The Greeks Had a Word for It* (1930); *O Evening Star* (1936); *Another Darling* (1950); and *The Swallow's Nest* (1950). Her later years were occupied with writing screenplays. Her 1935 dramatization of Edith Wharton's *The Old Maid* won her a Pulitzer Prize.

Judith Anderson and Robert Wallsten in *The Old Maid.* New York, Empire Theatre, 1935. [Photograph by Vandamm. Theatre Collection, The New York Public Library at Lincoln Center, Astor, Lenox and Tilden Foundations]

Zoë Akins's *The Greeks Had a Word for It*, with (l. to r.) Muriel Kirkland, Verree Teasdale, and Dorothy Hall. New York, Sam H. Harris Theatre, 1930. [Photograph by Vandamm. Theatre Collection, The New York Public Library at Lincoln Center, Astor, Lenox and Tilden Foundations]

Edward Albee
(1928 –)

Edward Franklin Albee, American dramatist, born on March 12, 1928, in Washington, was adopted as an infant by Mr. and Mrs. Reed A. Albee of the Keith-Albee theatre chain. He attended Trinity College in Hartford but left after a year and a half to work intermittently at such odd jobs as writing for a radio station and working as a counterman in a luncheonette. In 1952 he traveled to Florence, where he wrote a novel that has never been published. Returning to New York in 1955, he worked as a Western Union messenger until 1958, when he quit his job to write *The Zoo Story,* a one-act play.

Unable to interest Broadway in this two-character study, Albee sent the manuscript to a friend in Florence, David Diamond, who in turn forwarded it to Mrs. Stefani Hunzinger, the head of the drama department of a German publisher. Finally, in 1959, *The Zoo*

Toby Tompkins as Young Man and Barbara Bryne as Grandma in the Meadow Brook Theatre's 1969–1970 production of *The American Dream.* [Meadow Brook Theatre, Rochester, Mich.]

Edward Albee. [William Morris Agency]

Story, coupled with Samuel Beckett's *Krapp's Last Tape,* was presented at Berlin's Schiller Theater Werkstatt. Early in 1960 the two plays had their New York premiere Off Broadway, and in May, Albee received the Vernon Rice Award. His next play, *The Death of Bessie Smith,* was first presented in Berlin in 1960 and appeared Off Broadway with *The American Dream* in 1961. The combination won Albee the Lola D'Annunzio Award for sustained accomplishment in original playwriting. *See* BECKETT, SAMUEL.

In October, 1962, Albee made a successful Broadway debut with his first three-act play, *Who's Afraid of Virginia Woolf?* This vitriolic study of a decaying marriage established him as an important American playwright and won him an Antoinette Perry Award, the New York Drama Critics Circle award, and the Outer Circle Award. His later plays include *The Ballad of the Sad Café* (1963) and *Malcolm* (wr. 1965), both adaptations of novels; *Tiny Alice* (1964); *A Delicate Balance* (1966), for which he won the Pulitzer Prize; and *All Over* (1971), a play about death.

WORK

Edward Albee rose to prominence as a major American playwright in the 1960s, gaining initial recognition with a handful of one-act plays that examined a sterile world either suffused with cruelty or lacking in compassion and love. This attitude permeates all his subsequent plays, in which civilized institutions are represented as shams or sentimentalized conventions: family, school, marriage, and home exude false values.

Albee's work also displays his acute psychological perception. Cruelty is presented as a perverse form of communication, and trun-

Scene from *The Zoo Story*, with Scott Hylands (left) and Robert Goldsby, at the Marines' Memorial Theatre, San Francisco. [Courtesy American Conservatory Theatre, San Francisco, Calif. Photograph by Hank Kranzler]

cated characters love only the persons or things that may injure them, as in his adaptation of Carson McCullers's *The Ballad of the Sad Café* (1963). *See* MCCULLERS, CARSON.

In Albee's highly acclaimed first play, *The Zoo Story* (1959), Jerry, primitive and direct, desperately tries to make contact with Peter, rendered artificial and remote by affluence. Frustrated by the distance between them, Jerry tries to communicate but, unable to bear Peter's smug self-esteem, causes Peter to murder him. Thus the two are finally joined at the moment of death by a knife, the agent of death. *The American Dream* (1961) is a

burlesque satirizing the most respected American institutions: family, motherhood, marital love. Puncturing the complacent and self-congratulatory claims of an affluent society is basic strategy in Albee's moral assault. He sees America as a decadent culture supported by sterile institutions that extend from the conventional bourgeoisie, represented by Mommy and Daddy in *The American Dream,* to the intellectual community of *Who's Afraid of Virginia Woolf?* (1962). The latter play, Albee's first full-length drama, shocks through its suggestion that the principal couple, George and Martha, sustain their

marriage and themselves through continual mutually destructive acts of verbal and physical violence. In *Tiny Alice* (1964) a lay brother searches for the abstraction of God rather than the empty personification provided by the church.

Critics have asserted that Albee fails to balance the pretense and corruption he decries with positive values. Some, however, claim that positive values are implicit in such plays as *The Death of Bessie Smith* (1960), in which anger is directed against American racial prejudice as a great Negro singer dies when a Southern hospital refuses to admit her because she is black; and *Who's Afraid of Virginia Woolf?*, the conclusion of which intimates a redemptive beginning for an embattled couple. In the Pulitzer Prize-winning *A Delicate Balance* (1966), Tobias struggles to accept his friends as permanent guests and to live by the Christian principle of loving-kindness. Albee reveals a moralizing nature in his affinity for Christianity and its ritual, as demonstrated in the simulated crucifixions ending both *The Zoo Story* and *Tiny Alice*.

Crisp dialogue with changing tempos, crescendos, and diminuendos not only demonstrates Albee's mastery of both colloquial and recondite speech and tightly controlled form but also adds to the symbolic meaning of the plays. In *Who's Afraid of Virginia Woolf?* and *The Zoo Story,* for example, the changing rhythms of the dialogue match the mood and meaning of the plays.

Among Albee's other plays are *The Sandbox* (1960), a minor one-act forerunner of *The American Dream; Malcolm* (1966), an adaptation of the novel by James Purdy; and *Everything in the Garden,* based on the play by Giles Cooper concerning suburban wives and their realization that a few hours in a big-city brothel can solve their financial problems.

The Zoo Story (1959). Symbolic and realistic one-scene play set in a park where Peter, a conventional, "civilized" middle-class executive passing an inoffensive afternoon reading on a park bench is goaded by Jerry, the eternal outsider, into a conversation. As Jerry probes in vain for a point of contact with

Peter, he finds himself moving from a psychological confession to actual physical combat for the bench. He pushes Peter, whose indifference he has otherwise been unable to pierce, off the bench. Step by step, with blows and gibes, Jerry compels Peter to defend himself; finally he tosses an open knife at Peter's feet. As Peter, in rage and self-protection, clutches the knife, Jerry thrusts himself onto it. While his life ebbs, Jerry virtually blesses Peter, for by this act the two men have finally come together.

The American Dream (1961). Caricature satirizing life in middle-class America. Mommy and Daddy, paragons of inane convention, await the representative from the Adoption Service, who is to bring a replacement for the adopted child Mommy destroyed years before. Grandma, who expects to be carted off momentarily, makes ironic comments on their behavior. When a muscularly handsome young man dressed in the tee shirt and blue jeans familiar to motion-picture and television audiences enters in search of a job, Grandma dubs him "the American Dream." Despite his obvious indifference and coolness, he offers good looks and sexual prowess, and the family adopts him. As they celebrate with

a toast, Grandma wryly tells the audience, "Everybody's got what he thinks he wants."

Who's Afraid of Virginia Woolf? (1962). Realistic drama in three acts entitled "Fun and Games," "Walpurgisnacht," and "Exorcism," about the ritualized marital war between George, professor of history at New Carthage, and his wife Martha, daughter of the college president. Returning late from a faculty party, George discovers, to his irritation, that Martha has invited Nick, a new member of the science faculty, and his pregnant young wife Honey for a nightcap. George and Martha continue their verbal sparring with practiced familiarity, the young couple at first being only bewildered onlookers. But as the night wears on and liquor is consumed, the fun and games grow more vituperative and involve the guests as well. Despite George's cryptic warnings, Martha reveals the secret that has so long been a

Box-Mao-Box, with Jenny Egan (foreground), Lucille Patton (left), William Needles (right), and Conrad Yama (background). [Studio Arena Theatre, Buffalo, N.Y. Photograph by Greenberg-May Prod. Inc.]

Scene from *A Delicate Balance*, with Barbara Colby (left) and Ellen Geer, at the Marines' Memorial Theatre, San Francisco. [Courtesy American Conservatory Theatre, San Francisco, Calif. Photograph by Hank Kranzler]

Harry Frazier
(right) as the
Cardinal and
Paul Shenar
as Brother
Julian in *Tiny
Alice.* [Courtesy
American
Conservatory
Theatre, San
Francisco, Calif.
Photograph by
Hank Kranzler]

support of their lives together: they have a
son. Now the exchange of insults mounts
intensely, becoming a Walpurgisnacht of
mutual revilement. Martha taunts George
about his unpublished novel and flaunts her
seductive power over the compliant Nick. Finally, George's affected indifference goads
her into adultery with Nick, who fails to consummate the act. In retaliation for this last
attempt at emasculation, George invents a
telegram with news of their son's death.
Before divulging it, however, he urges Martha to recite a litany of their son's life while
he declaims, in counterpoint, the Mass for the
dead. With Martha's genuine collapse on
learning the news and her beseeching questions, Nick realizes that the child was an illusion sustained by the barren couple as a bond.
Nick and Honey then leave with a new
awareness of their insufficiencies, and Martha and George are left emotionally spent by
the exorcism.They accept the death of the illusion they had created, thus creating the
possibility of a new start without the aid of
illusions.

Tiny Alice (1964). Three-act play with
metaphysical overtones. After receiving an
offer of 2 billion dollars from Miss Alice, a
mysterious philanthropist, the Catholic
Church sends Julian, a lay brother, as its
emissary to complete the seemingly innocu-
ous business arrangements. In Miss Alice's
drawing room Julian finds that there is a
giant dollhouse replica of the manor. He is
subjected to a peculiar catechism by Miss
Alice's strange aides, a lawyer and a butler
who are her partners in a hieratical rite that
gradually involves Julian. Seduced by Miss
Alice, he marries her and discovers to his dismay that his bride was only the symbol of a
mystical presence that exists in the model
castle. He has been sacrificed, he realizes, to
that presence. When he refuses to accept this
sacrificial role, Miss Alice's lawyer shoots
him, and Julian is left to die before the dollhouse. As his life ebbs, the dollhouse seems to
come alive. A black formlessness engulfs him
while a giant heartbeat booms nearer and
nearer.

A Delicate Balance (1966). Drama set in
the living room of a wealthy suburban home
where Tobias drinks and grows increasingly
restless as his wife Agnes and her alcoholic
sister Claire argue. Tobias tolerates Claire's
drinking, as well as Agnes's invective against
her sister, with only an occasional mild
remonstration. Agnes exits to make a long-
distance telephone call to her daughter Julia
and returns to announce that Julia, having
left her fourth husband, is coming home the
next day. Harry and Edna, close friends of
Tobias and Agnes, arrive and ask to stay the
night because they feel the presence of a
nameless terror in their own home. The following evening, Julia complains bitterly
about having to share her room with Harry
and Edna. When their luggage arrives and it
becomes clear that they intend to remain in-
definitely, Julia becomes hysterical and
threatens the couple with a pistol. Edna declares that as friends they have a right to
stay. Forced to decide the matter, Tobias
agrees, but after everyone has retired for the
night, he stays behind, trying to reconcile
himself to the situation. The next morning,
Tobias tells Harry that the couple does have
the right to remain and begs him to assert
that right, even though he, Tobias, may not
want him to stay. Harry sadly declines, however, confessing that neither he nor Edna
could have accepted such a claim on friendship if the others had come to them, and so
they leave.

PLAYS

Unless otherwise noted, the plays were first performed
in New York.

1. *The Zoo Story.* Play, 1 scene. Written 1958. Published 1960. Produced West Berlin, Schiller Theater,
Werkstatt, Sept. 28, 1959; New York, Provincetown Playhouse, Jan. 14, 1960.

Paul Shenar and DeAnn Mears as Miss Alice in *Tiny Alice*. [Courtesy American Conservatory Theatre, San Francisco, Calif. Photograph by Hank Kranzler]

2. *The Death of Bessie Smith*. Play, 8 scenes. Written 1959. Published 1960. Produced West Berlin, Schlosspark Theater, Apr. 21, 1960; New York, Mar. 1, 1961.

3. *The Sandbox*. Play, 1 scene. Written 1959. Published 1960. Produced Jazz Gallery, Apr. 15, 1960.

4. *Fam and Yam*. Play, 1 act. Written 1960. Produced Westport, Conn., White Barn Theatre, Aug. 27, 1960; New York, Theatre de Lys, Oct. 25, 1960.

5. *The American Dream*. Play, 1 act. Written 1960. Published 1961. Produced York Playhouse, Jan. 24, 1961.

6. (With William Flanagan and James Hinton, Jr.). *Bartleby*. Play, 1 act. Produced York Playhouse, Jan. 24, 1961. Original companion piece to *The American Dream*, replaced by *The Death of Bessie Smith* on Mar. 1, 1961. Based on Herman Melville's *Bartleby the Scrivener* (1853).

7. *Who's Afraid of Virginia Woolf?* Play, 3 acts. Written 1962. Published 1962. Produced Billy Rose Theatre, Oct. 13, 1962.

8. (Adaptation). *The Ballad of the Sad Café*. Play, 1 act. Written 1963. Published 1963. Produced Martin Beck Theatre, Oct. 30, 1963. Based on the novel by Carson McCullers (1951).

9. *Tiny Alice*. Play, 3 acts. Written 1964. Published 1965. Produced Billy Rose Theatre, Dec. 29, 1964.

10. (Adaptation). *Malcolm*. Play. Written 1965. Published 1966. Produced Shubert Theatre, Jan. 11, 1966.

Based on the novel by James Purdy (1959).

11. *A Delicate Balance*. Drama. Written 1966. Published 1967. Produced Martin Beck Theatre, Sept. 22, 1966.

12. (Adaptation). *Everything in the Garden*. Play, 2 parts. Written 1967. Published 1968. Produced Plymouth Theatre, Nov. 29, 1967. Based on the play of the same title by Giles Cooper.

13. *Box-Mao-Box*. Collective title of two short plays: *Box* and *Quotations from Chairman Mao*. Published 1969. Produced Buffalo, Studio Arena Theatre, Mar. 6, 1968; New York, Billy Rose Theatre, Sept. 30, 1968.

14. *All Over*. Play. Produced New York, Martin Beck Theatre, Mar. 27, 1971.

EDITIONS

Collections.

The Zoo Story, The Death of Bessie Smith and The Sandbox, New York, 1960; *The American Dream, The Death of Bessie Smith and Fam and Yam*, New York, 1962; *The Zoo Story and Other Plays*, London, 1962; *The Zoo Story and The Sandbox*, New York, 1962; *The American Dream and The Zoo Story*, New York, 1963; *The Sandbox, The Death of Bessie Smith and Fam and Yam*, New York, 1963; *The Sandbox; The Death of Bessie Smith*, New York, 1964.

Individual Plays.

The American Dream. Coward-McCann, New York, 1961.

The Ballad of the Sad Café. Houghton Mifflin, Boston, 1963.

A Delicate Balance. Pocket Books, New York, 1968.

Everything in the Garden. Atheneum, New York, 1968.

Malcolm. Atheneum, New York, 1966.

The Sandbox. Published in *Modern Drama for Analysis,* ed. by P. M. Cubeta, 3d ed., Holt, New York, 1962.

Tiny Alice. Pocket Books, New York, 1966.

Who's Afraid of Virginia Woolf? Pocket Books, New York, 1963.

The Zoo Story. Published in *Famous American Plays of the 1950's,* ed. by L. Strasberg, Dell, New York, 1962; *Classics of the Modern Theater: Realism and After,* ed. by A. B. Kernan, Harcourt, Brace & World, New York, 1965; *Twentieth Century Drama: England, Ireland, the United States,* ed. by R. Cohn and B. Dukore, Random House, New York, 1966.

CRITICISM

R. E. Amacher, *Edward Albee,* New York, 1968; N. Vos, *Ionesco and Albee: Theatre of the Absurd,* Grand Rapids, Mich., 1968; M. E. Rutenberg, *Edward Albee: Playwright in Protest,* Drama Book Shop Publications, New York, 1969.

ALBERTI, Rafael (b. Puerto de Santa María, Cádiz Province, December 16, 1902). Spanish painter, poet, and dramatist who has been influenced by García Lorca. His drama *From One Moment to the Next* (*De un momento a otro,* 1936) reveals the difficulties experienced by a Spanish family in a time of social unrest. Because of the socially provocative nature of his work, Alberti left Spain after the Spanish Civil War, and he presently resides in Argentina. His other works include *The Game of Forfeits* (*La pájara pinta,* 1925); *St. Casilda* (*Santa Casilda,* 1930; now lost); *The Deserted Man* (*El hombre deshabitado,* 1931), which has elements of the classical picture of the "loner" and is done as a one-act religious drama; *Fermín Galán* (1931), a poetic work; *The South Coast of Death* (*Costa sur de la muerte,* 1936), showing the influence of social unrest in Spain; and *Cantata of Heroes and the Fraternity of Peoples* (*Cantata de los héroes y la fraternidad de los pueblos,* 1938), a salute to allied antifascist intellectuals. Among Alberti's works written in Argentina between 1940 and 1945 are *The Flowering Trefoil* (*El trébol florido*), a tragicomedy; *The Galliard* (*La gallarda*), a tragedy about cowboys; and *The Folly* (*El adefesio*), about love and old age. See GARCÍA LORCA, FEDERICO.

From One Moment to the Next (*De un momento a otro,* 1936). Drama that depicts the torment of the Spanish Civil War. Gabriel, an educated son of a wealthy family, joins the Republicans' struggle. He tries to convince his sister Araceli to do so too, and in their discussions the tragedy of turning against one's background to fight for ideals becomes very clear. His most obstinate enemies are his brother and an old school friend, and when at the end of the play Gabriel is killed, Araceli seems to fear that they are responsible.

ALECSANDRI, Vasile (1821–1890). Romanian dramatist, born in Bacău, who studied at home with French tutors and then at the Cuénim boarding school in Iaşi (Jassy). In 1834 he was sent to France for further studies in law and literature, studies that he pursued without taking a degree. Returning to his country in 1839 after travels through Great Britain, Italy, and Austria, he devoted himself to cultural and political activity. He made his literary debut in 1840 in the review *Literary Dacia* (*Dacia Literară*) with the story "The Flower Girl of Florence." With Mihai Kogălniceanu and Costache Negruzzi he managed the National Theatre in Iaşi from 1840 to 1842; then with Kogălniceanu and Ion Ghica he issued in 1844 the magazine *Progress: Scientific and Literary Paper* (*Propăsirea: Foaie stiintifică si literară*). Four years later he took part in the revolution in Moldavia, and in 1859, in the political struggle for the union of the principalities of Moldavia and Walachia. From 1885 to 1889 he served as Minister Plenipotentiary of Romania in Paris. Meanwhile, in 1867, he had become a member of the Romanian Literary Society, which evolved into the Romanian Academy in 1879.

Alecsandri's collection of Romanian folk poetry published in 1852 was the first of its sort to appear in his country. Subsequently

Vasile Alecsandri. [Editura Enciclopedică Română, Bucharest]

he wrote many poems evoking the Romanian people's tradition of struggle (the cycle *Legends*), the awakening of national consciousness (*Romania's Awakening*), the union of the principalities (*The Hora of the Union*), and the War of Independence (the cycle *Our Soldiers*), as well as picaresque stories (*The Story of a Ducat and a Farthing,* 1844) and travel memoirs (*Journey to Africa,* 1855). In addition, he was the founder of the national dramatic repertory theatre, which performed many of his plays. On January 18, 1844, *Iorgu from Sadagura* was successfully performed; on December 22, 1845, the play *Jassy in Carnival* was produced, followed by a cycle with Mme. Chiriţa as the main character, including *Chiriţa in Jassy* (1850) and *Chiriţa in the Provinces* (1852). In 1860 he took up residence on his estate in Mirceşti and announced that he had finished three plays, *The Leeches of the Village, The Wasteful Miser,* and *Cremene's Village, or Whitsuntide;* and two comical songs. On September 30, 1879, the drama *Voivode* (*Despot Vodă*), for which the Romanian Academy awarded him the Năsturel Herăscu Grand Prize in 1881, was presented at the National Theatre in Bucharest. On March 22, 1883, *The Fountain of Blanduzia* was staged in Bucharest, where it scored a great success. In 1890, feeling ill, Alecsandri retired to Mirceşti, where he died.

WORK

Working in a language still in its literary infancy, Alecsandri contributed to the progress of the Romanian theatre with his light, unpretentious comedies of manners. About the problems of language he wrote: "Romania's playwrights have to strive against four barely superable impediments: (1) the language, which is still that of infancy; (2) the public, which is akin to the language; (3) the actors, who are the same as the public; (4) the censorship." Specifying the social role of the theatre, he said: "Its purpose is to strike a blow at bad manners, which are a blemish in social life, and throw into bold relief the brilliant deeds in the history of the homeland, as well as the noblest feelings of mankind." *See* COMEDY OF MANNERS.

Alecsandri's comedies of manners are best exemplified by his Mme. Chiriţa cycle. *Jassy in Carnival,* through Mme. Chiriţa, satirizes Moldavian society of 1850, sometimes avoiding rigorous censorship by the use of satirical songs. The other plays continue to explore the character of Mme. Chiriţa, at the same time depicting her milieu with even sharper criticism.

Alecsandri's dramatic maturity began with *Voivode,* a play in the manner of Victor Hugo. Conflict, basic to Romanian historical drama, breaks out between the sixteenth-century Voivode's ambition, on the one hand, and the resistance interposed by tradition on the other. Peasants assume the role of a chorus, both hostile and impassive as witnesses to the hero's unrest. Despot is an adventurer of humble origin, ambitious, clever, and captivating, slightly formal and vainglorious in manner. His downfall comes as a result of these very qualities, which are incompatible with his utopian ideals and the actual state of affairs.

Another drama, *The Fountain of Blanduzia* (1883), debates, through Horatio, the relation between the poet and his epoch. Horatio undergoes Goethe's crisis: an exceptional spiritual vitality fighting against man's natural tragedy. In his verse drama *Ovid* (1885), Alecsandri meant to continue the genius's drama by treating the destiny of the famous Latin poet, who was exiled by the emperor Augustus and died on Romanian soil.

Vittorio Alfieri
(1749 — 1803)

Count Vittorio Alfieri, Italian poet, essayist, and dramatist, was born in Asti, Piedmont, on January 16, 1749. He was the son of a noble family of Savoyard descent that spoke French as its first language. From 1758 to

Vittorio Alfieri. [Italian Cultural Institute]

Antigone. [Federico Arborio Mella, Milan]

1766 he attended the Royal Academy of Turin, where he learned little except snatches of Italian literature. After leaving the academy, he spent six years traveling in continental Europe and England. During this period he discovered the works of Voltaire, Rousseau, Montesquieu, and other French writers and began to develop political convictions reflecting a hatred of tyranny and a love of freedom. His reading of Plutarch convinced him that he lived at a time and place inimical to greatness.

Alfieri bought a house in Turin in 1772. There he led the life of an aristocrat, writing his first works for the amusement of his friends. In the year 1774–1775, merely as a mental exercise, he wrote *Cleopatra,* a tragedy in bad Italian verse. Although the play was repudiated by the author and published only posthumously, under the title *Antony and Cleopatra* (*Antonio e Cleopatra*), it was well received at its first performance in

Turin in January, 1775. At last, Alfieri had found a purpose in life: to write great dramatic poetry in Italian. Because he knew more of French literature than of Italian and habitually thought in French—*Polynices* (*Polinice*) and *Philip II* (*Filippo*), which he wrote between 1775 and 1781, were actually first outlined in French prose—Alfieri had to prepare himself for this task. He went to Pisa to learn to think, write, and speak in Tuscan (literary Italian) and remained there for several months. After returning briefly to Turin, he moved to Florence, where he stayed three years. Between 1775 and 1790 he wrote twenty-one tragedies as well as a large number of sonnets; the five odes comprising *Free America* (*L'America libera*), a celebration of the American Revolution; a narrative poem; two prose treatises, *On Tyranny* (*Della tirannide*) and *Essays on Government and Literature* (*Del principe e delle lettere*); a dialogue; and some minor works.

In Paris, in 1777, Alfieri met Louise von Stolberg-Gedern, Countess of Albany and wife of Charles Edward Stuart, the Young Pretender. Although they never married, they were often together in Paris and Alsace, especially after her separation from Prince Charles Edward in 1780. In 1792 they fled from the French Revolution and settled in Florence, where they maintained a joint household for the last eleven years of Alfieri's life.

He continued to write until his death. His last tragedy, which he wrote in 1798, was *Alcestis* (*Alceste*), an adaptation of Euripides's drama (*see* EURIPIDES). Alfieri's hatred of tyranny was extended to the French as a result of the revolution's brutalities and the French occupation of Florence in 1799. His anti-French work *The Gallophobe* (*Il Misogallo,* 1793–1799), a mixture of prose and verse, was dedicated to Italy and the Italians. Ironically, it was the French and those Italians who were pro-French who admired him as a spokesman for freedom and who arranged for presentations of his republican tragedies.

On May 14, 1803, Alfieri finished the second portion of his autobiography, *Vita,* the first half having been completed in Paris in 1790 after his major plays had been written. In this now-classic work, he set himself the task of writing a "life" in the manner of Plutarch and of presenting a moral self-portrait in which he would attempt to establish the extent to which he had successfully adhered to his goals and ideals in both life and art. He died in Florence on October 8, 1803.

WORK

Alfieri wanted to restore Italian playwriting to a high level and undertook an intensive study of Tuscan Italian to aid him in creating dramas worthy of his heritage. He wrote twenty-eight plays, twenty-two of them tragedies, using classical, historical, Biblical, and romantic plots to present his major theme of freedom versus tyranny. His eleven-syllable blank-verse lines smoothly fuse his nondecorative style and spare structures. His tragedies, without local color and with minimal or no stage directions, observe complete unity of action and almost perfect unity of time and place. The few characters are motivated by strong passions, either for good or for evil, and none change during the course of the play. Tyranny is almost always presented as synonymous with royalty, the nobler passions being assigned to the common people and to the young. Rarely sentimental, Alfieri often achieves the sublime: a tragic vision emanating from his portrait of the darker side of human destiny. *See* UNITIES.

Alfieri's reputation rests on the national significance of his work as a vision rather than on particular plays. However, three tragedies may be singled out as superior examples of his dramatic art: *Antigone* (wr. 1777), in which the heroine is presented as intent on self-sacrifice; *Saul* (1794), depicting the last days of the King; and *Myrrha* (*Mirra;* wr. 1786, prod. 1819), a tragedy in which the classical theme of incest is treated romantically as the lyrical lines reinforce the drama of human frailty in the face of overwhelming passion. Other plays worth noting are *Philip II* (wr. 1775–1781, prod. 1825), in which Philip of Spain kills his son Carlos because he mistakenly believes the young man is plotting his murder to gain the throne; *Polynices* (wr. 1775–1781, prod. 1824), based on the Greek legend of the Seven Against Thebes, in which the brothers Polynices and Eteocles, rivals with Creon for the throne of Thebes, kill each other while Jocasta, their mother, looks on; *Virginia* (wr. 1778, prod. 1784), based on Livy, in which Virginia must be killed by her father to save her from the tyrant Appius Claudius, an act that incites the Romans to rebel; *Orestes* (*Oreste,* 1781), a recounting of Orestes' fate in avenging the murder of his father; *Agamemnon* (*Agamennone;* wr. 1778, prod. 1842), which like *Orestes* was inspired by a reading of Seneca rather than by the Greek tragedies (*see* SENECA); *Mary Stuart* (*Maria Stuarda,* wr. 1780), which Alfieri considered his weakest play but which contains interesting characterizations; *The Pazzi Conspiracy* (*La congiura de' Pazzi,* wr. 1779), a tangled tale of the revolt of a Florentine family against Lorenzo the Magnificent that results in the deaths of all the male members of the family; *Don Garcia* (*Don Garzia,* wr. 1779), the story of a fratricide based on an occur-

Oreste. [Federico Arborio Mella, Milan]

rence in the Medici family; *Sophonisba* (*Sofonisba;* wr. 1787, prod. 1824), in which the grandeur of the Queen is contrasted with the calculating coldness of Scipio; *The First Brutus* (*Bruto primo,* wr. 1787) and *The Second Brutus* (*Bruto secondo;* wr. 1787, prod. 1848), which present respectively the story of Junius Brutus, who expelled the Tarquins and sentenced his own sons to death when they conspired to restore the tyrants, and that of Marcus Brutus, who believed Julius Caesar would become a tyrant and helped assassinate him; and *Agis* (*Agide,* wr. 1786), dedicated to Charles I of England, about a Spartan king who was betrayed and killed.

Among plays of lesser interest are *Rosmunda* (wr. 1780, prod. 1841), a tragedy about a cruel medieval noblewoman; *Octavia* (*Ottavia,* wr. 1781), a tragedy about the heroine's pure love for the unworthy Nero; *Timoleon* (*Timoleone,* wr. 1781), a plea for freedom; *Merope* (wr. 1782), a hymn to maternal love and understanding, dedicated to Alfieri's mother; *Cleopatra* (wr. 1775), in which Cleopatra is cold and cruel, Augustus a weakling, and Antony noble; *Alcestis* (wr. 1798, prod. 1831), dedicated to the Countess of Albany, a tribute to the virtues of women that Alfieri based on Greek manuscripts he discovered; and *Abel* (*Abele,* wr. 1790), a *tramelogedia* (Alfieri's term for the fusion of tragedy and melodrama) about the murder of Abel by Cain, set in the Garden of Eden and the kingdom of Lucifer.

Alfieri's six verse comedies, written during the years 1799–1803, have been considered by some contemporary critics to have been unjustly overlooked. They deal mainly with political themes: monarchy in *The One* (*L'uno*); oligarchy in *The Few* (*I pochi*); democracy in *The Too Many* (*I troppi*); and, as a solution to the evils of all three, a moderate constitutional government in *The Antidote* (*L'antidoto*). *The Little Window* (*La finestrina*) is a work in the manner of Aristophanes (*see* ARISTOPHANES), and *Divorce* (*Il divorzio*) puts contemporary Italian customs and manners onstage.

Antigone (wr. 1777). Tragedy that closely follows Sophocles's plot but presents Antigone as being largely motivated by a desire for self-sacrifice to expiate the sins of her family. Determined to bury her slain brother Polynices, she is in no way deterred by her love for

Filippo, as produced at the Piccolo Teatro, Milan, in 1950. [Federico Arborio Mella, Milan]

Creon's son Haemon, who suffers through no fault of his own, being torn between love for Antigone and filial duty. Creon here is less loathsome than in Alfieri's *Polynices,* for his actions stem from the necessity to act as king and leader. He even attempts to save Antigone by agreeing to her marriage with Haemon, but she chooses death. *See also* SOPHOCLES.

Orestes (*Oreste,* 1781). Tragedy derived from Seneca, depicting the fatal destiny of the family of the Atrides. It recounts the death of Agamemnon after the sacrifice of Iphigenia has made him hateful to his wife Clytemnestra, who has already been seduced by Aegisthus. Orestes, born to kill his mother, does so inadvertently in his rage against Aegisthus. When he discovers his crime, he goes mad and wanders the world with his tormented sister Electra and his faithful friend Pylades.

Mary Stuart (*Maria Stuarda,* wr. 1780). Tragedy set in the court of Mary Stuart, Queen of Scotland. At the request of Queen Elizabeth of England, in order to safeguard the crowns of England and Scotland for her son, Mary agrees to forgive her husband Arrigo (Henry Stewart, Lord Darnley) for his crime of murder and to allow him to return from exile. On his return, however, Arrigo demands to be recognized as King and to control his son's education. As a result, Mary orders his strict supervision. Angered by this curtailment of his rights, Arrigo falsely accuses Mary of encouraging her son to commit treason and demands the execution of her confidant Botuello (Bothwell) and the exile of Ormondo (the Earl of Ormonde), Queen Elizabeth's envoy to the court of Scotland. When Ormondo reveals to Mary that Arrigo himself has asked the Queen of England to support his demands, Mary orders Arrigo's death. The order executed, Mary regrets it deeply and in a horrifying vision foresees her own destiny of imprisonment and decapitation.

Polynices (*Polinice;* wr. 1775–1781, prod. 1824). Tragedy based on the Greek legend of the Seven Against Thebes. To further his desire for the throne of Thebes, Creon undermines Jocasta's efforts to obtain peace for both Thebes and her family. Taking advantage of the lifelong hatred and jealousy of the brothers Polynices and Eteocles for one another, he spurs them on to distrust and war. Polynices mortally wounds Eteocles. Urged by Jocasta to embrace his dying brother, he is then himself treacherously stabbed to death by Eteocles.

Philip II (*Filippo;* wr. 1775–1781, prod. 1825). Drama about King Philip II of Spain, whose wife Isabella is in love with her stepson

Scene from *Saul.* [Federico Arborio Mella, Milan]

Don Carlos. Philip believes that Carlos wishes to murder him and gain the throne. Consequently, he imprisons Carlos and then orders his Council of Ministers to condemn the young man to death. A conversation between Isabella and Carlos in the prison reveals his son's loyalty, but the despotic King, now mad with jealousy, kills his son himself. Isabella then commits suicide.

Saul (wr. 1782, prod. 1794). During the last day and night of his life King Saul is haunted by visions of Samuel, who condemns him for disobedience to divine commands. Saul is also troubled by an evil spirit that makes him hate David and trust only the wicked counsel of Abner. Alone in his tent save for Michal, David's wife, and Jonathan, Saul receives David, who soothes him with lyrical songs of divine invocation, war, peace, and a vision of the future. Abner breaks the spell, and Saul attacks David, forcing him to flee. During the night the Philistines attack, rout the Israelites, and kill Jonathan and

Saul's other two sons. Finding himself alone, no longer a father, Saul wishes at least to die as a king. As he curses the approaching enemy, he falls on his own sword. Saul is masterfully characterized as a human being torn between conflicting emotions, a victim of psychological clashes and mental illness, alternately father and King, tyrant and friend, rebellious against God but ultimately to be crushed by His will.

Myrrha (*Mirra;* wr. 1786, prod. 1819). Tragedy based on a story by Ovid. Myrrha, daughter of the King and Queen of Cyprus, is an innocent girl cursed by the gods with an incestuous love for her father. As she prepares for her wedding to Pyrrhus, she cannot conceal her unhappiness from her puzzled parents. Myrrha hopes to forget her illicit passion once she and Pyrrhus are married and living far from Cyprus. She is unable, however, to go through with the wedding ceremony, and Pyrrhus commits suicide. The King insists that she tell him who it is she really loves. On hearing himself named, he recoils in horror. Myrrha seizes his sword and kills herself.

PLAYS

1. *Cleopatra**. Tragedy. Written 1775. Produced Turin, Teatro Carignano, Jan. 16, 1775.
2. *Antigone**. Tragedy. Written 1777. Published 1784.
3. *Oreste** (*Orestes*). Tragedy. Written 1778. Published 1784. Produced Rome, Teatro di Foligno, 1781.
4. *Agamennone** (*Agamemnon*). Tragedy. Written 1778. Published 1784. Produced Milan Teatro Re, 1842.
5. *Virginia**. Tragedy. Written 1778. Published 1784. Produced Turin, Teatro Carignano, 1784.
6. *Don Garzia** (*Don Garcia*). Tragedy. Written 1779. Published 1788.
7. *La congiura de' Pazzi** (*The Pazzi Conspiracy*). Tragedy. Written 1779. Published 1788.
8. *Rosmunda**. Tragedy. Written 1780. Published 1784. Produced Turin, Teatro Carignano, 1841.
9. *Maria Stuarda** (*Mary Stuart*). Tragedy. Written 1780. Published 1788.
10. *Polinice** (*Polynices*). Tragedy. Written 1775–1781. Published 1784. Produced Turin, Teatro Carignano, 1824.
11. *Filippo** (*Philip II*). Tragedy. Written 1775–1781. Published 1784. Produced Turin, Teatro Carignano, 1825.
12. *Ottavia** (*Octavia*). Tragedy. Written 1781. Published 1784.
13. *Timoleone** (*Timoleon*). Tragedy. Written 1781. Published 1784.
14. *Merope**. Tragedy. Written 1782. Published 1784.
15. *Saul**. Tragedy. Written 1782. Published 1788. Produced Florence, Teatro di Santa Maria, 1794.
16. *Agide** (*Agis*). Tragedy. Written 1786. Published 1788.
17. *Mirra** (*Myrrha*). Tragedy. Written 1786. Published 1789. Produced Bologna, Arena del Sole, 1819.
18. *Sofonisba** (*Sophonisba*). Tragedy. Written 1787. Published 1788. Produced Turin, Teatro Carignano, 1824.
19. *Bruto primo** (*The First Brutus*). Tragedy. Written 1787. Published 1788.
20. *Bruto secondo** (*The Second Brutus*). Tragedy. Written 1787. Published 1788. Produced Turin, Teatro Carignano, 1848.
21. *Abele** (*Abel*). Tragedy. Written 1790. Published 1804.
22. *Alceste* (*Alcestis*). Tragedy. Written 1798. Published 1804. Produced Turin, Teatro Carignano, 1831.
23. *L'uno* (*The One*). Comedy. Written 1802. Published 1804.
24. *I pochi* (*The Few*). Comedy. Written 1802. Published 1804.
25. *I troppi* (*The Too Many*). Comedy. Written 1802. Published 1804.
26. *L'antidoto* (*The Antidote*). Comedy. Written 1802. Published 1804.
27. *La finestrina* (*The Little Window*). Comedy. Written 1802. Published 1804.
28. *Il divorzio* (*Divorce*). Comedy. Written 1803. Published 1804.

EDITIONS

Collections.
Opere di Vittorio Alfieri, ed. by F. Maggini, Milan, 1940; *Tragedie e tragedie postume*, ed. by N. Bruscoli, Bari, 1946.
Individual Plays.
Myrrha. Published in *The Drama: Its History, Literature and Influence on Civilization*, ed. by A. Bates, vol. 5, Athenian Society, London, 1903–1904.
Saul. Published in *Gemme della letteratura italiane*, comp. by J. F. Bingham, Frowde, London, 1904; *World Drama*, ed. by B. H. Clark, vol. 2, Appleton, New York, 1933.

CRITICISM

M. Fubini, *Vittorio Alfieri: Il pensiero—La tragedia*, Florence, 1937; L. Russo, *Lettura lirica del teatro alfieriano*, Milan, 1944; G. Natali, *Vittorio Alfieri*, Rome, 1949.

ALFRED, William (1922–   ). American playwright, professor of English at Harvard, whose first professionally produced play was the highly acclaimed *Hogan's Goat* (1965). Alfred, born and raised in Brooklyn, uses this setting to tell of a first-generation Irish-American community. The drama, in verse, focuses on Matt Stanton, a poor immigrant, whose consuming political ambitions drive him to destruction.

ALLEGORY. Unified symbolic system in which characters, plots, or settings are used to represent abstract ideas or concepts. An allegory may be moral, political, or historical and is intended to instruct the audience in certain values. The moral allegory originated in classical drama and is associated particularly with the medieval mystery and morality plays. The Coventry cycle of mystery and miracle plays presented in England as early as 1416 included such characters as Justice, Truth, and Peace woven into the Bible stories. The morality plays of the late Middle Ages, allegorical fables invented to illustrate moral doctrines, included such allegorical personifications as Infidelity, Pride, and Concupiscence. The archetype of the form is the Dutch *Everyman* (ca. 1495), in which the virtues (Good Deeds, Beauty, Knowledge) vie with the vices (Worldly Goods, Death) for the possession of man's soul. *See* EVERYMAN; MORALITY PLAY; MYSTERY PLAY.

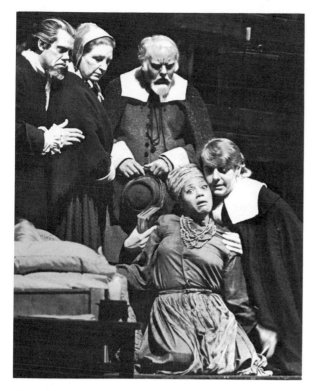

(Above) An example of a twentieth-century allegory: Arthur Miller's *The Crucible*, with (l. to r.) Ken Ruta, Ann Weldon, George Ede, Ruth Kobart, and John Schuck. [Courtesy American Conservatory Theatre, San Francisco, Calif. Photograph by Hank Kranzler]

Some time later, the political allegory made its appearance in such plays as *The Three Lords and Three Ladies of London* (ca. 1588). In this case the three ladies, Lucre, Love, and Conscience, are wooed by numerous gentlemen, English (Desire, Delight, Devotion) and Spanish (Pride, Ambition, Tyranny), with obvious parallels being drawn to the prevailing English-Spanish conflict that culminated in the defeat of the Spanish Armada. The historical allegory operated on a similar level.

Popular also in the baroque period, allegory lost favor in the nineteenth and early twentieth centuries but has reappeared in such plays as Arthur Adamov's *The Invasion* (1950), Max Frisch's *The Chinese Wall* (1946), and Arthur Miller's *The Crucible* (1953). *See* BAROQUE AGE.

ALLEN, Jay (1922–   ). American dramatist who became known for *The Prime of Miss Jean Brodie* (1967), her adaptation of Muriel Spark's novel. It was followed by *Forty Carats* (1968), an adaptation of Barillet and Grédy's *Quarante carats,* which had been produced in Paris the previous year. *See* BARILLET, PIERRE; GRÉDY, JEAN-PIERRE.

ÁLVAREZ, Alejandro Rodríguez. *See* CASONA, ALEJANDRO.

Jay Allen's *The Prime of Miss Jean Brodie,* with Zoe Caldwell as the schoolmistress. New York, Helen Hayes Theatre, 1968. [Friedman-Abeles]

Serafín and Joaquín Álvarez Quintero

(1871 – 1938; 1873 – 1944)

Serafín and Joaquín Álvarez Quintero, Spanish dramatists, were brothers, born on March 26, 1871, and January 20, 1873, respectively, in the small town of Utrera, near Seville. While the brothers were quite young, their well-to-do family moved to Seville, where they grew up. As adolescents, they began writing plays, the fruits of their collaboration being acted on the patio of their home. Their first play to be produced professionally was the farce *Fencing and Love* (*Esgrima y amor*), which was presented in Seville in 1888.

Joaquín and Serafín Álvarez Quintero. [Theatre Collection, The New York Public Library at Lincoln Center, Astor, Lenox and Tilden Foundations]

That year they left Seville to establish themselves in Madrid, where after some difficulty they produced a second farce, which failed. During the next nine years they wrote no significant plays, supporting themselves as minor officials in the Treasury. Then, in 1897 two one-act plays, *The Apple of His Eye* (*El ojito derecho*) and *The Grille* (*La reja*), attracted favorable attention. The following year, they achieved their long-awaited success with the production of *The Good Spirit* (*La buena sombra*), a musical play. For the next forty years Madrid saw the production of at least one new play annually by the Quinteros, usually an Andalusian *cuadro de costumbres* ("genre play"). The city of Seville honored them by dedicating a fountain and a library to them. In all, the brothers produced more than 200 dramas and sketches for the theatre.

Serafín died in Madrid on April 12, 1938, and Joaquín six years later, on June 14, 1944, also in Madrid. Joaquín was founder of the short-lived weekly *El Pobrecito Hablador* of Madrid, a founder and member of the Society of Spanish Authors, and a member of the Royal Spanish Academy.

WORK

Effervescent and sentimental, the Quinteros' vignettes and *sainetes* (one-act farces) presented their audiences with works far different from the realistic dramas then dominating the Spanish stage. The Quinteros painted halcyon landscapes with skies ever blue, people always charming and warmhearted, and life usually amusing and romantic. They represented onstage every pleasant aspect of Andalusian life, seldom venturing outside their native region, and then unsuccessfully. Their optimistic world is never burdened with ambiguity, profundity, or evil; rather, it is a simple place, with kindly inhabitants who delight in wholesome pleasures.

Two characteristic *sainetes, Don Abel Wrote a Tragedy* (*La musa loca*, 1905) and *The Merry Heart* (*El genio alegre*, 1906), prescribe laughter as the cure for all ills. Ordinary Andalusians are celebrated in two exemplary vignettes, *The Apple of His Eye* (1897), about a shrewd trader of donkeys; and *By Their Words Ye Shall Know Them* (*Hablando se entiende la gente*, 1913), about a dull shoemaker who wins the heart of a vain girl through his unwitting flattery.

The Quinteros' brand of romantic sentimentality permeates the bright dialogue of *A Sunny Morning* (*Mañana de sol*, 1905), in which an elderly couple's chance reunion becomes the occasion for an ironic recollection of their frustrated romance. The same emotion guides the plot of *The Prime of Life* (*La flor de la vida*, 1910), in which an innkeeper's son, who worships a duke's daughter from afar, rescues her from her dissolute husband and years later, when she is surrounded by her grandchildren, feels content to know that their relationship was innocent. Although more developed and satirical, *The Happiness of Others* (*La dicha ajena*, 1902) is still predominantly sentimental: the efforts of a young physician to establish an asylum for children are opposed by his cynical classmate, whose hardness melts when his idealistic friend saves his daughter's life.

A Hundred Years Old (*El centenario*, 1909), character study of Papa Juan, a hearty old man who greets each of life's milestones with renewed zest for the next. Celebrating his one-hundredth birthday, he makes plans to marry off some of his relatives so that their children will bring him pleasure.

Extravagant comedy often moves a play to its hilarious conclusion. In *The Women's Town* (*Puebla de las mujeres*, 1912), a young man visiting a town in which women far outnumber men is seized by gossips who steer him irrevocably to the girl of their choice. The hero of *Fortunato* (1912) innocently applies for a job with a woman who intends to use his body as the target in her shooting act. Filipe, the antihero of *The Lady from Alfaqueque* (*La Consulesa*, 1914), determined to coax his way into any likely household in order to secure the leisure in which to write poetry, deceives the lady from Alfaqueque by pretending to hail from her hometown.

The Quinteros also wrote some plays in a more nostalgic and serious vein. In *The Country Girl* (*La Zagala*, 1904), a widower, succumbing to tradition and pride, lets the harsh disapproval of his daughters drive away a beautiful but lowborn woman whom he loves. Another of this type is *Malvaloca* (1912), the Quinteros' best-known play, which makes an emotional plea for sympathy toward its heroine, a good woman who repents her aberrant past.

The Flowers (*Las flores*, 1901). Comedy in which María Jesús, a widow, grows flowers to support herself and her four daughters, Consuelo, María Rosa, Angeles, and Charito. Consuelo falls in love with Bernardo; María Rosa is pursued by Gabriel; and Angeles, who wants to be a nun, is loved by Juan Antonio. María Rosa elopes with Gabriel, who deserts her but then returns. Angeles gives up her goal of religious isolation and agrees to marry Juan Antonio. After keeping his love secret for two years, Bernardo proposes marriage to Consuelo and is accepted.

A Sunny Morning (*Mañana de sol*, 1905).

Comedy set in a park in Madrid on a sunny morning when Doña Laura, an elegant old lady, chances to meet Don Gonzalo, a crotchety old man. After initial wariness the two begin to talk, and in the course of their conversation they discover that they had been frustrated lovers in their youth. As each assumes the other's ignorance, they pretend to be merely acquainted with the lovers under discussion. They both fabricate colorful fictions to conceal the truth, and each realizes that the other is lying. Through this wistful, ironic conversation the two have become friends, and they agree to meet again in the park, on another sunny day.

The Merry Heart (*El genio alegre*, 1906). Comedy portraying the solitary Doña Sacramento Alcazar, Marchioness of Arrayanes, who lives in the past. Her easygoing son Julio returns home only when he needs money. Then Doña Sacramento's niece Consolación comes to live with her and changes everyone, the marchioness included, by her natural exuberance. Julio begins to spend more time at home and eventually proposes marriage to Consolación, who returns his love and accepts him.

Malvaloca (1912). Drama set in an Andalusian village. Leonardo goes to a convent to visit Salvador, his business partner in a brass foundry, who is recuperating from burns received from molten metal. In the waiting room Leonardo meets Malvaloca, Salvador's former mistress, a lovely lower-class woman, whom he had abandoned two years earlier, following the death of their child. Knowing that Salvador had sacrificed Malvaloca to his social ambition, Leonardo is moved by her concern for his partner. He falls in love with her but worries that her checkered past might jeopardize his social position too. Later, in a gesture of gratitude to the nuns, the two men agree to recast La Golondrina, the convent's long-silenced cracked bell. When Leonardo tells Salvador he has decided to marry Malvaloca, Salvador declares their partnership dissolved and leaves. As La Golondrina once again resounds across the village, Malvaloca feels that she too has been restored to life by a loving man.

PLAYS

Unless otherwise noted, the plays were first performed in Madrid.

1. *Esgrima y amor* (*Fencing and Love*). Comic trifle, 1 act. Produced Seville, Teatro de Cervantes, Jan. 30, 1888.

2. *Belén, 12, principal* (*Bethlehem, Street No. 12, Main Floor*). Comic trifle, 1 act. Produced Seville, Teatro de Cervantes, May 16, 1888.

3. *Gilito*. Comic trifle, 1 act. Produced Teatro de Apolo, Apr. 25, 1889. Music: José Osuna.

4. *Blancas y negras* (*Blacks and Whites*). Farce, 1 act. Written 1892? Produced Teatro Español, 1892.

5. *Viaje de recreo* (*Vacation Trip*). Farce, 1 act. Writ-

A Hundred Years Old, with Otis Skinner (seated). New York, Lyceum Theatre, 1929. [Photograph by Vandamm. Theatre Collection, The New York Public Library at Lincoln Center, Astor, Lenox and Tilden Foundations]

ten 1892? Produced Teatro de Lara, 1892.

6. *La media naranja* (*The Better Half*). Comic trifle, 1 act. Produced Teatro de Lara, Apr. 26, 1894.

7. *El tío de la flauta* (*The Old Flute Player*). Comic trifle, 1 act. Produced Teatro de la Comedia, Mar. 13, 1897.

8. *El ojito derecho* (*The Apple of His Eye*). Farce, 1 act. Produced Teatro de la Zarzuela, July 2, 1897.

9. *La reja* (*The Grille*). Comedy, 1 act. Produced Teatro Cómico, Dec. 4, 1897.

10. *La buena sombra* (*The Good Spirit*). Farce, 3 scenes. Produced Teatro de la Zarzuela, Mar. 4, 1898. Music: Apolinar Brull.

11. *El peregrino* (*The Pilgrim*). Musical comedy, 1 act. Produced Seville, Teatro del Duque, May 6, 1898. Music: Vicente Gómez.

12. *La vida íntima* (*Intimate Life*). Comedy, 2 acts. Produced Teatro de Lara, Oct. 15, 1898.

13. *Los borrachos* (*The Drunkards*). Farce, 4 scenes. Produced Teatro de la Zarzuela, Mar. 3, 1899. Music: Gerónimo Giménez.

14. *El chiquillo* (*The Kid*). Farce, 1 act. Produced Teatro de la Comedia, Mar. 11, 1899.

15. *Las casas de cartón* (*The Houses of Cardboard*). Comic trifle, 1 act. Produced Teatro de Lara, Apr. 14, 1899.

16. *El traje de luces* (*The Suit of Lights* (*The Bullfighter's Costume*). Farce, 3 scenes. Produced Teatro de la Zarzuela, Nov. 28, 1899. Music: Caballero and Mariano Hermoso.

17. *El patio* (*The Patio*). Comedy, 2 acts. Produced Teatro de Lara, Jan. 10, 1900.

18. *El motete* (*The Motet*). Farce, 1 act. Produced Teatro de Apolo, Apr. 24, 1900.

19. *El estreno* (*The First Performance*). Musical comedy, 3 scenes. Produced Teatro de Apolo, July 19, 1900. Music: Ruperto Chapí.

20. *Los galeotes* (*The Galley Slaves*). Comedy, 4 acts. Produced Teatro de la Comedia, Oct. 20, 1900.

21. *La pena** (*Grief*). Drama, 2 scenes. Produced Teatro Español, Jan. 6, 1901.

22. *La azotea* (*The Roof*). Comedy, 1 act. Produced Teatro de Lara, Feb. 7, 1901.

23. *El nido* (*The Nest*). Comedy, 2 acts. Produced Teatro de Lara, Oct. 31, 1901.

24. *Las flores* (*The Flowers*). Comedy, 3 acts. Produced Teatro de la Comedia, Dec. 4, 1901.

25. *Los piropos* (*The Compliments*). Farce, 1 act. Produced Teatro de Lara, Mar. 5, 1902.

26. *El flechazo* (*The Arrow Stroke*). Farce, 1 act. Produced Teatro de Lara, May 12, 1902.

27. *El amor en el teatro* (*Love in the Theatre*). Literary caprice; prologue and epilogue, 5 scenes. Produced Barcelona, Teatro de Novedades, June 25, 1902.

28. *¡Abanicos y panderetas, o A Sevilla en el "Botijo"!* (*Fans and Tambourines, or To Seville in "The Earthen Jar"!*). Humorous satire, 3 scenes. Produced Teatro de Apolo, July 10, 1902.

29. *La dicha ajena* (*The Happiness of Others*). Comedy, prologue and 3 acts. Produced Teatro de la Comedia, Nov. 4, 1902.

30. *Pepita Reyes.* Comedy, 2 acts. Produced Teatro de Lara, Jan. 30, 1903.

31. *Los meritorios* (*The Meritorious Ones*). Playlet, 1 act. Produced Teatro Español, Apr. 2, 1903.

32. *La zahorí* (*The False Seer*). Farce, 1 act. Produced Buenos Aires, Teatro Odeón, Sept. 5, 1903.

33. *La reina mora* (*The Moorish Queen*). Farce, 3 scenes. Produced Teatro de Apolo, Dec. 11, 1903. Music: José Serrano.

34. *Zaragatas* (*Quarrels*). Farce, 2 scenes. Produced Teatro de Lara, Dec. 31, 1903.

35. *La Zagala* (*The Country Girl*). Comedy, 4 acts. Produced Teatro Español, Jan. 17, 1904.

36. *La casa de García* (*The House of García*). Comedy, 3 acts. Produced Barcelona, Teatro Eldorado, June 8, 1904.

37. *La contrata* (*The Contract*). Comedy, 1 act. Produced Teatro de Apolo, July 19, 1904.

38. *El amor que pasa** (*Love Passes By*). Comedy, 2 acts. Produced Buenos Aires, Teatro Odeón, Sept. 10, 1904.

39. *El mal de amores* (*The Evil of Love*). Farce, 1 act. Produced Teatro de Apolo, Jan. 28, 1905. Music: José Serrano.

40. *El nuevo servidor* (*The New Servant*). Sketch, 1 act. Produced Teatro de Lara, Feb. 23, 1905.

41. *Mañana de sol** (*A Sunny Morning*). Comedy, 1 act. Produced Teatro de Lara, Feb. 23, 1905.

42. *Fea y con gracia* (*Ugly but Charming*). Sketch, 1 act. Produced Teatro Moderno, May 3, 1905. Music: Joaquín Turina.

43. (Adaptation). *La aventura de los galeotes* (*The Adventure of the Galley Slaves*). Comedy, 1 act. Produced Teatro Real, May 10, 1905. Based on an episode in Miguel de Cervantes' *Don Quixote.* (Part I, chap. XXII, 1605.)

44. *La musa loca** (*Don Abel Wrote a Tragedy*). Comedy, 3 acts. Produced Barcelona, Teatro de Novedades, July 4, 1905.

45. *La pitanza* (*The Pittance*). Farce, 1 act. Produced Teatro de la Zarzuela, Sept. 15, 1905.

46. *El amor en solfa* (*Love by Arrangement*). Literary caprice, prologue and 4 scenes. Produced Teatro de Apolo, Nov. 8, 1905. Second part of *El amor en el teatro.*

47. *Los chorros del oro* (*The Streams of Gold*). Farce, 1 act. Produced Teatro de Apolo, Mar. 8, 1906.

48. *Morritos.* Farce, 1 act. Produced Teatro de Lara, Mar. 12, 1906.

49. *Amor a obscuras* (*Love in the Dark*). Comedy, 1 act. Produced Teatro de Lara, Apr. 19, 1906.

50. *La mala sombra* (*The Evil Spirit*). Farce, 1 act. Produced Teatro de Apolo, Sept. 25, 1906. Music: Serrano.

51. *El genio alegre* (*The Merry Heart*). Comedy, 3 acts. Produced Buenos Aires, Teatro Odeón, Sept. 29, 1906.

52. *El niño prodigio* (*The Child Prodigy*). Comedy, 2 acts. Produced Teatro de Lara, Nov. 13, 1906.

53. *Nanita nana* (*Cradle Song*). Farce, 1 act. Produced Teatro de Apolo, February, 1907. Music: Serrano.

54. *La zancadilla* (*The Trick*). Farce, 1 act. Produced Teatro Español, Mar. 23, 1907.

55. *La bella Lucerito* (*Fair Lucerito*). Farce, 1 act. Produced Teatro de Apolo, Apr. 10, 1907. Music: Arturo Saco del Valle.

56. *La patria chica* (*Homeland*). Musical comedy, 1 act. Produced Teatro de la Zarzuela, Oct. 15, 1907. Music: Chapí.

57. *La vida que vuelve* (*Life that Returns*). Comedy, 2 acts. Produced Teatro de la Princesa, Dec. 20, 1907.

58. *A la luz de luna** (*In the Moonlight*). Comedy, 1 act. Produced Teatro Español, Jan. 21, 1908.

59. *La escondida senda** (*Peace and Quiet*). Comedy, 2 acts. Produced Teatro de Lara, Mar. 24, 1908.

60. *El agua milagrosa* (*Miraculous Water*). Comedy, 1 act. Produced Murcia, Teatro Romea, Mar. 28, 1908.

61. *Las buñoleras* (*The Waffle Makers*). Farce, 1 act. Produced Teatro de Lara, Apr. 20, 1908.

62. *Las de Caín* (*The Daughters of Cain*). Comedy, 3 acts. Produced Madrid, Teatro de la Comedia, Barcelona, Teatro Eldorado, Seville, Teatro de San Fernando, and Vigo, Teatro Rosalía de Castro, Oct. 3, 1908.

63. *Amores y amoríos* (*Loves and Intrigues*). Comedy, 4 acts. Produced Buenos Aires, Teatro Avenida, Oct. 10, 1908.

64. *Las mil maravillas* (*The Thousand Marvels*). Musical comedy, prologue and 4 acts. Produced Teatro de Apolo, Dec. 23, 1908. Music: Chapí.

65. *Cuatro palabras* (*Four Words*). Sketch, 1 act. Produced Teatro de la Comedia, Jan. 15, 1909.

66. *Sangre gorda* (*Rich Blood*). Farce, 1 act. Produced Teatro de Apolo, Apr. 30, 1909.

67. *El patinillo* (*The Little Courtyard*). Farce, 1 act. Produced Teatro de Apolo, Oct. 15, 1909. Music: Giménez.

68. *Doña Clarines** (*Lady Clarines*). Comedy, 2 acts. Produced Teatro de Lara, Nov. 5, 1909.

A Hundred Years Old, with Otis Skinner (right). New York, Lyceum Theatre, 1929. [Photograph by Vandamm. Theatre Collection, The New York Public Library at Lincoln Center, Astor, Lenox and Tilden Foundations]

69. *El centenario** (*A Hundred Years Old*). Comedy, 3 acts. Produced Teatro de la Comedia, Dec. 16, 1909.

70. *La muela del rey Farfán* (*The Molar of King Farfán*). Fantasy musical comedy for children, 1 act. Produced Teatro de Apolo, Dec. 28, 1909. Music: Amadeo Vives.

71. *Herida de muerte* (*Fatal Wound*). Comedy, 1 act. Produced Teatro de la Princesa, Mar. 14, 1910.

72. *El último capítulo* (*The Last Chapter*). Comedy, 1 act. Produced Teatro de la Comedia, Mar. 19, 1910.

73. *La flor de la vida** (*The Prime of Life*). Dramatic prose poem, 3 acts. Produced Buenos Aires, Teatro Odeón, June 23, 1910.

74. *La rima eterna* (*The Eternal Rhyme*). Comedy, 2 acts. Produced Teatro de Lara, Nov. 23, 1910.

75. *Carta a Juan soldado* (*Letter to Juan the Soldier*). Sketch, 1 act. Produced Teatro de la Princesa, Dec. 16, 1910.

76. *Solico en el mundo* (*Alone in the World*). Farce, 1 act. Produced Madrid, Teatro de Apolo, and Saragossa, Teatro Circa, Mar. 5, 1911.

77. *Palomilla* (*Little Dove*). Monologue, 1 act. Produced Teatro de la Comedia, Mar. 25, 1911.

78. *Rosa y Rosita* (*Rosa and Rosita*). Farce, 1 act. Produced Teatro de la Princesa, Apr. 30, 1911.

79. *El hombre que hace reir* (*The Man Who Makes You Laugh*). Monologue, 1 act. Produced Teatro de Cervantes, Dec. 6, 1911.

80. *Anita la risueña* (*Laughing Anita*). Musical comedy. Produced Teatro de Apolo, Dec. 23, 1911. Music: Vives.

81. *Puebla de las mujeres** (*The Women's Town*). Comedy, 2 acts. Produced Teatro de Lara, Jan. 17, 1912.

82. *Malvaloca**. Drama, 3 acts. Produced Teatro de la Princesa, Apr. 6, 1912.

83. *Sábado sin sol* (*Sunless Saturday*). Farce, 1 act. Produced Teatro de Lara, May 18, 1912. Music: Francisco Bravo.

84. *Las hazañas de Juanillo él de Molares* (*The Exploits of Juanillo de Molares*). Sketch, 1 act. Produced Palace of the Marquesa de Squilache, June 14, 1912.

85. *Mundo, mundillo* (*World, Little World*). Comedy, 3 acts. Produced Teatro de la Comedia, Oct. 5, 1912.

86. *Fortunato*. Historical tragicomedy, 3 scenes. Produced Teatro de Cervantes, Nov. 30, 1912.

87. *Nena Teruel*. Comedy, 2 acts and epilogue. Produced Teatro Español, Apr. 6, 1913.

88. *Sin palabras* (*Without Words*). Comedy, 1 act. Produced Teatro de la Comedia, May, 24, 1913.

89. *Hablando se entiende la gente** (*By Their Words Ye Shall Know Them*). Farce, 1 act. Produced Teatro Álvarez Quintero, Nov. 10, 1913.

90. *El amor bandolero* (*Love the Robber*). Musical comedy, 3 scenes. Produced Teatro de la Zarzuela, Nov. 27, 1913. Music: Bravo and Torres.

91. *Los leales* (*The Loyal Family*). Comedy, 3 acts. Produced Teatro Español, Jan. 21, 1914.

92. *La Consulesa** (*The Lady from Alfaqueque*). Comedy, 2 acts. Produced Teatro de Lara, Apr. 11, 1914.

93. *Chiquita y Benita* (*Chiquita and Benita*). Monologue, 1 act. Produced Seville, Teatro del Duque, May 2, 1914.

94. *Polvorilla, el Corneta* (*Polvorilla, the Bugle*). Monologue, 1 act. Produced Teatro Real, May 19, 1914.

95. *Dios dirá* (*God Will Say*). Comedy, 2 acts. Produced Teatro Esclava, Feb. 26, 1915.

96. *Isidrín, o Las cuarenta y nueve provincias* (*Isidrín, or The Forty-nine Provinces*). Farce, 1 act. Produced Teatro Cómico, Apr. 8, 1915. Music: Giménez.

97. *Becqueriana*. Operetta, 1 act. Produced Teatro de la Zarzuela, Apr. 9, 1915. Music: María Rodriga.

98. *El duque de Él* (*The Duke of Él*). Romantic comedy, 3 acts. Produced Seville, Teatro de Cervantes, Apr. 16, 1915.

99. *El ilustre huésped* (*The Illustrious Guest*). Satirical play; prologue and epilogue, 4 scenes. Produced Teatro de Cervantes, May 1, 1915.

100. *Diana Cazadora, o Pena de muerte al amor* (*Diana the Huntress, or Death Penalty for Love*). Musical comedy, 3 scenes. Produced Teatro de Apolo, Nov. 19, 1915.

101. *Cabrita que tira al monte . . .* (*One's Inner Nature Eventually Emerges*). Drama, 4 acts. Produced Teatro Español, Mar. 3, 1916.

102. *¿A quién me recuerda usted?* (*Of Whom Do You Remind Me?*). Comedy, 1 act. Produced Teatro de Lara, Apr. 29, 1916.

103. *El cerrojazo* (*Locked Out*). Farce, 1 act. Produced Teatro de Apolo, May 4, 1916.

104. (Adaptation). *Rinconete y Cortadillo*. Play, 2 scenes. Produced Teatro de Cervantes, May 18, 1916. Based on Cervantes' novella of the same name (1613).

105. (Adaptation). *Marianela*. Play, 3 acts. Produced Teatro de la Princesa, Oct. 18, 1916. Based on Benito Pérez Galdós's novel of the same name (1878).

106. *Los ojos de luto** (*Widow's Eyes*). Comedy, 1 act. Produced Teatro de la Infanta Isabel, Mar. 17, 1917.

107. *La casa de enfrente* (*The House Opposite*). Musical comedy, 1 act. Produced Teatro de Apolo, Mar. 20, 1917.

108. *Lo quetú quieras* (*That Which You Wish*). Comedy, 1 act. Produced Teatro de Lara, May 3, 1917.

109. *Lectura y escritura* (*Reading and Writing*). Farce, 1 act. Produced Teatro de Lara, Oct. 27, 1917.

110. *Así se escribe la historia* (*Thus History Is Written*). Comedy, 2 acts. Produced Teatro de la Infanta Isabel, Nov. 6, 1917.

111. *Pipiola*. Comedy, 3 acts. Produced Teatro de Lara, Feb. 7, 1918.

112. *La cuerda sensible* (*The Sensitive Chord*). Comedy, 1 act. Produced Buenos Aires, Teatro Odeón, Apr. 22, 1918.

113. *Los Marchosos* (*The Marchosos*). Farce, 1 act. Produced Teatro de la Infanta Isabel, May 3, 1918.

114. *Secretico de confesión* (*The Secret of Confession*). Farce, 1 act. Produced Teatro de la Comedia, June 15, 1918.

115. *Castañuela, arbitrista* (*Castañuela the Schemer*). Sketch, 1 act. Produced Seville, Teatro de San Fernando, June, 1918.

116. *La niña de Juana, o El descubrimiento de América* (*Juana's Daughter, or The Discovery of America*). Farce, 1 act. Produced Seville, Teatro de Cervantes, Oct. 5, 1918.

117. *Don Juan, buena persona* (*Don Juan, Good Fellow*). Comedy, 3 acts. Produced Teatro de la Comedia, Oct. 30, 1918.

118. *Pedro López*. Dramatic episode, 1 act. Produced Teatro del Centro, Nov. 21, 1918.

119. *La calumniada* (*The Slandered Woman*). Drama, 3 acts. Produced Teatro de la Princesa, Feb. 21, 1919.

120. *El corazón en la mano* (*The Heart in the Hand*). Comedy, 1 act. Produced Teatro Español, Apr. 12, 1919.

121. *Febrerillo el loco* (*Febrerillo the Mad*). Comedy, 2 acts. Produced Teatro de Lara, Oct. 28, 1919.

122. *El mundo es un pañuelo* (*The World Is a Kerchief*). Comedy, 2 acts and epilogue. Produced Teatro de la Infanta Isabel, Feb. 12, 1920.

123. *La flor en el libro* (*The Flower in the Book*). Comedy, 1 act. Produced Barcelona, Teatro de Novedades, Sept. 17, 1920.

124. *La del dos de Mayo* (*The Woman of May Second*). Farce, 1 act. Produced Teatro de Apolo, Nov. 5, 1920. Music: Tomás Barrera.

125. *Pasionera* (*The Singer of the Passion*). Comedy, 2 acts. Produced Teatro de Lara, Jan. 18, 1921.

126. *La seria* (*The Grave One*). Farce, 1 act. Produced Teatro Esclava, Feb. 5, 1921.

127. *Los pápiros* (*The Papyrus Trees*). Musical comedy, 3 acts. Produced Teatro de la Reina Victoria, Feb. 25, 1921. Music: Pablo Luna.

128. *La moral de Arrabales* (*The Moral of Arrabales*). Comedy, 1 act. Produced Teatro de Lara, Mar. 21, 1921.

129. *Ramo de locura* (*Insanity Ward*). Comedy, 3 acts. Produced Teatro del Centro, Apr. 26, 1921.

130. *La sillita* (*The Small Chair*). Farce, 1 act. Produced Teatro de la Infanta Isabel, Apr. 28, 1921.

131. *La prisa* (*Haste*). Comedy, 3 acts. Produced Teatro de la Infanta Isabel, Nov. 19, 1921.

132. *El mal ángel* (*The Bad Angel*). Farce, 1 act. Produced Teatro de Apolo, Nov. 25, 1921.

133. (With Benito Pérez Galdós). *Antón Caballero*. Comedy, 3 acts. Produced Teatro del Centro, Dec. 16, 1921. Pérez Galdós's incomplete play completed after his death by the Quintero brothers.

134. *El cuartito de hora* (*The Fifteen Minutes*). Farce, 1 act. Produced Teatro de Lara, Mar. 8, 1922.

135. *La quema* (*The Holocaust*). Comedy, 1 act. Produced Teatro Español, Apr. 28, 1922.

136. *Cabellos de plata* (*Silver Hair*). Farce, 1 act. Produced Teatro del Centro, May 6, 1922.

137. *Las benditas máscaras* (*The Masked Simpletons*). Comedy, 1 act. Produced Teatro del Centro, May 27, 1922.

138. *Las vueltas que da el mundo* (*The Turns of the World*). Comedy, 3 acts. Produced Teatro del Centro, Nov. 3, 1922.

139. *Cristalina*. Comedy, 3 acts. Produced Teatro Español, Feb. 7, 1923.

140. *Acacia y Melitón* (*Acacia and Melitón*). Farce, 1 act. Produced Teatro de Lara, Mar. 21, 1923.

141. *Ganas de reñir* (*Wishing to Quarrel*). Farce, 1 act. Produced Teatro Español, Mar. 24, 1923.

142. *Marianela*. Opera, 3 acts. Produced Barcelona, Gran Teatro del Liceo, Mar. 31, 1923. Music: Jaime Pahissa.

143. *Concha la limpia* (*Concha the Pure*). Comedy, 3 acts. Produced Valencia, Teatro Principal, Feb. 14, 1924.

144. *Mi hermano y yo* (*My Brother and I*). Comedy, 3 acts. Produced Teatro de Lara, Feb. 29, 1924.

145. *Dos pesetas* (*Two Pesetas*). Play, 1 act. Produced Teatro de Lara, Mar. 27, 1924.

146. *Vámonos* (*Let's Go*). Playlet, 1 act. Produced Teatro de Lara, Apr. 29, 1924.

147. *La suerte* (*The Chance*). Farce, 1 act. Produced Teatro de Apolo, May 17, 1924. Music: Ángel Barrios.

148. *Cancionera* (*The Songbook*). Dramatic verse poem, 3 acts. Produced Teatro de Lara, Nov. 4, 1924.

149. *Revoloteo* (*The Fluttering*). Monologue, 1 act. Produced Teatro Esclava, Nov. 13, 1924. Music: Manuel Font de Anta.

150. *Pepita y Don Juan.* (*Pepita and Don Juan*). Laudation, 1 act. Produced Teatro Español, Mar. 13, 1925.

151. *La boda de Quinita Flores* (*The Wedding of Quinita Flores*). Comedy, 3 acts. Produced Barcelona, Teatro Barcelona, July 8, 1925.

152. *El pie* (*The Foot*). Farce, 1 act. Produced Teatro de Lara, Sept. 18, 1925.

153. *Las muertes de Lopillo* (*The Death of Lopillo*). Farce, 3 acts. Produced Teatro de Apolo, Nov. 27, 1925. Music: Font de Anta.

154. *El último papel* (*The Final Paper*). Comedy, 1 act. Produced Teatro de la Latina, Jan. 8, 1926.

155. *Las de Ábel* (*The Daughters of Ábel*). Comedy, 3 acts. Produced Teatro de la Infanta Isabel, Apr. 3, 1926.

156. *Los grandes hombres, o El monumento a Cervantes* (*Great Men, or The Monument to Cervantes*). Laudation, 1 act. Produced Teatro Fontalba, Oct. 8, 1926.

157. *Barro pecador* (*Sinful Clay*). Comedy 3 acts. Produced Teatro Fontalba, Nov. 12, 1926.

158. *Cambio de suerte* (*Change of Luck*). Comedy, 1 act. Produced Teatro de la Infanta Isabel, Dec. 1, 1926.

159. *125 kilométros* (*125 Kilometers*). Farce, 3 acts. Produced Teatro Alházar, Dec. 21, 1926.

160. *La cuestión es pasar el rato* (*It's a Question of Passing the Time*). Comedy, 3 acts. Produced Valencia, Teatro Principal, June 9, 1927.

161. *Tambor y cascabel* (*Drum and Cascabel*). Comedy, 4 acts. Produced Teatro de la Reina Victoria, Nov. 23, 1927.

162. *Los mosquitos* (*The Mosquitos*). Comedy, 3 acts. Produced Teatro de Lara, Dec. 16, 1927.

163. *Novelera* (*The Newsmonger*). Comedy, 3 acts. Produced Teatro Fontalba, Dec. 7, 1928.

164. *Rondalla* (*The Fable*). Popular dramatic prose poem, 3 acts. Produced Saragossa, Teatro Principal, Dec. 14, 1928.

165. *Los duendes de Sevilla* (*The Phantoms of Seville*). Comedy, 3 acts. Produced Seville, Teatro de la Exposición, Oct. 11, 1929.

166. *El niño me retira.* Farce, 2 acts. Produced Teatro de la Zarzuela, Oct. 23, 1929.

167. *Cien comedias y un drama* (*A Hundred Comedies and One Drama*). Comedy, 3 acts. Produced Teatro de la Reina Victoria, Nov. 14, 1929.

168. *Mariquilla Terremoto.* Comedy, 3 acts. Produced Teatro de la Infanta Beatriz, Feb. 22, 1930.

169. *La esposa y la chismosa* (*The Wife and the Gossip*). Comedy, 1 act. Produced Teatro de la Infanta Isabel, May 27, 1930.

170. *Doña Hormiga.* Comedy, 3 acts. Produced Teatro de Lara, Oct. 29, 1930.

171. *Madreselva.* Dramatic verse poem, prologue and 3 acts. Produced Teatro Fontalba, Jan. 30, 1931.

172. *Noviazgo, boda y divorcio* (*Betrothal, Wedding, and Divorce*). Farce, 1 act. Produced Teatro de Lara, May 23, 1931.

173. *El peligro rosa* (*The Red Peril*). Comedy, 3 acts. Produced San Sebastián, Teatro de Príncipe, Sept. 11, 1931; Madrid, Teatro de la Infanta Isabel, Oct. 2, 1931.

174. *El nombre de un teatro* (*The Name of a Theatre*). Sketch, 1 act. Produced Teatro Figaro, Nov. 11, 1931.

175. *Visita de prueba* (*Trial Visit*). Comedy, 1 act. Produced Teatro María Guerrero, Dec. 22, 1931.

176. *Solera.* Comedy, 3 acts. Produced Teatro Fontalba, Jan. 13, 1932.

177. *Pitos y palmas* (*Catcalls and Hurrahs*). Musical comedy, 2 acts. Produced Teatro Calderón, Feb. 26, 1932. Music: Francisco Alonso.

178. *El rinconcito* (*The Little Corner*). Comedy, 3 acts. Produced Teatro de Lara, Apr. 8, 1932.

179. *Lo que hablan las mujeres* (*What the Women Are Saying*). Comedy, 3 acts. Produced Teatro de Lara, Oct. 21, 1932.

180. *La pícara vida* (*The Gay Life*). Comedy, 4 acts. Produced Teatro de la Avenida, Nov. 30, 1932.

181. *Los embustes de Pepitín* (*The Trinkets of Pepitín*). Monologue, 1 act. Produced Teatro Beatriz, Jan. 29, 1933.

182. *Un pregón sevillano* (*The Sevillan Hawker*). Farce, 1 act. Produced Teatro Español, Apr. 24, 1933.

183. *El susto* (*The Fright*). Comedy, 3 acts. Produced Teatro Fontalba, Apr. 28, 1933.

184. *La manga ancha* (*The Wide Sleeve*). Farce, 1 act. Produced Teatro Pavón, June 12, 1933.

185. *Juanito Arroyo se casa* (*Juanito Arroyo Gets Married*). Comedy, prologue and 3 acts. Produced Teatro Benavente, Oct. 26, 1933.

186. *Cinco lobitos* (*Five Little Wolves*). Comedy, 3 acts. Produced Teatro Cómico, Jan. 13, 1934.

187. *Las cosas claras* (*Cards on the Table*). Comedy, 1 act. Produced Barcelona, Teatro Poliorama, Mar. 22, 1934.

188. *Requiebros* (*Endearments*). Monologue, 1 act. Produced Teatro Cómico, Apr. 4, 1934.

189. *Colores y barro* (*Colors and Mud*). Musical comedy, 2 acts. Produced Coliseum, Sept. 4, 1934. Music: Jacinto Guerrero.

190. *La risa* (*The Laughter*). Comedy, 3 acts. Produced Seville, Teatro de Cervantes, Oct. 13, 1934.

191. *Para mal, el mío.* Comedy, 3 acts. Produced Teatro de Lara, Feb. 18, 1935.

192. *Martes, 13* (*Tuesday the Thirteenth*). Comedy, 3 acts. Produced Teatro Esclava, Apr. 20, 1935.

193. *Los restos* (*The Remaining Ones*). Burlesque comedy, 3 acts. Produced Barcelona, Teatro Barcelona, May 28, 1935.

194. *Seguidillas de baile* (*Danced Seguidillas*). Sketch, 1 act. Produced Teatro de la Comedia, May 29, 1935.

195. *La comiquilla* (*The Comedienne*). Comedy, 3 acts. Produced Teatro Benavente, Oct. 5, 1935.

196. *La inglesa sevillana* (*The Sevillan Englishwoman*). Comedy, 3 acts. Produced Teatro de la Zarzuela, Nov. 22, 1935.

197. *La venta de los gatos* (*The Sale of the Cats*). Dramatic verse poem, prologue and 3 acts. Produced Mexico City, Teatro Arbeu, July 10, 1937; Madrid, Teatro Español, May 14, 1940. Opera version: Produced 1943. Both versions are based on a short prose work by Gustavo Adolfo Bécquer.

198. *Los papaitos* (*The Little Fathers*). Comedy, 3 acts. Produced Montevideo, Teatro Solís, Nov. 4, 1937; Madrid, Teatro de la Comedia, Aug. 29, 1941.

199. *La Giralda* (*The Giralda*). Musical comedy, 3 acts. Produced Barcelona, Teatro Victoria, Sept. 22, 1939. Music: José Padilla.

200. *El maleficio* (*The Evil Spell*). Musical comedy, 3 acts. Produced San Sebastián, Teatro Victoria Eugenia, Sept. 30, 1939.

201. *Fifín II.* Caesarian comedy, 3 acts. Produced Bilbao, Teatro de Arriaga, Mar. 10, 1940.

202. *Siete veces* (*Seven Times*). Farce, 1 act. Produced Teatro Cómico, Mar. 23, 1940.

203. *La risa va por barrios* (*Laughter Makes the Rounds*). Burlesque comedy, 3 acts. Produced Teatro Cómico, Apr. 6, 1940.

204. *Tuyo y mío* (*Yours and Mine*). Comedy, 3 acts. Produced Teatro de la Reina Victoria, Jan. 16, 1941.

205. *¿A qué venía yo?* (*What Have I to Do With It?*). Farce, 1 act. Produced Teatro de la Reina Victoria, Feb. 28, 1941.

206. *Mañana de sombras* (*A Dark Morning*). Comedy, 1 act. Produced Teatro de la Zarzuela, July 3, 1941.

207. *La divina inventora* (*The Divine Inventor*). Comedy, 3 acts. Produced Teatro de Lara, Jan. 23, 1942.

208. *Burlona* (*Jester*). Comedy, 3 acts. Produced Teatro de Lara, Oct. 14, 1942.

209. *Olvidadiza* (*The Forgetful Woman*). Comedy, 3 acts. Produced Valencia, Teatro Esclava, Dec. 29, 1942.

210. *Azares del amor* (*Hazards of Love*). Farce, 1 act. Produced Teatro de la Infanta Beatriz, Jan. 8, 1943.

211. *Nidos sin pájaros* (*Nests Without Birds*). Comedy, 3

acts. Produced Vigo, Teatro García Barbón, Aug. 9, 1943; Madrid, Teatro de la Infanta Isabel, Apr. 8, 1944.

212. *Manantiales* (*Sources*). Comedy, 3 acts. Produced San Sebastián, Teatro Victoria Eugenia, Aug. 16, 1943.

213. *En mitad de la calle, o La prisa de las mujeres* (*In the Middle of the Street, or the Women's Quarrel*). Feminine colloquy, 1 act. Produced Radio Madrid, Nov. 12, 1943.

214. *Ventolera* (*The Gust of Wind*). Comedy, 3 acts. Produced Teatro Alházar, Dec. 6, 1944.

215. *El poetilla* (*The Poetaster*). Musical comedy, 1 act. Produced Elche, Gran Teatro, Apr. 20, 1945; Madrid, Teatro Rialto, July 4, 1945.

216. *Filosofía alcohólica* (*Alcoholic Philosophy*). Verse monologue, 1 act. Produced Córdoba, Argentina, Radio LUZ, November, 1945.

217. *El amor en un hito* (*Love in a Tourist Spot*). Comedy, 1 act. Produced Teatro Beatriz, July 1, 1946.

218. *Manolita Quintera.* Comedy, 3 acts. Produced Teatro Fontalba, September, 1946. Music: Alonso.

219. *Los burladores* (*The Jesters*). Musical comedy, 3 acts. Produced Teatro Calderón, Dec. 10, 1948. Music: Pablo Sorozábal.

220. *Entre sueños* (*Between Dreams*). Romantic verse comedy, 3 acts. Published 1953.

221. *El género ínfimo* (*The Lowest Class*). Playlet, 1 act. Music: Joaquín Valverde and Barrera.

222. *La historia de Sevilla.* Play.

223. *Pesado y medido.* Play.

224. *El otro peligro.* Play.

225. *Las rayas de la mano.* Play.

226. *El reparto de mujeres.* Play.

227. *Miel con miel.* Play.

228. *Pregón de flores* (*The Flower Hawker*). Operetta, 2 scenes. Music: Turina.

229. *El género chico* (*Light Comedy*). Play.

230. *Un día es un día* (*A Day Is a Day*). Play.

EDITIONS

Collections.
Four Plays, ed. and tr. by H. and H. Granville-Barker, Boston, 1928; *Four Comedies,* ed. and tr. by H. and H. Granville-Barker, New York, 1932; *Obras completas,* 7 vols., Madrid, 1947–1953.

Individual Plays.
By Their Words Ye Shall Know Them. Published in *Representative One-act Plays by Continental Authors,* ed. by M. J. Moses and tr. by J. G. Underhill, Boston, 1922.

A Hundred Years Old. Published in *Plays of To-day,* tr. by H. and H. Granville-Barker, vol. 3, London, 1925–1930.

In the Moonlight. Published in *Spanish One-act Plays in English,* ed. and tr. by W. K. Jones, Dallas, 1934.

Lady Clarines. Published in *Twentieth Century Plays,* ed. by F. W. Chandler and R. A. Cordell and tr. by H. and H. Granville-Barker, rev. ed., New York, 1939.

Malvaloca. Published in *Chief Contemporary Dramatists,* ed. by T. H. Dickinson and tr. by J. S. Fassett, 3d ser., Boston, 1930.

The Prime of Life (*The Fountain of Youth*). S. N. Baker, tr., New York, 1922.

A Sunny Morning. Published in *Thirty Famous One-act Plays,* ed. by B. Cerf and V. H. Cartmell and tr. by L. X. Floyd, New York, 1943.

The Women's Town. Published in *Contemporary Spanish Dramatists,* ed. and tr. by C. A. Turrell, Boston, 1919.

CRITICISM

Azorín (J. M. Ruiz), *Los Quintero y otras páginas,* Madrid, 1925; M. Carpi, *L'opera dei fratelli Quintero,* Rome, 1930; *Cuadernos de literatura contemporánea,* vols. XIII and XIV, Madrid, 1944; A. G. Climent, *Andalucía en los Quintero,* Madrid, 1956.

AMBROGINI, Angelo. *See* POLIZIANO, ANGELO.

AMIEL, Denys, pseudonym of Guillaume Roche (1884–   ). French dramatist who excelled in psychological portraits of women in love. His theatre continues the tradition of Georges de Porto-Riche and Henri Bataille, but it is distinguished by his use of the so-called intimist techniques found in the works of Jean-Jacques Bernard and other exponents of the "school of silence." Responding to the growing influence of Freud, Amiel contended that conventions of conversation were designed not to communicate the speaker's intention but to mask it. The intentions of his protagonists are therefore conveyed by what remains unspoken, implied, half-articulately expressed. *See* BERNARD, JEAN-JACQUES.

Close to Him (*Près de lui,* 1912), Amiel's first play, was successfully produced by André Antoine, who had introduced Paris audiences to the works of Porto-Riche, Brieux, and Curel. In the years immediately following World War I, Amiel abandoned the theatre, but in 1921 he collaborated with André Obey on what was to be his most successful play, *The Smiling Mme. Beudet* (*La souriante Madame Beudet*), the drama of a sensitive woman married to a kindly boor. In intimist fashion, Mme. Beudet's smile, taken by her husband and others as a sign of her contentment, masks the unexpressed desperation and unhappiness that eventually lead her to make an attempt on her husband's life. In *The Voyager* (*Le voyageur,* 1923), a woman transfers her affections from her current lover to his friend. While the three characters discuss at length travel, friends, and work, it becomes obvious that their minds are really occupied with their triangular relationship; their underlying emotions are conveyed by what remains unspoken under the constant stream of talk. *See* OBEY, ANDRÉ.

By and large, Amiel's following plays are variations on a theme. *The Couple* (*Le couple,* 1923) is a realistic examination of conjugal

Denys Amiel. [La Petite Illustration]

infidelity; *Mr. and Mrs. So-and-So* (*M. et Mme. Un Tel*, 1925) focuses on various aspects of middle-class life; and *The Image* (*L'image*, 1927) concerns two lovers who are separated by the memory of an ideal love. *Décalage* (1931) and *Three and One* (*Trois et une*, 1932) are comedies, the latter concerning a woman who has three children who were fathered by different men—a pianist, a sportsman, and a financier. *The Iron Age* (*L'âge de fer*, 1932) is somewhat of a departure from Amiel's usual themes in that it is a violent attack on the growing mechanization of society, but in *A Woman in Full Flower* (*La femme en fleur*, 1935) he returns to earlier themes and techniques with the study of an older woman jealous of her daughter. After World War II, Amiel wrote *Tierry's Return* (*Le retour de Tierry*, 1951), a drama of the French Resistance, but it was obvious that his theatre was too closely linked to the style of life that was gone forever to succeed with contemporary audiences.

ANAGNORISIS (Recognition Scene). Term used by Aristotle in his *Poetics* to denote the discovery of a character's true identity, as when Orestes is recognized by Electra in Euripides's *Electra*. Aristotle gives six ways in which this "change from ignorance to knowledge" may come about. They include signs or marks on the person, devices invented by the poet, awakened memory, reasoning, and erroneous reasoning that arrives at the correct solution. Best of all, according to Aristotle, is a discovery that grows in a logical manner from a play's incidents. Such a case is Oedipus's gradual progress toward self-recognition in Sophocles's *Oedipus the King*. Similarly, in the tragedies of Euripides the recognition frequently provides the moment when the action significantly changes course. Modern critics tend to use the term more broadly, applying it to any important discovery by a character of his or another's true state or condition. In New Comedy the *anagnorisis* was used as a comic device whereby the revelation of a character's true identity leads to a happy conclusion, as when a slave turns out to be a freeman and is therefore able to marry his mistress. *See* EURIPIDES; NEW COMEDY; SOPHOCLES.

Maxwell Anderson
(1888 – 1959)

Maxwell Anderson, American playwright and poet, was born in Atlantic, Pa., on December 15, 1888, the son of an itinerant Baptist minister. After attending schools in Pennsylvania, Ohio, Iowa, and North Dakota, he was graduated from the University of North Dakota in 1911, and in 1914 he earned a master's degree at Stanford University in California. During this period he taught at Whittier College and worked as an editorial writer on San Francisco newspapers. He was dismissed from these posts during World War I because of his stated pacifist beliefs.

In 1918 Anderson went to New York, where he first joined the staff of the *New Republic* and eventually became an editorial writer on the *World*. He wrote his first produced play, *White Desert*, in 1923, but it attracted little attention. Disappointed by the poor popular reception of this first attempt at verse drama (critics praised it), he joined with Laurence Stallings, a colleague on the *World*, in a short-lived collaboration that proved enormously successful with *What Price Glory?* (1924). Anderson and Stallings tried to reproduce the chemistry of this success with *First Flight* (1925), a historical play about Andrew Jackson, and *The Buccaneer* (1925), a swashbuckling play, but neither reached any degree of success, whereupon the partnership was dissolved. *See* STALLINGS, LAURENCE.

Although Anderson wrote many plays, poetry was his first love. In 1925 he published a book of lyric poems, *You Who Have Dreams*. He preferred the poetic medium in the theatre, and after several failures at verse drama with contemporary themes he turned to a historical subject: *Elizabeth the Queen* (1930) was one of the first successful American verse dramas to be presented. In 1933 he returned to prose in *Both Your Houses,* for which he won a Pulitzer Prize; but he persevered in blank verse and in 1935 had his first success with a contemporary subject in *Winterset,* which won the first New York Drama Critics Circle award. This award was presented to him again in 1937, for *High Tor,* a play combining blank verse and colloquial prose.

Maxwell Anderson. [Theatre Collection, The New York Public Library at Lincoln Center, Astor, Lenox and Tilden Foundations]

With the approach of World War II Anderson shifted to wartime themes, attacking fascism in all forms and praising the bravery of the French and the courage of American soldiers. After the war he dealt with other problems: marital infidelity in *Truckline Cafe* (1946) and racial prejudice in *Lost in the Stars* (1949).

Anderson also wrote radio plays, masques, and adaptations, many of which were sentimental and melodramatic. Several of his theatrical works were adapted as screenplays, among them *Winterset,* in 1936.

Anderson met his first wife, Margaret Haskett, while an undergraduate at the University of North Dakota and married her in 1911. She died in 1931, leaving him three sons. In 1933 he married Gertrude Maynard, by whom he had one daughter. It was she who encouraged him through his most creative years. After her death in 1953, Anderson married Gilda Oakleaf. Shortly thereafter his health began to fail, and after 1954 he did little writing. He died of a stroke in Stamford, Conn., on February 28, 1959.

WORK

Central to the plays of Maxwell Anderson was his great desire to create a poetic drama in the United States that would restore the theatre to a position of Shakespearean grandeur and raise it above the pedestrian reality of contemporary theatre to the heady atmosphere of poetry and universal truth. Yet his

lofty ambitions were not propelled by an infallible talent: strained, sometimes prosaic verse forms and vagueness of theme and conclusion caused failures despite his high purpose.

Although Anderson was successful in other forms of dramatic writing—*What Price Glory?* (1924) is a realistic portrayal of the emotional confusion of soldiers in combat, written in strong language of the battlefield never before heard onstage and exposing the vicious realities of war and love; and *Saturday's Children* (1927) is a domestic comedy, the pathetic tale of a young couple caught up in the problems imposed by poverty—poetry was the force that led to his singular influence on the American theatre. His romantic tragedies, all written at least partially in loose blank verse, began with a failure, *White Desert* (1923), describing a tragedy of infidelity and murder on the Dakota prairie. Nonetheless, with an increasingly unerring instinct for the current theatre, he managed, despite his use of familiar stories and themes and the newness of his verse forms on the stage, to enchant both audiences and critics with a whole series of poetic works—*Elizabeth the Queen* (1930), *Mary of Scotland* (1933), *Valley Forge* (1934), and *The Masque of Kings* (1937)—whose culmination was *Winterset* (1935) and *High Tor* (1937), both deeply felt and sensitively executed expressions of romanticism.

Thematically, with *Gods of the Lightning* (1928), a dramatic depiction of the Sacco-Vanzetti case written with Harold Hickerson, Anderson struck the chord that was to be repeated in each of his important succeeding works. The good and the innocent must inevitably succumb to "men who are hard . . . brigands in power who fight always for more power." As two innocent men are killed by the government in *Gods of the Lightning,* so in *Elizabeth the Queen* the righteous Essex is undone by ignoble forces behind the throne: "Those who are noble, free of soul, valiant and admirable—they go down in their prime, Always go down . . . the rats inherit the earth." So it is in *Mary of Scotland,* as Mary succumbs to the ruthless intrigues of Elizabeth; and in *Winterset,* as the anguished Mio and his innocent Miriamne are slaughtered by the corrupt forces they set out to expose. Only in *Valley Forge* do the meek inherit the earth, and Washington, after a brief disillusionment, is strengthened by the example of his valiant army to carry on the cause of the

(Opposite) *Mary of Scotland,* with Helen Hayes. New York, Alvin Theatre, 1933. [Photograph by Vandamm. Theatre Collection, The New York Public Library at Lincoln Center, Astor, Lenox and Tilden Foundations]

Elizabeth the Queen, with Alfred Lunt and Lynn Fontanne. New York, Guild Theatre, 1930. [Theatre Collection, The New York Public Library at Lincoln Center, Astor, Lenox and Tilden Foundations]

Revolution. *High Tor,* combining comic and tragic elements with political commentary, restates the inevitability of the victory of entrenched power over idealism.

The use of the Elizabethan period as the setting for some of these plays and the consequent imitation of Elizabethan language in the dialogue led some critics to compare Anderson with the poet-dramatists of the period. His verse, often prosaic and verbose, was criticized as a mechanical imitation of Shakespeare in its rhythms. At its best, however, its intensity compensates for its apparent archaism.

Anderson's political satires in a more contemporary vein earned him critical acclaim. *Both Your Houses* (1933) mounts an attack on corrupt politics. *Knickerbocker Holiday* (1938), a musical, satirizes the politics of the New York of Peter Stuyvesant; and *Key Largo*

Paul Muni and Uta Hagen in *Key Largo*. New York, Ethel Barrymore Theatre, 1939. [Photograph by Vandamm. Theatre Collection, The New York Public Library at Lincoln Center, Astor, Lenox and Tilden Foundations]

(1939), a poetic drama, concerns a defector from the Loyalist side in the Spanish Civil War who learns that there is no integrity without courage.

Anderson's work was more derivative in *The Wingless Victory* (1936) and *The Masque of Kings* (1937), about the tragedy at Mayerling. Then, as World War II grew closer, he wrote several plays devoted to the cause of fighting fascism. *Key Largo* drew a parallel between Spanish fascism and gangsterism in Florida; *Candle in the Wind* (1941) showed the gallantry of the French under German occupation; *The Eve of St. Mark* (1942) gave a lyrical picture of American soldiers on their entry into World War II; and *Storm Operation* (1944), a failure, was a heroic depiction of combat.

After the war Anderson returned to history with *Joan of Lorraine* (1946), an examination of Joan's character through a rehearsal for a play during which the actress portraying the saint and the director disagree on the interpretation of her role; *Anne of the Thousand Days* (1948), dealing with Anne Boleyn's maneuvers to ensure that her child Elizabeth will succeed Henry VIII on the throne of England; *Lost in the Stars* (1949), an adaptation of Alan Paton's novel *Cry, the Beloved Country* with music by Kurt Weill; and *Barefoot in Athens* (1951), about Socrates's choice of suicide over the loss of his integrity, the play Anderson considered the culmination of his career, an exposition of his philosophy couched in the genre he had championed all his life.

What Price Glory? (1924). Drama of a United States Marine company stationed in France during World War I. Sergeant Quirk arrives to assume the duties of his old enemy, Captain Flagg, the company commander, who is going on leave for eight days. At the farmhouse where they are quartered, Quirk takes up with a prostitute, Charmaine, unaware that Flagg is also interested in her. When Flagg returns, the two men are confronted by Cognac Pete, the girl's father, who wants his "deflowered innocent" married to the villain, Sergeant Quirk. Hatred between the two men flares up as Quirk, a confirmed bachelor, is threatened by Flagg with court-martial if he does not marry the girl. But just before the ceremony is to be performed, the company is ordered to the front. Quirk is then wounded and before long escapes from his hospital bed to make his way back to Charmaine. Flagg follows, and at Cognac Pete's tavern they play blackjack for the only gun, for they are determined to kill one another. Recall of the company to the fighting ends their private quarrel, and they depart together, leaving Charmaine alone.

Elizabeth the Queen (1930). Romantic historical drama in blank verse about the aging Queen Elizabeth I of England and the much younger Earl of Essex. Although Essex loves Elizabeth, he seeks to capture the throne, which Elizabeth will share with no one. Elizabeth's mistrust of Essex, nurtured by his rival Cecil and other foes while he is on a military campaign, strengthens her conviction that he is planning a rebellion. When he returns, she orders him arrested and executed for treason. As his execution nears, Elizabeth, wracked by grief, waits in vain for Essex to return a ring to her as a token promise that he will abandon his efforts to obtain the throne and so obtain his pardon. In the end she summons him, but Essex refuses to beg for his life, asserting that if he were free, he would again strive for power. The play ends as Elizabeth, grief-stricken, bows her head and clasps her hands to her ears as the clock gives the signal for Essex's death.

Both Your Houses (1933). Ironic comedy, satirizing congressional logrolling, in which Alan McLean, an idealistic freshman congressman, discovers the hard facts of political

Winterset, with (l. to r.) Theodore Hecht, Richard Bennett, Fernanda Eliscu, and Burgess Meredith. New York, Martin Beck Theatre, 1935. [Theatre Collection, The New York Public Library at Lincoln Center, Astor, Lenox and Tilden Foundations]

Both Your Houses. New York, Royale Theatre, 1933. [Photograph by Vandamm. Theatre Collection, The New York Public Library at Lincoln Center, Astor, Lenox and Tilden Foundations]

life when he is appointed to the Appropriations Committee. Members of his committee lobby for passage of a bill appropriating 200 million dollars that includes money for a number of unnecessary projects. Although 40 million dollars would be appropriated for a much-needed dam in his home state, fulfilling one of his campaign promises, McLean fights the bill because the contractors who were among his campaign supporters have submitted dishonest bids. Contact with his colleagues convinces him that they are less concerned with their constituents' welfare than with personal gain. To beat them at their own game he introduces a bill so flagrantly dishonest that he is certain it will be killed. Ironically, it passes both houses.

Mary of Scotland (1933).   Historical drama about Mary, Queen of Scots, daughter of King James V and Mary of Lorraine. At the age of six she was betrothed to the future King Francis II of France and, having spent her childhood in France, was married to him at the age of fifteen. As the play begins, four years later, Mary, now widowed, has returned to Scotland and presents her claim to the English throne. Because Mary is a Catholic,

Elizabeth fears she may in fact obtain enough support to take the throne. Playing on Mary's ingenuousness, Elizabeth contrives to have her marry Lord Darnley, a wastrel and drunkard, believing that he will aid in Mary's downfall. Mary has other powerful enemies: John Knox, the fanatical anti-Catholic clergyman; and the Scottish barons, greedy for power and jealous of the Earl of Bothwell, Mary's lover. When Mary marries Darnley, Bothwell exiles himself, leaving the politically naïve Queen without an ally. The barons initiate a civil war, and despite Bothwell's return with an army, Mary is beaten. She flees to England, still unaware of Elizabeth's enmity, and finds herself a prisoner. Finally recognizing Elizabeth's hand in her downfall, Mary denounces the Queen in a scene that seals her fate, proclaiming that she at least has known love and borne a child, while Elizabeth remains the Virgin Queen.

Winterset (1935).   Poetic tragedy in verse, inspired by a famous case in 1921 in which two Italian anarchists, Nicola Sacco and Bartolomeo Vanzetti, were condemned to death for a murder of which they denied all knowledge. Many people believed that they had been convicted because of their anarchist views. In the play Mio, whose idealistic and radical father was executed for a murder he did not commit, is determined to vindicate him. Learning that Garth Esdras knew that his father was innocent, Mio tracks him down in order to force him to testify. Rabbi Esdras and Miriamne, Garth's father and sister, are determined to prevent a confrontation between the two young men because they wish to protect Garth, who is under constant surveillance by the real murderer, a gangster named Trock. Garth's deteriorating emotional state places him in grave danger from the murderer. Meanwhile, Mio and young Miriamne fall in love. Knowing that exposure of the criminal would harm his beloved, Mio gives up his obsessive desire for revenge and refuses to call the police. In the end, Garth is safe, but because the star-crossed lovers know too much, they are killed by Trock's henchmen.

High Tor (1937).   Poetic fantasy in which Van Van Dorn, young owner of High Tor, a mountaintop overlooking the Hudson River, fights to keep corrupt land speculators away from his property. A large company sends two representatives who resort to threats in order to convince Van to sell his prized retreat. But he refuses to compromise his principles. Meanwhile, the company men find themselves trapped on the mountainside by nightfall and take refuge in a steam shovel overlooking a bluff. To their surprise they are hoisted aloft and held captive by the ghosts of Henry Hudson's crew, who have wandered the mountainside for three hundred years. Finally, a senior member of the firm ascends High Tor to find his men and offers Van a large sum of money for the property. Convinced that the mountain, like the ghostly crew, has vanished in the light of morning, Van accepts the offer.

PLAYS

Unless otherwise noted, the plays were first performed in New York.

1. *White Desert*. Drama, 4 acts; verse. Produced Princess Theatre, Oct. 18, 1923.
2. (With Laurence Stallings). *What Price Glory?* Drama, 3 acts; prose. Written 1924. Published 1926. Produced Plymouth Theatre, Sept. 3, 1924.
3. *Outside Looking In*. Play, 3 acts. Published 1929. Produced Greenwich Village Theatre, Sept. 7, 1925.
4. (With Stallings). *First Flight*. Play, 3 acts. Published 1926. Produced Plymouth Theatre, Sept. 17, 1925.
5. (With Stallings). *The Buccaneer*. Play, 3 acts. Published 1926. Produced Plymouth Theatre, Oct. 2, 1925.
6. *Sea Wife*. Play, 3 acts. Written ca. 1926. Produced Minneapolis, University of Minnesota, Dec. 6, 1932.
7. *Saturday's Children*. Comedy, 3 acts. Published 1927. Produced Booth Theatre, Jan. 26, 1927.
8. *Hell on Wheels*. Musical play. Written ca. 1928. Music: Jack Niles.
9. (With Harold Hickerson). *Gods of the Lightning*. Play, 3 acts. Published 1928. Produced Little Theatre, Oct. 24, 1928.
10. *Gypsy*. Play, 3 acts. Produced Klaw Theatre, Jan. 14, 1929.
11. *Elizabeth the Queen*. Drama, 3 acts; verse. Written 1930. Published 1932. Produced Guild Theatre, 1930.
12. *Night over Taos*. Play, 3 acts; verse. Published 1930. Produced 1932.
13. *Both Your Houses*. Drama, 3 acts. Written 1933. Published 1933. Produced Royale Theatre, Mar. 6, 1933.
14. *Mary of Scotland*. Historical drama, 3 acts; verse. Published 1934. Produced Alvin Theatre, Nov. 27, 1933.
15. *Valley Forge*. Drama, 3 acts; verse. Published 1934. Produced Pittsburgh, Guild Theatre, Dec. 10, 1934.
16. *Winterset*. Tragedy, 3 acts; verse. Published 1935. Produced Martin Beck Theatre, Sept. 25, 1935.
17. *The Wingless Victory*. Tragedy, 3 acts; verse. Published 1936. Produced Empire Theatre, Dec. 23, 1936.
18. *High Tor*. Comedy, 3 acts; verse and prose. Published 1937. Produced Martin Beck Theatre, Jan. 9, 1937.
19. *The Masque of Kings*. Tragedy, 3 acts; verse. Published 1937. Produced Shubert Theatre, Feb. 8, 1937.
20. *The Feast of Ortolans*. Radio play, 1 act; verse. Published 1938. Produced National Broadcasting Company (Blue Network), Sept. 20, 1937.
21. *The Star Wagon*. Dramatic fantasy, 3 acts. Published 1937. Produced Empire Theatre, Sept. 29, 1937.
22. *Second Overture*. Radio play, 1 act; verse. Published 1938. Produced New York, Station WEAF, Jan. 29, 1938.
23. *Knickerbocker Holiday*. Musical comedy, 2 acts. Published 1948. Produced Ethel Barrymore Theatre, Oct. 19, 1938. Lyrics: Maxwell Anderson. Music: Kurt Weill.
24. *Key Largo*. Drama, prologue and 2 acts; verse. Written 1939. Published 1939. Produced Ethel Barrymore Theatre, Nov. 27, 1939.
25. *Journey to Jerusalem*. Drama, 3 acts; verse. Written 1940. Published 1940. Produced National Theatre, Oct. 5, 1940.
26. *The Miracle of the Danube*. Radio play, 1 act. Published 1941. Produced Columbia Broadcasting System, 1941.
27. *Candle in the Wind*. Play, 2 acts. Published 1941. Produced Shubert Theatre, Oct. 22, 1941.
28. *The Eve of St. Mark*. Drama, 2 acts. Published 1942. Produced Cort Theatre, Oct. 7, 1942.
29. *Storm Operation*. Play; prologue and epilogue, 2 acts. Published 1944. Produced Belasco Theatre, Jan. 11, 1944.
30. *Joan of Lorraine*. Play; prologue and epilogue, 2 acts; prose. Published 1944. Produced Alvin Theatre, Nov. 18, 1946.
31. *Truckline Cafe*. Play. Produced Belasco Theatre, Feb. 27, 1946.
32. *Anne of the Thousand Days*. Historical drama, 2 acts; verse. Published 1948. Produced Shubert Theatre, Dec. 8, 1948.
33. *Lost in the Stars*. Musical play. Produced Oct. 30, 1949. Lyrics: Anderson. Music: Weill. Based on Alan Paton's novel *Cry, the Beloved Country* (1948).
34. *Barefoot in Athens*. Play, 2 acts. Published 1951. Produced Martin Beck Theatre, Oct. 31, 1951.
35. *The Bad Seed*. Play, 2 acts. Published 1955. Produced Dec. 8, 1954. Based on the novel of the same name by William March (1954).
36. *The Masque of Pedagogues* (*Being a Dream of President McVey's*). Published 1957.
37. (With Brendan Gill). *The Day the Money Stopped*. Play, 2 scenes. Written 1958? Produced Feb. 20, 1958.
38. *The Golden Six*. Play, 2 acts. Produced York Playhouse, Oct. 25, 1958.

EDITIONS

Collections.
Three American Plays, New York, 1926; *Eleven Verse Plays*, New York, 1940; *Four Verse Plays*, New York, 1959.

Individual Plays.

Anne of the Thousand Days. Published in *Best American Plays,* ed. by J. Gassner, 3d ser., New York, 1952.

The Bad Seed. Published in *Theatre,* ed. by J. Chapman, New York, 1955.

Both Your Houses. Published in *A New Edition of the Pulitzer Prize Plays,* ed. by K. Cordell and W. H. Cordell, New York, 1940.

Elizabeth the Queen. Published in *Aspects of Modern Drama,* ed. by M. W. Steinberg, New York, 1960.

The Feast of Ortolans. Published in *Adventures in Modern Literature,* ed. by R. M. Stauffer and W. H. Cunningham, New York, 1939.

Gods of the Lightning. (With Harold Hickerson). Published in *Twenty-five Best Plays of the Modern American Theatre,* ed. by J. Gassner, New York, 1949.

High Tor. Published in *Three Dramas of American Individualism,* ed. by J. E. Mersand, New York, 1961.

Journey to Jerusalem. Published in *Plays Without Footlights,* ed. by E. E. Galbraith, New York, 1945.

Key Largo. Published in *The Modern Omnibus,* ed. by F. P. Rolfe et al., New York, 1946.

Lost in the Stars. Published in *Famous American Plays of the 1940's,* ed. by H. Hewes, New York, 1960.

Mary of Scotland. Published in *The Theatre Guild Anthology,* New York, 1936.

The Masque of Kings. Published in *Representative American Dramas, National and Local,* ed. by M. J. Moses and J. W. Krutch, rev. ed., Boston, 1941.

Saturday's Children. Published in *Twenty-five Best Plays of the Modern American Theatre,* ed. by J. Gassner, New York, 1949.

Valley Forge. Published in *Representative Modern Plays,* ed. by R. Warnock, Chicago, 1952.

What Price Glory? (With Laurence Stallings). Published in *Famous American Plays of the 1920's,* ed. by K. Macgowan, New York, 1959.

The Wingless Victory. Published in *Modern Drama,* ed.

by E. J. Lovell and W. W. Pratt, Boston, 1963.

Winterset. Published in *Representative American Plays from 1767 to the Present Day,* ed. by A. H. Quinn, 7th ed., rev. and enl., New York, 1953.

CRITICISM

B. H. Clark, *Maxwell Anderson: The Man and His Work,* New York, Los Angeles, and London, 1933; M. D. Bailey, *Maxwell Anderson: The Playwright as Prophet,* London and New York, 1957.

ANDERSON, Robert [Woodruff] (b. New York, April 28, 1917). American dramatist best known for *Tea and Sympathy* (1953), the study of an adolescent who fears he is a homosexual. *All Summer Long* (1954) concerns a boy who, in the face of the apathy of his parents, tries in vain to build a levee to save his home from floodwater. *Silent Night, Lonely Night* (1959) is the story of two lonely people stranded in an inn on Christmas Eve. After a brief affair they go their separate ways with renewed strength and courage. Anderson's more recent plays are *The Days Between* (1966), concerning a teacher of writing who cannot write and his wife, who is attracted to a successful hack writer; *You Know I Can't Hear You When the Water's Running* (1967), a program of four one-act plays dealing humorously with subjects relating to sex; *I Never Sang for My Father* (1968), a drama in which a middle-aged man tries to establish affectionate contact with his father; and *Soli-*

Martin Balsam and Eileen Heckart in Robert Anderson's *You Know I Can't Hear You When the Water's Running.* New York, Ambassador Theatre, 1967. [Walter Hampden Memorial Library at the Players, New York]

taire/Double Solitaire (1971), two one-act plays, one set in a dehumanized future and the other in the present.

Tea and Sympathy (1953). Drama set in a New England boarding school in which Tom Lee, a lonely and sensitive adolescent, falls in love with the one person who understands him, Laura Reynolds, wife of the headmaster, in whose house he lives. Her husband Bill, a defensively masculine type, grows to dislike the sensitive boy. With Bill's tacit approval, the other boys come to believe that Tom is a homosexual and begin to persecute him relentlessly. To prove his manhood, Tom tries to have sexual relations with the town prostitute, but she is so distasteful to him that he runs away before touching her, convinced that he is a homosexual. Laura, finally rebelling against her husband's brutality, leaves him for his part in Tom's persecution and, at the end, gives herself to Tom to prove to him that he is a man. Produced New York, Ethel Barrymore Theatre, September 30, 1953.

Robert Anderson. [Theatre Collection, The New York Public Library at Lincoln Center, Astor, Lenox and Tilden Foundations]

Tea and Sympathy, with Deborah Kerr and John Kerr. New York, Ethel Barrymore Theatre, 1953. [Theatre Collection, The New York Public Library at Lincoln Center, Astor, Lenox and Tilden Foundations]

ANDRES, Stefan (1906–   ). German poet, novelist, and dramatist who spent the World War II years in exile and whose work reflects his concern with social and political issues. He first achieved worldwide fame with the dramatization of his novel *We Are Utopia* (*Wir sind Utopia*, 1943) under the title *God's Utopia* (*Gottes Utopia*, 1950), the story of a monk who leaves his monastery to become a political revolutionary in the Spanish Civil War. Andres's other plays include *Labyrinthian Dance* (*Tanz durchs Labyrinth*; wr. 1948, prod. 1956), a five-part mystery play that borrows from events in world history to show that Satan coexists with the good spirit in man; *Tourists* (*Touristen*, 1955), a burlesque comedy originally known as *Plato's Sons* (*Die Söhne Platons*, 1946), which deals with a modern Socrates opposed to tourism; and *Closed Zones* (*Sperrzonen*, 1958), a political tragedy concerning the Germans' war guilt. His work, colored by his early Catholic education and his sojourn in Italy during the war, reflects the mysticism of religious experience and is distinguished at the same time by clarity of style.

Andres is above all a gifted storyteller. In his more than twenty novels, including *The Marriage of Enemies* (*Die Hochzeit der Feinde*, 1947) and the ambitious trilogy *The Flood* (*Die Sintflut*, 1949–1959), and in his shorter prose works, he remains true to the theme of conflict between the moral law and the senses and he shows himself to be a master of form.

Leonid Nikolayevich Andreyev

(1871 — 1919)

Leonid Nikolayevich Andreyev, Russian short-story writer, playwright, and novelist, was born in Orel, the son of a provincial land surveyor, on August 21, 1871 (N.S.). In 1891 he entered the University of St. Petersburg, where he lived in great poverty. After his first term he attempted suicide following an unsuccessful love affair, left the university, spent a couple of years in restless idleness, and in 1893 resumed his law studies at the University of Moscow. He supported himself by selling the portraits he painted and by writing court reports and short stories for local papers. At the same time he took his law degree and in 1897 was admitted to the bar. By 1898 he had abandoned his law career and restricted himself to crime and court report-

ing for the newspaper *Kuryer* and to writing short stories. After reading the story "Bergamot i Garaska" (1898), Gorky encouraged Andreyev and began introducing him into influential literary circles; in 1901 Gorky's publishing firm, Znaniye, brought out Andreyev's first collection of short stories, which was instantaneously successful. The close friendship between the two men lasted until 1905, when Andreyev's own popularity far outstripped that of Gorky and he began to consider Gorky's social and humanitarian ideas naïve. *See* GORKY, MAXIM.

With a pathological history of several suicide attempts, a nervous breakdown, and neurotic fits of depression and paranoia, his literary style abruptly changed in 1902, the year he married Shura Veligorskaya. Following his marriage, Andreyev enjoyed his greatest popularity: every new story was a literary sensation, drawing either wild enthusiasm or strong condemnation. The failure of the 1905 Revolution and the death of his wife brought an emotional crisis in 1906 that changed his optimistic belief in social revolution to pessimism. These feelings of gloom and emptiness persisted and were reflected in Andreyev's subsequent writings, which include his best play, *The Life of a Man* (*Zhizn cheloveka*, wr. 1906). He became nihilistic in his political thinking, believing revolution and heroism in an evil world to be futile and freedom only an illusion.

After 1908 Andreyev's popularity and narrative ability began to wane. His novel *Sashka Zhegulyov* (1912), written during this period, attracted little attention. During the

Leonid Andreyev. [G. Lolivier, Paris]

years 1908–1916, Andreyev concentrated on writing for the theatre, but his plays reveal his creative decline.

World War I stimulated Andreyev to neurotic chauvinism, and his writings became highly patriotic and anti-German. In 1916 he accepted the editorship of the prowar newspaper *Russkaya Volya*. From 1917 onward he devoted himself to writing anti-Bolshevik pieces, the last of which was an emotional appeal, entitled *S.O.S.* (1919), to the Western Allies to save Russia. He then retired permanently to his villa in Kuokkala, Finland (now Repino, U.S.S.R.), where he died on September 12, 1919.

WORK

Andreyev's work is important as a historical gauge, showing the kind of experimentation prevalent in early-twentieth-century Russian theatre. His plays are rarely read, and they have never been performed on the Soviet stage. His style is fundamentally realistic with a heavy reliance on symbolist techniques. The themes of pessimism, the unrelieved gloom of life, the inevitability of brutality, heartlessness, and horror, and the falsity and vanity of humanity, which is doomed to insanity or death, are recurrent in Andreyev's drama. Gorky-influenced realism is seen in his first play, *To The Stars* (*K zvezdam,* 1906), a reaction to the failure of the 1905 Revolution. Following this, Andreyev experimented with symbolism and modernism. Most of the plays written between 1906 and 1910, although interesting, appear pretentious and contrived, employing personifications of abstractions such as death, hunger, and fate, and allegories and symbols to express "metaphysical" problems. Because of this tendency, many critics still refer to him as a pseudosymbolist. The most representative of the plays written during this period are *The Life of a Man* (1907), *Tsar Hunger* (*Tsar golod,* wr. 1906), *Black Masks* (*Chyornye maski,* wr. 1908), and *Anathema* (*Anatema,* 1909). *See* ALLEGORY; SYMBOLISM.

The Life of a Man is a synopsis of man's life from birth to death, introduced and narrated by Fate. Man's illusion of happiness is short, and he is destroyed by misfortune and death. The play was first staged in February, 1907, by the radical theatrical innovator Vsevolod Meyerhold. To indicate multidimensional time, Meyerhold used no sets. The walls, ceiling, and floor of the theatre were covered with gray draperies, and the stage was free from conventional props: the whole effect was dreamlike. In Konstantin Stanislavski's version later that year, the gloomy and mournful action of the drama was emphasized by a stage draped in black. Stanislavski's production initiated the use of "gloomy and grotesque impressionism" on the legitimate Russian stage. *Tsar Hunger,* a portrayal of a blind, brutal revolt of the hungry masses in which cities are destroyed and women and children are killed, was an experiment in the use of nightmarish imagery. The dimensions of insanity and life in the shadowy world of paranoia are explored in *Black Masks:* Duke Lorenzo, in the grip of the madness of a split personality, fights a duel with his double. *Anathema,* a pretentious allegory based on the Faustian theme, includes much philosophical abstraction. Humanity and compassion are represented by Leiser, a humble Jew who is given a fortune by Anathema (Satan) to tempt him. Leiser gives all his money to the poor and sick, and when it is gone, they kill him out of greed.

After 1910 Andreyev abandoned his extreme symbolist experiments and returned to realism; however, now his realistic style, infused with symbolism, produced many confused and inferior plays. The better plays of this period are *Professor Storitsyn* (1913); a dramatization of his story *Thought* (*Mysl,* 1913/14); and, best of all, *He Who Gets Slapped* (*Tot, kto poluchayet poshchechiny,* 1915). *Thought* is the story of a man who, believing himself superior to ordinary human beings, kills his lover's husband, simulates madness, and then kills the psychiatrist who must examine him. When he is confined to a mental institution, he begins to wonder if he is, in fact, mad. He in *He Who Gets Slapped,* a former intellectual who has become a circus clown, is a quasi-autobiographical character. The plays written after Andreyev's period of realism became increasingly melodramatic and are of comparatively poor quality.

To the Stars (*K zvezdam,* 1906). Drama reflecting the growing revolutionary spirit that was to engulf Russia after 1905. Sergius Ternovsky, a famous astronomer, has chosen to live in exile with his family. High in the mountains, away from life, he buries himself in his work. Life and reality intrude on him when his oldest son and best-loved child Nikolay is imprisoned for participating in a local rebellion. Nikolay's wife Marusia attempts to secure his release, but before she can succeed, there is an attempted prison break and Nikolay is nearly beaten to death. He survives but is left a mindless vegetable. The family is shattered by Nikolay's "death." Only Ternovsky is able to rise above his grief, in the realization that Nikolay's soul and ideals still live and that it is the duty of the living to carry on Nikolay's work.

Savva, or Fire Cures [*Savva (Ignis sanat),* 1906]. Drama based on a historical incident. Savva, an iconoclastic revolutionary, returns to his native village after being abroad. The town is famed for a nearby monastery that possesses a miracle-working ikon of Christ. Believing that religion is the opiate of the masses, Savva intends to blow up the ikon and free the people. He enlists the aid of Kondraty, a monk who has lost his faith. But Kondraty's courage fails, and he confesses the plot to the head of the monastery. The ikon is removed and, after the explosion, replaced. The people are convinced a miracle has occurred, and Kondraty, having regained his faith, now believes himself to be the implement of God's will. He denounces Savva as the Antichrist. The crowd, hysterical with religious fervor, turns on Savva and tears him to pieces, proclaiming at the same time that Christ has risen.

The Life of a Man (*Zhizn cheloveka,* 1907). Drama in five scenes, each scene depicting a stage in the life of Man, the central character. Fate, the narrator, is represented by the "Being in Gray," who, omnipresent and indifferent, conveys a pervading sense of man's

He Who Gets Slapped. New Orleans, Le Petit Théâtre du Vieux Carré, 1924. [Theatre Collection, The New York Public Library at Lincoln Center, Astor, Lenox and Tilden Foundations]

victimization and time's passage. In Scene I, Man is born after his mother's great travail. Scene II shows Man married, the object of his young wife's love and his neighbor's affection but tormented by poverty and distracted by fantasies of wealth and grandeur. In Scene III, Man achieves fame and fortune through a stroke of luck but finds that the realization of his fantasies has brought false friends and enemies. Scene IV follows Man through his loss of wealth and the death of his son, whereupon he curses God. Man's death in a barroom in Scene V contains a vision of horror telescoping memories of an ironic past. (Another version of Man's death appears in a variant Scene V in which the concept of succession is introduced by Man's "heirs," who actually force death upon him.)

Yekaterina Ivanovna (wr. 1912). Drama permeated by a sense of personal emptiness as well by the melancholy of a bored and moribund society. It depicts the moral disintegration of a sensitive woman because of her husband's unfounded jealousy. After George Stibelev has accused Yekaterina Ivanova, his wife, of infidelity and attempted to shoot her, she leaves him, but hurt and shock lead her into a brief affair with a man she despises. Six months later, George, realizing his wrong, begs Yekaterina's forgiveness, but although she returns to him, she never recovers from her initial blow. Having lost her moral equilibrium, Yekaterina becomes a woman in revolt who abandons herself to total dissipation.

Professor Storitsyn (1913). Realistic drama with symbolic overtones set in St. Petersburg and covering the last days of a Russian intellectual's life. Through a series of confrontations, the ailing Professor Storitsyn comes to realize that although his work in literature and aesthetics has inspired generations, his personal life is a failure. His wife is deceiving him with a boor on whom they are financially dependent, his sons are strangers to him, and a young woman student searching for truth and love finds him of no help. He dies broken in spirit, a victim of the world's crassness yet the agent of his own failure.

He Who Gets Slapped (*Tot, kto poluchayet poshchechiny,* 1915). Drama combining realistic and symbolic elements, set in a French city sometime before World War I. Into Papa Briquet's circus comes a cultured middle-aged man who wishes to become a clown. Although the man has no experience, with the help of the principal clown, Jackson, he conceives an identity and a routine for himself and is engaged. The new clown becomes known as He Who Gets Slapped, and his routine consists of being slapped. Later, it is revealed that He had been an important but little-known writer who lost his wife to a man who stole, vulgarized, and popularized his ideas. Thus, He's circus routine offers him the chance to satisfy two needs: to punish himself and to capture a mass audience for his satires.

Other members of the circus are Zinida, the lion tamer, married to Briquet; Bezano, the equestrian with whom Zinida is hopelessly in love; Consuelo, the silly equestrienne star of the circus, who because she is innocent, intuitive, and noncerebral, is the perfect artist, and whom Bezano loves. Consuelo is worshiped by He, but since the clown is unable to win her or to stop her father's selling her into a marriage with a wealthy baron, he poisons first Consuelo and then himself.

Samson in Chains (*Samson v okovakh*, wr. 1914/16). Tragedy revolving about Samson, the Biblical hero of Judea whom the Philistines feared and captured. Now blinded and confined to a dungeon, Samson receives a visit from Delilah, who still loves him, and her brothers Galial and Adoram. Galial, the agent who blinded Samson, stands in awe of the warrior and wishes to restore his power for Philistine exploitation and glory. Two Judean women, Samson's mother and a blind woman he once loved, beseech Samson to return to them; but he, pampered by the Philistines, now rages against his own people. Confounded by guilt, grief, and a might he can neither control nor understand, Samson becomes mad. During a ceremony at which he is to prostrate himself before the Philistines and Dagon, their god, he invokes the God of Israel and brings down destruction upon his captors and himself.

Revival of *He Who Gets Slapped*, with Susan Douglas and John Abbott. New York, Booth Theatre, 1946. [Theatre Collection, The New York Public Library at Lincoln Center, Astor, Lenox and Tilden Foundations]

PLAYS

1. *K zvezdam** (*To the Stars*). Drama, 4 acts. Written 1905. Published 1905. Produced Vienna, Freie Volksbühne, September, 1906; Terijoki, Finland, May 27, 1907.

2. *Savva* (*Ignis sanat*)* (*Savva, or Fire Cures*). Drama, 4 acts. Written 1906. Published 1906. Produced Feb. 10, 1906.

3. *Zhizn cheloveka** (*The Life of a Man*). Play, 5 scenes. Written 1906. Published 1907. Produced St. Petersburg, V. F. Kommissarzhevsky Theatre, Feb. 22, 1907; Moscow Art Theatre, Dec. 12, 1907.

4. *Tsar golod* (*Tsar Hunger*). Drama prologue and 5 scenes. Written 1906. Published 1907.

5. *Lyubov k blizhnemu** (*Love of One's Neighbor*). Farce, 1 act. Written 1908. Produced Odessa Theatre, Jan. 30, 1909.

6. *Dni nashey zhizni* (*Days of Our Life*). Drama, 4 acts. Written 1908. Published 1908. Produced St. Petersburg, Novy Theatre, Nov. 6, 1908; Odessa Theatre, Nov. 13, 1908.

7. *Chyornye maski** (*Black Masks*). Drama, 2 acts and 5 scenes. Written 1908.

8. *Anatema** (*Anathema*). Tragedy, 7 scenes. Written 1908/09. Published 1909. Produced Moscow Art Theatre, Oct. 2, 1909; St. Petersburg, Novy Theatre, Nov. 27, 1909.

9. *Anfisa* (*Anfissa*). Drama, 4 acts. Written 1909. Published 1909.

10. *Gaudeamus*. Comedy, 4 acts. Written 1909. Published 1910.

11. *Okean* (*The Ocean*). Tragedy, 7 scenes. Published 1911.

12. *Prekrasnye sabinyanki** (*The Beautiful Sabine Women*). Historical incident, 3 scenes. Published 1911.

13. *Chest* (*Stary graf*) (*Honor, or The Old Count*). Play, 1 act. Published 1912.

14. *Yekaterina Ivanovna**. Drama, 4 acts. Written 1912. Published 1912.

15. *Professor Storitsyn**. Drama, 4 acts. Written 1912. Published 1912. Produced St. Petersburg, Alexandrinsky Theatre, 1913; Moscow, Maly Theatre, 1913.

16. *Ne ubey* (*Thou Shalt Not Kill*); also called *Kainova pechat* (*The Brand of Cain*). Drama, 5 acts. Written 1913. Published 1914.

17. *Mysl* (*Thought*). Drama; 4 scenes or 6 tableaux. Produced Moscow Art Theatre, 1913/14.

18. *Popugay* (*The Parrot*). Comedy, 1 act. Written 1911/14.

19. *Proisshestviye** (*An Incident*); also called *Gore kuptsa Krasnobriukhova* (*The Sorrow of Merchant Krasnobriukhov*). Drama, 1 act. Written 1913/14.

20. *Korol, zakon i svoboda* (*The King, the Law, and Freedom*). Drama, 6 scenes. Written 1914. Produced Moscow, 1914.

21. *Tot, kto poluchayet poshchechiny** (*He Who Gets Slapped*). Circus comedy, 4 acts. Written 1914. Produced Moscow, Dramatic Theatre, Oct. 27, 1915; St. Petersburg, Alexandrinsky Theatre, Feb. 12, 1916.

22. *The Sorrows of Belgium.* Play, 6 scenes. Published 1915.

23. *Kon v senate* (*The Horse in the Senate*). Vaudeville from Roman history, 1 act. Written 1915. Published 1917, 1924 (2 versions).

24. *Mladost* (*Youth*). Dramatic scene. Written 1914/15. Published 1915.

25. *Samson v okovakh** (*Samson in Chains*). Tragedy. Written 1914/16. Published 1923/25.

26. *Sobachy vals** (*The Waltz of the Dogs*); also called *Poema odinochestva* (*A Poem of Loneliness*). Play, 4 acts. Written 1914/16. Published 1922.

27. *Milye prizraki* (*The Dear Ghosts*). Drama, 4 acts. Written 1916. Published 1917. Produced Petrograd, Alexandrinsky Theatre, Feb. 6, 1917; Moscow, K. N. Nezhobin Theatre, Feb. 21, 1917.

28. *Monument.* Comedy, 1 act. Written 1916. Published 1917. Produced Petrograd, Krivoye Zerkalo Theatre, Feb. 13, 1916.

29. *Dnevnik Satany* (*Satan's Diary*). Play: Published 1920/21. Produced Leningrad, Alexandrinsky Theatre, 1922/23. Dramatization of Andreyev's novel.

EDITIONS

Collections.
Savva; The Life of Man, tr. by T. Seltzer, New York, 1914; *Plays: The Black Maskers, The Life of Man, The Sabine Women,* tr. by C. L. Meader and F. N. Scott, New York and London, 1915; *Sobraniye sochineny L. Andreyeva,* 17 vols., Moscow, 1906–1916; *Sobraniye sochineny,* 4 vols., Moscow, 1954.

Individual Plays.
Anathema. H. Bernstein, tr., New York and London, 1910.

He Who Gets Slapped. G. Zilboorg, tr., New York, 1921; also published in *An Anthology of Russian Plays,* ed. and tr. by F. D. Reeve, vol. 2, New York, 1963; *20th Century Russian Drama,* ed. by J. Gassner and tr. by A. MacAndrew, New York, 1963.

An Incident. Published in *Representative One-act Plays by Continental Authors,* tr. by L. Pasvolsky, Boston, 1922.

The Life of a Man. C. J. Hogarth, tr., London and New York, 1915; also published in *Types of Philosophic Drama,* ed. by R. M. Smith and tr. by C. L. Meader and F. N. Scott, New York, 1928.

Love of One's Neighbor. J. West, tr., *The Dear Departing* (*Love of One's Neighbor*), London, 1916; T. Seltzer, tr., New York, 1914, 1917.

Professor Storitsyn. Published in *Masterpieces of the Russian Drama,* ed. by G. R. Noyes, vol. 2, New York, 1933.

Samson in Chains. H. Bernstein, tr., New York, 1923.

The Sorrows of Belgium. H. Bernstein, tr., New York and London, 1915.

To the Stars. M. Magnus, tr., London and New York, 1921.

The Waltz of the Dogs. H. Bernstein, tr., New York, 1922, London, 1924.

Yekaterina Ivanova. H. Bernstein, tr., New York and London, 1923.

CRITICISM

Russian. I. Basanov, *Leonid Andreyev kak khudozhnik psikholog i myslitel,* Kiev, 1907; *Kniga o Leonide Andreyeve,* Petrograd, 1922; A. V. Lunacharsky, *Kriticheskiye etyudy,* Leningrad, 1925; M. Gorky, *Literaturno-kriticheskiye statyi,* Moscow, 1937.

English. A. Kann, *Leonid Andreyev: A Critical Study,* New York, 1924; M. Gorky, *Reminiscences of Tolstoy, Chekhov, and Andreyev,* New York, 1968; J. B. Woodward, *Leonid Andreyev: A Study,* London, 1969.

ANNENSKY, Innokenty Fyodorovich (b. Omsk, August 20, 1856; d. St. Petersburg, November 30, 1909). Russian poet, critic, classical scholar, philologist, translator, and dramatist. While teaching and serving as the director of various secondary schools, Annensky engaged in literary pursuits. He wrote essays and papers on the technicalities of classical poetics, translated Euripides into Russian, made extensive studies of Homer and Herodotus, produced brilliant literary criticism of the Russian masters, and composed classical tragedies and many poems, all but one volume of which were published posthumously.

An erudite, disciplined scholar who had a thorough knowledge of the metaphysics and principles of poetic creativity of the classical Greek poets, he made use of this knowledge for the settings, plots, and themes of his own plays. Thus, within the context of the ancient world, he was able to explore contemporary problems of psychology and ethics. Although he experimented with ideological and mythological content in his plays, he adhered to the form of classical tragedy in all save one play, the only one to be staged. Annensky viewed tragedy as the universal form in which the eternal search for beauty and truth appears. He used irony in the classic sense, based on deep and genuine suffering, to present the truest picture of the essence of life, and the techniques of symbolism to bring the myths nearer "to our consciousness." *See* SYMBOLISM.

Melanippe the Philosopher (*Melanippa-filosof,* pub. 1901) explores the theme that men suffer without being guilty. In it Melanippe is blinded and imprisoned by her father when she confesses to being the mother of Aeolus and Beotus, her illegitimate sons by Poseidon, in order to save them from death. In *King Ixion* (*Tsar Iksion,* pub. 1902) the theme of the superman appears. Ixion is forgiven for his human crime, the murder of Dioneus, but when he tries to transcend human limitations by drinking nectar and pursuing Hera, he is punished by eternal torture. The lyrical tragedy *Laodamia* (pub. 1906) displays the poetic powers of Annensky in the depiction of Laodamia, who commits suicide to be with Protesilaus in the underworld.

For his sole departure from the restrictions of formal Greek tragedy, Annensky wrote *Thamyris, the Cither Player* (*Famira-kifared;* wr. 1906, prod. 1916), his last play and the only one to be seen by an audience. The unresolved conflict between art (the ideal) and life (reality) leads Thamyris to blind himself.

Thamyris, the Cither Player (*Famira-ki-fared;* wr. 1906, prod. 1916). Thamyris, son of the nymph Argiope and the Thracian king Philammon, after a twenty-year separation is found by his mother living in a humble hut alone with his cither and an old servant. By now absorbed in his music, Thamyris has little interest in his mother. Fearful of losing him again, Argiope tells him that she can let him hear the singing and playing of Euterpe, the Muse. The proud Muse, however, will only sing for a mortal in a contest. Eager to hear the purest art, Thamyris accepts the challenge, only to be rewarded for his impertinence with defeat and punishment: he will never again remember or hear music. In despair Thamyris blinds himself. Produced Moscow, Kamerny Theatre, November, 1916.

Jean Anouilh
(1910 –   )

Jean Anouilh, French dramatist, was born in Bordeaux on June 23, 1910. Because of his reluctance to grant interviews, not much is known about his personal life. His father was a tailor and his mother a violinist in the orchestra of a casino near Bordeaux. For three months in 1919, young Anouilh attended performances of stylized, artificial operettas, an experience reflected in many of his plays. At the age of twelve he started writing plays in the manner of Edmond Rostand, and he never afterward showed interest in any profession other than that of dramatist. However, after completing his early schooling in Paris, he did study law for a short time at the Sorbonne but soon left to work as a copywriter in an advertising firm, supplementing his income by writing publicity and comic scenes for the cinema. During this period he met the actress Monelle Valentin, whom he later married and eventually divorced. Their daughter Catherine is now an actress.

In 1929, while still in his teens, Anouilh collaborated with the screenwriter Jean Aurenche on his first play, *Humulus the Mute* (*Humulus le muet,* prod. 1948). He followed this with his own *Mandarine* (wr. 1929, prod. 1933). By 1931, as secretary to the company of the actor Louis Jouvet, he came into close contact with the theatrical world. Jouvet was not particularly interested in Anouilh's plays, but through the efforts of another actor, Pierre Fresnay, the young dramatist's first serious play, *The Ermine* (*L'ermine*), written soon after *Mandarine,* appeared in 1932 in a production by Aurélien-François Lugné-Poë. Although it ran for only thirty-seven performances, it attracted critical attention as a work of promise. It was followed by an even briefer production of *Mandarine.* Despite financial difficulties, Anouilh continued to write for the next three years, completing several plays that were produced considerably later. He had a comparative success with the production of *There Was a Prisoner* (*Y avait un prisonnier*) in 1935, and the sale of the film rights to Hollywood improved his financial status. For the next few years he wrote film scenarios while continuing to work on his plays.

The 1937 production of *Traveler Without Luggage* (*Le voyageur sans bagage*) marked the beginning of his successful theatrical career. Since then a new Anouilh play has been produced in Paris almost every season. In 1944, during the German occupation of France, his *Antigone* won a wide audience in Paris as a thinly disguised attack on the Nazis. After the war many of his plays were produced in London and New York. In 1953 he married Charlotte Chardon, but it was three years before the marriage was made public. Anouilh has always devoted himself to the production of his plays, attending the rehearsals assiduously and making his only public appearances at their premieres. In recent years he has written less and has directed some of his own plays as well as those of other authors.

Jean Anouilh.
[Photographer: Gertrude Fehr]

WORK

"Thanks to Molière," wrote Jean Anouilh, "the true French theatre is the only one that is not gloomy, in which we laugh like men at war with our misery and our horror. This humor is one of France's messages to the world." And continuing in the tradition of his acknowledged master, Anouilh offers a body of work in which even his most tragic plays are informed by the humor essential to Molière and the linguistic elegance that was polished to perfection by Marivaux, Musset, and Giraudoux. The result is often a mixing of genres that critics seem willing enough to accept in Shakespeare but find offensive or disturbing in Anouilh. But Anouilh undoubtedly has few contemporary peers in his mastery of stagecraft. *See* MARIVAUX, PIERRE CARLET DE; MOLIÈRE.

With few exceptions, Anouilh has described his plays as *pièces roses* ("rose plays"), in which fantasy dominates; *pièces noires* ("black plays"), in which realism and tragedy are emphasized; *pièces brillantes* ("brilliant plays"), which combine the two previous genres and tend to take place in aristocratic environments; *pièces grinçantes* ("grating plays"), in which the realism and tragedy of the "black plays" are emphasized by a corrosive humor; and *pièces costumées* ("costume plays"), in which historical personages are placed onstage. It seems, however, safe to say that no matter what the mood or the ostensible subject, Anouilh's themes remain constant: the impossibility for purity to survive in a world dominated by compromise; the insistence that happiness—often in the form of money, love, or both—is incompatible with purity; the clash between his characters' inner world and the real world that confronts them; and the conflict between the past and the present.

Anouilh's major moral concerns were announced in his first full-length play, *Mandarine* (wr. 1929, prod. 1933), in which the young wastrel of the title attracts the love and missionary zeal of a pure young girl. The play was a failure despite the fact that it elicited recognition of Anouilh's skill in creating character and handling dialogue.

Anouilh's first critical success was *The Ermine* (1932). In it Frantz kills the old Duchesse de Granat so that Monime, the girl he loves, will come into her inheritance. His ostensible reason is to acquire the money necessary to allow their love to be "beautiful . . . perfect." "To enable it to live I would have done more terrible things," he informs the horrified girl. But Frantz's vision of himself contrasts with the facts. Monime, who rejects him, belongs to "the more fortunate race, doubtless. . . ."

This use of the word "race" as contrasting rich and poor, heroic and nonheroic, also appears in the unproduced *pièce noire Jezabel* (*Jézabel,* wr. 1932). Jacqueline, rich and strong, seeks to help the poor and ineffectual Marc escape his wretched environment. "You can't stay here another day. *You* belong to another race," she tells him. But Marc is destined to sink deeper into the society of economic and moral outcasts.

Thieves' Carnival (*Le bal des voleurs;* wr. 1932, prod. 1938) is the first of Anouilh's *pièces roses*. Though the mood of this comedy ballet is gay, the themes remain essentially the same. "Bored as an old carpet," the aristocratic Lady Hurf arranges for the happiness of those about her by resolutely turning her back on reality.

One of Anouilh's most perfectly developed *pièces noires, The Restless Heart* (*La sauvage;* wr. 1934, prod. 1938), presents a heroine, Thérèse, who paradoxically retains her purity and integrity by accepting the past and the sordidness that surrounds her. She rejects the fortunate, easygoing Florent as belonging to another world, and, Antigone in the making, she goes off "to pit herself against the sharp corners of the world."

Anouilh published *There Was a Prisoner* (1935) apart from his regular series. In it a man released from prison after many years finds it impossible to accept the deceits and hypocrisies of the world from which he originally came. The relationship between people

Thieves' Carnival, with Dolores Mann (left) and Frances Sternhagen. [Theatre Collection, The New York Public Library at Lincoln Center, Astor, Lenox and Tilden Foundations]

and their past is also examined in Anouilh's *pièce noire, Traveler Without Luggage* (1937), in which an amnesia victim rejects a repugnant past and selects his future by having himself identified as belonging to a family other than his own.

Anouilh's two following *pièces roses, The Rendezvous at Senlis; Dinner with the Family* (*Le rendez-vous de Senlis;* wr. 1937, prod. 1941) and *Time Remembered* (*Léocadia,* 1940), deal, respectively, with a man who breaks with an ignoble past in which he was dependent on his rich wife and a young prince who is rescued from the prison of romantic memory and restored to the present by love. These plays were followed by four *pièces noires,* three of which take their inspiration from Greek mythology. In *Legend of Lovers; Point of Departure* (*Eurydice,* 1942), a modern Orpheus and Eurydice escape the compromises of life by choosing death. The same decision is made in *Antigone* (1944), in which the Greek heroine, who wants "everything, right now," rejects the attrition of life in favor of the purity of death. Because the play was produced during the Occupation, French audiences tended to identify Antigone with the Resistance and Creon with Vichy France, but this interpretation seems unlikely now. The theme of *Antigone* is repeated in *Romeo and Jeanette; Fading Mansions* (*Roméo et Jeannette,* 1946), in which young lovers decide on suicide. In *Medea* (*Médée;* wr. 1946, prod. 1953), the heroine, faced with a Jason who is weary of their criminal past and wants an orderly, conventional life, remains passionately true to herself and destroys both herself and the children who represent the past.

Ring Round the Moon (*L'invitation au château,* 1947) is the first of the *pièces brillantes.* In it a crippled old aristocrat indulges her sense of self-importance by cavalierly arranging the destinies of those around her. But behind the *marivaudage* of the comedy an intense battle goes on between the world of power and money and the world of poverty and purity. The influence of Marivaux's comedy is even more perceptible in *Cécile, or The School for Fathers* (*Cécile, ou L'école des pères;* wr. 1949, prod. 1954) though the title suggests Molière. The play ends in a double wedding, but one feels that the disillusions of a love lived out are not far behind. In *The Rehearsal* (*La répétition, ou L'amour puni,* 1950) Marivaux again sets the tone, and it is actually a play of his that is being rehearsed. Once more the conflict behind the brilliant comic dialogue is between purity and the artificiality of the aristocratic world. "I choose to live," says the Count. "This is always complicated and degrading." *Colombe* (*Mademoiselle Colombe,* 1951) presents the same contrast in terms of the false brilliance of the theatrical world and the unattractive puritanism of the heroine's idealistic husband.

In *The Waltz of the Toreadors* (*La valse des toréadors,* 1952), Anouilh reexamines characters introduced in the earlier *Ardèle; The Cry of the Peacock* (*Ardèle, ou La marguerite,* 1948), in which two hunchbacked lovers find "happiness" in death. Both works are *pièces grinçantes,* but in the latter we focus on the consequences of love gone sour, turned to mere possession. Life, we are told, is bearable only when it is not examined. In another play in the same genre, *Ornifle, or The Draft* (*Ornifle, ou Le courant d'air,* 1955), a modern-day Don Juan is smitten by death in the midst of a new act of selfishness. In *Poor Bitos, or The Masked Dinner* (*Pauvre Bitos, ou Le dîner de têtes,* 1956), however, a series of historical confrontations focuses attention on the division that has persisted in French society to this day. As in *The Fighting Cock* (*L'hurluberlu, ou Le réactionnaire amoureux,* 1959), we see Anouilh's essentially aristocratic disdain for and suspicion of the ambitious but graceless middle class pitted against a declining aristocracy dispossessed of function and place.

Le voyageur sans bagage, with Michel Vitold and Marguerite Jamois. [French Cultural Services]

Time Remembered, with Susan Strasberg (left) and Helen Hayes. New York, Morosco Theatre, 1957. [Walter Hampden Memorial Library at The Players, New York]

Money does not guarantee nobility of soul, but without it, his previous plays have told us, purity can be found only in death.

Becket, or The Honor of God (*Becket, ou L'honneur de Dieu,* 1959) is a work of the *pièces costumées* series introduced by *The Lark* (*L'alouette,* 1953), in which Anouilh put on stage France's national heroine, Joan of Arc. Joan chooses to die at the stake rather than live with the knowledge that she betrayed her faith, and Thomas Becket chooses

martyrdom rather than compromise with what, as a pastor, he owes to God. The last of this series, *Catch as Catch Can* (*La foire d'empoigne,* 1962), presents a Napoleon who is gross and egotistical and contrasts him with an idealized portrait of Louis XVIII. Once more the struggle for the soul and land of France is at stake, and idealism quickly degenerates in the world of action to selfishness and trickery.

The Cavern (*La grotte,* 1961), another play

assigned to no particular genre, presents a backstairs view of events behind the respectable facade of a fashionable Paris house. In a Pirandellian revolt the actors turn on the Author for being unable to decide how the play should end. The influence of Pirandello can also be seen in *Dear Antoine* (*Cher Antoine,* 1969), in which a play-within-a-play accurately predicts how a dramatist's friends and foes will react to the news of his death. *See* PIRANDELLO, LUIGI.

Anouilh's translations and adaptations include works by Shakespeare, Oscar Wilde, and Graham Greene. He has also written numerous film scenarios, one of which, *Little Molière* (*La petite Molière,* 1959), was successfully produced as a play. It focuses on the unhappy relations between Molière and his wife. The conclusion might sum up Anouilh himself: life is ugly and sad, made bearable only by laughter.

The Ermine (*L'ermine,* 1932). Drama in which Frantz believes the key to his future happiness with Monime is the acquisition of enough money to give her the same luxurious life her wealthy aunt and guardian, the old Duchess, provides for her. Frantz's business fails, and Monime, to affirm her love, offers to become his mistress. But their clandestine lovemaking seems to divide rather than unite them. Frantz decides to kill the Duchess so that Monime will come into her inheritance. He does so despite Monime's warning that crime is incompatible with their love and despite the arrival of a telegram offering him a position with a modest salary. Though the police suspect Frantz, he is saved by the confession of the Duchess's half-witted old manservant. Frantz's rejoicing in the freedom bought by the crime is cut short by Monime's announcement that she no longer loves him. Her willingness to go away with him to live out their guilty lives together in no way alleviates Frantz's despair. He gives himself up to the police, and this act rekindles Monime's love.

Jezabel (*Jézabel,* wr. 1932). Drama in which the wealthy Jacqueline attempts to rescue Marc, a poor young man, from his miserable environment because she believes that he is worthy of a better life. But Marc is weak and, through inaction, permits his mother, the Jezabel of the play, to murder his father. Thus he himself becomes cut off from society.

Maria Tucci as Antigone and Morris Carnovsky as Creon in a 1967 production of *Antigone.* [The American Shakespeare Festival Theatre, Stratford, Conn.]

Scene from *Médée.*
[French Cultural
Services]

Thieves' Carnival (*Le bal des voleurs;* wr. 1932, prod. 1938). *Comédie-ballet* in which three pickpockets and confidence men, Peterbono, Hector, and Gustave, insinuate themselves into the household of Lady Hurf and Lord Edgard by posing as Spanish grandees. Hector and Gustave become involved with Lady Hurf's nieces Eva and Juliette. Aware of the imposture from the beginning, Lady Hurf encourages them out of sheer boredom. The play revolves around Eva's inability to love Hector, despite all his attempts to please her, and the love of Gustave and Juliette, which is complicated by the pretense. Beneath the wit and lightheartedness is an undercurrent of sadness for those spectators incapable of participating in the excitement of life.

The Restless Heart (*La sauvage;* wr. 1934, prod. 1938). Thérèse is sincerely in love with Florent France, a successful and talented composer of good family. However, as the daughter of a third-rate bandleader whose wife is the mistress of the group's pianist, she feels that her life has been marked by a poverty and sordidness that can only end by soiling her love. She is ill at ease in the happy, comfortable atmosphere of the rich, whose money has enabled them to retain a kind of purity. After desperate attempts first to discourage Florent and then to adjust to his milieu, she runs away on the eve of her marriage.

There Was a Prisoner (*Y avait un prisonnier,* 1935). Ludovic, a former international financier recently released from fifteen years' imprisonment for fraud, finds that his superficially respectable family is more embarrassed than overjoyed at his return. Sickened by their attempts to make him conform to their hypocritical standards or be put away again as insane, he at first contemplates suicide. Eventually he decides to escape from the yacht on which the action takes place by swimming off with a mute prison companion, the Lamb, symbol of childhood.

Traveler Without Luggage (*Le voyageur sans bagage,* 1937). Drama centering on Gaston, who as the result of wounds received in World War I has been an amnesia victim for the succeeding eighteen years. Five families claim him as their long-lost son or nephew, but it gradually becomes certain that he is the son of the wealthy Renauds. During his interviews with them, however, they relate details of his childhood and youth that revolt him—he was cruel, dishonorable, selfish. To avoid assuming so repugnant an identity, Gaston contrives to have himself identified positively by one of the other claimants, a little boy who by an odd circumstance is the uncle of a missing soldier. The lad, like Gaston, remembers no family, his parents having died when he was a baby. Thus Gaston begins life again unburdened by any past and with a person who genuinely needs him.

The Rendezvous at Senlis; also **Dinner with the Family** (*Le rendez-vous de Senlis;* wr. 1937, prod. 1941). Comedy in which George, both his parents, his friend Robert, and Barbara, Robert's wife, all live together on the money provided by Henriette, George's wealthy wife (who never appears onstage). George is bored with Henriette and has taken Barbara as his mistress. However, he has recently fallen deeply in love with Isabelle, a young girl he met at the Louvre. He arranges a rendezvous with her at Senlis, where he rents a house and hires an actor and actress to impersonate his mother and father so that he can receive Isabelle in the imaginary, perfect home he never had. Because of complications in his Paris ménage, George is absent when Isabelle arrives and the actors tell her the truth of the situation. George's family also arrives, and after several mix-ups he decides to divorce Henriette, leaving his parasitic parents and friends without means of support. George and Isabelle then depart for her hometown in the Pyrenees.

Time Remembered (*Léocadia,* 1940). Romantic comedy in which Amanda, a young

Parisian milliner, is hired by the Duchess to come to her estate and impersonate, "bring back to life," Léocadia, the exotic ballerina who had had a three-day love affair with the Duchess's nephew Prince Albert and then had died abruptly, strangled by a scarf she was knotting around her neck. Albert relives over and over again his days with Léocadia, the locales of their romance—meeting place, nightclub, little inn—having been reconstructed on the Duchess's property. Amanda, who looks remarkably like Léocadia, falls in love with Albert and abandons her role as ghost to try to win him for herself. At first he resists giving up the past, but Amanda's flesh-and-blood beauty and tenderness bring him back to the real world, and he realizes that he is in love with her.

Legend of Lovers; also **Point of Departure** (*Eurydice,* 1942). Retelling of the Orpheus myth in a modern context. Orpheus, an itinerant accordionist, meets Eurydice, an actress with a second-rate company, in a provincial railway station. They immediately fall in love, swear eternal devotion, and go to Marseille to spend the night. The next day, when Orpheus is momentarily absent, Eurydice receives a note from the impresario of the troupe ordering her to return. Ashamed because for a year she has been the mistress of this boor, she runs away to avoid hurting Orpheus. Soon after, the impresario tells Orpheus about his relations with Eurydice, and the police bring word of her death in a bus accident. A mysterious M. Henri, who has followed the couple to the hotel, takes Orpheus back to the railway station and explains that Eurydice is there. He can speak to her but must not look at her until dawn. The lovers quarrel about Eurydice's affair with the impresario, and Orpheus looks at her too soon. M. Henri gives Orpheus a last choice: he can resume his musician's life, or he can join Eurydice. He chooses Eurydice and death.

Antigone (1944). The only play written by Anouilh that has been labeled a tragedy, it closely follows Sophocles. The chorus, or narrator, enunciates Anouilh's conception of tragedy: pure fatality wherein the characters, conscious of their destiny, shed all hope and are at peace. Creon, in this contemporary version, tries to save Antigone from the consequences of her efforts to bury her brother Polynices. He reminds her of her own lack of religious faith and points out that her brothers were both villainous characters, neither of whom was worth the sacrifice of her life. He has almost convinced her when his use of the word "happiness" brings to her mind the compromises she will have to make to assure happiness as the years go by. Finally, Anouilh's Antigone chooses death because of her fear of how compromises will distort and vilify life. Creon, bound first to protect the state against anarchy and civil war, goes on with the affairs of state "because there is work to be done." *See* SOPHOCLES.

Romeo and Jeanette; also **Fading Mansions** (*Roméo et Jeannette,* 1946). Drama presenting Anouilh's *Antigone* theme in middle-class terms. Jeanette, who refuses to accept the petty ugliness and compromise of middle-class life, meets Frederic, engaged to her sister Julia, paragon of middle-class virtues. Frederic and Jeanette fall in love, and Frederic realizes that the world he believed in has another, more attractive side. To preserve the perfection of love, Jeanette proposes double suicide, but Frederic insists that life must be lived and that death, too, is absurd. In the end, however, Frederic rejects the absurdity of his proposed life with Julia and accepts the absurdity of death with Jeanette.

Medea (*Médée;* wr. 1946, prod. 1953). Drama written in a prosaic tone, based on plays

Scene from *L'invitation au château.* [French Cultural Services]

Ardèle, ou La marguerite, Comédie des Champs-Élysées, Paris. [French Cultural Services]

by Euripides and Seneca. Ten years after helping Jason steal the Golden Fleece from her father's kingdom and killing her brother in order to escape, Medea learns that Jason is about to desert her and marry Creüsa, the young daughter of Corinth's King Creon. Now a sort of wandering gypsy, scorned everywhere because of the crimes she has committed for Jason's sake, she is consumed with hatred. Creon orders her immediate exile from Corinth but defends Jason's right to remain because he does not share the guilt of her barbaric actions. Jason arrives to explain that he is weary of adventure and crime and longs for the "oblivion and peace" of an orderly, conventional life, a life he cannot have until he breaks his ties with Medea. Now ready to express the pure evil she has embraced, Medea sends her children with a poisoned veil and diadem for the young bride; Creüsa and Creon meet agonizing deaths when they handle the gifts. Uncompromising to the end, Medea murders her children, symbols of her past life with Jason, and kills herself as well (a departure from the classical story). Jason prepares to rule in Creon's place and live in a rational world governed by law. *See* EURIPIDES; SENECA.

Ring Round the Moon (*L'invitation au château,* 1947). Comedy of identical twins—Frederic, an innocent romantic who has never grown up, and Horace, a Machiavellian cynic with the emotions of a child. The parts are meant to be played by the same actor. At a ball given by the twins' aristocratic aunt, Mme. Desmermortes, Horace amuses himself by trying to disrupt the engagement of Frederic to Diana Messerschmann. Horace hires a young actress, Isabelle, to attend the ball and, if possible, turn Frederic's head. But instead, Isabelle falls in love with Horace and suffers cruelly because of his impersonal attitude toward her. Finally, the twins' aunt intervenes, having guessed that Isabelle is in love only with Horace's facade and is likely to be happier with his double, the sincere Frederic. Sensing also that Horace and Diana are in love, she contrives to pair them off as well.

Ardèle; also ***The Cry of the Peacock*** (*Ardèle, ou La marguerite,* 1948). Drama, farcical and tragic, which centers on Ardèle, a hunchback spinster of forty-four who never appears onstage. Her brother, the General, has called a family conference to consider a startling situation: Ardèle and the family tutor, also a hunchback, have fallen in love. Ardèle's sister, the Countess, agrees with the General that the match is impossible, grotesque, scandalous. Her husband, the cuckolded Count, briefly defends Ardèle and her right to love, as does Nicholas, the General's idealistic son, who is in love with his childhood sweetheart, now his older brother's wife. As for the General, he long ago drove his own wife insane with his infidelities and is currently involved with one of the maids. It becomes obvious that though the love of Ardèle and her tutor is no more grotesque than the loves of the other members of the household, their physical deformity makes it unacceptable in what passes for a "normal" society. In a desperate move, the tutor sneaks into the house and barricades himself in Ardèle's room, where the unfortunate pair kill themselves. Some of the same characters appear in *The Waltz of the Toreadors.*

Cécile, or The School for Fathers (*Cécile, ou L'école des pères;* wr. 1949, prod. 1954). One-act comedy-satire focusing on the conflict between "duty and happiness." M. Orlas is infatuated with Araminthe, his daughter Cécile's young governess. Cécile and her suitor Chevalier, faced with paternal disapproval, decide to elope. Araminthe warns M. Orlas, who thinks her story is a cover-up for her own planned elopement with Chevalier. Together with Araminthe's father, M. Orlas plans to protect her honor. That night in the garden, M. Orlas sees Araminthe and urges her "to be a woman and to love." Actually, it is Cécile to whom he speaks. She reveals her true identity, and M. Orlas is enraged, for "there are laws in this country which protect a father's honor." Araminthe arrives with Chevalier, points out M. Orlas's hypocrisy, and pacifies her indignant father, who had been waiting in the bushes. She admits to loving M. Orlas and agrees to marry him. M. Orlas, in turn, consents to the marriage of Cécile and Chevalier. They then all retire to the banquet previously planned by Araminthe.

The Rehearsal (*La répétition, ou L'amour puni,* 1950). Modern drama employing the theatrical device of a play-within-a-play. Lucile, governess for the twelve wards of the Countess and Count (nicknamed Tiger), becomes entangled in the make-believe world of the upper classes. She and Tiger fall in love, and it is the latter's first experience of a simple and innocent passion unaffected by material or social considerations. Their feelings for each other are revealed to the other characters (the Countess; Hero, Tiger's drunkard friend who enjoys "breaking things"; Hortensia, Tiger's mistress; and Villebosse, the Countess's lover) at the rehearsal

Catherine Anouilh in the title role of *Cécile, ou L'école des pères.* Paris, Comédie des Champs-Élysées, 1954. [French Cultural Services]

Scene from *Pauvre Bitos*. Paris, Théâtre Montparnasse–Gaston-Baty, 1956. [French Cultural Services]

of a play, Marivaux's *Double Inconstancy,* to be presented at Tiger's ball. Alarmed by this sincere love which exposes the shallowness of their own loveless entanglements, the others plot to break up the romance. In the evening, Hero goes up to Lucile's attic room, convinces her that Tiger has never loved her, and seduces her. When Lucile fails to show up for rehearsal the next morning, Tiger runs after her in what will obviously be a vain attempt to cling to true love and free himself from the make-believe that surrounds him.

Mademoiselle Colombe (*Colombe,* 1951). Before entering military service, Julien, a stern realist, entrusts his wife Colombe and their infant son to his actress mother, Mme. Alexandra, the personification of love onstage but cold, mean, and petty in private life. When Julien returns on leave three months later, he discovers that Colombe too has become an actress, the darling of several men of the company, and the mistress of his own brother. She asserts her determination to pursue her career rather than resume a marriage rendered intolerable by what she considers Julien's perpetual jealousy, morose lectures on morality, and selfish insensitivity to her pleasure-loving nature. Julien's romantic hopes for a love that would last the rest of their lives, that would insulate them from the crudity and artificiality of the theatrical world around them, are shattered by Colombe's inability to accept reality and her preference for the theatrical world of make-believe.

The Waltz of the Toreadors (*La valse des toréadors,* 1952). Drama that reintroduces two characters from *Ardèle,* General Léon

Saint-Pé and his Amélie, as examples of marital incompatibility. Seventeen years before, Léon, a young officer, had danced the "Toreador Waltz" with Ghislaine and fallen in love with her. But their love remained unconsummated all this time because Léon, although hating his wife, has not had the courage to divorce her. The sudden reappearance of Ghislaine provokes a crisis during which Léon realizes that he is no longer the courageous young man he once was. Ghislaine falls in love again, this time with a younger man, and, too late, Léon confronts his wife. The last act is an ironic dialogue between husband and wife revealing that Amélie mentally has been as unfaithful to Léon as he to her. Yet she will not give him up since he belongs to her, as she to him, through marriage. Each selfishly condemns the other in self-defense, for each has had a few years of love and long years of regret, boredom, disgust, and self-dramatization.

The Lark (*L'alouette,* 1953). Drama de-

Suzanne Flon as Jeanne d'Arc in *L'alouette*, Théâtre Montparnasse–Gaston-Baty, Paris. [French Cultural Services]

The Lark, with (from left rear) Christopher Plummer, Roger De Koven, Michael Higgins, and Julie Harris. New York, Longacre Theatre, 1955. [Walter Hampden Memorial Library at The Players, New York]

Laurence Olivier
as Henry II in
Becket. New York,
St. James
Theatre, 1960.
[Friedman-
Abeles]

picting moments in the life of Joan of Arc. The dramatic framework is her courtroom trial, but as she is questioned, Joan steps back into her past for the answers. The audience sees her communing with her voices, arguing with her parents, and persuading the Dauphin to let her lead the armies. Hindsight colors many of the remarks made during her trial, and the eventual judgment of history and the church appears already to be known. After Joan's death at the stake, in a final juxtaposition of time she is seen on her "happiest day," Charles's coronation at Reims.

Ornifle, or The Draft (*Ornifle, ou Le courant d'air,* 1955). Drama analogous to Molière's *Don Juan* (1665). Ornifle, a successful versifier, is hypocritical and indifferent to the unhappiness his philandering causes. He is the despair of his ugly, adoring secretary Mlle. Supo and, to a lesser degree, of his understanding wife, who accepts him because she too is afraid of reality. He disposes of one of his mistresses by turning her over to Nachetu, his publisher, to simplify his plan for the seduction of Marguerite, his son's fiancée. Then, as he embarks on this adven-

Scene from a
German production
of *Ornifle.* [German
Information
Center]

L'hurluberlu.
Paris, Comédie des
Champs-Élysées,
1959. [French
Cultural Services]

ture, he dies of a heart attack, smitten, like
Don Juan, by God.

Poor Bitos, or The Masked Dinner
(*Pauvre Bitos, ou Le dîner de têtes,* 1956).
Drama in which Maxime, an aristocrat, sets
out to humble Bitos, the son of a washerwom-
an, who has risen to be deputy public prosecutor. Bitos's sin is uncompromising and narrow
devotion to duty: he has been unmerciful to
friends and unduly harsh on minor offenders.

Maxime has arranged a masquerade at
which each guest impersonates a figure from
the French Revolution—Bitos is Robespierre;
Maxime is Saint-Just. Speaking in character,
Maxime's highborn guests throw cruel barbs
at Bitos-Robespierre, for Bitos possesses many
of the unpleasant personal characteristics of
his historical counterpart. Old animosities
emerge: Bitos, having been a scholarship student at the same school as Maxime and some

of his friends, hates them for the taunts and slights he suffered there. Bitos narrowly escapes Robespierre's death at this thoroughly sinister party; he is saved, by one of the women, from the final humiliation of becoming intoxicated and going with the group to a local nightclub. He departs hoping to revenge himself someday.

The Fighting Cock (*L'hurluberlu, ou Le réactionnaire amoureux,* 1959). Resentful of the changes in contemporary France, the General has retired to the provinces after an ineffectual but heroic career in the Resistance during World War II. The play catches him in a moment of crisis in his life: his somewhat farcical conspiracy against the government has been exposed, and his tired conspirators are deserting his cause; Algaé, his young wife, has developed a disturbing interest in a local playboy; and Sophie, his daughter by a previous alliance, has become romantically involved with Mendigalès, a young man whose sophistication and modernity represent everything the General fears and hates in the contemporary world.

The action of the play centers in preparations to present a charity theatrical in the General's garden. The General's defeat by a world whose changes he is unable either to accept or to control is symbolized by his being apologetically but firmly knocked to the ground in a confrontation with Mendigalès, who has made Sophie his mistress even though he plans to marry a wealthy heiress. Seeing that his political life, his family life, and his love life are about to disintegrate, the General, "inconsolable and gay," prepares to play the role assigned to him in the play-within-a-play in order to try to please his wife. During the course of the play Anouilh indulges in some good-tempered satire on modern French antidrama.

Becket, or The Honor of God (*Becket, ou L'honneur de Dieu,* 1959). Drama depicting Thomas Becket's friendship with Henry II of England, their estrangement, and Becket's martyrdom. Becket, Henry's drinking and wenching companion, is also the man who taught him how to use his mind, and Henry holds him very dear, regarding him as his alter ego. When the Archbishop of Canterbury dies, Henry makes Becket, "his man," the new primate, thinking thus to ensure the cooperation of a competitive and jealous church. But he reckons without Becket's sense of honor, which compels him to defend God's cause even in opposition to the King. A violent clash of wills results in Becket's flight

Catherine Anouilh in *La petite Molière.* [French Cultural Services]

to France, where Henry later meets him and asks him to return. Becket does, but he refuses to compromise the honor of God in certain matters. Henry's peace of mind is shattered by the presence of a Becket with whom he no longer has any rapport, and in a hysterical outburst he asks if no one will rid him of this priest. Four of Henry's knights then slay Becket on the altar of Canterbury Cathedral. Henry does penance, wins the confidence of the people, and vows to seek out and punish Becket's murderers.

Catch as Catch Can (*La foire d'empoigne,* 1962). Drama about Napoleon's Hundred Days and Louis XVIII's return to power. The practical cynicism of King, Emperor, and Fouché, versatile Minister of Police under both rulers, is contrasted with the ineffectual idealism of Fouché's illegitimate son, young Lieutenant d'Assonville, a nobleman who has chosen to follow Napoleon, whom he idolizes. The King tries to persuade D'Assonville to serve him and help restore France to glory, but the young man begs Napoleon to let him accompany him into exile. The Emperor rejects the overemotional lad, reminds him that

(Opposite) Betty Field and Melvyn Douglas in *The Waltz of the Toreadors.* [Walter Hampden Memorial Library at The Players, New York]

politics is not a matter for tears, and advises him not to be sad. He then states the thesis of the play: "It's every man for himself and winner take all in this world."

The Cavern (*La grotte*, 1961). Drama whose title refers to the belowstairs kitchen in the Count's fashionable Paris house. Here the Coachman, a disgusting brute, has killed his mistress, the forty-seven-year-old Cook, who quarreled with him for making the ignorant young kitchen maid pregnant. The identity of the Cook's murderer is withheld from the audience until near the end, while the relationships among servants and masters are gradually revealed. The Cook, for example, turns out to have once been the Count's mistress and to have given birth to his illegitimate son, now a young seminary student. The Author, unable to decide how the play should proceed, addresses the audience directly, and the Police Superintendent investigating the crime tries to keep things moving toward its solution. Finally, the characters take over, ignore the protests of the Author, and bring the drama to its conclusion.

PLAYS

Unless otherwise noted, the plays were first performed in Paris.

1. (With Jean Aurenche). *Humulus le muet** (*Humulus the Mute*). Pièce rose. Written 1929. Published 1958. Produced Cité Universitaire, Sept. 18, 1948.

2. *Mandarine*. Play. Written 1929. Produced Théâtre de l'Athénée, 1933.

3. *L'ermine** (*The Ermine*). Pièce noire, 3 acts. Written 1929. Published 1934. Produced Théâtre de l'Oeuvre, Apr. 26, 1932.

4. *Attila le magnifique* (*Attila the Magnificent*). Play. Written 1930.

5. *Jézabel* (*Jezabel*). Pièce noire. Written 1932. Published 1946.

6. *Le bal des voleurs** (*Thieves' Carnival*). Pièce rose, 4 acts. Written 1932. Published 1938. Produced Théâtre des Arts, Sept. 17, 1938.

7. *La sauvage** (*The Restless Heart*). Pièce noire, 3 acts. Written 1934. Published 1938. Produced Théâtre des Mathurins, Jan. 10, 1938.

8. *Y avait un prisonnier* (*There Was a Prisoner*). Play. Written 1934. Published 1935. Produced Théâtre des Ambassadeurs, Mar. 21, 1935.

9. *Le petit bonheur* (*The Small Happiness*). Play. Written 1935.

10. *Le voyageur sans bagage** (*Traveler Without Luggage*). Pièce noire, 3 acts. Written 1936. Published 1937. Produced Théâtre des Mathurins, Feb. 16, 1937.

11. *Le rendez-vous de Senlis** (*The Rendezvous at Senlis;* also *Dinner with the Family*). Pièce rose. Written 1937. Published 1942. Produced Théâtre de l'Atelier, Feb. 30, 1941.

12. *Léocadia** (*Time Remembered*). Pièce rose, 2 acts. Written 1939. Published 1942. Produced Théâtre de la Michodière, Nov. 30, 1940.

13. *Eurydice** (*Legend of Lovers;* also *Point of Departure*). Pièce noire. Written 1941. Published 1942. Produced Théâtre de l'Atelier, Dec. 18, 1942.

14. *Antigone**. Pièce noire; tragedy. Written 1942. Published 1946. Produced Théâtre de l'Atelier, Feb. 4, 1944.

15. *Oreste* (*Orestes*). Fragment. Written 1942. Published 1945.

16. *Roméo et Jeannette** (*Romeo and Jeanette;* also *Fading Mansions*). Pièce noire, 4 acts. Written 1945. Published 1946. Produced Théâtre de l'Atelier, Dec. 3, 1946.

17. *Médée** (*Medea*). Pièce noire, 1 act. Written 1946. Published 1946. Produced Théâtre de l'Atelier, Mar. 26, 1953.

18. *L'invitation au château** (*Ring Round the Moon*). Pièce brillante, 4 acts. Written 1947. Published 1953. Produced Théâtre de l'Atelier, Nov. 4, 1947.

19. *Ardèle, ou La marguerite** (*Ardèle;* also *The Cry of the Peacock*). Pièce grinçante. Written 1948. Published 1949. Produced Comédie des Champs-Élysées, Nov. 3, 1948.

20. *Épisode de la vie d'un auteur** (*Episode in an Author's Life*). Play, 1 act. Written 1948. Published 1959. Produced Comédie des Champs-Élysées, Nov. 3, 1948.

21. *Cécile, ou L'école des pères** (*Cécile, or The School for Fathers*). Pièce brillante, 1 act. Written 1949. Published 1954. Produced Comédie des Champs-Élysées, Oct. 28, 1954.

22. *La répétition, ou L'amour puni** (*The Rehearsal*). Pièce brillante, 3 acts. Written 1950. Published 1950. Produced Théâtre Marigny, Oct. 25, 1950.

23. *Colombe** (*Mademoiselle Colombe*). Pièce brillante, 2 acts. Written 1950. Published 1953. Produced Théâtre de l'Atelier, Feb. 11, 1951.

24. *La valse des toréadors** (*The Waltz of the Toreadors*). Pièce grinçante. Written 1951. Published 1952. Produced Comédie des Champs-Élysées, Jan. 9, 1952.

25. *L'alouette** (*The Lark*). Pièce costumée, 2 acts. Written 1953. Produced Théâtre Montparnasse–Gaston-Baty, Oct. 14, 1953.

26. *Ornifle, ou Le courant d'air* (*Ornifle, or The Draft*). Pièce grinçante, 5 acts. Written 1955. Published 1956. Produced Comédie des Champs-Élysées, Nov. 4, 1955.

27. *Pauvre Bitos, ou Le dîner de têtes* (*Poor Bitos, or The Masked Dinner*). Pièce grinçante. Written 1956. Published 1956. Produced Théâtre Montparnasse–Gaston-Baty, Oct. 11, 1956.

28. *L'hurluberlu, ou Le réactionnaire amoureux** (*The Fighting Cock*). Play, 4 acts. Written 1958. Published 1959. Produced Comédie des Champs-Élysées, Feb. 5, 1959.

29. *Becket, ou L'honneur de Dieu** (*Becket, or The Honor of God*). Pièce costumée. Written 1958. Published 1959. Produced Théâtre Montparnasse–Gaston-Baty, Oct. 1, 1959.

30. *La petite Molière* (*Little Molière*). Play. Written 1959. Produced Bordeaux, Théâtre de France, June 14, 1959.

31. *La foire d'empoigne** (*Catch as Catch Can*). Pièce costumée, 1 act. Written 1960. Produced Comédie des Champs-Élysées, Jan. 11, 1962.

32. *La grotte** (*The Cavern*). Play. Written 1961. Produced Théâtre Montparnasse–Gaston-Baty, Oct. 5, 1961.

33. *L'orchestre** (*The Orchestra*). Play, 1 act. Produced Comédie des Champs-Élysées, Jan. 11, 1962.

34. *Le boulanger, la boulangère et le petit mitron* (*The Baker, the Baker's Wife, and the Baker's Apprentice*). Play. Published 1969. Produced Comédie des Champs-Élysées, Nov. 13, 1968.

35. *Cher Antoine* (*Dear Antoine*). Play. Produced Comédie des Champs-Élysées, Oct. 1, 1969.

36. *Les poissons rouges* (*The Goldfish*). Play. Produced Théâtre de l'Oeuvre, Jan. 21, 1970.

37. *Ne réveillez pas Madame* (*Don't Awaken Madame*). Play, 2 acts. Produced Comédie des Champs-Élysées, Oct. 21, 1970.

38. *Tu étais si gentil quand tu étais petit* (*You Were So Nice When You Were Little*). Play. Produced Théâtre Antoine, January, 1972.

EDITIONS

Collections.
La sauvage; L'invitation au château, French and European Publications, New York, 1961; *Le voyageur sans*

bagage; Le bal des voleurs, French and European Publications, New York, 1961; *Le rendez-vous de Senlis; Léocadia,* French and European Publications, New York, 1962; *Ardèle and Pauvre Bitos,* ed. by R. T. Riva, Dell, New York, 1965; *Five Plays,* vol. I, *Five Plays,* vol. II, *Seven Plays,* vol. III, Hill and Wang, New York, 1958–1967; *Théâtre,* 7 vols., Paris, 1951–1970.

Individual Plays.

Antigone. Published in *Makers of the Modern Theater* ed. by B. Ulanov and tr. by L. Galantière, McGraw-Hill, New York, 1961; *Masters of Modern Drama,* ed. by H. M. Block and R. G. Shedd and tr. by L. Galantière, Random House, New York, 1962; *The Creative Reader,* ed. by R. W. Stallman and R. E. Waters and tr. by L. Galantière, 2d ed., Ronald, New York, 1962.

Ardèle. Published in *The Off-Broadway Theatre,* ed. by R. A. Cordell and L. Matson and tr. by L. Hill, Random House, New York, 1959; as *Ardèle, ou La marguerite,* French and European Publications, New York, 1962.

Becket, or The Honor of God. New American Library, New York, 1964; also published in *Modern Drama for Analysis,* ed. by P. M. Cubeta and tr. by L. Hill, 3d ed., Holt, New York, 1962.

The Cavern. L. Hill, tr., Hill and Wang, New York, 1966; as *La grotte,* French and European Publications, New York, 1961.

Cécile, or The School for Fathers. Published in *From the Modern Repertoire,* ed. by E. R. Bentley and tr. by L. and A. Klein, vol. 3, Indiana University Press, Bloomington, 1949–1956; *One Act: Eleven Short Plays of the Modern Theatre,* ed. by S. Moon, Grove Press, New York, 1961; as *Cécile, ou L'école des pères,* French and European Publications, New York, 1954.

Colombe. French and European Publications, New York, 1963.

The Ermine. Published in *Plays of the Year,* ed. by J. C. Trewin and tr. by M. John, vol. 13, Elek, London, 1955.

Eurydice, or Legend of Lovers. Published in *Masterpieces of the Modern French Theatre,* ed. by R. W. Corrigan, Collier, New York, 1967.

La foire d'empoigne. French and European Publications, New York, 1962.

L'hurluberlu, ou Le réactionnaire amoureux. French and European Publications, New York, 1959.

The Lark. Published in *The Genius of the French Theater,* ed. by A. Bermel and tr. by C. Fry, New American Library, New York, 1961; *Eleven Plays: Introduction to Drama,* ed. by G. Weales, Norton, New York, 1964; *Drama and Discussion,* ed. by S. A. Clayes, Appleton-Century-Crofts, New York, 1967.

Léocadia. B. L. Knapp and A. M. Della Fazia, eds., French, New York, 1959.

Medea. Published in *Plays of the Year,* ed. by J. C. Trewin and tr. by L. Small, vol. 15, Elek, London, 1956; *The Modern Theatre,* ed. by E. R. Bentley and tr. by L. and A. Klein, vol. 5, Doubleday, Garden City, N.Y., 1957; *Medea: Myth and Dramatic Form,* ed. by J. L. Sanderson and E. Zimmerman, Houghton Mifflin, Boston, 1967.

Ornifle, ou Le courant d'air. French and European Publications, New York, 1953.

Pauvre Bitos, ou Le dîner de têtes. French and European Publications, New York, 1958.

Rehearsal. K. Black and P. H. Johnson, trs., Coward-McCann, New York, 1962.

Ring Round the Moon. C. Fry, tr., Oxford, New York, 1950; as *L'invitation au château,* ed. by D. J. Conlon, Cambridge, New York, 1962; French and European Publications, New York, 1962.

Thieves' Carnival. Published in *The Modern Theatre,* ed. by E. R. Bentley and tr. by L. Hill, vol. 3, Doubleday, Garden City, N.Y., 1955; *Masters of Modern Drama,* ed. by H. M. Block and R. G. Shedd and tr. by L. Hill, Random House, New York, 1962.

The Waltz of the Toreadors. Published in *Plays of the Year,* ed. by J. C. Trewin and tr. by L. Hill, vol. 8, Elek, London, 1953; *Deux pièces modernes,* ed. by T. Bishop, Harcourt, Brace & World, New York, 1965.

CRITICISM

J. Didier, *À la rencontre de Jean Anouilh,* Paris, 1946; H. Gignoux, *Jean Anouilh,* Paris, 1946; E. O. Marsh, *Jean Anouilh: Poet of Pierrot and Pantaloon,* London, 1953; J. P. Lassalle, *Jean Anouilh, ou La vaine révolte,* Paris, 1956; L. C. Pronko, *The World of Jean Anouilh,* Berkeley, Calif., 1961; J. Harvey, *Anouilh: A Study in Theatrics,* New Haven, Conn., and London, 1964; A. M. Della Fazia, *Jean Anouilh,* New York, 1969.

ANSKI, S., pseudonym of Shloyme Zanul Rappoport (1863–1920). Russian- and Yiddish-language folklorist, novelist, and dramatist who achieved worldwide acclaim with his mystical dramatic legend *The Dybbuk* (*Dybbuk;* wr. 1914, prod. 1920), also known as *Between Two Worlds* (*Tzvishen tzvei Velter*), which was written in both Yiddish and Russian. Born to a prominent Jewish family, Anski received a Hasidic education but turned to the Haskalah (the Jewish Enlightenment) at an early age, embracing the radical ideas prevalent among the Russian intelligentsia of his day. In his dramatic and narrative works he portrayed realistic scenes from Hasidic life —the suffering that Jews experienced in Russia following the Revolution of 1905 and in Eastern Europe during World War I. His plays include *Father and Son* (*Foter und Zon,* 1906), a one-act drama set in a small Jewish village during the Passover season of 1905; *The Grandfather* (*Der Zeideh,* 1906), another one-act play; and *Day and Night* (*Tog und Nacht*), left unfinished but completed by Alter Katzine and performed in 1921 in Warsaw.

Players of the Habimah troupe from Palestine in *The Dybbuk.* New York, Broadway Theatre, 1948. [Photograph by Vandamm. Theatre Collection, The New York Public Library at Lincoln Center, Astor, Lenox and Tilden Foundations]

ANTIMASQUE. Comic or grotesque counterpart of the festive masque popular with the English aristocracy during the sixteenth and seventeenth centuries. Antic masque and antemasque are variant forms of the term.

The antimasque customarily preceded the masque proper and was a jovial parody of its lofty sentiments and elaborate decor: whereas the masque was performed by members of the aristocracy, the antimasque was usually performed by hired actors. Perhaps inspired by the antic or grotesque elements in the dancing of the masque proper, Ben Jonson (1572–1637), court poet to the Stuarts and the author of numerous masques proper, wrote the first antimasque in 1609 as a preface to his allegorical *The Masque of Queens*, in which Queen Anne herself was to perform. In the masque proper the players represent twelve queens of antiquity, while the main figures in the antimasque are eleven witches. Similarly, in the antimasque to Jonson's *Neptune's Triumph* (1624), a cook serves as the counterpart to the poet of the main masque. To Jonson, ever the proponent of classical symmetry, the antimasque was a kind of negative mirror image of the masque proper. Jonson's rivals subverted the antimasque by eliminating its thematic connection with the masque. *See* JONSON, BEN; MASQUE.

ANTITHEATRE. Deliberate eschewing of conventional theatrical devices, such as climax and denouement, by such dramatists as Ionesco, Beckett, and Albee, usually for satirical purposes.

ANTONA-TRAVERSI, Camillo (1857–1934). Italian dramatist, literary critic, and theatre historian whose work focuses on the observation of contemporary social life. In *The Ronzeno Family* (*Le Ronzeno*, 1891), a young girl attempts to redeem herself from a corrupt society through true love, but she kills herself when her lover abandons her upon discovering that she is pregnant. *The Parasites* (*I parassiti*, 1899) is a satirical comedy depicting the dishonest resourcefulness of a family that preys on the gullibility of society. In *Albert's Marriage* (*Il matrimonio di Alberto*, 1881), the sophisticated Albert returns to his native city after years of absence and rediscovers his childhood friend Irene, who had idolized him while he was away.

ANTONA-TRAVERSI GRISMONDI, Giannino (1860–1939). Italian dramatist whose comedies deal with the shallow and frivolous lives led by members of Italian high society and, in particular, with the intrigues of their marital relations. He was, however, no didactic moralist, and his plays are noted for their deft construction and epigrammatic wit. In *The Martyrs of Work* (*I martiri del lavoro*, 1908), young married people find no time for each other because of their outside "duties." *The Coquette* (*La civetta*, 1894) is a character study of a countess who enjoys arousing desire but refuses to allow for its gratification. *The Friend* (*L'amica*, 1900) concerns the reasons for the impossibility of a simple friendship between a man and a woman. *The Happiest Days* (*I giorni più lieti*, 1903) suggests that the days following marriage are bound to be less happy those those that precede it. *An Honest Wife* (*Una moglie onesta*, 1907) is about an egotistical and sensual woman who persists in gratifying her desires regardless of those who are injured by her behavior.

ANTONELLI, Luigi (1882–1942). Italian critic and dramatist who opposed bourgeois realism in the theatre, substituting fantasy and ironic wit. Antonelli's best play, *The Man Who Met Himself* (*L'uomo che incontrò se stesso*, 1918), concerns a forty-five-year-old man who encounters himself as a youth and discovers that age does not prevent the repetition of his errors of inexperience. Antonelli's theatre prepared the way for that of Pirandello, but it was ideologically opposed to the Pirandellian conception of life, as is shown in *The Master* (*Il maestro*, 1933). Among Antonelli's other plays are *The Tale of the Three Wizards* (*La fiaba de tre maghi*, 1919) and *Bernardo the Hermit* (*Bernardo l'eremita*, 1920), in which the core of the drama is a confrontation between reality and fiction. *See* PIRANDELLO, LUIGI.

Ludwig Anzengruber
(1839 – 1889)

Ludwig Gruber, Austrian dramatist who wrote under the pseudonym Ludwig Anzengruber, was born on November 29, 1839, in Vienna. After the death of his father, a civil servant with literary ambitions, Anzengruber was brought up by his mother, who had a small pension. He attended the Piarist school in Vienna, then worked in a bookstore. Fascinated by the theatre, he became in 1860 an actor with a traveling company. At the same time he tried writing plays but without success. In 1869, after a period as a free-lance journalist for Viennese periodicals, he reluctantly joined the Vienna Police Department in order to earn a regular salary.

Anzengruber's life was radically changed

Ludwig Anzengruber. [Bildarchiv der
Österreichischen Nationalbibliothek]

WORK

Anzengruber finds his place as a dramatist among the German writers of the transition period between realism and naturalism. His plays are based upon the *Wiener Volksstück* ("Viennese folk play"), with its melodramatic effects. In their use of music, the plays draw equally upon the *Fastnachtsspiele* ("carnival plays") and the *Singspiele* ("musical comedies") of the German baroque period (*see* SINGSPIEL). Anzengruber's sharply etched characters vividly and unsentimentally portray the Austrian peasant world that was familiar to him from his own background. The dialogue represents a stylized version of the Bavarian-Austrian dialect and could hardly be appreciated outside this region.

The themes of Anzengruber's plays are closely related to the religious and social problems of the day and express his concern for religious tolerance as well as his struggle against narrow-mindedness, prejudice, and ignorance. Among his peasant dramas and

Ludwig Martinelli in the title role of *Der Meineidbauer.* [Bildarchiv der Österreichischen National-bibliothek]

by the unexpected success of his anticlerical play *The Parson of Kirchfeld* (*Der Pfarrer von Kirchfeld*), written and produced in 1870. Its popularity—due partly to its liberal sentiments, though it also had some literary merit—enabled Anzengruber to resign from the police and devote all his time to writing stories, novels, and plays. His mother, whom he dearly loved, died in 1873. That year he married Adelina Lipka, but the union ended in divorce in 1889, the year of his death.

In the formal world of the Viennese theatre, Anzengruber's earthy Tyrolean and Styrian peasants were a refreshing influence. His use of dialect and his presentation of folk figures as protagonists made his plays particularly attractive to audiences in southern Germany and Austria. Although he received the Schiller Award in 1878 and the Grillparzer Prize in 1886, he was unable to support himself solely as a dramatist and supplemented his income by editing several periodicals, including the Viennese humorous paper *Figaro*. On December 10, 1889, at the peak of his creative powers, he died of blood poisoning in Vienna.

Scene from *Die Kreuzelschreiber*, Berlin, 1905. [Theater-Museum, Munich]

tragedies are *The Parson of Kirchfeld* (1870), one of the most significant anticlerical works of the period of the Kulturkampf but artistically the weakest of Anzengruber's plays; and *The Farmer Forsworn* (*Der Meineidbauer*, 1871), a masterpiece of plot and characterization and the culmination of nineteenth-century folk drama. These rather somber dramas have comedy counterparts in *The Cross Markers* (*Die Kreuzelschreiber*, 1872), a variation of the *Lysistrata* theme; *The Worm of Conscience* (*Der G'wissenswurm*, 1874); and *The Double Suicide* (*Der Doppelselbstmord*, 1876).

As Anzengruber moves away from the peasant milieu, his dramatic power diminishes and his characters become less convincing. This is the case in his social drama *Elfriede* (1873) and in *The Usurer's Daughter* (*Die Tochter des Wucherers*, 1873). An outstanding exception is *The Fourth Commandment* (*Das Vierte Gebot*, 1877), which deals with the generations theme that later was frequently taken up by naturalistic writers. Through Otto Brahm's production in Berlin it gained great popularity outside Austria. Despite the weakness of many of his social dramas, however, they show his conviction that the theatre's role is to enlighten the audience. Anzengruber saw himself as a true teacher of the people who had a message to give and who bore a responsibility for the betterment of society.

Anzengruber was equally gifted as a nondramatic writer. Most of his other works were written in the later years of his creative period. He published two novels, *Der Schandfleck* (*The Blot of Shame*, 1876) and *Der Sternsteinhof* (*The Sternstein Farm*, 1876), and a collection of short stories, *Wolken und Sonnenschein* (*Clouds and Sunshine*, 1883), as well as a series of calendar stories.

The Farmer Forsworn (*Der Meineidbauer*, 1871). Folk drama with singing. After the death of the farmer Jakob Ferner, his brother Matthias has acquired the family farm by committing perjury and by burning the will in which the deceased has given the inheritance to his two illegitimate children Vroni and Jakob and their mother. Matthias's hope that the fraud can be kept a secret proves vain, for his son Franz has witnessed the destruction of the will. Moreover, when Vroni discovers in the papers of her dying brother a letter that testifies against Matthias, she resolves to fight for her rights and to take the case to court. In a wild hunt through the countryside Matthias tries in vain to retrieve the letter, first from Vroni and then from his son, and dies suddenly from a stroke. Vroni forgoes her accusation in court, burns the incriminating letter, and marries Franz. She thus acquires the farm through love instead of her claim.

The Cross Markers (*Die Kreuzelschreiber,* 1872).   Peasant comedy in three acts. To the great dismay of the village priest the illiterate peasants of Zwentdorf append their signatures, in the form of crosses, to a statement opposing the doctrine of papal infallibility. Supporting the priest, the peasants' wives agree to deny marital rights to their husbands until they have withdrawn the statement and returned from a penitential pilgrimage to Rome. The husbands agree to go to Rome, with the proviso that they be accompanied by a select group of village virgins. Infuriated, the wives abandon their demands, and reconciliation follows.

The Fourth Commandment (*Das Vierte Gebot,* 1877).   Folk drama in four acts. Hedwig Hutterer, who is in love with her piano teacher Robert Frey, is forced by her snobbish father into an unhappy marriage with the rich and irresponsible August Stolzenhalter. Stolzenhalter has been having an affair with the neighbors' daughter, Josefa Schalanter. Josefa's father is a drunkard, her mother is a procuress, and her brother Martin is trying to avoid the draft. A year goes by, and Hedwig, who is maltreated by her husband and whose baby is fatally ill, in her unhappiness tries to resume contact with Frey, who by now is a major in the army and Martin's hated superior. Martin and his father spy on their rendezvous, and in the ensuing argument Martin shoots Frey from behind and kills him. In prison and condemned to death, Martin curses his parents and their bad example, voicing the play's lesson that

Scene from Act III of *Das vierte Gebot.* [Bildarchiv der Österreichischen Nationalbibliothek]

parental morality is a precondition for observance of the Fourth Commandment.

PLAYS

1. *Der Pfarrer von Kirchfeld* (*The Parson of Kirchfeld*). Folk drama, 4 acts. Written 1870. Published 1872. Produced Vienna, Theater an der Wien, Nov. 5, 1870.

2. *Der Meineidbauer** (*The Farmer Forsworn*). Folk drama, 3 acts. Written 1871. Published 1872. Produced Vienna, Theater an der Wien, Dec. 9, 1871.

3. *Die Kreuzelschreiber* (*The Cross Markers*). Peasant comedy, 3 acts. Written 1872. Published 1872. Produced Vienna, Theater an der Wien, Oct. 12, 1872.

4. *Elfriede.* Drama, 3 acts. Written 1872. Published 1873. Produced Vienna, Carltheater, Apr. 29, 1873.

5. *Die Tochter des Wucherers* (*The Usurer's Daughter*). Drama, 5 acts. Written 1873. Published 1873. Produced Vienna, Theater an der Wien, Oct. 17, 1873.

6. *Der G'wissenswurm* (*The Worm of Conscience*). Peasant comedy, 3 acts. Written 1874. Published 1874. Produced Vienna, Theater an der Wien, Sept. 19, 1874.

7. *Hand und Herz* (*Hand and Heart*). Tragedy, 4 acts. Written 1874. Published 1875. Produced Vienna, Wiener Stadttheater, Dec. 31, 1874.

8. *Berta von Frankreich* (*Bertha of France*). Fragment. Tragedy, first act only. Written 1874. Published 1874.

9. *Der Doppelselbstmord* (*The Double Suicide*). Peasant farce, 3 acts. Written 1875. Published 1876. Produced Vienna, Theater an der Wien, Feb. 1, 1876.

10. *Der Ledige Hof* (*The Farm with an Unwed Master*). Drama, 4 acts. Written 1876. Published 1877. Produced Vienna, Theater an der Wien, Jan. 27, 1877.

11. *Das vierte Gebot** (*The Fourth Commandment*). Folk drama, 4 acts. Written 1877. Published 1878. Produced Vienna, Theater in der Josefstadt, Dec. 29, 1877.

12. *Ein Faustschlag* (*A Fist Blow*). Drama, 3 acts. Written 1877. Published 1878. Produced Vienna, Theater in der Josefstadt, Jan. 4, 1879.

13. *Das Jungferngift* (*The Poison of the Virgins*). Peasant comedy, 5 acts. Written 1878. Published 1878. Produced Vienna, Carltheater, Apr. 21, 1878.

14. *Alte Wiener* (*Old Viennese Gentlemen*). Folk drama, 4 acts. Written 1878. Published 1879. Produced Vienna, Ringtheater, Sept. 27, 1878.

15. *Die Trutzige* (*The Defiant One*). Peasant comedy, 3 acts. Written 1878. Published 1879. Produced Vienna, Theater an der Wien, Nov. 8, 1878.

16. *Die umkehrte Freit'* (*The Reversed Courtship*). Provincial sketch, 1 act. Written 1879. Published 1879. Produced Vienna, Theater an der Wien, Apr. 4, 1879.

17. *Aus'm gewohnten Gleis* (*Off the Beaten Track*). Farce, 5 acts. Written 1879. Published 1880. Produced Vienna, Theater an der Wien, Dec. 25, 1879.

18. *Brave Leut' vom Grund* (*Good Country Folks*). Folk drama, 3 acts. Written 1880. Published 1892. Produced Vienna, Internationales Ausstellungstheater im Prater, Sept. 3, 1892.

19. *Heimg'funden* (*The Prodigal's Return*). Christmas comedy, 3 acts. Written 1885. Published 1889. Produced Baden, Stadttheater, Dec. 26, 1885.

20. *Stahl und Stein* (*Steel and Stone*). Folk drama, 3 acts. Written 1886. Published 1887. Produced Vienna, Hofoperntheater, Nov. 6, 1887.

21. *Der Fleck auf der Ehr'* (*The Spot on the Honor*). Folk drama, 3 acts. Written 1889. Published 1889. Produced Vienna, Deutsches Volkstheater, Sept. 14, 1889.

EDITIONS

Collections.
Gesammelte Werke, 10 vols., Stuttgart, 1892; *Werke,* ed. by A. Bettelheim, 14 vols., Berlin, 1920; *Sämtliche Werke,* ed. by O. Rommel and R. Latzke, 15 vols., Vienna, 1921–1922.

Individual Plays.
The Farmer Forsworn. Published in *The German Clas-* sics of the Nineteenth and Twentieth Centuries, ed. by K. Francke and tr. by A. Busse, vol. 16, New York, 1913–1914.

The Fourth Commandment. Published in *German Plays of the Nineteenth Century,* ed. by T. M. Campbell, New York, 1930.

CRITICISM

A. Bettelheim, *Ludwig Anzengruber,* Berlin, 1897; A. Kleinberg, *Ludwig Anzengruber,* Stuttgart, 1921; F. Weber, *Anzengrubers Naturalismus,* Berlin, 1928; L. Koessler, *Ludwig Anzengruber,* Paris, 1943.

APOLLINAIRE, Guillaume, pseudonym of Wilhelm Apollinaris de Kostrowitzki (1880–1918). French poet, novelist, and art critic. *The Breasts of Tiresias* (*Les mamelles de Tirésias,* 1917), his only play, is essentially a manifesto of his artistic credo, and it was in relation to this work that Apollinaire coined the word "surrealist." He scorned art and drama that tried to imitate life, whose essence, he felt, could be conveyed only partially by the invention of new forms. *Tiresias* combines an outrageously farcical text with hilarious auditory and visual effects. When Thérèse decides to abandon her role as a woman and become Tiresias, her breasts, two balloons, literally float away; and her husband undertakes the task of turning out the children needed by France, doing so at the rate of 40,000 a day. Francis Poulenc used Apollinaire's play as the text for his comic opera of the same name (1945).

Apollinaire's poems are to some extent a literary translation of the techniques of cubism: odd juxtapositions, the use of chance elements, the inclusion of images reflecting the machine age, and unusual typographical effects. His major collections of poems are *Alcohols* (*Alcools,* 1913) and *Calligrammes* (1918).

ARAGOTO. Popular, highly stylized type of acting in Japanese drama, characterized by violent speech and gesture. *Aragoto* ("rough business") is found in the Kabuki dance drama, having been invented by Ichikawa Danjuro I, the great Kabuki actor of the seventeenth century. In its violence and energy and in its sharp, clear movements, *aragoto* is closely related to the style of the Japanese doll and puppet theatre. The *aragoto* character, who may be a warrior hero or a villain, is all masculinity, vigor, and strength. He shouts and swaggers. His face is painted a fearsome red and blue; his legs, arms, and hands are painted red and white to emphasize the tension of muscles, veins, and sinews. The sleeves of his kimono are bigger than anyone else's, and he wears a wig that increases the height and width of his head. If he carries an ax, it is four times life-size; if he is armed with swords, he carries three instead of the usual two. Some of the more refined actors called Danjuro's innovation ridiculous and refused to accept it, but audiences came to favor this hearty, masculine style, and it survives as the most popular in Japanese theatre. *See* KABUKI.

Alexey Arbuzov
(1908 —   )

Alexey Nikolayevich Arbuzov, Soviet actor, director, and dramatist, was born in Moscow on May 26, 1908 (N.S.), to a bank employee and his wife, the daughter of an engineer of Greek origin. Six years later the family moved to Petrograd, where the boy was sent to school. In 1917 family friction caused him to be withdrawn. Only two years later, his father deserted the family and his mother entered a hospital, where she remained for many years. Arbuzov eventually went to live with an aunt, and in 1922 he entered the Leningrad Conservatory, where he stayed for a year. Devoted to the theatre, he quickly at-

tached himself to a mime group, with which he worked as an extra; he found jobs as an actor and stage manager as well. In 1930 he and his friends organized a number of traveling theatrical companies, providing entertainment and at the same time disseminating Communist ideology. Soon he moved to Moscow and began an association with the Proletkult Theatre.

After working in a collective-farm theatre, Arbuzov began to write in earnest. His first play, a comedy entitled *Six Dear Ones* (*Shestero lyubimykh*) that he wrote in 1934, was to become one of his most popular. *The Long Road* (*Dalnyaya doroga*) was written in 1936, and *Tanya* in 1938. At the end of 1938, with the producer V. N. Pluchek he organized a collective theatre, the Moscow Theatrical Studio, which opened with his play *The Town at Daybreak* (*Gorod na zare*, 1940), highly praised by both critics and public. During World War II the studio moved its operations to the front, and Arbuzov continued to write and produce.

Since the war his reputation in the Soviet Union has continued to rise, what with the production of such plays as *The Twelfth Hour* (*Dvenadtsaty chas*, wr. 1958), and his most fa-

Scene from *The Town at Daybreak*. [*Moscow Theatres*]

Scene from *The
Years of
Wandering.*
[*Moscow Theatres*]

mous play, *The Irkutsk Story* (*Irkutskaya istoriya*, 1959).

WORK

Although the conflicts portrayed in Arbuzov's plays are usually enacted in personal
terms, often pivoting on a sparkling young
protagonist, the dramatist also addresses
himself to the collision between opposing abstractions, such as youth and old age or inexperience and experience. Dealing frequently
with common Soviet themes like the building
of a power plant or the mutual love of young
workers, his plays often begin in a gay, casual
setting but progress to a more serious arena
for the discussion of universal problems about
human existence, history, and other subjects
of interest to Communist youth. His characters, almost exclusively Russian, are not simple prototypes but more complex individuals
who confront problems of emotions in their
own ways. Motivation seems to spring from
within, and Arbuzov does not insist on providing solutions. On the whole, he maintains a
restrained hand over his material and does
not resort to melodrama. His style is characterized by a flowing lyricism into which lines
of familiar poetry and allusions to musical
compositions are introduced.

His most important plays are the enthusiastically received *The Irkutsk Story*
(1959), about the construction of a Siberian
power plant and how love helps build better
workers and Communists; and *Six Dear Ones*
(1935), which established him as one of the

leading Soviet socialist realist playwrights
and deals with a sentimental young worker's
nostalgia for medievalism. Among his other
plays of note are *Tanya* (1939), the portrait of
a complex woman; *Encounter with Youth*
(*Vstrecha s yunostyu*, wr. 1947), which centers
on an aging man; *The Years of Wandering*
(*Gody stranstvy*, 1954), which opens with a
spirited students' party and then delves into
philosophical questions; and *The European
Chronicle* (*Yevropeyskaya khronika*, 1952), set
in Denmark and France and showing the
effects of World War II on a variety of people.

Six Dear Ones (*Shestero lyubimykh*, 1935).
Stepan Gaydar, a young tractor worker of
the village of Samoylov, on the Volga River,
has a sentimental admiration for feudalism, symbolized by the pictures of medieval
knights he hangs on his wall. A streak of
anarchist individualism makes him a habitu-
al rebel against society and prompts him to
protest the loss of a flag he won in a competition. This year it is to be awarded to Lenka
Bogacheva, a girl from a neighboring village.
While they are waiting for Lenka to receive
her prize, Gaydar's friends, among them a
politician, a tractor driver, a middle-aged
woman, and a German Communist, try to
break down his convictions. Finally, Gaydar,
yielding to their entreaties, takes the medieval pictures from his wall and gives the flag
to Lenka.

The Long Road (*Dalnyaya doroga*, wr.
1936). Comedy about the building of the
Moscow subway. Living in a hostel are six

The Promise, with (l. to r.) Mark Bramhall, David Dukes, and Dana Larson. [Courtesy American Conservatory Theatre, San Francisco, Calif. Photograph by Hank Kranzler]

young workers of a labor brigade: Anton, the secretary of the brigade; Elena Lyashenko (Leshka), the leader of the girl workers; Topsik, her assistant; Lilya Bregman, a secretary; and two young workers, Ilya and Maksim. The first three, enthusiastic Communists, undertake the social reeducation of the others. Lilya, a Jew mourning the death of her infant son, has to learn to subordinate her private grief to higher responsibilities to the community; Maksim, lonely and unlucky in love, must resign himself to a collective existence; and Ilya, a hooligan, must be reintegrated into society. Leshka, while occupied with the enlightenment of her pupils, also becomes involved in a personal tragedy: Ilya, whom she loves, marries Lilya. She will, however, find happiness in following "the long and happy road to socialism."

PLAYS

1. *Shestero lyubimykh* (*Six Dear Ones*). Comedy, 3 acts. Written 1934. Published 1957. Produced Venyovsky Kolkhoz Theatre, 1935.

2. *Dalnyaya doroga* (*The Long Road*). Comedy, 3 acts. Written 1936. Published 1957. Produced Moscow, Central Theater of the Working Youth.

3. *Tanya*. Play, 2 parts. Written 1938. Published 1946. Produced Moscow, Theatre of the Revolution, 1939.

4. *Gorod na zare* (*The Town at Daybreak*). Play, 3 acts. Published 1957. Produced Moscow, Moscow Theatrical Studio, 1940.

5. *Domik na okraine* (*The Small House on the Out-*

skirts). Melodrama, 2 parts. First version: Written 1943. Second version: Published 1954. Produced Moscow, Mayakovsky Theatre, 1954.

6. *Vstrecha s yunostyu* (*Encounter with Youth*). Comedy, 3 acts. Written 1947. Published 1956. Produced Leningrad, Comedy Theatre.

7. *Yevropeyskaya khronika* (*The European Chronicle*). Drama, 2 parts. Written 1952. Published 1961. Produced Yermolova Theatre, 1952.

8. *Gody stranstvy* (*The Years of Wandering*). Drama, 2 parts. Written 1954. Published 1961. Produced Moscow, Theatre of the Leningrad Komsomol, 1954.

9. *Dvenadtsaty chas* (*The Twelfth Hour*). Tragicomedy, 3 acts. Written 1958. Published 1961. Produced Moscow, Vakhtangov Theatre, 1960.

10. *Irkutskaya istoriya** (*The Irkutsk Story*). Drama, 2 parts. Written 1959. Published 1959. Produced Moscow, Vakhtangov Theatre, 1959.

11. *Poteryanny syn* (*The Lost Son*). Melodrama, 3 acts. Written 1960. Published 1961. Produced Leningrad, Theatre of Drama, 1961.

12. *Moi bednyi Marat** (*The Promise*). Play. Published 1965.

EDITIONS

Collections.
Pyesy, Moscow, 1957; *Teatr*, Moscow, 1961.
Individual Plays.
The Irkutsk Story (*It Happened in Irkutsk*). Published in *Three Soviet Plays*, tr. by R. Prokofieva, Foreign Language Publishing House, Moscow, 1961.
The Promise. A. Nikolaeff, tr., Oxford, London, 1967.

ARCHIBALD, William (1924–1970). American singer, dancer, and choreographer whose varied career included writing *The Innocents*

(1950), an adaptation of Henry James's novelette *The Turn of the Screw* (1898).

ARDEN, John (b. Barnsley, Yorkshire, October 26, 1930). Technically one of the most Brechtian of the current British dramatists, Arden blends prose, verse, and ballads in his plays. Though they have strong underlying social and philosophical themes—pacifism in *Serjeant Musgrave's Dance* (1959), the welfare state in *Live Like Pigs* (1958)—Arden, no polemicist, effectively presents both sides of an argument. There are no heroes or villains, no good values or bad; there are only different people with differing values, which Arden refrains from judging. *See* BRECHT, BERTOLT.

His comedy *All Fall Down,* about the building of a railroad, was performed while he was studying architecture at Edinburgh before 1955. After his radio play *The Life of Man* was broadcast in 1956, the Royal Court Theatre selected *The Waters of Babylon* (1957) to inaugurate its low-budget Sunday-night productions. A satire on a bond system instituted by the British government, the play has as its central character a Polish *émigré* who works in an architect's office by day and runs a boarding house, tenanted by exploited foreigners and prostitutes whom he "manages," in his spare time.

Among Arden's other plays are *When a Door Is Not a Door,* a one-act play performed in 1958; *The Happy Haven* (1960), about an old people's home; *The Workhouse Donkey,* about political intrigue, performed at the Chichester Festival in 1963; *Ironhand,* performed by the Bristol Old Vic in 1963; *Armstrong's Last Goodnight,* produced in Glasgow in 1964; and *Left-Handed Liberty* (1965).

Serjeant Musgrave's Dance (1959). "Unhistorical parable" set in a bleak mining town in northern England in the 1880s at the height of British colonialism. In the midst of a mining strike the village is invaded by a small group of Her Majesty's soldiers led by the dour Serjeant Musgrave, ostensibly on a recruiting mission. In fact, the men are deserters, completely dominated by their leader's fierce pacifism, which has been transformed into a kind of maniacal religious fanaticism. When a squabble over a tavern girl results in the death of one of the soldiers, Musgrave delivers a tirade in the village square against the brutality of the country's

Scene from *Serjeant Musgrave's Dance,* Minneapolis, 1968. [The Guthrie Theater Company]

Paul Ballantyne and Roberta Maxwell in John Arden's *Serjeant Musgrave's Dance,* Minneapolis, 1968. [The Guthrie Theater Company]

colonial empire. Producing the skeleton of a local boy who was killed in the occupation of a foreign land, he tells how five other men were killed in reprisal. It is his intention, in order to teach the townspeople the horrors of war, to take the lives of five times as many of them. He is prevented from doing so by the arrival of a company of dragoons that takes the invaders into custody. Produced London, Royal Court Theatre, October 22, 1959.

ARENT, Arthur (1904–   ). American playwright who was one of the mainstays of socially conscious drama during the Depression of the 1930s and of the "living newspaper," a publication of documentary dramas sponsored by the Federal Theatre Project in that period. His *One Third of a Nation* (1938), an investigation of substandard housing and the slum problem, has come to typify that particular era of the American theatre. Arent was one of the collaborators of *Pins and Needles* (1937), a musical revue sponsored by the International Ladies Garment Workers Union, which applied the same techniques in a lighter vein to support the labor movement. Among his other plays are *Ethiopia* (1936), *Triple-A Plowed Under* (1936), *1935*

(1936), *Injunction Granted* (1936), *Power* (1937), and *It's Up to You* (1943).

Pietro Aretino
(1492 – 1556)

Pietro Aretino, Italian satirist and dramatist, was born in Arezzo on April 20, 1492, the son of a cobbler. After a few years in Perugia and Siena, he went to Rome, where he began writing his famous pasquinades, or lampoons, directed against rich and powerful figures of the day and commissioned by their equally rich and powerful rivals. Although he was under the protection of the Medici (including Pope Leo X) and the Chigi, he twice had to flee Rome, once after the election of Pope Hadrian VI, whom he had attacked, and again after an attempt on his life by Giovanni Matteo Giberti, a Curia official whom he had lampooned.

For a while Aretino enjoyed the protection of the Florentine *condottiere* Giovanni delle Bande Nere, but after Giovanni's death (1526) he moved to Venice, where he lived more or less unmolested, writing and enjoying the fruits of his friendship with Emperor Charles V, Pope Clement VII, Duke Cosimo I of Florence, and the painter Titian, who made a portrait of him. Aretino died in Venice on October 21, 1556.

WORK

In his five prose comedies, Aretino rejected a close imitation of Roman models in favor of a looser, more episodic form, which allowed him to include satirical and farcical scenes peripheral to the main action. He claimed that the freer form was better suited to de-

Pietro Aretino. [Federico Arborio Mella, Milan]

scribing Italian life of his own time, and it is true that his satirical talents are shown to great advantage in scenes of contemporary life interpolated in the plot. He seldom missed an opportunity to digress upon the follies and vices of the day, employing a racy, colloquial idiom that reflected the colorful rhythms of popular speech.

His two finest comedies, *The Courtesan* (*La cortigiana;* wr. 1526, prod. 1537) and *The "Horse Doctor"* (*Il marescalco,* 1526/27), are among the best of the century. Almost as successful is *The Hypocrite* (*Lo ipocrito,* 1545), based in part on Plautus's *The Twin Menaechmi* (*see* PLAUTUS). The hypocrite, a character not dissimilar to Molière's Tartuffe, presides over a complex tale of long-lost brothers and lovers, contributing an ironic and cynical air to an otherwise romantic tale (*see* MOLIÈRE). *Talanta* (*La Talanta,* wr. 1534), also based on *The Twin Menaechmi* as well as on Terence's *The Eunuch,* concerns three men contending for the attentions of a courtesan as well as two young people masquerading as members of the opposite sex (*see* TERENCE). Aretino's weakest comedy, *The Philosopher* (*Il filosofo,* wr. 1544) satirizes pedantry.

Aretino also wrote a tragedy, *The Horatii* (*Orazia,* pub. 1546), in which he refused to conform to the Aristotelian precepts generally observed by tragedians of his century.

Uninfluenced by contemporary literary theorists such as Giraldi Cinthio, Aretino sought to make his characterizations more realistic through the use of a free style and a loosely constructed plot. Although his tragedy had few followers in his time, because of the spontaneity and liveliness of its language it is considered by many present-day critics to be the best tragedy of the Italian sixteenth century. *See* GIRALDI CINTHIO, GIAMBATTISTA.

The Courtesan (*La cortigiana;* wr. 1526, prod. 1537). Satirical comedy in which two plots are loosely interwoven. In the first plot, the wealthy country bumpkin Maco, who desperately wishes to become a cardinal, falls into the clutches of Maestro Andrea, who insists that the first step is to become a courtier. The silly Maco, having suffered no end of pain and indignity, is finally proclaimed a courtier and then thoroughly humiliated for his presumption. The second plot concerns Parabolano, a foolish courtier who employs his rascally servant Russo to obtain the favors of the beautiful Donna Livia. Since the lady is inaccessible, Russo enlists the aid of the procuress Alvigia to substitute Togna, a baker's wife, for Donna Livia. The action culminates in a wildly farcical bedroom scene involving the baker himself. The play serves as a vehicle for Aretino's satirical observations on the contemporary Roman court and courtiers.

The "Horse Doctor" (*Il marescalco,* 1526/27). Comedy based upon Plautus's *Casina* and Machiavelli's *Clizia.* The homosexual Marescalco is forced into marriage by his patron, the Duke of Mantua. While some of his friends extol the benefits of marriage and others enumerate its horrors, Marescalco tries desperately to avoid the forthcoming nuptials. After the ceremony, in reality an elaborate hoax perpetrated by the members of the Duke's court, Marescalco discovers to his delight that his "wife" is a boy. The play was a source for Ben Jonson's *Epicoene. See* JONSON, BEN; MACHIAVELLI, NICCOLÒ.

PLAYS

1. *La cortigiana* (*The Courtesan*). Comedy, 5 acts; prose. Written 1526. Published 1534. Produced Bologna, 1537.

2. *Il marescalco* (*The "Horse Doctor"*). Comedy, 5 acts; prose. Written 1526/27. Published 1533. Produced Mantua, 1526/27.

3. *La Talanta* (*Talanta*). Comedy, 5 acts; prose. Written 1534. Published 1542.

4. *Lo ipocrito* (*The Hypocrite*). Comedy, 5 acts; prose. Written 1541/42. Published 1542. Produced Arezzo, 1545.

5. *Il filosofo* (*The Philosopher*). Comedy, 5 acts; prose. Written 1544. Published 1546.

6. *Orazia* (*The Horatii*). Tragedy, prologue and 5 acts; verse. Published 1546.

EDITIONS

Pietro Aretino: Teatro, ed. by N. Macarrone, Lanciano, 1914.

Frontispiece of the first edition of *Orazia.* [Federico Arborio Mella, Milan]

CRITICISM

Italian. G. M. Mazzuchelli, *La vita di Pietro Aretino,* Padua, 1741; A. Luzio, *Pietro Aretino nei suoi primi anni a Venezia e la corte dei Gonzaga,* Turin, 1888; E. Perito, *La Talanta di Pietro Aretino,* Girgenti, 1899; D. Grasso, *L'Aretino e le sue commedie,* Palermo, 1900; U. Fresco, *Le commedie di Pietro Aretino,* Camerino, 1901; F. Stacchiotti, *L'Orazia,* Camerino, 1907; B. Stocchi, *L'Orazia dell'Aretino e l'Horace del Corneille,* Naples, 1911; M. Bontempelli, *Verga, l'Aretino, Scarlatti e Verdi,* Milan, 1941; G. Petrocchi, *Pietro Aretino,* Milan, 1948.

English. J. Cleugh, *Divine Aretino,* New York, 1966.

Ludovico Ariosto

(1474 — 1533)

Ludovico Ariosto, Italian poet and dramatist, was born in Reggio Emilia on September 8, 1474, the son of Count Niccolò Ariosto. At the age of ten his family moved to Ferrara, where, somewhat against his inclination, he studied law from 1489 to 1494. Then, under the tutelage of the humanist scholar Gregorio de Spoleto, he began to study Latin and Greek language and literature. In 1500 his father died, and Ariosto assumed the management of the rather unprofitable family estates. In order to support the family, he became commander of the fort of Canossa in 1502, and in 1503 he entered the service of Ippolito Cardinal d'Este, with whom he remained until 1517. While in the service of the Cardinal, Ariosto began to write *Orlando Furioso,* his epic poem about the myth of Roland, which was published in Venice in 1516 in forty cantos.

In 1518 he entered the service of the Cardinal's brother, Duke Alfonso I of Ferrara, for whom he handled a delicate mission to Pope Julius II and acted as governor of the Garfagnana, spending two years in the wildest part of the Apennines dealing with rival factions and brigands. Around 1527 he secretly married the widow Alessandra Benucci, whom he had loved for some years. He spent the last part of his life revising and enlarging *Orlando Furioso,* which was republished in forty-six cantos in 1532. Ariosto died in Ferrara on July 6, 1533.

WORK

Ariosto was well versed in the classical tradition. As a member of a group organized to produce plays by Plautus and Terence at the Este court of Ferrara, he became especially familiar with their approaches to comedy, and their work later became the model for his own dramas. *See* PLAUTUS; TERENCE.

Because Italian dramatists of the late fifteenth century had not yet chosen between prose and verse as the major dramatic form, Ariosto sometimes wrote two versions of the same play. His five comedies, although not so skillfully executed as the chivalric poem *Orlando Furioso,* are equal to the best plays of the period. Their careful construction reflects Ariosto's keen sense of theatre. Totally involved in his plays, he not only acted in some of them but also directed them, and he even built the stage on which *The Chest (La cassaria;* prose version, 1508; verse version, 1531) was performed. If urbane wit is the mark of his poems, the comedies sparkle with sometimes cutting, sometimes good-humored irony. The playwright's empathy with his contemporaries is clearly illustrated in the relations between his realistically portrayed characters. They themselves are distinctive, and their speeches are painstakingly drawn.

Ariosto chose as his themes love and cunning and used comedy to define their relationship. In *The Chest,* two wily servants succeed in arranging desirable marriages for their masters. Much of the intrigue of *The Pretenders (I suppositi;* prose version, 1509; verse version, wr. 1528/31) also arises from the astuteness of a servant helping his master in the pursuit of love. In *The Necromancer (Il negromante,* wr. 1520), both fate and the cunning of a subordinate character, the necromancer, result in the happy marriages of two couples. All the comic theatrical devices of fate, intrigue, disguise, and discovery are employed in *The Students (I studenti,* wr. 1519), an unfinished comedy of frustrated love set in contemporary Ferrara. It was completed by his brother Gabriele about 1543 as *La scolastica* and by his son in 1556 as *L'imperfetta.* The realistic comedy *The Bawd Lena (La Lena,* 1528), which also portrays life in Ferrara, embarrassed the Este court by alluding to corruption among city officials.

The Chest *(La cassaria;* prose version 1508; verse version, 1531). Comedy that, although not derived directly from Plautus or Terence, exhibits many characteristics of ancient Latin comedy. The Greek youths Erofilo and Caridoro are in love with Eulalia and Corisca, slaves belonging to Lucrano. While Erofilo's father Crisobolo is away, his servant Volpino devises a plan for Erofilo to have Eulalia. Erofilo is to send a chest of spun gold to Lucrano, and Caridoro's father, a magistrate, will be told that Lucrano is a thief. Then Caridoro will intervene on Lucrano's behalf provided he frees the two slaves. But Crisobolo, returning unexpectedly, discovers Volpino's plot and puts him in prison. However, another servant, Fulcio, manages to placate Crisobolo and to collect enough money to free Eulalia and Corisca, who are joyfully united with their lovers.

Ludovico Ariosto; portrait by Titian. [Italian Cultural Institute]

The Pretenders (*I suppositi*, prose version, 1509; verse version, wr. 1528/31). Comedy, based on Terence's *The Eunuch* and Plautus's *The Captives*, in which Erostrato, a Sicilian youth studying in Ferrara, falls in love with Polinesta, daughter of Damone. In order to be near her he becomes Damone's servant and sends his own servant Dulippo to school in his place. Dr. Cleandro, an aging physician also in love with Polinesta, offers a very large dowry to gain her hand. The false Erostrato (Dulippo) offers an even larger dowry and further induces one of his friends to impersonate the real Erostrato's father, Filigono. When the real Filigono arrives, equivocal situations are created, but the play ends happily when Cleandro discovers that the false Erostrato is his long-lost son, abducted by the Turks during the sack of Otranto, and the true Erostrato marries Polinesta.

The Necromancer (*Il negromante*, wr. 1520). Verse comedy taking place in Cremona, in which Cinthio, adopted son of the rich Massimo, is secretly married to Lavinia, daughter of Fazio, a man of modest means.

The marriage is kept secret in order to preserve Cinthio's inheritance. Cinthio is forced by his father to marry Emilia but cannot consummate the marriage. Massimo requests the necromancer to cure Cinthio of his impotence, while Cinthio, wishing to have his second marriage annulled, appeals to the magician that he may remain impotent. The necromancer is also approached by Camillo, who is in love with Emilia. The necromancer profits from the involved situation until he is finally exposed. In the end Camillo marries Emilia, while Cinthio remains the happy spouse of Lavinia, whom Massimo has recognized as his long-lost daughter.

The Bawd Lena (*La Lena*, 1528). Comedy in five acts based on the story of Peronella in Boccaccio's *Decameron* (VII, ii). Flavio, in love with Licinia, tries to arrange a meeting with her at Lena's house, where Licinia goes for daily lessons in homemaking. Licinia's father Fatio is both Lena's landlord and one of her many lovers. Flavio's servant Corbolo cannot raise enough money to bribe Lena to arrange the meeting. Lena's husband therefore advises Flavio to sneak into the house in a wine cask. A usurer, however, demands the cask as settlement of a debt. Fatio puts the cask in his own house until the debt controversy is settled. When Flavio is discovered in the cask, his and Licinia's parents agree to allow the couple's marriage in order to avoid a scandal.

PLAYS

1. *La cassaria* (*The Chest*). Comedy, 5 acts. Prose version: Written 1507. Published 1508. Produced Ferrara, Teatro Ducale, Mar. 5, 1508. Verse version: Written 1530. Published 1530. Produced Ferrara, Teatro Ducale, Feb. 19, 1531.

2. *I suppositi* (*The Pretenders*). Comedy, 5 acts. Prose version: Written 1508. Produced Ferrara, Teatro Ducale, Feb. 6, 1509. Verse version: Written 1528/31.

3. *Gli studenti* (*The Students*). Comedy, 4 acts, 4 scenes. Written 1519. Uncompleted; completed as *La scolastica* and *L'imperfetta*.

4. *Il negromante* (*The Necromancer*). Comedy, 5 acts; verse. Written 1520.

5. *La Lena* (*The Bawd Lena*). Comedy, 5 acts; verse. Written 1528. Produced Ferrara, Carnival, 1528.

6. (Gabriele Ariosto). *La scolastica* (*The Academic Comedy*). Comedy, 5 acts; verse. Written ca. 1543. Completion of *Gli studenti*.

7. (Virginio Ariosto). *L'imperfetta* (*The Imperfect One*). Comedy, 5 acts; verse. Produced Ferrara, Torchiara Castle, July, 1556? Completion of *Gli studenti*.

EDITIONS

Commedie e satire di Ludovico Ariosto, ed. by G. Tortoli, Florence, 1856; *Le commedie*, edited by M. Catalano, 2d ed., rev. and enl., Bologna, 1940.

CRITICISM

E. G. Gardner, *King of the Court Poets: A Study of the Work, Life and Times of Lodovico Ariosto*, New York, 1906; B. Croce, *Ariosto, Shakespeare, and Corneille*, tr. by D. Ainslie, New York, 1920; M. Catalano, *Vita di Ludovico Ariosto ricostruita su nuovi documenti*, Geneva, 1931; C. Grabher, *Sul teatro dell'Aristo*, Rome, 1946.

Aristophanes

(ca. 445 — ca. 385 B.C.)

The date of Aristophanes's birth is uncertain. The little information that is available about his life comes from the ancient *Lives* (of which we have five), the scholia on his works and those of other authors, the remarks of the lexicographer Suidas, and the poet's own comments. Suidas tells us that Aristophanes was at the peak of his maturity in 404 B.C., the last year of the Peloponnesian War. Since in general Suidas considered men about forty years old mature, Aristophanes may have been born around 445 B.C. He is known to have produced his first play, *The Banqueters,* in 427 B.C. under a pseudonym and with it to have won second prize in one of the many drama festivals. In an allusion to this play Aristophanes wrote in *The Clouds* (*Nephelai,* lines 530–532; 423 B.C.): "Still a poetic virgin and not yet allowed to bear a child, I exposed my first-born for another to adopt, and you [Athenians] generously cherished and reared it." Furthermore, a scholium informing us that at the time of his authorship of *The Banqueters* Aristophanes was "a mere stripling" points unmistakably to his precocity.

Aristophanes was the son of Philippus and Zenodora, of the tribe of Pandion from the district of Cydathenaeon. In his lifetime it was rumored that he was a foreigner. His birthplace is variously given as Lindos or Camirus on Rhodes, Naucratis in Egypt, and Aegina. The demagogue Cleon brought Aristophanes to trial, accusing him of not being a legitimate Athenian citizen. The apparent reason for these stories was the ownership by his family of an estate on the island of Aegina; the property was probably granted them after the Athenian conquest of Aegina in 431 B.C.

The youth of Aristophanes corresponded to the ascendancy of Pericles (ca. 460–429 B.C.), the statesman who consolidated Athens's gains after the Persian Wars and made the city the political and cultural center of Greece. Pericles epitomized the qualities of the ideal ruler; he combined an incorruptible character with political talent, oratorical prowess, and a cultivated love of art and literature. By his skill in conducting affairs of state and his encouragement of intellectual and artistic achievement, he fostered the Golden Age of Athens. Thus, as a boy, Aristophanes became accustomed to an Athens constantly gaining power at the expense of the rest of Greece and proud of its cultural achievements.

In 431 B.C., the Peloponnesian War was initiated by the enemies of Athens, especially Sparta, which feared its influence and wealth. When the country people who lived under the protection of Athens rushed to the city for protection within the walls, overcrowding resulted in a plague (430 B.C.) that killed more than a quarter of the Athenian population and weakened the morale of the survivors. In 429 B.C., the plague killed Pericles, the only man capable of securing victory over Sparta and its allies. The conflict between Athens and Sparta continued until 404 B.C., when Athens surrendered. By the end of the war the ideals of Greek unity, of enlightened Athenian autonomy, and of classical art and letters were no longer supreme.

Aristophanes's productive period corresponds to the years of the Peloponnesian War and its aftermath. This war had fewer clearly defined causes than the Persian Wars, for which all Greece had united to preserve its cherished experiment in democracy against the threat of Persian tyranny. The uncer-

Bust of Aristophanes in the Capitoline Museum, Rome. [Alinari]

tainties of the Peloponnesian War fed the skepticism and materialism taught by the Sophists, professional philosophers who were less interested in sowing truth than in reaping profits. As old values were questioned, accepted art forms were subjected to experimentation and innovation. Aristophanes resented the Sophists because they advocated the breakdown of traditional standards, and he attempted to stem the tide of these new and liberal ideas by propounding a true conservatism. He ridiculed the speculations of the Sophists and the philosopher Socrates in *The Clouds* and parodied the new fashions in music and literature in *The Frogs* (*Batrachoi,* 405 B.C.). So outspoken was he against democratic leaders and policies that his critics believed him to be in the pay of the pro-Sparta faction. In *The Babylonians,* a lost play, Aristophanes criticized Athens's treatment of its allies by representing them as a chorus of branded slaves of the Athenians. This act of political courage resulted in the impeachment of the poet by Cleon. Aristophanes wanted greater Panhellenic harmony, and *Lysistrata* (*Lysistrate,* 411 B.C.) and *Peace* (*Eirene,* 421 B.C.) make apparent his genuine hope for peace with Sparta.

A charming sketch of the playwright survives in Plato's *Symposium.* Aristophanes is a guest at a banquet where after dinner there is a discussion on the nature of love. He constructs a myth concerning the primeval existence of sexually perfect beings. When these hermaphroditic creatures attacked the Olympian gods, they were punished by Zeus, who split their round, four-legged bodies in two. Since the division, each person has sought to be reunited with his other half, which may originally have been his male or female counterpart; when that other half is found, love results.

Of the plays attributed to Aristophanes, forty are authentic; four are spurious. Many works were produced under the names of his acquaintances Callistratus and Philonides. The last play that Aristophanes staged himself was *Plutus* (*Ploutos,* 388 B.C.). His last two plays, *Cocalus* and *Aeolosicon,* were produced posthumously under the name of his son Araros. For this reason, it is surmised that Aristophanes died about 385 B.C. Plato is said to have written this epitaph: "The Graces, seeking a shrine that would never fall, found the soul of Aristophanes."

WORK

Old Comedy, of which Aristophanes is the chief exponent, flourished at least as far back as 488–486 B.C., when it was first admitted to the Dionysian festivals. Its antecedent history may go back 100 years; the inventor of comedy, according to the Parian Chronicle (a marble tablet dating from 260 B.C. found on the island of Paros, which records the dates of important literary events and people), is said to have been Susarion of Megara, who lived in the early sixth century B.C. Very little is known of the ensuing development of comedy, except that it grew, probably by accretion, out of popular entertainment and religious rites. *See* OLD COMEDY.

Of the many writers of Old Comedy, only Aristophanes is known by more than fragmentary remains. With Cratinus and Eupolis, he formed the triad of great comic dramatists according to the Alexandrians. In fact, the little that we do know of his contemporaries and of earlier writers of Old Comedy (beyond what we read in the writings of Aristotle and other commentators) comes mainly from the parabasis (a direct address made by the chorus to the audience) of Aristophanes's own play *The Knights* (*Hippes,* 424 B.C.), in which he complains of the treatment accorded comic playwrights. The eleven extant plays of the forty he wrote are therefore the more precious as the sole representatives of the genre. They can be divided into three periods. The first, through 420 B.C., includes the plays in which political satire was used without restraint; the second, to 405 B.C., was characterized by plays written with more caution; the third, to 388 B.C., includes the two plays that mark the transition to Middle Comedy. That he was probably the greatest of his contemporaries can be inferred from the very survival of his plays, once given the probability that they were selected for their excellence by the copyists of Alexandria. *See* MIDDLE COMEDY.

The comedy of Aristophanes still reveals the origins of the form known as the *komos,* a popular ritual in which Dionysus was celebrated with licentious, mimic dance and bawdy song on occasions of legitimate communal hilarity such as carnivals. Often the parading revelers were masked and dressed as birds, frogs, or horses; this practice, with masks exaggerated in Aristophanes's time for purposes of caricature, was probably continued for the latitude it gave the disguised chorus to address members of the audience. The pungent asides, originating in the mocking of certain townspeople during an ancient rite, were formalized as the parabasis, a point occurring about midway through the play when the chorus turned to the audience, which it addressed directly. The farcical element derived from the town of Megara, Athens's neighbor, where burlesque sketches of a rudimentary sort were popular entertainment. The costumes of the principal actors, part also of a continuing tradition, con-

sisted of leggings, a short padded jerkin, and, just below it, an enormous phallus, which, according to some scholars, links the *komos* to a primitive fertility rite. To this rude admixture, Aristophanes brought great wit, a fantastic imagination, and an acute interest in current events. Through the alchemy of his lyrical genius, he produced comic plays that still remind readers at once of the social involvement of Shaw, the ribaldry of Rabelais, and the cleverness of Gilbert and Sullivan.

Aristophanes was a man of conservative temper, and he disliked the easy Sophism of the young intellectuals of his day. Believing, with some justification, that the tragedian Euripides often provided inadequate answers to the problems of intellect, Aristophanes made him the butt of many of his satirical fancies. *See* EURIPIDES.

In his first extant play, *The Acharnians* (*Acharnes,* 425 B.C.), most of Aristophanes's ideas are given expression. Chief among them is his displeasure over the Peloponnesian War. In this brilliant antiwar play the men-

tal attitudes of the warmongers, embodied in the Acharnian charcoal burners and their leader, General Lamachus, is contrasted unfavorably with the pragmatic, life-loving, and sensible Dicaeopolis, who has concluded a private peace with Sparta. The parabasis, which contains a sharp attack on Cleon, the popular demagogue, shows the extent to which the morale of Athenian democracy had been weakened: in the midst of war a strong attack of this nature could be made on the Athenian generals and head of state. Aristophanes's continued attack on Cleon in *The Knights* lacks the quicksilver wit of *The Acharnians*. The vituperation is unsparing; ancient commentators claim that the mask makers refused to make a mask of Cleon, so bitter did they consider the denunciation.

The Clouds (423 B.C.) even now stirs indignation among admirers of Socrates for its satire of the revered philosopher, who in the play represents the Sophists, hated by Aristophanes. In *The Wasps* (*Sphekes,* 422 B.C.), Cleon is attacked again, though indirectly, for the argument of the comedy centers on the unwieldy jury system of Athens. Aristophanes saw political danger in the practice of payment for jury service, which could allow demagogues to purchase adherents. This brilliant satire, in one of the funniest scenes in literature, depicts the trial of the house dog Labes, who has been caught stealing a Sicilian cheese. With *Peace* (421 B.C.), Aristophanes turned his attention again to the Peloponnesian War, decrying a struggle that was sapping the strength of both Athens and Sparta. Nonetheless, the play is filled with joyous humor and studded with exquisite choral odes praising the countryside. By the time *The Birds* (*Ornithes*, 414 B.C.) was produced, Athens stood bleakly at the turning point of the war, anxious about the fate of the fleet sent against Syracuse. Perhaps these circumstances moved Aristophanes to envision a fanciful world of his own, creating thereby one of his greatest comic fantasies. The theme of a utopia of birds, Cloud-Cuckoo-Land, contrasted with the disordered world of

men, foretells the use of similar satirical devices in many works of later Western literature. *Lysistrata* (411 B.C.) is as mirthful as its predecessor, if somewhat more serious, centering on a Panhellenic alliance of women who refuse all contact with their men unless the war is halted.

With *The Women at the Festival* (*Thesmophoriazousai*, 411 B.C.), another comedy about women, Aristophanes returned to the attack on Euripides begun fourteen years earlier in *The Acharnians*. With great good humor, he has Euripides use his theatrical tricks to aid Mnesilochus, who, as his advocate, had entered a conclave of women trying Euripides *in absentia* for depicting their faults in such plays as *Hippolytus*. Mnesilochus, in feminine attire, has defended Euripides too ardently, reminding his listeners of sins not revealed by Euripides, and is discovered and held captive as the women determine his punishment. Only when Euripides dresses up as an aged procuress, bringing with him two young girls to distract the guard, does Mnesilochus es-

Scene from The Knights, performed by the National Theatre of Greece. [Greek National Tourist Office]

cape. *The Frogs* (405 B.C.) again lampoons Euripides, with delightful comic invention. The action revolves about Dionysus, who fears that there are to be no more great dramas in Athens for his festival. Determined to bring the deceased Euripides back from Hades, he enlists Heracles's advice on how to get there. In amusing wordplay many suicidal measures are suggested. Finally, in Hades, Euripides and Aeschylus determine who is the weightier dramatist by placing individual lines in an enormous balance. Aeschylus is the victor. *See* AESCHYLUS.

In *The Women in Parliament* (*Ekklesiazousai,* 392? B.C.), the altered atmosphere resulting from Athens's defeat by Sparta is reflected in a descent from the high comedy of Aristophanes's earlier plays. Foreshadowing the coming decline of fantasy and freedom in Greek comedy, the parabasis, with its direct attack on politicians and citizenry alike, has been eliminated. The parody of a communist state run by women, a parody apparently of Plato's *Republic,* is still delightfully inventive, but the lyric spirit is now subdued and political references are introduced with caution. In *Plutus* (388 B.C.), Aristophanes's last extant play, which is essentially a morality play, the world of great comic invention no longer exists. Here blind Plutus, who represents wealth, is cured and able to see once again under the care of Chremylus, a noble Athenian citizen. Poverty, in female guise, would prove that she has been of more benefit to mankind, but she is vanquished in a debate, and Plutus, who is now able to discern the worthy from the unworthy, thenceforth will dispense his gifts more justly. In these last two plays the occasional flashes of wit and humor do not quite compensate for what every admirer of Aristophanes's earlier work must consider a decline in energy and spirit. This, given the circumstances, was perhaps inevitable both for the poet and for his city.

The Acharnians (*Acharnes; Acharniae,* 425 B.C.). Primarily a direct appeal for peace with Sparta, written during the Peloponnesian War. Dicaeopolis, an Athenian citizen, earnestly desires a truce with Sparta. When his pleas for negotiations are ignored by the Assembly, he sends his own ambassador to the enemy and concludes a private thirty-year truce for himself and his family, thereby incurring the wrath of the chauvinistic chorus of Acharnian charcoal burners, veterans of the Battle of Marathon. Then, in order to win them over to his way of thinking, he delivers a dramatic and eloquent defense of his position, impugning all justifications of the war and easily defeating his chief antagonist, the Acharnians' leader, General Lamachus. The chorus now praises the peace

National Theatre of Greece production of *The Knights,* with Christophoros Nezer (center). [Greek National Tourist Office]

movement to the audience. Dicaeopolis sets up shop in the marketplace, where he trades with a series of foreign citizens. With the chorus singing the praises of tranquillity, Diceaopolis goes off to a spring festival. Meanwhile, Lamachus has been ordered into combat, from which he now returns wounded and groaning. Dicaeopolis enters, reveling with courtesans, and the chorus celebrates his triumph.

The Knights (*Hippes; Equites,* 424 B.C.). The clearest expression of Aristophanes's political conservatism. The Athenian democratic extremist and demagogue Cleon is represented as a leathermonger, a slave who, by flattery and pandering, has won the favor of his master Demos (the people of Athens), much to the discomfort of two older slaves, Demosthenes and Nicias, who represent the Athenian generals of the same names. Con-

Scene from *The Clouds.* [Greek National Tourist Office]

sulting Cleon's book of oracles, they discover that he will be overthrown by a sausage-monger. When one of these appears, the elated generals quickly inform him of his divine mission, groom him as a demagogue, and present him with the chorus of Athenian knights, a conservative group longing for a return to "the good old days" of limited democracy and idealistic heroism. With the opposing forces thus aligned, the comedy becomes a prolonged battle between the sausagemonger, with the knights in support, and the wily, unscrupulous Cleon for the favors of Demos, who is not as stupid as they both believe and who plays them off one against the other to his own advantage.

Cleon is accused of being a cheat, a deceiver of his people and their allies; he retorts with summaries of the benefits he has bestowed upon his master. The sausagemonger finally defeats his opponent in a joint appeal to the Council, whose support he wins by playing upon the people's weaknesses. Triumphant, the sausagemonger, his name now revealed as Agoracritus ("Choice of the Agora"), boils Demos in magic herbs, transforming him into a figure from Athens's bygone days of glory and honor, and gives him a number of young and beautiful Peace Treaties, girls long locked up by Cleon's warlike policy. Cleon is left to his just deserts at the hands of Athens's allies.

The Clouds (*Nephelai; Nubes,* 423 B.C.). A hilarious attack on Socrates and the undermining of religious tradition and morality by the Sophists. An old Athenian, Strepsiades, much worried over the mounting debts of his chariot-racing son Pheidippides, would like the youth to enroll in Socrates's Thinkery, where he could gain enough skill in facile debate to avoid his creditors' imminent suits. When Pheidippides refuses, the old man enrolls himself in the Thinkery. There he finds Socrates suspended from the ceiling in a basket, necessary for lofty thinking, and is introduced to the chorus of clouds, goddesses of evasive rhetoric and antireligious scientific speculation. Willing to endure anything to be able to defeat his creditors, Strepsiades tries manfully to improve his intellect, but he is finally ousted by Socrates, who can no longer bear his stupidity and faulty memory.

Pheidippides, at his father's urging, consents at last to enroll in the school and is instructed by Just Reasoning and Unjust Reasoning, who vie for supremacy. Just

Reasoning, a stuffy upholder of old-fashioned ways, loses on a technicality to Unjust Reasoning, who personifies the current degenerate taste for material success, clever argument, and sexual license. The course is a great success, and Pheidippides, a brilliant student, delights his father by helping him talk down two moneylenders who have come to collect their debts. Immediately, however, the boy turns against his father, presents logical resoning to justify his act, and threatens to oppose his mother as well. Realizing, to his horror, that he has ruined his son, Strepsiades sets fire to the Thinkery, driving out Socrates and his followers.

The Wasps (*Sphekes; Vespae*, 422 B.C.). A satire of the Athenians' bellicosity and an indictment of the corruption of jurors by demagogues, especially Cleon. An old Athenian, Philocleon ("Lover of Cleon"), has a mania for jury duty. So obsessive is this passion that his temperate, level-headed son Bdelycleon ("Hater of Cleon") has imprisoned him at home, setting a guard at the door and surrounding the place with a net. Delirious in his efforts to get to court, Philocleon attempts a series of absurd escapes, consistently thwarted by his son and loyal slaves. A chorus of jurymen dressed as wasps arrives and, in their effort to rescue their fellow enthusiast, provoke a skirmish with Bdelycleon's slaves. A debate between father and son develops; Philocleon's arguments for the virtues and responsibilities of jurymen collapse before Bdelycleon's exposure of the courts as degrad-

Illustration on an antique vase of a scene from *The Frogs*. [Goethe House]

ed tools of the demagogue Cleon, an argument that convinces both Philocleon and the chorus but does not lessen their mania for trials.

Allowed to hold private court in his own home, the old man tries a dog for stealing a Sicilian cheese. After Bdelycleon's skillful defense, Philocleon is tricked into acquitting the defendant. He faints at having given such an unheard-of decision and when revived agrees to give up law for reveling. The chorus of jurymen, in the parabasis, praise Aristophanes and (sarcastically) the jury system. Philocleon, meanwhile, attends a banquet, where he behaves in a lecherous, disgraceful manner. He returns drunk, carrying a nude girl musician to whom he makes advances, much to the disgust of Bdelycleon. Philocleon, now accused of theft, assault and battery, and mischief, is carried into the house by his son, but he soon emerges again to join the chorus in a frenetic dance.

Lysistrata, as performed at the Epidaurus Festival. [Greek National Tourist Office]

Peace (*Eirene; Pax,* 421 B.C.). A plea for the cessation of warfare. An Athenian citizen, Trygaeus, deciding to take personal action to put an end to the war, flies to heaven on a dung beetle to consult Zeus. He discovers that Zeus and the Olympians, disgusted by the behavior of the Greeks, have moved farther away, leaving War and Tumult to rule in their vacated offices. Peace has been cast into a deep pit with stones piled on her. War intends to grind the cities of Greece in a huge mortar, though he still lacks a pestle. Anxious to rescue Peace, Trygaeus summons a chorus of laborers and farmers who, despite rivalry and confusion, succeed in releasing Peace from her pit, together with Opora (Harvest) and Theoria (Festival). Hermes promises Opora to Trygaeus in marriage, but first Theoria must be presented to the Senate. When this is accomplished, Trygaeus begins to enjoy the first fruits of peace. Despite ominous prophecies that the war will not end, a huge feast is prepared. A sickle maker, his business much improved, offers a sickle and casks to Trygaeus and his bride as wedding presents. A disgruntled armorer, a crest maker, a breastplate manufacturer, and others whose warlike business peace has undermined try to unload some war surplus, but they are driven off by Trygaeus, who joyfully signals the start of the wedding feast.

The Birds (*Ornithes; Aves,* 414 B.C.). A fantastic utopian escapade concerning the efforts of two war-weary Athenians, Peithetaerus and Euelpides, to find respite from strife and chaos. Guided by birds, they seek out Epops, the mysterious hoopoe, and explain their desires. When Epops is unable to offer a suitable suggestion, Peithetaerus is struck with a splendid notion: the birds will build their own kingdom midway between earth and sky in order to intercept the smoke from men's sacrifices, a strategy that will make them masters of both men and gods. The other birds are summoned and finally convinced by the two Athenians to begin the project. They accomplish the task with great enthusiasm, rejecting the impositions of various interlopers and fakes, including a poet, a prophet, a mathematician, and a government inspector. Peithetaerus and Euelpides sprout wings and christen the city Cloud-Cuckoo-Land, and the birds, now supreme, announce their divinity. The goddess Iris, trespassing in the new kingdom, brings threats from Zeus. Peithetaerus, ignoring her, orders the city closed and the smoke from men's sacrifices intercepted. The Titan Prometheus arrives, under an umbrella to hide himself from Zeus, and reveals that the famished gods are ready for a truce. He urges Peithetaerus to demand

the scepter of Zeus and the hand of Basileia (Royalty) in marriage. With Poseidon and Heracles acting as negotiators for the gods, these terms are accepted. The comedy ends as Peithetaerus, holding Zeus's thunderbolt and lightning, ascends with Basileia to Zeus's palace to the accompaniment of the birds' wedding song.

Lysistrata (*Lysistrate,* 411 B.C.). Probably the most popular and enduring of all Greek comedies. Disgusted with the Peloponnesian War and apprehensive over the future of Greece, Lysistrata, an Athenian woman, unites the females of her country in a general strike against their men until the combatants come to their senses. A chorus of old women succeeds in capturing the Acropolis with its war treasury, defending it successfully against the rival chorus of old men. The Acropolis becomes the center of contention for a while, as Lysistrata and her women repel another attack by a magistrate and his police. Following the hostilities a debate ensues between Lysistrata and the magistrate, wherein she brilliantly defends the rights of women and justifies their concern in politics and war, provoking a mock battle between the choruses.

Life away from their men has become unbearable for the women, however, and some attempt through various means to abandon the cause. But Myrrhine, a member of Lysistrata's high command, successfully resists the pleas of her husband to break the strike and tantalizes him beyond endurance. Soon a herald arrives from Sparta, announcing that there too the women's strike has been successful and that the men are ready to come to an agreement. Athenian and Spartan ambassadors unite in desperation to sue Lysistrata for a truce, and from her unassailable position she declares the value of women and the benefits of unifying peace. The ambassadors quickly concur, and the newly found tranquillity is celebrated in joyous dancing and revelry.

The Women at the Festival (*Thesmophoriazousai; Thesmophoriazusae,* 411 B.C.). Again Aristophanes uses the theme of revolution from the distaff side, this time directed against Euripides and his tragedies, which the women feel are an insult to their sex. The women of Athens have convened at the Thesmophoria (festival of Demeter) and are planning to put the great tragedian to death. Understandably terrified, Euripides pleads with the effeminate Agathon, another tragic poet, to infiltrate the meeting disguised as a wom-

(Opposite) *Lysistrata.* [Courtesy of Phoenix Theatre. Photograph by Friedman-Abeles]

Scene from
Lysistrata.
[Courtesy of
Phoenix Theatre.
Photograph by
Friedman-Abeles]

an and defend him. When Agathon refuses, Euripides's father-in-law Mnesilochus volunteers for the suicidal mission. Gaining entrance in woman's disguise borrowed from Agathon, Mnesilochus proceeds to defend Euripides before the surly group. The women turn on the apparent traitor and are punishing "her" violently when the renowned homosexual Clisthenes appears, also in female guise, and informs the conclave there is a man among them, a fact that is easily verified.

Captive now, bound to a post and guarded by a Scythian policeman, Mnesilochus tries to notify Euripides of his plight; he manages to summon the poet by reciting lines from his plays, to which Euripides responds in appropriate characterizations, first as Menelaus and then as Echo. The tragedian finally returns disguised as a procuress, accompanied by two young girls, and negotiates a peace with the women, promising to cease his slanders. Then, as the policeman amuses himself offstage with one of the girls, Euripides releases Mnesilochus. Both men escape as the women send the returning Scythian off in the wrong direction.

The Frogs (*Batrachoi; Ranae,* 405 B.C.). An extremely complex fantasy, the earliest Greek work (except for fragments) that deals predominantly with literary criticism. Dissatisfied with the present crop of tragedians and longing to see again the recently deceased Euripides, the god Dionysus disguises himself as Heracles and makes the long and difficult journey to Hades, intent on restoring a resuscitated Euripides to the tragic stage. Ferried across the River Styx by Charon to the accompaniment of a chorus of frogs and surviving a series of confusing encounters, he finds the great tragedian engaged in a controversy with Aeschylus over the privilege of dining at Hades' table, a place of great honor. To settle the argument a contest is arranged, with Dionysus as judge, wherein lines by each poet will be weighed in a scale.

As a preliminary the two giants of tragedy engage in a prolonged and detailed verbal battle, in reality Aristophanes's own weighing of the merits and defects of each writer's body of work. Euripides accuses Aeschylus of obscurity, repetition, pomposity, and warmongering. Aeschylus retorts by pointing out his rival's prosaic monotony, facile sophistry, and low moral tone; above all, he criticizes Euripides's debunking of the heroic, which appeals to the baser instincts of the audience and thus tends to corrupt their loftier aspirations.

The weighing of lines favors Aeschylus, but Dionysus still cannot make up his mind. To decide the issue, he asks each poet for practical advice in saving Athens from the disastrous Peloponnesian War. Aeschylus's forthright and manly urging that the war effort be strengthened is an obvious winner over Euripides's vague and effeminate sophistry, and Dionysus awards the victory to Aeschylus, resolving to take him rather than Euripides back to Athens.

The Women in Parliament (*Ekklesiazousai; Ecclesiazusae,* 392? B.C.). Comedy involving a female conspiracy. The Athenian woman Praxagora organizes other members of her sex to seize control of the Assembly by disguising themselves as men and simply voting themselves into power. Her scheme works superbly, and once securely in position, she proceeds to inaugurate a socialistic program in which private ownership is abolished, meals are to be taken in a common dining hall, and all women are to become public property. For fear that the law will cater to the prettiest girls and handsomest boys, it is stipulated that the elderly are always to be serviced first.

The Athenian citizen Chremes, while not intending to relinquish his property, nevertheless hurries off to enjoy the first public feast, while an Athenian youth who desires a beautiful young courtesan finds he must first make love to her older, heavily made-up counterpart. Almost rescued from this dreadful fate by his beloved, he is quickly intercepted by a hag even older than the first and then by another still older and even more hideous. The object of a vicious tug-of-war, he is finally dragged off by the old women, and the chorus joyfully invites the audience to the communal banquet.

Plutus (*Ploutos,* 388 B.C.). Utopian fantasy in which the dream of universal wealth is happily realized. Chremylus, an Athenian citizen, having consulted the Delphic oracle about his son's future success, has been instructed to follow the first person he meets, a blind and destitute old man. The ragged man reveals himself to be Plutus, god of wealth. He has been blinded by the envious Zeus and thus is unable to distinguish good from evil, which accounts for the rank injustice with which wealth seems to be distributed. Chremylus conceives the brilliant idea of restoring Plutus's sight, thus ending the injustices of life, since when only goodness is rewarded, all men will strive to be good.

The terrifying goddess Poverty appears and tries to dissuade Chremylus from his intent, pointing out that if all men are wealthy, they will do no work and nothing worthwhile will be produced. But Chremylus and his friend Blepsidemus reject her arguments and rush Plutus to the Temple of Asclepius, god of healing, where his sight is restored. The first just man appears, while Hermes descends with the news that the gods have lost their power since human beings no longer need to pray and sacrifice. Now out of a job, Hermes is converted to a faith in the new reigning god Plutus and is followed by a priest of Zeus, fallen on lean times now that his services are superfluous. The comedy ends with a procession to install the triumphant Plutus on the Acropolis.

PLAYS

In each case the first title given is a transliteration from the Greek; the first in parentheses is the Latin designation.

1. *Acharnes** (*Acharniae; The Acharnians*). 425 B.C. (Lenaea). Written under the pseudonym Callistratus.

2. *Hippes** (*Equites; The Knights*). 424 B.C.

3. *Nephelai** (*Nubes; The Clouds*). 423 B.C. (Great Dionysia).

4. *Sphekes** (*Vespae; The Wasps*). 422 B.C. (Lenaea). Written under the pseudonym Philonides.

5. *Eirene** (*Pax; Peace*). 421 B.C. (Great Dionysia).

6. *Ornithes** (*Aves; The Birds*). 414 B.C. (Great Dionysia). Written under the pseudonym Callistratus.

7. *Lysistrate** (*Lysistrata*). 411 B.C. (Lenaea). Written under the pseudonym Callistratus.

8. *Thesmophoriazousai** (*Thesmophoriazusae; The Women at the Festival*). 411 B.C. (Great Dionysia).

9. *Batrachoi** (*Ranae; The Frogs*). 405 B.C. (Lenaea). Written under the pseudonym Philonides.

10. *Ekklesiazousai** (*Ecclesiazusae; The Women in Parliament*). 392? B.C.

11. *Ploutos** (*Plutus*). 388 B.C.

EDITIONS

Collections.
Works, 2 vols., Loeb Classical Library, New York, 1924; *The Complete Greek Drama,* ed. by W. J. Oates and E. J. O'Neill, vol. 2, New York, 1938; *Great Books of the Western World,* ed. by R. M. Hutchins and tr. by B. Rogers, vol. 5, Chicago, 1952; *The Complete Plays of Aristophanes,* ed. by M. Hadas, New York, 1962.

Also published in *Greek Dramas,* ed. by B. Perrin and tr. by W. Hickie, New York, 1900; *Ten Greek Plays Translated into English,* tr. by J. Frere and D. Sandford, New York, 1930; *Fifteen Greek Plays Translated into English,* tr. by B. Rogers, New York, 1943; *Plays of the Greek*

Dramatists, New York, 1946; *Greek Literature in Translation,* ed. by G. Howe and G. A. Harrer and tr. by G. Murray and R. Cumberland, rev. ed., New York, 1948; *An Anthology of the Greek Drama,* ed. by C. A. Robinson, Jr., and tr. by B. Rogers, 2d ser., New York, 1954.

Individual Plays.

The Acharnians. W. J. M. Starkie, ed., London, 1909; C. E. Graves, ed., Cambridge, England, 1961; D. Parker, tr., Ann Arbor, Mich., 1961; also published in *Poetic Drama,* ed. by A. Kreymborg and tr. by J. Frere, New York, 1941; *Masters of Ancient Comedy,* ed. and tr. by L. Casson, New York, 1960.

The Birds. W. W. Merry, ed., 4th ed., New York, 1921; W. Kerr, tr., Washington, 1952; W. Arrowsmith, ed., Ann Arbor, Mich., 1961; also published in *Heath Readings in the Literature of Europe,* ed. by T. P. Cross and C. H. Silver and tr. by J. Frere, Boston, 1933; *Chief Patterns of World Drama,* ed. by W. S. Clark II and tr. by M. MacGregor, Boston, 1946; *Four Greek Plays,* ed. and tr. by D. Fitts, New York, 1960; *Comedy,* ed. by M. Felheim and tr. by D. Fitts, New York, 1962.

The Clouds. W. W. Merry, ed., New York, 1899; W. J. M. Starkie, ed., London, 1911; C. Barley, ed., New York, 1921; R. H. Webb, tr., Charlottesville, Va., 1960; W. Arrowsmith, tr., Ann Arbor, Mich., 1962; also published in *World Drama,* ed. by B. H. Clark and tr. by T. Mitchell, vol. 1, New York, 1933; *Greek and Roman Classics in Translation,* ed. by C. T. Murphy et al., New York, 1947; *Greek Drama for Everyman,* ed. and tr. by F. L. Lucas, London, 1954; *Eight Great Comedies,* ed. by S. Barnet et al. and tr. by B. Rogers, New York, 1958.

The Frogs. W. W. Merry, ed., New York, 1884; R. Lattimore, tr., Ann Arbor, Mich., 1962; W. B. Stanford, ed., 2d ed., New York 1963; also published in *Seven Famous Greek Plays,* ed. by W. J. Oates and E. J. O'Neill and tr. by G. Murray, New York, 1950; *Classics in Translation,* ed. by P. MacKendrick and H. M. Howe and tr. by J. Hawthorne, vol. 1, Madison, Wis., 1952.

The Knights. Published in *Dramatic Masterpieces by Greek, Spanish, French, German and English Dramatists,* tr. by J. Frere, vol. 1, New York, 1900.

Lysistrata. D. Parker, tr., Ann Arbor, Mich., 1963; R. H. Webb, tr., Charlottesville, Va., 1963; also published in *A Treasury of the Theatre,* ed. by B. Mantle and J. Gassner and tr. by G. Seldes, rev. ed., New York, 1940; *Greek Literature in Translation,* ed. by W. J. Oates and C. T. Murphy, New York, 1944; *An Anthology of Greek Drama,* ed. by C. A. Robinson, Jr., and tr. by C. Murphy, 1st ser., New York, 1949; *Ten Greek Plays in Contemporary Translations,* ed. by L. R. Lind and tr. by C. Murphy, Boston, 1957.

Peace. M. Platnauer, ed., Oxford, 1964; R. H. Webb, tr., Charlottesville, Va., 1964.

The Wasps. D. Parker, tr., Ann Arbor, Mich., 1962.

The Women at the Festival (Ladies' Day). D. Fitts, tr., New York, 1959.

The Women in Parliament (Congresswomen). D. Parker, tr., Ann Arbor, Mich., 1967.

CRITICISM

V. Ehrenberg, *The People of Aristophanes,* new ed., New York, 1962; L. E. Lord, *Aristophanes: His Plays and His Influence,* reprint, New York, 1963; G. Murray, *Aristophanes: A Study,* reprint, New York, 1964; C. H. Whitman, *Aristophanes and the Comic Hero,* Cambridge, Mass., 1964; L. Strauss, *Socrates and Aristophanes,* New York, 1966; D. Littlefield, ed., *Twentieth-century Interpretations of "The Frogs,"* New York, 1968; H. Dunbar, *Complete Concordance to the Comedies and Tragedies of Aristophanes,* reprint, New York, 1969.

ARNAUD, Georges, pseudonym of Henri Girard (1917–   ). French novelist and playwright, born in Montpellier. His writing is characterized by clever plots and exciting action rather than fine psychological detail. His first great success came with the novel *The Wages of Fear (Le salaire de la peur,* 1950), about a transport of nitroglycerin. He is also known for the naturalistic comedy *The Sweetest Vows (Les aveux les plus doux,* 1952).

ARNICHES Y BARRERA, Carlos (1866–1943). Prolific Spanish dramatist whose popularity was due mainly to his short comedy sketches, or farces, depicting the life of the lower classes in Madrid, the best of which are *The Stars (Las estrellas), Poor Valbuena (El pobre Valbuena),* and *The Saint of Isidra (El santo de la Isidra,* 1898). Arniches' first play, *The Publishing House (Casa editorial),* was produced in 1888, but it was not until the production of *The Legend of the Monk (La leyenda del monje)* on December 6, 1890, that his real success in the theatre began. Aided by his vast knowledge of theatrical technique, he continued to write at the rate of five or six plays a year, again winning acclaim in 1902 with the one-act musical comedy *The Handful of Roses (El puñao de rosas),* with music by Ruperto Chapí. Direct observation of the milieu about which he wrote and use of the language of the masses created in his plays an atmosphere of diversion and irony. Among such plays are *Watermelons and Cantaloupes (Sandías y melones,* 1900), *The Water of the Manzanares (El agua de Manzanares,* 1918), *He's My Man (Es mi hombre,* 1912), and *Sweet-smelling Roses (Rositas de olor,* 1924). Arniches also collaborated on many plays with Enrique García Álvarez, Celso Lucio y López, José López Silva, Carlos Fernández Shaw, and José Jackson Veyán.

Carlos Arniches y Barrera. [Biblioteca Nacional, Madrid]

ARNOUX, Alexandre (1884–   ). French poet, novelist, and playwright. His plays often include verse passages and sometimes, as in *Moriana and Galvan* (*Moriana et Galvan*, 1922), the dialogue for which is barely a page long, served as the basis for elaborate pantomimes. *Huon de Bordeaux* (1923), which like many of his earlier plays was staged by Charles Dullin, is based on the legend of the hero of a medieval *chanson de geste*. *Little Light and the Bear* (*Petite lumière et l'ourse*, 1924) is a modern fable in which children, distorting a conversation they have heard between their parents and an electrician, dream of the forces of electricity metamorphosed into live and threatening characters. *The Love of Three Oranges* (*L'amour des trois oranges*, 1947) is based on the life of Gozzi and shows the aged author dying surrounded by the characters his imagination had conjured up. *Must Joan Be Burned?* (*Faut-il brûler Jeanne?*, 1951), originally presented as a radio play, was staged soon after on the steps of the Rouen Cathedral. In this play God offers Joan her life if she will give up her voices. She is rescued from prison but, feeling deserted and useless, begs for her intended fate. She is therefore returned to prison, and the memory of her escape is erased from the minds of men. In addition to writing original dramas,

Scene from Alexandre Arnoux's *L'amour des trois oranges*. [French Cultural Services]

Arnoux adapted several plays by Calderón. *See* CALDERÓN DE LA BARCA, PEDRO; GOZZI, CARLO.

AROUET, François-Marie. *See* VOLTAIRE.

ARRABAL, Fernando (1932–   ). Spanish-born novelist and playwright whose works, written in French, are generally linked to the theatre of the absurd. He settled in France in 1954, and his plays first became known through publication rather than production. Even now they are more widely appreciated abroad than in his adopted country. Obsessed by childhood memories of the terror and betrayal that accompanied the Spanish Civil War, he projects a nightmare world populated by interchanging victims and executioners. "I dream of a theatre in which humor and poetry, fascination and panic, are one," he wrote. *See* THEATRE OF THE ABSURD.

Written in Spain in 1954, *Picnic on the Battlefield* (*Pique-nique en campagne*) introduced Arrabal to avant-garde Paris audiences in 1959, the year following the publication of the first of three collections of his plays. With nightmare intensity and humor, this antiwar satire contrasts the rhythm of family life

Alexandre Arnoux. [French Cultural Services]

Michael O'Sullivan
as the Emperor in
Fernando
Arrabal's
*The Architect and
the Emperor of
Assyria.* [Courtesy
American
Conservatory
Theatre, San
Francisco, Calif.
Photograph by
Hank Kranzler]

din des délices, 1969) was considered by some critics the most important drama presented in Paris since Genet's *The Screens.* Taking its title from Hieronymus Bosch's famous painting in the Prado, it presents the story of a world-weary actress's Dantesque investigation of the dark night of her soul. Employing bold sadomasochistic imagery, it shows her in moments of hallucination, humiliation, and ecstatic joy.

Among other Arrabal plays are *Fando and Lis* (*Fando et Lis;* pub. 1958, prod. 1964), *The Coronation* (*Le couronnement,* 1965), and *The Architect and the Emperor of Assyria* (*L'architecte et l'empereur d'Assyrie,* 1967). Arrabal has also published the novels *Baal Babylone* (1959) and *The Burial of the Sardine* (*L'enterrement de la sardine,* 1961) as well as a selection of surrealistic texts entitled *The Stone of Madness* (*La pierre de la folie,* 1963).

ARTAUD, Antonin (1896–1948). French actor, poet, director, and dramatist, born in Marseille. Because of his theoretical writings, especially *The Theatre and Its Double* (*Le théâtre et son double*), a collection of essays that appeared in 1938, Artaud became a central figure of the avant-garde European theatre. The influence of his conception of the theatre, which he called *le théâtre de la cruauté,* can be felt in the works of Ionesco, Audiberti, Genet, Schéhadé, Adamov, Beckett, and Tardieu. *See* THEATRE OF CRUELTY.

Artaud began as an actor; he was a student of Charles Dullin and acted and directed under Jacques Hébertot, Aurélien-Lugné-Poë, and Louis Jouvet. Along with André Breton, Roger Vitrac, and Louis Aragon he was one of the initiators of the surrealist movement. He contributed to the *Révolution Surréaliste* and the *Nouvelle Revue Française.* In 1928 he founded, together with Vitrac, his own theatre, which he called the Théâtre Alfred-Jarry, clearly expressing his indebtedness to Jarry. He acted in a number of important silent and speaking films of the 1920s and 1930s. In 1936 and 1937 he traveled to Mexico and Ireland. Burdened by nervous disorders that began early in his youth, he later had to be interned in various asylums until 1943. *See* JARRY, ALFRED; VITRAC, ROGER.

Artaud's work is the expression of his revolt against society and the rule of reason. Of the many pieces he planned to illustrate his theoretical writings he was able to complete only one, *The Cenci* (*Les Cenci,* 1935), based on works by Shelley and Stendhal. He saw in the theatre a metaphysical and social force and wanted to heal the sickness of society through an examination of the symptoms of the disease. The theatre was once again to become a vital necessity in the life of men. In

with that of a military operation. Unable to comprehend the ferocity of war, Zapo's parents visit him at the front and proceed to have a picnic. Zepo, a captured enemy soldier, joins the gay group, which is then slaughtered by a sudden burst of machine-gun fire. Chaplinesque innocence and sudden, unmotivated outbreaks of cruelty and violence characterize the inhabitants of Arrabal's world, who betray one another with the amorality and indifference of children. In *The Car Cemetery* (*Le cimetière des voitures;* pub. 1958, prod. 1967), the Christlike Emanou is betrayed, crucified on a police bicycle, and eventually murdered by those who, like himself, live in an abandoned car dump. *Guernica* (pub. 1961, prod. 1968) views the 1937 bombing of this Spanish city from the vantage point of two uncomprehending, childlike victims trapped under the rubble of a house and continuing their pathetic chatter as they await death. *The Garden of Delights* (*Le jar-*

order to achieve this, Artaud felt that the theatre had to go back to its mystical, ritualistic beginnings and shed the layers of civilized discourse and philosophical discussion. Words, he felt, had no intrinsic part in the theatrical performance. Rather, he emphasized the language of the body, the choreography of motion, and sound and light effects. His integral, total theatre was to combine all these to bring about an emotional catharsis, a purification from the perversions of social existence. The conscious and the unconscious, reality and dream, were to be freely mixed. Artaud compared the effect he wished to have to that of a volcano, of a catastrophe, of the plague:

> *If the theatre once again is to become a necessity, then it must give what crime, love, war and insanity are made up of. . . . Either we renew the central position and necessity of all the arts and find a correspondence in a brush-stroke, in the theatre and in the lava of a volcanic outbreak, or we ought to stop painting, talking, writing, or whatever else we are doing.*

He wanted a liberation of the instinctual force in man, spontaneity, originality, and an anarchic vitality. His work includes *L'ombilic des limbes* (1925), consisting of the parts *Ventre brûlé, ou La mère folle* and *Le jet de sang,* a piece that illustrates the disintegration of civilization's values and conventions through the destruction of temples and the decay of human bodies; *La coquille et le clergyman* (1927), a scenario; *La pierre philosophale* (1933), a pantomime with words; and *Atrée et Thyeste* (1934), an adaptation of Seneca's *Thyestes. See* SENECA.

ASCH, Sholem (1880–1957). Yiddish novelist and dramatist, one of the best-known and most prolific Yiddish literary figures. After having received a traditional Hebrew education in Kutno, Poland, Asch, at the age of eighteen, moved to Warsaw. There he came under the influence of I. L. Peretz and decided to write in Yiddish instead of Hebrew in order to reach the Jewish masses. In 1914 he moved to New York, where he began to achieve prominence. Although he split the ranks of his Jewish enthusiasts with three controversial novels centering in Jesus—*The Nazarene* (1939), *The Apostle* (1943), and *Mary* (1949)—it is generally conceded that Asch raised the standards of Yiddish literature to new heights and exerted a great influence upon the Yiddish stage. A student of German classics, he was also indebted to Dickens, Tolstoy, and especially Dostoyevsky. His plays, notwithstanding elements of mysticism and poetry, are essentially realistic in their portrayal of Jewish life.

Asch's first play, the two-act *Returned* (*Tzurikgekumen,* 1904), is set in a Jewish village in Poland at the turn of the century; composed in both Hebrew and Yiddish, it was produced the same year on the Polish stage. His subsequent plays include *The Time of the Messiah* (*Mashiach Tzeiten,* 1906), a three-act drama about contemporary Jewish life, which was also staged in Russian under the title *Na puti vayon;* and *God of Vengeance* (*Der Got vun Nekome,* 1907), a powerful and controversial drama dominated by the tragic figure of the "uncle" who clings to the illusion that he can raise a chaste daughter in his home, which is above the brothel he operates. The following year Asch wrote *Sabbatai Zevi,* a three-act tragedy with prologue and epilogue, depicting a seventeenth-century false messiah.

Among his other plays are *Pedigree* (*Yichus;* wr. 1909, prod. 1921), a satire about the Jewish bourgeoisie; *A String of Pearls* (*A Shnirl Perl;* wr. 1916, prod. 1925); *The Dead Man* (*Der toiter Mensch,* 1922); *Marranos* (*Maranen,* 1922), set in a seaport in 1492; *Our Faith* (*Unzer Gloybn,* pub. 1928*)*; and, both on Biblical themes, *The Destruction of the Temple* (*Churban Bet Hamikdash,* 1921) and *Jeph-*

Jacob Hochstein (left) and Leon Blank in *Our Faith,* by Sholem Asch. [Theatre Collection, The New York Public Library at Lincoln Center, Astor, Lenox and Tilden Foundations]

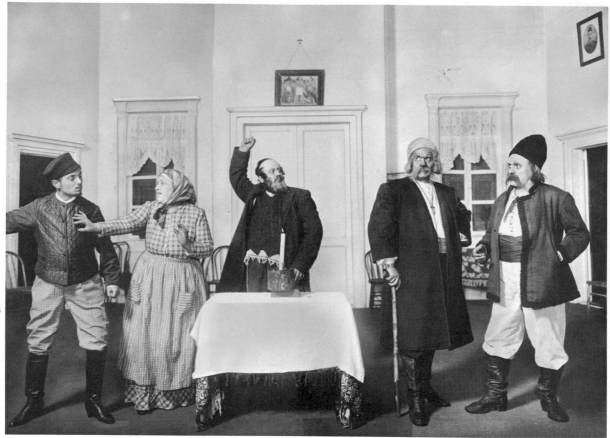

Scene from Sholem Asch's *Our Faith*, with Boris Thomashefsky (center). [Theatre Collection, The New York Public Library at Lincoln Center, Astor, Lenox and Tilden Foundations]

thah's Daughter (*Yiftachs Tochter*, 1922). He dramatized some of his own novels, including *Motke the Thief* (*Motke Ganev*, 1917), about the Polish underworld; *Uncle Moses* (1926), about early Jewish immigrants in America and their struggle to unionize the needle trades; *Holy Be Thy Name* (*Kiddush Ha-Shem*, 1928), a historical play describing the heroic martyrdom of Ukrainian Jews during the uprising against them in 1648; *Three Cities* (*Drei Shtet*, 1938); and *Salvation* (*Der T'hilim Yid*, 1939), a portrait of early-nineteenth-century Hasidism.

ASHTON, Winifred. *See* DANE, CLEMENCE.

ASIDE. Dramatic convention in which the actor's words are not heard by other actors on the stage with him; thus the audience is informed of a character's real thoughts or hidden intentions. Eugene O'Neill's *Strange Interlude* (1928) makes exhaustive use of this device.

ASPENSTRÖM, Werner (1918–   ). Swedish poet and playwright, author of more than thirty plays for radio, television, and theatre, most of them short, lyrical mood pieces executed in a Kafkaesque expressionistic style. The thematic emphasis in his work reflects a multiple sense of frustration, the frustration of a poet in an unpoetic age, the frustration of a postwar Scandinavian intellectual whose appeals for international understanding are unheard in the din created by the giant power blocs, and the frustration of a humanist in a dehumanized world. In his first play, *The Place Is Wrapped in Smoke* (*Platsen är inhöljd i rök*, 1948), the Big Giant and the Equally Big Giant argue over procedures for a meeting and fail to heed the Messenger's warning that the world is about to blow up. The destruction of the world is also the subject matter of *The Ark* (*Arken*, 1955), in which the validity of Noah's mission is challenged by skeptical leaders of the establishment. In the fairy-tale-like *The Poet and the Emperor* (*Poeten och kejsaren*, 1956) the Poet refuses to practice his art in the service of the imperialistic, warmongering Emperor. The simian characters in *The Apes Shall Inherit the Earth* (*Det eviga*, 1959) invade a lecture hall after mankind has disappeared and are amused by automatic audiovisual equipment that continues to spew forth random images of a lost civilization.

Throughout his work Aspenström has suggested the ambiguous role the poet must play: part creator, part Cassandra, and part clown. In *I Must Go to Berlin* (*Jag måste till Berlin*,

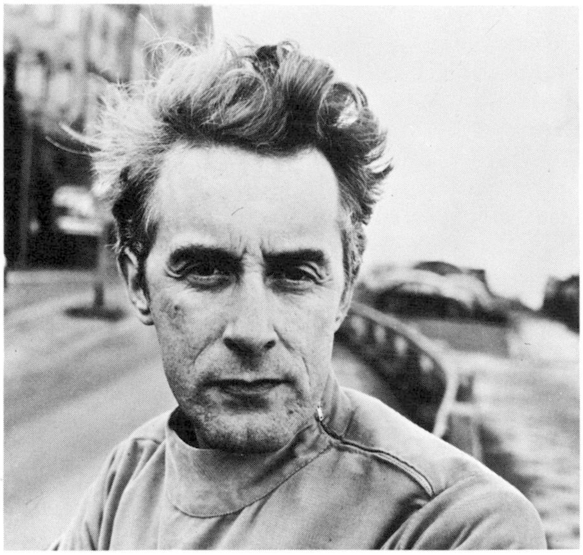

Werner Aspenström. [Swedish Information Service]

1967) an aging Isadora Duncan is accused by her young poet lover Sergei Jesenin of never having loved anything except her dancing. Her response to him is the question: "And you, what have you loved beyond your own poetry?"

EDITIONS

The Apes Shall Inherit the Earth. Published in *Tulane Drama Review,* November, 1961.
The Poet and the Emperor. Published in *Tulane Drama Review,* November, 1961.

CRITICISM

E. Törnqvist, "Poet in the Space Age: A Theme in Aspenström's Plays," *Scandinavian Studies,* February, 1967.

AUDEN, W[ystan] H[ugh] (b. York, England, February 21, 1907). Anglo-American poet, critic, and editor whose plays are composed mainly in a style that mingles poetic form with colloquial slang; their prevailing social and political satire is frequently colored by a kind of Eastern mysticism. Auden's collaboration with Christopher Isherwood resulted in two powerful dramas. The first, *The Dog Beneath the Skin, or Where Is Francis?* (1936), is a general satire on contemporary British and continental European culture, highly symbolic and occasionally obscure in its denunciation of middle-class values, pointing to individuality as the only path to salvation. The second, *The Ascent of F.6* (1937), equally symbolic and obscure, examines the psychological, political, and metaphysical forces that may drive a man to risk his life in a great endeavor. A less successful fruit of their collaboration was *On the Frontier* (1938), an antiwar drama. Auden's subsequent contributions to the theatre consisted for the most part in writing lyrics for music dramas and operettas. *See* ISHERWOOD, CHRISTOPHER.

The Dog Beneath the Skin, or Where Is Francis? (1936). Story presented in a pastiche of poetry, prose, and songs and set in a deceptively gentle English country hamlet called Pressan Ambo. The young Sir Francis Crewe, son of the town's deceased squire, has been missing for ten years, and annually one of the villagers is selected to set out in search of him. This year the choice falls on Alan Norman, who is shown passing through a number of deranged European states accompanied by Pressan Ambo's civic dog, a remarkably human canine who turns out to be none other than Francis Crewe, masquerading as the mongrel. Returning home, the pair find the hamlet suffocating in bickering, greed, and dullness. Finally, Francis, Alan, and a few of the citizens abandon the village, hoping to find a less oppressive place. Produced London, Westminster Theatre, January 30, 1936.

The Ascent of F.6 (1937). Poetic drama in which Michael Ransom, master mountain climber, leads an expedition of his countrymen up the unconquered slopes of the Himalayan mountain F.6 in competition with a group sponsored by a foreign power. Following a nightmarish vision in which Ransom realizes that he has been destroyed not only by his politician brother who urged him to the adventure but also by his mother who prompted him to accept the challenge, he dies on the peak. Produced London, Mercury Theatre, February 26, 1937.

W. H. Auden. [Theatre Collection, The New York Public Library at Lincoln Center, Astor, Lenox and Tilden Foundations]

Jacques Audiberti
(1899 – 1965)

Jacques Audiberti, French journalist, poet, novelist, and dramatist, was born in Antibes on March 25, 1899. After attending the Collège d'Antibes, he began his career as a journalist in southern France. He moved in 1925 to Paris, where he worked for *Le Journal* and, later, *Le Petit Parisien*. In 1929 he began to write the first of his seventeen novels and published his first volume of poems, which he described as "rigorously classical." Soon, however, he became intimately associated with the surrealist movement and drew the attention of a limited public when his second poetry collection, *Race of Men* (*Race des hommes*, 1937), was awarded the Mallarmé Prize by a jury that included Jean Cocteau, Paul Valéry, Charles Vildrac, and Paul Fort.

Audiberti's first play, *The Emperor* (*L'ampélour;* pub. 1937, prod. 1950), was awarded a prize as the best dramatic work by a new author, and with the production of *Quoat-Quoat* (1946) in a tiny Left Bank theatre he began to be more widely known. However, it was not until the production of *Evil Is Abroad* (*Le mal court*) in 1947 that Audiberti's reputation and success were firmly estabished.

Jacques Audiberti.
[French Cultural Services]

In addition to his own plays, Audiberti translated and adapted works by Valentino Bompiani, Beniamino Joppolo, and Shakespeare. In 1965 he was awarded the Grand Prix des Lettres and the Prix des Critiques. His last years were devoted to keeping a journal in which he depicted the progress of the fatal disease from which he died in Paris on July 10, 1965.

WORK

Audiberti once described himself as a man of the "indestructible" nineteenth century, "coexisting with a world of airplanes, telephones, and Sputniks." He felt that except for science fiction, literature had failed to keep pace with the technical evolution and that his own avant-garde label was simply a reflection of his audience's desire to place literature on an equal footing with science. He himself saw no moral or technical separation between his style and that of the Parnassians and naturalists who had written 100 years before him and though he admired the surrealists, he specifically disclaimed being a member of their school.

Indeed, the structure of his richly textured and fanciful plays is largely orthodox, and though his language is embellished with elaborate and often brilliant imagery, it in no way departs from conventional French syntax. However, one sometimes gets the impression of a self-indulgent talent unable to reject any clever idea or incident. The result is often a play so congested by willful paradox and minor incident that the general outlines tend to be obscured.

Audiberti sees man as a creature fallen from a state of grace, not the "grace" of the church, which is a corrupting influence, but the natural grace of the animal world, which is unburdened by the paraphernalia of civilization. His plays often show man fighting the corruption that surrounds and envelops him and trying desperately to reestablish contact with the magical forces of the natural and the supernatural.

In his first play, *The Emperor* (pub. 1937, prod. 1950), some Languedoc peasants have learned of Napoleon's escape, and each time there is a knock at the door they are sure it is he. Instead, they are visited by a priest, a blind man, and a butcher, three aspects of their Emperor.

Audiberti's best-known plays are *Quoat-Quoat* (1946), in which a romantic young man is used as a cat's-paw and chooses death rather than lose the identity he has accepted; *Evil Is Abroad* (1947), in which an innocent young girl encounters evil and decides to accept it rather than be destroyed by it; and *The Falcon* (*La hobereaute,* 1956), in which two inno-

Scene from *Quoat-Quoat*. [Courtesy of Centre Dramatique National Nord]

cent pagan lovers are destroyed by the corrupting influence of the so-called civilized world.

Maid (*Pucelle*, 1950) is an interesting retelling of the Joan of Arc story in which the Maid's double meets her death after being persuaded to participate in a theatrical re-enactment of the original burning at the stake. *The Black Feast* (*Le fête noire*, 1948) concerns a horrible beast, born of man's frustrated desire, that ravages the countryside and finally destroys the man who created it. *The Natives of Bordelais* (*Les naturels de Bordelais*, 1953) deals with a contemporary Don Juan, and in *Apple, Apple, Apple* (*Pomme, pomme, pomme,* 1962) a modern Adam and Eve are paradoxically driven from paradise in order that they may sin.

A latter-day Circe in search of a man capable of dominating her is the central character of *The Landlady* (*La logeuse*, 1960). Audiberti achieved something of a tour de force in *The "Cooler"* (*Le ouallou*, 1957), a one-act satire on police corruption that is written almost entirely in argot. He came closest to conventional boulevard comedy in *The Glapion Effect* (*L'effet Glapion*, 1959), in which the real and the imaginary are intermingled as a couple relive the Sunday on which they decided to marry. *See* BOULEVARD COMEDY.

Although Audiberti's plays rely heavily on the supernatural, he insisted in an interview given shortly before his death in 1965 that he never felt that he presented his audiences with anything more than a picture of how they might behave in an arbitrary situation he invented. "I never in any way tried to pro-

voke astonishment or to arouse irritation by inventing baroque situations."

Quoat-Quoat (1946).   Aboard a ship headed for Mexico, Amédée, a secret agent sent by Napoleon III to find Maximilian's lost treasure, is warned by the captain that the regulations forbid those on official missions to enter into serious relations with women passengers. But the ship is hardly out of port before Amédée has fallen in love with Clarisse, the captain's daughter. He invites her to join him on his mission, and in a brief transposition of time the two young people live through his future adventures and find the treasure. However, for having betrayed his secret, Amédée is sentenced to be shot in the morning. During the night a female Mexican agent enters his cabin and attempts to win the treasure for her revolutionary friends. She gives Amédée a portion of the stone containing the power of the old god Quoat-Quoat, but Amédée loyally turns both her and the stone over to the captain. Just as the latter is reluctantly preparing to have Amédée shot, another woman passenger appears and discloses that she is the true secret agent and Amédée only a decoy. Though pardoned by the captain, Amédée refuses life if it means the loss of his identity, and he races

Suzanne Flon (center) in *Le mal court*. Paris, Théâtre de Poche, 1947. [French Cultural Services]

Scenes from *Le mal court.* [Courtesy of Centre Dramatique National Nord]

out to face the firing squad. As the curtain descends, the captain (who may well be God), wary of the unhappiness caused by regulations he must obey, is about to use Quoat-Quoat's stone to destroy the ship.

Evil Is Abroad (*Le mal court*, 1947). Against the background of a fairy-tale eighteenth-century Europe, the play tells the story of the innocent Princess Alarica's first encounter with evil. On the eve of crossing into the kingdom of Occident to marry King Parfait, the Princess learns that the King has been forced by political necessity to reconsider the marriage scheduled for the next day. An agent has been sent by the King to seduce the Princess and so provide an excuse for him to break with her. In despair and confusion the Princess accepts the agent as her lover, only to learn that their night together has had no importance for him. Her disillusion is completed when she learns that her trusted governess is actually a spy in the employ of the King. Accepting the essential ignobility of the world, the Princess prepares to assume the ruthlessness necessary for her to carry out her role as the ruler of her own kingdom.

The Landlady (*La logeuse;* pub. 1956,

Les naturels du Bordelais. Paris, Théâtre La Bruyère, 1953. [French Cultural Services]

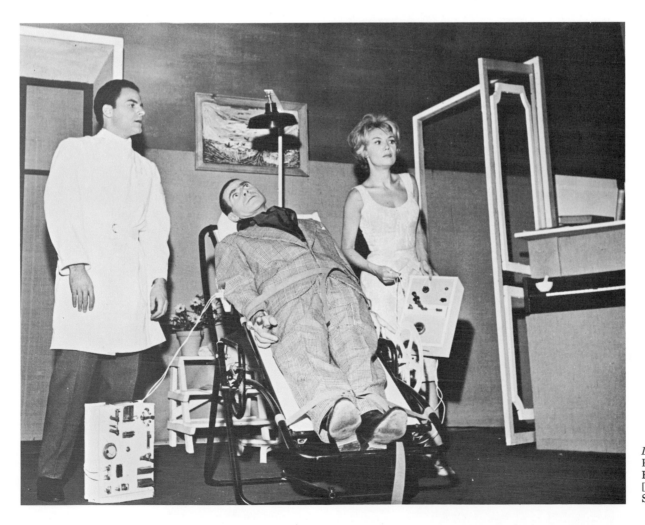

L'effet Glapion. Paris, Théâtre La Bruyère, 1959. [French Cultural Services]

Scene from *La
hobereaute*,
Théâtre du Vieux-
Colombier, Paris.
[French Cultural
Services]

prod. 1960). Mme. Cirqué, a landlady of
enigmatic charm, dominates the men who
surround her. For her sake, M. Cirqué has renounced politics and spends his days making
her hats, and her boarders have all been
induced to give up or change their careers
to serve her. As Tienne, a policeman, enjoys
his daily privilege of breakfast with Mme.
Cirqué, a former boarder who has become a
musician to please her plays the violin under
her window. Nevertheless, Tienne rouses himself sufficiently to have Mme. Cirqué arrested
when she induces her daughter's fiancé to
steal money from the bank he works in. During her brief imprisonment, everyone reclaims his own personality, but when Mme.
Cirqué is mysteriously freed by the police,
each again succumbs to her charm. Mme.
Cirqué, yearning to find a man who will dominate her, rids herself of all but the now-peni-

tent Tienne, whom she has retained to do the housework. As the play ends, she is welcoming a new boarder.

The Falcon (*La hobereaute*, 1956). Drama in which the struggle between good and evil is depicted through a conflict opposing nature and the church in ninth-century Burgundy. Though in love with the noble pagan knight Lotvy, the Falcon, a young girl with the attributes of a bird and a water nymph, is ordered by a Druid priest to marry the odious Baron Massacre. Her sacrifice is deemed necessary to discredit the church for sanctifying so unseemly a union. Stripped of her magical powers by her marriage, the Falcon lives a wretched and servile life with the baron. Meanwhile, Lotvy, driven mad by grief over his loss, declares war against the church, burning and pillaging convents. Disguised as a monk, he enters the baron's domain, but he is trapped in a hunting net and tied to a tree to be tortured. On seeing Lotvy die, the Falcon pours out her contempt for the baron and proclaims her lover the true son of God whose soul is the battlefield of good and evil. As she kneels before Lotvy, the Falcon is strangled by the enraged baron.

The title of the play was originally *Spoken Opera* (*Opéra parlé*), and it was published under that name.

PLAYS

Unless otherwise noted, the plays were first performed in Paris.

1. *L'ampélour* (*The Emperor*). Play, 1 act. Published 1937. Produced Théâtre des Noctambules, Feb. 17, 1950.
2. *La fête noire* (*The Black Feast*). Comedy, 3 acts. Published as *La bête noir* (*The Black Beast*), 1945; as *La fête noire*, 1948. Produced Théâtre de la Huchette, Dec. 3, 1948.
3. *Quoat-Quoat*. Play, 2 scenes. Published 1945. Produced Théâtre de la Gaîté-Montparnasse, Jan. 28, 1946.
4. *Sa peau* (*Her Skin*). Play. Produced Théâtre des Noctambules, 1947.
5. *Le mal court* (*Evil Is Abroad*). Play, 3 acts. Published 1947. Produced Théâtre de Poche, June 25, 1947.
6. *Les femmes du boeuf* (*The Ox's Women*). Play, 1 act. Published 1948. Produced Comédie-Française, Nov. 23, 1948.
7. (Adaptation). *Albertina*. Play, 1 act. Written 1948. Based on the play of the same name by Valentino Bompiani.
8. *Pucelle* (*Maid*). Play, 3 tableaux. Published 1950. Produced Théâtre de la Huchette, June 1, 1950.
9. *Les naturels du Bordelais* (*The Natives of Bordelais*). Play, 3 acts. Published 1953. Produced Théâtre La Bruyère, 1953.
10. *Le cavalier seul* (*The Lone Cavalier*). Play, 3 acts. Published 1955. Produced Lyon, Compagnie du Cothurne, January, 1964.
11. *La logeuse* (*The Landlady*). Play, 3 acts. Published 1956. Produced Théâtre de l'Oeuvre, Oct. 3, 1960.
12. *La hobereaute* (*The Falcon*). Play, 3 acts. Published as *Opéra parlé* (*Spoken Opera*), 1956; as *La hobereaute*, 1959. Produced Festival des Nuits de Bourgogne, 1956.
13. *Le ouallou* (*The "Cooler"*). Play, 1 act. Published 1956. Produced Théâtre La Bruyère, 1957.
14. *Altanima*. Lyric theme, prologue and 3 acts. Published 1956.
15. (Adaptation). *La mégère apprivoisée* (*The Taming of the Shrew*). Comedy, 3 acts. Published 1957. Produced Théâtre de l'Athénée, Oct. 10, 1957. Based on the play by William Shakespeare.
16. (Adaptation). *Les carabiniers* (*The Carabiniers*). Comedy. Produced Théâtre d'Aujourd'hui, 1958. Based on a play by Beniamino Joppolo.
17. *L'effet Glapion* (*The Glapion Effect*). Comedy, 2 acts. Published 1959. Produced Théâtre La Bruyère, Sept. 9, 1959.
18. *Coeur à cuir* (*Leather Heart*). Biography in seven moments; radio play. Published 1961.
19. *Le soldat Dioclès* (*Diocles the Soldier*). Radio play, 3 scenes. Published 1961.
20. *La fourmi dans le corps* (*Ant in the Body*). Play, 2 parts. Published 1961. Produced Darmstadt, Landestheater, 1961; Paris, Comédie-Française, May 30, 1962.
21. *Les patients* (*The Patients*). Poem for voices, 1 act. Published 1962.
22. *L'armoire classique* (*The Classical Cupboard*). Brief vaudeville, 1 act. Published 1962.
23. *Un bel enfant* (*A Beautiful Child*). Farce, 1 act. Published 1962.
24. *Pomme, pomme, pomme* (*Apple, Apple, Apple*). Comedy, 2 acts. Published 1962. Produced Théâtre La Bruyère, September, 1962.
25. *Bâton et ruban* (*Baton and Ribbon*). Sad comedy, 1 act. Published 1962.
26. *Boutique fermée* (*Closed Shop*). Farce, 1 act. Published 1962.
27. *La Brigitta* (*The Brigitta*). Play, 3 acts. Published 1962. Produced Théâtre de l'Athénée, September, 1962.
28. *L'opéra du monde* (*The Opera of the World*). Play, 1 act. Published 1965. Produced Théâtre du Lutèce, Oct. 13, 1965.
29. *La guérite* (*The Sentry Box*). Play. Produced Frankfurt am Main, 1967.

EDITIONS

Théâtre, 5 vols., Paris, 1948–1962.

CRITICISM

A. Deslandes, *Audiberti*, Paris, 1964; G. E. Wellwarth, *The Theater of Protest and Paradox*, New York, 1967.

Émile Augier
(1820 — 1889)

Guillaume-Victor-Émile Augier, French dramatist, was born in Valence on September 17, 1820. He received a law degree from the University of Paris in 1844 but was more interested in writing than in practicing law. He submitted a verse play, *Hemlock* (*La ciguë*), to the Théâtre-Français as soon as he had graduated. The play was rejected, and he then submitted it to the Théâtre de l'Odéon, where it was successfully presented in May, 1844. From that time on, Augier devoted himself solely to the writing of plays.

Between 1844 and 1853 he wrote seven plays in verse. Severely attacked in a theatrical review in 1853, Augier challenged his critic to a duel, from which both parties emerged unharmed. The same year he began to write in prose only, his plays supporting the

Émile Augier.
[G. Lolivier, Paris]

maintenance of bourgeois virtues at a time when the middle class was beginning to merge with the aristocracy. Having collaborated successfully with Musset in 1849 on *The Green Coat* (*L'habit vert*), he began to work with Labiche and Jules Sandeau, coauthoring plays with each over a period of years. *See* LABICHE, EUGÈNE; MUSSET, ALFRED DE; SANDEAU, JULES.

Although often criticized for his iconoclastic belittling of romantic ideals, Augier was elected to the Académie Française in 1857. But in 1861, with the appearance of *Faces of Brass* (*Les effrontés*), a political play concerning corrupt journalism, followed by another play, *Giboyer's Son* (*Le fils de Giboyer*, 1862), which portrayed political intrigue among the clergy, he aroused the fury of pamphleteers and defenders of the Catholic Church. Between 1861 and 1868 he was involved in a series of lawsuits and duels. He married a young actress named Laure Lambert during the 1870s. At this time his plays were concerned with social problems and the necessity for reform. In 1878, owing to a nervous ailment, Augier went into semiretirement at his home in Croissy, and he wrote less and less until his death there on October 25, 1889.

WORK

Augier and Dumas *fils*, both relying to a certain extent on Scribe's well-made play (*pièce bien faite*) techniques, laid the founda-

tions for modern realistic drama in France (*see* WELL-MADE PLAY). Augier began his career with seven verse plays written in a romantic vein; dealing as they did with fantasy and romance, they took place in exotic settings. He soon developed into a committed social dramatist, seriously portraying the life of the Second Empire and realistically analyzing a social crisis of his own time: the disintegration of bourgeois morality under the influence of growing materialism and the efforts of the middle class to merge with the aristocracy. He examined questions of status, money, family, marriage, divorce, and honor; and his moral position, favoring the preservation of bourgeois values, was always made clear. In the plays he wrote from 1853 on, he presented, without sermonizing, the dilemmas of his own time and place.

Two major themes of Augier's social dramas are the hypocrisy of the aristocracy and the materialistic corruption of the bourgeoisie. In *Olympe's Marriage* (*Le mariage d'Olympe,* 1855), a former courtesan marries into a good family but is unable to adjust to her new role in society; for menacing the family honor, she is killed. In this play Augier destroyed the romantic image of the life of a courtesan that had been presented in Dumas *fils*'s *Camille* (1852). *Monsieur Poirier's Son-in-law* (*Le gendre de M. Poirier,* 1854) depicts the problems generated in a marriage between an aristocrat and a wealthy young girl of middle-class origins. *Giboyer's Son* (1862) attacks the hypocrisies of politics and clericalism.

The decadence represented in Augier's drama is generally attributable to excessive financial or social ambition. *Faces of Brass* (1861) attacks unscrupulous journalists and the dishonest use of the power of the press. *Lions and Foxes* (*Lions et renards,* 1869) accuses the clergy of political intrigue and ambitions. An exposé of the shady dealings of the legal profession is presented in *Maître Guérin* (1864). Augier was also concerned with the decadence of bourgeois values within the family. This is particularly evident in his two plays dealing with divorce: *Jean de Thommeray* (1873) and *Madame Caverlet* (1876). Often Augier related the theme of materialism to the dissolution of the family. In *A False Step* (*Les lionnes pauvres,* 1858), a married woman of the petty bourgeoisie prostitutes herself to obtain luxuries. *The House of Fourchambault* (*Les Fourchambault,* 1878) is a powerful study of a family in financial difficulties.

Although Augier's inspiration was limited and the literary value of his work is modest, his dramas achieved success through their well-constructed plots and vigorous characterization of a society. In rejecting the myths and hypocrisies of his time as well as the idealizations of romanticism, Augier projected a lively and penetrating vision of an era that continues to interest modern audiences.

Monsieur Poirier's Son-in-law (*Le gendre de M. Poirier,* 1854). In a plot derived from a short story by Jules Sandeau, the ambitious M. Poirier, a rich tradesman who longs to gain a title, marries his only child, Antoinette, to the impoverished Marquis de Presles. Poirier supports the couple in luxury until he realizes that the marquis is simply using him. He informs the marquis that he will have to pay his own bills or give up his luxuries. With his source of income cut off, the marquis faces the necessity of either going to jail or fleeing to Africa. Frivolous but not without honor, the marquis is impressed by Antoinette's behavior during this crisis in their lives, and he truly falls in love with her. The situation is resolved by the generosity of Verdelet, Poirier's friend. The marquis takes a job, but Poirier, who has purchased his estates, still dreams of becoming a member of the nobility.

Olympe's Marriage (*Le mariage d'Olympe,* 1855). Pauline—in reality the ex-courtesan Olympe Taverny, who is believed to have died of yellow fever in San Francisco—tricks the young Comte de Puygiron into marrying her. Soon, however, she longs for the gay, carefree society she abandoned in order to secure her financial future. Seeking a way out of her marriage, she takes a rich, complaisant lover. However, though Pauline is bored with her husband, she wishes to retain the social and financial advantages that her marriage gives her. She therefore blackmails the family by threatening to make public a diary in which her husband's young niece has confided her love for him. When the head of the family, her husband's grandfather, cannot buy Pauline off, he shoots her, and he is preparing to kill himself as the play ends.

Giboyer's Son (*Le fils de Giboyer,* 1862). Realistic comedy in which the old aristocracy, represented by the Marquis d'Auberville, and the clerical faction are joined in common cause against the rising power of the Liberal party. The marquis has selected M. Giboyer to fill the post of speech writer for the Conservatives, aware that, in order to finance the education of his son Maximilien, Giboyer works for whatever cause pays him the most money. Maximilien, knowing Giboyer only as his tutor, is placed by the marquis as secretary to M. Maréchal, whom the marquis has selected to read the speech for the Conservative party against the Liberal party speaker. Maréchal, a rich bourgeois and former Liberal whose daughter Fernande is a protégée of

Drawing of a scene from *Le fils de Giboyer.* Paris, Comédie-Française, 1862. [Goethe House]

the marquis, anticipates a union of the old with the "new aristocracy." But when the clerical faction of the Conservative party decides to replace him, Maréchal, incensed, goes back to the Liberal party, and Maximilien, encouraged by Giboyer, prepares his retaliatory speech. Meanwhile, the marquis, a childless widower who does not wish to remarry, has selected the Comte d'Outreville, his young cousin, to continue his name as heir to his title and estates provided that he marries Fernande. The young man agrees, but because of the scandal over Maréchal's unexpected retaliation the marriage is called off. When the marquis learns that Fernande and Maximilien are in love and plan to marry, he offers to adopt Maximilien, who, however, declines the honor, having won Fernande despite his low birth.

PLAYS

All were first performed in Paris.

1. *La ciguë* (*Hemlock*). Comedy, 2 acts; verse. Produced Théâtre de l'Odéon, May 13, 1844.

2. *L'homme de bien* (*The Honest Man*). Comedy, 3 acts; verse. Produced Comédie-Française, Nov. 13, 1845.

3. *L'aventurière** (*The Adventuress*). Comedy, 4 acts; verse. Written 1848; revised 1860. Produced Comédie-Française, Mar. 23, 1848.

4. (With Alfred de Musset). *L'habit vert** (*The Green Coat*). Proverbe, 1 act; prose. Produced Théâtre des Variétés, Feb. 23, 1849.

5. *Gabrielle** (*Good for Evil*). Comedy, 5 acts; verse. Produced Comédie-Française, Dec. 13, 1849.

6. *Le joueur de flûte* (*The Flute Player*). Comedy, 1 act; verse. Produced Comédie-Française, Dec. 19, 1850.

7. (With Jules Sandeau). *La chasse au roman* (*In Pursuit of the Novel*). Comédie-vaudeville, 3 acts. Produced Théâtre des Variétés, Feb. 20, 1851.

8. *Sapho*. Libretto, 3 acts; verse. Produced Théâtre de l'Opéra, Apr. 16, 1851. Music: Charles Gounod.

9. *Diane*. Drama, 5 acts; verse. Produced Comédie-Française, Feb. 19, 1852.

10. *Les méprises de l'amour* (*Love's Misunderstandings*). Play. Published 1852.

11. *Philiberte.* Comedy, 3 acts; verse. Produced Théâtre du Gymnase, Mar. 19, 1853.

12. (With Sandeau). *La pierre de touche* (*Touchstone*). Comedy, 5 acts. Produced Comédie-Française, Dec. 23, 1853.

13. (With Sandeau). *Le gendre de M. Poirier** (*Monsieur Poirier's Son-in-law*). Comedy, 4 acts. Produced Théâtre du Gymnase, Apr. 8, 1854. Based on Sandeau's novel *Sacs et parchemins.*

14. *La ceinture dorée* (*Ill-gotten Gold*). Comedy, 3 acts. Produced Théâtre du Gymnase-Dramatique, Feb. 3, 1855.

15. *Le mariage d'Olympe** (*Olympe's Marriage*). Play, 3 acts. Produced Théâtre du Vaudeville, July 17, 1855.

16. *La jeunesse* (*Youth*). Comedy, 5 acts; verse. Produced Théâtre de l'Odéon, Feb. 6, 1858.

17. (With Édouard Foussier). *Les lionnes pauvres** (*A False Step*). Play, 5 acts. Produced Théâtre du Vaudeville, May 22. 1858.

18. (With Foussier). *Un beau mariage* (*A Good Match*). Comedy, 5 acts. Produced Théâtre du Gymnase-Dramatique, Mar. 5, 1859.

19. *Les effrontés** (*Faces of Brass*). Comedy, 5 acts. Produced Comédie-Française, Jan. 10, 1861.

20. *Le fils de Giboyer** (*Giboyer's Son*). Comedy, 5 acts. Produced Comédie-Française, Dec. 1, 1862.

21. *Maître Guérin.* Comedy, 5 acts. Produced Comédie-Française, Oct. 29, 1864.

22. *La contagion* (*The Infection*). Comedy, 5 acts. Produced Théâtre de l'Odéon, Mar. 17, 1866.

23. *Paul Forestier** (*Paul Forrester*). Comedy, 4 acts; verse. Produced Comédie-Française, Jan. 25, 1868.

24. *Le postscriptum** (*The Post-Script*). Comedy, 1 act. Produced Comédie-Française, May 1, 1869.

25. *Lions et renards* (*Lions and Foxes*). Comedy, 5 acts. Produced Comédie-Française, Dec. 6, 1869.

26. (With Sandeau). *Jean de Thommeray.* Comedy, 5 acts. Produced Comédie-Française, Dec. 29, 1873.

27. *Madame Caverlet.* Play, 4 acts. Produced Théâtre du Vaudeville, Feb. 1, 1876.

28. (With Eugène Labiche). *Le prix Martin* (*The Martin Prize*). Comedy, 3 acts. Produced Théâtre du Palais-Royal, Feb. 5, 1876.

29. *Les Fourchambault** (*The House of Fourchambault*). Comedy, 5 acts. Produced Comédie-Française, Apr. 8, 1878.

EDITIONS

Collections.
Théâtre complet, 7 vols., Paris, 1877–1878; *Four Plays,* tr. by B. H. Clark, New York, 1915.
Individual Plays.
Monsieur Poirier's Son-in-law. Published in *The Chief European Dramatists,* ed. by B. Matthews and tr. by B. H. Clark, Houghton Mifflin, Boston, 1916; *World Drama,* ed. and tr. by B. H. Clark, vol. 2, Appleton, New York, 1933; *Chief French Plays of the Nineteenth Century,* ed. by E. M. Grant, Harper, New York, 1934; *Seven French Plays,* ed. by C. Searles, Holt, New York, 1935.
Olympe's Marriage. Published in *Nineteenth Century French Plays,* ed. by J. L. Borgerhoff, Century, New York, 1931; *Camille and Other Plays,* ed. by S. S. Stanton and tr. by B. H. Clark, Hill and Wang, New York, 1957.

CRITICISM

H. Parigot, *Émile Augier,* Paris, 1894; H. G. de Champris, *Émile Augier et la comédie sociale,* Paris, 1910.

AUTO SACRAMENTAL. One-act allegorical verse drama based on the theme of the Eucharist. It was performed outdoors annually on the Feast of Corpus Christi in Spain and its colonies from the middle of the sixteenth through the middle of the eighteenth century.

This genre had its roots in the elaborate annual processions conducted through cities and villages by the church on the occasion of the Feast of Corpus Christi. During the sixteenth century the processions incorporated floats bearing religious *tableaux vivants,* the participants of which performed short musical dramas at given sites along the route. The various municipal governments soon assumed control of these presentations and encouraged their development by awarding prizes to the best among them.

The use of allegory as a vehicle for the dramatization of the rite of Communion was a result of the fact that no Biblical or evangelical text implicitly prescribed that the impersonators of Jesus Christ, the Virgin Mary, the Apostles, and others could enact the transubstantiation, as they could the stories of Christmas and Easter, which commemorated true events occurring in actual time. It was rather the central and timeless mystery of the Holy Sacrament that had to be conveyed through the personification and interaction of abstract theological concepts in an artificial temporal context. The authors of the *autos sacramentales* were able to cull religiously appropriate and dramatically viable allegorical dramas from the wealth of available narrative and descriptive literature, both religious and secular. *See* ALLEGORY.

The first extant examples of the *auto sacramental* are the anonymous *farsas sacramentales* (contained in the *Códice de autos viejos*), which were reworked by Juan de Timoneda in Valencia in the second half of the sixteenth century. The major authors of *autos sacramentales* in the seventeenth century, the Siglo de Oro (Spanish Golden Age), were Valdivielso and Lope de Vega; the greatest flowering of the Eucharistic drama occurred in the prolific output of Calderón. In the early eighteenth century dramatists tried to revive the dying medium of the *auto sacramental,* but in 1765 King Charles III banned future performances, believing them to be contrary to the spirit of the age of Enlightenment. Modern attempts to revive old *autos sacramentales* or to write new ones have met with only limited success, whereas in the Siglo de Oro they were extremely popular, appealing as they did to the people's heightened awareness of the mystical content of Catholicism. *See* CALDERÓN DE LA BARCA, PEDRO; SIGLO DE ORO; VALDIVIELSO, JOSÉ DE; VEGA CARPIO, LOPE DE.

AXELROD, George (1922–   ). American director and dramatist, author of light comedies such as his best-known work, *The Seven Year Itch* (1952), in which a man whose wife is out of town for the summer has a brief

George Axelrod's *The Seven Year Itch*, with Tom Ewell and Vanessa Brown. New York, Fulton Theatre, 1952. [Theatre Collection, The New York Public Library at Lincoln Center, Astor, Lenox and Tilden Foundations]

Marcel Aymé's *Les oiseaux de lune*, Théâtre de l'Atelier, Paris. [French Cultural Services]

affair with the girl upstairs and is then tortured by fantasies conjured up by his conscience. *Will Success Spoil Rock Hunter?* (1955) describes a young man's rise in show business with the help of his agent, the "devil"; and *Goodbye Charlie* (1959) recounts the trials of a dead playboy reincarnated in the body of a beautiful young woman.

AYMÉ, Marcel (b. Joigny, March 28, 1902); (d. Paris, October 14, 1967). French novelist, short-story writer, and dramatist. Like his well-known narrative writings—*The Green Mare* (*La jument verte*, 1933), *The Miraculous Barber* (*Travelingue*, 1941), *The Barkeep of Blémont* (*Uranus*, 1948)—his plays show a rich vein of Rabelaisian fantasy and satire. They are, by and large, completely independent of the themes and techniques that currently dominate the stage. *Lucienne and Her Butcher* (*Lucienne et son boucher*), Aymé's first play, was written in 1932 but was not produced until 1948. In it a tempestuous provincial lady induces her lover, a butcher, to kill her inoffensive husband; she then attempts to have the butcher guillotined for the murder. *Clérambard* (1950), a comedy in which the orientation of a proud man's tyranny is changed after a visitation from St. Francis, immediately established Aymé's in-

ternational reputation as a dramatist. It was followed by *Other People's Heads* (*La tête des autres*, 1952), a savage satire on the judiciary, in which a judge is faced with the dilemma of choosing between justice and public exposure of his wife's infidelity. *Moon Birds* (*Les oiseaux de lune*, 1956) features a school administrator who rids himself of overinquisitive government investigators by transforming them into birds. Other plays of interest are *Here Goes!* (*Vogue la galère*, 1936), *Home Truths* (*Les quatre vérités*, 1954), *The Blue Fly* (*La mouche bleue*, 1957), *Louisiana*

Scene from *Les maxibules.* [French Cultural Services]

Clérambard
(above). [French
Cultural Services]

(*Louisiane*, 1961), *The Maxibules* (*Les maxibules*, 1962), and *The Minotaur* (*Le minotaure*, 1963). Aymé has also translated Arthur Miller's *The Crucible* and *A View from the Bridge*. *See* MILLER, ARTHUR.

Clérambard (1950). Clérambard, a proud, tyrannical aristocrat and the sworn enemy of cats and dogs, retires to his ancestral château after suffering financial reverses. There he sternly sets his wife, son, and mother-in-law to work on textile looms. One day St. Francis appears to him and asks him why he persecutes people and animals. The result is an immediate and radical transformation in the nature of Clérambard's tyranny. Having himself seen the light, he drags everybody else toward it. Completely neglecting practical matters, he extends his "protection" even to the insects that infest the château and wants to marry his son to the local prostitute. After Clérambard has forced several remarkable conversions, St. Francis once more appears, and this time he is seen by all but the village priest. Clérambard and his family set out in a caravan to spread the saint's message. Produced Paris, Comédie des Champs-Élysées, 1950.

Louisiane (right).
[French Cultural
Services]

B

BABEL, Isaak Emanuilovich (b. Odessa, 1894; d. March 17, 1941). Russian- and Yiddish-language poet, short-story writer, and dramatist, whose fame rests mainly on the collection of short stories entitled *Cavalry Corps* (*Konarmiya,* 1926). The product of firsthand experience, the stories depict the savage bloodletting of the civil war in Russia. Babel's flair for the theatre is evident in *Marya* (prod. 1920, pub. 1935) and *Sunset* (*Zakat,* 1928), translated into Yiddish in 1929 as *Sonnenuntergang. Marya,* generally considered the more important, deals with the fate of those whom the Bolsheviks treated as "ideologically alien." Babel also wrote the scenario for the film *Benya Krik* (1926) and another scenario based on Sholem Aleichem's novel *Wandering Star.*

Marya (prod. 1920, pub. 1935). Drama in eight scenes depicting the effect of the Bolshevik victory on a Russian family. General Mukovnin's eldest daughter, Marya, has enthusiastically embraced the Bolshevik cause and left the family home in Petrograd. Her sister Ludmilla, bent on self-preservation, has become involved with a Jewish businessman turned black marketeer. Ludmilla's cousin Katya, in love with a young Bolshevik, hates the impersonality of Communist ideology and decides to escape to Kazan. Ludmilla's involvement in the black market results in her illness and arrest. The shock of discovering this drives her father mad and eventually causes his death. With the disintegration of her family, Katya leaves for Kazan. As the play ends, the flat Katya's family once occupied is being readied for its new tenants, a young worker and his pregnant wife, whose uncertainty of their own status in the changed social structure forebodes further disruption.

BAFFICO, Giuseppe (1852–1927). Italian journalist, novelist, and dramatist who created realistic dramas and bourgeois comedies. His plays include *The Deserters* (*I disertori,*

1898), a study of artistic temperament; and *The Broken Wing* (*Ala ferita,* 1898), a delightful idyll.

Hermann Bahr
(1863 – 1934)

Hermann Bahr, an Austrian critic, satirist, and dramatist, was born on July 19, 1863, in Linz. The son of a notary and Liberal deputy, he studied law, economics, and classical philology in Vienna, Czernowitz, and Berlin, but he did not take a degree. In his early twenties he was attracted first by the German nationalist movement and then by Marxism, both of which he later abandoned. From 1884 until 1887 he lived in Berlin and wrote theatrical criticism. In 1889 he visited Paris, where he came under the influence of Maurice Barrès. After traveling through Spain, Russia, and Switzerland, he settled in Vienna in 1891.

In Vienna, Bahr contributed to the magazine *Moderne Dichtung,* helped edit the liberal weekly *Die Zeit,* and wrote theatre reviews for the democratic *Neues Wiener Tageblatt.* During this period he discovered Eleonora Duse and drew attention to Walt Whitman. In a short time Bahr's stories, essays, and plays brought him fame. At the invitation of

Hermann Bahr.
[Bildarchiv der Österreichischen Nationalbibliothek]

Max Reinhardt, he became a stage director at the Deutsches Theater in Berlin in 1906–1907. In 1909 he married the singer Anna von Hildenburg, and in 1918 he and his wife moved to Salzburg.

During World War I Bahr was converted to Roman Catholicism, the faith of his childhood, and abandoned pan-German nationalism for Austrian patriotism. In 1918 he was appointed the first *Dramaturg* (artistic director) of Vienna's Burgtheater. Thereafter he made his home in Munich, where he died on January 15, 1934.

WORK

With a reformer's zeal, Bahr used his pen to fight the clichés, stagnation, and rigid conventions that he abhorred both in life and in the theatre. He sought to establish a theatre that would be meaningful enough to revitalize and improve modern man. Bahr's more than forty plays reflect the diverse artistic movements of his time: naturalism, impressionism, and expressionism. His work owes much to the tradition of the Viennese *Konversationsstück* ("conversation piece," a light play in an upper-class setting, with emphasis on witty, pointed dialogue), especially the plays of Eduard von Bauernfeld. His strength lies in his masterly dialogue and in his ability to temper irony with warmth.

Always concerned with showing truth in all its aspects, Bahr employed such varied forms as folk dramas, society comedies, and historical comedies, consistently managing to be one significant step ahead of contemporary fashion. His sensitivity to new literary movements can be seen in his essays *Zur Kritik der Moderne* (*Criticism of Naturalism,* 1890) and *Die Überwindung des Naturalismus* (*The Displacement of Naturalism,* 1891), in which he heralded a shift from naturalism at a time when that movement had not even reached its apex. Similarly, the essay *Expressionismus* (1914) deals with the dawn of another literary movement.

Bahr's comedy par excellence is *The Concert* (*Das Konzert,* wr. 1909), in which he expressed the idea that "in marriage it is necessary to set each other free in order to win each other again." Other notable plays are *The Star* (*Der Star,* wr. 1898), which concerns the incompatibility of the worlds of the theatre and the bourgeoisie; *Viennese Women* (*Wienerinnen,* wr. 1900), an exploration of the relations between men and women; *The Devil's Emissary* (*Der Krampus;* pub. 1901), one of Bahr's best character comedies; *The Master* (*Der Meister,* 1903), notable for its psychological analysis; *Helpless* (*Tschaperl,* 1897), a folk drama about a famous wife and an insignificant husband; *Josephine* (wr. 1897), which

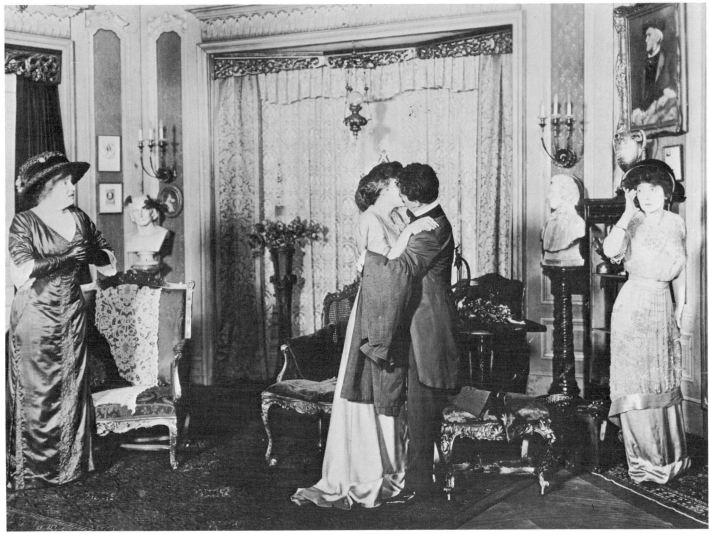

Scene from an adaptation of *The Concert* by Leo Ditrichstein. New York, Belasco Theatre, 1910. [Theatre Collection, The New York Public Library at Lincoln Center, Astor, Lenox and Tilden Foundations]

probes the human being behind the heroic image of Napoleon; and *The Voice* (*Die Stimme,* pub. 1916), an eloquent confirmation of Bahr's conversion to Catholicism.

The Concert (*Das Konzert,* wr. 1909). Comedy about the clandestine love affairs of Gustav Hein, an aging pianist, who seeks to maintain his youth by having affairs with his young pupils. On each occasion he tells his wife Marie that he is "giving a concert." Marie, an intelligent woman, pretends to be ignorant of these affairs until Eva, a pupil, learns that Gustav has taken a woman named Delphina to his cabin in the woods. In a fit of jealousy, Eva informs Delphina's husband Frank, who thereupon proposes to Marie that they encourage a marriage between Delphina and Gustav so that he, Frank, will be able to marry Marie. They go to the cabin to tell Gustav and Delphina of this decision, but when Marie starts to give Delphina detailed instructions on how to overcome the difficulties of living with a genius, Delphina hastily makes peace with Frank, and they leave. Gustav promises to reform, but upon Eva's arrival he automatically resumes his role of flatterer and seducer.

PLAYS

1. *Der fixe Punkt* (*The Fixed Point*). Farce, 1 act. Written 1882.

2. *Die Wunderkur* (*The Miracle Cure*). Farce, 1 act. Written 1883.

3. *Die neuen Menschen* (*The New Men*). Play, 3 acts. Written 1887. Published 1887.

4. *La Marquesa d'Amaëgui* (*The Marchioness of Amaëgui*). Conversation piece. Written 1887. Published 1888.

5. *Die grosse Sünde* (*The Great Sin*). Tragedy, 5 acts. Published 1888.

6. *Die Mutter* (*The Mother*). Play, 3 acts. Published 1891.

7. *Die häusliche Frau* (*The Domestic Woman*). Comedy, 4 acts. Written 1891. Published 1892. Produced Berlin, Lessingtheater, June 8, 1892.

8. (With Carl Karlweis). *Aus der Vorstadt* (*From the Suburbs*). Folk play, 3 acts. Published 1893. Produced Vienna, Deutsches Volkstheater, Mar. 11, 1893.

9. (Adaptation). *Die Nixe* (*The Mermaid*). Play, 4 acts. Published 1896. Based on a Russian play by H. V. Spashinsky.

10. *Juana.* Play. Published 1896.

11. *Josephine**. Play, 4 acts. Written 1897. Published 1898.

12. *Tschaperl** (*Helpless*). Play, 4 acts. Written 1897. Published 1898. Produced Vienna, Carltheater, Feb. 27, 1897.

13. *Der Star* (*The Star*). Play, 4 acts. Written 1898. Published 1899.

14. (With Karlweis). *Wenn es euch gefällt* (*If You Like It*). Revue, 3 scenes and prologue. Published 1899.

15. *Der Athlet* (*The Athlete*). Drama, 3 acts. Published 1899.

16. *Wienerinnen* (*Viennese Women*). Comedy, 3 acts. Written 1900. Published 1900.

17. *Der Franzl* (*Francis*). Play, 5 acts. Published 1901.

18. *Der Apostel* (*The Apostle*). Play, 3 acts. Published 1901.

19. *Der Krampus* (*The Devil's Emissary*). Comedy, 3 acts. Published 1901.

20. *Der liebe Augustin* (*Dear Augustine*). Pantomime. Published 1902.

21. *Der Meister** (*The Master*). Comedy, 3 acts. Written 1903. Published 1903. Produced Berlin, Deutsches Theater, Dec. 12, 1903.

22. *Unter sich* (*Among Themselves*). Poor people's play, 4 scenes. Published 1904.

23. *Die gelbe Nachtigall* (*The Yellow Nightingale*). Comedy, 3 acts. Published 1904.

24. *Sanna*. Play, 5 acts. Written 1904. Published 1905. Produced Berlin, Kleines Theater, Mar. 10, 1905.

25. *Die Andere* (*The Other Woman*). Play, 5 acts. Written 1905. Published 1906.

26. *Der arme Narr* (*The Poor Jester*). Comedy, 1 act. Published 1905.

27. *Ringelspiel* (*Merry-go-round*). Comedy, 3 acts. Published 1906. Produced Berlin, Deutsches Theater, 1906.

The following three plays were published under the joint title *Grotesken* (*Grotesques*).

28. *Der Klub der Erlöser* (*The Club of the Redeemers*). Grotesque, 1 act. Published 1907.

29. *Der Faun* (*The Satyr*). Grotesque, 1 act. Published 1907.

30. *Die tiefe Natur* (*The Deep Nature*). Grotesque, 1 act. Published 1907.

31. *Das Konzert** (*The Concert*). Comedy, 3 acts. Written 1909. Published 1909.

32. *Die Kinder* (*The Children*). Comedy, 3 acts. Published 1911.

33. *Das Tänzchen* (*The Little Dance*). Comedy, 3 acts. Published 1911.

34. *Das Prinzip* (*The Principle*). Comedy, 3 acts. Published 1912.

35. *Das Phantom* (*The Phantom*). Comedy, 3 acts. Published 1913.

36. *Der Querulant* (*The Complainer*). Comedy, 4 acts. Published 1914.

37. *Der muntere Seifensieder* (*The Jolly Soapmaker*). Farce. Written 1914. Published 1914.

38. *Die Stimme* (*The Voice*). Play, 3 acts. Published 1916.

39. *Der Augenblick* (*The Moment*). Comedy, 5 acts. Published 1917.

The following three plays were published under the joint title *Spielerei* (*Dalliance*).

40. *Der Unmensch* (*The Brute*). Play. Published 1919.

41. *Landpartie* (*Excursion*). Drama, 1 act. Published 1919.

42. *Ehelei* (*Wedlocking*). Comedy, 3 acts. Published 1920.

43. *Der Selige* (*The Blessed One*). Drama, 1 act. Published 1919.

44. *Der Umsturz* (*The Overthrow*). Farce, 1 act. Published 1919.

45. *Altweibersommer* (*Indian Summer*). Farce, 3 acts. Published 1924.

46. *Die Tante* (*The Aunt*). Comedy, 3 acts. Published 1928.

EDITIONS

The Concert. Published in *Chief Contemporary Dramatists,* ed. by T. H. Dickinson and tr. by B. Morgan, 2d ser., Boston, 1921.

CRITICISM

W. Handl, *Hermann Bahr,* Berlin, 1913; A. Bahr-Mildenburg, *Erinnerungen,* Vienna, 1921; M. Macken, *Hermann Bahr: His Personality and His Works,* Dublin, 1926; P. Wagner, *Der junge Hermann Bahr* (dissertation), Giessen, 1937; K. Bogner, *Hermann Bahr und das Theaterwesen seiner Zeit* (dissertation), Vienna, 1947; H. Nedomansky, *Der Theater-Kritiker Hermann Bahrs* (dissertation), Vienna, 1947; H. Kindermann, *Hermann Bahr: Ein Leben für das europäische Theater,* Graz, 1954.

BAKER, George Pierce (1866–1935). An American university professor and a writer of critical works on drama and the theatre, Baker made a significant contribution to the development of American drama through the instruction, encouragement, and inspiration he gave young writers in his 47 Workshop at Harvard. Through the years it was attended by such writers as Sidney Howard, Eugene O'Neill, John V. A. Weaver, Philip Barry, S. N. Behrman, John Mason Brown, Rachel Field, and Thomas Wolfe.

Baker was himself a student at Harvard; following his graduation in 1887 he joined the faculty, and in 1905 he was made a full

John Balderston's *Berkeley Square*, with Margalo Gillmore and Leslie Howard. New York, Lyceum Theatre, 1929. [Theatre Collection, The New York Public Library at Lincoln Center, Astor, Lenox and Tilden Foundations]

professor of English. He sponsored the Harvard Dramatic Club when it was established in 1908, and his course entitled English 47, on dramatic composition, developed into the 47 Workshop, which was to function as a laboratory where fledgling writers could stage their works without the pressures of the commercial theatre. It was his conviction that a dramatist must have a thorough knowledge of the living stage and its technical problems. Consequently, his students had to construct scenery as well as act and direct.

Since the unorthodox workshop was looked at askance at Harvard, Baker moved in 1925 to expanded quarters at Yale University, where he organized a department of drama and became director of the University Theatre. He retired in 1933, having published a number of works on the theatre, including *The Principles of Argumentation* (1895), *The Development of Shakespeare as a Dramatist* (1907), and *Dramatic Technique* (1919).

BALDERSTON, John Lloyd (1889–1954). American dramatist best known for his fantastic drama *Berkeley Square* (1929), written with J. C. Squire, which describes a romance that defies time, carrying the protagonist back to the eighteenth century as he inhabits the home of his ancestors and falls in love. The story was taken from *The Sense of the Past,* an unfinished novel by Henry James. Among Balderston's plays are *Dracula* (1927), written with Hamilton Deane, and *Red Planet* (1932), written with J. E. Hoare.

BALDWIN, James Arthur (1924–   ). American writer, author of fiction, essays, and drama, internationally known for his bold expression of black American life. He

James Arthur Baldwin. [Courtesy Dial Press]

has written two plays, *The Amen Corner* (wr. 1953, prod. 1965), dealing with the everyday life of a small church community in New York; and *Blues for Mr. Charlie* (1964), produced by the Actors Studio under the direction of Burgess Meredith, which decries racial discrimination. The latter play is based on a trial that took place in Mississippi in 1955. Following the murder of a black youth, the culprit is acquitted by the court.

BALE, John (1495–1563). English bishop of Ossory, Ireland, and a scholar noted for his vehement attacks upon the Catholic Church. He was the author of some twenty-two plays, five of which are extant. The best known is *King John* (*Kynge Johan,* wr. before 1536), a tedious seven-act tribute to a monarch whose opposition to the Pope resulted in his assassination by a monk. Because the play intermingles historical characters with such allegorical figures as Nobility and Sedition, it represents an important transition from the morality play to the secular and historical drama. Of the remaining four, three are miracle plays—*The Temptation of Our Lord* (1538), *A Tragedy or Interlude Manifesting the Chief Promises of God unto Man* (pub. 1538), and *A Brief Comedy or Interlude of John the Baptist Preaching in the Wilderness* (pub. 1538)—and the fourth, *The Three Laws of Nature, Moses, and Christ* (1538), a morality play by virtue of its allegorical characters. *See* MIRACLE PLAY; MORALITY PLAY.

BALZAC, Honoré de (b. Tours, May 20, 1799; d. Paris, August 18, 1850). French novelist and dramatist best known for *The Human Comedy* (*La comédie humaine*), a series of powerful realistic novels presenting a panoramic portrait of French life at the end of the First Empire and the beginning of the Restoration. One of Balzac's first works, however, was an unsuccessful tragedy based on the life of Cromwell. He thereafter turned to fiction, returning to the theatre only in later life when he was in desperate need of money because of his ruinous financial speculations. Beginning with *Vautrin* (1840), a drama extending the adventures of an attractive criminal rogue who appears in many of Balzac's novels, these ventures into the theatre proved equally ruinous. The play was attacked by the critics and closed by the police because the famous actor Frédérick Lemaître, who played Vautrin, costumed himself so as to resemble Louis Philippe. In 1842 Balzac tried his luck again with *The Resources of Quinola* (*Les ressources de Quinola*), an unsuccessful romantic drama set in Spain during the reign of Philip II. Quinola, a wily servant, saves his master, who has discovered

Bust of Honoré de Balzac by David d'Angers. [French Cultural Services]

struggle of two women, the general's daughter and her stepmother, for the love of the same man. Ironically, the play's success was cut short when the Revolution of 1848 caused all theatres to be shut down. Nevertheless, it showed that Balzac was beginning to understand the demands of the stage. Turning his back on the inanities inspired by romantic drama, Balzac returned in *Mercadet* to the realist comic tradition of plays such as Lesage's *Turcaret* (1708). Originally written in five acts, this fascinating portrait of a shrewd financier was adapted in three acts by Adolphe Dennery and produced in 1851, a year after Balzac's death, as *The Speculator* (*Le faiseur*). Many critics feel that it clearly indicates that, had he lived, Balzac might have

Théâtre National Populaire production of *Le faiseur*, with Jean Vilar (left). [French Cultural Services]

Drawing of the final scene of *Paméla Giraud.* Paris, Théâtre de la Gaîté, 1843. [New York Public Library Picture Collection]

the secret of the steamboat, from the tortures of the Inquisition. In *Paméla Giraud* (1843), Balzac recounted the story of a virtuous girl who saves her lover from prison by testifying that he was with her on the night he is accused of having participated in a political conspiracy. A Bonapartist general's hatred of those who forsook Napoleon brings ruin and death to young lovers in *The Stepmother* (*La marâtre,* 1848). The plot is complicated by the

produced a realistic drama on a par with his famous novels. *See* LESAGE, ALAIN-RENÉ.

Mercadet, or The Speculator (*Mercadet, ou Le faiseur,* 1851). Ever since his father-in-law Godeau absconded to America with the firm's funds, the financier Mercadet has existed by a series of daring ruses and speculations. The tide turns against him, however, and his creditors begin to hound him. Using all the resources of his wit, Mercadet fights for time in which to bring off a financial coup. He also hopes to mend his fortunes by marrying his daughter to De la Brive, a wealthy nobleman, but the latter turns out to be only a penniless fortune hunter named Michonnin. To dupe his creditors, Mercadet spreads the story that Godeau has recently returned from America, where he has amassed a fortune that will be placed at his son-in-law's disposal. Mercadet plans to palm off Michonnin as his father-in-law. However, when his wife announces to the assembled and angry creditors that Godeau has arrived, Mercadet discovers to his horror that one of them knows him well. It soon becomes apparent, however, that the real Godeau has returned. The latter, eager to atone for his previous behavior, pays Mercadet's debts. Produced Paris, Théâtre du Gymnase, August 24, 1851.

BANCES Y LÓPEZ-CANDAMO, Francisco Antonio (1662–1704). A favorite of King Charles II, Bances was the last major figure of the Siglo de Oro (Spanish Golden Age) drama and reflected its evolution toward the baroque. Very much a disciple of Calderón, Bances displayed a similar precision and complexity in his plots as well as a predilection for philosophical themes and extensive symbolism: magic and alchemy are often seen in his works. *See* CALDERÓN DE LA BARCA, PEDRO; SIGLO DE ORO.

Perhaps his best-known *comedia* is *The Slave in Golden Chains* (*El esclavo en grillos de oro*), which exemplifies his poetic lyricism (again a Calderonian trait) and his baroque stylization and imagery. Other notable *comedias* are *Macías, the Most Loving and Unfortunate Spaniard* (*El español mas amante y desgraciado, Macías*); *The Virgin of Guadalupe* (*La Virgen de Guadalupe*); *The Philosophers' Stone* (*La piedra filosofal*), based on Calderón's *Life Is a Dream;* and *The Avenger of Heaven* (*El vengador de los cielos*). In addition to his dramatic writings, Bances produced *Theatro de los theatros* (wr. 1690), a critical treatise that remained in manuscript until 1901.

BANVILLE, Théodore de (1823–1891). French poet, drama critic, and playwright. Banville's poetry is associated with the Parnassian school, whose leading lights were Charles-Marie Leconte de Lisle and Théophile Gautier. He wrote some twenty volumes of verse, the best known of which are *Les cariatides* (1842), *Odelettes* (1856), and *Les exilés* (1867). Though his production for the theatre was substantial, he is remembered today primarily for *Gringoire* (1866), a romantic prose play whose protagonist is an amalgam of François Villon and Pierre Gringoire, a poet who also appears in Victor Hugo's novel *Notre-Dame de Paris* (1831). Gringoire, an ugly and starving poet in medieval Paris's Court of Miracles, is under sentence of death for having written a poem mocking the King's justice. His only hope lies in winning the love and support of Loyse, a wealthy and beautiful young lady. To everyone's surprise, Loyse falls under the spell of the poet's genius

and champions him as the voice of man's conscience. *The Knavery of Nérine* (*Les fourberies de Nérine,* pub. 1864) is a verse comedy that owes a great deal to Molière's *The Rogueries of Scapin. The Kiss* (*Le baiser,* 1887), also in verse, was written for André Antoine's Théâtre Libre and enjoyed considerable success. Other plays of interest are *The Apple* (*La pomme, 1865*), *Florise* (pub. 1870), and *Socrates and His Wife* (*Socrate et sa femme,* pub. 1885). Banville also wrote several librettos for the lyric stage.

BARAKA, Imamu Amiri. *See* JONES, LEROI.

BARGAGLI, Girolamo (1537–1586). Italian poet, dramatist, and member of the Academy of the Intronati in Siena, called Il Materiale (The Materialist). His only work for the theatre is a prose comedy, *The Lady Pilgrim* (*La pellegrina;* wr. 1564, prod. 1583).

BARILLET, Pierre (1923–). French screenwriter and dramatist. Barillet's first plays were adaptations or works designed for radio, but in 1949 he collaborated with Jean-Pierre Grédy on *Adele's Gift* (*Le don d'Adèle*), a comedy about a housemaid with a talent for

Scene from Barillet and Grédy's *Ami-Ami.* [French Cultural Services]

Le bon débarras.
Paris, Théâtre
Daunou, 1952.
[French Cultural
Services]

prophecy. The play opened in Bordeaux and the following year was produced in Paris, where its success established Barillet and Grédy as writers of popular light comedy. Their best-known plays are *Cactus Flower* (*Fleur de cactus*, 1964), in which a bachelor dentist pretends to be married in order to safeguard his single state; and *Forty Carats* (*Quarante carats*, 1967), in which a woman of forty finds herself amorously involved with a man half her age. *Ami-Ami* (1950) deals with the confusions of two recently married couples; *Good Riddance* (*Le bon débarras*, 1952)

concerns a man who wearies of his nagging wife and mother-in-law and locks himself in a storeroom (*débarras*) for a month; *The White Queen* focuses on the confusions that result when a woman marries a Negro student who turns out to be a king in his own country; and *The Pen* (*La plume*, 1956) zeroes in on literary prodigies such as Françoise Sagan. Other comedies by this writing team, whose success recalls the turn-of-the-century popularity of Robert de Flers and Gaston de Caillavet, include *Gold and Straw* (*L'or et la paille,* 1956), *The Chinaman* (*Le chinois,* 1958), and *Four*

Rooms on a Garden (*Quatre pièces sur jardin*, 1969). They are also responsible for adaptations of a number of English and American plays. *See* GRÉDY, JEAN-PIERRE.

BARKER, James Nelson (b. Philadelphia, June 17, 1784; d. Washington, Mar. 9, 1858). A leading American dramatist of the first quarter of the nineteenth century. Of Barker's five extant plays (he wrote ten), three are on native American themes. The best of these, *Superstition* (1824), is a verse tragedy set in a Puritan village in New England; the other two are *Tears and Smiles* (1807), a comedy of manners set in contemporary Philadelphia, and *The Indian Princess, or La Belle Sauvage* (1808), about Pocahontas. The latter was the first play on an Indian theme written by an American to be performed, and probably the first American play to be produced, in England (1820). Barker's two other extant plays are *Marmion* (1812), a free adaptation of Scott's epic poem; and *How to Try a Lover* (wr. 1817, prod. 1836), a comedy based on the French novel *La folie espagnole* (1801), by Charles Pigault-Lebrun.

Superstition (1824).   Ravensworth, a Puritan clergyman, sets out to destroy Isabella Fitzroy and her son Charles, who have offended him. One day, on his way to the village, Charles encounters the Unknown (who is actually his grandfather, a fugitive from justice). The two reach their destination just as an Indian attack is in progress, and with great heroism they save the village. Since Charles is unharmed and the Unknown is considered to be supernatural, Ravensworth seizes the opportunity to charge Charles and his mother with witchcraft. Charles tries to enlist the aid of Ravensworth's daughter Mary, whom he loves, but is discovered with her and charged with rape. Charles is tried and executed, and Mary, mad with grief, falls dead at his bier. The Unknown, Isabella's father, appears and discloses too late that Charles is the son of the King. Produced Philadelphia, Chestnut Street Theatre, March 12, 1824.

Ernst Barlach
(1870 – 1938)

Ernst Barlach, German expressionist sculptor, poet, and dramatist, was born in Wedel on January 2, 1870, to a physician and his wife. He was orphaned while still a schoolboy, and his subsequent education was irregular.

Ernst Barlach. [German Information Center]

Nonetheless, he succeeded in entering the Hamburg Industrial Art School in 1888, and later, in 1891, the Dresden Academy of Arts, where he studied sculpture and design. Between 1895 and 1897 he lived and worked as a sculptor in Paris, laying the foundation of his later reputation as one of Germany's outstanding artists. He became noted especially for his wood carvings of peasant figures, which are reminiscent of Romanesque and early Gothic works.

Following his Paris days, Barlach traveled extensively, changing his residence frequently. In 1906 he visited Italy and Russia. He was greatly impressed with Russia, learning there what he called "Christian humility toward all things" and acquainting himself thoroughly with the works of Dostoyevsky and Tolstoy. In 1910 he settled permanently in Güstrow, an old Mecklenburg town famous for its cathedral. Having developed a deliberate sense of piety and seeking an "approximation to God," he turned to poetry and drama as a second medium for expressing his deeply religious view of life. Sculpture, however, remained his forte, and in 1930 he received a commission to execute a large war memorial at the Madgeburg Cathedral.

By 1937 the Nazis had classified Barlach as a dangerous and decadent artist. An exhibition of his works was forbidden, his name was struck from the membership list of the Prussian Academy of Arts, and, finally, all his works in public exhibitions were removed or destroyed. Outlawed and belittled, he lived in seclusion in Güstrow until his death on October 25, 1938. He left behind a detailed autobiography, *A Self-narrated Life* (*Ein selbsterzähltes Leben,* 1928), which is written in the baroque style that dominated his early prose.

WORK

Barlach, one of a rare breed of artist able to express himself forcefully through two media, shows the close interrelation of expressionism in art and literature. A principal exponent of the mystical-religious expressionist drama, he wrote plays of great poetic power, characterized by a brooding atmosphere and flashes of bizarre humor. The action is negligible: the creative impulse materializes in the search for God. The father-son conflict, central to expressionist drama, is treated by Barlach as a parable of the supernatural partnership uniting God with his creatures. Also implicit is the recognition that God can be reached only through the deliverance of the prodigal son, of sinning and guilty humanity. *See* EXPRESSIONISM.

Barlach's eight dramas, inspired by Gothic art, combine mysticism and realism and draw heavily on the attitudes of the inhabitants and on the landscape of his native northwest Germany. His settings, in particular, reflect that misty land, and his elemental characters seem to be born in the mist, from which they labor toward spiritual fulfillment. His reputation as a dramatist rests mainly on his later plays, which are progressively more realistic: characters become more sharply defined, settings less amorphous, and details more clearly etched. In *The True Sedemunds* (*Die echten Sedemunds,* 1921), for example, a satire on small-town Philistinism is enhanced by pungent character portraits and a scurrilous, earthy humor. *The Blue Boll* (*Der blaue Boll,* 1926) combines mysticism and grotesquerie

Berlin production of *Der blaue Boll,* 1930. [Theater-Museum, Munich]

but owes its dramatic effectiveness to the robust character of Boll, a boisterous country gentleman whose hedonistic ways are altered by strange experiences. *The Poor Cousin* (*Der arme Vetter,* 1919) is considered by some to be Barlach's most successful play. The young hero, a dreamer tired of his small-minded fellow townsmen, embarks on a search for God. Although he commits suicide in the end, he inspires a girl he meets on the way to seek a life of spiritual fulfillment. In *The Flood* (*Die Sündflut,* 1924), Barlach's Christianity finds its fullest expression with God's ultimate recognition of the inherent mixture of good and evil in man.

Among Barlach's other plays is the most purely expressionistic of his dramas, *The Dead Day* (*Der tote Tag;* wr. 1910, prod. 1919), in which a mother and son live in a vast hall in perpetual twilight. The strange struggle between the two, taking place against a background of obscure symbols (gnomes, spirits, a mystical presence), is resolved when the son recognizes that his quest for his father is also his search for God. *The Foundling* (*Der Findling;* wr. 1921, prod. 1928), in verse and prose, is an allegory depicting the redemption of man's brutal nature by faith. *Good Times* (*Die gute Zeit,* 1929), about an insurance company that will issue policies only to the rich, ends on a similarly redemptive note. In the posthumously published *The Count of Ratzeburg* (*Der Graf von Ratzeburg;* wr. 1927/37, prod. 1951), the ghosts of Moses, God, angels, and Crusaders take the stage in a play the author did not consider ready for publication or production.

The True Sedemunds (*Die echten Sedemunds,* 1921). Seven-part expressionistic drama dealing with the "genuine" and the "false." Revolted by his father's debauchery, young Sedemund becomes a political utopian. Called home because of his mother's death, which actually has been caused by his father, young Sedemund encounters an old friend, Grude, at a circus. Grude, who has been released from an insane asylum to attend the funeral, dedicates the day to persuading everyone that a lion is at large, for he believes in "a savage's conscience," in man's need for a "devourer" nipping at his heels. The symbolic lion takes on new meanings as the action unfolds into a kind of circus of man's corruption, moving from the circus through a beer garden, outside to the fairgrounds, through a graveyard, and into a chapel, and ending at the intersection before the churchyard. There, following Sedemund's father's grotesque parade to an organ-grinder's tune, the young Sedemund commits himself to the insane asylum. Thereupon, the newly released Grude, followed by his wife, dances on the gravestones, heralding "a new day and the genuine Grudes."

The Flood (*Die Sündflut*, 1924). Biblical play in five parts, presenting the opposing philosophies of its major characters, Noah and Calan. Noah's pure belief in a God who "is everything and the world nothing" contrasts with Calan's view of God as "a glimmering spark . . . who creates" and whose "creation creates him anew." Noah is blindly obedient, while Calan is a free spirit, taking full responsibility for his destiny. Noah's quarrelsome and self-centered sons contrast vividly with the loyalty and love of Calan's servant Chus. Calan's rigorous and independent honor contrasts with Noah's passive acceptance of events, of which he consequently is often the victim and which sometimes makes him the unwitting shield of evil. And when, in the end, Noah abandons Calan to the flood, one sees in the action a kind of betrayal and in Calan's subsequent courageous acceptance of death a tragic nobility.

The Blue Boll (*Der blaue Boll*, 1926). Expressionistic drama in seven scenes, unique for its use of broad humor and lusty grotesquerie. Its theme is self-acceptance, which in turn leads to a process through which one's spirit becomes greater and purer. This the author calls "becoming." Landowner Boll, "comfortable in the flesh," feels self-disgust and contemplates suicide, while Grete Greendale, despising the flesh, contemplates the murder of her children in order to transform them into pure spirit. Seeking poison, Grete begs it of Boll. Through a series of symbolic episodes the two becomes instruments of each other's salvation. An unconventional gentleman, a Christ figure, spurs Boll on "to suffer and to fight" in his "becoming." Grete becomes reconciled through a Satan figure, Elias, and his wife, a mammoth earth mother who envelops her in flesh. In their hell's kitchen Grete beholds visions of death in which she sees a younger and purer Boll as savior. Revolving about the "becoming" of the two antithetical central figures is the lesser "becoming" of the minor characters, to whom they are linked by a common humanity.

PLAYS

1. *Der tote Tag* (*The Dead Day*). Drama, 5 acts; prose. Written 1910. Published 1912. Produced Nov. 22, 1919.
2. *Der arme Vetter* (*The Poor Cousin*). Drama, 5 acts; prose. Written 1917. Published 1918. Produced Hamburg, Hamburger Kammerspiele, Mar. 3, 1919.
3. *Die echten Sedemunds* (*The True Sedemunds*). Drama, 7 scenes; prose. Written 1919. Published 1920. Produced Hamburg, Hamburger Kammerspiele, Mar. 23, 1921.
4. *Der Findling* (*The Foundling*). Drama, 3 parts; verse and prose. Written 1921. Published 1922. Produced Königsberg, Apr. 21, 1928.
5. *Die Sündflut* (*The Flood*). Drama, 5 parts; prose. Written 1923. Published 1924. Produced Stuttgart, Sept. 27, 1924.

Scene from *Die Sündflut*. [German Information Center]

6. *Der blaue Boll* (*The Blue Boll*). Drama, 7 scenes; prose. Written 1925. Published 1926. Produced Stuttgart, Oct. 13, 1926.
7. *Die gute Zeit* (*Good Times*). Drama, 10 acts. Written 1928. Published 1929. Produced Gera, Nov. 18, 1929.
8. *Der Graf von Ratzeburg* (*The Count of Ratzeburg*). Drama, 10 scenes; prose. Written 1927/37. Published 1951. Produced Nürnberg, Nov. 25, 1951.

EDITIONS

Das dichterische Werke, 3 vols., Munich, 1956–59; *Three Plays*, tr. by A. Page, Minneapolis, 1964.

CRITICISM

P. Fechter, *Ernst Barlach*, Gütersloh, 1957; W. Flemming, *Ernst Barlach*, Bern, 1958; H. Franck, *Ernst Barlach: Leben und Werke*, Stuttgart, 1961; P. Schurek, *Barlach: Eine Bildbiographie*, Munich, 1961; H. Meier, *Der verborgene Gott: Studien zu den Dramen Ernst Barlachs*, Nürnberg, 1963; A. Werner, *Barlach*, New York, 1966; E. M. Chick, *Barlach*, New York, 1967.

BAROQUE AGE. The baroque age grew out of the Renaissance revival of classical learning and aesthetics that spread from Italy to the rest of Europe in the fifteenth century. At the same time, an increase in wealth and power among the aristocracy and the merchant princes, who rivaled the clergy as patrons of the arts, fostered a taste for opulence, ornamentation, and extravagant spectacle that held sway in continental Europe from the late sixteenth to the late eighteenth century. Yet the theatre of the time was a truly popular one, attracting audiences from all classes. It was the period of *commedia dell'arte* in Italy, of Lope de Vega in Spain, of Corneille, Racine, and Molière in France, of Jakob Bidermann, Jakob Ayrer, and Christian Reuter in Germany, and of Kyd, Marlowe, Shakespeare, Jonson, and Dryden in England. But it was spectacle as much as literary quality that appealed to theatre audiences. Court theatres, like the churches and palaces of the day, were decked with gilded plaster nymphs, satyrs, and other figures from classical mythology. Music and ballet were employed even in tragedies, and it was at this time that opera made its appearance. Stage curtains and a system of painted side wings and backdrops made possible new technical effects. The Renaissance discovery of the principle of perspective was carried to elaborate extremes by scenic designers, whose backdrops were supplemented by grandiose dramatic spectacles of storms, battles, and natural disasters. Some designers, among them the Bibiena family, Bramante, Palladio, Peruzzi, Serlio, and Inigo Jones, became as famous as the writers and actors. The influence of such artists was felt far beyond the stage, for the spirit and style of their productions enriched and gave color to the society that supported them. The rise of the middle classes, with their leaden emphasis on prudence, good sense, and realism, finally put an end to the sumptuous age of the baroque.

Sir James Matthew Barrie
(1860 – 1937)

Sir James Matthew Barrie, Scottish dramatist and novelist, was born in Kirriemuir, a Lowland Scottish village, on May 9, 1860. He was the ninth of ten children, few of whom survived infancy. His father, David Barrie, was an impoverished weaver, and it was through the efforts of his mother, Margaret Ogilvy Barrie, that young James secured an education. Though an avid reader, he was a poor student and had to work hard to receive an M.A. degree from Edinburgh University in 1882.

In 1883 Barrie became a writer for the Nottingham *Journal* but left it in 1885 for London, where he earned a precarious living by free-lance writing under the name Gavin Ogilvy. His first novel, *Better Dead*, a satire on London life, was published in 1887. It was followed by *Auld Licht Idylls* (1888), a collection of stories about his native village that established him as a writer of repute. *The Little Minister* (1891) became a best seller and put Barrie on a firm financial footing. In 1891 his one-act burlesque on Ibsen, called *Ibsen's Ghost, or Toole up to Date*, was produced, followed the next year by his first full-length play, *Walker, London*. He later collaborated with Arthur Conan Doyle on the libretto of a comic opera, *Jane Annie, or The Good Conduct Prize*, produced by D'Oyly Carte in 1893. In 1897 he successfully dramatized *The Little*

Minister, and from then on he devoted himself almost entirely to the theatre.

With the production of *Quality Street* in Toledo, Ohio, in 1901 and *The Admirable Crichton* in England in 1902, Barrie's fame as a playwright was firmly established. Until 1920 he turned out approximately a play a year. Notable among them were *Peter Pan* (1904), *What Every Woman Knows* (1908), *The Twelve-Pound Look* (1910), *Dear Brutus* (1917), and *Mary Rose* (1920). From 1922 until 1936 Barrie remained silent as a dramatist. Then, in 1936 he presented his last two plays, *The Two Shepherds* and *The Boy David,* Biblical dramas unlike anything else he had written.

In 1894 Barrie married Mary Ansell, a young actress from whom he was divorced in 1907. He was made a baronet in 1913 and received the Order of Merit in 1922. In 1928 he served as president of the Society of Authors and in 1930 was made chancellor of Edinburgh University. He died in London on June 19, 1937.

WORK

James Barrie became best known for characteristics that began to develop early in his career. His vision of the world was unique. Deeply sensitive to the foibles of men, he pre-

James Matthew Barrie. [Walter Hampden Memorial Library at The Players, New York]

Maude Adams in *Peter Pan* (top left). Scene from *The Little Minister*, with Maude Adams and Robert Edeson (top right). Maude Adams in *Quality Street* (bottom left). [Brander Matthews Dramatic Museum, Columbia University]

George Crouse Tyler in the title role of *The Admirable Crichton* (bottom right). [Theatre Collection, The New York Public Library at Lincoln Center, Astor, Lenox and Tilden Foundations]

sented them sympathetically, albeit sentimentally. His sentimentality, however, was not maudlin, not a glossing over of reality but a consciously chosen attitude: his flights into fantasy served to outline more clearly the realities he saw.

Although *Peter Pan* (1904), the universal and ageless fantasy of eternal youth, is Barrie's most famous play, one of his best works is the social comedy *The Admirable Crichton* (1902). In it Barrie successfully combined fantasy with social comment. *Quality Street* (1902), a period romance, is saved from hopeless sentimentality by its lively heroine, who refuses to be the conventional Victorian. In *What Every Woman Knows* (1908) Barrie turned once again to social comedy, producing one of his best-drawn realistic plays, about a woman who makes a success of her insignificant husband.

Barrie also wrote a number of excellent one-act plays, the best known of which is probably *The Twelve-Pound Look* (1910), the story of Kate (strongly reminiscent of Maggie in *What Every Woman Knows*), who has left her wealthy husband and the barrenness of their life to find dignity and self-respect by working as a typist. *The Old Lady Shows Her Medals* (1917) is a touching story of loneliness in which an old charwoman, Mrs. Dowey, invents a soldier son. Suddenly her "son" appears, and through their mutual loneliness they forge a bond of true affection and love. *Shall We Join the Ladies?* (1921) is an intriguing murder mystery with a unique ending.

Among Barrie's many other full-length plays are *Dear Brutus* (1917), *Mary Rose* (1920), and *The Boy David* (1936). In *Dear Brutus,* Barrie offers a group of disgruntled people the opportunity to change their circumstances, but everyone remains as unhappy as he was before. *Mary Rose,* a fantasy reminiscent of *Peter Pan,* is based on a Celtic legend concerning a woman who returns to

Scene from *What Every Woman Knows*, with (l. to r.) Lumsden Hare, Selene Johnson, and Patricia Collinge. [Theatre Collection, The New York Public Library at Lincoln Center, Astor, Lenox and Tilden Foundations]

her home after having lived among the fairies. *The Boy David,* Barrie's last play and totally unlike anything that preceded it, is a drama about the young David's life at the time of his slaying of Goliath.

Quality Street (1901).   Comedy set during the Napoleonic Wars, in which Phoebe and Susan Throssel, two sisters living on Quality Street, expect Mr. Valentine to propose to Miss Phoebe. But Valentine enlists and goes off to fight Napoleon. Ten years later, he returns to Quality Street. He finds the sisters teaching classes and Phoebe rapidly becoming a tired spinster. Seeing his disappointment, Phoebe finds herself impersonating an imaginary niece, Miss Livvy. Through "Livvy," Valentine realizes that he loves Phoebe, proposes to her, and assists the ladies in disposing of the now-troublesome "niece."

The Admirable Crichton (1902).   Comedy in which Crichton, the perfect butler, is appalled by the insistence of his master, Lord Loam, that his servants be treated as equals once a month. Even a return to nature, Crichton feels, would not bring equality, only a new leader. His theory is proved when Lord Loam's yacht is shipwrecked on a desert island. Crichton's ability to ensure survival earns him not only the right to govern but also the love of Loam's daughter Mary. They are about to marry when the party is rescued. Returning to England, everyone reassumes his "proper" role; and Crichton, after securing the reputation of the family, leaves its service.

Peter Pan, or The Boy Who Would Not Grow Up (1904).   Fantasy in which the fanciful Peter Pan visits the Darling household in London, where he meets Wendy and her brothers, Michael and Peter. After teaching them how to fly, he takes them back to Never-Never-Land and to the tribe of lost boys. The boys gleefully accept Wendy, who happily becomes a mother to them. But dan-

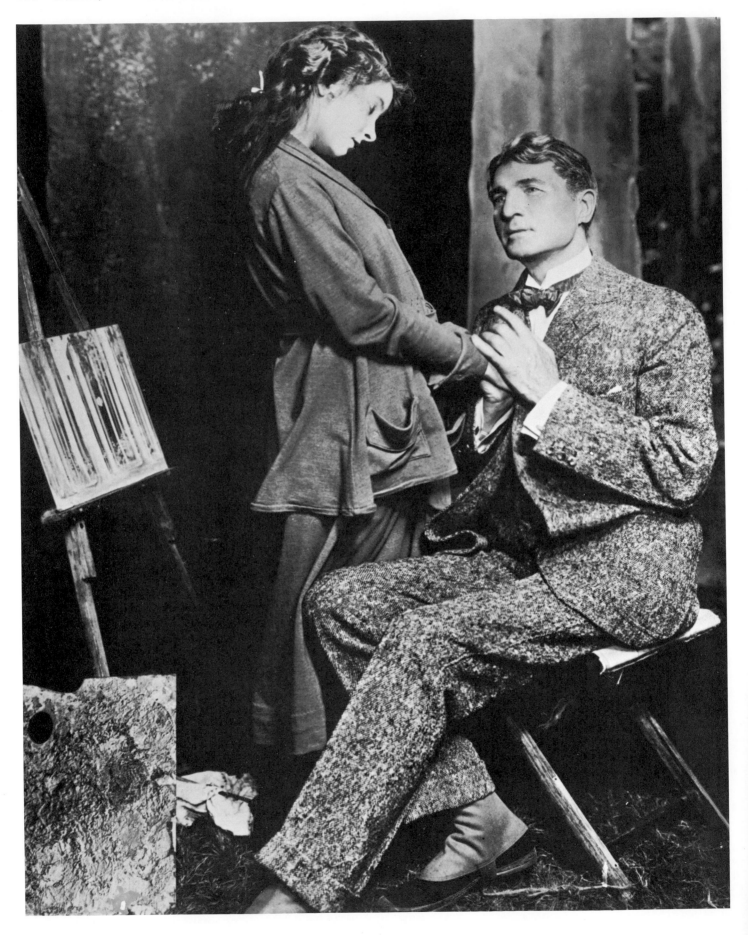

ger, in the person of the villainous Captain Hook, lurks in the background. Hook has a score to settle with Peter, for in a fight Peter had cut off Hook's arm and thrown it to a crocodile, who so enjoyed it that he has followed Hook around waiting for the rest of him. Through a dastardly ruse, Hook captures Wendy and the boys and is preparing to make them walk the plank when they are rescued by Peter. In the fight with Peter, Hook is defeated and ends by jumping into the waiting jaws of the crocodile. Wendy and her brothers then return home with the boys. She asks Peter to stay, too, but he chooses to remain a boy forever, because that is more fun.

What Every Woman Knows (1908). Comedy in which John Shand wants an education and Alick Wylie wants a husband for his daughter Maggie. So the two strike a bargain: John's education for Maggie's hand. Six years later they marry, just after John has been elected to Parliament. In London John falls in love with Lady Sybil, and Maggie forces him to make his choice between the two. John chooses Sybil. Then Maggie arranges for them to spend a month at the country house of Sybil's aunt, where John settles down to write the most important speech of his career. But his former brilliance is gone, and Sybil finds him a bore. He returns to Maggie, having learned that she has been his inspiration.

Dear Brutus (1917). Comedy in which Old Lob gathers an assorted group of men and women at his house. Outside the French windows lies a mysterious wood that offers, so Lob tells them, a magical second chance, the opportunity to relive their lives. One by one the guests venture into the wood. With each, the what-might-have-been happens. Each person in turn destroys his second chance, as surely as he destroyed the first. They return to the drawing room, to reality, and to their old lives, presumably with a better understanding of themselves. The title is taken from Shakespeare's *Julius Caesar:*

The fault, dear Brutus, is not in our stars,
But in ourselves, that we are underlings.

PLAYS

Unless otherwise noted, the plays were first performed in London.

1. *Caught Napping.* Comedy, 1 act. Published 1883.
2. *Becky Sharp.* Play, 1 act. Produced Terry's Theatre, 1891.

(Opposite) *Dear Brutus,* with Helen Hayes and William Gillette. New York, Empire Theatre, 1918. [Theatre Collection, The New York Public Library at Lincoln Center, Astor, Lenox and Tilden Foundations]

3. (With H. B. Marriott Wilson). *Richard Savage.* Drama, 4 acts. Published 1891. Produced Criterion Theatre, Apr. 16, 1891.
4. *Ibsen's Ghost, or Toole up to Date.* Burlesque, 1 act. Published 1939. Produced Toole's Theatre, May 30, 1891.
5. *Walker, London.* Comedy. Published 1907. Produced Toole's Theatre, Feb. 25, 1892.
6. *The Professor's Love Story.* Comedy. Published 1942. Produced New York, Star Theatre, Dec. 19, 1892; London, Comedy Theatre, June 25, 1894.
7. (With Arthur Conan Doyle). *Jane Annie, or The Good Conduct Prize.* Comic opera. Published 1893. Produced Savoy Theatre, May 13, 1893. Music: Ernest Ford.
8. *The Little Minister.* Comedy. Published 1942. Produced Haymarket Theatre, Nov. 6, 1897. Adapted from Barrie's novel.
9. *The Wedding Guest.* Comedy. Published 1900. Produced Garrick Theatre, Sept. 27, 1900.
10. *Quality Street.* Comedy. Published 1913. Produced Toledo, Ohio, 1901.
11. *The Admirable Crichton.* Fantasy. Published 1914. Produced Duke of York's Theatre, Nov. 4, 1902.
12. *Little Mary.* Uncomfortable play. Published 1942. Produced Wyndham's Theatre, Sept. 24, 1903.
13. *Peter Pan, or The Boy Who Would Not Grow Up.* Fairy play. Published 1928. Produced Duke of York's Theatre, Dec. 27, 1904.
14. *Alice-Sit-by-the-Fire.* Comedy. Published 1919. Produced Duke of York's Theatre, Apr. 5, 1905.
15. *Pantaloon.* Play, 1 act. Published 1914. Produced Duke of York's Theatre, Apr. 5, 1905.
16. *Josephine.* Political extravaganza. Produced Comedy Theatre, Apr. 6, 1906.
17. *Punch.* Toy tragedy, 1 act. Produced Comedy Theatre, Apr. 6, 1906.
18. *What Every Woman Knows.* Comedy. Published 1918. Produced Duke of York's Theatre, Sept. 3, 1908.
19. *Old Friends.* Play, 1 act. Published 1928. Produced Duke of York's Theatre, Mar. 1, 1910.
20. *The Twelve-Pound Look.* Comedy, 1 act. Published 1914. Produced Duke of York's Theatre, Mar. 1, 1910.
21. *A Slice of Life.* Play, 1 act. Produced Duke of York's Theatre, June 7, 1910.
22. *Rosalind.* Comedy, 1 act. Published 1914. Produced Duke of York's Theatre, Oct. 14, 1912.
23. *The Adored One (The Legend of Leonora).* Comedy. Produced Duke of York's Theatre, Sept. 4, 1913.
24. *The Will.* Comedy, 1 act. Published 1914. Produced Duke of York's Theatre, Sept. 4, 1913.
25. *Half an Hour.* Play, 1 act. Published 1928. Produced Hippodrome, Sept. 29, 1913.
26. *The Dramatists Get What They Want.* Sketch. Included in the revue *Hello Ragtime!* Produced 1913.
27. *Der Tag, or The Tragic Man.* Play. Published 1914. Produced London Coliseum, Dec. 21, 1914.
28. *The New Word.* Play, 1 act. Published 1918. Produced Duke of York's Theatre, Mar. 22, 1915.
29. *Rosy Rapture, the Pride of the Beauty Chorus.* Burlesque. Produced Duke of York's Theatre, Mar. 22, 1915. Music: Herman Darewski, Jerome Kern, and John Crook.
30. *A Kiss for Cinderella.* Fancy. Published 1920. Produced Wyndham's Theatre, Mar. 16, 1916.
31. *The Old Lady Shows Her Medals.* Play. 1 act. Published 1918. Produced New Theatre, Apr. 7, 1917.
32. *Seven Women.* Play, 1 act. Published 1928. Produced New Theatre, Apr. 7, 1917.
33. *Dear Brutus.* Comedy. Published 1923. Produced Wyndham's Theatre, Oct. 17, 1917.
34. *A Well-Remembered Voice.* Play, 1 act. Published 1918. Produced Wyndham's Theatre, June. 28, 1918.
35. *Echoes of the War.* Play. Produced 1918.
36. *Barbara's Wedding.* Play, 1 act. Published 1918. Produced Savoy Theatre, Aug. 23, 1927.
37. *The Truth About the Russian Dancers.* Play. Produced Coliseum, Mar. 16, 1920.

38. *Mary Rose.* Play. Published 1924. Produced Haymarket Theatre, Apr. 22, 1920.

39. *Shall We Join the Ladies?* Play, 1 act. Published 1927. Produced Royal Academy of Dramatic Art, Dec. 19, 1921.

40. *The Two Shepherds.* Biblical drama. Produced 1936.

41. *The Boy David.* Biblical drama. Published 1938. Produced His Majesty's Theatre, Dec. 14, 1936.

EDITIONS

Collections.
Representative Plays, Scribner, New York, 1954.
Individual Plays.
The Admirable Crichton. Published in *Favorite Modern Plays,* ed. by F. Sper, Globe Book, New York, 1953; *Representative Modern Plays,* ed. by R. Warnock, Scott, Foresman, Chicago, 1953; *Drama II,* ed. by C. E. Redmond, Macmillan, New York, 1962.
Dear Brutus. Published in *A Quarto of Modern Literature,* ed. by L. S. Brown and P. G. Perrin, Scribner, New York, 1935; *Contemporary Drama: European, English and Irish, American Plays,* ed. by E. B. Watson and B. Pressey, Scribner, New York, 1941; *Masterpieces of the Modern English Theatre,* ed. by R. W. Corrigan, Collier Books, New York, 1967.
The Little Minister. Grosset & Dunlap, New York, 1959.
What Every Woman Knows. Published in *Sixteen Famous British Plays,* ed. by B. A. Cerf and V. H. Cartmell, Garden City, New York, 1942.

CRITICISM

H. M. Walbrook, *J. M. Barrie and the Theatre,* Port Washington, N.Y., 1922; B. D. Cutler, *Sir James M. Barrie: A Bibliography with Full Collations of the American Unauthorized Editions,* New York, 1931; W. A. Darlington, *J. M. Barrie,* London, 1938; J. A. Roy, *James Matthew Barrie,* New York, 1938; R. L. Green, *J. M. Barrie,* New York, 1961; M. Elder, *The Young James Barrie,* New York, 1968.

Philip Barry
(1896 – 1949)

Philip James Quinn Barry, American dramatist, was born in Rochester, N.Y., on June 18, 1896, the third son of James Barry, a wealthy Irish businessman. The next year his father died, without mentioning his infant son in his will. The state of New York, however, claimed in the child's behalf a share of the inheritance, which eventually was to grow beyond the value of the whole estate. Barry described this unusual situation in his play *The Youngest* (1924).

Barry received his early education in both Roman Catholic and secular schools; in 1913 he entered Yale University, where he contributed to the newspaper and literary magazine. Rejected for military service during World War I, Barry left Yale in his senior year to work in the U.S. Department of State, serving at home and abroad. By the time he returned to Yale in 1919 his burgeoning interest in the theatre led him to join the Dramatic Club, for which he wrote a one-act play entitled *Autonomy.* Immediately after graduation, he enrolled in Professor George Pierce Baker's famous 47 Workshop, a course in playwrighting and production at Harvard University. He considered the workshop invaluable training; during his apprenticeship under Baker he wrote the play *A Punch for Judy,* which was produced in New York in 1921, partly through the efforts of Robert Sherwood. *See* BAKER, GEORGE PIERCE; SHERWOOD, ROBERT E.

In 1920 Barry left Harvard to work for an advertising firm, and during this period he married Ellen Marshall Semple. After writing *Jilts,* a play in which a young man faces the problem of giving up the prospect of financial security for the risks of becoming a dramatist, Barry himself decided to follow a career in the theatre. He returned to Harvard to see *Jilts,* produced in 1922, win the Harvard drama prize. The next year marked the beginning of Barry's long and successful theatrical career, with *Jilts* presented on Broadway as *You and I.*

During the 1920s Barry divided his time between suburban New York and Cannes, the latter providing the freedom from distraction

Philip Barry. [Courtesy of Mrs. Philip Barry]

Scene from *Holiday*. New York, Plymouth Theatre, 1928. [Theatre Collection, The New York Public Library at Lincoln Center, Astor, Lenox and Tilden Foundations]

that he needed. He continued, however, to write chiefly about Americans. *Cock Robin,* written in collaboration with Elmer Rice, was produced in New York in 1928, and there followed in the next decade eight plays, all of which had Broadway productions. The most successful, *The Philadelphia Story* (1939), was credited with saving the Theatre Guild from ruin. Barry's last five plays, written between 1940 and his death, were all produced in New York, one posthumously. He died of a heart attack in New York on December 3, 1949. *See* RICE, ELMER.

WORK

Barry, whose most successful plays are sophisticated comedies about the social elite, wrote for a generation newly concerned with the social and economic problems of the modern, urban world. His name suggests witty dialogue, amusing plots, and the high gloss usually associated with the comedy of manners, but in all his plays Barry was occupied with the universal questions of love, death, and the drive for individual fulfillment. *See* COMEDY OF MANNERS.

His early plays are comedies built on situations inspired by his own experience: *A Punch*

for Judy (1921), in which a foolish girl learns a lesson in love; *You and I* (1923), depicting the struggle between art and financial security; and *The Youngest* (1924), which deals with youthful revolt. Barry's next three plays, although financial failures, show the beginning of his interest in more complex themes: *In a Garden* (1925) is a comedy dramatizing the strong character of a girl who frees herself from both husband and lover; *White Wings* (1926), a fantasy, considers the plight of a street cleaner made obsolete by automobiles; and *John* (1927), a religious tragedy, describes the disciple's period of doubt.

But it was not until he returned to high comedy about the privileged class, in *Paris Bound* (1927), that Barry's reputation on Broadway was established, and only *Holiday* (1928) and *The Philadelphia Story* (1939) were to equal its success. Barry's two most interesting attempts at serious drama—*Hotel Universe* (1930), in which a party of Americans visiting a friend and her demented father near Toulon are carried back in memory, with the help of the father's visions, to events in their past and thus resolve their respective lives; and *Here Come the Clowns* (1938), a drama investigating man's search for spiritual truth and enlightenment—were popular failures.

Barry's remaining plays, though varied in quality, still follow the pattern of comedy laced with serious themes or dramas with comic overtones. They include *The Animal Kingdom* (1932), a comedy that focuses on the eternal triangle; *The Joyous Season* (1934), a comedy in which (as in *Hotel Universe*) one character resolves the lives of the others;

Leslie Howard and Lora Baxter in *The Animal Kingdom*. New York, Broadhurst Theatre, 1932. [Photograph by Vandamm. Theatre Collection, The New York Public Library at Lincoln Center, Astor, Lenox and Tilden Foundations]

Franchot Tone and Earle Larimore (holding fur) in *Hotel Universe.* New York, Martin Beck Theatre, 1930. [Photograph by Vandamm. Theatre Collection, The New York Public Library at Lincoln Center, Astor, Lenox and Tilden Foundations]

Bright Star (1935), a severe study of a selfish man; *Spring Dance* (1936), a farce; *Tomorrow and Tomorrow* (1931), a modern drama based on the story of Elisha and the Shunammite woman; *Liberty Jones* (1941), a political allegory; *Without Love* (1942), a political comedy about a marriage of convenience; *Foolish Notion* (1945), a fantasy; *My Name Is Aquilon*

(Opposite) Leslie Howard in *The Animal Kingdom.* New York, Broadhurst Theatre, 1932. [Photograph by Vandamm. Theatre Collection, The New York Public Library at Lincoln Center, Astor, Lenox and Tilden Foundations]

(1949), a comedy adapted from a play by Jean-Pierre Aumont; and *Second Threshold* (1951), revised by Robert Sherwood, about a disillusioned man who is saved by his daughter.

Paris Bound (1927). On their wedding day Jim and Mary Hutton, fashionable and rich, assure one another of their liberality concerning extramarital relations. They are disturbed later, however, when Jim's divorced parents reveal that, despite a similar vow, their marriage dissolved because Mrs. Hutton could not forgive her husband's involvement in a romantic affair. Years later, Mary discovers that on one of Jim's periodic trips abroad he visited an old sweetheart. Shocked, she determines to divorce him, despite her father-in-law's criticism and her own formerly tolerant views. Before Jim's return, however, Mary becomes aware of her own susceptibility to romance when a young composer whom she has befriended asserts his desire for her. By the time Jim arrives home, Mary has abandoned the idea of divorce and, convinced of his devotion, reaffirms their marital ties.

Holiday (1928).   Julia Seton, a millionaire's daughter, becomes engaged to Johnny Case, a hardworking young man who wants to enjoy himself when he is still young and work when he is older, rather than the reverse. Neither Julia nor her father can sympathize with Johnny's hopes; they plan to change his attitude by placing him in the family firm for two or three years. Linda,

Julia's nonconforming younger sister, falls in love with Johnny. Despite this, she urges him to follow his dreams. After he has left, Julia admits that she no longer cares for him, and Linda hurries away in his pursuit.

Hotel   Universe   (1930).   Experimental play in which mysticism is used to resolve the lives of a group of "lost Americans" visiting Ann Field and her father in southern France. Influenced by elderly Stephen Field and the timeless atmosphere of a small, deserted hotel, the characters reveal their pasts and decide on new futures: Lily Malone, a frustrated actress, decides to play Cordelia and forget her father; Tom and Hope Ames realize that Tom must, with Hope's support, renew his search for God; Norman Rose and Alice Kendall admit their mutual love; and Pat Farley, once Ann's lover but now guilt-stricken over another girl's death, decides to marry her. Stephen is struck by a cerebral hemorrhage, but knowing that Ann will now be happy, he

Van Heflin, Shirley Booth, and Katharine Hepburn in *The Philadelphia Story.* New York, Shubert Theatre, 1939. [Culver Pictures]

dies quietly believing he will be content in his life after death.

Here Come the Clowns (1938). Clancy, a stagehand who, after a series of misfortunes, had gone in search of God and an answer for all his suffering, returns to the Café des Artistes, which is peopled by the players from the adjoining variety theatre, symbolically called the Globe. He repudiates reports that his wife has cuckolded him, and the other vaudevillians present join him in denying truths about themselves. Max Pabst, an illusionist performing at the theatre, boasts that he can divine the truth. Out of curiosity the players, including a dwarf, a major, and a song-and-dance team, permit Pabst to stage his act. The results reveal wretched details from their pasts that torment their present existence. Clancy at last confronts his misery and believes that he has found, in Mr. Concannon, mysterious owner of the Globe, the God for whom he has been searching. Mr. Concannon's cynicism, however, reveals him as Pabst in disguise, and Clancy decides that it is man, not God, who is responsible for man's fate. Then, when Dickinson, a press agent, unable to bear Pabst's probing, tries to shoot him, Clancy interposes himself. He dies believing he has finally found the truth: the potential for good or evil exists in man's free will.

The Philadelphia Story (1939). Tracy Lord has divorced her husband, playboy Dexter Haven, because of his excessive drinking, and is about to marry the self-made but boorish George Kittredge. Mike, a newspaper reporter with some knowledge of the private lives of the Lords, has elicited permission to cover the wedding with his photographer as an inducement to keep Tracy's father's philanderings out of the press. Dexter arrives uninvited, and it becomes evident that Tracy is not indifferent to him. The evening before the wedding she gets drunk and, after swimming with Mike, collapses in his arms. George, seeing them together, concludes that Tracy has been unfaithful to him and stalks off to compose a note of regret. When Mike reveals the truth, George returns; but Tracy, angry at his prudery, will not have him, despite the fact that the wedding guests are waiting. Dexter decides to take George's place, and Tracy is finally content.

PLAYS

Unless otherwise noted, the plays were first performed in New York.

1. *A Punch for Judy.* Comedy, 3 acts. Written 1920. Produced Morosco Theatre, Apr. 18, 1921.
2. *You and I.* Comedy, 3 acts. Written 1922. Published 1925. Produced Belmont Theatre, Feb. 19, 1923. Original title: *Jilts.*
3. *The Youngest.* Comedy, 3 acts. Written 1922. Published 1925. Produced Gaiety Theatre, Dec. 22, 1924.
4. *In a Garden.* Comedy, 3 acts. Written 1925. Published 1926. Produced Plymouth Theatre, Nov. 16, 1925.
5. *White Wings.* Fantastic comedy, 4 acts. Written 1926. Published 1927. Produced Booth Theatre, Oct. 15, 1926.
6. *John.* Play, 5 scenes. Written 1927. Published 1929. Produced Klaw Theatre, Nov. 2, 1927.
7. *Paris Bound.* Comedy, 3 acts. Written 1927. Published 1929. Produced Music Box Theatre, Dec. 27, 1927.
8. (With Elmer Rice). *Cock Robin.* Comedy drama, 3 acts. Written 1928. Published 1929. Produced Forty-eighth Street Theatre, Jan. 12, 1928.
9. *Holiday.* Comedy, 3 acts. Written 1928. Published 1929. Produced Plymouth Theatre, Nov. 26, 1928.
10. *Hotel Universe.* Psychological drama, 1 long act. Written 1929. Published 1930. Produced Martin Beck Theatre, Apr. 14, 1930.
11. *Tomorrow and Tomorrow.* Drama, 3 acts. Written 1930. Published 1931. Produced Henry Miller's Theatre, Jan. 13, 1931.
12. *The Animal Kingdom.* Comedy, 3 acts. Written 1931. Published 1932. Produced Broadhurst Theatre, Jan. 12, 1932.
13. *The Joyous Season.* Comedy, 3 acts. Written 1932. Published 1934. Produced Belasco Theatre, Jan. 20, 1934.
14. *Bright Star.* Play, 3 acts. Produced Empire Theatre, Oct. 15, 1935.
15. (Adaptation). *Spring Dance.* Comedy, 3 acts. Written 1936. Published 1936. Produced Empire Theatre, Aug. 25, 1936. Based on a play by Eleanor Golden and Eloise Barrangon.
16. *Here Come the Clowns.* Drama, 3 acts. Written 1937. Published 1939. Produced Booth Theatre, Dec. 7, 1938.
17. *The Philadelphia Story.* Comedy, 3 acts. Written 1939. Published 1939. Produced Shubert Theatre, Mar. 28, 1939.
18. *Liberty Jones.* Allegory, 2 acts. Written 1941. Published 1941. Produced Shubert Theatre, Feb. 5, 1941.
19. *Without Love.* Comedy, 3 acts. Written 1941. Published 1943. Produced St. James Theatre, Nov. 10, 1942.
20. *Foolish Notion.* Comedy, 3 acts. Written 1944. Produced Martin Beck Theatre, Mar. 13, 1945.
21. (Adaptation). *My Name Is Aquilon.* Comedy, 2 acts. Written 1946. Produced Lyceum Theatre, Feb. 9, 1949. Based on Jean-Pierre Aumont's *L'empereur de Chine.*
22. (Revised by Robert Sherwood). *Second Threshold.* Play, 2 acts. Written 1947. Published 1951. Produced Morosco Theatre, Jan. 2, 1951.

EDITIONS

The Animal Kingdom. French, New York, 1931; also published in *Twenty Best Plays of the Modern American Theatre,* ed. by J. Gassner, Crown, New York, 1939.
Cock Robin. French, New York, 1929.
Here Come the Clowns. Coward-McCann, New York, 1939; also published in *Best American Plays,* ed. by J. Gassner, Crown, New York, 1961.
Holiday. French, New York, 1929; also published in *Comparative Comedies Present and Past,* ed. by R. K. Keyes and H. M. Roth, Noble, New York, 1935; *Famous American Plays of the 1920s,* ed. by K. Macgowan, Dell, New York, 1959; *Three Plays about Marriage,* ed. by J. E. Mersand, Washington Square, New York, 1962; *Representative American Dramas, National and Local,* ed. by M. J. Moses and J. W. Krutch, rev. ed., Little, Brown, Boston, 1941.
Hotel Universe. French, New York, 1930; also published in *Contemporary Drama: American Plays,* ed. by E. B. Watson and B. Pressey, Scribner, New York, 1931; *Plays for the College Theater,* ed. by G. H. Leverton, French, New York, 1934; *Representative Modern Dramas,* ed. by C. H. Whitman, Macmillan, New York, 1936; *The Theatre Guild Anthology,* Random House, New York, 1936.
In a Garden. Doran, New York, 1926; French, New York, 1926; also published in *Modern American and British Plays,* ed. by S. M. Tucker, Harper, New York, 1931; *Twenty-five Modern Plays,* ed. by S. M. Tucker, Harper, New York, 1931.
John. French, New York, 1929.
The Joyous Season. French, New York, 1935; also published in *Modern American Drama,* ed. by Sister Mary Agnes David, Macmillan, New York, 1961.
Liberty Jones. Coward-McCann, New York, 1943.
Paris Bound. French, New York, 1929; also published in *Twenty-five Best Plays of the Modern American Theatre,* ed. by J. Gassner, Crown, New York, 1949; *Representative American Plays from 1767 to the Present Day,* ed. by A. H. Quinn, 7th ed., rev. and enl., Appleton-Century-Crofts, New York, 1953.
The Philadelphia Story. French, New York, 1938; Coward-McCann, New York, 1939; also published in *Best Plays of the Modern American Theatre,* ed. by J. Gassner, 2d ser., Crown, New York, 1947; *Literature for Our Time,* ed. by L. S. Brown, H. O. Waite, and B. P. Atkinson, Holt, New York, 1947, 1953; *Literature for Our Time,* ed. by H. O. Waite and B. P. Atkinson, Holt, New York, 1958.
Second Threshold. Harper, New York, 1951.
Spring Dance. French, New York, 1936.
Tomorrow and Tomorrow. French, New York, 1931.
White Wings. Boni, New York, 1927; French, New York, 1929.
Without Love. Coward-McCann, New York, 1943.
You and I. Brentano, New York, 1923; French, New York, 1929; also published in *American Plays,* ed. by A. G. Halline, American Book, New York, 1935.
The Youngest. French, New York, 1925.

CRITICISM

J. P. Roppolo, *Philip Barry,* New York, 1965.

BASSANO, Enrico (b. Genoa, August 13, 1899). Italian dramatist and theatre critic whose plays reflect a leaning toward fantasy and symbolism at the expense of everyday reality. *One Sang for All (Uno cantava per tutti,* 1948) concerns two murderers whose past violence absolves them of their individual crimes and whose death is a sacrifice that may atone for the sins of all mankind. *Like a Thief in the Night (Come un ladro di notte,* 1953), a forceful antiwar statement, is an allegory in which a Christ figure is symbolically crucified by those whose hopes for a bet-

Enrico Bassano. [Federico Arborio Mella, Milan]

ter life are left unfulfilled. *The Rebellious Pelican* (*Il Pellicano ribelle,* 1953) deals with the fatal and uncomprehending condemnation by a brother and sister of their father, whose indifference has led their mother to embark upon an adulterous relationship.

Like a Thief in the Night (*Come un ladro di notte,* 1953). Set in a post-World War II gun emplacement atop a mountain, this allegorical drama of man's perpetual fall from grace centers upon the mysterious figure of the Man, a modern hermit who has retreated from the world untold years earlier. He is confronted by a number of lost, frightened, and victimized souls in flight from the valley below: two young veterans of the recent war; the proprietor of a brothel; a prostitute; a man and his wife running away from the nightmare of enemy soldiers who had raped her and tormented by the imminent birth of a child whose father is therefore indeterminable; and a salesman of toy weapons driven insane by his miraculous and undeserved escape from a firing squad. The salesman describes the end of the world as he imagines it about to take place and for which he feels personally responsible; the others are terrified by his apocalyptic vision but nevertheless believe him. Kneeling before the saintly figure of the Man, whom they have accepted

as Christ returned for the Apocalypse, they confess their sinful lives. The following morning, however, the earth remains unchanged. In a burst of savage temper, they turn on the Man, thinking that he has duped them, and attempt to crucify him. Save for the new mother, they all leave the mountaintop at the end. She, who has given birth and now holds up her infant, begs the Man's blessing for it.

BATAILLE, Henri (b. Nîmes, April 14, 1872; d. Malmaison, March 2, 1922). French poet and dramatist whose works are in the boulevard tradition of Georges de Porto-Riche's "theatre of love." His theoretical writings on drama stress the importance of revealing underlying truths by the use of indirect or unexpressed language, and so were highly influential on the "school of silence" represented by Jean-Jacques Bernard and Denys Amiel. In his own plays, however, the dialogue tends to be direct, declamatory, and often bombastic. His works feature psychological studies of women dominated by strong amorous passions. In *Maman Colibri* (1904), a middle-aged woman, nicknamed Maman Colibri (hummingbird) because of her ingenuousness, becomes the mistress of her son's friend. Faced with the evidence of her adultery, she proclaims her right to love and follows her lover to Algeria, where, after a few weeks of happiness, she realizes that he has tired of her. Accepting her fate as an "older woman," she returns to France and takes up her role as a grandmother. In *The Wedding March* (*La marche nuptiale,* 1905), a

Henri Bataille. [Theatre Collection, The New York Public Library at Lincoln Center, Astor, Lenox and Tilden Foundations]

romantic girl runs off with her piano teacher, only to find that she has bound herself to an essentially mediocre man. She commits suicide when she realizes that her pregnancy makes it impossible for her to leave him. *Poliche* (1906) presents a hero desperately in love with a woman who does not know her own heart and therefore repeatedly deserts him. *The Naked Woman* (*La femme nue*, 1908) focuses on the heartbreak of a woman deserted by her artist husband when success gives him an entree into a more fashionable world. *The Torches* (*Les flambeaux*, 1912) presents a hero whose devotion to science is troubled by the love of an ardent younger woman.

In the years following World War I, Bataille altered his themes somewhat and began to explore the relation between emotions and ideas in the trilogy made up of *The Amazon* (*L'amazone*, 1916), *The Animator* (*L'animateur*, 1920), and *Human Flesh* (*La chair humaine*, 1922). A satiric examination of a latter-day Don Juan is made in *The Man with the Rose* (*L'homme à la rose*, 1920), which shows the hero's powers of seduction to be completely dependent on the legend built up around him. Bataille's last two plays, *Tenderness* (*La tendresse*, 1921) and *Possession* (*La possession*, 1921), are explorations of the nature and power of sexual passion.

Poliche (1906). Deeply in love with Rosine, a rich widow, Poliche cynically takes to drink when she deserts him for the more attractive Saint-Vast. However, when Rosine is in turn deserted by Saint-Vast, she returns to Poliche, whose truly good nature has been revealed to her by one of his friends. The couple live quietly in the country until Rosine learns that Saint-Vast is once more available. Because he places his love for her above his personal happiness, Poliche gives her up. Rosine, unaware that it is Poliche she truly loves, leaves him again, probably only to discover that she has once more made a poor choice. Produced Paris, Comédie-Parisienne, December 10, 1906.

The Naked Woman (*La femme nue*, 1908). Bernier, an artist, wins fame and fortune with a nude painting of Lolette, his model and mistress during the years of poverty and struggle. In a burst of gratitude he marries her, and for a short time they are happy. But success makes available to Bernier a brilliant social world in which Lolette is ill at ease. He falls in love with a wealthy woman and asks Lolette for a divorce. Heartbroken, Lolette attempts suicide, and Bernier, overcome by remorse, decides to remain with her. Realizing that he does so only out of pity, Lolette runs off with a former lover. Produced Paris, Théâtre de la Renaissance, February 27, 1908.

BAX, Clifford (1886–1962). British dramatist, one of the founders of the Phoenix Society (1919–1926) and president of the Incorporated Stage Society. His plays include *The Poetasters of Ispahan* (1912); *The Marriage of the Soul* (1913); *Shakespeare* (1921), written in collaboration with Harold Rubinstein; *Polly* (1922), adapted from John Gay's opera of the same name; *The Insect Play* (1923), adapted from Karel Čapek's *From the Insect World* in collaboration with Nigel Playfair; *Midsummer Madness* (1924); *Up Stream* (1925); *Mr. Pepys* (1926); *Rasputin* (1929); *Socrates* (1929); *The Venetian* (1930); *The Immortal Lady* (1930); *The Rose Without a Thorn* (1932); *April in August* (1934); *The House of Borgia* (1935); *Golden Eagle* (1946); *The Buddha* (1947); and *A Day, a Night, and a Morrow* (1948). He also wrote several books on the theatre, including *Whither the Theatre. . .?* (1945) and *All the World's a Stage* (1949).

Pierre de Beaumarchais
(1732 – 1799)

Pierre de Beaumarchais, French dramatist, was born Pierre-Augustin Caron in Paris on January 24, 1732, one of ten children of André-Charles Caron, a clockmaker, and the former Louise-Nicole Pichon. He had little schooling but learned some Latin while attending a trade school in Alfortville. His family loved music, and as a child he developed his remarkable musical faculties, learning to play the violin, flute, and harp. His earliest employment was as a clockmaker in his father's shop, where he devised a system of regulating watches that earned him a patent from the French Academy of Sciences in 1754. The same year he presented himself at court, where his sale of a watch to Mme. de Pompadour won him the notice of King Louis XV.

In 1755 he purchased an annuity from a retiring court clerk, M. Franquet, thus gaining an official position at court. A year later, when Franquet died, Beaumarchais married his widow. In 1757 she died, leaving him a small property from which he took the name Beaumarchais. By now a court favorite, he was called upon to give music lessons to the King's daughters, to organize concerts, and to compose music for special occasions. During this time he became friendly with Joseph Paris-Duverney, financier and adviser to

Mme. de Pompadour, who initiated him into the world of high finance. By 1761 Beaumarchais was rich enough to buy the post of King's Secretary, which carried a title with it.

While in Spain on a financial mission for Paris-Duverney in 1764, Beaumarchais decided to resign his post and remain in Madrid, intending to devote himself to court and financial intrigues and to literature. He returned to Paris in 1767 to present *Eugénie,* his first play, and to make a serious attempt to launch a literary career.

In 1768 Beaumarchais married Geneviève-Madeleine Wattebled Lévêque, a widow, who died suddenly in 1770. *The Two Friends, or The Merchant of Lyons* (*Les deux amis, ou Le négociant de Lyon*) was presented the same year. A few months later Paris-Duverney died, and Beaumarchais sued his heir, the Count de la Blache, for money owed him by the estate. This began a succession of trials, judgments, appeals, and scandals lasting four years and bringing Beaumarchais temporary legal punishment but final exoneration, a felicity usually attributed to his four *Mémoires* (1773–1774), brilliant and popularly successful polemics challenging the unfair and corrupt decision against him.

Eager to ingratiate himself with the King once again, Beaumarchais volunteered to undertake a mission to London for the purpose of suppressing pamphlets libeling the French monarchy. With the death of Louis XV in May, 1774, and the accession of Louis XVI, new libelous publications sent Beaumarchais on similar missions to Amsterdam and again to London. Late in 1775, the same year that *The Barber of Seville, or The Useless Precaution* (*Le barbier de Séville, ou La précaution inutile*) was produced, Beaumarchais persuaded the King to aid the American rebels; by 1776 the dramatist, now firmly reinstated at court, was active in court operations that supplied arms to the American colonies. He also sent eleven of his own merchant ships to assist the new United States in its struggle against Great Britain.

Beaumarchais wrote *The Marriage of Figaro, or The Madness of a Day* (*La folle journée, ou Le mariage de Figaro*) during this period, but the King's declaration that the play was indecent caused its production to be postponed until 1784; even then the author paid for its appearance with a brief confinement in prison. After Voltaire died in 1778, Beaumarchais purchased his banned works and published them abroad (1785–1789). In 1785 he became one of the founders of the Water Company of Paris. In 1786 he took a third wife, Marie-Thérèse Willermaulas, who had borne him a daughter, Eugénie. He also wrote

Pierre de Beaumarchais. [New York Public Library Picture Collection]

his libretto for *Tarare,* which was presented in 1787 with music by Antonio Salieri. The same year he became involved in another lawsuit, which he eventually won, though not without damage to his reputation. *See* VOLTAIRE.

Through Figaro, his most famous character, Beaumarchais celebrated the irrepressible common man while satirizing an effete aristocracy. Beaumarchais's role in the founding of the first States-General for Dramatic Literature, in 1777 — an action springing from his dissatisfaction with the remuneration he received from the actors who had presented *The Barber of Seville* in 1775 — also revealed his revolutionary spirit. The organization, renamed the Société des Auteurs, enforced literary rights for authors and was given legal authority in 1791 by the revolutionary government. Nevertheless, as a titled and wealthy financier who had performed diplomatic services for two French kings, Beaumarchais stood in a somewhat precarious position with the new regime. Despite his writings and numerous liberal activities, his overall career and wealth provoked considerable antipathy among the new elite.

Beaumarchais's joy at the convocation of the States-General in 1789 turned to dread as the revolution continued. In 1792 he was charged mistakenly with storing weapons and was subsequently dispatched to the Abbaye Prison. After a brief incarceration he fled through England and Holland to Hamburg, where he settled as an *émigré*. Meanwhile, his family was imprisoned and his property seized. In 1796, two years after Robespierre's death, he returned to France and rejoined his family, now freed. His demand for the restoration of his property elicited no sympathetic response, and he was left destitute. Beaumarchais died of a stroke in Paris on May 17, 1799.

WORK

Although writing plays was but one facet of Beaumarchais's many-sided genius, in his best works he managed to synthesize the best elements of three comic traditions: the comedy of manners, of intrigue, and of character. Into this amalgam went an astringent dash of political satire, with the result that Beaumarchais figures as a transitional dramatist, grounded in the theatre of Molière and the *commedia dell'arte* but anticipating, from his distinctly critical approach, a more serious drama. His reputation as a dramatist, however, is due to his light touch, master-

ful construction, and sure comic flair. *See* COMEDY OF MANNERS; COMMEDIA DELL'ARTE; MOLIÈRE.

It was purely for fun that Beaumarchais wrote his first plays, slight entertainments called *Parades* (1760–1765?), which were performed privately at the home of Charles Lenormand d'Étoiles, husband of Mme. de Pompadour, before reaching the public at the Théâtre de la Foire. Little burlesques, or farces, these rather daring sketches were written in dialect, sprinkled with ribald verses, and designed for sheer amusement. One of them provided the basis for *The Barber of Seville*. A more serious intent lay behind Beaumarchais's full-length drama *Eugénie* (1767), in which he drew on his own sister's seduction and subsequent jilting to attack the rather cavalier manner of some members of the nobility with women of the middle and lower classes. Although Beaumarchais had given the play an English setting, certain noblemen protested its production; because of the growing influence of newspapers the matter soon became a European *cause*

Scene from *Le barbier de Séville.* [French Cultural Services]

célèbre. The dramatist went on to write *The Two Friends* (1770), another serious drama, but owing to its bourgeois tone and vaporous sentimentality it met with little success.

In his supreme theatrical achievements, *The Barber of Seville* (1775) and *The Marriage of Figaro* (wr. 1775/78, prod. 1784), Beaumarchais deployed an extraordinary constellation of characters in elaborate and witty entanglements, all presided over by his consummate comic persona, Figaro. Animating the intricate machinery of plot by his shrewd mind and quick tongue, Figaro masks beneath his frivolous surface a deeply sensitive intelligence. The embodiment of common sense, he possesses perspective and acute self-awareness. During the course of the two plays, the sprightly barber matures into an articulate spokesman of the common man's aspirations and resentment of privilege, and his famous monologue in *The Marriage* clearly announces the French Revolution. These comedies soar above the typical comedy of manners from which they derive. *Frailty and Hypocrisy* (*La mère coupable, ou L'autre Tartuffe*, 1792), also translated as *The Other Tartuffe, or The Guilty Mother*, completes the Figaro trilogy and concerns events occurring twenty years after those in the first two plays. In it, however, wit is replaced by sentiment, and invention by elaborate contrivance. Rossini's *The Barber of Seville* (1816) and Mozart's *The Marriage of Figaro* (1786) are brilliant operatic renditions that have contributed much to the perennial popularity of the two original comedies. Beaumarchais himself wrote a historical tragedy, *Tarare* (1787), which he hoped would be used as a libretto by Christoph Gluck. It was, however, set to music by Antonio Salieri and, having met with some success, continued to be performed until the middle of the nineteenth century.

Eugénie (1767). Melodrama set in London at the house of the Count of Clarendon, who has had his steward perform a ceremony secretly "wedding" him to Eugénie against her father's wishes. The fraudulent marriage was intended to permit the count to keep Eugénie's love and nevertheless be free to marry the woman chosen for him by his uncle. However, the steward repents his part in the scheme and sends a letter of confession to Eugénie's aunt. The count's efforts to conceal his duplicity fail. When Eugénie realizes that she is not legally the count's wife, she all but dies of shame. Eventually the count abandons his plans to marry another, Eugénie's father forgives her, and the way is clear for a genuine marriage. The plot of this play was inspired by an unfortunate incident in the life of Beaumarchais's sister.

The Two Friends, or The Merchant of Lyons (*Les deux amis, ou Le négociant de Lyon*, 1770). Drama in which two old friends, Melac and Aurelly, try in mutual secrecy to save one another from impending financial disgrace. Complicating their predicaments is a triangular love affair involving Aurelly's niece Pauline (who is eventually revealed to be his daughter), Melac's son, and Saint-Alban, a man to whom Aurelly owes money. Through the intervention of a countinghouse clerk named Dabins, the two friends are saved from scandal, their moves to assist each other are revealed, and Pauline is freed of Saint-Alban's suit.

The Barber of Seville, or The Useless Precaution (*Le barbier de Séville, ou La précaution inutile*, 1775). Comedy set in Seville. Count Almaviva is in love with Rosina, the ward of Dr. Bartholo, who plans to marry the girl himself. Almaviva enlists the aid of Figaro, Bartholo's barber, and is introduced into the house as Lindor, a soldier seeking lodgings. Before being driven off by the suspicious Bartholo, Almaviva manages to slip Rosina a love letter that wins her heart. With Figaro's help, Almaviva next appears at the house as the student Alonzo and claims to have been sent by Rosina's music teacher Don Bazile. On Don Bazile's sudden appearance, the count and Figaro are forced to flee. When Bartholo learns that Alonzo is an impostor, he arranges with Don Bazile to have a notary come and marry him to Rosina immediately. He then convinces the girl that Lindor-Alonzo actually means to abduct her for the "notorious" Count Almaviva. Unaware that Lindor-Alonzo is actually Count Almaviva, the terrified girl agrees to marry Bartholo and confesses that her lover has planned to carry her off that very night. Later, when Almaviva and Figaro enter her room by means of a ladder, she learns her lover's true identity and faints. Meanwhile, Bartholo removes the ladder and goes for the police. At this point Don Bazile appears with a notary ready to marry Rosina to Bartholo. Figaro cleverly convinces the notary that he has been summoned to marry Rosina and Almaviva, and Don Bazile is bribed into witnessing the contract. By the time Bartholo bursts in with the police, the ceremony is over. Bartholo is prevented from taking legal action against Almaviva by the threat of an investigation into his handling of Rosina's finances. As the play ends, Figaro tells Bartholo that an old man's precautions are no match for youth and love.

The Marriage of Figaro, or The Madness of a Day (*La folle journée, ou Le mariage de Figaro*; wr. 1775/78, prod. 1784). Comedy that reunites the characters of *The Barber of*

La folle journée, ou Le mariage de Figaro. Paris, Comédie-Française, 1946. [French Cultural Services]

Seville three years after Figaro has helped Count Almaviva marry Rosina, the ward of Dr. Bartholo. The fickle count now has designs on Suzanne, maid of Countess Almaviva (Rosina) and the betrothed of Figaro. Suspicious, Figaro resists Almaviva's attempts to send him off as a messenger to France. Figaro also has to find some way of getting out of a contract by which he has engaged either to pay his debts to Almaviva's old housekeeper Marceline or to marry her. Meanwhile, Almaviva discovers that his adolescent page Chérubin is in love with the countess and orders him to join his regiment, but the lovesick page does not.

Figaro sends Almaviva an anonymous letter telling him his wife is entertaining a lover. When Almaviva bursts in on the countess, Chérubin has already fled through the window and Almaviva is forced to beg his wife's pardon for his unjust suspicions. In order to win Almaviva's consent to her marriage, Suzanne has agreed to a tryst with him. However, unknown to Figaro, she has arranged with the countess to trick the count, who while Figaro looks on from hiding, woos his own wife, who has disguised herself as Suzanne. In a jealous rage, Figaro tries to make love to a woman he thinks is the countess but who turns out to be Suzanne in disguise. When he is slapped for his pains, he discovers that Suzanne has been true to him all along. As for Almaviva, when his wife discloses her disguise, he is sheepishly forced into admitting his dishonest intentions and agreeing to the marriage of Suzanne and Figaro.

In a subplot development, Figaro is freed of his obligation to Marceline when court records reveal that he is actually her illegitimate son and that Bartholo is his father. The latter is forced to marry Marceline, who now claims that it was the call of blood that attracted her to Figaro.

In a famous monologue, Figaro ruefully comments on feudal abuses of the common people, forecasting the coming revolution and the demise of the corrupt aristocracy.

Tarare (1787).   Opera, with music by Antonio Salieri, whose theme is that man's greatness depends not on rank but on character. The story concerns a Persian tyrant who attempts to seduce the wife of a soldier. The tyrant is killed, and the soldier becomes the ruler in his place. The play, written allegorically in the style popular at the time of the French Revolution, is critical of both the nobility and the church and lauds the revolution in a last act that was added after 1789.

Frailty and Hypocrisy; also ***The Other Tartuffe, or The Guilty Mother*** (*La mère coupable, ou L'autre Tartuffe,* 1792).   The chief characters of *The Barber of Seville* and *The Marriage of Figaro* are revisited twenty years later in a sentimental play intended to show Count Almaviva's transformation into a kindly man. The story concerns Florestine, Almaviva's illegitimate daughter, and Léon, illegitimate son of Countess Almaviva and Chérubin. (Chérubin is dead, having been killed in battle long ago.) The secrets of their births have been discovered by Bégearss, a latter-day Tartuffe, who tries to blackmail Almaviva into giving him Florestine's hand in marriage along with her fortune. He also tells Léon and Florestine, who love each other, that they are brother and sister. Figaro, aided by Suzanne, explains the situation, thereby reuniting the young couple and preserving the count's fortune. The count and the countess, equally guilty of infidelities, resolve to forgive and forget the past in the light of the joyous present.

Parades (1760–1765?).   Only five of these short verse plays have been preserved. *Colin et Colette* is a brief dialogue intended as a compliment to accompany the presentation of a bouquet of flowers. *The Seven-league Boots* (*Les bottes de sept lieues*) contains the story of two lovers who outwit their obtuse parents to gain their own ends. *The Deputies from Les Halles and Gros-Caillou* (*Les députés de la Halle et du Gros-Caillou*) is another brief compliment, in fishwife's slang, meant to accompany a gift of fish. *Leander, Relics Seller, Doctor and Flower Seller* (*Léandre, marchand d'agnus, médecin et bouquetier*) and *Stupid John at the Fair* (*Jean bête à la foire*) both tell the same story in similar words, but in the second play the character of Stupid John substitutes for that of the heroine's sister in the first play. Both relate stories of lovers who outwit their parents in order to obtain permission to marry. In *Stupid John,* apparently a second version of *Leander,* the dialogue and plot are more elaborately developed.

Although these five plays cannot be dated precisely, most critics believe they were composed between 1760 and 1765, a period during which Beaumarchais wrote under the encouragement of his friend Lenormand d'Étoiles. These works were staged as burlesque pieces at Lenormand's salon. They were never published during Beaumarchais's lifetime but were found among his papers when the Comédie-Française bought them in 1863.

PLAYS

All the works were first performed in Paris, and except *Tarare* are in prose. In addition, Beaumarchais wrote a group of sketches called *Parades* (1760–1765?).

1. *Eugénie.** Drama, 5 acts. Published 1767. Produced Comédie-Française, Jan. 25, 1767.

2. *Les deux amis, ou Le négociant de Lyon** (*The Two Friends, or The Merchant of Lyons*). Drama, 5 acts. Published 1770. Produced Comédie-Française, Jan. 13, 1770.

3. *Le barbier de Séville, ou La précaution inutile** (*The Barber of Seville, or The Useless Precaution*). Comedy, 4 acts. Written 1772. Published 1775. Produced Comédie-Française, Feb. 23, 1775.

4. *La folle journée, ou Le mariage de Figaro** (*The Marriage of Figaro, or The Madness of a Day*). Comedy, 5 acts. Written 1775/78. Published 1785. Produced Comédie-Française, Apr. 27, 1784.

5. *Tarare.* Libretto, 5 acts. Published 1787. Produced Théâtre de l'Académie Royale de Musique, June 8, 1787. Music: Antonio Salieri.

6. *La mère coupable, ou L'autre Tartuffe** (*Frailty and Hypocrisy; also The Other Tartuffe, or The Guilty Mother*). Comedy, 5 acts. Published 1797. Produced Théâtre du Marais, June 26, 1792.

EDITIONS

Collections.
Oeuvres complètes, 7 vols., Paris, 1809; *Oeuvres complètes,* 6 vols., Paris, 1828; *Théâtre,* Paris, 1846; *Théâtre,* Paris, 1861; *Théâtre,* Paris, 1866; *Théâtre,* 2 vols., Paris, 1872; *Théâtre,* Paris, 1934; *Théâtre complet,* Paris, 1952; *The Barber of Seville and The Marriage of Figaro,* tr. by J. Wood, Baltimore, 1964; *The Marriage of Figaro; The Barber of Seville,* tr. by V. Luciani, New York, 1965; *Theatre,* Odyssey, New York, 1966.

Individual Plays.
The Barber of Seville. Published in *Promenades littéraires et historiques,* ed. by A. G. Bovée et al., new ed., New York, 1948; *The Genius of the French Theater,* ed. and tr. by A. Bermel, New York, 1961; *Classical French Drama,* ed. and tr. by W. Fowlie, New York, 1962

The Marriage of Figaro. Published in *Eighteenth Century French Plays,* ed. by C. D. Brenner and N. A. Goodyear, New York, 1927; *Seven French Plays (1730–1897),* ed. by C. Searles, New York, 1935; *The Classic Theatre,* ed. by E. R. Bentley and tr. by J. Barzun, vol. 4, Garden City, N.Y., 1958–1961.

CRITICISM

French. P. Huot, *Beaumarchais en Allemagne,* Paris, 1869; L. de Loménie, *Beaumarchais et son temps,* Paris, 1856, 1873, 1888; A. Hallay, *Beaumarchais,* Paris, 1897; R. Dalsême, *La vie de Beaumarchais,* Paris, 1928; L. Lazarus, *Beaumarchais,* Paris, 1930; A. Bailly, *Beaumarchais,* Paris, 1945; S. Guitry, *Beaumarchais,* Paris, 1950; M. Pollitzer, *Beaumarchais: Le père de Figaro,* Paris, 1957.

English. L. de Loménie, *Beaumarchais and His Times,* tr. by H. S. Edwards, New York, 1857; E. S. Kite, *Beaumarchais and the War of American Independence,* 2 vols., Boston, 1918; J. Rivers, *Figaro: The Life of Beaumarchais,* London, 1922; R. Dalsême, *Beaumarchais, 1732–1799,* tr. by H. Bennet, New York and London, 1929; P. Frischauer, *Beaumarchais: Adventurer in the Century of Women,* tr. by M. Goldsmith, New York, 1935; M. L. Johnson, *Beaumarchais and His Opponents,* Richmond, Va., 1936; G. E. Lemaître, *Beaumarchais,* New York, 1949; J. B. Ratermanis and W. R. Irwin, *The Comic Style of Beaumarchais,* Seattle, 1961; C. Cox, *The Real Figaro: The Extraordinary Career of Caron de Beaumarchais,* New York, 1962.

German. A. Bettelheim, *Beaumarchais: Eine Biographie,* Munich, 1911; P. Frischauer, *Beaumarchais: Der Abenteurer im Jahrhundert der Frauen,* Zurich, 1935.

Francis Beaumont
(1584/85 — 1616)

Francis Beaumont, English dramatist, was born in either 1584 or 1585, probably at his family's ancestral estate of Gracedieu, in Leicestershire. He was the third son of Sir Francis Beaumont, a justice of the Court of Common Pleas. At the age of twelve, young Beaumont entered Oxford with his two brothers. Their father died the following year, and the older boys left the university; Francis may have stayed until 1600. Late that year, after leaving Oxford without taking a degree, he entered the Inner Temple and began to frequent London literary circles. Eventually he numbered among his friends Ben Jonson, George Chapman, and John Donne, and he undoubtedly knew Shakespeare, since he was associated with the Lord Chamberlain's Company. *See* CHAPMAN, GEORGE; JONSON, BEN; SHAKESPEARE, WILLIAM.

Beaumont may have met John Fletcher, his close friend and collaborator, in 1605, but the commendatory verses each contributed to Jonson's *Volpone* (pub. 1607) provide the first linking of their names. Beaumont's first play, *The Woman Hater,* was probably acted in 1606 and was followed by *The Knight of the Burning Pestle,* produced about 1607. It is thought that Fletcher and Beaumont began to share lodgings in 1608 and that they had begun to collaborate by 1607 or 1608. Between 1608 and 1610 they successfully pro-

duced their tragicomedy *Philaster, or Love Lies A-Bleeding* at the Globe and firmly established their joint reputation. Between 1608 and 1611 *The Maid's Tragedy* was also successfully acted at the Blackfriars. *See* FLETCHER, JOHN.

Beaumont's literary activities came to an end with his marriage to the heiress Ursula Isley in 1613 or 1614, although he wrote the masque presented by the members of the Inner Temple and of Gray's Inn as part of the wedding festivities of Princess Elizabeth in 1613 and had a hand in *The Scornful Lady* (1615/16). Soon afterward he probably retired to Kent, where he fathered two daughters, one of them born after his death in London on March 6, 1616. He was buried in the Poets' Corner of Westminster Abbey. *See* MASQUE.

WORK

Although scholars have found it extremely difficult to distinguish precisely between the respective contributions of Beaumont and Fletcher to the plays that are supposed to be their collaborations, most research indicates that Beaumont was the guiding spirit of the partnership. Reflecting the spirit of the new audiences of the Jacobean period, the collaborators laid moral questions aside and

Francis Beaumont. [New York Public Library Picture Collection]

aimed at providing pure entertainment. They found tragicomedy, a genre that Fletcher defined as drama in which some come close to death but none die, admirably suited to their purposes and skillfully developed plots that seem to be leading to tragedy but turn out happily through the introduction of a surprise ending. For example, in *A King and No King* (1611) the audience is shown a king in love with his sister and apparently destined to be ruined; in the last act it is revealed that she is not his sister, that, in fact, she is the Queen and he is not the King. In these tragicomedies themes of love, honor, and sensuality are played out in exotic settings by stock characters, sometimes humorous (the patient wife, the blunt friend, the noble hero, the lustful tyrant, the shiftless gallant, the wicked woman), who converse in refined, courtly speech. The plots are full of intrigue, mistaken identity, and chance meetings. *See also* TRAGICOMEDY.

Most modern scholars attribute to Beaumont alone *The Knight of the Burning Pestle* (ca. 1607), a burlesque of the Elizabethan audience and its tastes, and *The Woman Hater* (ca. 1606), a comedy utilizing Jonsonian structure and humorous characters. Beaumont's collaborations with Fletcher include *Philaster* (1608/10), a romantic tragicomedy; *A King and No King; The Maid's Tragedy* (ca. 1608/11), notable for a sustained mood of tension and exceptionally elevated language; *The Coxcomb* (ca. 1608/10), a comedy about a temporarily thwarted elopement; *Cupid's Revenge* (1612), a drama based on parts of Sir Philip Sidney's *Arcadia* (1590), depicting Cupid's retaliation for the desecration of his altars; and *The Scornful Lady* (1615/16), a comedy in which a lady who has banished her lover for a year jealously plots to win him back after he chooses another bride.

The Woman Hater (ca. 1606). Comedy set in Italy. On her way to meet her lover the Duke, Oriana accidentally takes shelter from the bad weather at the house of Gondarino, a widower and a staunch woman hater. A little later and for the same reason, the Duke and two companions also enter Gondarino's grounds. The gay young Oriana delights in plaguing Gondarino, and in angry retaliation he accuses her of unchastity before the Duke and Oriana's brother Count Valore. Despite his clever efforts to prove his accusation, Oriana withstands a test of her purity, and her reputation remains unsullied.

A subplot concerns Lazarillo, whose eccentricity is expressed in a passionate desire to taste all kinds of rare food. Hearing about an unusual fish head, he frantically chases after it as it passes from one owner to another. It finally rests at the house of a prostitute, and

Lazarillo finds he must promise to marry her in order to savor the fish. However, before he can taste the exotic new dish, he is arrested by two spies who have misinterpreted a conversation between him and Count Valore. Lazarillo is vindicated by the count and returns to his fish head and his future wife.

The Knight of the Burning Pestle (ca. 1607). Good-natured burlesque of the old-fashioned romantic plays beloved by contemporary London audiences, which were usually composed of shopkeepers and tradesmen. A love drama, *The London Merchant,* is about to be performed, but before it begins, a grocer and his wife in the audience insist on devising a play more to their liking; thus *The Knight of the Burning Pestle* is born and interwoven with scenes of the scheduled play.

The hero is played by Rafe, the Grocer's apprentice, while the Grocer and his wife direct and provide a running commentary on the outlandish drama. Rafe, a lad given to reading romances, sallies forth as the Knight of the Burning Pestle, doing good and correcting wrongs. Within the framework of *The London Merchant* he comes to grief, whereas another apprentice, the witty Jasper, wins the hand of his employer's daughter despite her father's hostility and Rafe's bungling intervention. As the Knight of the Burning Pestle, however, Rafe is more successful: he subdues the ugly giant Barbarosa, conducts a love affair with a Cracovian princess, and is finally crowned Lord of the May. But the Grocer and his wife, preferring a tragic ending, direct Rafe to die in a flood of tears with a forked arrow through his head.

Philaster, or Love Lies A-Bleeding (ca. 1608/10). Tragicomedy set in Sicily, where the young and popular Philaster, rightful heir to the throne usurped by the King of Calabria, is in love with Arethusa, the daughter of the King. Having been promised to Pharamond, the licentious Prince of Spain, Arethusa receives Philaster's page Bellario as go-between but as a result is accused of having an affair with Bellario. The rumors convince even Philaster, and he angrily leaves the court, followed by the faithful Bellario. The three meet by chance in a forest, where Philaster, in a fit of passion, wounds Arethusa. Bellario, seeking to assume his master's guilt, is arrested with him, and both are given by the King into Arethusa's custody. To the astonishment of all, the lovers reappear, reconciled and married.

At this point, when the rumor about Arethusa and Bellario is revived, Bellario reveals that he is really Euphrasia, daughter of a courtier, who has long been in love with Philaster. The King, afraid of a revolt by the people, who support Philaster, restores the throne of Sicily to his new son-in-law and also declares Philaster heir to the rest of his lands.

The Maid's Tragedy (ca. 1608/11). Tragedy set in Rhodes. A licentious king, in order to keep his liaison with the beautiful Evadne concealed, orders a noble young courtier, Amintor, to marry her. Intoxicated with what he believes to be this signal sign of royal favor, Amintor abandons his betrothed, Aspatia, and the wedding is richly celebrated. When the bride and the bridegroom retire, however, Evadne dismays and shocks her young husband by bluntly informing him that she is the King's mistress. Her callousness is overcome by his passionate words of recrimination; she falls in love with him and, thinking to win his esteem, murders the King. Almost universal tragedy ensues. Aspatia, distracted by grief, dresses as a man, goads Amintor into a duel, allows herself to be fatally wounded, reveals her identity, and dies. Evadne, finding that Amintor is horrified that she has dared to kill a king, commits suicide, and Amintor also stabs himself.

A King and No King (1611). Tragicomedy in which King Arbaces of Iberia, long absent on military expeditions, returns to his capital, where he meets his sister Panthea, whom he has not seen since she was a child. Because he is deeply attracted by Panthea, he humiliates and, without explanation, imprisons her. Though doubting his powers of self-restraint, he yields to the entreaties of Lord Protector Gobrias to visit his bewildered yet still devoted sister, and when he confesses his love for her, she also admits that she loves him. To justify his emotions, he blames Gobrias's letters praising Panthea and prepares to commit suicide. To save the life of his King, Gobrias reveals the truth: Arbaces is not the legitimate King; his mother was childless, and, fearing the disapproval of her royal husband, passed off Arbaces, a secretly adopted baby, as their son. Later, however, she bore Panthea, the legitimate heir. Relieved of his guilt, Arbaces gladly relinquishes the throne to Panthea and secures her promise to marry him.

PLAYS

All were first performed in London. An exact attribution is almost impossible. So popular were the plays of Beaumont and Fletcher that the collective term was frequently used in connection with plays written singly or in collaboration with others. The two folios of their "collected" plays (1647 and 1679) served to strengthen the belief that their collaboration was far more extensive than in fact it was.

See STATIONERS' REGISTER for an explanation of the term.

1. (With John Fletcher?). *The Woman Hater.* Comedy. Published 1607 (Stationers' Register, May 20, 1607); with subtitle *The Hungry Courtier,* 1649. Produced Children of St Paul's, ca. 1606. If Fletcher collaborated, his contribution was probably minor.

2. *The Knight of the Burning Pestle.* Comedy. Published 1613. Produced Queen's Revels, ca. 1607.

3. (With Fletcher?). *Wit at Several Weapons.* Comedy. Published 1647. Produced (?) ca. 1609/10? Possibly Beaumont and Fletcher's. Authorship is extremely doubtful. Thomas Middleton and William Rowley are probably the authors.

4. (With Fletcher). *Philaster, or Love Lies A-Bleeding.* Tragicomedy. Published 1620 (Stationers' Register, Jan. 10, 1620). Produced Globe Theatre (King's Men), ca. 1608/10.

5. (With Fletcher). *The Coxcomb.* Comedy. Published 1647. Produced Queen's Revels, ca. 1608/10. The extant text may have been revised by Philip Massinger or William Rowley.

6. (With Fletcher). *The Maid's Tragedy.* Tragedy. Published 1619 (Stationers' Register, Apr. 28, 1619). Produced King's Men, ca. 1608/11.

7. (With Fletcher). *A King and No King.* Tragicomedy. Published 1619. Produced King's Men, Dec. 26, 1611.

8. (With Fletcher). *The Captain.* Comedy. Published 1647. Produced at court (King's Men), ca. 1609/12. Beaumont's collaboration is extremely doubtful. Other possible collaborators are Ben Jonson, Massinger, and Rowley.

9. (With Fletcher). *Cupid's Revenge.* Tragedy. Published 1615. Produced Queen's Revels, Jan. 5, 1612. Based on parts of Sir Philip Sidney's *Arcadia* (1590).

10. (With Fletcher). *Four Plays, or Moral Representations in One: The Triumph of Honour, The Triumph of Love, The Triumph of Death, and The Triumph of Time.* Plays. Published 1647. Produced ca. 1612? Almost nothing is known about this group of masquelike pieces.

11. (With Fletcher). *The Honest Man's Fortune.* Tragicomedy. Published 1647. Produced Lady Elizabeth's Men (?), 1613. Beaumont's hand is doubtful. Robert Daborne, Nathan Field, Massinger, and Cyril Tourneur have also been suggested as Fletcher's possible collaborators.

The Maids Tragedie.

AS IT HATH BEENE

diuers times Acted at the *Black-Friers* by the Kings Maiesties Seruants.

Newly perufed, augmented, and inlarged, This fecond Impreffion.

ASPATIA.   AMINTOR.

Printed for *Francis Conftable,* and are to be fold at the White L I O N in *Pauls* Church-yard. 1622.

Title page of *The Maid's Tragedy,* published in London in 1622; now in the British Museum. [American Heritage]

12. (With Fletcher). *The Masque of the Inner Temple and Gray's Inn.* Masque. Published Stationers' Register, Feb. 27, 1613. Produced Whitehall, Feb. 20, 1613.

13. (With Fletcher). *The Scornful Lady.* Comedy. Published 1616 (Stationers' Register, Mar. 19, 1616). Produced Queen's Revels, 1615/16.

14. (With Fletcher). *The Tragedy of Thierry, King of France, and His Brother Theodoret.* Play, 5 acts. Published 1621. Produced King's Men. Indications of Beaumont are exceedingly slight. Daborne, Field, and Massinger have also been suggested as Fletcher's possible collaborators, Massinger as a reviser.

15. (With Fletcher?). *The Faithful Friends.* Comedy. Published 1812. Produced (?), 1604?/after 1621? Probably not by either Beaumont or Fletcher. Daborne, James Shirley, and Massinger and Field have been suggested.

16. (With Fletcher). *Love's Cure, or The Martial Maid.* Comedy. Published 1647. Probably extensively revised by Massinger. The play belonged to the repertory of the King's Men by 1641.

EDITIONS

Collections.
(With John Fletcher). *Works,* ed. by A. Glover and A. R. Waller, 10 vols., Cambridge, England, 1905–1912; *Selected Plays,* Dutton, New York, 1962; *Dramatic Works,* ed. by F. Bowers, vol. I, Cambridge, New York, 1966.

Individual Plays.
(With Fletcher). *A King and No King.* R. K. Turner, ed., *Regents Renaissance Drama Series,* University of Nebraska Press, Lincoln, 1963; also published in *Early Seventeenth Century Plays, 1600–1642,* ed. by H. R. Walley and J. H. Wilson, Harcourt, Brace, New York, 1930; *Beaumont and Fletcher,* vol. II, Hill and Wang, New York, 1950.

The Knight of the Burning Pestle. Published in *The Development of English Drama,* ed. by G. E. Bentley, Appleton-Century-Crofts, New York, 1950; *Six Elizabethan Plays,* ed. by R. C. Bald, Houghton Mifflin, Boston, 1963; *Elizabethan and Jacobean Comedy: An Anthology,* ed. by R. Ornstein and H. Spencer, Raytheon Education Company, Heath, Boston, 1964.

(With Fletcher). *The Maid's Tragedy.* Published in *Typical Elizabethan Plays,* ed. by F. E. Schelling and M. W. Black, rev. ed., Harper, New York, 1931; *Chief Patterns of World Drama,* ed. by W. S. Clark II, Houghton Mifflin, Boston, 1946; *Five Stuart Tragedies,* ed. by A. K. McIlwraith, Oxford, London, 1953.

(With Fletcher). *Philaster, or Love Lies A-Bleeding.* Published in *The English Drama,* ed. by E. W. Parks and R. C. Beatty, Norton, New York, 1935; *Representative English Plays,* ed. by J. S. P. Tatlock and R. G. Martin, 2d ed., Appleton-Century, New York, 1938; *Typical Elizabethan Plays,* ed. by F. E. Schelling and M. W. Black, 3d ed., Harper, New York, 1949.

CRITICISM

A. H. Thorndike, *Influence of Beaumont and Fletcher on Shakespeare,* New York, 1901; A. C. Sprague, *Beaumont and Fletcher on the Restoration Stage,* New York, 1926; J. H. Wilson, *The Influence of Beaumont and Fletcher on Restoration Drama,* Columbus, 1928; J. F. Danby, *Poets on Fortune's Hill: Studies in Sidney, Shakespeare, Beaumont and Fletcher,* Port Washington, N.Y., 1952; E. M. Waith, *The Pattern of Tragicomedy in Beaumont and Fletcher,* New Haven, Conn., 1952; B. Maxwell, *Studies in Beaumont, Fletcher, and Massinger,* New York, 1966; L. B. Wallis, *Fletcher, Beaumont & Company,* New York, 1968; C. M. Gayley, *Beaumont the Dramatist,* reprint, New York, 1969.

BECHER, Ulrich (1910–   ). German novelist and dramatist. A recipient of the first drama prize awarded by the German Stage Union (1955), Becher is considered by some a Hemingway on the stage because of his predilection for "the disinherited of this world." His first collection of short stories, *Men Make Mistakes* (*Männer machen Fehler,* 1932), was publicly burned in Germany a year after its appearance; and his first play, *Nobody* (*Niemand,* 1936), a "revolutionary Christ mystery," was banned in Berlin and eventually produced in Bern. He left Nazi Germany for Vienna, where he married the daughter of the humorist Roda Roda, and later emigrated to Brazil, not returning to Europe until after World War II. Becher, who views the theatre as a battleground against the dark forces in the world, writes "tragic farces" distinguished by their satirical tone. His plays include the antifascist work *The Fairy Tale of the Robber Who Became a Policeman* (*Das Märchen vom Räuber, der Schutzmann wurde,* 1945); *The Obstinate One* (*Der Bockerer,* 1949), a farce about Hitler's take-over of Austria written in collaboration with the Viennese actor Peter Preses; and *The Little Ones and the Big Ones* (*Die Kleinen und die Grossen,* 1955).

Samuel Beckett
(1906 –   )

Samuel Beckett, Irish-French poet, critic, novelist, and dramatist, was born near Dublin on April 13, 1906, of middle-class Protestant parents. He was educated at the Portora Royal School, Enniskillen, and at Trinity College, Dublin, where he took a B.A. degree in 1927, having specialized in French and Italian. For a short time he taught in Belfast, and in 1928 received a fellowship to the École

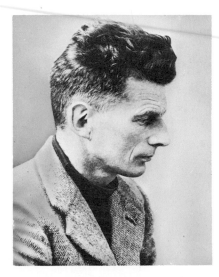

Samuel Beckett.
[French Cultural Services]

German
production
of *En attendant
Godot.* [German
Information
Center]

in Ireland, but he returned at once to Paris and worked in the French Resistance. Sought by the Nazis, he was compelled to flee from Paris to the south of France, where he wrote *Watt,* his second novel, which was not published until 1953. After World War II, he wrote for a time almost exclusively in French. In a burst of creativity, he translated *Murphy* into French; produced a novelistic trilogy— *Molloy* (1951), *Malone Dies* (*Malone meurt,* 1951), and *The Unnamable* (*L'Innommable,* 1953)—written in French and subsequently translated into English; and wrote two plays, *Eleutheria* (written ca. 1946/48 and never published or produced) and *Waiting for Godot* (*En attendant Godot,* 1953), as well as a group of tales entitled *Stories and Texts for Nothing* (*Nouvelles et textes pour rien,* 1953). The theatrical success of *Waiting for Godot* was followed by the production of a number of dramatic works for the stage, radio, and television, accompanied by Beckett's recognition as one of the leading influences in the theatre of the absurd. Beckett continues to reside in France. In 1969 he was awarded the Nobel Prize for Literature. *See* THEATRE OF THE ABSURD.

WORK

"My work is a matter of fundamental sounds made as fully as possible, and I accept responsibility for nothing else. If people want to have headaches among the overtones, let them," said Samuel Beckett, summing up his reaction to the critical exegeses inspired by his plays. The statement cannot help but bring to mind Beckett's first published work, *Whoroscope* (1930), a poem in which René Descartes is found soliloquizing in the musical accents of Dublin as he searches for self-identity. As some critics have pointed out, the "fundamental sounds" in Beckett's plays are actually the devices of a poet working in the French symbolist tradition that attempted to close the gap between language and music. By using imagery, rhythm, suggestion, pauses, and eventually the sound of silence itself, Beckett appeals directly to our senses and emotions, with the result that his message is often "felt" without being completely "understood." *See* SYMBOLISM.

Beckett was nearly fifty when he turned from verse, criticism, and fiction to the theatre, but the Paris production of *Waiting for Godot* (1953) immediately established him as one of the most controversial dramatists of his time and brought the so-called theatre of the absurd to popular attention. Jean Anouilh hailed the work as having "the importance of the first Pirandello presented in Paris," and the Spanish playwright Alfonso Sastre called it the first real tragicomedy,

Normale Supérieure in Paris. James Joyce, then living in Paris, became a friend of Beckett and exerted a profound influence on him. Under Joyce's supervision, Beckett helped translate into French a fragment of *Finnegans Wake,* and the relationship, often an uneasy one, lasted until Joyce's death in 1941. *See* JOYCE, JAMES.

Beckett's first published work, *Whoroscope,* a ninety-eight-line poem accompanied by seventeen footnotes, appeared in 1930. That same year he returned to Trinity College, where he took an M.A. degree and taught French until 1932, when he resigned to devote his time entirely to writing. Although he took up permanent residence in Paris, his first collection of short stories, *More Pricks than Kicks* (1934), and his first novel, *Murphy* (1938), written in English, were published in London.

When World War II broke out, Beckett was

"that mysterious situation before which we laugh, although horrified." And indeed one of the characters observes in *Endgame* (*Fin de partie*, 1957), "Nothing is funnier than unhappiness." This type of black humor occurs often in Beckett's work, providing momentary escape from the hopeless atmosphere of his plays and at the same time emphasizing the suffering of his characters. In addition, the bold, bare dramatic form he has developed seems peculiarly suited to expressing modern man's fundamental drama: an undefined sense of guilt, the feeling of hopelessness and anguish resulting from a loss of identity and purpose.

In *Waiting for Godot,* two clownish tramps on a naked plain graced only by a bare tree keep an indefinite appointment with the mysterious Godot, whom they have never seen. Like the anonymous A and B in Beckett's novel *Molloy* (1951), the tramps are essentially without identity since, though they appear on the cast list as Vladimir and Estragon, they address one another as Gogo and Didi, and when Godot's messenger arrives to announce that he, Godot, cannot come that day, he addresses Vladimir as "Monsieur Albert."

As the tramps wait, they draw whatever comfort they can from one another's presence, but like the disembodied Descartes of *Whoroscope* they cannot bear close contact with another being. "Don't touch me! Don't question me! Don't speak to me! Stay with me!" cries one in an anguished appeal. When Pozzo and Lucky pass along the road, we learn that their relationship is the less comforting and more degrading one of master and slave. After Godot's second failure to appear, the tramps make an unsuccessful effort to hang themselves. Then, unable to make up their minds to leave, they remain rooted to the spot. Christian interpreters have pointed out that the scattered sprouting leaves on the previously bare tree suggest that Godot has perhaps come and gone and not been recognized.

Endgame is a considerably more static play; by comparison, *Waiting for Godot* seems to abound in dramatic action. All the relationships represented by the four characters in the earlier work are here contained in Hamm and Clov, who are simultaneously friends, master and slave, and perhaps father and son. In *Waiting for Godot* dramatic contrast is provided by the fact that while Gogo and Didi cannot leave, Pozzo and Lucky cannot stay. In *Endgame,* Clov cannot sit, and Hamm cannot stir from his wheelchair. The setting is no longer an open plain but a closed room; the characters are no longer waiting since there is nothing left to wait for. Clov threatens to desert Hamm but seems unable or unwilling to face alone whatever may be outside. The "endgame" appears to have resulted in a stalemate.

In *Krapp's Last Tape* (*La dernière bande,*

Two scenes from a German production of *Fin de partie.* [German Information Center]

1958) the dramatic situation is even further reduced; here the "dialogue" is between an aged, dehumanized man and a tape recorder that plays back impressions he recorded thirty years before. As he laughs or responds in anger to his youthful idealism, we realize with horror that the past was only the present in embryo and that his life has been an ineluctable progression toward an animality stripped of mind and hope. The physical appetites remain, but the faculties have degenerated and the intellect can only respond with joy to the *sound* of the word "spool," a sound whose fascination was already obvious on a tape made long ago.

Though some critics feel that *Happy Days* (*Oh les beaux jours,* 1961) is Beckett's most pessimistic play, it is in many ways an exposition of the resourcefulness of the human spirit in the face of hopelessness. Nevertheless, it contains Beckett's clearest image of physical paralysis. While Gogo and Didi are only psychologically unable to leave the appointed

Ray Reinhardt as the only character in *Krapp's Last Tape.* [Courtesy American Conservatory Theatre, San Francisco, Calif. Photograph by Hank Kranzler]

rendezvous site and while Hamm is confined to his wheelchair in a closed room, Winnie is actually buried to the waist in earth that seems to be drawing her downward. Elaborately constructed routines occupy her time and her mind and make it possible for her to endure the hopelessness of her situation. In the second act Winnie is buried to her neck and must rely solely on the resources of her mind. The situation grotesquely echoes Descartes's famous "Cogito ergo sum" ("I think, therefore I am").

Like the characters in his novels, Beckett's dramatic characters lose the power to act progressively from play to play. His dramaturgy becomes more and more stripped as he successively isolates and emphasizes elements of dramatic construction such as the pause, entrances and exits, monologue and dialogue, movement and immobility.

Some of Beckett's shorter plays that were designed for radio gave him further scope for experimentation with "fundamental sounds" by excluding the visual. However, thematically they add nothing new to the works discussed above. Superficially, *All That Fall* (*Tous ceux qui tombent,* 1957) is the most realistic of Beckett's plays in that it offers bits of characterization and local color. But beneath the surface realism the words reveal that strange changes have taken place in the characters; for example, an old hag slowly becomes a suburban matron babbling about psychoanalysis. In *Embers* (*Cendres,* 1959) an old man sits by the sea endlessly telling himself stories. He is perhaps alone in the world. *Act Without Words, I* and *II* (*Acte sans paroles, I* and *II;* 1957, 1960) are both pantomimes in which language is suppressed, and *Come and Go* (*Va-et-vient,* pub. 1966) is a short dramatic action that consists of little more than a series of symbolic exits and entrances, the play being essentially composed of silences. Beckett has also written a script for television, *Eh Joe* (1966), and a movie pantomime, *Film* (1965), starring Buster Keaton. On March 8, 1970, Beckett's "play" entitled *Breath* was performed in New York. It spanned thirty seconds, during which time no words were spoken and no actors were present.

Waiting for Godot (*En attendant Godot,* 1953). Tragicomedy, in two acts, which was the first theatrical success of the theatre of the absurd. At dusk two tramps, Vladimir and Estragon, who call each other Gogo and Didi, meet near a bare tree on a country road to wait for the promised arrival of the elusive Godot. They pass the time in a variety of ways: trying to recall their past, quoting from the Bible, discussing the nearby tree, speculating about Godot, telling jokes, recounting dreams, eating, and urinating. Before night-fall, Pozzo, a capricious master, and Lucky, his brutalized servant, appear briefly. Their relationship as master and slave provides a sharp contrast with the friendly equality of the two tramps. Eventually Godot sends word that he will not come that day but will surely come the next. In Act II the tree has grown four or five leaves, but the state of Gogo and Didi has deteriorated. Their memories are even less dependable, and they find less and less to say. They are more conscious of their activities as pastime, or play. Pozzo and Lucky reappear briefly, the former now blind, the latter dumb. Once more Godot sends word that he cannot come that day. In despair, the tramps make an unsuccessful attempt to hang themselves. Then, as at the end of Act I, they declare their intention of leaving, but they do not move.

Endgame (*Fin de partie*, 1957). Long one-act drama of two couples: Nagg and Nell, an old husband and wife who remained fixed throughout in their respective ashcans; and their son Hamm and his companion Clov, who relates to Hamm as slave, friend, and, per-haps, son. Hamm cannot stand nor Clov sit, and Clov pushes Hamm about in a wheel-chair. The play opens as Clov ritualistically draws the curtains of two high, small win-dows, then removes dust sheets from the ash-cans and from Hamm's wheelchair. After that, Hamm and Clov converse about fini-tude, their fading view and failing health, love, and suffering. Nagg's request for bis-cuits is presently answered by Nell's appear-ance in her ashcan. Husband and wife chat about their deteriorating senses and chuckle over the accident that cost them their legs. Nagg tells Nell a story reflecting on the sorry state of God's world. Hamm and Clov busy themselves in a round of uninspired actions such as making a tour of the room, staring out the window, and killing an insect. Hamm bribes Nagg with the promise of plums to lis-ten to his story about a man seeking shelter for his son after a world holocaust; he then receives his father's curses when he confesses that he has no plums. Nell dies, and Clov con-ducts Hamm on another slow tour of the room. Clov threatens to leave and makes elaborate preparations for his departure. But at the closing curtain, Clov still stands mo-tionless at the door, while Hamm, his face veiled in a bloody handkerchief, also remains indifferent and immobile.

Happy Days (*Oh les beaux jours*, 1961). Two-act play that Beckett originally wrote in English and later translated into French. In Act I, Winnie is buried to the waist in earth; a scorching sun beats down. A bell summons Winnie to her day's activities, which begin with a prayer. As a defense against the infini-tude of time, she has devised a series of rou-tines: making an inventory of her possessions, doing her toilette, recalling the past, invent-ing stories, trying to remember snatches of poetry, and conversing with the generally unresponsive Willie, who dwells in a nearby hole just within her range of vision. Success-ful efforts of memory or an occasional word extracted from Willie convince her that it has been a happy day after all. The climax of this particular day comes when the sight of an ant stimulates Willie to a pun on "formi-cation," making the couple laugh. In Act II, Winnie is imbedded up to her neck, and her all-important physical routines are now im-possible. Her memory seems to have deteri-orated, but she perseveres in fabricating sto-ries and prattles on to the now-absent Willie. Because Winnie can no longer turn her head to see him, she may be unaware that he is gone, but soon he reappears dressed in morn-ing clothes and crawling toward her. Winnie

Bert Lahr in *Waiting for Godot.* [Walter Hampden Memorial Library at The Players, New York]

joyfully begins humming the "Merry Widow" waltz, but whether Willie means to kiss her or is merely groping for the revolver that lies on the nearby ground remains undisclosed as the curtain falls.

PLAYS

Since Beckett is equally fluent in French and English and acts as his own translator (unless otherwise noted), the first title in each listing below is the one under which the play first appeared.

1. *Eleutheria.* Play, 3 acts. Written ca. 1946/48.
2. *En attendant Godot** (*Waiting for Godot*). Play, 2 acts. Published 1952. Produced Paris, Théâtre de Babylone, Jan. 5, 1953; London, Theatre Arts Club, Aug. 3, 1955.
3. *Fin de partie** (*Endgame*). Play, 1 act. Published 1957. Produced London, Royal Court Theatre, Apr. 3, 1957; Paris, Studio des Champs-Élysées, May 2, 1957.
4. *Acte sans paroles, I** (*Act Without Words, I*). Pantomime, 1 act. Published 1957. Produced London, Royal Court Theatre, Apr. 3, 1957; Paris, Studio de Champs-Élysées, May 2, 1957.
5. *All That Fall** (*Tous ceux qui tombent*). Radio play. Published 1957. Produced London, BBC Third Programme, Jan. 13, 1957; Paris, Radiodiffusion Française, Jan. 26, 1963. French translation: Robert Pinget.
6. *Embers** (*Cendres*). Radio play. Published 1958. Produced London, BBC Third Programme, June 24, 1959. French translation: Beckett and Pinget.
7. *Krapp's Last Tape** (*La dernière bande*). Play, 1 act. Published 1959. Produced London, Royal Court Theatre, Oct. 28, 1958; Marseille, Théâtre Quotidien, 1959; Paris, Théâtre Récamier, Mar. 22, 1960.
8. *Act Without Words, II** (*Acte sans paroles, II*). Pantomime, 1 act. Published 1960. Produced London, London Institute of Contemporary Arts, 1960.
9. *Happy Days** (*Oh les beaux jours*). Play, 2 acts. Published 1961. Produced New York, Cherry Lane Theatre, Sept. 17, 1961; Paris, Théâtre de France, Oct 21, 1963.
10. *Words and Music** (*Mots et musique*). Radio play. Published 1962. Produced London, BBC Third Programme, Nov. 13, 1962. Music: John Beckett.
11. *Play** (*Comédie*). Play, 1 act. Published 1964. Produced Ulm, Ulmer Theater, June 14, 1963; New York, Cherry Lane Theatre, Jan. 4, 1964; Paris, Théâtre du Pavillon de Marsan, June 4, 1964.
12. *Cascando**. Radio play. Published 1964. Produced Paris, Radiodiffusion Française, 1964. Music: Marcel Mihalovici.
13. *Va-et-vient** (*Come and Go*). Dramaticule, 1 scene. Published 1966.
14. *Eh Joe**. Television play. Published 1967. Produced London, BBC Television, July 4, 1966.
15. *Breath.* Play. Produced New York, Mar. 8, 1970.

EDITIONS

Collections.
Endgame Followed by Act Without Words, Grove Press, New York, 1958; *Krapp's Last Tape and Embers,* Faber, London, 1959; *Krapp's Last Tape and Other Dramatic Pieces,* Grove Press, New York, 1960; *Play, and Two Short Pieces for the Radio,* Faber, London, 1964; *Comédie et actes divers,* Éditions de Minuit, Paris, 1966; *Eh Joe and Other Writings,* Faber, London, 1967; *Cascando and Other Short Dramatic Pieces,* New York, 1968.

Individual Plays.
All That Fall. Faber, London, 1957.
Come and Go: Dramaticule. Calder & Boyars, London, 1967.
Endgame. Published in *Masters of Modern Drama,* ed. by H. M. Block and R. G. Shedd, New York, 1962.
Happy Days. Grove Press, New York, 1961.
Waiting for Godot. Grove Press, New York, 1954; also published in *Seven Plays of the Modern Theatre,* with introduction by H. Clurman, Grove Press, New York, 1962.

CRITICISM

H. Delye, *Samuel Beckett, ou La philosophie de l'absurde,* La Pensée Universitaire, Aix, 1960; R. Cohn, *Samuel Beckett: The Comic Gamut,* Rutgers, New Brunswick, N.J., 1962; F. J. Hoffman, *Samuel Beckett: The Language of Self,* Southern Illinois University Press, Carbondale, 1962; H. Kenner, *Samuel Beckett: A Critical Study,* Grove Press, New York, 1962; R. Coe, *Samuel Beckett,* Grove Press, New York, Oliver & Boyd, Edinburgh, 1964; W. Y. Tindall, *Samuel Beckett,* Columbia, New York, 1964; *Samuel Beckett: A Collection of Critical Essays,* ed. by M. Esslin, Prentice-Hall, Englewood Cliffs, N.J., 1965; N. A. Scott, *Samuel Beckett,* Bowes and Bowes, London, Hillary House, New York, 1965; J. Jacobsen and W. R. Mueller, *The Testament of Samuel Beckett: A Study,* Hill and Wang, New York, 1964, Faber, London, 1966; J. Ludovic, *Pour Samuel Beckett,* Éditions de Minuit, Paris, 1966; P. Mélèse, *Beckett,* Seghers, Paris, 1966; *Beckett at Sixty: A Festschrift,* ed. by J. Calder, Calder & Boyars, London, 1967; J. Fletcher, *Samuel Beckett's Art,* Barnes & Noble, New York, 1967; I. H. Hassan, *The Literature of Silence: Henry Miller and Samuel Beckett,* Knopf, New York, 1968.

Henry Becque
(1837 — 1899)

Henry-François Becque, French journalist and dramatist, was born in Paris on April 18, 1837, the son of a government clerk. After graduating from the Lycée Bonaparte in 1850, he clerked in a railway office, but he eventually left to become private secretary

Henry Becque. [Theatre Collection, The New York Public Library at Lincoln Center, Astor, Lenox and Tilden Foundations]

and tutor in the household of a Polish diplomat. In 1867 he wrote the libretto for Victorin de Joncières's *Sardanapale*, an opera that was performed but gained little notice. About this time Becque became drama critic on *Le Peuple* and produced his first play, *The Prodigal Son* (*L'enfant prodigue*, 1868), a comedy. He interrupted his career to enlist in the army during the Franco-Prussian War, after which he returned to writing plays, eking out a living by working on the stock exchange and contributing articles to various publications.

In 1877 Becque completed *The Vultures* (*Les corbeaux*, 1882), but he had to wait five years before it was produced at the Comédie-Française. Although the play brought him some recognition, neither the critics nor the public truly accepted him and he still had to battle to have his works produced. Later he chronicled these difficult years in the vitriolic *Literary Quarrels* (*Querelles littéraires*, 1890) and *Recollections of a Dramatist* (*Souvenirs d'un auteur dramatique*, 1895). Some rewards did accrue to Becque, however: in 1886 he received the Legion of Honor; André Antoine, partly because of Becque's influence, provided a sympathetic home for naturalistic plays in the Théâtre Libre; and in 1893 Becque accepted an invitation to lecture in Italy, a land where his plays were enthusiastically received. But the financial difficulties that always plagued him worsened in 1894, when Becque's brother, who had sometimes supported him, died. Although Becque seems to have been irascible and rather misanthropic, his loneliness was alleviated by loyal friends. Becque suffered a shock after a fire broke out in his room and destroyed his belongings; he had to be sent to a sanatorium, where he died on May 12, 1899.

WORK

Becque was one of the most naturalistic of the nineteenth-century French realist dramatists who followed Alexandre Dumas *fils*. He found the slice-of-life technique congenial to his purposes and, reacting against the well-made play (*pièce bien faite*) as developed by Scribe, concentrated on constructing dramas in which individual scenes were powerfully true to life and contained elements of corrosive comedy. Instead of emphasizing plot, he focused on the development of character through the use of natural language free of rhetoric. As a social dramatist, he was particularly concerned with the effect produced by money. His pessimistic eye recorded the ironic maneuvers involved in acquiring and keeping money, and he rendered his observations in trenchant, often caustic, dialogue. His tough, hardheaded plays probably

La navette, Paris, 1961. [French Cultural Services]

represent the most incisive social thinking in the Parisian drama of his day. *See* WELL-MADE PLAY.

Becque's most notable and characteristic play is *The Vultures* (1882), which depicts a widow and her children being victimized by the rapacious partner, notary, and creditors of her deceased husband. Becque examines their predatory opportunism in scenes that convey his contempt and condemnation. With this play, Becque created the *comédie rosse* ("nasty comedy") that became a tradition of Antoine's Théâtre Libre, even though none of Becque's plays was ever presented there.

The Vultures was followed by *The Woman of Paris* (*La Parisienne*, 1885), a sophisticated, sardonic comedy in which Becque turned his interest from finance to affairs of the heart. In it he portrayed an outwardly respectable woman of fashion who actually lives according to a code of complete amorality. By dint of shrewd maneuvering, she escapes scandal and emerges unscathed from her amorous adventures.

Among other plays by Becque are *Michel Pauper* (1870), an early work that shows an imaginative worker's conflict with capitalism; *The Merry-Go-Round* (*La navette*, 1878), which was criticized for its "misanthropy"; *Virtuous Women* (*Les honnêtes femmes*, 1880), in which Becque, surprisingly, presented a completely endearing and irreproachable heroine; *The Departure* (*Le départ*), published in 1897 but not produced until 1924; and *The Buffoons* (*Les polichinelles*), an unfinished work on financial speculation.

The Vultures (*Les corbeaux*, 1882). Drama depicting the decline of a happy, prosperous middle-class family whose world begins to crumble when Vigneron, the head of the family and a businessman, dies. His partner Teissier and his notary Bourdon plunder his estate like vultures, taking ruthless advantage of Mme. Vigneron's naïveté concerning her husband's financial affairs. The desperate widow and her children soon find that penury exposes their lives to lamentable changes. Blanche, the youngest daughter, falls seriously ill when her fiancé's avaricious mother breaks the couple's engagement. Judith, the middle daughter, learns that her grasping music teacher has been misleading her regarding her talent. Gaston, the spoiled son of the house, joins the army to escape the family's ruin. Marie, the eldest and most resourceful daughter, tries to reclaim their affairs but is finally convinced that she can save the family's future only by accepting Teissier's proposal of marriage. Once she does so, Teissier begins to protect the family against the rapacity of other vultures.

The Woman of Paris (*La Parisienne*, 1885). Corrosive comedy in which a pretty and amoral woman, Clotilde du Mesnil, "protects" her husband's interests by taking and dropping lovers with complete indifference to the demands of sentiment. The opening scene in which Clotilde has a jealous quarrel with her lover Lafont brilliantly establishes the *ménage à trois* as the comedy's point of departure by leading the audience to assume that they are man and wife. To help her husband obtain a ministry post, Clotilde temporarily breaks with Lafont and takes a new lover, Simpson. However, once her husband is safely ensconced in his new job, Clotilde's notions of propriety and domestic tranquillity lead her to drop Simpson. To convince Lafont that he had been mistaken in his jealousy, Clotilde introduces Simpson to her husband. By the end of the play the original marital triangle has been reestablished. Clotilde's husband is

La Parisienne,
Théâtre Sarah-
Bernhardt, Paris.
[French Cultural
Services]

A Comédie-Française production of *La Parisienne*. [French Cultural Services]

presented as being fatuously unaware of his wife's maneuverings and convinced that she actually has a physical distaste for Lafont.

PLAYS

All were first performed in Paris.

1. *Sardanapale*. Opera, 3 acts. Published 1867. Produced Théâtre Impérial Lyrique, Feb. 8, 1867. Music: Victorin de Joncières. Based on Lord Byron's *Sardanapalus* (pub. 1821).

2. *L'enfant prodigue* (*The Prodigal Son*). Comedy, 4 acts. Published 1868. Produced Théâtre du Vaudeville, Nov. 6, 1868.

3. *Michel Pauper*. Drama, 5 acts. Published 1871. Produced Théâtre de la Porte-Saint-Martin, June 17, 1870.

4. *L'enlèvement* (*The Abduction*). Comedy, 3 acts. Published 1897. Produced Théâtre du Vaudeville, Nov. 18, 1871.

5. *La navette** (*The Merry-Go-Round*). Comedy, 1 act. Published 1878. Produced Théâtre du Gymnase, Nov. 15, 1878.

6. *Les honnêtes femmes* (*Virtuous Women*). Comedy, 1 act. Published 1880. Produced Théâtre du Gymnase, Jan. 1, 1880.

7. *Les corbeaux** (*The Vultures*). Play, 4 acts. Published 1882. Produced Comédie-Française, Sept. 14, 1882.

8. *La Parisienne** (*The Woman of Paris*). Comedy, 4 acts. Published 1882. Produced Théâtre de la Renaissance, Feb. 7, 1885.

9. *Veuve** (*Widowed*). Play, 1 act. Published 1897. Produced Théâtre de l'Odéon, June 11, 1914.

10. *Le domino à quatre* (*A Quiet Game*). Dialogue, 4 parts. Published 1897. Produced Théâtre de l'Odéon, June 1, 1908.

11. *Le départ* (*The Departure*). Play, 1 act. Published 1897. Produced Théâtre de l'Odéon, Mar 21, 1924.

12. *Une exécution* (*An Execution*). Play, 1 act. Published 1897.

13. *Les polichinelles* (*The Buffoons*). Uncompleted. Comedy, 5 acts. Published 1910. Act I produced Théâtre de l'Odéon, May 21, 1924.

EDITIONS

Collections.

Théâtre complet, 2 vols., Paris, 1890; *Théâtre complet,* 2 vols., Paris, 1909–1910; *Three Plays,* tr. by F. Tilden, New York, 1913; *Oeuvres complètes,* 7 vols., Paris, 1924.

Individual Plays.

The Vultures. Published in *Nineteenth Century French*

Plays, ed. by J. L. Borgerhoff, Century, New York, 1931; *Chief French Plays of the Nineteenth Century*, ed. by E. M. Grant, Harper, New York, 1934; *Omnibus of French Literature*, ed. by H. Steinhauer and F. Walter, vol. 2, Macmillan, New York, 1941.

The Woman of Paris. Published in *From the Modern Repertoire*, ed. by E. R. Bentley and tr. by J. Barzun, ser. 1, University of Denver Press, Denver, and Indiana University Press, Bloomington, 1949–1956; *The Modern Theatre*, ed. by E. R. Bentley and tr. by J. Barzun, vol. 1, Doubleday, Garden City, N.Y., 1955–1960; *Masterpieces of the Modern French Theatre*, ed. by R. W. Corrigan, Collier Books, New York, 1967.

CRITICISM

A. Got, *Henry Becque: Sa vie et son oeuvre*, Paris, 1920; E. A. Dawson, *Henry Becque: Sa vie et son théâtre*, Paris, 1923; Arnautović, *Henry Becque*, 3 vols., Paris, 1927; *id., Henry Becque, poète*, Paris, 1929; P. Blanchart, *Henry Becque: Son oeuvre*, Paris, 1930.

Richard Beer-Hofmann
(1866 — 1945)

Richard Beer-Hofmann, Austrian dramatist, was born in Vienna of Jewish parentage on July 11, 1866. Adopted by his uncle, he studied at the University of Vienna, from which he received a doctorate in law. In the 1890s he belonged, along with Hermann Bahr, Hugo von Hofmannsthal, and Arthur Schnitzler, to the Jung Wien (Young Vienna) literary movement; it was in 1893 that he first attracted public attention with his published stories. In 1905 he received the Schiller Award as a dramatist for *The Count of Charolais* (*Der Graf von Charolais*, wr. 1904). During a long stay in Berlin, he collaborated closely with Max Reinhardt in the staging of a number of plays. Returning to Vienna, he was active as a writer and stage director at the Burgtheater, where his production of Goethe's *Faust* was especially acclaimed. *See* GOETHE, JOHANN WOLFGANG VON.

A fervent Zionist, Beer-Hofmann was a friend of Theodor Herzl. In 1933, after the Nazi rise to power, his books were burned in Germany. Only one more performance of a Beer-Hofmann play was allowed in Berlin, in 1935, for spectators having at least one Jewish grandparent. In 1938 Beer-Hofmann escaped from Austria to the United States. Modest and withdrawn, he shunned publicity as well as political and literary coteries. He died in New York on September 26, 1945. A Beer-Hofmann society was established after his death.

WORK

Perhaps the most prominent figure in neoromantic Vienna after Hofmannsthal, Beer-Hofmann was chiefly concerned with problems of ethics and religion. The main virtues of his four plays are lyrical, not dramatic. His polished language, melodious and metaphorical, is drawn, in his major work, from the Bible. *The Count of Charolais* (1906), a tragedy loosely adapted from Massinger's *The Fatal Dowry*, though defective in construction, was an immediate success (*see* MASSINGER, PHILIP). The first play of a trilogy about King David, *Jacob's Dream* (*Jaákobs Traum;* wr. 1915, prod. 1919) combines impressionism and expressionism. It was followed by *The Young David* (*Der junge David*, wr. 1933) and *Prelude to the Theatre of King David* (*Das Vorspiel auf dem Theater zu König David*, pub. 1936). Inspired by a vision of Israel's mission and suffering, the trilogy gives artistic expression to Beer-Hofmann's Zionist convictions. In this attempt to create a myth of the Jewish people, he wrote one of the most beautiful Biblical dramas in German literature.

The Count of Charolais (*Der Graf von Charolais*, 1906). Verse tragedy in which the young Count of Charolais, burdened with a bankrupt estate, struggles to obtain a decent burial for his father, whose corpse is held in a debtors' tower. Old President Rochort is touched by the young man's devotion and pays the debt, thus clearing the way for the burial. In addition, he chooses Charolais as the husband for his beloved daughter Desirée. The couple marry, and their happiness seems assured. However, the President's

Richard Beer-Hofmann. [Bildarchiv der Österreichischen Nationalbibliothek]

young nephew Philip continues to woo Desirée and seduces her, taking advantage of her inexperience. When Charolais learns that his wife has been seen with Philip, he is enraged and kills Philip. He then forces the President, who begs him to be compassionate, to sign a death warrant for Desirée. After Charolais has rejected all Desirée's protestations of innocence, she takes her own life.

Jacob's Dream (*Jaákobs Traum;* wr. 1915, prod. 1919). Biblical verse drama retelling the Genesis story of Jacob and Esau (here called Edom). Old Isaac is dying, but Edom, his firstborn son, is away on a hunt and cannot receive his blessing. Issac's wife Rebecca arranges for the younger brother Jacob, a dreamer, to receive his father's blessing. When Edom returns, he swears a terrible vengeance and pursues his fleeing brother. But when they finally come face to face, Jacob's nobility and goodness subdue Edom's wrath, and the brothers are reconciled. Jacob then falls asleep and has a great dream in which his people's suffering destiny is disclosed. Jacob wrestles with Semal (Satan) and debates with God's messenger. He even challenges God, frightening the angels. When Jacob awakens, he is jubilant in the knowledge of his mission: to lead his people onward despite all hazards. His name is no longer Jacob but Israel.

PLAYS

1. *Der Graf von Charolais* (*The Count of Charolais*). Tragedy, 5 acts. Written 1904. Published 1904. Produced Berlin, Deutsches Theater, Mar. 8, 1906. Based on *The Fatal Dowry* (1616/19) by Philip Massinger and Nathan Field.

2. *Jaákobs Traum* (*Jacob's Dream*). Biblical drama, 1 act. Written 1915. Published 1918. Produced Vienna, Burgtheater, 1919.

3. *Der junge David* (*The Young David*). Biblical drama, 7 scenes. Written 1933. Published 1933.

4. *Das Vorspiel auf dem Theater zu König David* (*Prelude to the Theatre of King David*). Biblical drama, 1 act. Published 1936.

CRITICISM

E. Rader, *Beer-Hofmanns Graf von Charolais und seine Vorläufer*, Vienna, 1911; T. Reik, *Das Werk Richard Beer-Hofmanns*, Vienna, 1919; S. Liptzin, *Richard Beer-Hofmann*, New York, 1936; A. Werner, *Richard Beer-Hofmann: Sinn und Gestalt*, Vienna, 1936; O. Oberholzer, *Richard Beer-Hofmann: Werk und Weltbild*, Bern, 1947.

Brendan Behan
(1923 – 1964)

Brendan Francis Behan, Irish journalist and dramatist, was born on February 9, 1923, in Dublin, and reared in its slums. His family on both sides was traditionally anti-British; because of his involvement in the Irish uprising of 1916–1922, his father was in a British compound at his son's birth. One of his uncles, Peadar Kearney, was the author of the Irish national anthem, "Soldier's Song." Another uncle, P. J. Bourke, was the proprietor of a Dublin theatre, which young Behan attended regularly. Both the Behans and the Kearneys were interested in the early work of the Abbey Theatre.

Behan attended Catholic schools until he was expelled from the Irish Christian Brothers School in 1936. He then took up his father's trade of house painting. Having learned a trade, he next, in his association with the secret Irish Republican Army (IRA), learned the art of revolution. Since the age of nine he had been serving in the Fianna Eireann, a youth organization connected with the IRA, and in 1937 he was transferred to the IRA itself as a messenger boy.

In 1939 the IRA sent him to England, reportedly to help blow up a battleship in Liverpool harbor. He was arrested for carrying explosives and, after spending two months in a Liverpool jail, was sentenced to three years at a Borstal reform school. In 1958 he published *Borstal Boy,* a book recording his experiences in both the Liverpool jail and the Borstal school. It was banned in Ireland, as were several others of his books.

Soon after his release in 1942, Behan returned to Ireland. Arrested again, he was sentenced to fourteen years' imprisonment for the attempted murder of two detectives. He was freed under a general amnesty in 1946, but the next year he was arrested in Manchester and served a short term for al-

Brendan Behan. [Irish Tourist Board]

(Top left
and below)
Two scenes from
the Abbey Theatre
production of *The
Quare Fellow.*
[Dermot Barry
photographs]

(Top right) Frank McMahon's stage adaptation of
Borstal Boy. [Irish Tourist Board]

legedly helping an IRA prisoner to escape. He was next arrested in 1952 and this time was deported to France.

When not in jail, rousting about in pubs, or frightening off police, Behan worked as a house painter and as a free-lance journalist. He loved the sea and worked intermittently on ships, becoming a certified seaman in 1949. He lived a broad and ebullient life, shunning authority and smugness and befriending the boisterous, brawling people of the pubs and the ports.

Behan's first play, *The Quare Fellow,* based on his prison experiences, was refused by the Abbey Theatre and instead was presented at an avant-garde club in Dublin in 1954. It opened in London in 1956 and was highly praised by the critics. His second play, *The Hostage,* written in Gaelic under the title *An Gaill,* was first produced in Dublin in 1958. Brought to London, the English version was also highly successful.

In 1955 Behan married Beatrice ffrench-Salkeld, a painter and the daughter of a noted Dublin artist. He died in Dublin on March 20, 1964, of ailments resulting from his propensity for drinking.

WORK

Except for a number of one-act radio plays Behan's reputation as a dramatist of note rests solely on his two full-length plays, *The Quare Fellow* (1954) and *The Hostage* (1958). Both reveal an uncommon dramatic ability that enabled him to bring to the stage a true representation of the people in his world.

The Hostage, as produced by the American Conservatory Theatre (left), with Carol Teitel and Jay Doyle, and by the Abbey Theatre (right), with Maire Ni Ghrainna and Donal McCann as the hostage. [Courtesy American Conservatory Theatre, San Francisco, Calif., photograph by Hank Kranzler; Dermot Barry photograph]

Most critics have praised him for his insight and humanity; others fault his works for their naïveté and disjointedness.

The general tenor of Behan's work reflects his Irish Republican background. It is from the working class that he quarried most of his characters. Although he claimed not to have idealized the ordinary workingman, this character assumes a larger-than-life size and color and is made more human through the liberal application of anecdote, wit, and song. Thus, although Behan shows none of the romantic propensities of O'Casey, his work is in the tradition of O'Casey. *See* O'CASEY, SEAN.

The Quare Fellow takes its name from prison jargon for a condemned man. An expanded version of a radio play called *The Twisting of Another Rope*, it depicts the prisoners' world of manifold unkindness and few virtues, of relationships between warders and inmates, in such compassionate terms and with such realistically cruel detail that it becomes, with all its pettiness and humanity, the outside world in microcosm. Although characters wander in and out inconsistently, the play nevertheless is structured.

The Hostage shows greater control. Satirizing extremes of Irish nationalism and religious fervor, it is based on a true incident of the Irish Civil War of the 1920s and owes much with its interspersed songs to Irish balladry and the music hall.

In addition to the radio plays *A Garden Party* (pub. 1967) and *The Big House* (1963),

Behan is remembered for his brilliant autobiographical novel *Borstal Boy* (1958), which was adapted by Frank McMahon for the theatre and was first produced at the Abbey Theatre in 1967.

The Quare Fellow (1954). Comedy drama that presents a case for the abolition of capital punishment. The play depicts life in a Dublin prison during the twenty-four-hour period before a hanging and describes the impassive reaction of the inmates. The prisoners are getting ready for a visit from a government official when two new prisoners arrive. One of the "quare fellows" receives a reprieve, while the other is to be executed. Few distinctions are drawn between the prisoners, the officials, and the warders: brutality exists on both sides of the bars. Both the British and the Irish governments are objects of derision: the executioner comes over from England because no one in Ireland can meet the qualifications. Prison conditions are summarized by a prisoner who remarks: "The Free State didn't change anything more than the badge on the warders' caps."

The Hostage (1958). Tragicomedy employing farce, satire, and song and set in a disreputable Dublin lodging house, described by one of the characters as a "brockel." The house, owned by Monsewer, a former commander in the IRA, and run by Pat, who has served under him, is inhabited by religious eccentrics, prostitutes, and perverts. Their lives are disrupted by the arrival of a captive

English soldier whom the IRA intends to hold as a hostage for an Irishman sentenced to death by the British in Belfast. The hostage turns out to be a likable young man, confused and angry about his imprisonment. Everyone grows fond of him, including Teresa, a young serving girl, who falls in love with him; but Monsewer, Pat, and his girl Meg Dillon feel that loyalty to their cause demands his execution. The others want him to live, and they join together in an attempt to free him. A melee ensues when the British are led into the house, and the soldier is killed.

PLAYS

1. *The Quare Fellow.* Comedy drama, 3 acts. Published 1956. Produced Dublin, Pike Theatre, 1954; London, Theatre Royal, Stratford, May 24, 1956.

2. *The Hostage.* Play, 3 acts. Produced Dublin, Gaelic League (in Gaelic), 1958; London, Theatre Royal, Stratford, Oct. 14, 1958.

3. *The Big House.* Radio play. Published 1957. Produced London, Theatre Royal, Stratford, July 29, 1963.

4. *A Garden Party.* Radio play. Published 1967.

5. *Moving Out.* Radio play. Published 1967.

6. *Richard's Cork Leg.* Play. Under option to the Theatre Guild.

EDITIONS

Two Plays by Brendan Behan, Grove Press, New York, 1964.

The Quare Fellow. Published in *Seven Plays of the Modern Theatre,* with introduction by H. Clurman, Grove Press, New York, 1962.

CRITICISM

A. Simpson, *Beckett and Behan and a Theatre in Dublin,* New York, 1962; R. Jeffs, *Brendan Behan: Man and Showman,* Cleveland, 1966; S. McCann, ed., *The World of Brendan Behan,* New York, 1966; T. E. Boyle, *Brendan Behan,* New York, 1969.

BEHN, Aphra (1640–1689). The first woman to earn her living by writing, Aphra Behn (née Johnson), an Englishwoman, was a lively, ingenious poet, novelist, and dramatist. She is best known for her skillfully contrived tragicomedies of intrigue, influenced by the Spanish theatre, such as the popular *The Rover, or The Banish't Cavaliers* (two parts, 1677, 1681), in which, catering to the popular enthusiasm for the Italian *commedia dell'arte,* she used the characters Harlequin and Scaramouch. She also wrote tragedies, comedies, and plays dealing with moral problems, introducing unconventional ideas that appear modern even by twentieth-century standards. *See* COMMEDIA DELL'ARTE; TRAGICOMEDY.

From 1670, when her first play, *The Forc'd Marriage,* was produced, until her death, she contributed more than twenty plays to the stage, several of which proved successful, some remaining as stock pieces well into the eighteenth century. In addition to her work for the stage, she wrote numerous poems and pamphlets, and she also contributed to the novel when, in *Oroonoko* (1688), she made use of her early memories of life in the West Indies. Indirectly, this novel also made stage history, for Thomas Southerne's adaptation (1695) continued to appeal to audiences throughout the eighteenth century.

Among Mrs. Behn's other plays are *The Dutch Lover* (1673), a tragicomedy of intrigue based on a Spanish novel; *The Town Fop, or Sir Timothy Tawdrey* (1676); *Sir Patient Fancy* (1678), an intrigue play notable for the loose moral fiber of the characters; and *The Feign'd Curtizans, or A Night's Intrigue* (1679), another intrigue comedy, this time signaling Mrs. Behn's later work, which, save for a few problem dramas, was almost exclusively farce, in deference to the preferences of her audiences.

S. N. Behrman
(1893 –   )

Samuel Nathaniel Behrman was born in Worcester, Mass. on June 9, 1893. Early in his life he developed an interest in literature, and before the age of twenty he had written a vaudeville skit. He attended Harvard University, where he took part in the drama workshop, and graduated in 1916. A master's degree in English literature from Columbia University followed two years later. While trying to establish himself as a playwright,

S. N. Behrman. [Theatre Collection, The New York Public Library at Lincoln Center, Astor, Lenox and Tilden Foundations]

Lynn Fontanne
and Alfred Lunt in
The Second Man,
1927. [Photograph
by Vandamm.
Theatre Collection,
The New York
Public Library at
Lincoln Center,
Astor, Lenox and
Tilden
Foundations]

In the four decades since the appearance of *The Second Man,* Behrman has written twenty-two plays. *But for Whom Charlie* (1964), his most recent play, was produced by the Repertory Theatre of Lincoln Center for its initial season.

WORK

Behrman, a major representative of the American comedy of manners, examines with sophisticated humor the conventions of American upper-class life. His preeminence in the genre rests largely on his incisively drawn characters. Particularly skilled in depicting fashionable and perceptive women, Behrman uses them as instruments for social comment. At their best, his comedies are marked by a deft intermingling of philosophical comment with urbane and humorous dialogue. It has been said, however, that Behrman lacks the detachment necessary for the true comedy of manners and that he fails in his attempt to interweave serious matter with comic action. During the late 1930s, for example, when fascism was threatening, his plays became increasingly serious in tone, criticism breaking through the comic facade. *No Time for Comedy* (1939), about a writer torn between his talent for comedy and his inclination toward serious writing, could have been written about himself. *See* COMEDY OF MANNERS.

The plays most responsible for Behrman's success include the comedy *Biography* (1932), concerning Marion Froude, one of Behrman's sophisticated heroines, whose civilized and detached tolerance and wit present a devastating contrast to her zealous journalist lover, who must oppose evil at any cost; *The Second Man* (1927), in which a writer comes to realize that within him is the soul of a hedonist; *Rain from Heaven* (1934), a criticism of both fascism and those who are politically uncommitted, for Behrman an untenable point of view; and *End of Summer* (1936), a high comedy in which an idle rich lady escapes from an opportunistic psychiatrist into the arms of a young radical. Other plays of interest are *Meteor* (1929), a study of a successful and ruthless tycoon, Raphael Lord, who loses friends and family in the pursuit of success; *Jacobowsky and the Colonel* (1944), an adaptation of Franz Werfel's *Jacobowsky und der Oberst,* in which, against a World War II setting utilized both for comic

during the next nine years Behrman reviewed books for the *New York Times,* wrote short stories and articles, and collaborated with Kenyon Nicholson on two plays, *Bedside Manner* (1923) and *A Night's Work* (1924), both of which failed. Alone he wrote a comedy, *The Second Man,* which was successfully produced in 1927. Later plays, *Biography* (1932) and *End of Summer* (1936), also were well received.

In 1937 Behrman married Eliza Heifetz, sister of the violinist Jascha Heifetz. In 1938 the playwright, along with Maxwell Anderson, Robert Sherwood, Sidney Howard, and Elmer Rice, founded a producing organization, the Playwrights' Company, so that members could be both artistically and financially independent of Broadway producers.

(Opposite) Jay Fassett, Ina Claire, and Earle Larimore in *Biography,* 1932. [Photograph by Vandamm. Theatre Collection, The New York Public Library at Lincoln Center, Astor, Lenox and Tilden Foundations]

Ina Claire in two Theatre Guild productions: as Marion Froude in *Biography* (above left), New York, Guild Theatre, 1932; and as Leonie in *End of Summer*, New York, Guild Theatre, 1936. [Photographs by Vandamm. Theatre Collection, The New York Public Library at Lincoln Center, Astor, Lenox and Tilden Foundations]

effect and as a reflection of the underlying social comment, an anti-Semitic Polish colonel who is forced to flee the Nazis in the company of a resourceful Jew grows fond of the Jew despite himself; *Lord Pengo* (1962), a portrait of the idiosyncratic art dealer Duveen, based on Behrman's book *The Days of Duveen; Fanny* (1954), a musical adapted from Marcel Pagnol's *Marius* cycle; and *The Cold Wind and the Warm* (1958), an autobiographical play. Among other works are *Wine of Choice* (1938), *Brief Moment* (1931), *Dunnigan's Daughter* (1945), *Jane* (1952), *I Know My Love* (1949), and *But for Whom Charlie* (1964). Behrman's musical plays, adaptations, and comedies since World War II reflect a growing tendency toward sentimentality.

The Second Man (1927). Sophisticated comedy in which the ambivalent character of the novelist Clark Storey is explored. In his youth he had advocated socialism but had quickly abandoned it when experience taught

him that idealism is often accompanied by poverty. He then knowingly prostituted his talent by writing a biography glorifying a sweatshop proprietor, a book that launched his highly successful career. Now caught between his strong feeling for Monica Grey, a young woman passionately in love with him, and the indulgent love of Mrs. Kenneth Frayne, his former mistress and wealthy patroness, he chooses the latter. Having ensured an easy life, he recognizes within himself the existence of a "second man," one who would compromise his integrity rather than forgo a life of luxury.

Biography (1932). Urbane comedy dealing with the conflict between zealous commitment to ideals and tolerant acceptance. Marion Froude, a worldly and successful portrait painter and an intimate of great men, is approached by Richard Kurt, a muckraking editor who wants to publish her biography in his magazine. Leander Nolan, Marion's former lover, learns of the project and attempts to dissuade her from writing about her life, fearing that public knowledge of their affair will ruin his career. Pressed by Nolan's influential friends to suppress the biography, Kurt grows more determined than ever to publish it. Marion, trying to please everyone, is caught between Nolan's expedient self-interest and Kurt's fanatical idealism. She and Kurt fall in love, but his rabid intolerance of Nolan and of her own laissez-faire attitude moves Marion to destroy the manuscript, which she had written for her own pleasure. Kurt breaks with her, and Marion, having recognized their basic incompatibility, lets him go without recrimination.

Rain from Heaven (1934). Comedy of manners criticizing fascism and the politically disengaged. Rand Eldridge, a heroic explorer, visits the English manor of Lady Wyngate, whom he loves. He is accompanied by his wealthy older brother Hobart, who has two secret aims: to recruit an English Fascist for a Fascist youth movement in the United States and to destroy Rand's love for the liberal Lady Wyngate, thus driving his disillusioned brother to become the figurehead of the reactionary group. Arriving at the estate, Rand, who is peculiarly submissive to Hobart, explains to Lady Wyngate that he is deeply indebted to his brother for having financed his expeditions. Among the other guests, most of whom are fleeing from Communist and Nazi tyrannies, is Hugo Willens, a noted music critic who left Germany because of his Jewish ancestry. Soon Willens and Lady Wyngate discover a mutual attraction that Hobart uses to inflame Rand's jealousy. Then,

Theatre Guild presentation of *Wine of Choice*, with (l. to r.) Donald Cook, Claudia Morgan, Paul Stewart, Leslie Banks, Alexander Woollcott (seated), Theodore Newton, and Herbert Yost. New York, Guild Theatre, 1938. [Photograph by Vandamm. Theatre Collection, The New York Public Library at Lincoln Center, Astor, Lenox and Tilden Foundations]

(Above) John Halliday and Jane Cowl in *Rain from Heaven*. New York, Golden Theatre, 1934. [Photograph by Vandamm. Theatre Collection, The New York Public Library at Lincoln Center, Astor, Lenox and Tilden Foundations]

(Below) Osgood Perkins, Ina Claire, and Van Heflin in *End of Summer*. New York, Guild Theatre, 1936. [Theatre Collection, The New York Public Library at Lincoln Center, Astor, Lenox and Tilden Foundations]

Katharine Cornell and John Williams in *No Time for Comedy*. New York, Ethel Barrymore Theatre, 1939. [Theatre Collection, The New York Public Library at Lincoln Center, Astor, Lenox and Tilden Foundations]

when Rand hysterically attacks Lady Wyngate for her infidelity and calls Willens a "dirty Jew," she becomes aware of Rand's pettiness and of her own real love for Hugo. The philosophical Willens, feeling that he must aid the anti-Nazi movement, leaves, despite his love for Lady Wyngate, to work for the underground. Lady Wyngate vows to wait for him.

End of Summer (1936). Sophisticated comedy set in the Frothinghams' summer home in northern Maine during the Depression and suggesting by its title the impending end of the idle rich. Leonie Frothingham, beautiful millionairess and hedonist, is incapable of confronting the reality and challenge of a changing world. Estranged from her husband and dreading loneliness, she involves herself in a succession of affairs but never finds happiness. After an abortive affair with a Russian prince, she falls prey to Dr. Kenneth Rice, a mercenary psychoanalyst, and finally succumbs to Dennis McCarthy, an unscrupulous young radical who exploits her to finance a left-wing magazine. Meanwhile, her daughter Paula has fallen in love with Will Dexter, a penniless but uncompromising writer who is determined to succeed on his own. When Dexter leaves Paula, Leonie, keenly aware of the anguish of loneliness, urges Paula to follow him.

Laurence Olivier and Katharine Cornell in *No Time for Comedy*. New York, Ethel Barrymore Theatre, 1939. [Photograph by Vandamm. Theatre Collection, The New York Public Library at Lincoln Center, Astor, Lenox and Tilden Foundations]

PLAYS

Unless otherwise noted, the plays were first performed in New York.

Jason Robards, Jr., and Faye Dunaway in the Repertory Theatre of Lincoln Center production of *But for Whom Charlie.* New York, ANTA Washington Square Theatre, 1964. [Photograph by Martha Swope]

1. (With Kenyon Nicholson). *Bedside Manner*. Comedy, 1 act. Published 1924. Produced Threshold Theatre, 1923.

2. (With Nicholson). *A Night's Work*. Comedy, 1 act. Published 1926. Produced Peekskill, N.Y., Grand Theatre, June 7, 1924.

3. (With Owen Davis). *The Man Who Forgot*. Play.

4. *The Second Man*. Comedy, 3 acts. Published 1927. Produced Guild Theatre, Apr. 11, 1927.

5. (With Nicholson). *Love Is Like That*. Romantic comedy, 3 acts. Produced Cort Theatre, Apr. 18, 1927.

6. (Adaptation). *Serena Blandish*. Fabulous comedy, 2 acts. Published 1934. Produced Morosco Theatre, Jan. 23, 1929. Based on the novel by Enid Bagnold (1925).

7. *Meteor*. Comedy, 3 acts. Published 1930. Produced Guild Theatre, Dec. 23, 1929.

8. *Brief Moment*. Comedy, 3 acts. Published 1931. Produced Belasco Theatre, Nov. 9, 1931.

9. *Biography*. Comedy, 3 acts. Published 1933. Produced Guild Theatre, Dec. 12, 1932.

10. *A Love Story*. Play, 3 acts. Produced Philadelphia, Walnut Street Theatre, Dec. 13, 1933.

11. *Rain from Heaven*. Comedy, 3 acts. Published 1935. Produced John Golden Theatre, Dec. 24, 1934.

12. *End of Summer*. Comedy, 3 acts. Published 1936. Produced Guild Theatre, Feb. 17, 1936.

13. (Adaptation). *Amphitryon 38*. Comedy, prologue and 3 acts. Published 1943. Produced Shubert Theatre, Nov. 1, 1937. Based on Jean Giraudoux's play (1929).

14. *Wine of Choice*. Comedy, 3 acts. Published 1938. Produced Guild Theatre, Feb. 21, 1938.

15. *No Time for Comedy*. Comedy, 3 acts. Published 1939. Produced Ethel Barrymore Theatre, Apr. 17, 1939.

16. *The Talley Method*. Comedy, 3 acts. Published 1941. Produced Henry Miller's Theatre, Feb. 24, 1941.

17. (Adaptation). *The Pirate*. Comedy, 3 acts. Published 1943. Produced Martin Beck Theatre, Nov. 25, 1942. Music: Herbert Kingsley. Based on Ludwig Fulda's *Der Seeräuber* (1911).

18. (Adaptation). *Jacobowsky and the Colonel*. Comedy, 3 acts. Published 1944. Produced Martin Beck Theatre, Mar. 14, 1944. Based on Franz Werfel's *Jacobowsky und der Oberst* (1944).

19. *Dunnigan's Daughter*. Drama, 3 acts. Published 1946. Produced Golden Theatre, Dec. 26, 1945.

20. (Adaptation). *I Know My Love*. Comedy, 3 acts. Published 1952. Produced Shubert Theatre, Nov. 2, 1949. Based on Marcel Achard's *Auprès de ma blonde*.

21. *Let Me Hear the Melody*. Comedy. Produced Philadelphia, Walnut Street Theatre, Mar. 12, 1951.

22. (Adaptation). *Jane*. Comedy, 3 acts. Published 1952. Produced Coronet Theatre, Feb. 1, 1952. Based on W. Somerset Maugham's story.

23. (Adaptation). *Fanny*. Musical play, 2 acts. Published 1955. Produced Majestic Theatre, Nov. 4, 1954. Music and lyrics: Harold Rome. Based on Marcel Pagnol's *Marius* (1929), *Fanny* (1931), and *César* (1946).

24. *The Cold Wind and the Warm*. Play, 3 acts. Published 1959. Produced Morosco Theatre, Dec. 8, 1958.

25. *Lord Pengo*. Comedy drama, 3 acts. Published 1963. Produced Royale Theatre, Nov. 19, 1962. Based on Behrman's *The Days of Duveen*.

26. *But for Whom Charlie*. Play, 3 acts. Published 1964. Produced ANTA, Washington Square Theatre (Lincoln Center Drama Repertory Company), Mar. 12, 1964.

EDITIONS

Collections.
Three Plays, Farrar & Rinehart, New York, 1934; *Four Plays,* Random House, New York, 1955.
   Individual Plays.
   Amphitryon 38. Published in *Theatre Omnibus,* Hamilton, London, 1938.
   Biography. Published in *Sixteen Famous American Plays,* ed. by B. A. Cerf and V. H. Cartmell, Garden City, New York, 1941; *Representative Modern Plays,* ed. by R. Warnock, Scott, Foresman, Chicago, 1952; *American Dramatic Literature,* ed. by J. Y. Miller, McGraw-Hill, New York, 1961; *Best American Plays,* ed. by J. Gassner, Crown, New York, 1961.
   End of Summer. Published in *Twenty Best Plays of the Modern American Theatre,* ed. by J. Gassner, Crown, New York, 1939; *College Reader,* ed. by H. A. Watt and O. Cargill, Prentice-Hall, New York, 1948; *Famous American Plays of the 1930s,* ed. by H. Clurman, Dell, New York, 1959.
   Lord Pengo. Random House, New York, 1963.
   No Time for Comedy. Published in *Six Plays of 1939,* Hamilton, London, 1939; *The Pocket Book of Modern American Plays,* ed. by B. A. Cerf, Pocket Books, New York, 1942.
   Rain from Heaven. Published in *The Theatre Guild Anthology,* Random House, New York, 1936; *Twentieth Century Plays,* rev. ed., ed. by F. W. Chandler and R. A. Cordell, Nelson, New York, 1939.
   The Second Man. Published in *A Book of Dramas,* comp. by B. Carpenter, Prentice-Hall, New York, 1929; *Representative American Dramas, National and Local,* ed. by M. J. Moses and J. W. Krutch, rev. ed., Little, Brown, Boston, 1941; *Twenty-five Best Plays of the Modern American Theatre,* ed. by J. Gassner, Crown, New York, 1949.

BELASCO, David (b. San Francisco, July 25, 1853; d. New York, May 14, 1931). American dramatist whose work as a producer overshadowed his sentimental and often superficial melodramas. Noted for his managerial brilliance, his passion for mechanical innovations, particularly in the use of lighting, and his striving for realism in sets and costumes, Belasco worked with several companies as actor, stage manager, and director until 1907, when he built his own theatre in New York, known first as the Stuyvesant and finally as the new Belasco. His plays, most of which were written in collaboration, include adaptations of Dickens's novels, Goldsmith's *The Vicar of Wakefield,* plays and stories from the French and German, the work of other American playwrights, and even adaptations of his own earlier plays. His other works may be divided into melodrama, frontier drama, and fantasy plays. *See* GOLDSMITH, OLIVER.

Belasco's first major collaboration, with James A. Herne, resulted in a number of melodramas, notably *Within an Inch of His Life* (1879), in which a man attempts to end an affair before marriage; and *Hearts of Oak* (1879), based on the story of Enoch Arden (*see*

David Belasco. [Walter Hampden Memorial Library at The Players, New York]

HERNE, JAMES A.). With Henry C. de Mille he wrote a series of moral and romantic melodramas, among them *The Wife* (1887), about lovers separated through jealousy; and *The Charity Ball* (1889), in which sin causes intense suffering for the noble Rev. John van Buren and for his wastrel brother Dick, whose errors he attempts to correct. With Franklin Fyles, Belasco wrote *The Girl I Left behind Me* (1893), a sentimental western drama concerning an Indian girl who is accidentally killed while helping white people trapped in a Sioux uprising. Of his other frontier plays, the best known is *The Girl of the Golden West* (1905), made famous by Puccini, who used it as the basis for his opera of the same title.

Among Belasco's romantic melodramas, those written with John Luther Long are the most famous. They include *Madame Butterfly* (1900), later adapted as the libretto for one of Puccini's most famous operas; and *The Darling of the Gods* (1902), in which the Japanese princess Yo-San, who has fallen in love with the outlaw Kara against her father's will, meets her lover in heaven after both have committed suicide.

Belasco also wrote a few plays independently, of which the best is generally considered to be *The Return of Peter Grimm* (1911), a fantasy showing how the return of a spirit from the dead affects the living. Although the play is strongly sentimental, the theme of

Blanche Bates in
*The Girl of the
Golden West.*
[Theatre
Collection, The
New York Public
Library at Lincoln
Center, Astor,
Lenox and Tilden
Foundations]

the power of love raises it above the level of Belasco's other works.

Madame Butterfly (1900). Tragedy set in late-nineteenth-century Japan, based on a short story by John Luther Long. Madame Butterfly, mistress of Lieutenant Pinkerton of the United States Navy, has borne him a child and faithfully waited two years for him to return to Japan. The American Consul tries to persuade her to forget Pinkerton, but Butterfly clings to his promise to return "when the robins nest again." Hearing guns in the harbor, she realizes he has at last returned. Pinkerton, now married, is unable to face Butterfly and sends her some money through the Consul. His wife, after visiting Butterfly, urges him to see her. But Butterfly, true to her family's code "to die with honor when one can no longer live with honor," stabs herself and, as she dies, gives her child to the grief-stricken Pinkerton.

The Girl of the Golden West (1905). Drama epitomizing the spirit of the old West during the California gold rush. Although Minnie Falconer runs a saloon, she is respected by the community. When Dick Johnson, a highwayman, appears in town, Minnie falls in love with him. But Sheriff Rance, who is in love with Minnie, tells her that Johnson has committed a crime and is wanted by the law. Nevertheless, Minnie swears to stand by him, and when Johnson is wounded, she nurses him back to health. Now ready to pay the penalty for his crime, Johnson wishes to spare Minnie and surrenders secretly to a lynch mob. The members of the mob realize his willingness to repent and release him out of respect for Minnie's love. The play ends with Minnie and Johnson leaving California to start a new life.

BELCARI, Feo (1410–1484). Italian writer and dramatist, the earliest-known author of *sacre rappresentazioni* (mystery plays). The most important of these plays is *The Representation of Abraham and Isaac* (*Rappresentazione di Abramo ed Isac;* wr. ca. 1440, prod. 1443). The historical importance ascribed to it however, far exceeds its actual literary and dramatic merit. *See* MYSTERY PLAY.

BELLEMÈRE, Jean. *See* SARMENT, JEAN.

BELMONTE Y BERMÚDEZ, Luis de (1587?–?1650). Spanish poet and dramatist in the tradition of Lope de Vega, Belmonte is best known for *The Devil a Preacher* (*El diablo predicador,* 1623), although his authorship of this play is debated by scholars. Adapted from Lope's *Fray Diablo,* the play tells the story of Satan being forced by St. Michael to help a destitute Franciscan group. Only a few other plays attributed to Belmonte are extant, among them *The Apostate Woman of Valladolid* (*La renegada de Valladolid,* pub. 1652). *See* VEGA CARPIO, LOPE DE.

Jacinto Benavente
(1866 – 1954)

Jacinto Benavente y Martínez, Spanish dramatist and critic, was born on August 12, 1866, in Madrid, the only son of a distinguished pediatrician. As a child, Jacinto gave precocious evidence of his interest in the stage by writing short sketches for his own puppet theatre. He attended the San Isidro Institute, where he was an exceptional student, and later began to study law at the University of Madrid. However, after his father's death in 1885, Benavente left the university, determined to become a writer.

In the following years he began to attend theatre performances in Madrid and to read the works of the great dramatists, especially Shakespeare. He then joined a circus, eventually becoming its impresario, and with it toured France, Germany, and Russia. Next he decided to try his hand at acting: he joined the company of María Tubau, where he developed a love of the craft that was to endure all his life. In later years he performed whenever the opportunity arose, as, for example, in 1920, when he played the title role in Zorrilla's *Don Juan Tenorio*.

Benavente's first dramatic attempts took the form of a group of romantic fantasy plays published in 1892 under the title *Plays of Imagination* (*Teatro fantástico*). The following year he published a book of poetry and *Women's Letters* (*Cartas de mujeres*), a series of letters that reveal his unusual insight into feminine psychology. His first full-length play to be produced, *Another's Nest* (*El nido ajeno*, 1894), was not well received, but in 1896 the production of his *People of Importance* (*Gente conocida*) was an immediate success and launched a theatrical career that was to dominate the Spanish stage for the next half century. Benavente was early recognized as the foremost dramatist of the famous "generation of '98," a group of young writers, including Azorín, Valle Inclán, Baroja, and Unamuno, who following their country's defeat in the Spanish-American War publicly recognized the need for Spain's moral and cultural regeneration. *See* UNAMUNO, MIGUEL DE; VALLE INCLÁN, RAMÓN MARÍA DEL.

After 1900 Benavente began writing plays in rapid succession, and in the three years between 1901 and 1904 alone he wrote eighteen. *Saturday Night* (*La noche del sábado*, 1903) established his international reputation, and 1907 saw the production of *Bonds of Interest* (*Los intereses creados*), generally thought to be his critical masterpiece.

In 1913, after the enormous success of *The Passion Flower* (*La Malquerida*), Benavente was admitted to the Royal Spanish Academy. The same year the Société des Films Benavente was established in France with French and Spanish financial participation. However, after 1920, although there was scarcely a year in which he was not represented on the Madrid stage, his dramatic ability began to decline, and he produced no plays equal in quality to his earlier works.

Although Benavente did not marry and have children of his own, he inherited his father's intense interest in young people and eventually wrote numerous plays for them. In 1909 he and the actor Porredon founded a short-lived children's theatre that opened with a production of Benavente's *The Prince Who Learned Everything Out of Books* (*El príncipe que todo lo aprendió en los libros*), a fairy tale that was soon translated into many languages.

Between 1908 and 1912 Benavente wrote weekly articles for the newspaper *El Imparcial*. These were later collected in five volumes and published as *After-dinner Conversation* (*De sobremesa*). In addition, he published a series of papers on the theatre, translated plays by Shakespeare, Molière, Augier, and Dumas *père*, and edited the intellectual magazine *La Vida Literaria*.

During World War I, Benavente supported the German cause and even edited a symposium, *The Germanic Year* (*El año germanófilo*, 1916), in which he defended his position. In 1920 Benavente was named director of the Teatro Español, and in 1922 he was awarded the Nobel Prize for Literature.

At the outbreak of the Spanish Civil War, Benavente declared himself sympathetic to the Republican cause and left Madrid. There were conflicting stories of his whereabouts, but it is generally thought that he was captured in Valencia by Loyalist forces and taken back to Madrid, where he remained under house arrest. After the war Benavente made his peace with the Franco government and

Jacinto Benavente. [Biblioteca Nacional, Madrid]

was eventually the recipient of many official honors.

He continued to write plays, and his last to be produced was *The Brass Husband* (*El marido de bronce*, 1954). During his lifetime he was also regarded as one of Spain's outstanding literary critics. In June, 1954, while working on two new plays, Benavente became ill with a heart condition. He died in Madrid on July 14, 1954.

WORK

Benavente's plays set the tone for the Spanish stage during most of his lifetime and were for a time highly influential abroad. His enormous body of work, although occasionally mediocre, contains some of the best examples of twentieth-century Spanish drama. Inevitably, in the course of writing more than 175 plays and adaptations, he did not always maintain the same qualitative level: there are instances of repetition and lack of profundity. Though he was often criticized for his eclectic approach to contemporary European drama, he actually enriched the Spanish theatre by his introduction of themes and dramatic conventions that were being employed by the internationally famous playwrights of his day.

After an initial volume of short, lyrical dramatic sketches, *Plays of Imagination*

Rollo Peters (left) in *Bonds of Interest;* the first Theatre Guild production, April 19, 1919. [Theatre Collection, The New York Public Library at Lincoln Center, Astor, Lenox and Tilden Foundations]

(1892), Benavente began to satirize the decadent society of Madrid in dramas in which he tempered bitterness with romantic melancholy. Breaking, however, with the exaggerated nineteenth-century melodrama of José Echegaray and thus bringing the Spanish theatre up to date, Benavente adopted the attitude of the uninvolved, astute observer of life, at once tolerant and ironical. Nevertheless, during his long career, he did not limit himself to a single dramatic approach, and his protean production included short dialogues, comedies of manners, fairy tales, rural tragedies, imitations of the modes of the Oriental theatre, symbolic plays, and operetta libretti. As a leader of the generation of '98, he drew on sources outside the mainstream of Spanish tradition in an attempt to reinvigorate the national culture, upon whose decadence Spain's defeat in the Spanish-American War seemed to have set a seal. Though he was the critic and gadfly of contemporary mores in his early plays, there was essentially little of the social reformer about him, and the psychology of his characters appeared to interest him above all else. Therefore, even while his reputation was growing abroad, his works were subjected to more and more stringent criticism by his former comrades of the generation of '98, and Spain's younger writers objected strenuously when Benavente was awarded the Nobel Prize in 1922. By the end of his career, his theatre seemed to be almost an endorsement of the very society that he had mocked with wit and sharp observation.

Benavente's first successful play was *People of Importance* (1896), a loosely constructed but mordant satire concerning an impoverished aristocrat who seeks to rebuild his fortunes by marrying the illegitimate daughter of a successful businessman. This vein of social criticism was continued in *Bombastic Actors* (*La farándula*, 1897), in which the meaningless speeches of a provincial politician are compared to the empty histrionics of strolling actors; *The Wild Beasts' Banquet* (*La comida de las fieras*, 1898), in which a wealthy family suffers financial reverses and finds itself deserted by its former friends; *Vulgarity* (*Lo cursi*, 1901), the story of clumsy middle-class attempts at social elegance; and *The Governor's Wife* (*La gobernadora*, 1901), an exposé of the intrigues that control the cultural and political life of a provincial town.

Saturday Night (1903) established Benavente's reputation abroad. A highly complex and somewhat obscure work that Benavente described as "a novel for the stage," it is set on the Riviera and is a symbolic representation of the saturnalia of pre-World War I European aristocracy. In a mellower mood

Benavente put the same society and scene on-stage in *Princess Bebé* (*La princesa Bebé*, 1906), in which two democratically minded members of royalty find themselves at least temporarily thwarted by the social snobbery of their respective commoner lovers.

Benavente's acknowledged masterpiece is *Bonds of Interest* (1907), a delightful comedy in the *commedia dell'arte* style. In it love unites with material interest for the happy outcome. The mood is more pessimistic in a 1916 sequel, *The Joyous and Confident City* (*La ciudad alegre y confiada*), a philosophical drama in which the characters from *Bonds of Interest* suffer defeat and death but seem to enjoy a spiritual regeneration. *See* COMMEDIA DELL'ARTE.

Rustic tragedy is the theme of *The Passion Flower* (1913), one of Benavente's greatest international successes, in which a man's repressed passion for his stepdaughter explodes into violence and murder. Benavente returned to more traditional material in *Field of Ermine* (*Campo de armiño*, 1916); in this play a childless woman of noble birth learns to love and accept as her own a boy to whom she had originally been drawn under the mistaken assumption that he was her dead brother's illegitimate son. Benavente's intense interest in feminine psychology led to plays such as *A Lady* (*Una señora*, 1920), a "dramatic novel" about a woman abandoned by her ambitious lover; and *Autumnal Roses* (*Rosas de otoño*, 1905) and *Señora Ama* (1908), studies of monogamous women faced with the problem of philandering husbands.

Benavente also wrote several children's plays, the best known of which is *The Prince Who Learned Everything Out of Books* (1909). Other works of interest include plays in which Benavente made use of exotic locales: *The Fire Dragon* (*El dragón de fuego*, 1904), concerning an East Indian realm conquered by Europeans; and *The Yellow Jacket* (*La túnica amarilla*, 1916), an adaptation of an American play employing themes and techniques of the Oriental theatre.

Most critics agree that Benavente's later work, in which there was a growing commitment to more conventional ethics, is dramatically inferior to his earlier plays. Ironically enough, his "decline" began about the time he was awarded the Nobel Prize. He nevertheless continued to dominate the Madrid stage until his death. His last popular success was *Imprisoned Souls* (*Almas prisioneras*, 1953), a historical drama set in Mexico.

The Governor's Wife (*La gobernadora*, 1901). Satire in which a troupe of actors comes to a provincial city to present a play that is a point of controversy between conservatives and liberals. Josefina, wife of Governor Santiago, at first sides with the wealthy conservatives who protest that the play is immoral, and she persuades her husband to retract his permission for the performance. Manolo, secretary to the wealthy leader of the conservatives, Don Baldomero, and suitor of the latter's spoiled daughter, has long concealed a love for Josefina that began years before when she called upon him for a secret loan. Discovering that his long-lost brother is the theatrical troupe's manager, Manolo convinces Josefina that the play should be allowed, not only for his brother's sake but also because the town's majority is liberal.

To protect his interests, Baldomero attempts to blackmail Josefina with letters concerning her secret loan. When he publishes them in the newspaper, however, the citizens defend Josefina and accuse him of calumny. Santiago gives permission for the play's presentation as the town cheers him, and he is assured of a longer term in office.

Saturday Night (*La noche del sábado*, 1903). Drama focusing on the loves of functionless royalty and artistic bohemians in a Riviera winter resort. Imperia, an ambitious courtesan, has finally reached the top of the social ladder as the mistress of Prince Michael of Suavia. Her daughter Donina, the child of an earlier liaison, is a circus performer and the mistress of the clown Nunu. The corrupt Prince Florencio of Suavia, displaced as heir to the throne by the birth of a son to the reigning monarch, is attracted to Donina and purchases her from her unscrupulous lover. During an evening in a disreputable Riviera bar, Donina stabs Florencio, but his death is represented to the police as suicide. The murder coincides with the death of the infant heir to Suavia, and the way is now open for Prince Michael's accession to the throne. He refuses to rule without Imperia, but his mistress hesitates, feeling it her duty to remain with Donina. However, Donina dies begging Imperia to accompany Prince Michael. Free to follow "the only reality, the flight of our witches' spirits, as on Saturday night they turn to their ideal," Imperia leaves with Prince Michael to claim the destiny toward which her life had been tending.

Princess Bebé (*La princesa Bebé*, 1906). Satirical comedy contrasting royalty's aspiration for personal freedom and the common people's desire for privilege. Two cousins, Princess Helena (Bebé) and Prince Stephen, have been banished from Suavia by their uncle the Emperor, she for seeking a divorce and he for marrying a music-hall singer. But they cannot find freedom from the artificialities of court life because the world will not forget they are royalty. Neither Bebé's lover nor

Los intereses creados, as performed in Madrid by the Compañía Lope de Vega. [Courtesy Spanish Embassy]

Stephen's wife wishes to forgo the advantages of royal status. The royal cousins decide that the rare moments of happiness life brings can be obtained only by accepting life's disappointments and imposed responsibilities. It is perhaps not too late for them to love one another.

Autumnal Roses (*Rosas de otoño*, 1905). Comedy about marital infidelity and maturing love. Isabel, long-suffering wife of the philandering Gonzalo, and María Antonia, his daughter by his first wife, commiserate with each other about the infidelities of their husbands. When in desperation María pretends to have an affair, Isabel defends her right to do so. But Gonzalo asserts that both of them are wrong and that, despite his superficial relationships with other women, Isabel is the only one whom he has ever loved.

Bonds of Interest (*Los intereses creados*, 1907). Comedy in the style of the *commedia dell'arte* with many of its traditional characters: Columbine, Harlequin, Polichinelle, the Captain, and the Doctor. The handsome but impecunious Leander arrives in an Italian city with his crafty servant Crispin, who immediately plans to tap the wealth of the com-

munity. Leander at first resists Crispin's devious scheme but eventually gives way. Credit is obtained by convincing people that Leander is a wealthy aristocrat traveling incognito. Rumors of the distinguished visitor's arrival spread, and at a fete Leander meets and falls in love with Sylvia, daughter of the rich Polichinelle.

Leander, tortured by his deception, discloses his real identity to Sylvia, but Crispin, by making Polichinelle oppose the match, contrives for Sylvia to rebel against her father and flee to Leander's house. The wily Crispin then arouses public opinion against Polichinelle by spreading the rumor that he had attempted to have Leander murdered. He also convinces Leander's creditors that the young man's marriage to Sylvia is their only hope of payment. Eventually Crispin's deception is exposed. Confronted by Polichinelle and the law, he persuades the crowd that the lovers nevertheless belong together. Addressing the audience, Sylvia declares that although men are puppets controlled by bonds of interest, an ennobling thread of love winds through every heart.

Señora Ama (1908). Drama in which Dominica patiently endures her husband Feliciano's infidelity and even welcomes his illegitimate children and their mothers into her house. She had hoped that a child of their own would stop his philandering, but they have had no children. Then Dominica suddenly changes, and she refuses to accept the children and their mothers. When Feliciano is injured on his way to visit another woman, she upbraids him, finally announcing that she is pregnant. Feliciano is henceforth to stay at home and become a dutiful father. Feliciano promises to reform, and once again Dominica forgives him.

The School of Princesses (*La escuela de las princesas*, 1909). Comedy of manners set in an imaginary royal court. Princess Constanza is betrothed to Prince Albert of Suavia, but she is in love with Duke Alexander, one of her subjects. The King, her uncle, consents to her becoming affianced to Alexander because the match is popular with his restless subjects, and he offers Prince Albert the hand of Constanza's sister, Princess Felicia, instead. However, Constanza now finds Albert more attractive than her fiancé, whom she begins to regard as an ambitious upstart. The Prince dissuades Constanza from dismissing Alexander, convincing her that happiness is to be found in fulfilling responsibilities through sacrifice.

The Prince Who Learned Everything Out of Books (*El príncipe que todo lo aprendió en los libros*, 1909). Children's fantasy about a young prince who sets out to seek his fortune equipped only with a little knowledge from his tutor and some illusions from his parents. Although he encounters ogres, witches, woodchoppers, and beautiful princesses, none of them is what his fairy tales have led him to expect. He returns home safely with a beautiful princess as his bride, having gained experience of life through exposure to its deceptions and dangers.

The Passion Flower (*La Malquerida*, 1913). Drama set in the prosperous farmlands of Castile. Raimunda, wife of Esteban, announces the engagement of Acacia, her daughter by a previous marriage, to Faustino, but on his way home the latter is murdered. The primary suspect is Acacia's cousin Norbert, who had at one time been engaged to her. Norbert is tried and acquitted, but Faustino's family swears to hunt him down and kill him. He takes refuge in Raimunda's house, and she learns that Faustino was actually killed by Esteban's loyal servant Rubio. Raimunda begins to suspect that Esteban has long repressed a passion for Acacia, who for her part has always treated him with disdain, although the servant Juliana is convinced that Acacia unconsciously loves her

stepfather. Esteban confesses his secret lust to Raimunda, but she urges him not to reveal his feelings and so to dishonor her house. She plans to send her daughter away, but Acacia insists that Esteban be the one to go. However, as he is about to leave, Acacia suddenly confesses her love and begs that he be permitted to stay. Raimunda, knowing Esteban will protect Acacia, moves forward as though to kill her daughter but is shot by Esteban. As she dies, she forgives Acacia, content that the latter will never give herself to her mother's murderer.

Field of Ermine (*Campo de armiño*, 1916). Drama set in Madrid. On leaving boarding school, Gerardo, supposedly the illegitimate son of a deceased marquis, goes to live with his mother Natalia. However, his aunt Irene, out of maternal feelings for Gerardo, and affection for her brother the Marquis, soon takes Gerardo under her wing in order to pre-

Nance O'Neill in a scene from *The Passion Flower*, 1920. [Theatre Collection, The New York Public Library at Lincoln Center, Astor, Lenox and Tilden Foundations]

vent her family from disinheriting him. For the first time in his life Gerardo feels accepted. Then a certain Paco Utrillo visits Irene and offers to sell her letters from Natalia that establish that he, Utrillo, is Gerardo's father. Horrified by this disclosure, Irene sends the innocent Gerardo back to Natalia, but he runs away before reaching his mother's house. When Irene learns that he is missing, she is distracted with worry and realizes how much she loves the child. Gerardo returns and begs Irene to hire him as a servant, but she welcomes him as her son.

A Lady (*Una señora*, 1920). Tragedy about a woman's great love for a man who deserts her when she is no longer of use to him. Ever since his arrival, penniless, in Madrid, Enrique has been helped by a widow, Elisa. When her money eventually runs out, he marries a rich girl to help him in his political career. Inconsolable after her lover's betrayal and deserted by her friends, Elisa sinks into poverty. At length she receives a package of money. Recognizing Enrique's handwriting on the envelope, she flings the money away and dies, happy to have had this token from him.

Pepa Doncel (1928). Drama in which Felisa, after leading an adventurous life under the name Pepa Doncel, marries a wealthy man, who also adopts her daughter Genoveva. Upon her husband's death she goes to live in his native provincial city, where because of her late husband's wealth and social position she is able to buy her way into society. Pepa attempts to marry Genoveva to socially prominent Silverio, but Silverio learns that Genoveva is in love with another man. When Pepa herself proposes to him, he accepts. This incurs the wrath of the locally prominent families, and Pepa leaves the city. However, the community finds that it cannot live without Pepa's money, and so she returns. Genoveva marries her sweetheart, and Pepa lives on in the city as a great lady.

PLAYS

Unless otherwise noted, the plays were first performed in Madrid. Nos. 1 to 8 were published as *Teatro fantástico* (1892).

1. *Comedia italiana* (*Italian Comedy*). Comedy, 2 scenes. Written before 1892.

2. *El criado de Don Juan* (*Don Juan's Servant*). Play, 1 act. Written before 1892. Produced Teatro Español, Mar. 29, 1911.

3. *La senda del amor* (*The Path of Love*). Comedy for marionettes, 1 act. Written before 1892.

4. *La blancura de Pierrot* (*The Whiteness of Pierrot*). Pantomine, 1 act. Written before 1892.

5. *Cuento de primavera* (*Spring Story*). Comedy; prologue and epilogue, 2 acts. Written before 1892.

6. *Amor de artista* (*Artist's Love*). Panegyric, 1 act. Written before 1892.

7. *Modernismo* (*Modernism*). Play, 1 act. Written before 1892.

8. *El encanto de una hora** (*The Magic of an Hour*). Dialogue, 1 act. Written 1892. Produced Teatro de la Princesa, Dec. 30, 1905.

9. *El nido ajeno** (*Another's Nest*). Comedy, 3 acts. Produced Teatro de la Comedia, Oct. 6, 1894.

10. *Gente conocida* (*People of Importance*). Comedy, 4 acts. Produced Teatro de la Comedia, Oct. 21, 1896.

11. *El marido de la Téllez* (*The Téllez Woman's Husband*). Comedy, 1 act. Produced Teatro de Lara, Feb. 13, 1897.

12. *De alivio* (*On Comfort*). Monologue, 1 act. Produced Teatro de la Comedia, Feb. 27, 1897.

13. *Don Juan*. Comedy, 5 acts. Produced Teatro de la Princesa, Oct. 31, 1897. Based on the play by Molière.

14. *La farándula* (*Bombastic Actors*). Comedy, 2 acts. Produced Teatro de Lara, Nov. 30, 1897.

15. *La comida de las fieras* (*The Wild Beasts' Banquet*). Comedy, 3 acts. Produced Teatro de la Comedia, Nov. 7, 1898.

16. *Teatro feminista* (*Feminist Theatre*). Diversion, 1 act. Produced Teatro de la Comedia, Dec. 28, 1898. Music: Pablo Barbero.

17. (Adaptation). *Cuento de amor* (*Love Story*). Fantastic comedy, 3 acts. Produced Teatro de la Comedia, Mar. 11, 1899. Based on Shakespeare's *Twelfth Night*.

18. *Operación quirúrgica* (*Surgery*). Comedy, 1 act. Produced Teatro de Lara, May 4, 1899.

19. *Despedida cruel* (*Cruel Farewell*). Comedy, 1 act. Produced Teatro de Lara, Dec. 7, 1899.

20. *La gata de Ángora* (*The Angora Cat*). Comedy, 4 acts. Produced Teatro de la Comedia, Mar. 31, 1900.

21. *Viaje de instrucción* (*The Journey of Instruction*). Musical comedy, 1 act. Produced Teatro Alhambra, Apr. 6, 1900. Music: Amadeo Vives.

22. *Por la herida* (*Through Affliction*). Drama, 1 act. Produced Teatro de Novedades, July 15, 1900.

23. *Modas* (*Fashions*). Farce, 1 act. Produced Teatro de Lara, Jan. 18, 1901.

24. *Lo cursi* (*Vulgarity*). Comedy, 3 acts. Produced Teatro de la Comedia, Jan. 19, 1901.

25. *Sin querer* (*In Perfect Innocence*). Comic sketch, 1 act. Produced Teatro de la Comedia, Mar. 3, 1901.

26. *Sacrificios* (*Sacrifices*). Drama, 3 acts. Produced Teatro de Novedades, July 19, 1901.

27. *La gobernadora** (*The Governor's Wife*). Comedy, 3 acts. Produced Teatro de la Comedia, Oct. 8, 1901.

28. *El primo román* (*The First Roman*). Comedy, 3 acts. Produced Saragossa, Nov. 12, 1901.

29. *Amor de amar* (*Love of Loving*). Comedy, 2 acts. Produced Teatro de la Comedia, Feb. 24, 1902.

30. *¡Liberdad!* (*Liberty!*). Comedy, 3 acts. Produced Teatro de la Comedia, Mar. 17, 1902. Based on a play by Santiago Rusiñol y Prats.

31. *En tren de los maridos* (*In the Husbands' Retinue*). Comedy, 2 acts. Produced Teatro de Lara, Apr. 18, 1902.

32. *Alma triunfante* (*Triumphant Soul*). Drama, 3 acts. Produced Teatro de la Comedia, Dec. 2, 1902.

33. *El automóvil* (*The Automobile*). Comedy, 2 acts. Produced Teatro de Lara, Dec. 19, 1902.

34. *La noche del sábado** (*Saturday Night*). Novel for the stage, 5 acts. Produced Teatro Español, Mar. 17, 1903.

35. *Los favoritos* (*The Favorites*). Comedy, 1 act. Produced Seville, Mar. 20, 1903.

36. *El hombrecito* (*The Manikin*). Comedy, 3 acts. Produced Teatro de la Comedia, Mar. 23, 1903.

37. (Translation). *Mademoiselle de Belle-Isle*. Comedy, 5 acts. Produced Valladolid, Oct. 20, 1903. Based on the play of the same name by Alexandre Dumas *père*.

38. *Porqué se ama* (*Why One Loves*). Comedy, 1 act. Produced Teatro Español, Oct. 26, 1903.

39. *Al natural* (*No Affectation*). Comedy, 2 acts. Produced Teatro de Lara, Nov. 20, 1903.

40. *La casa de la dicha* (*The House of Happiness*). Drama, 1 act. Produced Barcelona, Teatro Íntimo, Dec. 9, 1903.

41. *No fumadores** (*No Smoking*). Farce, 1 act. Produced Teatro de Lara, Mar. 3, 1904.

42. (Translation). *Richelieu.* Drama, 5 acts. Produced Mexico City, Mar. 15, 1904. Based on the play of the same name by Edward Bulwer-Lytton.

43. *El dragón de fuego* (*The Fire Dragon*). Drama, 3 acts and epilogue. Produced Teatro Español, Mar. 16, 1904.

44. *La princesa Bebé** (*Princess Bebé*). Comedy, 4 acts. Written 1904. Produced Teatro Español, Mar. 31, 1906.

45. *Manon Lescaut.* Drama, 3 acts. Produced Teatro Español, Feb. 25, 1905.

46. *Rosas de otoño** (*Autumnal Roses*). Comedy, 3 acts. Produced Teatro Español, Apr. 13, 1905.

47. *El susto de la condesa* (*The Countess' Terror*). Dialogue, 1 act. Produced Teatro Español, Nov. 15, 1905.

48. *Cuento inmoral* (*Immoral Story*). Monologue, 1 act. Produced Teatro Español, Nov. 15, 1905.

49. *Los malhechores del bien** (*The Evil Doers of Good*). Comedy, 2 acts. Produced Teatro de Lara, Dec. l, 1905.

50. *La sobresalienta* (*The Understudy*). Lyrical farce, 1 act. Produced Teatro Español, Dec. 23, 1905.

51. *Las cigarras hormigas* (*The Harvest Flies*). Comedy, 3 acts. Produced Teatro de la Comedia, Dec. 24, 1905.

52. (Translation). *Buena boda* (*A Good Marriage*). Comedy, 3 acts. Produced Teatro de Sociedad, 1905. Based on Émile Augier's *Un beau mariage.*

53. *Más fuerte que el amor* (*Stronger than Love*). Drama, 4 acts. Produced Teatro Español, Feb. 22, 1906.

54. *El amor asusta* (*Love Shocks*). Comedy, 1 act. Produced Jan. 10, 1907.

55. *Los buhos* (*The Owls*). Comedy, 3 acts. Produced Teatro de Lara, Feb. 8, 1907.

56. *Abuela y nieta* (*Grandmother and Grandchild*). Dialogue, 1 act. Produced Teatro de Lara, Feb. 21, 1907.

57. *La copa encantada* (*The Enchanted Cup*). Musical comedy, 1 act. Produced Teatro de la Zarzuela, Mar. 16, 1907. Music: Vicente Lleó.

58. *La princesa sin corazón* (*The Heartless Princess*). Horror play, 1 act. Written 1907. Published 1908.

59. *Todos somos unos* (*All Are One*). Lyric farce, 1 act. Produced Teatro Esclava, Sept. 21, 1907.

60. *La historia de Otelo* (*The Story of Othello*). Comedy, 1 act. Produced Teatro de Apolo, Oct. 11, 1907.

61. *Los ojos de los muertos* (*The Eyes of the Dead*). Drama, 3 acts. Produced Teatro de la Princesa, Nov. 7, 1907.

62. *La sonrisa de Gioconda** (*The Smile of Mona Lisa*). Comedy, 1 act. Written 1907. Published 1908.

63. *El último minué.* (*The Last Minuet*). Comedy, 1 act. Written 1907. Produced Teatro Benavente, Oct. 23, 1909.

64. *Los intereses creados** (*Bonds of Interest*). Comedy, 3 acts. Produced Teatro de Lara, Dec. 9, 1907.

65. *Señora Ama.* Comedy, 3 acts. Produced Teatro de la Princesa, Feb. 22, 1908.

66. *De pequeñas causas . . .* (*From Small Beginnings . . .*). Comedy, 1 act. Produced Teatro de la Princesa, Mar. 14, 1908.

67. *El marido de su viuda** (*His Widow's Husband*). Comedy, 1 act. Produced Teatro del Príncipe Alfonso, Oct. 19, 1908.

68. *La fuerza bruta** (*Brute Force*). Comedy, 1 act. Produced Teatro de Lara, Nov. 10, 1908.

69. *Hacia la verdad* (*Near the Truth*). Comedy, 3 acts. Produced Teatro del Príncipe Alfonso, Dec. 23, 1908.

70. *Por las nubes** (*In the Clouds*). Comedy, 2 acts. Produced Teatro de Lara, Jan. 20, 1909.

71. *De cerca** (*At Close Range*). Comedy, 1 act. Produced Teatro de Lara, Apr. 10, 1909.

72. *¡A ver qué hace un hombre!* (*Let's See What a Man Does!*). Play, 1 act. Published 1909.

73. *La escuela de las princesas** (*The School of Princesses*). Comedy, 3 acts. Produced Teatro de la Comedia, Oct. 14, 1909.

74. *La señorita se aburre* (*The Señorita Is Bored*). Comedy, 1 act. Produced Teatro del Príncipe Alfonso, Dec. 1, 1909.

75. *El príncipe que todo lo aprendió en los libros** (*The Prince Who Learned Everything Out of Books*). Children's fantasy, 2 acts. Produced Teatro del Príncipe Alfonso, Dec. 20, 1909.

76. *Ganarse la vida* (*Earning a Living*). Comedy, 1 act. Produced Teatro del Príncipe Alfonso, Dec. 20, 1909.

77. *El nietecito* (*The Little Grandson*). Comedy, 1 act. Produced Teatro del Príncipe Alfonso, Jan. 27, 1910.

78. *Caridad* (*Charity*). Monologue, 1 act. Published 1918. Produced Teatro Real, Feb. 3, 1911.

79. *La losa de los sueños* (*The Graveyard of Dreams*). Comedy, 2 acts. Produced Teatro de Lara, Nov. 9, 1911.

80. (Translation). *El rey Lear* (*King Lear*). Prose tragedy, 5 acts. Published 1911. Based on the play by Shakespeare.

81. *La Malquerida** (*The Passion Flower*). Drama, 3 acts. Produced Teatro de la Princesa, Dec. 12, 1913.

82. (Translation). *El destino manda* (*Destiny Commands*). Drama, 2 acts. Produced Teatro de la Princesa, Mar. 25, 1914. Based on Paul Hervieu's *Le destin est maître.*

83. *El collar de estrellas* (*The Necklace of Stars*). Comedy, 4 acts. Produced Teatro de la Princesa, Mar. 4, 1915.

84. *La Verdad** (*The Truth*). Dialogue, 1 act. Published 1915. Produced Teatro de la Comedia.

85. *La propia estimación* (*Proper Esteem*). Comedy, 3 acts. Produced Teatro de la Comedia, Dec. 22, 1915.

86. *Campo de armiño** (*Field of Ermine*). Drama, 3 acts. Produced Teatro de la Princesa, Feb. 14, 1916.

87. (Translation). *La túnica amarilla* (*The Yellow Jacket*). Chinese fable, 3 acts. Produced Teatro de la Princesa, Apr. 22, 1916. Based on the play *The Yellow Jacket,* by George C. Hazelton and Harry Benrimo.

88. *La ciudad alegre y confiada* (*The Joyous and Confident City*). Comedy, prologue and 3 acts. Produced Teatro de Lara, May 18, 1916. Sequel to *Los intereses creados.*

89. *El mal que nos hacen* (*The Evil Done to Us*). Comedy, 3 acts. Produced Teatro de la Princesa, Mar. 23, 1917.

90. *Los cachorros* (*The Puppies*). Comedy, 3 acts. Produced Teatro de la Princesa, Mar. 8, 1918.

91. *La Mefistófela* (*Mephistopheles*). Comic operetta, 3 acts. Produced Teatro de la Reina Victoria, Apr. 29, 1918. Music: Prudencio Muñoz.

92. *La Inmaculada de los Dolores* (*Our Lady of Sorrows*). Dramatic novel, 3 acts. Produced Teatro de Lara, Apr. 30, 1918.

93. *La ley de los hijos* (*The Law of Children*). Drama, 3 acts. Produced Teatro de la Zarzuela, Dec. 23, 1918.

94. *Por ser con todos leal ser para todos traidor* (*Loyalty to All Through Treachery to All*). Drama, 3 acts. Produced Teatro del Centro, Mar. 5, 1919.

95. *La vestal de occidente* (*The Vestal of the West*). Drama, 4 acts. Produced Teatro de la Princesa, Mar. 29, 1919.

96. *La honra de los hombres* (*The Honor of Men*). Comedy, 2 acts. Produced Teatro de Lara, May 2, 1919.

97. (Adaptation). *El audaz* (*The Bold Man*). Drama, 5 acts. Produced Teatro Español, Dec. 6, 1919. Based on the novel of the same name by Benito Pérez Galdós.

98. *La Cenicienta* (*Cinderella*). Fairy tale, 3 acts. Produced Teatro Español, Dec. 20, 1919.

99. *Y va de cuento* (*And Once Upon a Time*). Fantasy, prologue and 4 acts. Produced Dec. 23, 1919.

100. *La fuerza bruta* (*Brute Force*). Musical comedy, 2 acts. Produced Teatro de la Zarzuela, 1919. Music: Chaves.

101. *Una señora** (*A Lady*). Dramatic novel, 3 acts. Produced Teatro del Centro, Jan. 2, 1920.

102. *Una pobre mujer* (*A Poor Woman*). Drama, 3 acts. Produced Teatro de la Princesa, Apr. 3, 1920.

103. *Más allá de la muerte* (*Beyond Death*). Drama, 3 acts. Produced Buenos Aires, August, 1922.

104. *Por que se quitó Juan de la bebida* (*Why Juan Quit*

Drinking). Monologue. Produced Montevideo, Teatro Soles, Aug. 30, 1922.

105. *Lecciones de buen amor* (*Lessons in Good Love*). Comedy, 3 acts. Produced Teatro Español, Apr. 2, 1924.

106. *Un par de botas* (*A Pair of Boots*). Comedy, 1 act. Produced Teatro de la Princesa, May 24, 1924.

107. *Alfilerazos* (*Pinpricks*). Comedy, 3 acts. Produced Buenos Aires, Teatro Avenida, June 18, 1924; Madrid, Teatro del Centro, Oct. 5, 1925.

108. *La otra honra* (*The Other Honor*). Comedy, 3 acts. Produced Teatro de Lara, Sept. 19, 1924.

109. *La virtud sospechosa* (*Suspect Virtue*). Comedy, 3 acts. Produced Teatro Fontalba, Oct. 20, 1924.

110. *Nadie sabe lo que quiere, o El bailarín y el trabajador* (*Nobody Knows What He Wants, or The Dancer and the Laborer*). Comedy, 3 acts. Produced Teatro Cómico, Mar. 14, 1925.

111. *¡Si creerás tú que es por mi gusto!* (*If You Think I Want It This Way!*). Dialogue, 1 act. Published 1925.

112. *El suicidio de Lucerito* (*Lucerito's Suicide*). Comedy, 1 act. Produced Teatro Alcázar, July 17, 1925.

113. *Los nuevos yernos* (*The New Sons-in-law*). Comedy, 3 acts. Produced Teatro Fontalba, Oct. 2, 1925.

114. *La mariposa que voló sobre el mar* (*The Butterfly That Flew over the Sea*). Comedy, 3 acts. Produced Teatro Fontalba, Sept. 22, 1926.

115. *El hijo de Polichinela* (*The Son of Pulchinella*). Comedy, prologue and 3 acts. Produced Teatro de Lara, Apr. 16, 1927.

116. *A las puertas del cielo* (*At the Gates of Heaven*). Dialogue, 1 act. Published 1927.

117. *La noche iluminada* (*The Illuminated Night*). Magical comedy, 3 acts. Produced Teatro Fontalba, Dec. 22, 1927.

118. *El demonio fué antes ángel* (*Angel before Devil*). Comedy, 3 acts. Produced Teatro Calderón, Feb. 18, 1928.

119. *¡No quiero, no quiero!* (*I Don't Want To, I Don't Want To!*). Comedy, 3 acts. Produced Teatro Fontalba, Mar. 10, 1928.

120. *Pepa Doncel.* Comedy, 3 acts. Produced Teatro Calderón, Nov. 21, 1928.

121. *Para el cielo y los altares* (*For Heaven and the Altars*). Drama, 3 acts and epilogue. Published 1929.

122. *Vidas cruzadas* (*Crossed Lives*). Screenplay, 2 parts. Produced Teatro de la Reina Victoria, Mar. 30, 1929.

123. *Los amigos del hombre* (*Man's Friends*). Farce, 4 acts. Produced Teatro de la Avenida, Nov. 3, 1930.

124. *Los andrajos de la púrpura* (*Purple Tatters*). Drama, 5 acts. Produced Teatro Muñoz Seca, Nov. 6, 1930.

125. *De muy buena familia* (*From a Very Good Family*). Comedy, 3 acts. Produced Teatro Muñoz Seca, Mar. 11, 1931.

126. *Literatura* (*Literature*). Comedy, 4 acts. Published 1931. Produced Teatro Alcázar, Apr. 4, 1931.

127. *La melodía del jazz-band* (*The Melody of the Jazz Band*). Comedy, prologue and 3 acts. Published 1931. Produced Teatro Fontalba, Oct. 30, 1931.

128. *Cuando los hijos de Eva no son los hijos de Adán* (*When Eve's Sons Are Not Adam's Sons*). Comedy, 3 acts. Produced Teatro Calderón, Nov. 5, 1931. Based on Margaret Kennedy's novel *The Constant Nymph* (1924).

129. *Santa Rusia.* Trilogy, 7 scenes, first part. Produced Teatro Beatriz, Oct. 6, 1932.

130. *La duquesa gitana* (*The Gypsy Duchess*). Magic comedy, 5 acts. Produced Teatro Fontalba, Oct. 28, 1932.

131. *La moral del divorcio* (*The Moral of Divorce*). Dialogue lecture, 3 parts. Produced Teatro de la Avenida, Nov. 4, 1932.

132. *La verdad inventada* (*The Invented Truth*). Comedy, 3 acts. Produced Teatro de Lara, Oct. 27, 1933.

133. *El rival de su mujer* (*His Wife's Rival*). Comedy, 3 acts. Produced Buenos Aires, Teatro Odeón, 1933.

134. *El pan comido en la mano* (*Bread Eaten from the Hand*). Comedy, 3 acts. Produced Teatro Fontalba, Jan. 12, 1934.

135. *Ni al amor ni al mar* (*Neither to Love nor to the Sea*). Drama, 4 acts and epilogue. Produced Teatro Español, Jan. 19, 1934.

136. *Memorias de un madrileño* (*Memoirs of a Madrid Man*). Moving tableaux, 5 acts. Produced Teatro de Lara, Nov. 8, 1934.

137. *La novia de nieve* (*The Snow Bride*). Comedy, prologue and 3 acts. Produced Teatro Español, Nov. 29, 1934.

138. *"No juguéis con esas cosas"* (*"Don't Play with Those Things"*). Comedy, 3 acts. Produced Teatro Esclava, Jan. 18, 1935.

139. *Cualquiera lo sabe* (*Anyone Knows That*). Comedy, 3 acts. Produced Teatro de la Comedia, Feb. 13, 1935.

140. *Lo increíble* (*The Incredible*). Comedy, 3 acts. Produced Teatro de la Comedia, Oct. 25, 1940.

141. *Aves y pájaros* (*Birds and Fowl*). Play, 2 parts. Produced Teatro de Lara, Oct. 30, 1940.

142. *Abuelo y nieto* (*Grandfather and Grandson*). Dialogue, 1 act. Produced San Sebastián, Teatro del Príncipe, Aug. 29, 1941.

143. *Y amargaba . . .* (*And It Was Bitter*). Comedy, 3 acts. Produced Teatro de la Zarzuela, Nov. 19, 1941.

144. *La última carta* (*The Last Letter*). Comedy, 3 acts. Produced Teatro Alcázar, Dec. 9, 1941.

145. *La honradez de la cerradura* (*The Integrity of the Lock*). Comedy, 3 acts. Produced Teatro Español, Apr. 4, 1942.

146. *La culpa es tuya* (*It's Your Fault*). Comedy, 3 acts. Published 1943. Produced San Sebastián, August, 1942; Madrid, Teatro de la Zarzuela, Sept. 17, 1942.

147. *Al fin, mujer* (*Finally, Woman*). Comedy, 3 acts. Produced San Sebastián, Teatro del Príncipe, Sept. 13, 1942; Madrid, Teatro Alcázar, Nov. 17, 1942.

148. *¡Hija del alma!* (*Daughter of My Soul!*). Play, 1 act. Produced Teatro de Lara, Sept. 17, 1942.

149. *La enlutada* (*The Mourner*). Play, 3 acts. Published 1943. Produced Saragossa, Teatro Principal, Oct. 16, 1942.

150. *El demonio del teatro* (*The Demon of the Theatre*). Comedy, 3 acts. Published 1943. Produced Teatro Cómico, Oct. 28, 1942.

151. *Don Magín él de las magias* (*Don Magín the Magician*). Comedy, 3 acts. Produced Barcelona, Teatro Barcelona, Mar. 26, 1944; Madrid, Teatro Alcázar, Jan. 12, 1945.

152. *Los niños perdidos en la selva* (*Children Lost in the Forest*). Dramatic novel, 4 acts. Produced Madrid, Teatro de la Infanta Beatriz, Apr. 14, 1944; San Sebastián, Teatro Principal, Oct. 14, 1944.

153. *Espejo de grandes* (*Mirror of the Great*). Historical play, 1 act. Produced Oct. 12, 1944; Madrid, Teatro de Lara, June 11, 1946.

154. *Nieve en Mayo* (*Snow in May*). Dramatic poem, 4 acts. Produced Teatro de la Zarzuela, Jan. 19, 1945.

155. *La ciudad doliente* (*The Suffering City*). Comedy, 3 acts. Produced Teatro de la Comedia, Apr. 14, 1945.

156. *Titania.* Comedy, 3 acts. Produced Buenos Aires, Sept. 25, 1945; Madrid, Teatro Calderón, Nov. 8, 1946.

157. *La infanzona* (*The Noblewoman*). Drama, 3 acts. Produced Buenos Aires, Dec. 6, 1945; Madrid, Teatro Calderón, Jan. 10, 1947.

158. *Al servicio de su majestad imperial* (*In the Service of His Imperial Majesty*). Comedy, 1 act. Published 1947.

159. *Abdicación* (*Abdication*). Comedy, 3 acts. Produced Teatro de Lara, Mar. 27, 1948.

160. *Divorcio de almas* (*Divorce of Souls*). Comedy, 3 acts. Produced Teatro Fontalba, Sept. 30, 1948.

161. *Adoración* (*Adoration*). Dramatic comedy, prologue and 2 acts. Produced Teatro Cómico, Dec. 3, 1948.

162. *Al amor hay que mandarlo al colegio* (*Love Should Be Sent to School*). Comedy, 4 episodes. Produced Teatro de Lara, Sept. 29, 1950.

163. *Su amante esposa* (*His Lover-Wife*). Comedy, 3 acts.

Produced Teatro de la Infanta Isabel, Oct. 20, 1950.

164. *Tu una vez y el diablo diez* (*You Once, the Devil Ten Times*). Comedy, 3 acts. Produced Valladolid, Teatro Lope de Vega, Oct. 23, 1950; Madrid, Teatro de la Infanta Isabel, Mar. 27, 1951.

165. *Mater imperatrix*. Dramatic comedy, 3 acts. Produced Barcelona, Teatro de la Comedia, Nov. 29, 1950; Madrid, Teatro de la Comedia, Jan. 30, 1951.

166. *La vida en verso* (*Life in Verse*). Comedy, 3 acts. Published 1953. Produced Teatro de la Infanta Isabel, Nov. 9, 1951.

167. *Ha llegado Don Juan* (*Don Juan Has Arrived*). Comedy, prologue and 2 acts. Produced Barcelona, Teatro de la Comedia, Apr. 12, 1952.

168. *El lebrel del cielo* (*The Hound of Heaven*). Comedy, 3 acts. Published 1953. Produced Teatro Calderón, Apr. 25, 1952. Based on Francis Thompson's poem of the same name (1893).

169. *Servir* (*To Serve*). Comedy, 2 acts and interlude. Produced Teatro María Guerrero, Jan. 22, 1953.

170. *El alfiler en la boca* (*A Pin in the Mouth*). Comedy, 3 acts. Produced Teatro de la Infanta Isabel, Feb. 13, 1953.

171. *Almas prisioneras* (*Imprisoned Souls*). Drama, prologue and 2 acts. Produced Teatro Álvarez Quintero, Feb. 26, 1953.

172. *Caperucita asusta al lobo* (*Little Red Riding-Hood Frightens the Wolf*). Comedy, 3 acts. Produced Teatro de la Infanta Isabel, Sept. 23, 1953.

173. *Hijos padres de sus padres* (*Sons Fathers of Their Fathers*). Comedy, 3 acts. Produced Teatro de Lara, Feb. 11, 1954.

174. *El marido de bronce* (*The Brass Husband*). Comedy, 3 acts. Produced Teatro de la Infanta Isabel, Apr. 23, 1954.

175. *El bufón de Hamlet* (*The Buffoon of Hamlet*). Play.

176. *Por salvar el amor* (*To Save Love*). Play.

EDITIONS

Collections.

Plays, ed. and tr. by J. G. Underhill, 4 vols., New York, 1917–1924; *Teatro,* 38 vols., Madrid, 1904–1931; *Obras completas,* 9 vols., Madrid, 1940–1950.

Individual Plays.

Another's Nest. Published in *Nineteenth Century Spanish Plays,* ed. by L. E. Brett, New York, 1935.

At Close Range. J. G. Underhill, tr., New York, 1936.

Bonds of Interest. Published in *Spanish Drama,* ed. by A. Flores and tr. by J. G. Underhill, New York, 1962.

Brute Force. J. G. Underhill, tr., New York, 1936.

His Widow's Husband. Published in *The Nobel Prize Treasury,* ed. by M. McClintock and tr. by J. G. Underhill, New York, 1948.

No Smoking. Published in *Adventures in World Literature,* ed. by R. B. Inglis and W. K. Stewart and tr. by J. G. Underhill, New York, 1936.

The Passion Flower. Published in *Twenty-five Modern Plays,* ed. by S. M. Tucker and A. S. Downer and tr. by J. G. Underhill, 3d ed., New York, 1953.

The Smile of Mona Lisa. J. A. Herman, tr., Boston, 1915.

CRITICISM

J. R. Sánchez, *Estudio crítico acerca de La Malquerida, drama de Jacinto Benavente,* Madrid, 1913; F. de Onís, *Jacinto Benavente: Estudio literario,* New York, 1923; W. Starkie, *Jacinto Benavente,* Oxford, 1924; A. Lázaro, *Jacinto Benavente: De su vida y su obra,* Madrid, 1925; *id., Biografía de Jacinto Benavente,* Madrid, 1930; J. Vila Selma, *El teatro de Benavente: Fin de siglo,* Madrid, 1952; S. Córdoba, *Benavente desde que le conocí,* Madrid, 1954; A. Guardiola, *Benavente: Su vida y teatro portentoso,* Madrid, 1954; F. C. Sáinz de Robles, *Jacinto Benavente,* Madrid, 1954; I. Sánchez Estevan, *Jacinto Benavente y su teatro,* Barcelona, 1954; M. C. Penuelas, *Jacinto Benavente,* New York, 1969.

Sem Benelli
(1877 – 1949)

Sem Benelli, Italian poet and dramatist, was born in Filettole di Prato, on August 10, 1877, to a family of poor artisans. His father's death interrupted his schooling, particularly his study of literature, and obliged him to seek employment as a craftsman. He also began to write for newspapers and to try other literary forms, producing a translation of *Oedipus the King* in 1898. Benelli wrote his first play in 1902, though he discarded his earliest attempts in his mature years. His first important poem was *A Son of the Times* (*Un figlio dei tempi,* 1905). He then began to write bourgeois comedies, which were well received. Greater acclaim came with neoromantic dramas such as *The Jest* (*La cena delle beffe,* 1909), based on a story by Antonio Francesco Grazzini from a collection of stories called *Suppers* (*Cene*).

Benelli served as an army officer in World War I and later became a Fascist deputy. He left the movement to protest the assassination of Matteotti (1924), only to return to it during the 1930s, when he fought in the Italo-Ethiopian War. His experiences in Ethiopia produced a book, *Africa and I* (*Io in Affrica,* 1936).

Sem Benelli.
[Federico Arborio Mella, Milan]

Benelli finally rejected fascism and emigrated to Switzerland. Repatriated after the fall of fascism, he published a bitter anti-Fascist polemic, *Slavery* (*Schiavitù*, 1946). He died in Zoagli, Genova Province, on December 18, 1949.

WORK

Benelli's dramatic works reflect a neoromantic reaction to the growing realism of the late nineteenth century. Many of the characters in his verse plays, which comprise the bulk of his thirty dramas, appear against spectacular, often melodramatic settings while absorbed in the deep inner conflict of reconciling an illusory ideal with the real world. In this Benelli continued the effort of D'Annunzio to detach Italian drama from the theatre of bourgeois realism. Benelli found much of the material for his historical plays in the intrigues of sixteenth-century Italy. *See* D'ANNUNZIO, GABRIELE.

His three major dramas, *The Mask of Brutus* (*La maschera di Bruto*, pub. 1908), *The Jest* (1909), and *The Love of the Three Kings* (*L'amore dei tre re*, 1910), describe tormented characters, such as Lorenzino de' Medici in *The Mask* and Gianetto in *The Jest*. The characters are elaborations of a type already established by Benelli in his prose comedy *The Bookworm* (*Tignola*, 1908), in which Giuliano Innocenti is a passive bookstore employee who dreams of being a man of the world. Realizing this ambition by falsely representing himself as a swashbuckler, he wins Adelaide, a desirable society woman, as his mistress and is ultimately wounded in a duel with her husband. His dream is punctured, forcing him back to the musty confines of the bookstore, where he accepts the reality of his true role.

Among the historical plays that reveal Benelli's romantic attraction to the past are *The Mantellaccio Society of Poets* (*Il Mantellaccio*, 1911), a love story set in the sixteenth-century academic world; *The Gorgon* (*La gorgona*, 1913), set in medieval Pisa; *The Wedding of the Centaurs* (*Le nozze dei centauri*, 1915), which concerns the conflict of the barbarian and Christian worlds, as does *Rosmunda* (1911); and *Florence* (*Fiorenza*, 1930) and *Caterina Sforza* (1934), which present historical portraits of great Renaissance figures and cities. Popular but less esteemed plays include a number of prose comedies, among them *The Spider* (*Il ragno*, 1935) and *The Elephant* (*L'elefante*, 1937), in which Benelli returned to his theme of the weak man who assumes the "mask" of strength. Benelli's last plays, *The Orchid* (*L'orchidea*, 1938), *The Party* (*La festa*, 1940), *Fear* (*Paura*, 1947), and the unpublished and unproduced *Virgin Gold* (*Oro vergine*, wr. 1949), are of minor importance.

The Jest (*La cena delle beffe*, 1909). Drama set in Florence in the time of Lorenzo the Magnificent. Gianetto has vowed vengeance on the brothers Neri and Gabriello, who stole his mistress Ginevra and caused his humiliation. At a banquet Gianetto encourages Gabriello to leave Florence. He gets Neri drunk and persuades him to oppose the Medici. He then proceeds to spread the rumor that Neri is mad and has him locked up. Clad in Gabriello's cloak, Gianetto visits Ginevra. Neri is judged harmless and, upon his release, learns that Gianetto will see Ginevra again. Leaving the young girl who has sheltered him, Neri goes to Ginevra's house, hides behind a tapestry, and mistakenly stabs his own brother, who also is Ginevra's lover. When he discovers his fratricide, Neri actually does become insane. Gianetto, feeling no remorse for what he has done, drops to his knees and recites a prayer of gratitude for the successful outcome of his vindictive scheme.

The Love of the Three Kings (*L'amore dei tre re*, 1910). Verse tragedy set in medieval times in an Italian castle forty years after a barbarian invasion. The play contrasts the untamed barbarism of the older generation (the original invaders) with the sensitivity of the younger generation, civilized by contact with Christian culture. The beautiful Flora, in love with her cousin Avito, has been sold into marriage with Manfredo, son of the fierce barbarian warrior Archibaldo, to ensure the freedom of her people. Archibaldo discovers her love for Avito and murders her. The old barbarian then places poison on the dead girl's lips, confident that Avito will go to kiss her as she lies in her coffin. In his despair, Manfredo also kisses her and dies beside his rival, as his cruel father bewails the loss of his beloved son. The play served as the libretto for Italo Montemezzi's opera of the same name (1913).

The Elephant (*L'elefante*, 1937). Comedy in which Sergio leaves his wife Nadia, a woman who dreams of owning a bank. He returns to his parents' home and enjoys life writing songs. Soon he discovers that Nadia, with the assistance of a conniving war profiteer whom she wishes to marry, has taken over her father-in-law's factory. Sergio puts his own considerable business acumen to work to get back everything his father has lost. For, like the elephant, Sergio will work if he has to, but only so that he may enjoy life.

PLAYS

1. *Ferdinando Lassalle*. Play. Published 1902.
2. *La terra* (*The Earth*). Play. Published 1903.
3. *Vita gaia* (*Happy Life*). Play. Published 1904.
4. (With Giulio de Frenzi). *La morale di Casanova* (*The Moral of Casanova*). Play. Published 1906.

An Arthur Hopkins production of *The Jest,* with Basil Sydney (standing) as Gianetto. New York, Plymouth Theatre, 1926. [Theatre Collection, The New York Public Library at Lincoln Center, Astor, Lenox and Tilden Foundations]

5. *Tignola* (*The Bookworm*). Comedy, 3 acts. Published 1908. Produced Genoa, Teatro Paganini, Feb. 10, 1908.

6. *La maschera di Bruto* (*The Mask of Brutus*). Play. Published 1908.

7. *La cena delle beffe** (*The Jest*). Dramatic poem, 4 acts. Published 1909. Produced Rome, Teatro Argentina, Apr. 16, 1909.

8. *L'amore dei tre re* (*The Love of the Three Kings*). Tragic poem, 3 acts; verse. Published 1910. Produced Rome, Teatro Argentina, Apr. 16, 1910.

9. *Il Mantellaccio* (*The Mantellaccio Society of Poets*). Dramatic poem, 4 acts. Published 1911. Produced Rome and Turin, Mar. 31, 1911.

10. *Rosmunda*. Tragedy, 4 acts. Published 1911. Produced Milan, Teatro Lirico, Dec. 20, 1911.

11. *La gorgona* (*The Gorgon*). Epic drama, 4 acts. Published 1913. Produced Trieste, Politeama Rossetti, Mar. 14, 1913.

12. *Le nozze dei centauri* (*The Wedding of the Centaurs*). Dramatic poem, 4 acts; verse. Produced Turin, Teatro Carignano, Apr. 17, 1915.

13. *Ali* (*Wings*). Drama, 4 acts. Produced Milan, Teatro Manzoni, Mar. 14, 1921.

14. *L'arzigigolo* (*The Enigma*). Play, 4 acts. Produced Rome, Teatro Costanzi, Oct. 17, 1922.

15. *La santa primavera* (*Holy Spring*). Play, 3 parts. Produced Turin, Parco del Valentino, July 21, 1923.

16. *L'amorosa tragedia* (*The Tragedy of Love*). Dramatic poem, 3 acts. Produced Rome, Teatro Valle, Apr. 14, 1925.

17. *Il vezzo di perle* (*The Pearl Necklace*). Comedy, 4 acts. Produced Milan, Teatro Olimpia, Mar 6, 1926.

18. *Con le stelle* (*With the Stars*). Mystery, prologue and 3 acts. Produced Milan, Teatro Manzoni, Feb. 26, 1927.

19. *Orfeo e Proserpina* (*Orpheus and Persephone*). Lyric drama, 4 acts. Published 1929. Produced Milan, Teatro Lirico, Dec. 18, 1928.

20. *Fiorenza* (*Florence*). Dramatic poem, 3 acts. Produced Milan, Apr. 16, 1930.

21. *Eroi* (*Heroes*). War drama, 1 act. Produced San Remo, Teatro del Casino Municipale, Jan. 22, 1931.

22. *Madre Regina* (*Mother Regina*). Drama of revolution, 1 act. Produced San Remo, 1931.

23. *Adamo ed Eva* (*Adam and Eve*). Fantastic comedy, 3 acts. Produced San Remo, Teatro del Casino Municipale, Feb. 1, 1932.

24. *Caterina Sforza*. Play. Produced Forlì, Teatro Comunale, Jan. 27, 1934.

25. *Il ragno* (*The Spider*). Comedy, 3 acts. Published 1935. Produced Milan, Teatro Odeon, Mar. 19, 1935.

26. *L'elefante* (*The Elephant*). Comedy, 3 acts. Produced 1937.

27. *L'orchidea* (*The Orchid*). Comedy, 3 acts. Published 1938. Produced San Remo, Teatro del Casino Municipale, Mar. 1, 1938.

28. *La festa* (*The Party*). Play. Produced Milan, Nov. 6, 1940.

29. *Paura* (*Fear*). Drama, 3 acts. Published 1947. Produced Florence, La Pergola, May 8, 1947.

30. *Oro vergine* (*Virgin Gold*). Play. Written 1949.

EDITIONS

The Love of the Three Kings. Published in *Chief Contemporary Dramatists*, ed. by T. H. Dickinson and tr. by H. Jones, 3d ser., Houghton Mifflin, Boston, 1930.

BENNETT, [Enoch] Arnold (1867–1931). Popular English novelist and short-story writer who produced only one outstanding play, *Milestones* (1912). Written in collaboration with Edward Knoblock, it is a novelistic comedy drama covering the behind-the-

Arnold Bennett.
[Theatre
Collection, The
New York Public
Library at Lincoln
Center, Astor,
Lenox and Tilden
Foundations]

scenes machinations, human and political, of an English industrial family through several generations. *The Great Adventure* (1911) is a comedy about a famous artist who allows his dead valet to be buried in his place. Among Bennett's other plays are *Cupid and Common Sense* (1908); *What the Public Wants* (1909); *The Honeymoon* (1911); *Rivals for Rosamund* (1914); *The Title* (1918); *Judith* (1919); *Sacred and Profane Love* (1919); *The Love Match* (1922); *Body and Soul* (1922); *London Life* (1924), with Knoblock; and *Return Journey* (1928).

BEOLCO, Angelo. *See* RUZZANTE, IL.

Hjalmar Bergman
(1883 – 1931)

Hjalmar Frederik Bergman, Swedish novelist, dramatist, poet, and screenwriter, was born in Örebro on December 19, 1883. He was educated there and in Västerås. (Later, in his works, he fused the two cities into the imaginary Wadköping.) His father, a well-to-do banker, supplied him with the means to spend ten years abroad; his travels took him to the Orient, Greece, and Italy. During this time he published a play, *Mary, Mother of Jesus* (*Maria, Jesu Moder*, 1905), and, in 1908, married Stina Lindberg, whose parents were both actors. In 1909 financial difficulties at home forced him to return and earn a livelihood from his writing.

Despite his prolific output during the years following his marriage and his return to Sweden, recognition came slowly. The collection *The Marionette Plays* (*Marionettspel*, pub. 1917) took him out of obscurity, but it was as a novelist, with the publication of *Markurells of Wadköping* (*Makurells i Wadköping*, 1919), that Bergman first gained a large following among the general public. That same year, *An Experiment* (*Ett experiment*), one of his most original plays, closed after only one performance. In 1923, at the invitation of the great Swedish film director Victor Sjöström, for whom he had written a number of screenplays before the latter's departure for Hollywood, Bergman left for the United States. Nothing came of the journey: his screenplays were rejected alternately by Sjöström's producers and the director himself, and Bergman returned to Sweden in less than a year. Consolation for the failure of his American trip was not long in coming, for *Swedenhielms,* a realistic comedy that he wrote in 1923, won him popularity as a dramatist. *Dollar* (pub. 1927), the polemical result of his

Hjalmar Bergman. [Swedish Information Service]

American experience; *The Rabble* (*Patrasket,* pub. 1928); and the stage adaptations of his most famous novels, *The Baron's Will* (*Hans nåds testamente,* 1931) and *Markurells of Wadköping* (1929), confirmed his position as a major Swedish dramatist.

Although in poor health during his final years, he continued writing vigorously until his death on New Year's Day, 1931, in Berlin. If he never achieved the greatness he sought, he remains a unique interpreter of the Swedish national temperament.

WORK

After an experimental, avant-garde period during which he wrote mostly one-act plays and failed to impress the general public, Bergman attained success with the productions of what have been called the two best-loved comedies in the Swedish language, *Swedenhielms* (1925) and *Markurells of Wadköping* (1929), both of which evoke the special qualities of small-town life in Sweden.

Before he wrote *The Marionette Plays* (pub. 1917), he was groping for a style. *Mary, Mother of Jesus* (wr. 1905, prod. 1961), a Biblical play in verse; *Savonarola* (1908), a historical play; and *Mrs. Vendla's Necklace* (*Fru Vendlas kedja,* 1908) all show disparate influences on the author, notably those of Maeterlinck, Strindberg, and Ibsen. *See* IBSEN, HENRIK; MAETERLINCK, MAURICE; STRINDBERG, AUGUST.

With *The Marionette Plays—Death's Harlequin* (*Dödens Arlekin*), *A Shadow* (*En skugga*), and *Mr. Sleeman Is Coming* (*Herr Sleeman kommer*)—Bergman, still influenced by Maeterlinck, began a series of realistic and poetic works appraising man's nature and the forces that guide him. The mature experimentation of an artist who had mastered his medium is obvious in plays such as *An Experiment* (1919), which contrasts a philosophizing scientist and a poor man who expatiates on the ways of the rich; and *The Door* (*Porton,* pub. 1923), a subtle Maeterlinckian drama.

Beginning with *Swedenhielms,* Bergman gave full vent to his genius for comedy. The eccentric members of the Swedenhielm family have been recognized by generations of Swedes as classic impersonations of national types. Subsequently, he produced some of the most charming plays in the Swedish repertoire, most notably the adaptations of his popular folk chronicles, *Markurells of Wadköping* (1929) and *The Baron's Will* (1931). Markurells is one of the great comic characters of the Swedish stage.

Mr. Sleeman Is Coming (*Herr Sleeman kommer,* pub. 1917). One-act drama belonging to *The Marionette Plays* (*Marionettspel*).

Anders de Wahl in *Swedenhielms,* Grand Theatre, Malmö. [Swedish Information Service]

Young Anne-Marie lives with her spinster aunts Bina and Mina, who have arranged a marriage between their niece and Mr. Sleeman, a wealthy businessman. The night before her fiancé is due to arrive, Anne-Marie escapes for a final idyll in the woods with her beloved Walter, a hunter. When she returns in the morning, she is ready to begin her new life as a married woman. Sleeman, middle-aged, bald, and partially lame, appears and expresses his love for her in words strangely similar to those of the hunter: "I shall have no friend but her. . . . I want to die the same day, the same hour, the same moment as Anne-Marie." Her response to Sleeman, ironically, reiterates what she had said to Walter: that she is so happy and that if she begins to cry, she will never stop.

Swedenhielms (1925). Comedy in four acts about the unorthodox family of a Nobel Prize winner. Swedenhielm, a widower and an eccentric inventor, has two spendthrift sons, Rolf (his assistant) and Bo (a lieutenant), and a daughter, Julia, an aspiring actress. The family is looked after by Marta Boman, Swedenhielm's sister-in-law. Old Swedenhielm is elated at winning the Nobel Prize, but his delight turns to misery when he learns that Bo appears to have forged his name to procure loans. Eventually Marta confesses that she is the forger, her aim having been to raise money to hold the eccentric family together.

Scene from *Herr Sleeman kommer,* Royal Dramatic Theatre, Stockholm. [Drottningholms Teatermuseum]

Markurells of Wadköping (*Markurells i Wadköping,* 1929).   The innkeeper Markurell has made himself the most powerful man in Wadköping so that the town will treat his son Johan better than it treated him. Johan is about to take matriculation examinations, and Markurell fears that the boy may be unable to pass. Thus he devises a plan to bribe the examiners, preparing a fantastic smorgasbord for them and making a large donation to the school. As the examiners enjoy his meal, they unwittingly reveal what the whole town (with the exception of Markurell) knows: Johan is really the son of Markurell's bitter enemy, Judge de Roche. Far from turning him into a monster, as everyone expects, the severity of the blow brings out the kindness Mrs. Markurell claims always lay dormant in her husband. He even gives the Countess de Roche, the judge's wife, incriminating papers with which he had planned to blackmail her husband. News is brought that De Roche's boy and Johan, who are very close friends, have fought because young De Roche called Markurell a swindler. Johan's quickness to defend Markurell's honor reassures Markurell that his boy's affection will always be his. When Johan brings home the news that he has succeeded at his matriculation, Markurell has quite forgotten his pain, and the play ends in a student celebration.

PLAYS

1. *Maria, Jesu Moder* (*Mary, Mother of Jesus*). Play. Written 1905. Produced 1961.
2. *Fru Vendlas kedja* (*Mrs. Vendla's Necklace*). Play. Produced 1908.
3. *Savonarola.* Play. Produced 1908.
4. *Parisina.* Play. Produced 1915.
5. *Marionettspel* (*The Marionette Plays*): *Dödens Arlekin* (*Death's Harlequin*); *En skugga* (*A Shadow*); *Herr Sleeman kommer* (*Mr. Sleeman Is Coming*). Three plays. Published 1917.
6. *Ett experiment* (*An Experiment*). Play. Published 1918. Produced 1919.
7. *Sagan* (*The Legend*). Play. Written 1919/20. Produced 1942.
8. *Vävaren i Bagdad* (*The Weaver of Bagdad*). Play. Published 1921. Produced 1936.
9. *Porton* (*The Door*). Play. Published 1923.
10. *Spelhuset* (*The Casino*). Play. Published 1923.
11. *Swedenhielms*.* Play. Written 1923. Produced 1925.
12. *Dollar.* Play. Published 1927.
13. *Patrasket* (*The Rabble*). Play. Published 1928.
14. *Markurells i Wadköping** (*Markurells of Wadköping*). Play. Published 1930. Produced 1929.
15. *Hans nåds testamente** (*The Baron's Will*). Play. Published 1930. Produced 1931.

EDITIONS

Collections.

Four Plays, ed. by W. Johnson, with introduction by
S. Bergman, University of Washington Press, Seattle,
1968.

Individual Plays.

Mr. Sleeman Is Coming. Published in *Scandinavian
Plays of the Twentieth Century,* tr. by H. Alexander, vol. 1,
Princeton, N.J., 1944–1951.

Swedenhielms. Published in *Scandinavian Plays of the
Twentieth Century,* tr. by H. Alexander and L. Jones, vol.
3, Princeton, N.J., 1944–1951.

CRITICISM

E. Sprinchorn, "Hjalmar Bergman," *Tulane Drama Review,* vol. VI, 1961.

BERLIN, Irving (1888–   ). A Russian-
born American composer and lyricist whose
many compositions, the first of which was
published in 1907, were written for musical
comedy, the revue stage, and films. Some of
the musical shows to which he contributed or
which he wrote in their entirety are *Watch
Your Step* (1914), *The Ziegfeld Follies of 1918,
Yip, Yip, Yaphank* (1918), a series of Music
Box revues (1921–1924), *The Cocoanuts* (1925),
Face the Music (1932), *As Thousands Cheer*
(1933), *Louisiana Purchase* (1940), *This Is the
Army* (1942), *Annie Get Your Gun* (1946), *Miss
Liberty* (1949), *Call Me Madam* (1950), and *Mr.
President* (1962). Berlin wrote original scores
for a number of films including *Top Hat*
(1935) and *Holiday Inn* (1942), and many of
his stage hits have been filmed. Some of his
song successes—"Easter Parade," "God Bless
America," and "White Christmas"—have
become standards in the American repertory
of popular music. *See* MUSICAL COMEDY.

Face the Music, by
Irving Berlin. New
York, New
Amsterdam
Theatre, 1932.
[Photograph by
Vandamm. Theatre
Collection, The
New York Public
Library at Lincoln
Center, Astor,
Lenox and Tilden
Foundations]

Jean-Jacques Bernard
(1888 −)

Jean-Jacques Bernard, French dramatist, was born in Enghien-les-Bains, near Paris, on July 30, 1888. He was educated in Paris, attending the Lycée Carnot and the Sorbonne. His father, Tristan Bernard, had a great facility for writing farces. Jean-Jacques did not inherit this gift, but by the time he was twenty-one he was sufficiently interested in the theatre to make his debut with the one-act *A Trip for Two* (*Le voyage à deux,* 1909). Three years later he wrote another one-acter, *The Joy of Sacrifice* (*La joie du sacrifice*, 1912), which revealed the sensitivity that was to permeate his future work. In January, 1914, before entering the army, he produced a collection of three short sketches under the title *The Grocer* (*L'épicier*). As France became embroiled in World War I, Bernard was writing war sketches from the front lines that were published in the newspaper *Excelsior* and later collected and published, after his release from the army, under the title *The Children Are Playing* (*Les enfants jouent*, 1919). *See* BERNARD, TRISTAN.

In addition to his articles for *Excelsior,* it was during the war that Bernard also wrote his first full-length play, *The House That Was Spared* (*La maison épargnée*), which was produced in 1919. In 1921 the drama *The Sulky Fire* (*Le feu qui reprend mal*), presented

Jean-Jacques Bernard. [Theatre Collection, The New York Public Library at Lincoln Center, Astor, Lenox and Tilden Foundations]

by the Escholiers, a private dramatic group, showed the continuing deep effect of the war upon Bernard.

With *Martine* (1922), Bernard for the first time in many years drew away from war themes and began what became known as *l'école du silence* ("the school of silence"). In the company of Gaston Baty, director of the avant-garde Compagnie de la Chimère, and his talented stable of playwrights, Bernard did much to revive the theatre in postwar France.

After the production of *Martine,* Bernard continued to write steadily for the theatre. *The Springtime of Others* (*Le printemps des autres*) and *Invitation to a Voyage* (*L'invitation au voyage*) appeared in 1924, *Denise Marette* in 1925, *The Unquiet Spirit* (*L'âme en peine*) and the one-act *The Poet's Secret* (*Le secret d'Arvers*) in 1926, *The Sisters Guédonec* (*Les soeurs Guédonec*) and *In Search of Hearts* (*À la recherche des coeurs*) in 1931, *National 6* (*Nationale 6*) in 1935, and *Madeleine* (*Le jardinier d'Ispahan*) in 1939. During the German occupation of France two of Bernard's plays were produced in Geneva: *Mary Stuart* (*Marie Stuart,* 1942) and *Louise de la Vallière* (1943).

During the winter of 1941 Bernard was arrested by the Nazis and interned at the Royallieu camp in Compiègne. He was released for reasons of health in March, 1942. His journal, *The Camp of Slow Death* (*Le camp de la mort lente,* 1945), tells of his ordeal and reflects the influences leading to his postwar conversion to Catholicism. After its appearance Bernard wrote a collection of short stories based on the occupation, *Red Bread* (*Le pain rouge,* 1947), and a novel entitled *Marie and the Vagabond* (*Marie et le vagabond,* 1949).

Bernard was beset by the cruelties of war all his life. He lost his oldest son in World War II when the latter was arrested for activities in the French Resistance movement and sent to the Mauthausen concentration camp in Austria. Bernard's father, also tired and broken by the war, died in 1947.

Bernard continues to write plays and also work with his brother in the film industry. His reflections on the theatre are contained in *My Friend the Theatre* (*Mon ami le théâtre,* 1958).

WORK

From the traditional rhetoric of classical theatre in France, from the classical emphasis on the written word—with gestures and scenery serving only to elaborate what is being spoken on the stage—Bernard and his contemporaries of the interwar period in France digressed to form a new school of

theatre sometimes called the school of silence. For Bernard, silence has great theatrical meaning: the quiet gesture, the unexpressed, and the half-expressed are, for him, often more interesting and profound than what can be uttered. Handling dialogue and character with great insight, Bernard prepares a dramatic atmosphere in which characters no longer need to express their emotions in words. Silence here becomes more effective and moving than the actual statement, and by it Bernard's characters more clearly express their innermost selves.

Bernard himself explains the theory as follows:

The theatre is above all the art of the unexpressed. It is less by lines than by the impact of the lines that the deepest sentiments reveal themselves. . . . Beneath the heard dialogue is an unspoken dialogue that has to be made audible. . . . The theatre has no worse enemy than literature, for literature expresses what should be merely suggested. . . . A sentiment commented on loses force. The logic of the theatre will not admit any sentiments that the situation does not impose. And if the situation imposes them, there is no need of expressing them. That is why less is said by a well-rounded poetic couplet than by some apparently casual remark.

Bernard carefully chooses the situations he can best elaborate with silence, and his crises are prepared for in advance so that a gesture or a facial expression may convey the true

Two scenes from a 1948 production of *Martine.* [French Cultural Services]

depth of meaning. In *The Sulky Fire* (1921), for example, the final decision of a returned soldier to stay with his young wife, who he suspects has been unfaithful with an American soldier, renders his wife almost speechless with the memory of her loneliness and suffering and with her present emotions. In *Martine* (1922), the heroine mutely endures her lover's departure with another woman, and when he cruelly asks her to recall their happy hours together, she merely says, "What is the use of recalling? . . . Is it not enough what you have done to me?"

Action is subordinated in Bernard's work. *The Poet's Secret* (1926), in a single scene, depicts unrequited love as expressed by a woman, the daughter of a famous man, who accepts with consummate disinterest the impassioned poem of her lover. *The Springtime of Others* (1924) pits mother against daughter as rivals for a man; the mother realizes in mute horror that she loves her daughter's husband. In *Invitation to a Voyage* (1924), the wife, loving a young admirer who has left for Argentina, becomes disillusioned when he returns and finally expresses her realization that she still loves her husband by playing his favorite tune on the piano.

Moving to fantasy, Bernard depicts in *The Unquiet Spirit* (1926) the vain struggle of people to find their true happiness. Yearning for her alter ego, her other self, a married woman crosses paths with him now and again, but they fail to recognize one another and never

speak. Finally he dies on her threshold, trying but failing to reach her. The heroine in *Denise Marette* (1925) sacrifices her identity and shows her love for her ailing father by passing off her work as his when he is no longer able to paint. After he dies, however, she sees him as a ghost, selfish and speaking only of himself.

In many instances, characters essential to the plot not only are mute but do not appear on the stage. Their presence is implied, as in the case of the American soldier in *The Sulky Fire* and the young lover in *Invitation to a Voyage.* The lover in *Denise Marette* and the lady's soul mate in *The Unquiet Spirit* appear fleetingly but are given only short speeches.

It can be said that Bernard's work is the subtle drama of inference and intention, of delicate nuance and intimate emotion.

The Sulky Fire (*Le feu qui reprend mal,* 1921). After being demobilized, André returns to his wife Blanche and discovers that during the war an American officer had been billeted in his house. Though Blanche has remained true to him for four lonely years, André is obsessed by jealousy and continues to plague his wife until she announces that she intends to leave him to rejoin the American, her life with André having become impossible. André's father intervenes and describes Blanche's lonely life during his son's absence. The description reawakens André's love and makes Blanche realize that she can never abandon André to the desolation that she herself had to endure. The couple are reunited, and their love for one another is rekindled.

Martine (1922). During a visit to his grandmother Mme. Mervan, Julien, a recently demobilized soldier, makes the acquaintance of Martine, a simple peasant girl who immediately falls in love with him. The idyll is interrupted by the arrival of Jeanne, an old sweetheart whom everybody has always assumed Julien would eventually marry. Their similar tastes and education lead Julien and Jeanne to renew their courtship, and to Martine's inarticulate despair their engagement is soon announced. Martine's suffering is increased when, during Julien's absence, Jeanne, eager to talk of her new love, makes the peasant girl her confidant. After the wedding, Julien and Jeanne move to Paris and Martine, on the advice of Mme. Mervan, who is aware of Martine's love, agrees to marry a local farmer. When Mme. Mervan dies, Julien returns briefly to sell his grandmother's house. He cruelly evokes for Martine the pleasure of their days together and almost wrings from her a confession of her love. Henceforth tied to a boorish husband, all she can look forward to are Julien's annual visits to his grandmother's grave.

PLAYS

Unless otherwise noted, the plays were first performed in Paris.

1. *Le voyage à deux* (*A Trip for Two*). Play. Produced Cercle Volney, Mar. 22, 1909; Théâtre Michel, Oct. 17, 1911.
2. *La joie du sacrifice* (*The Joy of Sacrifice*). Play, 1 act. Produced Comédie-Royale, Mar. 8, 1912.
3. *La maison épargnée* (*The House That Was Spared*). Play. Produced Théâtre Antoine, Nov. 5, 1919.
4. *Le feu qui reprend mal** (*The Sulky Fire*). Play. Produced Théâtre Antoine, June 9, 1921.
5. *Martine**. Play. Produced Théâtre des Mathurins, May 9, 1922.
6. *L'invitation au voyage** (*Invitation to a Voyage*). Play. Produced Théâtre de l'Odéon, Feb. 15, 1924; Théâtre de la Comédie, Oct. 17, 1926.
7. *Le printemps des autres** (*The Springtime of Others*). Play. Produced Théâtre Fémina, Mar. 18, 1924.
8. *Denise Marette*. Play. Produced Théâtre du Vieux-Colombier, Nov. 18, 1925.
9. *L'âme en peine** (*The Unquiet Spirit*). Play, 3 acts. Produced Monaco, Théâtre de Monte-Carlo, Jan. 12, 1926.
10. *Le secret d'Arvers** (*The Poet's Secret*). Play, 1 act. Produced Cercle de la Petite Scène, June 5, 1926.
11. *Le roi de Malousie* (*The King of Malousie*). Play. Produced Théâtre de l'Odéon, May 27, 1928.
12. *La Louise* (*Louise*). Play, 1 act. Produced Geneva, Théâtre de la Comédie, May 6, 1931.
13. *À la recherche des coeurs* (*In Search of Hearts*). Play. Produced Geneva, Théâtre de la Comédie, May 6, 1931.
14. *Les soeurs Guédonec* (*The Sisters Guédonec*). Play, 2 acts. Produced Studio des Champs-Élysées, Nov. 20, 1931.
15. *Jeanne de Pantin*. Play. Produced Théâtre de l'Odéon, Nov. 26, 1933.
16. *Nationale 6** (*National 6*). Play. Produced Prague, Sept. 23, 1935; Paris, Théâtre de l'Oeuvre, Oct. 18, 1935.
17. *Le jardinier d'Ispahan** (*Madeleine*). Play. Produced Théâtre de l'Oeuvre, Apr. 12, 1939.
18. *Marie Stuart* (*Mary Stuart*). Play. Produced Geneva, Théâtre de la Comédie, Nov. 12, 1942.
19. *Louise de la Vallière*. Play. Produced Geneva, Théâtre de la Comédie, Dec. 30, 1943.
20. *Notre Dame d'en haut* (*Our Lady on High*). Play. Produced Strasbourg, Théâtre Municipal, Feb. 5, 1951.
21. *La route de France* (*The Road of France*). Play. Produced 1951.

EDITIONS

Collections.
Théâtre, 7 vols., Paris, 1925–1949; *Sulky Fire and Other Plays*, tr. by J. L. Frith, London, 1939.
Individual Plays.
Invitation to a Voyage. Published in *Continental Plays*, ed. by T. H. Dickinson, Houghton Mifflin, Boston, 1935; also published as *Glamour* in *Eight European Plays*, comp. by W. Katzin, Brentano's, New York, 1927.
Martine. Published in *Eight European Plays*, comp. by W. Katzin, Brentano's, New York, 1927; *The Contemporary French Theatre*, ed. by S. A. Rhodes, Crofts, New York, 1942.
National 6. A. Y. Kroff and K. G. Bottke, eds., Appleton-Century-Crofts, New York, 1950.
The Poet's Secret. Published in *Four French Plays of the Twentieth Century*, ed. by E. M. Grant, Harper, New York, 1949.

BERNARD, Tristan, pseudonym of Paul Bernard (1866–1947). French author of novels and plays, whose fame derives mainly from his comedies of love. A master of dramatic technique with a gift for exact observation, he wrote plays abounding in situation comedy, disguises, concealments, and mistaken identities reminiscent of Plautus. He shunned

Tristan Bernard.
[New York Public Library]

the heroic and the larger-than-life, preferring to fill the stage with meek and timid characters whose weaknesses and failures are the subject of his plots. *See* PLAUTUS.

Bernard's plays include *Le fardeau de la liberté* (1898); *The Only Bandit of the Village* (*Le seul bandit du village,* 1898), in which a husband takes a thief for his wife's lover; *The Nocturnal Visitors* (*Une visite de nuit,* 1899); *The Touring Club Bride* (*La mariée du Touring Club,* 1899); *The Gang at Léon* (*La bande à Léon,* 1902), in which the husband takes his wife's lover for a thief; *The Mathieu Case* (*L'affaire Mathieu,* 1901); *Triplepatte* (1905), written with André Godfernaux and known in Clyde Fitch's adaptation as *Toddles; The Ambulant Flirt* (*Le flirt ambulant,* 1907); *The Twins of Brighton* (*Les jumeaux de Brighton,* 1908), which is modeled on *The Twin Menaechmi* of Plautus; *The Little Café* (*Le petit café,* 1911), in which a waiter inherits a fortune on condition that he serve his master for another twenty years; *The Soubigou Beacons* (*Les phares Soubigou,* 1912); and *Prince Charming* (*Le prince charmant,* 1914). Among his later plays are *Jules, Juliette et Julien, ou*

Two scenes from *Le petit café*, Théâtre Antoine, Paris. [French Cultural Services]

L'école du sentiment (1929); *Une amie d'Argentine* (1930), with Max Maurey; *Langrevin père et fils* (1930); and *Le sauvage* (1931).

BERNARD-LUC, Jean (1909–). French scenario writer and dramatist. Born in Guatemala City, he spent his childhood and

Tristan Bernard's *Le fardeau de la liberté*, Théâtre de la Madeleine, Paris. [French Cultural Services]

(Top) *Le complexe de Philémon*, Théâtre Montparnasse, Paris. [French Cultural Services] (Bottom) Robert Cummings and Ann Sothern in *Faithfully Yours*, adapted from *Le complexe de Philémon*. New York, Coronet Theatre, 1951. [Photograph by Vandamm]

student years in Paris. His first comedy, *Don José*, was performed in Brussels in 1936. His style is satirical, tending toward caricature, and the structure of his plays is reminiscent of vaudeville. Thematically he draws on Freud and Kinsey.

Among his other plays are a bourgeois drama entitled *The Family Dinner* (*Le dîner de famille*, 1944); a tragedy, *The Night of Men* (*La nuit des hommes*, 1950); the satirical comedies *The Philemon Complex* (*Le complexe de Philémon*, 1951) and *The Vine Leaf* (*La feuille de vigne,* 1953), the latter on the theme of sexual education; *Carlos and Marguerite* (1954); *Inexperienced Lovers* (*Les amants novices,* 1955); and *Hibernatus* (1957).

BERNSTEIN, Henry (1876–1953). French dramatist whose highly melodramatic works are solidly in the boulevard tradition of the "eternal triangle." He brought to the stage a taste for the violent passions and a sure sense of theatrical effect to which he willingly sacrificed psychological probability. *The Detour* (*Le détour,* 1902) concerns the daughter of a woman of dubious reputation; faced with narrow-minded provincial hostility, the girl eventually decides on the primrose path followed by her mother. In *The Whirlwind* (*La rafale,* 1905), a woman forced into a hateful marriage demands that her father compensate her by paying off the debts of her gambler lover. When her father refuses, she tries to obtain the money by prostituting herself—all to no avail, since her lover commits suicide. An unscrupulous married woman in *The Thief* (*Le voleur,* 1906) steals to buy clothes and jewels; when she is discovered, she persuades an impressionable young lover to announce that he has committed the theft.

As part of the aftermath of the Dreyfus affair, Bernstein wrote two plays dealing with anti-Semitism. In *Samson* (1907) he presented a Jewish financier whose gentile wife despises him until he deliberately causes his own financial ruin in order to bring about the downfall of her lover. *Israel* (1908) focuses on an anti-Semitic young aristocrat who, after publicly insulting a Jewish banker, finds that

Constance Collier as Agnès, Duchesse de Croucy, in *Israel* (left). New York, Criterion Theatre, 1909. [Theatre Collection, The New York Public Library at Lincoln Center, Astor, Lenox and Tilden Foundations]

Scene from *Victor* (below). Paris, Théâtre des Ambassadeurs, 1950. [French Cultural Services]

Henry Bernstein. [Theatre Collection, The New York Public Library at Lincoln Center, Astor, Lenox and Tilden Foundations]

Jean Forbes-Robertson, Cedric Hardwicke, Louise Platt, and Frank Lawton (l. to r.) in *Promise*, by Henry Bernstein. New York, Little Theatre, 1936. [Photograph by Vandamm. Theatre Collection, The New York Public Library at Lincoln Center]

the latter is actually his father. Following World War I, Bernstein, ever sensitive to fashions in taste, tried to produce works whose interest is in psychological motivation rather than dramatic plot twists. This departure was announced in *The Secret* (*Le secret*, 1913), in which a woman jealously tries to destroy the happiness of all who come into contact with her. In *To the Heights* (*L'elévation*, 1917), an adulterous wife learns from her dying soldier husband a lesson in sacrifice and devotion. *Judith* (1922) is a dramatic treatment of the Biblical heroine, and *The Hall of Mirrors* (*La galerie des glaces*, 1924) is a Freudian-type study of a painter whose feelings of inferiority lead him to doubt that he is really loved. *Venom* (*Le venin*, 1927) presents a hero whose life is dominated by his overriding sensuality. After World War II Bernstein abandoned psychological portraiture for a return, in *Thirst* (*La soif,* 1949) and *Victor* (1950), to plays whose interest centers on the

traditional lovers' triangle and whose effect depends on exotic plot turns.

Bernstein's other plays include *The Fold* (*Le bercail*, 1904), *The Claw* (*La griffe*, 1906), *After Me!* (*Après moi!*, 1911), *The Attack* (*L'assaut,* 1912), *The Messenger* (*Le messager,* 1933), *Promise* (*Espoir,* 1934), and *The Voyage* (*Le voyage,* 1937).

BERNSTEIN, Leonard (1918–   ). American composer who wrote the scores for the musicals *On the Town* (1944), *Wonderful Town* (1953), *Candide* (1956), and *West Side Story* (1957). His short opera *Trouble in Tahiti* (1952) is a satire on the middle-class values of suburbia. Bernstein's theatrical activities are only a part of a varied career that includes

(Opposite) Betty Comden and Adolph Green in *On the Town*. New York, Adelphi Theatre, 1944. [Photograph by Vandamm. Theatre Collection, The New York Public Library at Lincoln Center]

the composition of symphonies (*Jeremiah Symphony,* 1944; *The Age of Anxiety,* 1949), ballet music (*Fancy Free,* 1944), and, in 1971, a mass employing drama, dance, and chorus to celebrate the newly constructed Kennedy Center for the Performing Arts in Washington. For more than a decade he was conductor of the New York Philharmonic.

BERR, Georges (1867–1942). French actor, director, and dramatist who collaborated with Marcel Guillemaud and Louis Verneuil on gay, clever comedies such as *Le million* (1910), *Meet My Sister* (*Ma soeur et moi,* 1928), *Azaïs* (pub. 1926), and *Maître Bolbec et son mari* (pub. 1927). *See* VERNEUIL, LOUIS.

BERTOLAZZI, Carlo (b. Rivolta d'Adda, Milano Province, November 3, 1870; d. Milan, June 2, 1916). Italian dramatist and journalist. After serving as an officer of Alpine troops, he obtained a diploma that allowed him to work as a town clerk. He wrote his first play, *Ave Maria,* in 1887. About this time, he contributed dramatic criticism to the Milanese periodicals *Guerin Meschino* and *La Sera.* In 1888 his four-act drama *Mamma Teresa* was successfully produced in Milan by an amateur company. The following year his *Trilogy of Gilda* (*Trilogia di Gilda*), produced by a professional company, was a failure. In 1890 his dramatic monologue *The Lesson for Tomorrow* (*La lezione per domani*), interpreted by the child actress Dora Lambertini, was

Carlo Bertolazzi. [Italian Cultural Institute]

enthusiastically applauded by both public and critics. The same year, Bertolazzi produced his first play in Milanese dialect, *A Scene from Life* (*Ona scënna de la vita*). It was followed by two outstanding plays, both in dialect: *Our Milan* (*El nost Milan,* 1893) and *The Reflection* (*La gibigianna,* 1898), considered by many to be his best work. At the turn of the century Bertolazzi wrote two psychological dramas, *The Egoist* (*L'egoista,* 1900) and *Lulù* (1903), both received with great acclaim.

After 1900 Bertolazzi realized that the Milanese dialect was doomed to disappear as a spoken language. He therefore began writing his plays in standard Italian, though many of them were afterward translated into dialect. In spite of his relative success in the theatre, he was never able to earn his living as a dramatist. Plagued by illness, he was compelled in his last years to support himself as a notary.

The drama of Bertolazzi belongs to the movement in Italian literature known as *verismo,* initiated by Verga in the late nineteenth century and characterized by a realistic style akin to naturalism. While Verga and Capuana had portrayed peasant life and Giacosa and Praga the financial and social realities of the bourgeoisie, Bertolazzi was, with the Neapolitan Di Giacomo, the first to write veristic dramas about the urban proletariat. Although he also wrote plays concerning the upper and middle classes, the most striking realities of his dramas are those of the poor: the oppression of work and the despair of a closed future. The tragedy always present in his work stems essentially from the disastrous effects of unemployment, poverty, and illness. *See* VERGA, GIOVANNI.

In an effort to depict society realistically, Bertolazzi often set a play in a lively environment filled with a variety of secondary characters seemingly unrelated to the main story. He consistently used a nonliterary style, characterized by a rapid prose dialogue close to the everyday language of the people and often in the dialect of the lower classes. The best example of these techniques is *Our Milan.* A diptych of city life, it presents in two parts, *The Poor People* (*La povera gent*) and *The Gentlemen* (*I sciori*), contrasting views of the proletariat and noble classes. *The Poor People,* written in Milanese dialect, is a tragedy centering on the miserable life of circus performers. Another drama, this one dealing with artistic life, is *The Mask* (*La maschera,* 1896), in which Lina, the young star of an operetta company, is unwillingly pushed by her stepmother into a match with a wealthy count.

Poverty and selfish greed are dominant

themes in Bertolazzi's work. Two of his best dramas, *Lulù* and *The Reflection,* are psychological studies of young women who suffer tragic fates because of their inability to sacrifice material comfort for love. The drama *Lorenzo and His Lawyer* (*Lorenzo e il suo avvocato,* 1905) and the tragedy *The Spinster* (*La zitella,* 1915) depict the miserable existence of the poor, unequipped to deal with reality and incapable of resisting fate. In *The Egoist* a man causes misery and death to others in his selfish accumulation of wealth, which, in his guilt-ridden old age, he ultimately donates to a religious community. The young protagonist of *The House of Sleep* (*La casa del sonno,* 1902) scorns his humble provincial parents when he marries a Milanese heiress; but later, having squandered all his money, he is forced to flee from bankruptcy.

Among the Italian dramatists of the *verismo* school, Bertolazzi remains outstanding, not only for his unique portrayal of the proletariat but for his ability to combine piercing social criticism with wit and vitality.

Our Milan (*El nost Milan,* 1893). Diptych of Milanese life comprising two plays, *The Poor People* (*La povera gent*) and *The Gentlemen* (*I sciori*), which together follow the life of a single protagonist, Nina, through two levels of society. *The Poor People* takes place around 1890 in the periphery of Milan among the working and peasant classes. Nina, daughter of the poor but honest Peppon, falls in love with a circus clown who is too poor to marry her. In the end she sees him die of consumption. In her misery she allows herself to be exploited and abused by the rogue Carlone, who is eventually murdered by her father. In the second play, *The Gentlemen,* Nina has made her way into the corrupt society of Milanese nobility and adopted the name Hélène in an attempt to eradicate her past. The Marquis of Rivolta, having returned to Milan after fifteen years spent traveling and studying in Africa, finds himself disgusted by the decadence of the wealthy urban society. He is especially displeased by his brother, who has dissipated the family patrimony and now wishes to mend the family fortunes by inducing the Marquis to marry a rich but corrupt countess. The Marquis, however, is attracted by the simplicity and sincerity of Hélène and asks her to be his bride. Although Hélène loves the Marquis, remembrance of her past causes her to feel unworthy of him and to refuse his love.

Lulù (1903). Lulù has had a succession of lovers and is flagrantly unfaithful to her current lover, Mario. The latter's mother warns him against Lulù, but Mario is completely under the girl's spell. Lulù continues to make assignations with other men behind his back.

Eventually Mario discovers that his own father had been Lulù's lover and had committed suicide because of her. In his rage and disgust, Mario strangles Lulù.

BESCI, Kurt (1920–   ). Austrian critic and dramatist, proponent of a revolutionary Christianity (the theme of spiritual rebirth is an integral part of all his plays), whose writings reveal the influences of the Russian philosopher Nikolay Berdyayev. His modern mystery plays include *The German Passion Play* (*Deutsche Passion,* 1952); *Atom before Christ* (*Atom vor Christus,* 1952), an analysis of the guilt engendered by the bombing of Hiroshima; and *The Spanish Triangle* (*Spanisches Dreieck,* 1952), a historical drama on the Don Carlos theme that earned Besci the nickname "Christian Sartre" in Paris. In *The Salt March* (*Der Salzmarsch,* 1955), he dealt with Gandhi's passive resistance movement in India. Besci employed expressionistic devices in *Russian Easters* (*Russische Ostern,* 1959) and also choruses of Communists and Christians. In *Faust in Moscow* (*Faust in Moskau,* 1962), Ivan the Terrible and Faust are adversaries. His other recent plays include *The Night before Sarajevo* (*Die Nacht vor Sarajevo,* 1965) and *Party for Prophets* (*Party für Propheten,* 1965).

BESIER, Rudolph (b. Java, July, 1878; d. London, June 15, 1942). Dutch-English translator and dramatist who achieved international success with his historical drama *The Barretts of Wimpole Street* (1930). Toward the

Rudolph Besier. [Theatre Collection, The New York Public Library at Lincoln Center, Astor, Lenox and Tilden Foundations]

Katharine Cornell as Elizabeth Barrett in *The Barretts of Wimpole Street.* New York, Empire Theatre, 1931. [Photograph by Vandamm. Theatre Collection, The New York Public Library at Lincoln Center]

ber of plays, none of which succeeded in achieving great success: he collaborated with H. G. Wells to dramatize Wells's novel *Kipps* (1912), teamed with Hugh Walpole on *Robin's Father* (1918), and wrote a chronicle play, *Secrets* (1922), in collaboration with the novelist May Edginton. It was not until 1930, with the production of *The Barretts of Wimpole Street* at the Malvern Festival, after two rejections by London producers, that he soared to fame. The next year, the play was brought to New York, and after twenty-seven producers refused it, Katharine Cornell had it staged at the Hanna Theatre in Cleveland. She then took the play to New York, where it became a major success over the objections of the Barrett family, which resented the Freudian implications in the portrayal of Elizabeth's father.

The Barretts of Wimpole Street (1930). Drama about the love of Elizabeth Barrett and Robert Browning. Edward Moulton-Barrett, a widower, rules his family with a despotic, puritanical hand, determined to preserve his children from the evil influences of the world, including marriage. His eldest daughter, Elizabeth, an invalid who is confined to her room and to whom Edward shows uncommon affection, must act as a mother to her brothers and sisters. When Browning arrives on the scene, having made Elizabeth's acquaintance through a series of letters, he fills the house with an energy and love of life that infuse Elizabeth with new strength. Their friendship soon ripens into love; they secretly marry, and Elizabeth escapes forever from her plush Victorian prison. Produced Malvern Festival, 1930.

BESNARD, Lucien (1872–   ). French dramatist, author of subtle psychological comedies. He started writing for the theatre while still at the university and saw *The Bell* (*Le glas*), his first play, produced in 1896. Among his other plays are *Papa Dollivet* (1898); *The Master's Dogs* (*Les chiens du maître,* 1899); *The Rebel* (*La Fronde,* 1900); *The Estate* (*Le domaine,* 1902); *The Grisel Affair* (*L'affaire Grisel,* 1904); *Most in Love* (*La plus amoureuse,* 1906); *My Friend Teddy* (*Mon ami Teddy,* 1908), the story of an American who finally wins the woman he loves in Paris, written with André Rivoire; *The Devil Recluse* (*Le diable ermite,* 1909); *The Mad Bid* (*La folle enchère,* 1910); *I Want to Return to My Normandy* (*Je veux revoir ma Normandie,* 1913); *The Man Who Is No Longer with Us* (*L'homme qui n'est plus de ce monde,* 1924); *The Divided Heart* (*Le coeur partagé,* 1926), a study of a young wife's father complex; and *In the Shadow of the Harem* (*Dans l'ombre du harem,* 1927).

beginning of his career he gained a certain limited esteem in advanced circles by his first play, *The Virgin Goddess* (1906). Produced at the Adelphi Theatre, it was a classic tragedy that he had written during a visit to the United States. In 1909 he wrote *Olive Latimer's Husband.* The same year, the New Theatre in New York diverged from tradition by producing a comedy; Besier's *Don* was one of the few comedies ever to be seen in that theatre. In 1912 *Lady Patricia,* a satire on English affectations, was acted by Mrs. Minnie Maddern Fiske, her performance winning her tremendous acclaim.

For several years Besier turned out a num-

Ugo Betti
(1892 — 1953)

Ugo Betti, Italian magistrate, poet, novelist, and dramatist, was born in Camerino on February 4, 1892. In 1900 his father, a physician, was appointed director of the hospital in Parma, and Betti was educated there, studying the classics and then law.

As a young man he was interested chiefly in sports, but he found time to translate Catullus's *The Marriage of Thetis and Peleus*, which was published in 1910, when Betti was eighteen. When Italy entered World War I in 1915, Betti joined the army and became an officer in a light artillery regiment, receiving a medal before his capture by the Germans in 1917. During his stay in a prisoner-of-war camp, where his fellow prisoners were Bonaventura Tecchi and Carlo Emilio Gadda, Betti wrote his first book of poems, *The Thoughtful King* (*Il re pensieroso*, 1922). After the war he entered the judiciary and eventually became first a *pretore* ("magistrate") and then a judge in Parma. Meanwhile, he continued to write short stories and poems. In 1926 he won a dramatic competition with his play *The Mistress of the House* (*La padrona*), which was produced that year with outstanding success. He followed this over the years with twenty-five other plays, three of which appeared posthumously. Between 1941 and 1946 he wrote several film scenarios.

Betti remained a judge in Parma until 1930, the year of his marriage to Andreina Frosini, when he was appointed a magistrate of the High Court in Rome, a position that he held until a few years before his death. In 1944 he was made librarian of the Ministry of Justice, and in his last years he acted as legal counsel for the Theatrical Union.

Several of Betti's plays were awarded prizes at the time of their publication or production, and in 1949 he received the Italian National Institute of Drama Prize (Premio I.D.I.) for the body of his work. In 1953, a few days after completing his last play, *The Fugitive* (*La fuggitiva*), Betti learned that he was suffering from cancer. His friendship with Don Giuseppe de Luca, a scholarly priest, led to the dramatist's final reconciliation with the church shortly before his death in Rome on June 9, 1953.

WORK

Because of his wealth of imagination, diversified characterization, compact plot structure, and humanitarian approach to his major theme, the nature of evil, critics often consider Ugo Betti second only to Pirandello in the modern Italian theatre. Betti saw man as the victim of contradictory impulses, as a creature in need of judgment by other men and thirsting for a viable religion. Bringing his experience as a judge to bear, he often cast his plays in the form of an investigation into the nature of basic relationships. Although unrelenting in his indictment of evil, he never failed to temper his insistence on judgment with human understanding and compassion. *See* PIRANDELLO, LUIGI.

For the sake of convenience, his works can be divided roughly into an early, a middle, and a late period. His plays are indefinite as to location (the names of characters in some major works are un-Italian) and vaguely contemporary in time. A strong and easily recognizable Italian flavor may, however, be identified in family situations, relations between husbands and wives, the status of women, forms of bureaucracy, portrayals of city and country life, and attitudes toward religion.

The early plays (1926–1934) include two fairy-tale works, *The Wonderful Island* (*L'isola meravigliosa*, 1930) and *The Woman on the Shield* (*La donna sullo scudo*, 1927), the latter written in collaboration with Osvaldo

Ugo Betti. [Italian Cultural Institute]

Gibertini. They are closely allied in lyricism and fantasy to Betti's poems, and although more universal in theme, they have some of the magical aura of the best of Gozzi's fairy-tale plays (*fiabe; see* GOZZI, CARLO). Other plays of this period are *The Mistress of the House* (1926), *The Duck Hunter* (*Il cacciatore d'anitre;* wr. 1934, prod. 1940), and *Landslide* (*Frana allo scalo Nord;* wr. 1932, prod. 1936), one of his greatest plays and one that makes vivid use of his knowledge of legal procedure. Emphasizing Betti's belief that each man longs for human judgment and divine mercy, *Landslide,* the sixth of his plays to be produced, established his reputation with the critics.

Between 1934 and 1940, Betti wrote a group of comedies, of which the best known on the English-speaking stage is *Summertime* (*Il paese delle vacanze;* wr. 1937, prod. 1942). Others are *Our Dreams* (*I nostri sogni,* 1937) and *A Beautiful Sunday in September* (*Una bella domenica di settembre,* 1937). These plays have in common a gentle, dreamy atmosphere, a compassionate love of human nature, and sympathy with man's wish for happiness on earth. Some critics, however, have felt that they represent an attempt by Betti to avoid the issues arising from Fascist Italy's involvement in Ethiopia and Spain. The author himself called them a "diversion."

Betti wrote thirteen plays between 1941 and 1953. All tragedies, they are powerful indictments of evil and statements of his belief that the regeneration of man may come only through personal redemption and death. They stress the importance of both human and divine love, the one leading to self-realization and the other providing evidence of God's mercy. In *Corruption in the Palace of Justice* (*Corruzione al Palazzo di Giustizia,* 1949), considered by many Italian critics to be the most powerful play of the post-World War II period, it is human love that leads a guilty judge to confess his crimes just when his way to complete corrupt power seems finally unobstructed. Two vaguely political plays, *The Queen and the Rebels* (*La regina e gli insorti,* 1951), a realization of the nobility of the human spirit in moments of agony, and *The Burnt Flower-Bed* (*L'aiuola bruciata,* 1953), a severe indictment of the cynicism of politicians, indicate the dramatist's rejection of false gods and his sympathy for the individual struggling for good in a hostile world. Even the most hardened and corrupt need pity, forgiveness, and love—gifts from God that can be granted only in death. Cast in the mode of classical tragedy, *Goat Island* (*Delitto all'isola delle capre,* 1950) conveys a sense of destructive sexual passion at its most degrading. In the posthumously published *The Fugitive* (1953) the characters seem condemned to sinfulness by a malevolent fate. Led astray by the devil, they find peace only in the return to God after death.

Betti has been reproached by critics for his acceptance, however tenuous, of fascism. His plays, however, reflect no political point of view and were often censured by Fascist bureaucracy. Thematically, Betti's plays may best be characterized as moral, in that they focus on man and his contradictory impulses toward good and evil. The desire for free investigation into moral and religious questions—questions of human responsibility, free will, predestination, the immortality of the soul, and sexual morality—alienated Betti from the beliefs of orthodox religion until immediately before his death. However, many of Betti's plays represent a search for a divine justice that is above the ambiguity and fallibility of human justice.

The Mistress of the House (*La padrona,* 1926). Drama of the conflict between death-driven, consumptive Anna, daughter of a remarried widower, Pietro, and Marina, her life-oriented, attractive, and sexually provocative stepmother. At the wedding reception in Pietro's meanly furnished house, Anna's mordant presence casts a pall over the celebrants. As Pietro becomes intoxicated, his ambivalence in choosing between the attractively vital ways of his wife and his daughter's death wish is revealed with bitterly morbid cynicism. Increasingly ill, Anna rejects all tenders of friendship, whether from Marina or from Zoppo, a lame neighbor who loves her. Soon Marina becomes pregnant, and although Pietro would bind her to him by letting her run the house and his small store, her revulsion toward her surroundings makes her decide to leave. Her child is stillborn. In a spasm of hatred Anna tells her father that the child was not his and urges him to kill Marina. Overcome by his own impulses and Anna's persuasiveness, Pietro is about to do so when Anna's death releases him from her destructive influence.

The House on the Water (*La casa sull'acqua,* 1929). Drama in which Elli, a vivacious, lovely young woman, returns to her birthplace, a village on a lake whose mysterious waters erode and contaminate the lives as well as the land of all living nearby. She resides temporarily with a sullen childless couple, Francesco and Marta. Luca, Francesco's aimless artist brother, falls in love with Elli and with a new sense of life returns to his artistic endeavors. In love with Elli himself, Franco is stirred to jealousy by the sight of his brother painting again and escaping from his domination. When he vows to make the girl his own, both Marta and Elli disappear.

On the night of a local celebration, Marta reappears wet and bedraggled having unsuccessfully tried to drown Elli. Aware now of the enormity of his behavior, Francesco renounces his illicit passion and tells his brother to take Elli and go.

The Wonderful Island (*L'isola meravigliosa,* 1930). Ballet-drama written in the mode of Gozzi's *fiabe.* It tells the story of a king who neglects his kingdom and roams the world seeking happiness. He arrives at an island where a magician presents him with a young girl whom he at first loves and then rejects, for to him satisfaction means the end of desire. Nevertheless, the death of the maiden causes him great unhappiness. Thwarted in his wish for her return to life, he resumes his wandering in despair.

An Inn on the Harbor (*Un albergo sul porto,* 1933). Drama suggesting the possibility of redemption through love. A destitute young girl becomes the mistress of an innkeeper in order to provide shelter for her father and to escape prostitution. After Maria becomes pregnant, the young fisherman she loves returns and offers marriage, but ashamed, she rejects him. However, when her condition becomes known, the people of the inn find a new faith and unexpected goodness of heart. She is enabled to go away to bear and rear her child without disgrace to her father, who dies as soon as she leaves.

The Flood (*Il diluvio;* wr. 1931, prod. 1943). Farce about an unsuccessful attempt to rebel against a world out of joint. The moral "flood" that engulfs Professor Mattia sweeps away his honor, his wife, and his life when he agrees to help trap a millionaire into marrying his niece. He accidentally locks his wife instead of his niece into a bedroom with the longed-for bridegroom. To his horror he finds that his friends and neighbors applaud what they consider his courageous attempt to strike it rich.

Landslide (*Frana allo scalo Nord;* wr. 1932, prod. 1936). An investigation of the legal responsibility for a fatal landslide. Betti focuses attention not on the "facts" of the incident but on their "tragic vibrations." The investigation discloses a corrupt society in which each member accuses the other of having contributed to the disaster. Eventually, however, all concerned want to be punished for real crimes or personal guilt ranging from insensitivity to jealousy, lust, and cruelty. When the time comes to pronounce sentence, the judge, confronted with the complexity of human behavior, finds it impossible to assign responsibility. Only God can really judge men and thereby mercifully release them from guilt.

The Duck Hunter (*Il cacciatore d'anitre;*

Corruzione al Palazzo di Giustizia. Turin, Teatro Stabile di Torino, 1964. [Italian Cultural Institute]

wr. 1934, prod. 1940). Faustian drama about the corruption of a good man. Marco, an idealistic and solitary hunter, is tempted by Ignazio, the Mephistophelian secretary of a childless old merchant, to vie with his friend Aurelio for the old man's inheritance. He succeeds in winning the merchant's favor, but while he is celebrating his victory, Elena, his former sweetheart, appears with a child in her arms and accuses him of having abandoned her. He drives her away, but her threat of suicide obsesses him and he sets off in search of her. At a steep drop to the sea, he encounters the merchant, who accidentally falls from the cliff after having chided Marco for his deceit. Though before dying the merchant absolves Marco of guilt, Marco is brought to trial and condemned to prison after having refused freedom at the price of relinquishing his inheritance. Years later, Marco returns home to discover that the material goods he inherited have turned to dust. Marco is stabbed by the evil Ignazio after he turns on the latter and discharges him. As he lies dying, he hears the approach of the Regent, a distant ruler, whom he had long ago petitioned for justice.

A Beautiful Sunday in September (*Una bella domenica di settembre,* 1937). Comedy in which Adriana, the neglected wife of a busy civic councillor, having been deserted by her husband on her birthday, decides to make him jealous by spending an afternoon in a notorious café with Charles, one of his employees. When the police stage a surprise raid on the café, Adriana discovers to her dismay that her own daughter is among those rounded up with her. Later she tries in vain to make her husband jealous, but he insists in believing that she merely followed her daughter to the café out of concern for her safety. Only Adriana's threat to leave home makes her husband realize his neglect and beg her to stay. When Charles pleads with her to run away with him, she dismisses him and decides to remain with her husband and family, who need her.

Our Dreams (*I nostri sogni,* 1937). Comedy in which a poor young man impersonates a millionaire in order to indulge a poor young girl who dreams, as he does, of the pleasures of great wealth. Each discovers that the heart cannot be bought and that pretense does not bring happiness. The girl returns to the poor young man who loves her, and the man to a faithful friend who protects him from acts of folly.

Scenes from a French production of *Corruzione al Palazzo di Giustizia*. Paris, Théâtre du Studio des Champs-Élysées, 1953. [French Cultural Services]

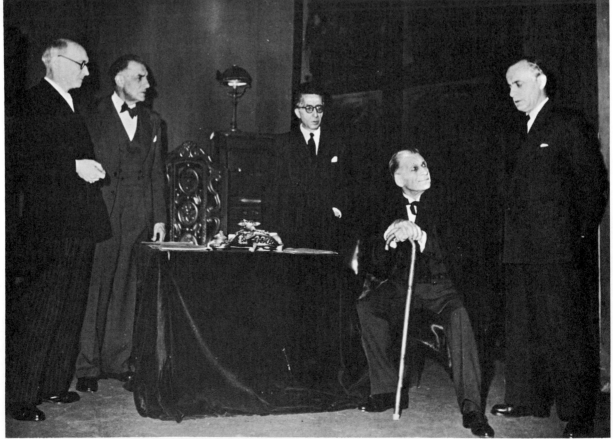

Summertime (*Il paese delle vacanze;* wr. 1937, prod. 1942).   Idyll about a clever young lady in love with a foolish young man who, having known her all his life, fails to see her as a desirable woman. A widow whom he has publicly compromised attempts, with the aid of her angry brother, to force him to marry her. After a series of complications during a picnic, the young woman thwarts the widow's plan and wins the young man.

Night in the House of the Rich Man (*Notte in casa del ricco;* wr. 1938, prod. 1942). Modern tragedy in which divine retribution is visited on the hero by means of a sacrificial victim. Valerio, a rich but lonely and guilty man, is sought out by Marco, whose life he ruined in a youthful escapade. To protect himself, Valerio brings about Marco's death. In the process, however, it is disclosed that Valerio's neglected daughter had become the mistress of one of his servants. Valerio's attempt to protect his respectability fails, and his daughter commits suicide.

Christmas Story (*Favola di Natale;* wr. 1940, prod. 1948).   Comedy in which a modern girl, desperately seeking marriage and security, finds her engagement broken when her fiancé's friend discovers her in a lie. However, seeing in her the purity and innocence of the child she once was, the friend falls in love with her himself. Pretending to speak for her former fiancé, he offers her the prospect of real love and a better future.

Night Wind (*Il vento notturno;* wr. 1941, prod. 1945).   Drama set in a huge modern apartment house. A man and a woman are torn between love and hate for one another. An older man, who the woman persists in believing is her father, gently leads her to rediscover in herself the lost paradise of her childhood and a desire for redemption.

The Inquiry (*Ispezione;* wr. 1941, prod. 1947).   Drama centering on a mysterious inspector's investigation of the lives of a family of war refugees who have applied to the authorities for repatriation. The family becomes a microcosm of human society as represented by the old avaricious mother, a middle-aged couple exhausted and debased by life, and a younger couple on the way to corruption. The impassive questioning of the inspector forces each member of the family to face his burden of guilt and shame. However, when the inspector leaves and the mother dies, they all return to the routine activities from which they have been momentarily distracted.

Husband and Wife (*Marito e moglie;* wr. 1943, prod. 1947).   Drama about marital love in which a wife, terrified of growing old, has an affair with a very young man. When her adultery is disclosed, she leaves her husband and is never heard from again. In an imagi-

Silvia Monfort in *Delitto all'isola delle capre*, Théâtre des Noctambules, Paris. [French Cultural Services]

nary trial aimed at the reconciliation of the couple, the husband explains that he had always thought he was protecting his wife but that now he realizes that it was she who was protecting him, from loneliness. He laments never having acknowledged that without her even salvation after death would be meaningless to him.

Corruption in the Palace of Justice (*Corruzione al Palazzo di Giustizia;* wr. 1944, prod. 1949).   The death of an adventurer and the subsequent destruction of compromising documents point to the possibility of corruption by one of three judges: Vanan, the aged and senile president of the tribunal; Croz, ambitious but mortally ill; and Cust, the true culprit. A government inspector soon finds that each is guilty to some degree and is eager to exculpate himself by accusing the others. Vanan's daughter Elena believes in her father's innocence, and when Cust, in an attempt to save himself, shakes this belief, she commits suicide. Vanan retires from the presidency, and Croz, though he has evidence of Cust's guilt, dies without exposing him in order to leave his rival for the presidency to the torments of conscience. Cust is now free to assume control of the tribunal, but redeemed by Elena's sacrifice of herself, he sees his corruption in a new light and freely confesses his guilt.

Struggle till Dawn (*Lotta fino all'alba;* wr. 1945, prod. 1949).   Drama set in 1945, immediately following the war. Giorgio and his wife Elsa return from northern Italy to a city in the south that they abruptly left on the first day of the war, after Giorgio had been seriously injured in an accident and required special medical treatment. Five years have passed, and Giorgio, under the pretense of settling a claim for compensation of war losses, has acquired legal assistance to trace his friends and possessions. In reality, Giorgio is motivated by an obsessive desire to complete the life he was leading at the time of the accident, when he and Delia, the wife of a close friend, Tullio, planned to run away together. During the years of his convalescence, Giorgio has been tormented by the remembrance of his past intentions. When he recalled the fantasy he and Delia shared of murdering their spouses, he was overcome with guilt. He decided to return to the south and find Tullio in order to make reparation. However, Tullio's jealousy over the past five years has made him insane.

Giorgio, realizing that his wrongs are irreparable, again feels compelled to complete his past. Fatalistically, he strives to acquire a sense of fulfillment by killing Tullio and preparing to depart with Delia. Elsa, realizing that this course can only bring him unhappiness, poisons her husband. As he is dying, Giorgio is inspired by Elsa to adopt a religious faith. She comforts him by the promise of regained innocence and salvation: after death Giorgio will no longer be tormented by the burden of self-judgment and will be subject only to divine justice.

Innocent Irene (*Irene innocente;* wr. 1946, prod. 1950).   Drama in which Ugo, a police officer, is made drunk by a local swindler and lured into the bed of Irene, the man's beautiful paralytic daughter. Irene falls in love with Ugo, but to avoid ruining his career she urges her father to take her away. Before they can leave, the angry townspeople intervene, and in despair Irene throws herself from the window. Recognizing her essential innocence, Ugo marries her in a deathbed ceremony.

Séance in the Old House (*Spiritismo nell'antica casa;* wr. 1946, prod. 1950). Drama posing the problem of whether death puts an end to spiritual as well as to carnal love. The heroine has seen her husband and children killed in an accident. She seeks comfort by attending séances and discovers that consolation cannot come in this world but only in an afterlife. The play ends with her suicide.

Goat Island (*Delitto all'isola delle capre,* 1950).   Drama of passion in which three women, condemned by circumstances to live out their lives on an isolated goat farm, are reduced to sexual bondage by a diabolical shepherd named Angelo. He first seduces Agata, who yields in defiance of her arid life; then Pia, her sister-in-law, who dreams of escape and a return to her teaching job; and finally Silvia, Agata's young daughter. The women are both fascinated and repelled by Angelo. When he is trapped in a dry well into which he has descended to fetch some wine, Agata decides to end his intolerable domination of them by letting him remain there. Frightened, Pia and Silvia protest but do nothing to save Angelo, since they are in essential agreement with Agata's decision. Eventually, Pia and Silvia flee the farm in horror, nevertheless aware that they are being offered a chance for a new life. Agata remains alone to await Angelo's death, triumphant in the knowledge that they are now bound together for eternity.

The Queen and the Rebels (*La regina e gli insorti,* 1951).   A group of travelers is detained by revolutionaries searching for the former Queen. Among them is Argia, a prostitute, who has come to join her lover Raim, who has opportunistically joined the insurgents. Recognizing the Queen, a weak and terrified woman now disguised as a peasant, Argia reveals her presence to Raim. Later, moved by pity, she arranges for the cringing Queen to escape and is herself mistaken by the rebels for the Queen. When Raim refuses to identify her, Argia asks that the peasant woman be brought back, and though the

A French production of *La regina e gli insorti,* Théâtre de la Renaissance, Paris. [French Cultural Services]

Scenes from *Il giocatore*. Paris, Théâtre de l'Atelier, 1953. [French Cultural Services]

Queen is recaptured, she commits suicide before revealing her identity. Argia then announces that she is indeed the Queen. Condemned to be shot, she is told that her life will be spared if she reveals the names of her "accomplices." Though Argia had previously learned these names from the real Queen, she takes her assumed role seriously and refuses. Rising to a dignity of which the real Queen was incapable, Argia rejects her humiliating life as a prostitute and goes to her death.

The Gambler (*Il giocatore*, 1951). Ennio returns to the town where he and his wife Iva were separated during the war to face charges that he is responsible for her death. At a hearing, his sister-in-law Alma accuses him of having taken advantage of wartime confusion to contrive Iva's death. As the circumstances of the fateful day are unraveled, Ennio is forced to admit that his wife was a burden to him. Determined to understand the true motivation of his behavior, he finds that he cannot accept the testimony given by witnesses. Meanwhile, Iva's ghost materializes in the hearing chamber and in Ennio's room, smiling sadly and telling of her love for him.

Ennio seduces Alma in order to get her to sign a retraction of her accusation, but he himself becomes convinced that he is guilty of unconsciously desiring his wife's death. The hearing ends in an acquittal, but as the word "acquitted" is pronounced, a somewhat otherworldly official says "condemned." Iva's ghost fades, but Ennio calls to her until her voice can be heard, and the official is forced to acknowledge the superior will of God's love.

Troubled Waters, or The Brother Who Protects and Loves (*Acque turbate, o Il fratello protegge e ama*, wr. 1951). To protect her brother Giacomo from the results of an investigation conducted by his former friend Gabriel, Alda is ready to seduce his accuser, her former lover. Giacomo, however, refuses to permit her sacrifice. He lures Alda and Gabriel into following him to a mountaintop. There he is accused by Gabriel of incestuous love for Alda. Giacomo loses his foothold and is in danger of falling into the gorge below. Clinging to a rock, he questions his own conduct toward his sister until he is forced to recognize the ambiguous nature of his "brotherly" love; then in despair he releases his hold and falls to his death.

The Burnt Flower-Bed (*L'aiuola bruciata*, 1953). The title refers to a world ruined by selfishness and deceit. Giovanni, a former political leader whose son committed suicide in revulsion at the world's evil, receives a delegation that asks him to return to political life and lead it in a dramatic frontier meeting designed to negotiate peace with a neighboring country. He is warned by Nicola, his former rival, that he will be killed and made a martyr to further national political aims. Nevertheless, Giovanni is persuaded by Rosa, the daughter of a man similarly martyred, to accept the challenge and so show young men like his son that the effects of evil can be overcome by goodwill and personal responsibility. As the delegation headed by Giovanni moves into the open, Rosa is killed when she seizes the truce flag and runs ahead. Holding Rosa's body in his arms, Giovanni continues to move forward, certain now that the men on both sides will finally acknowledge their mutual responsibilities and search for peace.

The Fugitive (*La fuggitiva*, 1953). In debt and unhappy, Daniele decides to abandon his neurotic and naïvely unfaithful wife Nina, who spends her time gambling with Giulio, a local official. During his absence on a supposed business trip, Nina, pressed for payment of her gambling debts, hysterically attempts to poison Giulio. Though far away, Daniele senses her panic and decides to return to her despite the urgings of a Mephistophelian doctor to continue his flight. At Nina's request, Daniele disposes of Giulio's body in the lake, unaware that Nina's poison was inefficacious and that Giulio may still be alive. He then decides to escape with Nina, although the doctor again urges him to abandon her. They reach a mountainous area, where they are mystically "visited" and absolved of guilt by all those involved in the tragedy. Both are forced to recognize that their guilt is a response to having failed something both within and beyond them. Nina, wounded during their flight, dies after having been redeemed by her grief. The doctor once more urges Daniele to abandon her, but he, sensing that they are bound by their mutual dissatisfaction and torment, blesses her and thereby finds his own salvation.

PLAYS

1. *La padrona* (*The Mistress of the House*). Drama, 3 acts. Written 1926. Published 1929. Produced Leghorn, Teatro Politeama, Aug. 14, 1926.

2. (With Osvaldo Gibertini). *La donna sullo scudo* (*The Woman on the Shield*). Drama, 3 acts. Written 1927. Published 1957. Produced Rome, Teatro Valle, Feb. 1, 1927.

3. *La casa sull'acqua* (*The House on the Water*). Comedy, 3 acts. Written 1928. Published 1929. Produced Salsomaggiore, Teatro Comunale, July 18, 1929.

4. *L'isola meravigliosa* (*The Wonderful Island*). Drama-ballet, 3 acts. Written 1929. Published 1936. Produced Milan, Teatro Manzoni, Oct. 3, 1930.

5. *Un albergo sul porto* (*An Inn on the Harbor*). Drama, 3 acts. Written 1930. Published 1943. Produced Turin, Teatro Alfieri, Dec. 23, 1933.

6. *Il diluvio* (*The Flood*). Farce, 3 acts. Written 1931. Published 1943. Produced Rome, Teatro Argentina, Jan. 28, 1943.

7. *Frana allo scalo Nord** (*Landslide*). Drama, 3 acts. Written 1932. Published 1935. Produced Venice, Teatro Goldoni, Nov. 28, 1936.

8. *Il cacciatore d'anitre* (*The Duck Hunter*). Modern tragedy, 6 scenes. Written 1934. Published 1940. Produced Milan, Teatro Manzoni, Jan. 24, 1940.

9. *Una bella domenica di settembre* (*A Beautiful Sunday in September*). Comedy, 3 acts. Written 1935. Published 1941. Produced Genoa, Teatro Margherita, Dec. 7, 1937.

10. *I nostri sogni* (*Our Dreams*). Comedy, 3 acts. Written 1936. Published 1941. Produced Parma, Teatro Regio, Nov. 7, 1937.

11. *Il paese delle vacanze** (*Summertime*). Idyll, 3 acts. Written 1937. Published 1942. Produced Milan, Teatro Odeon, Feb. 20, 1942.

12. *Notte in casa del ricco* (*Night in the House of the Rich Man*). Modern tragedy, prologue and 3 acts. Written 1938. Published 1942. Produced Rome, Teatro Eliseo, Nov. 15, 1942.

13. *Favola di Natale* (*Christmas Story*). Comedy, 3 acts. Written 1940. Published 1955. Produced Milan, Teatro Olimpia, Nov. 16, 1948.

14. *Il vento notturno* (*Night Wind*). Drama, 3 acts. Written 1941. Published 1946. Produced Milan, Teatro Olimpia, Oct. 17, 1945.

15. *Ispezione** (*The Inquiry*). Drama, 3 acts. Written 1941. Published 1947. Produced Milan, Teatro Odeon, Mar. 11, 1947.

16. *Marito e moglie* (*Husband and wife*). Drama. Written 1943. Published 1949. Produced Rome, Teatro delle Arti, Nov. 21, 1947.

17. *Corruzione al Palazzo di Giustizia** (*Corruption in the Palace of Justice*). Drama, 3 acts. Written 1944. Published 1949. Produced Rome, Teatro delle Arti, Jan. 7, 1949.

18. *Lotta fino all'alba** (*Struggle till Dawn*). Drama, 3 acts. Written 1945. Published 1949. Produced Rome, Teatro delle Arti, June 22, 1949.

19. *Irene innocente* (*Innocent Irene*). Drama, 3 acts. Written 1946. Published 1950. Produced Rome, Teatro Quirino, Mar. 23, 1950.

20. *Spiritismo nell'antica casa* (*Séance in the Old House*). Drama, 3 acts. Written 1946. Published 1950. Produced Rome, Teatro Eleonora Duse, Apr. 12, 1950.

21. *Delitto all'isola delle capre** (*Goat Island*). Drama, 3 acts. Written 1948. Published 1950. Produced Rome, Teatro delle Arti, Oct. 20, 1950.

22. *La regina e gli insorti** (*The Queen and the Rebels*). Drama, 4 acts. Written 1949. Published 1951. Produced Rome, Teatro Eliseo, Jan. 5, 1951.

23. *Il giocatore** (*The Gambler*). Drama, 3 acts. Written 1950. Published 1951. Produced Rome, Teatro Valle, Apr. 21, 1951.

24. *Acque turbate, o Il fratello protegge e ama* (*Troubled Waters, or The Brother Who Protects and Loves*). Drama, 3 acts. Written 1951. Published 1955.

25. *L'aiuola bruciata** (*The Burnt Flower-Bed*). Drama, 3 acts. Written 1952. Published 1953. Produced San Miniato, Chiesa di San Francesco, Sept. 24, 1953.

26. *La fuggitiva** (*The Fugitive*). Drama, 3 acts. Written 1953. Published 1953. Produced Venice, Teatro la Fenice, Sept. 30, 1953.

EDITIONS

Collections.
Teatro completo di Ugo Betti, Bologna, 1955; *Three Plays*, tr. by H. Reed, New York, 1958; *Three Plays on Justice: Landslide, Struggle till Dawn and The Fugitive*, tr. by G. H. McWilliam, San Francisco, 1964; *Ugo Betti: Three Plays*, ed. by G. Rizzo, New York, 1966.

Individual Plays.
Corruption in the Palace of Justice. Published in *The New Theatre of Europe*, ed. by R. W. Corrigan and tr. by H. Reed, New York, 1962; *Classics of the Modern Theater: Realism and After*, ed. by A. B. Kernan, New York, 1965.

Goat Island. H. Reed, tr., San Francisco, 1961; also published in *Masterpieces of the Modern Italian Theatre*, ed. by R. W. Corrigan, New York, 1967.

The Queen and the Rebels. Published in *Makers of the Modern Theater*, ed. by B. Ulanov and tr. by H. Reed, New York, 1961.

CRITICISM

E. de Michelis, *La poesia di Ugo Betti*, Florence, 1937; E. Barbetti, *Il teatro di Ugo Betti*, Florence, 1943; N. D. Aloisio, *Ugo Betti*, Rome, 1952; A. Fiocco, *Ugo Betti*, Rome, 1954.

BIBBIENA, Bernardo Dovizio da (b. Bibbiena, August 4, 1470; d. Rome, November 9, 1520). Italian man of letters of humble birth who became a cardinal. He is called Il Bibbiena. His diplomatic abilities were highly esteemed by Giovanni de' Medici, who, upon becoming Pope Leo X, rewarded him with high governmental positions. Bibbiena wrote *The Follies of Calandro* (*La Calandria*), a classicizing prose comedy revolving around the mistaken identities of the leading characters, which was first performed at the court of Urbino in 1513.

The Follies of Calandro (*La Calandria*, 1513). Prose comedy in five acts derived from Plautus's *The Twin Menaechmi* and *Casina* as well as from Boccaccio's *Decameron*

Bernardo Dovizio da Bibbiena; portrait by Raphael. [Federico Arborio Mella, Milan]

(II. 3, 9; VII. 9). Lidio, a boy, and Santilla, a girl, who are twins, have been separated since the invasion of their native city of Modon by the Turks. Lidio is believed dead, and Santilla, disguised as a boy, has fled with her nurse and a servant. The trio are rescued from a Turkish prison by Petrillo, who takes them to Rome and offers Santilla, still posing as a youth, his daughter in marriage. Meanwhile, Lidio, alive after all, makes his way to Rome and disguises himself as a girl to be free to make love to Fulvia, whose husband Calandro falls in love with him. After many ludicrous incidents, Lidio and Santilla recognize each other, don their proper clothes, and plan to leave Rome with their servants to live happily ever after. *See* PLAUTUS.

BICKERSTAFFE, Isaac (1735?–?1812). Irish dramatist, author of successful comic plays, most of which are adaptations. The best known of these is *The Maid of the Mill* (1765), based on Samuel Richardson's *Pamela* (1740). His other works include *Love in a Village* (1762), *Daphne and Amintor* (1765), *Love in the City* (1767), *Lionel and Clarissa* (1768), *The Absent Man* (1768), *The Padlock* (1768), *The Captive* (1769), *The Sultan* (1775), and the undated early play *The Hypocrite*.

Illustration from a 1786 edition of *The Hypocrite* by Isaac Bickerstaffe; Act IV, scene i, with Frances Abington as Charlotte. [Theatre Collection, The New York Public Library at Lincoln Center, Astor, Lenox and Tilden Foundations]

BIGOT, Sieur de. *See* PALAPRAT, JEAN.

BILLETDOUX, François (1927–). French director, journalist, novelist, and dramatist, influenced by the theatre of the absurd as well as by the boulevard tradition. He studied the humanities at the Sorbonne

François Billetdoux. [French Cultural Services]

and worked under Charles Dullin, the well-known producer and director. As a creative artist he has been interested in all means of artistic expression, has directed some of his own plays, and has worked in cabarets and performed as an actor. His plays are predominantly symbolic dramas characterized by brilliant, ironic dialogue, filled with humor. His main themes are the exploitation of men by men and the impossibility of communication between people. *See* BOULEVARD COMEDY; THEATRE OF THE ABSURD.

Billetdoux's plays include *Night at Night* (*À la nuit la nuit,* 1955); *Chin-Chin* (*Tchin-Tchin,* 1959), a highly successful comedy in which a man and a woman of widely different temperaments are brought together when their respective mates have an affair; *Chez Törpe* (*Va donc chez Törpe,* 1961), in which a police inspector is to investigate the suicide of five guests at Mme. Törpe's inn; *The Behavior of the Bredbury Couple* (*Le comportement des*

Scene from François Billetdoux's own production of *Le comportement des époux Bredbury.* Paris, Théâtre des Mathurins, 1961. [French Cultural Services]

époux Bredbury, 1960), based on an actual classified advertisement in which a wife offered her husband for sale; *Pour Finalie* (1962); *How Is the World, Môssieu? It Turns, Môssieu! (Comment va le monde, môssieu? Il tourne, môssieu!,* 1964), in which a deported French soldier and an American prisoner grope to recognize one another as human beings rather than objects; and *You Must Pass Through the Clouds (Il faut passer par les nuages,* 1964), in which a rich old woman, conscious of the fact that people are only after her money, liquidates her wealth in the hope of establishing some meaningful relationships but fails and is left alone. Billetdoux has been called a tragic optimist, who affirms life and love despite his negations.

BILLINGER, Richard (1893–1965). Austrian poet, novelist, and dramatist whose plays, resembling dramatic ballads, contrast pagan and Christian customs. Using realistic and surrealistic elements, he created a milieu bizarrely Dionysian, uniquely Austrian, yet universal. His hero, the peasant, represents the primitive world of magic and superstition, ever in conflict with the encroaching civilization. His plays include *Yule Night (Rauhnacht,* 1931), for which he received the Kleist

Award in 1932, concerning a pagan orgy on Christmas Eve; *Rosse* (1931), which was also made into an opera; *The Witch of Passau (Die Hexe von Passau,* 1935), about a beautiful country girl burned as a witch during the sixteenth-century Peasants' War; *The Giant (Der Gigant,* 1937), one of his most popular dramas, made into a film under the title *The Golden City (Die goldene Stadt,* 1942), in which the city is a source of evil; and *Paracelsus* (1943), a historical play ending with a dance of death. Billinger's main themes and devices are effectively recapitulated in *The Peasants' Passion Play (Bauernpassion,* 1960), an adaptation of a medieval mystery that interweaves pantomime, orgiastic dances, a reenactment of Christ's Passion, and the confrontation of God and the devil. Among his comedies are *Quiet Guests (Stille Gäste,* 1933) and *Gabrielle Dambrone,* the story of a Viennese seamstress who becomes a famous actress, which appeared in 1942 with two other dramas, *Melusine* (1941) and *The Fox Trap (Die Fuchsfalle,* 1942).

BIRABEAU, André (1890–). French dramatist and humorist, author of some thirty witty comedies about his native Paris. He is inventive in the creation of ever-new,

André Birabeau. [Theatre Collection, The New York Public Library at Lincoln Center, Astor, Lenox and Tilden Foundations]

unexpected situations, which he presents true to life, often in classical form. Among his plays are *Le coeur sur la main* (1919); *La peau* (1919), written in collaboration with Nicolas Nancey; *Le bébé barbu* (1920); *La femme fatale* (1920); *Une sacrée petite blonde* (1921), written with Pierre Wolff; *Un jour de folie* (1923); *On a trouvé une femme nue* (1923), with Jean Guitton; *La fleur d'oranger* (1924), written with Georges Dolley; *Un petit nez retroussé* (1924), with Nancey; *Le chemin des écoliers* (1924), a play depicting adults on a beach behaving like schoolboys; *Mon vieux* (1924), written with Henry Bataille; *Petit péché* (1924); *Un déjeuner de soleil* (1926), a hit as a Broadway musical; *L'eunuque* (1927), written with Henri Duvernois; *La fille et le garçon* (1927), with Dolley; *Votre sourire* (1928); *Un déjeuner d'amoureux* (1929), a one-acter; *Côte d'Azur* (1931), with Dolley; *Les baisers perdus* (1932), his first play to be performed at the Comédie-Française; *Soeur de luxe* (1933); *Tempête sur les côtes* (1933); *Fiston* (1936), a political comedy; *La chaleur du sein* (1937); *Pamplemousse* (1937), which shows the comic results of the appearance of a previously hidden illegitimate half-black child; *Le nid* (1938); *Plaire* (1941); *Le séducteur* (1945); and *Souviens-toi mon amour* (1954).

BIRD, Robert Montgomery (b. New Castle County, Del., February 5, 1806; d. Philadelphia, January 23, 1854). American novelist and dramatist; one of the pioneers of roman-

tic drama in the United States. Although Bird abruptly ceased writing plays in 1834, after a quarrel with the famous Shakespearean actor Edwin Forrest over rights and royalties, he produced four romantic dramas of some dramatic and literary importance. The most interesting of these are *The Broker of Bogotá* (1834), a domestic drama generally considered his best play; and *The Gladiator* (1831), a version of the story of Spartacus. *Oralloosa, Son of the Incas* (1832) is an account of the assassination of Francisco Pizarro in Peru, and *Pelopidas, or The Fall of the Polemarchs* (wr. 1830) is based on Plutarch's account of the revolt of Thebes against the tyranny of Sparta. Five other complete plays by Bird are extant: a pallid farce entitled *'Twas All for the Best, or 'Tis All a Notion* (wr. 1827); two romantic tragedies, *Caridorf, or The Avenger* (wr. 1827) and *The Cowled Lover* (wr. 1827); *News of the Night, or A Trip to Niagara* (wr. 1827/28), a farce; and a well-constructed comedy, *The City Looking-Glass* (wr. 1828).

The Gladiator (1831). Romantic tragedy notable for its antislavery stand. It is based on Plutarch's description of the revolt of the Roman gladiators under the Thracian Spartacus and his brother Pharsarius. The revolt is precipitated when the two meet in the arena and Spartacus refuses to fight his own brother. For a time the revolt is successful, but when the strength of the gladiators is undermined by the rashness and ineptitude of Pharsarius, they are divided and set upon by an overwhelming Roman force. In one last heroic gesture, Spartacus plunges into the hopeless battle and meets death at the hands of the Romans. Produced New York, Park Theatre, September 26, 1831.

The Broker of Bogotá (1834). Domestic tragedy that introduces a subtle Machiavellian character in the form of the unscrupulous hidalgo Cabarero. In eighteenth-century Bogotá, the engagement of Ramon, profligate son of Baptista Febro, to Juana Mendoza has been broken because of his irresponsible behavior. When Ramon falls in with Cabarero, he joins with him in a plot to rob Febro, his own father. After the robbery, the conspirators implicate Febro, who is then tried for burgling his own vaults. Ramon, by now completely in Cabarero's power, makes no attempt to help his father. He does, however, tell the truth about the theft to Juana, who rushes off to the Viceroy to clear Febro. After the charges against Febro are dismissed, he still refuses to believe in his son's complicity until Ramon confesses and then rushes out to commit suicide. Heartbroken, the old man dies. Produced New York, Bowery Theatre, February 12, 1834.

Bjørnstjerne Bjørnson
(1832 – 1910)

Bjørnstjerne Martinius Bjørnson, the eldest of six sons, was born on December 8, 1832, to the pastor of Kvikne, a small mountain parish in Norway. In 1837 his family moved to the parish of Noesset, and it was in this magnificent country that Bjørnson spent his youth. His headstrong, generous nature and his talent for storytelling were already evident in 1843 when he began grammar school at Molde. There he wrote his first poems, edited a handwritten newspaper, and manifested an interest in politics. In 1849 he left Molde to study in Christiania (now Oslo) in preparation for entering the university, which he did in 1852. By 1855, having been a regular contributor to various Christiania papers, he became the theatre reviewer for the newspaper *Morgenbladet.* His first stories appeared in *Illustreret Folkeblad,* of which he later became editor. During the next fifteen years, inspired by a visit to historic Uppsala, Sweden, he produced scores of folktales, saga dramas, and lyric poems and songs that form a memorable body of Norwegian peasant literature. One of his songs became Norway's national anthem, and his novel *Synnøve solbakken,* written the same year (1857) that saw his first play, *Between the Battles (Mellem slagene),* produced, influenced an entire generation of Norwegian writers.

From 1857 to 1859 Bjørnson was the director of the National Theatre (Den Nationale Scene) in Bergen, where he met Karoline Reimers, an actress whom he married. He continued to write poetry, and he was also active in liberal politics and edited a Bergen paper. Returning to Christiania in 1859 to edit the newspaper *Aftenbladet,* he founded the Society for Norwegian Culture and continued his political and literary activities. In 1860, forced to resign from the paper because of liberal and reformist articles, he set out on a government-financed tour of Europe; during his three years abroad he continued to write saga dramas and folktales. The dramatic trilogy *Sigurd the Bad (Sigurd Slembe)* was written in 1862 during a sojourn in Rome. When he returned home, his energy went into politics rather than writing, although from 1865 to 1867 he served as director of the Christiania Theatre and from 1866 to 1871 edited the *Norskt Folkeblad.*

From 1873 to 1876 Bjørnson was away from Norway. While in Rome, he came under the influence of Darwin and Georg Brandes. The late 1870s found him turning from folk themes to social questions such as women's rights, educational reform, sexual prohibitions, and political liberty. It was also at this time that he made known his rejection of formal religion. The reaction of his pious countrymen was critical, and his political positions brought on him the charge of high treason. Henceforth he spent much time abroad. During the 1880s he was principally concerned with individual ethics; he then campaigned for oppressed minorities and world peace. In 1903 he received the Nobel Prize for Literature and, although paralyzed on one side, continued working until his death in Paris on April 26, 1910. Ibsen's assessment of his friend and colleague was just and accurate: "His life was his greatest work." *See* IBSEN, HENRIK.

WORK

Bjørnson, Nobel Prize winner for literature, dramatist, novelist, and poet, was an untiring publicist for more than half a century, a powerful political figure, and the greatest Norwegian orator of his day. Had he never written a play, he would still be a national hero. Starting his literary career in the tradition of national romanticism, Bjørnson came to modern social drama by way of historical plays. His first important play, the one-act *Between the Battles* (1857), dealing with King Sverre

Bjørnstjerne Bjørnson. [Walter Hampden Memorial Library at The Players, New York]

(r. 1184–1202), was followed by *Lame Hulda* (*Halte Hulda,* pub. 1858); *King Sverre* (*Kong Sverre,* 1861); the best of his saga plays, the trilogy *Sigurd the Bad* (1863), centering on an obscure twelfth-century pretender to the Norwegian throne; and *Mary Stuart in Scotland* (*Maria Stuart i Skotland;* pub. 1864, prod. 1867).

In 1865, his historical series completed, Bjørnson wrote and produced *The Newly Married Couple* (*De nygifte*), a light problem play that foreshadowed the realism of his later work. After nearly a decade's absence, Bjørnson returned to the theatre in 1875 with *A Bankruptcy* (*En fallit*) and *The Editor* (*Redaktøren*), the first dealing with a dishonest businessman and the second attacking journalistic sensationalism. The spiritual and psychological crisis that caused Bjørnson to reject traditional religion led him to write the bold and controversial play *The King* (*Kongen;* pub. 1877, prod. 1902), which attacked the idea of monarchy and the narrowness of church dogma. A well-constructed and effective *pièce à thèse* ("thesis play"), it contains a curious blend of poetry and social philosophy, comedy and melodrama. In *A Gauntlet* (*En handske*, 1883), Bjørnson posed a simple question: why should a man not adhere to the same prenuptial chastity that he requires of his fiancée? *Beyond Our Power, I* (*Over aevne, I,* 1886), perhaps Bjørnson's best play, is a poignant study of a pastor whose "miraculous" cures fail to work on his own wife, leaving him to wonder whether her death was an answer to his own unconscious prayers. In *Love and Geography* (*Geografi og kjaerlighed,* 1885), Bjørnson satirized his own tendency to become preoccupied with personal interests. Although his plays are seldom performed today, at one time his influence on the drama of social problems, particularly in Germany, was second only to Ibsen's.

A Bankruptcy (*En fallit,* 1875). Drama describing the events leading to the bankruptcy of a well-to-do family and the effect on each of the people involved. The members of the Tjaelde family believe that they can never outlive the shame and scandal of the father's exposure as a speculator and supposedly "dishonest" businessman. But to their surprise they find that the ordeal strengthens them as a family and opens their eyes to the real values in life. The haughty daughter finally accepts the proposal of the family's hardworking but lowborn clerk, and the father lays the foundations of a new and sound business.

The Editor (*Redaktøren,* 1875). Drama in which Bjørnson attacks sensational journalism and the newspapermen whose invulnerable positions allow them to destroy reputations and careers without fear of retaliation. The editor of a newspaper of a Norwegian town tries to ruin one of the town's leading citizens by falsely accusing him of radical political leanings. When one of his venomous articles causes the death of an ailing young political leader, the tragedy forces the editor to recognize the responsibilities of his position, and he begs forgiveness from the people who would have been his victims.

A Gauntlet (*En handske,* 1883). Drama challenging the double standard of sexual morality for men and women. Following an affair that he now repents, Alfred Christensen is in love with Svava Riss. Despite his own vagaries, he is not willing to accept the same behavior in Svava, although she insists that men should be as chaste as they expect their brides to be. Her unprecedented stand unleashes a storm of debate and controversy between the Riss and Christensen families. Unfortunately, Svava inadvertently disturbs her own family's skeletons, and her father's affairs are exposed, completely dispelling her illusions. Although logic dictates that Svava break off her relationship with Alfred, her affection for him prevents such a drastic action. Alfred manages to extract from her a promise to wait for him until he can prove himself worthy of her love.

Beyond Our Power, I (*Over aevne, I,* 1886). Tragedy of a clerical family in a remote Norwegian parish. Pastor Sang has become famous for performing miracles having to do with healing the sick and raising the dead. Though his wife is an unbeliever, her devotion to him is such that she has sacrificed her health and is about to die. While the pastor prays for a miracle, a group of clergy meet to discuss the problem posed by Sang: have his cures been true miracles or have they been affected by the power of suggestion? They decide they must have a sign to prove the miracles. In order to give her husband the miracle he has wished for, Mrs. Sang apparently recovers, but as she leaves her bed, she dies in his arms. Disillusioned, Sang follows after her, unsure whether God has perhaps answered his unspoken prayer for his wife's death.

Love and Geography (*Geografi og Kjaerlighed,* 1885). Comedy that has as its protagonist one of Bjørnson's most charming creations, Professor Tygesen, the epitome of the impractical, ridiculous intellectual. A fanatic geographer, Tygesen tyrannizes his home with his obsession about his studies, and his eccentricities finally drive his desperate wife to leave him. Left to his own resources, he begins to realize what his wife really means to him. Finally, they are reconciled; he is a sadder and wiser man.

PLAYS

Unless otherwise noted, the plays were first performed in Christiania (now Oslo).

1. *Mellem slagene** (*Between the Battles*). Historical drama, 1 act. Published 1857. Produced Christiania Theatre, Oct. 27, 1857.

2. *Halte Hulda* (*Lame Hulda*). Historical drama, 3 acts; verse. Published 1858. Produced Copenhagen, Royal Theatre.

3. *Kong Sverre* (*King Sverre*). Historical drama, 3 acts; verse. Published 1861. Produced Norske Theatre, Oct. 9, 1861.

4. *Sigurd Slembe* (*Sigurd the Bad*). Dramatic trilogy, 3 acts; verse. Written 1862. Produced Trondheim Theatre, Sept. 30, 1863; Christiania Theatre, Aug. 27, 1865.

5. *Maria Stuart i Skotland** (*Mary Stuart in Scotland*). Historical drama, 5 acts. Published 1864. Produced Christiania Theatre, Mar. 29, 1867.

6. *De nygifte* (*The Newly Married Couple*). Play, 2 acts. Published 1865. Produced Copenhagen, Royal Theatre, Nov. 23, 1865; Christiania Theatre, Dec. 20, 1865.

7. *Sigurd Jorsalfar* (*Sigurd the Crusader*). Play, 3 acts. Published 1872.

8. *En fallit* (*A Bankruptcy*). Play, 4 acts. Written 1874. Published 1875. Produced Stockholm, Nya Theatre, Jan. 19, 1875; Christiania Theatre, Jan. 29, 1875.

9. *Redaktøren* (*The Editor*). Play, 4 acts. Published 1875. Produced Stockholm, Nya Theatre, Feb. 17, 1875; Christiania, Møllergatens Theatre, Apr. 28, 1875.

10. *Kongen* (*The King*). Play; prologue and epilogue, 4 acts. Published 1877. Produced National Theatre, Sept. 11, 1902.

11. *Det ny system** (*The New System*). Play, 5 acts. Published 1879. Produced Berlin, Residenztheater, Dec. 19, 1878; Christiania Theatre, Feb. 17, 1886.

12. *Leonarda**. Play, 4 acts. Published 1879. Produced Christiania Theatre, Apr. 22, 1879.

13. *En handske** (*A Gauntlet*). Play. Published 1883. Produced Hamburg, Stadttheater, Oct. 11, 1883; Christiania Theatre, October, 1886.

14. *Over aevne, I** (*Beyond Our Power, I*). Play. Published 1883. Produced Stockholm, Nya Theatre, Jan. 3, 1886; Paris, Théâtre de l'Oeuvre, 1894; Christiania, National Theatre, Oct. 21, 1899.

15. *Geografi og kjaerlighed** (*Love and Geography*). Play, 3 acts. Published 1885. Produced Christiania Theatre, Oct. 21, 1885.

16. *Over aevne, II** (*Beyond Our Power, II*). Play, 4 acts. Published 1895. Produced Christiania Theatre, Dec. 23, 1895.

17. *Paul Lange og Tora Parsberg* (*Paul Lange and Tora Parsberg*). Play, 3 acts. Published 1898. Produced Copenhagen, Dagmar Theatre, Apr. 28, 1901; Christiania, National Theatre, Sept. 6, 1901.

18. *Laboremus**. Play, 3 acts. Published 1901. Produced National Theatre, Apr. 29, 1901.

19. *Paa Storhove* (*At Storhove*). Drama, 3 acts. Published 1902. Produced National Theatre, Nov. 4, 1902.

20. *Daglannet* (*Dag's Farm*). Play, 4 acts. Published 1904. Produced National Theatre, Aug. 31, 1905.

21. *Naar den ny vin blomstrer** (*When the New Wine Blooms*). Play, 3 acts. Published 1909. Produced National Theatre, Sept. 29, 1909.

EDITIONS

Collections.

Gesammelte Werke, ed. by J. Elias, 5 vols., Berlin, 1911; *Samlede vaerker*, 12 vols., Christiania, 1910–1911; *Three Comedies*, tr. by R. F. Sharp, London and New York, 1912; *Samlede digter-verker*, ed. by F. Bull, 9 vols., Christiania, 1919–1920; *Samlede verker*, 5 vols., Oslo, 1960.

Individual Plays.

Between the Battles. Published in *The Nobel Prize Treasury*, ed. by M. McClintock and tr. by J. Weingarten, Garden City, N.Y., 1948.

Beyond Our Power. Published in *Chief Contemporary Dramatists*, ed. by T. H. Dickinson and tr. by L. Hollander, 1st ser., Boston, 1915; *Modern Continental Plays*, ed. by S. M. Tucker and tr. by E. Björkman, New York, 1929.

A Gauntlet. Published in *The Drama: Its History, Literature and Influence on Civilization*, ed. by A. Bates and tr. by O. Edwards, London, 1903–1904.

CRITICISM

J. Vibe, *Bjørnstjerne Bjørnson og den norsk poesi*, Christiania, 1876; G. Brandes, *Critical Studies of Ibsen and Bjørnson*, Copenhagen, 1899; G. Gran, *Bjørnstjerne Bjørnson*, Christiania, 1910; W. M. Payne, *Bjørnstjerne Bjørnson, 1832–1910*, Chicago, 1910; G. Neckel, *Ibsen und Bjørnson*, Berlin, 1921; C. C. D. Collin, *Bjørnstjerne Bjørnson haus barndom og ungdom*, 2d ed., 2 vols., Christiania, 1923; J. Marstrand, *Bjørnstjerne Bjørnson*, Copenhagen, 1923; C. C. D. Collin, *Bjørnstjerne Bjørnson*, 2 vols., Copenhagen, 1902–1907, 1924; C. Gierløff, *Bjørnstjerne Bjørnson*, Oslo, 1932; J. Lescoffier, *Bjørnson: La seconde jeunesse*, Paris, 1932; J. Nome, *Bjørnsons dikterproblem* (dissertation), Oslo, 1934; A. Farinelli, *Führende Geister des Nordens*, Stuttgart, 1940; H. Larsen, *Bjørnson: A Study in Norwegian Literature*, New York, 1945.

BLITZSTEIN, Marc (1905–1964). American composer and librettist whose *The Cradle Will Rock* (1937), a musical drama concerning the overpowering of an unscrupulous magnate by organized labor, caused much controversy. Because of antilabor political pressures, it received a stormy reception at its premiere, which was held without orchestra, scenery, or costumes. Blitzstein's Off Broadway adaptation of *The Threepenny Opera* (1955), by Bertolt Brecht and Kurt Weill, was

Marc Blitzstein. [Theatre Collection, The New York Public Library at Lincoln Center, Astor, Lenox and Tilden Foundations]

one of the most successful productions of the modern musical theatre and had one of the longest runs; it closed in 1961, after 2,611 performances. Among his other works are the music and libretto of the operas *No for an Answer* (1941); *Regina* (1949), adapted from *The Little Foxes,* by Lillian Hellman; *The Harpies* (1953); and *Juno* (1959). His incidental music enhanced innumerable Broadway, Hollywood, and television productions. *See* BRECHT, BERTOLT; HELLMAN, LILLIAN.

Aleksandr Aleksandrovich Blok
(1880 – 1921)

Aleksandr Aleksandrovich Blok, Russian symbolist poet and dramatist, was born on November 28, 1880 (N.S.), in St. Petersburg. His mother, unable to live with her neurotic and violent husband, took the boy and sought refuge with her father, the dean of the University of St. Petersburg. Thus Blok was brought up with the benefits of a cultivated artistic and intellectual environment. He studied philology at the university and took his degree in 1906, having married Lyubov Mendeleyeva, daughter of the famous Russian chemist, in 1903. His career began with

Aleksandr Aleksandrovich Blok. [New York Public Library Picture Collection]

his first collection of poems, *Verses about the Beautiful Lady* (*Stikhi o prekrasnoy dame,* 1902), which climaxed his symbolist worship of spiritual beauty, as distilled in the "Beautiful Lady." This collection marked the end of the period during which he was heavily influenced by the mystic philosophy of Vladimir Solovyov and lived and worked in the bohemian milieu of theatre and symbolist enthusiasts. *See* SYMBOLISM.

Blok's idealism was confronted with the harsh reality of the failure of the 1905 Revolution, which he had supported. As a result, he became disillusioned by his life, his friends, and his wife. The creative cycle generated by this rejection of his former life produced works filled with irony, pessimism, and suffering, among them the poetic collections *The Unknown Woman* (*Neznakomka,* 1906), *Earth's Rubles* (*Puzyri zemli,* 1905), *The City* (*Gorod,* 1904–1908), and *Masque of Snow* (*Snezhnaya maska,* 1907) and his first play, *The Puppet Show* (*Balaganchik,* 1906). In these works the world is not a bucolic dream but sensual, evil, and hungry. Blok was tormented and slowly driven mad by the unbridgeable gap between the life his aesthetic intellectual friends lived, discussing principles and abstractions, and the real, desperate world of the streets and gutters of Russia.

In 1908 two major themes began emerging in Blok's work: a merciless questioning of the validity of the culture created by his generation of aristocrats and intellectuals and the prediction of their imminent doom; and the displacement of the Beautiful Lady of his first period by Russia, symbolized as an irresistible but cruel woman. Blok foresaw not a sentimental national idyll but a great industrial transformation of Russia, as seen in the poem "The New America" ("Novaya Amerika," 1913). All the poems written on this second theme are found in his collection *Homeland* (*Rodina,* 1907–1916).

During World War I, in 1916, Blok declared himself a pacifist and served behind the lines. The next year he was appointed to investigate the Czar's ministers, and soon after he was assigned to the Theatre Section of the People's Commissariat of Enlightenment. He welcomed the Communist Revolution joyfully as the fulfillment of a dream. To it he addressed his masterpiece, the long poem *The Twelve* (*Dvenadtsat,* 1918), in which twelve Red Army soldiers on night duty in Petrograd bring with them not only death but the promise of resurrection.

From 1919 to 1921 Blok delivered lectures and wrote articles on literature and the theatre and translated books for Maxim Gorky's International Literature series. On February, 1921, at the Pushkin Festival, he made a last desperate plea for the "freedom of creation" required by a poet, without which he "can no longer breathe." Exhausted physically and spiritually and suffering from asthmatic attacks, scurvy, and a severe mental breakdown, Blok died shortly thereafter, on August 7, 1921, in Petrograd.

WORK

Blok's symbolist plays are dramatic extensions of his poetry. Although his first five plays were written during the years 1906–1908, a period of disenchantment, pessimism, and despair over the conditions of real life, his style is nevertheless akin to the romantic irony of Zhukovsky and Lermontov. His first play, *The Puppet Show* (1906), shows his own life and that of those around him as a Punch-and-Judy farce. In *The Unknown Woman* (*Neznakomka;* wr. 1906, prod. 1913), he allows the beautiful Sophia, the personification of Solovyov's "incorruptible eternal feminine," Blok's divine muse, to fall as a star to earth, where she becomes an ordinary prostitute. *See* LERMONTOV, MIKHAIL.

During this period Blok wrote very complex, highly symbolic plays that were hard to produce and were better understood when read as verse. The difficulty lay in his belief in the "principle of two kinds of time," chronological time and time unrestrained by conventional dimensions. The changing of time dimensions in Blok's drama caused Konstantin Stanislavski to reject *The Song of Fate* (*Pesnya sudby,* wr. 1908) for the Moscow Art Theatre; he felt the audience would be baffled by it. It was, nevertheless, one of the essential elements of Blok's symbolic drama. By not adhering to the restrictions of time, he was better able to create illusion, show the duality of characters and the trivia of the "real world" that make the beautiful grotesque, and present several planes of action, drawing an invisible dividing line between reality and dream-fantasy. The great producer at the Alexandrinsky Theatre, Vsevolod Meyerhold, believing that the laws of the theatre are very different from those of life, was able to express his leitmotif with Blok's tragic farce *The Puppet Show.* The Meyerhold production of this play in 1906 made Russian theatrical history, laying the basis for all future Meyerhold work, which may be the closest the Soviet theatre has ever approached the modern theatre of the grotesque.

By 1913 Blok was in a different poetical mood, and the two themes, the impending doom of his generation and the purification of Russia through mystical resurrection, that permeated his poetry during these years are seen also in *The Rose and the Cross* (*Roza i krest;* wr. 1913, prod. 1920–1921). In this play he compared thirteenth-century France to the period 1906–1914 in Russia and the young men of 1208 to the decadents of his own times. Throughout the play betrayals are transformed into profound affirmations of beauty and redemption.

Feeling that verse expressed his intense feelings and hopes better than drama, he wrote only one more play, *Ramzes* (*Ramses,* wr. 1919), a work of little dramatic value, executed for one of Gorky's educational projects.

The Puppet Show (*Balaganchik,* 1906). Play conceived at the request of several of Blok's friends, among them G. I. Chulkov and Meyerhold, and inspired by his poem "Balaganchik" (1905). It presents a sophisticated interplay between the author of the play, Death and other figures from the symbolist repertory (mystics, maskers, He, She, a clown), and three stock characters of the *commedia dell'arte,* Pierrot, Harlequin, and Columbine. The seemingly haphazard action escapes from the author's control, and he apologizes to the audience for the unwillingness of the actors to present his realistic drama. Throughout the play Pierrot tries to unite with his beloved Columbine, but misfortunes culminating in the sudden disappearance of all the actors condemn him to loneliness. *See* COMMEDIA DELL'ARTE.

The King in the Town Square (*Korol na ploshchadi,* wr. 1906). Drama based on Blok's optimistic cycle of poems, *Her Coming* (*Eyo pribytiye,* 1904), which voiced his ardent expectation of social revolution. The play, however, reflects Blok's disillusion after the Revolution of 1905, for although the characters in both the poems and the play hopefully await the arrival of ships, only in the poems do the ships actually arrive. The main characters are symbolic: an unrealistic poet; a magical architect with charismatic power over the masses; his beautiful, saintly daughter, who inspires man's dreams; a fool disguised as a priest; and a gigantic stone king who dominates the center of the town. The figures in the play drawn from everyday life speak on abstract topics, electing the exact opposite of their everyday condition ("What joy to die"). The abstract figures representing youth, virginity, secular power, and art talk about the goals toward which they strive ("I have a feeling that the ships are coming from afar") and are interrupted by representative ironies of everyday life (the vendor of roses is dying of hunger). Through art, love, and insight, secular power (the King) is transcended, the starving are fed, the ships arrive, and the poet and the architect's daughter experience the heavenly vision. At that ultimate moment, everything collapses.

The Unknown Woman (*Neznakomka;* wr. 1906, prod. 1913). Drama based on Blok's poem "Neznakomka" (1906) and expressing his wish to find and exalt the Unknown Woman of his early poetry. A poet who sees a star fall to earth discovers that it is the beautiful woman of his visions and follows her to a party, where he tries to talk to her but cannot. She vanishes, after which a beautiful star is again seen in the sky.

The Song of Fate (*Pesnya sudby;* first version, wr. 1908; second version, wr. 1918). Play related to Blok's cycle of poems *Faina* (1906–1908). Herman leaves his wife Elena in search of a richer life, which Faina, a carnival singer whose background is mystically connected with the Russian folk tradition, personifies. Faina treats Herman cruelly until she hears a folktale that she interprets as a command to love him. The two then live together, but during a snowstorm she abandons Herman so that he may return to Elena.

The Rose and the Cross (*Roza i krest;* wr. 1913, prod. 1920–1921). Drama set in the thirteenth century in Provence. Izora, the wife of Count Archimbaut, is locked away in a tower because of her husband's jealousy of an unknown lover whom Izora saw in a dream. Smitten by Izora, Bertrand, a young knight in the service of Archimbaut, goes out in search of the man in the dream and finds that he is an old troubadour. When he brings the old poet to Izora, she rejects him, for she does not recognize him as the knight of her dream. Now the castle is attacked by the enemies of Archimbaut. Bertrand valiantly defends his master and is mortally wounded. Then, despite his wounds he stands guard while Izora trysts with Aliskan, a young page to whom she has taken a fancy. His life ebbing, he uses his last strength to warn Izora of her husband's approach; Aliskan flees, Izora is saved, and Bertrand dies.

PLAYS

1. *Balaganchik** (*The Puppet Show*). Harlequinade, 1 act. Written 1906. Published 1906. Produced Moscow, V. F. Kommissarzhevskaya Theatre, Dec. 30, 1906.

2. *Korol na ploshchadi* (*The King in the Town Square*). Drama, prologue and 3 acts. Written 1906. Published 1907.

3. *O lyubvi, poezii i gosudarstvennoy sluzhbe* (*On Love, Poetry, and Government Service*). Dialogue, 1 act. Written 1906. Published 1907.

4. *Neznakomka* (*The Unknown Woman*). Drama, 3 scenes. Written 1906. Published 1907. Produced Moscow, Literary Artistic Circle, Feb. 3, 1913; St. Petersburg, studio of Vsevolod Meyerhold, April, 1914.

5. *Pesnya sudby* (*The Song of Fate*). Dramatic prologue, 7 scenes. Written 1908. Published 1909. Revised version: 7 scenes. Written 1918. Published 1919.

6. *Roza i krest* (*The Rose and the Cross*). Drama, 4 acts. Written 1913. Published 1913. Produced Kostroma, Kostromsky People's Theatre, 1920–1921.

7. *Ramzes* (*Ramses*). Scenes, 1 act. Written 1919. Published 1921.

EDITIONS

Sobraniye sochineny, 12 vols., Leningrad 1932–1936; *Sobraniye sochineny,* vols. 1–8, Moscow and Leningrad, 1960–1963.
The Puppet Show. Published in *An Anthology of Russian Plays,* ed. and tr. by F. Reeve, vol. 2, New York, 1961–1963.

CRITICISM

A. M. Beketova, *Aleksandr Blok,* Petrograd, 1922; A. Bely, *Vospominaniya ob A. A. Bloke,* Berlin, 1922–1923; E. F. Nikitina and S. V. Shuvalov, *Poeticheskoye iskusstvo Bloka,* Moscow, 1926; A. Y. Tsingovatov, *A. Blok,* Moscow and Leningrad, 1926; N. Volkov, *Aleksandr Blok i teatr,* Moscow, 1926; P. N. Medvedev, *Dramy i poemy Al. Bloka,* Leningrad, 1928; V. N. Orlov, *Aleksandr Blok,* Moscow, 1956; F. D. Reeve, *Aleksandr Blok: Between Image and Idea,* New York, 1962; V. M. Zhivmunsky, *Drama Aleksandra Bloka "Roza i krest,"* Leningrad, 1964.

BODEL, Jean or Jehan (d. ca. 1210). French poet and dramatist, born in Arras. The little that is known of Bodel's life comes from a work of his entitled *Farewell* (*Congé*), a poem in which, upon discovering that he is afflicted with leprosy, he takes leave of his friends before retiring to a leprosarium at Meulan. The form and theme of this work were to become traditional with medieval poets. Bodel is also the author of *La chanson des Saisnes,* an epic poem describing Charlemagne's expedition against the Saxons.

His only known dramatic work, *The Play of St. Nicholas* (*Le jeu de Saint Nicolas*), is an important transitional work in that it combines secular elements with the traditional miracle play. Its dialogue is often earthy and realistic, especially in the tavern scenes, where we are introduced to three comic characters—Pincedé, Rasoir, and Cliquet—who were often to be imitated by Bodel's successors. The scenes called for by the play include a splendid Oriental court, a pagan temple, a battlefield, a tavern, and a prison. The play may have been meant (somewhat unusually for medieval theatre) to be given without music, since only a closing *Te Deum* is indicated on the manuscript. *See* MIRACLE PLAY.

The Play of St. Nicholas (*Le jeu de Saint Nicolas*). Miracle play in which a Saracen leader is converted to Christianity. After a bloody battle a Crusader is taken prisoner by the Saracens as he prays before a statue of St. Nicholas. On being questioned, he claims that among the saint's powers is that of helping one recover possessions that have been lost or stolen. To test these claims, the Saracen chief orders the statue to be placed on his personal treasure, which is then to be left unguarded. Thieves immediately steal the treasure, and the Christian captive is sentenced to die. However, he prays to St. Nicholas with such fervor that the latter appears to the thieves and persuades them to restore the treasure. On finding that his treasure has been returned and doubled, the Saracen chief frees his Christian prisoner and announces his own conversion to Christianity.

George H. Boker
(1823 — 1890)

George Henry Boker, American poet and dramatist, was born in Philadelphia on October 6, 1823, the son of a successful banker. He was educated at the College of New Jersey (now Princeton University), graduating in 1842. In 1844 he married Julia Mandeville Riggs and spent some time touring Europe.

Although Boker had originally intended to practice law, he now turned to literature, publishing in 1848 a volume of verse, *A Lesson of Life,* and his first play, the verse tragedy *Calaynos.* The success of a pirated production of the play in England in 1849 convinced Boker that he should turn his attention to the stage. From 1850, when *The Betrothal* was produced, until 1857, he wrote steadily for the theatre. In the late 1850s he spent much of his time clearing the name of his deceased father from false charges of incompetence as a bank manager.

At the outbreak of the Civil War, Boker helped found the patriotic Union League in Philadelphia and became its secretary, a post he held until 1871. He was then appointed Minister to Turkey, serving in Constantinople until 1875, when he was named Envoy Extraordinary and Minister Plenipotentiary to Russia. In 1878 the Hayes administration recalled Boker. Returning to his native Philadelphia, he was active in local affairs until his death from heart disease on January 2, 1890.

WORK

The plays of Boker mark the culmination of romantic tragedy in the United States and the end of a period in which verse tragedy was a significant part of American drama. He was the first American dramatist whose work aroused interest abroad, and Allardyce Nicoll has called his masterpiece, *Francesca da Rimini* (1855), "as vigorous a dramatic work as any produced by the English poets of the age." Although this praise is mitigated somewhat by the general mediocrity of romantic drama, particularly in English-speaking lands, Boker's work is important and generally of good quality. Others of his romantic tragedies worthy of attention are *Leonor de Guzman* (1853), which recounts the plight of the mother of an unsuccessful claimant to the Spanish throne; *Glaucus* (wr. 1886), a

George H. Boker. [New York Public Library Picture Collection]

treatment of a traditional story of the last days of Pompeii; and *Calaynos* (1849), a drama of the conflict between Spanish Christians and Moors. Although Boker's forte was tragedy, two of his comedies, *The Betrothal* (1850) and *The Widow's Marriage* (wr. 1852), are of some interest.

Francesca da Rimini (1855). Romantic tragedy in blank verse, taking place in Italy about 1300, during the wars between the Ghibellines and the Guelphs. A marriage is arranged between Lanciotto of Rimini and Francesca of Ravenna to mend a political rift. The malformed Lanciotto, aware of his ugliness and crudity, hopes to avoid Francesca's scorn by sending his handsome brother Paolo as his emissary. Believing Paolo to be her betrothed, Francesca falls in love with him. Subsequently she and Lanciotto are married. When war threatens and Lanciotto goes off to fight, he is informed by a spiteful jester that in his absence Francesca has been deceiving him with Paolo. Inconsolable and torn between love and honor, he returns and kills both his brother and his wife.

PLAYS

1. *Calaynos.* Tragedy, 5 acts; verse. Written ca. 1848. Published 1848. Produced London, Sadler's Wells Theatre, May 10, 1849.

2. *Anne Boleyn.* Tragedy, 5 acts; verse. Written ca. 1849. Published 1850.

3. *The Betrothal.* Play, 5 acts; verse. Written ca. 1850. Published 1856. Produced Philadelphia, Walnut Street Theatre, Sept. 25, 1850.

4. *The World a Mask.* Comedy, 5 acts. Written 1851. Published 1940. Produced Philadelphia, Walnut Street Theatre, Apr. 21, 1851.

5. *The Podesta's Daughter.* Dramatic sketch, 1 act; verse. Written 1851. Published 1852.

6. *The Widow's Marriage.* Comedy, 5 acts; verse. Written 1852. Published 1856.

7. *Leonor de Guzman.* Tragedy, 5 acts; verse. Written 1852. Published 1856. Produced Philadelphia, Walnut Street Theatre, Oct. 3, 1853.

8. *Francesca da Rimini.* Tragedy, 5 acts; verse. Written 1853. Published 1856. Produced New York, Broadway Theatre, Sept. 26, 1855.

9. *The Bankrupt.* Comedy, 5 acts. Written 1853. Published 1940. Produced New York, Broadway Theatre, Dec. 3, 1855.

10. *Königsmark.* Tragedy, 5 acts; verse. Written before 1857? Published 1869.

11. *Nydia.* Tragedy, 5 acts; verse. Written 1885. Published 1929. Early version of *Glaucus.*

12. *Glaucus.* Tragedy, 5 acts; verse. Written 1886. Published 1940. A complete rewriting of *Nydia.*

EDITIONS

Collections.
Plays and Poems, 2d ed., 2 vols., Boston, 1857.
Individual Plays.
The Bankrupt. Published in *America's Lost Plays,* ed. by B. H. Clark, vol. III, Princeton, N.J., 1940.
Francesca da Rimini. Published in *A College Book of American Literature.* ed. by H. M. Ellis, L. Pound, and G. W. Spohn, vol. I, American Book, New York, 1939; *Representative American Plays from 1767 to the Present Day,* ed. by A. H. Quinn, Appleton-Century-Crofts, 7th ed., rev. and enl., New York, 1953; *Nineteenth-century American Plays,* ed. by M. Matlaw, Dutton, New York, 1967.
Glaucus. Published in *America's Lost Plays,* ed. by B. H. Clark, vol. III, Princeton, N.J., 1940.
The World a Mask. Published in *America's Lost Plays,* ed. by B. H. Clark, vol. III, Princeton, N.J., 1940.

CRITICISM

E. S. Bradley, *George Henry Boker, Poet and Patriot,* Philadelphia, 1927.

BOLT, Robert (b. Sale, August 15, 1924). English dramatist. Although Bolt rose to prominence during the English theatre renaissance

Robert Bolt. [Theatre Collection, The New York Public Library at Lincoln Center, Astor, Lenox and Tilden Foundations]

A Man for All Seasons, with Paul Scofield, Olga Bellin, and Carol Goodner. New York, ANTA Theatre, 1961. [Walter Hampden Memorial Library at The Players, New York]

begun by John Osborne, he is more closely allied to the traditional Rattigan school. His first stage play was the realistic drama *The Critic and the Heart,* produced by the Oxford Playhouse in 1957. The same year, *Flowering Cherry* was produced in London. An enormous success, the play describes the fate of an insignificant insurance salesman who vacillates between illusion and reality. When the time comes to make his dream of a flowering cherry orchard a reality, he abandons the dream. As a result his wife abandons him, having loved him for his dream. This play was followed by *The Tiger and the Horse* (1960), a sensitive examination of the way in which a cosmic problem, nuclear disarmament, can touch the lives of a middle-class family. The drama that earned Bolt an international reputation was *A Man for All Seasons* (1960), a chronicle play about Sir Thomas More. After the failure of his next play, *Gentle Jack* (1963), Bolt turned to drama for children and produced *The Thwarting of Baron Bolligrew* (1965). In writing the screenplays for *Lawrence of Arabia* (1962) and *Dr. Zhivago* (1965) and the radio play *The Drunken Sailor,* he found still other media for his considerable talent. A new play, *Vivat! Vivat Regina!,* was produced in the 1970–1971 season in London. *See* CHRONICLE PLAY.

A Man for All Seasons (1960). Drama depicting Sir Thomas More, intellectual of sixteenth-century England, scholar, lawyer, ambassador, Lord Chancellor, and Christian saint. Employing a loosely Brechtian technique, the drama revolves around More's clear-sighted and unwavering stand against Henry VIII's divorce from Catherine of Aragon. The divorce is opposed by the Pope, and More's refusal to support the King against the Pope eventually leads to his execution for treason. As his position grows increasingly dangerous, More, resisting the entreaties of his family and friends, is virtually alone in his steadfastness. Not simply a stubborn man, he tries to escape from his involvement, but he cannot be untrue to his own nature; it is this nature, this uncompromising sense of individual freedom, that sends him to his death. The narrator, the Common Man, who appears throughout the play in various characterizations, comments caustically on the action. In perfect contrast to More, the uncommon man, he serves himself, champions the cause that suits him, and changes in chameleon fashion to stay alive. Produced London, Globe Theatre, July 1, 1960.

Valentino Bompiani
(1898 –   )

Valentino Bompiani, Italian publisher and playwright, was born in Ascoli Piceno on September 27, 1898, of a noble family with its roots in Rome. He inherited the title of count. While still in his teens, Bompiani served with distinction in the Italian armed forces during World War I. After 1918 he studied law and was admitted to the bar. A keen student of world history and literature, he became secretary-general of the Mondadori publishing company and after several years accepted an executive post with the Unitas publishers. In 1929 he founded his own publishing company in Milan. From its inception the Bompiani firm showed a strong interest in modern literary trends and was responsible for introducing the works of such young Italians as Alberto Moravia, Elio Vittorini, and Vitaliano Brancati and for making available translations of André Gide, T. S. Eliot, and John Steinbeck.

Bompiani's first play, *The Virtuous Mistress* (*L'amante virtuosa*), was presented in Milan in 1931. However, it was not until after World War II that the Paris production of *Albertina* (1948) established him as a leading playwright. Since 1953 he has been the editor of *Sipario*, Italy's leading theatrical magazine.

WORK

Bompiani has defined his plays as "the theater of remorse, a search into the souls of our contemporaries." His major plays were written after World War II and reflect the postwar period's anguished investigation of the immediate past and its attempt to fix responsibility and reestablish a viable code of conduct.

One of Bompiani's favorite technical devices, the use of what he has called "dislocated" time, was first employed in *The Character's Delirium* (*Il delirio del personaggio*, 1937), which focuses on the dilemma of a mother who is abandoned by her children. Events are presented out of sequence as the mother's memories highlight and give psychological intensity to her present plight. Guilt and remorse are at the center of Bompiani's first major play, *Albertina* (1948), a postwar drama in which events are shown to be stronger than the ability of the human conscience to deal with them in terms of traditional morality. The war over, Albertina must redefine her relationship with her husband, to whom she was unfaithful with a man who helped her survive the terrible years during his absence in the army. Adulterous guilt is also at the heart of *Even the Fat Have Honor* (*Anchi i grassi hanno l'onore*, 1950). Personal revenge is shown to be point-

Valentino Bompiani.
[Federico Arborio Mella, Milan]

less and inhuman, as the sinner's own conscience will adequately mete out punishment.

Social problems of a more general nature are at the heart of *Fear of Myself* (*Paura di me*, 1951), in which an influential and successful man is confronted by problems involving his children and dependents. In it a young girl commits suicide to prevent her father from forcing his workers into a dangerous experiment. In *Teresa-Angelica* (1954) Bompiani offers a lyric drama of love. A young girl being urged toward corruption by her grasping mother finds in the idealistic devotion of a painter an awakening of her own will toward purity. Bompiani followed this work with *Orpheus's Lament* (*Il lamento d'Orfeo*, pub. 1961), an elegant fable that brings into sharp focus a view of love that had been implicit in previous works: love demands complete and absolute acceptance of the beloved as he or she is. In his retelling of the Greek myth, Bompiani has Orpheus lose Eurydice because he has remained blind to the truth of her innermost nature and would have been unable to accept her "less beautiful, less young, with the good and with the bad."

Albertina (1948). Alberto, married and childless, has taken his illegitimate child into his home. After the war he brings the child's mother, Albertina, to live with him and his wife. Forced to accept Alberto's help during the difficult war years, Albertina is now haunted by thoughts of her own husband, who disappeared during the war, and of her first child, who died in a bombing attack. Unable to adjust to life in Alberto's household, she eventually leaves. In a shabby hotel, Albertina finds her husband, Mario. As a pilot in the war, he was forced to inflict death and destruction on others. Consumed by guilt, he has now become despondent, and when he and Albertina return to their bombed-out house, his wife despairs of their ever being able to reestablish a life together. She asks Mario to kill her, but just as he lunges at her, the ruined structure of the house gives way beneath them. A desperate will to live reasserts itself, and Mario leads Albertina to safety.

PLAYS

1. *L'amante virtuosa* (*The Virtuous Mistress*). Play. Published 1931. Produced Milan, Teatro Arcimboldi, Apr. 24, 1931.

2. *Il delirio del personaggio* (*The Character's Delirium*). Play. Published 1938. Produced Rome, Teatro delle Arti, Dec. 30, 1937; Buenos Aires, Teatro del Pueblo, 1941.

3. *La conchiglia all'orecchio* (*The Shell Against the Ear*). Play. Published 1941. Produced Milan, Teatro Nuovo, Jan. 22, 1941.

4. *Albertina*. Play. Published 1945. Produced Paris, Théâtre de la Huchette, 1948; Bologna, Teatro Soffitta, Jan. 19, 1949.

5. *Anchi i grassi hanno l'onore* (*Even the Fat Have Honor*). Play. Published 1950. Produced Florence, Teatro La Pergola, 1950; Buenos Aires, Teatro Smart, 1953.

6. *Paura di me* (*Fear of Myself*). Play. Published 1950. Produced Radio Trieste, 1951; Buenos Aires, Teatro de Apolo, 1953.

7. *Teresa-Angelica*. Play. Produced Bergamo, Teatro Donizetti, 1954.

8. *Il lamento d'Orfeo* (*Orpheus's Lament*). Play. Published 1961.

BON, Francesco Augusto (1788–1858). Italian actor and dramatist whose prolific output of comedies includes his masterpiece, *The Trilogy of Ludro*, comprising *Ludro's Big Day* (*Ludro e la sua granda giornata*, 1832), *Ludro's Marriage* (*Il matrimonio di Ludro*, 1837), and *Ludro's Old Age* (*La vecchaia di Ludro*, 1837). Bon's popular comedies, written partially in Venetian dialect, reflect the influence of Goldoni as well as that of the French theatre of Molière and Beaumarchais. *See* BEAUMARCHAIS, PIERRE DE; GOLDONI, CARLO; MOLIÈRE.

Massimo Bontempelli
(1878 – 1960)

Massimo Bontempelli, Italian poet, novelist, literary critic, dramatist, musician, and journalist, was born in Como on May 12, 1878. His earliest writings, *Egloghe* (1904) and *Odi* (1910), were poetry in the neoclassicist style of Giosuè Carducci. After his first novel, *Seven Wise Men* (*Sette savi*, 1912), he continued to write poetry for another decade but concentrated on narrative prose and drama. During these years Bontempelli taught literature, first at a secondary school and then at a university. Influenced by the futurists and by Pirandello, he departed from the late-nineteenth-century literary tradition and joined in the anticlassicist polemics current at that time. In 1920 he published in the Milanese magazine *Primato* a series of articles expounding his theories on the drama. He later founded his own magazine, *Novecento* (1926–1929), which initiated the artistic movement known as *novecentismo*, characterized by a moderate anticlassicist orientation. In the year 1927–1928 he served as secretary of the Italian Writers Association. *See* PIRANDELLO, LUIGI.

Although Bontempelli had written a play, *The Little One* (*La piccola*), as early as 1913 and produced another, *Santa Teresa*, in 1915, his first important theatrical success was *Our Dea* (*Nostra Dea*), produced in May, 1925, by the Pirandello Company in Rome. He firmly established his reputation as a novelist with *The Son of Two Mothers* (*Il figlio di due ma-*

dri, 1929), followed by a number of other outstanding novels. Bontempelli continued to write plays, as well as short stories and novels, throughout his literary career. His work in the theatre was coupled with an interest in film, which led him to found the first Italian cinema club at the Hôtel de Russie, in Rome, on May 10, 1929. His theoretical writings on the theatre and film were collected and published as *The Twentieth Century Adventure* (*L'avventura novecentista*, 1939). A gifted musician, he composed symphonies, chamber music, and scores for several of his own plays. As a journalist, he published numerous articles on music and musicians.

Bontempelli was elected a senator in 1946. He died in Rome on July 21, 1960.

WORK

An important figure in the Italian theatre of the first half of the twentieth century, Massimo Bontempelli is best known for his original style, called magical realism, which he defined as an attempt to "discover surreality in reality." Although originally a classicist, Bontempelli was attracted to the futurists and to Pirandello, whose influence is particularly evident in his plays. His literary theories, expounded in his journal *Novecento* and highly influential in the 1920s, stressed the value of imagination. He superficially adapted Pirandello's ideas and dramatic forms to his own fantastic world. His style is characterized by the lucid presentation of unreal events, psychotic obsessions, and puppet personalities within the logical context of reality.

Two of Bontempelli's earliest plays deal with the tragic results of obsessive fantasies that have become reality to the protagonists. In *Watching for the Moon* (*La guardia alla luna*, 1916), a woman, having lost her fifteen-month-old daughter, imagines that the moon has stolen the child. In a delirious attempt to kill the moon, she climbs to the top of a high mountain where she dies of exposure. *Ingenuous Minnie* (*Minnie la candida*, 1929) deals with a simple girl who is jokingly told of the existence of robots who look exactly like men. Believing the story, she becomes obsessed by her inability to distinguish "real" men from robots. Eventually, she is driven to madness and suicide.

Two plays with clear Pirandellian motifs are *High Hedge in the Northwest* (*Siepe a nord-ovest;* wr. 1919, prod. 1923) and *Our Dea* (1925). Both exploit the Pirandellian theme of the dualism of face and mask, man and marionette. In *High Hedge,* men and puppets exist on the same level of reality while presenting vastly different interpretations of the same events. The protagonist of *Our Dea* is an automatonlike woman who changes her personality with each change of clothing. The play evidently satirizes contemporary psychological theories concerning the effect of environment on the individual.

Subdued anti-Fascist satire is discernible in *Hunger* (*La fame*), the story of a woman obsessed by the memory of severely suffered hunger. Written in 1943, *Hunger* was censored by the Fascist government and was not produced until 1949. The tragic fantasy *Cloud* (*Nembo*, 1935), centering on the theme of victimized childhood innocence, also has anti-Fascist overtones. These plays, however, are not direct political statements and owe their success largely to the author's ironic detachment. His only truly *engagé* play, *Venice Preserved* (*Venezia salva;* wr. 1927, prod. 1949), was less successful in its accent on political reality. Bontempelli's true originality and appeal lie rather in his ability to incorporate the force of realism in a fantasy world, as exemplified in *Cinderella* (*Cenerentola,* 1942), in which Cinderella refuses the Prince in order to marry a poor violinist.

Our Dea (*Nostra Dea,* 1925). Comedy in which the protagonist, Dea, is a woman whose personality is determined by the clothes she wears. One day while she is wearing a soft, feminine dress that has metamorphosed her into a meek and gentle girl, she meets the Countess Orsa. She promises to help Orsa arrange a meeting with her lover Dorante without arousing the suspicion of her husband. However, the next morning Dea is dressed in a lively, boyish costume that makes her per-

Massimo Bontempelli. [Federico Arborio Mella, Milan]

Laura Adani in
Cenerentola.
Florence, Teatro
La Pergola, 1942.
[Italian Cultural
Institute]

sonality aggressive and independent. Accordingly, she ridicules Orsa's romanticism and refuses to help her. Vulcano, a friend of the countess, learns the cause of Dea's eccentric behavior from a maid. He arranges to have Dea change back into more feminine clothing. Dea again consents to help Orsa by accompanying her to a ball that Dorante will attend, but at the ball she wears a dress designed in imitation of a serpent. The costume metamorphoses her into a diabolical creature. After causing a misunderstanding between Orsa and Dorante, she reveals the lovers' intrigue to Orsa's husband. When Dea returns home after the ball, her personality changes as each item of her clothes is removed. Finally, when she remains only in her underclothing, she is as static, vapid, and mechanical as a mannequin.

Cloud (*Nembo,* 1935). Symbolic anti-Fascist drama set in an unnamed town over which a malevolent fate hangs. Eight years earlier a cloud of unknown origin had ap-

peared, and simultaneously all the children of the town died. As Regina supervises children at play, Marzio and Felice, both in love with her, declare their love, but Regina can answer neither of them seriously because of the possible return of the cloud. As she teases her lovers, she is suddenly terrified at shouts warning that the cloud is again approaching. Regina, exhausted after trying to save the children, falls into a deathlike stupor and is placed with the other dead. Now the townspeople reveal their submissiveness and brutish instincts; one of them would even kill a child who inexplicably remains alive. Recovering from her trancelike state, Regina decides to test her lovers. Appearing before Felice, she rejects him after realizing that his love has been intensified by her imagined death. Marzio, however, affirms his faith in a flesh-and-blood love as opposed to an abstract ideal. Convincing Regina to set aside her insecurity, he wins her by the strength of his devotion.

PLAYS

1. *La piccola* (*The Little One*). Play. Written 1913.
2. *Santa Teresa.* Play. Produced Milan, Teatro Alfieri, May 15, 1915.
3. *La guardia alla luna* (*Watching for the Moon*). Play. 7 scenes. Produced Milan, Teatro Olympia, 1916.
4. *Siepe a nord-ovest* (*High Hedge in the Northwest*). Play. Written 1919. Produced Rome, Teatro degli Indipendenti, 1923.
5. *Nostra Dea* (*Our Dea*). Comedy. Produced Rome, Pirandello Company, May, 1925.
6. *Minnie la candida* (*Ingenuous Minnie*). Play. Written 1927. Produced Milan, Compagnia Italianissima, January, 1929.
7. *Venezia salva* (*Venice Preserved*). Play. Written 1927. Produced 1949.
8. *Valoria, o La famiglia del fabbro* (*Valoria, or The Blacksmith's Family*). Play. Written 1931. Produced San Remo, Compagnia Picasso, December, 1932.
9. *Bassano padre geloso* (*Bassano, the Jealous Father*). Play. Written 1932. Produced Milan, Teatro Odeon, Feb. 5, 1934.
10. *Nembo* (*Cloud*). Play. Produced 1935.
11. *Cenerentola* (*Cinderella*). Play. Produced 1942.
12. *La fame* (*Hunger*). Play. Written 1943. Produced Rome, Teatro dell'Ateneo, 1949.

BOOTHE, Clare (1903–   ). American journalist, politician, and dramatist. For several years an editor of *Vanity Fair,* she later became a free-lance journalist and foreign correspondent. Her first novel, *Stuffed Shirts,* a satire of New York high society, was published in 1931. There followed *The Women* (1936), a play with an all-female cast, in which Mary Haines, having lost her husband to a conniving woman, employs the same ruthless tactics to win him back. The play exposes the sophisticated sham of idle rich women. Other plays are *Kiss the Boys Goodbye* (1938), a satire on the making of a movie star; and *Margin for Error* (1939), an anti-Nazi play about a Jewish policeman in New

Sam Levene as Officer Finkelstein in Clare Boothe's *Margin for Error*. New York, Plymouth Theatre, 1939. [Photograph by Vandamm. Theatre Collection, The New York Public Library at Lincoln Center, Astor, Lenox and Tilden Foundations]

York assigned to guard a Nazi official.

She became active in the Republican party in the 1940s and served as a congresswoman from Connecticut from 1943 to 1947 and as Ambassador to Italy between 1953 and 1956. Her entry into the Roman Catholic Church is reflected in the religious theme of the play *Child of the Morning* (1958). She is the widow of the publisher Henry R. Luce.

BORCHERT, Wolfgang (b. Hamburg, May 20, 1921; d. Basel, November 20, 1947). German actor, short-story writer, poet, and dramatist. He is best known for his expressionist drama *The Man Outside* (*Draussen vor der Tür,* 1947), which was first performed the day after Borchert died of a disease contracted during World War II. The play reveals the dramatist's deep sense of disillusionment and despair in the face of conformity and tyranny and reflects his own experience of a German military prison, where he spent eight months under sentence of death for anti-Nazi statements he made on the Russian front. Borchert's vivid prose sketches, *Lantern, Night and Stars* (*Laterne, Nacht und Sterne,* 1946), among them several excellent short stories, are remarkable for their style, and they too reflect the desolation of Germa-

Scene from Wolfgang Borchert's *Draussen vor der Tür*, produced in West Berlin. [German Information Center]

Wolfgang Borchert. [German Information Center]

ny in the early postwar years. *See* EXPRESSIONISM.

The Man Outside (*Draussen vor der Tür,* 1947). "A play [in the words of Borchert] that no theatre will produce and no public will want to see." Beckmann, a corporal and German prisoner of war for several years in Russia, returns home lame and hungry only to be rejected by his wife, who has a lover. Desolate and alone, he attempts to drown himself in the Elbe, but the river, which appears to him as both mother and fishwife, refuses to take him. In a number of dream sequences Beckmann is rejected seemingly by all society. A young woman finding him on the shore takes him home with her, but he is thrown out by her husband. Beckmann then goes to his former colonel, who once gave him full responsibility for a patrol at Stalingrad. Beckmann, the sole survivor of that fatal mission, is burdened by the guilt of his fellow soldiers' deaths and asks the colonel to take back his responsibility for the men. Again, he is shut out. Beckmann seeks employment at a cabaret but is told by the producer that audiences are not interested in hearing about the war experience, the horrors and senseless killings. Having had every door slammed in his face, Beckmann takes to wandering and comes upon God, a helpless old man in whom no one believes any longer, and Death in his function as undertaker, belching from overwork. Produced Hamburg, Kammerspiele, November 21, 1947.

Dion Boucicault
(1820/22 – 1890)

Dionysius Lardner Boucicault, Irish-American actor, producer, and dramatist, was born in Dublin on either December 26, 1820, or December 20, 1822, to Anne Darley Boursiquot, who had divorced her husband, Samuel Smith Boursiquot, in 1819. Her son's paternity is in doubt, but his father may have been Dionysius Lardner, a writer who financed Boucicault's education. By 1840 Boucicault had left the University of London, and the next year he scored his first dramatic success with *London Assurance* (1841). A few years later he married and traveled to France, where he remained from 1845 to 1847 and where his wife died. Returning to London, he was made an assistant to Charles Kean at the Princess's Theatre in 1848. Soon after he married an actress in the Kean company, Agnes Robertson, by whom he had four children.

In 1853 Boucicault sailed for the United States, where he lectured and toured with

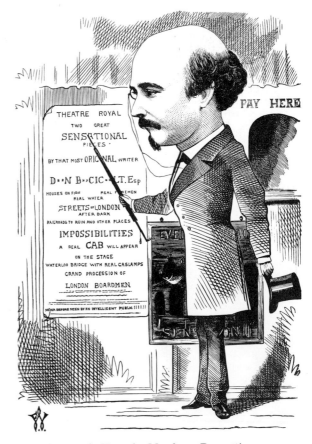

Dion Boucicault. [Brander Matthews Dramatic Museum, Columbia University]

Revival of *The Streets of New York (The Poor of New York)*. New York, Forty-eighth Street Theatre, 1931. [Photograph by Vandamm. Theatre Collection, The New York Public Library at Lincoln Center, Astor, Lenox and Tilden Foundations]

The Young Actress, a musical interlude of his own starring himself and his wife. During this first stay in the United States he wrote and produced *The Poor of New York* (1857), *Jessie Brown* (1858), *The Octoroon* (1859), *Dot* (1859), and *The Colleen Bawn* (1860). In addition, he joined Boker and Bird in their attempt to get Congress to enact the nation's first dramatic copyright law (1856). *See* BIRD, ROBERT MONTGOMERY; BOKER, GEORGE H.

In 1858 he purchased a theatre in Washington with William Stuart, and the next year he acquired the Winter Garden in New York. The success of the *The Colleen Bawn* in New York inspired Boucicault to take his play, cast and all, to London in 1860, thus initiating the traveling company. Five years later, in 1865, he created, with the actor Joseph

Jefferson, *Rip Van Winkle,* which was to become, after years of playing the role, Jefferson's own creation. In 1872 Boucicault returned to New York, where he produced *The Shaughraun* (1874), his last American triumph, preceded by *Belle Lamar* (1874), the first play written about the American Civil War.

In his later years, wishing to marry the American actress Louise Thorndike, Boucicault denied his former marriage, declaring that Agnes Robertson had been only a common-law wife. His marriage to Louise took place in 1888, two years before his death in New York on September 18, 1890. By the time of his death, his fortunes had declined and he was teaching in a New York acting school.

Dorothy Gish in *The Streets of New York (The Poor of New York).* New York, Forty-eighth Street Theatre, 1931. [Theatre Collection, The New York Public Library at Lincoln Center, Astor, Lenox and Tilden Foundations]

WORK

Boucicault, who is believed to have written more than 120 plays, most of them adaptations, was an acknowledged master of melodrama, a style of theatre ideally suited to the temper of the pre-Civil War United States. It was exciting drama, though certainly simpleminded, usually with a moral lesson implied or tacked on at the end. In retrospect, melodrama proved to have a substantial effect on the growth of the realistic drama, if only as a genre against which new playwrights could react. Boucicault contributed, though slightly, to the stream of realism by alluding to social problems and by introducing increasingly sophisticated character delineation. *See* MELODRAMA.

Although his dramas hardly reflect the most serious problems of burgeoning industrialization, some of them indicate his scientific and social interests. For example, the novel and celebrated plot device on which hinges the denouement of his most famous play, *The Octoroon* (1859), is a photograph of the villain in the act of committing the crime, accidentally taken by a jostled camera. *The Poor of New York* (1857), another notable melodrama, contains, amid sensational events, implied social criticism of the poverty resulting from the financial panic of 1857.

Beyond these two plays, Boucicault's reputation rests in large measure on his plays about Irish subjects, a genre he is said to have introduced. These plays were not about the Irish in the United States but presented indigenous Irish for the first time with understanding, compassion, and humor. Such attempts at realistic portraiture, however, are often submerged in a more conventional depiction of the stage Irishman. In the best known of Boucicault's Irish plays, *The Shaughraun* (1874), for example, the unifying character Conn, a tipsy wanderer described in a program note as "the life of every funeral, the first fiddle at all weddings and parties," is undeniably a stock portrait. Other important Irish plays, notable for their movement, however slight, from the vaudeville stereotype to an emphasis on character, are *The Colleen Bawn* (1860), about a peasant girl who is reconciled to her husband despite his attempt to murder her; *Arrah-na-Pogue* (1864), noted for its portrait of Colonel Bagenal O'Grady and based on the capture and escape of an Irishman after the Fenian revolt; and *The O'Dowd* (wr. 1873, prod. 1880), concerning the sacrifice by a Galway Celtic chieftain of the hard-won soil of his ancestors for the sake of his prodigal son.

Among Boucicault's many other plays are numerous adaptations from the French, such as *Mimi* (1873), based on Murger's *Scènes de la vie de bohème,* and *Led Astray* (1873), taken from Feuillet's *La tentation,* a love triangle transferred from France to Ireland; the American Civil War drama *Belle Lamar* (1874), in which three officers, two Northern and one Confederate, appearing at the Southern heroine's trial for espionage, try to outdo each other in self-sacrifice; *Jessie Brown or the Relief of Lucknow* (1858), based on a supposedly true story of a Scottish girl who kept up the soldiers' spirits in the besieged garrison of Lucknow; and a famous reworking of *Rip Van Winkle* (1865), commissioned by the actor Joseph Jefferson.

The Poor of New York (1857). Melodrama depicting the rise and fall of Gideon Bloodgood during the financial panics of 1837 and 1857. Paul Fairweather, who has deposited $100,000 in Bloodgood's bank, hears a rumor the following day that the bank is about to fail and rushes back to withdraw his money. When Bloodgood refuses to give him the money, the incensed Fairweather attacks him but is stricken suddenly with apoplexy and dies. As he falls, the deposit slip drops and is surreptitiously pocketed by Tom Badger, a clerk who had witnessed the deposit being made. The next day Fairweather's body is found in a gutter. Twenty years later, in the middle of the panic of 1857, the Fairweather family is shown as destitute, while the Bloodgoods are living luxuriously on the stolen funds. Meanwhile, Badger, who has been blackmailing Bloodgood, is arrested at the banker's request in an attempt to recover the deposit slip. When the slip is not found on Badger's person, Bloodgood sets fire to the clerk's rooming house in order to destroy it. After being rescued by the police, Badger accuses Bloodgood of arson and incriminates him in Fairweather's death. With Bloodgood's arrest, the money will be returned to the Fairweathers. When this play appeared in other cities, it was reworked and retitled accordingly; for example in London, it became *The Poor of London.*

The Octoroon, or Life in Louisiana (1859). Melodrama dealing with tense pre-Civil War social issues, based on *The Quadroon* (1856), a novel by Mayne Reid. George Peyton inherits his uncle's financially failing Louisiana plantation and falls in love with Zoe, a handsome slave girl, who is one-eighth Negro. She returns his affection but refuses his proposals of marriage, recognizing the insurmountable barrier to their union. Money that has been sent to save the plantation is intercepted by Jacob McClosky, a New England overseer who wishes to take George's place as owner. As he kills the Negro mail messenger and takes the funds, a camera re-

Juliet Randall, Robert Blackburn, and Bette Henritze in *The Octoroon.* New York, Phoenix Theatre, 1961. [Courtesy of Phoenix Theatre. Photograph by Henry Grossman]

cords his actions. Meanwhile, although George could marry his neighbor, the wealthy Dora Sunnyside, and thus save his property, he refuses to do so because of his love for Zoe. Dora, however, convinces her father to buy the auctioned plantation and attempts to buy Zoe, who is also up for auction. But McClosky's bid wins the plantation and Zoe. When the accidentally exposed photographic plate reveals McClosky as thief and murderer, he is hunted down and killed. Meanwhile, Zoe, unaware of McClosky's end, takes poison to avoid his loathed embrace.

The Colleen Bawn (1860). Melodrama set near Lake Killarney. Mrs. Cregan attempts to save her family's impoverished estate by encouraging a marriage between her son Hardress and his wealthy cousin Anne Chute. Hardress, although secretly wed to the lovely peasant girl Eily O'Connor, makes advances to Anne to save his estate. One night Anne mistakes Hardress, as he sets off across the lake to visit Eily, for her lover Kyrle Daly; in a fit of pique at Kyrle's appar-

The Octoroon, with Ray Reinhardt (top) and John Heffernan. New York, Phoenix Theatre, 1961. [Courtesy of Phoenix Theatre. Photograph by Henry Grossman]

ent duplicity and on learning of the Cregans' financial plight the next day, she agrees to marry Hardress. Danny Mann, Hardress' evil servant, hearing about Eily, pretends to take her across the lake to meet Hardress and tries to drown her lest she prevent the wedding. At that moment Danny is shot by Myles na-Coppaleen, a rogue whose former love for Eily, though vain, still endures. Meanwhile, as the wedding of Hardress and Anne is about to take place, police officers accompanied by the dying Danny intrude; Danny falsely accuses Hardress of killing Eily. Just then, Eily appears, having been hidden after her rescue by the loyal Myles. Finally, Mrs. Cregan accepts Eily as her daughter, Anne and Kyrle are reconciled, and Anne saves the Cregan estate by paying off the mortgage.

Rip Van Winkle (1865). Folk drama based on the Washington Irving story. Having drunk his wealth away, lighthearted Rip Van Winkle narrowly escapes capitalist Der-

rick von Beekman's scheme to trick him out of the deed to his land. Rip swears to give up drinking but succumbs one last time. On his return home, his wife turns him out. Rip sadly marches off into the snow, where he encounters an elfin crew and drinks himself into a stupor that lasts for twenty years. He returns unrecognized to find his wife married to Derrick, who maltreats her, claims Rip's son is dead, and is trying to force Rip's daughter to marry his nephew in order to obtain Rip's property. But the son reappears, and Rip reveals his identity, proving it with the deed he had carried with him ever since Derrick's attempt to get it years earlier.

The Shaughraun (1874). In Ballyraggett, Ireland, a lad named Conn, a generous, lovable, and irresponsible wanderer, is known as a shaughraun, who though careless of his own safety values that of his friends. When his friend Robert Ffolliott is transported to Australia because of his opposition to British rule, Conn helps him return to Ireland. During Robert's absence his sister Claire falls in love with Molyneux, the English officer sent to capture Robert. Also during his absence, Claire and Arte O'Neale, Robert's betrothed, have been reduced to poverty by the machinations of Kinchela, an envious trustee of Robert's estate. Conn helps them survive. Soon after Robert's return, Kinchela has him rearrested, but he is granted an amnesty. Before he learns of the pardon, however, Robert is tricked into a foolhardy escape by Kinchela, who plans to kill him in order to take over his estate and marry Arte. The Shaughraun rescues his friend and is himself shot by Kinchela. Later, when Kinchela attempts to kidnap Arte and Claire, Conn, pretending to be dead, overhears the plan at his own wake and rescues the two women. Kinchela is then arrested, Robert and Arte are free to live unmolested, and Claire is restored to Molyneux. The reckless Conn decides to settle down with Moya, a priest's daughter.

PLAYS

Since some plays remain in manuscript, this list is necessarily incomplete.

1. *London Assurance*. Play. Produced London, Covent Garden, Mar. 4, 1841. Written under the pseudonym Lee Morton.
2. *Alma Mater, or A Curse for Coquettes*. Play. Produced London, Haymarket Theatre, 1842.
3. *A Lover by Proxy*. Play. Produced London, Haymarket Theatre, 1842.
4. *The Irish Heiress*. Play. Produced London, Covent Garden, 1842.
5. *The Old Guard*. Play. Produced London, Princess's Theatre, 1843.
6. *Woman*. Play. Produced London, Covent Garden, 1843.
7. *Old Heads and Young Hearts*. Play. Produced London, Haymarket Theatre, 1844.
8. *Used Up*. Farce. Produced London, Haymarket Theatre, Feb. 6, 1844.

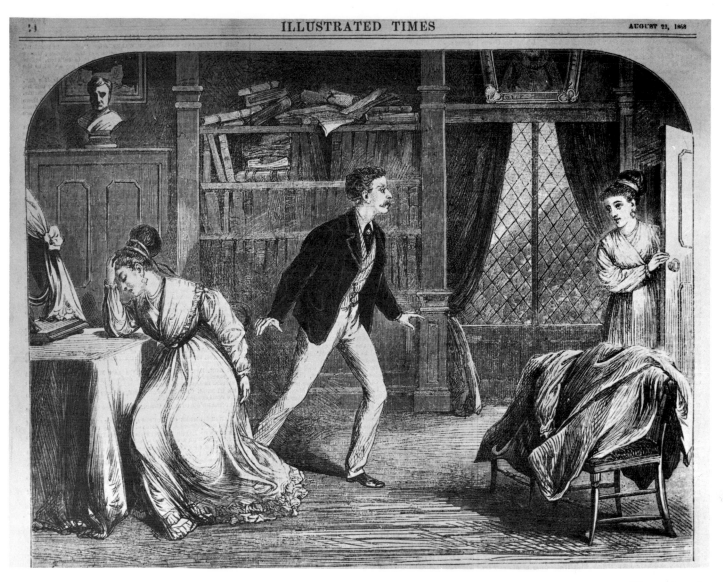

Illustration of *After Dark* from the *Illustrated Times*, August 22, 1868. New York, Princess's Theatre, 1868. [Theatre Collection, The New York Public Library at Lincoln Center, Astor, Lenox and Tilden Foundations]

9. *The School for Scheming.* Comedy. Produced London, Haymarket Theatre, 1847.

10. *Confidence.* Comedy. Produced London, Haymarket Theatre, 1848.

11. *The Knight of Arva.* Play. Produced London, Haymarket Theatre, 1848.

12. (Adaptation). *The Willow Copse.* Play. Written 1849. Produced London, Adelphi Theatre, Nov. 26, 1849. Based on Frédéric Soulié's *La closerie des genêts.*

13. (With Ben Webster). *Giralda or The Miller's Wife.* Play. Written 1850.

14. (With J. V. Bridgeman). *The Broken Vow.* Play. Written 1851.

15. *Dame de Pique.* Play. Produced London, Drury Lane Theatre, 1851.

16. *Love in a Maze.* Play. Produced London, Princess's Theatre, Mar. 6, 1851.

17. (Adaptation from the French). *The Corsican Brothers.* Melodrama. Produced London, Princess's Theatre, 1852.

18. *The Prima Donna.* Farce. Produced London, Princess's Theatre, 1852.

19. (Adaptation from the French). *The Vampire.* Melodrama. Produced London, Princess's Theatre, 1852.

20. (Adaptation from the French). *Genevieve or The Reign of Terror.* Play. Produced London, Adelphi Theatre, 1853.

21. *The Fox Hunt.* Play. Produced New York, Burton's Theatre, 1853.

22. *The Young Actress.* Musical interlude. Produced New York, Burton's Theatre, 1853.

23. (Gaelic adaptation). *Andy Blake.* Play. Produced Boston Museum, 1854. Based on Jean-François-Alfred Bayard's *Gamin de Paris.*

24. *Faust.* Play. Produced 1854.

25. (Adaptation). *Janet Pride.* Play. Produced Buffalo, 1854. Based in part on Adolphe Dennery and Julien de Mallian's *Marie Jeanne.*

26. (Adaptation from the French). *Pierre the Foundling.* Play. Produced London, Adelphi Theatre, 1854.

27. (Adaptation from the French). *Eugenie or A Sister's Vow.* Produced London, Drury Lane Theatre, 1855.

28. *Grimaldi or The Life of an Actress.* Play. Produced Cincinnati, 1855. Based on *La vie d'une comédienne,* by Théodore Barrière and Auguste Anicet-Bourgeois.

29. (Adaptation from the French). *Louis XI.* Play. Produced 1855.

30. *Una.* Play. Produced 1856.

31. (Adaptation). *Wanted, a Widow.* Play. Produced 1857. Based on the vaudeville *Monsieur Jovial,* by M.-E.-G.-M. Théaulon de Lambert and Adolphe Choquart.

32. (Adaptation). *The Poor of New York.* Melodrama. Produced New York, Wallack's Theatre, Dec. 8, 1857.

Based on *Les pauvres de Paris,* by Édouard-Louis-Alexandre Brisebarre and Eugène Nus.

33. (Adaptation). *Pauvrette.* Play. Produced 1858. Based on Dennery's *Bergère des Alpes.*

34. *The Pope of Rome.* Play. Produced 1858. Revised version of *The Broken Vow.*

35. *Jessie Brown or The Relief of Lucknow.* Play. Produced New York, Wallack's Theatre, Feb. 22, 1858; London, Britannia Theatre, 1859.

36. (Adaptation). *Dot.* Play. Produced 1859. Based on Charles Dickens's *The Cricket on the Hearth* (1845).

37. (Adaptation). *Nicholas Nickleby.* Play. Produced 1859. Based on Dickens's novel (1838–1839).

38. (Adaptation). *The Octoroon, or Life in Louisiana.* Melodrama. Produced New York, Winter Garden, Dec. 5, 1859. Revised version: Produced London, Adelphi Theatre, 1861. Based on Mayne Reid's novel *The Quadroon* (1856).

39. (Adaptation). *The Trial of Effie Deans.* Play. Written 1860. Based on Sir Walter Scott's novel *The Heart of Midlothian* (1818).

40. (Adaptation). *Vanity Fair.* Play. Written 1860. Based on *Les fanfarons du Vise,* by Philippe Dumanoir and Edmond Desnoyers de Biéville.

41. (Adaptation). *The Colleen Bawn.* Melodrama. Produced New York, Laura Keene's Theatre, Mar. 29, 1860; London and Dublin, 1860. Based on the novel *The Collegians* (1829), by Gerald Griffin.

42. (With John Oxenford). *The Lily of Killarney.* Opera libretto. Produced 1862. Music: Sir Julius Benedict.

43. *How She Loves Him.* Play. Produced New York, 1863.

44. *Arrah-na-Pogue, or The Wicklow Wedding.* Play, in Gaelic. Produced Dublin, 1864.

45. *The Poor of Liverpool* and *The Streets of London.* Produced London, 1864. Revision of *The Poor of New York.*

46. *Omoo, or The Sea of Ice.* Play. Written 1864.

47. (Adaptation; with Joseph Jefferson). *Rip Van Winkle.* Folk drama. Written 1865. Produced London, Adelphi Theatre, 1865. Based on the story by Washington Irving (1819).

48. *The Flying Scud or Four-Legged Fortune.* Play. Written 1866.

49. (Adaptation). *The Long Strike.* Play. Written 1866. Based on novels by Elizabeth Gaskell.

50. *The Parish Clerk.* Play. Written 1866.

51. *The Two Lives of Mary Leigh.* Play. Written 1866.

52. (Adaptation). *A Wild Goose;* also known as *The Scamp.* Play. Written 1867. Based on *Rosedale* (1863), by Lester Wallack.

53. *After Dark, a Tale of London Life.* Play. Written 1868.

54. (With Charles Reade). *Foul Play.* Play. Written 1868.

55. *Formosa or The Railroad to Ruin.* Play. Written 1869.

56. (With Henry James Byron). *Lost at Sea, a London Story.* Play. Written 1869.

57. *Presumptive Evidence;* also known as *Mary Dodd.* Play. Written 1869.

58. *Seraphine or A Devotee.* Play. Written 1869.

59. *Jezebel or The Dead Reckoning.* Play. Written 1870.

60. *Paul La Farge or Self Made.* Play. Written 1870.

61. *The Rapparee or The Treaty of Limerick.* Play. Written 1870.

62. *Elfie or The Cherry Tree Inn.* Play. Written 1871.

63. (Adaptation from the French). *Night and Morning.* Play. Written 1871.

64. (With James Planché). *Babil and Bijou, or The Lost Regalia.* Play. Produced London, Covent Garden, 1872.

65. (Adaptation). *John Bull.* Play. Written 1872. Based on George Colman's play of the same name (1803).

66. (Adaptation). *Led Astray.* Play. Written 1873. Produced New York, Union Square Theatre, 1873. Based on Octave Feuillet's *La tentation.*

67. (Adaptation). *Mimi.* Play. Written 1873. Based on *Scènes de la vie de bohème* (1851), by Henri Murger.

68. (Gaelic adaptation). *The O'Dowd.* Play. Written 1873. Produced London, 1880. Based on *Les crochets du père Martin,* by Eugène Cormon and Eugène Grangé.

69. *Belle Lamar.* Play. Produced New York, Booth's Theatre, Aug. 10, 1874. Revised as *Fin Maccoul.*

70. *The Shaughraun.* Play. Produced New York, Wallack's Theatre, 1874.

71. *Forbidden Fruit.* Play. Written 1876.

72. *Marriage.* Play. Written 1877. Produced London, 1880, as *A Bridal Tour.*

73. (Adaptation). *Clarissa Harlowe.* Play. Written 1878. Based on Samuel Richardson's novel (1747–1748).

74. *Norah's Vows.* Play. Written 1878.

75. *Contempt of Court.* Play. Written 1879.

76. *Rescued or A Girl's Romance.* Play. Written 1879.

77. *The Amadan.* Play. Produced Boston, 1883.

78. (Adaptation). *Vice Versa.* Play. Written 1883. Based on *Le truc d'Arthur,* by Henri-Alfred Duru and Henri-Charles Chivot.

79. *Robert Emmett.* Play. Written 1884.

80. (Adaptation). *The Jilt.* Play. Produced Boston, 1885. Based on a story by Hawley Smart.

81. (Adaptation). *The Spae Wife.* Play. Written 1886. Based on Scott's novel *Guy Mannering* (1815).

82. *Fin Maccoul.* Play. Produced London, 1887. Revised version of *Belle Lamar.*

83. (Adaptation; with Webster). *Don César de Bazan.* Play. Produced London, Adelphi Theatre. Based on the play of the same name by Dumanoir and Dennery.

84. (With Webster). *The Fox and the Goose or The Widow's Husband.* Operetta. Produced London, Adelphi Theatre.

EDITIONS

Collections.
Forbidden Fruit and Other Plays, ed. by A. Nicoll and F. T. Clark, Princeton, N.J., 1940, Bloomington, Ind., 1963.

Individual Plays.
Belle Lamar. Published in *Plays for the College Theater,* ed. by G. H. Leverton, French, New York, 1934.

The Colleen Bawn. Published in *Nineteenth Century Plays,* ed. by G. Howell, Oxford, London, 1953.

Dot. Published in *America's Lost Plays,* ed. by B. H. Clark, vol. I, Princeton, N.J., 1940–1941.

The Flying Scud or Four-legged Fortune. Published in *America's Lost Plays,* ed. by B. H. Clark, vol. I, Princeton, N.J., 1940–1941; *Favorite American Plays of the Nineteenth Century,* ed. by B. H. Clark, Princeton, N.J., 1943.

Forbidden Fruit. Published in *America's Lost Plays,* ed. by B. H. Clark, vol. I, Princeton, N.J., 1940–1941.

London Assurance. Published in *Representative British Dramas, Victorian and Modern,* ed. by M. J. Moses, Little, Brown, Boston, 1931; *The Development of English Drama,* ed. by G. E. Bentley, Appleton-Century-Crofts, New York, 1950; *Masterpieces of British Drama: The Nineteenth Century,* ed. by R. W. Corrigan, Dell, New York, 1967.

Louis XI. Published in *America's Lost Plays,* ed. by B. H. Clark, vol. I, Princeton, N.J., 1940–1941.

The Octoroon, or Life in Louisiana. Published in *Representative American Plays from 1767 to the Present Day,* ed. by A. H. Quinn, Appleton-Century-Crofts, New York, 1953; *The Black Crook, and Other Nineteenth Century American Plays,* ed. by M. Matlaw, Dutton, New York, 1967.

Presumptive Evidence. Published in *America's Lost Plays,* ed. by B. H. Clark, vol. I, Princeton, N.J., 1940–1941.

Rip Van Winkle. Published in *The Most Successful Plays in the History of the American Stage,* ed. by B. Cerf and V. H. Cartmell, Doubleday, Garden City, N.Y., 1944; *Representative American Plays from 1767 to the Present*

Day, ed. by A. H. Quinn, Appleton-Century-Crofts, New York, 1953.

Robert Emmett. Published in *America's Lost Plays,* ed. by B. H. Clark, vol. I, Princeton, N.J., 1940–1941.

CRITICISM

T. Walsh, *The Career of Dion Boucicault,* New York, 1915.

BOULARAN, Jacques. *See* DEVAL, JACQUES.

BOULEVARD COMEDY. Term applied to the popular comedy written and performed in France since about 1850. Emerging as a reaction to the serious social satire and thesis plays of the nineteenth century, boulevard comedy aims at attaining commercial success by presenting light entertainment for as many people as possible. Therefore, it is usually performed in the large boulevard theatres of Paris, though it also appears off the boulevards in smaller but equally elegant theatres known as *bonbonnières.* Invariably the cast includes a famous star among the handome and well-groomed actors and actresses. The plays are generally rather short and begin late in order to accommodate the after-dinner audience. They follow the conventions of realism and psychological analysis, though the latter never reaches any great depth. Frequently what they lack in literary quality is compensated for in superb craftsmanship.

Among the classics of the genre are plays by Alexander Dumas *fils* and, in the present century, *Marius* (1929) and *Fanny* (1931), by Marcel Pagnol. Other leading writers of boulevard comedy since 1900 are Georges Feydeau, Sacha Guitry, Louis Verneuil, Alfred Savoir, Jacques Deval, and André Birabeau.

BOURDET, Édouard (b. Saint-Germain-en-Laye, October 26, 1887; d. Paris, January 16, 1945). French dramatist and theatrical director (he was administrator of the Comédie-Française from 1936 to 1940) who is known especially for his acute psychological analyses of sexual attitudes and for his mordant social satires. Because Bourdet was content to present his observations without comment, his plays were often attacked as lacking a clear moral point of view. It must be noted, however, that though his subjects are often titillating, his treatment is never salacious or brutal but is distinguished by ironic and intelligent detachment.

Bourdet's interest in sexual mores is demonstrated in his successful first play, *The Rubicon* (*Le Rubicon,* 1910), in which a bride's conjugal apprehensions are drowned in champagne. Deviant sexual attitudes are examined in *The Captive* (*La prisonnière,* 1926), a

dramatic study of lesbian passion; and *The Snobs* (*La fleur des pois,* 1932), a comic treatment of the manners and mores of upper-class homosexuals. The hit of the 1929 Paris theatrical season was *Le sexe faible* (literally *The Weaker Sex,* but presented in New York as *The Sex Fable*), which cleverly inverts the traditional scheme of things by presenting a situation in which handsome but impecunious young men are hotly pursued by lusty,

Scene from *Fric-Frac,* by Edouard Bourdet. Théâtre Antoine, Paris. [French Cultural Services]

Édouard Bourdet. [New York Public Library]

Yvonne Printemps
and Pierre Fresnay
in *Hyménée*
(above). Paris,
Théâtre de la
Michodière, 1952.
[French Cultural
Services]

wealthy women. Incest is the theme of *Margot* (1935), a historical drama that examines the relationship between Margaret of Navarre and her brother. Two of Bourdet's best plays on broadly social themes are *Best Sellers* (*Vient de paraître*, 1927) and *Hard Times* (*Les temps difficiles*, 1934; adapted by Louis Bromfield as *Times Have Changed*). In the former he examined the decadence of literary and publishing circles in which human and moral considerations are forced to give way to commercial exigencies. *Hard Times* is a mordant drama that focuses on an upper-class family willing to ensure its financial fortunes by marrying an innocent young girl to a wealthy imbecile.

Among Bourdet's other plays are *The Open Cage* (*La cage ouverte*, 1913); *Lovers' Hour* (*L'heure du berger*, 1922); *The Chained Man* (*L'homme enchaîné*, 1923); *Fric-Frac* (1936), which was made into an enormously successful film starring Fernandel, Michel Simon, and Arletty; *Father* (*Père*, 1942); and *Marriage* (*Hyménée*, 1944).

The Captive (*La prisonnière*, 1926). To explain her unwillingness to accompany her father to Rome, Irène de Montcel tells him that she is in love with Jacques Virieu and

Le sexe faible, as
presented by the
Comédie-
Française. Paris,
Salle Luxembourg,
1957. [French
Cultural Services]

wants to remain in Paris in order to be near him. Jacques, however, knows that Irène is not in love with him. Believing her to be in love with Georges Aiguines, he confronts the latter and discovers that it is actually Mme. Aiguines with whom Irène is having an affair. Irène admits her unnatural passion and begs Georges to help her conquer her inclinations. Irène and Georges are married, and after their return from their honeymoon Irène tries to avoid Mme. Aiguines. However, her struggle is undermined by Jacques's discontent with their marriage, and eventually Irène is once more ensnared by Mme. Aiguines. Produced Paris, Théâtre Fémina, 1926.

The Sex Fable (*Le sexe faible*, 1929). The title literally means "The Weaker Sex," and the play concentrates on a world of upper-class gigolos whose aim in life is to make a "good" marriage. Isabelle Leroy-Gomez, an impecunious but ambitious socialite, schemes to marry her handsome sons to wealthy women. Two of them have already been "established," but Jimmy proves to be a somewhat more difficult case and insists on his romance with Nicole, a working girl, in spite of the fact that Isabelle has arranged a match for him with an American heiress. An amusing counterpoint to Isabelle's efforts is provided by the pathetic situation of Carlos, a handsome Spaniard who becomes somewhat *déclassé* because he has allowed himself to be seduced by a wealthy woman who now refuses to marry him. Jimmy decides to put pragmatic considerations before love after Isabelle points out to him that he need only stay married long enough to accumulate a nest egg before returning to Nicole.

BOURGEOIS DRAMA. Term applied to the type of late-eighteenth-century French drama that emphasized middle-class morality and extolled the virtues of middle-class life. It was inspired initially by the *comédie larmoyante* ("tearful comedy") of Nivelle de La Chaussée (1692–1754), whose popularity with middle-class audiences was based on a frank appeal to sentimentality, pathos, and priggish morality. A typical feature was the bourgeois affinity, shared by dramatist and audience alike, for the happy ending in which virtue and family life emerge triumphant and evildoers are led to righteousness. *See* LA CHAUSSÉE, PIERRE-CLAUDE NIVELLE DE.

The bourgeois dramatists, foremost of whom was the playwright and encyclopedist Denis Diderot (1713–1784), combined the seriousness of tragedy with the middle-class concerns of comedy. Sharing the bourgeois belief in the fundamental goodness of man and pity for man's suffering, they attributed man's shortcomings to social causes rather than to the individual. Consequently, their dramas were concerned less with the psychological aspects of man's existence than with his condition as a social being, which they treated with gravity. Their prime interest was in improving man's moral and spiritual condition by portraying his corrupt relations with his family and with the rest of the world. Unlike the seventeenth- and early-eighteenth-century comedy of manners of Molière and Marivaux, the bourgeois drama had the serious intent of encouraging social reform. This was a new element in the French theatre, and the Parisian journalist Melchior von Grimm declared optimistically that the new drama might even bring back morality to France. *See* COMEDY OF MANNERS; DIDEROT, DENIS.

Diderot's *The Natural Son* (pub. 1757, prod. 1771) and *The Father of the Family* (1761) were, as their titles suggest, the epitome of the new serious genre. More than his plays, however, it was his critical essay *Conversations on "The Natural Son,"* published with the play, that had a major influence on the drama that followed. In these *Conversations* he argued for a relaxation of the oppressive conventions of declamatory playwriting and acting. The emphasis of the drama, he said, should be on the realistic expression of the passions and tragedies of everyday life, with a clear moral lesson implied. Diderot's argument and the popularity of bourgeois drama turned the art of acting and the drama generally in a more subtle and emotional direction.

BOURSAULT, Edme (b. Mussy l'Évêque, Aube, October, 1638; d. Paris, September 15, 1701). French dramatist whose reputation rests upon *The Comedy Without a Title, or "Le Mercure Galant"* (*La comédie sans titre, ou "Le Mercure Galant,"* 1683). Frequently embroiled in controversy and sensing some real or imagined slight in Molière's *The School for Wives Criticized* (1663), Boursault responded with his own *Portrait of the Painter* (*Le portrait du peintre*, 1663), which prompted Molière to reply with *The Versailles Impromptu*. Later, in reaction to certain criticisms made by Nicolas Boileau, Boursault wrote the biting one-act play *The Satire of Satires* (*La satire des satires*, pub. 1669), which was never performed. Eventually, he was reconciled with both men. *See* MOLIÈRE.

Boursault's best plays belong to his later years, when he wrote the comic spectacle *Phaeton* (1691) and a lively one-act play, *Fashionable Words* (*Les mots à la mode*, 1694). *Aesop* (*Ésope*, 1690), a loosely constructed moralistic comedy, belongs to this period. Its success brought forth a sequel, *Aesop at Court*

(*Ésope à la cour*), which was adapted into English by John Vanbrugh. Boursault's earlier and far less successful plays are the tragedies *Germanicus* (1673), an adaptation of Mme. de La Fayette's novel *La Princesse de Clèves* set in Rome in deference to popular taste, and *Mary Stuart* (*Marie Stuart*, 1683); the comedies *Les Cadenats* (1660), *The Living Dead Man* (*Le mort vivant*, 1661), *Les Nicandres* (1663), and *The Flying Doctor* (*Le médecin volant*, 1664); and the pastoral *The Eyes of Phyllis* (*Les yeux de Philis*, 1664).

The Comedy Without a Title, or "Le Mercure Galant" (*La comédie sans titre, ou "Le Mercure Galant"* 1683). Comedy that supposedly takes place in the office of the well-known seventeenth-century French periodical *Le Mercure Galant*. Oronte has persuaded his friend Licidas, editor of the publication, to let him pose as editor for one day. His purpose is to impress his sweetheart's father, M. de Boisluisant, a great admirer of the periodical. Naturally, Boisluisant readily agrees to a match between his daughter Cécile and the "editor."

Within this loosely constructed framework are thirteen vignettes of typical contemporary Parisians, all of whom want something from the editor. Two sisters, for example, claim to have mastered the art of remaining silent from an article they read in the *Mercure*. They ask Oronte to judge which is the more proficient, whereupon they fall into an argument and babble on incessantly. Produced Paris, Comédie-Française, March 5, 1683.

BOYLE, William (b. County Louth, April 4, 1853; d. Dulwich, England, March 6, 1923). Irish poet, patriot, versifier, and dramatist. He grew up during the agitation for Irish Home Rule, becoming a strong supporter of Parnell, then, during World War I, of John Redmond, and finally of the government of the Irish Free State. He first made his mark in Irish letters with a book entitled *A Kish of Brogues* (1899), taking his title from the shoe stalls at Irish fairs. He describes the contents as "sketches in prose and verse of rural life in Ireland."

Boyle's substantial comic talent won him a special place in the early Abbey Theatre, since many of the other playwrights were exclusively serious. His first and best comedy for the Abbey was *The Building Fund* (1905); it was followed by *The Eloquent Dempsey* (1906), a comedy depicting a small-town publican with political ambitions who tries to maneuver between the partisans of Home Rule and the Unionists. His next comedy, *The Mineral Workers* (1906), about an energetic Irish-American who disrupts an Irish farm by digging for iron in the pasture, was produced by the Abbey; soon after, Boyle strenuously objected to the theatre's production of *The Playboy of the Western World* and Synge's portrayal of Irish life. A break in his dramatic activity, which occurred after *The Mineral Workers*, lasted until the production of *A Family Failing* (1912), also set on an Irish farm. However, none of his later plays, except perhaps *A Family Failing*, display comic scenes as skillfully executed as some of his first efforts.

The Building Fund (1905). Comedy of Irish farm life in which Michael O'Callaghan and Daniel MacSweeney arrive at the Grogan farm to solicit a contribution to the building fund for the new parish church. Shan Grogan, living with his despotic and miserly mother, pleads that he is virtually destitute and refuses them anything more than a shilling. Worried that his niece might share in his mother's estate, Shan urges his mother to make a will, which she does just before she dies. After the funeral, to the surprise of all, Mrs. Grogan is discovered to have left everything to the parish priest. Shan is allowed to stay on merely as farm manager. Produced Dublin, Abbey Theatre, April 25, 1905.

BRACCO, Roberto (b. Naples, November 10, 1861; d. Sorrento, April 20, 1943). Italian journalist, poet, critic, short-story writer, and dramatist. Influenced by Maeterlinck and Ibsen, Bracco was a representative of modern

Roberto Bracco. [Italian Cultural Institute]

Alla Nazimova in *Comtesse Coquette.* New York, Bijou Theatre, 1907. [Photograph by Bruguiere. Theatre Collection, The New York Public Library at Lincoln Center, Astor, Lenox and Tilden Foundations]

psychological drama who advocated women's rights. A liberal politician and member of the Parliament, he was persecuted by the Fascist regime, and his books were forbidden to be published. After writing several plays, such as *The Unfaithful* (*Infidèle,* 1894), a realistic comedy later produced in New York under the title *Comtesse Coquette,* and *Don Pietro Caruso* (1895) in the style of southern Italian popular melodrama, he turned to the genre of drawing-room comedy, in which he treated his themes realistically, concentrating not on plot but on motivation and feeling, with compassion for those who suffer and understanding for those who sin. Bracco's attempts to illuminate the workings of the unconscious mind were not always satisfactory, but he was able to describe the nature of female psychology in such plays as *Motherhood* (*Maternità,* 1903) and *The Little Fountain* (*La piccola fonte,* 1905), an investigation of the marital relations of a poet and his simple, devoted wife. Bracco's most famous play, *The Little Saint* (*Il piccolo santo,* 1909), concerns a humble priest unable to escape the passions of his youth. His most coherent works are one-act plays in Neapolitan dialect, such as *Lost in the Dark* (*Sperduti nel buio,* 1907), in which he gave free expression to his social conscience.

The Little Fountain (*La piccola fonte,* 1905). Teresa, a simple woman, lives only for her husband Stefano, a poet. When critical success and another woman enter his life, the realization that she is not everything to him causes Teresa to lose her mind. Believing himself to be the cause of Teresa's insanity, Stefano can no longer write, and in desperation he finally decides to run away, although he no longer loves the other woman. He gets as far as the railroad station but is irresistibly drawn back to Teresa, who, in a last burst of love and perhaps lucidity, commits suicide, thus freeing Stefano.

The Little Saint (*Il piccolo santo,* 1909). Drama in five acts concerning Don Fiorenzo Barsi, a parish priest who is loved and admired for his exemplary religious conduct. One day his brother Giulio returns home after a long stay in South America. Giulio falls in love with Anita; the daughter of a woman now dead, once loved by Don Fiorenzo, she wishes to become a nun. Don Fiorenzo urges her to marry Giulio. At first she resists, then accedes to his wish. Following the marriage to Giulio, her love for him grows. Anita and Giulio decide to leave secretly for South America, and when their intention is discovered, it is sanctioned by Don Fiorenzo. However, Barbarello, a presumed half-wit who was once saved from death by the priest, having vaguely understood Don Fiorenzo's unconscious love for Anita, murders Giulio.

Vitaliano Brancati
(1907 — 1954)

Vitaliano Brancati, Italian poet, novelist, and dramatist, was born in Pachino, Sicily, on July 24, 1907. During his childhood, his family moved to Catania, where the cultural environment stimulated his interest in literature and his desire to write. Between 1924 and 1926 he wrote his first work, the dramatic poem *Fedor,* published in 1928. At this time, Brancati enthusiastically supported the new Fascist regime, initially attractive to him as an expression of youthful vigor. His second drama, *Everest,* successfully produced in Rome in 1930, and his first novel, *The Friend of the Victor* (*L'amico del vincitore,* 1932), revealed Brancati's ideals as decidedly pro-Fascist. He received a university degree in 1932 and produced his third play, *Piave,* the same year in Rome. In 1933 he was appointed a professor at the Rome Normal Institute. About this time he began to doubt the ethical and civil aims of the Fascist regime. His play *Don Juan in Spite of Himself* (*Don Giovanni involontario*), censored in 1933 because of its antitotalitarian allusions, marked the beginning of a new anti-Fascist attitude in his work.

In 1933 Brancati returned to Sicily, and in 1935, after the narrative *Strange Adventure on a Journey* (*Singolare avventura di viaggio,* 1934), he repudiated all his previous works. He soon returned to the literary scene, however, with a one-act farce, *This Marriage Must Be Made* (*Questo matromonio si deve fare,* pub. 1939), and in the following years published two of his best novels, *The Lost Years* (*Gli anni perduti,* 1941) and *Don Juan in Sicily* (*Don Giovanni in Sicilia,* 1941). Returning to Rome in 1941, he produced the politically *engagé* one-act play *The Eustachian Tubes* (*Le trombe d'Eustachio*) the following year. He also began an active career as a writer of motion-picture scenarios. Again in Sicily in 1943, he published two volumes of essays, *Pleasures* (*I piaceri,* 1943) and *The Fascists Are Aging* (*I fascisti invecchiano,* 1946). His satirical drama *Raphael* (*Raffaele,* pub. 1948) mocked Fascist society.

Brancati won the Vendemmia Prize in 1948 for his short story "The Old Man with the Boots" ("Il vecchio con gli stivali," 1944), which he rewrote as a screenplay for the film *The Difficult Years* (*Anni difficili,* 1948), directed by Luigi Zampa. His most successful novel, *Handsome Antonio* (*Il bell' Antonio,* 1949), was awarded the Bagutta Prize in 1950. Hampered by illness, Brancati was unable to complete his last literary work, the novel *Passionate Paul* (*Paolo il caldo*), begun in 1954. He died in Turin on September 25 of that year.

WORK

Although better known as a novelist, Brancati is widely recognized as one of the most vocal dramatists of Fascist and postwar Italy. His earliest plays, *Fedor* (wr. 1926), *Everest* (1930), and *Piave* (1932), were inspired by Fascist ideology. Brancati's moral and intellectual maturation later caused him to repudiate his first plays and adopt an anti-Fascist position. His growing awareness of the oppressive nature of the regime and its consequent demoralizing effect on society determined the satirical style of his dramas, in which he attempted to liberate the Italian mentality by exposing the corruption and hypocrisy of its values.

He most frequently chose provincial Sicilian society as a subject for critical analysis, but his ideals of freedom and sincerity give universal significance to his work. Although his dramas have a fundamentally pessimistic tone, owing to his relentless portrayal of the suffocating rigidity of social tradition, they are permeated by a melancholy aspiration to innocence. His characteristic protagonist lives in a grotesquely depicted, static society to which he forces himself to conform. While he is aware of the absence of personal freedom, he is unable to comprehend the conflict within himself.

The dominant themes of Brancati's dramas are politics, generally approached from a negatively satirical point of view, and sensuality, which in a repressive society is often represented by lust or impotency. His outstanding plays on political themes are *The Eustachian Tubes,* a satirical critique of Fascist political society that was enthusiastically applauded by the Roman public in 1942; and *Raphael* (pub. 1948), based on the conflict between two brothers, one timid and apathetic, the other actively searching for truth. Plays dealing with sexual repression in provincial Sicilian families are *Don Juan in Spite of Himself* (1943), which centers on the theme of *gallismo* (the virile pride of a Don Juan); and *The Governess* (*La governante;* pub. 1952, prod. 1965), in which a lesbian is compelled to commit suicide in the face of rigid social mores and her own moral hypocrisy.

Raphael (*Raffaele,* pub. 1948). This play is both a comedy of manners about fascism and a satire aimed at political opportunists. In an Italian mountain village Raphael Scarmacca lives with his brother Giovanni. Raphael is a timid and a narrow-minded bourgeois who is most concerned with maintaining the peace and quiet of his own life. Giovanni, in direct contrast, is a fanatic for truth and a leading figure of the opposition. He believes that he is always right and attempts to convert everyone to his position. Shortly before the end of World War II Raphael is elevated to the office of secretary of the federal government, a post he had sought long before the war in order to appear a loyal member of the party. The Allied Powers occupying Italy bring Raphael to trial for his Fascist activities. An English officer has apparently condemned Raphael to death and placed him before a firing squad just as Giovanni appears to engage the Englishman in a heated discussion about democracy. Raphael is saved and immediately falls at the feet of the new representatives of authority.

The Governess (*La governante;* pub. 1952, prod. 1965). Employed as a governess by the Platanias, a wealthy Sicilian family living in Rome, Caterina Leher is admired for her intellectualism and high moral character. Therefore, when she hints to Leopoldo, the grandfather, that Jana, a young housemaid brought north by the family, is sexually perverse, the adolescent girl is sent back to Sicily in disgrace. Jana is replaced by Francesca, a girl of Caterina's choice, who soon arouses the erotic interest of Bonivaglia, a literary friend of the Platanias. Caterina furiously attacks both the personal life and the writings of Bonivaglia for their libertine nature, and she is applauded by the Platanias for her fine moral stand.

Long after Jana is assumed to be back in Sicily, word comes that the girl has been injured in a Naples train accident. Oddly upset, Caterina denounces herself for having given Jana money to stop off at Naples to visit members of her family. Leopoldo sees in the incident only the unfortunate results of misguided generosity. Later, seeking Caterina with news of Jana's subsequent death, he finds her in a compromising situation with Francesca. Caterina admits that she misrepresented Jana's innocent affection. Disclosing her struggle against her own lesbian nature, she pleads with Leopoldo to be allowed to stay with the Platanias. Leopoldo is ready to agree, but when Caterina learns that Jana died blessing her, she hangs herself.

PLAYS

1. *Fedor.* Dramatic poem. Written 1926. Published 1928.

2. *Everest.* Play, 1 act. Produced Rome, Salone Margherita, Teatro dei Giovani, 1930.

3. *Piave.* Play. Published 1932. Produced Rome, Teatro Valle, October, 1932.

4. *Il viaggiatore dello sleeping n. 7 era forse Dio?* (*The Traveler in Pullman No. 7 Was Perhaps God?*). Play. Published 1933. Produced Genoa, March, 1935.

5. *Questo matrimonio si deve fare* (*This Marriage Must Be Made*). Play, 1 act. Published 1939.

6. *Le trombe d'Eustacio* (*The Eustachian Tubes*). Play, 1 act. Published 1942. Produced Rome, Teatro dell'Università, January, 1942.

7. *L'orecchio de Dionisio* (*Dionysius' Ear*). Play, 1 act. Published 1957. Produced Rome, Teatro delle Arti, March, 1943.

8. *Don Giovanni involontario* (*Don Juan in Spite of Himself*). Play, 3 acts. Published 1954. Produced Rome, Teatro delle Arti, March, 1943.

9. *Raffaele* (*Raphael*). Play, prologue and 3 acts. Published 1948.

10. *Una donna di casa* (*A Housewife*). Play, 4 acts. Published 1950.

11. *Il tenore sconfitto* (*The Defeated Tenor*). Verse libretto. Produced Rome, Teatro Eliseo, 1950. Music: Vincenzo Tommasini.

12. *La governante* (*The Governess*). Play, 3 acts. Published 1952. Produced Genoa, Compagnia Proclemer-Albertazzi, 1965.

EDITIONS

Teatro, Milan, 1957.

Bertolt Brecht
(1898 — 1956)

Eugen Berthold Friedrich Brecht, one of the most influential dramatic figures of this century, was born on February 10, 1898, in Augsburg, southern Germany. He was the first of two sons and was baptized in his mother's Protestant faith. His father, a Cath-

Bertolt Brecht with Paul Dessau (foreground), who wrote the songs for *Mutter Courage und ihre Kinder.* [German Information Center]

olic, was an able salesman, and Brecht's childhood and early education were typically bourgeois. After finishing elementary school (1904–1908), he was sent to the Königliches Realgymnasium and soon became known as an *enfant terrible,* shy, taciturn, and intellectually independent. Probably the seeds of his lifelong hatred of "people of my own class" were sown in this middle-class milieu, which he detested.

Brecht's first poems were published in 1914, three years before he graduated from secondary school. Although launched as a poet and fast becoming interested in the theatre, he decided to study medicine and science at the Ludwig Maximilian University in Munich after his graduation. In 1918 he was drafted as a medical orderly and served at Augsburg military hospital. His direct experience of human suffering formed the basis of his lifelong and impassioned pacifism.

During the Bavarian revolutionary turmoil of 1918, Brecht wrote his first play, *Baal,* conceived as an antipiece to Hanns Johst's drama about Grabbe, *The Lonely One* (1917). His association with communism began in 1919, when he joined the Independent Social Democratic party in Munich and was a member of the Augsburg Soldiers Council. The same year marked the beginning of his friendship with the German writer Lion Feuchtwanger, who encouraged the young dramatist and advised him on the discipline of playwriting (*see* FEUCHTWANGER, LION). Also in that year, as a result of a brief affair with a Fräulein Bie, Brecht's son Frank was born. While sporadically continuing his studies, which he finally gave up in 1921, Brecht began writing drama criticism for the Independent Socialist (later Communist) *Augsburger Volkswille.*

By 1920 Brecht was named *Dramaturg* (chief adviser on play selection) at the Munich Kammerspiele. His association at this time with the dialect comedian Karl Valentin, an exponent of Bavarian folk comedy, was an important event in his development. Brecht could often be seen during these years in Munich's literary cafés, delivering his ballads to his own banjo accompaniment.

The publication of his first short story in 1921 made his name known in Berlin as well as in Munich. In 1922, the same year that he married the actress Marianne Zoff, he received the Kleist Prize for *Drums in the Night* (*Trommeln in der Nacht*). A daughter, Hanne Marianne, was born in 1923.

In the spring of 1924 Brecht staged *Edward II* (*Leben Eduards des Zweiten von England*), the first of his many productions. He moved to Berlin in the autumn, to become, along with Carl Zuckmayer, a dramatist in Max Reinhardt's Deutsches Theater, and was immediately drawn into the city's cultural life. In the three years that followed, three of his plays and a collection of poems appeared in book form. During this period he also helped the director Erwin Piscator to adapt Hašek's novel *The Good Soldier Schweik* (1920–1923) for the stage. Piscator influenced Brecht in the formulation of the concept of epic theatre (*see* EPIC THEATRE). Subsequently, Brecht's collaboration with the composer Kurt Weill resulted in several musical plays and led to fame and financial success with the production of *The Threepenny Opera* (*Die Dreigroschenoper*) in 1928.

In 1927 Brecht divorced Marianne Zoff, and a year later he married the actress Helene Weigel, a convinced Communist. She gave brilliant interpretations on the stage of his chief feminine characters. Appalled by the economic and political crises wracking Germany after World War I, Brecht had undertaken an intensive and systematic study of Marxist philosophy and economics and concluded that the only solution to the problems besetting both his country and the world was communism. The crystallization of his political consciousness is evident in his *Lehrstücke,* didactic pieces with music by Paul Hindemith and Kurt Weill, which Brecht first staged as amateur productions in 1929.

For his increasingly dogmatic plays, Brecht found a new musical collaborator in Hanns Eisler, with whom in 1930 he wrote and produced his first overtly Communist play, *The Measures Taken (Die Massnahme).* The same year his daughter Maria Barbara was born. Brecht also worked with Eisler on a Communist propaganda film, *Kuhle Wampe* (name of an area on the outskirts of Berlin where the unemployed lived in shacks), which was released in 1932 and banned shortly afterward.

With the rise of Nazi power, production of Brecht's plays became difficult. Performances were interrupted by the police or summarily forbidden. On February 28, 1933, the day after the Reichstag fire, Brecht fled from Germany with his family. The Paris performance of *The Seven Deadly Sins; Anna-Anna (Die sieben Todsünden der Kleinbürger)* in June, 1933, marked his last collaboration with Kurt Weill. Before the year was over, Brecht had settled in Denmark.

Europe, outside of Germany, accepted Brecht respectfully but did not readily provide stages for his plays. In 1934 his only novel, *The Threepenny Novel (Der Dreigroschenroman),* based on *The Threepenny Opera,* was published in the Netherlands. On June 8, 1935, still in exile, he was officially deprived of his German citizenship by the Nazi regime. By the following November he was in New York to attend a performance of his play *The Mother (Die Mutter,* wr. 1930/32), based on Gorky's novel of the same name. *See* GORKY, MAXIM.

Active in political propaganda against the Third Reich, Brecht became coeditor of the German-language periodical *The Word (Das Wort),* published in Moscow in 1936, although he himself did not live there. Several of his plays written during this period contained strong indictments of Nazism and fascism.

Some of Brecht's biographers see a link between the first successful splitting of the uranium atom in 1938 and Brecht's treatment of the theme of a scientist's conscience in his play *Galileo (Leben des Galilei),* begun in the same year. This play initiated a series of less doctrinaire dramas, written mostly during the war, including *Mother Courage and Her Children (Mutter Courage und ihre Kinder)* in 1939 and ending with *The Cauca-*

French production of *Im Dickicht der Städte*, Studio des Champs-Élysées, Paris. [French Cultural Services]

sian Chalk Circle (Der kaukasische Kreidekreis) in 1945.

In the summer of 1939, anticipating Germany's entry into Denmark, Brecht left for Sweden and in 1940 arrived in Finland, where he found a temporary home at the estate of the writer Hella Wuolijoki. On May 3, 1941, he received an immigration visa from the United States Consul in Helsinki. In June, Brecht and his family traveled across the U.S.S.R. and at Vladivostok took a freighter bound for San Pedro, Calif., where they arrived on July 21, 1941. After they settled in Santa Monica, Brecht tried to write for Hollywood in order to earn some money, but with little success. The only script that found partial acceptance was written for the war film Hangmen Also Die (United Artists), released in 1942. In California Brecht met many old friends from Germany and made new ones, including Charlie Chaplin and the critic Eric Bentley, who became one of his foremost champions in the English-speaking world.

American audiences were reluctant to accept Brecht's disturbing plays; his best reception was in university theatres. Joseph Losey, a director, made plans to launch Brecht in

the commercial theatre with a production of Galileo. Charles Laughton, who was to play the leading part, helped Brecht adapt the play into English. The premiere took place in Hollywood on July 30, 1947, and was well received by the critics but not by audiences.

In October, 1947, Brecht was called to testify about his Communist party affiliations before the House Un-American Activities Committee; he evaded the committee's questions and denied Hanns Eisler's statement that he had joined the Communist party in 1930. The next month, without waiting for the opening of Galileo in New York, he flew to Switzerland.

The Züricher Schauspielhaus, which had produced three of Brecht's plays during World War II, welcomed him. There he staged his own adaptation of Antigone in 1948, with a design provided by Caspar Neher, a friend from his Augsburg days. He also codirected some of his other plays. Brecht's only volume of short stories, Calendar Tales (Kalendergeschichten), was published in 1948.

By now Brecht was looking toward his divided homeland. The choice between East and West Germany was probably made easier by the offer from East Germany of a theatre and an almost unlimited subsidy. In October, 1948, he decided to settle permanently in East Germany.

Brecht now plunged himself into stage activity, setting out to establish a company for the production of his own plays. The Berliner Ensemble, composed of his veteran co-workers and new talent, made its debut on November 12, 1949, with Mr. Puntila and his Hired Man, Matti (Herr Puntila und sein Knecht Matti, wr. 1940/41). The Ensemble was directed by Helene Weigel, but Brecht, officially the Dramaturg, was its moving spirit and handled every detail of staging. The Ensemble developed into one of the world's best theatre companies and became the embodiment of Brecht's theatrical philosophy.

Brecht's main theoretical treatise, Little Organum for the Theatre (Kleines Organon für das Theater), and fragments from his unfinished novel, The Business Deals of Mr. Julius Caesar (Geschäfte des Herrn Julius Cäsar), were published in 1949. At this time the Suhrkamp publishing house in West Germany, which Brecht entrusted with the copyright of his works, resumed publication of his collected plays, entitled Projects (Versuche), all publication activity having been interrupted in 1933.

After writing The Days of the Commune (Die Tage der Commune) in 1948/49, Brecht completed no more plays. He excelled as a stage manager, and the operation of the theatre consumed much of his time. Party re-

Scene from Im Dickicht der Städte, Munich, 1923. [Theater-Museum, Munich]

strictions took their toll. East German authorities were eager to make political capital out of Brecht's fame but frowned on his "formalism." In April, 1950, to assure for himself freedom of travel, Brecht took out Austrian citizenship. His pacifist opera *The Trial of Lucullus* (*Das Verhör des Lukullus,* wr. 1939), with music by Paul Dessau, was withdrawn after one performance at the Berlin State Opera, on March 17, 1951, and Brecht was persuaded by East German authorities to prepare a new version that justified defensive wars against imperialism. He was awarded the East German State Prize on October 7, 1951.

The anti-Communist revolt in East Berlin on June 17, 1953, came as a shock to Brecht, as some of his poems and statements suggest. A letter written by him to the government of East Germany criticizing conditions there was published after being censored; only his expression of allegiance to communism was left intact. This incident led to a short-lived boycott of Brecht's plays in West Germany.

Nevertheless, Brecht maintained his allegiance to the Communist cause and continued to participate in various public functions organized by the East German regime. In 1954 the Berliner Ensemble was given a permanent home in the renovated Theater am Schiffbauerdamm, where, a quarter century earlier, *The Threepenny Opera* had scored its initial success. However, the party organ *Neues Deutschland* ignored the German premiere of *The Caucasian Chalk Circle,* which was staged there.

Although Brecht's plays (except *The Threepenny Opera,* staged in 1930) were not performed in the U.S.S.R., he was awarded the Stalin Peace Prize on May 25, 1955. The growing realization of his importance as a major dramatist transcended political barriers. A Brechtian vogue swept Europe and the United States. His collected works appeared in both East and West Germany, and a number of his plays were published in the United States.

The stormy applause that greeted Brecht at the Paris International Theatre Festival in 1955 was a mark of the recognition he had

Jo Sullivan, Scott Merrill, and Lotte Lenya in *The Threepenny Opera.* New York, Theatre de Lys, 1954. [Theatre Collection, The New York Public Library at Lincoln Center, Astor, Lenox and Tilden Foundations]

achieved. He continued to adapt and stage plays at his own theatre, relying mainly on established works by George Farquhar, Gerhart Hauptmann, Jakob Lenz, and Shakespeare.

In the spring of 1956 Brecht contracted a lung inflammation. He died of a coronary thrombosis on August 14, 1956, in East Berlin.

WORK

Although Brecht enjoyed some renown in Germany during the 1920s and thereafter among German-speaking people not living under the Nazi regime, his achievement did not become widely recognized until after World War II. Since then his reputation has grown to the point where he is generally considered one of the great dramatists of the twentieth century. Moreover, his influence on other dramatists of the mid-century period shows no signs of diminishing. He contributed to the theatre some forty plays, a number of adaptations and fragments, and the essays that present his revolutionary theories on the function of theatre and on staging.

Of his voluminous theoretical writings,

the one that most clearly summarizes his thoughts is the *Little Organum for the Theatre* (1948). Additional notes on his developing ideas, with interesting pictorial material, are contained in the "model books" for his productions, which include *Theatre Work (Theaterarbeit,* 1952). Against the "magic" and emotionalism of the traditional theatre he pits the clarity, simplicity, and objectivity of a didactic stage.

The most widely known of Brecht's theoretical concepts are those of epic theatre and *Verfremdung* ("alienation"). Epic theatre was partly inspired by Erwin Piscator's staging techniques in the early 1920s. It was, in Brecht's words, a "Theater for Learning," narrating a sequence of events and communicating information to the spectator; man on the epic stage was an object of inquiry. The epic theatre was to appeal to the spectator's reason and to instill in him a questioning attitude. To this end Brecht advocated and used such didactic devices as subtitles and slide projections. By *Verfremdung*, inadequately rendered in English as "alienation," he meant the portrayal of an event in a new and unfamiliar light, intended to discourage the spectator from projecting himself into the action to achieve the emotional catharsis traditionally offered by the theatre. Instead, the spectator was to be induced to regard the event with critical detachment. Brecht's early insistence on a strictly "anti-illusory" and "antihypnotic" theatre mellowed with time, and in the late 1940s he also accepted, though with wry comment, emotional involvement and entertainment as functions of the theatre.

Brecht's productions of his own plays often ran contrary to his theory. Though he insisted that spectators ought not to identify themselves with Mother Courage, he had created a character so richly human that audiences were involved despite his intentions. In fact, the bourgeois audience that witnessed *Mother Courage and Her Children* (1941) for the first time in Zurich admired the leading character for her indomitable spirit in wartime and her capitalist ability to survive. Actually, Brecht intended no such audience identification. There is a similar discrepancy between his drama and his political philosophy. Marxism and communism were the principal economic-political doctrines of his life and art, but he was never able to stay within the confines of the orthodox party ideology. Never fully accepted by the Communist literary establishment, Brecht was constantly reprimanded for his "formalism," for "abstract" treatment of the masses, and for his obsession with the "conversion of the bourgeois to leftism."

In the skeptical world of Brecht's plays, one

of the main conflicts is between goodness and evil, with evil triumphant. But the dramatist's faith in change through political action and his contemplation of the "temptation of goodness," though goodness cannot survive in a corrupt society, counterbalance his pessimistic fears and his deep-seated mistrust of human emotions and instincts.

Brecht was a total theatre artist whose final statement was his own production of his play. Although he borrowed ideas and entire plots from other writers, he created works uniquely his own. *Edward II* (1924) is a free adaptation from Marlowe, *Baal* (wr. 1918, prod. 1923) is influenced stylistically by Büchner's *Woyzeck,* and *The Days of the Commune* (wr. 1948/49, prod. 1956) is shaped by Nordahl Grieg's *The Defeat* (*see* BÜCHNER, GEORG; GRIEG, NORDAHL). Many of the early plays hold echoes of Wedekind, Rimbaud, and Villon. In the later didactic plays, characteristics of the medieval morality plays and of the Reformation and Jesuit theatre of the sixteenth and seventeenth centuries are discernible, with techniques inspired by the stylized Oriental theatre. From the Japanese Nō plays he adopted the use of a narrator and also the technique of making the actor himself narrate as well as perform, introducing his actions to the audience and criticizing the course of events (*see* NŌ). From this source, too, Brecht developed the use of a chorus that interrupted and commented upon the play and of an orchestra placed in full view of the audience. Other influences were the Austrian and Bavarian folk comedy, especially the plays of Karl Valentin, and the films of Chaplin, Keaton, and the Marx Brothers. Brecht's belief in the necessary and desirable mutability of the world and mankind may help to explain his delight in parody and his tendency to use as source material the works of other writers, often giving old themes a contemporary relevance. He felt no compunction about using for his own ends the words of Shakespeare, Schiller, Goethe, and other classic authors as well as numerous Biblical quotations. The satirical and the grotesque, so prevalent in Brecht's plays, are weapons against the existing social order and tools for the ultimate transformation of the world.

This literary eclecticism contributes to the structural complexity of Brecht's dramas. They consist of short scenes strung loosely together with a minimal concern for the neoclassical unities of space and time and interspersed with songs and narrative sequences. Prologues and epilogues have an explanatory function, and the occasional interruptions of the chorus serve to reinforce the drama's central message. The plays proceed through episodic thrusts and, indicating

Brecht's interest in dialectics, through the constant clash of opposing ideas. The result is often an apparent inconsistency, which is in fact an ironic contrast.

Music and song play important roles in Brecht's dramas, many of which were intended as semioperatic works. His attitude to stage production is anti-Wagnerian: there is no fusion of music, text, and decor into a single unified mood; instead, the different elements set each other off in a strange and unfamiliar light. For Brecht, music in drama must be "antihypnotic" and *gestisch,* that is, expressive of basic underlying attitudes. He used songs to provide interludes for reflection, to make historical and philosophical comment, and to summarize the significance of the action.

To create his unique stage idiom Brecht integrated such varied sources as the German vernacular, popular songs, the language of the Lutheran Bible, and Kipling. One of his aims was to depart as far as possible from the bombastic rhetoric of the traditional German theatre. He infused variety by mixing verse with prose, bureaucratic jargon with colloquial and dialect forms; he parodied blank verse

Die Dreigroschenoper, Berlin, 1929. [Theater-Museum, Munich]

*Mother Courage
and Her Children*,
with (l. to r.)
Charlotte Glenn,
Judy London, and
Greg Abels.
Princeton,
McCarter Theatre,
1965. [McCarter
Theatre,
Princeton, N.J.]

with hexameters. His language is an effective instrument on the stage, concrete in detail but echoing with allusions, and thus difficult to translate.

Brecht was a master at characterization even though his plays are full of one-dimensional characters, caricatures such as Peachum, reflecting solely a particular class and environment and governed by a single dominant trait, like the humors of Ben Jonson. The individual, for Brecht, is second in importance to the social group. He gives his characters social, not psychological, motivation, and the theme of the extinction of personality runs through many of his plays, such as *The Measures Taken* (1930) and *A Man's a Man* (*Mann ist Mann,* 1926). Brecht's dialectical way of thinking sometimes manifests itself in giving characters a literally split personality, like the good Shen Te and the expedient Shui Ta in *The Good Woman of Setzuan* (*Der gute Mensch von Sezuan,* 1943) and the businesslike Anna I and the artistic Anna II in *The Seven Deadly Sins* (1933). His outstanding creations, however, transcend such limitations. Azdak, Galileo, and Mother Courage

are not mere abstractions, illustrating the author's theories or representing "forces of history," but complex and profoundly human individuals.

Following Brecht's belief that "truth is concrete," his plays are full of concrete details. Yet the themes of his plays, through their oversimplification of political doctrines, often display a certain remoteness from reality and its complexity. His settings frequently show disregard for literal representation, for example, when he invents a mythical Anglo-American never-never land or a fairy-tale Orient. Often, however, Brecht's careful attention to selected details—the wagon of Mother Courage, for example—create the apposition of illusion and reality. Unconcerned with historical accuracy, he constructs historical plays as parables of contemporary events. External improbabilities and anachronisms do not concern him, for the story is only the mechanism by which momentum is achieved.

Brecht's plays may be divided roughly into early expressionistic pieces, didactic plays (*Lehrstücke*), musical plays, realistic dramas, and the later masterpieces. The early plays, for example, *Baal* (wr. 1918, prod. 1923), *Drums in the Night* (1922), and *In the Jungle of the Cities* (*Im Dickicht der Städte*, 1923), bear the imprint of German expressionism. Violence, squalor, and depravity of all kinds invest these plays with a contemporary exoticism, jazz and rape becoming complementary. They are often shrill but can also be sensuous and poetic. *A Man's a Man* marks a movement away from expressionism and toward the austere didacticism found in *The Didactic Play of Baden: On Consent* (*Das Badener Lehrstück vom Einverständnis*, 1929), *The Measures Taken, The Exception and the Rule* (*Die Ausnahme und die Regel;* wr. 1930, prod. 1947), and *The Mother* (1932). *The Threepenny Opera* (1928) and *Rise and Fall of the City of Mahagonny* (*Aufsteig und Fall der Stadt Mahagonny,* 1930) are outstanding examples of Brecht's musical plays. *The Private Life of the Master Race* (*Furcht und Elend des dritten Reiches,* 1938) and *Senora Carrar's Rifles* (*Die Gewehre der Frau Carrar,* 1937) employ more traditionally naturalistic and realistic devices than his other works.

In Brecht's masterpieces the lyrical, didactic, musical, and realistic elements are combined. *Mother Courage and Her Children, Galileo* (wr. 1938/39, prod. 1943), *The Good Woman of Setzuan,* and *The Caucasian Chalk Circle* (1948) are marked by a fertile interplay of idea and action and contain most of Brecht's greatest characters. *Saint Joan of the Stockyards* (*Die heilige Johanna der Schlachthöfe,* 1932) and the comically inventive *Mr. Puntila and His Hired Man, Matti* (wr. 1940/41, prod. 1948) are generally thought to rank second to his masterworks.

Brecht is also one of Germany's important modern poets, his verse ranging from mordant satire to lyrical nature pieces of folksong simplicity. The most representative collection of his poems is *Verses and Songs* (*Gedichte und Lieder,* 1956). Brecht's prose consists of short stories, written during his early career, *The Threepenny Novel* (1934), and fragments of other novels.

Baal (wr. 1918, prod. 1923). Twenty-one–scene prose drama parodying and refuting the romantic concept of the poet's martyrdom in the philistine world. Baal, a wandering minstrel, is a ruthless and selfish drunkard and brawler who defies every norm of society in post-World War I Germany, attracting, seducing, and then abandoning women wherever he goes. Ekart, a composer, befriends him and accompanies him on his wild journeys. Baal's former mistress Sophie follows them and in despair drowns herself. The two friends then compete for a waitress they both like, and Baal kills Ekart. Hunted by the po-

lice, Baal flees to the forests, where, after staying with some woodcutters, he dies alone in a hut.

The Wedding (*Die Hochzeit;* wr. 1919, prod. 1926). One-act play in the style of a Bavarian folk comedy. A wedding reception gradually disintegrates as the furniture, made by the bridegroom, collapses, the guests forget their manners, the bride reveals that she is pregnant, and the bridegroom accuses her of infidelity. When the guests depart, however, the newlyweds make peace.

The Beggar, or The Dead Dog (*Der Bettler, oder Der tote Hund,* wr. 1919). Brief allegorical dialogue in which a king, on the way to a victory celebration, strikes up a conversation with a beggar, who reveals to him the people's contempt for his royal doings. The beggar concludes that a dead dog is more important than the king. At the end it is discovered that the beggar is blind.

He Exorcises a Devil (*Er treibt einen Teufel aus,* wr. 1919). One-act farce in the Bavarian popular tradition. A Bavarian girl

Leben des Galilei, Städtische Bühnen, Frankfurt am Main.

Die Dreigroschenoper: (above) Berliner Ensemble, 1960; (left) Städtische Bühnen, Frankfurt am Main. [German Information Center]

and her lover are interrupted in their love-making outside the girl's home by her father. The lover visits the girl at night, but her father takes his ladder away, whereupon they retreat to the roof.

Light in Darkness (*Lux in Tenebris*, wr. 1919). Farce about bourgeois hypocrisy. An exhibition showing the effects of venereal disease is organized in a red-light district by Paduk, who delivers rousing speeches on immorality. Shortly afterward he becomes a partner in running a brothel across the street.

Drums in the Night (*Trommeln in der Nacht*, 1922). Dark comedy condemning the choice by a young man of bourgeois safety over revolution. Returning to Berlin from a war prisoners' camp after World War I, Andreas Kragler finds that his fiancée Anna is engaged to a profiteer, Friedrich Murk. Uninvited he goes to the engagement party in the Piccadilly Bar and demands her back. Outside shots are heard as the abortive Spartacist Communist uprising begins. Although pregnant by Murk, Anna still loves Kragler and cannot bring herself to tell him about

her condition. She begs him to leave, and Kragler storms out into the night, gets drunk, and almost joins the revolt. It is dawn when Anna finds him. He vents his anger on her but finally chooses her in preference to the revolution.

In the Jungle of the Cities (*Im Dickicht der Städte*, 1923). In Brecht's words, a play about an "inexplicable wrestling match between two men." The ring is the giant city of Chicago; the contestants are Shlink, a Malayan timber merchant, and George Garga, a librarian. Shlink employs every means to possess Garga's soul but meets with stubborn resistance. The merchant turns Garga's mistress, Jane, and his sister, Marie, into prostitutes and eventually turns his business over to Garga, who destroys it and consequently goes to prison. Then Garga exposes Shlink to a lynch mob by accusing the merchant of ruining Jane and Marie. Garga is released, and both men escape the mob. In a final confrontation Shlink says that he fought for the sake of a spiritual contest, while Garga discloses that he fought to survive. Shlink dies, and Garga sets fire to the timber business and leaves for New York.

Edward II (*Leben Eduards des Zweiten von England,* 1924). The plot outline of Marlowe's *Edward II* is transformed into a historical ballad. By favoring Gaveston, Edward alienates his lords, the church, and his wife. War breaks out and Edward is captured by Mortimer and eventually killed. Edward's son then has Mortimer hanged and imprisons the Queen in the Tower. In Brecht's version the plot is simplified, motives are altered, and the relationship between Edward and Gaveston is more overtly homosexual than that in Marlowe's. *See* MARLOWE, CHRISTOPHER.

A Man's a Man (*Mann ist Mann,* 1926). Comedy set in India in 1925, based on Kipling's *Barrack-Room Ballads* (1892). Four British soldiers try to loot a temple and free one of their number, Jeriah Jip. Afraid of being discovered, they decide to substitute for the missing soldier the Irish docker Galy Gay, who is unable to say no and who wishes to please everyone. By means of threats and blackmail, Gay is forced to renounce his wife and his earlier existence. While the missing soldier Jip is presented as a miracle-working deity in the temple, Gay is subjected to a transformation ritual, implicated in a nonexistent black-market deal, and executed with blank bullets. Gay becomes convinced that he is Jip and delivers an oration at his own fake funeral. Armed with his new identity, he becomes a military monster and subdues a fortress single-handed. Galy Gay has become the perfect soldier.

The Elephant Calf (*Das Elefantenkalb,* wr. 1924/25). Surrealistic interlude "to be played in the foyer" during the intermission of *A Man's a Man.* A baby elephant, portrayed by the actor who plays Galy Gay in *A Man's a Man,* is charged with the murder of its mother and found guilty, even though the alleged victim is found to be alive and not to be its mother.

Warren Hastings (*Kalkutta, 4 Mai,* wr. 1925). Revision by Brecht and Lion Feuchtwanger of the latter's play *Warren Hastings, Governor of India.* Commissioners of the East India Company investigate the conduct of Hastings as Governor-General. Though they are shocked by his cruelty and cynicism, they find he has no selfish motives and is moved solely by his civilizing zeal.

The Threepenny Opera (*Die Dreigroschenoper,* 1928). Adaptation of John Gay's *The Beggar's Opera* (1728), with music by Kurt Weill. The plot is basically the same as that of *The Beggar's Opera,* although little of the original text remains and the setting is that of late-nineteenth-century Soho. By marrying Polly Peachum, the robber Macheath incurs the wrath of Polly's father, the king of beggars, who plans to have him arrested. But the chief of police, Tiger Brown, is an old army friend of Macheath and hesitates to arrest him. Macheath, however, is betrayed by a prostitute and arrested at his favorite brothel. Soon after, he escapes from jail with the help of Brown's daughter, whom he has assured of his love. Now Peachum's threat to spoil a royal procession through the city by sending hordes of beggars in its path forces Tiger Brown to act. Macheath is arrested again at the same brothel, condemned to death, and sent to the scaffold. At the last moment a messenger arrives with the Queen's pardon and the promise of a title and a pension for Macheath. The moral: the bourgeois and the criminal are two of a kind. *See* GAY, JOHN.

Happy End (1929). Play written in collaboration with Elisabeth Hauptmann, with music by Kurt Weill. In contemporary Chicago, Lillian Holiday, a Salvation Army lieutenant, comes to "Bill's Ballhaus" in order to convert a band of gangsters. Bill Creaker,

Helene Weigel as Frau Carrar in *Die Gewehre der Frau Carrar.* [German Information Center]

Aufstieg und Fall der Stadt Mahagonny, Städtische Bühnen, Frankfurt am Main.

der to cheat gold prospectors of their money. Newcomers, however, find the town dull, the rules and prohibitions too confining. On the eve of a hurricane, Paul Ackermann suggests a formula for happiness: all restrictions must be abolished. Within a year loose living is the law in Mahagonny, and one by one Paul's friends meet their ruin. He himself squanders all his money on drink and a tart named Jenny and is arrested, condemned, and electrocuted for incurring debts, the only crime punishable by death in Mahagonny. Demonstrations and flames signal the destruction of the city. Mahagonny burns, and its inhabitants show themselves to be members of a society totally dependent upon the accumulation of material wealth.

The Didactic Play of Baden: On Consent (*Das Badener Lehrstück vom Einverständnis,* 1929). Didactic cantata in which four airmen have crash-landed and ask mankind for help. In considering their request, the "skilled" and the "mass" choruses sift evidence to see whether man does help man. As evidence, a scene between three clowns is presented in which one, an ailing giant clown, Herr Schmitt, is cured by the other two. In curing him, however, they saw off all the diseased limbs and even tear off his head. From this the choruses conclude that man does not help man. Until the world is changed, power, and not help, is what counts. The pilot of the group refuses to accept the verdict and is annihilated for his individualism. The other three, who are mechanics, accept the inevitability of the historical process and are saved from destruction.

He Who Says Yes (*Der Jasager,* 1930). Opera for schoolchildren after the Japanese Nō play *Taniko,* with music by Kurt Weill. A teacher leads an expedition to the mountains to get medicine for the victims of a village epidemic. With him is a boy whose mother is ill. On the way the boy himself falls ill and is asked whether he will agree to be left behind as custom dictates. He answers yes and, in accordance with his own wish, is hurled into the valley by the other members of the party.

Saint Joan of the Stockyards (*Die heilige Johanna der Schlachthöfe,* 1932). Play in classical blank verse, prose, and irregular unrhymed verse. The meat kings of Chicago are locked in fierce competition with one another. Joan Dark, a member of a Salvation Army group, the Black Straw Hats, tries to help the poor stockyard workers. She pleads with Pierpoint Mauler, the canned-meat king, to improve their lot and prevent unemployment. Her idealism moves Mauler, but he continues to speculate, forcing canning factories to close down and finally overextending himself so that the whole meat market crashes. When

proprietor of the establishment and a member of the gang, falls in love with Lillian. As a result, he is thrown out of the gang and she is dismissed from the Salvation Army. The gang descends on a Salvation Army meeting to murder Bill, whereupon their leader, the Lady in Gray, recognizes Hannibal Jackson, another Salvation Army lieutenant, as her missing husband. In the end the gang and the Salvation Army unite to establish a bank.

Lindbergh's Flight (*Der Flug der Lindberghs,* 1929). Didactic radio play for children in which Lindbergh, by means of a chorus, tells the story of his flight across the Atlantic in 1927. Although fog, snowstorms, and exhaustion impede his progress, he perseveres and asserts his aim to defeat the primitive forces of nature. Eventually he reaches his destination, and the play concludes with praise of man's achievements and progress.

Rise and Fall of the City of Mahagonny (*Aufstieg und Fall der Stadt Mahagonny,* 1930). "Epic opera" with music by Kurt Weill. A band of thieves escaping from the police establishes the city of Mahagonny in or-the meat-packers try to enlist the Black Straw Hats in a scheme to divert the unemployed from their plight, Joan drives the meat-packers away and is in turn expelled from the Black Straw Hats. She considers allying herself with the Communists, but realizing that they will not hesitate to use violence, she deliberately fails to deliver an important letter calling on them for a general strike. The leaders of the stockyard workers are arrested, and Mauler is able to reopen his factories. Joan, now disillusioned, dies of pneumonia. With her last breath she rejects God and maintains that force is necessary to change the present system of exploitation. Her radical words are drowned by a chorus of meat-packers, stockbreeders, and the Black Straw Hats.

He Who Says No (*Der Neinsager,* wr. 1930). Basically the same play as *He Who Says Yes,* written with a different ending in response to critical remarks from school audiences and Communists alike. A boy becomes ill on the journey of a group across the mountains and is told that an ancient custom demands that whoever is abandoned at the place where they have stopped must be thrown into the abyss. But the boy refuses to be killed and asks for the institution of a new custom, "that one must think afresh in every new situation."

The Measures Taken (*Die Massnahme,* 1930). Didactic play in the form of a dramatic cantata, with music by Hanns Eisler. Four political agitators who have returned to the Soviet Union from a clandestine mission to China report to the Communist party's "control chorus" that they had to eliminate a young member of their group. Reenacting the events, each taking a turn at the Young Comrade's part, they show how he joined them at the frontier as a guide and agreed to remain completely anonymous but that, once in China, his emotional humanitarian attitude led him to immediate involvements that endangered the long-range benefits of the mission. After admitting the error of his ways, he asked to be killed; his comrades shot him and returned to their work. The control chorus approves their action as having been taken in the interest of the party.

The Exception and the Rule (*Die Ausnahme und die Regel;* wr. 1930, prod. 1947). Short didactic play. A merchant, hurrying

Aufstieg und Fall der Stadt Mahagonny, Städtische Bühnen, Frankfurt am Main.

across a desert in order to overtake a competitor, dismisses his guide for being too friendly with a coolie porter, whom the merchant mistreats. The merchant and his coolie lose their way and run out of water. When the coolie approaches the merchant and offers him a water bottle, the merchant mistakes this gesture of kindness for an attempt to kill him and shoots the coolie. At the merchant's subsequent trial for murder it is established that the act of the coolie was one of kindness, not hate. However, since the merchant believed that the coolie hated him and had no reason to believe the gesture was friendly, the court decides that the merchant acted in self-defense, conducting himself according to the rule rather than the exception, and that he was therefore justified in killing the coolie.

The Mother: Life of the Revolutionary Pelagea Vlassova from Tver (*Die Mutter: Leben der Revolutionärin Pelagea Wlassowa aus Twer*, 1932). Didactic adaptation of Maxim Gorky's novel *The Mother* (1907). Pelagea Vlassova is shocked to discover that her son Pavel is engaged in secret revolutionary activities against the czarist regime. However, she helps him in order to protect him and finds herself drawn into the movement. She takes part in a demonstration in which Pavel is arrested; her new involvement inspires her to learn to read and write, and she begins work as a party agitator. Meanwhile, Pavel is sent to Siberia and is shot while trying to escape. The incident hardens Pelagea in her new views. In the winter of 1916 she carries a red flag at the head of a demonstration of strikers, thus showing that her revolutionary education is complete.

The Seven Deadly Sins; Anna-Anna (*Die sieben Todsünden der Kleinbürger*, 1933). Ballet cantata in verse, with music by Kurt Weill. Two sisters, Anna I (the singer) and Anna II (the dancer), set out into the world to earn money to build a house for their family in Louisiana. In each of the seven cities they visit, Anna II is tempted by one of the deadly sins—transgressions in a capitalist society but, according to Brecht, basic human virtues, such as sloth (when it comes to making money) and anger (at social injustices). She avoids all temptations, which would have ruined her, and the two Annas return home with enough money to build the house.

The Roundheads and the Peakheads (*Die Rundköpfe und die Spitzköpfe*, 1936). Free adaptation of Shakespeare's *Measure for Measure* in the form of an "atrocity story" in which racial doctrines are superimposed on the realities of the class struggle. To prevent an uprising of tenant farmers in the land of Yahoo, the Viceroy puts Angelo Iberin, a demagogic politician, at the helm. Iberin accomplishes his task by proclaiming the racial superiority of the Roundheads over the Peakheads, thus confusing the economic class struggle. De Guzman, a Peakhead landlord, is sentenced to death for seducing the daughter of his tenant Callas, a Roundhead. The sentence, however, is never carried out; the Viceroy returns, and the landlord is released. Rich Peakheads and Roundheads join together again to exploit the poor.

The Horatians and the Curatians (*Die Horatier und die Kuriatier;* wr. 1934, prod. 1958). Short didactic play for children about military and political strategy. In the manner of the Chinese classical theatre, each army is represented by actors carrying pennants denoting the respective military strengths, while two choruses comment on the battle. The Curatians attack the city of the Horatians and win the engagements between the bowmen and the pikemen. By a strategic retreat, the Horatians split up the Curatians and their swordsmen gain a decisive victory. The chorus of the Horatians summarizes the tactical lessons of the battle.

Senora Carrar's Rifles (*Die Gewehre der Frau Carrar*, 1937). Free adaptation of J. M. Synge's one-act play *Riders to the Sea* (1903), set in Spain. All wars are abhorrent to Teresa Carrar; her husband, a fisherman, was killed in the workers' revolt of 1934. She refuses to let her sons join the Republican Army during the Spanish Civil War and hides from her brother a cache of rifles that had been concealed by her husband. One night, the Carrar family is waiting for the oldest son to return home with his boat. In a heated argument with her younger son, brother, and neighbors, Teresa alone defends neutrality. When the fishermen finally appear with the body of her son, shot by the Nationalists, Teresa abandons her neutrality and, together with her brother and her younger son, takes the hidden rifles and leaves for the front. *See* SYNGE, J. M.

The Private Life of the Master Race (*Furcht und Elend des dritten Reiches*, 1938). (There is also a shorter version known in English under the literal translation *Fear and Misery in the Third Reich.*) Sequence of twenty-eight scenes, four as yet unpublished, forming a spectacle of the reign of terror during the first five years of Nazi domination in Germany. The style, although fragmented, is that of a realistic, conventional play, atypical of Brecht. Though characters vary from scene to scene, unity is maintained by the limitations of time and place. In *The Jewish Wife*, a Jewess decides to leave her Aryan husband and go abroad because they are ostracized and his career is in danger. The husband pretends that she will be gone only until the persecution by the Nazis ceases, but in fact he knows that he will never see her again. In *The Informer*, middle-class parents criticizing the regime are terrified when they realize that their schoolboy son has gone out, possibly to inform on them. The protagonist of *The Old Nazi*, a butcher and supporter of the Nazi party, has forced his son to join the storm troopers, but this display of loyalty wins him no favors from the party. Instead, he is persecuted for not following the rules for storekeepers, and he hangs himself in his shopwindow. In *In Search of Justice*, a judge has to try a case of robbery from a Jewish jeweler. He wrestles with his conscience. Nazi storm troopers are clearly implicated, yet to administer justice would clearly invite his own death. In other sketches, two drunken SS officers start shooting wildly in a "suspicious" area of the city; a maid sees her Nazi boyfriend transformed into a fiend; fear compels two physicists to dismiss Einstein's work as "Jewish cleverness"; and a middle-class couple listens in fear to the sounds of a man being arrested because of remarks the two have made.

Galileo (*Leben des Galilei;* wr. 1938/39, prod. 1943). Drama in fifteen scenes, loosely based on the astronomer's life and indicating various paradoxes within it. Galileo lives on a pittance he receives as lecturer in the republic of Venice, freely indulging his excessive appetite for knowledge and food. His closest companions are his daughter Virginia and Andrea Sarti, a boy with a great talent for science. Galileo, using a Dutch telescope, which he claims as his own invention, tries to prove that the earth is only one of many planets and not the center of the universe. Despite his freedom to work, Galileo is poor, and he seeks to increase his stipend by accepting an invitation to the court of the Grand Duke of Florence. Meanwhile, the Chief Astronomer of the Papal College in Rome confirms Galileo's theory concerning the earth's position in the universe. But believing that the theory must lead to the questioning of all established authority, the Church frowns upon it, denounces Galileo's teachings as absurd and heretical, and orders him to abandon them. Galileo, afraid of being burned at the stake, remains silent for eight years.

Then Cardinal Barberini, a noted mathematician, becomes Pope Urban VIII, and Galileo's hopes are revived. The Inquisition, however, convinces the new Pope that the teaching of Galileo's theories would have disastrous consequences for the Church, and Galileo, shown the inquisitor's instruments of torture, agrees to renounce his theories.

Furcht und Elend des dritten Reiches, Städtische Bühnen, Frankfurt am Main.

Disgusted with his master's "cowardice," Andrea leaves Galileo. Virginia, whose prospects for marriage had previously been ruined by Galileo's heresy, continues to attend her aging father.

After a long interval Andrea visits Galileo, now living under strict supervision dictated by the Inquisition. Galileo reveals to him that he has secretly completed a new foundation of physics, his *Discorsi*. Andrea now realizes that his master had recanted only to gain time. But Galileo confesses that he was simply afraid of physical pain and condemns himself before Andrea for betraying his vocation, even if by doing so he gained time to complete his work. He sees in his failure the seeds of an increasing alienation of science from humanitarian goals, a selling out of science to the existing political powers. Andrea smuggles the *Discorsi* out of Italy.

Mother Courage and Her Children (*Mutter Courage und ihre Kinder,* 1941). Chronicle play of the Thirty Years' War, based on Hans Jakob Grimmelshausen's picaresque novel *Simplicissimus* (1669), with music by Paul Dessau. Anna Fierling is a vivandière (canteen manager), nicknamed Mother Courage because of her daring in saving her goods under enemy fire. Her children, the daredevil Eilif, the honest Swiss Cheese, and the retarded but sensitive Kathrin who loves children, were born of different fathers. Together they cross many lands, drawing a canteen wagon behind them. Soon Mother Courage loses Eilif to the Swedish Protestant Army, where his bravery immediately earns him fame. Swiss Cheese becomes an army paymaster, but his honesty leads to his undoing when he tries to hide the regimental funds from the enemy. Mother Courage forfeits the chance to buy his life with a bribe by haggling too long over the ransom price of her wagon. Later she shields a Protestant chaplain from the Catholic enemy by disguising him as her handyman. Although she curses the war, Mother Courage continues to subsist because of it. In fact, during a brief spell of peace she fears that her business will be ruined. What was bravery during the war is crime in peacetime, and Eilif is executed for plundering. Now only Mother Courage, Kathrin, and their companion, a cook, are left. The cook, having inherited a small inn in Holland that will support only one or two people, proposes to Mother Courage. Unable to leave Kathrin behind as the cook insists, Mother Courage rejects his offer. Mother and daughter now draw the wagon by themselves. As they near Halle, Kathrin overhears a Catholic plan to seize the city. Realizing that children may be killed in the attack, she climbs on the roof of a peasant cottage and beats a drum to warn the citizens. Soldiers shoot her down, but the town is already awakened. Mother Courage, having lost all her children, goes on pulling the wagon alone. War, having deprived her of everything but her wagon, continues to provide her with a means of survival.

The Trial of Lucullus (*Das Verhör des Lukullus;* wr. 1939, prod. 1951). Libretto for an opera, with music by Paul Dessau; originally written as a radio play. The great Roman general Lucullus, conqueror of the East, has died and awaits trial in the underworld. Figures from his triumphal past appear as witnesses in the trial. The victims of his victo-

ries, his pillaging, and his hauling of slaves testify to the suffering and misery he has caused. The only testimony offered in his favor—his introduction of the cherry tree into Europe—is not enough to balance 80,000 deaths. The verdict sends Lucullus "into the Nothingness."

The Good Woman of Setzuan (*Der gute Mensch von Sezuan,* 1943). Parable play examining the dilemma of how to be virtuous and at the same time survive in a capitalist world. In a "half-Europeanized" province of China, three gods come down to Setzuan searching for a truly virtuous human being. Shen Te, a penniless prostitute, is the only person who offers them hospitality. They reward her with money, with which she buys a tobacco shop. The news of her good fortune brings a pack of parasitic relatives upon her. In order to escape their demands, she disguises herself as a man, her ruthless and imaginary cousin Shui Ta, to put her importunate relatives in their place.

Meanwhile, she saves an unemployed pilot, Yang Sun, from suicide and falls in love with him. They plan to marry, but their plans founder when he confides to Shui Ta that he is merely interested in Shen Te's money so that he can get a job as a pilot. After breaking with Yang Sun, Shen Te finds herself alone and pregnant and on the verge of losing her shop because of the heavy debts she has incurred.

To reestablish herself she again disguises herself as Shui Ta and starts a tobacco factory, through which her fortune is restored. She employs Yang Sun as foreman, but he exploits the workers ruthlessly. Shen Te's apparent absence for so long a period draws suspicion on Shui Ta, who is arrested for having murdered his "cousin." At the trial the gods act as judges. Shen Te tells the gods that their injunction to be good and yet live in a harsh world tore her like lightning, in two. She confesses that she had to assume a second identity in order to survive. In response to her plea for a solution to her problems, the gods absolve her of all charges and, instructing her to continue to be virtuous, vanish in a cloud.

Mr. Puntila and His Hired Man, Matti (*Herr Puntila und sein Knecht Matti;* wr. 1940/41, prod. 1948). Folk play based on stories by the Finnish writer Hella Wuolijoki. Puntila, a rich farmer, has a split personality: when drunk, he is generous and kind; when sober, mean and selfish. Sober, Puntila wants his daughter Eva to marry a Foreign Office diplomat; drunk, he leads her to his chauffeur and drinking companion, Matti. Although Eva prefers Matti, she fails to attract him, and a party is arranged to celebrate her engagement to the diplomat. During the party Puntila gets drunk and insults the diplomat, who leaves. Puntila now wants Matti to marry Eva. Matti puts her to the test to see if she is good enough to be a proletarian's wife, but she fails to meet his requirements, and Matti leaves to join his working-class comrades.

The Resistible Rise of Arturo Ui (*Der aufhaltsame Aufstieg des Arturo Ui;* wr. 1941, prod. 1958). Comic parable play concerning the Nazis' rise to power, set in Chicago's gangland. Ui (Hitler), a gang leader, sells "protection" to Chicago's vegetable merchants and blackmails the mayor, Dogsborough (Hindenburg). The resulting testament from Dogsborough, naming Ui as his successor, causes friction among the gangsters. But Ui, undaunted, paves the way to power by having those who challenge him— Roma and Dullfeet—murdered. Thus the vegetable merchants of Cicero (Austria) are terrorized into asking for Ui's protection. Ui now sets his sights on the world beyond Chicago and Cicero.

The Visions of Simone Machard (*Die Gesichte der Simone Machard;* wr. 1941/43, prod. 1957). Play written in collaboration with Lion Feuchtwanger and based on the latter's novel. During the German invasion of France in 1940, Simone, a teen-age girl, is a servant in a hotel in central France. Absorbed by the story of Joan of Arc, she dreams that her brother, a French soldier, has called upon her to save France. In dream interludes she identifies herself with Joan, seeing the people around her as historical figures. Inspired by a sense of mission, she feeds hungry refugees and, when the Germans arrive, sets fire to the hotel's gasoline supplies to prevent them from falling into the enemy's hands. At last she has a vision of being tried and sentenced to death; in fact, she is seized and sent to a mental institution.

Schweyk in the Second World War (*Schweyk im zweiten Weltkrieg;* wr. 1941/43, prod. 1957). Play based on the title character in Jaroslav Hašek's picaresque novel *The Good Soldier Schweik.* The "good soldier" of World War I, incarnation of the indestructible little man, now reemerges in Nazi-

Lincoln Center Repertory Theatre production of *The Good Woman of Setzuan*, with Colleen Dewhurst. New York, Vivian Beaumont Theatre, 1970. [Photograph by Martha Swope]

Herr Puntila und sein Knecht Matti, Städtische Bühnen, Frankfurt am Main.

occupied Prague. He becomes involved with informers, patriots, the Gestapo, and the SS without ever betraying whether his stupidity is real or assumed. On the trail of a handsome dog that he has been sent to steal for an SS leader, Schweyk finds himself in a German army unit fighting near Stalingrad. In brief interludes Hitler appears to express his concern about the attitudes of the common man. In the end Schweyk and Hitler meet on the battlefield of Stalingrad, both of them quite lost.

The Ginger Jar (*Leben des Konfutse;* wr. before 1944, pub. 1958). Play written to be acted by children. The only scene published shows the young Confucius teaching his playmates how to subdue their instincts by means of self-control.

The Caucasian Chalk Circle (*Der kaukasische Kreidekreis,* 1948). Parable play based on the Chinese drama *The Circle of Chalk,* proclaiming that ownership should be decided by merit, not law. In a prologue, members of two Soviet communes, goat breeders and fruit growers, meet in a war-shattered village to discuss who should have a certain valley, the ownership of which is disputed. The problem is settled in favor of the fruit growers, and to

celebrate the decision a storyteller recounts through song and dance an old legend, which the fruit growers perform. In the legend strife breaks out on Easter Sunday in feudal Grusinia between the Grand Duke and his princes. The Grand Duke's governor Abashwili is murdered, and his wife flees from the palace, leaving her baby son Michael behind. The child is rescued by a maid, Grusha, who takes him across the mountains to the safety of her brother's farm. To protect the child and to give him a name, she agrees to marry a rich farmer who is apparently dying but subsequently discloses that he has feigned illness to avoid being drafted into the army. Once the war is over, the governor's wife goes to court to reclaim her son in order to get her husband's estate.

In a flashback, the story reverts to the Easter Sunday on which the trouble began. Azdak, a disreputable village scribe, is the unwitting rescuer of the Grand Duke, having hidden him from the police. The rebel soldiers appoint Azdak judge, a post he occupies for two years, accepting bribes but also administering justice. When the fighting ends, Azdak is seized as an enemy and is to be hanged, but the Grand Duke shows his gratitude by spar-

Herr Puntila und sein Knecht Matti, Städtische Bühnen, Frankfurt am Main.

ing him. And so it is Azdak who hears the case brought before him by the governor's wife.

A circle of chalk is drawn on the floor, and Azdak orders the child to be placed in the middle of it. Azdak tells both the mother and the maid Grusha that the one who drags him out of the circle will be his true mother. The mother pulls violently, but Grusha lets the child go. In a Solomon-like decision, Azdak awards the child to Grusha, because she acted as a true mother should. He also grants her a divorce so that she can marry her soldier fiancé Simon. Azdak then disappears, never to be seen again.

The Antigone of Sophocles (*Die Antigone des Sophokles*, 1948). Adaptation of the Greek tragedy, based on a translation by the German poet Hölderlin. The prologue presents an incident in Berlin in April, 1945: two sisters find the body of their brother, who has been hanged as a military deserter, and they debate whether to risk being seen cutting him down by the SS. In the play itself the tyrant Creon covets the iron ore of Argos, and Polynices deserts Creon's army in protest against the attack on Argos in which his brother has been killed. Antigone also shares Polynices' opposition. Tiresias offers a pessimistic analysis of the present situation, and the ordinarily reserved chorus eventually turns against Creon. Antigone and Haemon die, and the fall of Creon and his city of Thebes is imminent.

The Days of the Commune (*Die Tage der Commune;* wr. 1948/49, prod. 1956). Critical and extensive reworking of *The Defeat,* a play by the Norwegian dramatist Nordahl Grieg, with music by Hanns Eisler. Set at the time of the Paris Commune (1871), the play has as its heroes a group of simple workers from Montmartre, who resist Thiers's efforts to disarm the National Guard and who dance and banter in the streets. The liberal prejudices and outdated notions of legality held by the leaders of the Commune, who have seized

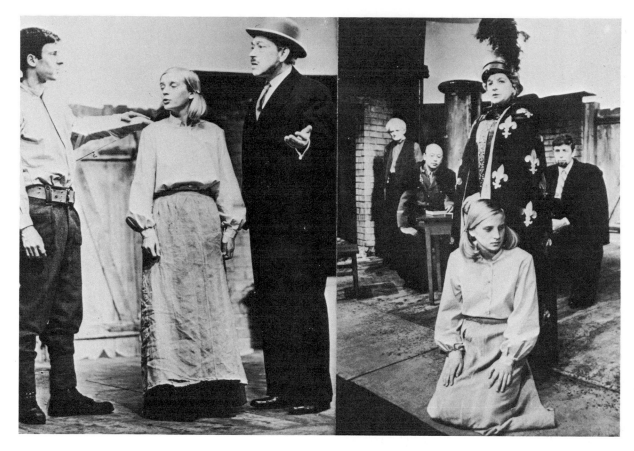

Two scenes from a Hamburg production of *Die Gesichte der Simone Machard*, starring thirteen-year-old Karin Lamster. [German Information Center]

power at the Hôtel de Ville, cause them to make mistakes. Instead of following the radical revolutionary road, they restrain the masses, respect the inviolability of the Bank of France, and fail to impose discipline on their ranks. The enemies of the Commune include Bismarck, bent on "pacifying" Paris, Thiers, and the French aristocrats and bourgeois who abandon the Communards and, at a safe distance, watch them die on the barricades.

The Private Tutor (*Der Hofmeister*, 1950). Adaptation of a play by Jakob Lenz, an eighteenth-century German writer. Läuffer earns a meager living as a tutor to a retired major's two children. The daughter seduces Läuffer and becomes pregnant by him. Pursued by the major and his friends, Läuffer runs away and takes refuge with a village schoolmaster. There he becomes attracted to the schoolmaster's goddaughter and, to prevent repetition of the previous disaster, castrates himself. He then finds he is acceptable to all, and eventually he marries the girl. Läuffer is acclaimed as the perfect teacher and entrusted with the education of Germany's youth. Brecht's portrayal of the private tutor and his self-castration is a representation of the moral collapse of German intellectuals and educators during the Nazi era. *See* LENZ, JAKOB.

The Resistible Rise of Arturo Ui, with Robin Gammell (foreground) as Arturo Ui, Minneapolis, 1968. [The Guthrie Theater Company]

Zoe Caldwell as Grusha in *The Caucasian Chalk Circle*, Minneapolis, 1965. [The Guthrie Theater Company]

1. *Baal**. Play, 21 scenes. Written 1918. Published 1922. Produced Leipzig, Altes Theater, Dec. 8, 1923. Revised version: Produced Berlin, Deutsches Theater, Feb. 14, 1926.

2. *Die Hochzeit* (*The Wedding*). Farce, 1 act. Written 1919. Published under the title of the later version, *Die Kleinbürgerhochzeit* (*The Petit Bourgeois Wedding*), 1953. Produced Frankfurt am Main, Schauspielhaus, Dec. 11, 1926.

3. *Der Bettler, oder Der tote Hund* (*The Beggar, or The Dead Dog*). Play, 1 act. Written 1919. Published 1953.

4. *Er treibt einen Teufel aus* (*He Exorcises a Devil*). Comedy, 1 act. Written 1919. Published 1953.

5. *Lux in Tenebris* (*Light in Darkness*). Farce, 1 act. Written 1919. Published 1953.

6. *Trommeln in der Nacht** (*Drums in the Night*). Comedy, 5 acts. Written 1918/20. Published 1922. Produced Munich, Kammerspiele, Sept. 23, 1922.

7. *Im Dickicht der Städte* (*In the Jungle of the Cities; In the Swamp*). Play, 11 scenes. Written 1921/23. Published 1927. Produced Munich, Residenztheater, May 9, 1923.

8. (With Lion Feuchtwanger). *Leben Eduards des Zweiten von England** (*Edward II*). History, 21 scenes; verse. Written 1923/24. Published 1924. Produced Munich, Kammerspiele, Mar. 18, 1924. Based on Christopher Marlowe's *Edward II* (1594).

9. *Mann ist Mann** (*A Man's a Man*). Comedy, 11 scenes. Written 1924/25. Published 1927. Produced Darmstadt, Landestheater, Sept. 25, 1926.

10. *Das Elefantenkalb** (*The Elephant Calf*). Farce, 1 act. Written 1924/25. Published 1927.

11. (With Feuchtwanger). *Kalkutta, 4 Mai** (*Warren Hastings*). Colonial history, 4 acts. Written 1925. Published 1927. Based on Feuchtwanger's *Warren Hastings, Gouverneur von Indien* (wr. 1915).

Report from Herrnburg (*Herrnburger Bericht*, 1951). Brief propaganda play, with songs by Paul Dessau. Some West German youths returning from a Communist rally in East Germany are stopped by West German police at the frontier. The policemen harass them, try to take their names, and forbid them to sing while marching through Lübeck. The youths taunt the police.

Coriolanus (*Coriolan*, wr. 1952/53). Adaptation of Shakespeare's *Coriolanus*, about the Roman miltary leader. Brecht emphasizes class struggle rather than what he calls the bourgeois theatre's depiction of Coriolanus as a hero and of the plebeians as merely comic figures. For Brecht, Coriolanus's tragedy rests mainly in his belief that he is irreplaceable.

Trumpets and Drums (*Pauken und Trompeten*, 1956). Adaptation of George Farquhar's comedy *The Recruiting Officer*, with new songs by Brecht and music by Rudolf Wagner-Regeny. During the American Revolution, Captain Plume and Sergeant Kite attempt to recruit unwilling Americans. Their antics in doing so are refracted through an anti-imperialist and anticolonialist prism. *See* FARQUHAR, GEORGE.

PLAYS

Plays are in prose unless otherwise noted.

A 1964 production of *Coriolan*, performed by the Berliner Ensemble, with Ekkehard Schall as Coriolanus and Helene Weigel as Volumnia. [German Information Center]

12. *Die Dreigroschenoper** (*The Threepenny Opera*). Ballad opera, prelude and 3 acts. Written 1928. Published 1929. Produced Berlin, Theater am Schiffbauerdamm, Aug. 31, 1928. Music: Kurt Weill. Based on John Gay's *The Beggar's Opera* (1728).

13. (With Elisabeth Hauptmann). *Happy End*. Musical play, prelude and 3 acts. Written 1928/29. Produced Berlin, Theater am Schiffbauerdamm, Aug. 31, 1929. Music: Weill.

14. *Der Flug der Lindberghs** (*Lindbergh's Flight*). Didactic radio play for children. Written 1928/29. Published 1929. Produced Baden-Baden, July, 1929. Music: Weill and Paul Hindemith.

15. *Aufstieg und Fall der Stadt Mahagonny** (*Rise and Fall of the City of Mahagonny*). Epic opera, 20 scenes. Written 1928/29. Published 1929. Produced Leipzig, Mar. 9, 1930. Music: Weill.

16. *Das Badener Lehrstück vom Einverständnis** (*The Didactic Play of Baden: On Consent*). Didactic play; 11 short sections, 1 interpolated scene, and short section of film. Written 1928/29. Published 1930. Produced Baden-Baden, July 28, 1929. Music: Hindemith.

17. *Der Jasager** (*He Who Says Yes*). School opera. Written 1929/30. Published 1931. Produced Berlin, June 23, 1930. Music: Weill. Based on the Japanese Nō play *Taniko*.

18. *Die heilige Johanna der Schlachthöfe** (*Saint Joan of the Stockyards*). Play, 11 scenes. Written 1929/30. Published 1931. Produced Berlin Radio, Apr. 11, 1932; Hamburg, Deutsches Schauspielhaus, Apr. 30, 1959.

19. *Der Neinsager** (*He Who Says No*). School opera. Written 1930. Published 1931. Music: Weill. Revision of *Der Jasager*.

20. *Die Massnahme** (*The Measures Taken*). Didactic

Berliner Ensemble production of *Die Tage der Commune*, 1963. [German Information Center]

play, 8 sections. Written 1930. Published 1931. Produced Berlin, Grosses Schauspielhaus, Dec. 10, 1930. Music: Hanns Eisler.

21. *Die Ausnahme und die Regel** (*The Exception and the Rule*). School play; prologue and epilogue, 9 sections. Written 1930. Published 1937. Produced Paris, Théâtre des Noctambules, 1947. Music: Paul Dessau.

22. *Die Mutter: Leben der Revolutionärin Pelegea Wlassowa aus Twer** (*The Mother: Life of the Revolutionary Pelegea Vlassova from Tver*). Didactic play, 15 scenes. Written 1930/32. Published 1932. Produced Berlin, Theater am Schiffbauerdamm, Jan. 15, 1932. Music: Eisler. Based on Maxim Gorky's novel *Mat* (1907).

23. *Die sieben Todsünden der Kleinbürger* (*The Seven Deadly Sins; also known as Anna-Anna*). Ballet cantata, 7 sections. Written ca. 1933. Published 1959. Produced Paris, Théâtre des Champs-Élysées, June 7, 1933. Music: Weill. Choreography: George Balanchine.

24. *Die Rundköpfe und die Spitzköpfe** (*The Roundheads and the Peakheads*). Atrocity story, 11 scenes. Written 1931/34. Published 1936. Produced Copenhagen, Riddersalen Theatre, Nov. 4, 1936. Music: Eisler. Based on William Shakespeare's *Measure for Measure*.

25. *Die Horatier und die Kuriatier** (*The Horatians and the Curatians*). Didactic play for children about dialectics, introduction and 3 episodes. Written 1934. Published 1938. Produced Halle, Theater der Jungen Garde, Apr. 26, 1958. Music: Kurt Schwaen.

26. *Die Gewehre der Frau Carrar** (*Senora Carrar's Rifles*). Play, 1 act. Written 1937. Published 1937. Produced Paris, Salle Adyar, Oct. 16, 1937; Berlin, Hebbel Theater, after 1945. Free adaptation of J. M. Synge's *Riders to the Sea* (1903).

27. *Furcht und Elend des dritten Reiches** (*The Private Life of the Master Race; Fear and Misery in the Third Reich*). Play, 28 scenes. Written 1935/38. Published 1945. Produced Paris (selected scenes), May 21, 1938; Los Angeles, Wheeler Auditorium, June 7, 1945.

28. *Leben des Galilei** (*Galileo*). Play, 15 scenes. Written 1938/39. Published 1955. Produced Zurich, Schauspielhaus, Sept. 9, 1943. Music: Eisler.

29. *Mutter Courage und ihre Kinder** (*Mother Courage and Her Children*). Chronicle play, 12 scenes. Written 1939. Published 1949. Produced Zurich, Schauspielhaus, Apr. 19, 1941; Berlin, Deutsches Theater, Jan. 11, 1949. Music: Dessau. Based on Hans Jakob Grimmelshausen's novel *Simplicissimus* (1669).

30. *Das Verhör des Lukullus** (*The Trial of Lucullus*). Radio play, 14 sections. Written 1939. Published 1940. Broadcast by Studio Bern, May 12, 1940. Also produced as opera, East Berlin, Staatsoper, Mar. 17, 1951. Revised version: *Die Verurteilung* (*The Condemnation of Lucullus*). Opera. Produced East Berlin, Staatsoper, Oct. 12, 1951. Music (for both versions of opera): Dessau.

31. *Der gute Mensch von Sezuan** (*The Good Woman of Setzuan*). Parable; prologue and epilogue, 10 scenes. Written 1938/40. Published 1953. Produced Zurich, Schauspielhaus, Feb. 4, 1943.

32. *Herr Puntila und sein Knecht Matti** (*Mr. Puntila and His Hired Man, Matti*). Folk play; prologue and epilogue, 12 scenes. Written 1940/41. Published 1951. Produced Zurich, Schauspielhaus, June 5, 1948. Music: Dessau. Based on stories by Hella Wuolijoki.

33. *Der aufhaltsame Aufstieg des Arturo Ui** (*The Resistible Rise of Arturo Ui*). Parable, prologue and 16 scenes; verse. Written 1941. Published 1957. Produced Stuttgart, Nov. 10, 1958.

34. (With Feuchtwanger). *Die Gesichte der Simone Machard* (*The Visions of Simone Machard*). Play, 4 acts. Written 1941/43. Published 1956. Produced Frankfurt am Main, Mar. 8, 1957.

35. *Schweyk im zweiten Weltkrieg** (*Schweyk in the Second World War*). Play; prelude, and postlude, 8 scenes. Written 1941/43. Published 1957. Produced Warsaw (in Polish), Polish Army Theatre, Jan. 17, 1957; Erfurt (in German), March, 1958. Music: Eisler. Based on Jaroslav Hašek's novel *The Good Soldier Schweik* (1920–1923).

36. *Leben des Konfutse** (*The Ginger Jar*). Play. Written before 1944. Published 1958 (only 1 scene).

37. *Der kaukasische Kreidekreis** (*The Caucasian Chalk Circle*). Play, prelude and 5 acts. Written 1944/45. Published 1949. Produced Northfield, Minn. (in English), Carleton College, May 4, 1948; Berlin, Theater am Schiffbauerdamm, June 15, 1954. Music: Dessau. Based on the Chinese play *The Circle of Chalk*.

38. *Die Antigone des Sophokles* (*The Antigone of Sophocles*). Prologue and play of 1,300 lines; verse. Written 1947/1948. Published 1948. Produced Chur, Switzerland, Stadttheater, Feb. 15, 1948. Based on the Hölderlin translation of the Sophocles play.

39. *Die Tage der Commune* (*The Days of the Commune*). Play, 14 scenes. Written 1948/49. Published 1957. Produced Chemnitz, Nov. 17, 1956. Music: Eisler. Based on Nordahl Grieg's *The Defeat*.

40. (Adaptation). *Der Hofmeister* (*The Private Tutor*). Play, 5 acts. Written 1950. Published 1951. Produced East Berlin, Berliner Ensemble, Apr. 15, 1950. Adaptation of Jakob Lenz's *Der Hofmeister* (1778).

41. *Herrnburger Bericht* (*Report from Herrnburg*). 10 songs and commentary, 2 film fragments. Written 1951. Published 1951. Produced East Berlin, Deutsches Theater, Aug. 6, 1951. Music: Dessau.

42. *Der Prozess der Jeanne d'Arc zu Rouen 1431* (*The Trial of Joan of Arc at Rouen, 1431*). Play, 16 scenes. Written 1952. Published 1959. Produced East Berlin, Berliner Ensemble, Nov. 23, 1952. Based on the radio play by Anna Seghers.

43. *Don Juan*. Play, 4 acts. Written 1952. Published 1959. Produced East Berlin, Berliner Ensemble, Nov. 16, 1953. Based on Molière's *Don Juan* (1665).

44. *Coriolan* (*Coriolanus*). Play. Written 1952/53. Published 1959. Adaptation of Shakespeare's *Coriolanus*.

45. *Turandot oder Der Kongress der Weisswäscher* (*Turandot, or The Congress of Whitewashers*). Play, 10 scenes. Written 1950–1954. Produced Zurich, 1970. Music: Eisler.

46. (With Elisabeth Hauptmann and Benne Besson). *Pauken und Trompeten** (*Trumpets and Drums*). Play, 12 scenes. Written 1955. Published 1959. Produced Berlin, Theater am Schiffbauerdamm, 1956. Music: Rudolf Wagner-Regeny. Adaptation of George Farquhar's *The Recruiting Officer* (1706).

EDITIONS

Collections.
Versuche, vols. 1–7, Berlin, 1930–1933; *Gesammelte Werke*, 2 vols., London, 1938; *Parables for the Theater*, tr. by E. and M. Bentley, Minneapolis, 1948, London, 1956; *Versuche*, vols. 7–15, Berlin and Frankfurt am Main, 1949–1957; *Stücke*, 12 vols., Berlin, 1956–1959; *Plays*, London, 1961; *Seven Plays*, ed. by E. Bentley, New York, 1961; *The Jewish Wife and Other Short Plays*, tr. by E. Bentley, New York, 1965; *Jungle of the Cities and Other Plays*, New York, 1966; *Stücke*, 13 vols., Berlin and Frankfurt am Main, 1953–1966; *Gesammelte Werke*, 20 vols., Frankfurt am Main, 1967; *Collected Plays*, ed. by R. Manheim and J. Willett, vol. 1, New York, 1971.

Individual Plays.
The Exception and the Rule. Published in *New Directions in Prose and Poetry*, ed. by J. Laughlin and tr. by E. Bentley, Norfolk, Conn., 1955.

Galileo. Published in *From the Modern Repertoire*, ed. by E. Bentley and tr. by C. Laughton, vol. 2, Bloomington, Ind., 1949–1956.

The Good Woman of Setzuan. Published in *Drama: An Introductory Anthology*, ed. by O. Reinert and tr. by E. Bentley, Boston, 1961.

The Measures Taken. Published in *The Modern Theatre*, ed. and tr. by E. Bentley, vol. 6, Garden City, N.Y., 1955–1960.

Mother Courage and Her Children. Published in *Char-*

acter and Conflict: An Introduction to Drama, ed. by A. B. Kernan and tr. by E. Bentley, New York, 1963.

The Private Life of the Master Race. Published in *A Treasury of the Theatre,* ed. by J. Gassner and tr. by E. Bentley, rev. ed., vol. 2, New York, 1951.

Saint Joan of the Stockyards. Published in *From the Modern Repertoire,* ed. by E. Bentley and tr. by F. Jones, vol. 3, Bloomington, Ind., 1949–1956.

The Threepenny Opera. Published in *From the Modern Repertoire,* ed. by E. Bentley and tr. by D. Vesey and E. Bentley, vol. 1, Bloomington, Ind., 1949–1956.

The Trial of Lucullus. Published in *German Literature since Goethe,* ed. by E. Feise and H. Steinhauer, vol. 2, Boston, 1958.

CRITICISM

German. C. Tolksdorf, *John Gays Beggar's Opera und Bert Brechts Dreigroschenoper,* Rheinberg, 1934; H. Lüthy, *Vom armen Bert Brecht,* Frankfurt am Main, 1952; G. Grosz, *Ein kleines Ja und ein grosses Nein,* Hamburg, 1955; E. Schumacher, *Die dramatischen Versuche Bertolt Brechts 1918–33,* Berlin, 1955; G. Zwerenz, *Aristotelische und Brechtsche Dramatik,* Rudolstadt, 1956; V. Klotz, *Bertolt Brecht: Versuch über das Werk,* Darmstadt, 1957; S. Melchinger, *Drama zwischen Shaw und Brecht: Ein Leitfaden durch das zeitgenössische Schauspiel,* Bremen, 1957; K. Fassman, *Brecht: Eine Bildbiographie,* Munich, 1958; O. Mann, *Bertolt Brecht—Mass oder Mythos?,* Heidelberg, 1958; R. Grimm, *Bertolt Brecht: Die Struktur seines Werkes,* Nürnberg, 1959; W. Hinck, *Die Dramaturgie des späten Brecht,* Göttingen, 1959; H. Jhering, *Bertolt Brecht und das Theater,* Berlin, 1959; M. Kesting, *Bertolt Brecht,* Hamburg, 1959; C. Niessen, *Brecht auf der Bühne,* Cologne, 1959; A. Bronnen, *Tage mit Bertolt Brecht: Geschichte einer unvollendeten Freundschaft,* Munich, 1960; H. Jhering, *Von Reinhardt bis Brecht: Vier Jahrzehnte Theater und Film,* 3 vols., Berlin, 1958–1960; B. Reich, *Bertolt Brecht: Ein Abriss seines Schaffens,* Moscow, 1960; J. Goldhahn, *Das Parabelstück Bertolt Brechts,* Rudolstadt, 1961; R. Grimm, *Bertolt Brecht und die Weltliteratur,* Nürnberg, 1961; *Das Ärgernis Brecht,* ed. by W. Jaeggi, Basel and Stuttgart, 1961; W. Hecht, *Brechts Weg zum epischen Theater,* Berlin, 1962; H. Kaufmann, *Bertolt Brecht: Geschichtsdrama und Parabelstück,* Berlin, 1962; W. Hecht et al., *Bertolt Brecht: Leben und Werk,* Berlin, 1963; H. O. Munsterer, *Bert Brecht: Erinnerungen aus den Jahren 1917–1922,* Zurich, 1963; F. Sternberg, *Der Dichter und die Ratio: Erinnerungen an Bertolt Brecht,* Göttingen, 1963; H. Mayer, *Bertolt Brecht und die Tradition,* rev. ed., Munich, 1965; H. J. Schrimpf, *Lessing und Brecht: Von der Aufklärung auf das Theater,* Pfullingen, 1965; W. Zimmermann, *Brechts "Leben des Galilei,"* Düsseldorf, 1965; H. Rischbieter, *Bertolt Brecht,* 2 vols., Velber bei Hannover, 1966; D. Schmidt, *"Baal" und der junge Brecht,* Stuttgart, 1966; G. Szczesny, *Das Leben des Galilei und der Fall Bertolt Brecht,* Frankfurt am Main and Berlin, 1966; K.-D. Müller, *Die Funktion der Geschichte im Werk Bertolt Brechts,* Tübingen, 1967; W. van der Will, *Pikaro heute: Metamorphosen des Schelms bei Thomas Mann, Döblin, Brecht, Grass,* Stuttgart, 1967.

English. M. Esslin, *Brecht: A Choice of Evils,* London, 1959; J. Willett, *The Theatre of Bertolt Brecht,* Philadelphia, 1959; M. Esslin, *Brecht: The Man and His Work,* Garden City, N.Y., 1961; R. Gray, *Bertolt Brecht,* New York, 1961; *Brecht: A Collection of Critical Essays,* ed. by P. Demetz, Englewood Cliffs, N.J., 1962; D. I. Grossvogel, *Four Playwrights and a Postscript: Brecht, Ionesco, Beckett, Genet,* Ithaca, N.Y., 1962; W. Weideli, *The Art of Bertolt Brecht,* New York, 1963; D. I. Grossvogel, *Blasphemers: Theatre of Brecht, Ionesco, Beckett, Genet,* Ithaca, N.Y., 1965; F. Ewen, *Bertolt Brecht: His Life, His Art, and His Times,* New York, 1967; M. Spalter, *Brecht's Tradition,* Baltimore, 1967; W. Haas, *Bertolt Brecht,* New York, 1968; C. R. Lyons, *Bertolt Brecht: The Despair and the Polemic,* Carbondale, Ill., 1968; G. Szczesny, *Case Against Brecht,* tr. by A. Gode, New York, 1968.

Manuel Bretón de los Herreros
(1796 — 1873)

Manuel Bretón de los Herreros, Spanish poet, prose writer, and dramatist, was born in Quel, Logroño Province, on December 19, 1796, into that middle class he was later to satirize in his theatre. At the age of sixteen he enlisted in the army. He fought against the French in the Peninsular War and remained in the army until 1822. He then settled in Madrid and began to engage in journalism and politics. In 1824 his first work, which includes lyrical and satirical poetry, critical prose, and political articles, was published; the same year his first play, *Old-age Folly* (*A la vejez viruelas,* wr. 1817), was produced and acclaimed. Subsequently he produced an immense body of varied work.

In 1835 Bretón began a querulous dialogue with his good friend the critic and dramatist Mariano José de Larra, because the latter had condemned one of his plays. His comedy *I Am Leaving Madrid* (*Me voy de Madrid,* 1835) was taken by some as an exposé of Larra's affair with a married woman and a retaliation to Larra's criticism. The quarrel was finally terminated, with great emotion, at a celebration of Bretón's appointment as second

Manuel Bretón de los Herreros. [Biblioteca Nacional, Madrid]

librarian at the Royal Library in 1836. *See* LARRA, MARIANO JOSÉ DE.

Heavily and sometimes even dangerously involved in politics, Bretón eventually found himself in favor with the regime and was given the post of director of the government printing office and editor in chief of the *Gaceta,* or register of laws and decrees. In 1847 another political shift of the wind made him Director of the National Library. Later he was made permanent secretary of the Royal Spanish Academy, an honor he held almost until his death in Madrid on November 8, 1873.

WORK

Although the romantic movement dominated Bretón's era, he remained faithful to the neoclassical tradition of his predecessor and idol, Fernández de Moratín. He fathered the Spanish realistic comedy of manners (*costumbrista*) and the drama of social satire, and he influenced both his contemporaries and the next generation of Spanish dramatists. *See* FERNÁNDEZ DE MORATÍN, LEANDRO.

Bretón's 175 stage works, comprising 103 original plays, 62 translations from French and Italian, and 10 *refundiciones* ("adaptations") of Golden Age dramas by Lope de Vega, Tirso de Molina, and Calderón, offer a satirical yet benign view of the social customs of the day. Madrid's middle classes are portrayed with facile irony and a jovial lightness, for never did Bretón censure or indict the public for its ways, and his plays are curiously unreflective of the currents of social change already beginning to be felt. Written to formula, most of his plots concern the matchmaking efforts of middle-class mothers who want wealthy husbands for their daughters; although there are some variations, one play is much like another. However, graceful versification, coherence of theme, and occasional and refreshing grotesque characters serve to redeem his work from charges of superficiality and repetitiveness.

Bretón's most famous dramas are *Marcela, or Which One of the Three?* (*Marcela, o ¿Cuál de los tres?,* 1831), a typical social comedy; *Die and You Will See!* (*¡Muérete y verás!,* 1837), which contrasts inconstancy and true devotion; and *I Am Going Back to Madrid* (*A Madrid me vuelvo,* 1828), which mocks the custom of arranged marriages. Other representative plays are *A Fiancé for the Little Girl* (*Un novio para la niña,* 1834), a matchmaking comedy; *All the World Is a Sham* (*Todo es farsa en este mundo,* 1835), in which the wrong suitor is chosen; and *Fools Come in Pairs* (*Dios los cría y ellos se juntan,* 1841), another matrimonial comedy.

I Am Going Back to Madrid (*A Madrid me vuelvo,* 1828). Verse comedy which, like Moratín's *When a Girl Says Yes* (*El sí de las niñas,* 1806), criticizes the practice of arranged marriages. Bernardo, tired of the aimless court life in Madrid, joins his brother Baltasar in a village in the Sierra de Cameros. However, he finds no peace there, for Baltasar is planning the marriage of his daughter Carmen, against her wishes, to wealthy Esteban, and Bernardo cannot stand by indifferently while Carmen is separated from Felipe, the man she really loves. Comic incidents follow one another until Esteban's mother suddenly forbids her son to marry Carmen, whom she deems unworthy, and Esteban, emotionally dependent on his mother, cancels the marriage. Baltasar, after considerable ranting, becomes convinced that Felipe is the right man for his daughter. Bernardo, disconcerted by the strange tenor of village life and the unexpected turn of events, declares that he is "going back to Madrid."

Marcela, or Which One of the Three? (*Marcela, o ¿Cuál de los tres?,* 1831). Comedy in three acts in which Marcela, a beautiful and rich young widow, is encouraged by her uncle, with whom she is living, to remarry. She is courted by three suitors, the egocentric and effeminate Don Agapito; Don Amadeo, a timid poet; and Don Martín, a gregarious captain. Marcela enjoys the attentions of all three, but she must decide between them when she receives three notes of proposal on the same day. She brings the suitors together to give her reply. She first refuses Agapito, advising him to take up more masculine pursuits if he wants a wife. She tells Amadeo that although she will be his friend forever, she cannot marry him because of the difference in their characters. It now seems certain that she has chosen Don Martín, but she refuses him too, explaining that she is not sure of his love. In fact, she is not yet ready to give up her freedom.

Die and You Will See! (*¡Muérete y verás!,* 1837). Drama set in Saragossa during the First Carlist War. Don Pablo, an army officer, departs for war, leaving behind his fiancée Jacinta, a superficial and fickle girl; her sister Isabel, who secretly loves him; their brother Don Froilán; and Don Elías, a moneylender to whom Pablo is in debt. When they receive word that Pablo has died in battle, Isabel is the only one to show any grief. Don Matías, a surviving officer who had been Pablo's friend, asks Jacinta to marry him. At the same time Don Pablo, not dead at all, returns to Saragossa, planning to surprise Jacinta. He learns that memorial services are being held for him at that very moment but that Jacinta is attending a ball with Matías. Pablo also overhears Froilán declare his indifference to Pablo's supposed demise and his scorn for Isabel's devotion. Finally Pablo appears at Jacinta's wedding disguised as a ghost. Then he pays his debt to Elías and marries Isabel, declaring that there is no better lesson in living than to "die" and observe the reactions of others.

PLAYS

This list includes only Bretón's original plays. Unless otherwise noted, all were first performed in Madrid.

1. *A la vejez viruelas* (*Old-age Folly*). Comedy, 3 acts; prose. Written 1817. Produced Teatro del Príncipe, Oct. 14, 1824.

2. *Los dos sobrinos* (*The Two Nephews*). Comedy, 5 acts; verse. Produced Teatro del Príncipe, May 30, 1825.

3. *A Madrid me vuelvo* (*I Am Going Back to Madrid*). Comedy, 3 acts; verse. Published 1836. Produced Teatro del Príncipe, Jan. 25, 1828.

4. *El rival de sí mismo* (*His Own Rival*). Comedy, 1 act; prose. Produced Teatro del Príncipe, Aug. 11, 1828.

5. *El ingenuo* (*The Naïve Boy*). Comedy, 5 acts; verse. Produced Teatro del Príncipe, Nov. 13, 1828.

6. *El templo de Himeneo* (*The Temple of Hymen*). Comedy, 1 act; verse. Produced Teatro del Príncipe, Dec. 12, 1829.

7. *La falsa ilustración* (*The False Explanation*). Comedy, 5 acts; verse. Produced Teatro de Sevilla, Feb. 10, 1830; Madrid, Teatro de la Cruz, May 30, 1830.

8. *La sorpresa* (*The Surprise*). Comedy, 1 act; prose. Produced Teatro de Sevilla, July 24, 1830.

9. *Achaques a los vicios* (*The Lure of Vice*). Comedy, 3 acts; prose. Produced Teatro de Sevilla, July 24, 1830.

10. *El ensayo* (*The Test*). Comedy, 1 act; prose. Produced Teatro de Sevilla, July 24, 1830.

11. *Marcela, o ¿Cuál de los tres?* (*Marcela, or Which One of the Three?*). Comedy, 3 acts; verse. Produced Teatro del Príncipe, Dec. 30, 1831.

12. *El músico y el poeta* (*The Musician and the Poet*). Comedy, 1 act; prose. Produced Teatro del Príncipe, May 30, 1833.

13. *El templo de la gloria* (*The Temple of Glory*). Comedy, 1 act; prose. Produced Teatro de la Cruz, June 23, 1833.

14. *El triunfo de la inocencia* (*The Triumph of Innocence*). Comedy, 1 act; prose. Produced Teatro del Príncipe, June 25, 1833.

15. *Un tercero en discordia* (*A Third Party in Disagreement*). Comedy, 3 acts; verse. Produced Teatro de la Cruz, Dec. 25, 1833.

16. *Un novio para la niña o la casa de huéspedes* (*A Fiancé for the Little Girl or The Boardinghouse*). Comedy, 3 acts; verse. Produced Teatro del Príncipe, Mar. 30, 1834.

17. *Los carlistas en Portugal* (*The Carlists in Portugal*). Comedy, 1 act. Produced Teatro del Príncipe, Apr. 15, 1834.

18. *Elena*. Drama, 5 acts; verse. Produced Teatro del Príncipe, Oct. 23, 1834.

19. *Un hombre gordo* (*A Fat Man*). Comedy, 1 act; prose. Produced Teatro del Príncipe, Jan. 6, 1835.

20. *Mérope*. Tragedy, 3 acts; verse. Produced Teatro del Príncipe, Apr. 26, 1835.

21. *Todo es farsa en este mundo* (*All the World Is a Sham*). Comedy, 3 acts; verse. Produced Teatro del Príncipe, May 13, 1835.

22. *El plan de un drama o la conspiración* (*The Outline of a Play or The Conspiracy*). Comedy, 1 act; prose. Produced Teatro de la Cruz, Oct. 22, 1835.

23. *Otro diablo predicador o el liberal por fuerza* (*Another Fiendish Preacher or The Liberal in Spite of Himself*). Comedy, 1 act; prose. Produced Teatro de la Cruz, Nov. 16, 1835.

24. *1835 y 1836 o lo que es y lo que será* (*1835 and 1836 or What Is and What Will Be*). Comedy, 1 act; prose. Produced Teatro del Príncipe, Dec. 5, 1835.

25. *Me voy de Madrid* (*I Am Leaving Madrid*). Comedy, 3 acts; verse. Produced Teatro de la Cruz, Dec. 21, 1835.

26. *La redacción de un periódico* (*The Editing of a Newspaper*). Comedy, 5 acts; verse. Produced Teatro del Príncipe, July 5, 1836.

27. *El amigo mártir* (*The Martyred Friend*). Comedy, 4 acts; verse. Produced Teatro del Príncipe, Oct. 10, 1836.

28. *Las improvisaciones* (*The Improvisations*). Comedy, 1 act; prose. Produced Teatro del Príncipe, Jan. 30, 1837.

29. *Una de tantas* (*One of Many*). Comedy, 1 act; verse. Produced Teatro del Príncipe, Mar. 2, 1837.

30. *¡Muérete y verás!* (*Die and You Will See!*). Comedy, 4 acts; verse. Produced Teatro del Príncipe, Apr. 26, 1837.

31. *Don Fernando el emplazado* (*Don Fernando on Trial*). Drama, 5 acts; verse. Produced Teatro del Príncipe, Nov. 30, 1837.

32. *Medidas extraordinarias o los parientes de mi mujer* (*Extraordinary Measures or My Wife's Relatives*). Comedy, 1 act; verse. Produced Teatro de la Cruz, Dec. 24, 1837.

33. *Ella es él* (*She Is He*). Comedy, 1 act; verse. Produced Teatro del Príncipe, Feb. 15, 1838.

34. *El poeta y la beneficiada* (*The Poet and the Beneficiary*). Comedy, 2 acts; verse. Produced Teatro del Príncipe, Mar. 15, 1838.

35. *El pro y el contra* (*The Pros and the Cons*). Comedy, 1 act; verse. Produced Teatro del Príncipe, Mar. 24, 1838.

36. *El hombre pacífico* (*The Peace-loving Man*). Comedy, 1 act. verse. Produced Teatro del Príncipe, Apr. 7, 1838.

37. *Flaquezas ministeriales* (*Ministerial Foibles*). Comedy, 5 acts; verse. Produced Teatro del Príncipe, Oct. 26, 1838.

38. *El qué dirán y el qué se me da a mí* (*What They Will Say and What They Will Attribute to Me*). Comedy, 4 acts; verse. Produced Teatro del Príncipe, Nov. 29, 1838.

39. *Un día de campo o el tutor y el amante* (*A Day in the Country or The Guardian and the Lover*). Comedy, 3 acts; verse. Produced Teatro del Príncipe, Mar. 4, 1839.

40. *El novio el concierto* (*The Bridegroom and the Agreement*). Musical comedy, 1 act; verse. Produced Teatro del Príncipe, Mar. 22, 1839.

41. *No ganamos para sustos* (*We Won't Win by Frightening*). Comedy, 3 acts; verse. Produced Teatro del Príncipe, May 12, 1839.

42. *¡Una vieja!* (*An Old Woman!*). Comedy, 4 acts; verse. Produced Teatro del Príncipe, Nov. 30, 1839.

43. *Vellido Dolfos*. Drama, 4 acts; verse. Produced Teatro del Príncipe, Dec. 13, 1839.

44. *El pelo de la dehesa* (*Rustic Ancestry*). Comedy, 5 acts; verse. Produced Teatro del Príncipe, Feb. 19, 1840.

45. *Lances de carnaval* (*The Time of Revelry*). Comedy, 1 act; verse. Produced Teatro del Príncipe, Mar. 21, 1840.

46. *Pruebas de amor conyugal* (*Conjugal Love Test*). Comedy, 2 acts; verse. Produced Teatro del Liceo, Apr. 8, 1840; Teatro del Príncipe, 1842.

47. *La ponchada* (*The Bowl of Punch*). Comedy, 1 act; prose. Produced Teatro del Príncipe, Oct. 1, 1840.

48. *El cuarto de hora* (*A Quarter of an Hour*). Comedy, 5 acts; verse. Produced Teatro del Príncipe, Dec. 10, 1840.

49. *Dios los cría y ellos se juntan* (*Fools Come in Pairs*). Comedy, 3 acts; verse. Produced Teatro del Príncipe, Feb. 11, 1841.

50. *Cuentas atrasadas* (*Late Accounts*). Comedy, 4 acts; verse. Produced Teatro del Príncipe, Mar. 6, 1841.

51. *Mi secretario y yo* (*My Secretary and I*). Comedy, 1 act; verse. Produced Teatro del Príncipe, Apr. 11, 1841.

52. *¡Qué hombre tan amable!* (*What An Obliging Man!*). Comedy, 3 acts; verse. Produced Teatro del Príncipe, May 5, 1841.

53. *Lo vivo y lo pintado* (*Naturalness and Artificiality*). Comedy, 3 acts; verse. Produced Teatro del Príncipe, Oct. 22, 1841.

54. *La pluma prodigiosa* (*The Miraculous Feather*). Play, 3 acts; verse. Produced Teatro del Príncipe, Nov. 3, 1841.

55. *La batelera de Pasages* (*The Ship Stewardess from*

Pasages). Drama, 4 acts; verse. Produced Teatro del Príncipe, Jan. 13, 1842.

56. *La escuela de las casadas* (*The School for Married Women*). Comedy, 4 acts; verse. Produced Teatro del Príncipe, Apr. 1, 1842.

57. *El editor responsable* (*The Responsible Publisher*). Comedy, 3 acts; verse. Produced Teatro del Príncipe, May 3, 1842.

58. *Los solitarios* (*The Hermits*). Musical comedy, 1 act; verse. Produced Teatro del Príncipe, Jan. 9, 1843.

59. *El carnaval de los demonios* (*The Devils' Carnival*). Play, 1 act; verse. Produced Teatro del Príncipe, Jan. 9, 1843.

60. *¡Estaba de Dios!* Comedy, 3 acts; verse. Produced Teatro del Príncipe, Jan. 19, 1843.

61. *Un novio a pedir de boca* (*A Bridegroom to His Heart's Content*). Comedy, 3 acts; verse. Produced Teatro del Príncipe, Mar. 23, 1843.

62. *Un francés en Cartagena* (*A Frenchman in Cartagena*). Comedy, 2 acts; verse. Produced Teatro del Príncipe, Apr. 28, 1843.

63. *Por no decir la verdad* (*For Not Telling the Truth*). Comedy, 1 act; verse. Produced Teatro del Príncipe, May 30, 1843.

64. *Finezas contra desvíos* (*Kindness Against Indifference*). Comedy, 4 acts; verse. Produced Teatro del Príncipe, Nov. 2, 1843.

65. *La sombra de Isabel I* (*The Ghost of Isabel I*). Comedy, 1 act; verse. Produced Teatro del Príncipe, Nov. 8, 1843.

66. *Una noche en Burgos o la hospitalidad* (*A Night in Burgos or Hospitality*). Comedy, 3 acts; verse. Produced Teatro del Príncipe, Dec. 19, 1843.

67. *Pascual y Carranza* (*Pascual and Carranza*). Comedy, 1 act; prose. Produced Teatro del Príncipe, Dec. 24, 1843.

68. *La independencia* (*Independence*). Comedy, 4 acts; prose. Produced Teatro del Príncipe, Jan. 19, 1844.

69. *A lo hecho pecho* (*Making the Best of a Bad Bargain*). Comedy, 1 act; verse. Produced Teatro de la Cruz, Sept. 11, 1844.

70. *¡Cuidado con las amigas!* (*Beware of Friends!*). Comedy, 3 acts; verse. Produced Teatro del Príncipe, Sept. 23, 1844.

71. *Aviso a las coquetas* (*Advice to Flirts*). Comedy, 1 act; verse. Produced Teatro del Príncipe, Nov. 21, 1844.

72. *La minerva o lo que es vivir en buen sitio* (*The Printing Press or What It Means to Live in a Good Location*). Comedy, 1 act; verse. Produced Teatro del Príncipe, Dec. 24, 1844.

73. *Don Frutos en Belchite* (*Don Frutos in Belchite*). Comedy, 3 acts; verse. Produced Teatro del Príncipe, Jan. 27, 1845.

74. *Frenología y magnetismo* (*Phrenology and Magnetism*). Comedy, 1 act; verse. Produced Teatro de la Cruz, Dec. 24, 1845.

75. *Errar la vocación* (*To Miss One's Calling*). Comedy, 3 acts; verse. Produced Teatro del Príncipe, Jan. 16, 1846.

76. *Mi dinero y yo* (*My Money and I*). Comedy, 3 acts; verse. Produced Teatro del Príncipe, Jan. 16, 1846.

77. *Un enemigo oculto* (*A Concealed Enemy*). Comedy, 4 acts; verse. Produced Teatro del Príncipe, Jan. 14, 1848.

78. *Memorias de Juan García* (*Juan García's Memoirs*). Comedy, 3 acts; verse. Produced Teatro del Príncipe, Sept. 16, 1848.

79. *El intendente y el comediante* (*The Manager and the Actor*). Comedy, 1 act; verse. Produced Teatro del Príncipe, Oct. 20, 1848.

80. *¿Quién es ella?* (*Who Is She?*). Comedy, 5 acts; verse. Produced Teatro Español, Dec. 7, 1849.

81. *Los tres ramilletes* (*The Three Bouquets*). Comedy, 1 act; verse. Produced Teatro Español, Mar. 13, 1850.

82. *Una ensalada de pollos* (*Chicken Salad*). Comedy, 1 act; verse. Produced Teatro Español, Oct. 25, 1850.

83. *Por poderes* (*Marriage by Proxy*). Comedy, 1 act; verse. Produced Teatro de la Drama, Dec. 14, 1851.

84. *La escuela del matrimonio* (*The School for Marriage*). Comedy, 3 acts; verse. Produced Teatro de la Drama, Jan. 14, 1852.

85. *El novio pasado por agua* (*The Parboiled Fiancé*). Musical comedy, 3 acts; verse. Produced Teatro del Circo, Mar. 18, 1852.

86. *El valor de la mujer* (*The Worth of Woman*). Drama, 5 acts; verse. Produced Teatro de Variedades, Oct. 16, 1852.

87. *La cabra tira al monte* (*Nature Will Out*). Comedy, 3 acts; prose. Produced Teatro de Variedades, Apr. 2, 1853.

88. *El duro y el millón* (*The Spanish Dollar and the Million*). Comedy, 3 acts; verse. Produced Teatro del Príncipe, Nov. 19, 1853.

89. *La niña del mostrador* (*The Girl at the Counter*). Comedy, 3 acts; verse. Produced Teatro del Príncipe, Mar. 15, 1854.

90. *Cosas de Don Juan* (*A Matter of Don Juan*). Musical comedy, 3 acts; verse. Produced Teatro del Circo, Sept. 9, 1854.

91. *Al pie de la letra* (*To the Letter*). Comedy, 3 acts; verse. Produced Teatro del Príncipe, Dec. 13, 1855.

92. *Por una hija* (*For a Daughter*). Comedy, 1 act; verse. Produced Teatro del Príncipe, Dec. 13, 1856.

93. *Mocedades* (*Youth*). Comedy, 3 acts; verse. Produced Teatro de Novedades, Oct. 29, 1857.

94. *La hipocresía del vicio* (*Hypocrisy of Vice*). Comedy, 3 acts; verse. Produced Teatro del Príncipe, Oct. 15, 1859.

95. *Entre dos amigos* (*Between Two Friends*). Comedy, 3 acts; verse. Produced Teatro del Príncipe, Jan. 11, 1860.

96. *Elvira y Leandro o el premio* (*Elvira and Leandro or The Reward*). Comedy, 5 acts; verse. Produced Teatro del Príncipe, Nov. 30, 1860.

97. *El peluquero y el cesante* (*The Hairdresser and the Pensioner*). Comedy, 1 act; verse. Published 1860.

98. *Entre santa y santo* (*Between Two Saints*). Comedy, 1 act; verse. Published 1860.

99. *La hermana de leche* (*The Foster Sister*). Comedy, 3 acts; verse. Produced Teatro de Variedades, January, 1862.

100. *María y Leonor* (*Maria and Leonor*). Comedy, 3 acts; verse. Produced Teatro del Príncipe, Jan. 16, 1863.

101. *Cuando de cincuenta pases* (*When You're over Fifty*). Comedy, 3 acts; verse. Produced Teatro del Príncipe, Dec. 24, 1864.

102. *El abogado de pobres* (*The Poor People's Lawyer*). Comedy, 3 acts; verse. Produced Teatro del Circo, Jan. 26, 1866.

103. *Los sentidos corporales* (*The Senses*). Comedy, 3 acts; verse. Produced Teatro Jovellanos, Jan. 16, 1867.

EDITIONS

Obras, 5 vols., Madrid, 1883–1884.
Die and You Will See! Published in *Nineteenth Century Spanish Plays*, ed. by L. E. Brett, New York, 1935.

CRITICISM

Marqués de Molins, *Bretón de los Herreros: Recuerdos de su vida y de sus obras*, Madrid, 1883; G. Le Gentil, *Le poète Manuel Bretón de los Herreros et la société espagnole de 1830 à 1860*, Paris, 1901; E. Piñeyro, "Manuel Bretón de los Herreros," in *The Romantics of Spain*, tr. by E. A. Peers, Liverpool, 1934.

James Bridie
(1888 – 1951)

Osborne Henry Mavor, a Scottish dramatist who wrote under the pseudonym James Bridie, was born on January 3, 1888, in Glasgow, the son of an engineer. His father encouraged him to read Shakespeare, the Bible, Ruskin, and Darwin and introduced him to artistic circles in Glasgow. As an undergraduate at the University of Glasgow, Bridie quickly earned a reputation for wit and nonconformity. He edited the university magazine, wrote student plays, and from 1910 to 1912 was cartoonist for *Scots-Pictorial.* After nine years of study he qualified as a doctor in 1913, at the age of twenty-five, becoming house physician at the Glasgow Royal Infirmary. He entered the British Army the following year. His experience as an army doctor from 1914 to 1919 in France, Mesopotamia, Persia, and the Caucasus is the subject of *Some Talk of Alexander* (1926), his first book.

On his return to Scotland in 1919, he joined the staff of the Victoria Infirmary as assistant and visiting physician and began to write plays in his spare time. He established a private practice in Glasgow and in 1923 married Rona Locke Bremmer. His first produced play was *The Sunlight Sonata,* written under the pseudonym Mary Henderson and staged in 1928. A year later, with the Birmingham Repertory Theatre production of *The Switchback,* Dr. Mavor's career as James Bridie began. In the next twenty-two years he became one of the most prolific dramatists in Europe, author of more than forty plays, some of the best of which were written during his last seven years.

James Bridie. [Raymond Mander and Joe Mitchenson Theatre Collection]

At the outbreak of World War II in 1939, Bridie reenlisted in the Royal Army Medical Corps, with the rank of major. He continued with his writing throughout this period and returned to civilian life before the war's end. *Holy Isle* (1942) marked his return to the theatre; it was followed by *Mr. Bolfry* (1943); *It Depends What You Mean* (1944); *The Forrigan Reel* (1945); and *Daphne Laureola* (1949), which had its Broadway premiere in 1950.

Bridie lived in Scotland all his life, practicing medicine until he was fifty and leading a double life as physician-playwright. Eventually, when his dual identity caused a decline in the enthusiasm of his patients, he gave up medicine to devote himself to writing. His autobiography, *One Way of Living,* appeared in 1939, and in 1949 he wrote the screenplay of *Under Capricorn* for Warner Brothers.

Bridie worked long and hard to create a Scottish national theatre and led in the formation of the Glasgow Citizens' Theatre (1943). In 1950 he founded the first College of Dramatic Art in Scotland. Bridie died of a vascular ailment in Edinburgh on January 29, 1951, at the age of sixty-three.

WORK

Introduced to the world of drama by the Scottish National Theatre Society, James Bridie did much to further the development of Scottish drama. In the 1930s, however, his great talent turned outward toward the financial and artistic support of the English theatre, for Scottish audiences were small. Bridie was the first Scottish dramatist to be accepted by a European audience. His work encompassed elements of both Shaw and Ibsen. Nevertheless, his talent was unique, rivaling Shaw's in devising comic twists to serious subjects. He was graced with a whimsy that found expression in his characters and humor, but the same whimsy was the cause of so many of his plays' coming to no conclusion at all. Strong beginnings characteristically fade gradually into weak endings, concluding scenes that exasperated audiences and critics alike for their ambiguity and looseness. *The Switchback* (1929), for example, has a magnificent first act that is not supported by the succeeding acts. The penetrating study of life in Edinburgh that begins *The Anatomist* (1930), a historical play about Dr. Knox, a devoted anatomical scientist who discovers the seamy aspect of science when he buys cadavers from the notorious Burke and Hare, is not sustained to the end. *See* IBSEN, HENRIK; SHAW, GEORGE BERNARD.

Not concerned with social questions, Bridie was interested in problems of religion and the church, treating them both seriously and humorously. Biblical overtones are present in

Scenes from *A Sleeping Clergyman*, starring Ruth Gordon. New York, Guild Theatre, 1934. [Photographs by Vandamm. Theatre Collection, The New York Public Library at Lincoln Center, Astor, Lenox and Tilden Foundations]

The Amazed Evangelist (1932); and in *A Sleeping Clergyman* (1933), in which he refuted the fatalistic theory of inherited evil (the theory of the "bad seed") and suggested that genius may pass mysteriously in a following generation to great evil and thence, in yet another generation, to great good. *Tobias and the Angel* (1930) and *Susannah and the Elders* (1937) treat Biblical themes. The former describes Tobias's meeting and marriage with Sarah while on a journey with the archangel Raphael; the latter modernizes the Susannah story by placing it in a Scottish university. *The Dragon and the Dove* (1942) raises questions about God, man, and the devil.

Bridie's unbounded imagination and his love of fantasy were the forces that created such works as *Mr. Bolfry* (1943), in which a proud Scottish devil disguised as Mr. Bolfry engages in theological debate with a Presbyterian minister in the Highlands; and *Daphne Laureola* (1949), a modern version of the Greek myth about a nymph transformed into a laurel tree. *Jonah and the Whale* (1932) combines Bridie's interest in the Bible with his sense of fantasy; a fairy tale based on the Biblical story, it includes at the same time symbolism and satire. In *The King of Nowhere* (1938) he conjured a modern world in which a madman can easily become a Hitler.

The Queen's Comedy (1950) and *The Baikie Charivari* (1952), the latter about Pounce-Pellott, a metaphorical character representing Pontius Pilate and Punch, are companion pieces written near the end of Bridie's life. In *The Baikie Charivari* there are comedy and tragedy, satire and allegory, prose and verse. Ideas clash in a dialectical interplay, and the resolution is as powerful as anything Bridie ever wrote.

Complex and imaginative, Bridie's works run the gamut from fantasy to history, from seriousness to humor. That many of his plays are marred by unsuccessful endings yet are admired as works of great worth, witty, versatile, and dramatically valid, is a tribute to their brilliance.

Tobias and the Angel (1930). Drama based on the Book of Tobit in the Apocrypha. Tobias is the son of Tobit, a blind old Jewish beggar who lives in a hovel in Nineveh with his wife Anna. The disguised archangel Raphael, who has been hospitably received by Tobit, volunteers to accompany Tobias on a journey to Media. They stop in Ecbatana at the home of Sarah, whom Tobias marries despite a warning that seven previous bridegrooms were murdered by the demon Asmoday (Asmodeus). After driving off this menace, Raphael escorts the couple to Nineveh, where he cures Tobit's blindness. Raphael then reveals himself as the mighty Archangel and disappears.

Jonah and the Whale (1932). Drama in which Jonah appears as an egotistical, urbane philosopher in the year 825 B.C. He is highly regarded by all the people of his village, Gittah Hepher, except the commercial traveler Bilshan, who considers him impractical and unworldly. Jonah claims to have saved Gittah Hepher from the Lord's wrath when he rid it of the foul state of adultery and idolatry. Now he feels that the city of Nineveh must be saved also, but he is afraid to tackle the job. He tries to escape the problem by taking a sea voyage, but the ship runs into trouble, and Jonah, who has had a revelation from God, convinces the crew and passengers to throw him overboard in order to save the others. This done, Jonah is swallowed by a whale and lectured for the three days of his confinement. When the whale opens its mouth to swallow water, Jonah is cast out onto land.

The final act shows Jonah in Nineveh

Ruth Gordon and Ernest Thesiger in *A Sleeping Clergyman.* New York, Guild Theatre, 1934. [Photograph by Vandamm. Theatre Collection, The New York Public Library at Lincoln Center, Astor, Lenox and Tilden Foundations]

Cecil Parker and Dame Edith Evans in *Daphne Laureola*. New York, Music Box Theatre, 1950. [Theatre Collection, The New York Public Library at Lincoln Center, Astor, Lenox and Tilden Foundations]

warning the populace of the city's destruction, but when nothing happens, Jonah is mortified and says he should have heeded the whale. He cries out that he will never prophesy again, curses his fate, and realizes that he is only an ordinary man.

A Sleeping Clergyman (1933). Melodrama in which Providence is described as the Sleeping Clergyman who can change evil to good in three generations. The opening scene depicts the Clergyman fast asleep while two doctors are discussing the tawdry history of the Marshall Cameron family, a story of crime and genius, which is then reenacted. After Charlie Cameron, a brilliant but wild medical student, has died from phthisis, his mistress Harriet, who is the sister of his friend Dr. Marshall, gives birth to Wilhelmina. Dr. Marshall fosters the child. Wilhelmina becomes pregnant by John Hannah, a poor medical student, whom she murders. The scene returns to the doctors, who tell about the murder trial and Wilhelmina's pregnancy. After giving birth to twins six months later, Wilhelmina commits suicide, leaving the orphans in Marshall's care. Ironically, the twins become persons of genius and saviors of mankind during a mysterious plague. They have come full circle, inheriting the genius of their ancestor Charlie Cameron.

The Baikie Charivari or The Seven Prophets (1952). Two-act miracle play that adopts a common Scottish theme, mortal man's struggle against the devil and his works. The play has a dual character as it takes on the two planes of reality and fantasy. The inhabitants of the Scottish sea resort Baikie Charivari, in about 1930, are at one and the same time real people and Punch and

Judy characters operated by the devil. Sir James MacArthur Pounce-Pellot, representing Punch and Pontius Pilate, who recently retired from a life of civil service in India as Knight Commander of the Indian Empire, has settled here with his etiquette-minded wife and adolescent daughter, hoping to adapt himself to the twentieth century in the West. To achieve his aim, he consults various neighbors for guidance. The Reverend Beadle acts as spiritual guide; Mr. Mascara, as modern aesthetics adviser; and Dr. Pothecary, a female psychologist, as an emotional adviser.

Action continues on a supernatural level at intervals throughout the play, with Mrs. Crowe and Dr. Pothecary, modern soothsayers, dancing to a chant dedicated to Satan. Sir James's daughter Baby, who as a child was saved from drowning by Ketch, a Communist and the town councillor, has been promised magical powers by Mr. Mascara, who has persuaded her to join Satan's group.

The central action of the play is the attempt to save Baby, who ends by marrying an apprentice plumber to escape the theoreticians. Sir James fights off temptation in his quest for the truth, but dialectical interplay between Communist Ketch and the Reverend Beadle leads him to realize he has "sold his God for order." In the end, Punch symbolically kills off all foes with his stick and exorcises the devil with his incantation but still is no closer to truth. However, he can still joke and maintains hope that there is an answer to be found.

PLAYS

1. *The Sunlight Sonata, or To Meet the Seven Deadly Sins.* Farce-morality; prologue and epilogue, 3 scenes. Produced Glasgow, Lyric Theatre (Scottish National Players), Mar. 20, 1928.

2. *The Switchback.* Play, 3 acts. Produced Birmingham Repertory Theatre, Mar. 9, 1929.

3. *What It Is to Be Young.* Play, 3 acts. Produced Birmingham Repertory Theatre, Nov. 2, 1929.

4. *The Anatomist.* Drama, 3 acts. Published 1931. Produced Edinburgh, Lyceum Theatre, July 6, 1930; London, Westminster Theatre, Oct. 7, 1931.

5. *The Girl Who Did Not Want to Go to Kuala Lumpur.* Comedy, 3 acts. Produced Glasgow, Lyric Theatre (Scottish National Players), November, 1930.

6. *Tobias and the Angel.* Comedy, 3 acts. Published 1931. Produced Cambridge, Festival Theatre, Nov. 20, 1930.

7. *The Pardoner's Tale.* Morality, 1 act. Published 1930. Based on Geoffrey Chaucer's tale.

8. *The Dancing Bear.* Comedy, 3 acts. Produced Glasgow, Lyric Theatre (Scottish National Players), Feb. 2, 1931.

9. *The Amazed Evangelist.* Comedy, 1 act. Published 1931. Produced London, Westminster Theatre, Dec. 12, 1932.

10. *Jonah and the Whale.* Play, prologue and 3 acts. Produced London, Westminster Theatre, Dec. 12, 1932.

11. *A Sleeping Clergyman.* Play, 2 acts. Produced Malvern, Festival Theatre, July 29, 1933.

12. *Marriage Is No Joke.* Melodrama, 2 acts. Produced Glasgow, King's Theatre, January, 1934; London, Globe Theatre, Feb. 6, 1934.

13. *Colonel Witherspoon, or The Fourth Way of Greatness.* Comedy, 3 acts. Published 1934. Produced Glasgow, Lyric Theatre (Scottish National Players), Mar. 23, 1934.

14. (With Claude Gurney). *Mary Reed.* Play, 3 acts. Produced London, His Majesty's Theatre, Nov. 21, 1934.

15. *The Black Eye.* Comedy, 2 acts. Published 1935. Produced London, Shaftesbury Theatre, October, 1935.

16. (Adaptation). *Storm in a Teacup.* Play. Produced London, Royalty Theatre, Feb. 5, 1936. Based on Bruno Frank's *Sturm in Wasserglas.*

17. *Susannah and the Elders.* Play, 3 acts. Produced London, Duke of York's Theatre, Oct. 31, 1937.

18. *The King of Nowhere.* Play, 3 acts. Published 1938. Produced London, Old Vic, Mar. 15, 1938.

19. *Babes in the Wood.* Quiet farce, 2 acts. Published 1938. Produced London, Embassy Theatre, June 13, 1938.

20. *The Last Trump.* Play, 2 acts. Published 1938. Produced Malvern, Festival Theatre, Aug. 5, 1938; London, Duke of York's Theatre, Sept. 13, 1938.

21. *The Kitchen Comedy.* Radio play, 1 act. Produced Glasgow, British Broadcasting Corporation, Nov. 18, 1938.

22. *The Letter Box Rattles.* Play. Published 1938.

23. *What Say They?* Play, 2 acts. Produced Malvern, Festival Theatre, Aug. 7, 1939.

24. *The Sign of the Prophet Jonah.* Radio play. Produced British Broadcasting Corporation, 1942. Version of *Jonah and the Whale.*

25. *The Dragon and the Dove or How the Hermit Abraham Fought the Devil for His Niece.* Play, 2 acts. Produced Glasgow, Lyric Theatre, August, 1942; London, Arts Theatre, Mar. 9, 1943.

26. *Jonah 3.* Play. Produced Manchester, November 1942. Revised version of *Jonah and the Whale.*

27. *Holy Isle.* Play, 3 acts. Produced London, Arts Theatre, Dec. 11, 1942.

28. *A Change for the Worse.* Play. Produced London, Arts Theatre, Mar. 9, 1943.

29. *Mr. Bolfry.* Play, 4 scenes. Produced London, Westminster Theatre, Aug. 3, 1943.

30. *It Depends What You Mean.* Play, 3 acts. Published 1949. Produced London, Westminster Theatre, Oct. 12, 1944.

31. *The Forrigan Reel.* Ballad opera, 2 acts. Published 1949. Produced London, Sadler's Wells Theatre, Oct. 24, 1945.

32. *Lancelot.* Play, 2 acts. Published 1945.

33. *Paradise Enow.* Play, 1 act. Published 1945.

34. *Dr. Angelus.* Play, 3 acts. Published 1949. Produced Edinburgh, June 23, 1947; London, Phoenix Theatre, July 30, 1947.

35. *John Knox.* Play, 3 acts. Published 1949. Produced Glasgow, Citizens' Theatre, Aug. 18, 1947.

36. *Gog and Magog.* Play. Produced London, Arts Theatre, December, 1948.

37. *Daphne Laureola.* Play, 4 acts. Published 1949. Produced London, Wyndham's Theatre, Mar. 23, 1949.

38. *The Golden Legend of Shults.* Play, 3 acts. Produced Perth, Scotland, Perth Theatre, July 24, 1949.

39. *Mr. Gillie.* Play, prologue and 2 acts. Published 1950. Produced Glasgow, Feb. 13, 1950; London, Garrick Theatre, Mar. 9, 1950.

40. *The Queen's Comedy.* Play. Produced Edinburgh, Lyceum Theatre, Aug. 21, 1950.

41. *The Baikie Charivari or The Seven Prophets.* Miracle play, 2 acts. Published 1953. Produced Glasgow, Citizens' Theatre, Oct. 6, 1952.

42. (With Archibald Batty). *Meeting at Night.* Play. Produced Glasgow, Citizens' Theatre, May, 1954.

43. *The Pyrate's Den.* Play.

44. *The Tragic Muse.* Play.

45. (Adaptation). *The Wild Duck.* Play. Based on Henrik Ibsen's *Vildanden.*

46. (Adaptation). *Liliom.* Play. Based on Ferenc Molnár's play of the same name (1909).

47. (Adaptation). *Hedda Gabler.* Play. Based on Ibsen's play of the same name.

48. (Adaptation). *The Misanthrope.* Play. Based on Molière's *Le misanthrope.*

CRITICISM

W. Bannister, *James Bridie and His Theatre,* London, 1955; U. Gerber, *James Bridies Dramen,* Bern, 1961; G. Weales, *Religion in Modern English Drama,* Philadelphia, 1961; H. L. Luyben, *James Bridie: Clown and Philosopher,* Philadelphia, 1965.

Eugène Brieux
(1858 — 1932)

Eugène Brieux, French journalist and dramatist, was born in Paris on January 19, 1858. After attending elementary school, he became an apprentice cabinetmaker in his father's workshop, but he attended classes at night, studied Latin and Greek on his own, and spent his small earnings on books. He began writing plays while still quite young, and *Bernard Palissy,* a one-act verse play he wrote in collaboration with Gaston Salandri, was performed in 1879.

Brieux gave up cabinetmaking to become a journalist in Rouen, where he eventually became editor in chief of the *Nouvelliste de Rouen.* He continued to write plays, and his efforts were rewarded when, in 1890, *Artists' Homes (Ménages d'artistes)* was produced by André Antoine at the Théâtre Libre. In 1897 Brieux returned to Paris, where he continued to work as a journalist on *Le Figaro* and oth-

Eugène Brieux. [Theatre Collection, The New York Public Library at Lincoln Center, Astor, Lenox and Tilden Foundations]

er papers until 1908. That year, his reputation as a dramatist firmly established, he left Paris to live in Agay, near Cannes, but was so harassed by inquisitive tourists that he moved to a farm in the Loiret Department. He later became a cantonal delegate and also gave examinations for school-leaving certificates.

With his election to the Académie Française in 1910, Brieux attained a lifelong ambition. He continued to write plays on social and moral problems until shortly before his death in Nice on December 6, 1932.

WORK

As a journalist turned playwright, Brieux naturally became an important exponent of the "useful theatre," since he was a dramatic propagandist who described social evils and offered remedies for them in areas ranging from politics to public health. The first of his

plays to receive public attention was *Artists' Homes* (1890), which was produced at Antoine's Théâtre Libre. This was followed by other successes: *Duramé's Daughter* (*La fille de Duramé,* 1890), *Monsieur de Réboval* (1892), and *Blanchette* (1903). Perhaps the most widely acclaimed of these initial dramatic ventures was *Blanchette;* in this play Brieux attacked the French teacher-training schools, which turned out socially uprooted young women for whom society could find no employment.

Other plays show the range and diversity of Brieux's themes: *The Nest* (*La couvée,* 1893) points to domestic corruption, while *The Machine* (*L'engrenage,* 1894) exposes political corruption; *The Philanthropists* (*Les bienfaiteurs,* 1896) shows the defects of institutional philanthropy. He opposed both marriages of convenience and divorce in *The Three Daughters of M. Dupont* (*Les trois filles*

Act III of *La robe rouge,* produced by the Comédie-Française. [G. Lolivier, Paris]

Scene from
Damaged Goods.
New York, Fulton
Theatre, 1913.
[Theatre
Collection, The
New York Public
Library at Lincoln
Center, Astor,
Lenox and Tilden
Foundations]

de M. Dupont, 1897), *Suzette* (1909), and *The Woman Who Deserted* (*La déserteuse*, 1904).

Brieux's use of dramatic form to advocate social change is best seen in *The Three Daughters of M. Dupont*, a semididactic study of a marriage of convenience; *The Red Robe: The Letter of the Law* (*La robe rouge*, 1900), an aggressive attack on the lack of ethics in the legal profession; *Maternity* (*Maternité*, 1903), a plea for birth control; and *Damaged Goods* (*Les avariés*, 1902), in which the stage is used as a means of presenting the latest medical findings on the cure and prevention of syphilis and of urging the necessity for public health legislation. In *Maternity* and *Damaged Goods*, the dramatist in Brieux gave way entirely to the social critic and the characters are didactically manipulated within a minimal plot.

In *False Gods* (*La foi*, 1909), Brieux departed somewhat from his concern with immediate social problems and examined the question of religion's place in life. Occasionally he gave his fancy freer rein, as in *The June Bugs* (*Les hannetons*, 1906), a rueful comedy about a love affair, but he always came back to using the theatre as a forum for social ideas. For example, in one of his last plays, *The Child, or Pierrette and Galaor* (*L'enfant, ou Pierrette et Galaor*, 1923), he dealt with an economically independent woman's right to maternity without marriage.

George Bernard Shaw's judgment that Brieux was France's "greatest writer since Molière" seems strange today. However, even if only a few of Brieux's plays survive, he will certainly be remembered for introducing, into a French theatre preoccupied with frivolous and vaguely immoral themes, a drama concerned with serious problems requiring reform. Perhaps he himself best explained his method: "Had I lived in the seventeenth century I would have been a preacher, but now I write plays."

The Three Daughters of M. Dupont (*Les trois filles de M. Dupont*, 1897).   Drama set in a French provincial town. M. Dupont, the bourgeois proprietor of a printing establishment, arranges a marriage between his youngest daughter, Julie, and Antonin Mairaut, the son of a banker. Dupont has two older daughters by a previous marriage: Caroline, a frustrated spinster who has turned to religion, and Angèle, who has become a prostitute after having been turned out of the house because of a youthful indiscretion. Hoping that the Mairauts will influence an uncle in the prefectural government to direct government printing contracts his way, Dupont promises to provide Julie with a large

Damaged Goods.
New York, Fulton
Theatre, 1913.
[Culver Pictures]

dowry. However, he is unable to produce the money, and it is discovered that Antonin's uncle has actually recently lost his government position. Julie has no real affection for her new husband, and she gradually realizes that they have been the pawns of their ambitious parents. Once the Mairauts and Duponts discover their mutual deception, Antonin, who has become increasingly tyrannical, tells Julie that she must not have children because they are unable to afford it. Since this denies one of Julie's deepest aspirations, she leaves him. After a conversation with her sisters, however, she becomes convinced that any marriage is preferable to the lonely struggles of a spinster or a prostitute, and so she returns to her husband.

The Red Robe: The Letter of the Law

(*La robe rouge,* 1900). Drama in which Vagret, magistrate of Mauléon, has long hoped to be promoted to councillor, but the red robe signifying that honor has always been

awarded to someone else. When his appointment at last seems imminent, he is in the midst of trying Etchepare, a Basque peasant, for the murder of an old man to whom he owed money. Mouzon, a ruthless examining magistrate who also aspires to the red robe, is assigned to assist Vagret. He intimidates the defendant's wife Yanetta by uncovering a former lover with whom, before her marriage, she was arrested for the possession of stolen goods. She had not told her husband about her arrest because she knew he could never accept her guilt; when her secret is revealed during the trial, their marriage is irreparably damaged. Vagret begins to believe that Etchepare is innocent of the murder, and he confides his doubts to the jury, swaying them toward acquittal. Even though it is Mouzon who is given the coveted promotion, Vagret has no regrets, since he has saved a possibly innocent man. When Etchepare refuses to forgive Yanetta and deprives her of her home and children, she kills Mouzon with a knife he had proudly saved as a souvenir from an earlier murder conviction.

Damaged Goods (*Les avariés*, 1902). Drama set in Paris in the early 1900s. When Georges Dupont discovers that he has contracted syphilis after a night of carousing, his physician warns him not to marry for three or four years. However, unwilling to risk losing his fiancée Henriette, the daughter of Loches, a well-known deputy, he waits only six months before marrying. A sickly daughter is born to the couple. After Georges's mother brings the child and her nurse back from a stay in the country, the same doctor reveals that the baby has congenital syphilis. The doctor warns that the wet nurse must discontinue breast-feeding the child lest she herself contract the disease and spread it further. Georges is helpless with sorrow, and his mother, fearing that the infant will not survive on bottle feeding, decides to bribe the nurse to resume her service without knowledge of the jeopardy to her health. When the doctor angrily objects to this arrangement, the wet nurse learns of her danger. She attempts to blackmail the Duponts, and Henriette, learning her husband's secret, returns to her family with the child. Loches requests documentation of Georges's disease in order to institute divorce proceedings, but the doctor refuses and argues for the reconciliation of the couple. He urges the deputy to use his influence to have laws passed making premarital syphilis tests mandatory.

PLAYS

Unless otherwise noted, the plays were first performed in Paris.

1. (With Gaston Salandri). *Bernard Palissy*. Drama, 1 act. Published 1880. Produced Théâtre Cluny, Dec. 21, 1879.

2. (With Salandri). *Le bureau des divorces* (*The Divorce Bureau*). Vaudeville, 1 act. Published 1880.

3. *Ménages d'artistes** (*Artists' Homes*). Comedy, 3 acts. Published 1890. Produced Théâtre Libre, Mar. 21, 1890.

4. *La fille de Duramé* (*Duramé's Daughter*). Drama, 5 acts. Published 1890. Produced Rouen, Théâtre Français, Mar. 25, 1890.

5. *Monsieur de Réboval*. Play, 3 acts. Published 1892. Produced Théâtre de l'Odéon, Sept. 20, 1892.

6. *Blanchette**. Comedy, 3 acts. Published 1892. Produced Comédie-Française, Oct. 9, 1903.

7. *La couvée** (*The Nest*). Comedy, 3 acts. Published 1904. Produced Rouen, 1893 (privately); Paris, Coopération des Idées, Université Populaire du Faubourg Saint-Antoine, July 9, 1903.

8. *L'engrenage* (*The Machine*). Comedy, 3 acts. Published 1894. Produced Théâtre de la Comédie-Parisienne, May 16, 1894.

9. *La rose bleue* (*The Blue Rose*). Comédie-vaudeville, 1 act. Published 1895. Produced Geneva, Grand Théâtre July 26, 1895.

10. *Les bienfaiteurs** (*The Philanthropists*). Comedy, 4 acts. Published 1897. Produced Théâtre de la Porte-Saint-Martin, Oct. 22, 1896.

11. *L'évasion** (*The Escape*). Comedy, 3 acts. Published 1897. Produced Comédie-Française, Dec. 7, 1896.

12. *Les trois filles de M. Dupont** (*The Three Daughters of M. Dupont*). Comedy, 4 acts. Published 1899. Produced Théâtre du Gymnase, Oct. 8, 1897.

13. *L'école des belles-mères* (*The School for Mothers-in-law*). Comedy, 1 act. Published 1898. Produced Théâtre du Gymnase, Mar. 25, 1898. Based on Brieux's *La couvée*.

14. *Résultat des courses!* (*Racing Results!*) Comedy, 6 tableaux. Published 1898. Produced Théâtre Antoine, Dec. 10, 1898.

15. *Le berceau* (*The Cradle*). Comedy, 3 acts. Published 1898. Produced Comédie-Française, Dec. 19, 1898.

16. *La robe rouge** (*The Red Robe: The Letter of the Law*). Play, 4 acts. Published 1900. Produced Théâtre du Vaudeville, Mar. 15, 1900.

17. *Les remplaçantes* (*The Substitutes*). Play, 3 acts. Published 1901. Produced Théâtre Antoine, Feb. 15, 1901.

18. *Les avariés** (*Damaged Goods*). Play, 3 acts. Written 1901. Published 1902. Produced Liège, Théâtre du Gymnase, Mar. 6, 1902; Paris, Théâtre Antoine, Feb. 22, 1905.

19. *La petite amie* (*The Girl Friend*). Play, 3 acts. Published 1902. Produced Comédie-Française, May 3, 1902.

20. *Maternité** (*Maternity*). Play, 3 acts. Published 1904. Produced Théâtre Antoine, Dec. 9, 1903.

21. (With Jean Sigaux). *La déserteuse* (*The Woman Who Deserted*). Play, 4 acts. Published 1904. Produced Théâtre de l'Odéon, Oct. 15, 1904.

22. *L'armature* (*The Armature*). Play, 3 acts. Published 1905. Produced Théâtre du Vaudeville, Apr. 19, 1905. Based on Paul Hervieu's novel *L'armature*.

23. *Les hannetons** (*The June Bugs*). Comedy, 3 acts. Published 1906. Produced Théâtre de la Renaissance, Feb. 3, 1906.

24. *La française* (*The Frenchwoman*). Comedy, 3 acts. Published 1907. Produced Théâtre de l'Odéon, Apr. 18, 1907.

25. *Simone**. Play, 3 acts. Published 1908. Produced Comédie-Française, Apr. 13, 1908.

26. *La foi** (*False Gods*). Play, 5 acts. Published 1912. Produced Monte Carlo, Apr. 10, 1909; Paris, Théâtre de l'Odéon, May 22, 1912.

27. *Suzette*. Play, 3 acts. Published 1909. Produced Théâtre du Vaudeville, Sept. 28, 1909.

28. *La femme seule** (*The Woman on Her Own*). Comedy, 3 acts. Published 1913. Produced Théâtre du Gymnase, Dec. 22, 1912.

29. *Les américains chez nous* (*Americans among Us*). Comedy, 3 acts. Published 1920. Produced Théâtre de l'Odéon, Jan. 9, 1920.

30. *Trois bons amis* (*Three Good Friends*). Comedy, 3 acts. Published 1921. Produced Théâtre de l'Odéon, May 7, 1921.

31. *L'avocat** (*The Lawyer*). Comedy, 3 acts. Published 1922. Produced Théâtre du Vaudeville, Sept. 22, 1922.

32. *L'Enfant, ou Pierrette et Galaor* (*The Child, or Pierrette and Galaor*). Comedy, 3 acts. Published 1923. Produced Théâtre du Vaudeville, Sept. 20, 1923.

33. *La famille Lavolette* (*The Lavolette Family*). Comedy, 3 acts. Published 1926. Produced Théâtre des Nouveautés, Sept. 11, 1926.

34. *Puisque je t'aime* (*Because I Love You*). Comedy, 1 act. Published 1929. Produced Comédie-Française, May 6, 1929.

35. *La régence* (*The Regency*). Play, 5 acts. Published 1929.

EDITIONS

Collections.
Three Plays, New York, 1911; *Blanchette and The Escape*, Boston, 1913; *The Woman on Her Own, False Gods and The Red Robe*, New York, 1916; *Théâtre complet*, 9 vols., Paris, 1921–1929.

Individual Plays.
False Gods. Published in *Modern Continental Plays*, ed. by S. M. Tucker, Harper, New York, 1929.

The Red Robe. Published in *Chief French Plays of the Nineteenth Century*, ed. by E. M. Grant, Harper, New

York, 1934; *Continental Plays,* ed. by T. H. Dickinson and tr. by F. Reed, vol. II, Houghton Mifflin, Boston, 1935; *Representative Modern Dramas,* ed. by C. H. Whitman and tr. by F. Reed, Macmillan, New York, 1936.

The Three Daughters of M. Dupont. Published in *Nineteenth Century Plays,* ed. by J. L. Borgerhoff, Century, New York, 1931; *French Plays,* ed. by T. G. Bergin and T. Anderson, American Book, New York, 1941.

CRITICISM

A. Bertrand, *Eugène Brieux,* Paris, 1910; P. V. Thomas, *The Plays of Eugène Brieux,* London, 1913, Boston, 1915; W. H. Scheifley, *Brieux and Contemporary French Society,* New York, 1917; G. Möller, *Henry Becque und Eugène Brieux,* Breslau, 1937.

BRIGHOUSE, Harold (b. Eccles, Lancashire, July 26, 1882; d. London, July 25, 1958). English novelist, critic, and playwright, one of the most notable of the so-called Manchester school of dramatists, a small group of young men, including Brighouse, Stanley Houghton, and Allan Monkhouse, whose plays were introduced by Annie Elizabeth Horniman at her repertory theatre in Manchester. A master of Lancashire dialect and a student of provincial humor, Brighouse reached the height of his talent for characterization in the comedy *Hobson's Choice* (1915), a minor masterpiece about the blustering Lancashire owner of a shoe store and his rebellious, aging daughter. Social and political disruption, particularly among the lower classes, is the subject of several plays: *Dealing in Futures* (1909) delved into labor-management relations, and *Garside's Career* (1914) took a comic look at politics.

Brighouse was the author of many one-act plays that appear in some fifty anthologies. The plays that were produced at the Gaiety Theatre in Manchester include *The Doorway* (1909), *Dealing in Futures* (1909), *The Polygon* (1911), *Lonesome Like* (1911), and *Spring in Bloomsbury* (1911). He also wrote *The Price of Coal* (1911); *The Oak Settle* (1912); *The Odd Man Out* (1912); *Little Red Shoes* (1912); *The Game* (1913); *The Northerners* (1914); *The Road to Raebury* (1915); *Followers* (1915); *The Hillary's* (1915), with Houghton; *Converts* (1915); *The Clock Goes Round* (1916); *Zack* (1916); *Maid of France* (1918); *The Bantam V.C.* (1919); *Other Times* (1920); *Once a Hero* (1923); *A Marrying Man* and *Mary's John* (1924); *The Happy Hangman* (1925); *What's Bred in the Bone* (1927); *When Did They Meet Again?* (1927); *It's a Gamble* (1928); *Safe among the Pigs* (1929); *A Coincidence* (1930); *Mr. Somebody* (1936), an adaptation of a play by Ferenc Molnár; and *British Passport* (1939).

Hobson's Choice (1915). Comedy in four acts that depicts the maneuverings of Henry Horatio Hobson, owner of a prosperous shoe store, to keep his eldest daughter Maggie an

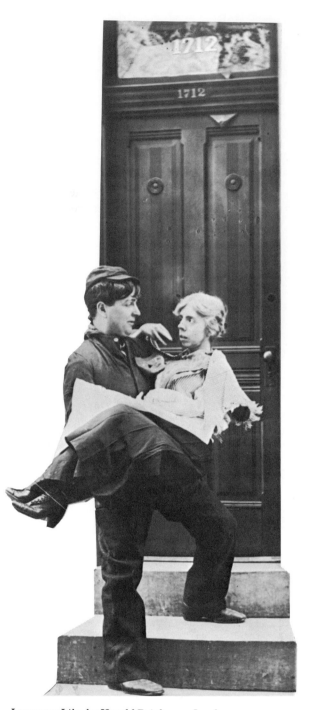

Lonesome Like, by Harold Brighouse, London, 1915. [Theatre Collection, The New York Public Library at Lincoln Center, Astor, Lenox and Tilden Foundations]

old maid. Despite her father, the thirty-year-old Maggie beguiles the shy, ignorant Willie Mossop, Hobson's gifted shoemaker, into marriage, and together they set up a rival shoe shop. By inspiring Willie with her own self-confidence, Maggie turns him into a successful businessman. By another cunning device, she virtually blackmails Hobson into providing dowries for her two younger sisters. An alcoholic, Hobson finally collapses, and Maggie and Willie become partners in his business. Produced New York, Princess Theatre, November 2, 1915; London, Apollo Theatre, June 22, 1916.

BROD, Max (1884–1968). German-language composer, poet, novelist, essayist, theatre director, and dramatist who is best known in the theatre for his dramatization of Kafka's novels *The Castle* (*Der Schloss,* 1953) and *America* (*Amerika,* 1956). An ardent Zionist, Brod lived from 1939 on in Tel Aviv, where he was director of the Habimah Theatre, a company formed in Moscow for the production of plays in Hebrew and permanently resident in Israel since 1931. His own dramatic works include *The Forger* (*Der Fälscher,* 1920), in which love is preferred to politics as a means of achieving happiness on earth; the frequently performed *Adventures of the Good Soldier Schweyk* (*Die Abenteuer des braven Soldaten Schweyk,* 1923), adapted, in collaboration with Hans Reimann, from Jaroslav Hašek's novel; *Lord Byron Is No Longer in Fashion* (*Lord Byron kommt aus der Mode,* 1929); and *Reubeni* (1929), a Hebrew translation and dramatization of Brod's novel *Reubeni, Prince of the Jews* (*Reubeni, Fürst der Juden,* 1925).

Richard Brome
(ca. 1590 — ?1652/53)

Richard Brome, English dramatist, was born probably about 1590. Little is known of his early life, except that he had been Ben Jonson's servant and that he had received aid and encouragement from his master. As early as 1614 Jonson had stated in the Induction to *Bartholomew Fair* (1614) that Brome was "his man." In this occupation Brome began his writing career, and it was as the master's servant and disciple that he was best known to the seventeenth century. Years later, Brome himself referred to *The City Wit* (ca. 1629?) as having been written at a time "when it bore just judgement, and the seal of Ben." The success in 1629 of *The Lovesick Maid* (lost) at Blackfriars firmly established Brome as a dramatist and, incidentally, incurred the temporary pique of Jonson, who had just suffered the failure of his *The New Inn* at the same theatre. *See* JONSON, BEN.

Brome's later life is as shadowy as his beginnings, although his name was periodically connected with several of the contemporary London theatrical companies. Before 1635 he wrote for the Red Bull Theatre, after which he contracted to write exclusively for the Salisbury Court Theatre. After three years the Cockpit Theatre lured him away, and he began to write for that company. He undoubtedly suffered when the theatres were shut down temporarily during the plague of 1636–1637, and he was ruined after the Puritans closed the theatres in 1642. It is believed that he died in 1652 or 1653 after more than a decade of abject poverty.

WORK

Brome, together with James Shirley and Sir William Davenant, represents the last phase of the first great age of English drama, which had begun almost 100 years before in the reign of Elizabeth I and continued through the reigns of James I and Charles I. Brome had a genius for chronicling, in an animated, realistic comic manner, the life of the bourgeois and lower-class society of the Caroline period, much as Shirley's work records the life of the upper classes of the time. Although Brome's work is merely a reflection of the more robust comic efforts of his mentor, Ben Jonson, and has little originality or depth, the best of it is lively and filled with genuine fun. His two best-known plays, *The Jovial Crew* (1641), in which country girls run off to join a band of sportive gypsies, and *The City Wit* (ca. 1629?), a Jonsonian comedy of London life, abound with clever satirical portraits. *See* DAVENANT, WILLIAM; SHIRLEY, JAMES.

A similar comic flair is evident in several of Brome's other works: *The Weeding of the Covent Garden* (1632), known more for its satirical characters than for its complex plot; *The Sparagus Garden* (1635), which draws much of its humor from the notion that asparagus is an aphrodisiac; *A Mad Couple Well Matched* (1637?/39), in which a debauchee succeeds in marrying a rich widow; *The Northern Lass* (1629), a dark comedy in which an innocent country lass, sent to London to be married, wins the man of her choice; and *The Antipodes* (1638), an almost farcical work in which persons of opposing humors are eventually brought together.

The City Wit, or The Woman Wears the Breeches (ca. 1629?). Comedy in which Crasy, a merchant, finding he cannot settle financial accounts by honest means, decides to use trickery to attain his goals. Disguises enable him to terrify Sarpego, a tutor, into paying his debt; to learn from a widow, Tryman, that her wealth is a hoax designed to win her a choice suitor; to swindle cash from Tryman's suitor, Linsy-Wolsy; to fool Mister Sneakup and his wife Pyannet, Crasy's derisory parents-in-law; and to implicate Josina,

Crasy's lecherous wife, in a brawl. After Sarpego has convinced Pyannet, who has matched Tryman with her son Toby and is preparing the wedding, that they should entertain themselves by staging the play of the Prodigal, Crasy reveals his identity and charges the scoundrels with their chicanery. As Sarpego's play continues, Tryman's acting of the whore becomes increasingly bawdy, provoking Pyannet's disgust and a plea that Toby be released from the marriage. Bribed by a gold chain, Tryman acquiesces, but she demands as a final condition that as Pyannet is so tyrannical, she put on breeches. Finally Tryman astonishes the guests by revealing that she is actually Jeremy, Crasy's apprentice, in disguise. All offenses forgiven, Pyannet promises to mend her domineering ways.

The Jovial Crew, or The Merry Beggars

(1641). Comedy poking gentle fun at the gay life of the gypsy. Jovial Squire Oldrents, usually the merriest of men, is brooding because of a prediction that his daughters will be beggars. Depressed by the sudden gloom of the household, his two girls, Meriel and Rachel, prevail upon their sweethearts, Vincent and Hilliard, to join them in a lark. They accompany their father's steward, Springlove, a former beggar, who is about to take his annual vacation with a "jovial crew" of beggars. The four young innocents soon discover the realities of vagabondage. Plagued by lice and hunger, they beg with style but no success. They are joined by Justice Clack's runaway niece Amie, who is eloping with Clack's clerk. By the time the runaways are discovered, however, Amie has fallen in love with Springlove. Learning this, Oldrents discloses that Springlove is his natural son; the squire then gives Springlove an annuity and pardons the runaways, and the play ends happily.

PLAYS

All were first performed in London.

1. *The Northern Lass.* Comedy, 5 acts; verse. Published 1632 (Stationers' Register, Jan. 2, 1632). Produced Globe Theatre (King's Men), July 29, 1629 (entry in notebook of the Master of the Revels).

2. *The City Wit, or The Woman Wears the Breeches.* Comedy, 5 acts; verse. Published 1653. Produced Salisbury Court Theatre (?), ca. 1629?

3. *The Queen's Exchange.* Tragicomedy. Published 1657 (Stationers' Register, Nov. 20, 1656); under title *The Royal Exchange,* 1661. Produced Blackfriars Theatre (King's Men)?, 1631/32?

4. *The Novella.* Comedy, 5 acts; verse. Published 1653. Produced Blackfriars Theatre (King's Men), 1632.

5. *The Weeding of the Covent Garden, or The Middlesex Justice of Peace.* Comedy, 5 acts; verse. Published 1658 (Stationers' Register, Aug. 4, 1640). Produced 1632.

6. (With Thomas Heywood). *The Late Lancashire Witches.* Comedy, 5 acts; verse. Published 1634 (Stationers' Register, Oct. 28, 1634). Produced Globe Theatre (King's Men), 1634.

7. *The Sparagus Garden.* Comedy, 5 acts; verse. Published 1640 (Stationers' Register, Mar. 19, 1640). Produced Salisbury Court Theatre, 1635.

8. *The English Moor, or The Mock Marriage.* Comedy, 5 acts; verse. Published 1658 (Stationers' Register, Aug. 4, 1640). Produced Salisbury Court Theatre (Queen Henrietta's Men)?, 1637.

9. *The Damoiselle, or The New Ordinary.* Comedy, 5 acts; verse. Published 1653. Produced Salisbury Court Theatre (Queen Henrietta's Men), 1637/38?

10. *The Antipodes.* Comedy, 5 acts; verse. Published 1640 (Stationers' Register, Mar. 19, 1640). Produced Salisbury Court Theatre (Queen Henrietta's Men), 1638.

11. *The Queen and Concubine.* Comedy. Published 1659. Produced Salisbury Court Theatre (King's Revels)?, 1635/39?

12. *A Mad Couple Well Matched.* Comedy, 5 acts; verse. Published 1653. (Stationers' Register, June 11, 1659). Produced Cockpit Theatre (Beeston's Boys)?, 1637?/39.

13. *The Lovesick Court, or The Ambitious Politique.* Comedy, 5 acts; verse. Published 1658 (Stationers' Register, Aug. 4, 1640). Produced ca. 1632/40.

14. *The Court Beggar.* Comedy, 5 acts; verse. Published 1653. Produced Cockpit Theatre (Beeston's Boys), 1639/40.

15. *The New Academy, or The New Exchange.* Comedy, 5 acts; verse. Published 1658 (Stationers' Register, Aug. 4, 1640). Produced not later than 1640.

16. *The Jovial Crew, or The Merry Beggars.* Comedy, 5 acts; verse. Published 1652. Produced Cockpit Theatre (Beeston's Boys), 1641.

EDITIONS

Collections.
Dramatic Works, ed. by R. H. Shepherd, 3 vols., London, 1873.
Individual Plays.
The Antipodes. A. Haaker, ed., University of Nebraska Press, Lincoln, 1966; also published in *Representative English Comedies,* ed. by C. M. Gayley, vol. III, Macmillan, New York, 1903–1936; *Six Caroline Plays,* ed. by A. S. Knowland, Oxford, London, 1962.
A Jovial Crew. A. Haaker, ed., University of Nebraska Press, Lincoln, 1968; also published in *Shakespeare and His Fellow Dramatists,* ed. by E. H. C. Oliphant, vol. 2, Prentice-Hall, 1929; *Elizabethan Dramatists Other than Shakespeare,* ed. by E. H. C. Oliphant, Prentice-Hall, New York, 1931.
A Mad Couple Well Matched. Published in *Early Seventeenth Century Plays, 1600–1642,* ed. by H. R. Walley and J. H. Wilson, Harcourt, Brace, New York, 1930; *Six Caroline Plays,* ed. by A. S. Knowland, Oxford, London, 1962.

CRITICISM

H. F. Allen, *A Study of the Comedies of Richard Brome, Especially as Representative of Dramatic Decadence,* Ann Arbor, Mich., 1912; C. E. Andrews, *Richard Brome: A Study of His Life and Works,* New Haven, Conn., 1913; R. J. Kaufmann, *Richard Brome: Caroline Playwright,* New York and London, 1961.

BRONNEN, Arnolt (1895–1959). Austrian dramatist, son of the Austrian-Jewish dramatist Ferdinand Bronner (who wrote under the pseudonym Franz Adamus). Bronnen lived in Berlin and was acclaimed as an exponent of the new generation's outlook. He began as an extreme expressionist and then turned to stark realism, though signs of the explosive diction and crude dramatic effects characteristic of expressionism run through all his works. In 1933 he threw in his lot with the Nazi movement, pronouncing himself the illegitimate son of an Aryan, and emerged from the war a Communist. *See* EXPRESSIONISM; REALISM.

Bronnen's first play, *The Birth of Youth* (*Die Geburt der Jugend;* wr. 1914, prod. 1922), in which roving bands of boys and girls on horseback trample the older generation to dust, was followed by his greatest successes: *Parricide* (*Vatermord;* wr. 1915, prod. 1920); *The Excesses* (*Die Exzesse,* 1923), a farce rising to a sexual paroxysm of unbelievable brutality; *Anarchy in Sillian* (*Anarchie in Sillian,* 1924), which features a "superman" engineer; and *Catalaunian Battle* (*Katalaunische Schlacht,* 1924), mingling crude eroticism with the idea of the war's continuation after its end. *The Rhine Rebels* (*Rheinische Rebellen,* 1925) and the comedy *Reparations* (*Reparationen,* 1926) contain unmistakable pre-Nazi references to the "great German nation." After a confused one-man play called *Journey to the East Pole* (*Ostpolzug,* 1926), Bronnen wrote *Michael Kohlhaas* (1929), *Sunny Hill* (*Sonnenberg,* 1934), *N* (1938; *N* stands for Napoleon), *Gloriana* (1941), *Kette Kolin* (1950), *Kaprun* (1955), and *The Youngest Night* (*Die jüngste Nacht*), a comedy about Americans.

BROWNING, Robert (1812–1889). English poet and playwright. Primarily a lyricist, Browning turned to the stage through the encouragement he received from the actor William Charles Macready (1793–1873), who had become manager of Covent Garden in 1837. That year Macready produced Browning's

Robert Browning. [Library of Congress]

first play, *Strafford,* but it ran for only four nights. The very qualities that were to make Browning's dramatic monologues memorable—his subtle understanding of complex psyches, his lyricism, and the rhetorical quality of his works—marred his productions for the stage. All of them, those written for production and those written as closet dramas, are in effect dramatic lyrics and lack dramatic action. *See* CLOSET DRAMA.

Strafford was followed by the poetic *Pippa Passes* (pub. 1841); *King Victor and King Charles* (pub. 1842), considered his best play; *The Return of the Druses* (pub. 1843); *A Blot in the 'Scutcheon* (1843); *Colombe's Birthday* (pub. 1844, prod. 1853); *Luria* (pub. 1846); *A Soul's Tragedy* (pub. 1846); and *In a Balcony* (pub. 1855). Despite Browning's intention to revitalize the theatre, an interest and purpose shared by many of the poets of the age, only three of his plays reached the stage.

Ferdinand Bruckner
(1891 — 1958)

Ferdinand Bruckner, Austrian dramatist, was born Theodor Tagger in Vienna on August 26, 1891, to an Austrian industrialist and a Frenchwoman. After studying German language and literature in Vienna and music and history in Paris and Berlin, he made an early debut in the literary world with poetry, prose, and articles on music and sociology. In 1917 he founded the avant-garde magazine *Marsyas.* He and his wife, Bettine Neuer, moved in 1923 to Berlin, where he established the Renaissancetheater, serving as its manager and stage director until 1929. The premiere of his play *The Malady of Youth* (*Krankheit der Jugend*), written in 1924 under the pseudonym Bruckner, was an enormous success.

With Hitler's rise to power in 1933, Bruckner left for Austria; he lived briefly in France and in 1936 went to the United States. After a short time in Hollywood, he moved to New York, where he taught European literature at New York University. Eventually he became an American citizen. Meanwhile, he continued his literary activities, writing plays, adapting plays (among them Arthur Miller's *Death of a Salesman*) for the Austrian stage, and translating American Negro spirituals into German. He returned to Europe in 1951 and was appointed director of the Schiller-und-Schlosspark-Theater in West Berlin, where he died on December 5, 1958.

Ferdinand Bruckner. [Theatre Collection, The New York Public Library at Lincoln Center, Astor, Lenox and Tilden Foundations]

WORK

Always a critical observer of contemporary society and its ills, Bruckner dealt with many subjects and experimented with several different forms in his twenty-one plays. His early dramas focus on the anarchy in Europe following World War I, particularly the personal problems of young people and the collapse of middle-class values. Although these works of the 1920s and early 1930s show a degree of psychological insight and an expressionistic style, Bruckner in those days was closest to the Neue Sachlichkeit ("new reality" or "new matter-of-factness") school of functional drama, a naturalistic movement that depicted "things as they are." After 1933, however, his method of presentation became more involved and subtle, and he often employed historical drama as a means of criticizing current situations. Also, from then on elements of epic theatre emerged in his work that brought him to the creation of an existential kind of tragedy. These plays of the 1950s, less nihilistic and didactic than his earlier works, are as near as Bruckner came to realizing his aim of a "permanent tragic substance," that is, the expression of the essence of drama, which he described in 1955 as the internal conflict of man as an individual and as a member of the community. Bruckner termed this conflict insoluble, and he therefore offered no solutions in his plays. *See* EPIC THEATRE.

The most notable of his plays are two early works, *The Malady of Youth* (1926) and *The Criminals* (*Die Verbrecher*, 1928), which explore sexual problems and questions of personal ethics; the historical drama *Elizabeth of England* (*Elisabeth von England*, 1930), a pessimistic work distinguished for its skillful use of a divided stage; and *The Races* (*Die Rassen*, 1933), about racial persecution among German students. Other important and representative plays are *Napoleon the First* (*Napoleon der Erste*, 1937) and *Heroic Comedy* (*Heroische Komödie;* wr. 1942, prod. 1946), historical dramas about Napoleon through which Bruckner criticizes modern dictators; the two-part tragedy *Simon Bolivar* (Part I, wr. 1942, prod. 1957; Part II, prod. 1945), in which he weighs democracy and dictatorship; *The Creature* (*Die Kreatur,* 1930), a comic treatment of middle-class ethics and adult sex dilemmas; and the later existential tragedies *Pyrrhus and Andromache* (*Pyrrhus und Andromache,* 1952) and *The Earthen Cart* (*Das irdene Wägelchen, 1957*).

The Malady of Youth (*Krankheit der Jugend,* 1926). Drama about a group of students who, in their search for the meaning of life and for regeneration, plunge into sexual experimentation and corruption. Sexually jaded Desirée, vital and humane Marie, and typically middle-class Irma-Irene become entangled with the brutal and dynamic Freder, the writer Petrell, and the mature Alt. Freder seduces all three girls and also guides the plain-looking maid Lucy into theft and prostitution. Finally, Desirée poisons herself, while Freder proposes to Marie, whom he then rapes and murders.

The Criminals (*Die Verbrecher,* 1928). Drama depicting both overt and concealed "criminals" who go unpunished while innocent people suffer. In a private house in Berlin, the cook Ernestine Puschek, in love with the unemployed waiter Tunichtgut, craves children but is unable to have any. She takes care of the pregnant secretary Miss Nagerle, whose child she hopes to adopt. In a fit of jealousy Ernestine strangles her rival for Tunichtgut's affections, the tavern keeper Kudelka, and contrives to have Tunichtgut accused of the crime. In a court in which all cases end in miscarriages of justice, he is sentenced to death. The courts of justice are "totally removed from life," says Kummerer, the chorus and *raisonneur* of the play.

Elizabeth of England (*Elisabeth von England,* 1930). Historical drama in twelve scenes, dealing with the relationship of Elizabeth to the young Earl of Essex and to King Philip II of Spain. Essex, proud and ambitious, courts the middle-aged Elizabeth in the hope of gaining control over her. When this fails, he plots her overthrow. Arrested while attempting to take her prisoner, he is tried and executed. Philip is portrayed as a religious bigot tormented by the presence of a Protestant on the English throne. He is determined to wage war with England, against the advice of his ministers, while Elizabeth is urged, against her will, to declare war on Spain. Philip launches his Armada against England, and the news of its destruction causes his death.

The Races (*Die Rassen,* 1933). Tragedy set in a small German university town immediately before and after Hitler's take-over. Karlanner, a young medical student in love with Helene, a Jewess, is urged by his friend Tessow to join the Nazi party. Although repelled intellectually by the party, Karlanner is attracted to it emotionally, and he joins. After Hitler's election, the persecution of the Jews begins; Karlanner at first takes part but soon becomes disenchanted. He is sent to arrest Helene but instead warns her to leave the country, thus becoming a traitor to the party. He waits until she is safely gone and then allows himself to be arrested. The play ends as Karlanner is led off to be executed for having "betrayed" Germany.

PLAYS

1. *Annette.* Comedy. Published 1920. Produced Vienna, Kammerspiele, Dec. 16, 1920.

2. *Harry oder die Komödie der Untergang der Welt* (*Harry or The Comedy of the World's Downfall*). Comedy. Published 1920. Produced Halle, Stadttheater, Dec. 23, 1920.

3. *Kapitän Christoph* (*Captain Christopher*). Play. Written 1921.

4. *Te Deum.* Play, 1 act. Produced Berlin, Neues Theater, Feb. 1, 1922.

5. *Krankheit der Jugend** (*The Malady of Youth*). Play, 3 acts. Written 1924. Published 1928. Produced Breslau, Lobetheater, and Hamburg, Kammerspiele, Oct. 16, 1926.

6. *Die Verbrecher** (*The Criminals*). Play, 3 acts. Written 1928. Published 1928. Produced Berlin, Deutsches Theater, Oct. 23, 1928.

7. *Die Kreatur* (*The Creature*). Play, 3 acts. Published 1929. Produced Berlin, Komödie, Mar. 10, 1930.

8. *Elisabeth von England* (*Elizabeth of England*). Historical drama, 5 acts. Published 1930. Produced Berlin, Deutsches Theater, and Bremen, Hamburg, and Leipzig, Nov. 1, 1930.

9. (Adaptation). *Timon.* Tragedy. Written 1931. Published 1932. Produced Vienna, Burgtheater, Jan. 23, 1931. Based on Shakespeare's *Timon of Athens.* New versions: 1948, 1956.

10. (Adaptation). *Die Marquise von O.* (*The Marchioness of O.*). Play. Published 1933. Produced Darmstadt, Feb. 25, 1933. Based on the novella by Heinrich von Kleist.

11. *Die Rassen** (*The Races*). Play, 3 acts. Written 1933. Published 1933. Produced Zurich, Schauspielhaus, Nov. 30, 1933.

12. *Napoleon der Erste** (*Napoleon the First*). Comedy, 3 acts. Written 1935. Published 1936. Produced Prague, Národní Divadlo, Mar. 9, 1937.

13. *Heroische Komödie* (*Heroic Comedy*). Comedy, 3 acts. Written 1942. Published 1948. Produced Vienna, Volkstheater, 1946.

14. *Denn seine Zeit ist kurz* (*For His Time Is Short*). Play. Written 1942. Published 1945. Produced Mexico City, Sept. 30, 1943.

15. *Simon Bolivar*.* Historical drama, 2 parts. Part I: *Der Kampf mit dem Engel* (*The Fight with the Angel*). Written 1942. Published 1957. Produced Brunswick, Sept. 4, 1957. Part II: *Der Kampf mit dem Drachen* (*The Fight with the Dragon*). Published 1945. Produced Dresden, Staatstheater, 1945.

16. *Die Befreiten* (*The Liberated*). Documentary discussion play. Written 1944. Produced Zurich, Schauspielhaus, Sept. 13, 1945.

17. *Fährten* (*Tracks*). Play. Written 1947. Published 1948. Produced Vienna, Burgtheater, May 8, 1948.

18. *Pyrrhus und Andromache* (*Pyrrhus and Andromache*). Tragedy. Written 1951. Published 1956. Produced Zurich, Schauspielhaus, Feb. 16, 1952.

19. *Früchte des Nichts* (*Fruits of Nothingness*). Play. Produced Mannheim, National Theater, Apr. 19, 1952.

20. *Der Tod einer Puppe* (*The Death of a Doll*). Modern tragedy. Published 1957. Produced Bochum, Oct. 15, 1956.

21. (Adaptation). *Das irdene Wägelchen* (*The Earthen Cart*). Play. Written 1956. Produced Mannheim, Oct. 29, 1957. Based on the Sanskrit play *Mṛcchakaṭikā* (*The Little Clay Cart*), by King Shūdraka.

EDITIONS

Collections.
Gesammelte Werke, 3 vols., Berlin, 1948.
Individual Plays.
Elizabeth of England. A. Dukes, tr., London, 1931.
The Races. R. Langner, tr., New York, 1934.

CRITICISM

E. Rieder-Laska, *Ferdinand Bruckner* (dissertation), Vienna, 1949.

BRUEYS, David-Augustin de (b. Aix, 1640; d. Montpellier, November 25, 1723). French dramatist best known for the plays he wrote in collaboration with Jean Palaprat. Their most successful work, *The Grumbler* (*Le grondeur,* 1691), was written primarily by Brueys and reveals his considerable talent for dramatic structure. The plays Brueys wrote alone were not nearly so successful; nevertheless, *The Empiricists* (*Les empiriques,* 1697) is an entertaining farce about medical quacks, and *Lawyer Patelin* (*L'avocat Patelin,* 1706)— though inferior to its medieval source, *The Farce of Master Pathelin*—has charm and was for many years in the repertory of the Comédie-Française. His other plays are *Important Man at Court* (*L'important de cour,* 1693), *The Stubborn Man* (*L'opiniâtre,* 1722), and *Gabinie* (1699), an inferior tragedy.

For plays written in collaboration, *see* PALAPRAT, JEAN. *See also* FARCE OF MASTER PATHELIN, THE.

The Grumbler (*Le grondeur,* 1691). Comedy by Brueys and Palaprat in which Grichard, a querulous old physician, is about to marry his daughter Hortense to a young gentleman named Mondor, and his son Térignan to Clarice, daughter of Saint-Alvar. Clarice, in order to win favor with her future father-in-law, pretends to be as severe a grouch as he and finds, to her horror, that he has decided to marry her himself. With the help of Lolive, a clever valet whom Grichard has dismissed, the young people begin to play on the old man's weaknesses. When Clarice pretends to be extravagant, the old man breaks the engagement immediately. Finally, he is duped into offering to sail to Madagascar, but he backs down at the last minute. Faced with a breach-of-promise suit and a sea captain who is about to press him into service, Grichard substitutes Térignan for himself in the marriage contract, and the captain (really Mondor) is given the hand of Hortense. Produced Paris, Comédie-Française, February 3, 1691.

BRUNO, Giordano (b. Nola, 1548; d. Rome, February 17, 1600). Italian philosopher whose prolific writings include only one play, the acerbic comedy, *The Candle Bearer* (*Il candelaio*, 1582), which is one of the most significant dramatic works of the sixteenth century. Bruno, a Dominican monk, possessed a keen, inquiring mind and a stubborn will that soon brought him into conflict with the church. He fled from Naples about 1567 to avoid persecution. After traveling widely in Italy and in Catholic and Protestant Europe, where he was the object of constant notoriety, he appeared in Venice about 1592 and was soon arrested as a heretic by the Inquisition. After seven years of imprisonment, he was excommunicated and burned at the stake.

The Candle Bearer (*Il candelaio*, 1582). Satirical comedy in five acts that recounts the adventures of Bonifacio, a simpleton, who lusts after Vittoria, a courtesan; Bartolomeo, a miser who wishes to practice alchemy; and Manfurio, a pedant who believes himself to be a great scholar. A rendezvous with Vittoria, arranged by Bonifacio with the aid of the dishonest necromancer Scaramurè, is kept instead by his wife Carubina, who vindicates herself by seducing her own husband. Bartolomeo gives 600 scudi to the alchemist Cericio but gets nothing in return, while his wife Martha, bored with her absent and senile spouse, takes young Barro as her lover. Manfurio is ridiculed by the clever Ottaviano, whom he had sought to impress with his magniloquence. The three fools are finally arrested by practical jokers disguised as police, are beaten soundly, and presumably return home sadder if not wiser than they began.

Georg Büchner
(1813 — 1837)

Georg Büchner, German playwright and physician, was born on October 17, 1813, in Goddelau, near Darmstadt. The father, who wanted young Büchner to follow him in a medical career, encouraged his son's interest in science but disparaged his literary inclinations. After completing his studies at the Darmstadt Gymnasium, Büchner began studying medicine in Strasbourg in 1831. He moved to the University of Giessen in 1833 and there broadened his field of study to include philosophy and history. In 1834 he became engaged to Minna Jaegle, the daughter of a parson in whose house he had lived during his stay at Strasbourg.

At Giessen, Büchner's interest in politics quickened under the influence of the Junge Deutschland (Young Germany) movement, of which the playwright Karl Gutzkow, one of Büchner's few contemporary admirers, was an adherent. Most of the adherents of the movement put their faith in the educated classes; Büchner, however, believed that Germany's regeneration would come from the peasants. In 1834 he founded a secret club, the Gesellschaft der Menschenrechte (Society for the Rights of Man), which aimed at revolutionary change in the Grand Duchy of Hesse. In a passionate and biting pamphlet, *The Hessian Courier* (*Der hessische Landbote*, 1834), he urged the peasants to use force to secure their rights. When the society was unmasked, Büchner was forced to flee Giessen and returned home. There, under the constant threat of arrest, he worked feverishly to

Giordano Bruno.
[Italian Cultural Institute]

complete his first play, *Danton's Death* (*Dantons Tod;* wr. 1835, prod. 1902). *See* GUTZKOW, KARL FERDINAND; JUNGE DEUTSCHLAND.

In 1835 Büchner was to receive a doctorate in the natural sciences from the University of Zurich and to obtain an academic position there. Because of political restrictions on his travel, he was awarded his first degree *in absentia* in September, 1836. Once an advocate of force as the only means of achieving social justice, he now asserted that revolutionary tactics were useless, for he recognized that at that particular time revolutionary activity was in vain. He concentrated instead on *Lenz* (wr. 1835), a work based on the life of the dramatist Jakob Lenz (1751–1792), and translated two of Hugo's plays, *Mary Tudor* and *Lucretia Borgia*. One of the plays Büchner wrote at this time, *Pietro Aretino,* was destroyed by his fiancée, who thought it indecent. *See* HUGO, VICTOR; LENZ, JAKOB.

In October, 1836, Büchner was allowed to enter Switzerland and was appointed lecturer in comparative anatomy at the University of Zurich, where he taught a course on the nervous system of the brain. There he completed his comedy *Leonce and Lena* (*Leonce und Lena;* wr. 1836, prod., 1885) and worked on his tragedy *Woyzeck* (wr. 1836, prod. 1913). His pessimism and determinism unabated, Büchner died of typhoid fever in Zurich on February 19, 1837, at the age of twenty-three.

WORK

Three plays written hurriedly in 1835 and 1836 established Büchner as one of the great seminal figures of world drama. Although his immediate impact was negligible, some fifty years after his death his work began to influence German drama. With the years both his influence and his reputation have grown to the point where his work is considered central to the development of modern drama. His influence, for example, can be felt in such figures of German drama as Hauptmann and Brecht. *See* BRECHT, BERTOLT; HAUPTMANN, GERHART.

His plays are characterized by an extensive use of historical documents. Büchner felt that the greatest task of the dramatic poet "is to come as close as possible to history as it actually was." He admired Goethe and Shakespeare but not Schiller, for Schiller wanted to present the world as it ought to be, not as it is.

Many of the trends that were to appear in Western drama were anticipated in his writing: naturalism, expressionism, surrealism, epic theatre, theatre of the absurd, and documentary theatre (*see* EPIC THEATRE; EXPRESSIONISM; THEATRE OF THE ABSURD). Moreover, the plays embody many of the themes that

Georg Büchner; lithograph by A. Hoffmann. [Theater-Museum, Munich]

were to recur in the drama of the twentieth century: man's essential loneliness, his inability to communicate, his helplessness before the events of history and the conditions of society, and the terror and foolishness of a world without God.

Danton's Death (wr. 1835, prod. 1902), Büchner's first play and often called the finest first play ever written, illustrates the theme of man's lack of free will. Although Büchner was influenced by Shakespeare's histories and by German plays of the *Sturm und Drang* period and although he also bor-

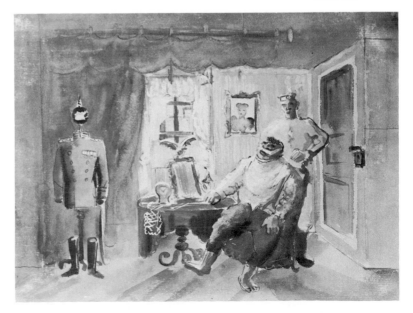

Sketch of a scene from *Woyzeck*, Düsseldorf, 1930. [Theater-Museum, Munich]

Two productions of *Woyzeck*: (left) Frankfurt am Main, Städtische Bühnen; (right) Hamburg, Hamburgische Staatsoper, 1953.

rowed extensively from Thiers's *History of the French Revolution,* he expressed in *Danton's Death* his own fatalistic determinism and introspection in somberly melodious language. The brief scenes are in turn realistic, lyrical, grotesque, and parodistic. The dialogue shifts from aphoristic brevity to broad rhetoric. *See* STURM UND DRANG.

Büchner said in *The Hessian Courier* that "the life of an aristocrat is a long Sunday." In *Leonce and Lena* (wr. 1836, prod. 1885), a severe attack on most of the injustices and stupidities prevalent in the Germany of his time, he portrayed royalty as self-indulgent and ignorant of the reality of life. His Italian titles for the kingdoms of Prince Leonce and Princess Lena—Popo and Pipi—are sarcastically aimed at producing a childish and degrading image of royalty. The ideal of the philosopher-king is satirized in the person of King Peter. As a ruler, Peter is oblivious of the people and concerned only with pomp. However, when Prince Leonce becomes king, Peter decides to devote his old age to "uninterrupted thought" in solitude. Alfred de Musset's *Fantasio* (wr. 1833) and Clemens Brentano's *Ponce de Leon* (1804) are the play's main influences. *Leonce and Lena,* which is also greatly indebted to Shake-spearean drama, parodies German idealistic and romantic faith in progress and is infused with the bitter fatalism of history. *See* MUSSET, ALFRED DE.

In *Woyzeck* (wr. 1836, prod. 1913), which was influenced by Lenz's play *The Soldiers* (*Die Soldaten,* wr. 1775), Büchner chose as his protagonist a downtrodden member of the lower classes, a congenital victim of the immutability and pervasive influence of a hostile environment. To achieve his effect, Büchner employed cold naturalistic detail to underscore the plight of his central character. His method was to use abrupt, densely atmospheric autonomous scenes, resembling ballad stanzas, in order to achieve a cumulative impact. In 1920 the composer Alban Berg wrote an opera version of the play, entitled *Wozzeck.*

Büchner has been criticized for haste, ambiguity, and loose construction. His plays are devoid of the traditional dramatic paraphernalia; there is no clash between strong personalities, no gradual unfolding of an idea. His method, particularly in *Danton's Death* and *Woyzeck,* was to place his central figure in a series of loosely connected scenes that focus on the character's state of mind or pinpoint his relation to the world around him.

Danton's Death (*Dantons Tod;* wr. 1835, prod. 1902). Chronicle play of the French Revolution. Its many episodes contrast the intrigues of the National Convention's leaders with philosophic and lyrical interludes. Danton and Robespierre, the two protagonists of the revolution, have drifted apart. Realizing that the revolution has not achieved its goals and that the iron laws of history cannot be changed, Danton sinks into fatalism and gives way to sensuous pleasures. The dogmatic and merciless Robespierre, meanwhile, plans another bloodbath of "enemies of the revolution." Danton senses the danger to himself but still believes that his contribu-tions to the revolutionary cause and his popularity will protect him. He tells Robes-pierre that the executions must stop and that too many innocent people have already died. Robespierre retorts that virtue must reign by fear. After this abortive discussion with Danton, Robespierre declares that he must be liquidated.

Danton's friends advise him to act quickly, but he does nothing and is eventually arrest-ed at night in his home. Legendre defends Danton before the National Convention, but Robespierre rallies the deputies to his side. Danton's eloquent self-defense, however, arouses the spectators. General Dillon plots to

A French production of *Dantons Tod*, Théâtre National Populaire, Paris. [French Cultural Services]

Lili Darvas in a German production of *Dantons Tod.* [Theater-Museum, Munich]

free Danton and his friends from jail, but the plot is discovered and the egregious deputy Saint-Just uses it to incriminate Danton. The people in the mob in front of the Palais de Justice are not convinced of their idol's guilt, although they are swayed by the contrast between Danton's luxurious style of living and Robespierre's asceticism. Danton's wife Julie sends him a lock of her hair with assurances that he will not die alone. His last night in prison among his friends is spent in trying to console his comrade Desmoulins, distracted with grief about his wife Lucille, who presently appears outside the window and goes insane. As the prisoners are led to their execution, Julie takes poison. On the scaffold Danton and his friends exchange farewells.

Leonce and Lena (*Leonce und Lena*; wr. 1836, prod. 1885). Büchner's only comedy, a satire of the vapid and uncommitted life of the aristocracy. Prince Leonce of the kingdom of Popo leads an idle and meaningless life, unable to see any purpose in his present role as prince or his future role as king. Detached from reality, he attributes all human activity to the boredom that motivates his own life. Similarly, Princess Lena of the kingdom of Pipi, betrothed to Leonce, whom she has never seen, lives in an unreal world of romantic fantasy. Both of them, spoiled and childlike, are opposed to the arranged marriage, which is incompatible with their romantic image of falling in love. Both decide to run away, Leonce to Italy in search of adventure and the ideal woman, "infinitely beautiful and infinitely unintellectual," and Lena in search of a wandering prince who can satisfy

her image of a romantic lover. While traveling, they meet at an inn and, each unaware of the other's identity, fall in love. The royal couple decide to wed, and it is only after the marriage that they learn each other's true identity. Disappointed to find that they have realized the political wedding they sought to avoid, they decide to romanticize at least their reign by leading an even more idyllic and unreal life, while reducing the role of the populace to that of puppets existing only for the royal pleasure.

Woyzeck (wr. 1836, prod. 1913). Play based on the case of Johann Christian Woyzeck, a soldier who murdered his mistress in a jealous rage, and the ensuing medical controversy as to whether or not he was insane. There is no definitive text of the play, as Büchner failed to number his scenes or organize them into acts. The central character is depicted as a man who is basically kind and good-hearted but is surrounded by tormentors. His Captain and the Doctor provoke him physically and psychologically, while his mistress Marie, by having an affair with a handsome Drum Major, inflames his jealousy and his sense of sin. Woyzeck is deeply religious, and Marie's affair reveals to him not only her sin but his own and that of the world. Büchner presents the tragic image of a man trapped by his environment and by the strength of his vision.

The events of the play have no firm chronological sequence but are actually a series of related incidents. Woyzeck and Marie go to a carnival; Woyzeck wanders in the fields, talks with his friend Andres, and watches Marie and the Drum Major dance at an inn, while all the time his emotions build toward Marie's murder and his own death, which Büchner purposely couches in ambiguous terms. We cannot be certain whether the death is suicide, an accident, or an act of God.

PLAYS

1. *Dantons Tod** (*Danton's Death*). Drama, 3 acts. Written 1835. Published 1835 (abridged version), 1850 (complete version, in *Nachgelassene Schriften,* ed. by Ludwig Büchner). Produced Berlin, Belle-Alliance Theater, Jan. 5, 1902.

2. *Leonce und Lena** (*Leonce and Lena*). Comedy, 3 acts. Written 1836. Published 1838 (abridged version), 1850 (complete version). Produced Biederstein, near Munich, Intimes Theater, May 31, 1885.

3. *Woyzeck**. Drama (incomplete), 1 long act. Written 1836. Published 1879. Produced Munich, Residenztheater, Nov. 8, 1913.

EDITIONS

Collections.
Gesammelte Schriften, ed. by P. Landau, 2 vols., Berlin, 1909; *Sämtliche Werke und Briefe,* ed. by F. Bergemann, Leipzig, 1922; *Plays,* tr. by G. Dunlop, London, 1927; *Gesammelte Werke,* ed. by C. Seelig, Zurich, 1944; *Werke und Briefe,* Stuttgart, 1948; *Werke und Briefe,* ed. by F. Bergemann, Wiesbaden, 1958; *Complete Plays and*

Prose, tr. by C. R. Mueller, New York, 1963; *Sämtliche Werke*, ed. by H. J. Meinerts, Gütersloh, 1963.

Individual Plays.

Danton's Death. Published in *From the Modern Repertoire*, ed. by E. R. Bentley and tr. by S. Spender and G. Rees, ser. 1, Bloomington, Ind., 1949; *A Treasury of the Theatre*, ed. by J. Gassner and tr. by S. Spender and G. Rees, rev. ed., vol. 1, New York, 1951; *The Modern Theatre*, ed. by E. R. Bentley and tr. by J. Holmstrom, vol. 5, Garden City, N.Y., 1955–1960; *Classical German Drama*, ed. and tr. by T. H. Lustig, New York, 1963.

Leonce and Lena. Published in *From the Modern Repertoire*, ed. and tr. by E. R. Bentley, ser. 3, Bloomington, Ind., 1956.

Woyzeck. Published in *The Modern Theatre*, ed. by E. R. Bentley and tr. by T. Hoffman, vol. 1, Garden City, N.Y., 1955–1960.

CRITICISM

M. Zobel von Zobeltitz, *Georg Büchner: Sein Leben und sein Schaffen*, Berlin, 1915; H. Mayer, *Georg Büchner und seine Zeit*, Wiesbaden, 1946; E. Diehm, *Georg Büchners Leben und Werk*, Heidelberg, 1948; K. Viëtor, *Georg Büchner: Politik, Dichtung, Wissenschaft*, Bern, 1949; A. H. J. Knight, *Georg Büchner*, Oxford, 1951; J. Auger-Duvignaud, *Georg Büchner, dramaturge*, Paris, 1954; G. Baumann, *George Büchner: Die dramatische Ausdruckswelt*, Göttingen, 1961; H. Lindenberger, *Georg Büchner*, Carbondale, Ill., 1964.

BUCKINGHAM, 2d Duke of. *See* VILLIERS, GEORGE.

Antonio Buero Vallejo
(1916 –   )

Antonio Buero Vallejo, Spanish painter and dramatist, was born on September 9, 1916, in Guadalajara. At an early age the boy showed an interest in painting, which his father, a military engineer, encouraged by sending him to study at the Academy of Fine Arts following his graduation from secondary school. However, his education was interrupted in 1936 by the outbreak of the Spanish Civil War, and Buero Vallejo left the academy to serve as a medical aide on the Loyalist side. Because of his political activity (*adhesión a la rebelión*), he was arrested by the Franco government after the war; his imprisonment, after commutation of a death sentence, lasted until 1946.

Although he continued to paint, he turned to writing as a career, and his importance as a dramatist was established in 1949 with *Story of a Staircase* (*Historia de una escalera*, wr. 1947), for which the municipality of Madrid awarded him the Lope de Vega Prize. Also in 1949, he received the Quintero Prize for his one-act play *Words in the Sand* (*Palabras en la arena*). The following year he experienced another triumph on the stage with *In the Burning Darkness* (*En la ardiente oscuridad*,

Antonio Buero Vallejo. [New York Public Library]

wr. 1946). The serious and introspective plot of *The Dream Weaver* (*La tejedora de sueños*), produced in 1952, failed to arouse the interest of critics and public alike.

Buero Vallejo's popularity was revived in 1953 with the production of *Daybreak* (*Madrugada*). In 1956 he was awarded the María Rolland Prize for his play *Today Is a Holiday* (*Hoy es fiesta*). Despite his ambivalent attitude toward the Franco government, his plays have continued to win considerable critical acclaim in Spain. In 1962 he received a prize for his dramatic parable *The Concert on St. Ovid's Day* (*El concierto de San Ovidio*).

WORK

Buero Vallejo is generally recognized as one of the most important social dramatists of the contemporary Spanish theatre. He has renewed the concept of tragedy, giving it a simplicity and a realism relevant to the modern world. His work focuses upon the essential and tragic realities of human life and is particularly effective in its portrayal of the poor and weak. In his hands contemporary Spanish drama has turned from banal sentimentality toward a sober, universal expression of man's pain. His method, called transcendental realism, stresses the complexity of human relations, often in a poetically symbolic context. Aware of the delicate interaction of reality and illusion, he avoids facile solutions and dogmatic conclusions. While not strictly pessimistic, his works are permeated by the anxiety and disillusionment of everyday life, relieved only by a vague hope for the future and belief in the redemptive power of love.

His best-known plays are *Story of a Staircase* (1949), a drama depicting the endless misery and futile hopes of the poor in Madrid; *In the Burning Darkness* (wr. 1946, prod. 1950), which deals with psychological tensions among the blind; and *The Dream Weaver*

(1952), a modern version of the legend of Ulysses and Penelope that universalizes the loneliness and frustration of the heroine.

Among his other plays are *Today Is a Holiday* (1956), which depicts the misery and futile sacrifice involved in resisting the "system"; *The Cards Face Down* (*Las cartas boca abajo*, 1957), which portrays the mendacity of middle-class Madrid; *Daybreak* (1953), a psychological drama concerning the trials of a sincere young lover in a hypocritical world; *A Dreamer for the People* (*Un soñador para un pueblo*, 1958), about an aristocrat's failure to initiate reforms—an ambiguous evocation of the past designed to raise questions about the present; *Words in the Sand* (1949), a one-act dramatic comedy dealing with the theme of adultery; *Irene, or The Treasure* (*Irene, o El tesoro*, 1954), a subtle fusion of humor and melancholy which questions the desirability of escaping a sordid fate through insanity; *The Ladies-in-waiting* (*Las meninas*, 1960), depicting Velázquez as a man of spirit subjected by society to enormous pressure; and *The Concert on St. Ovid's Day* (1962), a blind man's rebellion against the false charity of society.

In the Burning Darkness (*En la ardiente oscuridad;* wr. 1946, prod. 1950). Drama of Ignacio, who has been blind since birth and is embittered by his handicap. When he goes to a school for the blind, his unhappy spirit disrupts the tranquillity of the school and disturbs the other students with the exception of a girl named Juana. Carlos, Juana's sweetheart, becomes jealous of Ignacio and asks him to leave the school. Ignacio refuses, and Carlos kills him. With Ignacio's death, which is generally believed to have been accidental, tranquillity returns. Only Doña Pepita, wife of the director, knows the truth, having seen Carlos kill Ignacio. Now she sees Carlos nurturing the same bitterness about his blindness that had tormented Ignacio.

Story of a Staircase (*Historia de una escalera*, 1949). Drama about the lives of poor families in a tenement house in Madrid over the course of thirty years. As the play opens, Fernando, Elvira, and Carmina are dreaming of their plans for the future. Both girls love Fernando, who, although he loves Carmina, later marries Elvira, while Carmina marries Urbano. Elvira and Fernando have a son, Fernandito; Carmina and Urbano, a daughter. Both marriages are unhappy, and the friends drift far apart. As the children grow up, they fall in love and begin to entertain the same optimistic but futile dreams that their parents shared. As the play ends, the cycle is beginning to repeat itself.

The Dream Weaver (*La tejedora de sueños,* 1952). Three-act drama that presents the legend of Ulysses and Penelope in modern terms. Penelope, angry that Helen of Troy's frivolity has provoked a war which has deprived her and so many other wives of their husbands, decides to avenge herself on her suitors. As she weaves by day and unravels her work by night, she dreams of her gentle suitor Amphion, who truly loves her in contrast with the other, false suitors who are despoiling Ulysses' kingdom. Ulysses returns in disguise to spy upon Penelope, and he discovers her method of putting off the suitors. To resolve matters, Ulysses suggests a contest in which the suitors will attempt to draw the bow that none but he can draw. Penelope secretly offers to help Amphion, but despite his love he nobly declines. Ulysses kills the suitors after they fail the test and then reveals his identity. As the chorus chants of her loyalty, Penelope turns on her husband, condemning Ulysses for abandoning her and then returning surreptitiously; and she prays that men will someday behave, as Amphion had, with compassion and patience.

PLAYS

1. *En la ardiente oscuridad** (*In the Burning Darkness*). Drama, 3 acts. Written 1946. Published 1951. Produced Madrid, Teatro Nacional María Guerrero, Dec. 1, 1950.

2. *Historia de una escalera** (*Story of a Staircase*). Drama, 3 acts. Written 1947. Published 1950. Produced Madrid, Teatro Español, Oct. 14, 1949.

3. *Palabras en la arena* (*Words in the Sand*). Tragedy, 1 act. Written 1949? Published 1952. Produced Madrid, Teatro Español, Dec. 19, 1949.

4. *La tejedora de sueños** (*The Dream Weaver*). Drama, 3 acts. Written 1952? Published 1952. Produced Madrid, Teatro Español, Jan. 11, 1952.

5. *La señal que se espera* (*The Expected Sign*). Dramatic comedy, 3 acts. Written 1952? Published 1952. Produced Madrid, Teatro de la Infanta Isabel, May 21, 1952.

6. *Casi un cuento de hadas* (*Almost a Fairy Tale*). Variation on Perrault, 3 acts. Written 1953? Published 1953. Produced Madrid, Teatro Alcázar, Jan. 9, 1953.

7. *Madrugada* (*Daybreak*). Dramatic episode, 3 acts. Written 1953? Published 1954. Produced Madrid, Teatro Alcázar, Dec. 9, 1953.

8. *Irene, o El tesoro* (*Irene, or The Treasure*). Written 1954? Produced Madrid, Teatro Nacional María Guerrero, Dec. 14, 1954.

9. *Hoy es fiesta* (*Today Is a Holiday*). Drama. Published 1960. Produced Madrid, Teatro Nacional María Guerrero, Sept. 20, 1956.

10. *Las cartas boca abajo* (*The Cards Face Down*). Drama. Published 1959. Produced Madrid, Teatro de la Reina Victoria, Nov. 5, 1957.

11. *Un soñador para un pueblo* (*A Dreamer for the People*). Historical drama. Produced 1958.

12. *Las meninas* (*The Ladies-in-waiting*). Historical drama. Produced 1960.

13. *El concierto de San Ovidio* (*The Concert on St. Ovid's Day*). Dramatic parable, 3 acts. Produced Madrid, Teatro Goya, Nov. 16, 1962.

14. *Aventura en lo gris* (*Adventure in Grayness*). Drama, 2 acts and interlude.

15. *El terror inmovil* (*Motionless Terror*). Tragedy, 6 scenes.

16. *El sueño de la razón* (*Reason's Dream*). Play, 2 acts. Produced Madrid, Teatro de la Reina Victoria, Feb. 6, 1970.

EDITIONS

Collections.
Colección Teatro, Ediciones Alfil, Madrid, various dates.
Individual Plays.
The Dream Weaver. Published in *Teatro español 1951–1952,* ed. by F. C. Sáinz de Robles, Aguilar, Madrid, 1953.
In the Burning Darkness. S. A. Wofsy, ed., New York, 1954; also published in *Teatro español 1950–1951,* ed. by F. C. Sáinz de Robles, Aguilar, Madrid, 1952.
Story of a Staircase. Scribner, New York, 1955; also published in *Teatro español 1949–1950,* ed. by F. C. Sáinz de Robles, Aguilar, Madrid, 1951.

Mikhail Afanasyevich Bulgakov

(1891 — 1940)

Mikhail Afanasyevich Bulgakov, Soviet Russian dramatist, novelist, and short-story writer, was born in Kiev on May 14, 1891 (N.S.). The son of a professor of the Kiev Theological Academy, he attended the First Gymnasium and graduated with distinction from the College of Medicine of Kiev University in 1916. During the next two years he recorded his first serious studies of the human character and temperament, which he used later in *Notes of a Young Doctor (Zapiski yunogo vracha,* 1925–1926), while serving in a district hospital in the village of Nikolsky. In 1918, while Kiev was still under the German puppet government, Bulgakov returned home, but the revolution soon came to the Ukraine. One night in 1919, Bulgakov, without a destination in mind, boarded a train that took him to Vladikavkaz (now Dzaudzhikan), in the Caucasus. There he worked in the arts subsection of the district literary organization and began to write seriously. Bulgakov ridiculed some of these early efforts, especially his play *The Mullah's Sons (Synovya mully,* 1920), in his collection of short stories *Notes Written on the Cuff (Zapiskakh na manzhetakh,* 1923).

In 1921, his medical career abandoned, he moved to Moscow, where he lived for the rest of his life. For the next four years he earned his living as a free-lance journalist, contributing articles, short stories, and feuilletons to some of the most influential periodicals of the time. During this period he also wrote his first novel, *The White Guard (Belaya gvardiya,* 1924), based on his experiences in Kiev during the revolution. His first serious drama, *The Days of the Turbins (Dni Turbinykh,* 1926) is an adaptation of that novel, written with the encouragement of Pavel Alexandrovich Markov, the artistic director of the Moscow Art Theatre. The extraordi-

nary success of the Moscow Art Theatre production caused the play to remain in the repertory until 1929, when it was banned as counterrevolutionary. In 1925 a collection of Bulgakov's satirical short stories was published under the title *Devilry (Dyavoliada);* it included three of his most famous longer stories: "Fatal Eggs" ("Rokovye yaytsa"), "Devilry," and "The Adventures of Chichikov" ("Pokhozhdeniya Chichikova"), in which Gogol's Chichikov from *Dead Souls* finds himself in Soviet Russia and adapts rapidly.

Starting about 1927, most of Bulgakov's plays either did not reach production or were closed after a few performances. By 1930 an official ban was placed on his "neobourgeois" works. Faced with "ruin, the street, and death," he nevertheless refused to alter his writing style. Instead he appealed to Stalin, in a letter dated March 28, 1930, to be allowed either to leave Russia or, if he "should be sentenced to lifelong silence in the U.S.S.R.," to be given some kind of employment in the theatre. Stalin refused him permission to leave but granted him a position in the Moscow Art Theatre. Thus, from 1930 on Bulgakov worked as an assistant producer under Konstantin Stanislavski until a disagreement regarding the production of Bulgakov's *The Cabal of Hypocrites (Kabala svyatosh,* wr. 1930–1936) in 1936 caused him to leave. He then worked as a literary consultant for the Bolshoy Theatre and wrote the opera libretti for *Minin i Pozharsky, The Black Sea (Chyornoye more),* and *Peter the Great (Pyotr veliky).* Like Pasternak and others, he became a master of the Soviet genre of "desk drawer" literature.

Bulgakov's death was not reported in the *Literary Gazette,* and his name was omitted from literary histories until the "rehabilitation" in 1955 of writers whose person and works had disappeared under Stalin. His date of death has been established as March 10, 1940.

WORK

It is estimated that Bulgakov wrote almost thirty-six plays, most of which were unpublished and unproduced and are believed to be either still extant in old NKVD vaults or to have been burned when the German Army was approaching Moscow in 1941. The few available dramas, however, point to Bulgakov as one of the most creative playwrights Soviet Russia has produced.

The Days of the Turbins (1926), like the novel from which it was adapted, is written in the classical Tolstoyan realistic style and portrays landowning aristocrats sympathetically. Their way of life disappearing before them, the Turbin family and their friends who survive the civil war reevaluate their feelings about the new regime and, like Dr. Zhivago, wish only to be left in peace.

In 1925 Bulgakov began to change his style to a mixture of allegorical satire and Gogolian fantastic realism, which enabled him better to describe his world. His satirical humor derived from an understanding of the world as a place in which external circumstances may change radically but the basic foibles of mankind remain the same. Thus we "laugh through tears" at the peasant, the bureaucrat, and the poet, whether they exist under the Czar or the People's Soviets; in either case they are victims not only of their world but also of their humanity.

Zoyka's Apartment (*Zoikina kvartira*, 1926), set in a brothel, satirizes not only the housing problems of the 1920s but also the new Soviet philistines. It was withdrawn from the Vakhtangov Theatre after a few performances. *The Purple Island* (*Bagrovy ostrov*, 1928) is a gay satire on the propaganda potboilers approved by party members of the Glavrepertkom (Censorship Committee).

On the Run (*Beg;* wr. 1928, prod. 1957), banned by the Glavrepertkom, is a continuation of *The Days of the Turbins* and describes the fate of those Russians who, unlike the Turbins, decide to emigrate. Bulgakov is sympathetic with their disillusionment, alienation, and disintegration and describes the strength needed to endure exile. *The Cabal of Hypocrites* (1936), finally produced without the sanction of Stanislavski, is one of three plays in which Bulgakov used the theme of the persecuted creative and independent person who is ultimately crushed by a "cabal of hypocrites" who think they alone possess the truth. The two other plays, both produced posthumously, are *Don Quixote* (*Don Kikhot;* wr. 1938, prod. 1941) and *The Last Days* (*Posledniye dni;* wr. 1934/35, prod. 1943), which describes the final days of Pushkin before he was shot in a duel. The heroes of all three plays are ill-fated men tormented by the government and society.

The Days of the Turbins (*Dni Turbinykh*, 1926). Artillery Colonel Aleksey Turbin, his brother Nikolay, a cadet, and their sister Elena belong to a once-prosperous landowning family now threatened by the peasant revolt accompanying the revolution in Kiev in 1918. They are caught between the advancing Bolshevik armies and Simon Petlyura's Ukrainian nationalists; Kiev is temporarily held by the German-backed regime of Hetman Skoropadsky. The hetman and the White General Staff, which includes Elena's husband Colonel Talberg, soon realize the futility of their resistance and abandon Aleksey and his soldiers to defend Kiev alone.

Colonel Talberg deserts Elena and the Whites to flee to Berlin. Finally, Aleksey orders his men to go home. They barely escape the attacking Ukrainians, who kill Aleksey and cripple Nikolay for life.

In the final act two months later, the Turbins and their friends, grateful to be still alive and happy to see Petlyura defeated, have decided to reconcile themselves to the existence of the Bolsheviks (Reds). Their joy is temporarily marred by Colonel Talberg, who, on his way to join the White resistance on the Don, has stopped in Kiev to get Elena and discovers that he is rejected by his former friends and will soon be divorced by his wife. The attitude of the Turbins and their circle is now represented by the practical Lieutenant Myshlayevsky, who declares that he is sick of the fighting that has been going on since 1914 and of the imperial generals who have abandoned their troops and who probably will emigrate. He feels he would not be able to endure the lonely and insecure life of an *émigré* and hence will stay in Russia, come what may. Only the romantic Captain Studzinsky holds that Russia is doomed and that while for some these events may be a prologue to a new historical drama, for others they are an epilogue.

The Cabal of Hypocrites (*Kabala svyatosh;* wr. 1930–1936, prod. 1936). Drama also known as *Molyer* (*Molière*), symbolic of Bulgakov's position in Stalin's Russia. Molière, at the peak of his fame, is reviled by the church and the court, both of which he criticized in his comedy *Tartuffe*. The Archbishop of Paris, aided by a popular preacher, Father Barthélemy, some noblemen, and Jesuits, forms the Cabal of the Holy Writ to destroy Molière. Having discovered that Molière's young and unfaithful wife, Armande Béjart, is passing as the sister of Madeleine Béjart, Molière's old mistress, but in fact is her daughter by her first husband, they conceal certain facts and make it appear that Molière has married his own daughter, thus hoping to turn Louis XIV against him. Their plan is effective: Louis banishes Molière from the court and withdraws his protection; *Tartuffe* is forbidden. Molière grows old and sick, enduring persecution, disgrace, and humiliation until he finally dies of a broken heart during a performance of *The Imaginary Invalid*.

PLAYS

1. *Dni Turbinykh* (*The Days of the Turbins*). Drama, 4 acts. Written 1926. Published 1926. Produced Moscow Art Theatre, Oct. 5, 1926.

2. *Zoikina kvartira* (*Zoika's Apartment*). Comedy. Written 1926. Published 1926. Produced Moscow, Vakhtangov Theatre, 1926.

3. *Beg* (*On the Run*). Drama, 4 acts. Written 1928. Published 1955. Produced Volgograd, Gorky Theatre, May 18, 1957.

4. *Bagrovy ostrov* (*The Purple Island*). Play. Written 1928. Produced Moscow, Kamerny Theatre, 1928.

5. *Myortvye dushi* (*Dead Souls*). Play. Produced Moscow Art Theatre, 1932. Dramatic adaptation of Nikolay Gogol's novel (1842).

6. *Poloumny Zhurden* (*Half-witted Jourdain*). Comedy, 3 acts. Written 1932. Variant of *Kabala svyatosh*.

7. *Poslednie dni* (*The Last Days*); also called *Pushkin*. Drama, 4 acts. Written 1934/35. Published 1943. Produced Moscow Art Theatre, Apr. 10, 1943.

8. *Kabala svyatosh* (*The Cabal of Hypocrites*); also called *Molyer* (*Molière*). Drama, 4 acts. Written 1930–1936. Published 1965. Produced Moscow Art Theatre, Feb. 15, 1936.

9. *Ivan Vasilyevich*. Fantastic comedy, 3 acts. Written 1936. Published 1965. Scheduled to appear in Theatre of Satire, Moscow, Mar. 9, 1936; première canceled and play forbidden.

10. *Don Kikhot* (*Don Quixote*). Play, 4 acts. Written 1938. Produced Leningrad, Pushkin Academic Theatre, Mar. 13, 1941.

11. *Batum*. Drama. Written 1939.

12. *Blazhenstvo* (*Bliss*). Fantastic comedy. Written 1930s.

EDITIONS

Dramy i komedii M. Bulgakova, Moscow, 1965.

The Days of the Turbins. Published in *Six Soviet Plays,* ed. by E. Lyons, Houghton Mifflin, Boston, 1934; *An Anthology of Russian Plays,* ed. and tr. by F. D. Reeve, vol. 2, Vintage Books, New York, 1961–1963.

CRITICISM

V. Kaverin, *Zametki o dramaturgii Bulgakova,* in *Teatr,* 1956.

BULWER-LYTTON, Edward George Earle Lytton. *See* LYTTON, 1ST BARON.

BUONARROTI, Michelangelo (b. Florence, 1568; d. 1642).

Italian man of letters and dramatist (called Il Giovane), nephew of Michelangelo. *Constanza* (*La Tancia,* 1611), a rustic comedy in verse, expresses the author's longing for a return to nature. *The Fair* (*La fiera;* wr. 1619, pub. 1726) is a comedy in twenty-five acts, divided into five days (*giornate*) of five acts each, during which the numerous inhabitants of an imaginary city, Pandora, celebrate at a fair. Buonarroti's work also includes a number of mythological "scene poems" that superficially derive from the tradition of pastoral drama. The first of these, *Hercules's Birthday* (*Il natal d'Ercole,* 1605), was followed by *The Judgment of Paris* (*Il giudizio di Paride,* 1608) and *The Syrinx* (*La siringa,* 1634). *See* PASTORAL DRAMA.

Constanza (*La Tancia,* 1611). Rustic comedy in which two country girls, Tancia (Constanza) and Cosa (Nicolosa) are besieged by suitors, Tancia by a young man from the city and one from the country and Cosa by a shy peasant. Cosa's simple romance permits the use of peasant vocabulary, which creates a rustic atmosphere. Tancia, finally choosing the country lover, proves the thesis that it is necessary, given the corrupt society of the cities, to return to nature.

BURGGRAF, Waldfried. *See* FORSTER, FRIEDRICH.

BURLESQUE.

Play offering a comic imitation of another dramatic or literary form. The burlesque first appeared early in the seventeenth century as a reaction to the types of plays then current and all too familiar. The word itself comes from the Italian *burlesco,* meaning "mockery." One of the first types of drama to be made the target of burlesque was the popular romance of Shakespeare's time. The chivalry and daring of the Elizabethan romances were parodied by Francis Beaumont in *The Knight of the Burning Pestle* (ca. 1607). Another early master of the form was George Villiers, Duke of Buckingham, whose *The Rehearsal* (1671) poked fun at Dryden and the heroic drama. During the eighteenth century burlesque achieved great popularity, the most common form being the rehearsal in imitation of Buckingham. Henry Fielding and Richard Brinsley Sheridan, great wits of the day, were the foremost writers of burlesque. Fielding's *Tom Thumb: A Tragedy* (1730) satirized the conventions of heroic drama, and Sheridan's *The Critic* (1779) was a takeoff on the sentimental dramatic and literary tastes of the period. *See* FIELDING, HENRY; HEROIC PLAY; SHERIDAN, RICHARD BRINSLEY.

During the nineteenth century a new type of burlesque flourished, one that relied less

Michelangelo Buonarroti. [Italian Cultural Institute]

heavily on the audience's knowledge of literary and dramatic forms. It was a lighter, more absurd burlesque and often included song and dance. In this form it survived until well into the twentieth century. American burlesque originated in the mid-nineteenth century as a bawdy song-and-dance show made up of comedy skits, monologues, chorus numbers, acrobatics, music by instrumentalists or sentimental singers, and an occasional political satire. The show ended with an "extra added attraction," usually the display of a girl in tights. The striptease, introduced in the 1920s, came to dominate the show; then prohibition, police cleanups, and motion pictures all but put an end to American burlesque.

BUTTI, Enrico Annibale (b. Milan, February 19, 1868; d. there, November 29, 1912). Italian author and dramatist whose plays have a mystic, religious content that does not belong to the mainstream of early-twentieth-century Italian drama. His first important play, *The Vortex* (*Il vortice*, 1892), was followed by others in which passive characters are forced to react to sudden crises by which they are ultimately defeated. In *The Race for Pleasure* (*La corsa al piacere*, 1900), an unfaithful husband must face the psychological consequences of his actions when his mother dies. In *Utopia* (*L'utopia*, 1894), Dr. Serchi, a vociferous supporter of infanticide, emphatically reverses his convictions when his own baby becomes ill. In *Lucifer* (*Lucifero*, 1900), a father must accept the fact of his son's conversion to atheism. The protagonist of *A Tempest* (*Una tempesta*, 1901) must face the indifference of the beneficiaries of his assassination of an absentee landlord. Butti's vague religious aspirations, set forth in *The Castle of the Dream* (*Il castello del sogno*, 1910), are more thoroughly explored in his earlier play *Flames in the Shadows* (*Fiamme nell'ombra*, 1904), in which an ambitious young priest assumes the responsibility of saving his sister from an ultimate fall from grace.

Flames in the Shadows (*Fiamme nell'ombra*, 1904). Drama set in the home of a priest, Antonio, to which his sister Elizabeth returns after years of estrangement. Antonio's anger at her for having eloped at the age of fourteen had become hatred when the ensuing scandal shattered his hopes for advancement. Now that she is ill, however, having been abandoned years earlier to a life of hardship by her lover, her presence reawakens the affection he had felt while raising her after the death of their parents. Soon, however, life in the parish house grows dull for Elizabeth. One day, she meets a childhood friend, imagines a great love dawning, and

involves herself again in a passionate affair. Her lover, however, is dependent on the wishes of his parents. When they intercept a letter from her in which she tells him that she is pregnant, they confront the priest with it, demanding that he keep her from their son. Embittered by this new event, having given up the chance to become a bishop when he took his sister in, Antonio now determines to throw her out. While preparing to leave, Elizabeth tries to make her brother understand her dream of an ideal love and how she had struggled unsuccessfully to keep her illegitimate child alive. Touched at last, Antonio renounces worldly ambition, accepts a small parish in the mountains, and takes Elizabeth to live with him.

BYRON, George Gordon (b. London, January 22, 1788; d. Missolonghi, Greece, April 19, 1824). In 1798, on the death of his great-un-

George Gordon Byron. [New York Public Library Picture Collection]

Scene from *Werner*
showing Werner
and Josephine in
the hall of a
decayed palace.
[Theatre
Collection, The
New York Public
Library at Lincoln
Center, Astor,
Lenox and Tilden
Foundations]

cle, he became the 6th Baron Byron. Among the major poets of the early nineteenth century, many of whom tried their hands at drama, Byron came closest to success in this medium, his plays possessing greater impact and a more extensive knowledge of theatrical conventions than those of his fellow poets. The entire body of his theatrical work consists of eight plays, three of which, *Manfred* (pub. 1817, 1834), *Cain, a Mystery* (pub. 1821), and *Heaven and Earth* (pub. 1822), are almost purely speculative closet dramas. The remaining five, although written in rhetorical language, show signs of having been written for stage production, despite Byron's constant claim in his prefaces that his plays are "not for the stage." *See* CLOSET DRAMA.

His creative spirit was both more intense than that of his compatriots and more closely in touch with real life, and his personal qualities lent themselves to the creation of tragic heroes. Conforming to the custom of romantic writers, Byron put much of himself in his writing, the result being, in *Manfred* for example, a Faustian figure, a brooding epitome of the Gothic hero, burdened by some unnameable guilt, lonely and isolated. Although theatrically weak, *Manfred* exhibits this Faustian character with great impact, indicating the hero's desire for knowledge, his misanthropy, and his isolation. This theme was to be developed by Byron in his other speculative plays, all dealing with the conflicts of the Faustian hero, his brooding desire for knowledge, and his isolation from society.

Byron's other dramas are historical, dealing with Venetian subjects. With Otway as his model in *Marino Faliero, Doge of Venice* (pub. 1821), the only play produced in Byron's lifetime, he aired his political beliefs, pitting an honorable old autocrat against a newly instituted but corrupt commonwealth in an effort to reconcile aristocratic qualities with liberal government. *The Two Foscari* (pub. 1821) describes the conflicts of a father forced to sit in judgment on his son. *Sardanapalus* (pub. 1821, 1834) presents the martyrdom of a voluptuous Assyrian Emperor whose sincere efforts to create a peaceful realm are met with ingratitude and insurrection. *Werner, or The Inheritance* (pub. 1822, 1830), which proved Byron's greatest success in the theatre, is a tragedy modeled on Schiller, depicting the sins of a father visited on an errant son. *The Deformed Transformed* (pub. 1824), a fragment of a drama set in ancient Rome, has the qualities of both Byron's historical plays and his speculative plays, dealing with ancient Rome and at the same time incorporating a Faustian hero. *See* OTWAY, THOMAS; SCHILLER, FRIEDRICH VON.

Manfred (pub. 1817, 1834). Dramatic poem set in the Swiss Alps. Manfred, who communicates with the spirits of the universe, after brooding about his life commands them to appear in his castle. When the spirits finally arise and ask his wishes, he requests forgetfulness even if it means his death. But the spirits cannot accomplish this, and despairing over the failure of his magical powers, Manfred goes into the mountains. There he encounters a hunter who prevents him from jumping to his death and offers to change places with him. Manfred refuses and descends into the valley, where he summons the Witch of the Alps. He tells her that his life has been lonely and that he has been happy only once, when he loved a girl, Astarte, who had good qualities where his were lacking. But his love, he says, destroyed her. The Witch promises to help him, but only if he will bind himself to her. Manfred refuses and moves on to the Hall of Arimanes, where the three Destinies and Nemesis are gathered. Nemesis agrees to call Astarte from the dead and does so, but Astarte can only prophesy that Manfred's despair will end within a day.

Filled with the calm of acceptance, Manfred returns to his castle, where the Abbot arrives to save him from his own magic. Manfred refuses his offer of help, preferring to go on alone. As Manfred awaits his death, the Abbot makes a second appeal; however, he is helpless as Manfred dies, possessed neither by spirits nor by mortals.

C

CAILLAVET, Gaston de (1869–1915). French journalist and playwright. Caillavet was the son of Mme. de Caillavet, mistress of Anatole France, whose salon dominated French literary society at the turn of the century. For some fifteen years he collaborated with Robert de Flers on sentimental and satirical comedies that were the delight of the boulevard audiences. For further details, *see* FLERS, ROBERT DE. *See also* BOULEVARD COMEDY.

Pedro Calderón de la Barca
(1600 – 1681)

Pedro Calderón de la Barca, poet and dramatist of the Siglo de Oro (Spanish Golden Age), was born in Madrid on January 17, 1600, to Diego Calderón de la Barca, an aristocratic and wealthy Castilian employed as secretary to the Royal Treasury, and the former Ana María de Henao y Riaño, who was of Flemish ancestry. At the age of eight, he entered the Colegio Imperial de los Jesuitas; two years later his mother died. In 1614 Don Diego married Juana Freyre, and when he died the following year, his widow contested his will and eventually was awarded the major portion of the family estate. Though the dispute is said to have caused great bitterness, Calderón, his two brothers, and his sister were amply provided for. *See* SIGLO DE ORO.

After briefly attending the University of Alcalá de Henares, in 1615 Calderón entered the University of Salamanca, where he studied canon law and theology and otherwise occupied himself by writing poetry and plays. In about 1620, having completed or abandoned his studies, he decided to devote himself entirely to writing. Juan de Vera Tassis,

Pedro Calderón de la Barca. [Library of Congress]

his day, he was involved in many amorous escapades, and some of his activities gave rise to scandal. In 1629, when his brother Diego was wounded by an actor, Calderón pursued the latter into a convent in which he had sought sanctuary. The nuns were said to have been molested, and Calderón was publicly reproved by the court preacher. He replied by inserting in *The Constant Prince* (*El príncipe constante*, wr. 1629) several lines parodying the preacher's bombastic style.

In 1635, following the death of Lope de Vega, Calderón began to write plays for the court, and the next year was made a knight of Santiago. When Philip IV's new Buen Retiro Palace was completed, Calderón wrote to celebrate the event *Love, the Greatest Enchantment* (*El mayor encanto, amor,* wr. 1635), which was given a spectacular production on an elaborate stage in the lake while the King and his entourage watched from the shore. Another royal palace was later to be the scene of some of Calderón's most charming works, the zarzuelas, or operettas, that took their name from the Zarzuela Palace built in the woods near Madrid. The best known of these early musicals is *Echo and Narcissus* (*Eco y Narciso*, wr. 1661).

In 1636 and 1637, Diego Calderón issued two volumes containing twenty-four of his brother's plays, including *Life Is a Dream* (*La vida es sueño,* wr. ca. 1631/32). Calderón participated in 1640 in a military expedition sent to put down a rebellion in Catalonia and was wounded in the hand. It may be that the experience of this campaign against rebellious peasants is reflected in *The Mayor of Zalamea* (*El alcalde de Zalamea,* wr. 1640/44), one of his greatest plays, but evidence on the play's date is ambiguous at best.

Two years later, ill health forced him to retire from all military duties, and he was given an infrequently paid royal pension. For a time he was in the service of the Duke of Alba. These years were depressing ones for Calderón. Deaths in the royal family curtailed dramatic entertainments, and his two brothers were killed. During this time he had a love affair with an unknown woman, probably an actress, who died in bearing him a son in 1647. In 1651 Calderón took holy orders and thereafter confined his literary activities to writing plays for special court occasions and *autos sacramentales* for Madrid's Corpus Christi celebrations. *See* AUTO SACRAMENTAL.

Philip IV had in 1653 appointed Calderón chaplain of Los Reyes Nuevos, in Toledo, but the poet's frequent absence from court saddened the monarch, who called Calderón to Madrid in 1663 and made him his private chaplain. The third, fourth, and "unauthorized" fifth collected volumes of his plays ap-

one of his first biographers, credits him with having written a play entitled *The Chariot of Heaven* (*El carro del cielo*) at the age of thirteen, but no trace of such a work has been found. His literary activities first won public attention in 1620 and 1622, when verses entered in a competition held in celebration of St. Isidore, Madrid's patron saint, won the praise of Lope de Vega. Calderón is said to have collaborated with Juan Pérez de Montalbán and Antonio Coello on a play, but the first work to appear in his own name was *Love, Honor, and Power* (*Amor, honor y poder*), which was performed in Madrid in 1623. *See* VEGA CARPIO, LOPE DE.

Beginning in 1625 he intermittently saw service with the Spanish Army in Italy and Flanders, and the surrender of Breda, which he probably witnessed, was the inspiration for one of his early plays, *The Siege of Breda* (*El sitio de Bredá,* wr. 1625).

Despite his absences on military campaigns, Calderón was frequently in Madrid, and this was one of the periods of his greatest productivity. Like most young gentlemen of

peared in 1664, 1672, and 1677, respectively. Shortly before his death, Calderón was asked to compile a list of his works, and on it he included 111 plays and 70 *autos*. However, many other works were ascribed to him, and he is sometimes credited with more than 200. He died in Madrid on May 25, 1681, while working on the two *autos* scheduled for that year, *Isaiah's Lamb* (*El cordero de Isaías*) and *To Love and Be Loved, or The Divine Philothea* (*Amar y ser amado y divina Filotea*).

WORK

The theatre of Calderón dominated the Spanish stage during the latter part of Spain's Golden Age, just as the plays of Lope de Vega had set the tone for the first years. However, when after the death of his illustrious predecessor Calderón became the principal dramatist at the court of Philip IV, Spain was already in a period of national and political decline. The great burst of national vigor, which in Lope de Vega and others had given birth to new artistic forms, was over. A view of life and a code of conduct that to the earlier playwrights had been self-evident was being challenged by the forces of social change and concomitant economic and political currents. It was Calderón's unconscious task to objectify and insist on a concept of man and society that was beginning to lose unquestioning adherence.

Faith and honor were Calderón's essential themes, and the vehicle for discussing them was the popular *comedia* form developed by his predecessors. Calderón, like his great contemporaries, was not attached to academic theories of dramatic composition: he was not a neoclassic writer. But his dramatic craftsmanship was of a high order, and he used the techniques of his time brilliantly to produce a series of masterpieces in which these techniques found their best expression. His theatre, generally classified as baroque, is distinguished by strict and detailed development of plot. Characterization, as in much of Golden Age drama, is sketchy, however, and Calderón's power and intensity are to a large extent due to his lyric and graceful verse. Many modern critics tend to look upon his major plays as dramatic poems whose essential themes are conveyed by vivid and sometimes elaborate imagery. In this area, Calderón was influenced by Spain's great Golden Age poet Luis de Góngora. A man of great learning, wit, and sophistication, Góngora revolutionized Spanish poetry by introducing elegant forms and a style based on the use of highly polished imagery, metaphors drawn from various sources, neologisms, and a Latinized vocabulary studded with mythical and classical allusions. This style came to be known as *gongorismo,* which found its prose equivalent in the *conceptismo* exemplified in the writings of the contemporary novelist, essayist, and poet Quevedo. Calderón drew upon both these stylistic approaches but generally managed to avoid excesses that might have endangered the immediacy of his communication with theatre audiences. *See* COMEDIA.

The themes of Calderón's plays vary widely, ranging from the *comedia de capa y espada* to the *auto sacramental.* Modern audiences and readers are perhaps most familiar with his *Life Is a Dream* (wr. 1631/32), a *comedia filosófica* that deals with problems of free will and the impossibility of distinguishing between illusion and reality. Life, Calderón suggests, is the dream from which we shall awake at death to the reality of judgment. To the same philosophical category belongs the lesser-known *In This Life Everything Is Both True and False* (*En esta vida todo es verdad y todo mentira,* wr. 1659).

Among the plays generally classified as *comedias de pundonor,* or honor plays, are *The Surgeon of His Honor* (*El médico de su honra,* wr. 1635), *Secret Vengeance for a Secret Insult* (*A secreto agravio, secreta venganza,* wr. 1635), *Three Judgments at a Blow* (*Las tres justicias en una,* wr. ca. 1636/37?) and *The Painter of His Own Dishonor* (*El pintor de su deshonra,* wr. ca. 1648/50). In all, strict adherence to the rigid honor code results in the tragic death of the innocent, even when, as in *Secret Vengeance,* the protagonist bemoans the tyranny of this code. Typically, in these

Scene from a German production of *La dama duende.* [Goethe House]

plays a husband will kill his wife in order to restore his own honor and will be pardoned by the King for his act. There is an unresolved dilemma in the interpretation of these plays. Did Calderón approve of the honor code despite its harshness? Or was his object to show the excesses to which it drove decent people? Or, again, did he wish to represent a tragic moral dilemma, between the dictates of Christian morality and medieval honor, which he himself could not resolve? Calderón's manifest Christianity in other aspects of his work has led recent critics to feel that these plays are a condemnation of the honor code; yet if that is the case, it marks a rather curious break from the convention under which the final dispensation of royal or paternal justice is supposed to represent the "correct" version of morality.

Though often classified as a *comedia histórica, The Mayor of Zalamea* (wr. 1640/44) is closely related in theme to the traditional honor play. Here, however, the protagonist is not a nobleman but a proud peasant, and his claims to honor are treated as ridiculous pretensions by the noble captain who has ravished his daughter. Calderón's characterization of Pedro Crespo, the mayor, is perhaps one of the best in a rich gallery of individual portraits. This play is said to have been inspired by a real incident. Calderón originally called the play *The Best Garroting Ever Carried Out* (*El garrote más bien dado*). To the same historical genre, again enriched by legend and tradition, belongs *The Constant Prince* (wr. 1629), which deals with the imprisonment and death of Prince Ferdinand of Portugal at the hands of the Moors. However, because Ferdinand chooses a martyr's death instead of allowing a Christian city to be surrendered to the infidels in exchange for his freedom, this play is often considered among the religious dramas.

In the latter category, often identified as *comedias de santos,* is the magnificently moving *Devotion to the Cross* (*La devoción de la cruz,* wr. ca. 1633). Though the play ends in a series of miracles, in many ways its chief dramatic force is derived from the demonstration of how a noble father's monstrous pride is castigated. *The Wonder-working Magician* (*El mágico prodigioso,* wr. 1637) is based on a Faustian legend of St. Cyprian of Antioch, in which Cyprian is converted to Christianity after the devil is shown to be incapable of subverting a beautiful young Christian girl for whom the pagan philosopher was willing to sell his soul. Shelley was so moved by the play that he translated portions of it. (To some extent it was due to the enthusiasm of the romantic poets and critics, beginning with the Schlegel brothers in Germany, that Calderón was rediscovered by moderns.) Shelley also highly praised the religious play *Absalom's Hair* (*Los cabellos de Absalón,* wr. ca. 1634), a Biblical drama based on the tragic ambitions of David's son. *See* SHELLEY, PERCY BYSSHE.

The Great Prince of Fez (*El gran príncipe de Fez,* wr. 1668) deals with the conversion of an infidel prince. *The Purgatory of St. Patrick* (*El purgatorio de San Patricio,* wr. ca. 1634) shows Patrick winning the pagan King of Ireland to Christianity by resurrecting his daughter and allowing him to glimpse the souls in purgatory.

The dramatic genre known as the *comedia de capa y espada,* or cloak-and-sword play, reached its finest development with Calderón. The purpose here was frankly to amuse the audience with an exciting tale of intrigue, misunderstandings, jealous lovers, overzealous brothers, and wily but pure young ladies. The plots generally concern an attempt to prevent or force a marriage and conclude

German production of *La vida es sueño,* Hamburg, 1953. [Goethe House]

with a solution that manages to be a triumph for love as well as for honor and morality. Perhaps the best examples of this genre are *The Phantom Lady* (*La dama duende,* wr. 1629), *A House with Two Doors Is Difficult to Guard* (*Casa con dos puertas, mala es de guardar,* wr. 1629), and *Beware of Still Water* (*Guárdate del agua mansa,* wr. 1649).

During his lifetime, Calderón was probably better known for his *autos sacramentales* than his *comedias.* These are one-act religious dramas concerned with the mystery of the Eucharist. They were meant for open-air street performances during the Corpus Christi festival, and after Calderón's "retirement" in 1651 he provided Madrid with two *autos* annually until his death in 1681. The *autos,* originally designed for performance in public, combined comic and theological elements. By Calderón's time they had evolved into quite complex allegories, suitably sophisticated for performance at court. Abstract ideas were presented by incorporating them in allegorical figures such as Beauty, Vanity, and Idolatry, and the scenic effects employed became more and more elaborate. Lope de Vega had helped establish the contemporary popularity of the genre, but Calderón was to surpass him and show an ingenious skill in adapting a variety of subjects from the Bible, legends, history, and so on and relating them to the Eucharist. Perhaps the best known of his *autos* are two earlier works, *Belshazzar's Feast* (*La cena del rey Baltasar,* wr. 1634) and *The Great Theatre of the World* (*El gran teatro del mundo,* wr. 1635?). In the latter play, Calderón developed a conceit in which the world itself is a stage whose best actors will eventually dine with the Manager, or Head, of the troupe. An *auto* based on the theme of *Life Is a Dream* (wr. 1673) substitutes abstractions such as Man, Free Will, and Grace for the characters in the play, and Calderón allegorized several other secular plays as well.

A final word should be said about the zarzuelas, which Calderón derived and elaborated from earlier forms of musical theatre. These dramatic pieces, which made extensive use of music, singing, dancing, and elaborate scenic effects, took their name from the rustic Zarzuela Palace (which in turn got its name from the *zarzas,* or brambles, that grew nearby), where they were presented as entertainments for the court. They were generally presented to mark a special court occasion. Often, as in *Echo and Narcissus* (wr. 1661), they were based on classical legends that were freely adapted to the occasion. Examples of this genre are *The Laurel of Apollo* (*El laurel de Apolo,* 1658) and *The Purple of the Rose* (*La púrpura de la rosa,* 1660).

The Constant Prince (*El príncipe con-*

Scene from a French production of *La devoción de la cruz,* translated by Albert Camus. Paris, Deuxième Festival d'Art Dramatique, 1953. [French Cultural Services]

stante, wr. 1629). *Comedia histórica* in which the Portuguese Army, led by Prince Ferdinand, engages the Moors in battle near Tangier. The Portuguese are defeated, and Ferdinand is taken prisoner. The King of Fez demands the city of Ceuta as his ransom, but Ferdinand refuses to let a Christian city be given to the Moors. The King orders Ferdinand to be treated as a slave, forced to do manual work, and starved. Eventually Alfonso, King of Portugal, comes with his army to free the Prince but is too late. Ferdinand has died, but his spirit leads the army. The King of Fez's daughter is captured and returned to the Moors in exchange for the body of Ferdinand.

A House with Two Doors Is Difficult to Guard (*Casa con dos puertas, mala es de guardar,* wr. 1629). *Comedia de capa y espada* in which Don Félix, whose friend Lisardo is staying with him, hides his sister Marcela so that Lisardo will not know of her presence. However, Marcela has been meeting Lisardo outside the house, although he does not know who she is. Marcela now arranges to meet Lisardo in the house of a friend, Laura, who is Félix's beloved. Both houses have two doors (front and side), and as one character comes in one door, another leaves by the other. After a series of comings and goings, Félix is convinced that Lisardo is after Laura, and Lisardo believes that Marcela is Félix's mistress. Laura finally explains everything, and the two couples are happily and correctly paired.

The Phantom Lady (*La dama duende,* wr. 1629). *Comedia de capa y espada* in which Angela, a capricious young widow, lives in Madrid with her brothers Juan and Luis. However, in order to preserve her chastity and their honor, they keep her presence a secret. When Angela slips out to see the entertainments in the palace grounds, she is pursued by her brother Luis, who fails to recognize her. She appeals to a stranger for help. A duel follows during which Angela escapes. It is stopped only by the arrival of Juan, who recognizes the stranger as his friend Don Manuel. The latter is invited to stay with Juan and Luis and is given a room next to Angela's. A false wall of mirrors hides a connecting door through which Angela, curious about her rescuer, visits the room in Manuel's absence and leaves mysterious tokens of her presence. Manuel's servant is convinced that a phantom is at work. After much confusion, misunderstanding, and arguing about honor, Angela and Manuel are happily united. Juan is to marry Angela's

La devoción de la cruz. Paris, Deuxième Festival d'Art Dramatique, 1953. [French Cultural Services]

friend and confidant Beatriz, but Luis remains unpaired and frustrated.

Life Is a Dream (*La vida es sueño,* wr. ca. 1631/32). *Comedia filosófica* in which Basilio, King of Poland, having read in the stars that his newly born son Segismundo is fated to be a tyrant, decides to have him brought up in solitary imprisonment. Locked in a mountain tower where he sees only his adviser and jailer Clotaldo, Segismundo has after twenty years become a mixture of man and beast. In a famous monologue he envies the freedom of animals. The aged King, concerned over the succession to his throne, now determines to test the predictions of the stars and see whether free will can triumph over predestination. He decides to have Segismundo drugged and brought to court while still asleep. If when he awakens, Segismundo shows himself capable of controlling his passions, he will be allowed to reign. If he proves to be a cruel man, he will be drugged and returned to prison, where he will be told that his experiences in the palace were a dream.

When Segismundo awakens in the palace, he is for the first time told of his royal birth. Having been brought up like a beast, he proceeds to behave as one. He attempts to kill Clotaldo, defenestrates a servant who tries to intervene, and forces his attentions on Rosaura, a woman who has come to court in search of her seducer, the Duke of Muscovy. Drugged and returned to his prison, Segismundo awakens and ponders the nature of reality. Had the court been a dream, or is the present prison a dream?

Basilio must choose as his successor either the Duke of Muscovy or the visiting Princess Estrella. When he decides on the Duke, his soldiers rebel against the notion of a foreign ruler. Freeing Segismundo, they proclaim him King. Segismundo is tempted to revenge himself on Basilio, but experience has taught him prudence. After first reproving his father, he throws himself at his feet and begs his forgiveness. With princely justice, he then compels the Duke of Muscovy to marry Rosaura, who is discovered to be nobly born and the daughter of Clotaldo, and he himself asks for the hand of Princess Estrella. Though his happiness now seems complete, Segismundo is haunted by the possibility that he may once more be dreaming and that he will again awaken in prison.

Devotion to the Cross (*La devoción de la cruz,* wr. ca. 1633). *Comedia de santos* in which Eusebio loves Julia but is prevented from marrying her because of his low birth. When he persists in courting her, Eusebio is challenged to a duel by her brother Lisardo. Eusebio explains that though he was an abandoned child who was found at the foot of a cross, the symbol of which he bears in his flesh, his devotion to the Cross has several times caused his life to be miraculously saved. He therefore considers that he has acquired nobility. Lisardo, however, insists on a duel and is mortally wounded. Eusebio secretly visits Julia but is forced to hide when her father Curcio enters. The latter berates Julia for her behavior, comparing it to that of her mother, who after he struck her in a jealous rage gave birth to her and to a now-lost brother at the foot of a cross.

Lisardo's body is brought in, and Julia, learning that Eusebio killed her brother, sends her lover away in despair. She is forced by Curcio to enter a convent; Eusebio becomes a bandit. One day he saves the life of a priest, who promises in return to come and confess him when he is dying. Unable to forget Julia, Eusebio breaks into her convent, intending to rape her. When, however, he sees the sign of the Cross on her breast, he flees in horror. Julia now resolves to follow him, and disguising herself as a man joins the bandits. Eusebio pleads with her to return to the convent. Eventually, Curcio tracks down Eusebio and mortally wounds him. As Eusebio dies, Curcio sees the cross on his breast and realizes that this is his long-lost son.

True to his promise, the priest arrives to confess Eusebio, who miraculously returns to life long enough to be shriven. Learning that Eusebio is her brother, Julia despairingly confesses her sins. When Curcio raises his arm to strike her, she takes refuge at the foot of the cross near Eusebio's grave. She and the cross are miraculously lifted to heaven.

Belshazzar's Feast (*La cena del rey Baltasar,* wr. 1634). *Auto sacramental* in which King Belshazzar has wedded Vanity and Idolatry. Daniel is sent by God to warn Belshazzar to repent, giving him three warnings; on each occasion Belshazzar almost repents but cannot give up his brides. At a feast given by Belshazzar, Daniel comes as a guest, accompanied by Death disguised as his attendant. Death gives Belshazzar a poisoned drink to kill his soul, then draws his knife to slay his body. They fight, and Belshazzar is dragged away by Death. He calls to Vanity and Idolatry to help him, but they are powerless.

The Purgatory of St. Patrick (*El purgatorio de San Patricio,* wr. ca. 1634). *Comedia de santos* in which St. Patrick is shipwrecked on the shores of pagan Ireland with a wicked companion, Ludovico. Captured by Egerio, the King, the two men are imprisoned by the pagans; but Ludovico is set free by the King's daughter Polonia, who has fallen in love with him. St. Patrick escapes to Rome but returns to attempt the conversion of Ireland. Ludovico, having seduced and then killed Polonia, is confronted by St. Patrick, who resurrects the girl and converts the hardened criminal by his miracles. Although St. Patrick has allowed the King to witness the miracle that

La cena del rey Baltasar, as performed by the Compañía Lope de Vega, 1954. [Courtesy Spanish Embassy]

converted Ludovico, the monarch remains unconvinced of the existence of life after death. After an angel reveals purgatory and hell to Egerio through an underground cavern, he accepts Christianity for himself and for Ireland.

Love, the Greatest Enchantment (*El mayor encanto, amor*, wr. 1635). *Comedia mitológica* based on Homer's story of Ulysses, who in his wanderings is trapped by the beauty of Circe. In a romantic, exotic, and lavish setting, Ulysses and his entire crew fall in love with Circe. Eventually, however, Ulysses and his men regretfully trick her into letting them escape. Her attempt to bring them back causes her ruin and the destruction of the magic island. Calderón's exuberant portrayal of the mythical Circe may owe something to Ariosto's Alcina and Tasso's Armida, both seductive witches who abduct young knights and hold them captive on magic islands. *See* ARIOSTO, LUDOVICO; TASSO, TORQUATO.

Secret Vengeance for a Secret Insult (*A secreto agravio, secreta venganza*, wr. 1635). *Comedia de pundonor* in which Doña Leonor, a Castilian lady, agrees to a proxy marriage with Don Lope de Almeida of Portugal, after she learns that Don Luis, her true love, has been killed. On her arrival in Portugal, Leonor learns that Luis is alive and determined to win her back. Torn between love and duty, Leonor receives Luis during her husband's absence and attempts to persuade him to leave Portugal. Lope, his suspicions aroused, returns unexpectedly and surprises the lovers. Upon the advice of a friend, he pretends to accept Luis's explanation of his presence in the house. In his own surly way, Lope truly loves Leonor, but he accepts the demands of the unbending code of honor. To avoid an open scandal over this secret insult, Lope plans a secret revenge. Meanwhile, Leonor has determined to dismiss Luis forever. Before she can do so, Lope arranges for Luis to be drowned in what will appear to be an accident. He than stabs Leonor and sets fire to the house so that her death will also seem accidental. The King, learning the truth behind these deaths, approves of Lope's behavior.

The Surgeon of His Honor (*El médico de su honra*, wr. 1635). *Comedia de pundonor* in which Don Gutierre breaks his engagement with Doña Leonor to marry Doña Mencía, who loves and is loved by Prince Enrique, the King's brother. But Enrique is away on military duty, and in compliance with her father's wishes Doña Mencía marries Don Gutierre. Upon his return, Enrique pursues her, but she honorably rejects his advances. The Prince persists in his attempts to see her, and Don Gutierre begins to suspect his wife's fidelity. In disguise he slips into her room at night. Thinking that only Enrique would have such audacity, Mencía addresses him as

Scene from *El gran mercado del mundo*, performed in Einsiedeln, Switzerland. [Swiss National Tourist Office]

"Your Highness" and convinces her husband that his suspicions are well founded. Don Gutierre vows to become the "surgeon of his own honor" and kills his wife. This he does by having her bled to death by a blood-letter. He is pardoned by the King and is reunited with Leonor.

The Great Theatre of the World (*El gran teatro del mundo*, wr. 1635?). *Auto sacramental* in which all humanity is called before "the sovereign *Autor*," or Stage Manager. The world is a stage, and men are the actors. The best actors will dine with God, and each performer will receive his due. Divine Grace demands that each man do good works because "God is God," but only Discretion and the Poor Man listen. The others, such as the Rich Man, occupy themselves with their pleasures. At judgment, all repent their sins except the Rich Man, who is thereby condemned to hell. The King, Farmer, and Peasant go to purgatory; the Poor Man and Discretion to heaven; and the Stillborn Child to limbo, where there is neither pain nor glory. The elect partake of the sacred Eucharist from the hands of God.

The Wonder-working Magician (*El mágico prodigioso*, wr. 1637). *Comedia de santos* in which the Devil comes to Antioch determined to corrupt Cyprian, a serious young student, and Justina, a young girl renowned for her virtue. In an attempt to seduce Justina, the Devil climbs her balcony and is seen by two of her suitors, Lelius and Florus. Each thinks it was the other, and they fight a duel but are stopped by Cyprian, who has also fallen in love with Justina. Believing the Devil to be a magician, Cyprian asks for his help in winning her. The Devil agrees to help on condition that Cyprian sell him his soul. Having bought Cyprian, the Devil turns to Justina, but her purity protects her from lies and spells, and as he cannot induce her to go to Cyprian, he sends a phantom instead. The phantom is disguised as Justina, but when Cyprian hazards an embrace, he finds only a skeleton in his arms.

Disillusioned, Cyprian seeks consolation and truth in Christianity. A year later, he discovers Justina in prison, where she has been sentenced for being a Christian. Cyprian, brought before the Governor, defends Christianity, and the Governor orders him and Justina beheaded. After their execution, the Devil appears, and is forced by God to clear Justina's name and announce Cyprian's redemption by his sacrifice.

The Mayor of Zalamea (*El alcalde de Zalamea*, wr. 1940/44). *Comedia histórica* in which Pedro Crespo, a wealthy peasant, has Don Álvaro, a young captain of noble birth, billeted in his home. An extremely proud man, Crespo will yield to no man when his

French production of *El alcalde de Zalamea*. Paris, Théâtre National Populaire, 1961. [French Cultural Services]

honor is at stake. Álvaro conceives a passion for Crespo's daughter Isabel, whom he abducts and rapes. Crespo is determined to avenge his honor, but before he is able to do so, he is elected mayor and magistrate of Zalamea. Forced to place justice above revenge, he goes to Álvaro and humiliates himself by begging him to marry Isabel and restore her honor. Álvaro contemptuously refuses, and Crespo arrests him. A dispute ensues between Crespo and Don Lope de Figueroa, Álvaro's general, who threatens to storm the prison and free Álvaro. Violence is averted by the arrival of King Philip II. The King listens to the case and demands to see Álvaro, but Crespo has already had him executed. Impressed by Crespo's steadfastness and agreeing that the penalty was just, the King appoints Crespo mayor for life.

Beware of Still Water (*Guárdate del agua mansa*, wr. 1649). *Comedia de capa y espada* concerning two sisters, Clara and Eugenia, the one serious and silent, the other worldly and talkative. Their widowed father Alonso wishes to marry one of them to the head of the family, a simple rustic hidalgo. The latter eventually decides on the flighty Eugenia, but she tries desperately to palm him off on Clara, who is the elder of the two. Meanwhile, Eugenia has been encouraging Don Juan and Don Pedro to rival each other for her hand. Their friend Don Félix mistakes Clara for Eugenia and gives her a letter asking that she choose between them in order to avoid disharmony. As an excuse for seeing Félix, Clara pretends to believe that the letter was addressed to Eugenia only as a cover that would allow Félix to approach her. When Eugenia dismisses both Juan and Pedro, the latter learn of the exchange between "Eugenia" and Félix, and they become jealous. Still pretending to be Eugenia, Clara appoints a rendezvous with Félix. Juan and Pedro break in, and a brawl ensues in which Alonso and the hidalgo join. Clara then explains her stratagem, and the plan ends with the marriage of Clara to Félix and of Eugenia to Juan. The character of the head of the family is close to the caricature types found in the *comedias de figurón.*

The Painter of His Own Dishonor (*El pintor de su deshonra,* wr. ca. 1648/50). *Comedia de pundonor* in which Don Juan Roca of Barcelona, a gifted painter, has married his much younger cousin Serafina, whom he loves passionately. Serafina, however, does not love him and has married him only after the reported death of Don Álvaro, to whom she had been secretly engaged. The couple visit the Governor of Naples, Álvaro's father, whose daughter Porcia is Serafina's best friend. Serafina confides that she is unhappy and unable to forget Álvaro. Álvaro suddenly appears with the Prince of Ursino, by whom he has been rescued from a shipwreck. Though still in love with him, Serafina is determined not to dishonor her marriage. However, her tears and confused emotions mislead Álvaro into thinking there is still hope for him. The Prince of Ursino, Porcia's suitor, catches a glimpse of Serafina and falls in love.

Serafina returns home, resigned to being Juan's faithful wife. When he is briefly absent from the house, Álvaro enters but meets Serafina's determined resistance. Juan returns unexpectedly, and Álvaro narrowly escapes. At a carnival party Álvaro, in disguise, dances with Serafina, and she again rejects him. Fire breaks out, and in the confusion Álvaro abducts Serafina and makes her a prisoner at his father's country estate. There the Prince of Ursino accidentally meets her. Still attracted to her, he commissions a painter whose works he has been buying to hide in the bushes and paint her portrait. The artist is Juan. From his hiding place he recognizes his wife, and as Álvaro woos her, Juan shoots both of them. He offers the sight of bloody corpses as the "painting of his own dishonor," and the fathers of the slain couple can find no fault with a man "who defends his honor."

Echo and Narcissus (*Eco y Narciso,* wr. 1661). Zarzuela based on a Greek myth. While hunting, the shepherd Antaeus captures Liriope, a strange creature clothed in skins, and brings her as a trophy to Echo, a beautiful maiden with whom he is in love. Liriope recounts that a magician had prophesied that her son Narcissus would die because of "a voice and a beauty"; she had therefore raised him in a cave, far from society. To find her absent son, she now asks everyone to sing, and Narcissus eventually appears. He has fallen in love with Echo's voice but in obedience to his mother gives her up and wanders off into the mountains. Liriope deprives Echo of the normal use of her voice. Wandering in the mountains, Echo finds Narcissus leaning over a pool. He speaks to the image, and Echo replies, but she can only repeat his last one or two words. Narcissus learns that there is no beautiful nymph in the water and that he has fallen in love with his own image; he dies, destroyed by his love of his own beauty and his hatred of a voice that echoes his despair. Narcissus is changed into a flower, and Echo turns to air when an amorous shepherd tries to embrace her.

The Great Prince of Fez (*El gran príncipe de Fez,* wr. 1668). *Comedia de santos* in which Muley Mahomet, Prince of Fez, is beset by religious doubts because of a reference in the Koran; his teacher Cide Hamet fails to clarify it for him. While the Prince sleeps, an Evil Genie and a Good Genie vie for domination over him. During the next day's battle with the King of Morocco, the Prince falls

German production of *El alcalde de Zalamea,* Berlin, 1961. [Goethe House]

from his horse and is stunned, but his wife Zara takes command and defeats the Moroccans. The unconscious Prince is once more fought over by the two genies. On his recovery, the Prince undertakes a pilgrimage to Mecca but is captured and taken to Malta by the Christian leader Don Baltasar. In the latter's library the Prince finds an account of the life of St. Ignatius of Loyola.

Ransomed through the efforts of Zara, the Prince sails for Mecca. However, when a storm threatens the ship, it is the Virgin Mary he invokes. She appears and advises him to return to Malta, where he is baptized before setting out on a pilgrimage to Rome. When Zara learns of his conversion, she is enraged, but she is comforted by the King of Morocco, who now hopes to marry her. Cide Hamet, humiliated, makes an unsuccessful attempt to poison the Prince with a deadly bouquet. The play ends with the apotheosis of the saintly Prince and the triumph of the Good Genie.

PLAYS

The following alphabetized lists of plays of Calderón have been compiled from the *Obras completas de don Pedro Calderón de la Barca* (Aguilar, Madrid, 1952–1956).

Dramas and Comedias.

1. *El acaso y el error* (*Chance and Error*). Play. Written ca. 1635/36?
2. *Afectos de odio y amor* (*Feelings of Love and Hate*). Play. Written 1658.
3. *Agradecer y no amar* (*Gratitude Without Love*). Play. Written 1650.
4. *El alcaide de sí mismo* (*His Own Judge*). Play. Written 1636.
5. *El alcalde de Zalamea** (*The Mayor of Zalamea*). Play. Written 1640/44.
6. *Amado y aborrecido* (*Loved and Hated*). Play. Written ca. 1650/52. Published ca. 1656 (2d printing).
7. *Amar después de la muerte o El Tuzaní de la Alpujarra** (*Love after Death, or Tuzaní of Alpujarra*). Play. Written 1633.
8. *Amigo, amante y leal* (*Friendship, Love, and Loyalty*). Play. Written ca. 1629/36 (?1629/31). Published 1653.
9. *Amor, honor y poder* (*Love, Honor, and Power*). Play. Produced June 29, 1623. Based on a story by Matteo Bandello.
10. *Antes que todo es mi dama* (*My Lady First of All*). Play. Written ca. 1636. Published 1662.
11. *Apolo y Climene* (*Apollo and Clymene*). Play. Written 1661. Part I of *El hijo del sol, Faetón*.
12. *Argenis y Poliarco* (*Argenis and Poliarco*). Play. Written ca. 1634.
13. *Las armas de la hermosura* (*Weapons of Beauty*). Play. Written 1652.
14. *A secreto agravio, secreta venganza** (*Secret Vengeance for a Secret Insult*). Play. Written 1635.
15. *El astrólogo fingido* (*The Feigned Astrologer*). Play. Written ca. 1624/25. Published 1633.
16. *Auristela y Lisidante* (*Auristela and Licidante*). Play. Written ca. 1653/60. Published 1663.
17. *La aurora en Copacabana* (*Dawn in Copacabana*). Play. Written ca. 1661.
18. *La banda y la flor* (*The Scarf and the Flower*). Play. Written 1631.
19. *Basta callar* (*It Is Enough to Keep Silent*). Play. Written ca. 1660/61.
20. *Bien vengas, mal, si vienes solo* (*Welcome, Trouble, if You Come Alone*). Play. Written 1635.

21. *Los cabellos de Absalón* (*Absalom's Hair*). Play. Written ca. 1634. Act 2 taken from Tirso de Molina's *La venganza de Tamar*.
22. *Cada uno para sí* (*Everyone for Himself*). Play. Written 1652.
23. *Las cadenas del demonio* (*The Devil's Chains*). Play. Written ca. 1635/36.
24. *Casa con dos puertas, mala es de guardar** (*A House with Two Doors Is Difficult to Guard*). Play. Written 1629. Published 1636.
25. *El castillo de Lindabridis* (*The Castle of Lindabridis*). Play. Written 1661/63?
26. *Celos, aun del aire, matan* (*Even Jealousy of the Air Kills*). Play. Written 1662?
27. *La cisma de Ingalaterra* (*The English Schism*). Play. Written ca. 1634.
28. *El conde Lucanor* (*Count Lucanor*). Play. Written ca. 1650/51. Published 1661.
29. *Con quien vengo, vengo* (*I Come with Whom I Come*). Play. Written ca. 1634/35.
30. *¿Cuál es mayor perfección?* (*Which Is the Greatest Perfection?*). Play. Written ca. 1650/52. Published 1663.
31. *La dama duende** (*The Phantom Lady*). Play. Written 1629.
32. *Darlo todo y no dar nada* (*Give Everything or Nothing*). Play. Written 1651.
33. *Dar tiempo al tiempo* (*Give Time to Time*). Play. Written 1650.
34. *La desdicha de la voz* (*Her Voice Her Misfortune*). Play. Written 1639.
35. *De una causa, dos efectos* (*From One Cause, Two Effects*). Play. Published 1671 (1658?).
36. *De un castigo, tres venganzas* (*A Punishment in Three Acts of Revenge*). Written ca. 1628. Published 1634.
37. *La devoción de la cruz** (*Devotion to the Cross*). Play. Written 1633.
38. *Dicha y desdicha del nombre* (*The Good and Bad Fortune in a Name*). Play. Written ca. 1660/61. Published 1662.
39. *Los dos amantes del cielo* (*The Two Lovers of Heaven*). Play. Written ca. 1636. Published 1636.
40. *Duelos de amor y lealtad* (*Duels for Love and Loyalty*). Play. Written 1678.
41. *Eco y Narciso** (*Echo and Narcissus*). Play. Written 1661.
42. *Los empeños de un acaso* (*Obliged by Chance*). Play. Written 1639.
43. *El encanto sin encanto* (*Enchantment Without Enchantment*). Play. Written 1650/52. Published (licensed) 1672.
44. *En esta vida todo es verdad y todo mentira* (*In This Life Everything Is Both True and False*). Play. Written 1659.
45. *El escondido y la tapada* (*The Hidden Man and the Veiled Woman*). Play. Written 1636.
46. *La estatua de Prometeo* (*The Statue of Prometheus*). Play. Written 1669.
47. *La exaltación de la cruz* (*The Exaltation of the Cross*). Play. Written 1648.
48. *La fiera, el rayo y la piedra* (*The Beast, the Thunderbolt, and the Rock*). Play. Written 1652.
49. *Fieras afemina amor* (*Love Tames the Wild Beasts*). Play. Written 1669.
50. *Fineza contra fineza* (*Favor Against Favor*). Play. Written ca. 1669/72.
51. *Fortunas de Andrómeda y Perseo* (*The Fortunes of Andromeda and Perseus*). Play. Written 1653.
52. *Fuego de Dios en el querer bien* (*The Fire of God in Loving Well*). Play. Written ca. 1640/44. Published 1660.
53. *El galán fantasma* (*The Phantom Courtier*). Play. Written ca. 1634/36.
54. *El golfo de las sirenas* (*The Gulf of the Sirens*). Play. Written 1656.
55. *La gran Cenobia* (*The Great Zenobia*). Play. Written ca. 1634.

56. *El gran príncipe de Fez** (*The Great Prince of Fez*). Play. Written 1668.

57. *Guárdate del agua mansa** (*Beware of Still Water*). Play. Written 1649.

58. *Gustos y disgustos son no más que imaginación* (*Pleasure and Displeasure Are Only Imagination*). Play. Written ca. 1634. Published 1656. Produced Valencia, 1638 (first performance?).

59. *Hado y divisa de Leonido y Marfisa* (*The Destiny and Emblem of Leonido and Marfisa*). Play. Written 1680.

60. *La hija del aire, Parte I* (*The Daughter of the Air, Part I*). Play. Produced by Adrián López, 1653.

61. *La hija del aire, Parte II* (*The Daughter of the Air, Part II*). Play. Produced by Adrián López, 1653.

62. *El hijo del sol, Faetón* (*Phaeton, the Son of the Sun*). Play. Written 1661.

63. *Los hijos de la fortuna, Teágenes y Ćariclea* (*The Children of Fortune, Theagenes and Chariclea*). Play. Written ca. 1651/53.

64. *El hombre pobre todo es trazas* (*Poverty Sharpens the Wits*). Play. Written 1628.

65. *El jardín de Falerina* (*The Garden of Falerina*). Play. Written 1648? Based on Matteo Maria Boiardo's *Orlando innamorato*.

66. *El José de las mujeres* (*The Female Joseph*). Play. Written ca. 1640/44. Published 1660.

67. *Judas Macabeo* (*Judas Maccabaeus*). Play. Published 1636.

68. *Lances de amor y fortuna* (*The Turns of Love and Fortune*). Play. Written 1624/25. Published 1635.

69. *El laurel de Apolo* (*The Laurel of Apollo*). Play. Written 1657. Produced Mar. 4, 1658.

70. *Luis Pérez el Gallego* (*Luis Pérez the Galician*). Play. Written 1628.

71. *El maestro de danzar* (*The Dancing Master*). Play. Written ca. 1651/52.

72. *El mágico prodigioso** (*The Wonder-working Magician*). Play. Written 1637.

73. *Mañanas de abril y mayo* (*Mornings in April and May*). Play. Written ca. 1637.

74. *Mañana será otro día* (*Tomorrow Is Another Day*). Play. Written 1636.

75. *Las manos blancas no ofenden* (*White Hands Do Not Offend*). Play. Written 1640.

76. *El mayor encanto, amor** (*Love, the Greatest Enchantment*). Play. Written 1635.

77. *El mayor monstruo del mundo* (*No Monster Like Jealousy*). Play. Written ca. 1634.

78. *El médico de su honra** (*The Surgeon of His Honor*). Play. Written 1635.

79. *Mejor está que estaba* (*Fortune Mends*). Play. Written 1631.

80. *El monstruo de los jardines* (*The Monster of the Gardens*). Play. Written ca. 1650/53.

81. *Mujer, llora y vencerás* (*Woman, Cry and You Will Conquer*). Play. Written 1660.

82. *Nadie fié su secreto* (*Keep Your Own Secret*). Play. Written ca. 1623/24.

83. *Ni Amor se libra de amor* (*Not Even Love* [i.e., Cupid] *Is Free from Love*). Play. Written 1662.

84. *La niña de Gómez Arias* (*The Daughter of Gómez Arias*). Play. Written ca. 1637/39.

85. *No hay burlas con el amor* (*No Jesting with Love*). Play. Written ca. 1631/32. Published 1650.

86. *No hay cosa como callar* (*There Is Nothing Like Silence*). Play. Written 1638/39.

87. *No siempre lo peor es cierto* (*Don't Always Believe the Worst*). Play. Written ca. 1648/50. Published 1652.

88. *Origen, pérdida y restauración de la Virgen del Sagrario* (*Origin, Loss, and Restoration of the Virgin of the Sagrario* [*of Toledo*]). Play.

89. *Para vencer amor, querer vencerle* (*To Conquer Love, Want to Conquer It*). Play. Written ca. 1633. Published 1654. Produced 1650.

90. *Peor está que estaba* (*From Bad to Worse*). Play. Written 1630.

91. *El pintor de su deshonra** (*The Painter of His Own Dishonor*). Play. Written ca. 1648/50. Published 1650.

92. *El postrer duelo de España* (*The Last Duel in Spain*). Play. Written ca. 1651/53.

93. *Primero soy yo* (*First Am I*). Play. Written ca. 1640/42.

94. *El príncipe constante** (*The Constant Prince*). Play, 3 acts; verse. Written 1629. Published 1636.

95. *La puente de Mantible* (*The Bridge of Mantible*). Play. Written 1632.

96. *El purgatorio de San Patricio** (*The Purgatory of St. Patrick*). Play. Written ca. 1634.

97. *La púrpura de la rosa* (*The Purple of the Rose*). Play. Written 1659. Produced Jan. 17, 1660.

98. *Saber del mal y del bien* (*Knowledge of Good and Evil*). Play. Written 1625.

99. *El secreto a voces* (*The Open Secret*). Play. Written 1642.

100. *El segundo Escipión* (*The Second Scipio*). Play. Written 1677.

101. *La señora y la criada* (*The Lady and the Maidservant*). Play. Written ca. 1636. Published 1679.

102. *La síbila de Oriente* (*The Sibyl of the Orient*). Play. Written ca. 1634/36.

103. *El sitio de Bredá* (*The Siege of Breda*). Play. Written 1625.

104. *También hay duelo en las damas* (*Women, Too, Have Honor to Defend*). Play. Written ca. 1648/50. Published 1664.

105. *Los tres afectos de amor* (*The Three Sentiments of Love*). Play. Written 1658.

106. *Las tres justicias en una* (*Three Judgments at a Blow*). Play. Written ca. 1636/37?

107. *Los tres mayores prodigios* (*The Three Greatest Marvels*). Play. Written 1636.

108. *La vida es sueño** (*Life Is a Dream*). Play. Written ca. 1631/32. Published 1636.

Autos Sacramentales.

1. *A Dios por razón de estado* (*To God* [or, punning, *Good-bye*] *for Reasons of State*). Play. Written 1650–1660?

2. *Los alimentos del hombre* (*The Nourishment of Man*). Play. Written 1676.

3. *A María el corazón* (*His Heart for Mary*). Play. Written 1664.

4. *Amar y ser amado y divina Filotea* (*To Love and Be Loved, or The Divine Philothea*). Play. Written 1681.

5. *Andrómeda y Perseo* (*Andromeda and Perseus*). Play. Written 1680.

6. *El año santo de Roma* (*The Holy Year in Rome*). Play. Written 1650.

7. *El año santo en Madrid* (*The Holy Year in Madrid*). Play. Written 1652.

8. *El árbol del mejor fruto* (*The Tree with the Best Fruit*). Play. Written 1661.

9. *El arca de Dios cautiva* (*The Ark of the Covenant in Captivity*). Play. Written 1673.

10. *La cena del rey Baltasar** (*Belshazzar's Feast*). Play. Written 1634.

11. *El cordero de Isaías* (*Isaiah's Lamb*). Play. Written 1681.

12. *El cubo de la Almudena*. Play. Written 1651.

13. *La cura y la enfermedad* (*Cure and Sickness*). Play. Written 1658.

14. *La devoción de la misa* (*Devotion to Mass*). Play. Written 1637?

15. *El diablo mudo* (*The Mute Devil*). Play. Written 1660.

16. *El día mayor de los días* (*The Greatest of All Days*). Play. Written 1678.

17. *El divino Jasón* (*The Divine Jason*). Play. Written before 1630.

18. *El divino Orfeo* (*The Divine Orpheus*). Play. Second version: Written 1663.

19. *Los encantos de la culpa* (*The Sorceries of Sin*). Play. Written ca. 1645?

20. *En valle de la zarzuela* (*In the Valley of the Zarzuela*). Play. Written ca. 1655?
21. *Las espigas de Ruth* (*The Wheat Tassels of Ruth*). Play. Written 1663.
22. *El gran duque de Gandía* (*The Grand Duke of Gandía*). Play. Written 1639?
23. *El gran mercado del mundo* (*The Great Marketplace of the World*). Play. Written 1634/35?
24. *El gran teatro del mundo** (*The Great Theatre of the World*). Play. Written 1635?
25. *La hidalga del valle* (*The Noblewoman of the Valley*). Play. Written 1634?
26. *La humildad coronada de las plantas* (*The Crowned Humility of the Plants*). Play. Written 1644.
27. *La iglesia sitiada* (*The Church Besieged*). Play. Written before 1630.
28. *El indulto general* (*The General Pardon*). Play. Written 1680.
29. *La inmunidad del sagrado* (*The Immunity of Consecrated Ground*). Play. Written 1664.
30. *El jardín de Falerina* (*Falerina's Garden*). Play. Written 1675.
31. *El laberinto del mundo* (*The Labyrinth of the World*). Play. Written 1677.
32. *La lepra de Constantino* (*Constantine's Leprosy*). Play. Written ca. 1660/63.
33. *El lirio y la azucena* (*The Iris and the White Lily*). Play. Written ca. 1660.
34. *Llamados y escogidos* (*The Called and the Chosen*). Play. Written 1649?
35. *Lo que va del hombre a Dios* (*That Which Goes from Man to God*). Play. Written 1640?
36. *El maestrazgo del toisón* (*The Master of the Order of the Fleece*). Play. Written 1659.
37. *Los misterios de la misa* (*The Mysteries of the Mass*). Play. Written 1640.
38. *Mística y real Babilonia* (*Mystical and Royal Babylon*). Play. Written 1662.
39. *La nave del mercader* (*The Merchant's Ship*). Play. Written 1674.
40. *No hay instante sin milagro* (*There Is No Moment Without a Miracle*). Play. Written 1672.
41. *No hay más fortuna que Dios* (*There Is No Other Fortune than God*). Play. Written 1653?
42. *El nuevo hospicio de pobres* (*The New Shelter of the Poor*). Play. Written 1668.
43. *El nuevo palacio del Retiro* (*The New Palace of Buen Retiro*). Play. Written 1634.
44. *El orden de Melchisedech* (*The Order of Melchizedek*). Play. Written ca. 1662/63.
45. *Las órdenes militares* (*Military Orders*). Play. Written 1662.
46. *El pastor fido* (*The Faithful Shepherd*). Play. Written 1677?
47. *La piel de Gedeón* (*Gideon's Skin*). Play. Written 1650.
48. *El pintor de su deshonra* (*Painter of His Own Dishonor*). Play. Written ca. 1644/50.
49. *El pleito matrimonial del cuerpo y el alma* (*Matrimonial Dispute Between the Body and the Soul*). Play. Written 1631?
50. *La primer flor del Carmelo* (*The First Flower of Carmel*). Play. Written before 1650.
51. *Primero y segundo Isaac* (*The First and Second Isaac*). Play. Written before 1659?
52. *El primer refugio del hombre y probática piscina*. Play. Written 1661.
53. *La protestación de la fe* (*The Confession of Faith*). Play. Written 1656.
54. *Psiquis y Cupido* (*Psyche and Cupid*). Play. Written 1640.
55. *¿Quién hallará mujer fuerte?* (*Who Will Find a Strong Woman?*). Play. Written 1672.
56. *La redención de cautivos* (*The Redemption of Prisoners*). Play. Written ca. 1672.

57. *El sacro Parnaso* (*Sacred Parnassus*). Play. Written 1659.
58. *El santo rey Don Fernando, Primera parte* (*The Saint King Ferdinand, Part I*). Play. Written 1671.
59. *El santo rey Don Fernando, Segunda parte* (*The Saint King Ferdinand, Part II*). Play. Written 1671.
60. *La segunda esposa y triunfar muriendo* (*The Second Wife, or Triumph in Death*). Play. Written 1649?
61. *La semilla y la cizaña* (*The Seed and the Weed*). Play. Written 1651.
62. *La serpiente de metal* (*The Metal Serpent*). Play. Written 1676.
63. *La siembra del Señor* (*The Sowing of God*). Play. Written before 1655.
64. *El socorro general* (*The Common Relief*). Play. Written 1644.
65. *Sueños hay que verdad son* (*There Are Dreams that Are True*). Play. Written 1670.
66. *El tesoro escondido* (*The Hidden Treasure*). Play. Written 1679.
67. *La torre de Babilonia* (*The Tower of Babylon*). Play. Written ca. 1650.
68. *Tu prójimo como a ti* (*Thy Neighbor as Thyself*). Play. Second version: Written before 1674.
69. *La vacante general* (*The Common Vacancy*). Play. Written 1649.
70. *El veneno y la triaca* (*Poison and Antidote*). Play. Written 1634.
71. *El verdadero Dios Pan* (*Pan, the True God* [in Spanish the title puns between Pan, the pagan god, and the bread, or *pan*, of the Eucharist]). Play. Written 1670.
72. *El viático cordero* (*The Eucharistic Lamb*). Play. Written 1665.
73. *La vida es sueño* (*Life Is a Dream*). Play. Second version: Written 1673.
74. *La viña del Señor* (*The Vineyard of the Lord*). Play. Written 1674.

EDITIONS

Collections.
Obras, 5 vols., Madrid, 1636–1677; *Obras*, ed. by J. de Vera Tassis y Villarroel, 9 vols., Madrid, 1682–1691; *Autos sacramentales*, ed. by P. Pando Mier, 6 vols., Madrid, 1717; *Comedias completas*, ed. by J. E. Hartzenbusch, 4 vols., Madrid, 1848–1850; *Select Plays of Calderón*, ed. by N. MacColl, London, 1888; *Six Dramas of Calderón*, tr. by E. Fitzgerald, London, 1909; *Autos sacramentales*, ed. by Á. Valbuena Prat, Madrid, 1926/27; *Obras completas*, 3 vols., Madrid, 1952–1956; *Four Plays*, tr. by E. Honig, New York, 1961.

Individual Plays.
Belshazzar's Feast. Published in *The Drama: Its History, Literature and Influence on Civilization*, ed. by A. Bates and tr. by D. MacCarthy, vol. 4, London, 1903–1904.
Beware of Still Water (*Keep Your Own Secret*). Published in *Western World Literature*, ed. by H. W. Robbins and W. H. Coleman and tr. by E. Fitzgerald, New York, 1938.
The Constant Prince. Published in *World Drama*, ed. by B. H. Clark and tr. by D. MacCarthy, vol. 2, New York, 1933.
Don't Always Believe the Worst. Published in *Cuarto comedias*, ed. by J. M. Hill and M. M. Harlan, New York, 1941.
The Great Theatre of the World. Published in *Masterpieces of the Spanish Golden Age*, ed. by A. Flores and tr. by M. Singleton, New York, 1957.
Life Is a Dream. Published in *Spanish Drama*, ed. by A. Flores and tr. by E. and E. Huberman, New York, 1962.
Love after Death. Published in *The Classic Theatre*, ed. by E. R. Bentley and tr. by R. Campbell, vol. 3, Garden City, N.Y., 1958–1961.
The Wonder-working Magician. Published in *The Clas-*

sic Theatre, ed. by E. R. Bentley and tr. by P. Shelley, vol. 3, Garden City, N.Y., 1958–1961.

CRITICISM

H. Breymann, *Calderon-Studien, vol. I, Die Calderon-Literatur: Eine bibliographische-kritische Übersicht,* Munich and Berlin, 1905; C. Pérez Pastor, *Documentos para la biografía de D. Pedro Calderón de la Barca,* Madrid, 1905; E. Cotarelo y Mori, *Ensayo sobre la vida y obras de D. Pedro Calderón de la Barca, Part I,* Madrid, 1924 (Part II not published); S. de Madariaga, *Shelley and Calderón,* 1935; Á. Valbuena Prat, *Calderón: Su personalidad, su arte dramático,* Barcelona, 1941; A. A. Parker, *The Allegorical Drama of Calderón,* Oxford, 1943; E. Frutos, *La filosofía de Calderón en sus autos sacramentales,* Saragossa, 1952; N. D. Shergold, "The First Performance of Calderón's *El Mayor Encanto Amor,*" *Bulletin of Hispanic Studies,* vol. XXXV, pp. 24–27, 1958; A. E. Sloman, *The Dramatic Craftsmanship of Calderón,* Oxford, 1958; E. Schwarz, *Hofmannsthal und Calderón,* Cambridge, Mass., 1962; B. W. Wardropper, ed., *Critical Essays on the Theatre of Calderón,* New York, 1965; E. W. Hesse, *Calderón de la Barca,* New York, 1968; *Allegorical and Metaphorical Language in the Autos Sacramentales of Calderón,* Catholic University of America Studies in Romance Languages and Literatures Series, New York, 1969.

CALVO-SOTELO, Joaquín (1905–). Spanish lawyer, lecturer, journalist, and dramatist. Since his first play, *To Land 500,-000 Kilometers* (*A la tierra kilómetros, 500,-000,* 1932), he has written almost forty dramas that, although they deal with everyday problems of contemporary Spain, cut beneath the surface of reality into the realm of the abstract, the philosophical, and the moral. *The Impasse* (*La muralla,* 1954), his most famous play, portrays a religious man's struggle to save his soul in the face of his family's incomprehension. In *Story of a Re-sentful Man* (*Historia de un resentido,* 1955), the protagonist, gnawed by envy and dissatisfaction at his own lack of success, seeks revenge by murdering a famous author and then dies himself, hating the world. In *Miracle in the Plaza del Progreso* (*Milagro en la Plaza del Progreso,* 1953), the intimate bonds of good and evil are revealed in the activities of a bank employee who steals money and then gives it to the poor.

Criminal of War (*Criminal de guerra,* 1951) is one of several plays in which Calvo-Sotelo treats the philosophical and moral problems of war; another is *The Inheritance* (*La herencia,* 1957), which concerns the profound effects of warfare and hatred on the minds of young children. The themes of dictatorship, power, and the intrinsic nature of man are developed in *The Chief* (*El jefe,* 1953), in which a group of escaped criminals who have fled to a deserted island recognize the necessity for law and order, without which they cannot survive. The light comedy *The Little Girl from Valladolid* (*Una muchachita de Valladolid,* 1957) concerns a young lady from the provinces of an imaginary South American country who is married to a worldly diplomat. Calvo-Sotelo's recent contributions to the Spanish stage include *Micaela* (1962) and *The Christ of the Forecasts* (*El Cristo de las Quinielas,* 1970).

CAMPTON, David (1924–). British dramatist whose principal work and success have been in the provinces. Campton wrote about twenty plays before *Going Home* was accepted for publication in 1949. Thereafter he enjoyed a modest success as a writer of one-acters. In 1955 his play *The Laboratory* was televised; his first full-length play, *The Cactus Garden,* was produced in Reading; and his comedy *Dragons Are Dangerous* was produced at the Theatre-in-the-Round, Scarborough.

Campton's later writings follow the line of the absurd and resemble the works of Pinter, although his most notable play, *The Lunatic View,* was produced in 1957, a year before Pinter's *The Birthday Party. The Lunatic View,* which Campton calls "a comedy of menace," is comprised of four sketches or "playlets . . . linked by spoof television announcements." The first, *A Smell of Burning,* details the invasion of a humdrum household by a sinister government agent; the second, *Memento Mori,* centers on the aging owner of a house under the floor of which he has buried his wife. *Getting and Spending,* the third, reveals the aimless existence of a married couple; and the fourth, *Then . . .,* concerns the two survivors of a nuclear explosion. Among his other plays are *Ring of Roses*

Joaquín Calvo-Sotelo. [Biblioteca Natcional, Madrid]

(1958), a light comedy; *The Gift of Fire* (1959), an adaptation of *Frankenstein;* and *A View from the Brink* (1960?), a comedy of menace similar in form to *The Lunatic View.* Campton also wrote a number of radio plays and some notable revue sketches. *See* PINTER, HAROLD; THEATRE OF THE ABSURD.

Albert Camus
(1913 – 1960)

Albert Camus, French journalist, essayist, novelist, and dramatist, was born on November 7, 1913, in Mondovi, Constantine Department, Algeria. After his father, an agricultural worker, was killed in World War I, his mother, of Spanish descent, moved to Algiers. There, while she worked as a servant, Camus attended community schools and in 1923 won a scholarship for the Lycée d'Alger. To earn pocket money, he spent his spare time working at a racetrack. In 1930, the year of his graduation, it was discovered that he had tuberculosis. Nevertheless, he went on to the University of Algiers, where he majored in philosophy while working at various jobs to support himself. He was married in 1933 and divorced in 1934, joined the Communist party, organized an amateur theatrical group, Le Théâtre de Travail, and toured Algeria with the theatre wing of Radio Algiers. By 1935 he had received his degree in philosophy, but in 1937 he was too ill to take his doctoral examinations. Beginning in that year he became associated as actor and director with a theatrical group known as L'Équipe. Later, he went to France and spent about a year in the Savoy mountains recuperating from an attack of tuberculosis. During this period he was inspired by his reading of Suetonius's *Lives of the Caesars* to write his first play, *Caligula,* which was not, however, to be produced until 1945.

Returning to Algiers, Camus began to work as a journalist for *L'Alger Républicain.* In 1939 he tried to enlist in the army but was rejected because of his health. The next year he remarried and went to Paris, where he worked for *Paris-Soir.* After the fall of France, he returned to Algeria and for the following two years taught in a private school in Oran. Back in Paris in 1942, he joined the Resistance and published *The Stranger* (*L'étranger*), a short philosophical novel that was to establish him as one of the leaders of the postwar French literary scene. *The Misunderstanding,* also translated as *Cross Purposes* (*Le malentendu,* 1944), was the first

Albert Camus in 1951. [Photo Hachette]

of his plays to be produced, and the same year, as editor in chief, he published the first issue of the then-clandestine newspaper *Combat,* which he edited until 1947.

The publication of Camus's second novel, *The Plague* (*La peste,* 1947), was an international literary event. The allegorical theme, in which a city in the grip of an epidemic is compared to a country under totalitarian rule, was taken up in different form in the play *State of Siege* (*L'état de siège,* 1948). Camus toured South America in 1950, but the following year he was forced by illness to give up all activities except writing. In 1953 he broke with his friend Jean-Paul Sartre after the latter had criticized his philosophical essay *The Rebel* (*L'homme révolté,* 1951), an analysis of the phenomenon of revolution, on what Camus regarded as narrow Communist party lines. *See* SARTRE, JEAN-PAUL.

The publication of *The Fall* (*La chute,* 1956), a short novel, was taken by some critics as an indication that Camus had reached a new stage in his ideological development and was trying to establish for a guilt-stricken war generation a new basis for action. Camus received the Nobel Prize for Literature in 1957 and the same year published a short-story collection entitled *Exile and the Kingdom* (*L'exil et le royaume*). He was killed in an automobile accident near Sens on January 4, 1960.

WORK

Although Camus's plays are inferior to his essays and fiction, they are representative of his thought and reflect a world view shared by many of his generation. As a writer associated with the philosophy of existentialism, Camus was concerned with the basic "absurdity" of life and the dilemma of the individual who must establish an identity for himself and find a meaning for his life in a world in which he is essentially alone. His plays are dramatizations of this dilemma, but they are weakened by Camus's predilection for creating characters who tend to be vehicles for his philosophy rather than convincing human beings.

Of his plays, the most successful is *Caligula* (wr. 1938, prod. 1945), in which the Roman Emperor uses his unlimited powers to explore the outermost limits of freedom. The merciless application of logic turns the pensive Emperor into a monstrous tyrant who eventually finds that "one cannot destroy everything without destroying oneself." His attempt to be free of others and faithful only to his personal logic ends in a "superior suicide," since he forces the hand of those who eventually kill him.

State of Siege (1948), similar in subject matter to Camus's novel *The Plague* (1947), is an allegory about totalitarianism, symbolized by the plague, and the crushing effects of the tyranny of fear on man's search for freedom. It reflects Camus's belief that fascism and Nazism were not mere cultural and political phenomena but recurrent and ever-present possibilities in human experience.

Among other plays by Camus are *The Misunderstanding* (1944), which tells of the return of a man to an inn run by his mother and sister in a gloomy, hopeless land. The two women, unaware of his identity and eager to obtain money that will enable them to begin their dismal lives over again in some new and sunny country, kill him and throw his body into the river. An attempt at tragedy in contemporary language, the play uses a situation first employed by George Lillo in *The Fatal Curiosity* (1736), a work that influenced the rise of *Schicksalstragödie* ("fate tragedy") in Germany. *The Just Assassins* (*Les justes,* 1949) deals with Russian revolutionaries who in 1905 decide to assassinate the Grand Duke. Camus's humanistic philosophy clearly emerges in a scene in which one of the revolutionaries explains how the unexpected presence of a child kept him from tossing his bomb at the critical moment. *The Possessed* (*Les possédés,* 1959) is a dramatic adaptation of Dostoyevsky's novel of the same name, a work that all his life Camus felt to be prophetic because it not only prefigured contemporary nihilism but also presented protago-

Scene from *Caligula,* with Gérard Philipe (front center). Paris, Théâtre Hébertot, 1945. [French Cultural Services]

Maria Casarés and Yves Brainville in *Les justes*.
Paris, Théâtre Hébertot, 1949. [French Cultural
Services]

nists "wanting to believe and yet unable to do
so—like those who people our society and our
spiritual world today."

Caligula (wr. 1938, prod. 1945). Camus
described this play as a "tragedy of the intelligence." After the death of his sister-mis-
tress Drusilla, Caligula, the young Emperor
of Rome, becomes aware of the intolerable
truth that "Men die; and they are not happy." He decides to use his power to free himself from the human condition and to awaken
others to the necessity of rebelling against its
absurdity. But his faulty conception of liberty
leads him to a systematic perversion of all
human values: pursuing individual freedom
to its logical extreme, he eventually alienates
himself from all mankind. Caligula orders
the execution of his friends, establishes merit
badges for brothel clients, impersonates
Venus, and holds stop-whistle poetry contests.
These events dramatize the arbitrariness of
death and suffering and the logical absurdity
of morality, love, and art. By endangering the
desire of the intellectual Chaerea for security, even at the expense of logic, and by flout-
ing the poetic Scipio's love for humanity,
Caligula estranges the two men closest to him
in spirit. Finally, he feels compelled to kill
Caesonia, his faithful mistress, because she is
the last link to any human emotion in him.
After Caligula finally understands that he

has not attained the freedom he sought, that
by destroying everything about him he has
also destroyed himself, he "accepts" death at
the hands of conspirators led by Chaerea and
Scipio.

State of Siege (*L'état de siège*, 1948).
Satire indicting bureaucratic totalitarianism
and utilizing a variety of theatrical techniques including pantomime, farce, lyrical
monologue, and chorus. When a comet appears in the sky over the fortified city of Cádiz, Nada, the nihilistic town drunkard,
warns that it is an evil omen. The stir among
the people is quashed by a government edict
forbidding them to acknowledge that they
have seen a comet, and a chorus parrots
"Nothing is happening, nothing will happen."
The Plague and his secretary appear in the
form of a man and a woman, usurp the governor's post, and put into effect an insidious
bureaucratic program in which all sentiment
and emotion are replaced by organization.
Death becomes a matter of logic and efficien-
cy, and certificates of existence are prerequi-
sites for living. Diego, a young man in love
with Victoria, tries to defy the authority of
the Plague. Victoria is stricken by the
Plague, and Diego sacrifices his life to save
her. Eventually, the Plague is expelled, personal courage having been demonstrated to
be the only means of combating the devastating effects of totalitarianism.

PLAYS

Unless otherwise noted, the plays were first performed
in Paris.

1. *Caligula**. Play, 4 acts. Written 1938. Published
1944. Produced Théâtre Hébertot, 1945.

2. *Le malentendu** (*The Misunderstanding;* also *Cross
Purposes*). Play, 3 acts. Published 1944. Produced
Théâtre des Mathurins, 1944.

3. (Adaptation). *Les esprits* (*The Ghosts*). Play. Produced originally 1946; Château d'Angers, June 16, 1953.
Based on Pierre de Larivey's play of the same name.

4. *L'état de siège** (*State of Siege*). Play, 3 parts. Published 1948. Produced Théâtre Marigny, Oct. 27, 1948.

5. *Les justes** (*The Just Assassins*). Play, 5 acts. Published 1950. Produced Théâtre Hébertot, Dec. 15, 1949.

6. (Adaptation). *La dévotion à la croix* (*Devotion to the
Cross*). Play. Produced Château d'Angers, June, 1953.
Based on Pedro Calderón de la Barca's *La devoción de la
cruz*.

7. (Adaptation). *Un cas intéressant* (*An Interesting
Case*). Play. Produced Théâtre La Bruyère, 1955. Based
on Dino Buzzati's play *Un caso clinico* (pub. 1953).

8. (Adaptation). *Requiem pour une nonne* (*Requiem for
a Nun*). Play. Produced Théâtre des Mathurins, 1956.
Based on William Faulkner's novel *Requiem for a Nun*
(1951).

9. (Adaptation). *Les possédés** (*The Possessed*). Play, 3
parts. Published 1959. Produced Théâtre Antoine, Jan.
30, 1959. Based on Fyodor Dostoyevsky's novel *The Possessed* (1871).

EDITIONS

Collections.
Récits et théâtre, Paris, 1958; *Caligula and Three Other
Plays*, tr. by S. Gilbert, New York, 1958.

Individual Plays.

Caligula. Published in *Masters of Modern Drama,* ed. by H. M. Block and R. G. Shedd and tr. by S. Gilbert, New York, 1962.

The Misunderstanding. Published in *The French Theater since 1930,* ed. by O. F. Pucciani, Boston, 1954.

CRITICISM

A. Maquet, *Albert Camus, ou L'invincible été,* Paris, 1956; R. Quilliot, *La mer et les prisons: Essai sur Albert Camus,* Paris, 1956; T. Hanna, *The Thought and Art of Albert Camus,* Chicago, 1958; A. Maquet, *Albert Camus: The Invincible Summer,* tr. by H. Briffault, New York, 1958; J.-C. Brisville, *Camus,* Paris, 1959; J Cruickshank, *Albert Camus and the Literature of Revolt,* London, 1959; P. Thody, *Albert Camus: A Study of His Work,* London and New York, 1959; R. de Luppé, *Albert Camus,* 6th ed., rev., Paris, 1960; G. Brée, *Camus,* New Brunswick, N.J., 1959, 1961; G. Brée, ed., *Camus: A Collection of Critical Essays,* Englewood Cliffs, N.J., 1962; P. Thody, *Albert Camus, 1913–1960,* New York, 1962; A. King, *Camus,* New York, 1964; C. Petersen, *Camus,* New York, 1969; N. A. Scott, *Camus,* 2d rev. ed., London, 1969.

CAÑIZARES, José de (1676–1750). Spanish dramatist. A prolific writer with more than 100 plays attributed to him, Cañizares imitated the great dramatists of the Siglo de Oro (Spanish Golden Age), especially Calderón de la Barca. He is best known for the ironic and highly comical *comedia de figurón* ("grotesque comedy") *Lucas the Fool* (*El dómine Lucas*), after Lope de Vega, generally acknowledged to be one of the best plays of this genre. A well-constructed parody of characters and situations, it is outstanding for its caricatured portrayal of the grotesque protagonist Lucas and his foolish fiancée Melchora. Other plays are *The Little Rogue in Spain* (*El picarillo en España*); *Honor Brings Understanding* (*El honor da entendimiento*); *The Most Distinguished Kitchenmaid* (*La más ilustre fregona*), after Cervantes; *The Lawsuit of Hernán Cortés* (*El pleito de Hernán Cortés*); and *The Sacrifice of Iphigenia* (*El sacrificio de Ifigenia*). Cañizares also wrote several *comedias de magia* ("magic plays"), which were very popular in his time. *See* SIGLO DE ORO.

CANTICUM. In Roman comedy, any part that was sung or accompanied by music. Roman comedies were composed of spoken parts (*diverbia*), written in the six-foot iambic line, and parts sung or declaimed with flute accompaniment (*cantica*). The declamatory *cantica,* melodramatic recitals performed by one or more actors, were written in trochaic or iambic lines of six or seven and one-half feet, the latter being the most common meter. The lyric *cantica,* usually sung by one actor but occasionally by two or more, were written in a variety of meters. An actor wanting to save his voice often mimed the *cantica* while a substitute sang from a concealed place. *See* ROMAN COMEDY.

Karel Čapek
(1890 — 1938)

Karel Čapek, Czech novelist, essayist, journalist, and dramatist, was born on January 9, 1890, in Malé Svatoňovice, in the Sudetenland section of Bohemia (now Czechoslovakia), the youngest of the three children of Antonín Čapek, the village doctor, and his neurotic and intellectual wife, Božena Čapková. A sensitive, precocious, and somewhat sickly child, pampered by his mother, Karel enjoyed a happy, normal childhood in large measure because of the healthy influence of his older brother Josef, who was his close friend and occasional collaborator for the rest of his life. Karel began to write verses, fairy tales, and short stories while in high school in Hradec Králové, Brno, and Prague. Even before he entered Charles University in Prague (1909), he had begun to collaborate with Josef in the composition of stories for Czech newspapers.

Karel continued his studies (primarily in

Karel Čapek. [Courtesy Czechoslovak Society of Arts and Sciences]

Tyrone Guthrie adaptation of *The Makropoulous Secret*. New York, Phoenix Theatre, 1957. [Friedman-Abeles]

philosophy) at Berlin University (1910) and in Paris (1911), finally obtaining a doctorate in philosophy at Charles University in 1915. During this period the brothers continued to write, producing their first book, *Zářivé hlubiny* (*The Luminous Depths*), a collection of tales published in 1916. That year Karel accepted a post as tutor to the son of Count Vladimir Lažanský, an outspoken Czech nationalist. During the next three years he worked as a journalist, meanwhile publishing a treatise on pragmatism and a volume of French poetry in translation.

In 1920 his play *The Outlaw* (*Loupežník*) was produced. The principal role was understudied by a young Czech actress, Olga Scheinpflugová, with whom Čapek fell in love. Poor health, however, prevented him from marrying her until 1935. The appearance of *R.U.R.: Rossum's Universal Robots* in 1921 established Čapek not only as the foremost

Czech writer of his time but as the first to enjoy an international reputation. For the next two years he was extremely active in the theatre. *From the Insect World* (*Ze života hmyzu*), which was a collaboration with Josef, was produced at the National Theatre in 1922, and *The Makropoulous Secret* (*Věc Makropulos*) was performed the same year at the Prague Municipal Theatre, of which Čapek was director between 1921 and 1923.

He seemed to tire of the theatre, however, and, except for another collaboration with his brother, *Adam the Creator* (*Adam stvořitel*, pub. 1927), wrote no more plays until 1937. He devoted his energies to journalism and the writing of novels: *Hordubal* (1933), *Meteor* (*Povětroň*, 1934), *An Ordinary Life* (*Obyčejný život*, 1934), and *The War with the Newts* (*Válka s mloky*, 1936). He had become increasingly involved in politics, supporting the liberal nationalism of Tomáš Masaryk and Eduard Beneš, and was one of the first and most eloquent opponents of Nazism. His last two plays, *The White Plague* (*Bílá nemoc,* 1937) and *The Mother* (*Matka,* 1938), reveal an intense concern with the horrors of totalitarianism.

The settlement of Munich in September, 1938, and the establishment of a new right-wing Czech government were severe blows to him. As Čapek came under continuous scurrilous attack, his health deteriorated, and he died in Prague on December 25, 1938, of a lung inflammation, less than three months before Nazi soldiers entered the city. The death of this champion of Czechoslovak nationalism and liberalism was widely regarded as symbolic, both in his own country and abroad.

WORK

From the Insect World. Prague, National Theatre, 1965. [Czechoslovak Center of the International Theatre Institute]

Although Čapek cannot be characterized precisely as an expressionist, his plays bear certain marked similarities to those of this school. Like expressionist dramatists, he was little concerned with the realistic representation of everyday life, preferring to deal with the larger issues of man's condition and fate.

Consequently, his characters tend to be archetypes, broadly sketched rather than created in careful detail. Although a certain flatness of characterization is produced, this quality is a deliberate and logical extension of Čapek's theme rather than a dramatic flaw. Similarly, his plots are highly experimental, often employing fantastic elements to point up his vision of the world.

Concern over the progressive mechanization and dehumanization of man pervades his work, dramatic and nondramatic alike. This is informed by three principal and fundamental motifs, delineated by William Harkins: (1) "destruction," often the total destruction of mankind as a result of the unleashing of forces that man is unable to control; (2) the "siege" of the individual by implacable and insurmountable external forces; and (3) Čapek's "anxiety concerning the reality of human personality," resulting in an insoluble conflict between naturalness and artificiality, individuality and civilization—forces that are opposed but mutually dependent.

The first of Čapek's plays, *The Fateful Game of Love* (*Lásky hra osudná;* wr. 1910, prod. 1930), is a one-act comedy in the

commedia dell'arte tradition, written with his brother Josef. In this brief ironic satire, the Čapeks use a traditional *commedia* love plot as the facade behind which they reveal the reality and vulgarity of real life. *See* COMMEDIA DELL'ARTE.

In *The Outlaw* (1920), comedy also covers pain: in the course of the Outlaw's fight for the lady he loves we are led to understand the past tragedies that cause her parents and her elder sister to want to protect the girl from the consequences of truth and love. *The Outlaw* was followed by *R.U.R.: Rossum's Universal Robots* (1921). This drama of the consequences of technology, which culminates in the take-over of the world by robots, was given widely differing interpretations throughout the world. This led Čapek to state that in the play, which reflected the times, "Human truth is opposed to another truth no less human, ideal against ideal, positive worth against positive worth."

From the Insect World (1922) is also a parable of the human condition, but from the timely analysis of the effects of the technological revolution Čapek (and his brother Josef) pass to a description of man's timeless vices, personified as insects. *The Makropoulous Secret* (1922) compounds the impression of pessimism produced by *From the Insect World,* as it endeavors to prove that immortality is a curse which renders what few blessings life may offer pallid and distasteful. Death is compassionate, for it comes before illusions have been lost and life's meaning has disappeared.

Čapek's last two plays are clear reflections of his fear of impending war and his opposition to dictatorship. *The White Plague* (1937) deals with a doctor who has discovered a cure for a mysterious white plague. Inadvertently the cure becomes the instrument of peace, lost when the doctor is killed by a war-crazy mob. *The Mother* (1938) is essentially a dialogue between a mother (the life force) and the ghosts of her husband and sons, who have all died in the service of a cause. When an approaching army is reported to be killing innocent women and children, she arms her last son herself.

From the Insect World (*Ze života hmyzu,* 1922).   Parable in two acts with prologue and epilogue. A tramp falls asleep in the woods. In the first of three dreams two female butterflies flirt alternately with two males and a poet. At length one of the males is killed, the two females fly off with the male in pursuit, and the poet is left behind to work. In the second dream Mr. and Mrs. Beetle's carefully laid-up store of dung is stolen by another beetle; a chrysalis announces that the world will be reborn through its birth; and an ambitious

Kathlene MacDonell and Louis Calvert in *R.U.R.* New York, Garrick Theatre, 1922. [Theatre Collection, The New York Public Library at Lincoln Center, Astor, Lenox and Tilden Foundations]

fly kills two crickets and is, in turn, devoured by a parasite. In the third dream rival colonies of ants struggle for power, and as the winners claim their victory, the Tramp crushes their leader. On awakening, the Tramp notices sudden silences in the forest and realizes that death has come. The morning light reveals his body to a woodcutter and his pregnant wife, who covers the body with leaves, commenting that there are always enough people in the world.

R.U.R.: Rossum's Universal Robots (1921).   Three-act symbolic fantasy. Helen Glory, of the Humane League, visits Rossum's Universal Robots island factory, marries its manager, Harry Donin, and remains on the island with the factory's small group of humans and their robot workers. Dr. Goll, who is still experimenting with the robots' manufacture, adds to their completely mechanical qualities the ability to feel pain. Then, urged by Helen, he further "humanizes" them. The years pass, robots replace men as workers, and wars begin to break out. As if in revolt, men stop propagating. This so shocks Helen that she secretly burns the robot formula. The island's robots, part of an international union, surround the house and kill all but one of the humans, Alquist, spared because he is the last human to work with his hands. Pressed by the robots, Alquist vainly tries to re-create the lost formula. Exhausted, he falls asleep, awakening to find that two robots, Helen and Primus, have just discovered love. Alquist, the last of his line, realizes the formula is now unnecessary, for a new Adam and Eve exist.

The White Plague (*Bílá nemoc,* 1937). Drama of a doctor in a totalitarian state who has discovered a cure for the "white plague." a deadly disease that attacks only people over forty. Pressed to reveal the cure, Dr. Galen refuses to do so unless the nations of the world agree to ban war. The dictator of Galen's own country contracts the disease and so is forced to agree to end his war preparations. But the lust for war has grown too great. On his way to treat the dictator, Galen is killed by a war-mad mob. The cure is lost, and with it the instrument for peace.

The Mother (*Matka,* 1938). Expressionistic drama of a mother who loses a husband and five sons, all of whom are killed fighting for or attempting to achieve something in which they strongly believe. In each there is a heroic imbalance, a single-minded devotion to some idea that borders on rigidity. This contrasts with the mother's feminine devotion to the perpetuation and preservation of life and her belief in balancing opposites. Much of the play is in the form of conversations between the mother and the ghosts of her dead loved ones. In the end, an approaching army is reported to be killing women and children. The mother hands her last and youngest son a gun so that he may join the fight against the invader.

PLAYS

1. (With Josef Čapek). *Lásky hra osudná* (*The Fateful Game of Love*). Comedy, 1 act. Written 1910. Produced Prague, Studio of National Theatre, May 15, 1930.
2. *Loupežník** (*The Outlaw*). Play. Produced Prague, National Theatre, Mar. 2, 1920.
3. (With Josef Čapek). *Ze života hmyzu** (*From the Insect World; The World We Live In; And So Ad Infinitum*). Parable; prologue and epilogue, 2 acts. Published 1920. Produced Prague, National Theatre, Mar. 8, 1922.
4. *Věc Makropulos** (*The Makropoulos Secret*). Play. Published 1920. Produced Prague, Municipal Theatre, Nov. 21, 1922.
5. *R.U.R.: Rossum's Universal Robots**. Play, 3 acts. Produced Prague, National Theatre, Jan. 25, 1921.
6. (With Josef Čapek). *Adam stvořitel** (*Adam the Creator*). Play. Published 1927.
7. *Bílá nemoc** (*The White Plague*). Play. Produced 1937.
8. *Matka** (*The Mother*). Play. Produced 1938.

EDITIONS

Collections.
R.U.R., and The Insect Play, London, 1961.
Individual Plays.
Adam the Creator. Published in *Dramas of Modernism and Their Forerunners,* ed. by M. J. Moses and O. J. Campbell and tr. by D. Round, rev. ed., Boston, 1941.
From the Insect World (*The Life of the Insects*). Published in *Chief Patterns of World Drama,* ed. by W. S. Clark II and tr. by P. Selver, Boston, 1946.
R.U.R.: Rossum's Universal Robots. Published in *Twenty-five Modern Plays,* ed. by S. M. Tucker and A. S.

Downer and tr. by P. Selver, 3d ed., New York, 1953.

CRITICISM

W. E. Harkins, *Karel Čapek,* New York, 1962; A. Matuška, *Karel Čapek: An Essay,* tr. by C. Alan, Prague, 1964.

CAPUANA, Luigi (b. Mineo, May 28, 1839; d. Catania, November 29, 1915). Italian novelist, critic, and playwright who belonged to the literary movement *verismo* ("realism") and whose best plays were written in Sicilian dialect. *Enchantment* (*Malìa,* 1895) is the rustic story of a young girl's passion for her brother-in-law. In *In Cavaliere Pidagna's Family* (*Lu Cavalieri Pidagna,* 1909), Capuana portrayed a gullible Sicilian ladies' man deceived by a sophisticated adventuress. The protagonist in *A Matchmaker* (*Un paraninfu,* 1914) avidly seeks husbands for all the spinsters in his village.

Enchantment (*Malìa,* 1895). Drama of suppressed sexual desire, superstition, and violence in a small Sicilian town. The action centers on Jana, a young woman who, although she is engaged to Nino, has conceived a violent passion for her brother-in-law Cola. Suppressing her desire with difficulty, Jana grows ill. Pallid and restless, she ultimately succumbs to bouts of hysteria verging on delirium. These attacks, as well as the revulsion she feels at the sight of Nino, lead the townspeople to believe she is the victim of an

Luigi Capuana. [Federico Arborio Mella, Milan]

evil spell. Soon Jana herself begins to believe this, and in a fervent prayer for help she casts herself at the foot of a statue of the Virgin Mary. Her torment, however, remains undiminished. One day, during a religious procession, she scandalizes the townsfolk by cursing aloud. Believing herself irretrievably lost, she confesses her passion to Cola, whose own lust is aroused. Once satisfied, Jana's desire turns to remorse. Gradually her tender feeling for Nino returns, and when she confesses her sin to him, he still wants to marry her. Cola, however, has been awakened by her love and attempts to prevent the marriage. In a violent fight with Nino he is killed, and at last the spell is broken.

CAPUS, Alfred (b. Aix, November 25, 1858; d. Neuilly, November 1, 1922). French novelist, journalist, and playwright whose ironic realism and independent heroines gave him for a time a reputation as the poor man's Ibsen. However, Capus's talent lay essentially in lighthearted social satires, and his occasional attempts at serious drama were failures. His protagonists accept life as a bad bargain and then proceed to make the best of it, convinced that with a little luck things can be made tolerably comfortable. His best-known play, *Brignol and His Daughter (Brignol et sa fille,* 1894), presents a typical Capus rascal whose faith that "something will come along" is justified when his pretty daughter becomes the wife of his chief creditor's nephew, thereby saving her father from ruin and imprisonment. In another major work, *Luck (La veine,* 1901), an unsuccessful lawyer patiently awaits his "big chance," and with the connivance of his mistress eventually gets his first important case. Rising rapidly in the world, he temporarily abandons his mistress, but because he is a basically decent fellow, he returns and marries her. *Rosine* (1897), *The Little Functionary (La petite functionnaire,* 1901), *The Two Schools (Les deux écoles,* 1902), and *The Passersby (Les passagères,* 1906) all present typically plucky and independent heroines who manage to arrive at successful compromises with the hard facts of life. Though most of Capus's twenty-five plays end happily, their mood is one of sophisticated, ironic pessimism, so dear to the French heart.

Brignol and His Daughter (*Brignol et sa fille,* 1894). Comedy revolving around Brignol, who spends his life dodging creditors and thinking up schemes to "get rich quick." His irresponsibility catches up with him when Commandant Brunet, who has entrusted Brignol with 30,000 francs, which Brignol has spent, demands his money. The commandant brings his wealthy nephew Maurice to confront Brignol, but Maurice falls in love with Brignol's daughter Cécile. Taking advantage of Maurice's feelings, Brignol then borrows money from him to pay the commandant and other debtors. Maurice has had no intention of marrying Cécile, but when he learns that she plans to go away, he proposes. Brignol happily agrees to her marriage with Maurice, and the commandant concludes that once Brignol is rid of his creditors, he will make a perfect father-in-law. Produced Paris, Théâtre du Vaudeville, November 23, 1894.

Ion Luca Caragiale
(1852 — 1912)

Ion Luca Caragiale, Romanian journalist, dramatist, and short-story writer, was born on January 30, 1852, in the tiny village of Haimanale, near Ploeşti. His was a theatrical family: two uncles were actors who also wrote for the stage, and his father had been an actor prior to a career as a lawyer and judge. He was raised in Ploeşti, but in 1868 he left for Bucharest to attend classes at the acting academy of his uncle Costache Caragiale. On the death of his father in 1870, Caragiale's

Ion Luca Caragiale. [Editura Enciclopedică Română, Bucharest]

mother and sister became dependent on him, and for the next thirty-odd years he was engaged in a continual financial struggle. In addition to his job as prompter with his uncle's acting company, Caragiale tutored privately, proofread for two newspapers, and translated French literature. In 1877 he worked as a journalist on a conservative paper and for a short period served on the editorial staff. Before his own plays appeared, he had established himself as a theatre critic with articles published in *România Liberă*.

His career as a dramatist began in 1879 with the very successful production of his comedy *A Stormy Night, or Number 9 (O noapte furtunoasă sau numărul 9)*. He reached his zenith as a playwright in 1884 with the comedy *The Lost Letter (O scrisoare pierdută)* and wrote the tragedy *False Witness, or Woe (Năpasta)* in 1890. It has been aptly said of Caragiale that "he made more reputation than money." Though he wrote only eight plays, he is considered Romania's greatest dramatist.

During his years as a playwright he continued to work as a journalist; in addition, he served as an inspector of schools between 1881 and 1884. In 1888 he was appointed director general of the National Theatre in Bucharest, a post he held only a few months. The same year he married and again was confronted with problems of finances; between 1889 and 1904 he struggled to support

Dandanache, a character in *A Stormy Night*. [Embassy of the Socialist Republic of Romania]

The Lost Letter. [Embassy of the Socialist Republic of Romania]

his family, working as a civil servant, tending a restaurant, and even running a tavern. In 1904, however, he received a share of an inheritance and used the money to move to Berlin—a self-inflicted exile motivated in large part by the deliberate neglect of his literary achievements by his countrymen. There Caragiale died on June 9, 1912.

WORK

Considered Romania's most important dramatist, Caragiale has been said to have done for Romania what Mark Twain did for the Mississippi River Valley. The first four of his major plays are parodies of Romanian life in the late nineteenth century. Set in Bucharest, they satirize the mores and social hypocrisies of the petty bourgeoisie. His perceptions of contemporary Romanian life were acute, his characters vividly drawn, his plots imaginative, and his satire biting. His talent was denied the recognition it deserved.

The production of his first play, *A Stormy Night, or Number 9* (1879), caused a furor similar to the reception Dublin gave Synge's *The Playboy of the Western World;* Caragiale was summarily denounced as immoral and unpatriotic. The satire in his next play, *Mr. Leonida and the Reactionaries (Conul Leonida față cu reacțiunea;* pub. 1880, prod. 1912), was so pointed that theatre officials changed the two main characters from a member of the privileged aristocracy (representing the ruling class) and his mistress to an old provincial and his wife; thus the satire was reduced to farce, and the characters became comic types

at whom the audience could laugh. *The Lost Letter* (1884), Caragiale's masterpiece, is a particularly sharp satire exposing the corrupt political customs of the day. It was followed by *Carnival Scenes* (*D'ale carnavalului*, 1885), a milder satire emphasizing the comic. With *False Witness, or Woe* (1890), Caragiale departed from his usual style and attempted a psychological peasant drama of murder and revenge. Anca, suspecting her second husband Dragomir of having murdered her first husband, carefully and coldly plots her revenge and his downfall.

A Stormy Night, or Number 9 (*O noapte furtunoasă sau numărul 9*, 1879). Comedy in which Dumitrache, a petty tyrant and bully, is intensely jealous of his wife Veta. Since he is head of the civil guard and often must make nightly rounds, he is fearful for his honor. Therefore he has his assistant Chiriac guard the house while he is away, completely unaware that Chiriac is Veta's lover. At the same time, Veta's sister Zita is carrying on a clandestine relationship with Rica, a journalist and law student, who blunders into Dumitrache's house thinking he is visiting Zita. There he is caught by Dumitrache and Chiriac, both of whom threaten to kill him. However, Zita arrives, and the matter is straightened out. Dumitrache is placated when he becomes convinced that his honor and his wife's virtue are still intact.

Mr. Leonida and the Reactionaries (*Conul Leonida față cu reacțiunea*; pub. 1880, prod. 1912). Before retiring to bed, Mr. Leonida tells his wife Efimița about Romania's great revolution, many years earlier, and of the establishment of the republic, which lasted

Scenes from *The Lost Letter*, National Theatre "Ion Luca Caragiale," Bucharest. [Editura Enciclopedică Română, Bucharest]

Emil Botta in *False Witness*. [Embassy of the Socialist Republic of Romania]

three whole weeks. His idea of a republic is a superutopian state in which there are no taxes and the government pays everyone a fair wage. Later that night the couple are awakened by gunfire. Efimița insists this must be the revolution, but Leonida declares that a revolution is impossible, for firearms are prohibited. As the gunfire persists, Leonida becomes convinced that the reactionaries are taking over and that his life is in danger —after all, he's a well-known republican. The couple barricade the door but are told by the maid Safta that the "reactionaries" are merely some townspeople, led by the local policeman, celebrating Shrove Tuesday.

The Lost Letter (*O scrisoare pierdută*, 1884). Comedy set in the capital of a mountain province where an election is to be held. One of the candidates, Stepan Tipătescu, discovers that his opponent, Cațavencu, has a love letter that Tipătescu had written to Zoe Trahanache, wife of Tipătescu's friend. If the letter were published, the resulting scandal would cost Tipătescu the election. His efforts to recover the letter are in vain, as are the attempts he and Zoe make to bribe Cațavencu. Offered any job he wants in Tipătescu's cabinet, Cațavencu wants all or nothing. At this point the government makes known its wish to have Agamemnon Dandanache elected. Tipătescu throws his support to Cațavencu and determines to fight the government. In the meantime, Cațavencu loses the letter. It is found by the town drunk and finally retrieved by Zoe. Dandanache wins the election, and the play ends with a scene of reconciliation and celebration.

Carnival Scenes (*D'ale carnavalului*, 1885). Intricately plotted comedy set against the background of carnival time in Bucharest. Mița is deceiving her lover Mache with the barber Nae Girimea, who is also having an affair with Didine, who in turn is deceiving her lover Pompon. Mița discovers Nae's infidelity and tells Pompon, already suspicious of Didine, that his mistress is having an affair with her lover. The confusion is compounded when Pompon is told that Mache is Mița's lover and proceeds to beat up the befuddled Mache. This merry mix-up continues until Nae finally convinces both cuckolded lovers that their mistresses are faithful. Then, as the repentant lovers abjectly apologize to their mistresses, the irrepressible Nae surreptitiously makes assignations with both women for that night.

PLAYS

All were first performed in Bucharest.

1. *O noapte furtunoasă sau numărul 9** (*A Stormy Night, or Number 9*). Comedy, 2 acts. Published 1879. Produced National Theatre, Jan. 18, 1879.

2. *Conul Leonida față cu reacțiunea** (*Mr. Leonida and the Reactionaries*). Farce, 1 act. Published 1880. Produced National Theatre, 1912.

3. *O soacra.* Farce-fantasy, 1 act. Published 1894. Produced National Theatre, Feb. 17, 1883.

4. *O scrisoare pierdută** (*The Lost Letter*). Comedy, 4 acts. Published 1885. Produced National Theatre, Nov. 13, 1884.

5. *D'ale carnavalului** (*Carnival Scenes*). Comedy, 3 acts. Published 1885. Produced National Theatre, Apr. 8, 1885.

6. *Năpasta* (*False Witness, or Woe*). Drama, 2 acts. Published 1890. Produced National Theatre, Feb. 3, 1890.

7. *1 Aprilie* (*April First*). Monologue. Published 1896. Produced National Theatre, Sept. 6, 1912.

8. *Incepem.* Play, 1 act. Published 1909. Produced Bucharest, Leon Popescu Theatre, Sept. 12, 1909.

EDITIONS

The Lost Letter, and Other Plays, tr. by F. Knight, London, 1956; *Opere,* ed. by A. Rosetti, 3 vols., Bucharest, 1959–1962; *Opere,* 4 vols., Bucharest, 1962.

CRITICISM

H. P. Petrescu, *Ion Luca Caragiales Leben und Werke,* Leipzig, 1911; A. Colombo, *Vita e opere di Ion Luca Caragiale,* Rome, 1934; P. Bujor, *Amintiri de A. Vlahață și Ion Luca Caragiale,* Bucharest, 1938; B. Jordan and L. Predescu, *Caragiale,* Bucharest, 1939; S. Iosifescu, *Caragiale,* Bucharest, 1951; W. Siegfried, *Personaje și decoruri din teatrul lui Caragiale,* Bucharest, 1956; M. Anghelescu, *Trei fețe caragialești,* Bucharest, 1958.

CARETTE, Louis. *See* MARCEAU, FÉLICIEN.

CARO, Annibale (1507–1566). Italian man of letters, poet, and author of the prose comedy à clef *The Comedy of the Ragamuffins* (*La comedia degli straccioni,* ca. 1544), which was largely inspired by Achilles Tatius's fourth-century Greek romance *The Adventures of Leucippus and Cleitophon*.

CAROLINE DRAMA. English drama written during the reign of Charles I (1625–1649).

CARON, Pierre-Augustin. *See* BEAUMARCHAIS, PIERRE DE.

Paul Vincent Carroll
(1900 – 1968)

Paul Vincent Carroll, Irish dramatist, was born on July 10, 1900, in Blackrock, County Louth, where until the age of thirteen he was educated by his father, a schoolmaster. After three years at St. Mary's College, Dundalk, he went to Dublin. While studying to be a teacher at St. Patrick's Training College, he became involved in the Irish Rebellion. At the same time, he learned the rudiments of drama at the Abbey Theatre. After graduating, to avoid the pervasive influence of the Irish clergy he went to Glasgow to teach. He was later to remark, "In religion I cling by conviction to Catholicism, but God save me from its administrators." In 1923 he married Helena Reilly, a dress designer, with whom he had three daughters.

While teaching in Glasgow, he began his "reeducation" in the world of literature, rediscovering the Greeks, Shakespeare, and the romanticists and finally falling under the influence of Swift, Hardy, Ibsen, and Synge.

His first play, *The Watched Pot* (1931), was followed by *Things that Are Caesar's,* which won the Abbey Theatre Award for 1932. But it was not until the international success of *Shadow and Substance* (wr. 1934), which won the 1938 New York Drama Critics Circle award for the best foreign play, that he achieved recognition as a dramatist. The Abbey Theatre, bowing to clerical strictures, refused to produce *The White Steed* (wr. 1938), which was performed with success in the United States in 1939. During World War II Carroll was active in the British repertory movement, founding, in partnership with James Bridie, the Glasgow Citizens' Theatre in 1943 (*see* BRIDIE, JAMES). Declaring himself apolitical, he stated, "I like a system of government that leaves me alone to do what I want to do." Carroll lived near Glasgow until his death on October 20, 1968.

WORK

Despite an auspicious beginning, Paul Vincent Carroll did not achieve a major position among contemporary dramatists. His important successes came early in his career, with *Shadow and Substance* (1937) and *The White Steed* (1939), both of which won the New York Drama Critics Circle award. Thereafter he wrote no drama of comparable quality.

Locked in conflict with the Catholic Church, Carroll used his plays to present his arguments. He first took issue with the church in his second play, *Things that Are Caesar's* (1932). Written in collaboration with Teresa Deevey, it depicts a struggle between a bigoted mother and a freethinking father over their daughter's happiness. Subsequent plays include *The Coggerers* (1936), about the Easter Rebellion; *Shadow and Substance* (1937), depicting the conflict between the church and a renegade, which causes the

Paul Vincent Carroll. [Theatre Collection, The New York Public Library at Lincoln Center, Astor, Lenox and Tilden Foundations]

Cedric Hardwicke and Julie Haydon in *Shadow and Substance.* New York, Golden Theatre, 1938. [Photograph by Vandamm. Theatre Collection, The New York Public Library at Lincoln Center, Astor, Lenox and Tilden Foundations]

death of an innocent girl; *The White Steed* (1939), taken from an Irish folk legend and pitting rigid morality and secular law against one another; *The Strings, My Lord, Are False* (1942), about the place of the Catholic Church in modern war; and *The Devil Came from Dublin* (1953), an uninhibited but belabored farce about a district justice from Dublin who wisely and unsuccessfully tries to curtail the smuggling carried on by the residents of Chuckeyhead, on the Northern Ireland border.

Shadow and Substance (1937). Drama presenting the conflicting forces in Ireland, which finally cause the death of an innocent girl. Canon Skerritt, a man of taste and intelligence, is extremely proud and feels himself superior to his parishioners. He is in constant conflict with Dermot O'Flingsley, the liberal-thinking schoolmaster, whom he regards as a troublemaker. The only thing the two men have in common is their affection for Canon's Skerritt's servant Brigid, who, in turn, loves them both. A devout, ingenuous girl, Brigid has confided to O'Flingsley that St. Brigid ap-

Act III, scene ii, of *Shadow and Substance*, with Henry Sothern, Len Doyle, Cedric Hardwicke, Julie Haydon, Lloyd Gough, and Sara Allgood. New York, Golden Theatre, 1938. [Theatre Collection, The New York Public Library at Lincoln Center, Astor, Lenox and Tilden Foundations]

pears to her in visions. Sympathizing with her, he urges her to tell the canon, but when she does so, the canon refuses to believe her. Meanwhile, the canon discovers that the schoolmaster is the author of a controversial book and discharges him. Because of the book, the townspeople's rage against O'Flingsley builds up dangerously, and Brigid sees in a vision that there will be violence. She rushes out to prevent trouble but is killed by a rock thrown at the schoolmaster. As Canon Skerritt and O'Flingsley stare at her body, each realizes that he shares responsibility for her death.

The White Steed (1939). Comedy drama in which Father Shaughnessy, an intolerant moralist, temporarily replaces Canon Matt Lavelle, whose legs have been paralyzed by a stroke. Father Shaughnessy forms a vigilance committee to stamp out sin, which in his view includes drinking, courting, and interfaith marriages. Through his committee

he breaks up the engagement of schoolmaster Denis Dillon to a Protestant girl and discharges librarian Nora Fintry because she has been seen with a man. Denis is intimidated, but Nora is determined to fight the priest. She and Denis fall in love, and through her Denis finds the strength to stand up to the priest. Inspector Toomey, who has tried to protect the secular rights of those oppressed by the vigilance committee, threatens to arrest the priest, and a mob gathers to prevent him from doing so. Then Canon Lavelle appears, miraculously walking. He calms his parishioners, sends them home, and rebukes Father Shaughnessy for his hotheadedness and "spiritual snobbery." The canon's offer of reinstatement is rejected by Denis, who declares his independence and goes off to find his strength and love, Nora.

PLAYS

1. *The Watched Pot*. Drama. Produced 1931.
2. (With Teresa Deevey). *Things that Are Caesar's*.

Drama, 3 acts. Produced Dublin, Abbey Theatre, Aug. 15, 1932.

3. *Shadow and Substance.* Drama. Written 1934. Produced Dublin, Abbey Theatre, Jan. 25, 1937.

4. *The Coggerers (The Conspirators).* Play, 1 act. Published 1939. Produced Dublin, Abbey Theatre, November, 1936.

5. *The White Steed.* Play, 3 acts. Written 1938. Published 1939. Produced New York, Cort Theatre, Jan. 10, 1939.

6. *Beauty Is Fled.* Play, 1 act. Published 1938.

7. *Kindred.* Play. 1939.

8. *The Old Foolishness.* Play. Written 1940. Produced London, Arts Theatre, May 5, 1943.

9. *The Strings, My Lord, Are False.* Drama of the Clydeside air raids, 4 scenes. Written 1942. Produced Dublin, Olympia Theatre, Mar. 16, 1942.

10. *The Wise Have Not Spoken.* Play. Written 1944. Produced London, 1946.

11. *The Chuckeyhead Story.* Play, 3 acts. Written 1950. Published 1958. Produced Bournemouth, Pavilion Theatre, Oct. 9, 1950. Revived under title *The Devil Came from Dublin.* Produced 1953.

12. *Green Cars Go East.* Play. Written 1951.

13. *Interlude.* Play, 1 act.

EDITIONS

Three Plays, London, 1944; *Irish Stories and Plays,* New York, 1958.

Shadow and Substance. Published in *Five Great Modern Irish Plays,* ed. by G. J. Nathan, New York, 1941.

CASELLA, Alberto (b. Prato, November 1, 1891). Italian writer, critic, and dramatist in whose "tragic fable" *Death Takes a Holiday* (*La morte in vacanza,* 1923), Death lures a young girl from high society into his domain. The suggestive quality of the conception recalls German romanticism at its peak, but the underlying polemic against the frivolity of the milieu portrayed makes the play contemporary.

Death Takes a Holiday (*La morte in vacanza,* 1923). Supernatural fantasy comedy that takes place at a house party in the castle of Duke Lambert, whose son Corrado is in love with Grazia. As the party begins, Grazia feels a cold wind in the garden and is terrified. The guests discuss various near-fatal accidents of the past few hours. When Death confronts the Duke and announces his intention to live as a mortal and take a gay holiday, the reason for these mysterious occurrences is made clear. Death, called Prince Sirki for the duration of his stay, falls in love with Grazia and she with him. The Duke is appalled and finally reveals the secret to his son and some of the guests. Nothing can be done, however, for Death, although impressed by mortal man's courage, is omnipotent, and Grazia, having always been enamored of Death, now joins him forever.

CASEY, John. *See* O'CASEY, SEAN.

Alejandro Casona
(1903 — 1965)

Alejandro Rodríguez Álvarez, Spanish poet and dramatist who wrote under the pseudonym Casona, was born on March 23, 1903, in the Asturian village Besullo, the third of five children of Gabino Rodríguez and the former Faustina Álvarez. His parents, both teachers, wished to prepare their children to be teachers as well, and to find proper schooling to this end they moved the family often. Alejandro studied in Gijón and Palencia before earning his baccalaureate in Murcia in 1919. In 1922, following two years at the University of Murcia, financial problems forced his transfer to the Escuela Superior del Magisterio, a pedagogical institution in Madrid, from which he graduated in 1926, the year his first volume of poetry, *The Pilgrim with the Flowing Beard* (*El peregrino de la barba florida*), appeared.

In 1928, Casona and his bride, the former Rosalía Martín, were sent by the Primo de Rivera dictatorship to the Valle de Arán, in the Pyrenees, where he served as superintendent of an elementary school. During his two years there, Casona published a book of

Rose Hobart and Philip Merivale in Alberto Casella's *Death Takes a Holiday.* New York, Ethel Barrymore Theatre, 1929. [Theatre Collection, The New York Public Library at Lincoln Center, Astor, Lenox and Tilden Foundations]

Alejandro Casona.
[New York Public
Library]

poems, *The Flute of the Toad* (*La flauta del sapo,* 1930), founded the children's theatre called the Painted Bird (*El Pájaro Pinto*), and wrote a fantasy, *The Siren Castaway* (*La sirena varada;* wr. 1929, prod. 1934).

In 1930 Casona became superintendent of an elementary school in León and in 1931 won a competitive examination to become superintendent of schools in Madrid. Later that year he was made director of the Teatro del Pueblo of the Misiones Pedagógicas, a government project designed to bring culture to the rural populace. His assignments included the writing and arranging of plays for touring companies as well as the organizing and directing of the Teatro del Pueblo. About the same time he produced three one-act plays: *Interlude of the Cripple Who Married a Fierce Woman* (*Entremés del mancebo que casó con mujer brava*), about the taming of a shrew; *Sancho Panza on the Island of Barataria* (*Sancho Panza en la isla Barataria*), a dramatization of episodes taken from *Don Quixote;* and *The Ballad of Atta Troll* (*Balada de Atta Troll*), an adaptation from Heine later incorporated in *Our Natacha* (*Nuestra Natacha,* 1935).

The Siren Castaway won the Lope de Vega Prize in 1934, and its subsequent performance in Madrid met with great success. In 1935

Casona's revision of another fantasy, *The Devil Again* (*Otra vez el diablo*), originally written eight years earlier, was produced to critical acclaim. His next success, *Our Natacha,* about student reformers confronting reactionary indifference, subsequently caused the Franco regime to ban his works. In 1937 Casona left Spain for Paris, where he became director of a touring theatre company that traveled to all the Spanish-speaking countries in the Americas, and in 1939 he settled in Buenos Aires, where he continued to write. Among the major plays written during his exile are *No Suicide Allowed in Spring* (*Prohibido suicidarse en primavera,* 1937), *The Lady of the Dawn* (*La dama del alba,* 1944), and *The Boat Without a Fisherman* (*La barca sin pescador,* 1945). He remained in Buenos Aires until 1963, when he returned to Spain. Casona died in Madrid on September 17, 1965, as the result of a heart attack that occurred during preparations for the Spanish premiere of *The Three Perfect Married Women* (*Las tres casadas perfectas,* 1941).

WORK

Because of his forced exile, Alejandro Casona became more a part of the mainstream of modern European theatre than did Federico García Lorca, his distinguished contemporary who was killed in 1936 by the same extremists who banned Casona's works. Like Lorca, Casona explored the chasm between dreams and reality, but his aim was to awaken his countrymen, whom he saw as committed to isolation, reaction, and inertia. He possessed the curious ability to mix fantasy with sociopolitical themes and thereby to produce highly personalized dramas that contain serious underlying messages. With psychological insight he deliberately destroyed the comfortable illusions of his characters and propelled them into the flesh-and-blood world of responsibilities and demands. His plays are strongly poetic, as many of the titles suggest. While most of his work has a distinctly Spanish quality, the implications of his plays are universal rather than local. The majority, written after his exile, show the influence of Pirandello and exhibit Casona's basic humanitarian concerns. See PIRANDELLO, LUIGI.

Casona's most notable works are *The Siren Castaway* (wr. 1929, prod. 1934), about the return to sanity of a girl who had taken refuge in madness; *The Lady of the Dawn* (1944), which focuses upon the mystery of the cycle of death and rebirth; and *The Trees Die Standing* (*Los árboles mueren de pie,* 1949), concerning a scheme designed to preserve an old lady's illusion about her criminal grandson, whom she believes to be an architect.

La dama del alba.
[Consulate General of Spain]

Among other important plays are an overt social drama, *Our Natacha* (1935), a criticism of rigid methods of education and a plea for academic reform; *The Boat Without a Fisherman* (*La barca sin pescador*, 1945), which depicts the birth of conscience in a shameless capitalist who is ready to kill in order to satisfy his greed; *The Devil Again* (wr. 1927, prod. 1935), a fantasy morality play in which a young man enlists the devil's aid to make an amorous conquest but repudiates Satan at the crucial moment; and *The Crown of Love and Death* (*Corona de amor y muerte;* also known as *Doña Inés de Castro*, 1955), about the tragic love of Inés de Castro and Prince Pedro of Portugal. Other notable plays by Casona are *The Wife of the Miller of Arcos* (*La molinera de Arcos*, 1947), a reworking of Pedro Antonio de Alarcón's *The Three-cornered Hat* (1874); and *No Suicide Allowed in Spring* (1937), in which a number of men intent upon suicide decide to live.

While in Buenos Aires, Casona made a number of motion pictures, including *Our Natacha* (1943) and *The Mary Celeste* (1944), which are adaptations of his own plays. He also wrote stories, essays, articles, and lecture texts.

The Siren Castaway (*La sirena varada;* wr. 1929, prod. 1934). Comedy drama of Ricardo, an eccentric young millionaire, who invites to a "haunted" house half a dozen men of drastically different backgrounds and beliefs. His idea is to found a republic of individuals who have nothing in common. While he is waiting for Samy, an old clown, to arrive, a strange, beautiful girl appears; she claims that her name is Sirena and that she is a mermaid. Ricardo is captivated and becomes her lover. Samy finally arrives and tells Ricardo that Sirena is his daughter María and that she is mad. Don Florín, a doctor, takes her under his care and restores her to sanity by forcing her to confront certain grim facts of her past. Ricardo, however, wanting to spare her pain and preferring her as she was, tries to re-create her madness. But María clings to sanity, and Ricardo finally realizes that he can love her as much as he had loved "Sirena."

The Lady of the Dawn (*la dama del alba*, 1944). Called a ballad by its author, this drama has the lyric and mystical qualities of a legend. The Pilgrim, a beautiful young woman, symbol of death, arrives at the rural home of a grandfather who lives with his three grandchildren and their mother. The Pilgrim has come for the visitor, young Martín, who a few years before married Angelica, the eldest granddaughter. After three days of marriage, Angelica was said to have drowned in the river. Only Martín knows that in fact she did not drown but sailed to the other bank of the river, where a stranger was wait-

La barca sin pescador. Madrid, Teatro Bellas Artes, 1963. [New York Public Library Picture Collection]

self. But his grandmother has already discovered it, though she pretends to know nothing. She sends him away, however, and eventually says good-bye to the two impersonators. Their visit has been the happiest time of her life, and she prefers to keep her illusions.

PLAYS

1. *Otra vez el diablo* (*The Devil Again*). Morality play, prologue and 3 acts. Written 1927. Published 1935. Produced Madrid, Teatro Español, Apr. 26, 1935.

2. *La sirena varada* (*The Siren Castaway*). Comedy, 3 acts. Written 1929. Published 1934. Produced Madrid, Teatro Español, Mar. 17, 1934.

3. *Sancho Panza en la isla Barataria* (*Sancho Panza on the Island of Barataria*). Comedy, 1 act. Written 1931? Produced Teatro del Pueblo (Misiones Pedagógicas). Based on *Don Quixote,* by Miguel de Cervantes.

4. *Entremés del mancebo que casó con mujer brava* (*Interlude of the Cripple Who Married a Fierce Woman*). Comedy, 1 act. Written 1931? Published 1941. Produced Teatro del Pueblo (Misiones Pedagógicas).

5. (With Alonso Hernández-Catá). *El misterio del Maria Celeste* (*The Mystery of the Mary Celeste*). Comedy, 3 acts. Written 1935? Produced Madrid, Teatro de la Zarzuela, July, 1935.

6. *Nuestra Natacha* (*Our Natacha*). Comedy, 3 acts. Written 1935? Published 1936. Produced Barcelona, 1935. Based on an earlier adaptation from Heinrich Heine entitled *Balada de Atta Troll* (*The Ballad of Atta Troll,* wr. ca. 1931).

7. *Prohibido suicidarse en primavera* (*No Suicide Allowed in Spring*). Comedy, 3 acts. Written 1937. Published 1941. Produced Mexico City, Teatro Arbeu, June 12, 1937.

8. *El crimen de Lord Arturo* (*The Crime of Lord Arthur*). Drama, 3 acts. Written 1938? Produced Havana, 1938.

9. *Romance de Dan y Elsa* (*Romance of Dan and Elsa*). Romantic comedy, 3 acts. Written 1938? Produced Caracas, Teatro Nacional, June 17, 1938.

10. *Sinfonía inacabada* (*Unfinished Symphony*). Romantic historical drama, 3 acts. Written 1939. Produced Montevideo, Teatro Solís, May 21, 1940.

11. *María Curie* (*Marie Curie*). Dramatic biography. Written 1940? Produced Buenos Aires, Teatro Smart, 1940.

12. (Adaptation). *Las tres casadas perfectas* (*The Three Perfect Married Women*). Comedy, 3 acts. Written 1941? Produced Buenos Aires, Teatro Avenida, May, 1941. Based on a play by Arthur Schnitzler.

13. *La dama del alba** (*The Lady of the Dawn*). Ballad, 4 acts. Written 1944? Published 1944. Produced Buenos Aires, Teatro Avenida, Nov. 3, 1944.

14. *La barca sin pescador* (*The Boat Without a Fisherman*). Comedy, 3 acts. Written 1945? Produced Buenos Aires, Teatro Liceo, July 24, 1945.

15. *La molinera de Arcos* (*The Wife of the Miller of Arcos*). Musical interlude, 5 scenes. Written 1947? Produced Buenos Aires, Teatro Argentino, June 19, 1947.

16. *Los árboles mueren de pie** (*The Trees Die Standing*). Comedy, 3 acts. Written 1949? Produced Buenos Aires, Teatro Ateneo, Apr. 1, 1949.

17. *Fablilla del secreto bien guardado* (*Little Fable of the Well-kept Secret*). Comedy, 1 act. Written 1949? Published 1949.

18. *Farsa del cornudo apaleado* (*Farce of the Thrashed Cuckold*). Comedy, 1 act. Written 1949? Published 1949. Based on Giovanni Boccaccio's *Decameron.*

19. *Farsa y justicia del corregidor* (*Farce and Justice of the Magistrate*). Play, 1 act. Written 1949? Published 1949.

20. *La llave en el desván* (*The Key in the Loft*). Comedy, 3 acts. Written 1951? Produced Buenos Aires, Teatro Ateneo, June 1, 1951.

ing for her. Weary, the Pilgrim oversleeps, missing the hour she was to have departed with Martín, and so she must leave without him. Later Martín rescues Adela, a homeless and desperate young girl, from drowning herself and brings her to the home of the grandfather, where she is welcomed. Adela and Martín fall in love, and Martín, knowing that Angelica is still alive, wishes to depart. Now Angelica, broken and defeated by life, returns, as does the Pilgrim. Taking the prodigal Angelica lovingly in her arms, the Pilgrim carries her to the river, there to find eternal peace. In this way death, personified by the "Lady of the Dawn," makes way for the flowering of new life.

The Trees Die Standing (*Los árboles mueren de pie,* 1949). Comedy in which Balboa's grandson Mauricio, an international criminal living abroad, cables Balboa to say he is returning home. Soon after, news arrives that he has been drowned at sea. Believing that the news may kill his wife, Balboa enlists the help of a "personal problem" bureau. Its director and his assistant agree to impersonate Mauricio and Mauricio's wife. Presently the real Mauricio arrives and blackmails Balboa by threatening to reveal the truth about him-

21. *¡A Belén, pastores!* (*To Bethlehem, Shepherds*). Play. Written 1951? Produced Montevideo, Parque Rodó, December, 1951.

22. *Siete gritos en el mar* (*Seven Cries in the Sea*). Comedy, 3 acts. Written 1952? Produced Buenos Aires, Teatro Politeama, Mar. 14, 1952.

23. *La tercera palabra* (*The Third Word*). Comedy, 3 acts. Written 1953? Produced Buenos Aires, Teatro Odeón, May 29, 1953.

24. *Corona de amor y muerte; Doña Inés de Castro* (*The Crown of Love and Death*). Dramatic legend, 3 acts. Written 1955? Produced Buenos Aires, Teatro Odeón, Mar. 8, 1955.

25. *La casa de los siete balcones* (*The House with Seven Balconies*). Comedy, 3 acts. Written 1957? Produced Buenos Aires, Teatro Liceo, Apr. 12, 1957.

26. *Carta de una desconocida* (*Letter of an Unknown Woman*). Dramatic monologue. Written 1957? Produced Brazil, Porto Alegre, Teatro São Pedro, May 9, 1957.

27. *Tres diamantes y una mujer* (*Three Diamonds and a Woman*). Play. Written 1961? Produced Buenos Aires, 1961.

28. *El lindo Don Gato* (*The Handsome Mr. Gato*). Play, 1 act.

29. *El caballero de las espuelas de oro* (*The Gentlemen with the Gold Spurs*). Play.

30. *Retablo jovial.* Play.

EDITIONS

Obras completas, 3 vols., ed. by F. C. Sáinz de Robles, Buenos Aires and Madrid, 1964–1965.

The Boat Without a Fisherman. Published in *The Modern Spanish Stage: Four Plays,* ed. by M. P. Holt, New York, 1970.

The Lady of the Dawn. Published in *The Genius of the Spanish Theater,* ed. by R. O'Brien and tr. by B. Roman and R. O'Brien, New York, 1964.

CRITICISM

J. Rodríguez Richart, *Vida y obra de Alejandro Casona,* Oviedo, 1963.

THE CASTLE OF PERSEVERANCE. Earliest extant English morality play, probably performed in the opening years of the fifteenth century (the extant manuscript has been dated about 1440). It is one of the three so-called Macro moralities. A heavily didactic work of some 3,500 lines by an unknown author, it chronicled the life of Humanum Genus (Mankind) from birth to divine judgment. Beset immediately after birth by World, Flesh, and the Devil, Mankind resists the strenuous counteraction of the Good Angel and sides with the World. Later, however, the Good Angel, aided by Penitence and other Virtues, wins him over, and Mankind finds sanctuary in the Castle of Perseverance. A great battle ensues in which the Vices and the Virtues contend for his soul. As old age approaches, Mankind succumbs to the blandishments of Avarice and Covetousness, thereby incurring the loss of salvation. When he sees his worldly goods vanish and death drawing near, he is terrified and begs for salvation. During a momentous debate, Justice urges that Mankind be damned, but Mercy prevails, and he is saved. *See* MACRO MORALITIES; MORALITY PLAY.

Guillén de Castro y Bellvís
(1569 — 1631)

Guillén de Castro y Bellvís, Spanish poet and dramatist, was born in Valencia in 1569, to a distinguished family. In 1591, at the age of twenty-three, he became a member of the literary society Nocturnos. Castro is credited with having written twenty-four poems and four discourses while a member of the society, which disbanded in 1594. In 1595 his marriage to Doña Marquesa Girón de Rebolledo, a union that ended unhappily, took place. This was also the year when Lope de Vega arrived in Valencia for a two-year sojourn, during which time Castro became his friend and follower. *See* VEGA CARPIO, LOPE DE.

In 1604 Castro left Valencia to become a soldier. He found his way to Italy, where in 1607 he was appointed Governor of Stigliano by the Count of Benavente, Viceroy of Naples. The position was honorary rather than political, and Castro returned to Valencia in 1609.

Title page of *Las mocedades del Cid,* by Guillén de Castro y Bellvís. [New York Public Library Picture Collection]

Ten years later he established himself in Madrid in the service of the Marquis of Peñafil, who bestowed on him the house and lands of Casablanca, which he in turn gave to his sister Magdalena in 1620. At this time he was admitted to the Academy of Poetry, whose members included many famous dramatists and poets. In 1623 he became a knight in the military Order of Santiago. The following year he was accused of complicity in the murder of a rival; judicial investigation failed to establish his guilt, and the case was dismissed for lack of evidence. Then, in 1626, he married Doña Angela María Salgado, but again marriage brought him only unhappiness.

Though he was a celebrated poet, his remaining years were spent in poverty. Enfeebled by pain, scarcely able to write, and abandoned by his friends, he died in Madrid on July 28, 1631.

WORK

Castro's perceptive portrayals of human nature place his work only slightly behind the ranks of the three major dramatists of the Siglo de Oro (Spanish Golden Age): Lope de Vega, Calderón, and Tirso de Molina. An admirer and imitator of Lope (who praised him publicly on several occasions), Castro derived the themes for his plays from Spanish history, popular ballads, and folk legends. By transplanting these to the stage, he breathed fresh life into the heroic traditions of Spain. The twenty-seven plays whose authorship is undisputed have well-constructed plots, vigorous imagery, and harmonious verse, and many stress basic values such as duty and honor. *See* SIGLO DE ORO.

Castro's reputation rests mainly on *The Youthful Adventures of the Cid* (*Las mocedades del Cid,* 1612?/18?) and its sequel, *The Exploits of the Cid* (*Las hazañas del Cid,* 1610?/15?), both of which derive from popular ballads about the Cid's youth. *The Youthful Adventures of the Cid,* his best-known work, profoundly influenced European drama (it is, for example, the direct source of Corneille's masterpiece, *Le Cid*). The characters in both these works, in addition to being full of the vigor of the heroic age, reflect the ideals of the courtly life of Castro's own time. *See* CORNEILLE, PIERRE.

Most of Castro's plays take the form of the *comedia,* the special type of drama that flourished in Spain in the late sixteenth century and in the first half of the seventeenth. Although his plays made no original contribution to the *comedia* as a national form of drama, they are marked by their individuality and diversity of subject matter and method of treatment. Among them are *comedias* of character and customs, plays of chivalry and romance, "cloak-and-dagger" comedies (*comedias de capa y espada*), historical plays, and tragicomedies. *See* COMEDIA; TRAGICOMEDY.

His most realistic plays are the *comedias* of character and customs, such as *The Mismatched of Valencia* (*Los mal casados de Valencia,* 1595?/1604?) and *The Force of Habit* (*La fuerza de la costumbre,* 1610?/20?). To be included in this category are the *comedias* based upon incidents drawn from Castro's own experiences and observation and portraying the social life of his time. Of this group, *Dandy in His Opinion* (*El narciso en su opinión,* 1612?/15?) was the model for *Don Diego the Fop* (1662), one of Moreto's masterpieces of comedy. *See* MORETO Y CABAÑA, AGUSTÍN.

Mythology and classical literature provided Castro with the material for *Dido and Aeneas* (*Los amores de Dido y Eneas,* 1613?/16?) and *Procne and Philomena* (*Progne y Filomena,* 1608?/12?). From the ballads and romances of chivalry he obtained the plots of several plays. *The Impertinent Meddler* (*El curioso impertinente,* 1605/08?), *Don Quijote de la Mancha* (1605/08?), and *The Power of Blood* (*La fuerza de la sangre,* 1613/14) indicate his indebtedness to the great novels and the *Novelas ejemplares* of Cervantes. *See* CERVANTES, MIGUEL DE.

Castro distinguished himself by his vigorous portrayal of unrestrained passions, and his individuality as a dramatist is founded primarily upon the unbounded energy and sometimes the brutality that he imparted to many of his characters. Although he was widely praised as a dramatist in his lifetime, there are few enthusiasts for the majority of his plays today. Involved plots, abrupt and illogical endings, and superfluous characters and incidents that retard the action can all be said to have contributed to his decline in popularity in modern times. Nevertheless, among his many plays great scenes stand out to demonstrate the poetic and dramatic genius of their author.

His many other works include *Count Alarcos* (*El conde Alarcos,* 1600?/02), a robust tragedy; *To Pay Back in Kind* (*Pagar en propia moneda,* before 1623); *Mercy in Justice* (*La piedad en la justicia,* 1615?/20?); *Proud Humility* (*La humildad soberbia,* 1595?/1605?); and *The Count of Irlos* (*El conde de Irlos,* 1600?/10?); all of which illustrate Castro's preoccupation with the preservation of values. Others are *Deceived While Deceiving* (*Engañarse engañado,* 1620?/24), *The Would-be Pauper* (*Pretender con pobreza,* 1620?/24), and *The Perfect Gentleman* (*El perfecto caballero,* 1610?/15?)—all examples of Castro's "dramatic comedies" (*comedias dramáticas*);

The Hostile Brothers (*Los enemigos hermanos,* 1615?/20?), a cloak-and-dagger comedy; and *Tragedy Through Jealousy* (*La tragedia por los celos,* 1622) and *Ingratitude for Love* (*Ingratitud por amor,* 1620?/28), both dealing with infidelity and jealousy.

The Youthful Adventures of the Cid
(*Las mocedades del Cid,* 1612?/18?). Drama of the early deeds of El Cid, the legendary Spanish hero. Diego Laínez has been insulted by Count Lozano and tests his three sons to discover who will best avenge his honor. He finds that only Rodrigo has pride enough to assert himself when insulted. Rodrigo, however, is in love with Jimena, the daughter of Count Lozano, and thus his loyalties are divided. But the obligation to avenge his father's honor prevails, and he kills the count. Although Jimena returns Rodrigo's love, she asks King Ferdinand to avenge her loss. Before the King, Diego defends Rodrigo's action, since it was taken to protect paternal honor. He advises Rodrigo, however, to serve the King and fight the Moors. Rodrigo does so and in time becomes so redoubtable that a Moorish king dubs him *el mio Cide* ("my lord"). One day a leper begs Rodrigo and his men for food, and while the soldiers are disgusted, Rodrigo shows him kindness. The leper then reveals that he is really St. Lazarus, the patron saint of Spain, and promises to help Rodrigo achieve greatness.

Impelled by filial duty and honor to bring Rodrigo to justice, although in her heart she still loves him, Jimena promises to marry her suitor Don Martín of Aragon if he will defeat Rodrigo in a duel and bring back to her his severed head. Don Martín fights Rodrigo but is himself beheaded. Following false reports of his death, Rodrigo returns with Don Martín's head and demands Jimena's hand. After some hesitation she consents, and the two become betrothed.

The Exploits of El Cid
(*Las hazañas del Cid,* 1610?/15?). Sequel to *The Youthful Adventures of the Cid,* in which Don Sancho, now King of Castile, is at odds with his sister Urraca and his brother Don Alfonso. Because Rodrigo (El Cid) is unconvinced that Sancho's stand is just, he vows to defend only the person of his King and not to fight otherwise. Arias Gonzalo, Urraca's faithful servant, and his five sons swear to defend her honor. When Don Sancho determines to seize Zamora, which is ruled by Urraca, Arias warns him to abandon his plan. Even the spirit of King Ferdinand calls upon his son to relinquish the idea. Bellido de Olfos of Zamora, winning Don Sancho's confidence, persuades the King to follow his advice to capture Zamora, but in so doing Don Sancho is killed. Rodrigo avenges the king's death. When Don Diego Ordóñez, a loyal follower of Don Sancho, attacks Zamora, three of Arias's sons are killed defending Urraca. Zayda, a Moorish woman, helps Don Alfonso, whom the Moors have been holding prisoner in Toledo, to escape. She later is converted to Christianity, and when Don Alfonso ascends the throne vacated by his brother's death, he makes Zayda his queen. Don Alfonso pardons Arias Gonzalo, and Rodrigo vows to serve the new King.

PLAYS

The dating of the plays is based on that given by Courtney Bruerton, "The Chronology of the *Comedias* of Guillén de Castro," *Hispanic Review,* April, 1944.

1. *El amor constante* (*Constant Love*). Play, 3 acts. Published 1608. Produced 1596?/99?
2. *El desengaño dichoso* (*The Happy Ending*). Play. Published 1618. Produced ca. 1599.
3. *El nacimiento de Montesinos* (*The Birth of Montesinos*). Play. Published 1618. Produced 1595?/1602?
4. *El conde Alarcos* (*Count Alarcos*). Play. Published 1618. Produced 1600?/02.
5. *Los mal casados de Valencia* (*The Mismatched of Valencia*). Play, 3 acts. Published 1618. Produced 1595?/1604?
6. *El caballero bobo* (*The Foolish Gentleman*). Play. Published 1608. Produced 1595?/1605?
7. *La humildad soberbia* (*Proud Humility*). Play. Published 1618. Produced 1595?/1605?
8. *El curioso impertinente* (*The Impertinent Meddler*). Play. Published 1618. Produced 1605/08?
9. *Don Quijote de la Mancha.* Play. Published 1618. Produced 1605/08 (probably 1605/06?).
10. *El conde de Irlos* (*The Count of Irlos*). Play. Published 1618. Produced 1600?/10? (probably 1605?/08?).
11. *Progne y Filomena* (*Procne and Philomena*). Play. Published 1618. Produced 1608?/12?
12. *La verdad averiguada o El engañoso casamiento* (*The Truth Investigated or The Deceitful Marriage*). Play. Published 1625. Produced 1608?/12?
13. *La fuerza de la sangre* (*The Power of Blood*). Play. Published 1625. Produced 1613/14.
14. *Las hazañas del Cid* (*The Exploits of the Cid*). Play. Published 1618. Produced 1610?/15?
15. *El perfecto caballero* (*The Perfect Gentleman*). Play. Published 1618. Produced 1610?/15?
16. *El narciso en su opinión* (*Dandy in His Opinion*). Play, 3 acts. Published 1618. Produced 1612?/15?
17. *Los amores de Dido y Eneas* (*Dido and Aeneas*). Play. Published 1625. Produced 1613?/16?
18. *Las mocedades del Cid* (*The Youthful Adventures of the Cid*). Play. 3 acts. Published 1618. Produced 1612?/18? (1612?/15?).
19. *La fuerza de la costumbre* (*The Force of Habit*). Play. 3 acts. Published 1625. Produced 1610?/20? (probably 1610?/15?).
20. *Los enemigos hermanos* (*The Hostile Brothers*). Play. Published 1625. Produced 1615?/20? (1615?).
21. *La piedad en la justicia* (*Mercy in Justice*). Play. 3 acts. Published 1625. Produced 1615?/20?
22. *El mejor esposo san José* (*St. Joseph, Ideal Husband*). Play. Published 1625. Produced 1617/20?
23. *La tragedia por los celos* (*Tragedy Through Jealousy*). Play. Published 1622. Produced 1622.
24. *El vicio en los extremos* (*Vice in the Extremes*). Play. Published 1625. Produced ca. 1623.
25. *Cuánto se estima el honor* (*The Price of Honor*). Play. Published 1625. Produced 1615?/24 (1622?/24).
26. *Engañarse engañando* (*Deceived While Deceiving*). Play. Published 1625. Produced 1620?/24 (1622?/24).
27. *Pretender con pobreza* (*The Would-be Pauper*). Play. Published 1625. Produced 1620?/24.

Comedias Probably by Castro.

1. *Donde no está su dueño, está su duelo* (*Where There Is No Master, There Is Grief*). Play. Published 1634. Produced 1610?/20?

2. *El ayo de su hijo* (*His Son's Tutor*). Play. Published 1906. Produced 1620?/23.

3. *Ingratitud por amor* (*Ingratitude for Love*). Play. Published 1899. Produced 1620?/28 (perhaps 1624?/28).

Doubtful Comedias.

1. *El renegado arrepentido* (*The Repentant Renegade*). Play. Published 1887. Produced 1592?/1600?

2. *Nieto de su padre* (*Grandson of His Father*). Play. Published 1658. Produced 1620/22.

3. *Pagar en propia moneda* (*To Pay Back in Kind*). Play. Produced before 1623.

4. *Las maravillas de Babilonia* (*The Wonders of Babylon*). Play. Published 1652. Produced ca. 1623?

5. *Quien no se aventura* (*Nothing Ventured . . .*). Play. Published 1878. Produced 1625?/31?

6. *El cerco de Tremecén* (*The Siege of Tremecén*). Play. Published 1638.

7. *La manzana de la discordia o El robo de Elena* (*The Apple of Discord or The Abduction of Helen*). Play. Published 1927.

8. *El pobre honrado* (*The Honest Pauper*). Play.

EDITIONS

Obras completas, ed. by E. Juliá Martínez, 3 vols., Madrid, 1925–1927; *Comedias,* ed. by R. de Mesonero Romanos, *Biblioteca de autores españoles,* vol. XLIII, Madrid, 1951.

The Youthful Adventures of the Cid. G. W. Umphrey, ed., New York, 1939; also published in *Diez comedias del siglo de oro,* ed. by H. Alpern and J. Martel, New York, 1939.

CRITICISM

Baron Holland, *Some Account of the Lives of Lope Félix de Vega Carpio and Guillén de Castro,* London, 1817; J. B. Segall, *Corneille and the Spanish Drama,* New York, 1902; H. Mérimée, *Pour la biographie de don Guillén de Castro,* Montpellier, 1907; id., *L'art dramatique à Valencia,* Toulouse, 1913; B. Matulka, *The Cid as a Courtly Hero, from the Amadís to Corneille,* New York, 1928.

CAVACCHIOLI, Enrico (1885–1954). Italian dramatist and journalist who aspired to create an avant-garde theatre in Milan. *She Who Resembles You* (*Quella che t'assomiglia,* 1919) is based on the theme of the dichotomy between appearance and reality in the human personality. *The Bird of Paradise* (*L'uccello del paradiso,* 1919) is a drama in which a single personage controls the other characters through his suggestive power. Cavacchioli's other plays, such as *The Belly Dance* (*La danza del ventre,* 1921) and *The Oasis* (*L'oasi,* 1935), concern the conflict between the spiritual and the sensual.

CECCHI, Giovan Maria (1518–1587). Italian dramatist who wrote a variety of classical comedies, farces, moral comedies, and religious dramas as well as the intermezzi in prose and verse for which he is best remembered. Cecchi's middle-class heritage and his participation in the public life of Medicean Florence made him aware of the pettiness of bourgeois virtue, which contrasted sharply with the austere ancients he studied and which served as the object of satire in his early theatrical productions. *The Cuckold* (*L'assiuolo,* 1549), a burlesque farce of student life, is Cecchi's most important play. Later in life, he stood self-accused of the merciless dissection of religion in his early works and turned away from the imitation of classical authors to create exclusively spiritual dramas.

CENTLIVRE, Susannah (ca. 1667–1723). English dramatist and actress, friend of Nicholas Rowe, George Farquhar, and Richard Steele. Although she was known chiefly for her ingenious and successful comedies of intrigue, her last dramatic works were comedies of manners and of humors. *See* COMEDY OF HUMORS; COMEDY OF MANNERS.

Her plays include *The Perjur'd Husband* (1700), a blank-verse tragedy; *The Beau's Duel* (1702); the cleverly contrived *The Stolen Heiress or The Salamanca Doctor Outplotted* (1702); *Love's Contrivance or Le Médecin Malgré Lui* (1703), a farcical adaptation of Mo-

Henry Woodward playing Marplot in Susannah Centlivre's *The Busie Body.* [Theatre Collection, The New York Public Library at Lincoln Center, Astor, Lenox and Tilden Foundations]

Susannah Centlivre. [Theatre Collection, The New York Public Library at Lincoln Center, Astor, Lenox and Tilden Foundations]

lière's *The Doctor in Spite of Himself; The Gamester* (1705), a sentimental comedy of manners attacking gambling; *The Busie Body* (1709), a very successful and well-characterized comedy of intrigue; *The Man's Bewitch'd or The Devil to Do about Her* (1709), a comedy with conventional characters but cleverly devised situations; *A Bickerstaff's Burying, or Work for the Upholders* (1710), a farce; and *The Wonder! A Woman Keeps a Secret* (1714), a skillfully constructed and popular comedy that was performed well into the nineteenth century.

Miguel de Cervantes
(1547 — 1616)

Miguel de Cervantes Saavedra, Spanish poet, novelist, and dramatist, was born in Alcalá de Henares in 1547, the fourth of seven children of Rodrigo de Cervantes, an unsuccessful apothecary-surgeon. The poverty Miguel knew as a boy was to haunt him all his life. Little is known of his schooling, but it is thought to have been scant. In either 1568 or 1569 he studied in Madrid with the humanist Juan López de Hoyos, but left Spain in 1569 to seek his fortune in Italy. He served as a gen-

tleman-in-waiting in the household of Cardinal Aquaviva in Rome, then left his service to join a Spanish regiment in Naples.

His military career lasted from 1570 to 1575, during which time he fought in several campaigns against the Turks and Moors. As a result of his part in the naval battle of Lepanto in 1571, he was commended for bravery. During that same battle he lost the use of his left hand and thereafter was nicknamed *el manco de Lepanto* ("the cripple of Lepanto"). In 1575, having been recommended for a commission, he set sail for Spain to present himself at court, but his ship was captured by pirates under Arnaute Mami. Cervantes and his brother Rodrigo, who had been serving with him, were sold into slavery in Algiers. Because of some papers he was carrying, Cervantes was thought to be an important personage; thus a high ransom was demanded for him. Rodrigo was soon ransomed, but Cervantes spent five years in Algiers, where he became a leader among the Christian slaves. With them he planned at least five conspiracies to escape, all of which were betrayed. In 1580 his ransom was raised, and Cervantes returned to Spain.

In Madrid Cervantes found that the government had forgotten his services and that his family had been left penniless after paying his ransom. Hoping to help them by distinguishing himself as a playwright, he wrote his first play, *The Commerce of Algiers* (*Los tratos de Argel*), which was probably presented not long after his return to Spain in 1580. At that time, however, the genius of the younger Lope de Vega, which had recently burst upon the Spanish stage, overshadowed Cervantes' efforts. A liaison of this period with an actress, Ana Franca de Rojas, produced a daughter, Isabel Saavedra. In 1584, however, he married Catalina de Palacios Salazar, the daughter of a well-to-do peasant. The marriage was childless and is thought to have been unhappy. In 1585 the publication of Cervantes' first novel, *La Galatea,* brought him some esteem but no money. *See* VEGA CARPIO, LOPE DE.

In 1587 Cervantes was appointed a commissioner in Andalusia to purchase wheat and oil for the Spanish Armada. It was a thankless task, and at one point he was excommunicated for having appropriated some wheat belonging to the clergy of Seville. Cervantes was honest but not a businessman, and his affairs soon became so entangled that in 1592 he was imprisoned for debt to the state. After his release he resumed office until 1594. In 1597, and probably again in 1602, he was imprisoned for the same debt. It was during one of these incarcerations that he began to write *Don Quixote.*

Miguel de
Cervantes.
[Biblioteca
Nacional, Madrid]

By 1603 Cervantes and his family were living a penurious existence in Valladolid, then the capital of Spain. In 1605, Part I of *Don Quixote* was published in Madrid. Its success was immediate. Cervantes, however, did not reap any immediate monetary benefit from its sales, and bad luck continued to dog him. Later in the same year a dissolute nobleman, wounded on the street in front of Cervantes' house and nursed by his sister, died. There followed a bitter lawsuit, during which Cervantes and the women of his household were jailed on suspicion of having had a hand in the nobleman's death. Although they were shortly released, they continued in poverty, and for some time thereafter Cervantes wrote little. In 1613 he published his *Novelas ejemplares,* containing some of his best prose work. The next year saw the publication of the burlesque poem *Viaje del Parnaso,* and in 1615 there appeared a collection of his dramatic efforts titled *Ocho comedias y ocho entremeses nuevos.* This collection shows the rather sharp distinction between his failure when attempting, in the *comedias,* the style of Lope (whom he knew well), and his success in the more permissive and spontaneous medium of the *entremeses* (interludes). *See* COMEDIA; ENTREMÉS.

Meanwhile, the success of the *Quixote* had led to the publication in 1614 of a sequel by one Alonso Fernández de Avellaneda, prefaced with taunts at Cervantes. Impelled by the affront, Cervantes, now failing in health, completed his own sequel late in 1615.

He had moved to Madrid with the royal court a few years previously, and it was there that he spent his last years. His final document is a moving dedication to the Count of Lemos of his prose work *Los trabajos de Persiles y Sigismunda.* Despite noble sponsors and his growing fame abroad, Cervantes remained a poor man. He died in Madrid on April 23, 1616.

WORK

Cervantes' achievement as a dramatist in no way ranks with his accomplishment as a novelist. Although he longed for success in the theatre and complained when it was denied him, he exhibited a theatrical talent that except in one instance was slight, and he deserved little more dramatic recognition than he received during his lifetime. His authentic dramatic significance consists in his occupying a transitional position between Lope de Rueda and Lope de Vega. *See* RUEDA, LOPE DE.

Cervantes' finest play, *The Siege of Numantia* (*El cerco de Numancia,* wr. ca. 1585/87), bears scant resemblance to any of his other plays or to most contemporaneous Spanish drama. Usually Cervantes' full-length plays are discursive in style, with only a rudimentary dramatic structure. They are occasionally redeemed by insights into character that indicate a novelistic more than a dramatic genius. *The Siege of Numantia* is an exception, being not only a fine drama based on classical models but a rare example, for the Spanish Renaissance, of tragedy. It manifests Cervantes' early espousal of neoclassical dramatic theory, as distinguished from the spirit of Spanish *comedia,* which matured in the plays of Lope de Vega. In *Don Quixote* Cervantes deplored the "excesses" of the *comedia* and called for plays written in conformity with classical models.

Cervantes' only other meritorious full-length play is *The Commerce of Algiers* (after 1580), which, although structurally weak, contains realistic scenes remarkable for their time. The best of Cervantes' other full-length plays are *Pedro, the Artful Dodger* (*Pedro de*

Urdemalas, pub. 1615), a picaresque play; and *The Prisons of Algiers* (*Los baños de Argel,* pub. 1615), whose theme and treatment recall *The Commerce of Algiers.*

The most popular of Cervantes' plays are his eight *entremeses,* which include *The Wonder Show* (*El retablo de las maravillas,* wr. ca. 1598/1600?), in which two rascally actors, feigning a show of wonders, forestall criticism of their bogus marvels by ascribing illegitimacy or Jewish descent to those who cannot see them; *The Cave of Salamanca* (*La cueva de Salamanca,* wr. ca. 1611?), in which a cuckold returns home to find his wife sporting with lovers and is persuaded to believe they are devils in the process of being exorcised; *The Basque Imposter* (*El vizcaíno fingido,* wr. ca. 1611?), in which a courtesan is tricked; *The Hawk-eyed Sentinel* (*La guarda cuidadosa,* wr. ca. 1611?), in which a soldier lets no one approach his beloved's home; and *The Jealous Old Husband* (*El viejo celoso,* pub. 1615), another play about a cuckold.

The Commerce of Algiers (*Los tratos de Argel,* after 1580). Comedy based on Cervantes' experiences as a Moorish captive. The main plot revolves around Aurelio and Silvia, lovers who have been captured by the Moors and then separated. A subplot deals with the fate of other Christians imprisoned by the Moors. Aurelio is owned by Izuf, whose wife Zara loves Aurelio. Izuf falls in love with and buys Silvia. Izuf then pleads with Aurelio to win Silvia's heart for him, while Zara exhorts Silvia to do the same with regard to Aurelio. The reunited lovers hope to secure their release but while embracing are discovered by Izuf and Zara. Before Izuf can revenge himself, the King intervenes and offers to liberate the lovers if Aurelio will pledge a ransom of 3,000 ducats. Aurelio agrees, and as he and Silvia celebrate their freedom, a priest arrives from Spain with money to ransom the other prisoners.

The Siege of Numantia (*El cerco de Numancia,* wr. ca. 1585/87). Tragedy set in Spain during the Roman siege of Numantia in 134 B.C. Scipio the Younger, the general, reproves his troops for their lackluster performance in battle but rejects all conciliatory

Pedro de Urdemalas, Teatro Español, Madrid. [Courtesy Spanish Embassy]

efforts made by the Numantines, including a proposal to have the respective champions of the two sides compete in a joust the outcome of which would decide the city's fate. Behind the walls of Numantia there are famine and foreboding. Marquino, a magician, predicts that Numantia will be destroyed not by Romans but by "the sword of friends." Marandro, a young man, dashes across the Roman lines to steal bread for his sweetheart and is killed. The men of Numantia favor a daring frontal assault on the enemy but reject the idea when they consider the consequences for their women and children. Eventually, crazed by hunger and resolved not to surrender to the Romans, they kill their families and themselves. Scipio and his officers note the silence shrouding the city and, looking over the walls, see a lake of blood. Only one Numantine, the young Baratius, survives, having hidden himself in a tower. He throws himself off the ramparts rather than be taken hostage. Scipio prepares a hero's funeral for the boy, while Fame sings the praises of the brave Numantines, from whose ashes a proud and victorious Spain will arise.

PLAYS

There is no adequate chronology of Cervantes' dramatic work; thus the listing below is alphabetical by category: full-length plays and *entremeses*. Of the full-length plays, all but No. 3 are *comedias*. All the plays known to have been by Cervantes except Nos. 3 and 10 were included in his *Ocho comedias y ocho entremeses nuevos* (pub. 1615).

Full-length Plays.
1. *Los baños de Argel* (*The Prisons of Algiers*). Published 1615.
2. *La casa de los celos y selvas de Ardenia* (*The House of Jealousy or The Forests of Arden*). Published 1615.
3. *El cerco de Numancia* (*The Siege of Numantia*). Tragedy, 4 acts. Written ca. 1585/87. Published 1784.
4. *La entretenida* (*The Amusing Woman*). Published 1615.
5. *El gallardo español* (*The Gallant Spaniard*). Published 1615.
6. *La gran sultana, doña Catalina de Oviedo* (*The Great Sultana, Doña Catalina de Oviedo*). Published 1615.
7. *El laberinto de amor* (*The Labyrinth of Love*). Published 1615.
8. *Pedro de Urdemalas* (*Pedro, the Artful Dodger*). Published 1615.
9. *El rufián dichoso, Cristóbal de Lugo* (*The Happy Ruffian, Cristóbal de Lugo*). Published 1615.
10. *Los tratos de Argel* (*The Commerce of Algiers*). Published 1784. Produced after 1580.

Entremeses.
1. *La cueva de Salamanca* (*The Cave of Salamanca*). Written ca. 1611? Published 1615.
2. *La elección de los alcaldes de Daganzo* (*Choosing a Councilman in Daganzo*). Published 1615.
3. *La guarda cuidadosa* (*The Hawk-eyed Sentinel*). Written ca. 1611? Published 1615.
4. *El juez de los divorcios* (*The Divorce Court Judge*). Published 1615.
5. *El retablo de las maravillas* (*The Wonder Show*). Written ca. 1598/1600? Published 1615.
6. *El rufián viudo llamado Trampagos* (*Trampagos, the Pimp Who Lost His Moll*). Published 1615.

7. *El viejo celoso* (*The Jealous Old Husband*). Published 1615.
8. *El vizcaíno fingido* (*The Basque Imposter*). Written ca. 1611? Published 1615.
Three other *entremeses* have been attributed to Cervantes: *La cárcel de Sevilla* (*The Seville Jail*), *Los habladores* (*Two Chatterboxes*), and *El hospital de los podridos* (*The Hospital for Complainers*).

EDITIONS

Collections.
Voyage to Parnassus, Numancia and The Commerce of Algiers, tr. by G. W. J. Gyll, London, 1870; *Entremeses*, ed. by E. Cotarelo y Mori, *Nueva biblioteca de autores españoles*, vol. XVII, Madrid, 1911; *Entremeses*, ed. by A. Bonilla y San Martín, Madrid, 1916; *Obras completas*, ed. by R. Schevill and A. Bonilla y San Martín, 19 vols., Madrid, 1914–1941; *Entremeses*, ed. by M. Herrero García, Madrid, 1945; *The Interludes of Cervantes*, tr. by S. G. Morley, Princeton, N.J., 1948; *Interludes*, tr. by E. Honig, New York, 1964.

Individual Plays.
The Cave of Salamanca. Published in *World Drama*, ed. by B. H. Clark and tr. by M. Jagendorf, vol. 2, New York, 1933.
The Hawk-eyed Sentinel (*The Vigilant Sentinel*). Published in *Spanish Drama*, ed. by A. Flores and tr. by A. Flores and J. Liss, New York, 1962.
The Jealous Old Husband. Published in *Eight Spanish Plays of the Golden Age*, ed. and tr. by W. Starkie, New York, 1964.
The Siege of Numantia. Published in *The Classic Theatre*, ed. by E. R. Bentley and tr. by R. Campbell, vol. 3, Garden City, N.Y., 1958–1961.

CRITICISM

Spanish.
A. Cotarelo y Valledor, *El teatro de Cervantes*, Madrid, 1915; A. Bonilla y San Martín, *Cervantes y su obra*, Madrid, 1916; A. Castro, *El pensamiento de Cervantes*, Madrid, 1925; A. Maldonado Ruiz, *Cervantes: Su vida y sus obras*, Madrid, 1947; J. Casalduero, *Sentido y forma del teatro de Cervantes*, Madrid, 1951; A. Castro, *Hacia Cervantes*, Madrid, 1957.

English.
J. Fitzmaurice-Kelly, *Miguel de Cervantes Saavedra: A Memoir*, Oxford, 1913; R. Schevill, *Cervantes*, New York, 1913; W. J. Entwistle, *Cervantes*, Oxford, 1940; A. F. G. Bell, *Cervantes*, Norman, Okla., 1947; E. C. Riley, *Cervantes's Theory of the Novel*, Oxford, 1962.

George Chapman
(ca. 1560 — 1634)

George Chapman, English dramatist, poet, and classical scholar, was born in Hitchin, Hertfordshire, about 1560. His father was Thomas Chapman, yeoman and copyholder. Nothing is known of the younger Chapman's education, but his knowledge of the classics suggests that he attended one of the universities. He left England for the Continent about 1585 and served under Sir Francis Vere in the Low Countries before returning to London about 1591.

In 1594 Chapman published his first work,

the poem *The Shadow of Night*. His first play, *The Blind Beggar of Alexandria*, a popular comedy written for the theatre manager Philip Henslowe, was produced by the Lord Admiral's Men in 1596. *All Fools* (wr. 1599?), originally called *The World Runs on Wheels* and considered one of his best plays, followed *An Humourous Day's Mirth* (1597). In 1599 Chapman's name disappeared from Henslowe's *Diaries* and began to appear as the author of a series of plays written for the Children of St. Paul's Chapel (later known as the Children of the Queen's Revels). During this period it is thought that he began to work on his translations of Homer as well. In 1605 Chapman, with Ben Jonson and John Marston, wrote *Eastward Ho!*, a comedy of city life. For satirical references to the Scots, and by implication to James I, the playwrights were imprisoned in the Tower of London. In 1607 Chapman's popular tragedy *Bussy d'Ambois* was published. *See* JONSON, BEN; MARSTON, JOHN.

Chapman's most important work, winning him distinction as a classical scholar, was his translation of the complete works of Homer, published in installments. The first twelve books of *The Iliad* appeared in 1609 and the rest by 1611; he then began *The Odyssey*. The translation of the complete works was finished in 1616. It is perhaps best known as the subject of Keats's famous poem "On First Looking into Chapman's Homer" (1816). In 1618 Chapman published a translation of Hesiod's *Works and Days*.

Despite his popularity and high reputation, Chapman remained poor throughout his life, and he died in poverty in London on May 12, 1634. His tomb in St. Giles-in-the-Fields, designed by the famous architect Inigo Jones, still stands.

WORK

George Chapman's love of classical learning, experimentation with comedy, use of Senecan techniques, and interest in history and philosophy are evidence of his kinship with Ben Jonson. But his unrestrained style, with its flamboyant metaphysical figures and "the elegant, sententious excitation to virtue" that he calls (in his dedication to *The Revenge of Bussy d'Ambois*, ca. 1610) a necessity for tragedy, mark him as a more romantic Elizabethan.

After experimenting with "comedy of humors," which in fact he originated, since his *An Humourous Day's Mirth* (1597) antedates Jonson's famous *Every Man in His Humour*, Chapman used two plays of Terence as a source for his comic masterpiece, *All Fools* (wr. 1599?, prod. 1604?). The comedy is a penetrating study of folly and intrigue, as is

George Chapman. [New York Public Library Picture Collection]

the later *May Day* (ca. 1609). In other comedies, *The Gentleman Usher* (ca. 1602?), *Monsieur d'Olive* (1604), and *The Widow's Tears* (1603/09), complicated classical devices such as mistaken identity (altered and influenced by Renaissance intrigue) are used to express Chapman's own philosophical concerns and his dismay at the pretensions of society. *See* COMEDY OF HUMORS.

Of Chapman's tragedies, only *The Wars of Pompey and Caesar* (wr. ca. 1612/13) has an ancient Roman theme; the others deal with contemporary French history. The hero of *Bussy d'Ambois* (1604), for instance, is based on Seigneur Louis de Bussy-d'Amboise. The play's Bussy (whom Chapman introduces as poor and neglected, unlike the actual Bussy) is, like Tamerlane, an ideal Renaissance hero, with lofty ambition, limitless aspiration, strength, valor, and passion; he is less than ideal, however, in his hypocrisy and arrogance. The play has been viewed by scholars as a Christian tragedy, a Senecan tragedy, and the prototype for a heroic tragedy. *See* HEROIC PLAY; SENECAN DRAMA.

The Revenge of Bussy d'Ambois presents a different hero, Bussy's brother-avenger, Clermont. Chapman drew heavily on a Latin translation of Epictetus for his characterization of Clermont, a Stoic. The two parts of *The Conspiracy and the Tragedy of Charles, Duke of Byron* (1608) and *Chabot, Admiral of France* (wr. 1621/22?, rev. 1635, with James Shirley as collaborator) are based on French incidents altered to portray Chapman's tragic intent.

Chapman's verse often tends to be obscure: he adapted philosophical discourse to the blank-verse line and laced it with proliferating images, parenthetical phrases, and ellipses. However, his wit is brilliant, and the verse itself is surging and powerful.

All Fools (wr. 1599?, prod. 1604?). Comedy of intrigue with a complex plot concerning the efforts of two pairs of lovers to make the course of love run smooth. Valerio, though a profligate, is believed by his father to be the epitome of virtue. He has married Gratiana secretly, fearing his father's censure of the match. Valerio's sister Bellanora is loved by Fortunio, whose brother Rinaldo convinces their father that it is really Fortunio and Bellanora who are secretly married. The deception enables both couples to live together under one roof, ostensibly so that Fortunio may learn "virtue" from Valerio. The difficulties that follow are eventually resolved to the satisfaction of all parties, with a truce declared in the battle between the generations.

The Gentleman Usher (ca. late 1602?). Comedy in which Lady Margaret is the object of many gentlemen's attentions. The most influential and oldest of her suitors is Alphonso, but his son Vincente is Margaret's favorite. Vincente arranges a private meeting with Margaret through her father's usher and becomes Margaret's lover. Alphonso is enraged. After attempting to send Vincente away and seeing that Margaret wishes to go with him, Alphonso decides to let them have their way.

Bussy d'Ambois (1604). Chronicle of the career of the Duke of Alençon, personification of the Renaissance adventurer and gallant: "the bravest man the French earthe bears." Bussy d'Ambois, introduced to the court of Henry III by Monsieur, the King's brother, rises rapidly and incurs the enmity of the Duke of Guise and the jealousy of Monsieur himself. Bussy embarks on a love affair with Tamyra, Countess Montsurry (with whom Monsieur is in love), and thus provides his enemies with a weapon for their revenge. They hasten to inform the countess's husband and, despite ghostly warnings, Bussy dies at the hand of assassins hired by Montsurry. His death expiates Tamyra's sin and reconciles her with her husband.

The Revenge of Bussy d'Ambois (ca. 1610). Tragedy in which the task of avenging the death of Bussy d'Ambois is laid on the shoulders of his brother Clermont, a "Senecal man" and akin to "Rome's Brutus." When Clermont fails to take his revenge of Count Montsurry to the satisfaction of his sister

Charlotte, her husband takes charge and arranges for Clermont's arrest. Clermont, however, belongs to the Duke of Guise's Catholic faction at court, and the Duke secures his release. After prolonged delays and proddings by the ghost of Bussy d'Ambois, Clermont kills Montsurry in a duel. Guise falls victim to a plot of the King, and Clermont kills himself in a fit of melancholy, leaving Montsurry's widow and Charlotte to enter a cloister.

PLAYS

The plays were first performed in London.

1. *The Blind Beggar of Alexandria.* Comedy, 10 scenes. Published 1598 (Stationers' Register, Aug. 15, 1598). Produced Rose Theatre (Lord Admiral's Men), Feb. 12, 1596.

2. *An Humourous Day's Mirth.* Comedy, 14 scenes. Published 1599. Produced Rose Theatre (Lord Admiral's Men), May 1, 1597.

3. *All Fools.* Comedy, 5 acts. Written 1599(?), as *The World Runs on Wheels.* Published 1605. Produced Blackfriars Theatre, 1604?

4. (Sometimes doubtfully attributed to Chapman). *Charlemagne, or The Distracted Emperor.* Play. Exists in Egerton manuscript. Produced ca. 1600. Cyril Tourneur, John Marston, and Thomas Dekker also have been suggested as possible authors.

5. *The Gentleman Usher.* Comedy. 5 acts. Published 1606 (Stationers' Register, Nov. 26, 1605). Produced ca. late 1602?

6. *Sir Giles Goosecap.* Comedy, 5 acts. Published 1606 (Stationers' Register, Jan. 10, 1606). Produced Children of St. Paul's Chapel, ca. late 1601/early 1603.

7. (Attribution to Chapman seriously questionable). *Alphonsus, Emperor of Germany.* Tragedy, 5 acts. Written before 1604?, revised before 1630? Published 1654. Produced Blackfriars Theatre (King's Men), 1630?

8. *Bussy d'Ambois.* Tragedy, 5 acts. Published 1607 (Stationers' Register, June 3, 1607. Produced Children of St. Paul's Chapel, 1604.

9. *Monsieur d'Olive.* Comedy, 5 acts. Published 1606. Produced Blackfriars Theatre (Children of the Queen's Revels), 1604.

10. (With Ben Jonson and John Marston). *Eastward Ho!* Comedy, 5 acts. Published 1605 (Stationers' Register, Sept. 4, 1605). Produced Blackfriars Theatre (Children of the Queen's Revels), 1605.

11. *The Conspiracy and the Tragedy of Charles, Duke of Byron,* Part I, conspiracy, 5 acts. Part II, tragedy, 5 acts. Published 1608 (Stationers' Register, June 5, 1608). Produced Blackfriars Theatre, 1608.

12. *May Day.* Comedy, 5 acts. Published 1611. Produced Blackfriars Theatre, ca. 1609.

13. *The Widow's Tears.* Comedy, 5 acts. Published 1612 (Stationers' Register, Apr. 17, 1612). Produced Blackfriars or Whitefriars Theatre (Children of the Queen's Revels), 1603/09.

14. *The Revenge of Bussy d'Ambois.* Tragedy, 5 acts. Published 1613 (Stationers' Register, Apr. 17, 1612). Produced Whitefriars Theatre, ca. 1610.

15. *The Wars of Pompey and Caesar.* Tragedy, 5 acts. Written ca. 1612/13. Published 1631. (Stationers' Register, May 18, 1631).

16. *The Middle Temple and Lincoln's Inn Masque.* Stationers' Register, Feb. 27, 1613. Produced Whitehall, Feb. 15, 1613.

17. (With James Shirley). *Chabot, Admiral of France.* Tragedy, 5 acts. Written 1621/22?, revised 1635. Published 1639 (Stationers' Register, Oct. 24, 1638). Produced Phoenix Theatre (Queen's Men), 1635 (licensed Apr. 29, 1635).

EDITIONS

Collections.
Tragedies, ed. by T. M. Parrott, 2 vols., New York, 1910; *Comedies,* ed. by T. M. Parrott, 2 vols., New York, 1914.
Individual Plays.
Bussy d'Ambois. Published in *Five Stuart Tragedies,* ed. by A. K. McIlwraith, London, 1953.
The Revenge of Bussy d'Ambois. Published in *Early Seventeenth Century Plays, 1600–1642,* ed. by H. R. Walley and J. H. Wilson, New York, 1930.

CRITICISM

E. S. Rees, Jr., *The Tragedies of George Chapman: Renaissance Ethics in Action,* Cambridge, Mass., 1955; G. de F. Lord, *Homeric Renaissance: The Odyssey of George Chapman,* New Haven, Conn., 1956; E. M. Waith, *The Herculean Hero in Marlowe, Chapman, Shakespeare and Dryden,* New York, 1962; M. MacLure, *George Chapman,* Toronto, 1966; C. Spivak, *George Chapman,* New York, 1967; J. W. Wieler, *George Chapman: The Effect of Stoicism upon His Tragedies,* New York, 1969.

CHASE, Mary Coyle (b. Denver, February 25, 1907). American dramatist best known for the comedy-fantasy *Harvey* (1944), about a gentle and whimsical inebriate who finds solace and companionship in a giant-sized invisible rabbit named Harvey. The best of her other plays are *Mrs. McThing* (1952), in which, as a result of witchcraft, a woman

Frank Fay (right) as Elwood P. Dowd and Fred Irving Lewis in *Harvey.* New York, Forty-eighth Street Theatre, 1944. [Photograph by Vandamm. Theatre Collection, The New York Public Library at Lincoln Center, Astor, Lenox and Tilden Foundations]

James Stewart and Helen Hayes in a Phoenix Theatre production of *Harvey,* staged by the University of Michigan Professional Theatre Program. Ann Arbor, Mendelssohn Theatre, 1970. [Professional Theatre Program, University of Michigan]

stops trying to idealize her son and accepts his real qualities; and *Bernadine* (1952), in which Wormy, an ineffectual adolescent, tries to translate the values of his gang's dream fantasies into everyday life. Among Mrs. Chase's other plays are *Now You've Done It* (1937) and *Midgie Purvis* (1961).

Harvey (1944). Comedy of Elwood P. Dowd, a lovable alcoholic whose constant companion is an imaginary 6-foot white rabbit named Harvey. The invisible Harvey is a source of embarrassment for Elwood's sister Veta, and she tries to have Elwood committed to Chumley's sanatorium. But after hearing her story, the doctor commits her instead. When the mistake is discovered, Elwood is gone. Finally Elwood is found and returned to the sanatorium, where he is to be given an injection that will drive Harvey from his mind. When Veta realizes Elwood will change into a penny-pinching grouch, she stops the doctor; and she, Elwood, and Harvey happily return home. Produced New York, Forty-eighth Street Theatre, November 1, 1944.

CHAYEFSKY, Paddy (1923–   ). American director and writer for television, radio, films, and stage. Having graduated from the City College of New York in 1943, during World War II, he served in the United States Army and was wounded. While convalescing in England he wrote the libretto and lyrics for the musical comedy *No T.O. for Love* (London, 1954). This was followed by *Middle of the Night* (New York, 1956), a play about a romance between a lonely widower and a girl nearly thirty years his junior. In 1959 he wrote *The Tenth Man*, a play set in a shabby store, now used as a synagogue, where a group of devout Jews have met to pray. So that the exorcism of a dybbuk (demon spirit) possessing young Evelyn may take place, a tenth man is brought in from the street to make up the number required for prayer. Estranged from his religion and on the verge of suicide, the tenth man is freed of his bitterness by the ceremony and enabled to feel love for Evelyn. *Gideon* (1961), drawn from the Book of Judges, tells how a humble wheat thresher is chosen by the Lord to save the people of Israel from the persecution of the Midianites. *The Passion of Josef D.* (1964) deals with the life of Stalin. *The Latent Heterosexual* (1968) is Chayefsky's latest play. He has also written a number of screenplays, including *The Great American Hoax, Marty* (1955), *The Bachelor Party* (1957), *The Americanization of Emily* (1964), and *Hospital* (1970).

Anton Pavlovich Chekhov
(1860 — 1904)

Anton Pavlovich Chekhov was born in Taganrog, a commercial town on the Sea of Azov in southern Russia, on January 29, 1860 (N.S.; January 17, 1860, O.S.). His father, the son of an enterprising serf who had bought

Gena Rowlands and Edward G. Robinson in *Middle of the Night*, by Paddy Chayefsky. New York, ANTA Theatre, 1956. [Walter Hampden Memorial Library at The Players, New York]

his freedom, was a harsh disciplinarian to his six children and his wife, a gentle woman. Chekhov spent much of his childhood working in his father's grocery store, which by 1876 was declared bankrupt, a result of unwise investments. The family sold their home and left for Moscow, leaving Anton in Taganrog for three years to complete his studies at the local Gymnasium while supporting himself by tutoring. These three years were important in the formation of Chekhov's personality; living by his wits taught him independence, responsibility, and a contempt for pettiness and meanness.

In August, 1879, the young Chekhov arrived in Moscow, planning to enter the Medical School of Moscow University on a scholarship. Soon after his arrival, he assumed the role of head of the family, for which his father was now too weak. This moral and financial responsibility remained with him for the rest of his life.

Encouraged by his older brother Aleksandr, Chekhov began sending short pieces to humorous magazines in order to earn money. In March, 1880, his first tale was published, in St. Petersburg's *Strekoza* (*Dragonfly*): it was "A Letter from the Don Landowner Stepan Vladimirovich N." ("Pismo donskogo pomeshchika Stepana Vladimirovicha N."), a parody of the popular concept of scientific knowledge held by the pretentious, poorly educated gentry. For the next four years, drawing his characters and themes from the streets of Moscow, Chekhov contributed hundreds of anecdotes, sketches, tales, jokes, articles, and dramatic scenes to the humorous magazines of Moscow and St. Petersburg. His choice of commonplace people for his characters was not to change throughout his career.

Chekhov's first two serious stories appeared in 1882: "The Lady of the Manor" ("Barynya") and "Late-blooming Flowers" ("Tsvety zapozdalye"), both of which show the ironic and compact style of the mature Chekhov. In June, 1884, he received his medical degree and began the practice of his new profession. His patients, however, were poor, and writing became increasingly important to him as a means of support. In addition, he became aware that he was infected with tuberculosis, to which he was predisposed by heredity.

During the years 1883 to 1886, Chekhov wrote more than 300 pieces for Nikolay Leykin, the owner of the journal *Oskolki* (*Fragments*). Among them were "Fragments of Moscow Life," a column in which he attacked many aspects of city life. Although he chafed under Leykin's editorial restrictions, the subject matter strengthened his relation to reality and sharpened his powers of observation, and the stories he contributed at this time to

Anton Pavlovich Chekhov. [New York Public Library]

the *Petersburg Gazette* showed a maturing talent. It was during these formative creative years that Chekhov concluded that life's pathos is to be found in everyday existence.

In December, 1885, upon visiting Leykin in St. Petersburg, Chekhov discovered to his amazement that he was a kind of celebrity among influential people in the publishing world and that his stories were favorites among the reading public and were admired in literary circles. During this visit he was introduced to A. S. Suvorin, editor of the influential periodical *Novoye Vremya* (*New Times*). In March, 1886, Chekhov received a letter from the celebrated novelist Dmitri Grigorovich, who urged him not to squander his talents and to publish under his own name and not pseudonyms. Thus, he gave up writing for comic journals and began publishing his stories in Suvorin's *Novoye Vremya*. Some of his most famous stories appeared in this periodical: "Sergeant Prishibeev" ("Unter Prishibeyev"), "The Hunter" ("Yeger"), and "Grief" ("Gore"). In March, 1888, Chekhov made his debut in the world of "thick" intellectual monthlies with the publication of the story "The Steppe" ("Step") in the *Severny Vestnik* (*Northern Messenger*). For a time he became interested in Tolstoy's philosophy of nonresistance to evil. *See* TOLSTOY, LEO.

After one schoolboy attempt at playwriting, *Platonov* (*Pyesa bez nazvaniya*, wr. 1878/

81), Chekhov began his career in this field with several one-act comedies and his first produced play, *Ivanov* (wr. 1887). There followed his popular one-act plays, or "jokes," *The Bear* (*Medved,* 1888) and *The Marriage Proposal* (*Predlozheniye,* wr. 1888), and several dramatic one-act studies. *The Wood Demon* (*Leshy,* 1889) was his first attempt at a lyrical play. Tolstoyan in tone, it resembles a morality play. After its failure Chekhov gave up playwriting for several years and concentrated on short stories written in the light of the Tolstoyan *Weltanschauung* ("world view"). His stories of this period as well as some of the earlier ones were published in four volumes: *Motley Stories* (*Pyostrye rasskazy,* 1886); *Innocent Speeches* (*Nevinnye rechi,* 1887); *In the Twilight* (*V sumerkakh,* 1887), for which he was awarded the Pushkin Prize by the Russian Academy of Sciences; and *Stories* (*Rasskazy,* 1889).

In 1890, dissatisfied with his life, Chekhov traveled across Siberia by coach to Sakhalin Island to take a census of the penal colonies. With his book *Sakhalin* (1893), which was responsible for prison reforms, he completely renounced Tolstoyan philosophy. Now restless and agitated, he left with Suvorin to tour Western Europe in March, 1891. Six weeks later Chekhov was anxious to return home and work. "The Duel" ("Duel," 1891) and "Ward No. 6" ("Palata No. 6") were two of his most powerful stories in refutation of Tolstoy's concepts of Christian love and nonresistance to evil. Chekhov's Sakhalin experience had aroused in him the desire to do something practical about the evils of Russian society. He grew increasingly impatient with the philosophizing, do-nothing Russian intelligentsia—the "Moscow Hamlets"—who were incapable of improving the lot of others.

In the spring of 1892, Chekhov acquired Melikhovo, an estate near Moscow, where he hoped to live with his family and write in peace. But he soon became involved in treating peasants in the surrounding area during a cholera epidemic. Two years later, because of the worsening of his tubercular condition, he was forced to go to Yalta. Meanwhile, he began work on *The Sea Gull* (*Chayka*). The play was given at the Alexandrinsky Theatre in St. Petersburg, on October 17, 1896, but neither the director nor the actors were sympathetic to Chekhov's concept of drama in which mood and talk prevail over plot and action, and it was a complete failure. Hurt, Chekhov turned once again to short-story writing. His health continued to decline, and in March, 1897, he had his first lung hemorrhage. That year, the year the Dreyfus case was reopened, he went to France with Suvorin. Chekhov became a strong supporter of Zola and the French liberals, bringing him into conflict with the more conservative Suvorin and cooling their long friendship.

On his return to Melikhovo in 1898, Chekhov was persuaded by his doctors to spend his winters in a mild climate. Thus, after his father's death he sold the estate and moved with his mother and sister to Yalta in 1899. Having contracted with the St. Petersburg publisher Fyodor Marks to publish a complete edition of his works, he began three years of editing, revising, and in some cases rewriting his stories in preparation for publication. Although he continued to write new and powerful stories for the rest of his life, continually refining his techniques, the years 1895 to 1904 are particularly noted for his great work as the innovator of modern Russian drama. With the formation of the Moscow Art Theatre by Chekhov's friend Vladimir Nemirovich-Danchenko and Konstantin Stanislavski, Chekhov began what was to be the most important association of his last years. Having extracted permission from Chekhov to include a new production of *The Sea Gull* in their first season's repertoire, they proceeded with rehearsals, some of which Chekhov was able to attend before leaving Moscow. It was at these rehearsals that he first met Olga Knipper, the actress who played Mme. Arkadina and who later became his wife. The 1898 production of *The Sea Gull* proved to be an enormous success. The next year Stanis-

V. I. Kachalov playing the title role in a Moscow Art Theatre production of *Ivanov.* New York, Jolson's Fifty-ninth Street Theatre, 1923. [Theatre Collection, The New York Public Library at Lincoln Center, Astor, Lenox and Tilden Foundations]

Scene from a Moscow Art Theatre production of *Ivanov*, with A. K. Tarasova and V. I. Kachalov. New York, Jolson's Fifty-ninth Street Theatre, 1923. [Theatre Collection, The New York Public Library at Lincoln Center, Astor, Lenox and Tilden Foundations]

lavski successfully produced *Uncle Vanya* (*Dyadya Vanya*), and in 1900 the troupe traveled to the Crimea so that Chekhov could see his play performed. This gave him the opportunity to renew his relationship with Olga Knipper, and on May 6, 1901, they were married. The couple spent only their summers together: at Chekhov's insistence his wife continued her career and remained in Moscow during the theatre season, while he spent that time in the south. Although he felt himself exiled from the intellectual life of Moscow, his warm friendships with Gorky and Tolstoy, who were living in the Crimea at the time, were a compensation for him. In fact, two years after his election in 1900 as an honorary member of the Russian Academy of Sciences, Chekhov resigned in protest when Gorky's election was denied at the behest of the Czar. *See* GORKY, MAXIM.

Chekhov continued to write for the Moscow Art Theatre, which in 1901 presented *The Three Sisters* (*Tri sestry*). However, his strength continued to ebb, and the enormous effort required to finish *The Cherry Orchard* (*Vishnyovy sad,* wr. 1903) and to attend Moscow rehearsals, despite his doctor's admonitions, brought about a complete collapse in the winter of 1903–1904. His wife took him to Badenweiler, a health resort in southern Germany, to recuperate, but Chekhov died there on July 15, 1904 (N.S.).

WORK

A hard childhood, heavy family responsibilities in his student years, the discovery in his mid-twenties of a disease that he knew would cut his life short, and the listlessness of prerevolutionary Russia were the exterior forces that shaped the work of Chekhov. Within him were the compassion, understanding, optimism, humor, and gentleness of a man less severely beset by personal difficulties. These are the qualities that motivate his writing and make it both warm and foreboding, hopeful and realistic, sad and funny.

Of his first play, *Platonov* (wr. 1878/81), rejected for production at the Maly Theatre,

Platonov, produced
by the Théâtre
National
Populaire, with
Georges Wilson
(left) and Jean
Vilar as Platonov,
Théâtre National
du Palais de
Chaillot, Paris.
[French Cultural
Services]

duced. *The Swan Song* (*Lebedinaya pesnya,* 1888), also a dramatic study adapted from another of Chekhov's own stories, "Kalkhas," depicts the quiet, despairing acceptance by an aging once-popular actor of his obscure future.

Chekhov's other early dramatic efforts sprang from his love of vaudeville and French farce. Permeating the pure merriment of these one-act jokes is his deep understanding of and compassion for people. *The Bear* (1888) relates the story of a widow and a young landlord whose argument over the payment of the lady's debt terminates in a marriage proposal. *The Marriage Proposal* (1890) shows a landowner and the girl he wants to marry in constant battle over a worthless piece of land, even after he finally proposes. *The Wedding* (*Svadba,* wr. 1889) looks in on a bridal feast that is marred by the pompous and wearisome presence of a retired ship's captain. *The Anniversary* (*Yubiley,* wr. 1891) concerns the disrupted fifteenth-anniversary celebration of a bank manager.

Ivanov, though a critical failure, contained the seeds of the mature Chekhov. The well-drawn characters foreshadow other Chekhovian characters, and the plot reveals the author's later-developed theory of tragedy, in which defeat is considered to come from within rather than from external conflict. Thus, almost ten years later Chekhov won his first real triumph with *The Sea Gull* (1896), in which, rather than centering on the tragedy of one individual, he concentrated on a group, the wasting intelligentsia of provincial Russia. Although the environment of the characters is static, within themselves they are active: they dream, worry, rebel, and reach out to fulfill their desires, yet do nothing. So it is in *Uncle Vanya* (1899), in which the futilities and frustrations of existence in the provinces eat away at the lives of the dreamers. Again, in *The Three Sisters* (1901), tragedy comes from unfulfilled dreams: the characters waste their lives in seeking but never finding fruition. Perhaps the most complex of Chekhov's plays, it expresses one of his overriding ideas, that "Life is all right if you don't waste it." In *The Cherry Orchard* (1904), Chekhov's crowning achievement, the aristocratic world of Mme. Ranyevskaya comes to an end when workmen begin to chop down her cherry orchard. In the boarded and abandoned house is left an old servant, a forgotten symbol of a passing and lovely world, to die.

Thematically, Chekhov's plays contrast life, seen in beauty, health, reality, compassion, tolerance, useful work, love, and nature, with death, represented by greediness, self-delusion, boredom, vanity, trivia, gluttony, hypocrisy, and *poshlost* (banality, vulgarity,

only a rough draft exists. Long, clumsy, and somewhat melodramatic, it lacks the typically Chekhovian delicate and intricate structure but possesses in embryonic form all the character prototypes, themes, symbols, and techniques such as pauses, silences, and the use of nature in setting a mood that appear in the later plays. *Ivanov* (1887), about a more sophisticated and older Platonov, is more compact and structured, but there is still much external action. Nevertheless, in *Ivanov* Chekhov established his character types and continued his experiments in setting sensitive moods through the use of dialogue and psychological symbols.

Prior to his vaudevillelike character sketches, or "jokes," Chekhov wrote or adapted from his own stories one-act plays that, though touched with laughter, are gloomy. *On the Highroad* (*Na bolshoy doroge,* wr. 1884), his first composition for the theatre, was a stage version of his story "In the Autumn" (1883). In its new form it became a dramatic study in which an assortment of down-and-out characters interact under the eaves of a roadside inn. Submitted to the censor in 1885, it was rejected and was never pro-

and pettiness). Two intrinsic human traits can destroy a man or, at best, force him to lead a wasted life: the tendency to hide from painful truth by fantasizing and rationalizing and the propensity to *poshlost*. The substance of Chekhovian style is a sense of irony that reveals the absurdity of life and society. So skillful and subtle is Chekhov's irony that his plays, especially if they are not performed well, are often mistakenly interpreted as tragic. Instead, each play, maintaining the delicate balance between pathos and comedy, examines self-delusion and *poshlost* by means of techniques that Chekhov perfected: indirect action, inner dialogue, anticlimactic endings, the creation of moods, and intricate character types. By the time he wrote *The Cherry Orchard*, a perfectly constructed play,

he was able to convey characters, motive, and action without any overt dramatic action having taken place or any traditional character development.

His experiences in Sakhalin taught Chekhov the importance of illusion to the human psyche under duress. But whereas illusion helped the unfortunates of Sakhalin to survive, the heavy reliance on illusion by the gentry of St. Petersburg served as a destructive force, their inability to face reality rendering them ineffectual. Wanting to reveal these illusions, characters as they truly "are" (inner action) and not as they merely "appear to be" (outer action), Chekhov developed the technique of indirect action: important dramatic events take place offstage and are felt or seen through the reactions of the charac-

A French production of *The Marriage Proposal*. [French Cultural Services]

ters onstage. These reactions are recorded by means of inner dialogue; that is, two persons conversing do not participate in a dialogue but rather in two monologues, neither communicating with the other but both revealing the inner being that is hidden from the other. Double-level speech, whereby outer thoughts are spoken in one tone of voice while inner thoughts directly follow in *sotto voce,* accompanied by a change in facial expression, is another character-revealing technique.

Time in Chekhov's plays appears stagnant or suspended but, in fact, is not. The passage of time and the wasting of it are indicated by external action (taking place offstage), which is reported to the players onstage, for example, the change of seasons, the growth of children, the sale of an orchard.

Certain characters sometimes recur in Chekhov's plays, their recognizable traits sparking subtle interactions peculiar to each

Scene from an American Conservatory Theatre production of *The Sea Gull,* with Ellen Geer and Ramon Bieri. [Theatre Collection, The New York Public Library at Lincoln Center]

work. One character reflects reality with comparative faithfulness, so that the audience has a standard against which it can measure the self-delusion of the other characters. He also serves as a Greek chorus and makes comments on the action, the characters, or society in general. In some plays this role is filled by a physician. In *The Cherry Orchard* the servant Firs represents the past, and Lopakhin the future. Another character, a shallow, self-centered woman who busies herself with insignificant, egotistical affairs, refuses to acknowledge the disintegration of her life; Mme. Arkadina (*The Sea Gull*) and Mme. Ranyevskaya (*The Cherry Orchard*) exemplify the type. There is also a mediocre man with pretensions, who speaks in the fashionable jargon of the day, is concerned with his image, and is impressed by his own "originality" and achievement; he is seen in the playwright Trigorin (*The Sea Gull*) and Professor Serebryakov (*Uncle Vanya*). Bureaucrats are represented by many of the supporting characters—landowners, impoverished gentry, civil servants, and merchants—all of whom are absorbed in *poshlost.* Their only enjoyment is found in food, drink, and evening parties where they can sit and discuss trivialities. They are devoid of both mental and physical vigor. Still another character, a young woman determined to "martyr" herself either for a cause or for a man, is typified by Nina (*The Sea Gull*), Masha (*The Three Sisters*), and Sophie (*Ivanov*). And last there is the intelligent, well-educated character who, while knowing well the pitfalls of self-delusion and *poshlost,* ultimately succumbs to his stifling environment because of weakness and either wastes his life or dies. He can be seen in Platonov, Ivanov, Uncle Vanya, Treplyov (*The Sea Gull*), Vershinin and Andrey (*The Three Sisters*), and Trofimov (*The Cherry Orchard*).

Platonov (*Pyesa bez nazvaniya,* wr. 1878/ 81). Platonov, a landowner who has squandered his fortune, looks to love and sex as consolations. Though he has promised his wife Sasha to begin a new life as a schoolteacher, he wastes much of his time on the neighboring Voynitsev estate, where he gently rejects the advances of General Voynitsev's widow Anna and casually arouses the passions of Marya Grekov, an unattractive scientist. Anna's stepson Sergey is married to Sonia, who had once been in love with Platonov. Platonov compulsively arouses Sonia's old feelings for him and eventually succeeds in making her his mistress. Once more he is tempted to begin a new life, and he and Sonia plan to run off together. Sasha reproaches her husband for breaking up another man's home. She makes an unsuccessful attempt to poison herself, and Platonov decides to repent and return to his wife. Sonia's distress fills Platonov with self-revulsion, and he briefly contemplates suicide. But then Marya enters the room, and Platonov is soon compulsively drawn toward her. Discovering the two in an embrace, Sonia shoots Platonov to death.

On the Highroad (*Na bolshoy doroge*, wr. 1884). Dramatic study that takes place in a roadside tavern sheltering pilgrims, workers, and thieves. Bortsov trades a locket for a desperately needed drink. The coachman Kuzma enters and recognizes in Bortsov his former employer. As the others listen, Kuzma tells how Bortsov, betrayed by his wife and cheated by his brother-in-law, turned to drink and dissipated his vast estate. All are moved by the story, but the tramp Merik seems especially stirred as it arouses memories of how he himself has been betrayed by a woman. Coincidence forces Bortsov's wife to take refuge in the tavern after her carriage has broken down. When Bortsov sees her, he drunkenly pleads for her love. Merik, recognizing her from the portrait in the locket, hysterically tries to attack her with an ax and so revenge both himself and Bortsov for what they have suffered at the hands of women. However, with the help of her coachman Bortsov's wife escapes into the night.

The Swan Song (*Lebedinaya pesnya*, 1888). Dramatic study in which the aging actor Svetlovidov awakens from a drunken stupor in an empty theatre late at night after a performance for his benefit. Looking back over his life and feeling the approach of old age and death, Svetlovidov blames his deterioration as a man and as an actor on the woman he loved, who would not marry an actor. Remembering his great moments on the stage, he regains some of his self-esteem. He tries to comfort himself with the notion that "where there is art, where there is talent, there is no old age, there is no solitude or sickness, and even death is not half so frightening," but he is forced to realize that he has wasted his talent and that he is now only a lonely old man.

On the Harmfulness of Tobacco (*O vrede tabaka*, wr. 1886–1903). Dramatic monologue in which Nyukhin, a henpecked husband, has been "volunteered" by his wife to deliver a charity lecture on the evils of tobacco. However, unable to concentrate on anything except his own misery, he rambles on about his unhappy life with his shrewish wife and his seven daughters. Fluctuating between self-pity and self-contempt, his eye twitching nervously, he is often all but incoherent. Finally, spotting his wife in the wings, he begs the audience not to report any of his comments about her but to say that he has performed his assignment with success and

Richard Basehart and Lois Smith in *Uncle Vanya*. [Center Theatre Group, Mark Taper Forum, Los Angeles, Calif.]

dignity. Chekhov wrote six versions of this short work.

Ivanov (1887). Highly intelligent, overimaginative, restless, but incapable of decisive action, Ivanov cannot bear spending his evenings at home with his wife Anna, who is dying of tuberculosis. To the brutally honest but stuffy and unimaginative Dr. Lvov, Ivanov admits that though he loved his wife at the time he won her against the wishes of her Jewish family, the thought of her approaching death now leaves him unmoved. Despite Anna's pleading, Ivanov goes to the neighboring Lyebedev estate, where he finds companionship, cards, and gossip. Young Sasha Lyebedev, a romantic and intelligent girl

Scene from
Uncle Vanya,
with (l. to r.)
Pamela Tiffin,
Joseph Wiseman,
and Richard
Basehart. [Center
Theatre Group,
Mark Taper
Forum, Los
Angeles, Calif.]

weary of her milieu, is drawn to Ivanov when he talks to her of his loneliness, guilt, and frustration. Confessing her love for him, she urges Ivanov to go to America with her. Then Dr. Lvov arrives with Anna, who surprises Ivanov and Sasha in an embrace. Reproached by his wife, who accuses him of having married her for her money, Ivanov cruelly tells her that she is dying.

In the final act, some months after Anna's death, Ivanov has reluctantly agreed to marry Sasha, even though he feels that her attempt to arrest his moral deterioration is futile. When Dr. Lvov arrives and publicly denounces Ivanov, Sasha accuses the doctor of extraordinary insensitivity, disguised as honesty. Ivanov declares that he has "been going downhill long enough" and runs into the garden to shoot himself.

The Bear (*Medved,* 1888). "Joke" in which Yelena Popova, recently widowed, receives an unwelcome visit from Smirnov, a landowner to whom her late husband was in debt. Though Yelena's grief is obviously tempered by memories of her husband's meanness and cruelty and by the knowledge that he had been unfaithful to her, she insists on remaining "true to the grave." Smirnov demands immediate payment, but Yelena says he must wait a day or two. On Smirnov's rude insistence, a quarrel ensues. Enraged, Smirnov challenges the widow to a duel. She agrees but asks that he first show her how to fire a pistol. Even as they continue to argue, they discover and reluctantly admit that they have fallen in love with each other.

The Marriage Proposal (*Predlozheniye,* 1890). "Joke" in which Lomov, who suffers from nervous palpitations, comes to ask his neighbor Chubukov for the hand of his daughter Natalya. When Lomov and Natalya are left alone, they immediately begin quarreling over a parcel of land. Chubukov rejoins them, and the dispute becomes more intense as he takes his daughter's side. Lomov stalks off in anger. Only now does Natalya learn that Lomov had come to propose. She pleads with her father to bring Lomov back. Lomov returns, but soon he and Natalya are arguing so furiously over the merits of their respective hunting dogs that he has a fit and swoons. On being revived, he is informed that his proposal has been accepted. The couple exchange a hasty kiss and renew their argument as Chubukov calls for champagne.

The Tragedian in Spite of Himself (*Tragik po nevole,* wr. 1889). "Joke" in which Tolkachov, laden down with a variety of articles and packages, arrives at his friend Murashkin's house and dramatically asks to borrow a pistol so that he can kill himself. He explains that he can no longer bear being imposed upon by his wife and his neighbors, who will not let him have a quiet minute. He specifically complains of being forced to make purchases and run errands every time he travels from his country house to his job in the city. Murashkin listens with apparent sympathy but eventually asks Tolkachov to deliver a sewing machine to a woman who lives near Tolkachov's house. Tolkachov turns purple and starts chasing Murashkin around the room, shouting "I want blood!"

The Wedding (*Svadba,* wr. 1889). Farce set at the wedding reception of Aplombov and his bride Dashenka. A group has gathered to celebrate the wedding, and a variety of arguments develop between family members and guests. The bridegroom is annoyed with his new in-laws, and one of his complaints is the absence of a general, whose attendance had been promised to add distinction to the wedding. The "general" finally does arrive, but he proceeds to bore everyone with a lecture on seamanship because he is really a retired ship's captain. When it becomes known that the friend of the bride's father who was entrusted with 25 rubles to buy the presence of the "general" has pocketed the money instead, the feast turns into pandemonium.

The Anniversary (*Yubiley,* wr. 1891). "Joke" based on a short story entitled "A Helpless Creature." Shipuchin, an incompetent but ambitious bank manager, has arranged to have the bank's shareholders commemorate his fifteenth year in office by presenting him with a silver cup he himself has provided. Khirin, his hardworking but misogynist clerk, is struggling to finish a report Shipuchin is to deliver at the celebration when Mrs. Shipuchin comes in and starts babbling about her recent trip to her mother's house. On her heels comes an old woman who insists on presenting Shipuchin with a petition that in no way concerns the bank. As Shipuchin nervously tries to deal with these

A Comédie-Française production of *Uncle Vanya.* [French Cultural Services]

women, Khirin loses his head and starts chasing them around the room. At the height of the confusion, the shareholders' committee arrives to present Shipuchin with the cup meant to honor him for his efficiently run organization.

The Sea Gull (*Chayka*, 1896). Comedy of frustrated lives. Accompanied by her lover, the celebrated novelist Trigorin, Mme. Arkadina, a successful but aging actress, visits the country estate of her brother Sorin. Her son Konstantin, hoping to impress his mother, arranges with his sweetheart Nina to stage a symbolist drama he has written, but his mother's thoughtlessly mocking comments cause him to suspend the performance and stalk off in a rage. Nina, introduced to Trigorin, is dazzled by his fame and sophistication, and in the days that follow her relationship with Konstantin cools. Konstantin kills a sea gull and reproachfully lays it at her feet, dramatically indicating his readiness to commit suicide. To Nina the killing of the sea gull is another example of Konstantin's moodiness; to Trigorin it suggests the possibility of a story about a free-spirited girl who is thoughtlessly destroyed by a man seeking escape from boredom. In his despair Konstantin does attempt suicide, and Mme. Arkadina, fearful of losing Trigorin, abruptly decides to end their stay in the country. Nina declares her love to Trigorin, and Trigorin makes an ineffectual attempt to break with Mme. Arkadina. Still, when Nina tells him she is going to Moscow to be an actress, he arranges to meet her.

Two years elapse. Mme. Arkadina and Trigorin are once more at Sorin's estate. Konstantin has published some pieces, but his life is blighted by the loss of Nina, now an actress with provincial companies. She has briefly been Trigorin's mistress, but he has returned to Mme. Arkadina. Now, while the others are at dinner, Nina slips into Konstantin's study. Feverish, incoherent, repeatedly referring to herself as a sea gull, she tells Konstantin of her hard life and of her struggle to become a great actress. When he begs her to stay with him, she confesses that she is still in love with Trigorin. After she has left, Konstantin destroys his manuscripts and shoots himself, while in the next room, unaware of what has happened, Mme. Arkadina is playing cards with her friends.

Uncle Vanya (*Dyadya Vanya*, 1899). Professor Serebryakov, a pretentious minor scholar, has for years been supported by the drudgery of his daughter Sonia and his brother-in-law Ivan (Uncle Vanya), who have managed the estate left by his first wife. Serebryakov is now married to Yelena, a young, beautiful girl who was dazzled by his imagined fame. Both Vanya and Yelena begin to recognize Serebryakov's essential mediocrity, Vanya regretting the years wasted supporting the professor's intellectual activities and Yelena finding herself trapped in a loveless marriage to an old, egotistical man. Vanya is increasingly drawn to Yelena and bitterly realizes that if he had not been busy working for the professor's benefit, he might have won Yelena for himself.

Yelena's restlessness and Serebryakov's egoism disrupt the work routines of the estate. A physician, Dr. Astrov, is attracted by Yelena and becomes a frequent visitor, using as an excuse his ministrations to the hypochondriacal professor, but it is Sonia who falls helplessly in love with Astrov. She appeals to Yelena to speak to the doctor for her, and Yelena makes an honest attempt, but her talk with Astrov only forces her to recognize that she herself is drawn to him. Astrov rejects the idea of marriage to Sonia, suggesting instead that he and Yelena have an affair.

The tense situation on the estate is brought to a climax when Serebryakov announces that he wants to sell the land and use the money to live in the city. At the thought that his labors and Sonia's inheritance are to be squandered to support a pedant, Vanya loses control and tries to kill Serebryakov. Yelena now persuades her husband to leave the estate. After their departure, Astrov takes his

Ralph Richardson as Vershinin in a London production of *The Three Sisters.* [Theatre Collection, The New York Public Library at Lincoln Center, Astor, Lenox and Tilden Foundations]

Konstantin Stanislavski as Vershinin in *The Three Sisters*. [Theatre Collection, The New York Public Library at Lincoln Center, Astor, Lenox and Tilden Foundations]

leave, announcing that he will no longer be able to visit quite so frequently. Vanya and Sonia return to their drudgery for the benefit of others, and Sonia reassures the despondent Vanya that in the next world, where life will be beautiful, they will finally be able to "rest."

The Three Sisters (*Tri sestry,* 1901). In a provincial garrison town, the gentle, highly cultured Prozorov sisters long for the stimulation and excitement of Moscow, which they left eleven years before. Olga is constantly exhausted by her unrewarding work as a schoolmistress; Masha, who at eighteen married a man she considered an intellectual giant, bitterly realizes that he is a dull pedagogue; and Irina dreams of a romantic future and rejects both the sincere love of Lieutenant Tuzenbakh, an unattractive but kindly man, and the advances of Staff Captain Vasi-

ly Vasilyevich Solony. To the garrison officers who form the sisters' and their brother Andrey's circle of friends is added Vershinin, a lieutenant colonel who has once lived in Moscow. He enchants them with his glowing vision of a cultural millennium "in two or three hundred years." Masha is especially drawn to Vershinin, who, like herself, is unhappily married.

The Prozorovs and their friends recognize the frustration and uselessness of their lives, but hope in some vague future keeps their spirits high. The atmosphere changes when Andrey marries and brings into the house a crude and grasping local girl, Natasha. The sisters' immediate prospects of a return to Moscow are dashed. Irina tries to find relief in work, but her job in the telegraph office offers only tiresome routine. The sisters are virtually dispossessed of their home as Natasha inexorably moves toward assuming the role of mistress of the household. Andrey takes refuge in gambling and mortgages the house he and his sisters own jointly.

News that the garrison is to be transferred

A French production of *The Three Sisters*, Théâtre de l'Oeuvre, Paris. [French Cultural Services]

A French production of *The Cherry Orchard*, with (l. to r.) Jean-Louis Barrault, Madeleine Renaud, Pierre Bertin, and Simone Valère, Théâtre Marigny, Paris. [French Cultural Services]

brings depressing prospects for the future, and Irina decides to escape into marriage with Tuzenbakh, who resigns his army commission in the hope of finding more meaningful work. As Masha and Vershinin, who have become lovers, bid each other good-bye and the regiment prepares to leave, word comes that Tuzenbakh has been killed by Solony in a duel over Irina. The sisters cling to one another for consolation, but as the band strikes up, the infectious gaiety of the music inspires them to hope that their suffering was meaningful and that there is a new life in store for them.

The Cherry Orchard (*Vishnyovy sad,* 1904). After five years abroad, the widowed Mme. Ranyevskaya returns to her estate to find that it has been heavily mortgaged to pay for her extravagances and that it is to be auctioned. Generous and scatterbrained, she seems incapable of recognizing her desperate situation. A halfhearted attempt is made to collect money owed the family by Pischin, a neighboring landowner, but he himself is in financial straits. Gaev, Madame Ranyevskaya's brother, makes some impractical suggestions, but his chief hope lies in an uncertain legacy or a rich marriage for Anya, Mme. Ranyevskaya's young daughter. The only apparently feasible proposal comes from Lopakhin, a merchant whose father was once a serf of the Ranyevskaya family. He suggests cutting down the famous cherry orchard and dividing the land into plots for summer cottages. The idea of destroying such beauty is rejected as a sacrilege, and with no specific plan in mind for saving the estate, the family drifts aimlessly but hopefully toward the day set for the auction. On that very evening, Mme. Ranyevskaya gives a party that she can ill afford. In the midst of the festivities Lopakhin arrives and happily announces that he has acquired the estate and intends to carry out his suggested plan for cutting down the orchard. The estate and the orchard now gone, the family prepares to leave. Forgotten in the confusion is the very old and ailing Firs, the devoted former family serf, and as the sound of an ax rings from the cherry orchard, he lies down to rest and soon is motionless.

PLAYS

1. *Pyesa bez nazvaniya** (known in English as *Platonov, or A Country Scandal*). Play, 4 acts. Written 1878/81. Published 1923. Since the original title page was destroyed, the correct title has never been determined.
2. *Na bolshoy doroge** (*On the Highroad*). Dramatic study, 1 act. Written 1884. Performance forbidden by censor in 1885. Adapted from Chekhov's short story "In the Autumn" (1883).
3. *Lebedinaya pesnya** (*The Swan Song*). Dramatic study, 1 act. Written 1886. Published 1887. Produced Moscow, Korsh Theatre, Feb. 19, 1888. Adapted from Chekhov's short story "Kalkhas."
4. *O vrede tabaka** (*On the Harmfulness of Tobacco*). Dramatic monologue, 1 act. Written 1886–1903 (six versions). Published 1903.
5. *Ivanov**. Drama, 4 acts. Written 1887. Published 1887. Produced Moscow, Korsh Theatre, Nov. 19, 1887; St. Petersburg, Alexandrinsky Theatre, Jan. 31, 1889.
6. *Medved** (*The Bear*). Joke, 1 act. Written 1888. Published 1888. Produced Moscow, Korsh Theatre, Oct. 28, 1888.
7. *Predlozheniye** (*The Marriage Proposal*). Joke, 1 act. Written 1888. Published 1889. Produced Moscow, Maly Theatre, 1890.
8. *Leshy** (*The Wood Demon*). Comedy, 4 acts. Written 1889. Produced Moscow, Abramova Theatre, Dec. 27, 1889. Early version of *Dyadya Vanya*.
9. *Tatyana Repina**. Play, 1 act. Written 1889.
10. *Tragik po nevole** (*The Tragedian in Spite of Himself*). Joke, 1 act. Written May, 1889. Published 1890.
11. *Svadba** (*The Wedding*). Farce, 1 act. Written October, 1889. Published 1902.
12. *Yubiley** (*The Anniversary*). Joke, 1 act. Written 1891 (revised 1902). Published 1902. Based on the short story "A Helpless Creature."
13. *Chayka** (*The Sea Gull*). Comedy, 4 acts. Written 1896. Published 1897. Produced St. Petersburg, Alexandrinsky Theatre, Oct. 17, 1896; Moscow, Moscow Art Theatre, Dec. 17, 1898.
14. *Dyadya Vanya** (*Uncle Vanya*). Play, 4 acts. Written 1896. Published 1897. Produced Moscow, Moscow Art Theatre, Oct. 26, 1899. Based on *Leshy*.
15. *Tri sestry** (*The Three Sisters*). Drama, 4 acts. Written 1900. Published 1901. Produced Moscow, Moscow Art Theatre, Jan. 31, 1901.
16. *Vishnyovy sad** (*The Cherry Orchard*). Comedy, 4 acts. Written 1903. Published 1904. Produced Moscow, Moscow Art Theatre, Jan. 17, 1904.

EDITIONS

Collections.
Polnoye sobraniye sochineny A. P. Chekhova, 6 vols., St. Petersburg, 1900–1904; *Neizdannaya pyesa A. P. Chekhova*, ed. by N. F. Belchikov, Moscow, 1923; *Russian Text of Three Plays*, New York, 1946; *Polnoye sobraniye sochineny i pisem A. P. Chekhova*, 20 vols., Moscow, 1946–1948; *Best Plays*, tr. by S. Young, New York, 1956; *Plays and Stories*, New York, 1958; *Nine Plays of Chekhov*, New York, 1959; *Plays*, tr. by E. Fen, Baltimore, 1959; *Six Plays of Chekhov*, tr. by R. W. Corrigan, New York, 1962; *Chekhov: The Major Plays*, tr. by A. Dunnigan, New York, 1964; *Chekhov*, ed. by R. Hingley, vol. 2, New York, 1967; *Four Great Plays by Chekhov*, New York, 1968; *The Oxford Chekhov*, vol. 1, *Short Plays*, ed. by R. Hingley, New York, 1968.
Individual Plays.
The Anniversary (The Jubilee). Published in *Five Russian Plays, with One from the Ukrainian*, tr. by C. E. B. Roberts, New York, 1916.

The Bear (The Boor). Published in *Interpreting Literature*, ed. by K. L. Knickerbocker and H. W. Reninger and tr. by B. Clark and H. Banknage, rev. ed., New York, 1960.
The Cherry Orchard. Published in *Masters of Modern Drama*, ed. by H. M. Block and R. G. Shedd and tr. by S. Young, New York, 1962.
Ivanov. Published in *Makers of the Modern Theater*, ed. by B. Ulanov and tr. by E. Winer, New York, 1961.
The Marriage Proposal. Published in *The Arts of Reading*, ed. by R. G. Ross et al. and tr. by T. Hoffman, New York, 1960.
The Sea Gull. Published in *The Art of the Play*, ed. by A. S. Downer and tr. by S. Young, New York, 1955.
The Swan Song. Published in *Repertory*, ed. by W. Blair and J. Gerber and tr. by M. Fell, Chicago, 1960.
The Three Sisters. Published in *Drama: An Introductory Anthology*, ed. by O. Reinert and tr. by E. Fen, Boston, 1961.
Uncle Vanya. Published in *Contemporary Drama*, ed. by S. A. Clayes and D. G. Spencer and tr. by S. Young, New York, 1962.
The Wedding. Published in *Comedy*, ed. by M. Felheim and tr. by E. Bentley, New York, 1962.

CRITICISM
Chekhov: Ego zhizn i sochineniya, ed. by V. I. Pokrovsky, Moscow, 1905; I. F. Annensky, *Drama nastroyeniya "Tri sestry,"* St. Petersburg, 1906; D. Magarshack, *Chekhov the Dramatist*, New York, 1960; E. J. Simmons, *Chekhov: A Biography*, Boston, 1962; T. Winner, *Chekhov and His Prose*, New York, 1966.

CHESTER CYCLE. See MYSTERY PLAY.

Luigi Chiarelli
(1880 — 1947)

Luigi Chiarelli, Italian journalist, short-story writer, and dramatist, was born in Trani on July 7, 1880, and raised in Rome. He contemplated entering the University of Rome, but the sudden death of his father prevented his doing so. He showed precocious talent, beginning to write poems and articles for newspapers when he was only fifteen. Until 1910 he was a regular contributor to *L'Alfieri* and *La Patria;* then, in 1911, he moved to Milan and became the editor of *Il Secolo*. During these early years he wrote and destroyed some eight plays, but he persisted, and his professional debut came in 1912 with the production of two one-act plays, *A Night of Love* (*Una notte d'amore*) and *The Policeman* (*Er gendarme*). Shortly thereafter Chiarelli became the editor of the literary review *Armi e Politica*, continuing to serve in this capacity until Italy's entry in World War I in 1915, when he was inducted into the army. He was permitted, however, to continue his literary and theatrical activities as a noncombatant, and in 1916 he became the stage director of the Dramatic Theatre of Rome.

Luigi Chiarelli.
[Federico Arborio
Mella, Milan]

many notable productions, in particular Goldoni's *The Mistress of the Inn* (*La locandiera*) and Morselli's *Glaucus* (*Glauco*). He became drama critic for the *Corriere Italiano* of Rome in 1923 and was elected president of the Syndicate of Dramatists in 1925. He held many honorary positions, presided at numerous international conferences of authors, and also served as counselor of the Italian Theatre Corporation from 1941 to 1945.

In addition to his original dramas, Chiarelli provided the Italian stage with many translations, including Shakespeare's *The Merry Wives of Windsor* (1921), François Mauriac's *Asmodeus* (1939), and Zorrilla's *Don Juan Tenorio* (1946). He wrote one of the first plays for Italian radio, *The Ring of Teodosio* (*L'anello di Teodosio*), in 1929. Chiarelli died on December 20, 1947.

WORK

Chiarelli is noted principally as the developer of the *teatro del grottesco* ("theatre of the grotesque"), which is characterized by bizarre occurrences, abstract characters, and often a distinctly expressionistic mode. The themes of grotesque drama frequently deal with life as illusion and parallel in many instances the theatre of Pirandello. *See* PIRANDELLO, LUIGI.

La maschera e il volto. Turin, Teatro Stabile di Torino, 1956. [Teatro Stabile di Torino]

With the production of his famous "grotesque" play *The Mask and the Face* (*La maschera e il volto*) in 1916, Chiarelli's reputation was established. In 1918 he formed his own acting company, Ars Italica, and staged

Chiarelli's fame rests largely on five grotesque comedies, beginning with his enor-

Humphrey Bogart and Judith Anderson in Somerset Maugham's translation of *The Mask and the Face.* New York, Guild Theatre, 1933. [Photograph by Vandamm. Theatre Collection, The New York Public Library at Lincoln Center, Astor, Lenox and Tilden Foundations]

mously successful and brilliantly conceived *The Mask and the Face* (1916), which established the genre. Going beyond the ironic humor of this drama, *Chimeras* (*Chimere*, 1920) takes on a more tragic coloring: Claudio and Marina vow that their lives will always be founded on the purest principles. External reality, however, in the form of financial disaster, forces them into distasteful compromises and reveals the superficial nature of their ideals. With Claudio's consent Marina becomes the mistress of a banker who promises to save Claudio from financial ruin. In *The Silken Ladder* (*La scala de seta*, 1917) the almost allegorical presentation of character types establishes a link with the *commedia dell'arte* tradition in its tale of an unprincipled rascal's climb to success. *See* COMMEDIA DELL'ARTE.

The mocking irony of *The Mask and the Face* is recaptured in *The Lovers' Death* (*La morte degli amanti*, 1921), in which a suicide pact between an unfaithful wife and her lover is thwarted when the husband enters and innocently turns off the gas. Thus, the romantic death is frustrated by practical economy.

Fireworks (*Fuochi d'artificio*, 1923), in a manner that is reminiscent of Benavente's *Bonds of Interest* (1907), recounts the picaresque adventures of two emigrants who return destitute to Italy. One, posing as the other's secretary, spreads the rumor that his employer is a millionaire; even when the latter confesses the hoax, the townspeople insist on believing he is rich and eventually make him so. In this transformation of falsehood into truth, the world of Pirandello is again seen. *Fireworks* has generally been considered to be the last of Chiarelli's grotesque dramas. *See* BENAVENTE, JACINTO.

Chiarelli's other plays include the humorous political satire *The Sedan Chair* (*La portantina*, 1917); *The Magic Circle* (*Il cerchio magico*, 1937), about the fantasies of an unhappy wife; and *To Be* (*Essere*, 1953), an allegorical drama in which Chiarelli seems to turn his back on his earlier philosophical premises and insist on the demands of objective reality.

The Mask and the Face (*La maschera e il volto*, 1916). Grotesque comedy in which Paolo, after having publicly declared that if

Scene from *The Mask and the Face,* with Leo G. Carroll (left) and Shirley Booth. New York, Guild Theatre, 1933. [Photograph by Vandamm. Theatre Collection, The New York Public Library at Lincoln Center, Astor, Lenox and Tilden Foundations]

his wife Savina were ever unfaithful, he would kill her, discovers that she has a lover. His instinct is to forgive her, but fearing ridicule from his friends, he contrives an elaborate scheme in which she is sent abroad while he announces that he has killed her and thrown her body into the lake. After a trial at which he is exonerated, Paolo becomes a local hero and the darling of the ladies. He is revolted by this ludicrous turn of events.

One day a woman's body is found in the lake, and everyone insists that it is Savina. Paolo is forced to go through the farce of a funeral at which the penitent Savina herself turns up and is recognized. Husband and wife are reconciled, but Paolo now faces arrest for perjury and contempt of court. "I killed her and they exonerated me. . . . I didn't kill her and they send me to jail," he complains. The

lovers decide that they are not accountable to society for their acts, and they flee abroad.

The Silken Ladder (*La scala di seta,* 1917). Grotesque comedy contrasting the fates of Roberto, an honest man doomed to failure, and Desiré, a vain and unscrupulous dancer whose connivances enable him effortlessly to ascend the silken ladder of success. About the two protagonists revolves a greedy group of confidence men and prostitutes, for whose deviousness only Desiré is a match. Eventually the dancer marries a millionaire's daughter and blackmails his way to a post as Minister of State. As he is acclaimed by the foolish crowd that has come to hear his ministerial speech, Desiré hears the distant sound of a waltz, and though he continues to spout homilies about freedom, truth, and justice, his feet cannot resist the temptation to go into their dance. The play cynically implies that only those who view life as a playful dance can succeed.

PLAYS

1. *Una notte d'amore* (*A Night of Love*). Comedy. 1 act. Produced Bologna, Teatro Verdi, 1912.

2. *Er gendarme* (*The Policeman*). Play. In Romansh: Produced Milan, Teatro Fossati, Sept. 21, 1912. In Italian: Produced Chioggia, Teatro Garibaldi, 1913.

3. *Extra Dry*. Play, 1 act. Published 1926. Produced Milan, Teatro Olimpia, Jan. 24, 1914.

4. *La maschera e il volto** (*The Mask and the Face*). Grotesque, 3 acts. Published 1917. Produced Rome, Teatro Argentina, May 31, 1916.

5. *La scala di seta* (*The Silken Ladder*). Grotesque. Published 1922. Produced Rome, Teatro Argentina, June 28, 1917.

6. *La portantina* (*The Sedan Chair*). Political satire. Produced Milan, Teatro Manzoni, Oct. 3, 1917.

7. *Le lacrime e le stelle* (*The Tears and the Stars*). Drama, 3 acts. Published 1918. Produced Rome, Teatro Argentina, Jan. 23, 1918.

8. *La morte degli amanti* (*The Lovers' Death*). Grotesque, 3 acts. Written 1919. Published 1924. Produced Rome, Teatro Valle, Jan. 27, 1921.

9. *Chimere* (*Chimeras*). Grotesque, 3 acts. Published 1921. Produced Turin, Teatro Carignano, Feb. 6, 1920.

10. *Fuochi d'artificio* (*Fireworks*). Grotesque, 3 acts. Written 1922. Published 1923. Produced Turin, Teatro Alfieri, Feb. 7, 1923.

11. *Les tripes à la mode de Caen* (*Tripe Caen-style*). Comedy, 1 act. Published 1925. Produced Milan, Teatro Arcimboldi, Oct. 24, 1925.

12. *Jolly*. Comedy, 3 acts. Written 1928. Published 1929. Produced Milan, Teatro Manzoni, Feb. 8, 1928.

13. *La providente Lucilla* (*The Provident Lucille*). Play, 1 act. Published 1928.

14. *Ciclo delle noci di cocco* (*Cycle of Coconuts*). Play. 1 act. Written 1928.

15. *Il libro nero* (*The Black Book*). Play, 1 act. Written 1928.

16. *Don Juan*. Play, 1 act. Published 1929.

17. *L'anello di Teodosio* (*The Ring of Teodosio*). Radio play. Written 1929.

18. *La reginetta* (*The Little Queen*). Play, 1 act. Published 1929. Produced Milan, Teatro Arcimboldi, 1931.

19. *Leggere e scrivere* (*To Read and Write*). Comedy, 1 act. Published 1929. Produced Milan, Teatro Arcimboldi, 1931.

20. *K. 41*. Dramatic representation, 3 acts. Published 1930. Produced Nov. 2, 1929.

21. *L.E.F.* Comedy, 1 act. Published 1930.

22. *L'errore necessario* (*The Necessary Error*). Play. Published 1930.

23. *Scaramanzia* (*Exorcism*). Comedy; 5 scenes, 1 act. Published 1931. Produced Milan, Teatro Arcimboldi, 1931.

24. *Un uomo da rifare* (*A Man to Remake*). Drama, 3 acts. Written 1931. Published 1932. Produced Milan, Teatro Manzoni, Jan. 27, 1932.

25. *Clara ha ragione* (*Clara Is Right*). Comedy, 1 act. Published 1932.

26. *Carne bianca* (*White Flesh*). Play. Published 1934.

27. *La follia dell'oro* (*The Folly of Gold*). Play, 1 act. Published 1935.

28. *Una più due* (*One Plus Two*). Comedy, 3 acts. Published 1935. Produced San Remo Casino, May 16, 1935.

29. *Il cerchio magico* (*The Magic Circle*). Comedy, 3 acts. Published 1937. Produced San Remo Casino, Feb. 17, 1937.

30. *Enea come oggi* (*Aeneas as Today*). Play. Published 1938.

31. *Moneta falsa* (*Counterfeit Money*). Play. Written 1939.

32. *Pulcinella*. Comedy; 3 acts. Published 1939.

33. *Ninon*. Dramatic allegory. Published 1940.

34. *Enrico VIII* (*Henry VIII*). Play. Written 1940. Published 1941.

35. *Il teatro in fiamme* (*The Theater in Flames*). Play. Produced Rome, Teatro Quirino, Mar. 16, 1945.

36. *Natale* (*Christmas*). Play, 1 act. Written 1945.

37. *Essere* (*To Be*). Dramatic allegory. Published 1953. Produced Rome, Teatro Pirandello, June 3, 1953.

38. *Scandalo* (*Scandal*). Play.

EDITIONS

Varietà, 2 vols., Turin, 1934.
The Mask and the Face. Published in *International Modern Plays*, tr. by V. Beamish, London, 1950.

CRITICISM

M. Lo Vecchio Musti, *L'opera di Luigi Chiarelli*, Rome, 1942.

CHIKAMATSU MONZAEMON, pseudonym of Sugimori Nobumori (b. Echizen Province, 1653; d. Osaka, January 6, 1725). Japanese playwright of the Genroku period of Japanese art. The use of the term "Genroku" roughly corresponds to the use of the term "Elizabethan" in histories of English drama. Extending from about 1688 to 1703, Genroku represents one of the most dynamic periods of Japanese art, a period that also witnessed the upsurge of the middle class. Chikamatsu is

The Love Suicides at Sonezaki, 1970. [Japanese Government]

often referred to as the Shakespeare of Japan.

Born into a minor samurai family, Chikamatsu began his career by writing for the Kabuki, or popular theatre, but established his fame through his collaboration with the famous chanter (*jōruri*) Takemoto Gidayū (1650–1714), who had opened a puppet theatre (*bunraku*) in the fast-growing mercantile city Osaka. Chikamatsu found his powerful imagination liberated by the puppets and wrote his most famous plays for them. *See* KABUKI.

His plays fall into two groups, the heroic quasi-historical plays (*jidaimono*), such as *The Battles of Coxinga* (*Kokusenya Kassen*, 1715), which deals with a military expedition of the Japanese into China; and the domestic plays (*sewamono*), such as *The Love Suicides at Sonezaki* (*Sonezaki Shinjū*, 1703), a three-act later version of which may be taken as a fine example of the genre. Called *The Love Suicides at Amijima* (*Shinjū ten no Amijima*, 1720), this version tells of a man who, having fallen in love with a courtesan, deserts his wife and family. In the last act the two lovers make their journey to a deserted spot in the countryside to perform their ceremonial death scene. These plays became so popular and had such a powerful effect on the audiences that in 1772, in order to stem the rash of suicides among young lovers, the government found itself forced to ban all plays with the term "love suicides" in the title.

Chikamatsu's style, a unique combination of realism and fantasy, of journalism and highly conscious, sophisticated art, is especially apparent in the *sewamono* type of plays. His language is opulent and pungent, prose alternates with verse, and the vocabulary closely reflects character and milieu. Humor, dialect, double meanings and puns, popular songs, and contemporary references abound.

Among Chikamatsu's other well-known plays are *The Courier for Hades* (*Meido no hikyaku*, 1711); *The Fair Ladies at a Game of Poem Cards* (*Kaoyo utagaruta*, 1714); *The Old Almanac of Daikyōji* (*Daikyōji mukashi-goyomi*, 1715), later renamed *The Almanac of Love* (*Koi hakke hashiragoyomi*); *The Soga Revenge* (*Soga Kaikeizan*, 1718); *Kojorō of Hakata and the Pirates* (*Hakata Kojorō nami-makura*, 1718); and *The Tethered Steed* (*Kan hasshu tsunagi uma*, 1724).

The Love Suicides at Sonezaki (*Sonezaki Shinjū*, 1703).   One-act tragedy based on an actual happening in Osaka in 1703. The first play on the theme of the double suicide of lov-

Scene from *The Battles of Coxinga*, 1970. [Japanese Government]

Two scenes from
*The Love Suicides
at Amijima*, 1970.
[Japanese
Government]

(Opposite) *The Battles of Coxinga* (above) and *The Courier for Hades* (below), 1970. [Japanese Government]

ers and a model for all later ones, it explores the conflict between personal inclination and social obligation.

The play opens to the courtesan O-Hatsu's complaints that her lover Tokubei has stayed away for ten days. When Tokubei appears, he says that his uncle, who is also his employer, has chosen him to marry his daughter. Despite his refusal, his stepmother has already accepted part of the dowry and Tokubei must repay it at once. Since the refusal cost him his job, his only hope of making the repayment lies in getting back the money he has lent to a friend, Kuheiji. However, Kuheiji denies that he has borrowed the money, and when Tokubei shows him his own seal on the note, he maintains that Tokubei stole it from him. Unable to prove that Kuheiji borrowed the money and unable to pay his uncle, Tokubei resolves to die to save his honor. O-Hatsu begs to be permitted to die with him. The two flee to the shrine at Sonezaki, where he kills her and then himself.

The Love Suicides at Amijima (*Shinjū ten no Amijima*, 1720). Three-act domestic tragedy. The owner of a stationery shop in Osaka, Jihei, who is married to his cousin Osan, has fallen in love with the courtesan Koharu. A rich merchant tries to come between the lovers but is refused by Koharu. However, Jihei is too poor to buy her freedom. The resulting conflicts lead to the resolution of a double suicide. The dramatic tension is heightened by the behavior of both heroines. The wife is ready to sell her belongings so as to help Jihei buy Koharu's freedom; Koharu, on the other hand, is ready to relinquish her love in order to spare Osan further pain.

CHLUMBERG, Hans (1897–1930). Austrian dramatist known for his tragic-grotesque play *Miracle at Verdun* (*Das Wunder um Verdun*, 1930), about the resurrection of German and French World War I dead. His other plays include *The Leaders* (*Die Führer*, 1919), *Someday* (*Eines Tages*, 1922), and *The Blue of the Sky* (*Das Blaue vom Himmel*, 1929).

CHODOROV, Jerome (1911–   ). American playwright, director, and screenwriter, best known for plays written in collaboration with Joseph Fields: *Schoolhouse on the Lot* (1938); *My Sister Eileen* (1940), based on the stories of Ruth McKenney; *Junior Miss* (1941); *The French Touch* (1945); *Anniversary Waltz* (1954); and *The Ponder Heart* (1956). Chodorov and Fields also wrote the books for the musicals *Pretty Penny* (1940); *Wonderful*

David Wayne and Sarah Marshall in Jerome Chodorov's *The Ponder Heart*. New York, Music Box Theatre, 1956. [Theatre Collection, The New York Public Library at Lincoln Center, Astor, Lenox and Tilden Foundations]

Town (1953), which obtained the New York Drama Critics Circle award; and *The Girl in Pink Tights* (1954). Alone, Chodorov wrote the book for the musical *I Had a Ball* (1964); and a comedy, *3 Bags Full* (1966). See FIELDS, JOSEPH.

CHORUS. Lyrical component of ancient Greek drama, composed of a number of singer-actors who performed in unison under the direction of a leader. According to Aristotle, the origin of the drama is to be found in the ritual celebration in Athens of the god Dionysus with ecstatic choral odes. The Greek historian Herodotus records that in the seventh century B.C. Arion of Lesbos interspersed dialogue, spoken by the leader of the chorus, in the lyrical context of the performance. A second and then a third actor were introduced into the drama by Aeschylus and Sophocles, and consequently, as in the tragedy of Euripides and the comedy of Aristophanes and Menander, the importance of the chorus was significantly lessened. The chorus itself had been reduced in size from about fifty members to twelve or fifteen. By the time of Plautus and Terence, the chorus had completely disappeared from comedy, while in tragedy it served only to observe and comment rather than participate in the action. *See* AESCHYLUS; ARISTOPHANES; EURIPIDES; MENANDER; SOPHOCLES.

Originally the choral hymn, the dithyramb, was chanted in honor of Dionysus, but as time went on, it was also sung in honor of other deities as well as human heroes. The director of the entire ritual performance was called the *choregus,* and the leader of the chorus *coryphaeus.* The sections spoken by the second actor in the early plays, which interrupted the chanted odes, were known as episodes, and there was no division into acts. As the drama developed, the situation was reversed, and the lyrical interruptions of the dialogue brought about the separation of the play into scenes and acts. The choral chant was divided into the *parados,* or entrance song; the *stasima,* or formal odes; and the *exodos,* or concluding song. There were also informal spoken and musical exchanges between actors and chorus, in which sometimes the actors sang solo (monody) or the choral leader spoke.

CHRONICLE PLAY. Type of play that employs subject matter drawn from the historical records of a nation, the events of whose past are seen as relevant to the resolution of current sociopolitical problems. The chronicle play flourished in Elizabethan and Stuart England between the late 1580s and the 1630s. It was often revived and was imitated or adapted in other countries.

Traditionally it is taken from historical surveys, or chronicles, and although originality of plot is not essential, facts are often altered for dramatic or aesthetic effect. This kind of play flowers in the eras of a people's history in which a strong emphasis is laid on national pride. It serves to augment this sense of popular self-awareness by apposite allusions to the events of the past in terms of their significance for the present, but this intentionally propagandistic purpose is often subordinated to the purely theatrical qualities inherent in the plot. In Elizabethan England the transition from the didactic religious and allegorical history of mystery and morality plays to the secular history of the chronicle play, still didactic in intent, was easily effected, especially since there existed an abundance of nontheatrical historical writing that exhibited a strong sense of national unity. The so-called Tudor myth, which evolved in the fifteenth century, propounded the concept of divine kingship, and this endowed secular history with a spiritual relevance second only to religion.

The first close antecedent of the chronicle play was John Bale's *King John* (wr. before 1536), which was still largely allegorical. A three-part play in Latin, *Richard Tertius,* was written by Thomas Legge of Cambridge in 1579. Chronicle plays in the English language became popular in the late 1580s. The earliest, which are of disputed authorship, include *The Famous Victories of Henry V, The True Tragedy of Richard III,* and *The Troublesome Reign of John King of England.* Christopher Marlowe wrote the chronicle play *Edward II,* but the high point of the success of chronicle plays came in the work of Shakespeare. Other Elizabethan authors of chronicle plays were George Peele (*Edward I,* ca. late 1592/early 1593), Thomas Dekker and John Webster (who collaborated on *Sir Thomas Wyatt,* 1602), Thomas Heywood (*Edward IV,* 1599), and John Ford (*Perkin Warbeck,* 1622/32).

During the Restoration and in the eighteenth century there were numerous adaptations of Shakespeare, such as Colley Cibber's *The Tragical History of Richard III* (1699). New plays also were written, by Roger Boyle (*The Black Prince,* 1667), John Bancroft (*Edward III,* 1690), Nicholas Rowe (*The Tragedy of Lady Jane Gray,* 1715), and Henry Brooke (*The Earl of Essex,* 1750). In the nineteenth century Alfred Tennyson wrote a trilogy of

Colley Cibber; portrait by Jean-Baptiste Van Loo. [Theatre Collection, The New York Public Library at Lincoln Center, Astor, Lenox and Tilden Foundations]

chronicle plays on the making of England (*Harold*, 1877; *Becket*, 1893; and *Queen Mary*, 1876), and Algernon Swinburne composed a trilogy concerning Mary, Queen of Scots (*Chastelard*, 1865; *Bothwell*, 1874; and *Mary Stuart*, 1881). Even in the twentieth century certain authors have devoted themselves to major protagonists of English history, such as Oliver Cromwell, in the play of the same name by John Drinkwater (1923), and Sir Thomas More, in *A Man for All Seasons* by Robert Bolt (1960).

Non-English history plays, although frequently called chronicles, often take other forms: in France they are usually romanticized versions of history; in Germany, historical tragedies; in Russia, polemically propagandistic dramas; and in the United States, historical pageants. Only Spain and Scandinavia have created a genre of history play that comes close to the English chronicle play as it has been defined. August Strindberg, in fact, wrote more than twenty magnificent plays of this type chronicling Swedish history. He took as his prototype the historical plays of Shakespeare.

Colley Cibber
(1671 – 1757)

Colley Cibber, English actor, Poet Laureate, and dramatist, was born in London on November 16, 1671, the son of a Danish sculptor and his second wife, an Englishwoman. He went to school at Grantham in Lincolnshire between 1682 and 1687, and in 1688, having failed to win entry to Winchester College, joined a company of volunteers raised by the Earl of Devonshire to aid William of Orange. Then, after vainly petitioning the earl for patronage, he returned to London, where he became interested in the theatre. In 1690 he was engaged as an actor in Thomas Betterton's company at the Drury Lane. Although Cibber gradually gained a reputation as a character actor and comedian, he was extremely hard pressed for money. In 1693 or 1694 he married, but he soon found that he could not support a rapidly growing family on an actor's salary. So, in 1696, to supplement his income he wrote a comedy, *Love's Last Shift*, which established him as a dramatist.

Cibber now began writing in earnest, although he continued to act, mainly at Drury Lane. He produced at this time a long series of plays, several of which proved very popular, most notably *She Wou'd and She Wou'd Not* (1702) and *The Careless Husband* (1704).

In 1706 he joined the company of actors at the Haymarket Theatre, but he soon returned to the Drury Lane as a shareholder. In 1711, along with Robert Wilks and Thomas Doggett, he became a member of the managerial triumvirate at that playhouse. A lively and informative autobiographical record of these activities appears in his well-known *An Apology for the Life of Mr. Colley Cibber* (1740), the first work of its kind in English theatrical history.

Cibber was an ardent Whig, and the Whigs repaid his support handsomely. He won notoriety with *The Non-Juror* (1717), a political play attacking Jacobites and supporting the Hanoverians, and possibly because of this was made Poet Laureate in 1730. But these political interests involved him in many controversies as well, particularly one with Alexander Pope. Pope's opposition and contempt for Cibber were expressed in the 1741 revision of *The Dunciad*, in which he pilloried Cibber as the prime Prince of Dullness.

In 1733 Cibber announced his retirement from the stage, although he continued to make occasional appearances until his last in 1754. Two of his children, Theophilus and Charlotte, were, concurrently with their father, personages of some notoriety on the theatrical scene, Theophilus as a scandalous actor and manager of the Haymarket Theatre, and Charlotte as a quarrelsome and disreputable actress and writer. Theophilus was the husband of the accomplished tragic actress Susannah Maria Cibber, and Charlotte married Richard Charke, a violinist from whom she was soon separated. Their father died in London, on December 11, 1757, of heart disease, and is buried in the British and Foreign Sailors' Church in London.

WORK

The Restoration comedy of manners had hardly reached its zenith point of brilliance in the last quarter of the seventeenth century when pressures from the burgeoning middle class forced its decline and introduced as its successor the sentimental comedy. By the time Cibber wrote his first play, there were signs of this new mood in the theatre. Adroitly Cibber grasped the mood of the time, and his first play, *Love's Last Shift* (1696), having the general frame and characters of the earlier comedy of manners, concludes, somewhat artificially, with the licentious hero promising to reform his ways. *See* COMEDY OF MANNERS.

Cibber's succeeding comedies lacked the luster of *Love's Last Shift*, and it was not until he wrote *The Careless Husband* in 1704 that he achieved real fame as a dramatist. He followed this success with *The Lady's Last*

Illustration from a 1777 edition of *The Careless Husband*, with Frances Abington in the role of Lady Betty Modish. [New York Public Library Picture Collection]

Stake in 1707, but most of his work, although eminently theatrical, is of little importance except as a barometer of what was happening in the playhouses of the time. If his comedies are mediocre, his tragedies are bad. Nevertheless, his adaptation (1699) of Shakespeare's *Richard III* is noteworthy because it remained the chief acting text of the play well into the nineteenth century. His other use of Shakespeare, in *Papal Tyranny in the Reign of King John* (1745), was purely political, building on the much earlier style of *The Non-Juror* (1717), taken from Molière's *Tartuffe* in which Cibber mixed political ideas with sentimental humor. *See* MOLIÈRE; SHAKESPEARE, WILLIAM.

Although far from great, Cibber's plays are interesting, and several, such as *The Lady's Last Stake* and *The Refusal* (1721), remained long on the popular stage. Most of the plays exploit the licentious "intrigue" material typical of the earlier comedy of manners and combine it with a flavor of the sentimental, the final reformation, as it were, palliating all sins.

Love's Last Shift; or, The Fool in Fashion (1696). Comedy in which Amanda, who was abandoned six months after her marriage to Loveless, learns from Young Worthy that her husband has returned after eight years of wandering and believes her to be dead. Promising Amanda to help her win back Loveless, Young Worthy proceeds with his other undertakings: courting Hillaria for his brother, the Elder Worthy, and seeking the hand of Narcissa, Hillaria's cousin, for himself. He tricks Loveless into an affair with Amanda; Loveless discovers her identity and vows to reform. Then he dupes Narcissa's father, Sir William Wisewoud, who wants his daughter to marry the Elder Worthy, into signing a marriage contract with him, and the Elder Worthy finally wins the hand of Hillaria.

The Careless Husband (1704). Comedy in which an inconstant husband finally reforms. Sir Charles Easy, having won a beautiful wife, finds she no longer interests him. He betrays her with her maid Mrs. Edging, but at the same time he is plagued by his mistress Lady Graveairs, in whom he has also lost interest. His feminine counterpart is Lady Betty Modish. Assured that she has won the heart of Lord Morelove, Lady Betty scorns and torments him by playing the coquette with Lord Foppington. Lady Easy, aware of her husband's betrayals, has kept silent, forbearing to reproach him. When Sir Charles learns that his wife knows of his dalliance, he suddenly awakens to her remarkable virtues and promises to reform. Then, together they convince Lady Betty that she may lose Morelove, whereupon she immediately repents and agrees to marry him.

PLAYS

All were first performed in London.

1. *Love's Last Shift; or, The Fool in Fashion*. Comedy. Published 1696. Produced Drury Lane Theatre, January, 1696.

2. *Woman's Wit; or, The Lady in Fashion*. Comedy. Published 1697. Produced Drury Lane Theatre, ca. December, 1696.

3. *Xerxes*. Tragedy. Published 1699. Produced Drury Lane Theatre, ca. February, 1699.

4. *The Tragical History of King Richard III*. Tragedy. Published 1700. Produced Drury Lane Theatre, ca. December, 1699. Adapted from William Shakespeare's *Richard III*.

5. *Love Makes a Man; or, The Fop's Fortune*. Comedy. Published 1701. Produced Drury Lane Theatre, Dec. 13, 1700.

6. *She Wou'd and She Wou'd Not; or, The Kind Impostor*. Comedy. Published 1703. Produced Drury Lane Theatre, Nov. 26, 1702.

7. *The School Boy; or, The Comical Rivals*. Farce. Published 1707. Produced Drury Lane Theatre, 1702.

8. *The Careless Husband*. Comedy. Published 1705. Produced Drury Lane Theatre, Dec. 7, 1704.

9. *Perolla and Izadora*. Tragedy. Published 1706. Produced Drury Lane Theatre, Dec. 3, 1705.

10. *The Comical Lovers*. Comedy. Published 1707. Produced Haymarket Theatre, Feb. 4, 1707. First acted as *Marriage à la Mode; or, The Comical Lovers*. Made up of scenes from two of John Dryden's plays.

11. *The Double Gallant; or, The Sick Lady's Cure*. Comedy. Published 1707. Produced Haymarket Theatre, Nov. 1, 1707.

12. *The Lady's Last Stake, or The Wife's Resentment.* Comedy. Published 1708. Produced Haymarket Theatre, Dec. 13, 1707.

13. *The Rival Fools.* Comedy. Published 1709. Produced Drury Lane Theatre, Jan. 11, 1709.

14. *The Rival Queens, with The Humours of Alexander the Great.* Burlesque. Published 1729. Produced Haymarket Theatre, June, 1710.

15. *Hob, or The Country Wake.* Farce. Published 1715. Produced Drury Lane Theatre, Oct. 6, 1711. Based on a play by Thomas Doggett. Attribution is doubtful.

16. *Ximena; or, The Heroick Daughter.* Tragedy. Published 1719. Produced Drury Lane Theatre, Nov. 28, 1712.

17. *Venus and Adonis.* Masque. Published 1715. Produced Drury Lane Theatre, Mar. 12, 1715.

18. *Myrtillo.* Masque. Published 1715. Produced Drury Lane Theatre, Nov. 5, 1715.

19. *The Non-Juror.* Comedy. Published 1718. Produced Drury Lane Theatre, Dec. 6, 1717. Based on Molière's *Tartuffe.*

20. *The Refusal; or, The Ladies' Philosophy.* Comedy. Published 1721. Produced Drury Lane Theatre, Feb. 14, 1721.

21. *Caesar in Aegypt.* Tragedy. Published 1725. Produced Drury Lane Theatre, Dec. 9, 1724.

22. (With John Vanbrugh) *The Provok'd Husband; or, A Journey to London.* Comedy. Published 1728. Produced Drury Lane Theatre, Jan. 10, 1728. Cibber completed Vanbrugh's play.

23. *Love in a Riddle.* Ballad opera. Published 1729. Produced Drury Lane Theatre, Jan. 7, 1729.

24. *Damon and Phillida.* Ballad opera. Published 1729. Produced Haymarket Theatre, Aug. 16, 1729.

25. *Papal Tyranny in the Reign of King John.* Tragedy. Published 1745. Produced Covent Garden Theatre, Feb. 15, 1745.

26. *The Lady's Lecture.* Theatrical dialogue between Sir Charles Easy and his marriageable daughter. Published 1748.

EDITIONS

Collections.
Dramatic Works, ed. by D. E. Baker, 5 vols., London, 1777.

Individual Plays.
The Careless Husband. Published in *British Plays from the Restoration to 1820,* ed. by M. J. Moses, vol. 1, Boston, 1929; *British Dramatists from Dryden to Sheridan,* ed. by G. H. Nettleton and A. E. Case, Boston, 1939.

Hob, or The Country Wake. Published in *Ten English Farces,* ed. by L. Hughes and A. H. Scouten, Austin, Tex., 1948.

Love's Last Shift; or, The Fool in Fashion. Published in *Representative English Dramas from Dryden to Sheridan,* ed. by F. Tupper and J. W. Tupper, new and enl. ed., New York, 1934; *Plays of the Restoration and Eighteenth Century,* ed. by D. MacMillan and H. M. Jones, New York, 1938.

The Provok'd Husband; or, A Journey to London. Published in *The Drama: Its History, Literature and Influence on Civilization,* ed. by A. Bates, London, 1903–1904; *Restoration Dramatists,* ed. by F. J. Tickner, London, 1930.

CRITICISM

D. C. Croissant, *Studies in the Work of Colley Cibber,* Lawrence, Kans., 1912; D. M. E. Habbema, *Appreciation of Colley Cibber,* Amsterdam, 1928; R. H. Barker, *Mr. Cibber of Drury Lane,* New York, 1939; L. R. N. Ashley, *Colley Cibber,* New York, 1964.

CID QUARREL. The popular success of the production of Corneille's *Le Cid* (December, 1636/January, 1637) drew immediate fire from the "classicists," who perceived in this work of genius, despite its formal adherence to classical restraints, the individualism and freedom of spirit that could disrupt the movement toward harmony and order in drama which they believed necessary. The first step was a violent attack by Georges de Scudéry (*Observations sur le Cid,* 1637), which provoked Corneille's emotional response, *Lettre apologétique* (1637). In the proliferation of charges and countercharges, Jean Mairet, champion of the "classical" position, joined in the attack, while Jean de Rotrou, next to Corneille the most illustrious dramatist of the time, sided with the latter. The dispute was sent to the newly formed Académie Française, where, under the jealous anti-Corneillian eye of Cardinal Richelieu, Jean Chapelain formulated *Les sentiments de l'Académie Françoise sur la tragi-comédie du Cid* (1637), which, despite Chapelain's efforts to cloak Richelieu's bias in a mantle of fairness, repudiated the play and tacitly enforced this official position with the authority of Richelieu. This defeat forced Corneille, who was not out of sympathy with the classical movement, to focus his broad talents in a circumscribed area. *See* CORNEILLE, PIERRE; MAIRET, JEAN; ROTROU, JEAN DE.

Although *Le Cid* continues to be the most popular of Corneille's plays, the result of the controversy was the imposition of an authoritarian, classical orthodoxy, not only upon the great Corneille but upon the timid and fledgling dramatists of his time. Even after Richelieu's death (1642) the Cardinal's dead hand, the Académie Française, maintained a tight grip on the drama in general and on tragedy in particular.

CINI, Giovanni Battista (d. 1586). Italian poet and dramatist whose lively verse comedy *The Widow* (*La vedova*) was first performed in Florence in 1569. Cini was also a composer of intermezzi.

CINTHIO, Giambattista Giraldi. *See* GIRALDI CINTHIO, GIAMBATTISTA.

Paul Claudel
(1868 – 1955)

Paul-Louis-Charles-Marie Claudel, French diplomat, poet, essayist, and dramatist, was born August 6, 1868, at Villeneuve-sur-Fère, a small village in the Champagne country. His family was well known in the town; his great-uncle, curé of the village. In 1869, after the death of the curé, the family moved to Bar-le-Duc, in the Vosges, and there Claudel went to school until 1876. In 1881 the family moved again, this time to Paris, where Claudel attended the Lycée Louis-le-Grand until 1885.

Claudel, who abhorred the philosophy of Renan and Kant, reached a turning point in his life in 1886, when he read the symbolist poet Rimbaud's *Illuminations* and *A Season in Hell* (see SYMBOLISM). He relates in *My Conversion* (*Ma conversion*, 1909) how on Christmas Day, during the singing of the Magnificat at a mass in Notre Dame, he was suddenly and mystically converted to Catholicism, a conversion that was not made formal until 1890. For the first time Claudel began to read the Bible, and he plunged into Pascal, Bossuet, Dante, Aristotle, Thomas a Kempis, and Dostoyevsky, making the discovery that poetry and religion were inextricably linked.

In 1890, exactly four years from the date of his revelation, Claudel received Communion in the Catholic Church, and that same year he entered the diplomatic service. He had already begun to have his writings published, and in 1892 he wrote the first version of *The Maid Violaine* (*La jeune fille Violaine*), which after a second version was to be finally revised and produced in 1912 as *The Tidings Brought to Mary* (*L'annonce faite à Marie*). His first diplomatic post was that of Acting Consul in New York (1893), and in 1894 he

Paul Claudel. [Theatre Collection, The New York Public Library at Lincoln Center, Astor, Lenox and Tilden Foundations]

went to Boston to become director of the consulate there. From this date until his retirement from the diplomatic service at the age of sixty-five, Claudel wrote constantly, publishing poetry, prose poems, essays, and plays.

In 1895 he was sent to China, where he remained, moving between Foochow and Shanghai, until 1900. He also visited Japan. After returning to France by way of Syria and Palestine, he spent a month in a Benedictine monastery in Ligugé. Claudel's Catholicism was always mystical and passionate, and the influence of church literature, especially that of Thomas Aquinas, is reflected in everything he wrote.

He returned to China in 1901 and remained there until 1909. During this period Claudel is thought to have met and fallen in love with a married woman, who served as the inspiration for Ysé in *Break of Noon* (*Partage de midi;* wr. 1905, prod. 1948) and Prouhèze in *The Satin Slipper* (*Le soulier de satin;* wr. 1919–1924, prod. 1943). In 1905 he temporarily returned to France and married Reine Perrin. On the completion of his tour of duty in China, he was sent to Prague, then to Frankfurt, and finally to Hamburg, from which he was expelled by the Germans when World War I broke out. In 1915 he undertook an economic mission to Rome, and in 1917 he became Ambassador to Argentina, where his secretary was Darius Milhaud, the composer. He was next posted to Copenhagen, in 1921, to Tokyo, in 1922, and to Washington, where he remained from 1926 until 1933. During his stay in the United States, Claudel received many honorary degrees from American universities, among them Yale, Princeton, Columbia, and Chicago. In Washington he was instrumental in the drawing up and signing of the Kellogg-Briand Pact (1928), and he conferred with President Franklin D. Roosevelt on the problem of French war debts. His last ambassadorial post was Brussels (1933–1935), after which ill health forced his retirement from the diplomatic service.

Claudel's diplomatic career was a distinct factor in the development of his writing. Although he found time to produce an enormous body of work, he was also able to develop other interests, among them English literature, Dutch and Italian painting, Chinese drama, and Japanese poetry. To these must be added familiarity with the Greek and Latin classics and with Japanese ideograms. Claudel's interest in modern music stemmed from his association with Milhaud, who supplied music for *Proteus* (*Protée*, wr. 1913) and *The Book of Christopher Columbus* (*Le livre de Christophe Colomb*, 1930).

In 1939 he was sent to Rome as a special ambassador to the coronation of Pope Pius

Tête d'Or. [French
Cultural Services]

XII. During the German occupation of France, actor Jean-Louis Barrault received Claudel's permission to present a revised stage version of the playwright's masterwork, *The Satin Slipper.* Claudel was so pleased with the results that he eventually granted Barrault permission to produce other works, including *Break of Noon,* which because of its intense personal significance he had long withheld from the stage.

Claudel was elected to the Académie Française in 1947, after having been rejected in 1935. His sponsor was François Mauriac, the eminent Catholic writer. The publication in 1949 of the correspondence (1900–1926) between Claudel and André Gide, in which Claudel outlined his Christian beliefs and attempted to convert Gide, provides one of the most interesting documents in twentieth-century French literature.

From 1935 on Claudel's writing was confined almost entirely to essays, Biblical commentary, and translations of Chinese poetry and of Francis Thompson, Chesterton, Poe, and Thomas Lovell Beddoes. Claudel died on February 23, 1955, at the age of eighty-six.

WORK

One of the foremost French dramatists of the twentieth century, Claudel in his poetic dramas broke not only with naturalism but with the formal verse tradition represented in his time by Edmond Rostand. He created a

Murder scene in *Tête d'Or,* with Alain Cuny and Jean-Louis Barrault as the King, Théâtre de l'Odéon, Paris. [French Cultural Services]

structurally loose dramatic form that is largely dependent for its power on the musical and symbolic features of language. Given the mystical nature of his Catholic themes, Claudel felt they could not be directly communicated to the understanding, and he therefore used the resources of the symbolist poet to assault the heart and win its consent. All else—dramatic structure, individual characterization, and historical accuracy— was generally sacrificed to this goal. Like his ideological antithesis, Bertolt Brecht, Claudel favored an epic approach to theatre, the creation of characters larger than life, a bold didacticism, alienation effects, and the establishment of conflicts that transcended the individual. *See* BRECHT, BERTOLT; ROSTAND, EDMOND.

From *Tête d'Or* (wr. 1889, second version prod. 1919) to *The Satin Slipper* (wr. 1924, prod. 1943), Claudel's plays may be seen as stages in a search for Christian salvation that was initiated with his mystical conversion to Catholicism in 1886. Catholic doctrine informs all his works, and they show the intensity of his struggle to make an overwhelmingly strong ego submit to what he conceived of as the will of Divine Providence.

Tête d'Or was written at the height of Claudel's fascination with Rimbaud, and the playwright called it "the drama of the possession of the earth." In it a semibarbarous young conqueror, drawing his strength from the void created by the death of a loved one, attempts to dominate the world. But as in *The City* (*La ville;* wr. 1890, second version prod. 1926) and *The Exchange* (*L'échange;* wr. 1893–1894, prod. 1914), we are given a demonstration of the futility of human endeavor that is not touched by grace. In one of Claudel's most popular plays, *The Tidings Brought to Mary* (wr. 1892, prod. 1912) the conflict is between the demands of human love and aspirations toward God. The theme of salvation through renunciation is repeated throughout Claudel's work. *Tidings* was based on an earlier and twice-revised play entitled *The Maid Violaine* (wr. 1892, second version prod. 1944) and was itself revised into a "definitive stage version." Each version further emphasized Claudel's conception of the play as "an opera with purely verbal music" and changed the personal drama of Violaine into something closely resembling a medieval miracle play. *See* MIRACLE PLAY.

The play in which Claudel sacrificed verbal music to formal plot structure to the greatest degree is *The Hostage* (*L'otage;* wr. 1909, prod. 1914). Originally staged by Aurélien-François Lugné-Poë, it is the first part of a trilogy which includes *Crusts* (*Le pain dur;* wr. 1914, prod. 1949) and *The Humiliation of the Father* (*Le père humilié;* wr. 1916, prod. 1928). In this trilogy Claudel presents his version of how France's traditional Catholic aristocracy was supplanted by the forces liberated by the French Revolution. Lugné-Poë is said to have first requested permission to stage *Crusts* in 1914, but despite his high moral fervor Claudel was concerned about the repercussions on his diplomatic career of the anti-Semitic portraits contained in that play.

Though written some twenty years apart and different in form and superficial subject matter, *Break of Noon* (wr. 1905, prod. 1948) and *The Satin Slipper* are connected by an essential theme, the role of human love in the workings of Divine Providence. The female protagonists of both these intensely lyrical dramas are said to have been inspired by Claudel's unhappy love affair with a married woman. In both plays love is shown to be the instrument of man's salvation, but since Claudel's God is essentially the jealous deity of the Old Testament, it is through the anguish of love that man is drawn to Him, and we are made to see that "even sin" plays a part in the "economy of grace." *The Satin Slipper* is often considered Claudel's most distinguished play, and it is certainly his most ambitious. A summary of all his poetic and dramatic works, it is also a résumé of his views on Catholic theology. "The scene of this drama is the world," we are told; more especially, it is the world of late-sixteenth-century Catholic Spain. Driven by the unattainability of Doña Prouhèze, Rodrigue, a Spanish conquistador, makes it possible for Christ's message to be brought to the New World when he wins that world for the King of Spain. Requiring nine hours of performance time in its original version, *The Satin Slipper* is by turn wildly burlesque, deeply moving, and verbosely didactic. It nevertheless contains some of the greatest lyric passages written in this century. "Listen carefully," a narrator warns. "It is what you fail to understand that is the best . . . it is what you will not find amusing that is the funniest." Firm in his faith, Claudel has no hesitation in explaining the ways of God to man.

But despite the inner serenity that Claudel had achieved, he still retained a restlessness which he compared in 1927 to that of an explorer searching for a new world. It is not surprising, therefore, that one of his last major works was *The Book of Christopher Columbus* (1930). Carelessly distorting history, Claudel presents not so much a portrait of the explorer, some critics feel, as a psychological portrait of his own life, his inner struggles, and his final submission to divine will. To discover the New World, Columbus uses all means at his disposal, justifying his behavior with a cry that contains a weird echo of the Marxist adage of the end justifying the means: "I promised to pull the world out of darkness; I did not promise to take away suffering."

Many of Claudel's plays have been revised several times (consult the play list), and in his struggle to find new poetic forms he created his own verse form, *le verset claudélien,* which is inspired essentially by Biblical prose and is regulated by the natural demands of respiration.

Claudel brought to his work a profound knowledge of Oriental poetry and drama as well as of Greek tragedy. He translated Aeschylus's *Agamemnon, The Eumenides,* and *The Libation Bearers;* his *The Woman and Her Shadow* (*La femme et son ombre;* wr. 1922, revised version prod. 1923) makes excellent use of elements of Japanese Nō drama (*see* AESCHYLUS; NŌ). In addition, his work has inspired some of the finest musicians of our time: Arthur Honegger wrote the score for his dramatic oratorio *Joan of Arc at the Stake* (*Jeanne d'Arc au bûcher;* wr. 1933–1935, prod. 1939), and Darius Milhaud used *The Book of*

Christopher Columbus as the libretto for an opera in 1930 and provided completely new incidental music for Jean-Louis Barrault's 1953 stage production. To Barrault goes the credit for having brought Claudel's dramatic work to an increasingly wider audience by his remarkable productions of *Break of Noon, The Satin Slipper, Columbus,* and *Tête d'Or.* Difficult to perform and, at times, to understand, Claudel's plays possess a lyrical quality and a depth and breadth that make them a towering achievement in modern drama.

The Slumberer (*L'endormie,* wr. 1883). One-act lyrical play set in a forest inhabited by dancing and cavorting nymphs and four-legged creatures. This lively fable tells the story of a fickle poet upon whom an old faun and a young goat play a joke. The theme and the characters in this play reappear in somewhat altered form in Claudel's *The Moon in Search of Herself* (*La lune à la recherche d'elle-même,* 1947), an "extravaganza for radio."

Tête d'Or (wr. 1889, second version prod. 1919). Three-part lyrical drama taking as its theme the vanity of all earthly aspiration and power unrelated to spiritual ends. Part I opens in a timeless, nameless universe as Simon Agnel returns home from his wander-

L'annonce faite à Marie, Saint-Étienne, 1954. [Comédie de Saint-Étienne]

Two scenes from
L'échange.
[Courtesy of
Centre
Dramatique
National Nord]

ings with the body of his wife. As he is burying her in a field, he meets Cébès, a childhood friend, who asks for his protection. As a sign of eternal fidelity Simon spills his blood over Cébès, who reciprocates the oath. In Part II Simon, now a powerful conqueror known as Tête d'Or (Golden Head), begins a new life when the gentle Cébès mysteriously dies, symbolically carrying away with him the conqueror's nobler nature. Electing to gain undisputed mastery over men and things, Tête d'Or slays the monarch whose kingdom he has been protecting and drives the King's daughter into exile. In Part III Tête d'Or, having conquered Europe, is on the doorstep of Asia. Wounded in combat, he asks to be left to die on a high pass. There he finds the exiled Princess crucified upon a tree. Tête d'Or, pulls out the binding nails with his teeth, while the Princess proclaims her love for him as they both expire.

The City (*La ville;* wr. 1890, second version prod. 1926). Three-act drama set in modern, industrial times. Isidore de Besme, disillusioned master builder of a city fallen into corruption, is about to turn it over to his politically oriented brother Lambert, the opponent of Avare, a nihilist. The aging Lambert will accept control only if his adopted daughter Lâla will agree to marry him. She is about to accept when she encounters Coeuvre, a poet. Overwhelmed by Coeuvre's youth and vision, she falls in love with him and becomes his bride. In the second act, Lâla, finding Coeuvre unable to share his vision with just one person, leaves him after bearing his son Ivors. Seeking to rejoin Lambert, she discovers him digging his own grave. Eventually, Besme, Avare, and Coeuvre join them at the grave site, and the men exchange opposing views of life and the city. Leaving Lambert to his death and Besme to his disillusionment, Lâla goes off with Avare, and together they bring about the destruction of the corrupt city. In the third act, Besme, faced with imminent execution, discovers the divine mystery of life. Coeuvre returns and announces that he has found his answer in religion. Avare, his mission of destruction over, cedes the rebuilding of the city to Ivors, and Lâla remains to help.

The Tidings Brought to Mary (*L'annonce faite à Marie;* wr. 1892, revised version prod. 1912). Parable in four acts and a prologue, set in medieval France. Anne Vercors, having fulfilled his earthly duties, betroths his favorite daughter, Violaine, to Jacques Hury, leaves his farm and family in Jacques's keeping, and departs for the Holy Land. At about the same time, Pierre de Craon, a cathedral builder afflicted with leprosy, departs on a mission of his own, the building of God's

churches. Violaine, in the fullness of her own joy and in pity for Pierre, who once tried to rape her, gives him a compassionate kiss of farewell. The kiss is seen by her jealous sister Mara and misrepresented to Jacques, so that when on their wedding eve Violaine shows symptoms of leprosy, Jacques believes Mara's slander, sends Violaine away, and marries Mara. Stories of Violaine's saintliness begin to circulate, and when Mara's infant, Aubaine, dies on Christmas Eve, she goes to Violaine, now blinded by leprosy and living in a cave, to plead for a miracle. Violaine declares her helplessness, but Mara insists on her sister's saintliness. Then, as Mara reads the Christmas service while Violaine clutches the dead child to her bosom, life stirs in Aubaine, whose eyes open to reveal that they are no longer brown but blue, like Violaine's. Mara does not disclose the miracle to Jacques but claims for herself the credit for the child's revival. Soon afterward, Anne returns from his pilgrimage to find that Violaine, having been led into a sandpit through Mara's treachery, is close to death. Violaine spends her last moments at home, where Jacques, now convinced of the innocence of the kiss she gave Pierre, a kiss that has miraculously cured his leprosy, begs her forgiveness. Itself based on the earlier *The Maid Violaine, Tidings* was revised by Claudel in 1948.

Rest on the Seventh Day (*Le repos du septième jour;* wr. 1896, prod. 1928). A wise Chinese Emperor makes a journey through the underworld, where he encounters his mother, a disembodied soul caught in a timeless night. He then meets the Devil, who describes hell and explains evil as a product of man's poor stewardship of the earth and his failure to adhere to the divine image. The Angel of the Lord suggests that man must rest on the seventh day and revere God. The Emperor returns to earth a leper, his imperial scepter transformed into a cross. He turns over earthly rule to his son, whom he exhorts to believe that man's salvation lies in faith, suffering, and sacrifice.

Break of Noon (*Partage de midi;* wr. 1905, prod. 1948). Lyrical verse drama of sin and redemption through love. On a ship headed for the Orient are Ysé, a passionate, spiritually demanding woman; De Ciz, her shallowly pragmatic husband; Almaric, her former lover, a sanguine, realistic man; and Mesa, a tormented would-be priest, who claims to have "given up the world." Ysé and Mesa are immediately drawn to one another but struggle against this attraction, she because she feels that he belongs to God and he because she is married to De Ciz. As they pass the ocean's midpoint, the ship's bell sounds noon.

In the second act the protagonists are in Hong Kong. Ysé indirectly appeals to De Ciz to defend her against her attraction to Mesa, but her husband fails to understand. In combined exhilaration and despair she replies to Mesa's passion.

In the third act we are in a Chinese city besieged by rebels intent on murdering its white inhabitants. Ysé is now living with Almaric, but we learn that she and Mesa previously lived together adulterously for a year. Ysé abandoned Mesa in despair of ever possessing that portion of his being which she feels is reserved for God. To avoid torture by the rebels, Almaric and Ysé have decided to commit suicide by setting a time bomb. Mesa appears to reclaim Ysé, having understood her sufferings through his own. He is stunned into unconsciousness by Almaric, who steals his pass through the rebel lines and escapes with Ysé, leaving Mesa to die when the bomb explodes. However, Ysé soon returns to die with Mesa. Accepting the fact that their love can be realized only in death, Mesa and Ysé blissfully await the detonation that will bring the eternal reunion for which they hope by God's mercy.

The Hostage (*L'otage;* wr. 1909, prod. 1914). First play in a trilogy that traces the fate of the Coûfontaine family under the Napoleonic Empire. Synge de Coûfontaine and her cousin Georges personify the dispossessed aristocracy, whose successors are represented by the police prefect Toussaint Turelure, son of a former peasant on the Coûfontaine estate. Georges has freed Pope Pius VII from his Napoleonic captors in the hope of enlisting his help against the revolution, but the Pope refuses to become involved in politics. Meanwhile, Turelure learns of the Pope's whereabouts; intent on merging his authority with that of the old order, Turelure proposes marriage to Synge, promising a safe-conduct for the Pope in return for her consent. Though she finds Turelure repulsive and has sworn fidelity to Georges, Synge consents on the advice of a priest, who convinces her that her duty lies in securing the Pope's safety. After her marriage a son, Louis-Agénor Napoléon Turelure, is born, and his future is guaranteed when Turelure betrays the revolution

and surrenders the city of Paris to King Louis XVIII. Realizing that Turelure intends to retain the real power, Georges tries to assassinate him; but Synge intercepts the bullet meant for Turelure, who kills Georges. Synge dies without confession in order to avoid having to pardon Turelure, who is made a count by the new King. In a variant ending Claudel implies Synge's forgiveness.

Proteus (*Protée;* wr. 1913, revised version prod. 1955). Lyric farce, based on Claudel's poem of the same name and eventually presented with music by Darius Milhaud. On the island of Naxos, the nymph Brindosier and her troop of satyrs are prisoners of the sea-god Proteus, who has now become a supplier for the fashion industry. When, after the fall of Troy, Helen and Menelaus stop at Naxos, Brindosier disguises herself as Helen, with the latter's connivance, and she and her satyrs depart for Greece with Menelaus, leaving the real Helen to be Proteus's bride. But Proteus is only a "sixth-rate god," and his Olympian superiors reclaim Helen and make a star of her.

Crusts (*Le pain dur;* wr. 1914, prod. 1949). The second play of the Coûfontaine-Turelure trilogy, in which Synge's sacrifice is avenged, is written against the background of the Industrial Revolution and the rise of colonial empires during the nineteenth century. The aim of Lumir, a fanatical Polish idealist and the fiancée of Turelure's son Louis, is to regain the money which she lent Louis to finance his Algerian colonial schemes but which really belongs to the Polish nationalists. Opposing her is Sichel, Turelure's Jewish mistress, who schemes to inherit Turelure's fortune. Sichel's usurer father, Ali Habenichts, meanwhile is buying up the Coûfontaine domains from Turelure. In the course of events Turelure dies as the result of a fight with his son, leaving his money to Sichel. Lumir is repaid, but feeling herself an alien in Louis's materialistic milieu, she abandons him and plans to return to Poland and the service of her people. Louis offers to marry Sichel, both because he wants to regain his lost possessions and because he realizes that her ruthlessness complements his own. In a final scene, he sells to Habenichts a bronze crucifix that had belonged to the Coûfontaines and had been painfully reconstructed by Synge after it was smashed to pieces during the French Revolution.

Christmas Night, 1914 (*La nuit de Noël de 1914,* wr. 1915). One-act lyrical drama which opens in a small village near Reims that has been burned by the Germans and continues in a supernatural realm. The meaning of their violent death is revealed to two young soldiers as they enter that realm:

God has taken them, in the manner of the children massacred by Herod, to spare them a life of suffering on earth. The play ends with an outburst of French messianism.

The Humiliation of the Father (*Le père humilié;* wr. 1916, prod. 1928). The final play of the Coûfontaine-Turelure trilogy is set in Rome during the turbulent years 1869–1871. Pensée, the blind and beautiful daughter of Louis Turelure (now the Comte de Coûfontaine, Ambassador of France in Rome) and of his Jewish wife Sichel, loves Orian (who stands for light), a nephew of Pope Pius IX. Although Orian is attracted to the religious life, he is irresistibly drawn to darkness in Pensée. Isolated by the majesty of his office and seeing his temporal power ebbing under the assaults of Italian nationalism, the Pope counts on Orian to take to a hostile world his message of God's joy. But Orian feels that the debt the papacy owes the Coûfontaine family for Synge's sacrifice should be paid; he therefore offers himself to Pensée. Pensée is left with child as Orian departs with his brother Orso to serve with the French in the Franco-Prussian War. Before he is killed, Orian requests Orso, who also loves Pensée, to marry her so that the child may have an honorable name. The souls of Orian and Pensée, the light and the darkness, can be united only in eternity.

The Bear and the Moon (*L'ours et la lune,* wr. 1917). A lyrical farce set in the infirmary of a German prison camp during World War I. A French prisoner dreams of his dead wife Maria, his dead son, and his grandchildren, who have been left as orphans in the care of strangers. Moonlight envelops the prisoner, and he enters a world of marionettes. Here he is able to see his children. In their room is a fur bear sleeping in bed between two dolls. As the bear relates that he was a banker who went wrong, an aviator with amputated legs (probably the son of the prisoner) appears. His girl friend Rhodo, a charming young girl who works in a munitions plant, is seen with her father, Le Rhabilleur (The Fixer). The banker-bear does all in his power to seduce Rhodo, but it soon becomes time for the dream to end. All the marionettes are chased away by the announcement of the arrival of Bourguignon (Sun). Dawn then enters, lifting the veils of muslin the moon has wrapped around the prisoner, who awakens whispering the words "Day is dawning."

Man and His Desire (*L'homme et son désir,* wr. 1917). Extremely short scenario of a ballet in which the theme is the passage of time, expressed by a slow-moving line of hours. As the moon and its reflection in the water move across the stage, a sleeping man appears. With him is the ghost of a dead woman. The ghost and its double pull and push the man forward, turning him around until they envelop him in their veils. The moon and its reflection disappear, and the black hours of night become the early white hours of dawn. Movement and rhythm alone comprise the action, and no costumes are used.

The Woman and Her Shadow (*La femme et son ombre;* wr. 1922, revised version prod. 1923). Scenario for a mimed drama with a Japanese setting. The ancient warrior and his suite arrive at the "border between two worlds." Behind a screen burns a memorial lantern to his lost love. Suddenly, the warrior sees the shadow of a woman. As he pursues the shadow, a woman arrives in a palanquin and attempts to persuade the warrior that the shadow is a figment of his imagination. Each movement of the woman is duplicated by the shadow. The warrior pulls out his sword, and in a swift blow cuts the line that seems to join the woman and the shadow. The woman falls, but the shadow moves away, the warrior following. He succeeds in striking the shadow with his sword, and when he pulls out the blade, it is covered with blood. The woman screams and dies. The warrior and his suite withdraw in horror.

The Satin Slipper (*Le soulier de satin, ou Le pire n'est pas toujours sûr;* wr. 1924, prod. 1943). Mystical drama in which two lovers, Don Rodrigue and Doña Prouhèze, are brought to salvation through acts of sacrifice and the denial of their worldly love. The play compresses epochs, events, and geographical areas into four "days" (*journées*); the sphere of action is the world, but primarily Catholic Spain of the late sixteenth or early seventeenth century. In the opening scene a Jesuit priest, tied to a shipwrecked mast symbolic of the Cross floating in the Atlantic, prays that his brother Rodrigue, who has strayed from his heavenly path in search of worldly glory, may, through a pure and unconsummated human love, be led back to God.

Rodrigue is in love with Prouhèze, the childless wife of an aged judge, Don Pelage. Prouhèze returns Rodrigue's love and feels that their passion is heaven-inspired. However, she offers one of her satin slippers to a statue of the Virgin, praying that if she attempts to rejoin Rodrigue, at least it will be be with a "clipped wing." Meanwhile, in his pursuit of Prouhèze Rodrigue has ignored the King's command that he become Viceroy to the New World. Don Pelage, aware of his wife's temptation and her capacity for self-sacrifice, suggests that she go to Mogador, in North Africa, to represent the King to Don Camille, the renegade who has captured the territory from the infidels. Prouhèze accepts the position, and Rodrigue eventually departs on his mission to the New World. In the ensuing decade Rodrigue founds a Spanish empire in Latin America. Prouhèze, her husband dead, voluntarily marries Camille in an attempt to bring him to salvation.

In Panama, Rodrigue receives a desperate letter written by Prouhèze ten years earlier and cast into the sea in a bottle. Unaware that she has since married Camille and borne him a daughter, Rodrigue deserts his post and sets out to find her.

In Mogador, meanwhile, Prouhèze converses in a dream with her guardian angel, who informs her that Rodrigue's unsatisfied desire for her will in the end lead him to God. When Rodrigue's fleet arrives at Mogador, Camille, now become a Moslem, believes that

Rodrigue has been sent by the King of Spain. Camille offers Rodrigue Prouhèze in return for sparing the city. However, Prouhèze demands of Rodrigue a renunciation equal to her own. Rodrigue's fleet departs, and Prouhèze returns to Camille.

In the epilogue, a humble Rodrigue, lame, mocked, and bound as a traitor, is befriended by nuns in whose convent he will serve as a scullion. Emptied of his desires, his temporal trial over, he awaits a new, eternal destiny.

Wisdom, or The Parable of the Feast (*La sagesse, ou La parabole du festin;* wr. 1935, as the second version of a 1926 work). A dramatic and musical interpretation of the parable of St. Luke (Luke 14: 16–24), set in a ruined temple. A woman is lying between two pillars. Two voices offstage talk of how God's children have turned away from Him. The

A Comédie-Française production of *Le soulier de satin.* [French Cultural Services]

Partage de midi (left), produced at the Théâtre de France by Jean-Louis Barrault, who also appeared in a leading role. [French Cultural Services]

voices ask the woman, who is the personification of God's divine wisdom, to make man remember his Father. Wisdom begins her search for man, accompanied by the Latin singing of the choir. She soon sees the fruitlessness of her efforts, for vanity's influence is too great. Only the poor and the afflicted are ready to follow her. Wisdom then prepares a great feast in her new house, set on seven pillars. The righteous poor are praised, and the *Hymn of the Apocalypse* is sung.

The Book of Christopher Columbus (*Le livre de Christophe Colomb;* wr. 1927, prod. 1930). Two-part lyrical drama. As Part I begins, a narrator reads from a book about the life and voyages of Columbus, who is then seen as a poverty-stricken old man being dunned by an innkeeper in Valladolid. Embodying the voice of posterity, the narrator summons Columbus to join him and a chorus and to watch while a second Columbus figure reenacts the events of his life. We see Columbus ruthlessly sacrificing everything to his desire to find a passage to the Indies. He is eventually given the means by Queen Isa-

Edwige Feuillère and Jean-Louis Barrault in *Partage de midi* (right). [French Cultural Services]

Le livre de Christophe Colomb. [French Cultural Services]

bella, who recognizes on his finger a ring that, on a childish impulse, she once confided to the beak of a dove. On the voyage, driven by his inner compulsion, Columbus heartlessly taunts his terrified crew, who are about to mutiny when land is sighted.

In Part II, Columbus, having failed to find the Indies, is on his third voyage. During a storm a demoniac cook taunts him with visions of the future and with probings into his conscience. Columbus is made to see that he has not found the East but a new continent that will not even bear his name, a continent to which he will have brought suffering and slavery. On his return to Spain, Columbus finds that Isabella, his friend and only supporter in the court, has died. We then return to Valladolid, where the innkeeper confiscates Columbus's mule in payment for debt. To compensate him for this loss, the first Columbus figure abandons the narrator and the chorus and joins with the second Columbus figure onstage. In a final scene, Isabella is about to make her entrance into heaven astride the old mule ceded to her by Columbus. Darius Milhaud used the play as the libretto for an opera (1930) and also wrote incidental music for a dramatic production (1953).

Under the Rampart of Athens (*Sous le rempart d'Athènes,* 1927). A short play written in celebration of the hundredth anniversary of the birth of the celebrated French chemist Marcelin Berthelot. To a fictitious Greek philosopher named Hermas are attributed the fundamental ideas of Berthelot. Two pilgrims have come from afar to visit the burial place of Hermas. Under the rampart of Athens, each witnessed by a shadow, they hold a philosophical discussion about his ideas.

Joan of Arc at the Stake (*Jeanne d'Arc au bûcher;* wr. 1935, prod. 1939). Oratorio with music by Arthur Honegger, centering on the beatification of Joan of Arc. Joan awaits her fate tied to the stake. Father Dominique, who had been present at her trial, reads from a book of Joan's deeds as her life is enacted in medieval allegory. Suddenly, Joan is alone. As the flames rise, she recognizes that hope, faith, joy, and God are stronger than the chains that bind her. Her immortal soul is freed from the prison of her body while voices proclaim: "There is no greater love than to give one's life for those one loves."

Stone Throwing (*Le jet de pierre,* wr. 1938). Plastic suite in twelve movements. The suite opens in a château, the House of the Poets, that has been closed for the winter. Aliki, having returned from a trip, has just

Scene from *L'otage*, Théâtre du Vieux-Colombier, Paris. [French Cultural Services]

opened the château. Nada arrives, and they discuss the idea of poetry. They reach the conclusion that the essence of a poem is like a stone that is thrown. The poet is working toward beauty, but he only reaches fame, for beauty is so far away that no dart lanced or stone thrown can reach this goal.

Tobias and Sara (*L'histoire de Tobie et Sara;* wr. 1938, prod. 1947). Morality play in three acts using music, cinema, mime, two choruses, and three narrators to make of the apocryphal Book of Tobit a lyrical drama by way of illustrating the truth of Matthew 18: 19–20. Although Tobit, a virtuous Jew exiled in Nineveh, is poor, blind, and harassed by a shrewish wife, he unfailingly performs his ritual obligations. His adventurous young son Tobias undertakes a journey to faraway Media to reclaim from Raguel the 10 talents entrusted to him by Tobit long ago. His guide,

Le père humilié.
[French Cultural Services]

Azarias, tells him that he is destined to marry Raguel's comely daughter Sara. To win her, Tobias must frighten away Asmodeus, an evil and jealous demon who has successively murdered Sara's seven bridegrooms on their wedding nights. Tobias is successful and returns to Nineveh a wealthy man; his wife Sara is with child. He restores his aged father's sight, while Azarias reveals himself to be the archangel Raphael. The family bursts into a hymn of praise to God, who in His love heard the cries of Sara and the prayers of Tobit.

The Rape of Scapin (*Le ravissement de Scapin,* wr. 1949). A farcical comedy based on Molière's *Les fourberies de Scapin.* As the play begins, a group of actors are drinking, joking, and quarreling. Suddenly, someone appears with a large basket filled with costumes and theatrical wigs. The actors are instantly inspired, and in a flash each is ready to act a condensation of Molière's play. The takeoff begins with Argante and Géronte having unexpectedly returned from a trip. Scapin, a valet, attempts to extort money from them, but his double dealings are discovered and he is lifted up by his feet through a trapdoor in the ceiling. *See* MOLIÈRE.

PLAYS

Unless otherwise noted, the plays were first performed in Paris.

1. *L'endormie* (*The Slumberer*). Play, 1 act. Written 1882/83. Published 1925. Early version of *La lune à la recherche d'elle-même.*

2. *Tête d'Or**. Play, 3 acts; verse. Written 1889. Published 1890. Second version: Written 1895. Published 1901. Produced Théâtre du Gymnase, Mar. 30, 1919.

3. *La ville** (*The City*). Play, 3 acts; verse. Written 1890. Published 1893. Second version: Written 1897. Published 1901. Produced Brussels (in Dutch), Salle Patria, Feb. 24, 1926; Paris, Palais de Chaillot, Dec. 2, 1955.

4. *La jeune fille Violaine* (*The Maid Violaine*). Play, 4 acts; verse. Written 1892. Published 1926. Second version: Written 1898. Published 1901. Produced Salle d'Iéna, Mar. 14, 1944. Early version of *L'annonce faite à Marie.*

5. *L'annonce faite à Marie** (*The Tidings Brought to Mary*). Parable, 4 acts and a prologue. Written 1892 (rev. 1910, 1948). Published 1912. Produced Théâtre de l'Oeuvre, Dec. 20, 1912. Based on *La jeune fille Violaine.*

6. *L'échange** (*The Exchange*). Play, 3 acts. Written 1894. Published 1901. Produced Théâtre du Vieux-Colombier, Jan. 22, 1914. Second version: Written 1951. Published 1954. Produced Théâtre Marigny, Dec. 13, 1951.

7. *L'Agamemnon d'Eschyle* (*The Agamemnon of Aeschylus*). Play. Written 1894. Published 1896 (rev. 1951).

8. *Le repos du septième jour* (*Rest on the Seventh Day*). Play, 3 acts. Written 1896. Published 1901. Produced Warsaw, Narodny Theatre, Dec. 10, 1928.

9. *Partage de midi** (*Break of Noon*). Play, 3 acts; verse. Written 1905. Published 1906. Produced Théâtre Marigny, Dec. 16, 1948.

10. *L'otage** (*The Hostage*). Play. Written 1909. Published 1911. Produced Théâtre de l'Oeuvre, June 5, 1914.

11. *Protée* (*Proteus*). Play, 2 acts. Written 1913. Published 1914. *Second version:* Written 1926. Published 1927. Produced Amsterdam, Muncipal Theatre, Apr. 4, 1933; Paris, Comédie de Paris, February, 1955.

12. *Le pain dur** (*Crusts*). Play. Written 1914. Published 1918. Produced Théâtre de l'Atelier, Mar. 12, 1949.

13. *La nuit de Noël de 1914* (*Christmas Night, 1914*). Play, 1 act. Written 1915. Published 1915.

14. *Le père humilié** (*The Humiliation of the Father*). Play. Written 1916. Published 1919. Produced Dresden, Schauspielhaus, Nov. 26, 1928; Paris, Théâtre des Champs-Élysées, May 10, 1946.

15. *Les Choéphores d'Eschyle* (*The Libation Bearers of Aeschylus*). Play. Written 1916. Published 1920. Produced Brussels, Théâtre de la Monnaie, Mar. 27, 1935.

16. *Les Euménides d'Eschyle* (*The Eumenides of Aeschylus*). Play. Written 1916. Published 1920. Produced Brussels, Théâtre de la Monnaie, Mar. 27, 1935.

17. *L'ours et la lune* (*The Bear and the Moon*). Play. Written 1917. Published 1919.

18. *L'homme et son désir* (*Man and His Desire*). Ballet scenario. Written 1917. Published 1917.

19. *La femme et son ombre* (*The Woman and Her Shadow*). Mime drama. Written 1923. Published 1956. Produced Tokyo, Imperial Theatre, March, 1923. An earlier sketch was written and published in 1922.

20. *Le soulier de satin, ou Le pire n'est pas toujours sûr** (*The Satin Slipper, or The Worst Is Not Sure*). Play. Written 1924. Published 1928–1929 (stage version 1944). Produced Comédie-Française, Nov. 27, 1943.

21. *La parabole du festin* (*The Parable of the Feast*). Parable. Written 1926. Published 1926. Second version: *La sagesse, ou La parabole du festin* (*Wisdom, or The Parable of the Feast*). Written 1935. Published 1939.

22. *Le livre de Christophe Colomb** (*The Book of Christopher Columbus*). Play, 2 acts. Written 1927. Published 1933. Produced Berlin, Staatsoper, May 5, 1930; Paris, Théâtre Marigny, Oct. 1, 1953. Music: Darius Milhaud.

23. *Sous le rempart d'Athènes* (*Under the Rampart of*

Athens). Play. Written 1927. Published 1927. Produced Palais de l'Élysée, 1927.

24. *Jeanne d'Arc au bûcher* (*Joan of Arc at the Stake*). Oratorio. Written 1935. Published 1939. Produced Orléans, Théâtre Municipal, May 6, 1939.

25. *Le jet de pierre* (*Stone Throwing*). Suite, 12 movements. Written 1938. Published 1956.

26. *L'histoire de Tobie et Sara** (*Tobias and Sara*). Play, 3 acts. Written 1938. Published 1942. Produced Avignon, Sept. 5, 1947.

27. *La lune à la recherche d'elle-même* (*The Moon in Search of Herself*). Radio extravaganza. Written 1947. Published 1956. Based on *L'endormie*.

28. *Le ravissement de Scapin* (*The Rape of Scapin*). Play. Written 1949. Published 1952.

EDITIONS

Collections.
Three Plays, tr. by J. Heard, Boston, 1945; *Théâtre*, 2 vols., Paris, 1947–1948; *Oeuvres complètes*, 13 vols., Paris, 1950–1958.

Individual Plays.
The Satin Slipper. Published in *Writers of the Western World*, ed. by C. A. Hibbard and H. Frenz and tr. by J. O'Connor, Boston, 1954.

The Tidings Brought to Mary. Published in *Modern Continental Dramas*, ed. by H. H. Hatcher and tr. by L. Sill, New York, 1941.

Tobias and Sara. Published in *Port-Royal, and Other Plays*, ed. by R. Hayes and tr. by A. Fiske, New York, 1962.

CRITICISM

French. G. Duhamel, *Paul Claudel*, Paris, 1913; J. de Tonquédoc, *L'oeuvre de Paul Claudel*, Paris, 1917; F. Lefèvre, *Les sources de Paul Claudel*, Paris, 1927; L. Chaigne, *Le chemin de Paul Claudel*, Paris, 1931; J. Madaule, *Le génie de Paul Claudel*, Paris, 1933; V. Bindel, *Claudel*, Paris, 1934; J. Madaule, *Le drame de Paul Claudel*, Paris, 1936; H. Colleye, *La poésie catholique de Claudel*, Liège, 1945; A. Moliton, *Aspects de Paul Claudel*, Paris, 1945; G. Truc, *Paul Claudel*, Paris, 1945; C. Chonez, *Introduction à Paul Claudel*, Paris, 1947; J. Samson, *Paul Claudel, poète-musicien*, Geneva, 1947; L. Barjon, *Paul Claudel*, Paris, 1953; J. Andrieu, *La foi dans l'oeuvre de Paul Claudel*, Paris, 1955; H. Guillemin, *Claudel et son art d'écrire*, Paris, 1955; J. Madaule, *Paul Claudel, dramaturge*, Paris, 1956; J. Bastien, *L'oeuvre dramatique de Paul Claudel*, Reims, 1957; H. J. W. van Hoorn, *Poésie et mysticisme: Paul Claudel, poète chrétien*, Geneva, 1957; E. Beaumont, *Le sens de l'amour dans le théâtre de Claudel: Le thème de Béatrice*, Paris, 1958; J.-C. Berton, *Shakespeare et Claudel*, Geneva, 1958; S. Fumet, *Claudel*, Paris, 1958; R. Farabet, *Le jeu de l'acteur dans le théâtre de Claudel*, Paris, 1960; H. Mondor, *Claudel plus intime*, Paris, 1960; L. Chaigne, *Vie de Paul Claudel et genèse de son oeuvre*, Tours, 1961.

English. M. Ryan, *Introduction to Paul Claudel*, Cork, 1951; E. Beaumont, *The Theme of Beatrice in the Plays of Claudel*, London, 1954; J. Chiari, *The Poetic Drama of Paul Claudel*, New York, 1954; L. Chaigne, *Paul Claudel: The Man and the Mystic*, tr. by P. de Fontnouvelle, New York, 1961.

CLOSET DRAMA. Play intended to be read rather than performed. Its Greek origins are to be found in Plato's dialogues about the death of Socrates. In Rome, Julius Caesar Strabo and Quintus Cicero wrote plays meant for private perusal, and the dramas of Seneca were meant to be recited among friends. In the Elizabethan Renaissance, the closet drama was popular with the literary elite;

the most important example of the genre was Sir Fulke Greville's *Mustapha* (1603–1608). In the seventeenth century, John Milton's verse tragedy *Samson Agonistes* (1671) was specifically written to be read rather than staged. The closet drama was also preferred by the English and French romantic and Victorian poets, such as Byron (*Manfred,* pub. 1817), Shelley (*Prometheus Unbound,* 1820; *The Cenci*), Musset (*Comédies et proverbes*), Browning (*A Soul's Tragedy,* pub. 1846), and Hardy (*The Dynasts*). *See* BROWNING, ROBERT; BYRON, GEORGE GORDON; MUSSET, ALFRED DE; SHELLEY, PERCY BYSSHE.

Jean Cocteau
(1889 — 1963)

Jean Cocteau, French poet, novelist, artist, critic, cinematographer, and dramatist, was born on July 5, 1889, in Maisons-Lafitte, 10 miles from Paris. Though his father, a wealthy lawyer and an amateur painter, died when Cocteau was ten, he had a lasting influence on his son. Cocteau's childhood was

Jean Cocteau.
[French Cultural Services]

Jean Cocteau as he appeared in the role of Heurtebise in a 1927 production of *Orphée*. [French Cultural Services]

where he was deeply moved by the silent and dreamlike precision of the dancers. Because of his family's connections he had no difficulty in being introduced to Diaghilev. Cocteau's admiration for the Russian resulted in a significant friendship. Not only did the poet begin writing ballets, but he himself said that he was born at twenty when Diaghilev said to him, "Surprise me." And, in fact, from that day on Cocteau began his versatile career, a career in which his primary aesthetic principle was to surprise and shock his audience.

Cocteau's literary life ceased with the outbreak of World War I. He was rejected for active service by the French Army but joined a civilian ambulance unit. His extraordinary difficulties and experiences at the front were used several years later as the basis for his novel *The Impostor Thomas* (*Thomas l'imposteur*, 1923). Toward the end of the war, he began to frequent Montparnasse and there joined a creative avant-garde that included the poets Guillaume Apollinaire and Blaise Cendrars. He became friendly with Pablo Picasso, and they collaborated with the composer Erik Satie to write *Parade*, "a realistic ballet." Produced in May, 1917, it was a complete failure; only in retrospect has it proved to be one of the most daring and modern ballets of the twentieth century.

Immediately after the war Cocteau met the brilliant writer Raymond Radiguet, another important figure in his development as a dramatist. Radiguet pointed Cocteau away from the avant-gardists. "He taught me an attitude of astonishing novelty," wrote Cocteau in 1947, "an attitude which consisted in not appearing original. . . . It was he who taught me how to lean on nothing." When, in 1923, three years after their first meeting, twenty-year-old Radiguet died of typhoid fever, Cocteau was inconsolable without his teacher, lover, and friend. He started to take opium, and though he became addicted, he never stopped writing. His first completely original play, *Orpheus* (*Orphée*), was produced in 1926; the next year he collaborated with Stravinsky on *Oedipus-Rex*, an opera-oratorio. In 1929 Cocteau was hospitalized for opium poisoning. At the clinic he met Jacques Maritain, the anti-Bergsonian Catholic philosopher, who succeeded in returning him (temporarily, it would seem) to religion. Their eventual open exchange of letters on Catholicism caused considerable intellectual excitement in France.

In the early 1930s Cocteau turned his attention to the only theatrical medium he had not tried: motion pictures. Among his best-known films are *The Blood of a Poet* (*Le sang d'un poète*, 1932), *Beauty and the Beast* (*La belle et la bête*, 1945), and *Orpheus* (*Orphée*,

stormy, and his family had great difficulty in keeping him at the Lycée Condorcet, for he boasted of being ineducable and of detesting school. His real education came from the artistic and literary atmosphere of his home and from his regular attendance at the theatre.

In 1906, when Cocteau was seventeen, his literary talents first became evident. His friends included such writers as Catulle Mendès, Léon Daudet, Marcel Proust, and the Comtesse de Noailles. Édouard de Max, a leading actor of the time, arranged for Cocteau to participate in a reading of his own poems at the Théâtre Fémina; by 1909 he succeeded in publishing his first book, *Aladdin's Lamp* (*La lampe d'Aladin*), a collection of poems written in a traditional manner. Shortly thereafter he attended a performance of the Ballet Russe, directed by Serge Diaghilev,

1950), all surrealistic works on the theme of fatality. In 1936 Cocteau, as the result of a bet with the newspaper *Paris-Soir,* succeeded in completing the itinerary imagined by Jules Verne in *Around the World in Eighty Days. My First Voyage* (*Mon premier voyage,* 1936) is the brilliant account of his travels.

Cocteau began a new and notorious phase of his professional career and personal life in 1937, when young Jean Marais played the lead in his *The Knights of the Round Table* (*Les chevaliers de la table ronde,* 1937); from then on the two men became inseparable. Cocteau was unconcerned with the gossip to which their relationship gave rise, and he designed roles especially for Marais in nearly all his succeeding works.

In the beginning of World War II, Cocteau took a pacifist stand, protesting only when the Germans began bombing Parisian monuments. During this period he returned to the cinema and wrote five films in the next five years. Marais was the hero of four of them.

In 1949 Cocteau made a trip to the United States and a theatrical tour of the Middle East. The following year he made the film version of his famous 1929 novel *Les enfants terribles* (sometimes known in English as *The Holy Terrors,* but not to be confused with *Les monstres sacrés,* his 1940 play known by the same English title). He continued leading an active life until 1953, when ill health forced him into semiretirement. In 1955 Cocteau was elected to the Belgian Academy and the Académie Française; a year later he was granted an honorary degree by Oxford University. Cocteau spent his last seven years painting as well as writing. He died in Milly, outside Paris, on October 11, 1963.

(Left) *La voix humaine,* as presented at the Festival d'Aix-en-Provence in 1960. [French Cultural Services]

WORK

It would be hard to imagine a more versatile artist than Jean Cocteau, and in the years following World War I this *enfant terrible* of the French avant-garde was incredibly active, turning out poems, novels, criticism, ballets, and plays that were to scandalize—and so delight—"tout Paris." Cocteau always considered himself first and foremost a poet, and in every field in which he worked it was the poet who spoke. Like his close friend Pablo Picasso, he seemed to be intent on creating an art founded not on the representation of objects but on evocation by poetic analogies and equivalents. His technique in the theatre as well as in other genres relied heavily on the element of surprise, by which the specta-

Jean Marais and Jeanne Moreau in *La machine infernale,* Théâtre des Bouffes-Parisiens, Paris. [French Cultural Services]

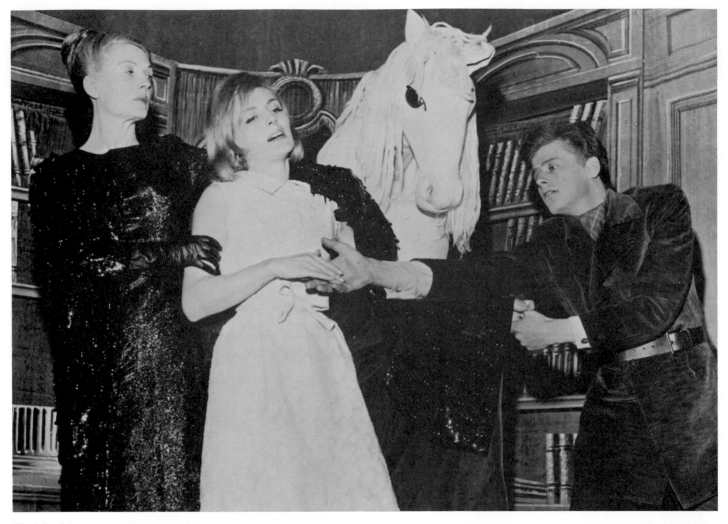

(Top) *Orphée,* Théâtre Hébertot, Paris. (Below left) *Les chevaliers de la table ronde,* as presented by the Centre Dramatique de l'Ouest at the Théâtre de L'Athénée, Paris. (Below right) A 1964 production of *Les parents terribles,* with Jean Marais. [French Cultural Services]

tor was startled into a fresh perception of familiar material seen in a new light or from an unexpected point of view.

Cocteau's earliest theatrical works were refreshing ballet scenarios—*The Blue God* (*Le dieu bleu,* 1921), *Parade* (1917), and *The Ox on the Roof, or The Nothing-Doing Bar* (*Le boeuf sur le toit, ou The Nothing-Doing Bar,* 1920)—with scores by such then-unknown composers as Reynaldo Hahn, Erik Satie, and Darius Milhaud. His most famous work in this category is *The Wedding on the Eiffel Tower* (*Les mariés de la Tour Eiffel,* 1921), in which he strove to invent "a machine" for communicating poetry to the stage. In line with his theory of poetically transforming the banal, he took as his subject a wedding party at the photographer's shop in the Eiffel Tower. Two actors dressed as phonographs comment on the action mimed and danced by the other performers. In the course of the "spectacle," an ostrich, the newlyweds' future child, a Trouville bathing beauty, and a man-eating lion all emerge and reenter the camera—the lion not until he has devoured a general, who believes the beast to be an illusion and so fails to hide. Music for this attempt at full-bodied "poetry of the theatre" was supplied by Georges Auric, Germaine Tailleferre, Arthur Honegger, Francis Poulenc, and Darius Milhaud, all members of the now-famous Groupe des Six.

A new phase in Cocteau's development was launched by a reasonably faithful adaptation of Sophocles's *Antigone* (1922) in a production largely dependent upon unusual staging techniques intended to adapt the Greek tragedy "to the rhythm of our times." Similar but more drastic treatment was given Shakespeare's *Romeo and Juliet* in Cocteau's adaptation, *Roméo et Juliette* (1924). The lyrical passages were suppressed in favor of symbolic stage action in which black-clothed actors performed against a black-velvet backdrop actions that had previously been rehearsed to music.

Turning once more to Greek mythology, Cocteau wrote his first completely original play, *Orpheus* (1926), often considered his masterpiece. Mixing all genres in this often hilariously funny "tragedy," he investigated the relation of the poet to his source of inspiration. Surrealistic in form, the play presents a bickering modern Orpheus and Eurydice, a horse that supplies spirit messages, a talking head, and death in the form of a beautiful and expensively gowned woman.

In 1927 Cocteau turned to the Oedipus legend and collaborated with Igor Stravinsky on an opera-oratorio entitled *Oedipus-Rex.* In order to "spare" audiences the "effort of listening or remembering," Cocteau's French text was translated into Latin and a French-speaking narrator recalled the basic story. Cocteau drew on this work for his *Oedipus the King* (*Oedipe-Roi;* wr. 1928, prod. 1937), a free adaptation of Sophocles. In 1962 he revised the work into an attempt at "total theatre" in which all the arts—recitation, choral singing, dancing, mime, and music—made their contribution to this "lyric tragedy."

Oedipus also provided the theme for another of Cocteau's major works, *The Infernal Machine* (*La machine infernale,* 1934), in which he investigated his growing preoccupation with the problem of free will. A brash and ambitious Oedipus uses the oracle's warning as an excuse to leave his supposed parents and go out to seek his fortune. But his every gesture and those of the other characters only serve to advance the "machine" set up by the cruel gods to crush him. In essence the play points an accusing finger at the "base treachery" of the powers above.

In 1937 Cocteau turned to a new source of mythology and presented *The Knights of the Round Table,* a study of the conflict between good and evil. In his version of the Celtic legend, after freeing the inmates of King Arthur's castle from Merlin's enchantment, Galahad finds that many of them cannot survive without the illusions they have known. The endless struggle between the opposing forces is symbolized by Galahad's departure with Merlin for a new battleground.

Intimate Relations (*Les parents terribles,* 1938) is a play whose basic inspiration is Greek but whose superficial form seems to be drawn from boulevard comedy. Written with great economy, it is a new departure in that it is completely independent of scenic effects for its interest. In this investigation of the relations of the members of a single family, audiences saw an attack on middle-class decadence, but once more Cocteau seems to have been basically concerned with the opposing forces of order and disorder. Paradoxically, purity is shown to reside in the impulsive and innocent disorder of the spoiled protagonist and his frantically possessive mother rather than in the sensible and possibly calculating aunt. *The Holy Terrors* (1940), another play with a contemporary background, successfully challenged popular theatre on its own ground. A famous theatrical couple find their relationship threatened by an ambitious young actress; their response is to strike a series of dramatic poses. The play ends happily, however, and the wife successfully reclaims her straying husband. *See* BOULEVARD COMEDY.

During the Occupation, Cocteau presented *Renaud and Armide* (*Renaud et Armide,* 1943), a romantic verse tragedy in which he

experimented with verbal opera. The structure of musical composition may have been Cocteau's preoccupation in *The Eagle Has Two Heads* (*L'aigle à deux têtes*, 1946), since he described the play as a fugue in which the separate themes of the first two acts are combined in the third. As was basically intended, this play provided magnificent roles for Edwige Feuillère and Jean Marais as the Queen and her would-be assassin.

Cocteau's last full-length play, *Bacchus* (1951), is probably the most conventional in form, but it aroused enormous scandal because of its attack on the abuses of organized religion and provoked a bitter denunciation by the Catholic novelist François Mauriac. The scene of the play is Reformation Germany; Hans, a seeming idiot who has been elected the Bacchus of a local festival, attempts to use his temporary power to return the church to its primitive purity.

Other plays of interest by Cocteau include *The Human Voice* (*La voix humane*, 1930), a tour de force in which a woman holds an agonizing telephone conversation with her faithless lover; *The Indifferent Lover* (*Le bel indifférent*, 1940), written for Edith Piaf, in which a woman berates her silent and contemptuous lover; and *The Typewriter* (*La machine à écrire*, 1941), a full-length play ostensibly about a provincial poison-pen scandal but actually concerned chiefly with the relations among members of a household.

Cocteau's film achievements are by no means his least significant. He often made his own film versions of his stage plays—*Intimate Relations* and *The Eagle Has Two Heads,* for example—and sometimes treated the same subjects in radically different manners that coincided with his current interests and the special potential of the movie camera. Thus, the treatment of the Orpheus legend in his film (1950) bears no relation to its handling in his 1926 play of the same name.

Orpheus (*Orphée*, 1926). A modern Orpheus and Eurydice quarrel because the poet's inspiration comes from a horse, the devil, that taps out messages. Eurydice consults Heurtebise, a glazier, but loses confidence in him when she sees him standing in midair. After attempting to poison the horse, Eurydice is herself killed when she licks an envelope poisoned by the Bacchantes. Death appears in the form of a beautiful woman, feeds the horse Eurydice's poison, and after surgi-

Scene from a German production of *Bacchus.* [German Information Center]

cally preparing Eurydice's body for entrance into Hades through the mirror, departs, forgetting her gloves. At Heurtebise's urging, Orpheus puts them on and, passing through the mirror, manages to bring Eurydice back, only to lose her again when, in a moment of irritation, he deliberately looks at her. In order to rejoin Eurydice, Orpheus allows himself to be killed by the Bacchantes; he repasses through the mirror, leaving his head behind. A confused police commissioner arrives to question Heurtebise about Orpheus's death, and the head identifies itself as "Jean Cocteau." In a final scene Orpheus, Eurydice, and Heurtebise reenter through the mirror what is now paradise. Heurtebise is revealed as the guardian angel of the couple, who have now both attained salvation, she by her devotion to love and he by his devotion to poetry. Orpheus now requests that Eurydice and not Heurtebise pour his wine.

The Infernal Machine (*La machine infernale*, 1934).   After having used this theme in an opera-oratorio (1927) and a free adaptation of Sophocles's version of the Oedipus legend, Cocteau here retells the story in modern terms. A voice replaces the traditional chorus

(Left) *La machine à écrire*, at the Comédie-Française, Salle du Luxembourg. (Above) *L'épouse injustement soupçonnée*, at the Théâtre de la Gaîté-Montparnasse. (French Cultural Services)

and recalls the basic story to the audience. In a scene reminiscent of *Hamlet,* two guards on the ramparts of Thebes have seen Laius's ghost and caused the Queen, Jocasta, to appear. She, however, is unable to see or hear the ghost, which tries vainly to warn her of Oedipus's approach. Oedipus, a callow youth, encounters the Sphinx in the form of a young girl who, in an attempt to make him love her, reveals the solution to her riddle. Unaware that the old man he recently killed is Laius, his true father, Oedipus tells how he left Corinth so that he would not fulfill the oracle's warning that he would kill the King and marry the Queen, assumedly his parents. Ambitious and ungrateful, Oedipus proceeds to Thebes and claims Jocasta as his reward for defeating the Sphinx. On his wedding night he is visited by Tiresias, the blind seer, who predicts a troubled future. Oedipus then has a nightmare and is maternally soothed by Jocasta. The final portion of the play closely follows Sophocles except that, after Oedipus has blinded himself, the ghost of Jocasta appears to him. Purified by death, she is no longer the wife but only the mother. The proud Antigone may think she is leading her

father, but Oedipus can "see" Jocasta's ghost, which will serve as his real guide.

Intimate Relations (*Les parents terribles,* 1938). In an untidy apartment that reflects the emotional disorder of its inhabitants, Yvonne is informed by Leonie, her orderly spinster sister, that her son Michael is in love and her husband George has been unfaithful. A hysterically possessive mother, Yvonne resents losing Michael; the situation is further complicated when George realizes that he himself is involved with Madeleine, the girl Michael loves. At the instigation of Leonie, George threatens Madeleine with exposure unless she breaks with his son. She agrees and tells Michael that she is in love with someone else. But Leonie's motives are complicated by the fact that she had formerly sacrificed her own love for George. Seeing Madeleine's distress, Leonie changes tactics and now plays on George's emotions until he agrees to tell Michael that Madeleine's story was a lie. The happiness of the reunited young people is, however, blasted by the suicide of Yvonne, who cannot give up her son. Leonie is now free to impose order on those about her.

Scene from
Bacchus, as
performed at the
Théâtre Marigny,
with stage and
costume designs
by the author.
[French Cultural
Services]

The Eagle Has Two Heads (*L'aigle à deux têtes,* 1946).   Play taking its theme from the inexplicable murder of Empress Elizabeth of Austria by a madman. Extremely melodramatic, highly romantic, and so complicated as to be confusing, the play introduces a veiled and widowed Queen into whose bedroom comes a young man, Stanislas or Azrael, angel of death, bearing a remarkable resemblance to the dead King. Sheltered by the Queen, Stanislas, an anarchistic poet, falls in love with her. His love is reciprocated. The Queen has never really ruled but now plans, with her lover's aid, to take her rightful place upon the throne. Implausible political machinations make this plan impossible. In a gesture of love, Stanislas takes poison and then stabs the Queen as she stands at her window to review her troops.

PLAYS

Unless otherwise noted, the plays were first performed in Paris.

1. *Le dieu bleu* (*The Blue God*). Ballet. Produced 1912. Music: Reynaldo Hahn.
2. *Parade.* Realistic ballet, 1 act. Written 1916. Published 1919. Produced Théâtre du Châtelet, May, 1917. Music: Erik Satie.
3. *Le boeuf sur le toit, ou The Nothing-Doing Bar* (*The Ox on the Roof, or The Nothing-Doing Bar*). Farce, 1 act. Written 1920. Published 1920. Produced Comédie des Champs-Elysées, Feb. 21, 1920. Music: Darius Milhaud.
4. *Les mariés de la Tour Eiffel** (*The Wedding on the Eiffel Tower*). Spectacle, 1 act. Written 1921. Published 1923. Produced Théâtre des Champs-Élysées, June 18, 1921. Music: Georges Auric, Arthur Honegger, Germaine Tailleferre, Darius Milhaud, and Francis Poulenc.
5. *Antigone**. Tragedy, 1 act. Written 1922. Published 1928. Produced Théâtre de l'Atelier, Dec. 21, 1922. Based on Sophocles's play.
6. *Les biches* (*The Does*). Ballet, 1 act. Written 1924. Published 1924. Produced Théâtre de Monte-Carlo, Jan. 6, 1924.
7. *Le train bleu* (*The Blue Train*). Ballet. Written 1924. Produced Théâtre de Monte-Carlo, 1924.
8. *Roméo et Juliette* (*Romeo and Juliet*). Pretext for a production after Shakespeare; 5 acts, 23 tableaux. Written 1924. Published 1926. Produced Théâtre de la Cigale, June 2, 1924.
9. *Orphée** (*Orpheus*). Tragedy; 1 act, 1 interval. Writ-

ten 1925. Published 1927. Produced Théâtre des Arts, June 15, 1926.

10. *Le pauvre matelot* (*The Poor Sailor*). Complaint, 3 acts. Written 1927. Published 1927.

11. *Oedipus-Rex*. Opera-oratorio, 2 acts. Written 1927. Published 1928. Produced Théâtre Sarah-Bernhardt, 1927. Music: Igor Stravinsky.

12. *Oedipe-Roi* (*Oedipus the King*). Play. Written 1928. Published 1928. Produced Nouveau Théâtre Antoine, June, 1937. Revised version: Produced Lyon Festival, 1962. Free adaptation of Sophocles's play.

13. *La voix humaine** (*The Human Voice*). Monologue, 1 act. Written 1930. Published 1930. Produced Comédie-Française, Feb. 18, 1930.

14. *La machine infernale** (*The Infernal Machine*). Play, 4 acts. Written 1932. Published 1934. Produced Théâtre Louis-Jouvet, Apr. 10, 1934.

15. *L'école des veuves* (*The School for Widows*). Comedy, 1 act. Written 1936. Published 1936. Produced A.B.C. Cabaret, 1936.

16. *Les chevaliers de la table ronde** (*The Knights of the Round Table*). Play, 3 acts. Written 1937. Published 1937. Produced Théâtre de l'Oeuvre, Oct. 14, 1937.

17. *Les parents terribles** (*Intimate Relations*). Play, 3 acts. Written 1938. Published 1938. Produced Théâtre des Ambassadeurs, Nov. 14, 1938.

18. *Les monstres sacrés** (*The Holy Terrors*). Play, 3 acts. Written 1940. Published 1940. Produced Théâtre Michel, Feb. 17, 1940.

19. *Le bel indifférent* (*The Indifferent Lover*). Monologue, 1 act. Written 1940. Published 1940. Produced Théâtre des Bouffes-Parisiens, 1940.

20. *La machine à écrire** (*The Typewriter*). Play, 3 acts. Written 1941. Published 1941. Produced Théâtre Hébertot, Apr. 29, 1941.

21. *Renaud et Armide* (*Renaud and Armide*). Verse tragedy, 3 acts. Written 1943. Published 1943. Produced Comédie-Française, Apr. 13, 1943.

22. *L'aigle à deux têtes** (*The Eagle Has Two Heads*). Play, 3 acts. Written 1946. Published 1946. Produced Brussels, Théâtre des Galeries, Oct. 3, 1946; Paris, Théâtre Hébertot, Dec. 20, 1946.

23. *Le jeune homme et la mort* (*Death and the Young Man*). Ballet, 1 act. Written 1946. Published 1957. Produced Paris, Opéra, 1946.

24. (Adaptation). *Un tramway nommé Désir* (*A Streetcar Named Desire*). Play, 3 acts. Written 1949. Published 1949. Produced Théâtre Édouard VII, Oct. 15, 1949. Based on Paule de Beaumont's translation of the play by Tennessee Williams.

25. *Le fantôme de Marseille* (*The Ghost of Marseille*). Monologue, 1 act. Published 1949. Produced Compiègne, Mar. 19, 1952.

26. *L'épouse injustement soupçonnée* (*The Unjustly Suspected Wife*). Play, 1 act. Produced Théâtre de la Gaîté-Montparnasse, Mar. 4, 1950.

27. *Phèdre* (*Phaedra*). Choreographic tragedy. Written 1950. Published 1950. Produced Paris, Opéra, 1950.

28. *Bacchus**. Play, 3 acts. Written 1951. Published 1952. Produced Théâtre Marigny, Dec. 20, 1951.

29. *La dame à la licorne* (*The Lady and the Unicorn*). Ballet, 1 act. Written 1953. Published 1957. Produced Munich, Theater am Gärtnerplatz, May 9, 1953.

30. *L'impromptu de Palais-Royal* (*The Palais-Royal Impromptu*). Divertissement, 6 scenes. Written 1961. Published 1962. Produced Japan, Compagnie de la Comédie-Française, 1962.

EDITIONS

Collections.
Théâtre, 2 vols., Paris, 1948; *Théâtre de poche*, Paris, 1949; *Oeuvres complètes*, 11 vols., Geneva, 1946–1951; *Théâtre complet*, 2 vols., Paris 1957; *Nouveau théâtre de poche*, Monaco, 1960; *Five Plays*, New York, 1961; *Four Plays*, London, 1962; *The Infernal Machine and Other Plays*, Norfolk, Conn., 1963.

Individual Plays.
The Infernal Machine. Published in *International Modern Plays*, tr. by C. Wildman, London, 1950.
Intimate Relations, Published in *From the Modern Repertoire*, ed. by E. R. Bentley and tr. by C. Frank, ser. 3, Bloomington, Ind., 1949–1956.
Orpheus. Published in *Masters of Modern Drama*, ed. by H. M. Block and R. G. Shedd and tr. by C. Wildman, New York, 1962.
The Wedding on the Eiffel Tower. Published in *New Directions in Prose and Poetry*, ed. by J. Laughlin and tr. by D. Fitts, Norfolk, Conn., 1937.

CRITICISM

French.
C. Mauriac, *Jean Cocteau, ou La vérité du mensonge*, Paris, 1945; J.-P. Millecam, *L'étoile de Jean Cocteau*, Monaco, 1952; P. Dubourg, *Dramaturgie de Jean Cocteau*, Paris, 1954; M. Meunier, *Méditerranée, ou Les deux visages de Jean Cocteau*, Paris, 1959; J.-J. Kihm, *Cocteau*, Paris, 1960; A. Fraigneau, *Cocteau par lui-même*, Paris, 1966.

English.
M. Crosland, *Jean Cocteau*, London, 1955, New York, 1956; N. Oxenhandler, *Scandal & Parade: The Theater of Jean Cocteau*, New Brunswick, N.J., 1957; W. Fowlie, *Jean Cocteau: The History of a Poet's Age*, Bloomington, Ind., 1966; F. Brown, *An Impersonation of Angels: A Biography of Jean Cocteau*, New York and London, 1968; E. Sprigge and J.-J. Kihm, *Jean Cocteau: The Man and the Mirror*, London and New York, 1968; F. Steegmuller, *Cocteau*, Boston, 1970.

COELLO Y OCHOA, Antonio (b. Madrid, October 26, 1611; d. there, October 20, 1652). A collaborator of several major dramatists of the Siglo de Oro (Spanish Golden Age), Coello is best known for a powerful *comedia histórica, The Earl of Essex, or To Give One's Life For One's Lady* (*El conde de Sex, o Dar la vida por su dama*; prod. 1633, pub. 1638), the first of several plays to deal with the romance between Queen Elizabeth and the 2d Earl of Essex; and *The Jealous Estremenian* (*El celoso extremeño*, 1634), adapted from Cervantes' *novela* of the same name (1613). His other plays, mainly in the tradition of Calderón, include *No Sooner Said than Done* (*Lo dicho hecho*, pub. 1650), *The Adulteress Punished* (*La adúltera castigada*), *Peor es hurgallo, The Two Ferdinands of Austria* (*Los dos Fernandos de Austria*, pub. 1646), and *The Adventures of Six Hours* (*Los empeños de seis horas*). See CALDERÓN DE LA BARCA, PEDRO; SIGLO DE ORO.

The Earl of Essex, or To Give One's Life for One's Lady (*El conde de Sex, o Dar la vida por su dama*; prod. 1633, pub. 1638). *Comedia histórica*, a much-distorted version of the relationship between Elizabeth I of England and the 2d Earl of Essex. The play opens with Essex foiling an attempted assassination of Queen Isabela (Elizabeth), whom he does not recognize. Essex has been in love with Blanca, whose parents were put to death by the Queen for supporting Mary Stuart. Essex, who has by this time fallen in love with Isabela, nevertheless remains constant to

Blanca and promises to help her take her revenge on the Queen. In fact, he plans to foil the plot in a way that will protect both Isabela and Blanca. However, both women become suspicious, and Blanca tries to shoot the Queen herself. Essex deflects the pistol, saving the Queen. Then he proclaims his own and Blanca's innocence. He is arrested as Blanca flees.

COHAN, George Michael (1878–1942). American actor, songwriter, dramatist, director, and producer. Appearing in the family vaudeville act "The Four Cohans" as a child, he soon began writing vaudeville skits, songs, and plays, becoming a successful manager, dramatist, and stage director. He wrote more than forty plays, including *Forty-five Minutes from Broadway* (1906), *Fifty Miles from Boston* (1908), *The Yankee Prince* (1908), *The American Idea* (1908), *Get-Rich-Quick Wallingford* (1910), *Broadway Jones* (1912), *Seven Keys to Baldpate* (1913), *The Miracle Man* (1914), *Hit-the-Trail Holiday* (1915), *A Prince There Was* (1918), *The Voice of McConnell* (1918), *The Song and Dance Man* (1923), and *Gambling* (1929). It was his role as the "Yankee Doodle Boy" in *Little Johnny Jones,* a play he produced in 1904, that was thereafter as-

sociated with him. In addition, his patriotic song "Over There" became a theme song for Americans during World War I. "Give My Regards to Broadway," "I'm a Yankee Doodle Dandy," "Grand Old Flag," and "Mary Is a Grand Old Name" were equally popular and identifiable as the songs of Broadway's "favorite song-and-dance man."

George M. Cohan and Irene Rich in a revival of *Seven Keys to Baldpate.* New York, National Theatre, 1935. [Photograph by Vandamm. Theatre Collection, The New York Public Library at Lincoln Center, Astor, Lenox and Tilden Foundations]

COLLIN-BARBIÉ DU BOCAGE, Louis. *See* VERNEUIL, LOUIS.

COLMAN, George, the elder (1732–1794). English barrister, theatre manager, and dramatist who essayed almost every dramatic form. Among some forty works are scattered numerous adaptations and translations. Although Colman wrote at a time when sentimental comedy was in full flower, his work is generally free of the worst excesses of sentimentalism, and, in fact, he frequently mocked the sentimental tradition. *See* SENTIMENTAL COMEDY.

His best-known plays are *The Jealous Wife* (1761), a comedy of manners based in part on Henry Fielding's novel *Tom Jones* (1749); and *The Clandestine Marriage* (1766), written with David Garrick. Also of interest are the farces *Polly Honeycombe* (1760), with a heroine whose head is filled with romantic rubbish; and *The Deuce Is in Him* (1763). *The*

Fred Niblo and Katherine La Salle in George M. Cohan's *Hit-the-Trail Holiday.* New York, Astor Theatre, 1915. [Theatre Collection, The New York Public Library at Lincoln Center, Astor, Lenox and Tilden Foundations]

George Colman, the elder. [Theatre Collection, The New York Public Library at Lincoln Center, Astor, Lenox and Tilden Foundations]

English Merchant (1767), adapted from Voltaire's *The Café, or The Scotswoman* (1760), is a successful attempt at sentimental comedy. Colman's plays also include *Man and Wife, or The Shakespeare Jubilee* (1769) and *The Man of Business* (1774). His son, George Colman

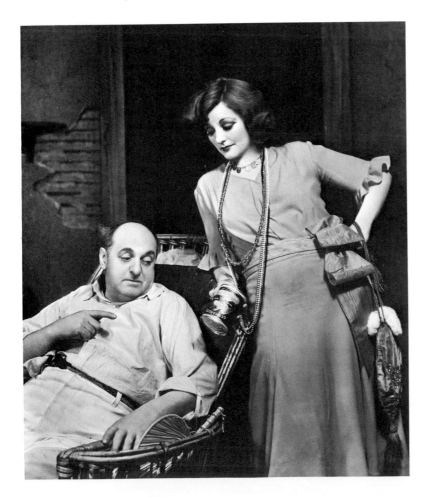

Granville Bates and Tallulah Bankhead in a revival of *Rain*, by John Colton and Clemence Randolph. New York, Music Box Theatre, 1935. [Photograph by Vandamm. Theatre Collection, The New York Public Library at Lincoln Center, Astor, Lenox and Tilden Foundations]

the younger, was also a dramatist. *See* GAR-RICK, DAVID; VOLTAIRE.

COLTON, John (b. Minnesota, December 13, 1889; d. Gainesville, Fla., December 28, 1946). Anglo-American dramatist, author of a number of highly theatrical plays, including *Rain* (with Clemence Randolph, 1922), an adaptation of "Miss Thompson," a short story by Somerset Maugham (*see* MAUGHAM, SOMERSET). His other plays are *The Shanghai Gesture* (1926), a melodrama in which a Chinese madam takes her revenge on an Englishman who betrayed her years earlier; *Saint Wrench* (1933); and *Nine Pine Street* (with Carleton Miles, 1933), a play based on the sensational Lizzie Borden murder case, which took place in Massachusetts in 1892.

Rain (1922). Drama in which Sadie Thompson, an ebullient, good-natured prostitute, is stranded in Pago Pago. Among her companions are the Reverend and Mrs. Davidson, militant missionaries whose marriage is spiritual, not physical. Davidson sees in Sadie an errant soul to be saved and arranges for her to be returned to the United States, the one thing she fears the most, for a prison term awaits her there. Sadie calculatingly pleads for mercy, but slowly her resistance to Davidson's proselytizing crumbles. As her spirituality emerges, so does Davidson's lust. Eventually he rapes her and then commits suicide. Sadie, disillusioned, agrees to leave for Australia with Marine Sergeant O'Hara in the hope that they will be able to start a new life together. Produced New York, Maxine Elliott Theatre, November 7, 1922.

COLUM, Padraic (b. Longford, Ireland, December 8, 1881; d. Enfield, Conn., January 11, 1972). Irish scholar, poet, folklorist, and dramatist who contributed to the surge of realism that developed in the course of the Irish renaissance. He joined the Irish Literary Theatre, and it was not long before his tragedy *Broken Soil* (1903) was produced by that company. In 1905 the same group, now the Abbey Theatre, produced *The Land*, which deals with the conflict between the generations of an Irish family and their responses to the appeal of the city vis-à-vis the strong appeal of the land. After the Abbey's production of Synge's *The Playboy of the Western World*, Colum withdrew his works in protest, and a revision of *Broken Soil*, entitled

Padraic Colum.
[Library of
Congress]

The Fiddler's House, was produced by the Theatre of Ireland Company in 1907. However, by 1910 the Abbey was once again producing his plays. The starkly naturalistic *Thomas Muskerry* appeared that year, revealing the drabness of small-town life. It proved to be the last of Colum's notable plays. Later, with Mrs. F. E. Washburn Freund, he wrote *Grasshopper* (1922), a melodrama adapted from a work by Eduard von Keyserling; and *Balloon* (1929), a comedy satirizing modern industrial society.

In 1914 Colum emigrated to the United States with his wife Mary Maguire, also a writer, and thereafter devoted himself mainly to the writing of children's stories, lecturing, and literary criticism. With his wife he wrote *Our Friend James Joyce* (1958) and *Moytura: A Play for Dancers* (wr. 1963), a play in the manner of the Japanese Nō dramas, concerning Sir William Wilde, father of Oscar Wilde. *See* NŌ.

The Fiddler's House (1907). Drama of the fiddler Conn Hourican, who has been forced to settle down by his daughters Maire and Anne. Living in the house left to Maire by her grandmother, Conn tries to work the land. But since he is no farmer, he lives only for his fiddling and longs for the open road. Meanwhile, Anne is being courted by a young man whose father wants him to marry a girl with a large dowry. Knowing this, Maire secures Anne's future by deeding the farm to her. Then, handing her father the fiddle that she has been denying him, she prepares to accompany him to the fairs.

COMEDIA. In Spain, the principal dramatic form of the Siglo de Oro (Golden Age), which began early in the sixteenth century as a primitive imitation of Italian tragicomedy. The form as used by Bartolomé de Torres Naharro was divided into five acts, or *jornadas* (lit. "resting places"), and was written in verse. Torres Naharro describes two types of *comedia* into which his own work might be divided, the *comedia a noticia* ("realistic play") and the *comedia a fantasia* ("romantic play"). Later in the sixteenth century the number of acts was reduced to four, and then, with the work of Cristóbal de Virués and Juan de la Cueva in the 1580s, cut to three. Cueva also introduced the comedy of manners and was the first to use Spanish history as dramatic material. During this period the term *jornada* was revived and came into general use. *See* SIGLO DE ORO; TORRES NAHARRO, BARTOLOMÉ DE.

Lope de Vega endowed the *comedia* with certain characteristics that set it apart from other forms of comedy: the mingling of comic and tragic elements; a complex, suspenseful plot in three acts; the use of a variety of verse forms; a disregard for the classical unities; and verisimilitude of language and action. *See* UNITIES; VEGA CARPIO, LOPE DE.

The *comedia* developed in the most firmly orthodox of all Roman Catholic countries; consequently the power and prestige of the church is reflected in the form itself. The church not only suppressed all dramatic material that was either heretical or inimical to its prevailing attitudes but provided a background and an atmosphere basic to the form. Thus the *comedia* is an accurate dramatic reflection of life in a Christian universe.

Characteristic of the *comedia* is its subordination of character to action. A. A. Parker in *The Approach to the Spanish Drama of the Golden Age* (1957) says:

> *The Spanish drama works on the assumption — which after all has the authority of Aristotle behind it — that the plot and not the characters is the primary thing. We can then judge the action in its own right and see what it has to offer us in terms of human values. This does not mean that the characters are unimportant. What it does mean is that since the dramatists are out to present, within a strict limitation of time, an action that is full of incident, they generally have no time to elaborate their characters, and must confine their characteristics to brief touches. They left it to the audience to fill in, from these hints and touches, the psychology of the characters.*

The *comedia* differs from other contemporary forms in many ways. Unlike other plays of the time, it consists of three acts, usually of equal length, running some 3,000 lines. The comedia is somewhat shorter than the Elizabethan play but, with the addition of the various *loas, entremeses,* and other interludes, probably took about the same length of time to perform. *See* ENTREMÉS.

Since all full-length plays of the Siglo de Oro were *comedias,* the great mass of surviving material was unwieldy and confusing to students of the period. As a result, scholars divided *comedias* into categories. However, because this sorting and labeling was a later development imposed on the *comedia,* many plays fit into several categories or into none at all. The categories, nevertheless, are useful and provide a rough guide to the range and achievements of the period.

Comedia bíblica. Play dealing with a Biblical subject or story. Tirso de Molina's *The Vengeance of Tamar* and Antonio Mira de Amescua's *The Harp of David* are typical.

Comedia de capa y espada. One of the lightest of *comedia* forms; a play that derives its name from the traditional street dress of the Spanish lower nobility and upper bourgeoisie. This genre deals with the intrigues of the upper classes, which, although usually treated in a romantic and conventional way, are here portrayed with wit and masquerade and numerous turns of plot. As in most Spanish secular plays, love and honor are the principal themes, although the treatment is much less serious and severe than in the *comedias históricas* and *comedias de pundonor.* The *comedia de capa y espada* shares many characteristics with the well-made play as practiced by the nineteenth-century French dramatist Eugène Scribe and his followers. *See* WELL-MADE PLAY.

One of the most frequently used forms of the *comedia,* this category includes some of the finest plays of the period: Lope's *The Dog in the Manger, The Idiot Lady,* and *The Waters of Madrid;* Tirso's *The Man in Green Breeches* and *The Balconies of Madrid;* Juan Ruiz de Alarcón's *Privileged Bosoms;* Pedro Calderón de la Barca's *The Phantom Lady, Beware of Still Water,* and *A House with Two Doors Is Difficult to Guard;* Francisco de Rojas Zorrilla's *Obliged though Offended;* and Agustín Moreto y Cabaña's *It Cannot Be, or A Woman Cannot Be Guarded.*

Comedia de carácter. Play with a stronger emphasis on character than is usual in the *comedia.* Tirso and Ruiz de Alarcón excelled in this genre, but their approaches were dissimilar. Tirso tended toward a full, rounded depiction of character, whereas Alarcón emphasized certain peculiar traits of character, as Molière was to do later. The finest examples of this genre are Tirso's *The Trickster of Seville,* Ruiz de Alarcón's *The Truth Suspected,* and Moreto's *Scorn for Scorn.* Others are Tirso's *Martha the Pious* and Ruiz de Alarcón's *The Test for Husbands* and *The Walls Have Ears.*

Comedia divina (Comedia devota). Religious *comedia* not to be confused with the *auto sacramental,* which is a different form. This category is subdivided into the *comedias bíblicas, comedias de santos,* and *comedias teológicas. See* AUTO SACRAMENTAL.

Comedia de enredo. The most extreme type of *comedia de intriga* in which all other elements are distinctly subordinate to the machinations of a fantastically complicated plot. Rojas Zorrilla's *What Women Are* and Moreto's *The Look-Alike at Court* are examples of this form.

Comedia de figurón. Extension of the *comedia de carácter* into the realm of caricature. The finest examples are Moreto's *Don Diego the Fop* and Rojas Zorrilla's *The Sport of Fools, or Don Lucas del Cigarral.*

Comedia filosófica. Philosophical play. The best is Calderón's *Life Is a Dream,* which dramatizes the theme:

> *What is life? A thing that seems,*
> *A mirage that falsely gleams,*
> *Phantom joy, delusive rest*
> *Since is life a dream at best*
> *And even dreams are themselves dreams.*

Comedia histórica. Play based on material drawn from history, usually Spanish history. Since Spanish dramatists were artists and not historians, their plays often ran counter to historical fact. Excluding those historical plays which are also categorized as *comedias palaciegas* and *comedias villanescas,* the outstanding examples of this genre are Tirso's *Prudence in Woman* and *King Pedro in Madrid, or The Nobleman of Illecas;* Lope's *The Knight from Olmedo, A Certainty for a Doubt,* and *The Girl with Money;* and Calderón's *The Constant Prince.*

Comedia de intriga. Play that depends upon "intrigue" or plot for its principal impact. The *comedia de capa y espada* and *comedia de enredo* have similar characteristics.

Comedia mitológica. Play drawn from classic myth. Most *comedias mitológicas* were written for performance at court, where they were elaborately produced with musical accompaniment. From this *comedia* developed a musical form, similar to the operetta, known as the zarzuela. Examples are Calderón's *Love, the Greatest Enchantment* and *Echo and Narcissus. See* ZARZUELA.

Comedia novelesca. Play derived from a work of fiction by such authors as Bandello, Boccaccio, and Cervantes. Examples are Tirso's *Words and Feathers* and *The Lovers of*

Teruel, Lope's *Doña Blanca's Glove*, and Calderón's *The Bridge of Mantible*.

Comedia palaciega. Play dealing with life at court, its intrigues and amours. Tirso's *The Timid Fellow at Court* is one of the finest examples of this type. Others are Tirso's *The Punishment of Thoughtlessness* and *Jealousy Cures Jealousy* and Calderón's *The Scarf and the Flower*.

Comedia de pundonor. Play based upon a serious treatment of the Spanish "code of honor." The word *pundonor* is a contraction of *punto de honor* ("point of honor"). The code, an anomaly in a nation with a strong monarchy and a powerful church, runs counter to both institutions. It substitutes personal revenge for the legal judicial processes of the state and a harsh "eye for an eye" attitude for Christian morality and ethics, flaunting ecclesiastical authority in the process. Although similar to the codes of personal honor that existed in other countries for years, the Spanish code was considerably more rigid and severe.

The severity of the code and its popularity as a dramatic subject have led critics to denounce for their insensitivity and disregard for human decency both the audiences of the time and the dramatists who used the genre. Professor Parker (*op. cit.*) has countered this point of view by noting, in a discussion of Calderón's *The Surgeon of His Honor:*

> *When at the end of the play the husband's murder of his innocent wife is apparently condoned by the King as an act of justice, we are not entitled to assume, as nearly all critics have done, that Calderón wishes us to approve of the murder because the King condones it. On the contrary, since he has presented the King as inhuman and cruel, he wishes us thereby to see that the justice which honor claims to exact is an inhuman and cruel one. There are many indications of this kind in the play, all pointing to the fact that Calderón is seeking to arouse our horror and not our approval for the murder of an innocent wife.*

Other examples of the genre are Calderón's *Secret Vengeance for a Secret Insult* and *The Painter of His Own Dishonor* and Rojas Zorrilla's *None But the King*.

Comedia de santos. Religious play about the life, conversion, or martyrdom of a saint. Examples are Calderón's *The Wonder-working Magician*, Mira de Amescua's *The Devil's Slave*, and Lope's *The Outrageous Saint*.

Comedia teológica. A play dealing with a theological question or some aspect of Catholic doctrine. Tirso's *Damned for Doubt* is supreme in this genre.

Comedia villanesca. Play peopled with peasants and often dramatizing their relationship to the nobility and the King. Some of Lope's finest plays fall into this category: *Peribáñez and the Commander of Ocaña*, *Fuenteovejuna*, and *The King the Greatest Alcalde*. Tirso's *Mari-Hernández the Galician* is another good example of the genre.

COMEDY. Historically, one of the two basic forms of drama, differing from tragedy in that it is generally light in tone and has a happy ending. It deals with themes of everyday life rather than with the heroic, with the real rather than the ideal. Today the meaning of the term has been broadened to include any play written in a light style and having a happy ending.

The word "comedy," deriving from the Greek *komoidia*, which itself derives from *komos*, "a processional celebration," tells much of the origins of this type of drama. Comedy apparently evolved from ancient Dionysian rites and celebrations of song and revel, during which actors, dressed as satyrs, with masks and huge leather phalli, paraded about obscenely, making impromptu jests and mocking the spectators. Eventually poets began composing "phallic verses" for the jesters to recite, and from these, according to Aristotle, the stage comedy of Athens derived, the first being performed in the fifth century B.C. as part of the city's competitive festival.

The earliest of the Greek comedies, known as Old Comedy, followed the exuberant tradition of the Dionysian comedians in ridiculing prominent people and events. The chorus, the mime, and even perhaps the leather phallus of the street comedies were also retained. The most famous of the writers of Old Comedy, and the only one whose work survives, is Aristophanes, whose delight in the use of fantasy was equaled only by the pleasure he derived in launching the most obscene and savage attacks on well-known Athenians, including Socrates. Aristophanes's later plays mark the beginning of the period of Middle Comedy, in which the emphasis of the satire was turned to social rather than political themes and in which the bawdy tone and the use of the chorus was more subdued. *See* ARISTOPHANES; CHORUS; MIDDLE COMEDY; OLD COMEDY.

New Comedy made its appearance with the poet Menander, and again the emphasis shifted, this time to ridicule of social types, to plots of intrigue and romance, and to a concern generally with private and domestic rather than public themes. It was the style, the attitudes, the subject matter, and even the stock characters of New Comedy that were adopted by the Roman playwrights, of whom Plautus and Terence were the most outstanding. The Romans, however, revived some of the comedy's original lively and boisterous spirit, while continuing to steer clear of political satire. Eventually, Roman comedy split in two; theatrical drama was replaced by mime and pantomime while literary drama was written only to be read and became, therefore, the province of the educated classes. *See* MENANDER; NEW COMEDY; PLAUTUS; ROMAN COMEDY; TERENCE.

Such was the state of comedy when the theatre was suppressed by the church in the middle of the sixth century. But laughter and comedy could not be quashed altogether. During the Middle Ages minstrels, mummers, and acrobats maintained the comic tradition, and gradually, as such secular influences began to be felt in the church, dramatic comedy began to reappear in the medieval mystery plays, in which the lofty figures of saints and patriarchs mingled with lowly peasants and shepherds. By the time secular stage drama reappeared in the Renaissance there was still some degree of separation between popular and literary drama, as in Italy, where popular farce (the improvisational *commedia dell'arte*) and the closet drama of Ariosto and Machiavelli existed side by side. However, such distinctions began to blur as the Renaissance progressed, and comedy diverged in several directions. *See* CLOSET DRAMA; COMMEDIA DELL'ARTE; MYSTERY PLAY.

In England, the very distinction between tragedy and comedy began to break down, as Shakespeare freely mingled elements of both genres in his plays. In Spain, Lope de Vega was writing love intrigues that were not especially comical but avoided violence and had happy endings. At the same time Ben Jonson was returning to the Roman conception of comedy as a "pleasant and ridiculous" means of correcting the petty and ill-mannered individual. It was this comedy of manners—calling forth laughter by presenting the follies of mankind—that dominated the French and English stage in the seventeenth century, reaching its height in the plays of Corneille, Molière, Wycherley, and Congreve. In the eighteenth century yet another type of comedy appeared, the comedy of sentiment, the "weeping comedy" in which virtue and true feeling are beset by difficulty and pretense but finally emerge triumphant. In England this type of comedy was at its best not on the stage but in the novels of Fielding and Smollett. It appeared in France in the plays of Marivaux and in Germany in those of Lessing. *See* COMEDY OF MANNERS; SENTIMENTAL COMEDY.

Nineteenth-century egalitarianism and the trend toward naturalism in the arts produced the social comedy of Dumas *fils*, the comedy of ideas of Shaw, and the ironic and semitragic comedy of Chekhov. In rebellion perhaps against the serious tone of such plays there also developed the broader low comedy of the music hall and vaudeville, which depended less on character and dialogue than on the incongruities and exaggerated buffoonery so popular with the audiences of Aristophanes and Plautus. By the twentieth century rebellion was also occurring in the literary comedy, with Synge, O'Casey, and others seeking to replace drab realism with poetry and fantasy. Later, a new type of comedy appeared in the works of Beckett, Pirandello, and Ionesco, who portrayed the absurdity of modern existence with bleak humor. By mid-century man's view of his world had so altered that the heroic seemed comic, the comic seemed heroic, and pure tragedy and pure comedy no longer seemed possible. *See* HEROIC PLAY; THEATRE OF THE ABSURD; VAUDEVILLE.

COMEDY OF HUMORS. Kind of comedy built upon dominant traits in most of the characters. One trait—jealousy, greed, braggadocio—usually predominates in each character and is often employed to make him appear ridiculous. The form is based upon the Middle Ages and Renaissance psychology of humors.

COMEDY OF MANNERS. Play that satirizes the behavior, moral code, and philosophy of life of the socially elite. It was originated by Molière in the mid-seventeenth century and developed by him into the comedy of morals. *See* MOLIÈRE.

While such comedies of social criticism flourished in France, a more delicate form of the comedy of manners, characterized by the stereotyping of the protagonists according to their dominant traits and the exchange of witty repartee, flowered in Restoration England. Among its major practitioners were Sir George Etherege (*The Man of Mode*, 1676), John Dryden (*Marriage à la Mode*, 1672), William Wycherley (*The Country Wife*, 1675; *The Plain Dealer*, 1677), and William Congreve (*Love for Love*, 1695; *The Way of the World*, 1700). The comedy of manners waned in the early eighteenth century after the death of George Farquhar (*The Beaux' Stratagem*, 1707), but it was briefly revived later in the century by Richard Sheridan (*The School for Scandal*, 1777).

The expression is sometimes used to describe the light comedy and social comedy of such modern dramatists as Noel Coward, Philip Barry, and S. N. Behrman.

COMMEDIA DELL'ARTE. Dramatic form, developed by companies of professional actors, that flourished in Italy and throughout Western Europe from the middle of the sixteenth to the middle of the eighteenth century. The origins of the *commedia dell'arte,* or comedy of "artists," are obscure. Only the briefest scenarios were recorded, making it difficult to trace any literary antecedents for this theatrical mode, which required the improvisation of a stage performance from a scenario that engaged a number of stock characters in a series of standard plot devices. Evidence suggests, however, that the players' improvisations drew heavily on classical Greek and Roman comedy and mime. The minstrels and jesters of the Middle Ages and the farces included in the medieval mystery plays probably also provided inspiration. But, far from merely imitating these diverse elements, the *commedia dell'arte* players combined them and reshaped them into a unique art, a lively, lusty theatrical show that included mime, acrobatics, jokes, tirades, slapstick, soliloquies, tricks, romance, dance, and music. *See* MYSTERY PLAY; ROMAN COMEDY.

Like the mystery plays, the *commedia* was usually performed on a platform set up in the street, with a simple backdrop to suggest the setting. Starting with only a brief plot outline, the troupe improvised dialogue and routines, using a set of stock characters, jokes, repartee, and comic devices. Thus, *commedia dell'arte* was very much an actor's medium.

The first *commedia dell'arte* appeared in Italy in the early 1500s, one of its illustrious practitioners being the actor Angelo Beolco, whose stage name was Il Ruzzante. The form remained experimental and loosely organized until about 1550, when some professional actors organized companies, often taking up permanent residence in one town; others formed itinerant troupes. One of the earliest and most famous of these was the Gelosi ("zealous"), led by Francesco Andreini and his wife Isabella. Other prominent troupes were the Desiosi, the Confidenti, and the Uniti. *See* RUZZANTE, IL.

Known by their masks and costumes, some dozen stock characters were the mainstay of the *commedia* repertoire. Their later incorporation into the plays of Shakespeare, Molière, and others has made many of them immortal: the *zannis* (buffoons) Scaramuccia, Arlecchino (Harlequin), and Pulcinello (Punch); the grave elderly parent Pantalone (Pantaloon) and his pedantic friend Gratiano, the *dottore;* the servant girl Columbine; and the clown Pierrot. Another standard character, known by a variety of names depending on which troupe was giving the performance, was the alien captain, a braggart and a coward, usually Spanish or Greek. The romantic hero and heroine, who alone appeared without masks and who were usually the palest of the characters, were also known by several

names. The hero might be Fortunio, Aurelio, Ortensio, Fulvio, or Valerio; the heroine was perhaps Isabella, Flaminia, Sylvia, Olivetta, or Valeria. Some actors were so famous for their portrayals of these characters that they were known to the public (and to subsequent theatre history) by their stage names. *See* MOLIÈRE; SHAKESPEARE, WILLIAM.

A company of Italian players is known to have visited England as early as 1546, and by the end of the century the appearance of Italian troupes was fairly common. Queen Elizabeth witnessed a performance in 1602. Traveling players brought the *commedia dell'arte* to France in the mid-sixteenth century; the rollicking good humor and liveliness of the *commedia all'italiana* was so well received, both in Paris and in the provinces, that France became its second home. An Italian company established in Paris in 1716 was so heartily embraced by French playwrights and actors that it eventually lost its Italian element altogether, becoming the Opéra Comique in 1763. The Italians also brought the *commedia dell'arte* to Spain in the mid-sixteenth century, and in the second half of the seventeenth century several troupes traveled to the German principalities and to Poland and Russia.

The gaiety, the swift pace, the wit, and the antics of the *commedia dell'arte* were infectious not only with audiences but also with playwrights. Everywhere the *commedia* appeared it left its mark on the native drama. Shakespeare borrowed *commedia* characters, pranks, and settings for his comedies and delighted in using Italian plot devices: fantasy, masquerade, mistaken identity, and young people who turn out to be long-lost sister and brother were all devices used in the original *commedias.* The works of Ben Jonson, George Chapman, and other English playwrights also bear the unmistakable stamp of this particular form. *See* CHAPMAN, GEORGE; JONSON, BEN.

In France Molière's long association in a theatre with an Italian troupe was reflected in his dramatic characters and techniques. Ultimately the *commedia dell'arte* of Italy gave stimulus and direction to the embryonic *comedia nueva* of Spain, while it also spurred the development of indigenous theatre in Eastern Europe. *See* COMEDIA.

The *commedia dell'arte* gradually lost its original impetus, and its stock characters and situations grew away from their sources in the actual lives of the people to whom they had once appealed. It was the Venetian playwright Goldoni who progressively revitalized the content of the *commedia dell'arte* while stripping it of its outmoded means of formal expression. He did so by creating realistic comedy from the idiosyncrasies of humanity that the *commedia dell'arte* had so acutely perceived but had rendered in nonrealistic fashion on the stage. Finally, in the twentieth century, the slapstick comedy of the early American cinema and the European puppet theatre both attest to the vitality of the *commedia dell'arte* as a viable dramatic form. *See* GOLDONI, CARLO.

CONFIDANT. Secondary character in a play whose main function is to provide a leading character with a friend to whom he can entrust confidences. The usual purpose, of course, is dramatic exposition. *See* DRAMATIC EXPOSITION.

William Congreve
(1670 – 1729)

William Congreve, English comic dramatist of the Restoration period, was born in Bardsey, a Yorkshire town near Leeds, on January 24, 1670. He was the son of Lieutenant William Congreve, a descendant of Staffordshire gentry, and his wife, the former Mary Browning. After four years spent in London and the Low Countries, Congreve went to Ireland, where he attended school in Kilkenny from 1682 to 1685. He then studied at Trinity Col-

lege, Dublin, from 1685 to 1688, there becoming a close friend of Jonathan Swift, his elder by two years.

During the conflict between James II and William of Orange, Trinity College was closed; Congreve moved to Staffordshire and then, in 1690, to London to study law at the Middle Temple. The literary life of the time excited him, and he soon began to take an active part in it, publishing, in 1692, *Incognita, or Love and Duty Reconciled,* a short novel he had written while at Trinity College. Although there was little merit in this effort, the verses he had begun to write attracted the attention of John Dryden, and the two became close friends. *See* DRYDEN, JOHN.

The same year, his twenty-second, Congreve completed his first play, *The Old Bachelor,* which was successfully produced in March, 1693. One of the actresses in this production was Anne Bracegirdle, with whom Congreve fell deeply in love. Although they never married, they remained close friends for the rest of their lives. She played leading roles in most of his plays, some, if not all, of which were written especially for her.

Congreve's next play, *The Double Dealer* (1693), although less successful than *The Old Bachelor,* was well received. His two succeeding plays, *Love for Love* (1695) and *The Mourning Bride* (1697), his only tragedy, were also popular. In 1698 Jeremy Collier published his famous Puritan attack on the theatre, entitled *Short View of the Immorality and Profaneness of the English Stage;* this provoked Congreve to defend the theatre in a retort that, unfortunately, lacked his usual brilliance and added nothing to his reputation. In 1700, when the last and finest of his plays, *The Way of the World,* was coolly received, Congreve wrote no more plays. His only other dramatic compositions were a masque and the libretto for an opera. In 1705 he briefly joined Sir John Vanbrugh in the management of the Queen's Theatre in the Haymarket, but he does not appear to have been very active. *See* VANBRUGH, JOHN.

Apart from a few occasional verses and poetical translations, Congreve's last twenty years yielded little. He lived on royal sinecures and property he had acquired. Eventually his health and eyesight began to fail, and he suffered increasingly from gout. When Voltaire visited him toward the end of his life, he was repelled by the irascibility of the ailing wit. On January 19, 1729, Congreve

William Congreve; painting by Sir Godfrey Kneller. [National Portrait Gallery, Washington]

(Opposite) John Gielgud, Cyril Ritchard, and George Hayes in *Love for Love.* New York, Royale Theatre, 1947. [Photograph by Vandamm. Theatre Collection, The New York Public Library at Lincoln Center, Astor, Lenox and Tilden Foundations]

died in London of injuries sustained in a coach accident.

WORK

Congreve surpassed his predecessor George Etherege and all his own contemporaries to become the preeminent writer of the English Restoration's comedy of manners. Dryden considered him Shakespeare's equal, saying: "Heaven, that but once was prodigal before/To Shakespeare gave as much; she could not give him more." This is perhaps praise that would not be endorsed by all critics, but the brilliance of Congreve's wit, which Macaulay likened to a "sort of jewelry," and his exquisite prose phrasings have

Pamela Brown as Angelica in *Love for Love*. New York, Royale Theatre, 1947. [Photograph by Vandamm. Theatre Collection, The New York Public Library at Lincoln Center]

been universally admired. *See* ETHEREGE, GEORGE.

Congreve's plays reflect the libertine world of Restoration aristocracy, which had discarded puritanical commandments for worldly pleasures: amorous intrigues, fashionable dress, and stylish manners. Into this atmosphere of sensuality and indolence Congreve infused his sparkling dialogue, delicate style, and brilliant wit.

Although influenced by Etherege, Congreve's plays are concerned less with plot and more with dialogue and style. When serious emotion intrudes upon wit or when realistic characters or events encroach upon the artifices of his sumptuous world, Congreve falters; his genius was not to mirror reality but to present a polished and refined version of it.

Although the plot of *The Old Bachelor* (1693) centers on the surly bachelor Heartwell, whom Silvia, Vainlove's discarded mistress, nearly entraps, its chief delight lies in the romantic banter between Vainlove and his sweetheart Araminta. The villainy of Maskwell and Lady Touchwood casts *The Double Dealer* (1693) in a darker tone, but again it is the fiery dialogue, not the plot, that interests the audience; as Mellefont and Cynthia stalk one another to certain marriage, it is their crackling verbal fancies that raise the comedy to its particular excellence. Congreve approached the full mastery of comic dialogue in *Love for Love* (1695), whose plot consists of Valentine's pursuit of the sharp-tongued Angelica while he is also attempting to prevent his father from disinheriting him. In *The Way of the World* (1700), widely considered the finest comedy of manners ever written, Congreve is at his best. A complicated and confusing plot serves mainly as a prop for the sprightly badinage of the lovers Millamant and Mirabell. The "proviso," or "condition," scene, in which Millamant agrees to "dwindle into a wife," is one of the most famous in English comedy. *The Mourning Bride* (1697), Congreve's only tragedy, although popular on the stage in its own time and in the greater part of the eighteenth century, is hardly remembered now save for its opening line, "Music has charms to sooth a savage breast," and for the heroine's admission that "Heaven has no rage like love to hatred turned, nor hell a fury like a woman scorned." Clearly Congreve was no great writer of tragedy; only in the sheer brilliance of his wit and comic style does he stand as a true master.

The Old Bachelor (1693). Comedy in which Heartwell, a confirmed bachelor, falls in love with the prostitute Silvia. Unaware of her profession, he "marries" her but is saved when it turns out that the service was performed by his friend Bellmour disguised as a minister. Around this central plot, Congreve presents a varied picture of current London society peopled with elegant, witty, and amoral characters: the genial Bellmour, who pursues pleasure and any opportunity for an elaborate jest; the country squire, Sir Joseph Wittol, whose gullibility leaves him an easy prey for urban pranksters; Captain Bluffe, whose boasts of great military exploits are belied by his cowardice; the elderly banker Fondlewife, who tries in vain to avoid being cuckolded by his young wife; and Vainlove, whose passion for his beloved Araminta cools when he is led to believe that, contrary to the code of society, she is becoming too ardent in her attentions to him, and who gladly marries her when this proves to be false.

The Double Dealer (1693). Lady Touchwood is trying to destroy her husband's nephew Mellefont because he has resisted her amorous advances. To accomplish this she forms an alliance with the evil Jack Maskwell, to whom she gives herself. Maskwell tells Lord and Lady Plyant that Mellefont's attentions to their stepdaughter Cynthia are a ruse to seduce Lady Plyant. Meanwhile, he tricks Mellefont into hiding in Lady Touchwood's bedchamber, where he is conveniently discovered by the outraged Lord Touchwood, who then agrees to make Maskwell his heir and help him gain Cynthia's hand. Discovering that Maskwell has betrayed her, Lady Touchwood plans to take Cynthia's place in an abduction of the girl that has been planned by Maskwell and the unsuspecting Mellefont. However, Lord Touchwood discovers her plan and overhears a quarrel between Lady Touchwood and Maskwell in which their villainy is revealed. At last, Mellefont and Cynthia are united.

Of particular interest is the character of Jack Maskwell, a classic Machiavellian who disguises his villainy by pretending to be a plain dealer and by telling partial truths (V, iv):

No mask like open truth to cover lies,
As to go naked is the best disguise.

Love for Love (1695). Valentine Legend has squandered his money and is in danger of being disinherited for his profligate ways by his father, Sir Sampson Legend. In desperation, the young man agrees to sign a preliminary bond relinquishing his inheritance to his sailor brother Ben in return for an immediate settlement of £4,000. Since his father will not help him, Valentine pretends insanity each time the lawyer, Buckram, brings him the final papers to sign. Meanwhile, these machinations have upset Valentine's beloved, Angelica, niece of the old fool Foresight. She approaches Sir Sampson with a plan whereby she and Sir Sampson will pretend to marry in order to bring Valentine to his senses. Sir Sampson counters this with a proposal that they should in fact marry and produce an heir in order to disinherit his son. Angelica uses this proposal to win a declaration of love from Valentine and then informs Sir Sampson that she always intended to marry his son. The old man relents, and the two lovers are united.

The Mourning Bride (1697). Tragedy concerning Almeria, daughter of King Manuel of Granada, who had been captured by her father's enemy, King Anselmo of Valencia. Anselmo had been kind to her and intended her to marry his son Alphonso, thus ending the strife between the two kingdoms. Before the wedding could take place, however, King Manuel attacked and captured Anselmo. Alphonso and Almeria, much in love, fled aboard a ship and were secretly married just before they were shipwrecked off the shore of Africa. Each had been saved separately and believed the other lost.

The play opens almost a year after Almeria, mourning the loss of her husband, has been returned to her father's court. King Manuel, returning in triumph from fighting off invading Moors, orders Almeria to put off her gloomy clothes and manner and marry Garcia, a young nobleman. Among the Moorish captives are Zara, their Queen, and Osmyn, to whom the Queen is attracted but does not know to be Alphonso. He and Almeria are briefly and secretly reunited. When Alphonso is cool toward Zara, she has Manuel, who is infatuated with her, imprison him. Uprisings against Manuel in Valencia and rumors that Alphonso has returned throw Manuel's court into disorder. Osmyn is implicated, and his death is ordered, but various twists of events bring about his escape, the gory death of Manuel, and Zara's suicide. Manuel's forces are defeated by Alphonso and his countrymen, and Alphonso is at last reunited with his bride.

The Way of the World (1700). Comedy of manners interesting chiefly for its brilliant and witty dialogue. The plot, one of the most difficult to follow of all the comedies of the time, develops around Millamant, a coquette whose wit is matched by none of her numerous beaux except Mirabell, a consummate gallant. The two wish to marry but are denied permission by Millamant's aunt, Lady Wishfort, who detests Mirabell because he once falsely pretended love to her. Mirabell therefore contrives a scheme in which his servant Waitwell is to impersonate a rich suitor for Lady Wishfort's hand. Calculating that she will be duped into signing a marriage con-

Jessica Tandy (left) as Lady Wishfort and Nancy Wickwire as Mistress Marwood in *The Way of the World*, Minneapolis, 1965. [The Guthrie Theater Company

5. *The Way of the World*. Comedy, 5 acts. Published 1700. Produced Lincoln's Inn Fields Theatre, early March, 1700.

6. *The Judgment of Paris*. Masque. Published 1701. Produced Dorset Garden Theatre, March, 1701.

7. *Semele*. Opera, 3 acts. Published 1710.

EDITIONS

Collections.
Complete Works of William Congreve, ed. by M. Summers, 4 vols., New York, 1923; *William Congreve: Complete Plays*, ed. by A. C. Ewald, New York, 1956; *Comedies*, ed. by B. Dobrée, London, 1959; *Complete Plays of William Congreve*, ed. by H. Davis, Chicago, 1967.

Individual Plays.
Love for Love. Published in *The Development of English Drama*, ed. by G. E. Bentley, New York, 1950.

The Way of the World. Published in *Introduction to Drama*, ed. by R. C. Roby and B. Ulanov, New York, 1962.

CRITICISM

J. C. Hodges, *William Congreve: The Man*, New York, 1944; E. I. Avery, *Congreve's Plays on the Eighteenth Century Stage*, New York, 1951; N. Holland, *The First Modern Comedies: The Significance of Etherege, Wycherley and Congreve*, Cambridge, Mass., 1959; J. Loftis, *Comedy and Society from Congreve to Fielding*, Stanford, Calif., 1959; H. T. E. Perry, *The Comic Spirit in the Comedy of Etherege, Wycherley, Congreve, Vanbrugh, and Farquhar*, reprint, New York, 1962; D. C. Taylor, *William Congreve*, reprint, New York, 1963; B. Dobrée, *Congreve*, New York, 1964; J. C. Hodges, ed., *William Congreve: Letters and Documents*, New York, 1964; D. Schmid, *William Congreve*, reprint, New York, 1965; K. M. Lynch, *Congreve's Gallery*, New York, 1966; W. H. Van Voris, *Cultivated Stance: The Designs of Congreve's Plays*, Chester Springs, Pa., 1966.

CONNELLY, Marc (b. McKeesport, Pa., December 13, 1890). American director, producer, and playwright who won the Pulitzer Prize for his charming fantasy *The Green Pastures* (1930), a Negro folk conception of God, heaven, and the sinfulness of the world adapted from a short story by Roark Bradford. Connelly's collaboration with George S. Kaufman resulted in a series of successful comedies, among them *Dulcy* (1921), about a brainless but well-meaning young lady; *To the Ladies* (1922), a study of illusions; *Merton of the Movies* (1922), a satire on Hollywood; and *Beggar on Horseback* (1924), a dream play. See KAUFMAN, GEORGE S.

The Green Pastures (1930). All-black fable play based on the stories of the Old Testament as told by a rural Negro preacher to his students in a Louisiana church. The scene shifts to heaven, where the Lord, a kind-hearted Negro patriarch, is enjoying a fish fry with His angels. Having just created earth and man, God mingles among His creatures and becomes angered by their sins. He sends the unrepentant Cain wandering, in the hope that he will find a girl and settle down to raising a family. Generations later the Lord drops in on earth and finds sin still rampant: a descendant of Cain has committed murder over his flashy girl friend Zeba, and what seems to be a prayer meeting is in

tract with Waitwell, Mirabell plans to expose the impostor at that time and through this apparent rescue to win both her gratitude and her consent to wed Millamant. The scheme is put into action, and after a flurry of events, accusations, misunderstandings, and artifices, Lady Wishfort yields her consent for Mirabell to marry Millamant.

PLAYS

All were first performed in London.

1. *The Old Bachelor*. Comedy, 5 acts. Published 1693. Produced Drury Lane Theatre, March, 1693.

2. *The Double Dealer*. Comedy, 5 acts. Published 1694. Produced Drury Lane Theatre, October, 1693.

3. *Love for Love*. Comedy, 5 acts. Published 1695. Produced Lincoln's Inn Fields Theatre, Apr. 30, 1695.

4. *The Mourning Bride*. Tragedy, 5 acts. Published 1697. Produced Lincoln's Inn Fields Theatre, Feb. 20, 1697.

Marc Connelly. [Theatre Collection, The New York Public Library at Lincoln Center, Astor, Lenox and Tilden Foundations]

fact a group of kneeling dice players. In anger the Lord sends down the Deluge, sparing only Noah and his family. But wickedness continues to prevail, and God promises Abraham's descendants, the only righteous people left, to have Moses lead them out of Egyptian bondage. Ages hence, when corruption has spread among the chosen people, the Lord renounces man. In the end, however, the belief of one man, Hezdra, in a compassionate God, and the suffering of Jesus for all men move the Lord to become a God of love and mercy. Produced New York, Mansfield Theatre, February 26, 1930.

CONRAD, Robert Taylor (1810–1858). American poet, journalist, and dramatist whose only extant play is the romantic verse tragedy *Jack Cade* (1835), which deals with the English rebellion of 1450.

CONTAMINATION. Term that originally referred to the practice of mixing two plots from Greek drama to produce a single play, as in Plautus. It was extended to include the use of multiple plots in one play, as in Shakespeare's *Merchant of Venice*.

COOLUS, Romain, pseudonym of Max-René Weil (1868–1952). French dramatist whose ironical characterizations revealed his empathy with free and unconventional attitudes toward love. His plays include *The Brésile Household* (*Le ménage Brésile,* 1893), a one-acter; *Raphaël* (1896); *The Sick Child* (*L'enfant malade,* 1897); *Lysiane* (1897); *Coeurblette* (1899); *Le marquis de Carabas* (1900); *The Lovers of Sazy* (*Les amants de Sazy,* 1901); *Spontini Street* (*Rue Spontini,* 1901); *Lucette* (1903); *Yvonne Dines in Town* (*Yvonne dîne en ville,* 1903); *Les pieds qui remuent* (1903); *The Kangaroo* (*Le kanguroo,* 1903); *Antoinette Sabrier* (1903); *Little Pest* (*Petite peste,* 1905); *The Cherished Child* (*L'enfant chérie,* 1906); *Heart to Heart* (*Coeur à coeur,* 1907); *Four Times Seven Equals Twenty-eight* (*Quatre fois sept=vingt-huit,* 1909); *Mirette a ses raisons* (1909); *Effets d'optique,* 1909); *The Risk* (*Le risque,* 1909); *A Woman Passed By* (*Une femme passa,* 1910); *Les bleus de l'amour* (1910); *Les jeux de l'amour et de la confidence* (1910); *The Coast of Love* (*La côte d'amour,* 1912); *The Red Roses* (*Les roses rouges,* 1913); *Les jeux de l'amour et de la conférence* (1913); *L'amour buissonnier* (1914); *The Eternal Masculine* (*L'éternel masculin,* 1920); *Born on a Sunday* (*Né un dimanche,* 1924); *La fifille à sa mémère* (1925); *Les vacances de Pâques* (1926); *La guêpe* (1928); *Mad* (1931); and *Boby-Chéri* (1932).

Coolus also collaborated with Maurice Hennequin on such plays as *Love, When You Hold Us* (*Amour quand tu nous tiens,* 1919), *The Alarm Bell* (*La sonnette d'alarme,* 1922), *The Ostrich* (*L'autruche,* 1923), and *Jim* (1924), and with André Rivoire on *The Kisses of Panurge* (*Les baisers de Panurge,* 1925) and *Pardon, Madame* (1930).

COPEAU, Jacques (1879–1949). French dramatist and director. One of the most important modern directors, Copeau created a new style in staging, emphasizing an austere simplicity coupled with a poetic, rather than a realistic, interpretation of life. Along with André Gide and Jean Schlumberger, he founded the *Nouvelle Revue Française* in 1909 and was its chief editor from 1912 to 1914. In 1913 he founded the experimental Théâtre du Vieux-Colombier, which he directed until 1924. Without utilizing the "star" system, he succeeded in welding together a fine ensemble counting among its members such important figures as Charles Dullin and Louis Jouvet. In 1921 he established the École du Vieux-Colombier in Burgundy, where he trained actors in all the theatre arts. The Compagnie des Quinze, an experimental theatre company founded in 1930, was an outgrowth of this school to which Copeau devoted all his energies after 1924. In 1936 he became a producer at the Comédie-Française and in 1940 was named its president. His plays include an adaptation of Dostoyevsky's *The Brothers*

Jacques Copeau.
[French Cultural
Services]

Karamazov (*Les frères Karamazov*, 1911), *The Birthplace* (*La maison natale*, 1923), and several translations of Shakespeare's plays.

COPPÉE, François (b. Paris, January 26, 1842; d. there, May 23, 1908). French poet, novelist, and dramatist. Although Coppée was technically a member of the Parnassian school headed by Leconte de Lisle, his sentimental concern with the life of the poor soon established an individual and popular ap-

François Coppée.
[Walter Hampden
Memorial Library
at The Players,
New York]

proach that won him the title *poète des humbles*. His first collection of poems, *The Reliquary* (*Le réliquaire*), appeared in 1865, and four years later he scored an enormous success with his first and best-known play, *The Passerby* (*Le passant*), a delightful if somewhat facile and superficial verse idyll. It was followed by a series of now-forgotten plays perhaps the most interesting of which is *Do What's Necessary* (*Fais ce que dois*, 1871). Inspired by France's defeat in the Franco-Prussian War, it is an intensely patriotic and nationalistic statement that prefigures themes in his later work as well as his anti-Dreyfusard stand in the notorious Dreyfus case. *The Hundred Years' War* (*La Guerre de Cent Ans*, 1878), written in collaboration with Armond d'Artois, was the first of his later historical verse dramas of somewhat larger conception. In the same vein are *Madame de Maintenon* (1881); *Severo Torelli* (1883); *The Jacobites* (*Les Jacobites*, 1885); and *For the Crown* (*Pour la couronne*, 1895), a drama in which patriotism leads to parricide. Coppée was made a member of the Académie Française in 1884. Although he was one of the most popular poets of the time of the Third Republic, his dramatic work has failed to withstand the test of time.

The Passerby (*Le passant*, 1869). One-act romantic verse drama concerning the beautiful Silvia, who is disturbed by her inability to respond to the passions she arouses. She meets the young minstrel Zanetto, who enthusiastically recounts the joys he is able to extract from his poverty-stricken life. Silvia is determined to make him love her and to love him in turn. Zanetto confesses that he fears that love will rob him of his free life, but he nevertheless wants to stay with her. Moved by his naïveté, Silvia drives Zanetto away lest she make him suffer. He leaves, carrying with him a flower that has fallen from her hair, and Silvia weeps with joy because at last her heart has been touched by love. Produced Paris. Théâtre de l'Odéon, January 14, 1869.

Pierre Corneille
(1606 – 1684)

Pierre Corneille, French dramatist, was born in Rouen on June 6, 1606, the son of Pierre and Marthe Lepesant Corneille. He was the eldest of six children and the older brother of the playwright Thomas Corneille. Most of the men in his family were lawyers or magistrates, and Corneille was destined for a similar career. After attending a Jesuit school where he twice received prizes for his proficiency in Latin and verse composition, Corneille studied law and on June 18, 1624, was admitted to the bar. In 1629 he purchased the position of attorney general in a government department, a post he held for more than twenty years. *See* CORNEILLE, THOMAS.

Corneille's literary inclinations were revealed early and were nurtured by his surroundings. Rouen, a publishing center with its own literary and dramatic interests, was well known for its Jesuit academy, the Puy des Palinods, which encouraged poets and awarded literary prizes.

Although Corneille had followed the family tradition by becoming a lawyer, he had, according to his nephew Fontenelle, no taste for the law and no success in it. His real career started with the production of his first play, *Mélite, or The False Letters* (*Mélite, ou Les fausses lettres*), a comedy performed in Paris by the actor Mondory, probably in early February, 1630. This was an immediate success.

Between 1630 and 1636 Corneille wrote seven plays (five comedies, a tragicomedy, and a tragedy) and became sufficiently celebrated to attract the notice of Cardinal Richelieu, who invited him to become a member of a group of dramatists engaged in writing a play under the Cardinal's supervision. There were already four members—Guillaume Colletet, François de Boisrobert, Claude de L'Estoile, and Jean de Rotrou—each of whom was assigned an act and given one month to complete it. Corneille was given the third and most important act. Corneille, however, changed the Cardinal's plot, thereby causing a dispute that resulted in his resignation. However, the play, *The Comedy of the Tuileries* (*La comédie des Tuileries,* 1635), bears his name. *See* ROTROU, JEAN DE.

During this period Corneille became interested in Spanish literature and read the contemporary drama *The Youthful Adventures of the Cid* by Guillén de Castro. The Spanish play inspired Corneille to write *The Cid* (*Le Cid,* 1636/37), a tragicomedy depicting the tension between love and honor in two young lovers. A nonacademic work only partially observing classical dramatic rules, it was directed to the general public rather than the learned elite. The popularity of this new play on the stage revolutionized the French theatre, but not without provoking attacks from Corneille's rivals, led by Richelieu. The result was the famous Cid quarrel, in which Corneille's failure to adhere to classical rules was severely criticized. His opponents accused him of employing a nonclassical form, the tragicomedy, and of taking excessive liberties

Pierre Corneille.
[French Cultural Services]

with classical conventions such as the unities, an ordered succession of scenes, and the essentiality of plot and character. His verse was also criticized as irregular; Richelieu demanded that the Académie Française criticize the play's style and grammar. It is possible that Richelieu may have been embittered by Corneille's earlier clash with him or that he was jealous of the play's popularity. As Spain was at war with France, there may also have been political reasons for castigating a play that glorified Spanish chivalry. Whatever Richelieu's motive, *The Cid* received a great deal of critical censure, and Corneille, who had originally defended the play, retired submissively to Rouen, where he spent three years without writing. *See* CASTRO Y BELLVÍS, GUILLÉN DE; CID QUARREL; TRAGICOMEDY; UNITIES.

His next play, the tragedy *Horatius* (*Horace*), did not appear until 1640. Corneille apparently reacted to the Cid quarrel in writing this play, which adheres strictly to the unities of time and place and draws its subject from ancient Roman history. All Corneille's later tragedies were written according to

Two players in a Comédie-Française production of *Le Cid.* [French Cultural Services]

classical rules. The year *Horatius* was produced he married Marie de Lampérière, whose family had the same legal background as his own. The next five years were the brightest of Corneille's life. During this period he produced most of his greatest plays: *Cinna, or The Clemency of Augustus* (*Cinna, ou La clémence d'Auguste*), *Polyeuctes* (*Polyeucte*), *The Death of Pompey* (*La mort de Pompée*), *The Liar* (*Le menteur*), *Sequel to The Liar* (*La suite du menteur*), and *Rodogune, Princess of Parthia* (*Rodogune, Princesse des Parthes*). *Rodogune,* one of Corneille's favorites, was at the time extremely popular for its suspenseful dramatic action but was later regarded as one of his lesser plays. He was at this time also an active member in the social life at the Hôtel de Rambouillet, the home of Catherine de Vivonne de Rambouillet, who conducted one of the foremost literary salons of the time, one fostering the *préciosité* ridiculed by Molière in *The Affected Ladies* (1659). Corneille contributed verses to the *Guirlande de Julie,* a collection of verses published by the habitués of Mme. de Rambouillet's salon. The only shadow cast on his success was his rejection by the Académie Française, first in 1644 and then in 1646, on the ground that he was not a resident of Paris. But in 1647 he was finally admitted. *See* MOLIÈRE.

By this time Corneille's success had begun to wane. *Theodora, Virgin and Martyr* (*Théodore, vierge et martyre,* 1645), depicting the violent death of a virgin martyr, shocked his audience. *Heraclius* (*Héraclius,* 1646/47) and *Don Sancho of Aragon* (*Dom Sanche d'Aragon,* 1649), though popular then, are inferior to his other tragedies. *Nicomedes* (*Nicomède,* 1650/51) is considered the last of his great plays. His next tragedy, *Pertharites, King of the Lombards* (*Pertharite, roi des Lombards,* 1651), failed so decisively (it had only two performances) that Corneille retired to Rouen for the next seven years. There he became warden of his parish and devoted himself to a verse translation of the *Imitation of Christ* (*De imitatione Christi,* 1426) by Thomas à Kempis. In all, Corneille wrote close to 25,000 verses, translated either from liturgical Latin or from the Latin of the *Imitation.*

There seem to be two reasons for Corneille's emergence from his retirement: his enthusiasm for the theatre, which was rekindled by a performance by Molière's company in Rouen in 1658, and the determination of the finance minister Nicolas Fouquet, an enthusiastic patron of the arts, to bring Corneille back to the theatre. Fouquet proposed three subjects from which Corneille should choose one, and as a result, on January 24, 1659, *Oedipus* (*Oedipe*) delighted the audience at the Hôtel de Bourgogne. Corneille now began to work with renewed enthusiasm, writing a play a year.

Racine, a new playwright then rising to prominence, was beginning to overshadow the old master. This was bitterly resented by Corneille. The two dramatists clashed openly on the stage in 1670, when both produced tragedies on the classic love story of Titus and Berenice; Racine was clearly the victor. With the failure of Corneille's *Titus and Berenice* (*Tite et Bérénice*) it was obvious, even to his most loyal admirers, that his powers were declining. He wrote only three more plays, one, *Psyche* (*Psyché,* 1671), in collaboration with Molière and Quinault. In 1674 he retired from the theatre. *See* QUINAULT, PHILIPPE; RACINE, JEAN.

Little is known of Corneille's private life. He was a plain man with simple tastes, a good husband and father, and a devoted member of the Catholic Church. Although his plays contain brilliant poetry, his contemporaries found his conversation dull, and he was known as a shy man.

Of his six children very little is known. Pierre, the eldest son, was a cavalry officer who died before his father. By her marriage to Jacques-Adrien de Farcy, the eldest daughter, Marie, became the ancestress of

Charlotte Corday, who assassinated Marat in the wake of the French Revolution.

Corneille spent his last years in poverty. For unknown reasons his pension was suspended from 1674 until, it is thought, 1683. Only an occasional poem addressed to Louis XIV reminded the public that he was still alive. He died in Paris on October 1, 1684, and was buried there in the Church of St-Roch. No monument marked his grave until 1821.

WORK

Corneille, the first of the great French neoclassical dramatists, wrote thirty-four plays in a wide variety of genres: tragedy, tragicomedy, comedy, heroic comedy, and tragedy ballet. Unlike the plays of his great contemporary Racine, with which they are frequently compared, Corneille's plays represent a somewhat earlier approach to the drama not dissimilar to that of the English Elizabethans and the Spanish playwrights. His plays and the verse in which they are written are thus more robust and straightforward in approach and more heroic in concept. The plots are frequently more complex, in terms of incident, than most neoclassical plays, leading some critics to conclude that Corneille's achievement would have been greater had he not been forced to observe the rules, particularly the unities, of neoclassicism. His heroic approach to characterization led La Bruyère to state that Corneille depicts "people as they should be," while Racine shows them "as they are." Sartre later challenged this notion, asserting another view of reality by his insistence that the opposite was true. *See* SARTRE, JEAN-PAUL.

Corneille expounded his theories of drama in his three *Discourses on Dramatic Poetry* (*Discours,* 1660) and his *Scrutinies* (*Examens,* 1660). Tragedy, for Corneille, requires as its subject a "renowned, extraordinary, serious action" taken from history or legend. The main characters must be noble in rank (kings, princes) or of heroic stature (saints, warriors). Tragic action requires dignity, which demands "some great interest of state, some passion that is nobler and more virile than love." Consequently, love generally plays a lesser role in Corneille's drama than in that of Racine. Tragic conflict, Corneille insists, must pit "the impetuousness of passion against the laws of duty." Thus, in *Poly-*

Le Cid, Comédie-Française. [French Cultural Services]

euctes (1641/42) the hero struggles against his love for Pauline to fulfill his Christian duty, the sacrifice of all earthly affections to God. Love in Corneille's plays is frequently mutual, based on reason, and when linked to honor, is related to the ideals of medieval chivalry. When literally applied, as in some minor works, his theories prove impractical and impede the spontaneous creation that renders many of his other plays so rich and varied.

The distinction between his tragedies and comedies is not marked. Comedies for him were plays that deal with less exalted members of society or with persons of high rank who face lesser dangers. Many of his "tragedies" are actually tragicomedies with happy endings. In comedy, Corneille refined the farcical crudity of his predecessors, substituting naturalness, truthfulness, and action rooted in character.

There is a great variety of character types in Corneille's plays. He makes extensive use of "great souls"—strong personalities without a touch of mediocrity—who seek the fullest self-realization; his ideal hero is one whose stoic self-mastery is stronger than fate. The conflict, although sometimes between charac-

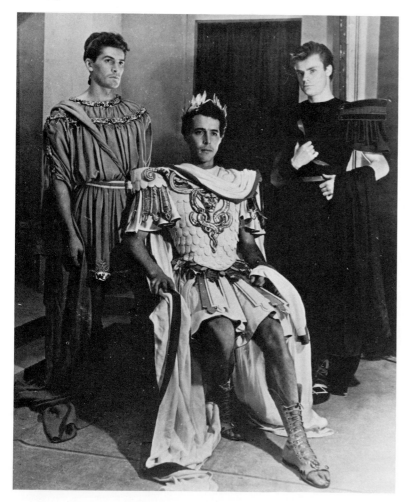

Horace. Paris, Théâtre Charles de Rochefort, 1945. [French Cultural Services]

ters, is often engendered within the hero's heart as a struggle between passion and duty.

Because in Corneille's plays "man is his own Prometheus" (Michelet), the dramatist has been criticized for his "cult of heroes" and for extolling "supermen," the representatives of "inhuman humanity" (Barère). However, his heroes, though great, have many human qualities. Their virtues are a combination of classic, Christian, and knightly ideals.

Corneille's verse, varied and flexible, covers a wide range of emotions, from Roman grandeur to tender love. He excelled in rhetorical debate and in the soliloquy, and the tragic rhythm in his plays is often punctuated by lyrical stanzas. His dramatic models were principally the Spaniards (*The Cid, The Liar*) and the Romans, especially Seneca (*Medea, Cinna*) and Lucian (*Pompey*). *See* SENECA.

Mélite (1630), his first play and virtually the first seventeenth-century French comedy, launched a series of comedies of intrigue dealing with separated and then reunited lovers. Complicated and artificial though the plots may be, Corneille sought to provoke laughter without recourse to stock grotesque characters and unrealistic dialogue. His early tragicomedy *Clitandre* (1631?) and the tragedy *Medea* (*Médée,* 1634/35) are marred by excessive pathos and insufficient humanity.

With *The Comic Illusion* (*L'illusion comique,* 1635/36) and the character of Matamore, a braggart soldier typical of Spanish comedy, Corneille foreshadowed in a comic key the heroics to come later in *The Cid* (1636/37). The production of *The Cid* marks one of the key dates in the history of French theatre. The play is outstanding for the dramatic quality and beauty of its verse, for its well-constructed action, which is interior and psychological, and for the high idealism and humanity of its characters, who are responsible for their own destiny. Revolutionary in its independence of classical rules, the play was defined by Corneille in its first edition in 1637 as a tragicomedy and as a tragedy. But because of its happy ending and its derivation from a contemporary Spanish play, it is more properly labeled a tragicomedy. The play's failure to comply with the strict rules of neoclassicism subscribed to by the Académie Française subjected it to fierce critical attacks despite its immense popularity on the stage.

In *Horatius* (1640) and *Cinna, or The Clemency of Augustus* (1640/41), Corneille tried to follow the rules rigorously. These two plays on Roman themes are simpler and more austere. Their characters, less human than those of *The Cid,* display a rigid and abstract con-

L'illusion comique, presented by the Théâtre National de Belgique at the Hôtel de Sully, Paris. [French Cultural Services]

ception of heroism. *Polyeuctes,* considered by some to be the best of Corneille's works, presents a more modern approach to tragedy in that the action results not from overpowering fate or divine influence but from the conflict of the free will of the characters. The religious orientation of the protagonist, an early Christian martyr, is complex, blending Roman, Christian, and Stoic virtues.

In a number of Corneille's works modern themes prevail over classical elements. With *The Liar* (1643), his outstanding comedy, he returned to a plot of intrigue, fusing elements of both French and Spanish comedy. Excessive artificiality weakens the tragedies *Rodogune* (1644/45) and *Heraclius* (1646/47), in which Corneille introduced romantic and melodramatic themes into the tragic genre. A similar melodramatic tone, centering in a pathetic and gentle heroine, pervades *Theodora, Virgin and Martyr* (1645), a tragedy of martyrdom that failed to repeat *Polyeuctes'* success. Corneille departed even further from classical norms in the two spectacular tragedies *Andromeda* (*Andromède,* 1650) and *The Golden Fleece* (*La toison d'or,* 1660). Both are characterized by supernatural action, frequent and erratic changes of scenery, and elaborate stage machinery.

The plays of Corneille's old age are complex and show his increasing preoccupation with political and social motives. The dialogue is intellectual, and conflict is represented on a psychological level. Thus the dramatist was drifting away from changing public taste, moving toward greater subtlety and polish. Gentleness, which Corneille eschewed in earlier decades, adds a lyrical charm to the tragedy ballet *Psyche* (1671) and tempers the heroic, uncompromising tenor of the tragedy *Surenas* (*Suréna,* 1674).

Corneille's plays were extremely popular during his lifetime, but they fared less well in the eighteenth century. One of the most damning criticisms was made by Schiller, who spoke of "poverty of invention, the meagerness and dryness in the handling of characters, the coldness of passions, the lameness and stuffiness in plot development." French critics frequently contrast Corneille with Racine in simple parallels, with references to Corneille's "heroic" approach to the psychological as opposed to Racine's human approach. In such comparisons, Racine has usually emerged the greater of the two. But this in no way diminishes Corneille's place in French drama. The best of his plays are among the finest in the French language. Moreover, no other man was as responsible for the rise of French tragedy as "le grand

Corneille." *See* SCHILLER, FRIEDRICH VON.

Mélite, or The False Letters (*Mélite, ou Les fausses lettres,* 1630). Comedy in which Éraste loves Mélite but cannot win her love. His friend Tircis loves no one and believes he is invulnerable to such passions. However, when Éraste introduces him to Mélite, he falls in love with the girl and she reciprocates his love. In revenge Éraste decides to destroy not only the love between Tircis and Mélite but also the love between Chloris, Tircis's sister, and her fiancé Philandre. He forges a letter from Mélite, saying she is in love with Philandre, and sends it to Philandre, who decides to betray Chloris with Mélite. Philandre shows the letter to Tircis in order to discourage his rival. Tircis faints at the thought of losing his love, and Mélite, believing him dead, also falls into a swoon. Éraste receives an erroneous report that both Tircis and Mélite have died, their hearts broken. Driven insane by remorse, he believes himself dead and in hell. The lovers, having recovered and learned the truth, forgive Éraste and arrange for his betrothal to Chloris, who has rejected the unfaithful Philandre.

Clitandre (1631?). Tragicomedy concerning the lovers Rosidor and Caliste. They are opposed by Dorise, who loves Rosidor; Pymante, who loves Dorise and is jealous of Rosidor; and Clitandre, who loves Caliste. Pymante tries to kill Rosidor but fails and is eventually arrested with the help of Dorise. In the end it is made clear that Rosidor and Caliste will wed, as will Clitandre and Dorise.

The Widow, or The Betrayer Betrayed (*La veuve, ou Le traître trahi,* 1631/32). Comedy in which Philiste loves the widow Clarice, who is also loved by Alcidon. Alcidon's friend Celidon, under the impression that he is assisting him to win Philiste's sister Doris, helps Alcidon abduct Clarice. When he discovers what has happened, Celidon restores Clarice to Philiste and is rewarded with the hand of Doris, whom he has secretly loved for a long time.

The Palace Corridor, or The Rival Friend (*La galerie du palais, ou L'amie rivale,* 1632). Comedy in which lovers test one another. Lysander and Célide are in love. But Lysander is loved also by Hippolyte, who in turn is loved by Dorimant. Célide decides to test Lysander's affections by pretending to love Dorimant, with the result that she loses Lysander. Eventually, however, she wins him back, and Hippolyte accepts Dorimant.

The Maidservant (*La suivante,* 1633). Comedy in which Théante is tired of Amarante (the *suivante*) and loves her mistress Daphnis. He brings Florame, a friend, to meet Amarante, but Florame falls in love with Daphnis, and she with him. Amarante's attempts to win Florame for herself lead to fantastic complications, as do those of Théante, who eventually abandons his attempts to win Daphnis. When Amarante's machinations are revealed, she confesses and there are no further impediments to the marriage of Daphnis and Florame.

Place Royale, or The Extravagant Lover (*La place royale, ou L'amoureux extravagant,* 1633/34). Comedy in which Angélique is loved by Doraste, Cléandre, and Alidor, the extravagant lover. She loves Alidor, but he prefers his freedom and so agrees to help Cléandre win her. They try to abduct her but capture Doraste's sister by mistake. She and Cléandre fall in love. Although Alidor finally offers to marry Angélique, she refuses and vows to enter a convent.

Medea (*Médée,* 1634/35). Drama based on Seneca's *Medea.* The role of Jason is here enlarged so that he is almost as important as Medea. Although still an ingrate and a philanderer, Jason is devoted to his children. In this version of the story, Creon's daughter Creüsa appears onstage, where she, Creon, and Jason die. Medea, however, murders her children offstage.

The Comedy of the Tuileries (*La comédie des Tuileries,* 1635). Comedy written with Boisrobert, Colletet, L'Estoile, and Rotrou. Aglante and Cléonice are betrothed but have never met. Following an accidental meeting they fall in love. In the belief that each is destined to marry another, they both attempt to commit suicide. Finally, however, the truth is revealed by their relatives and they are married.

The Comic Illusion (*L'illusion comique,* 1635/36). Comedy in which Clindor, having years before left his home because of his father's abusive treatment, is now the servant of Matamore, a braggart soldier. Clindor's father, remorseful for having mistreated his son and ignorant of his whereabouts, consults a magician in the hope of obtaining knowledge of the young man's fate. The magician enables the father to envision his son's present existence. He sees Clindor as the agent of Matamore, sent to woo Isabelle in his master's name. Clindor falls in love with the girl himself and wishes to marry her, but he is thwarted by her servant Lise and Isabelle's father, who has him imprisoned. Lise repents and frees Clindor with the help of the jailer, who is in love with her. Later, with the help of the magician, Clindor's father has another vision in which he sees both his son and Isabelle lose their lives. He is overcome with despair until the vision reveals that Clindor and Isabelle, as well as Lise and the jailer, have run away with a company of actors and that the death he witnessed was merely a scene in

Cinna. [French Cultural Services]

a tragedy. The play, having emphasized the theatrical illusion of reality indicated in the title, ends with a defense of the acting profession.

The Cid (*Le Cid,* 1636/37). Romantic tragicomedy based on Guillén de Castro's *The Youthful Adventures of the Cid*. The Infanta, daughter of the King of Spain, loves Rodrigue but, because he is of lower rank, cannot marry him. She has therefore encouraged an attachment between him and Chimène. But a complication arises when the King names Rodrigue's father Don Diègue tutor to the Prince. The Count de Gormas, Chimène's father, feels the position should be his. In a bitter quarrel, Gormas unjustly accuses Don Diègue of gaining the King's favor through flattery and deceit, and Gormas strikes him. Diègue calls upon Rodrigue to uphold his family's honor. Rodrigue, torn between love and duty, eventually challenges the count to a duel and kills him.

Chimène still loves Rodrigue but also hates him for her father's murder. She seeks justice from the King, but before he makes a decision he is interrupted by news that the Moors have attacked the city. The Spanish Army, led by Rodrigue, routs the Moors, and as a reward the King gives him the title of Cid, a Moorish word meaning "lord." But Chimène, still seeking redress, insists on her right to have a champion to defend her family's honor in single combat. Don Sancho, hoping to win Chimène for himself, offers his services and challenges Rodrigue, and the King decrees that Chimène must marry the victor. Rodrigue offers to let himself be killed, but Chimène begs him to defend himself and he defeats Sancho.

After the duel, Rodrigue sends his sword to

Chimène with Sancho. When Chimène sees Rodrigue's sword in Sancho's hand, she believes Rodrigue to be dead. She therefore hurries to the King and begs him not to force her to marry her lover's slayer. The King explains Rodrigue's victory over Sancho and insists that she shall marry Rodrigue. But Chimène protests, saying she cannot bury her father and marry his murderer on the same day. The King, understanding her plea, decrees that Rodrigue shall continue to fight the Moors for a year, and at the end of that time Rodrigue and Chimène shall be married.

Horatius (*Horace*, 1640). Tragedy in which Alba Longa and Rome, previously friendly, are at war. Sabina, wife of Horatius, is divided in her loyalties between the city of her birth, Alba Longa, where her brothers live, and Rome, the city of her husband. Curiatius, one of her three brothers, is betrothed to her sister-in-law Camilla, who is likewise torn between the two cities. The issues at stake are to be decided by armed combat between three heroes from each side. Curiatius and his brothers are to represent Alba Longa; Horatius and his brothers, Rome. Camilla and Sabina beg them both to avoid the battle for the sake of their homes and families; Horatius and Curiatius, however, defend the cause of honor and patriotism. Rome emerges victorious from the fight after Curiatius's brothers, the Curiatii, kill Horatius's brothers and he in turn slays the Curiatii. Horatius then returns in triumph to Camilla. She calls him a murderer, and a dispute follows in which Horatius accuses her of disloyalty and kills her with Curiatius's sword. Brought before King Tullius, Horatius explains his conduct as an act of excessive patriotism and asks to be put to death. Sabina offers to die in his place. Tullius says he cannot judge Horatius and will pardon him, leaving final judgment to the gods.

Cinna, or The Clemency of Augustus (*Cinna, ou La clémence d'Auguste*, 1640/41). Drama about Cinna and Emilia, daughter of the emperor Augustus's tutor, who are in love. Emilia refuses to marry Cinna unless he agrees to slay the Emperor, whom she blames for the death of her father, which took place during Augustus's rise to power. Cinna and his friend Maximus therefore become leaders of a conspiracy against the Emperor, whom they denounce as a bloodthirsty tyrant. In the second act, however, the Emperor is revealed as a temperate, conscientious ruler whose closest advisers are Maximus, to whom he offers the governorship of Sicily, and Cinna, to whom he offers Emilia as a wife. His resolve shaken, Cinna appeals to Emilia, but she still insists that he avenge her father.

Meanwhile, Maximus, who is also in love with Emilia, is appalled to discover that she and Cinna are in love and decides to betray the conspirators and flee with Emilia. His plan fails when she refuses to accompany him and goes instead to the Emperor, asking to be allowed to die with Cinna. Maximus, plagued by feelings of guilt for having betrayed both his friend Cinna and his master Augustus, then enters and confesses his duplicity. Augustus announces that he forgives the conspirators, awards the Sicilian governorship to Maximus, and promises that Cinna and Emilia shall be married the next day.

Polyeuctes (*Polyeucte*, 1641/42). Tragedy concerning Polyeuctes, an Armenian nobleman who is married to Paulina, daughter of Felix, the Roman Governor of Armenia. Unknown to his wife and her father, Polyeuctes has recently been converted to Christianity. With his friend Nearchus, he plans to enter the temple, interrupt a service, and destroy the pagan images. Meanwhile, Felix is apprehensive because of the reappearance of Paulina's former suitor Severus. Felix had previously not allowed him to court Paulina, for he had neither money nor position, but now he is a famous general and in great favor with the Emperor. Paulina, on hearing that Polyeuctes has defiled the temple and that Nearchus has been put to death, pleads with her father for her husband's life. Felix consents to spare him only if he will renounce Christianity, fearing that Severus may otherwise use the incident to ruin him. Polyeuctes refuses to renounce his new faith, and Severus, impressed with his rival's steadfastness, also pleads for Polyeuctes' life, saying that the Emperor, though hating Christians, also admires them. Felix, believing that Severus is trying to trick him, has Polyeuctes executed. After witnessing the execution, Paulina tells her father that she too has become a Christian, whereupon Felix himself is converted. Severus, declaring the conversion to be a miracle, swears to return to Rome and intercede with the Emperor for the Christians.

The Death of Pompey (*La mort de Pompée*, 1642/43). Tragedy in which Pompey, a Roman general who has helped Ptolemy retain the throne of Egypt, is later defeated by Julius Caesar and the Roman Army. Ptolemy has Pompey slain and presents Caesar with his head. Caesar is angered by Ptolemy's treachery, though its victim was his own enemy, and he spares Ptolemy solely out of regard for his sister Cleopatra. Ptolemy and his advisers now plan to murder Caesar, but Cornelia, Pompey's widow, learns of the plot and warns Caesar. Although she blames Caesar for Pompey's death and desires Caesar's death in retaliation, she tells him she wants to bring about his death herself. The plot-ters are slain, and Caesar crowns Cleopatra Queen of Egypt.

The Liar (*Le menteur*, 1643). Comedy based on Ruiz de Alarcón's *The Truth Suspected*. Dorante, a liar, woos women with tales of his military exploits and friends with tales of his amatory conquests. He almost loses both his closest friend and his ladylove before the truth is revealed. *See* RUIZ DE ALARCÓN, JUAN.

Sequel to The Liar (*La suite du menteur*, 1644/45). Comedy, based on Lope de Vega's *To Love Without Knowing Whom*, in which Dorante is in trouble again, having been wrongly arrested for killing a man in a duel. He protests his innocence, saying that he is reformed and no longer lies. In the course of the play, however, he does lie to protect a lady's honor and to save his friend Cléandre, who actually fought the duel. *See* VEGA CARPIO, LOPE DE.

Rodogune, Princess of Parthia (*Rodogune, Princesse des Parthes*, 1644/45). Tragedy in which Demetrius Nicator, King of Syria, has been taken prisoner by the Parthians and reported dead. His wife Cleopatra marries his brother, who later dies. She then learns that Demetrius is still alive. He will not forgive her for having remarried, and he plans to wed Rodogune, the young sister of the Parthian King. But when he brings Rodogune to Syria, the jealous Cleopatra attacks

the cortege. Demetrius Nicator is killed and Rodogune enslaved.

As the play opens, Cleopatra is forced by the Parthian Army to sign a treaty arranging for Rodogune's marriage to the elder of her twin sons Antiochus and Seleucus. With him Rodogune will ascend the Syrian throne. Only Cleopatra knows which of her sons was born first. She declares that she will name as heir the son who will kill Rodogune, but both refuse. Instead they both propose to Rodogune, who answers that she will marry the one who will slay his mother. Cleopatra feigns a reconciliation with Rodogune and agrees that she shall marry Antiochus. She then secretly slays Seleucus and prepares poison for Rodogune and Antiochus. Before the wedding news arrives of Seleucus's death, and suspicion is cast on the two women. Not wanting to find out which of them has murdered his brother, Antiochus prepares to kill himself but is thwarted in the attempt. He then announces that he will marry Rodogune anyway, whereupon Cleopatra, frustrated after all, poisons herself.

Théodora, Virgin and Martyr (*Théodore, vierge et martyre*, 1645). Tragedy in which Placidius, son of Valens, Roman Governor of Antioch, is engaged to his stepsister but is in love with Theodora. His stepmother Marcella, discovering that Theodora is a Christian who has taken a vow of chastity, sends her to a

A Comédie-Française production of *La mort de Pompée*. [French Cultural Services]

Le menteur, produced by the Comédie-Française on the occasion of the 350th anniversary of Corneille's birth. [French Cultural Services]

brothel. She is rescued by Didymas, another Christian, but he is captured by Marcella, and Theodora surrenders in order to share his martyrdom. They are both murdered by Marcella, who then commits suicide, after which Placidius stabs himself.

Heraclius (*Héraclius,* 1646/47). Tragedy beginning with the seizure of the Eastern Roman throne in Byzantium by Phocas and his execution of the emperor Mauricius and his sons. Leontina, a noblewoman, saves Mauricius's infant son Heraclius by exchanging him for her own child. Phocas gives his son Martian into her keeping, and she again exchanges children so that Phocas raises Heraclius as his own son "Martian" and Leontina raises Martian as her son "Leontinus." "Martian" knows his identity, but "Leontinus" is led to believe he is Heraclius. Phocas wishes "Martian" to marry Pulcheria, daughter of the late emperor Mauricius. Since this would be incest, "Martian" reveals that he is Heraclius, Pulcheria's brother. Meanwhile, "Leontinus" also claims to be Heraclius. In anger and confusion, Phocas nearly murders them both. When the boys' true identities are made

known, Heraclius ascends the throne.

Andromeda (*Andromède,* 1650). Tragedy based on the legend of Andromeda and Perseus told by Ovid. The important difference in Corneille's play is that after Andromeda is rescued from the sea monster, Perseus gives her the freedom to choose her own husband, and she chooses him in preference to the coward Phineus, to whom she was betrothed.

Don Sancho of Aragon (*Dom Sanche d'Aragon,* 1649). Heroic comedy, based on Mira de Amescua's *The Confused Palace.* Like *Heraclius,* this play centers on hidden identity. Carlos, a young soldier whose valor has made him the hero of Castile, believes he is the son of a humble fisherman; but in fact he is Don Sancho, rightful heir to the throne of Aragon. He is in love with and is loved by both Isabella, Queen of Castile, and Elvira, Princess of Aragon, his sister. When his true identity is revealed, thus explaining his love for Elvira as brotherly, the path becomes clear for his marriage to Isabella. *See* MIRA DE AMESCUA, ANTONIO.

Nicomedes (*Nicomède,* 1650/51). Tragedy about Nicomedes, the son of Prusias, King of Bithynia, a great soldier and popular hero. Arsinoë, the King's second wife, hates her stepson and wants her own son Attalus to succeed to the throne. To achieve this, Arsinoë plots with Flaminius, the Roman envoy, to discredit Nicomedes with his father and to wed Attalus to Laodice, Queen of Armenia, to whom Nicomedes is betrothed. Arsinoë convinces Prusias that Nicomedes is plotting against her. Confronted with this accusation by his father, Nicomedes so angers him that Prusias declares that Attalus shall be his heir and sends Nicomedes to Rome as a prisoner. Hearing this, the people revolt and, led by Laodice, demand to have Nicomedes as their king. Prusias attempts to have him smuggled aboard a Roman galley, but a masked friend slays the guards, allowing Nicomedes to escape and restore order. Nicomedes then makes peace with Prusias and Arsinoë and assures Attalus that he will conquer a kingdom for him to rule. Attalus then reveals that it was he who helped Nicomedes to escape, thus proving himself worthy of being a king.

Pertharites, King of the Lombards (*Pertharite, roi des Lombards,* 1651). Tragedy in which Grimoald has defeated and supposedly killed Pertharites, King of the Lombards, and now wants to marry his wife Rodelinde. When Pertharites returns, he is willing to yield the throne to Grimoald if allowed to keep his wife. Grimoald is impressed by Pertharites' magnanimity and gives him back both kingdom and wife.

Oedipus (*Oedipe,* 1659). Tragedy based on

the *Oedipus the King* of Sophocles, in which Oedipus discovers that he has unwittingly killed the late King of Thebes, Laius, whose widow, Jocasta, he has married. He further learns that Jocasta is actually his mother and Laius was his father. Jocasta, horrified on learning of the patricide and incest, kills herself; Oedipus, overcome with guilt and grief, puts out his eyes and goes into voluntary exile.

Corneille has expanded the original action of the play to include a complicated subplot concerning the love of Dirce, daughter of Laius and Jocasta, and Theseus, King of Athens. The two lovers wish to marry, but their plans are thwarted, first by Oedipus, because Dirce's marriage would give Theseus a rightful claim to the throne, and then by Theseus himself, who, by misunderstanding an oracular statement, believes he is Laius's missing son. The discovery of Oedipus as Laius's true son, which causes his exile, permits Theseus to marry Dirce and ascend the throne. *See* SOPHOCLES.

The Golden Fleece (*La toison d'or*, 1660). Tragedy written to celebrate the marriage of Louis XIV to Marie Thérèse of Spain. To the tale of Jason and the Golden Fleece Corneille

Edwige Feuillère and Roger Marion in *Rodogune*. Paris, Théâtre Sarah-Bernhardt, 1960. [French Cultural Services]

added another story, that of Hypsipyle's love for Jason. In the end Hypsipyle marries Medea's brother Absyrtus.

Sophonisba (*Sophonisbe*; wr. 1660, prod. 1663). Tragedy in which Sophonisba, daughter of the Carthaginian general Hasdrubal, despite her love for Masinissa, King of East Numidia, marries his rival Syphax, King of West Numidia, in order to gain him as an ally for Carthage. She keeps Syphax at war against Rome, but he is eventually defeated and captured by Masinissa, who has joined the Roman side. Sophonisba now marries Masinissa, hoping to win him over to the side of Carthage. She fails, however, and finally commits suicide.

Sertorius (1662). Tragedy concerning a Roman Governor in Spain, Sertorius, who is the leader of the faction opposed to the dictatorship of Sulla in Rome and his army leader Pompey. A truce has been declared, and Pompey has come to Spain to talk to Sertorius. Meanwhile, Sertorius plans to wed Pompey's divorced wife Aristia to win the support of her family in Rome. He asks Viriata, Queen of Lusitania, who loves him and whom he loves, to marry Perpenna, his lieutenant and a nobleman of Rome. When Viriata refuses, Perpenna becomes jealous of Sertorius and kills him. He in turn is killed by Pompey. Then Pompey is reunited with Aristia and agrees to join forces with Viriata to fight against Sulla.

Otho (*Othon*, 1664). Drama of intrigue set in ancient Rome, revolving around the machinations of the various characters to get their candidate named as the aged emperor Galba's successor. The action centers on Otho. Although he is engaged to Plautina, both she

Scene from Antoine Bourseiller's production of *Rodogune*. Paris, Théâtre Sarah-Bernhardt, 1960. [French Cultural Services]

and her father Vinius convince him that it is in their mutual interest for him to marry the Emperor's niece Camilla and thus be named heir to the throne. When Galba agrees to Otho's marriage to Camilla but offers the throne to his rival Piso, Otho balks. Convinced by Vinius that he has the support of the people, Otho seizes power and sets a trap to capture Galba. It is successful, and Galba and Vinius are killed. Otho informs Plautina that he has been named Emperor and protests his innocence of her father's death. She believes him, and it is suggested that after a period of mourning they will marry.

Agesilaus (*Agésilas*, 1666). Tragedy concerning Agesilaus, King of Sparta, who fears his powerful minister Lysander. Learning that Lysander is plotting against him, he renounces the woman he loves and marries one of Lysander's daughters.

Attila (1667). Drama in which Attila, King of the Huns, must choose as a wife one of two princesses, Honoria, sister of the Roman Emperor, or Ildione, sister of the King of the Franks. The princesses are both already in love with others: Honoria loves Valamir, King of the Ostrogoths, and Ildione loves Ardaric, King of the Gepidae. However, each wishes to marry Attila in order to outdo her rival. Being princesses, both feel a responsibility to obtain such a powerful ally. Attila at first chooses Ildione, but political events make Rome seem the preferable ally, and he decides to marry Honoria. He asks Ildione to reject his suit. She does and then tells Honoria that she is to marry the man she rejected. Insulted, Honoria refuses Attila, revealing her love for Valamir and Ildione's for Ardaric. Angered, Attila summons the two princes and tells them that the one who kills the other may marry his choice. The dilemma is solved when Attila unexpectedly dies of a hemorrhage. The two princesses are thus released and are free to marry the men they love.

Titus and Berenice (*Tite et Bérénice*, 1670). Heroic comedy in which Titus, Emperor of Rome, is betrothed to Domitia, daughter of an influential Roman general. Berenice, Queen of Palestine, arrives unexpectedly in Rome and revives Titus's past love for her. The situation embarrasses Titus and is further complicated by Berenice's jealousy of Domitia, who is actually in love with Titus's brother Domitian. Berenice wishes to marry Titus but realizes that she might disgrace him and weaken his position by preventing him from marrying Domitia. Consequently, she leaves Rome. Titus, aware that Domitia does not love him, surrenders her to his brother.

Psyche (*Psyché*, 1671). Hasty collaboration between Molière (outline, first act, and two scenes), Corneille (remaining scenes), Quinault (song lyrics), and Lully (music). In vers libre, the comedy ballet is an adaptation of the Cupid and Psyche myth, based largely on the story from *The Golden Ass* of Apuleius. All the classical elements are brought into play: Psyche's beauty, the jealousy of her sisters and of Venus, Cupid's love, and Psyche's breach of faith, punishment, and eventual happiness. Cupid is disguised as a young man, and he sorrowfully reveals the truth as a proof of his love.

Pulcheria (*Pulchérie*, 1672). Tragedy in which duty to the state triumphs over desires of the heart. Pulcheria, newly crowned Empress of the Byzantine Empire, must choose a husband. She loves Leo, a young soldier, but realizes that her other suitors, older men of higher birth and achievement personified by the unscrupulous Aspar, might denounce him. She therefore makes a marriage of convenience with Marcianus, an elderly and respected general and statesman who loves her, but arranges for Leo to marry Marcianus's

A Comédie-Française production of *Nicomède*. [French Cultural Services]

daughter, so that he will be heir to the throne.

Surenas (*Suréna*, 1674). Tragedy of love and jealousy in which Surenas, a Parthian general, has secretly fallen in love with Eurydice, an Armenian princess, while acting as an envoy at her father's court during the unsuccessful campaign of the Roman army of Crassus against Parthia. After the war, however, Eurydice is promised in marriage to Pacorus, son and heir of King Orodes of Parthia, who wishes his own daughter Mandane to wed Surenas. Eurydice's coldness persuades Pacorus that he has a rival, and he forces her to reveal his identity. Finally she agrees to marry Pacorus, but she wants Surenas to marry no one, not even Mandane. Meanwhile, Surenas is murdered by the minions of Pacorus, and Eurydice collapses saying that she, too, will die. Palmis, Surenas's sister, vows to avenge his death.

PLAYS

1. *Mélite, ou Les fausses lettres* (*Mélite, or The False Letters*). Comedy, 5 acts; verse. Written 1629. Published 1633. Produced Paris, Berthault Tennis Court (Lenoir Company), early 1630.

2. *Clitandre*. Tragicomedy, 5 acts; verse. Published 1632. Produced Paris, Berthault Tennis Court, 1631?

3. *La veuve, ou Le traître trahi* (*The Widow, or The Betrayer Betrayed*). Comedy, 5 acts; verse. Published 1634. Produced Berthault Tennis Court(?), 1631/32.

4. *La galerie du palais, ou L'amie rivale* (*The Palace Corridor, or The Rival Friend*). Comedy, 5 acts; verse. Published 1637. Produced Paris, Berthault Tennis Court(?), 1632.

5. *La suivante* (*The Maidservant*). Comedy, 5 acts; verse. Published 1637. Produced Paris, Fontaine Tennis Court, 1633.

6. *La place royale, ou L'amoureux extravagant* (*Place Royale, or The Extravagant Lover*). Comedy, 5 acts; verse. Published 1637. Produced Paris, Fontaine Tennis Court(?), 1633/early 1634.

7. *Médée* (*Medea*). Tragedy, 5 acts; verse. Published 1639. Produced Paris, Théâtre du Marais, end 1634/early 1635. Based on Seneca's *Medea*.

8. (With François de Boisrobert, Guillaume Colletet, Claude de L'Estoile, and Jean de Rotrou). *La comédie des Tuileries* (*The Comedy of the Tuileries*). Comedy, 5 acts; verse. Published 1638. Produced Paris, Louvre, February, 1635. Corneille probably wrote the third act.

9. *L'illusion comique* (*The Comic Illusion*). Comedy, 5 acts; verse. Published 1639. Produced Paris, Théâtre du Marais, 1635/36.

10. *Le Cid** (*The Cid*). Tragicomedy, 5 acts; verse. Published 1637. Produced Paris, Théâtre du Marais, December, 1636/January, 1637. Based on Guillén de Castro's *Las mocedades del Cid*.

11. *Horace** (*Horatius*). Tragedy, 5 acts; verse. Published 1641. Produced Paris, Hôtel de Bourgogne(?), before Mar. 9, 1640.

12. *Cinna, ou La clémence d'Auguste** (*Cinna, or The Clemency of Augustus*). Tragedy, 5 acts; verse. Published 1643. Produced Paris, Hôtel de Bourgogne(?), late 1640/early 1641.

13. *Polyeucte** (*Polyeuctes*). Tragedy, 5 acts; verse. Published 1643. Produced Paris, Théâtre du Marais, late 1641/early 1642.

14. *La mort de Pompée** (*The Death of Pompey*). Tragedy, 5 acts; verse. Published 1644. Produced Paris, Théâtre du Marais(?), December, 1642/February, 1643.

15. *Le menteur** (*The Liar*). Comedy. Published 1644. Produced Paris, Théâtre du Marais, early 1643. Based on Juan Ruiz de Alarcón's *La verdad sospechosa*.

16. *La suite du menteur* (*Sequel to The Liar*). Comedy, 5 acts; verse. Published 1645. Produced Paris, Théâtre du Marais, late 1644/early 1645. Based on Lope de Vega's *Amar sin saber a quién*.

17. *Rodogune, Princesse des Parthes** (*Rodogune, Princess of Parthia*). Tragedy, 5 acts; verse. Published 1647. Produced Paris, Théâtre du Marais(?), late 1644/early 1645.

18. *Théodore, vierge et martyre* (*Theodora, Virgin and Martyr*). Tragedy, 5 acts; verse. Published 1646. Produced Paris, Théâtre du Marais(?), 1645.

19. *Héraclius** (*Heraclius*). Tragedy, 5 acts; verse. Published 1647. Produced Paris, Théâtre du Marais(?), December, 1646/January, 1647.

20. *Andromède* (*Andromeda*). Tragedy, 5 acts; verse. Written 1647. Published 1650. Produced Paris, Théâtre Royal de Bourbon, early 1650.

21. *Dom Sanche d'Aragon** (*Don Sancho of Aragon*). Heroic comedy, 5 acts; verse. Published 1650. Produced Paris, Théâtre du Marais(?), late 1649. Based on Antonio Mira de Amescua's *El palacio confuso*.

22. *Nicomède** (*Nicomedes*). Tragedy, 5 acts; verse. Published 1651. Produced Paris, Théâtre du Marais(?), late 1650/early 1651.

23. *Pertharite, roi des Lombards* (*Pertharites, King of the Lombards*). Tragedy, 5 acts; verse. Produced Paris, Théâtre du Marais(?), late 1651.

24. *Oedipe* (*Oedipus*). Tragedy, 5 acts; verse. Published 1659. Produced Paris, Hôtel de Bourgogne, Jan. 24, 1659. Based on Sophocles's *Oidipous Tyrannos*.

25. *La toison d'or* (*The Golden Fleece*). Tragedy. Published 1661. Produced Paris, Théâtre du Marais, November, 1660.

26. *Sophonisbe* (*Sophonisba*). Tragedy, 5 acts; verse. Written 1660. Published 1663. Produced Paris, Hôtel de Bourgogne, January, 1663.

27. *Sertorius.** Tragedy, 5 acts; verse. Published 1662. Produced Paris, Théâtre du Marais, February, 1662.

28. *Othon** (*Otho*). Tragedy, 5 acts; verse. Published 1665. Produced Paris, Hôtel de Bourgogne, July 31, 1664.

29. *Agésilas* (*Agesilaus*). Tragedy, 5 acts; verse. Published 1666. Produced Paris. Hôtel de Bourgogne, Feb. 26, 1666.

30. *Attila.** Tragedy, 5 acts; verse. Published 1667. Produced Paris, Palais-Royal, Mar. 4, 1667.

31. *Tite et Bérénice* (*Titus and Berenice*). Heroic comedy, 5 acts; verse. Published 1671. Produced Paris, Palais-Royal, Nov. 28, 1670.

32. (With Molière and Philippe Quinault). *Psyché** (*Psyche*). Comedy ballet, 5 acts; verse. Published 1671. Produced Paris, Salle des Machines, Jan. 17, 1671. Music: Jean-Baptiste Lully.

33. *Pulchérie** (*Pulcheria*). Heroic comedy, 5 acts; verse. Published 1673. Produced Paris, Théâtre du Marais, Nov. 14, 1672.

34. *Suréna** (*Surenas*). Tragedy, 5 acts; verse. Published 1675. Produced Paris, Hôtel de Bourgogne, October/ November 1674.

EDITIONS

Collections.

Théâtre, 3 vols., Paris, 1660; *Théâtre*, 2 vols., Paris, 1663–1664; *Oeuvres*, 10 vols., Paris, 1759; *Théâtre*, 12 vols., Geneva, 1765; *Théâtre*, 8 vols., Geneva, 1774; *Théâtre*, 10 vols., Geneva, 1776; *Théâtre*, 12 vols., Paris, 1797; *Oeuvres*, with commentary by Voltaire, 12 vols., Paris, 1801, 1817, 1821–1822; *Théâtre de Pierre et Thomas Corneille*, 2 vols., Paris, 1859; *Oeuvres*, ed. by C. J. Marty-Laveaux, 12 vols., Paris, 1862–1907; *Six Plays by Corneille and Racine*, ed. by P. Landis, New York, 1931; *Chief Plays*, tr. by L. Lockert, Princeton, N.J., 1957; *Moot Plays*, tr. by L. Lockert,

Nashville, 1957; *Oeuvres complètes*, ed. by A. Stegmann, Paris, 1963.

Individual Plays.

The Cid. Published in *Classical French Drama*, ed. and tr. by W. Fowlie, New York, 1962.

Cinna. Published in *Poetic Drama*, ed. by A. Kreymborg and tr. by P. Landis, New York, 1941.

Horatius. Published in *Nine Classic French Plays*, ed. by J. Seronde and H. Peyre, Boston, 1936.

The Liar. Published in *Eight French Classic Plays*, ed. by J. C. Lyons and C. Searles, New York, 1932.

Polyeuctes. Published in *Three Great French Plays*, ed. by V. Loggins and tr. by T. Constable, Greenwich, Conn., 1961.

CRITICISM

French. F.-P.-G. Guizot, *Corneille et son temps*, Paris, 1813; J.-A. Taschereau, *Histoire de la vie et des ouvrages de Pierre Corneille*, 2d ed., Paris, 1855; C. J. Marty-Laveaux, *Lexique de la langue de P. Corneille*, 2 vols., Paris, 1868; É. Picot, *Bibliographie cornélienne*, Paris, 1876; J. Lemaître, *Corneille et la Poétique d'Aristote*, Paris, 1888; G. Lanson, *Corneille*, Paris, 1898; R. Le Brun, *Corneille devant trois siècles*, Paris, 1906; P. Le Verdier and É. Pelay, *Additions à la bibliographie cornélienne*, Rouen, 1908; A. Dorchain, *Pierre Corneille*, Paris, 1918; E. Renan, *Sur Corneille, Racine et Bossuet*, Paris, 1926; L. Batiffol, *Richelieu et Corneille*, Paris, 1936; A. Le Corbeiller, *Pierre Corneille, intime*, Paris, 1936; L. Rivaille, *Les débuts de Pierre Corneille*, Paris, 1936; J. Madaule, *Pierre Corneille*, Paris, 1941; R. Schneider, *Grandeur de Corneille et de son temps*, tr. by M. de Gandillac, Paris, 1943; L. Lemonnier, *Corneille*, Paris, 1945; G. C. May, *Tragédie cornélienne, tragédie racinienne*, Urbana, Ill., 1948; O. Nadal, *Le sentiment de l'amour dans l'oeuvre de Pierre Corneille*, Paris, 1948; G. Couton, *La vieillesse de Corneille*, Paris, 1949; *id.*, *Corneille et la Fronde*, Clermont-Ferrand, 1951; L. Herland, *Corneille par lui-même*, Paris, 1955; B. Dort, *Pierre Corneille, dramaturge*, Paris, 1957; G. Couton, *Corneille*, Paris, 1958; R. Brasillach, *Pierre Corneille*, Paris, 1961; M. Descotes, *Les grands rôles du théâtre de Corneille*, Paris, 1962; S. Dubrovsky, *Corneille et la dialectique du héros*, Paris, 1963; J. Maurens, *La tragédie sans tragique: Le néostoïcisme dans l'oeuvre de Pierre Corneille*, Paris, 1966.

English. F.-P.-G. Guizot, *Corneille and His Times*, London and New York, 1852; L. D. Lodge, *Study in Corneille*, 1891; L. H. Vincent, *Corneille*, Boston and New York, 1901; J. B. Segall, *Corneille and the Spanish Drama*, New York, 1902; D. F. C. Fisher, *Corneille and Racine in England*, New York, 1904; L. M. Riddle, *Genesis and Sources of Pierre Corneille's Tragedies from Médée to Pertharite*, Baltimore, 1925; M. Barras, *The Stage Controversy in France from Corneille to Rousseau*, New York, 1933; W. L. Schwartz, *The Sententiae in the Dramas of Corneille*, Stanford, Calif., and London, 1939; M. Turnell, *The Classical Moment: Corneille, Molière and Racine*, London, 1947; R. J. Nelson, *Corneille: His Heroes and Their Worlds*, Philadelphia, 1963; A. W. H. West, *The Cornelian Hero*, Auckland, 1963; P. J. Yarrow, *Corneille*, London and New York, 1963; B. Croce, *Ariosto, Shakespeare and Corneille*, tr. by D. Ainslie, new ed., New York, 1966; R. J. Nelson, *Corneille and Racine: Parallels and Contrasts*, Englewood Cliffs, N.J., 1966; H. Fogel, *The Criticism of Cornelian Tragedy*, New York, 1967.

CORNEILLE, Thomas (b. Rouen, August 20, 1625; d. Les Andelys, October 8, 1709). French dramatist and younger brother of the famous tragedian Pierre Corneille, Thomas was educated at the Jesuit school of Rouen and at the University of Caen, becoming a lawyer in 1649. Deeply influenced by his brother, who guided his education and career, Thomas went so far as to marry the sister of Pierre's wife. The brothers seem to have divided the dramatic genres between them; Pierre wrote no comedies after Thomas began to do so, and Thomas wrote nothing but comedies until Pierre retired in 1651. In later life Thomas gained a reputation as a journalist, grammarian, translator, and encyclopedist. The author of some forty plays and a number of opera libretti, Thomas excelled in tragicomedies, of which his most successful was *Timocrates* (*Timocrate*, 1656). *See* CORNEILLE, PIERRE; TRAGICOMEDY.

Though, following the fashion of the times, he preferred to draw the subjects for his tragedies from the legends and history of classical antiquity, one of his best tragic works is *The Earl of Essex* (*Le Comte d'Essex*, 1678), which recounts the ill-fated love of Queen Elizabeth and Essex. Among other tragedies and tragicomedies are *Laodice, Queen of Cappadocia* (*Laodice, Reine de Cappadoce*, 1668), *Ariadne* (*Ariane*, 1672), *Camma, Queen of Galatia* (*Camma, Reine de Galatie*, 1661), *Maximian* (*Maximien*, 1662), and *The Death of the Emperor Commodus* (*La mort de l'Empereur Commode*, 1657). His comedies were largely influenced by Spanish models; the most famous of them are *Fashionable Love* (*L'amour à la mode*, 1653) and *His Own Jailer* (*Le geôlier de soy-mesme*, 1656). *The Stone Statue's Feast* (*Le festin de pierre*, 1677) is a verse version of Molière's comedy *Don Juan*.

Timocrates (*Timocrate*, 1656). Tragicomedy based on the novel *Cassandre* by Gauthier de Costes de La Calprenède. While the army of Timocrates of Crete besieges the capital of the widowed Queen of Argos, he introduces himself into her court disguised as Cleomenes, a soldier of fortune. As Cleomenes, he quickly becomes the Queen's friend and adviser, undertaking the defense of the city his own army is besieging. Cleomenes-Timocrates succeeds in winning the love of the Queen's daughter Eriphyla, and soon an ambassador arrives from Timocrates offering the Queen peace in exchange for her daughter's hand. The Queen instead decides to award Eriphyla to whoever vanquishes Timocrates. After a complicated series of events, the real identity of Cleomenes is disclosed, the Queen abdicates, and Eriphyla and Timocrates marry, thereby uniting their two countries in peace.

Laodice, Queen of Cappodocia (*Laodice, Reine de Cappodoce*, 1668). Tragicomedy in which Laodice has ruthlessly contrived to retain the throne of Cappadocia for herself by killing five of her sons and by postponing her daughter's marriage. When her surviving son

Ariarathes, who was raised in Rome, comes to her court disguised as Orontes, the Queen falls in love with him, as does Axiana, Princess of Sicily. The Roman Ambassador forces Ariarathes to reveal his true identity to Laodice, who then commits suicide. Ariarathes succeeds to the throne and announces his intention to marry Axiana. Produced Hôtel de Bourgogne, February, 1668.

The Earl of Essex (*Le Comte d'Essex,* 1678). Tragedy based on Queen Elizabeth's struggle to decide between her love for the Earl of Essex and her duty to the state. Essex is accused of plotting against the Crown, but his real intention had been to overthrow the Queen's minister, with whose wife Henrietta he is in love. Brought before the Queen, he affirms his innocence but proudly refuses to disclose the real explanation of his behavior. Essex is sentenced to death but refuses to throw himself on the Queen's mercy, though she herself pleads with him to do so. The Queen eventually brings herself to pardon him of her own accord, but the reprieve arrives too late. Overcome by remorse, the Queen hopes for her own death. Produced Hôtel de Bourgogne, January 7, 1678.

COSSA, Pietro (b. Rome, January 20, 1830; d. Leghorn, August 30, 1881). Italian dramatist who, in fifteen plays, all except one in verse, sought to re-create and reinterpret historical fact in terms of an epic conception. Cossa's work marks the evolution away from romantic drama toward realism in Italian literature. Considered his masterpieces are *Nero* (*Nerone*, 1872), in which the Roman Emperor is portrayed as a weak figure fearful of his subjects and controlled by the woman who loves him; and *Messalina* (1876), in which the female protagonist is shown to be the victim of her uncontrollable passions. Cossa's other plays, notably *Plautus and His Century* (*Plauto e il suo secolo*, 1873), *Cleopatra* (1877), and *The Neapolitans of 1799* (*I napoletani del 1799*, 1881), lack dramatic unity and reveal the playwright's fundamental inability to analyze the psychology of his characters. Cossa's contribution to the theatre is now largely considered to fulfill a purely historical function.

Nero (*Nerone*, 1872). Verse drama presenting the emperor Nero against the colorful background of imperial Rome's working-class neighborhood by day and the vulgar splendors of his court by night. The poor look upon him as the terrifying and mighty symbol of majesty. At the palace, however, he is a weak and ignoble individual torn between two women, Egloge, a young courtesan, and Atte, whose unbounded passion for him is offered as a justification for her murder of Egloge. It

Pietro Cossa.
[Italian Cultural Institute]

is Atte who urges Nero to take poison when she realizes that he cannot be saved from the uprising of the populace and that his life is empty and decadent. The play ends in a climax of Nero's terror as death approaches.

COUP DE THÉÂTRE. French term meaning "stroke of the theatre." A sudden, startling turn of the plot used to effect great surprise, the *coup de théâtre* occurs most often in melodrama.

Georges Courteline
(1858 — 1929)

Georges-Victor-Marcel Moineaux, French journalist, novelist, short-story writer, and dramatist who used the pseudonym Georges Courteline, was born in Tours on June 25, 1858. His father was Jules Moineaux, a novelist and the author of *Comic Tribunals* (*Tribunaux comiques*), a celebrated series of vaudeville skits on which his son was later to draw for several of his own plays. Courteline went to school in Paris until 1870, when the family fled from the Prussians to Meaux.

Georges
Courteline.
[French Cultural
Services]

There the undisciplined but imaginative Courteline, more interested in student theatricals than his studies, completed his education. In 1878 Moineaux enlisted his still-unsettled son in the 13th Cavalry Squadron at Bar-le-Duc, where Courteline spent fourteen miserable months before being discharged for reasons of health. This experience provided material for works of fiction, *Squadron Gaities* (*Les gaîtés de l'escadron*, 1886) and *The 8:47 Train* (*Le train de 8h.47*, 1888), that were afterward used as a source for some of his plays.

Having failed his entrance examinations for the Sorbonne, Courteline found through his father a post in the Ministry of Culture. Though it was an undemanding job, he paid half his salary to a needy co-worker who performed his duties for him. Using the freedom thus obtained to pursue a literary career, he contributed stories, poems, and sketches to *Les Petites Nouvelles Quotidiennes* almost daily until 1890. His first book of sketches appeared in 1884, and in 1890 he began to write for *L'Écho de Paris*, signing his work Jean de la Butte. In 1894 he resigned from the Ministry and devoted himself exclusively to writing; however, his experiences had supplied him with material for his novel *The Bureau-*

crats (*Messieurs les ronds-de-cuir*, 1893) and a celebrated skit, *Badin the Bold* (*Monsieur Badin*, 1897).

Initially Courteline gave little importance to his dramatic skits, which were often acted in a Montmartre cabaret and seemed designed solely for the amusement of his friends. However, in 1891 *Lidoire*, a one-acter based on his military experiences, was given as a curtain raiser at André Antoine's Théâtre Libre, and his dramatic career was officially launched. Two years later, *Boubouroche*, often considered his masterpiece, was given at the same theatre. In 1895 Courteline collaborated with Édouard Norès on *Squadron Gaities*, drawn from his novel of the same name. There followed a series of one-act plays and skits satirizing various aspects of the law, the army, and middle-class domestic life. In 1909 Courteline collaborated with Pierre Wolff on *The Dolt* (*La cruche*), his last play of any importance.

Courteline was married twice, first to the former actress Suzanne Berty, whom he met when he acted for a time with Les Bouffes Parisiens, and after her death to Marie-Jeanne Brécourt, also a former actress. In 1912 his literary output slackened, but he continued writing until 1925, when his right leg was amputated. He spent his remaining years as an invalid and died during a second leg-amputation operation in Paris on June 25, 1929.

WORK

Though Courteline is little known abroad, in his native France his popularity and reputation as a comic dramatist are second only to those of Molière. This is because the average Frenchman can very easily identify with Courteline's hero or, more properly speaking, antihero, a man locked in all but mortal combat with the unyielding irrationalities of bureaucracy, the law, the military, and the frustrations of middle-class domesticity. To Courteline belongs the credit of having successfully reanimated the traditional *esprit gaulois*, just as shortly afterward Giraudoux was to give new life to that other component of French comedy, *l'esprit précieux*. See GIRAUDOUX, JEAN; MOLIÈRE.

Courteline's great strength was derived from the fact that he almost never departed from his own experience in choosing the themes of his plays. An inveterate café sitter himself, he reported with unerring precision and sidesplitting hilarity the life that boiled and bubbled in the Parisian turn-of-the-century cafés, which provided society for the bachelor and a refuge for the married man. In his masterpiece, *Boubouroche* (1893), the title character, prototype of the small French *rentier,* comfortably spends in the cafés' relaxing male atmosphere what time he can spare from his mistress Adèle.

In *An Important Customer* (*Un client sérieux,* 1896) Courteline combined two of his favorite themes, café life and the law. Courteline's interest in the courts and legal procedures can no doubt be traced to his father's comic writings. However, he approached the topic with an infectious verve all his own, often choosing a character named La Brige as his explosively frustrated Everyman caught in the toils of legal red tape. In one of the most successful of his comedies, *Article 330* (*L'article 330,* 1900), La Brige, comfortably disrobed within the privacy of his home, finds himself imprisoned for indecent exposure upon the evidence of 13,687 Peeping Toms. In *The Scales* (*Les balances,* 1901) La Brige's attempt to retire to a quiet country retreat brings him into conflict with various branches of the law.

Courteline's experiences in the cavalry supplied the material for his first play, *Lidoire* (1891), and for his ever-popular *Squadron Gaities* (1895). Domestic friction is the theme of *Afraid to Fight* (*La peur des coups,* 1894) and *Peace at Home* (*La paix chez soi,* 1903), in which fascinating and sharp-tongued women quickly reduce the Gallic rooster to something more like a capon. The theme is perhaps most successfully expressed in the second half of *Boubouroche,* with its uncanny echoes of Molière's *The Misanthrope.* That his illustrious predecessor's masterpiece preyed on Courteline's mind can be seen from an uncharacteristic verse play, *The Conversion of Alceste* (*La conversion d'Alceste,* 1905), in which he tried to supply it with a sequel.

Many of Courteline's plays are so short that they are barely more than sketches. In his last important play, *The Dolt* (1909), however, he provided a sympathetic two-act portrait of a woman who is the eternal victim of the male ego.

Boubouroche (1893). Kindhearted, sentimental, and credulous, Boubouroche divides his time between his café friends and his mistress Adèle, of whose fidelity he boasts. One day an elderly café habitué informs Boubou-

Les gaîtés de l'escadron. Paris, Théâtre de la Renaissance, 1947. [French Cultural Services]

roche that Adèle has consistently been unfaithful to him. Bourbouroche rushes off to confront his mistress, who pretends indignation at her lover's accusations, maintaining this attitude even when the presence of a young man hidden in a large sideboard is accidentally revealed. To Bourbouroche's demands for an explanation, she merely replies that the circumstance is due to a "family secret" which she cannot reveal because it concerns "another woman's honor." Before long Bourbouroche is so much impressed by her seeming nobility of spirit that he humbly implores her pardon. Relieved not to have lost Adèle and the comfort of his routine, Bourbouroche vents his frustration by trouncing the old man who informed him of Adèle's infidelity. The play is based on an earlier *récit* of the same name.

Squadron Gaities (*Les gaîtés de l'escadron*, 1895). Based on Courteline's prose sketches of the same name, these nine almost plotless tableaux deal with various aspects of cavalry life in peacetime. Courteline humorously exposes the hardships and gripes of a conscript army: bad food, incompetent officers, and dehumanizing regulations. Two of the main characters are the immortal and brutal Adjutant Flick, terror of his men, and the gruff but kindhearted Captain Hurluret, who has risen from the ranks and is totally devoted to his men. When a general makes a surprise inspection, he is somewhat startled by Captain Hurluret's laxity about regulations but recognizes the unit's basic *esprit de corps*.

An Important Customer (*Un client sérieux*, 1896). Comedy dealing with the pomposities and stupidities of lawyers, judges, and courtroom procedure. Café owner Alfred brings assault charges against Lagoupille, a customer who spends all day at the café over a single cup of coffee and who immediately commandeers all the newspapers and cards. In despair at seeing his other customers desert him, one day Alfred attempted to eject Lagoupille from his café and was given a black eye by his indignant and only remaining customer. Though Alfred proves that Lagoupille ruined a once-flourishing business, he loses his case and is obliged to pay court costs.

Article 330 (*L'article 330*, 1900). Under Article 330 of the Penal Code, La Brige is hauled into court upon the complaint of 13,687 witnesses for having affronted public morality by indecently exposing his posterior. La Brige explains that he was in his apartment searching for a coin he had dropped. The witnesses, who were on a moving sidewalk built by the Paris Exposition on a level with his windows, were actually invading his privacy by peering in. The court, though conceding that he was within his rights, nevertheless condemns him to a fine and imprisonment.

Peace at Home (*La paix chez soi*, 1903). As Trielle, a penny-a-liner, is completing the daily installment of his serial novel, his wife Valentine enters and demands her monthly household money. Trielle explains that he is withholding 150 francs as a fine for her various infractions of domestic peace. Valentine alternately pleads and threatens, but she only obtains the additional 150 francs when Trielle learns to his horror that she needs them to pay off a bank draft to which she has forged his name. Mellowed by her victory and Trielle's concern for her, Valentine momentarily cuddles in her husband's arms. As she leaves, Trielle adds to his manuscript, "To be continued."

The Dolt, or I've Had Enough of Margot (*La cruche, ou J'en ai plein le dos de Margot*, 1909). Margot, the young mistress of the ill-tempered and egotistic Lauriane, remains with her middle-aged lover because she is pathetically unable to assert her will. Lauriane, momentarily bored with her, forces Margot into the arms of his friend, the painter Lavernié, whom Margot sincerely loves. Then, terrified by the solitude to which he has condemned himself, Lauriane reclaims Margot with a promise of marriage. Unable to resist

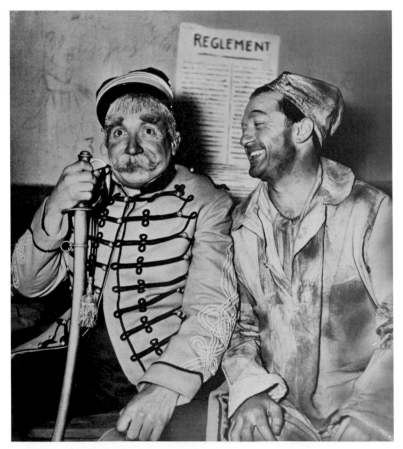

Les gaîtés de l'escadron. Paris, Théâtre de la Renaissance, 1947. [French Cultural Services]

the force of his appeal and suspecting that her happiness with Lavernié is only temporary, Margot wearily agrees to Lauriane's proposal. Lavernié is briefly stunned but soon happily returns to his painting.

PLAYS

Unless otherwise noted, the plays were first performed in Paris.

1. *Lidoire.* Military tableau, 1 act. Published 1891. Produced Théâtre Libre, June 6, 1891.

2. (With Catulle Mendès). *Les joyeuses commères de Paris.* Fantasy, 5 acts. Published 1892. Produced Nouveau Théâtre, 1892. Music: Alfred Rabuteau and Gabriel Pierné.

3. *Boubouroche*.* Comedy, 2 acts. Published 1893. Produced Théâtre Libre, Apr. 27, 1893.

4. (With Louis Marsolleau). *Les grimaces de Paris.* Revue, 3 acts. Produced Théâtre des Nouveautés, Oct. 26, 1894.

5. *La peur des coups** (*Afraid to Fight*). Saynète ("short play"), 1 act. Published 1895. Produced Théâtre d'Application, Dec. 14, 1894.

6. (With Édouard Norès). *Les gaîtés de l'escadron.* (*Squadron Gaieties*). Scenes from barracks life. Published 1905. Produced Théâtre Ambigu, Feb. 18, 1895.

7. *La cinquantaine* (*The Fifty*). Popular scene, 1 act. Published 1895. Produced Théâtre du Carillon, Nov. 22, 1895.

8. *Petin, Mouillardbourg et Consorts* (*Petin, Mouillardbourg, and Associates*). Judiciary fantasy, 1 act. Produced Théâtre du Carillon, May 5, 1896.

9. *Le droit aux étrennes* (*The Right to New Year's Gifts*). Vaudeville, 1 act. Published 1896. Produced Théâtre du Grand Guignol, May 13, 1896.

10. *Un client sérieux* (*An Important Customer*). Comedy, 1 act. Published 1898. Produced Théâtre du Carillon, Aug. 24, 1896.

11. *Une lettre chargée* (*The Registered Letter*). Saynète, 1 act. Published 1898. Produced Théâtre du Carillon, Jan. 10, 1897.

12. *Hortense, couche-toi!** (*Hold On, Hortense*). Saynète, 1 act. Published 1898. Produced Théâtre du Grand Guignol, Mar. 15, 1897.

13. *Monsieur Badin** (*Badin the Bold*). Scene from office life, 1 act. Published 1897. Produced Théâtre du Grand Guignol, Apr. 13, 1897.

14. *L'extra-Lucide* (*Extra-Lucide*). Saynète, 1 act. Published 1897. Produced Théâtre du Carillon, May 17, 1897.

15. *Théodore cherche des allumettes* (*Theodore Looks for Matches*). Saynète, 1 act. Published 1898. Produced Théâtre du Grand Guignol, Oct. 10, 1897.

16. *Gros chagrins* (*Heavy Sorrows*). Saynète, 1 act. Published 1898. Produced Théâtre du Carillon, Dec. 2, 1897.

17. *La voiture versée* (*The Overturned Vehicle*). Comedy, 1 act. Published 1898. Produced Théâtre du Carillon, Dec. 2, 1897.

18. *Les Boulingrin** (*Those Cornfields*). Vaudeville, 1 act. Published 1898. Produced Théâtre du Grand Guignol, Feb. 7, 1898.

19. (With Norès). *Le gendarme est sans pitié* (*The Officer Is Pitiless*). Comedy, 1 act. Published 1899. Produced Théâtre Antoine, Jan. 27, 1899.

20. (With Pierre Véber). *L'affaire champignon* (*The Champignon Affair*). Judiciary fantasy, 1 act. Published 1899. Produced Théâtre Scala, Sept. 8, 1899. Based on Jules Moineaux's *Tribunaux comiques.*

21. (With Véber). *Blancheton père et fils* (*Blancheton and Son*). Judiciary fantasy, 1 act. Published 1900. Produced Théâtre des Capucines, Oct. 26, 1899. Based on Moineaux's *Tribunaux comiques.*

22. *Panthéon-Courcelles.* Musical fantasy, 1 act. Produced Théâtre du Grand Guignol, Nov. 2, 1899.

23. (With Jules Lévy). *Le commissaire est bon enfant** (*The Commissioner Is a Good Guy*). Comedy, 1 act. Published 1900. Produced Théâtre du Gymnase, Dec. 16, 1899.

24. *L'article 330** (*Article 330*). Comedy, 1 act. Produced Théâtre Antoine, Dec. 12, 1900.

25. *Sigismond.* Fantasy, with chorus, 1 act. Produced Tréteau de Tabarin, Feb. 10, 1901.

26. *Les balances* (*The Scales*). Comedy, 1 act. Published 1902. Produced Théâtre Antoine, Nov. 26, 1901.

27. *Victoires et conquêtes* (*Victories and Conquests*). Fantasy, 1 act. Published 1902. Produced Théâtre des Mathurins, Apr. 15, 1902.

28. *La paix chez soi* (*Peace at Home*). Comedy, 1 act. Published 1903. Produced Théâtre Antoine, Nov. 25, 1903.

29. *La conversion d'Alceste* (*The Conversion of Alceste*). Comedy, 1 act; verse. Published 1905. Produced Comédie-Française, Jan. 15, 1905.

30. (With Dominique Bonnaud). *Les mentons bleus* (*The Blue Chins*). Scenes from stage life, 1 act. Published 1906. Produced Boîte à Fursy, Jan. 1, 1906.

31. (With Pierre Wolff). *La cruche, ou J'en ai plein le dos de Margot* (*The Dolt, or I've Had Enough of Margot*). Comedy, 2 acts. Published 1909. Produced Théâtre de la Renaissance, Feb. 27, 1909.

EDITIONS

Collections.
Théâtre, 2 vols., Paris, 1918; *Oeuvres complètes illustrées,* 8 vols., Paris, 1930; *Plays,* tr. by A. Bermel and J. Barzun, New York, 1961; *Théâtre complet,* Paris, 1961.

Individual Plays.
The Commissioner Is a Good Guy. Published in *Four Modern French Comedies,* ed. by W. Fowlie and tr. by A. Bermel, New York, 1960.

Those Cornfields. Published in *Let's Get a Divorce! and Other Plays,* ed. and tr. by E. R. Bentley, New York, 1958.

CRITICISM

R. LeBrun, *Georges Courteline,* Paris 1906; J. Dessuet, *Georges Courteline, l'humoriste français,* Paris, 1928; M. Richards, *Le comique de Courteline,* Montreal, 1950; A. Dubeux, *La curieuse vie de Georges Courteline,* Paris, 1958.

COVENTRY CYCLE. See MYSTERY PLAY.

Noel Coward
(1899 –   )

Noel Pierce Coward, English actor, director, producer, composer, and dramatist, was born in Teddington on December 16, 1899. He left school at an early age to begin acting and made his first professional appearance as Prince Mussel in *The Goldfish,* a fairy play for children, performed at the Little Theatre in London. Thereafter he was steadily employed as a child actor; he appeared, for example, in a musical comedy by C. Mills and J. Ramsey, *Where the Rainbow Ends,* and played the part of Slightly in two different productions of *Peter Pan.* He joined the army's Artists' Rifles in the winter of 1918 and was back onstage two years later as Ralph in Francis Beaumont's *The Knight of the Burning Pestle. I'll Leave It to You* (1920), his first produced

Noel Coward.
[Theatre
Collection, The
New York Public
Library at Lincoln
Center, Astor,
Lenox and Tilden
Foundations]

play, met with some approval, but his first real success came in 1924 with *The Vortex,* a drama of the post-World War I period. After *The Vortex,* Coward began to produce the sophisticated comedies and farces that came to be typical of the postwar generation. In 1925 five plays by Noel Coward, including *Hay Fever, Fallen Angels, Easy Virtue,* and *On with the Dance,* were running simultaneously in London.

Other triumphs in which Coward combined the talents of actor, singer, composer, lyricist, stage manager, and director were *This Year of Grace!* (1928), a revue; and *Bitter-Sweet* (1929), for which he composed some of his most memorable songs. Having achieved financial as well as artistic success, Coward began traveling extensively. It was in Shanghai in 1929 that he wrote the comedy *Private Lives,* which was produced in London in 1930, starring himself and Gertrude Lawrence. Soon after he wrote *Cavalcade* (1931); *Design for Living* (1933), in which he starred with Alfred Lunt and Lynn Fontanne; and *Tonight at 8:30* (1935–1936). *Blithe Spirit,* his last big success, was produced in Manchester and London in 1941.

During World War II Coward toured with *This Happy Breed* (1942). He also produced, codirected, wrote, and starred in the motion picture *In Which We Serve* (1943), a tribute to the Royal Navy; made numerous appearances to raise funds and sell government bonds; and entertained Allied troops with his extraordinarily diverse talents. Although

Coward continued to write for the theatre after the war, he never again achieved the popularity he enjoyed during the 1920s and 1930s. A three-act play, *Waiting in the Wings,* was staged in London in 1960. The next year Coward went to the United States to stage *Sail Away,* an unsuccessful musical for which he wrote the book, lyrics, and music.

Coward's other activities are myriad: he has made numerous nightclub and television appearances; he wrote the score for a ballet; and he composed many songs, the best of which are included in *Noel Coward's Song Book* (1953). He has written two autobiographies, *Present Indicative* (1934) and *Future Indefinite* (1954); the novel *Pomp and Circumstance* (1960); and two volumes of short stories. His name still appears regularly in the annals of theatrical productions, as it has since his beginnings in the 1920s. In 1963 he wrote the music and lyrics for *The Girl Who Came to Supper,* a musical by Harry Kurnitz. The next year a musical called *High Spirits,* based on his *Blithe Spirit,* was produced.

WORK

Although Coward's work for the theatre includes serious and sentimental dramas, his fame as a dramatic craftsman is based most-

Jane Cowl and Robert Harris as Larita and John in *Easy Virtue.* New York, Empire Theatre, 1925.
[Culver Pictures]

Tammy Grimes
and Brian Bedford
in *Private Lives.*
Ann Arbor,
Mendelssohn
Theatre, 1969.
[Professional
Theatre Program,
University of
Michigan]

ly on his witty and acerbic comedies and revue sketches. Imaginative plots, natural, witty dialogue, and clever songs characterize
these works, which, for all their "lightness,"
have proved to be remarkably durable.

Hay Fever (1925) was the first of the Coward comedies to achieve a notable success; it
is supposed to have been based on a weekend
Coward spent with the family of an American
actress. He followed it with several comedies
that reflected the gaiety and abandon of the
1920s, culminating in *Private Lives* (1930).
His next comedy, *Design for Living* (1933),
shocked some of its audiences with its conclusion in a happy *ménage à trois*.

The work that demonstrates the full range
and diversity of Coward's talent is *Tonight at
8:30,* a collection of nine one-act plays, all
first produced in 1935 or 1936, which he wrote
as vehicles for himself and Gertrude Lawrence. His best single work is *Blithe Spirit*
(1941), which had a record run for a nonmusi-
cal play in England. Here a touch of delicacy
has been added to the brittle wit, and the humor is more mature than in his other works.

Other important plays by Coward are *The
Vortex* (1924), a realistic study of post-World
War I decadence, in which a mother loses her
young lover to the sweetheart of her drug-
addicted son; *Fallen Angels* (1925), a comedy
famous for the drinking scene in which two
young wives, awaiting the arrival of a man
both had known in Italy, confess that each
has had an affair with him; and the patriotic
drama *Cavalcade* (1931), about England from
the Boer War to armistice night in 1918.

Hay Fever (1925). Comedy in which four
guests arrive to spend the weekend at the
country home of the eccentric Bliss family.
They are Sandy, a young man infatuated
with Mrs. Bliss, who is an actress; Jackie, a
young flapper whom Mr. Bliss wants to study
for a novel; and Richard and Myra, guests of
Sorel and Simon, the Blisses' daughter and
son. During the weekend the Blisses quarrel
with each other and their guests, mother and
daughter exchange men, and father and son
exchange women. Finally, the bewildered
guests sneak out of the house, leaving the
Blisses happily arguing at the breakfast table.

Private Lives (1930). Comedy in which
Elyot Chase, honeymooning in France with
his second wife, Sibyl, discovers that his first
wife Amanda is in the same hotel honeymooning with her new husband Victor. Recalling their marriage, Elyot and Amanda
decide to leave their new spouses and elope to
Paris. Once there in Amanda's apartment,
however, they begin arguing again. Sibyl and
Victor arrive and witness the final explosion.
The next morning, the four discuss the pros
and cons of divorce. Soon Sibyl and Victor are
fighting with each other. As Sibyl slaps Victor and he begins shaking her, Elyot and
Amanda wink at each other, pick up their
suitcases, and depart.

Design for Living (1933). Comedy about

Scene from a South
African production
of *Hay Fever.*
[Theatre
Collection, The
New York Public
Library at Lincoln
Center, Astor,
Lenox and Tilden
Foundations]

Design for Living, with (l. to r.) Noel Coward, Ethel Borden, Alfred Lunt, Alan Campbell, Gladys
Henson, and Lynn Fontanne. New York, Ethel Barrymore Theatre, 1933. [Photograph by
Vandamm. Theatre Collection, The New York Public Library at Lincoln Center, Astor, Lenox and
Tilden Foundations]

The Lunts and
Noel Coward in
Design for Living.
New York, Ethel
Barrymore
Theatre, 1933.
[Photograph by
Vandamm. Theatre
Collection, The
New York Public
Library at Lincoln
Center, Astor,
Lenox and Tilden
Foundations]

Gertrude Lawrence and Noel Coward in three plays from *Tonight at 8:30:* "*Red Peppers*" (top left); *We Were Dancing* (top right); *Ways and Means* (bottom). New York, National Theatre, 1936. [Photographs by Vandamm. Theatre Collection, The New York Public Library at Lincoln Center, Astor, Lenox and Tilden Foundations]

the *ménage à trois* of Gilda, Otto, and Leo. Gilda, living in Paris with Otto, a painter, is visited by Leo, a successful playwright. They have an affair, and Otto leaves her. While living with Leo in London, Gilda is visited by the now-successful Otto, who spends the night. Then, feeling that neither man needs her, Gilda goes off with Ernest. Eighteen months later, Gilda, now married to Ernest, has become a successful decorator in New York. Her well-ordered life is disrupted by the arrival of Otto and Leo, who have come to take her back with them. Bored by her conventional life in New York, she leaves with them willingly.

We Were Dancing (1935). Light episode in which Louise Charteris and Karl Sandys meet and fall in love while dancing. They decide to elope, but instead of doing so at once they explain the situation to Louise's husband. The night is spend discussing the affair, and by morning the enchantment is gone. Karl goes away, and Louise returns to her husband.

The Astonished Heart (1935). Drama in which Christian Faber, an eminent psychiatrist, falls in love with his wife's friend Leonora Vail. At first, he and his wife treat the attachment as a passing affair. Then Christian finds himself obsessed by Leonora. His love becomes so possessive and jealous that he destroys Leonora's love for him. Eventually, she leaves him, and he commits suicide.

"Red Peppers" (1935). Vaudeville sketch in which George and Lilly Pepper, music-hall performers, are happy onstage in their comedy routine. But in their dressing room between scenes they argue with each other, the musical director, the fading actress in the next room, and the manager, who discharges them. Finally, they dash back onstage, just in time for their second number.

Hands across the Sea (1935). Satire on hospitality. Lady Maureen Gilpin invites the people she meets on her world travels to visit her in London, but she never remembers them later. Thus, when the Wadhursts arrive, she thinks they are another couple. She discovers and corrects her mistake in time, and as the confused Wadhursts leave, she cheerfully invites them to return.

Fumed Oak (1935). Comedy in which Henry Gow, a middle-aged clerk, revolts after fifteen years of marriage to a nagging wife. After telling her, her mother, and his daughter exactly what he thinks of them, he walks out to begin a life of his own.

Shadow Play (1935). Musical fantasy in which the marriage of Victoria and Simon Gayforth is about to break up. To sedate herself, Victoria takes too many sleeping pills and in her drugged state relives her relation-

Gertrude Lawrence and Noel Coward in *Tonight at 8:30.* [Photographs by Vandamm. Theatre Collection, The New York Public Library at Lincoln Center, Astor, Lenox and Tilden Foundations]

Peggy Wood, Clifton Webb, and Leonora Corbett (l. to r.) in *Blithe Spirit*. New York, Morosco Theatre, 1941. [Photograph by Vandamm. Theatre Collection, The New York Public Library at Lincoln Center]

ship with her husband. She wakes to find him waiting anxiously at her side. The fear of losing her has brought him back and saved their marriage.

Family Album (1935). Satire on Victorian hypocrisy. The bereaved Featherways children and their spouses gather to mourn the loss of their father. As they recall the past, they remember that the old man was a cruel, spiteful philanderer and discover that they are all glad he is dead.

Ways and Means (1936). Farce in which Stella and Toby Cartwright have overstayed their welcome at a house on the Riviera. Their hostess has asked them to leave, but they have no money. Their problem is resolved by an amateur burglar who invades their room. At their direction he robs a wealthy fellow guest and splits the proceeds with them.

Still Life (1936). Drama that was later adapted for the famous British postwar film *Brief Encounter* (1946). Laura Jesson and Alec Harvey meet by chance in a railway sta-

tion. Though both are married, they fall in love and have an affair but realize they must eventually part. Alec finally breaks the relationship by accepting a job in Africa, and they see each other for the last time in the railway station where they met.

Blithe Spirit (1941). Comedy in which Charles Condomine, in order to gather material for a book, holds a séance, conducted by Madame Arcati, in his home. Unexpectedly the spirit of Elvira, Charles's first wife, materializes and begins to make life difficult for Charles and Ruth, his second wife. Elvira decides not to leave the house unless she takes Charles with her. But her plan misfires, and Ruth, not Charles, is killed. Charles again summons Madame Arcati, who, while trying to exorcise Elvira, brings back Ruth. Finally, Madame Arcati manages to exorcise both wives but advises Charles, for safety's sake, to take a long trip. As he prepares to leave, he addresses himself to the seemingly empty living room and tells Ruth and Elvira, in case they are listening, that he is glad to be rid of them both. As he departs, the furious spirits begin to dismantle the room.

Present Laughter (1942). Light comedy in which matinee idol Garry Essendine, catered to by his small entourage of friends and business associates, lives a life of sophisticated sexual freedom. He is separated from his wife, but they maintain a mutual friendship and forbearance. Attractive to most women, he submits to their adoration with great gusto. When, however, the wife of his best friend arrives at his flat proclaiming an irresistible passion for him, he fights her off feebly and finally submits to her adoring logic. The play ends with Garry revealing to his associates that their own sexual exploits compare favorably with his own. Then, to avoid the importunities of yet another young female admirer, he goes off with his wife.

PLAYS

Unless otherwise noted, the plays were first performed in London.

1. *The Rat Trap.* Play, 4 acts. Written 1918. Published 1924. Produced Hampstead, Everyman Theatre, Oct. 18, 1926.

2. *I'll Leave It to You.* Light comedy, 3 acts. Written 1919. Published 1920. Produced Manchester, Gaiety Theatre, May 3, 1920; London, New Theatre, July 21, 1920.

3. *The Young Idea.* Comedy of youth, 3 acts. Written 1920. Published 1924. Produced Bristol, Prince's Theatre, Sept. 25, 1922; London, Savoy Theatre, Feb. 1, 1923.

4. *Sirocco.* Play, 3 acts. Written 1921; revised 1927. Published 1927. Produced Daly's Theatre, Nov. 24, 1927.

5. *The Better Half.* Comedy, 1 act. Written 1921. Produced Little Theatre, May 31, 1922.

6. *Mild Oats.* Play, 1 act. Written 1922. Published 1931.

7. (With Ronald Jeans). *London Calling.* Revue, 2 parts. Written 1923. Portions published in various collections. Produced Duke of York's Theatre, Sept. 4, 1923. Music and lyrics: Noel Coward.

8. *Weatherwise.* Comedy, 2 scenes. Written 1923. Published 1931. Produced Malvern, Festival Theatre, Sept. 8, 1932.

9. *Fallen Angels.* Comedy, 3 acts. Written 1923. Published 1924. Produced Globe Theatre, Apr. 21, 1925.

10. *The Vortex.* Play, 3 acts. Written 1923. Published 1925. Produced Hampstead, Everyman Theatre, Nov. 25, 1924.

11. *Hay Fever.* Comedy, 3 acts. Written 1924. Published 1925. Produced Ambassadors Theatre, June 8, 1925.

12. *Easy Virtue.* Play, 3 acts. Written 1924. Published 1926. Produced New York, Empire Theatre, Dec. 7, 1925; Manchester, Opera House, May 31, 1926; London, Duke of York's Theatre, June 9, 1926.

13. *On with the Dance.* Revue, 2 parts. Written 1925. Portions published in various collections. Produced Manchester, Palace, Mar. 17, 1925; London, Pavilion, Apr. 30, 1925.

14. *The Queen Was in the Parlour.* Play, 3 acts. Published 1926. Produced Martin's Theatre, Aug. 24, 1926.

15. *"This Was a Man."* Comedy, 3 acts. Written 1926. Produced New York, Klaw Theatre, Nov. 23, 1926.

16. *The Marquise.* Comedy, 3 acts. Published 1927. Produced Criterion Theatre, Feb. 16, 1927.

17. *Home Chat.* Play, 3 acts. Published 1927. Produced Duke of York's Theatre, Oct. 25, 1927.

18. *This Year of Grace!* Revue. Written 1928. Portions published in various collections. Produced Manchester, Palace, Feb. 28, 1928; London, Pavilion, Mar. 22, 1928. Book, music, and lyrics: Coward.

19. *Bitter-Sweet.* Operetta, 3 acts. Published 1929. Produced Manchester, Palace, July 2, 1929; London, His Majesty's Theatre, July 18, 1929.

20. *Private Lives.* Intimate comedy, 3 acts. Written 1929. Published 1930. Produced Edinburgh, King's Theatre, Aug. 18, 1930; London, Phoenix Theatre, Sept. 24, 1930.

21. *Post-Mortem.* Play, 8 scenes. Written 1930. Published 1931.

22. *Some Other Private Lives.* Playlet, 1 act. Published 1931. Produced London, Hippodrome, Dec. 8, 1930.

23. *Cavalcade.* Play, 3 parts. Published 1932. Produced Drury Lane, Oct. 13, 1931.

24. *Words and Music.* Revue, 2 parts. Published 1939. Produced Manchester, Opera House, Aug. 25, 1932; London, Adelphi Theatre, Sept. 16, 1932. Book, lyrics, and music: Coward.

25. *Design for Living.* Comedy, 3 acts. Published 1933. Produced New York, Ethel Barrymore Theatre, Jan. 24, 1933; London, Haymarket Theatre, Jan. 25, 1939.

26. *Conversation Piece.* Romantic comedy with music, 3 acts. Published 1934. Produced His Majesty's Theatre, Feb. 16, 1934.

27. *Point Valaine.* Play, 3 acts. Published 1935. Produced New York, Ethel Barrymore Theatre, Jan. 16, 1935; Liverpool, Playhouse, Oct. 18, 1944; London, Embassy Theatre, Sept. 3, 1947.

The following nine plays (Nos. 28–36) were designed to be presented in various combinations of three bills of three plays each under the collective title *Tonight at 8:30.*

28. *We Were Dancing.* Comedy, 2 scenes. Published 1936. Produced Manchester, Opera House, Oct. 15, 1935; London, Phoenix Theatre, Jan. 29, 1936.

29. *The Astonished Heart.* Play, 6 scenes. Published 1936. Produced Manchester, Opera House, Oct. 15, 1935; London, Phoenix Theatre, Jan. 9, 1936.

30. *"Red Peppers."* Interlude with music, 1 scene. Published 1936. Produced Manchester, Opera House, Oct. 15, 1935; London, Phoenix Theatre, Jan. 9, 1936.

31. *Hands across the Sea.* Light comedy, 1 scene. Published 1936. Produced Manchester, Opera House, Oct. 18, 1935; London, Phoenix Theatre, Jan. 13, 1936.

32. *Fumed Oak.* Unpleasant comedy, 2 scenes. Published 1936. Produced Manchester, Opera House, Oct. 18, 1935; London, Phoenix Theatre, Jan. 13, 1936.

33. *Shadow Play.* Play with music, 1 scene. Published 1936. Produced Manchester, Opera House, Oct. 18, 1935; London, Phoenix Theatre, Jan. 13, 1936.

34. *Family Album.* Victorian comedy with music, 1 scene. Published 1936. Produced Birmingham, Theatre Royal, Dec. 9, 1935; London, Phoenix Theatre, Jan. 9, 1936.

35. *Ways and Means.* Comedy, 3 scenes. Published 1936. Produced Phoenix Theatre, May 5, 1936.

36. *Still Life.* Play, 5 scenes. Published 1936. Produced Phoenix Theatre, May 18, 1936.

37. *Star Chamber.* Light comedy, 1 act. Produced London, Phoenix Theatre, Mar. 21, 1936.

38. *Operette.* 2 acts. Published 1938. Produced Manchester, Opera House, Feb. 17, 1938; London, His Majesty's Theatre, Mar. 16, 1938.

39. *Set to Music.* Revue, 2 acts. Produced New York, Music Box Theatre, Jan. 18, 1939. Book, lyrics, and music: Coward.

40. *Blithe Spirit.* Improbable farce, 3 acts. Published 1941. Produced Manchester, Opera House, June 16, 1941; London, Piccadilly Theatre, July 2, 1941.

41. *Present Laughter.* Play, 3 acts. Published 1943. Produced Blackpool, Grand Theatre, Sept. 20, 1942; London, Haymarket Theatre, Apr. 29, 1943.

42. *This Happy Breed.* Play, 3 acts. Published 1943. Produced Blackpool, Grand Theatre, Sept. 21, 1942; London, Haymarket Theatre, Apr. 30, 1943.

43. *Sigh No More.* Revue, 2 parts. Portions published in various collections. Produced Manchester, Opera House, July 11, 1945; London, Piccadilly Theatre, Aug. 22, 1945. Writer and composer: Coward.

44. *Pacific 1860.* Musical romance, 3 acts. Published 1958. Produced Drury Lane, Dec. 19, 1946.

45. *Peace in Our Time.* Play, 2 acts. Published 1947. Produced Brighton, Theatre Royal, July 15, 1947; London, Lyric Theatre, July 22, 1947.

46. *Ace of Clubs.* Musical play, 2 acts. Portions published in various collections. Produced Manchester, Palace Theatre, May 16, 1950; London, Cambridge Theatre, July 7, 1950.

47. *Island Fling.* Light comedy, 3 acts. Published 1956. Produced Westport, Conn., Country Playhouse, July 22, 1951; Manchester, Opera House, Mar. 19, 1956; London, Lyric Theatre, Apr. 25, 1956.

48. *Relative Values.* Light comedy, 3 acts. Published 1952. Produced Newcastle, Theatre Royal, Oct. 15, 1951; London, Savoy Theatre, Nov. 28, 1951.

49. *Quadrille.* Romantic comedy, 3 acts. Published 1952. Produced Manchester, Opera House, July 15, 1952; London, Phoenix Theatre, Sept. 12, 1952.

50. *After the Ball.* Musical play, 3 acts. Portions published in various collections. Produced Liverpool, Royal Court Theatre, Mar. 1, 1954; London, Globe Theatre, June 10, 1954. Based on Oscar Wilde's *Lady Windermere's Fan.*

51. *Nude with Violin.* Light comedy, 3 acts. Published 1957. Produced Dublin, Olympia Theatre, Sept. 24, 1956; London, Globe Theatre, Nov. 7, 1956.

52. *Look after Lulu!* Comedy, 3 acts. Published 1959. Produced Royal Court Theatre, July 29, 1959. Based on Georges Feydeau's *Occupe-toi d'Amélie.*

53. *Waiting in the Wings.* Play, 3 acts. Published 1960. Produced Duke of York's Theatre, Sept. 7, 1960.

54. *Sail Away.* Musical, 2 acts. Produced New York, Broadhurst Theatre, Oct. 3, 1961. Book, lyrics, and music: Coward.

55. *The Girl Who Came to Supper.* Musical, 2 acts. Produced New York, Broadway Theatre, Dec. 8, 1963. Based on Terence Rattigan's *The Sleeping Prince.* Book: Harry Kurnitz. Music and lyrics: Coward.

56. *High Spirits.* Musical, 2 acts. Produced New York, Alvin Theatre, Apr. 7, 1964. Based on Coward's *Blithe Spirit.* Book, lyrics, and music: Hugh Martin and Timothy Gray.

57. *Come into the Garden Maud.* Light comedy, 1 act.

Published 1966. Produced Queen's Theatre, Apr. 14, 1966.

58. *Shadows of the Evening*. Play, 2 scenes. Published 1966. Produced London, Queen's Theatre, Apr. 14, 1966.

59. *A Song at Twilight*. Comedy, 2 acts. Published 1966. Produced London, Queen's Theatre, Apr. 25, 1966.

EDITIONS

Collections.
Three Plays, New York, 1965.
Individual Plays.
Blithe Spirit. Published in *Drama and Theatre, Illustrated by Seven Modern Plays*, ed. by A. R. Fulton, New York, 1946; *Seven Plays of the Modern Theater*, ed. by V. Wall and J. P. McCormick, New York, 1950; *A Treasury of the Theatre*, ed. by J. Gassner, rev. ed., New York, 1951; *Cavalcade of Comedy*, ed. by L. Kronenberger, New York, 1953; *Representative Modern Plays, British*, ed. by R. Warnock, Chicago, 1953.
Cavalcade. Published in *Sixteen Famous British Plays*, ed. by B. Cerf and V. H. Cartmell, New York, 1942; *Four Good Plays to Read and Act*, ed. by H. A. Voaden, Toronto, 1944.
Conversation Piece. Published in *Seven Plays*, London, 1935.
Design for Living. Published in *Six Plays*, London, 1934.
Easy Virtue. Published in *Representative British Dramas, Victorian and Modern*, ed. by M. J. Moses, Boston, 1931.
Fumed Oak. Published in *This Generation*, ed. by G. K. Anderson and E. L. Walton, Chicago, 1949; *Preface to Drama*, ed. by C. W. Cooper, New York, 1955.
Hay Fever. Published in *Modern Plays*, London, 1937; *My Best Play*, London, 1934.
Point Valaine. Published in *Six Plays of Today*, London, 1939.
Private Lives. Published in *Twentieth Century Plays*, ed. by F. W. Chandler and R. A. Cordell, New York, 1939; *Twentieth Century Plays, British*, ed. by F. W. Chandler and R. A. Cordell, New York, 1941.
Still Life (Brief Encounter). Published in *Introduction to Imaginative Literature*, ed. by B. D. N. Grebanier and S. Reiter, New York, 1960.
The Vortex. Published in *Modern American and British Plays*, ed. by S. M. Tucker, New York, 1931.
Ways and Means. Published in *Contemporary Drama, Eleven Plays: American, English, European*, ed. by E. B. Watson and B. Pressey, New York, 1956.
The Young Idea. Published in *Great Modern British Plays*, ed. by J. W. Marriott, London, 1932.

CRITICISM

P. Braybrooke, *Amazing Mr. Noel Coward*, London, 1933; R. Greacen, *The Art of Noel Coward*, Aldington, Kent, 1953; R. Mander and J. Mitchenson, *Theatrical Companion to Coward*, London, 1957; J. R. Taylor, *The Rise and Fall of the Well-made Play*, New York, 1967; M. Levin, *Noel Coward*, New York, 1968.

COXE, Louis O. (b. Manchester, N.H., April 15, 1918). American educator, poet, and dramatist known in the theatre for the drama *Billy Budd* (1951), an adaptation (with Robert Chapman) of Herman Melville's novella *Billy Budd, Foretopman* (wr. ca. 1890).

Billy Budd (1951). Drama that deals with the confrontation between good and evil aboard a British man-of-war in 1798. Billy Budd, a young foretopman, personifies all that is good and admirable in man. His presence antagonizes Claggart, the ship's master-at-arms, who is his antithesis. Claggart's efforts to destroy the young seaman result in Billy's accidentally causing Claggart's death. Despite his innocence, Billy is charged with murder and convicted. The ship's philosophical master, Captain Vere, is reluctantly forced by law to order Billy's execution. Produced New York, Biltmore Theatre, February 10, 1951.

Prosper Jolyot de Crébillon
(1674 – 1762)

Prosper Jolyot, French tragic dramatist who wrote under the pseudonym Crébillon, was born on January 13, 1674, in Dijon, the son of the master clerk to the Chambre des Comptes of that city. He was educated by the Jesuits at Dijon, and after studying law in Besançon, went to Paris to live in the home of a counsel to Parliament named Prieur. Prieur may have encouraged Crébillon to try his hand at neoclassical tragedy: in 1703 *La mort des enfants de Brutus* (*The Death of Brutus's Children*), now lost, was rejected by the Comédie-Française. In 1705, however, his *Idomeneus* (*Idoménée*) was accepted and successfully performed, to the dismay of his father, who died in 1707 leaving him no inheritance. *See* NEOCLASSICISM.

For the next six years Crébillon was the most popular tragic dramatist in Paris, but his successes led him to abandon his work in favor of the pleasures of society. Although his money ran low, he did nothing to help himself financially. He married in 1707, but his wife died soon afterward, leaving him a son, Claude-Prosper Jolyot de Crébillon (1707–1777), who was later to become famous as the author of witty, licentious novels. The elder Crébillon's progressively deteriorating financial status soon turned to ruin, and he lived a number of years in seclusion and poverty. Despite his reclusive ways, in 1731 he was elected to the Académie Française and four years later was named royal censor, a post that won him many enemies, among them Voltaire. In 1745 Mme. de Pompadour came to his aid, and he was given a pension and a position at the Bibliothèque du Roi. On June 17, 1762, he died in Paris at the age of eighty-eight.

WORK

Next to Voltaire, Crébillon was the finest French tragic dramatist of the eighteenth century, although the sorry state of French tragedy at the time makes the distinction a dubious one. Crébillon's particular skills were the construction of effective theatrical scenes and the creation of perceptively drawn, passionate characters. On the other hand, his plays sometimes betray a certain crudity, through the confusion of the tragic with the merely melodramatic. This tendency, coupled with Crébillon's unswerving devotion to the classical unities, led him to develop situations that strain credulity. In addition, his verse is consistently pedestrian. Despite his faults, Crébillon was an important figure, marking the transition from the passionate eloquence of Racine to the elegant intellectualism of Voltaire. Since Crébillon wrote in a dying form, it is an achievement that he succeeded at all. *See* UNITIES.

The best of his eight plays is *Rhadamisthus and Zenobia* (*Rhadamiste et Zénobie*, 1711), a well-paced tragedy that was performed until its impressive theatrics were surpassed by the melodramatics of romanticism. Another notable work is *Electra* (*Électre*, 1708), an original treatment of the famous myth in which Orestes, unaware that he is Agamemnon's son, falls in love with the daughter of Aegisthus. Orestes' discovery of his true identity makes a very effective scene. Also of interest are *Atreus and Thyestes* (*Atrée et Thyeste*, 1707), a horrific version of the bloody tragedy; *Idomeneus* (1705), a work of grim dignity; and *Pyrrhus* (1726), Crébillon's last play of any merit.

Rhadamisthus and Zenobia (*Rhadamiste et Zénobie*, 1711).

Tragedy telling the story of Rhadamisthus, son of Pharasmane, the authoritarian King of Iberia. Rhadamisthus was brought up by his uncle Mithradates, King of Armenia, whom he slew in order to marry his daughter Zenobia. Escaping from Armenia, Rhadamisthus stabs his wife to prevent her from being possessed by another man. She survives, however, and eventually appears at the court of Pharasmane, where she attracts the love of both the King and his other son, Arsame. Meanwhile, Rhadamisthus has been living among the Romans, who eventually send him as Ambassador to his father's court.

As the play begins, Zenobia, in love with Arsame but fearful of incurring the anger of his father, decides to seek the counsel of the Roman Ambassador. Discovering his true identity, she agrees to flee with him. But the two are caught by Pharasmane, and Rhadamisthus is killed. Stricken with remorse, Pharasmane gives Zenobia to Arsame and makes him ruler of Armenia.

PLAYS

All were first performed in Paris.

1. *Idoménée* (*Idomeneus*). Tragedy, 5 acts; verse. Published 1706. Produced Comédie-Française, Dec. 29, 1705.

2. *Atrée et Thyeste** (*Atreus and Thyestes*). Tragedy, 5 acts; verse. Published 1709. Produced Comédie-Française, Mar. 14, 1707.

3. *Électre* (*Electra*). Tragedy, 5 acts; verse. Published 1709. Produced Comédie-Française, Dec. 14, 1708.

4. *Rhadamiste et Zénobie** (*Rhadamisthus and Zenobia*). Tragedy, 5 acts; verse. Published 1711. Produced Comédie-Française, Jan. 23, 1711.

5. *Xercès* (*Xerxes*). Tragedy, 5 acts; verse. Published 1749. Produced Comédie-Française, Feb. 7, 1714.

6. *Sémiramis*. Tragedy, 5 acts; verse. Published 1717. Produced Comédie-Française, Apr. 10, 1717.

7. *Pyrrhus*. Tragedy, 5 acts, verse. Published 1726. Produced Comédie-Française, Apr. 21, 1726.

8. *Catalina*. Tragedy, 5 acts; verse. Published 1749. Produced Comédie-Française, Dec. 20, 1748.

9. *Le triumvirat, ou La mort de Cicéron* (*The Triumvirate, or The Death of Cicero*). Tragedy, 5 acts; verse. Published 1755. Produced Comédie-Française, Dec. 23, 1754.

EDITIONS

Oeuvres complètes, 3 vols., Paris, 1823; *Théâtre complet*, ed. by A. Vitu, Paris, 1885.

Rhadamisthus and Zenobia. Published in *The Chief Rivals of Corneille and Racine*, ed. and tr. by L. Lockert, Nashville, 1956.

CRITICISM

M. Dutrait, *Étude sur la vie et le théâtre de Crébillon*, Bordeaux, 1895.

CROISSET, Francis de, pseudonym of Frantz Wiener (1877–1937). French dramatist, author of successful boulevard pieces. He collaborated with Emmanuel Arène, Robert de Flers, and Maurice Leblanc and also wrote clever, sentimental comedies of his own, dealing chiefly with the theme of love. Some of his plays are *Chérubin* (1901); *The Gangplank* (*La passerelle*, 1902), written with Mme. Fred

Francis de Croisset. [Italian Cultural Institute]

Gressac; *Happiness, Ladies* (*Le bonheur, mesdames*, 1905); *Paris–New York* (1907), written with Arène; *Arsène Lupin* (1908), a detective story written with Leblanc; *The Borrowed Fire* (*Le feu du voisin*, 1910); *The New Secretary* (*Le coeur dispose*, 1912); *From One Day to Another* (*D'un jour à l'autre*, 1917); *Vineyards of the Lord* (*Les vignes du Seigneur*, 1923), with De Flers; and *Pierre or Jack* (*Pierre ou Jack*, 1931), a play that contrasts the sentimental young man of the pre-World War I type with the bolder sort typical in contemporary motion pictures and radio. His best-remembered drama is *The Hawk* (*L'épervier*, 1914). *See* FLERS, ROBERT DE.

Fernand Crommelynck
(1885 – 1970)

Fernand Crommelynck, Belgian actor and dramatist, was born in Brussels on November 19, 1885. His mother was French, and his father a Belgian of French descent. Crommelynck attended school until the age of twelve, when he went to work in a stockbroker's office. But his father and uncle were actors, and Crommelynck felt that his real

vocation lay in the theatre. He did a little acting and taught himself to write for the stage. Writing in French, he turned out his first play, *The Sculptor of Masks* (*Le sculpteur de masques*, wr. 1905), when he was twenty. This play and his next, *We Shall Go to the Woods No More* (*Nous n'irons plus au bois*, 1906), were one-act verse plays, but *The Sculptor of Masks* was revised and produced as a three-act prose play in 1911.

About this time, Crommelynck went to Paris and was engaged as an actor at the Théâtre des Bouffes-Parisiens, where he remained until 1920, when *The Magnificent Cuckold* (*Le cocu magnifique*) established him as a successful prose dramatist. Crommelynck lived in Paris from 1920 on, writing plays that were successfully produced. When World War II broke out, he returned to Brussels, where he remained until 1944. He then went back to France and lived there until his death, on March 17, 1970, in Saint-Germain-en-Laye.

WORK

Although Crommelynck calls some of his plays farces, others dramas, and others simply plays, the distinctions are arbitrary. Whether or not laughter is present in any given work, pain always is. It is the pain felt by characters living in a world where happiness, often a reality at the outset, is quickly destroyed by irrationalism, self-deception, and obsession. As in the works of his compatriot Ghelderode, the process of destruction may be farcical but the outcome never is. Indeed, in the case of his most popular and important play, *The Magnificent Cuckold* (1920), the author specifically declared that the work may be done as either farce or tragedy. *See* GHELDERODE, MICHEL DE.

The ambiguity of Crommelynck's theatre is probably traceable to the ambivalence of his artistic roots. While he early displayed a strong taste for the heavy, almost plodding type of farce usually associated with the Flemish stage, as a young man he was also influenced by the fashionable literary movement of the time, symbolism. The unproduced one-act verse version of his first play, *The Sculptor of Masks* (wr. 1905, rev. 1911), was introduced to the reading public by Émile Verhaeren, Belgium's leading symbolist poet, and the dramatist significantly chose to call it a "tragic symbol in one act." Though still reflecting the influence of the successful poetic drama of his fellow Belgian Maeterlinck, it introduced the themes of destructive sensuality and carnality that were to dominate Crommelynck's theatre. The protagonist, Pascal, a maker of larger-than-life dramatic masks, in his longing to integrate the de-

Fernand Crommelynck.
[Consulate General of Belgium]

A 1959 Brussels
production of *Le
cocu magnifique*.
[Consulate General
of Belgium]

mands of fleshly passion with beauty projects the problems of art and life as seen by the playwright. It is significant that the use of both real and illusory masks was to be an important element in Crommelynck's plays. *See* MAETERLINCK, MAURICE; SYMBOLISM.

Crommelynck's next produced play was *The Merchant of Regrets* (*Le marchand de regrets*, 1913), in which an antiquary's obsession with antiques leads him to neglect his young wife, who eventually runs off with the village miller. In 1920 came the spectacularly successful *The Magnificent Cuckold*, which was to bring the author international success. In it, Bruno, obsessed by jealousy, is destroyed by the inventions of his fevered brain. Unlike Shakespeare's trusting Othello, Bruno is an innately jealous man who needs no Iago to stimulate his imaginings. The ambiguousness of his wife's nature, however, is perhaps suggested by the mask he forces her to wear.

The Childish Lovers (*Les amants puérils*, 1921), also cast in the form of tragic farce, contrasts the love of two adolescents and a once-handsome pair of lovers fallen into the decrepitude of age and desperately clinging to the mask of youth. In *Golden Guts* (*Tripes d'or*, 1925), Crommelynck invented a Flemish parallel of Molière's Harpagon, presenting a miser so obsessed by his gold that he ends by eating it. Costumed like Louis XIV, Pierre-Auguste dies on his *chaise percée* when the gold literally bursts his guts. The inability of innocence to adjust to the world's corruption is the theme of *Carine, or The Girl in Love with Her Soul* (*Carine, ou La jeune fille folle de son âme*, 1929), but in *A Woman Whose Heart Is Too Small* (*Une femme qu'a le coeur trop petit*, 1934), love conquers implacable and meddlesome virtue. In *Hot and Cold, or Monsieur Dom's Idea* (*Chaud et froid, ou L'idée de Monsieur Dom*, 1934), the theme is cuckoldry again and, paradoxically, the protagonist is able to obtain his wife's fidelity only as a result of a misunderstanding that arises after his death.

The mixture of buffoonery and tragedy characteristic of Crommelynck's theatre extends to his prose style, which presents the most outrageous, gross situations in a language of such beautifully sensuous imagery that it often caused his audiences to burst into applause. Many of his plays were revived after World War II with great success.

The Magnificent Cuckold (*Le cocu magnifique*, 1920). Grotesque farce. So great is the admiration of the scribe Bruno for his lovely wife Stella that, to prove the perfection of her charms, he exposes her bosom to her cousin Petrus. However, sensing Petrus's lust, Bruno is immediately seized by feelings of jealousy and suspicion and decides to keep his wife masked and under lock and key. Tormented by his doubts, Bruno eventually forces Stella and Petrus to sleep together so that his suspicion may be an actuality. Stella complies in the hope of curing her husband's madness, but Bruno soon convinces himself that she and Petrus only pretended to make love. He therefore forces Stella to take as lovers the village menfolk. Though she is obediently unfaithful, her husband continues to believe that she is pretending in order to conceal a secret lover. Bruno himself visits her in disguise, and when she yields to him, he becomes enraged but soon convinces himself that she has recognized him. After a vengeful ducking by the village women, Stella, feeling purified, decides to disobey her husband by refusing to accept as a lover a local cowherd who truly loves her. As a result, Bruno becomes convinced that the cowherd must be her secret lover, and he prepares to kill him. To save the cowherd's life, Stella accepts him as a lover. She goes off to live with him, asking only that she be permitted to remain faithful. Bruno remains convinced that this is "but another of her tricks." Although the tone of the play is farcical throughout, the agony of Bruno is profound and pathetic.

Golden Guts (*Tripes d'or*, 1925). Satirical farce about a modern Midas. When Pierre-Auguste inherits a large estate from an uncle, his first reactions are benevolence and joy. He can now marry his beloved Azelle, and he decides to give away a pile of gold coins found in his uncle's strongbox, intending to keep for himself merely 150 gold pieces that seem to bear a likeness of Azelle. But when these coins become mixed with the rest, all of them look alike. At this point, Pierre-Auguste turns avaricious and retracts his generous decision. He then begins to worry constantly about losing his gold. Advised jestingly by a doctor to eat it, thus absorbing it into his body, he does just that, mixing it with dog food. For a moment, he is "Golden Guts," reveling in his riches and forgetting Azelle, who weeps at the change in him. Finally, in a farcical scene, Mother Nature takes over, and Pierre-Auguste, enthroned on his toilet seat, explodes, dying in a great burst of liberating laughter.

Carine, or The Girl in Love with Her Soul (*Carine, ou La jeune fille folle de son âme*, 1929). Drama in which a sheltered and sensitive girl fails to adjust to the harsh truth she discovers about the people around her. On the morning after their marriage, Carine and Frédéric, deeply and truly in love, are briefly separated. During this interval Carine is confronted with a series of shocking truths that she cannot accept, since she has always been idealistic, unaware of her milieu, in which lies resemble truth and love is at best a masquerade and at worst a cynical pastime. The sudden knowledge of her mother's illicit love affair and of Frédéric's intimate relations with her best friend, as well as the advances of both a lesbian and her own uncle, chill her to the bone. In her bewilderment she alienates Frédéric and then commits suicide before he can grasp what has happened. Carine cannot be like other women, and it is too late for Frédéric to protect her with his love.

A Woman Whose Heart Is Too Small (*Une femme qu'a le coeur trop petit*, 1934). Comedy in which Balbine, the newly married second wife of Olivier, is an "implacable allegory of Domestic Virtue" and a virtuous prude. Her heart, too small to encompass warmth, gentleness, compassion, or love, fails her each time she is confronted with any form of human weakness. After upsetting everyone around her—her servants, her stepdaughter, her brother-in-law, and the villagers—and driving her husband to drink, she finally accepts the advice of a woman whose heart is too big. Balbine is miraculously cured by the simple act of sharing her husband's bed, and order is restored as she becomes a real woman and ceases to meddle.

Hot and Cold, or Monsieur Dom's Idea (*Chaud et froid, ou L'idée de Monsieur Dom*, 1934). Grotesque farce in which, after the death of Monsieur Dom, a colorless, noncommittal cuckold, a rumor spreads throughout the town that on his deathbed Dom had a marvelous idea. Since the nature of the "idea" is unknown, there is nothing to prevent every faction and philistine in town from becoming its resolute champion. Thus the drab Monsieur Dom, by virtue of having carried his idea with him to the grave, becomes a great "spiritual" force in the town. His adulterous wife Léona not only becomes entrapped as the loving widow of this paragon of virtue but discovers that her late husband had a mistress who is eager to commit suicide in order to claim the place beside him in the tomb as provided in his will. To forestall this, Léona manages to throw the mistress into the arms of her own current lover. Thus unencumbered, Léona prepares to take her place as sole proprietress of her husband's memory and to preside over the museum which the town creates as a shrine for his idea.

PLAYS

1. *Le sculpteur de masques* (*The Sculptor of Masks*).

Play, 1 act; verse. Written 1905. Published 1908. Revised version: 3 acts; prose. Written 1911. Published 1918. Produced Paris, Théâtre du Gymnase, Feb. 1, 1911.

2. *Nous n'irons plus au bois* (*We Shall Go to the Woods No More*). Play, 1 act, verse. Written 1906. Published 1906. Produced Brussels, Théâtre du Parc. Apr. 28, 1906.

3. *Chacun pour soi* (*Every Man for Himself*). Play. Written 1907. Published 1907.

4. *Le marchand de regrets* (*The Merchant of Regrets*). Play. Written 1913. Published 1913. Produced Brussels, Théâtre du Parc, 1913.

5. *Le cocu magnifique** (*The Magnificent Cuckold*). Grotesque farce, 3 acts, Written 1920. Published 1921. Produced Paris, Théâtre de l'Oeuvre, Dec. 20, 1920.

6. *Les amants puérils* (*The Childish Lovers*). Play, 3 acts. Written 1921. Produced Paris, Comédie Montaigne, Mar. 14, 1921.

7. *Tripes d'or* (*Golden Guts*). Play, 3 acts. Written 1925. Published 1930. Produced Paris, Comédie des Champs-Élysées, Apr. 29, 1925.

8. *Carine, ou La jeune fille folle de son âme* (*Carine, or The Girl in Love with Her Soul*). Drama, 1 act. Written 1929. Published 1930. Produced Paris, Théâtre de l'Oeuvre, Dec. 19, 1929.

9. *Une femme qu'a le coeur trop petit* (*A Woman Whose Heart Is Too Small*). Comedy, 3 acts. Written 1934. Published 1934. Produced Brussels, Palais des Beaux-Arts, Jan. 11, 1934.

10. *Chaud et froid, ou L'idée de Monsieur Dom* (*Hot and Cold, or Monsieur Dom's Idea*). Play, 3 acts. Written 1934. Published 1936. Produced Paris, Comédie des Champs-Élysées, Nov. 24, 1934.

11. *Le chevalier à la lune, ou Sir John Falstaff* (*Knight of the Moon, or Sir John Falstaff*). Comedy, 5 acts. Written 1954. Published 1954. Based on Shakespeare.

Other Known Titles.

L'ange qui pleure (*The Weeping Angel*).

Le chemin des conquêtes (*The Road of Conquests*).

Le cimitière des belles amours (*The Cemetery of Beautiful Love Affairs*).

Le coeur volant (*The Flying Heart*).

La gourgandine (*The Strumpet*).

Maison fondée en 1550 (*Establishment Founded in 1550*).

Le matin du troisième jour (*The Morning of the Third Day*).

Va mon coeur (*Go, My Heart*).

EDITIONS

Théâtre complet, 1 vol. to date, Paris, 1956; *Théâtre*, 3 vols., Paris, 1967–1968.

CRITICISM

M. Arland, *À la rencontre de Fernand Crommelynck*, Liège, 1947; D. I. Grossvogel, "Crommelynck," *The Self-conscious Stage in Modern French Drama*, New York, 1958.

Rachel Crothers
(1878 – 1958)

Rachel Crothers, American dramatist, was born on December 12, 1878, in Bloomington, Ill., the daughter of two physicians, Dr. Eli Kirk Crothers and Dr. Marie Louise De Pew Crothers. While still a child, she showed an interest in the theatre, amusing herself with the production of plays of her own composition. After graduating from the Illinois State Normal School in 1892, she moved to New York, where she enrolled in the Wheatcroft School of Acting, later becoming a member of the faculty. During this period she enjoyed a brief career as a professional actress. Her one-act play *The Rector* was produced professionally in 1902. The successful production of *The Three of Us* in 1906 established her reputation as a dramatist, and thereafter her life was mainly a chronicle of her activity in the theatre.

By World War I Miss Crothers's reputation had grown considerably. She directed her own plays and, in 1920, played the lead in a revival of *He and She*. In 1925, at the height of her career, she produced John Kirkpatrick's *The Book of Charm*. The failure of the play brought financial disaster, and she spent the following years paying the debts she had incurred.

After 1926 she wrote only six plays, but they include those for which she is chiefly remembered: *Let Us Be Gay* (1929); *As Husbands Go* (1931); *When Ladies Meet* (1932); and, after a five-year absence from the theatre, her last play, *Susan and God* (1937). Thereafter, although retired from the

Rachel Crothers. [Theatre Collection, The New York Public Library at Lincoln Center, Astor, Lenox and Tilden Foundations]

theatre, she was active in theatrical and war relief organizations. She spent her retirement at her home in Redding, Conn., where she died on July 5, 1958.

WORK

Some twenty-three full-length plays written over more than three decades established Rachel Crothers as one of the leading American practitioners of the comedy of manners during the early twentieth century. Expert in the composition of the well-made play, she used her skill to depict the varying social roles of the American woman during the years in which she wrote. Thus her approach changes from an interest in the emancipation of women to a growing concern with the responsibilities imposed by this new freedom. Addressed to these problems, her mildly satirical plays contain shrewd observation and well-drawn characters. *See* COMEDY OF MANNERS; WELL-MADE PLAY.

Most of her better plays were written after 1925. These include *Susan and God* (1937), in

Roman Bohnen and Catharine Doucet in *As Husbands Go.* New York, John Golden Theatre, 1931. [Theatre Collection, The New York Public Library at Lincoln Center, Astor, Lenox and Tilden Foundations]

which a woman espouses a religious philosophy concerned with the power of love yet neglects her husband and child; *As Husbands Go* (1931), which deals with two American women who become amorously involved with two European men; *When Ladies Meet* (1932), a comedy of a confrontation between a man's wife and his mistress; and *Let Us Be Gay* (1929), a comedy in which a divorced man and wife become reconciled.

Of particular interest among her earlier plays are *A Man's World* (1909), in which a woman who has determined to destroy the father of an illegitimate child she has raised discovers that it is the man she loves; *He and She* (1911), which depicts the marital problems of a husband and wife who compete as sculptors; *Nice People* (1920), a portrait of "flaming youth"; *Mary the Third* (1923), the study of three generations of women; and *Expressing Willie* (1924), in which a naïve young man is saved from the clutches of a sophisticated but shallow woman.

As Husbands Go (1931). Comedy in which Lucille Lingard falls in love with a young English poet, Ronald Derbyshire, on a trip to Paris, while her widowed friend Emmie falls in love with a Continental gentleman, Hippolytus Lomi. Returning to break with her husband Charles in Iowa, Lucille hesitates because of his kindness and obvious love for her. When Ronald arrives, although they try to keep their intentions secret, Charles becomes aware of the situation. He becomes friendly with Ronald, gets him drunk, and leads him to confess that he conceives of a wife as an adjunct to his own genius. Realizing the selfishness of his infatuation, Ronald departs, leaving Charles and Lucille together. Meanwhile, overcoming the objections of her grown daughter, Emmie decides to marry Hippolytus.

When Ladies Meet (1932). Comedy in which Mary Howard, an attractive author, is trying to convince Jimmie Lee, who is in love with her, that the novel she is writing is realistic. In her book, a "proper" woman, who is in love with a married man, confronts the man's wife and explains that since they are in love, it is only right that the wife surrender her husband to the mistress. When Mary is invited to spend the weekend at a friend's house, she requests that an invitation be extended to her publisher, Rogers Woodruff, with whom she has fallen in love. The invitation proffered and the weekend in progress, Jimmie, unknown to anyone, has lured Rogers from the house with an urgent call for him to return to New York. Then, with Rogers out of the house, he arrives with Claire, Rogers's wife, under the pretext that they are lost. Jimmie introduces Claire as his cousin,

Scene from *When Ladies Meet,* with Walter Abel and Frieda Inescort. New York, Royale Theatre, 1932. [Theatre Collection, The New York Public Library at Lincoln Center, Astor, Lenox and Tilden Foundations]

explaining to Claire that her presence with him will make Mary jealous. Because of a storm, Claire and Jimmie are forced to spend the night. While the others are asleep, Mary and Claire discuss Mary's novel. Speaking from experience, Claire contests the reality of the book. Mary disagrees because she knows she would act like the mistress in the story. With Rogers's return, Claire suddenly realizes Mary's relationship with him, and Mary discovers Claire's true identity. Mary thinks this is the proper time for Rogers to tell his wife about their affair, but he hesitates and she realizes that he does not love her. Claire, who formerly took Rogers back after his escapades, has decided to leave him. For the first time she has seen the suffering Rogers inflicts on the women he loves and leaves.

Susan and God (1937). Social comedy in which the lovable and featherbrained Susan Trexel returns from Europe and announces that while in England she has found a new religion of love. At the estate of her friend Irene, where her husband, daughter, and friends have assembled to welcome her, Susan preaches her shallow morality, which is sheer hypocrisy when seen in the light of her personal relations. Blossom, her gawky daughter, has been shut up in boarding schools and camps for years, while Barrie, her husband, is an alcoholic whom she thinks of divorcing. However, in her euphoric homecoming mood, she strikes a bargain with Barrie: if he stays sober, they will live together for the summer for Blossom's sake. At his first drunken breath he is to give her a divorce. By summer's end, Barrie has remained faithful to his promise, save for one drunken spree provoked by her, and Susan has recognized that strength and determination are the instruments for changing people, not empty prayer. "God," she says, "is here—in

Gertrude Lawrence (seated) and Nancy Coleman in *Susan and God*. Cleveland, Hanna Theatre, 1939. [Theatre Collection, The New York Public Library at Lincoln Center, Astor, Lenox and Tilden Foundations]

us." Realizing the joy of being with those who need and love her, she gives up the idea of divorce and determines to stay with her adoring family.

PLAYS

Unless otherwise noted, the plays were first performed in New York.

1. *The Rector.* Play, 1 act. Published 1905. Produced Madison Square Theatre, Apr. 3, 1902.
2. *Criss-Cross.* Play, 1 act. Published 1904.
3. *The Three of Us.* Play, 4 acts. Published 1916. Produced Madison Square Theatre, Oct. 17, 1906.
4. *The Coming of Mrs. Patrick.* Play, 4 acts. Produced Madison Square Theatre, Nov. 6, 1907.
5. *Myself Bettina.* Play, 4 acts. Produced Chicago, Powers Theatre, January, 1908; New York, Daly's Theatre, Oct. 5, 1908.
6. *Katy Did.* Play, 1 act. Published 1909.
7. *Mrs. Molly.* Play, 1 act. Published 1909.
8. *A Man's World.* Play, 4 acts. Published 1915. Produced Washington, National Theatre, Oct. 18, 1909; New York, Comedy Theatre, Feb. 8, 1910.
9. *He and She.* Play, 3 acts. Published 1933. Produced Poughkeepsie, N.Y., 1911; Boston, Plymouth Theatre, Feb. 5, 1912, as *The Herfords;* New York, Little Theatre, Feb. 12, 1920.
10. *Ourselves.* Play, 1 act. Produced Lyric Theatre, New York, Nov. 13, 1913.
11. *Young Wisdom.* Play. Produced Criterion Theatre, Jan. 5, 1914.
12. *The Heart of Paddy Whack.* Comedy, 3 acts. Published 1925. Produced Baltimore, Oct. 5, 1914; New York, Grand Opera House, Nov. 26, 1914.
13. *Old Lady 31.* Comedy, prologue and 3 acts. Published 1923. Produced Schenectady, N.Y., Sept. 4, 1916; New York, Thirty-ninth Street Theatre, Oct. 30, 1916.
14. (With Kate Douglas Wiggin). *Mother Carey's Chickens.* Little comedy of home, 3 acts. Published 1925. Produced Cort Theatre, Sept. 25, 1917.

15. *Once upon a Time.* Comedy, 4 acts. Published 1925. Produced Atlantic City, N.J., October, 1917; New York, Fulton Theatre, Apr. 15, 1918.
16. *A Little Journey.* Comedy, 3 acts. Published 1923. Produced New York, Little Theatre, Dec 26, 1918.
17. *39 East.* Comedy, 3 acts. Published 1924. Produced Broadhurst Theatre, Mar. 31, 1919.
18. *Nice People.* Play, 3 acts. Published 1924. Produced Atlantic City, N.J., Dec. 26, 1920; New York, Klaw Theatre, Mar. 2, 1921.
19. *Everyday.* Comedy drama, 3 acts. Published 1930. Produced Atlantic City, N.J., Oct. 27, 1921; New York, Bijou Theatre, Nov. 16, 1921.
20. *Mary the Third.* Comedy, prologue and 3 acts. Published 1923. Produced Thirty-ninth Street Theatre, Feb. 5, 1923.
21. *Expressing Willie.* Comedy, 3 acts. Published 1924. Produced Forty-eighth Street Theatre, Apr. 16, 1924.
22. *Peggy.* Play, 1 act. Published 1924.
23. *A Lady's Virtue.* Play, 3 acts. Produced Selwyn Theatre, Chicago, October, 1925; New York, Bijou Theatre, Nov. 23, 1925.
24. *The Importance of Being Clothed.* Play, 1 act. Published 1925.
25. *The Importance of Being Nice.* Play, 1 act. Published 1925.
26. *The Importance of Being Married.* Play, 1 act. Published 1925.
27. *The Importance of Being a Woman.* Play, 1 act. Published 1925.
28. *What They Think.* Play, 1 act. Published 1925.
29. *Venus.* Comedy, 3 acts. Produced Masque Theatre, Dec. 26, 1927.
30. *Let Us Be Gay.* Comedy, 3 acts. Published 1929. Produced Little Theatre, Feb. 21, 1929.
31. *As Husbands Go.* Comedy, 3 acts. Published 1931. Produced John Golden Theatre, Mar. 5, 1931.
32. *Caught Wet.* Comedy, 3 acts. Published 1932. Produced John Golden Theatre, Nov. 4, 1931.
33. *When Ladies Meet.* Comedy, 3 acts. Published 1932. Produced Royale Theatre, Oct. 6, 1932.
34. *Susan and God.* Drama, 3 acts. Published 1938. Produced Plymouth Theatre, Oct. 7, 1937.

EDITIONS

Collections.
Mary the Third, Old Lady 31 and *A Little Journey,* New York, 1923; *Expressing Willie, Nice People* and *39 East,* New York, 1924; *Six One-act Plays,* Boston, 1925.

Individual Plays.
As Husbands Go. Published in *Twentieth Century Plays,* ed. by F. W. Chandler and R. A. Cordell, New York, 1934.

Expressing Willie. Published in *Representative Modern Plays,* ed. by R. A. Cordell, New York, 1929.

He and She. Published in *Representative American Plays from 1767 to the Present Day,* ed. by A. H. Quinn, 7th ed., rev. and enl., New York, 1953.

Mary the Third. Published in *Twenty-five Modern Plays,* ed. by S. M. Tucker, New York, 1931.

Nice People. Published in *Representative American Dramas, National and Local,* ed. by M. J. Moses and J. W. Krutch, rev. ed., Boston, 1941.

CROUSE, Russel (1893–1966). American journalist and dramatist. Beginning as a reporter on the *Cincinnati Commercial Tribune* at the age of seventeen, Crouse had an active career in journalism before turning to the theatre. His collaboration with Howard Lindsay produced a series of highly successful plays: *Anything Goes* (1934); *Red, Hot and Blue* (1936); *Hooray for What?* (1937); *Life with Father* (1939), based on the book by Clarence Day (1935); *Strip for Action* (1942); *State of the Union* (1945), a satire on American politics for which they received the Pulitzer Prize the following year; *Life with Mother* (1948); *Call Me Madam* (1950); *Remains to Be Seen* (1951); *The Prescott Proposals* (1953); *The Great Sebastians* (1956); *Happy Hunting* (1956); *Tall Story* (1959), based on Howard Nemerov's novel *The Homecoming Game* (1957); *The Sound of Music* (1959); and *Mr. President* (1962). Crouse produced the libretti for the musicals *The Gang's All Here* (1931; music by Lewis Gensler); and *Hold Your Horses* (1933), with Carey Ford. *See* LINDSAY, HOWARD.

CROWLEY, Mart (1935–   ). American dramatist whose first professionally produced play, *The Boys in the Band* (1968), is a sensitive study of personal relationships among homosexuals.

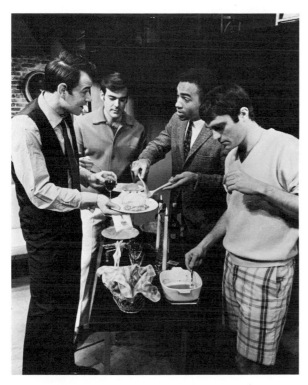

Scene from Mart Crowley's *The Boys in the Band*. [Friedman-Abeles]

CROWNE, John (ca. 1640–ca. 1703). English playwright whose dramas and comedies of intrigue, although typical of the Restoration, nevertheless show signs of the sentimentalism that was to become prevalent later in the eighteenth century. After several experiments in the tragic-heroic style, Crowne turned to comedy in 1676 with *The Countrey Wit,* based on Molière's *The Sicilian, or Love Makes the Painter.* While containing a fore-

taste of moral sentimentalism, *The Countrey Wit* is a typical Restoration piece, complete with a young girl deceiving her fiancé for love of a rake. Although it was successful, Crowne continued, with but few exceptions (one of which was his major success), in the style with which he had begun his career. His next play was *City Politiques* (1683), a comedy satirizing prominent Whigs, and it was followed by *Sir Courtly Nice, or It Cannot Be* (1685). This comedy, based on a Spanish piece which, it is said, Charles II asked Crowne to adapt, proved to be his longest-enduring success: for the greater part of the eighteenth century it remained a popular stock piece. His last plays, save perhaps for *The English Frier, or The Town Sparks* (1690), are of little significance. They consist of a couple of comedies, some neoclassical tragedies, and several heroic dramas with historical settings, such as *The Destruction of Jerusalem by Titus Vespasian* (two parts, 1677), attacking the Puritans, and *The History of Charles the Eighth of France, or The Invasion of Naples by the French* (1671). His *Calisto, or The Chaste Nymph* (1675), a masque commissioned by the Earl of Rochester and performed at court, although lacking particular merit, is nonetheless notable as the only attempt during this period to carry on the court-masque tradition that was so strong before 1640. *See* MASQUE; SENTIMENTAL COMEDY.

Ramón de la Cruz
(1731 – 1794)

Don Ramón de la Cruz Cano y Olmedilla, Spanish dramatist, translator, and poet, was born on March 28, 1731, in Madrid. He was the eldest of four sons of a modest family that evidently had never been successful financially or socially. He studied the humanities at a school in Madrid, and when his father died in 1744, he appealed to relatives for money to continue his education. But their help was short-lived, and he probably never attended a university. He began writing at the age of thirteen; by fourteen he was writing tragedies.

Between 1748 and 1759, Cruz devoted himself to writing poetry and verse plays and translating French works, among them those of Racine and Voltaire, into Spanish. But success eluded him. In 1759 he obtained employment as a bookkeeper in a government office for the collection of fines. Shortly thereafter he married Doña Margarita Beatriz de Magán. In 1764 Cruz finally found his expression

Ramón de la Cruz.
[Biblioteca
Nacional, Madrid]

Cruz died in Madrid on March 5, 1794, from a recurrence of pneumonia, leaving some 542 works, of which 300 were *sainetes*. During the three decades of his prolific career he had been alone among his contemporaries in appealing both to the general public and to learned classicists with his lively works.

WORK

Cruz successfully fought the neoclassical mainstream of his day and returned national forms such as the *sainete* and *entremés* (interlude), as well as a piquant Hispanic realism, to the Spanish stage. Extraordinarily prolific, he had resources and energy that led critics to liken him to Lope de Vega. While he was little appreciated by nineteenth-century critics, modern dramatic historians value his preservation and continuance of Spanish dramatic traditions. His often-quoted motto was "Truth dictates and I write," and his depictions of court and back-alley life are compared in fidelity, artistic merit, and satirical thrust to the tapestries of Goya. Thus Cruz is also a precursor of the realistic and assertively Spanish theatre of the late nineteenth century. *See* ENTREMÉS.

The forms for which Cruz is best known, the *sainete* and the *entremés,* were somewhat moribund at the time he took them up. These forms are similar in that they are meant as preludes or interludes to more serious works. They had been used by such earlier authors as Lope de Rueda. The zarzuela, somewhat more elaborate, being a more extended production and leaning heavily though not exclusively on musical material, had been used by Calderón and Lope de Vega, and it, too, found an echo in the late nineteenth century. Cruz contributed to the form chiefly by substituting genre characters for the previously favored gods and goddesses. As he developed these forms and profited by them, he agonized in print over his forced abandonment of such conventions as the three classical unities but was apparently not deterred by these doctrinal qualms. He wrote in verse, using mostly the eight-syllable line with balanced lines rhyming in assonance. Even his best plays, however, show him to be a minor poet. *See* UNITIES.

Among the most representative and successful of Cruz's *sainetes* are *Manolo I* and *Manolo II* (ca. 1769), two tragic burlesques; *Pride's Fall* (*La presumida burlada*, 1768), mocking feminine pretensions; and *The Dance of the Lamp* (*El fandango del candil*, wr. 1768), a series of character vignettes. The *Manolo* plays are in a lower-class Madrid setting and mock the pointless brutality of life in those surroundings. The action consists of feuds and love quarrels that are a kind of

and his success through the *sainete* (a short, often satirical sketch, performed between the acts of full-length plays). Although throughout his career he occasionally produced full-length tragedies and comedies, it was for his *sainetes* and other short pieces that he became known and is remembered today. In fact, by 1770, despite criticism of the *sainete* form by intellectuals, its popularity had grown and Cruz had become a celebrated author, admired even by former critics.

Though he remained in his government position, he became a friend and protégé of the Dukes of Alba and Osuna and of the Duchess of Benavente, in whose house he lived until his death. The usual jealousies and controversies of a literary career were not lacking in his life. His most illustrious contemporary and literary rival in Madrid was Nicolás Fernández de Moratín (father of the more renowned Leandro Fernández de Moratín), an accomplished lyricist who seems to have resented the popularity of Cruz on the stage. Moratín was unable to win acceptance for his own efforts at comedy and tragedy, and his criticism of Cruz finally led the latter to write a *sainete* mocking his rival's desire to be a jack-of-all-trades. *See* FERNÁNDEZ DE MORATÍN, NICOLÁS.

burlesque of the *comedia de pundonor,* just as the bawdily comic names of the protagonists are a foil to the lords and ladies of the serious *comedias* being performed on the same stage. *Pride's Fall* ridicules the airs of a servant girl who, upon marrying her widowed master, tries to claim noble antecedents. She is humbled by the appearance of her peasant mother. *The Dance of the Lamp* depicts, through the device of a dance hall, a variety of Madrid characters including toughs and dandies, young girls, two older women, and a fop. The insubstantial plot culminates in the outbreak of a brawl and the arrival of the police. The brilliance of all these pieces rests not on masterful plotting or depth of feeling but on their fast pace, clever and colloquial dialogue, and telling commentary on daily life in Madrid. *See* COMEDIA.

EDITIONS

Sainetes, 2 vols., ed. by A. Durán, Madrid, 1843; *Sainetes inéditos,* ed. by C. Cambronero, Madrid, 1900; E. Cotarelo y Mori, ed., "Sainetes . . . en su mayoría inéditos," *Nueva biblioteca de autores españoles,* vol. XXIII, Madrid, 1915.

CRITICISM

E. Cotarelo y Mori, *Don Ramón de la Cruz y sus obras,* Madrid, 1899; A. Hamilton, *A Study of Spanish Manners, 1750–1800, from the Plays of Ramón de la Cruz,* Urbana, Ill., 1926; J. Vega, *Don Ramón de la Cruz, el poeta de Madrid,* Madrid, 1945.

Gergely Csíky
(1842 – 1891)

Gergely Csíky, the father of modern social drama in the Hungarian theatre, was born in Pankota (Pâncota), Transylvania, on December 8, 1842. His father, a physician, died at an early age, but not before arousing an enthusiasm for the theatre in his son by writing occasional plays for children. Csíky's mother, however, wanted her son to enter the priesthood. Therefore, in 1859 Csíky graduated from the Catholic Gymnasium in the town of Arad and entered the seminary in Temesvár (Timişoara). After three years the Bishop of Csanád County sent his brilliant student of theology to the central seminary in Pest. Csíky was ordained into the priesthood in 1865 and then received his doctorate in theology at the St. Augustine Seminary in Vienna. In 1868 he returned to Temesvár to teach religion in the Gymnasium. He was assigned to the seminary of Temesvár, as professor of ethics, canon law, and ecclesiastical history in 1870.

Since his early school days Csíky had been writing numerous poems, novels, and dramas under various pen names. A collection of his short stories and a volume of his poems were published under an assumed name in 1872. By 1875 he had received the Teleki Prize of the Hungarian Academy of Sciences for his play *The Prophecy* (*Jóslat*), which appeared under his own name. He received the same prize in 1877 for *The Rebel Pagan* (*Janus*), a tragedy, but it was his play *The Proletarians* (*A proletárok*), produced in 1880, that established his fame.

It was not long before his activities in the theatre stimulated harsh criticism from the Catholic hierarchy. After the success of *The Proletarians* his bishop asked Csíky to give up the theatre. Rather than comply, he left the priesthood, became a Lutheran, and married Amanda Bakody, the widow of Ernő Villecz, in 1881. For the next decade Csíky dominated the Hungarian stage. He wrote thirty-five plays, published numerous novels, translated Plautus and Sophocles, and edited the Hungarian edition of the *Collected Works of Shakespeare*. In addition, he taught the theory and history of the drama in the School of Dramatic Art, was the *Dramaturg* (artistic adviser) of the Hungarian National Theatre (Magyar Nemzeti Szinház), and held the post of secretary in the Kisfaludy Society, a famous literary stronghold.

Csíky had chronic heart trouble that caused his death, on November 19, 1891, at the age of forty-eight, in Budapest.

WORK

Csíky was the first major Hungarian playwright to depict social problems realistically. He used the popular formulas and theatrical

Gergely Csíky.
[Interfoto MTI, Budapest]

Ferenc Naday in
Fancy Misery.
[Interfoto MTI,
Budapest]

devices of French playwrights such as Dumas
fils, Sardou, and Augier. In such comedies as
The Title Hunter (*Mukányi,* 1880), *Bubbles*
(*Buborékok,* 1884), and *The Legacy Hunters*
(*Az atyafiak,* 1891) he ridiculed with sardonic
humor every shade of snobbery as well as the
practices of buying love, respect, or a title
with money and of turning social status into
cash.

In *The Proletarians* (1880), Csíky's first major success, the word "proletarian" is used
ironically to refer to certain segments of
Hungarian society which, as in the days of
the Roman Empire, without property or assured income subsisted by means of parasitic
scheming. In *Fancy Misery* (*Cifra nyomoruság,* 1881), he mocked the attempts of low-
paid state bureaucrats to live up to their titles by living far beyond their means.

After the publication of his study entitled
Catholic Matrimonial Law in 1874, Csíky was
considered an authority on divorce, and many
of his plays deal with this problem. In *Cecilia's Marriage* (*Cecil házassága,* 1883) he offered a practical rather than a religious solution.

Csíky was also preoccupied with maternal
love. In *The Stomfay Family* (*A Stomfay család,* 1882) a mother gives up happiness for
her daughter; *Evil Love* (*Bozóthy Márta,* 1883)
depicts a mother protecting her family
through dishonesty; *Anna* (1882) is about a

mother who reveals her secret to prevent her
daughter from repeating the same mistake;
and in *Eternal Law* (*Örök törvény,* 1890) a
mother wants to see the child she abandoned
fifteen years earlier. One of Csíky's most
popular plays, *The Grandmother* (*A nagymama,* 1891), portrays a grand old lady who
straightens out the love affairs of her grandchildren.

The Iron Man (*Vasember,* 1888) is a modern
social tragedy written in the genre of the
classical Greeks. The story was influenced by
Schiller's *Love and Intrigue;* the dramatic
concept, by Sophocles's *Antigone.*

The Proletarians (*A proletárok,* 1880).
Drama exposing the decadent morals of the
contemporary bourgeoisie. Mrs. Kamilla Sze-
dervári, masquerading as the widow of a
heroic colonel of the 1848 War of Independence, solicits gifts for herself in a businesslike manner. Timót, a rich sheep farmer impressed by the reputation of the imaginary
dead colonel, visits Kamilla to help her overcome her bereavement. There he meets and
falls in love with Kamilla's only daughter,
Irén. Timót mistakenly confides his feelings
for the girl to Zátonyi, who suddenly shows
an interest in the girl and tells the widow
that he will unmask her scheme if she refuses
to let him marry Irén. Meanwhile, Irén and
Darvas, a penniless lawyer whom she truly
loves, are planning to marry as soon as Darvas gets a job. But, to save her mother from
jail after Kamilla tells her of the blackmail,
Irén marries Zátonyi, and Darvas is given a
good job with Timót.

Right after the marriage Zátonyi leaves his
wife on the pretense of business, and his former wife spreads rumors about Irén and Timót. After his return Zátonyi plays the understanding husband and offers a quick
divorce from Irén if Timót will pay a large
sum of money. Irén now realizes that Zátonyi
married her only to profit by a quick divorce.
She breaks off with Zátonyi and also with her
mother, even though Kamilla tells Irén that
her scheme was the only way to assure her a
decent upbringing. After the marriage is dissolved, the lovers are reconciled and Irén
marries Darvas.

Fancy Misery (*Cifra nyomoruság,* 1881).
Drama about the money-conscious Hungarian bourgeoisie. Sodró, a minor clerk in the
state bureaucracy, is bankrupt, the yearly interest on his debt being twice as large as his
annual salary. His orphaned niece Eszter, for
whom he is responsible, is being courted by
two men, Poprádi, an irresponsible young
man who with various schemes has succeeded
in putting off the auctioning of Sodró's belongings, and Bálint, Commissioner of Audit
in the state bureaucracy, a decent but re-

served person. Eszter marries Bálint, but after six months their marriage is in trouble because of the underhanded machinations of Poprádi, who intends to ruin Eszter's husband. Eszter's foster father is forced to borrow money at an exorbitant interest rate in order to pay the debt. Luckily Tarcali, a friend whom Eszter once loved, appears on the scene. Tarcali has now fallen in love with Eszter, but she refuses his advances. When she wanted the rich Tarcali, he would not have a poor girl. Now, at a private meeting, Eszter tells him that she no longer loves him. Suddenly Bálint arrives, misinterprets the meeting, and forces Tarcali to sign a statement that he will marry Eszter. After their divorce, Bálint and Eszter meet once more, the misunderstanding is resolved, and they remarry.

PLAYS

Unless otherwise noted, the plays were first performed in Pest (Budapest).

1. *Jóslat* (*The Prophecy*). Comedy in iambics, 5 acts. Published 1875. Produced Magyar Nemzeti Szinház, Oct. 11, 1875.
2. *Janus* (*The Rebel Pagan*). Tragedy in iambics, 5 acts. Published 1877. Produced Magyar Nemzeti Szinház, Oct. 15, 1877.
3. Special-event play for the opening of the theatre in Arad, Transylvania, in 1877.
4. *Theodora*. Historical tragedy. 1877.
5. *A mágusz* (*The Magus*). Tragedy, 1 act. Published 1878. Produced Magyar Nemzeti Szinház, Jan. 11, 1878.
6. *Az ellenállhatatlan* (*The Irresistible Knight*). Comedy in verse, 3 acts. Published 1878. Produced Magyar Nemzeti Szinház, Oct. 11, 1878.
7. *Bizalmatlan* (*The Distrustful*). Comedy in verse, 3 acts. Written 1879.
8. *A proletárok* (*The Proletarians*). Play, 4 acts. Published 1882. Produced Magyar Nemzeti Szinház, Jan. 23, 1880.
9. *Mukányi* (*The Title Hunter*). Comedy, 4 acts. Published 1882. Produced Magyar Nemzeti Szinház, Oct. 22, 1880.
10. *Anna*. Play, 1 act. Published 1880. Produced Magyar Nemzeti Szinház, Apr. 28, 1882.
11. *Cifra nyomoruság* (*Fancy Misery*). Play, 4 acts. Published 1882. Produced Magyar Nemzeti Szinház, Oct. 28, 1881.
12. *A kaviár* (*Caviar*). Comedy, 3 acts. Published 1882. Produced Magyar Nemzeti Szinház, Mar. 24, 1882.
13. *Szép leányok* (*Beautiful Girls*). Play, 3 acts. Published 1882. Produced Magyar Nemzeti Szinház, May 4, 1882.
14. *A Stomfay család* (*The Stomfay Family*). Play, 3 acts. Published 1883. Produced Magyar Nemzeti Szinház, Oct. 20, 1882.
15. *Bozóthy Márta* (*Evil Love*). Play, 3 acts. Published 1883. Produced Magyar Nemzeti Szinház, Feb. 23, 1883.
16. *Cecil házassága* (*Cecilia's Marriage*). Play, 3 acts. Published 1883. Produced Magyar Nemzeti Szinház, Nov. 23, 1883.
17. *Buborékok* (*Bubbles*). Comedy, 3 acts. Published 1884. Produced Magyar Nemzeti Szinház, Apr. 18, 1884.
18. *Nóra* (*Nora*). Drama, 4 acts. Published 1884. Produced Magyar Nemzeti Szinház, Oct. 22, 1884.
19. *A sötét pont* (*The Dark Secret*). Drama, 3 acts. Published 1885. Produced Magyar Nemzeti Szinház, Nov. 20, 1885.
20. *Spartacus*. Tragedy, 5 acts. Published 1886. Produced Magyar Nemzeti Szinház, Apr. 9, 1886.
21. *Petneházy*. Play, 3 acts. Published 1886. Produced Operaház, Sept. 1, 1886.
22. *Királyfogás* (*King's Gambit*). Musical comedy, 3 acts. Published 1886. Produced Népszinház, Oct. 29, 1886. Music: József Konti.
23. *A komédiás* (*The Comedian*). Historical comedy, 1 act. Published 1886. Produced Magyar Nemzeti Szinház, Feb. 25, 1887.
24. *A jó Fülöp* (*Good Old Philip*). Comedy, 3 acts. Published 1887. Produced Magyar Nemzeti Szinház, Jan. 7, 1887.
25. *A vadrózsa* (*The Wild Rose*). Play, 3 acts. Published 1887. Produced Magyar Nemzeti Szinház, Aug. 26, 1887.
26. Special-event play for the fiftieth anniversary of the Hungarian National Theatre (Magyar Nemzeti Szinház) in 1887.
27. *Vasember* (*The Iron Man*). Drama, 3 acts. Published 1888. Produced Magyar Nemzeti Szinház, Jan. 14, 1888.
28. *Divatkép* (*Moral Fashions*). Play, 3 acts. Published 1888. Produced Magyar Nemzeti Szinház, Oct. 26, 1888.
29. *Suhanc* (*The Youngster*). Musical comedy, 3 acts. Produced Népszinház, 1888. Music: Konti.
30. *Örök törvény* (*Eternal Law*). Play, 3 acts. Published 1890. Produced Magyar Nemzeti Szinház, Feb. 7, 1890.
31. *A nagyratermettek* (*The Climbers*). Comedy, 3 acts. Published 1890. Produced Magyar Nemzeti Szinház, Nov. 2, 1890.
32. *A nagymama* (*The Grandmother*). Comedy, 3 acts. Published 1891. Produced Magyar Nemzeti Szinház, Mar. 8, 1891.
33. *Az atyafiak* (*The Legacy Hunters*). Play, 3 acts. Published 1891. Produced Magyar Nemzeti Szinház, Nov. 27, 1891.
34. *Két szerelem* (*Two Loves*). Tragedy, 3 acts. Published 1893. Produced Magyar Nemzeti Szinház, Nov. 19, 1892.
35. *Citerás* (*The Zither Player*). Musical comedy, 3 acts. Produced Népszinház, 1898. Music: Konti. Completed posthumously by Károly Murai.

EDITIONS

Szinmüvei, 18 vols., Budapest, 1882–1894.

CRITICISM

Gedeon, *Csíky Gergely mint drámairó*, 1889; J. Janovics, *Csíky Gergely élete és müvei*, 2 vols., 1900–1902.

CSOKOR, Franz Theodor (1885–1969). Austrian novelist, poet, and dramatist, exiled from 1938 to 1944. His early expressionistic plays, *The Red Street* (*Die rote Strasse*, 1918) and *The Hour of Dying Away* (*Die Stunde des Absterbens*, 1916), show the influence of Strindberg and Wedekind. In the play *Society for Human Rights* (*Gesellschaft für Menschenrechte*, 1929), which depicts Georg Büchner as a revolutionary, Csokor turned to realism. Political and social problems are discussed in his "European" trilogy, consisting of *Occupied Territory* (*Besetztes Gebiet*, 1930), *Third of November 1918* (*Der dritte November 1918*, 1923), and *The Prodigal Son* (*Der verlorene Sohn*, 1946). Another ambitious trilogy, *Olympus and Golgotha* (*Olymp und Golgotha*), extolling the revolutionary power of Christianity, includes the plays *Kalypso* (1942), *Pilatus* (1949), and *Caesar's Widow* (*Cäsars Witwe*, 1953). Social criticism and metaphysical ideas mingle in *Remove the Stone* (*Hebt den Stein ab*, 1957), a grotesque comedy; and *The Writing on the Wall* (*Das Zeichen an der*

Franz Theodor Csokor. [Bildarchiv der Österreichischen Nationalbibliothek]

Wand, 1962), an indictment of fascist war criminals.

CUBILLO DE ARAGÓN, Álvaro (b. Granada, 1596?; d. Madrid, October 21, 1661). Spanish poet and dramatist. Although unoriginal and at times pretentious, Cubillo was a scrupulously precise and clever craftsman, excelling in the refined comedy of manners. *Marcela's Dolls* (*Las muñecas de Marcela,* 1634), a charming comedy unusual in its portrayal of adolescent love, is generally considered Cubillo's best work. Among his other comedies are *Father Christmas* (*El señor de noches buenas,* 1635); *El rayo de Andalucía o Genízaro de España* (1632), about the legendary bastard Mudarra and the Infante de Lara; *The Count of Irlos* (*El conde de Irlos*); *The Commanders of Córdoba* (*Los comendadores de Córdoba,* 1658); and *El invisible príncipe del baúl* (1636). *See* COMEDY OF MANNERS.

Marcela's Dolls (*Las muñecas de Marcela,* 1634). Comedy in which Carlos, having killed Valerio's son in a duel, is forced to flee Valerio's vengeance. He takes refuge in the home of Marcela. They fall in love, but her sister Victoria tells him that Marcela is promised to Octavio. He leaves the house and meets Octavio, who, mistaking him for Marcela's brother Luis, tells him that Feliciana, Carlos's sister, has given birth to Luis's child. A final confrontation of all the characters resolves the situation happily: Marcela becomes betrothed to Carlos, Luis to Feliciana, and Octavio to Victoria.

Juan de la Cueva
(1550? — 1610)

Juan de la Cueva, Spanish poet and playwright about whose personal life very little is known, was born in Seville, about 1550, into a family of supposedly noble ancestry, as he himself recorded in *The History and Heritage of the Cueva* (*Historia y sucesión de la Cueva*). After a trip (1574–1577) with his brother Claudio to Mexico, during which he wrote nostalgic verse expressing his longing to return to Spain, he went back to Seville and began to write plays and poetry. Since his flawed plays were quickly surpassed by the work of contemporaries, Cueva's chief importance is historical, for he was an innovator—the first to use Spanish history and legend as dramatic sources, the first to use Italian meters, the first to employ the themes and rhythms of popular ballads in his plays. Legend and history influenced such plays as *The Seven Princes of Lara* (*Los siete infantes de Lara,* 1579); *The Liberation of Spain by Bernardo del Carpio* (*La libertad de España por Bernardo del Carpio,* wr. 1579?); *The Sack of Rome and Death of Borbón* (*El saco de Roma y muerte de Borbón,* wr. 1579?); and *The Death of King Don Sancho and Challenge of Zamora* (*La muerte del rey don Sancho y reto de Zamora,* 1579), based on a portion of the legend of the Cid. His contribution to the development of the Spanish comedy of manners can be seen in *The Defamer* (*El infamador,* 1581) and *The Man Beheaded* (*El degollado*). Among his plays that deal with classic themes are *The Tragedy of Ajax Telamon* (*La tragedia de Ayax Telemón,* pub. 1588), *The Death of Virginia* (*La muerte de Virginia,* pub. 1588), and *The Liberation of Rome by Mucius Scaevola* (*La libertad de Roma por Mucius Scévola*).

Cueva was among the playwrights who tried to create tragic drama in sixteenth-century Spain. But important though his contributions were, his craftsmanship was weak. Although the intrusion of elements of horror reflects at times the influence of Seneca, Cueva's *comedias* more closely resemble poetic narratives in dialogue than dramas: they have a paucity of action, too much declamation, and an overabundance of irrelevancies of both character and event. The *comedia nueva* of Lope de Vega and his school soon eclipsed Cueva, and in 1583 he stopped writing plays, although several were published in 1588. In 1606 he wrote a treatise dealing with the drama (*Exemplar poetico,* pub. 1774), in which he endorsed Lope's work while still insisting upon his own position as an innovator. *See* COMEDIA; VEGA CARPIO, LOPE DE.

Among Cueva's other plays, most of which were written between 1579 and 1581, are *The Constancy of Arcelina* (*La constancia de Arcelina*), *The Tyrant Prince* (*El príncipe tirano*), *The Tutor* (*El tutor*), and *The Comedy of the Infatuated Old Man* (*La comedia del viejo enamorado*).

The Seven Princes of Lara (*Los siete infantes de Lara*, 1579). Tragedy in which Ruy Velázquez takes as his prisoners his brother-in-law Gonzalo Bustos and his seven nephews, Gonzalo's sons. He turns Gonzalo over to the Moorish king Almanzor but, at the instigation of his wife Doña Lambra, slays the seven princes. Presented with their heads, Gonzalo is in such despair that Almanzor is touched and sets him free. Before Gonzalo departs, Almanzor's sister Zayda, with whom he has been intimate, tells him that she is pregnant. He gives her a ring, requesting her to give it to their child and to send him to him when he comes of age. Sixteen years later Zayda sends her son Gonzalo Mudarra to his father. The boy is converted to Christianity and sent out to avenge the death of his half brothers. Mudarra fights Velázquez and kills him. Doña Lambra locks herself in her house, but Gonzalo Mudarra sets fire to it, and she is burned alive.

Juan de la Cueva. [Italian Cultural Institute]

The Defamer (*El infamador*, 1581). Comedy of manners in which Leucino believes that for money no woman will remain virtuous. Indeed, only one woman, Eliodora, has refused him. Even the intervention of the goddess Venus has not caused Eliodora to yield to Leucino. Finally Leucino tries to abduct Eliodora, but she resists him and in the process kills his servant Ortelio. Leucino then accuses Eliodora of having killed Ortelio because the latter had spurned her unwelcome attentions and informed his master of her behavior. Eliodora is arrested and sentenced to death. The goddess Diana comes to her rescue, proclaiming her innocence and purity. Brought face to face with Eliodora, Leucino confesses his guilt. Eliodora is freed, and Leucino is condemned to be buried alive.

PLAYS

1. *Los siete infantes de Lara* (*The Seven Princes of Lara*). Tragedy, 4 acts. Written 1579. Produced Seville, Huerta de Doña Elivra, 1579.
2. *La libertad de España por Bernardo del Carpio* (*The Liberation of Spain by Bernardo del Carpio*). Historical drama. Written 1579?
3. *El saco de Roma y muerte de Borbón* (*The Sack of Rome and Death of Borbón*). Historical drama. Written 1579?
4. *La muerte del rey don Sancho y reto de Zamora* (*The Death of King Don Sancho and Challenge of Zamora*). Historical drama. Written 1579? Produced Seville, Huerta de Doña Elivra, 1579.
5. *El infamador* (*The Defamer*). Comedy of manners. Written 1581? Produced Seville, Huerta de Doña Elivra, 1581.
6. *El príncipe tirano* (*The Tyrant Prince*). Drama. Written 1581?
7. *La constancia de Arcelina* (*The Constancy of Arcelina*). Drama. Written 1581?
8. *La comedia del viejo enamorado* (*The Comedy of the Infatuated Old Man*). Comedy. Written 1579–1581?
9. *El tutor* (*The Tutor*). Play. Written 1581?
10. *La tragedia de Ayax Telemón* (*The Tragedy of Ajax Telamon*). Tragedy. Published 1588.
11. *La muerte de Virginia* (*The Death of Virginia*). Drama. Published 1588.
12. *La libertad de Roma por Mucius Scévola* (*The Liberation of Rome by Mucius Scaevola*). Historical drama.
13. *El degollado* (*The Man Beheaded*). Comedy of manners.
14. *El vil amador* (*The Base Lover*). Play.

CUMBERLAND, Richard (b. Cambridge, February 19, 1732; d. London, May 7, 1811). Most important sentimental dramatist of the late eighteenth century in England. His prolific career in this genre began in 1769 with *The Brothers,* in which he sought to wring pathetic tears from an artificially contrived situation describing a father who turns his affections toward his son's beloved. Despite its manifest weaknesses, it appealed to the public, and two years later Cumberland, pursuing the same path, achieved his greatest success with *The West Indian* (1771), which proved to be one of the landmarks of the sentimental drama: its hero Belfour, a careless

Richard Cumberland; painting by George Romney. [National Portrait Gallery, Washington]

mentalizing. It was not until two years and several comedies later that a play of Cumberland's came up to the standards of *The Wheel of Fortune*. That play was *False Impressions* (1797), a dramatization of his own novel *Henry*. It signaled the merging of sentimental drama and melodrama at the close of the century. Cumberland wrote a considerable number of other works including some tragedies, a few musical pieces, none of which were significant, and several tending toward melodrama, typical of which are *The Days of Yore* (1796) and *Joanna of Montfaucon* (1800). See SENTIMENTAL COMEDY.

The West Indian (1771). Comedy. Belfour, a Jamaican visiting London for the purpose of discovering his father's identity, is a guest at the home of Stockwell, a merchant who confides to his servant that the young man is his son. Soon after his arrival Belfour meets Louisa Dudley, a beautiful girl who astonishes the West Indian by withholding her identity and by repulsing his ardent advances. In time, and after numerous entanglements, the hero is reunited with his long-sought father and, promising to mend his libertine ways, is accepted by Louisa. They marry even though he believes she is poor, and he is rewarded for his righteousness by the discovery that she is, in fact, a wealthy heiress.

CUMMINGS, E[dward] E[stlin] (b. Cambridge, Mass. October 14, 1894; d. North Conway, N.H., September 3, 1962). American poet whose work as novelist, painter, and dramatist was overshadowed by his poetry, in which he experimented with unusual spellings and typography. His penchant for experimentation with form and technique extended to his first play, *Him* (1928), a surrealistic phantasmagoria whose protagonist, Him, defines himself as "the sort of man who is writing a play about a man who is writing a sort of play." This looking-glass effect is exemplified by the intrusion of incidents and episodes apparently taken from a play written by another Him in the mirror. The concern of Him about the problem of identity and the uncertainty of reality is reflected in the uncertain relationship between Him and his girl friend, Me. Cummings's poetic drama *Tom* (wr. 1935) is based on *Uncle Tom's Cabin*, and his one-act *Santa Claus* (wr. 1946) is a contemporary morality play. See MORALITY PLAY.

Him (1928). Surrealistic play in which the Three Weirds, old crones symbolizing the Fates, appear intermittently and make nonsensical comments about life while Him discusses the play he is writing with his girl friend, Me. He dramatizes possible scenes for her, presenting three drunken men and a vir-

libertine endowed with tender sentiments, served as a model for future writers of this genre. Cumberland's next play, *The Fashionable Lover* (1772), was equally sentimental, this time about an ill-treated ward who escapes seduction. *The Choleric Man* (1774) was not quite so successful, but *The Natural Son* (1784), in which the rake hero has a heart of gold, was a worthy successor to *The West Indian*. With *The Impostors* (1789), based on Farquhar's *The Beaux' Stratagem,* Cumberland moved somewhat away from the sentimental style, and he continued in this new vein in *The School for Widows* (1789) and *The Box-Lobby Challenge* (1794), a comedy of low manners. Sentimentalism, however, still held him in thrall, and in *The Jew* (1794) it led him into the sphere of propaganda. The hero, no longer a softhearted rake, is a Jew, Sheva, reviled but good-hearted, ultimately the kindest, most honest character in the play. *The Wheel of Fortune* (1795), a superior comedy with lifelike characters, treats the theme of repentance when Woodville forgoes his vengeance at the sight of his loved one's son. *First Love* (1795), which appeared soon after, was marred by propaganda and oversenti-

E. E. Cummings. [Library of Congress]

gin, a street-corner orator haranguing a crowd, and a gathering of epicene Romans and a burlesqued Mussolini, but these fragmentary scenes displease Me and lead the two of them to a discussion of art and life. Then, Him appears in a Paris restaurant in which some of his own characters are seated. On his return home to Me, he extols the wonders he has seen and seems closer to some undefinable truth about himself. He remarks that their lives seem an "illusion" that they "inhabit." Suddenly a carnival scene unfolds, and Him appears on the edge of a sideshow crowd. As the last "freak" faces front, Him utters a cry of rage when he sees that it is Me. Back once again in their room, Him and Me face the audience, admitting its presence and its attempt to believe that Him and Me are real. Produced New York, Provincetown Playhouse, April 18, 1928.

François de Curel
(1854 – 1928)

Vicomte François de Curel, French novelist and dramatist, was born to a wealthy family in Metz on June 10, 1854. After primary schooling he entered the École Centrale des Arts et Manufactures to study engineering in

order to manage his mother's share of the Wendel steel mills. Upon his graduation in 1876, however, he discovered that he could not return to conquered Lorraine until he had passed military age, and he spent the following nine years completing his literary education and writing short stories. His first novel, *The Summer of the Dry Fruits* (*L'été des fruits secs*), appeared in 1885, and he continued to write novels and short stories until 1889.

Contemporary critics like Charles Maurras insisted that Curel's fiction indicated a strong flair for the theatre. Curel began writing plays in 1891 with *Rescued from the Water* (*Sauvé des eaux*), which over the years was revised first as *Love Embellishes* (*L'amour brode,* 1893) and then as *The Dance before the Mirror* (*La danse devant le miroir,* 1914). Also in 1891 he wrote *The Nettle* (*L'ortie*), which, after being refused by the Théâtre de l'Odéon and the Comédie-Française, was revised and produced as *A False Saint* (*L'envers d'une sainte*) in 1892 at Antoine's Théâtre Libre. Though it established Curel's reputation, the critic Jules Lemaître complained that it was more of a novel in dialogue form and that it would have been fine "if it had been signed Ibsen."

In 1894 Curel was permitted to return to his family home in German-occupied Lorraine. He divided his time between Lorraine and Paris, interrupting his gentlemanly life

François de Curel. [G. Lolivier, Paris]

of leisure only occasionally to work on a play. These years saw the production of *The New Idol* (*La nouvelle idole;* pub. 1895, prod. 1899), *The Lion's Meal* (*Le repas du lion,* 1897), and *The Savage Girl* (*La fille sauvage,* 1902). After completing *The Beat of the Wing* (*Le coup d'aile,* 1906) Curel temporarily ceased writing and did not produce a new play for thirteen years. Three days before World War I broke out, in August, 1914, he had to leave Lorraine to spend the war years in Switzerland. Upon his return to France, he was elected to the Académie Française (1919). The success of *The Soul Gone Mad* (*L'âme en folie,* 1919) encouraged Curel to follow it with several more new plays and caused many of his previous plays to be revived. His last plays, *The Lively Woman and the Half-dead Man* (*La viveuse et le moribond,* 1926) and *Mystical Storm* (*Orage mystique,* 1927), were disappointing. On December 27, 1927, Curel was struck by an automobile, and he never completely recovered his previously robust health. He died suddenly of a heart attack, while sitting at his desk in Paris, on April 25, 1928.

WORK

Although Curel wrote at a time when the *pièce à thèse* ("thesis play") was the fashion and many serious French dramatists were busy exposing the ills of society and indicating remedies, his drama is of a different order. He rejected the assumption, implicit in much of the contemporary thesis drama, that legislative or sociological reform is a universal panacea to be expounded on the stage. Rather, he was interested in the effect of social ills on character. That social ills exist is understood without question; that they work on every soul in a different way is brought out in the plays of Curel, in which social drama is fused with prose tragedy and symbolic comedy to form the drama of ideas. This idea drama differs from the thesis play in emphasis; the action is not engineered by the dramatist in order to expound certain ideas; rather, the action emanates naturally from the characters and vice versa.

Action in Curel's dramas is sparked by the clash of character with religious, sentimental, and intellectual passions. In his early works, sentiments and passions dominate. A young nun in *A False Saint* (1892) retains the murderous resentment she once had for a rival in a love affair; she returns to the convent as self-punishment for her lack of contrition.

Later Curel's plays began to be motivated to a greater degree by ideas. Clashes take place between characters and society, between a character's inner law and the external codes of society. In *The New Idol* (pub. 1895, prod. 1899), an atheistic scientist conducts his research by inoculating moribund patients with cancer-producing serum. When he realizes that but for his experiments a young girl would have made a complete recovery, he injects the serum into himself. In the final scenes he attempts to understand the nature of his remorse. *The Lion's Meal* (1897) deals with aristocratic attitudes toward the working class. *The Savage Girl* (1902) shows the inability of civilization to tame or inspire a savage girl. *The Fossils* (*Les fossiles,* 1892) portrays the struggle of aristocrats to retain their code of conduct in a world that no longer has any use for them.

After World War I, Curel turned to satire. *The Soul Gone Mad* (1919), Curel's only popular success, compares human and animal behavior. The instinct to love is traced from pure animal attraction to the glories of human passion; but when the lonely heroine, Blanche, is dying of heart failure, her thoughts are of the love derived from the beast. In *The Wise Man's Intoxication* (*L'ivresse du sage,* 1922), Hortense is loved by a professor who philosophizes about love and a rustic baron who is convinced that the instincts of beast and man are similar. Representing the intoxication of ideas, the philosopher loses Hortense to his rival, the intoxication of love.

Curel's great personal wealth freed him from the financial necessity to court his audiences, and he was able to produce a substantial body of work which, although it elicited considerable critical esteem, rarely won popular success. The reasons for this are not hard to find. While Curel's plays possess a uniqueness and a richness of vision worthy of a great dramatist, he chose a muted approach that failed to win the enthusiasm of any but the most perceptive audiences.

The Fossils (*Les fossiles,* 1892; revised 1900). This, Curel's best-known play, is a thoughtful and sympathetic portrayal of the plight of the aristocrat in the modern world: while his trappings and prerogatives are out of date, he must still live up to aristocratic tradition. Robert, the last duke of the Chantemelle line, is near death. He beseeches his family to allow him to marry Hélène, a working-class girl who has borne a son Robert believes to be his. After the marriage he learns that the child is actually his father's, but his ideals and concern for the aristocracy triumph over a desire for vengeance. After his death his will is found to contain instructions that his stepson, the future duke, be educated to contribute to the world the noblest qualities of the aristocracy.

The New Idol (*La nouvelle idole;* pub. 1895, prod. 1899). In his fanatic devotion to science, "the new idol," Dr. Donnat secretly

Scene from *La fille sauvage*. [G. Lolivier, Paris]

inoculates with cancer those of his patients whom he believes to be suffering from incurable diseases. He hopes in this way to be able to study the development of cancer and so find a cure. However, when Antoinette, a convent-raised orphan, recovers from the tuberculosis that caused her hospitalization, Donnat realizes that if she dies now, it will be as a direct result of his experiments. In remorse, he inoculates himself with the cancer-producing serum. Then, as his horrified and devoted wife looks on, he tries to understand why a scientist like himself, a man who believes in neither God nor the immortal soul, should experience remorse. Antoinette reveals that she had been aware of his experiments on her and had submitted in the hope that the results would save many others. Donnat realizes that, like himself, she is capable of dying for an ideal. He also recognizes and accepts his wife's devotion to him. Eventually he understands that all three are actually serving morality under its various names: religion, love, and concern for the truth. Science is shown to be only one path to some "unknown splendor."

The Lion's Meal (*Le repas du lion*, 1897; revised version, 1920). To atone for causing the death of one of his workmen, Jean de Miremont, an aristocrat, devotes his life to philanthropic works. He wishes to reconcile the old feudal nobility and the working classes. He is not by nature self-sacrificing, however, and he soon envies the position of his brother-in-law, who runs the family mines, builds factories, and provides a living for thousands of workers. Jean wishes for a share in the lion's larger portion of the feast. He recognizes similarities between feudalism and big business and decides to command his factories as his ancestors commanded armies, for his own glory.

The Savage Girl (*La fille sauvage*, 1902). Paul Moncel rescues from death a girl belonging to a savage African tribe. He brings her to Paris in order to civilize and educate her so that she may return to Africa to rule as an ally of France. She proves a responsive pupil, but by the time her education is finished she has fallen in love with Paul. Her enforced return to Africa prevents her from practicing her newfound faith or fulfilling her love. Embittered, she reverts to her savage instincts, making use of her education and ruling position to outwit both savages and missionaries.

PLAYS

Unless otherwise noted, the plays were first performed in Paris.

1. *Sauvé des eaux* (*Rescued from the Water*). Play. Written 1891. Early version of *L'amour brode*.

2. *L'ortie* (*The Nettle*). Play. Written 1891. Early version of *L'envers d'une sainte*.

3. *L'envers d'une sainte** (*A False Saint*). Play, 3 acts. Published 1892; revised 1921. Produced Théâtre Libre, Jan. 25, 1892. Revision of *L'ortie*.

4. *Les fossiles** (*The Fossils*). Play, 4 acts. Published 1892; revised 1900. Produced Théâtre Libre, Nov. 29, 1892; revised version, Comédie-Française, May 21, 1900.

5. *L'invitée* (*The Guest*). Comedy, 3 acts. Published 1893. Produced Théâtre du Vaudeville, Jan. 19, 1893.

6. *L'amour brode* (*Love Embellishes*). Play, 3 acts. Published 1893. Produced Comédie-Française, Oct. 12, 1893. Revision of *Sauvé des eaux*.

7. *La nouvelle idole* (*The New Idol*). Play, 3 acts. Published 1895. Produced Théâtre Antoine, Mar. 11, 1899.

8. *La figurante* (*The Supernumerary*). Comedy, 3 acts. Published 1896. Produced Théâtre de la Renaissance, Mar. 5, 1896.

9. *Le repas du lion* (*The Lion's Meal*). Play, 4 acts. Published 1919. Produced Théâtre Antoine, Nov. 26, 1897; revised version, Comédie-Française, Mar. 20, 1920.

10. *La fille sauvage* (*The Savage Girl*). Play, 5 acts. Published 1902; revised 1919. Produced Théâtre Antoine, Feb. 17, 1902.

11. *Le coup d'aile** (*The Beat of the Wing*). Play, 3 acts. Written 1905; revised 1922. Produced Théâtre Antoine, Jan. 10, 1906.

12. *La danse devant le miroir* (*The Dance before the Mirror*). Play, 3 acts. Published 1914. Produced Théâtre du Nouvel-Ambigu, Jan. 17, 1914. Revision of *Sauvé des eaux*.

13. *La comédie du génie* (*The Comedy of Genius*). Play, 3 acts. Published 1918. Produced Théâtre des Arts, Mar. 16, 1921.

14. *L'âme en folie* (*The Soul Gone Mad*). Dramatic comedy, 3 acts. Published 1920. Produced Théâtre des Arts, Dec. 23, 1919.

15. *L'ivresse du sage* (*The Wise Man's Intoxication*). Comedy, 3 acts. Published 1921. Produced Comédie-Française, Dec. 6, 1922.

16. *Terre inhumaine* (*Inhuman Land*). Drama, 3 acts. Published 1923. Produced Théâtre des Arts, Dec. 13, 1922.

17. *La viveuse et le moribond* (*The Lively Woman and the Half-dead Man*). Comedy, 3 acts. Published 1926. Produced Monte Carlo, Dec. 29, 1926; Paris, Théâtre des Arts, Jan. 6, 1926.

18. *Orage mystique* (*Mystical Storm*). Play, 3 acts. Published 1927. Produced Théâtre des Arts, Dec. 1, 1927.

EDITIONS

Collections.
Théâtre complet, 6 vols. Paris, 1919–1924.
Individual Plays.
A False Saint. Published in *Nineteenth Century French Plays,* ed. by J. L. Borgerhoff, New York, 1931.

The Fossils. Published in *Contemporary Drama: European Plays,* ed. by E. B. Watson and B. Pressey and tr. by B. Clark, vol. 1, New York, 1931–1934.

The Lion's Meal. Published in *The Contemporary French Theatre,* ed. by S. A. Rhodes, New York, 1942.

CRITICISM

R. LeBrun, *François de Curel,* Paris, 1905; P. Blanchart, *François de Curel; Son oeuvre,* Paris, 1924; A. G. de Voisins, *François de Curel,* Paris, 1931; E. Pronier, *La vie et l'oeuvre de François de Curel,* Paris, 1935.

DAGERMAN, Stig (1923–1954). Swedish novelist and dramatist whose promising career was tragically cut short by suicide. Receiving critical acclaim while still in his early twenties, Dagerman gave eloquent expression to the sense of angst that was a sign of the frustration and disillusionment felt by young intellectuals in neutral Sweden during World War II as well as a reflection of the preoccupation with existential terror that had its roots in the works of Kafka and Strindberg. *See* STRINDBERG, AUGUST.

Expressionistic echoes of Strindberg resound in Dagerman's first play, *The Condemned (Den dödsdömde,* 1947): a man wrongly sentenced to death and set free only because of a quirk of justice attends a bizarre gathering in his honor that has an atmosphere reminiscent of *The Ghost Sonata*. In *The Shadow of Mart (Skuggan av Mart,* 1948), a young man living in the shadow of a brother who died a hero's death fighting for the underground is bitter because during the war

Stig Dagerman.
[Swedish
Information
Service]

the family profited from a factory run for the Germans.

The influence of Dagerman's experience as a syndicalist journalist is evident in *The Climber* (*Streber,* 1949), which shows how a cooperative working-class business enterprise is destroyed by the selfish ambition of one of the partners. *No One Goes Free* (*Ingen går fri,* 1949), an adaptation of Dagerman's novel *Burned Child* (*Bränt barn,* 1948), is a psychological study of mendacity centered on a young man's problems with his parents.

EDITIONS

The Condemned. Published in *Scandinavian Plays of the Twentieth Century,* tr. by H. Alexander and L. Jones., vol. 3, Princeton, N.J., 1951.

CRITICISM

A. Gustafsson, *A History of Swedish Literature,* Minneapolis, 1961.

DALY, [John] Augustin (b. Plymouth, N.C., July 20, 1838; d. Paris, June 7, 1899). Prolific American dramatist, drama critic, stage manager, and producer-director. An autocratic and dictatorial manager, he presented to American audiences the best theatre of the day, and he won international acclaim when he took an American stage company to England, France, and Germany. Daly's importance as a playwright lies in his role as a transitional figure, for his plays show both the romanticism of his predecessors and the realism of his followers. In all, he wrote or adapted approximately ninety productions, of which only five or six are original dramas.

Augustin Daly.
[Brander Matthews
Dramatic Museum,
Columbia
University]

His first play, *Leah the Forsaken* (1862), an adaptation, deals with the persecution of the Jews in an eighteenth-century Austrian village. Leah, a Jewish girl, is forsaken by her Christian lover and after much unhappiness learns to accept her lot. Daly's first original play, *Under the Gaslight* (1867), is a sensational melodrama with a realistic setting in which the identity of a young girl is in question. When Laura Courtland's status as protégée of the rich Courtlands is in doubt, she becomes a homeless waif, only to be identified finally as their true daughter. The climax of the play depicts Laura rescuing the faithful Snorkey from an oncoming full-sized locomotive, which appears onstage. *Horizon* (1871), Daly's best original play, is a realistic frontier drama with melodramatic turns of plot showing the priority of local law over federal law on the western frontier. Among Daly's other plays are *Divorce* (1871) and *Pique* (1875), early social-problem plays; and the adaptations *Pickwick Papers* (1868) and *Frou-Frou* (1870).

Horizon (1871). Frontier drama in five acts. Alleyn, the adopted son of a New York society woman, Mrs. Van Dorp, learns from a lawyer that Wolf Van Dorp abandoned his wife years ago and disappeared with his daughter. Having recently received a military commission to serve in the West, Alleyn sets out on his overland journey with his friend Sundown Rowse, who is heading west to take over land that has become his by an act of Congress. In the woods of Colorado Alleyn falls in love with a "backwoods Venus" named Med, who he later learns is Mrs. Van Dorp's lost daughter. Med's father, Wolf, is killed by Wannemucka, a surly Indian who wishes to have Med for himself, but not before Med has been placed by her father in the care of Loder, his gambling friend. In a series of scenes Rowse explores his western lands with Med, Loder, Alleyn, and others; in the interim Med and Rowse are captured by Wannemucka. Just as they are about to be killed, Alleyn and Loder arrive, rescue Med from a jealous squaw's knife, and shoot Wannemucka.

DANCOURT, Florent Carton (1661–1725). French actor and dramatist remembered for his performances at the Comédie-Française and for some entertaining comedies in which he satirized contemporary mores and offered representative portraits of social types. Educated to be a lawyer, Dancourt married, against the wishes of his family, the daughter of the actor François Lenoir de la Thorillière and thereafter devoted himself exclusively to the theatre, winning great acclaim for his comic roles, especially that of Alceste in Molière's *The Misanthrope.* His own major

Florent Carton Dancourt. [Italian Cultural Institute]

play is considered to be *The Modish Cavalier* (*Le chevalier à la mode*, 1687), in which a fashionable but penniless libertine decides to mend his fortunes by marrying a wealthy older woman. Given the lady's age, he feels free to carry on several other romances simultaneously, and eventually he is found out.

Many of Dancourt's plays deal with problems of the impoverished nobility and the social climbing of the middle classes, but he also depicted the loves and intrigues of village life. His best-known works include *The Country House* (*La maison de campagne*, 1688), *The Fashionable Ladies* (*Les bourgeoises à la mode*, 1692), *Ladies of Quality* (*Les bourgeoises de qualité*, 1700), and *The Gallant Gardener* (*Le galant jardinier*, 1704). It has now been established that not all the works that bear his name, some sixty in number, were actually written by him.

DANE, Clemence, pseudonym of Winifred Ashton (1888–1965). English actress, novelist, and dramatist who began her versatile career in 1913 when she appeared on the stage under the name Diana Cortis. Her first play, *A Bill of Divorcement* (1921), is a powerful treatment of the effects of World War I on a man's life and, in turn, his impress on his

family. Its great success advanced the burgeoning career of the soon-to-be-famous Katharine Cornell. *Will Shakespeare* appeared the same year; written in blank verse, it attempts to throw light on the man by portraying him among his family and friends. *Wild Decembers* (1932) dramatizes the lives of Emily and Charlotte Brontë. The question of self-sacrifice in human relationships is treated seriously in *The Way Things Happen* (1924). *Naboth's Vineyard* (1925) is a dramatization of the Biblical story of Jezebel, Jehu, and Naboth. *Granite* (1926) and *Mariners* (1927) have the sea as their setting and central theme.

Miss Dane wrote two musical plays for which Richard Addinsell produced the music: *Adam's Opera* (1928), a social satire; and *Come of Age* (1934), based on the life of the English poet Thomas Chatterton. She also adapted Rostand's *L'Aiglon,* Beerbohm's *The Happy Hypocrite,* and Hebbel's *Herod and Mariamne. The Saviours,* consisting of short plays with a religious theme, was produced in 1942, after which she wrote adaptations of Schiller's *Don Carlos* and *Mary Stuart* for the radio and two television plays, *Scandal at Coventry* (1961) and *Till Time Shall End* (1961).

Gabriele D'Annunzio
(1863 – 1938)

Gabriele D'Annunzio, Italian poet, novelist, and dramatist, was born March 12, 1863, in Pescara. The son of a clerk who later became mayor of the town, he was a precocious child, writing verses in secondary school which his father published as *Primo vere* (1879). Shortly after establishing himself in Rome in 1881 to study literature at the university, he began contributing to newspapers, particularly *Fanfulla della Domenica, Capitan Fracassa,* and *Cronaca Bizantina,* and was soon a member of various literary groups. His fame as a poet was established with the publication of *New Song* (*Canto novo,* 1882), a volume of poems celebrating the Abruzzi region. In Rome he met Maria, daughter of the Duke of Gallese-Hardouin, and eloped with her in 1883. The couple had three sons, but eventually a separation was arranged. Meanwhile, D'Annunzio produced much hack work in order to support his titled wife: popular stories, light verse, and even a society column, all under pseudonyms. He also wrote a sensational book of poems, *Intermezzo of Rhyme* (*L'intermezzo di rime,* 1884), in which he depicted frankly

Gabriele
D'Annunzio.
[Walter Hampden
Memorial Library
at The Players,
New York]

his romance with Maria, and made what
might be considered his first attempt at playwriting in *The Cantata of the Calends of April*
(*La cantata di calen d'aprile*), a staged dialogue, in 1886. With the publication of his
novel *Child of Pleasure* (*Il piacere,* 1889), he
gained a worldwide reputation.

In 1894, after a long liaison with another
titled woman, the Countess Gravina Auguis-
sola (whose husband cited him as co-
respondent in a separation suit), D'Annunzio
met the celebrated actress Eleanora Duse
and soon began a liaison famous in theatrical
history. For her he wrote many of his best
plays, including *La Gioconda* (1899) and
Francesca da Rimini (1901), although he offered *The Dead City* (*La città morta,* 1898)
to Sarah Bernhardt. His novel *The Flame of
Life* (*Il fuoco,* 1900) is a fictionalized account
of his love affair with Duse and aroused considerable scandal on its publication. Their relationship ended in 1910, when D'Annunzio's
attention wandered to the Marchioness Alessandra di Rudini-Carolotti.

By this time, without Duse to perform in
them, his plays were no longer in demand,
and D'Annunzio entered a lean period. Living
nonetheless with his usual extravagance, he
was soon forced to flee from his creditors to
France. He remained there until shortly
before Italy's entry into World War I in 1915.
Returning with great patriotic fervor, he
made speeches and wrote articles exhorting
his countrymen to assist the Allied cause. He

then joined the air force and became one of
Italy's most celebrated heroes. During a
forced landing he was blinded in the left eye
by a splintered propeller fragment.

After the war, furious over the Allies' broken promise to restore Fiume to Italy, D'Annunzio mustered a group of volunteers in September, 1919, and "captured" the city. He was
relieved as self-declared commandant when
regular army troops marched into Fiume in
January, 1921. Then, with government approval, he retired to a Lake Garda villa,
which he remodeled and renamed Vittoriale
degli Italiani. On March 15, 1924, with Mussolini's approval, D'Annunzio was granted a
patent of nobility as Prince of Montenevoso.
In 1937 he was made president of the Italian
Royal Academy. On March 1, 1938, he died
suddenly of a cerebral hemorrhage while
writing in his villa.

WORK

After several decades of *verismo* ("realism"), the Italian stage at the turn of the
twentieth century experienced a short-lived
return to romanticism in the poetic and highly charged dramas of Gabriele D'Annunzio.
Although he seems to have possessed little
knowledge of Nietzsche's philosophy, he believed fervently in the Nietzschean superman
and embodied that concept in a series of

Poster advertising the premiere of *La figlia di Jorio*.
[Italian Cultural Institute]

heroes who act outside the law, their amorality justified by their superhuman capabilities. It has been said that these characters are in large measure reflections of aspects of D'Annunzio's personality. It was with a handful of plays in which such characters figure, beginning with *The Dead City* (1898), that D'Annunzio's popular success and reputation were established. In *The Dead City* he displayed brilliantly his ability to evoke a brooding atmosphere, in this instance the fateful aura cast over modern lovers by the violent history of the house of Atreus. *La Gioconda* (1899) is a symbolic drama in which the amoral compulsiveness of the artist is contrasted with the conventional morality of his wife. In *Francesca da Rimini* (1901), D'Annunzio turned to a well-known story of medieval Italy for a plot of overt sensuality. Although he is held by critics to be a more accomplished lyric poet and novelist than dramatist, his considerable theatrical talent is revealed in *The Daughter of Jorio* (*La figlia di Jorio,* 1904). The play's setting among the Abruzzi peasants, with whom his first and perhaps most notable book of poetry also deals, lends

the tragedy a pastoral quality.

Other interesting plays elaborating the superman motif are *Glory* (*La gloria,* 1899), centering on Ruggero Flammo, a political giant who becomes a Roman dictator and rules until he is assassinated; *More than Love* (*Più che l'amore,* 1906), which depicts an explorer hero who turns out to be a cheat and the seducer of his best friend's sister; and *The Ship* (*La nave,* 1908), in which D'Annunzio presented Marco Gatico as a hero who is not bound to the moral standards of lesser mortals. Similar attitudes are expressed in *Phaedra* (*Fedra,* 1909), derived from Racine's verson of Euripides's tragedy; *The Torch under the Bushel* (*La fiaccola sotto il moggio,* 1905), which presents the downfall of the Sangro family and is judged the equal of *The Daughter of Jorio* in lyric strength; and *The Martyrdom of St. Sebastian* (*Le martyre de Saint Sébastien,* 1911), which was written in archaic French for Ida Rubinstein, the famous dancer and mime, during the author's exile, and is notable for its commingling of sensuality and saintliness in the presentation of early Christian times. The musical setting was composed by Claude Debussy. Plays of little importance include historical dramas and nationalistic pieces that, for the most part, revel in gratuitous brutality, lust, and sensationalism.

The Dead City (*La città morta,* 1898). Play set in Greece near the ruins of Mycenae. The site is "thirsty," and the ruins are "rich in gold"; the atmosphere is one of breathless heat and thirst for the riches of Maria Bianca's love and beauty. Maria Bianca's brother Leonardo, an archeologist, loves her incestuously. His friend Alessandro, a young poet, is willing to abandon his blind wife Anna for Maria Bianca and so secure for himself "the unity of life which will give him the strength to pursue his art." Maria Bianca, torn between devotion to Anna, a natural affection for her brother, and growing love for Alessandro, allows herself to be led into a tomb that Leonardo has opened, where he murders

Ida Rubinstein in *Le martyre de Saint Sébastien.* Paris, Châtelet, 1911. [Italian Cultural Institute]

her. In rushing to help her, Anna falls down a flight of stairs and is killed.

La Gioconda (1899). Tragedy in which Lucio Settala, a sculptor, having attempted suicide, is recovering in the home of his wife Silvia, whom he had abandoned. His recovery brings with it the realization that he is still passionately in love with his mistress and creative inspiration, La Gioconda. In a confrontation between the two women in Lucio's studio, La Gioconda tries to destroy Lucio's masterpiece and Silvia's hands are smashed as she saves it. Her sacrifice is useless, for Lucio returns to his art and his mistress. D'Annunzio's treatment of the theme implies that artists are necessarily extreme egoists.

Francesca da Rimini (1901). Lyrical verse tragedy based on the pathetic stanzas found in Dante (*Inferno* V, 88–142), with the addition of an elaborate and learnedly constructed medieval background. Francesca Polenta, betrothed to the ugly Gianciotto Malatesta, mistakes his handsome brother Paolo for her intended bridegroom and falls in love with him. After her marriage to Gianciotto, his younger brother Malatestino, one-eyed and cruel, spies upon Francesca and in jealousy informs Gianciotto of his wife's infidelity. Gianciotto, in attempting to slay Paolo, mortally wounds Francesca, who has placed herself between the two brothers. Mad with grief and rage, Gianciotto stabs Paolo and breaks his bloody sword across his knee.

The Daughter of Jorio (*La figlia di Jorio,* 1904). Verse tragedy set in the Abruzzi in ancient times. Mila, a prostitute and the daughter of a sorcerer, is received in the hut of Lazaro after his son Aligi has rescued her from a group of lusting peasants. With her is her younger sister Ornella, a symbol of innocence. Aligi falls in love with Mila (although he is already betrothed to another girl) and goes to live with her in the mountains where the sheep are pastured for the summer. They live together for a while, and one day during Aligi's absence Lazaro comes to their cave to bring his son home. When Mila is threatened with violence, she calls for help. Aligi returns and during the ensuing quarrel with his father kills him. Aligi is condemned to death and has already received extreme unction when Mila claims that she bewitched him and so is solely responsible for Lazaro's murder. She is led away to be burned at the stake, cursed by Aligi, and shown sympathy only by her sister.

PLAYS

1. *Sogno d'un mattino di primavera* (*The Dream of a Spring Morning*). Tragic poem, 1 act; prose. Published 1897. Produced Paris, Théâtre de la Renaissance, June 15, 1897; Rome, Teatro Valle, Jan. 11, 1898.

2. *Sogno d'un tramonto d'autunno* (*Dream of an Au-*

tumn Sunset). Tragic poem, 1 act; prose. Published 1898. Produced Leghorn, Teatro Rossini, Dec. 2, 1905.

3. *La città morta** (*The Dead City*). Tragedy, 5 acts; prose. Published 1898. Produced (in French as *La ville morte*) Paris, Théâtre de la Renaissance, Jan. 21, 1898; Milan, Teatro Lirico, Mar. 20, 1901.

4. *La Gioconda**. Tragedy, 4 acts; prose. Published 1899. Produced Palermo, Teatro Bellini, Apr. 15, 1899.

5. *La gloria* (*Glory*). Tragedy, 5 acts; prose. Published 1899. Produced Naples, Teatro Mercadante, Apr. 27, 1899.

6. *Francesca da Rimini**. Tragedy, 4 acts; verse. Published 1902. Produced Rome, Teatro Costanzi, Dec. 9, 1901.

7. *La figlia di Jorio** (*The Daughter of Jorio*). Pastoral tragedy, 3 acts; verse. Published 1904. Produced Milan, Teatro Lirico, Mar. 2, 1904.

8. *La fiaccola sotto il moggio* (*The Torch under the Bushel*). Tragedy, 4 acts; verse. Published 1905. Produced Milan, Teatro Manzoni, Mar. 27, 1905.

9. *Più che l'amore* (*More than Love*). Tragedy, 2 episodes; prose. Published 1907. Produced Rome, Teatro Costanzi, Oct. 29, 1906.

10. *La nave* (*The Ship*). Tragedy, prologue and 3 episodes; verse. Published 1908. Produced Rome, Teatro Argentina, Jan. 11, 1908.

11. *Fedra* (*Phaedra*). Tragedy, 3 acts; verse. Published 1909. Produced Milan, Teatro Lirico, Apr. 10, 1909.

12. *Le martyre de Saint Sébastien* (*The Martyrdom of St. Sebastian*). Mystery, 5 acts; in French. Published 1911. Produced Paris, Châtelet, May 27, 1911; Milan, La Scala, Mar. 4, 1926.

13. *Parisina*. Lyric tragedy, 4 acts. Published 1913. Produced Milan, La Scala, Dec. 15, 1913.

14. *Le chèvrefeuille* (*The Honeysuckle*). Tragedy, 3 acts; in French. Published 1914. Produced Paris, Théâtre de la Porte-Saint-Martin, Dec. 14, 1913; Turin, Teatro Carignano, Jan. 27, 1914.

15. *La crociata degli innocenti* (*The Children's Crusade*). Published 1920. Produced Rome, Teatro delle Arti, Oct. 1, 1948.

EDITIONS

The Daughter of Jorio. Published in *Representative Continental Dramas, Revolutionary and Transitional*, ed. by M. J. Moses and tr. by C. Porter et al., Boston, 1924.

The Dead City. Published in *The Eleonora Duse Series of Plays*, ed. by O. M. Say and tr. by G. Mantellini, New York, 1923.

Francesca da Rimini. Published in *Continental Plays*, ed. by T. H. Dickinson and tr. by A. Symons, vol. 1, Boston, 1935.

La Gioconda. Published in *Types of Domestic Tragedy*, ed. by R. M. Smith and tr. by A. Symons, New York, 1928.

DAUDET, Alphonse (b. Nîmes, May 13, 1840; d. Paris, December 16, 1897). French novelist and dramatist whose reputation rests on narrative writings such as *Letters from My Mill* (*Lettres de mon moulin*, 1869), *Jack* (1876), and *The Nabob* (*Le nabab*, 1877). His only notable stage work is *The Arlesienne* (*L'Arlésienne*, 1872), which is based on a story in *Letters from My Mill*. Originally a failure, the play was revived in 1885, at which time, largely owing to Georges Bizet's by then familiar incidental music, it was well received and went on to become a minor classic. Some critics, however, prefer his dramatization of his novel *Sapho* (1885). Written in collaboration with Adolphe Belot, it tells the story of two lovers who are unable to break off a rela-

Alphonse Daudet. [Italian Cultural Institute]

tionship that has long ceased to be satisfactory to either of them. Daudet collaborated with various authors on plays drawn from his novels and stories—*Jack* and *The Nabob*, for

Bernard Noël and Annie Ducaux in Daudet's *Sapho* (below). [French Cultural Services]

example. His original dramas include *The Older Brother* (*Le frère aîné*, 1865), *Lise Tavernier* (1869), and *The Obstacle* (*L'obstacle*, 1890).

Daudet was the father of the right-wing journalist and novelist Léon Daudet (1868–1942), founder of the newspaper *L'Action Française*.

The Arlesienne (*L'Arlésienne*, 1872). Poetically realistic drama of life in Provence, in which the tormented love of Frederick Castelet for a girl from Arles—who never appears onstage—is contrasted with the healthy, patriarchal peasant life of his family and friends. Learning that his betrothed has a lover, Frederick breaks off his engagement but nevertheless remains obsessed by his love. He decides to marry Vivette, a childhood sweetheart, but on the eve of his betrothal he imagines he hears the Arlesienne and her lover riding away together. His mind unhinged, he plunges from an open window.

A subplot involves Frederick's retarded younger brother Innocent, who, as has been prophesied, "awakens" on the day on which Frederick meets his tragic end.

Scenes from a 1951 Comédie-Française production of *L'Arlésienne*. [French Cultural Services]

William Davenant
(1606 – 1668)

Sir William Davenant, English theatre manager and dramatist, was baptized in Oxford on March 3, 1606. He was the son of a well-to-do vintner and tavern keeper who became mayor of Oxford, and his wife, the former Jane Shepherd. Tradition has it that Shakespeare, a family friend who frequented their tavern, the Crown, was the child's godfather. When Davenant was sixteen, his father died, leaving him little money and instructions that he be sent to London as an apprentice to a merchant. Davenant had apparently been occupied with studies at Lincoln College, Oxford; he left there to go to London, where instead of entering into an apprenticeship, he became a page to the Duchess of Richmond. He later served in the household of Fulke Greville, Lord Brooke, until Greville's death in 1628. Sometime prior to 1624 he took a wife, Mary, who bore him at least two children but otherwise remains obscure.

Davenant's first drama, *Albovine, King of the Lombards*, an unacted tragedy, was written a few years before it was published in 1629. His first play to be performed was *The Cruel Brother*, acted by the King's Men at the Blackfriars Theatre in 1627. During the early 1630s Davenant's life was marked by two unfortunate events: he was seriously stricken by syphilis (his nose was ultimately disfigured), and as a result of a fatal attack on a tapster he was forced to leave London until pardoned by King Charles I.

The Temple of Love, a masque produced in 1635 for Queen Henrietta Maria, won her favor and was the beginning of Davenant's professional attachment to the court, for which he became the principal writer of masques. In 1638 he was named Poet Laureate to succeed Ben Jonson. Two years later he was appointed manager of the child actors at the Cockpit Theatre in Drury Lane in place of William Beeston, who had been incarcerated by the King for presenting an unlicensed and objectionable play. *See* MASQUE.

During the Bishops' Wars (1639–1640) Davenant served the King as a soldier in combat and as a paymaster. In 1643, during the Civil War, he was knighted by Charles at the siege of Gloucester. Between 1642 and 1649 he negotiated numerous royal missions in the Netherlands and France, and while on one of his French assignments in 1646 he is supposed to have been converted to Roman Catholicism. In May, 1650, the royal cause lost, Davenant joined the Queen in Paris, was appointed Lieutenant Governor of Maryland to replace Lord Baltimore, who favored the Commonwealth, and set sail for America. But his ship was seized in the Channel by the Puritans, who imprisoned him first in Cowes Castle and then in the Tower of London, during which time he wrote and published *Gondibert*. Released from the Tower in October, 1652, he shortly thereafter married Dame Anne Cademan, a rich widow. He was pardoned by Cromwell in 1654. In 1655, six months after his second wife's death, Davenant traveled to France and married Henrietta Maria du Tremblay; returning with his third wife to London, he took up residence at Rutland House.

By May, 1656, he had begun staging in Rutland House productions that he described as "operas" involving "music and instruction," thereby evading the Puritan ban on theatrical performances. His success at circumventing legal prohibition was sufficient to permit him in 1658 to transfer the enterprise to the Cockpit Theatre. The most memorable of these productions, *The Siege of Rhodes* (1656, 1659?), is generally considered the first English opera as well as the first production in England to employ movable canvas scenery and a female performer.

After the Restoration, Davenant and Thomas Killigrew each obtained patents from Charles II to run the two theatres that were to be permitted to operate. Davenant's troupe, known as the Duke's Company,

William Davenant. [New York Public Library Picture Collection]

gained a reputation for being expertly managed and trained, and it schooled many of the Restoration's finest actors. At the Lincoln's Inn Fields Theatre (also called Lisle's Tennis Court or the Duke's Theatre), Davenant's productions included adaptations of Shakespeare's plays that were tailored to contemporary taste and, like his other presentations, gave new emphasis to elaborate stage machinery, ballet, and music.

Davenant died in his quarters in the Lincoln's Inn Fields Theatre on April 7, 1668. He was buried two days later in Westminster Abbey.

WORK

Davenant's importance as a dramatist was twofold. As a playhouse director, he anticipated the type of theatre that was to become characteristic of the late seventeenth century. As a writer of plays before, after, and even during the Commonwealth, a time when theatrical performances were officially forbidden, his work formed a bridge between the Caroline and Restoration stages and, despite its limitations, foreshadowed the more brilliant drama that was to follow. Three plays serve to illustrate the range and transitional nature of his work. *Love and Honor* (1634), produced during the Caroline period, owed much to the tragicomedy of John Fletcher while anticipating, and in fact serving as a propelling force toward, the development of heroic "love and honor" plays of the Restoration period as typified by John Dryden. The two-part *The Siege of Rhodes* (1656, 1659?), called an opera to elude the prohibition of the production of plays, combines music and exotic spectacle in a manner designed to be as inoffensive as possible to the Puritan authorities. *The Play-House to Be Let* (1663), performed shortly after the Restoration, is a potpourri of four playlets, a sort of sampler of wit and heroics for an audience just reintroduced to the theatre after an eighteen-year hiatus. Except for this last curiosity, however, Davenant produced nothing of note after the Restoration. *See* DRYDEN, JOHN; FLETCHER, JOHN.

His best work, written before the closing of the theatres, comprises a group of cleverly constructed comedies distinguished by an epigrammatic, sometimes fantastic, wit. *The Wits* (1634) portrays the farcical misadventures of two country gentlemen intent on making their way in London by their brains. *News from Plymouth* (1635) is a briskly realistic comedy. *The Platonic Lovers* (1635) is a romantic comedy set in an imaginary Sicilian court, elevated in tone and gracefully executed, satirizing the contemporary Caroline vogue favoring platonic love. *Salmacida*

Spolia (1640), one of Davenant's finest court masques, was the last of these entertainments to be presented before Charles I.

Love and Honor (1634). Tragicomedy with heroic and romantic overtones. During a war between the houses of Milan and Savoy, Princess Evandra of Milan, in company with her champion Leonell, is captured by Prospero, a soldier of Savoy. To protect her from the vengeful Duke of Savoy, his friend Alvaro's father, Prospero hides Evandra in a cave. But the Duke is determined to take the life of any Milanese and threatens Prospero and his son with death unless they produce Evandra. To avoid this tragedy, Evandra and Leonell's sister Melora, who has joined them in the cave, both present themselves to the Duke, each insisting that she is the Princess. The Duke then resolves to have both put to death, and Evandra's three suitors, Leonell, Alvaro, and Prospero, despair for her life as well as Melora's. Just in time, however, the Duke discovers that his brother, thought to have been killed by the Prince of Milan, is alive, and vengeance is no longer necessary. Leonell claims Evandra, Alvaro wins Melora, and Prospero goes off to war.

The Siege of Rhodes (1656, 1659?). Historical play in two parts, a musical extravaganza followed by a drama in five acts and several scenes, based on the Turkish siege of the Christian fortress on Rhodes in 1522. Ianthe, the virtuous bride of Alphonso, one of the Christian defenders of the fort, has been captured by the Turks during an attempt to join her husband in battle. Moved by the young woman's courage, Sultan Solyman permits her to pass through the Turkish camp unscathed. But when she finally reaches Alphonso, he suspects that she has won her release through infidelity with Solyman. Later, however, Alphonso repents, and the Christians dispatch Ianthe to discuss peace with the Turks, whose assault has all but vanquished Rhodes. Although Roxolana, Solyman's wife, is initially annoyed by her husband's admiration for Ianthe, she later discerns the girl's worth and effects her reunion with Alphonso during a last, desperate Christian effort to rescue her. Solyman sends the couple back to Rhodes, leaving to Ianthe all the arrangements for surrendering the fortress.

PLAYS

All were first performed in London.
See STATIONERS' REGISTER for an explanation of the term.

1. *Albovine, King of the Lombards.* Tragedy. Written ca. 1626. Published 1629.

2. *The Cruel Brother.* Tragedy. Published 1630 (Stationers' Register, Jan. 10, 1630). Produced Blackfriars Theatre (King's Men), early 1627 (licensed Jan. 12, 1627).

3. *The Siege.* Comedy. Published 1673 (Stationers'

Register, as *The Colonel*, Jan. 1, 1630). Produced Cockpit Theatre (?), 1629? (licensed July 22, 1629, as *The Colonel*, believed but not certain to be the same play).

4. *The Just Italian*. Play. Published 1630 (Stationers' Register, Jan. 10, 1630). Produced Blackfriars Theatre (King's Men), late 1629 (licensed Oct. 2, 1629).

5. *The Wits*. Comedy. Published 1636 (Stationers' Register, Feb. 4, 1636). Produced Blackfriars Theatre (King's Men), Jan. 22, 1634 (licensed Jan. 19, 1634).

6. *Love and Honor;* also entitled *The Courage of Love; and the Nonpareilles,* or *The Matchless Maids*. Tragicomedy. Published 1649 (Stationers' Register, Sept. 4, 1646). Produced Blackfriars Theatre (King's Men), before Dec. 12, 1634 (licensed Nov. 20, 1634).

7. *The Temple of Love*. Masque. Published 1635. Produced Whitehall, Feb. 10, 1635. Settings: Inigo Jones.

8. *News from Plymouth*. Comedy. Published 1673 (in folio). Produced Globe Theatre (King's Men), summer, 1635 (licensed Aug. 1, 1635).

9. *The Platonic Lovers*. Tragicomedy. Published 1636 (Stationers' Register, Feb. 4, 1636). Produced Blackfriars Theatre (King's Men), late 1635 (licensed Nov. 16, 1635).

10. *The Triumphs of the Prince D'Amour*. Masque. Published 1636 (Stationers' Register, Feb. 19, 1636). Produced Middle Temple, Feb. 23/24, 1636.

11. *Britannia Triumphans*. Masque. Published 1638 (licensed for publication Jan. 8, 1638). Produced Whitehall, Jan. 7, 1638.

12. *Luminalia, or The Festival of Light*. Masque. Published 1638. Produced Whitehall, Feb. 6, 1638. Settings: Jones.

13. *The Unfortunate Lovers*. Tragedy. Published 1643. Produced Blackfriars Theatre (King's Men), Apr. 23, 1638 (licensed Apr. 16, 1638).

14. *The Fair Favorite*. Tragicomedy. Published 1673 (in folio). Produced Cockpit Theatre (King's Men), Nov. 20, 1638 (licensed Nov. 17, 1638).

15. *The Distresses;* probably also entitled *The Spanish Lovers*. Comedy. Published 1673. Produced King's Men, late 1639 (licensed Nov. 30, 1639).

16. *Salmacida Spolia*. Masque. Published 1640. Produced Whitehall, Jan. 21, 1640.

17. *The First Day's Entertainment at Rutland House*. Entertainment. Published 1657. Produced Rutland House, May 23, 1656.

18. *The Siege of Rhodes, Part I*. Opera. Published 1656. Produced Rutland House, September, 1656.

19. *The Cruelty of the Spaniards in Peru*. Opera. Published 1658 (Stationers' Register Nov. 30, 1658). Produced Cockpit Theatre, 1658.

20. *The Siege of Rhodes, Part II*. Opera. Published 1663 (Stationers' Register, May 30, 1659). Produced Cockpit Theatre (?), 1659?

21. *The History of Sir Francis Drake*. Opera. Published 1659. Produced Cockpit Theatre, 1659.

22. *The Law Against Lovers*. Tragicomedy. Published 1673. Produced Lincoln's Inn Fields Theatre, Feb. 5, 1662.

23. *The Play-House to Be Let*. Comedy. Published 1673. Produced Lincoln's Inn Fields Theatre, ca. August, 1663.

24. *The Rivals*. Comedy. Published 1668 (Stationers' Register, Nov. 9, 1668). Produced Lincoln's Inn Fields Theatre, before September, 1664. A revision of John Fletcher's *The Two Noble Kinsmen*.

25. *Greene's Tu Quoque*. Comedy. Produced Lincoln's Inn Fields Theatre, Sept. 12, 1667.

26. (Adaptation; with John Dryden). *The Tempest, or The Enchanted Island*. Comedy. Published 1670 (Stationers' Register, Jan. 8, 1670). Produced Lincoln's Inn Fields Theatre, Nov. 7, 1667. Based on William Shakespeare's play.

27. *The Man's the Master*. Comedy. Published 1669 (Stationers' Register, June 8, 1669). Produced Lincoln's Inn Fields Theatre, Mar. 26, 1668.

28. (Adaptation). *Macbeth*. Dramatic opera. Published 1674. Produced Dorset Garden Theatre, Feb. 18, 1673. Based on Shakespeare's play.

EDITIONS

Collections.
Dramatic Works, ed. by J. Maidment and W. H. Logan, 5 vols., Edinburgh, 1872–1874, New York, 1964.
Individual Plays.
Love and Honor. Published in *Early Seventeenth Century Plays, 1600–1642,* ed. by H. R. Walley and J. H. Wilson, New York, 1930.
The Siege of Rhodes, Part I. Published in *Plays of the Restoration and Eighteenth Century,* ed. by D. MacMillan and H. M. Jones, New York, 1938.
The Wits. Published in *Six Caroline Plays,* ed. by A. S. Knowland, London, 1962.

CRITICISM

A. Kinross, *Davenant,* New York, 1907; A. Harbage, *Sir William Davenant, Poet Venturer, 1606–1668,* Philadelphia and Oxford, 1935; A. H. Nethercot, *Sir William D'Avenant, Poet Laureate and Playwright-Manager,* Chicago, 1938.

DAVIES, David Ivor. *See* NOVELLO, IVOR.

DAVIES, Robertson (1913–   ). Canadian novelist and playwright; former Old Vic actor, now master of Massey College, University of Toronto. Davies's one-act *Eros at Breakfast* won the Barry Jackson Trophy for the best Canadian play of 1948. A three-act play, *Fortune My Foe,* about the need for maintaining one's integrity under financial pressures as well as lures, earned him the trophy the following year. *Leaven of Malice* (1960), an adaptation of Davies's novel about a small-town journalist, was seen in New York in a production by Tyrone Guthrie. Among his other plays are *Hope Deferred* (1948), based on the banning of Molière's *Tartuffe* in Quebec in 1693; *At My Heart's Core* (1950); *A Masque of Aesop* (1952); and *A Jig for the Gypsy* (1954).

DAVIS, Owen (b. Portland, Me., January 29, 1874; d. New York, October 14, 1956). American playwright whose large body of work caused the critic George Jean Nathan to call

Owen Davis.
[Walter Hampden Memorial Library at The Players, New York]

Ruth Gordon and Raymond Massey in *Ethan Frome*, by Owen Davis. New York, National Theatre, 1936. [Photograph by Vandamm. Theatre Collection, The New York Public Library at Lincoln Center]

her with compassion. She has sent for Ben, Mother Jordan's youngest son and favorite, who some time ago had left home to avoid imprisonment for arson. When it is revealed that Mother Jordan has left her entire estate to Jane, who loves Ben, the horrified relatives depart. Only Ben remains, after Jane pays his bail bond, to help on the farm. But when Jane discovers Ben in the arms of another girl, she decides to leave, having effected his freedom from imprisonment and given him the farm and all the money, as his mother had wished. Not too late, Ben realizes he loves Jane and cannot do without her, and they announce their impending marriage. Produced New York, Sam Harris Theatre, February 10, 1923.

Ethan Frome (1936). Drama of northern New England depicting the tragedy of Ethan Frome, a poor farmer, trapped in an unhappy marriage with the nagging, unsympathetic Zeena. Ethan falls in love with Mattie Silver, the young cousin who comes to work as a hired hand. Realizing what has happened, Zeena insists that Mattie leave the house. Although desperately in love, Ethan cannot ignore his duty to his wife, and he undertakes to take Mattie to the station on a sled. On the way, Ethan and Mattie declare their love, and Ethan steers the sled toward certain disaster. Denied the deaths they desired, Ethan finishes his life disfigured and crippled, and Mattie, her mind affected, is a whining invalid. Both are dependent on the ministrations of Zeena. Produced New York, National Theatre, January 21, 1936.

him "the Lope de Vega of the American theatre." The majority of almost 300 plays were admittedly produced solely for financial gain and are of little consequence, but when Davis turned to his native New England for inspiration, he won a Pulitzer Prize with *Icebound* (1923), a grim drama about the stultifying effects of puritanical morals and attitudes on a hard-bitten family. Davis's feeling for New England life also resulted in *Ethan Frome* (1936), adapted from Edith Wharton's tragic novel. Outstanding among his other plays are *The Detour* (1921), a realistic portrayal of frustrated ambition that besets a mother and her daughter; and an adaptation of Pearl Buck's *The Good Earth* (1932).

Icebound (1923). Drama set on a farm in northern New England, where Mother Jordan's relations cynically await her death and their consequent inheritance. Only the poor Jane Crosby, a distant relative who has been Mother Jordan's companion, watches over

Eduardo De Filippo
(1900 –   )

Eduardo De Filippo, poet, actor, and dramatist, was born in Naples on May 24, 1900, into a family of actors. While still adolescents, he, his brother Peppino, and his sister Titina—all three the illegitimate children of Eduardo Scarpetta—joined the famous Scarpetta acting company and became principal performers. They separated shortly thereafter, and Eduardo joined the company of L. Carini as utility man, character actor, and author. He then moved into the field of musical comedy as a member of Peppino Villani's company, but by 1929 he was reunited with his brother and sister in the Molinari Company. During his two years there, Eduardo, using many pseudonyms, collaborated with other writer members of the company, composing variety sketches and his first one-act plays. The De

Eduardo De Filippo in his *Le voci di dentro* (above). [Federico Arborio Mella, Milan]

Filippo family then formed its own company, I De Filippo, in Naples, performing at the Kursaal and the Cinema Reale in a number of one-act plays written by Eduardo in collaboration with Peppino. The company toured Italy in 1933 and 1934 with great success. In the ensuing years, they made a number of films, beginning in 1932 with *Three Men in Tails* (*Tre uomini in frak*). In 1937 Eduardo attracted attention as a writer with his first screenplay, *I Did It!* (*Sono stato io!*). The De Filippo family performed together intermittently during the war years, but in 1945 they separated again. Soon Eduardo began producing his own works, among them the well-known *Millionaire Naples* (*Napoli milionaria!*, 1945), a drama about the black market. With the success of *These Ghosts!* (*Questi fantasmi!*, 1946), followed by *Filumena Marturano* (1946), Eduardo's reputation as a playwright was firmly established. He published a highly acclaimed volume of poetry, *Naples, the Country of Pulcinella* (*Il paese di Pulcinella*, 1951), and in 1954 reopened the celebrated Teatro San Ferdinando of Naples. He continued to write, to direct films, and to act.

(Below) Scene from a French production of *Questi fantasmi!* Paris, Théâtre du Vieux-Colombier, 1957. [French Cultural Services]

WORK

One of the most gifted dramatists of the contemporary Italian theatre, De Filippo in his more than fifty plays discloses a fine craftsmanship that owes a great deal to his acting experience. The many sketches and one-act comedies he wrote for his own troupe and for others during his apprentice years grounded him in a twofold sense, in the practical knowledge of what works in the theatre and in a tragicomic awareness of the fine line between illusion and reality. Influenced by Pirandello, De Filippo wrote dramas that develop the idea of a fiction which, created as an evasion of life, assumes an autonomy of its own. There is, however, less negativism, less tragic sense than in Pirandello; the view of life is more buoyant and zestful. Mostly written in Neapolitan dialect, the plays are invested with the infectious spirit of Pulcinella, with a core of matter-of-fact earthiness, a compound of love and mockery that characterizes the Neapolitan temperament and the same folk spirit that gave rise to the *commedia dell'arte* tradition. *See* COMMEDIA DELL'ARTE; PIRANDELLO, LUIGI.

Reality is the principal substructure of De Filippo's dramas; there is little overt symbolism or social or political criticism. Instead, the inherently self-critical characters reveal through interaction their lives and condition. Among De Filippo's best-known plays are *Filumena Marturano* (1946), which focuses on a former prostitute's successful efforts to assure the financial future of her three illegitimate children by maneuvering her middle-aged lover into marriage; *The Big Magic* (*La grande magia,* 1949), in which the "little magic" of a charlatan is contrasted with the "larger magic" that is life itself; *These Ghosts!* (1946), the most eerie of his plays, in which, unlike Pirandello, De Filippo sweeps illusions aside by explanations that hint at the reality just below the surface; *Inner Voices* (*Le voci di dentro,* 1948), written in seventeen hours, in which he elaborates the provocative theme that dreams are forms of reality since they project our unrealized potential for good or evil; and *My Darling and My Love* (*Bene mio e core mio,* 1955), an investigation into the nature of family affection. In 1961 he presented *Vincenzo De Pretore* (*De Pretore Vincenzo*), drawn from an earlier poem, in which a young Neapolitan thief believes himself to be under the special protection of St. Joseph. The somewhat irreverent treatment of the saint in this play scandalized some Italians.

De Filippo's other plays include the realistic *Millionaire Naples* (1945), depicting the moral corruption of the family of a businessman involved in the black market; the comedy *Fear Number One* (*La paura numero uno,* 1950), in which Matteo Generoso uses his fear of World War III as a subterfuge for preventing his daughter's marriage; and the Pirandellian drama *The Truth That Was Never Revealed* (*Le bugie con le gambe lunghe,* 1948), whose title literally means "long-legged lies" and is a reversal of the Italian proverb "Le bugie hanno le gambe corte" ("Lies have short legs"). This play shows how by tacit consent a lie can come to be accepted for the truth. *The Boss of the Sanità District* (*Il sindaco di rione Sanità,* 1960) is a grotesque "comedy" in which Antonio Barrancono, an old boss of the local Mafia, withdraws after thirty-five years of unlawful activity in favor of a man who challenges his authority and by whom he is eventually killed. De Filippo's earlier comedies include *Sik-Sik, the Magic Craftsman* (*Sik-sik, l'artefice magico,* wr. 1930) and *Christmas at the Cupiellos'* (*Natale in casa Cupiello,* wr. 1931), a play about a childishly innocent man's encounter with evil.

These Ghosts! (*Questi fantasmi!,* 1946). Comedy of a man forced by poverty to accept free rent for himself and his young wife in an apartment said to be haunted. He becomes convinced that the apartment is haunted by a benevolent ghost whom he sees, but in reality the "ghost" is his wife's rich lover. The latter is so touched by the husband's good

Yves Deniaud and Valentine Tessier in a French production of *Filumena Marturano.* Paris, Théâtre de la Renaissance, 1952. [French Cultural Services]

A Russian
production of
*Filumena
Marturano*.
Moscow,
Vakhtangov
Theatre, 1957.
[*Moscow Theatres*]

faith that he goes away, leaving on a table the money he had accumulated in order to run away with the wife.

Filumena Marturano (1946). Neapolitan comedy about Filumena, a former prostitute, who for twenty-five years has been the mistress of the wealthy Don Domenico Soriano. When she discovers that he is about to marry a younger woman, she pretends to be dying and tricks him into marrying her in a death-bed ceremony. She then reveals that she has three grown sons who do not know their mother's identity but whom she has been supporting with money stolen from Don Domenico. By virtue of the marriage, Domenico is now their legal father. Having seen through her deception, in a fury he swears to have the marriage annulled. As a parting shot, however, Filumena tells him that he is the father of one of her sons. Ten months later, a much-chastened Domenico has wooed, won, and remarried Filumena; however, she still refuses to tell him which son is his: they must all be equal in his affection.

Inner Voices (*Le voci di dentro*, 1948). Alberto Saporiti dreams one night that the members of the Cimmaruta family have murdered his friend Aniello. Once awake, he remains under the influence of the dream, and confusing it with reality, he denounces the Cimmarutas to the police. When, however, Aniello turns out to be very much alive, the police release the Cimmarutas from custody and Saporiti realizes that he must have dreamed it all. He expects the family to reproach him for his calumnies, but to his surprise the various members of the Cimmaruta family come to see him and accuse one another of the crime. Saporiti realizes that his "dream" was actually an intuition of what the Cimmarutas were capable of.

The Big Magic (*La grande magia*, 1949). Comedy developing the idea that life is a game. A conspiracy of friends helps Marta join her lover Mariano by eluding the watchful attention of her jealous husband Calogero. They enlist the aid of Otto, a visiting magician, who uses Marta as the subject in a disappearing act. But instead of returning in fifteen minutes, as stipulated, Marta runs off with Mariano. To save face before his audience, the magician gives the confused Calogero a small box from which his wife can be produced, but only if Calogero has complete faith in her fidelity. Holding stubbornly to the illusion that time has not passed but that he is still living before the moment when Otto is to bring back Marta, Calogero keeps the box closed for four years. Coaxed by the guilt-ridden Otto, he finally decides to open it, though his faith is not complete. He counts, "one, two . . . ," when Marta comes back, a moment too soon. The box is still closed, and Calogero's faith has not been tested; therefore he cannot accept Marta but clings to the unopened box.

De Filippo (center) in his *La grande magia.* [Federico Arborio Mella, Milan]

Vincenzo De Pretore (*De Pretore Vincenzo,* 1961). Vincenzo De Pretore, raised as a foundling, has sworn to be "somebody" but for the moment is only a thief. His friend Ninuccia convinces him to appeal to St. Joseph for protection, but Vincenzo's understanding of the arrangement is that the saint is to protect him from the law and point out easy touches in exchange for votive candles and flowers on the altar. Convinced that he has the saint's protection, Vincenzo becomes careless and is shot while trying to make off with a bank messenger's briefcase. In a dream, he appears at the gates of paradise only to find that St. Joseph disclaims all knowledge of the bargain. Indignant, Vincenzo argues that a bargain is a bargain and forces his acceptance by the hosts of heaven. But the last scene takes us back to the hospital, where Vincenzo dies still arguing for his admission into paradise.

PLAYS

1. *Ho fatto il guaio? Riparerò* (*I Did Wrong? I'll Fix Things*). Play, 3 acts; Neapolitan dialect. Written 1926.
2. (With Peppino De Filippo). *Prova generale* (*Final Dress Rehearsal*). Play, 1 act; Neapolitan dialect. Written 1929.
3. *Sik-Sik, l'artefice magico* (*Sik-Sik, the Magic Craftsman*). Play, 1 act; Neapolitan dialect. Written 1930. Published 1932.
4. *L'opera dei pupi* (*Puppet Play*). Play. Written 1931.
5. *Ogni anno, punto e da capo* (*Every Year, from the Beginning*). Revue. Written 1931.
6. *Ombre della città* (*Shadow of the City*). Revue. Written 1931.
7. *C'era una volta Napoli* (*Once There Was Naples*). Revue. Written 1931.
8. *L'ultimo bottone* (*The Last Button*). Play, 1 act; Neapolitan dialect. Written 1931.
9. *Natale in casa Cupiello* (*Christmas at the Cupiellos'*). Comedy, 2 acts, revised as 3 acts; Neapolitan dialect. Written 1931. Published 1943.
10. *Pulcinella principe in sogno* (*Pulcinella, Dream Prince*). Revue. Written 1932.
11. *E s'è 'nfucato o' sole* (*The Sun's Caught Fire*). Play; Neapolitan dialect. Written 1932.
12. (With C. Mauro). *Cento di questi giorni* (*A Hundred of Such Days*). Play. Written 1932.
13. *Farmacia di turno* (*Pharmacy Open on Alternate Sundays*). Play, 1 act; Neapolitan dialect. Written 1932.
14. *La voce del padrone* (*His Master's Voice*). Play, 1 act. Written 1932.
15. *Quei figuri di trent'anni fa* (*Those Faces of Thirty Years Ago*). Play, 1 act; Neapolitan dialect. Written 1932.
16. *Addio Nico!* (*Good-bye, Nico!*). Play, 1 act. Written 1932.
17. *Gennariello.* Play, 1 act; Neapolitan dialect. Written 1932.
18. *Io, l'erede* (*I, the Heir*). Play, 3 acts; Neapolitan dialect. Written 1932. Published 1942.
19. *Tre mesi dopo* (*Three Months Later*). Play, 1 act; Neapolitan dialect. Written 1932.
20. *Chi è cchiù felice'e me!* (*Who's Happier than I Am!*). Play, 2 acts; Neapolitan dialect. Written 1932.
21. *Ditegli sempre sí* (*Always Tell Him Yes*). Play, 2 acts; Neapolitan dialect. Written 1932.
22. *Requie all'anima sua* (*Peace to Him*). Play, 1 act; Neapolitan dialect. Written 1932.
23. (With M. Scarpetta). *Parlate al portiere* (*Speak to the Porter*). Play, 1 act. Written 1932.
24. *Una bella trovata* (*A Fine Expedient*). Play, 1 act. Written 1932.
25. *Noi siam navigator* (*We Are Navigators*). Play, 1 act. Written 1932.
26. *Cuoco cuoco della mala cucina* (*Cook, Cook of the Bad Kitchen*). Play, 1 act. Written 1932.
27. *Il thè delle cinque* (*Five O'Clock Tea*). Play, 1 act. Written 1932.
28. *Uomo e galantuomo* (*Man and Gentleman*). Play, 3 acts; Neapolitan dialect. Written 1933.
29. *Il dono di Natale* (*Christmas Gift*). Play, 1 act; Neapolitan dialect. Written 1934.
30. *Sentiteci ad ogni costo* (*Listen at All Costs*). Play, 1 act. Written 1935.
31. *Quinto piano, ti saluto!* (*Good-bye, Fifth Floor!*). Play, 1 act, Neapolitan dialect. Written 1935.
32. (With G. Riva). *La speranza ha trovato un alloggio* (*Hope Has Found a Lodging*). Play, 3 acts; Neapolitan dialect. Written 1936. Produced Milan, Teatro Olimpia, Apr. 15, 1936.
33. *L'abito nuovo* (*The New Clothes*). Play, 3 acts. Written 1937. Adapted from a scenario of Luigi Pirandello.
34. *Uno coi capelli bianchi* (*Someone with White Hair*). Play, 3 acts; Neapolitan dialect. Written 1938. Published 1938.
35. *Pericolosamente* (*Dangerously*). Play, 1 act; Neapolitan dialect. Written 1938.
36. *Non ti pago* (*I Won't Pay You*). Play, 3 acts; Neapolitan dialect. Written 1940. Published 1941.
37. *La parte di Amleto* (*Hamlet's Part*). Play, 1 act; Neapolitan dialect. Written 1940. Published 1940.
38. *In licenza* (*On Leave*). Play. Written 1941.
39. (With A. Curcio and R. De Angelis). *La fortuna con l'effe maiuscola* (*Fortune with a Capital F*). Play, 3 acts; Neapolitan dialect. Produced Turin, Teatro Alfieri, Mar. 24, 1942.

40. *Napoli milionaria!* (*Millionaire Naples*). Play, 3 acts. Published 1951. Produced 1945.

41. *Questi fantasmi!* (*These Ghosts!*). Play, 3 acts. Published 1946. Produced Rome, Teatro Eliseo, Jan. 12, 1946.

42. *Filumena Marturano**. Play, 3 acts. Published 1947. Produced Naples, Nov. 7, 1946.

43. *San Carlino 1947*. Farce, 1 act. Produced Milan, Mediolanum, Apr. 8, 1947.

44. *Le bugie con le gambe lunghe* (*The Truth That Was Never Revealed*). Play, 3 acts. Published 1948. Produced Rome, Teatro Eliseo, Jan. 14, 1948.

45. *Le voci di dentro* (*Inner Voices*). Play, 3 acts. Published 1949. Produced Milan, Teatro Nuovo, Dec. 11, 1948.

46. *La grande magia* (*The Big Magic*). Play, 3 acts. Published 1950. Produced Naples, Teatro Mercadante, Dec. 14, 1949.

47. *La paura numero uno* (*Fear Number One*). Play, 3 acts. Published 1951. Produced Venice, Teatro la Fenice, July 29, 1950.

48. *Amicizia* (*Friendship*). Play, 1 act. Published 1956. Produced Rome, Ridotto del Teatro Eliseo, May 9, 1952.

49. *I morti non fanno paura* (*The Dead Are Harmless*). Play, 1 act. Published 1956. Produced Rome, Ridotto del Teatro Eliseo, May 9, 1952.

50. *Il successo del giorno* (*The Outcome of the Day*). Play, 1 act. Produced Rome, Ridotto del Teatro Eliseo, May 9, 1952.

51. *Mia famiglia* (*My Family*). Play, 3 acts. Published 1956. Produced Perugia, Teatro Morlacchi, Jan 16, 1955; Rome, Teatro Eliseo, Jan 18, 1955.

52. *Bene mio e core mio* (*My Darling and My Love*). Play, 3 acts. Published 1956. Produced Rome, Teatro Eliseo, Nov. 11, 1955.

53. *Sabato, domenica e lunedì* (*Saturday, Sunday, and Monday*). Play, 3 acts; Neapolitan dialect. Produced Rome, Teatro Quirino, Nov. 6, 1959.

54. *Il figlio di Pulcinella* (*The Son of Pulcinella*). Play. Written 1959.

55. *Dolore sotto chiave* (*Grief under Lock and Key*). Play, 1 act. Produced Milan, Teatro San Erasmo, Mar. 5, 1960.

56. *Il sindaco del rione Sanità* (*The Boss of the Sanità District*). Play, 3 acts. Published 1961. Produced Rome, Teatro Quirino, Dec. 9, 1960.

57. *De Pretore Vincenzo* (*Vincenzo De Pretore*). Play, 2 parts. Produced Genoa, Teatro Politeama, Dec. 3, 1961.

58. *Filosoficamente* (*Philosophically*). Play.

59. *Occhiali neri* (*Dark Glasses*). Play.

CRITICISM

F. Frascani, *La Napoli amara di Eduardo de Filippo,* Florence, 1958.

Thomas Dekker

(ca. 1572 – 1632)

Thomas Dekker, English dramatist, was a Londoner, born probably about 1572. Most of the information about his early life is conjectural. Evidence of some knowledge of French, Latin, and Dutch in his plays indicates that he may have received some formal education, but there is no record of his ever having attended a university. A first child of a "Thomas Dycker" (Dykers, or Dicker) was baptized in 1594. From this and other similar evidence it has been conjectured that Dekker

married shortly before that date and fathered two more daughters between 1598 and 1602.

By January, 1598 (perhaps even earlier), he had begun writing for the theatre, for his name appears in Philip Henslowe's diary that month in connection with work done on a lost play, *Phaethon*. Until his regular association with Henslowe ended in 1602, he produced plays at a prodigious rate—some forty-four alone or in collaboration with others, including *Old Fortunatus* (1599) and *The Shoemaker's Holiday* (1600). During this period he wrote *Satiromastix* (1601) for a rival company, the Lord Chamberlain's Men, and for private performance by the Children of St. Paul's; this play, an attack on Ben Jonson, figured in the War of the Theatres. *See* JONSON, BEN.

After 1602 he divided his time between playwriting and the composition of pamphlets that appear to have won him more recognition from his contemporaries than did his plays. Many of these pamphlets, particularly *The Gull's Hornbook* (1609), drew upon his experiences as a dramatist and thus reflect the theatre of the times. His dramatic works of the next ten years include *The Honest Whore, Part I* (ca. 1604; with Middleton), *The Honest Whore, Part II* (ca. 1605); *Westward Ho!* (1604; with Webster), *Northward Ho!* (1605; with Webster), *The Roaring Girl* (ca. 1610; with Middleton), and *The Virgin Martyr* (1620?; with Massinger). *See* MASSINGER, PHILIP; MIDDLETON, THOMAS; WEBSTER, JOHN.

Possibly falling into debt in 1613, Dekker seems to have spent seven years in King's Bench Prison. After his release in 1619 he was relatively inactive for the rest of his life. There is strong evidence that he is the

Thomas Dekker. From a woodcut in *Dekker His Dreame,* published in Nathan Drake's *Shakespeare and His Times,* vol. II; Folger Library. [American Heritage]

"Thomas Decker" who was buried in St. James's Parish, Clerkenwell, London, on August 25, 1632.

WORK

Although there are more than forty plays on which Thomas Dekker is known to have collaborated, only *The Shoemaker's Holiday* (1600), *Old Fortunatus* (1599), and probably *The Honest Whore, Part II* (ca. 1605) are definitely his alone; but his humor, tenderness, pathos, and realism suggest his hand in the extant collaborations. Centering his plays on contemporary life at home and abroad, Dekker merged Elizabethan romance with everyday realism, homely virtue, and a new interest in the merchant class.

The Shoemaker's Holiday, Dekker's best-known play, is a rowdy comedy wherein three plots are successfully woven together against a background of contemporary Elizabethan life. In *The Honest Whore* Dekker again used his knowledge of London life, this time less exuberantly than in *The Shoemaker's Holiday* but still with sympathy and humor; it is a fascinating tragicomedy with an underplot involving humorous characters. It is believed, but not certain, that Middleton had a small share in *The Honest Whore, Part I,* as may be indicated by its intrigue plot. This play, like *Patient Grissell* (1600), a domestic piece written with Henry Chettle and William Haughton and the first of the Elizabethan patient-wife plays, inaugurated its own vogue, that of the young blade mixing with the rising merchant class. *Old Fortunatus,* an old-fashioned piece related to the morality plays, is believed by some scholars to be Dekker's first romance.

Dekker answered Jonson's ridicule in *The Poetaster* with the nearly incoherent *Satiromastix, or The Untrussing of the Humourous Poet* (1601). Although some scholars hold that Marston had a hand in the writing of *Satiromastix,* it is not a confirmed fact and therefore held doubtful by others. Two more realistic plays, *Westward Ho!* (1604) and *Northward Ho!* (1605), both possibly written with Webster, followed, and then came a series of collaborations: with Middleton, *The Roaring Girl* (ca. 1610), about the notorious Moll Cutpurse; with Massinger, *The Virgin Martyr* (1620?), about the legend of a St. Dorothea; with Ford, Rowley, and Webster, *The Late Murder of the Son upon the Mother, or Keep the Widow Waking* (1624), a play, now lost, about a contemporary London matricide; with Ford, *The Sun's Darling* (1624), a masque that was probably popular at court and was also performed in theatres; and with Ford and Rowley, *The Witch of Edmonton* (1621), based on an account of the trial of a woman burned as a witch earlier that year, a play notable for two remarkable characters, the lovely, simple Susan, murdered by her husband, and Mother Sawyer, the witch, persecuted into a pact with the devil. Dekker's sympathetic treatment of this woman, even though he believed her to be a witch, gives the play a tragic dimension. *See* FORD, JOHN; MARSTON, JOHN; MASQUE; ROWLEY, WILLIAM.

Dekker has been criticized for the use of hackneyed devices, structural carelessness, and hasty writing, but he has often been praised for the beauty of his lyric verse and for his vigorous, dramatic prose.

Old Fortunatus (1599). "Pleasant comedy," a combination of allegorical moralities, masquelike pageantry, and fairy-tale magic, that shifts its setting from Cyprus to Babylon to England. While wandering in the woods, an old beggar, Fortunatus, encounters the goddess Fortune, who offers him his choice of her many gifts. He selects wealth, and after granting him an inexhaustible purse, Fortune rebukes him for his choice and sends him on his way. Fortunatus returns home to his sons, the virtuous Ampedo and the covetous Andelocia, tells of his good fortune, and leaves forthwith to meet the great men of the world. In Babylon, Fortunatus beguiles the Sultan and steals his magical hat, a hat that will transport its wearer anywhere he wishes. Fortunatus wishes himself back to Cyprus, where, having been told by Fortune that his death is imminent, he bequeathes to his sons the hat and purse, to be kept together and shared equally. But Andelocia makes off with the purse to England, where he hopes his wealth will entice the beautiful princess Agripyne. A wily adversary, she tricks him out of the purse and finally of the hat (which he has stolen from his brother) as well. To retrieve his treasures from Agripyne, he feeds

Michael Moriarty and Helen Carey in a 1967 production of *The Shoemaker's Holiday.* [The Guthrie Theater Company]

Scene from *The Shoemaker's Holiday* with Grace Keagy, 1967. [The Guthrie Theater Company]

her Vice's fruit, causing horns to grow on her and her courtiers. Ampedo now burns the hat, and the purse falls into the hands of two courtiers, who revenge themselves on the brothers by clapping both of them in the stocks, where they soon perish. Now the courtiers argue over the purse, but the goddesses and members of the court intercede and restore it to Fortune. A contest between Vice and Virtue awaits resolution, and Virtue prevails upon Queen Elizabeth to judge which is superior. Vice vanishes before her royal presence, while Fortune and Virtue pay homage to the Queen.

The Shoemaker's Holiday, or The Gentle Craft (1600).   Comedy presenting a lusty, often coarse picture of Elizabethan life in London as seen by Simon Eyre, "the true shoemaker of Tower Street and a gentleman of the gentle craft." Interwoven with the scenes of citizen life are two love stories. In one, Ralph, Eyre's assistant journeyman, is wrested from his newly acquired wife Jane when pressed into service as a soldier. He returns just in time to rescue Jane from marriage to Hammon, a rich citizen who had convinced her that Ralph was dead. The other love tale centers on the nobly born Rowland Lacy, who is in love with Rose Otley, daughter of the Lord Mayor of London. He is about

to be packed off to the French wars by his uncle, the Earl of Lincoln, who is opposed to the match. Having no intention of leaving his beloved, Rowland retains a portion of the expense money and, disguised as Hans Meulter, a Flemish cobbler, enters the service of Simon Eyre.

The ebullient Simon prospers: owing to an investment of money borrowed from "Hans," he suddenly finds his fortunes on the rise and progresses from alderman to sheriff. At the dinner celebration for the latter honor, Rose meets "Hans" and recognizes him as Rowland; the two decide to elope despite the efforts of Rowland's uncle, who has guessed the truth. Meanwhile, Simon rises to the position of Lord Mayor, attracting the attention of the King when he proclaims Shrove Tuesday a holiday for all shoemakers. The delighted King pardons Rowland for his dereliction of duty and joins the new Lord Mayor in banqueting and sport.

The Honest Whore, Part I (ca. 1604). Comedy depicting the conversion to virtue and chastity of the notorious courtesan Bellafront. Her transformation comes about when her amorous advances are refused by the virtuous Milanese nobleman Hippolito, a melancholy count who is pining away in the mistaken belief that his beloved, Infelice, is dead.

Bellafront falls in love with Hippolito and embraces chastity for his sake. Actually, however, Infelice has been hidden in the country by her father, Trebazzi, Duke of Milan, who then commissions the good Dr. Benedict to poison Hippolito, whom he finds unsuitable to marry his daughter. Dr. Benedict merely pretends to poison Hippolito; informing him of Infelice's whereabouts, he arranges for them to meet in a country monastery.

Bellafront, in despair over the rejection by Hippolito, feigns madness and is sent to the madhouse of the same monastery. But Hippolito and Infelice are married before her father can arrive to prevent the nuptials, and Bellafront is wed to Hippolito's friend Matheo, the young rake who first started her on the road to sin.

A subplot concerns Viola, shrewish wife of the draper Candido, and her efforts to ruffle her husband's even temper, which has survived the most outlandish practical jokes of his customers. Imperturbable, Candido is finally committed by his wife to the same monastery as Infelice and Bellafront, from which, still patient and unscathed, he is freed by the Duke.

The Honest Whore, Part II (ca. 1605). Sequel to *The Honest Whore, Part I,* picking up where Part I ended. The reformed Bellafront now suffers a kind of martyrdom in her forced marriage to the spendthrift rake Matheo, recently imprisoned for murder. She appeals for help to Hippolito, now married to Infelice, but that nobleman's nature has changed, and he now embarks on a vigorous campaign to seduce the former courtesan whom he once had scorned. Bellafront's stern father Orlando Friscobaldo, who outwardly rejects his daughter, enters the scene in the disguise of "Pacheco," a servant, engages himself to her and Matheo, and informs Infelice of her husband's philandering.

Although Matheo continues to sink deeper and deeper into debt and misery, Bellafront virtuously refuses Hippolito's offers, which could alleviate their financial straits. The Duke of Milan, at the instigation of Pacheco, finally has everyone arrested. Hippolito pleads his innocence, Matheo is released with a stern warning by the Duke and returns to his wife's forgiving arms, and Friscobaldo gives them his blessing.

The subplot continues the story of Candido, who, phlegmatic as ever, has been left a widower. His marriage to a woman even more temperamental than Viola results in vows to tame this shrew, and with the help of his friend Lodovico he succeeds. His arrest and incarceration in Bridewell Prison with all the others is revealed to be a mistake, and he is quickly freed by the Duke.

PLAYS

All were first performed in London.

See STATIONERS' REGISTER for an explanation of the term.

1. *Old Fortunatus.* Comedy, 5 acts. Published 1600 (Stationers' Register, Feb. 20, 1600). Produced at court (Lord Admiral's Men), Dec. 27, 1599. The play is probably based on an earlier two-part play (*Fortunatus*) by Dekker, Part I of which was performed at court by the Lord Admiral's Men between Feb. 3 and May 24, 1596.

2. *The Whore of Babylon.* Allegory, 5 acts. Published 1607 (Stationers' Register, Apr. 20, 1607). Produced Prince Henry's Servants, 1606/07. This may be a revision of Dekker's play *Truth's Supplication to Candlelight* (wr. before January, 1600).

3. *The Shoemaker's Holiday, or The Gentle Craft.* Comedy, 5 acts. Published 1600. Produced at court (Lord Admiral's Men), Jan. 1, 1600.

4. (With Henry Chettle and William Haughton). *Patient Grissell.* Comedy, 5 acts. Published 1603 (Stationers' Register, Mar. 28, 1600). Produced Lord Admiral's Men, 1600.

5. (With John Marston?). *Satiromastix, or The Untrussing of the Humourous Poet.* Comedy, 5 acts. Published 1602 (Stationers' Register, Nov. 11, 1601). Produced Globe Theatre (Lord Chamberlain's Men), and Children of St. Paul's, 1601.

6. (With John Webster and, possibly, Chettle, Thomas Heywood, and Wentworth Smith). *Sir Thomas Wyatt.* Famous history, 5 acts. Published 1607. Produced Worcester's Men, 1602.

7. (With Thomas Middleton). *The Honest Whore, Part I.* Comedy, 5 acts. Published 1604 (Stationers' Register, Nov. 9, 1604). Produced Prince's Men, ca. 1604.

8. (With Webster). *Westward Ho!* Comedy, 5 acts. Published 1607 (Stationers' Register, Mar. 2, 1605). Produced Children of St. Paul's, 1604.

9. *The Honest Whore, Part II.* Comedy, 5 acts. Published 1630 (Stationers' Register, Apr. 29, 1608). Produced ca. 1605.

10. (With Webster). *Northward Ho!* Comedy, 5 acts. Published 1607 (Stationers' Register, Aug. 6, 1607). Produced Children of St. Paul's, 1605.

11. (With Middleton). *The Roaring Girl, or Moll Cutpurse.* Comedy, 5 acts. Published 1611. Produced Fortune Theatre (Prince's Men), ca. 1610.

12. *If It Be Not Good, the Devil Is in It.* Comedy, 5 acts. Published 1612. Produced Red Bull Theatre (Queen's Men), 1610/12.

13. *Match Me in London.* Tragicomedy, 5 acts. Published 1631 (Stationers' Register, Nov. 8, 1630). Produced Queen Anne's Men (?), ca. 1611/12? (licensed, as an "old play," Aug. 21, 1623).

14. (With Philip Massinger). *The Virgin Martyr.* Tragedy, 5 acts. Published 1622 (Stationers' Register, Dec. 7, 1621). Produced Red Bull Theatre (King's Revels), 1620? (licensed Oct. 6, 1620).

15. (With John Ford and William Rowley). *The Witch of Edmonton.* Tragicomedy, 5 acts. Published 1658. Produced Cockpit Theatre (Prince's Men), 1621; at court, Dec. 29, 1621.

16. *The Wonder of a Kingdom.* Comedy, 5 acts. Published 1636 (Stationers' Register, May 16, 1631). Produced before 1631. Some scholars believe John Day's *Come See a Wonder* (licensed Sept. 18, 1623) to be the same play.

17. (With Ford). *The Welsh Ambassador, or a Comedy in Disguises.* Comedy, 5 acts. Published 1620. Produced ca. 1623?

18. (With Ford). *The Sun's Darling.* Moral masque, 5 acts. Published 1656. Produced Cockpit Theatre (Lady Elizabeth's Men), 1624 (licensed Mar. 3, 1624).

19. *The Noble Soldier [The Noble Spanish Soldier], or A Contract Broken, Justly Revenged.* Tragedy, 5 acts. Published 1634, as by S.R. [Samuel Rowley?] (Stationers'

Register, May 16, 1631, as by Dekker). Produced 1622/31. Most scholars attribute this play to Dekker despite the initials S.R. on the 1634 quarto. Some consider Day a possible collaborator.

Masques.

1. *The Magnificent Entertainment Given to King James.* Published 1604 (Stationers' Register, Apr. 2, 1604). Produced Mar. 15, 1603.

2. *Troia Nova Triumphans.* Published 1612 (Stationers' Register, Oct. 21, 1612). Produced Oct. 29, 1612.

3. *Britannia's Honor.* Published 1628. Produced Oct. 29, 1628.

4. *London's Tempe, or The Field of Happiness.* Published 1629? Produced Oct. 29, 1629.

EDITIONS

Collections.

The Dramatic Works of Thomas Dekker, ed. by R. H. Shepherd, 4 vols., London, 1873; *Dramatic Works,* ed. by F. Bowers, 4 vols., New York, 1953–1960.

Individual Plays.

The Honest Whore, Parts I and II. Published in *The Chief Elizabethan Dramatists, Excluding Shakespeare,* ed. by W. A. Neilson, Boston, 1911; *Elizabethan Plays,* ed. by H. Spencer, Boston, 1933.

Old Fortunatus. Published in *Typical Elizabethan Plays,* ed. by F. E. Schelling and M. W. Black, rev. and enl. ed., New York, 1931.

The Shoemaker's Holiday. Published in *Four Great Elizabethan Plays,* ed. by J. Gassner, New York, 1960; *Six Elizabethan Plays,* ed. by R. C. Bald, Boston, 1963; *Elizabethan and Jacobean Comedy,* ed. by R. Ornstein and H. Spencer, Boston, 1964.

CRITICISM

M. L. Hunt, *Thomas Dekker,* New York, 1911, reprint, New York, 1964; J. H. Conover, *Thomas Dekker: An Analysis of Dramatic Structure,* The Hague, 1969; G. R. Price, *Thomas Dekker,* New York, 1969.

DELANEY, Shelagh (b. Salford, Lancashire, 1939). English playwright. Associated with Joan Littlewood's theatre workshop in Stratford, Miss Delaney, at the age of seventeen, having had little education and no training in dramatic writing, wrote the realistic *A Taste of Honey* (1958), a study of a girl's relationship with her mother, her mother's lover, and a homosexual boyfriend. Free of moralistic overtones, the play is remarkable for its lifelike characterizations. *The Lion in Love* (1960), Miss Delaney's other play, is a somewhat more symbolic treatment of a disturbed and unhappy family and focuses on the mismatch of an entrapped father and his alcoholic wife.

A Taste of Honey (1958). Drama about a young girl, Jo, who follows the promiscuous behavior of her mother, Helen, while retaining the innocence of a sensitive child. Although planning to leave her mother and the life that has been thrust upon her, Jo cannot hide her jealousy of the obnoxious playboy boyfriend whom her mother marries, leaving Jo alone. Desolate, Jo consummates a "schoolgirl" affair with Jimmy, a Negro sailor. When he leaves for sea duty, she finds a job and a friend in Geoffrey, whose homosexuality alternately fascinates and annoys her. She

Nigel Davenport and Angela Lansbury in Shelagh Delaney's *A Taste of Honey.* New York, Lyceum Theatre, 1960. [Walter Hampden Memorial Library at The Players, New York]

wearily accepts his loving attention during her pregnancy. But when her insensitive mother, hearing of her pregnancy, returns and drives Geoffrey away, she resigns herself to his absence and her mother's presence out of fear of her approaching labor.

DELAVIGNE,   Casimir-Jean-François (1793–1843). French poet and playwright whose literary reputation was established with the publication of *The Messinian Women (Les Messéniennes,* 1815), a series of patriotic odes in which he captured the nationalistic fervor that swept France following Napoleon's defeat at Waterloo. His tragedies represent a compromise between the ideas of neoclassicism and those of the emerging romanticism. Influenced by Shakespeare and Walter Scott, he avoided the legends of classical antiquity and chose his subjects from European history. His first tragedy, *Sicilian Vespers (Les vêpres siciliennes,* 1819), is an account of a thirteenth-century uprising in Sicily. In *Marino Faliero* (1829), borrowing a theme previously treated by his literary mentor Lord Byron, he dealt with the rise and fall of a fourteenth-century Venetian doge. Produced shortly before Dumas *père*'s *Henry III and His Court* and a full year before the celebrated premiere of Hugo's *Hernani,* the play interestingly foreshadowed the local color, mixture of tragic and comic genres, and abandonment of the unities that were to be the hallmark of romantic drama. Delavigne made clearer and more definite use of these romantic components in *Louis XI* (1832), generally considered his tragic masterpiece; and *Edward's Children (Les enfants d'Édouard,* 1833), which was generously inspired by Shakespeare's *Richard III. See* UNITIES.

Though Delavigne's theatre failed to satisfy either the classicists or the romantics, it was enormously successful with the public. In *The Daughter of the Cid (La fille du Cid,* 1840), he even dared to take up a theme treated by the great Corneille. In addition to his tragedies, Delavigne wrote several comedies of manners—*The School for Graybeards (L'école des vieillards,* 1823), *La princesse Aurélie* (1828), and *Popularity (La popularité,* 1838)—which were extremely well received in their day. In 1831 he collaborated with Scribe on the libretto for Giacomo Meyerbeer's *Robert the Devil.* Delavigne was elected to the Académie Française in 1825. *See* SCRIBE, EUGÈNE.

DELAVRANCEA, Barbu, pseudonym of Barbu Ştefănescu (b. Bucharest, April 5, 1858; d. Iaşi, April 29, 1918). Romanian play-

Barbu Delavrancea. [Editura Enciclopedică Română, Bucharest]

wright who, after graduating from the Faculty of Law at the University of Bucharest in 1882, went to Paris to finish his studies. He made his literary debut in 1877 with a poem published in the daily *România Liberă.* In 1884, back in Romania, he entered politics, making a name for himself as a journalist in the newspaper *Epoca.* His active commitment to the system of two parties, Liberal and Conservative, and his impassioned speeches delivered in Parliament, at the bar, and on public platforms supporting the two-party system led to his reputation as an orator of some note. In 1894 he became a deputy and in 1899 lord mayor of the capital. In 1910–1911, soon after his trilogy *Sunset* (1909), *The Blizzard* (1909), and *The Morning Star* (1910) appeared, he served as Minister of Public Works. In 1912 he was admitted to the Romanian Academy, where he delivered a remarkable reception speech about folk poetry (published under the title *The Aesthetics of Folk Poetry,* 1913). He died in Iaşi toward the end of World War I.

WORK

Delavrancea's trilogy *Sunset, The Blizzard,* and *The Morning Star* is a great dramatic work of historical evocation while at the same time it presents three pathetic dramas of personality. The first play is devoted to the valiant Prince Stephen the Great of Moldavia (r. 1457–1504); the others concern two of his descendants, Stefăniţă, his grandson (r. 1517–1527), and Petru Rareş, his illegitimate son (r. 1527–1538; 1541–1546). These are three hypostases of power, in three distinct historical moments. The first is an example of the triumphant hero on the political and social scene, dominating history. Yet, apprehending his end (the "sunset" of the title), Stephen critically estimates the alternatives of his succession and, aware of his own singularity and genius, is beset by the fear that everything he has built up may crumble with his death. He therefore tries vainly to protect his work with unimpugnable laws and testaments. In *The Blizzard,* Stefăniţă matches his predecessor's valor but lacks his political, military, and administrative wisdom. In him genius is replaced by ambition; the leader is a puppet in the hands of the various factions and dies poisoned by the boyars. The third of the line, Petru Rareş, in *The Morning Star,* recalls his illustrious precursor in wisdom and bravery but not in decisiveness or foresight. A victim of foreign intervention in his first reign, he ends by exiling himself in his second reign. The greatness of their ancestor has raised both his successors, but at the same time it has crushed them.

The play in the trilogy that arouses the

(Left) *Sunset.*
[Embassy of
the Socialist
Republic of
Romania]

deepest response is *Sunset.* Prince Stephen, now aged, realizes that his strength has diminished, that his body is no longer that of the hero; yet his soul is still young. When he embarks on a battle, he seems to forget about his illness and age; the *man* has grown old, has lost the superb physical condition of his prime, while the *Voivode* has preserved his youthful spirit and noble ardor for the good of the country and the community. Hence, the psychological conflict in *Sunset.* Another conflict in the play, less discussed, involves the relations between the Hospodar, the boyars, and the people and the Voivode's collision with those who want to betray him. Stephen reveals himself as the perfect Hospodar, filled with love for his country, righteous, wise, and valiant.

The Blizzard, written almost simultaneously with *Sunset,* is the most "theatrical," perhaps also the most dramatic, in a "scenic" sense, of Delavrancea's plays. The development of violent conflict, the collision of characters of equal value, and the lively dialogue all add to the force of the play. The stormy, tempestuous Stefăniță is not, like Prince Stephen, the only personage thrown in bold relief, the only "character" in the play; his per-

Scene from a production of *Sunset* at the National Theatre, Bucharest. [Editura Enciclopedică Română, Bucharest]

sonality does not eclipse all the others. Instead, the patriotic boyars headed by Luca Arbore, Princess Tana, and Oana are all dramatic personages. In Stefăniţă, Delavrancea portrayed a typical feudal tyrant: vainglorious, vindictive, and hateful, setting his personal interests above the country's and experiencing the frenzy of blood, like Macbeth or Richard III.

In *The Morning Star,* Delavrancea recreated the years of Petru Rareş's reign, which to a certain extent recall Stephen the Great's glorious epoch. Lacking a well-knit conflict, individualized characters, clearly defined action, and strong dramatic movement, *The Morning Star* is a dull play. Petru Rareş is a pale copy, a shadow, not rising much above the level of good intentions.

Delavrancea's love for the theatre led him to transpose a short story into the social drama *Irinel* in 1912. In 1913 his satirical comedy *Hagi Tudose* appeared; an enormous success, it was also initially a short story. Its chief character is a miser like that of Molière, belonging, nonetheless, to the Balkan environment, a perfect egoist to the point of tragic grotesqueness.

Obsessed with the destiny of artistic work, Delavrancea wrote the play *The Second Consciousness* (pub. 1923), a remote re-creation of the myth of Pygmalion and Galatea. The main character, Rudolph, a young and gifted intellectual, is haunted by the famous image of Leonardo da Vinci's *Gioconda,* before which he fancies that he acquires a "second consciousness." Meeting Mélanie, his wife's cousin, a woman of angelic beauty, he undergoes a violent crisis of second consciousness, culminating in his suicide.

Only three of the six plays Delavrancea wrote are in the national repertory. His name is linked with *Sunset, The Blizzard,* and *Hagi Tudose,* which enjoy large audiences.

Giambattista Della Porta
(1535 – 1615)

Giambattista Della Porta, Italian scientist and dramatist, was born in Naples in 1535 of an upper-class family. A precocious youth, he began at the age of fifteen to study "natural magic," a subject that interested him for the rest of his life. While still a young man, he published the first draft of his treatise *Natural Magic* (*Magia naturalis,* 1558), which won him European renown but also a reputation

for witchcraft, for which he was accused but proved innocent before the Inquisition. However, when the charge was repeated in 1581 by Jean Bodin, he was forced to close the Academy of the Secrets, which he had founded in Naples. He then traveled extensively in Italy, France, and Spain, gained the patronage of Luigi Cardinal d'Este, and helped revive the Accademia dei Lincei in Rome. Della Porta is credited with several important scientific observations, and his experiments with magnetism and optical instruments have proved valuable. He devoted his leisure to writing plays. Della Porta died in Naples on February 4, 1615.

WORK

Although Della Porta was the last important writer of the *commedia erudita,* his work differs appreciably in approach and tone from that of the earlier writers. He was the principal exponent of *commedia grave* ("serious comedy"), a development of the *commedia erudita* that was strongly influenced by Giraldi Cinthio's theories and the resulting rise of tragicomedy. Della Porta's comedies are often almost indistinguishable from tragicomedy, since their action is usually quite serious and the characters endure countless trials before the happy ending. However, unlike tragicomedy, they are written in prose and make use of the stock characters of Italian comedy (the rascally servant, the braggart captain, the fraudulent

Giambattista Della Porta. [Federico Arborio Mella, Milan]

savant), and they are frequently enlivened by comic horseplay. Thus in *The Sister* (*La sorella,* 1589), while Attilio agonizes over his passion for a wife whom he believes to be his long-lost sister, the antics of his servant Trinca provide comic relief. *See* GIRALDI CINTHIO, GIAMBATTISTA; TRAGICOMEDY.

Of Della Porta's fourteen extant prose comedies, *The Sister, The Moor* (*Il moro,* pub. 1607), and *The Astrologer* (*L'astrologo,* wr. 1570) are representative of his range. Whereas the first is generally typical of Della Porta's style, the other two represent his most serious and his lightest sides respectively. Other comedies are *The Maidservant* (*La fantesca,* wr. 1592), which treats the humiliation of two braggart captains; *The Madwoman* (*La furiosa,* pub. 1600), in which separated lovers lose their powers of reason; *The Two Rival Brothers* (*I due fratelli rivali,* pub. 1601), in which brothers love the same woman; and *Olympia* (*L'Olimpia;* wr. 1550, prod. 1588), in which a girl seeks her long-lost father in order to avoid a distasteful marriage. It is a curious fact that, despite the serious tone of his comedies, Della Porta was widely plundered by the scenarists of the *commedia dell'arte. See* COMMEDIA DELL'ARTE.

In addition to his comedies, Della Porta wrote a traditional tragedy, *Ulysses* (*Ulisse,* wr. 1612); two "sacred" tragedies, only one of which, *St. George* (*Giorgio,* 1611), survives; and *Penelope* (wr. before 1585), a tragicomedy.

The Astrologer (*L'astrologo,* wr. 1570). Prose comedy in which Pandolfo and Guglielmo, widowers, have promised to marry each other's daughters. When Guglielmo is thought to be drowned, his son Lelio expresses the desire to marry Pandolfo's daughter Sulpizia in his father's place and to arrange for his sister Artemisia to wed not Pandolfo, but his son Eugenio. Pandolfo still desires Artemisia, however, and is persuaded by the astrologer-magician Albumazar that he can restore Guglielmo to life so that their marital bargain can be kept. Albumazar, in reality a confidence man, merely steals Pandolfo's gold and makes a fool of one of his servants. When Guglielmo finally returns, he supports his children's marital plans and persuades Pandolfo to do the same. Albumazar is unmasked, and Pandolfo's treasure is restored.

The Sister (*La sorella,* 1589). Prose comedy that takes place some years after Attilio, sent by his father Pardo to ransom his mother and sister from the Turks, falls in love with and marries Sofia, a slave girl, and uses the ransom money to free her. On his return to his home in Nola, he passes her off as his sister Cleria and informs his father that his mother is dead. To the consternation of At-

tilio and his rascally servant Trinca, Pardo prepares to marry the false Cleria to Captain Trisimaco while arranging a match for Attilio with Sulpizia. Meanwhile, Pedolitro, a friend of Pardo, arrives from Turkey with a letter from Constanza, Pardo's wife. Attilio swears that his mother is dead and that Pedolitro is lying, but when she arrives in Nola, her son confesses his subterfuge to his mother. Then, to his dismay, she identifies Sofia as her daughter, the real Cleria. Faced with the fact that he has married his own sister, Attilio almost goes insane. At the last minute, Sulpizia's nurse announces that Sulpizia and Cleria were exchanged as babies and proves Sulpizia's true identity by a birthmark. The happiness of Attilio and Cleria is matched by the union of Sulpizia and her lover Erotico.

The Moor (*Il moro,* pub. 1607). Prose comedy that takes place years after the wedding night of Pirro and Oriana, during which Captain Parabola had arranged to have a servant discovered under the lady's bed. Pirro had immediately deserted his wife and is believed to be dead. Now, the faithful Oriana is being urged to marry Erone, nephew of the Governor of Capua. Pirro, disguised as a Moor, meanwhile returns and, learning the truth about Parabola's trick, tries to kill Erone to prevent the wedding but succeeds only in causing his own imprisonment. Pirro's brother Filadelfo, unaware of Pirro's return, also tries to prevent the wedding, by challenging Erone to a duel. Rescued from prison by Erone, Pirro offers to take his place in the duel with Filadelfo. He then defeats his brother but spares his life. At last, still disguised as the Moor, he meets Oriana, tells her of Parabola's trick and informs her that he, Pirro, is dead. Oriana's dismay is proof of her constancy. Finally, Pirro reveals his identity to all, enlists the aid of Erone, spares the life of Parabola, and is reunited with Oriana.

PLAYS

1. *L'Olimpia* (*Olympia*). Comedy, 5 acts; prose. Written 1550. Published 1589. Produced Naples, 1588.

2. *L'astrologo** (*The Astrologer*). Comedy, 5 acts; prose. Written 1570. Published 1606.

3. *La turca* (*The Turkish Woman*). Comedy, 5 acts; prose. Written 1572. Published 1606.

4. *Penelope.* Tragicomedy, 5 acts; verse. Written before 1585. Published 1591.

5. *La sorella* (*The Sister*). Comedy, 5 acts; prose. Written 1589. Published 1604. Produced Naples, residence of Francesco Blanco, 1589.

6. *La Cinthia* (*Cinthia*). Comedy, 5 acts; prose. Written 1592. Published 1592.

7. *La fantesca* (*The Maidservant*). Comedy, 5 acts; prose. Written 1592. Published 1592.

8. *La trappolaria* (*The Snare*). Comedy, 5 acts; prose. Published 1596. Produced Ferrara, 1614.

9. *La Chiuppinaria* (*Chiappino, the Bear*). Comedy, 5 acts; prose. Written after 1598. Published 1609.

10. *La furiosa* (*The Madwoman*). Comedy, 5 acts; prose. Published 1600.

11. *I due fratelli rivali* (*The Two Rival Brothers*). Comedy, 5 acts; prose. Published 1601.

12. *I due fratelli simili* (*The Two Similar Brothers*). Comedy, 5 acts; prose. Published 1604.

13. *La carbonaria* (*Black Face*). Comedy, 5 acts; prose. Published 1606.

14. *Il moro* (*The Moor*). Comedy, 5 acts; prose. Published 1607.

15. *Giorgio* (*St. George*). Sacred tragedy, 5 acts; verse. Written before 1608. Published 1611. Produced 1611.

16. *La tabernaria* (*The Tavern Play*). Comedy, 5 acts; prose. Published 1612.

17. *Ulisse* (*Ulysses*). Tragedy, 5 acts; verse. Written 1612. Published 1614.

EDITIONS

Della commedie di Giovanbattista de la Porta napolitano, ed. by G. Muzio, 4 vols., Naples, 1726; *Le commedie,* ed. by V. Spampanato, 2 vols., Bari, 1910–1911.

CRITICISM

H.-G. Duchesne, *Notice historique sur la vie et les ouvrages de J. B. Porta, gentilhomme napolitain,* Paris, 1801; F. Colangelo, *Raconto istorico della vita di Giovanni Battista Della Porta filosofo napolitano con un'analisi delle sue opere stampate,* Naples, 1813; C. Fornari, *Di G. B. della Porta e delle sue scoperte,* Naples, 1871; G. Campori, *Giovan Battista della Porta e il Cardinale Luigi d'Este,* Modena, 1872; L. G. Chubb, *Giambattista Della Porta, Dramatist,* Princeton, N.J., 1965.

Federico Della Valle
(ca. 1560 – 1628)

Federico Della Valle, Italian dramatist, was born about 1560 in the region of Asti. Little is known of his life until he appeared at the court of the Duke of Savoy in Turin in 1587. He served as quartermaster of the cavalry of Duchess Catherine, daughter of Philip II of Spain and wife of Duke Charles Emmanuel I of Savoy. Early in his career he tried his hand at poetry but received little recognition for his efforts. He did produce many laudatory pieces, including a madrigal, a nuptial song, some sonnets, and other minor works that reflect the milieu of the court of Savoy. In 1595, on the occasion of the arrival of Archduke Albert of Austria at the court, Della Valle composed the tragicomedy *Adelonda of Phrygia* (*Adelonda di Frigia*), one of his major works. After the death of the Duchess in 1597, Della Valle followed her Spanish retinue to Milan. There, in addition to writing several funeral orations, he worked on his major plays, the three tragedies *Judith* (*Iudit,* wr. 1590/1600), *Esther* (wr. 1590/1600), and *The Queen of Scotland* (*La reina di Scozia,* wr. ca. 1591/1600). He died in Milan in 1628.

WORK

Della Valle has been called one of the greatest dramatic authors of seventeenth-century Italy, unique in the tragic theatre of the baroque age. His tragedies were written not long after the Counter Reformation and are imbued with a somber and moralistic religiosity. The sobriety and restraint evident in his major work stand in contrast to the flamboyant style prevalent in much baroque literature. Educated in the classics and influenced by the lyricism of Petrarch, Della Valle also drew inspiration from the Bible. In addition, his work reflects the stern piety of Spanish Catholicism; the mood is one of brooding melancholy. Men are weak, subject to the vicissitudes of fortune, and women, the protagonists in all the tragedies, alternate between "fear" and "hope," two thematic words that run through the plays of Della Valle. *See* BAROQUE AGE.

Adelonda of Phrygia (1595) has elements of the pastoral lyric, which Della Valle adapted to fit the requirements of a tragicomedy. The play recounts the plight of Adelonda, Queen of Phrygia, who is shipwrecked on the island of the Amazons. After she has been taken captive and forced to become a priestess at the ritual sacrifice of the men the Amazons capture, she contrives her escape with one of the prisoners, her lover Mirmirano, and the play ends on a happy note. *The Queen of Scotland* (wr. ca. 1591/1600) is concerned with the imprisoned Mary Stuart, in the last hours before her execution. In it, the certainty of death dictates the mood, which becomes more intensely melancholy as the play draws to its conclusion. *Esther* (wr. 1590/1600), the least successful of Della Valle's plays, is based on the Biblical story of Esther, the Jewish wife of Ahasuerus, who saves the Israelites from slaughter. *Judith* (wr. 1590/1600), the most complex of the tragedies and also a great poetic work, is the story of the Old Testament heroine who slays Holofernes, the Assyrian general, to save her people.

Judith (*Iudit,* wr. 1590/1600). Tragedy based on the Biblical story of Judith, who saves the city of Bethulia by killing Holofernes, the general of the besieging Assyrian Army. Leaving the city under cover of night, she presents herself to Holofernes, whom she pretends to love. Attracted by her beauty, Holofernes plans to delay seizing the city until he has spent a night with Judith. A sumptuous feast is ordered even though Holofernes' captains insist that Bethulia is ripe for capture. Blind to everything except his lust, Holofernes insists on postponing the battle. After the feast, the inebriated Assyrian captains return to their tents and Holofernes retires to his chamber with Judith. She takes advantage of his drunken stupor to murder him and returns to Bethulia with his severed head, which is placed on the city's walls. Encouraged by Judith, the Hebrews attack the Assyrian camp. Finding their leader dead, the Assyrians retreat in confusion.

Esther (*Ester*, wr. 1590/1600). Tragedy based on the Biblical story of Esther. Ahasuerus, King of Persia, has fallen in love with and married his servant, the beautiful Jewish maiden Esther. Since the Jews are a captive people in Persia, Mordecai, Esther's uncle and guardian, has advised her to keep her faith a secret. Ahasuerus has rewarded the service of his minister Haman by entrusting him with the royal seal. In his pride and vanity, Haman demands for himself the treatment accorded the King. When Mordecai refuses to bow to him, Haman vows revenge. Without the King's knowledge, he issues an edict condemning all Jews to death, and he plans to hang Mordecai from a high cross even though Mordecai enjoys the King's favor. Learning of the edict, Esther reveals Haman's plot to the King and tells him that she herself is Jewish. Ahasuerus, horrified and outraged by his minister's treachery, repeals the edict and condemns Haman to be hanged on the cross intended for Mordecai. The King then divides between Esther and Mordecai the land and wealth he promised to Haman.

The Queen of Scotland (*La reina di Scozia*, wr. ca. 1591/1600). Tragedy dramatizing the last hours of Mary Stuart, Queen of Scotland. The play is set in the English prison where Mary has been held for twenty years. As Mary and her lady-in-waiting lament their unhappy fate, a messenger brings her hope of liberation. James VI of Scotland, Mary's son, has threatened to invade England with the help of Spanish arms, and it is thought that Queen Elizabeth may release Mary in order to forestall a war. Although still unsure of her fate, Mary regains hope and nostalgically recalls the beauties of Scotland. However, as the price for granting Mary's freedom, Elizabeth sends word that Mary must renounce her succession to the English throne, abdicate the Scottish throne in favor of her son, and discourage the diffusion of Catholicism in Scotland. Mary consents only to the first demand, and she is condemned to immediate execution. Turning to her faith for strength, with saintly humility she resigns herself to death.

PLAYS

1. *Adelonda di Frigia* (*Adelonda of Phrygia*). Tragicomedy, 5 acts; verse. Written 1595. Published 1629. Produced Turin, Nov. 18–27, 1595.

2. *Iudit* (*Judith*). Tragedy, prologue and 5 acts; verse. Written 1590/1600. Published 1627.

3. *Ester* (*Esther*). Tragedy, prologue and 5 acts; verse. Written 1590/1600. Published 1627.

4. *La reina di Scozia* (*The Queen of Scotland*). Tragedy, prologue and 5 acts; verse. Written ca. 1591/1600.

Published 1628. An early manuscript of the play, entitled *Maria la reina,* is dated 1591.

EDITIONS

Tragedie, ed. by C. Filosa, Bari, 1939; *Tutte le opere,* ed. by P. Cazzani, Milan, 1955.

DENISON, Merrill (1893–   ). Canadian playwright, the first dramatist of note to appear in Canada. His plays are short, satirical, and critical in a realistic manner. Among them are *Balm* (pub. 1926) and *The Prizewinner* (pub. 1928). A collection entitled *Unheroic North* (pub. 1923) includes *Brothers in Arms, From Their Own Place, The Weather Breeder,* and *Marsh Hay.*

DESCAVES, Lucien (1861–1949). French novelist and dramatist whose interest focused on everyday life and whose sympathies lay with simple people and their troubles. Early his gift of observation produced uncompromisingly realistic drama; later he turned to a more detached manner of presentation combining sentimentality with irony. In 1889 his novel *Noncommissioned Officer* (*Sous-offs*), a powerful satire of military life, caused a scandal that resulted in a court action. Subsequently, although absolved of guilt, Descaves was viewed with some suspicion by middle-class audiences. Nonetheless, he wrote several thousand often very aggressive newspaper articles on social and moral issues, thus creating many lifelong enemies. He collaborated with Georges Darien on the antibourgeois comedy *The Capons* (*Les chapons,* 1890) and with Maurice Donnay on the social satires *The Clearing* (*La clairière,* 1900) and *Birds of Passage* (*Oiseaux de passage,* 1904). He also wrote *The Cage* (*La cage,* 1898), concerning a family reduced by poverty to suicide; and *The Dazzled Heart* (*Le coeur ébloui,* 1926), a comedy about students on the eve of World War I. *See* DONNAY, MAURICE.

A member of the Académie Goncourt for four years, Descaves was elected its president in 1944.

DESMARETZ DE SAINT-SORLIN, Jean (1595–1676). French poet and dramatist known for his comedy *The Visionaries* (*Les visionnaires,* 1637). One of the best comedies of the period before Molière, it anticipated the latter's attack on preciosity. Desmaretz was induced to begin writing plays by his patron, Cardinal Richelieu, and at his insistence wrote seven plays, one each year from 1636 until the cardinal's death in 1642. Except for *The Visionaries,* only the tragicomedy *Scipio* (*Scipion,* 1638) is of interest. The others are the comedy *Aspasie* (1636); the tragicomedies *Roxane* (1639), *Mirame* (1641), and *Érigone* (1641); and the *comédie héroïque Europe*

(1642). Desmaretz was one of Richelieu's "Cinq Auteurs" and a founding member of the Académie Française.

Philippe Néricault Destouches
(1680 – 1754)

Philippe Néricault Destouches, French diplomat, government official, and dramatist, was born in Tours on April 9, 1680. At the age of seventeen he left home and school to join a troupe of strolling players, remaining with them until 1703, when he became secretary to a M. de Puysieux, a Frenchman living in Switzerland, who encouraged him to write his first plays. Destouches became sufficiently well known through private performances of these early works to be appointed secretary to Abbé Guillaume Dubois, who was attached to the French Embassy in London. Destouches remained in London as embassy secretary, secretly marrying an English girl before returning to Paris in 1723. Upon his return to France, he was elected a member of the Académie Française, more for his diplomatic accomplishments than for his writing skills, as his best works came after his admission to the academy.

Destouches, preoccupied with his government career rather than with his reputation as a dramatist, bought the fiefs and seigneuries of Vosnes and Fortoiseau in 1727, the year that saw the production of one of his

Le glorieux. [New York Public Library Picture Collection]

most popular plays, *The Married Philosopher, or The Husband Ashamed to Be One* (*Le philosophe marié, ou Le mari honteux de l'être,* wr. ca. 1722), which was based on his own secret marriage. In 1728, for a large sum, he bought the charge of the King's gate, a privilege that exempted him from taxes. In 1735 he again purchased a position, this time the governorship of Melun, and he settled down in his château at Fortoiseau, writing plays, attending to his various public duties, and leading a model life of pious devotion until his death on July 4, 1754.

WORK

The plays of Destouches may be considered to bridge the gap between Molière's comedies of manners and La Chaussée's *comédies larmoyantes* (sentimental comedies). Though more obviously intent than Molière on edifying and improving his audiences, Destouches, unlike La Chaussée, did not strive to move his public to sentimental tears. His plays, though often sentimental in the extreme, are essentially dissertations upon the condition and disposition of mankind: in all situations the characters philosophize and apply moral maxims. The resulting comedy is subtle and interior rather than broad. Destouches depicted the weaknesses of human beings, their fantasies and caprices, their inclinations toward good or evil. The virtuous characters always triumph, the half-bad are converted to good, and the bad are made to seem shameful. Plots and situations are believable and not unduly complicated; dialogue is lively and pointed. Nevertheless, Destouches's incessant moralizing is in the final analysis boring, and his characters tend to be mere abstractions of virtue and vice.

The titles of Destouches's first plays, written before he went to England, indicate the individual types he attacked: *The Ingrate* (*L'ingrat,* 1712), *The Irresolute Man* (*L'irrésolu,* 1713), and *The Slanderer* (*Le médisant,* 1715). *The Married Philosopher* (wr. ca. 1722, prod. 1727) and *The Conceited Count* (*Le glorieux,* 1732) are considered his best works, the first showing the influence of English comedy in its characterizations and the second, his masterpiece, focusing on the conflict between the traditional power of the aristocracy and the forces of change represented by the rising middle class. *The Night Drummer, or The Wizard Husband* (*Le tambour nocturne, ou Le mari devin;* pub. 1736, prod. 1762) is an adaptation of Addison's *The Drummer.*

The plays of Destouches's later years failed to find favor with the public. However, *False Agnes, or The Rustic Poet* (*La fausse Agnès, ou Le poète campagnard,* wr. 1727), which was first produced in 1759, five years after his death, was given almost 500 performances, more than any of his other works.

The Married Philosopher, or The Husband Ashamed to Be One (*Le Philosophe marié, ou Le mari honteux de l'être;* wr. ca. 1722, prod. 1727).

Although Ariste is happily married and lives with his wife Mélite, he wishes to keep the marriage a secret because he is ashamed of having succumbed to matrimony and is afraid of losing an inheritance from his disagreeable uncle Géronte. But Mélite, who is being pursued by the Marquis de Lauret, wishes to halt his advances by announcing the marriage. Ariste is adamant in spite of the indiscreet remarks of Celiante, Mélite's sister, and Finette, the maid. But when his uncle appears and plans Ariste's marriage to his rich stepdaughter, the truth has to be told. The marquis marries the heiress, the uncle is reconciled to Ariste's marriage, and Celiante accepts the proposal of Ariste's friend Damon.

The Conceited Count (*Le glorieux,* 1732).

Comedy in which the interest is focused on the struggle between Lisimon, a rich bourgeois, and the Count de Tufière, representative of an illustrious and dying past. While Lisimon is interested in providing his daughter Isabelle with a noble husband, he resents the behavior of the count, whose arrogance has won him the nickname "le glorieux." Lisimon's wife promotes the marriage of Isabelle to Philinte, a timid and awkward bourgeois. A subplot involves the love of Valère, Lisimon's son, for Lisette, the family maid, whose conviction that she is out of place as a domestic is encouraged by the mysterious beggar Lysandre. The latter turns out to be an aristocrat in disgrace at the court and is also revealed to be the father of both Lisette and the count. When the count renounces Isabelle so that he can devote himself to his newly found sister and father, his disinterested generosity wins Isabelle's heart. Lisimon, aware that the count will now be dependent on him and his wealth, consents to the marriages of the count and Isabelle and of Valère and Lisette.

PLAYS

Unless otherwise noted, the plays are in prose and were first performed in Paris.

1. *Le curieux impertinent* (*The Impertinent Curious Man*). Play, 5 acts; verse. Written ca. 1704. Published 1710. Produced Comédie-Française, Nov. 17, 1710.

2. *L'ingrat* (*The Ingrate*). Play, 5 acts; verse. Published 1712. Produced Comédie-Française, Jan. 28, 1712.

3. *L'irrésolu* (*The Irresolute Man*). Comedy, 5 acts; verse. Published 1713. Produced Comédie-Française, Jan. 5, 1713.

4. *Le médisant* (*The Slanderer*). Comedy, 5 acts; verse. Published 1715. Produced Comédie-Française, Feb. 20, 1715.

5. *Le triple mariage* (*The Triple Marriage*). Comedy, 1 act. Published 1716. Produced Comédie-Française, July 7, 1716.

6. *L'obstacle imprévu, ou L'obstacle sans obstacle* (*The Unforeseen Obstacle, or The Obstacle Without Obstacle*). Comedy, 5 acts. Published 1718. Produced Comédie-Française, Oct. 18, 1717.

7. *Le philosophe marié, ou Le mari honteux de l'être.* (*The Married Philosopher, or The Husband Ashamed to Be One*). Comedy, 5 acts; verse. Written ca. 1722. Published 1727. Produced Comédie-Française, Feb. 15, 1727.

8. *La fausse Agnès, ou Le poète campagnard* (*False Agnes, or The Rustic Poet*). Comedy, 3 acts. Written before 1727. Published 1736. Produced Comédie-Française, Mar. 12, 1759.

9. *L'envieux, ou La critique du philosophe marié* (*The Envious Man, or The Married Philosopher Criticized*). Comedy, 1 act. Written 1727. Published 1736. Produced Comédie-Française, May 3, 1727.

10. *Les philosophes amoureux* (*The Amorous Philosophers*). Comedy, 5 acts; verse. Published 1730. Produced Comédie-Française, Nov. 26, 1729.

11. *Le glorieux** (*The Conceited Count*). Comedy, 5 acts; verse. Written 1729. Published 1732. Produced Comédie-Française, Jan. 18, 1732.

12. (Adaptation). *Le tambour nocturne, ou Le mari devin* (*The Night Drummer, or The Wizard Husband*). Comedy, 5 acts. Published 1736. Produced Comédie-Française, Oct. 16, 1762. Based on Joseph Addison's *The Drummer.*

13. *Le dissipateur, ou L'hônnete friponne* (*The Spendthrift, or The Honest Minx*). Comedy, 5 acts; verse. Published 1736. Produced Comédie-Française, Mar. 23, 1753.

14. *Le dépôt* (*The Deposit*). Comedy, 1 act; verse. Written after 1736. Published 1757.

15. *L'archi-menteur, ou Le vieux fou dupé* (*The Archliar, or The Old Fool Duped*). Comedy, 5 acts; verse. Written after 1736. Published 1757.

16. *Le mari confident* (*The Husband Confidant*). Comedy, 5 acts; verse. Written after 1736. Published 1757.

17. *L'ambitieux et l'indiscrète* (*The Ambitious Man and the Indiscreet Woman*). Tragicomedy, 5 acts; verse. Published 1737. Produced Comédie-Française, June 14, 1737.

18. *La belle orgueilleuse, ou L'enfant gâté* (*The Proud Beauty, or The Spoiled Child*). Comedy, 1 act; verse. Published 1741. Produced Comédie-Française, Aug. 17, 1741.

19. *L'amour usé* (*Threadbare Love*). Comedy, 5 acts. Published 1742. Produced Comédie-Française, Sept. 20, 1741.

20. *Le trésor caché* (*The Hidden Treasure*). Comedy, 5 acts. Written ca. 1736/45. Published 1757. Produced Théâtre Italien, 1745.

21. *La force du naturel* (*The Force of Nature*). Comedy, 5 acts; verse. Published 1750. Produced Comédie-Française, Feb. 11, 1750.

22. *Le jeune homme à l'épreuve* (*The Young Man on Trial*). Comedy, 5 acts. Written ca. 1745/51. Published 1751.

23. *L'homme singulier* (*The Singular Man*). Comedy, 5 acts; verse. Written 1736/53. Published 1765. Produced Comédie-Française, Oct. 29, 1764.

EDITIONS

Oeuvres dramatiques, 10 vols., Paris, 1774; *Oeuvres dramatiques,* 6 vols., Paris, 1811; *Chefs-d'oeuvre dramatiques,* 2 vols., Paris, 1822.

The Conceited Count. Published in *French Comedies of the XVIIIth Century,* tr. by R. Aldington, London, 1923.

CRITICISM

M. G. W. Lüdermann, *Über Destouches Leben und Werke,* Greifswald, 1895; J. Hankiss, *Philippe Néricault Destouches,* Debrecen, 1918.

DEUS EX MACHINA.

Latin term meaning "god from machine." Originally it denoted a stage apparatus that served to lower onto the proscenium an actor playing a god, whose function was to bring about cleanly and efficiently the denouement of an intricate plot. Foremost among the ancient playwrights who employed the *deus ex machina* was Euripides. For this he was roundly parodied by Aristophanes, and in a more serious vein Aristotle condemned the artificiality stemming from the undiscriminating use of the device. *See* ARISTOPHANES; EURIPIDES.

In modern usage, the expression characterizes any inorganic and arbitrary resolution of the plot of a play, and it is even extended to apply to any improbable solution of the complex events of real life.

DEVAL, Jacques, pseudonym of Jacques Boularan (b. Paris, June 27, 1894). French screenwriter and dramatist known primarily for sophisticated light comedies such as *Her Cardboard Lover* (*Dans sa candeur naïve,* 1926) and *Tovarich* (*Tovaritch,* 1933). Following the success of his first play, *A Weak Woman* (*Une femme faible,* 1920), a comedy dealing with a woman unable to make up her mind about a suitor, Deval's original plays and many adaptations of foreign dramas became staples of the Paris theatrical season. His early plays show powers of keen, satirical observation, but after the failure of *Prayer for the Living* (*Prière pour les vivants,* 1933), Deval seemed to avoid serious social comment and turned his attention almost exclusively to well-constructed but facile comedies. In

Marta Abba and John Halliday in Jacques Deval's *Tovarich.* New York, Plymouth Theatre, 1936. [Photograph by Vandamm. Theatre Collection, The New York Public Library at Lincoln Center, Astor, Lenox and Tilden Foundations]

spite of its failure to please the pre-World War II public, *Prayer for the Living,* a naturalistic drama covering three generations in the life of an egotistical and cynical French family, was accepted into the repertoire of the Comédie-Française in 1964.

Deval's major works include *Étienne* (1930), the drama of an adolescent caught between conflicting loyalties to his pompous father and his long-suffering mother; *Mademoiselle* (1932), the story of an old maid whose maternal longings lead her to accept another woman's illegitimate child as her own; and *Tonight at Samarkand* (*Ce soir à Samarcande,* 1950), a poetic speculation on predestination. *Her Cardboard Lover,* a comedy about a woman who falls in love with a man she hires to prevent her from once more coming under the spell of her persistent ex-husband, established Deval's international reputation. Its success was equaled by that of *Tovarich* (adapted in 1935 by Robert E. Sherwood), which hilariously contrasts a French middle-

Jacques Deval. [French Cultural Services]

class family with an aristocratic White Russian couple torn between their love for Russia and their hatred of the present Communist regime. In 1934 Deval adapted his novel *Marie Galante,* written three years earlier, into the libretto for a musical by Kurt Weill, who was then living in exile in Paris. *See* SHERWOOD, ROBERT E.

Deval has written some forty plays in all, including adaptations of Terence Rattigan's *O Mistress Mine* and *The Front Page* by Ben Hecht and Charles MacArthur. Among his most recent plays are *Charming Evening* (*Charmante soirée,* 1955), a jaundiced view of man's potential for foul behavior; and *What about Hell, Isabelle?* (*Et l'enfer, Isabelle?,* 1963), a drama in which a murderess goes free because of the law's inability to establish legal proof against her.

Tovarich (*Tovaritch,* 1933). Grand Duchess Tatiana and her husband, Prince Mikhael, White Russian *émigrés* living in Paris, are trustees of a Romanov fortune deposited under the prince's name in the Bank of France. Unwilling to use this money, which they dream of someday turning over to a new Czar, they take jobs as domestic servants in the home of a Socialist deputy. At a dinner given by their employers, the duchess and the prince wait on table and are recognized by a Soviet Commissar who has come to

France to arrange a financial deal with representatives of the Banks of England and of France. The Commissar follows them to the kitchen and explains that in order to obtain the money needed for famine relief the Soviet government has empowered him to grant Britain and France concessions in the Ural oilfields. Their love for Russia overcoming their hatred of its present rulers, the aristocratic *émigrés* sign over the Romanov fortune to the Soviet government to prevent foreign powers from establishing themselves on Russian soil. Produced Paris, Théâtre de Paris, October 13, 1933.

Leslie Howard and Jeanne Eagels in Deval's *Her Cardboard Lover.* New York, Empire Theatre, 1927. [Photograph by Vandamm. Theatre Collection, The New York Public Library at Lincoln Center, Astor, Lenox and Tilden Foundations]

Scene from Deval's *Ce soir à Samarcande.* Paris, Théâtre de la Renaissance, 1950. [French Cultural Services]

DIAMANTE, Juan Bautista (1625–1687). Like the plays of other dramatists of the late Siglo de Oro (Spanish Golden Age), Diamante's work is characterized by a lack of originality and an excessively ornate and affectedly elegant style. Of more than fifty *comedias* attributed to him, the best known is *The Jewess of Toledo* (*La judía de Toledo,* 1667), based on *Unfortunate Rachel* of Mira de Amescua and serving as the source for the more famous *Raquel* of García de la Huerta. His other plays include *El honrador de su padre* (1657), *The Siege of Zamora* (*El cerco de Zamora,* 1685), *Queen Mary Stuart* (*La reina*

Maria Estuarda, 1660), and *Valor Has No Age, or Samson of Estremadura* (*El valor no tiene edad y Sansón de Extremadura*, pub. 1704). Diamante also excelled in the zarzuela (musical comedy) form, as in *Alfeo and Arethusa* (*Alfeo y Aretusa*, 1678). *See* SIGLO DE ORO.

DICENTA Y BENEDICTO, Joaquín (b. Calatayud, February 3, 1863; d. Alicante, February 20, 1917). Spanish novelist and dramatist who laid the foundation for the social drama in Spain with his most successful and best-remembered play, *Juan José* (1885), a limited but intensely violent portrait of workmen's lives in Madrid. Dicenta did not attack any one social class but rather rebelled against a general decay of moral values which he saw pervading his generation, although he did feel that this decay was manifested to its greatest degree in the bourgeoisie. His later dramas, in which Dicenta turned his attention from the workmen to the bourgeoisie, are of less interest. Among his other plays are *The Feudal Lord* (*El señor feudal,* 1896), concerning a young peasant dishonored by her master and then avenged by her brother; *The Suicide of Werther* (*El suicidio de Werther,* 1888); *The Irresponsible Ones* (*Los irresponsables,* 1890); *Aurora* (1902); *Daniel* (1906); *To Keep Living* (*Sobrevivirse,* 1911), the tragedy of a dramatic author who loses his ability to write; and *The Wolf* (*El lobo,* 1913).

Juan José (1895). Drama of Juan José, a laborer who is in love with Rosa. Although she lives with him, she does not love him, and Juan José is afraid of losing her. To fulfill her constant demands for money, he commits a robbery but is caught and sentenced to eight years at hard labor. While in prison he learns that Rosa is living with Paco, a factory owner. Beside himself with jealousy, Juan José escapes and seeks out and kills Paco. Rosa begins calling for help, and to silence her he strangles her. His friend Andrés urges him to flee, but Juan José says that he no longer has a reason for living.

Denis Diderot
(1713 – 1784)

Denis Diderot, French encyclopedist, essayist, novelist, critic of art and literature, and dramatist, was born in Langres on October 5, 1713. His father was a cutler, but Diderot, who showed no signs of mechanical ability, was sent to a Jesuit college. He received the tonsure in 1726 and continued his studies in the hope of receiving an inheritance from an uncle who was an influential churchman. Diderot then studied at the University of Paris, receiving a master of arts degree in 1732. Unsure of his dedication to the church, he remained in Paris from 1733 to 1735 and earned his living as a notary's clerk, much to the chagrin of his father. In 1743 he married Antoinette Champion, a devout Catholic who escaped from a convent to which she had been sent by her father. She bore him four children, three of whom died in infancy. The marriage was an unhappy one.

During this period the young Diderot turned to translating; by 1745 he had published a free translation of Lord Shaftesbury's *Inquiry Concerning Virtue or Merit*. In 1746 his *Philosophic Thoughts* (*Pensées philosophiques*) was condemned by an act of the French Parliament. His *Letter on the Blind* (*Lettre sur les aveugles,* 1749) resulted in his imprisonment for several months because of its bold application of the principle of relativity to the concept of God. It was about this time that he became friendly with Jean-Jacques Rousseau and the intellectual circle that surrounded him.

For the next fifteen years Diderot was occupied in the writing of his *Encyclopedia*, novels, and essays. At the same time, his vigorous opposition to the persecution of philosophical thought by the government, the

Denis Diderot; portrait by Dmitri Levitski. [Giraudon]

Jesuits, and others led to equally vigorous attacks on him. Diderot was advised to leave France, but he refused to abandon his family.

His only daughter was married in 1772. Since he had not received the sinecures that were traditionally given to needy intellectuals, his financial status forced him to sell his library to provide his daughter's dowry. Empress Catherine II of Russia, through her emissary in Paris, bought the library and requested Diderot to maintain the collection as librarian for an annual salary.

The next year Diderot traveled to Russia to thank the Empress. There he wrote two educational texts for Catherine, and though pressed to remain, he returned to France and to his writing. *The Paradox on Acting* (*Paradoxe sur le comédien*, 1773; rev. 1778) brilliantly challenged the contemporary notion that only an actor in the grip of a passion can communicate his emotion to the audience. The most successful acting, Diderot maintained, is done by "cold" actors, whose detachment from their material allows them to attain mastery of the techniques by which emotion is simulated on the stage.

In 1783 Diderot was deeply affected by the deaths of Sophie Volland, his mistress since 1757, and Jean d'Alembert, his close friend and collaborator on the *Encyclopedia*. Worn out by constant persecution for his advanced ideas and by the struggle to support his family, Diderot died in Paris on July 31, 1784.

WORK

Known primarily for his labors on the *Encyclopedia* and for his other philosophical and scientific writings, Diderot was also an astute dramatic theorist. He outlined requirements for a realistic bourgeois drama growing out of La Chaussée's *comédies larmoyantes*. His ideas greatly influenced Lessing and Hebbel as well as such nineteenth-century dramatists as Augier and Dumas *fils*. Diderot expounded his theories in *Discourse on Dramatic Poetry* (*Le discours sur la poésie dramatique*, 1758), *Conversations about the Natural Son* (*Les entretiens sur le fils naturel*, 1757), *The Paradox of Acting* (1773), and the prefaces to some of his plays. According to him, the existing forms of classical tragedy and light comedy should be supplemented by serious drama concerned with middle-class problems and persons. He thought prose better than verse for rendering this social milieu and urged that realistic scenery, symbolic gestures, exaggerated movements, and striking stage groupings be used as aids to communication. *See* BOURGEOIS DRAMA; LA CHAUSSÉE, PIERRE-CLAUDE NIVELLE DE.

Diderot's plays, however, reveal that he was unable to convert his ideas into dramas that could command the attention of audiences. Technically, his plays are slow, almost static. A tableau quality in many scenes is perhaps the unconscious by-product of the hours he spent scrutinizing paintings in the role of art critic. Above all, there is the deliberate striving after pathos, and the inevitable moral.

Diderot's two best-known plays are *The Natural Son, or The Proofs of Virtue* (*Le fils naturel, ou Les épreuves de la vertu*; pub. 1757, prod. 1771), with a complex plot and a heavy burden of pathos and sentiment (note that Dumas *fils* used the same title years later); and *The Father of the Family* (*Le père de famille*, 1761), a sentimental piece in which love prevails over monetary concerns. *Is He Good? Is He Bad?, or Informal Banterer, or He Who Serves All and Pleases No One* (*Est-il bon? Est-il méchant?, ou L'officieux persifleur, ou Celui qui les sert tous et qui n'en contente aucun*; wr. 1781, prod. 1951), the most humorous and least didactic of Diderot's plays, was probably performed privately, but the manuscript was not discovered until 1834.

The Natural Son, or The Proofs of Virtue (*Le fils naturel, ou Les épreuves de le vertu*; pub. 1757, prod. 1771). Moralistic play in which the characters outdo one another in noble behavior, thus complicating their lives and loves. Dorval, son of an unknown father, loves Rosalie, the fiancée of his best friend Clairville. Dorval is in turn loved by both Rosalie and Constance, Clairville's sister. Rosalie wishes to break her engagement, while Clairville, grateful for Dorval's intercession in his behalf when he is nearly killed in a fight, offers him Constance's hand. Further entanglements are provided by Dorval's efforts to make Constance scorn him for his illegitimacy and his determination to give up Rosalie for the sake of his friend. The play ends in an effusion of sentiment when Rosalie's father returns and discloses that Dorval is his son and the rightful heir to his fortune.

The Father of the Family (*Le père de famille*, 1761). Domestic comedy posing the problem of marriage for love versus marriage for money. Saint-Albin, son of Orbesson, wishes to marry Sophie, a mysterious stranger. When his love affair is discovered, Saint-Albin is ready to give up a possible inheritance from his pompous uncle, the Commander, in order to live happily with his love. Cécile, Saint-Albin's sister, loves the penniless Germeuil, of whom the Commander also disapproves. The Commander attempts to force his will upon the family but is thwarted by Germeuil. The play ends with the two pairs of lovers engaged, the uncle irate, and Orbesson content, for he believes his children should marry for love.

A Comédie-
Française
production of
*Est-il bon? Est-il
méchant?* [French
Cultural Services]

Is He Good? Is He Bad?, or Informal Banterer, or He Who Serves All and Pleases No One (*Est-il bon? Est-il méchant?, ou L'officieux persifleur, ou Celui qui les sert tous et qui n'en contente aucun;* wr. 1781, prod. 1951). Written in 1781 as *The Play and the Prologue* and left in a drawer for ten years, this play was then rewritten with a change of title but never publicly staged until 1951. It deals with a play written to order and produced with a cast selected at random. M. Hardouin, the hero, is Diderot himself: hardworking, clever, indiscreet, seductive, generous, a poet and a philosopher, ready to be useful and equally ready to quarrel. Fascinated by himself, he wonders about his behavior and whether he is better or worse than he appears. In spite of many petty misdeeds, he manages to do good for everyone.

PLAYS

All were first performed in Paris.

1. *Le fils naturel, ou Les épreuves de la vertu** (*The Natural Son, or The Proofs of Virtue*). Drama. Published 1757. Produced Comédie-Française, Sept. 26, 1771.

2. *Le père de famille** (*The Father of the Family*). Drama. Published 1758. Produced Comédie-Française, Feb. 18, 1761.

3. *Les pères malheureux* (*The Unhappy Fathers*). Little prose tragedy, 1 act. Written 1770. Published 1875. Based on Salomon Gessner's *Éraste*.

4. *Est-il bon? Est-il méchant?, ou L'officieux persifleur, ou Celui qui les sert tous et qui n'en contente aucun* (*Is He Good? Is He Bad?, or Informal Banterer, or He Who Serves All and Pleases No One*). Play, 4 acts. Written 1781. Published 1834. Produced Salle Valhubert, Mar. 30, 1951.

5. *La pièce et le prologue, ou Celui qui les sert tous et qui n'en contente aucun* (*The Play and the Prologue, or He Who Serves All and Pleases No One*). Play, 1 act. Published 1820. Early version of *Est-il bon? Est-il méchant?*

NOTE: In addition, there are a number of fragments and outlines for projected works.

EDITIONS

Oeuvres, 15 vols., Paris, 1800; *Oeuvres complètes*, 20 vols., Paris, 1875–1877; *Diderot's Writings on the Theatre*, ed. by F. C. Green, Cambridge, England, 1936.

The Father of the Family. Published in *Eighteenth Century French Plays*, ed. by C. D. Brenner and N. A. Goodyear, New York, 1927.

CRITICISM

A. Billy, *Diderot*, Paris, 1932; A. Cresson, *Diderot: Sa vie, son oeuvre*, Paris, 1949; L. G. Crocker, *The Embattled Philosopher*, East Lansing, Mich., 1954.

Salvatore Di Giacomo

(1860 – 1934)

Salvatore Di Giacomo, Italian poet, short-story writer, historian, and playwright, was born in Naples on March 12, 1860. He spent most of his life in his native city, whose history and daily scene were to provide the subject of his best scholarly and creative work. Abandoning the study of medicine in 1880, he embarked upon a career in journalism, contributing to a number of magazines and newspapers including the *Corriere del Mattino, Pungolo,* and, later on, the *Corriere di Napoli.* A passionate student of various aspects of Neapolitan culture, particularly the theatre of the eighteenth century, Di Giacomo served for many years as director of the Lucchesi-Palli Theatrical Library and was also associated with the San Pietro a Maiella Library and the Archivi dei Filippini.

His scholarly interests and activities resulted in numerous articles on music and musicians; in a rich and imaginative history of Naples in thirty-four volumes, in which journalistic items are frequently used as the basis for historical reminiscence; and in an important account of the Neapolitan theatre, *History of the San Carlino Theatre (Storia del Teatro San Carlino,* 1891). Despite the value of these scholarly publications, Di Giacomo is known primarily for his poems, stories, and plays. His first collection of poems, *Antique Sonnets (Sonette antiche),* appeared in 1884. By the time a collected edition of his poems was published in 1907, his reputation was international. Written in Neapolitan dialect, his lyrics, many of which were set to music by such popular composers as Tosti, Costa, and Pizzetti, are considered by critics such as Benedetto Croce to be among the finest of their kind. Di Giacomo's short stories are written in standard Italian (as were all his prose works), but like his dialect poetry and plays they are impregnated with the color and drama of the Neapolitan scene. "The Vow" ("Il voto") provided the basis for his first play, *Underworld (Malavita),* written in collaboration with Goffredo Cognetti and published in 1881. Di Giacomo, who was elected to the Italian Academy when it was formed in 1929, devoted the last years of his life to scholarly research and the preparation of final editions of his works. He died in Naples on April 5, 1934.

WORK

Di Giacomo began writing at the time when the naturalistic movement begun in France by Zola and De Maupassant had spread to Italy and given birth to the literary school known as *verismo* ("realism"). He is generally considered a representative of the regionalist and verist tradition (whose most important exponent was Giovanni Verga) because his stories and plays concentrate on characters drawn from the lower classes and emphasize the pathological, macabre, or horrifying aspects of life. *See* VERGA, GIOVANNI.

Like the French naturalists, Di Giacomo made use of historical and journalistic documentation, but his approach tended to be one of emotional lyricism rather than cold analysis. The dramatic significance of the events he portrays is due essentially to the mood evoked by choral comments and to the response of secondary characters whose reactions highlight the tragic situations of the protagonists.

Di Giacomo collaborated with Goffredo Cognetti on *Underworld* (pub. 1881, prod. 1888), which was based on one of his own short stories. The three-act play, essentially a series of interconnected and colorful scenes from Neapolitan popular life, was afterward translated by him into dialect and published under the title *'O voto (The Vow).* It was followed by *In San Francisco Prison (A "San Francisco,"* 1896), an evocation of life in the famous Naples prison. Giovanni Accietto, imprisoned for the murder of his unfaithful wife, discovers that a new inmate is her lover, Peppe Pazzia. The two men confront one another, and Peppe is stabbed to death.

The Marian Month ('O mese mariano, 1898), one of Di Giacomo's best dramas, is based on his short story "Without Seeing Him" ("Senza Vederlo"). An unfortunate mother arrives at a home for the poor to see her child, unaware that he has died the previous night. The attendants try to keep this fact from her, acting out of a combination of sympathy and guilt. The woman's plight attains tragic proportions less by an analytical disclosure of the situation than by a synthetic revelation of her increasing anxiety as she confronts the realities of her environment and intuitively comes to grasp the truth.

Di Giacomo's masterpiece is generally considered to be *Assunta Spina* (1909), which Allardyce Nicoll called a "powerfully drawn portrait of a woman led by her instincts to betray two men." Enormously successful, the play, with its realistic setting and dialogue, was considered a distinct reaction to the theatre of D'Annunzio. But its interest lies less in an analysis of Assunta's tragic wavering between two men than in the lyric and picturesque evocation of Naples street life and the intrigues that dominate the dispensation of justice at the city's Castelcapuano Tribunal. *See* D'ANNUNZIO, GABRIELE.

Quand l'amour meurt (When Love Dies, 1911), a one-act comedy (written in Italian despite the French title), is generally considered one of Di Giacomo's less successful works. In *Settecento (Eighteenth Century;* pub. 1907, prod. 1920), also known as *L'Abbé Péru* and *Olivetta,* Di Giacomo paid a delightful tribute to the life of his beloved eighteenth-century Naples, the time of Pergolesi, Scarlatti, and Cimarosa. In addition, Di Giacomo wrote the libretti for several operas, some of them based on works originally presented as prose dramas.

Assunta Spina (1909). Realistic tragedy set among the lower classes of Naples. Michele Boccadifuoco is sentenced to two years in prison for knife wounds he has inflicted on his mistress, Assunta Spina, in a jealous rage. Assunta, who has forgiven her lover, fears she will be unable to see him for the length of his term if he is sent to a distant jail. Federigo Funelli, a vice-chancellor of the court, decides to take advantage of Assunta's weakness in order to seduce her. He promises to use his influence to keep Michele in Naples if she will become his mistress. Assunta reluctantly consents. One night, three months before Michele's prison term is to be completed, Assunta awaits the arrival of Federigo at her home. Michele enters unexpectedly and joyfully announces that he has obtained an early release. His sincere affection increases Assunta's guilt: she confesses her infidelity, and Michele immediately realizes Federigo has been her lover. As footsteps approach the house, Michele seizes a knife and leaves by the window. A scream is heard, and Federigo enters clutching his side. He falls dead as two police officers arrive. Assunta, in her guilt and in her love for Michele, steps forward and declares herself the murderess.

PLAYS

1. (With Goffredo Cognetti). *Malavita (Underworld);* translated into Neapolitan dialect as *'O voto (The Vow).* Play, 3 acts. Published 1881. Produced Naples, Teatro Nuovo, 1888.
2. *A "San Francisco" (In San Francisco Prison).* Play, 1 act. Published 1897. Produced Naples, Teatro San Ferdinando, 1896.
3. *'O mese mariano (The Marian Month).* Play, 1 act. Published 1900. Produced Naples, Teatro Verdi, 1898.
4. *Assunta Spina.* Tragedy, 2 acts. Published 1920: Produced Naples, Teatro Nuovo, Mar. 27, 1909.
5. *Quand l'amour meurt (When Love Dies).* Play, 1 act. Published 1920. Produced Naples, Teatro Nuovo, Jan. 14, 1911.
6. *Settecento (Eighteenth Century);* also known as *L'Abbé Péru* and *Olivetta.* Play. Published 1907. Produced Naples, Teatro Sannazaro, May 15, 1920.
7. *La stessa voce (The Same Voice).* Dramatic fragment.

EDITIONS

Teatro, 2 vols., Lanciano, 1920; *Opere,* ed. by F. Flora and M. Vinciguerra, 2 vols., Milan, 1946.

DIKĒ. Ancient Greek concept of justice, seen particularly as a working out of the proper order of things in the universe.

Ludovico Dolce
(1508 — ?1568)

Ludovico Dolce, Italian poet, biographer, and dramatist, was born in Venice in 1508, of a noble but impoverished family. His parents managed to send him to the university in Padua, a traditional practice for Venetian aristocrats. Soon after graduation Dolce permanently solved his financial problems by entering the service of the Giolito family, Venetian painters and booksellers, who through the years published his enormous literary output.

Dolce is perhaps best known as an educator because of his treatise *On the Education of Women (Dialogo della istruzione delle donne,* 1547). His lyric poems, imitative of Pietro Bembo, were widely anthologized in his day. They are classicistic, as are his biographies of Charles V (1561) and Ferdinand the Catholic (1566). His epic poems include *The First Enterprises of Roland* (1572), *Palmerino d'Oliva* (1561), and *Primaleone, Son of King Palmerino* (1562). He also adapted and translated a number of classical writers, from Homer to Pliny. Dolce died in Venice, probably in 1568, leaving many unfinished works.

WORK

Dolce's present reputation as a dramatist rests on his *Mariamne (Marianna,* 1565), one of the better tragedies of his time. His output —five comedies and eight tragedies—was so prolific for his era that it exerted an influence among his contemporaries well beyond its actual literary merit. A follower of Giambattista Giraldi Cinthio, Dolce devoted himself primarily to the neoclassical tragedy, based upon the Senecan model, so that even when his sources were Greek, he used Latin translations, which gave his plays a Roman flavor. *See* GIRALDI CINTHIO, GIAMBATTISTA; SENECA.

Mariamne, a tragedy of repentance for an impetuous act, exhibits a talent for characterization and language that is rarely found in his other work. His only other original tragedy is *Dido* (*Didone*, pub. 1547), which he based in part upon Giraldi Cinthio's work on the same topic; Virgil's *Aeneid* was their common source. Of his six other tragedies drawn from Euripides, Seneca, or both, only *Jocasta* (*Giocasta*, wr. 1549) is of interest.

Dolce's five comedies, while less successful than his two original tragedies, are interesting if only because they are less slavish imitations of antiquity than most of his other work. The most original is *The Play of Fabrizio* (*La Fabrizia*, pub. 1549), in which a youthful scholar wins the hand of a young girl in rivalry with an elderly pedant. The others are *The Boy* (*Il ragazzo*, pub. 1541), an amalgam of Plautus's *Casina*, Machiavelli's *Clizia*, and Aretino's *The "Horse Doctor"*; *The Captain* (*Il capitano*, pub. 1545), taken from Plautus's *The Braggart Warrior*; *The Husband* (*Il marito*, pub. 1545), from Plautus's *Amphitryon*; and *The Pimp* (*Il rofiano*, pub. 1551/52), from Il Ruzzante's *Piovana*. *See* ARETINO, PIETRO; MACHIAVELLI, NICCOLÒ; PLAUTUS; RUZZANTE, IL.

Mariamne (*Marianna*, 1565). Verse drama in five acts with two prologues, one spoken by Tragedy and the other by Pluto and Jealousy, and a number of choruses. The story concerns the tyrant Herod of Judea and his wife Mariamne, who loves him against her better judgment. Herod, upon returning from a journey, is angered at Mariamne's unceremonious welcome and her seemingly inadequate gratitude for the gifts he has brought her. His annoyance makes him receptive to the accusations of Salome and some of his advisers against Mariamne and deaf to the pleas of innocence of his wife and her friends in the palace. He orders that Mariamne, her mother, and his children by his wife be killed. Too late he realizes that he will repent their execution for the rest of his life.

PLAYS

1. *Il ragazzo* (*The Boy*). Comedy; prose. Published 1541.
2. *Il capitano* (*The Captain*). Comedy; verse. Published 1545.
3. *Il marito* (*The Husband*). Comedy; verse. Published 1545.
4. *Didone* (*Dido*). Tragedy, 5 acts; verse. Published 1547. Based upon Giambattista Giraldi Cinthio's *Dido*.
5. *La Fabrizia* (*The Play of Fabrizio*). Comedy; prose. Published 1549.
6. *Giocasta* (*Jocasta*). Tragedy, 5 acts; verse. Written 1549. Published 1560. Adapted from Euripides's *The Phoenician Women*.
7. *Il rofiano* (*The Pimp*). Comedy; verse. Published 1551/52.
8. *Hecuba.* Tragedy, 5 acts; verse. Published 1560. Adapted from Euripides's *Hecuba*.
9. *Ifigenia* (*Iphigenia*). Tragedy, 5 acts; verse. Published 1560. Adapted from Euripides's *Iphigenia in Aulis*.
10. *Medea.* Tragedy, 5 acts; verse. Published 1560. Based on the *Medea* of Euripides and of Seneca.
11. *Thieste* (*Thyestes*). Tragedy, 5 acts; verse. Published 1560. Adapted from Seneca's *Thyestes*.
12. *Marianna* (*Mariamne*). Tragedy, 2 prologues and 5 acts; verse. Published 1565. Produced Ferrara, Palazzo Ducale, 1565.
13. *Le troiane* (*The Trojan Women*). Tragedy, 5 acts; verse. Published 1567. Based on *The Trojan Women* of Euripides and of Seneca.

CRITICISM

A. Salza, *Delle commedie di Ludovico Dolce*, Melfi, 1889.

DONNAY, Maurice (b. Paris, October 12, 1859; d. there, March 31, 1945). French dramatist who began his career by writing sketches for Le Chat Noir, the famous turn-of-the-century Montmartre cabaret. After the success of *Elsewhere* (*Ailleurs*, 1891), "a symbolic revue in twenty scenes," he turned to the legitimate theatre with a clever modern adaptation of Aristophanes's *Lysistrata* (1892). In 1895 he wrote what is generally considered his masterpiece, *Lovers* (*Amants*), a bittersweet account of two civilized Parisians who manage to navigate the shoals of love without losing sight of the fact that practical considerations are eternal while love is ephemeral.

Most of Donnay's subsequent work is strictly within the traditions of "the theatre of love," to which he brought a sophisticated and humorous acceptance of the torments that accompany the pleasures of dalliance. However, he occasionally tried to include wider social considerations within his theme. *The Clearing* (*La clairière*, 1900) and *Birds of Passage* (*Oiseaux de passage*, 1904), both written in collaboration with Lucien Descaves, respectively satirize radicalism and feminism. *The Return from Jerusalem* (*Le retour de Jérusalem*, 1903) focuses on a liaison between a gentile and a Jew who are eventually forced to part because of differences in tradition and temperament. In 1907 Donnay was elected to the Académie Française. *See* DESCAVES, LUCIEN.

After World War I he tried to adapt his themes to changing times by showing in *The Manhunt* (*La chasse à l'homme*, 1919) the wild scramble for men in a country where women outnumbered them by 2 million. He continued writing on into the mid-1930s but met with little success because, as he put it, "the public was no longer gay." His other plays include *The Torrent* (*Le torrent*, 1899), *The Other Danger* (*L'autre danger*, 1902), *Appearances* (*Paraître*, 1906), *The Education of the Prince* (*L'éducation du prince*, 1906), and *The Women Scouts* (*Les éclaireuses*, 1912).

Lovers (*Amants*, 1895). As the mistress of Count Ruyseux, former actress Claudine Rozay has achieved a stable financial situation and an emotional life free from the jealous torments of love. When, however, she falls in love with Georges Vetheuil, her life is immediately invaded by jealousy and suspicion. Unwilling to put up with Ruyseux as a rival even though he knows that Claudine's relation with the count is based on strictly pragmatic considerations, Georges makes a vain attempt to break with Claudine. Later, the couple manage to spend an idyllic interlude in Italy. As they are preparing to return to Paris, Georges reaffirms his intention to leave Claudine. Though anguished, she eventually accepts his reasoning that it is best for them to part while their love is at its height. Fourteen months later, the lovers meet again. Claudine is now the count's wife, and Georges is about to marry an heiress. Their passion having cooled to quiet affection, both lovers are able to smile at their recent torment. Produced Paris, Théâtre de la Renaissance, November 5, 1895.

DORSET, 1st Earl of. *See* SACKVILLE, THOMAS.

DORST, Tankred (1925–   ). German dramatist whose works are characterized by a great variety of style and theme. He began his theatrical career with a revised version of Tieck's *Puss in Boots* for Munich's Puppet Theatre. Tieck's ironic use of the conventions of illusionary theatre, as well as Dorst's own experience with marionettes, has had a lasting influence. His first play, *Party in Autumn* (*Gesellschaft im Herbst,* 1960), uses relics of the romantic past to satirize contemporary society. Unfounded rumors of a hidden treasure are cleverly exploited by a financier to bring a family to financial ruin and thus enable him to secure its house cheaply. The financier stands above and beyond the other characters and pulls the strings like a puppet master. *Freedom for Clemens* (*Freiheit für Clemens,* 1960) employs similar stylistic elements but deals with the existential restrictions of human existence as represented by Clemens, the man in the cell, who attempts to build his world in that constricted environment. *The Bend in the Road* (*Die Kurve,* 1960) is a farce in the tradition of Beckett. Two clownlike brothers set up a funeral business at the side of a road in order to profit from the many car accidents that occur there. An official who is sent to investigate is murdered with exaggerated gestures, and business continues. The brothers quiet their consciences by sending numerous payments to a distant ministry. The play, with its idyllic atmosphere, is a parody of the attitude that all is well in the world if business is good. In *The Great Diatribe at the City Wall* (*Grosse Schmährede an der Stadtmauer,* 1961), Dorst tried his hand at a parable play reminiscent of Brecht. *The Moor* (*Die Mohrin,* 1964) is a

parody of Büchner's *Leonce and Lena.*

Important among Dorst's latest plays is the semidocumentary *Toller* (1968). The play, making use of a simultaneous stage, depicts scenes from a German revolution, the Munich Räterepublik of 1919, with the expressionist poet Ernst Toller as the central figure. It was acclaimed by critics and public alike, not least because it deals with the relation of the idealistic artist to the realities of politics, a much-debated theme in current German literature. Dorst has also made several adaptations, among them *The Judge from London* (*Der Richter von London,* 1964), based on a play by Thomas Dekker; and *Rameau's Nephew* (*Rameaus Neffe,* 1966), based on a play by Diderot. His theories of aesthetics are presented in the essays *Das Geheimnis der Marionette* (1958), *Auf kleiner Bühne* (1959), and *Die Bühne ist der absolute Ort.*

DRAMATIC EXPOSITION. Presentation to the audience of relevant background information which it must have in order to understand the action that follows. Historically this presentation makes varying approaches to and departures from realism. The prologues of some Greek and Roman plays are completely unrealistic; the bald exchange of information between characters in Elizabethan drama is somewhat less so. Most modern playwrights try to hide the exposition in natural, casual dialogue, but the opening telephone conversation or exchange between servants will not always stand close skeptical analysis.

DRAME. Originally a French term for serious plays that, unlike French classical tragedy, include some comic touches. More recently, the term has often been used to refer to serious plays that do not conclude tragically.

DRAYTON, Michael (1563–1631). English poet and dramatist. Raised among the country gentry, Drayton later could count among his patrons many members of the nobility. His lifelong series of ambitious poems, however successful, did not preclude his trying his hand at dramatic writing. He turned to the stage for the short period between 1597 and 1602. Records of the period show him to have been actively associated with other authors on numerous plays, in the contemporary tradition of multiple collaboration. He is found to have joined Anthony Munday and Robert Wilson in working on *Sir John Oldcastle* (ca. 1599). That he was acquainted with Shakespeare (whose birthplace, Warwickshire, he shared) is likely; in fact, tradition holds that he was present at the drinking session that led to Shakespeare's demise.

John Drinkwater
(1882 – 1937)

John Drinkwater, English poet, biographer, critic, and dramatist, was born in Leytonstone, Essex, on June 1, 1882. In 1897 he began working for an insurance company in Nottingham. In 1901 the company transferred him to Birmingham, where he met Barry (later Sir Barry) Jackson. A wealthy young man who had become deeply interested in the theatre, Jackson had formed the Pilgrim Players and was to employ Drinkwater as an actor and producer.

Before that, in 1903, Drinkwater paid to have a volume of poetry published. Although the verses were undistinguished, they marked the beginning of his literary career. By 1909, having gradually risen to a position of some responsibility in the insurance business while developing an abiding enthusiasm for the theatre, Drinkwater had left the insurance field to devote himself to writing. His early plays were staged by the Pilgrim Players under his direction. In 1913 the Pilgrim Players became the famous Birmingham Repertory Theatre, with Drinkwater as the general manager. Drinkwater proceeded to write an average of one play a year, but it was not until 1918, with *Abraham Lincoln,* that he achieved fame as a playwright, although he had already established himself as a prolific writer of poetry, biographies, and criticism.

In 1924 Drinkwater married the violinist Daisy Kennedy; the couple had one daughter. A collection of essays called *The Muse in Council,* his *Collected Plays,* and a study of Byron, *The Pilgrim of Eternity,* appeared in 1925. His autobiography was published in two volumes, *Inheritance* (1931) and *Discovery* (1932). Drinkwater died in London on March 25, 1937.

WORK

Like many other early-twentieth-century playwrights, Drinkwater sought to escape from the trammels of the currently popular realistic play by turning to historical and imaginative themes. His first play in this vein was *Rebellion* (1914), an allegorical work, written in verse and set in an imagined land, which protested the standards of Victorianism. *The Storm* (1915) was inspired by Synge's *Riders to the Sea. X=O: A Night of the Trojan War* (1917), written in verse, commented on the bitterness of war and glorified peace.

In 1918 Drinkwater's reputation as a dramatist soared with the appearance of

John Drinkwater. [New York Public Library Picture Collection]

Abraham Lincoln, an episodic historical play in prose, which became his most popular and successful work. The formula for the chronicle play developed in *Abraham Lincoln,* the rise of a man or woman above the commonplace, was repeated, although less successfully, in *Mary Stuart* (1921), which deals with the familiar tale of Bothwell and Darnley and achieves some fine poetic and dramatic moments; *Oliver Cromwell* (1923); *Robert E. Lee* (1923); and *Robert Burns* (pub. 1924). In each of these works Drinkwater chose a protagonist who, confronted with a crisis, assumes heroic qualities. *See* CHRONICLE PLAY.

The only play that enjoyed a popular success equal to that of *Abraham Lincoln* was the pleasant but slight comedy about ordinary people, *Bird in Hand* (1927). Of his later plays, *A Man's House* (1931) is the most significant. It deals with the effects on the world of the coming of Jesus as seen in one Jewish household. Although Drinkwater's poetry is merely competent, he helped bring the modern poetic drama to a wider audience.

Abraham Lincoln (1918). Episodic drama in verse and prose, exploring six turning points in the life of Abraham Lincoln that delineate his character, humanity, uncertainties, and humility. The episodes are introduced by two chroniclers who act as a Greek chorus. The play begins when Lincoln is offered the Republican nomination and decides to accept it. There follow his refusal to com-

Frank McGlynn (left) and Albert Phillips in John Drinkwater's *Abraham Lincoln.* New York, Cort Theatre, 1919. [Theatre Collection, The New York Public Library at Lincoln Center, Astor, Lenox and Tilden Foundations]

promise with the South about secession, his doubts about the Civil War, the strengthening of his resolve to sign the Emancipation Proclamation, his determination that there should be no retaliation against the South, and, finally, his assassination by John Wilkes Booth.

PLAYS

1. (Adaptation). *Ser Taldo's Bride.* Verse play, 1 act. Produced Birmingham, Pilgrim Players, Jan. 21, 1911. Based on the prose play by Barry Jackson.

2. *Cophetua.* Verse play, 1 act. Published 1911. Produced Birmingham, Pilgrim Players, Nov. 18, 1911.

3. *Puss in Boots.* Play, 5 scenes. Published 1911. Produced Birmingham, Pilgrim Players, Dec. 30, 1911.

4. *An English Medley.* Choruses with music. Published 1911. Produced Bournville, 1911. Music: Rutland Boughton.

5. *The Pied Piper: A Tale of Hamelin City.* Play. Published 1912. Produced Bournville, 1912. Music: S. W. Sylvester.

6. *The Only Legend: A Masque of the Scarlet Pierrot.* Play. Published 1913. Produced Bournville, July 10, 1913. Music: J. Brier.

7. *Rebellion.* Verse play, 3 acts. Published 1914. Produced Birmingham Repertory Theatre, May 2, 1914.

8. *Robin Hood & the Pedlar.* Play. Published 1914. Produced Bournville, June 25, 1914. Music: Brier.

9. *The Storm.* Play, 1 act. Published 1914. Produced

Birmingham Repertory Theatre, May 8, 1915.

10. *The God of Quiet.* Play, 1 act. Published 1916. Produced Birmingham Repertory Theatre, Oct. 7, 1916.

11. *X=O: A Night of the Trojan War.* Play. Published 1917. Produced Birmingham Repertory Theatre, Apr. 14, 1917.

12. *Abraham Lincoln.* Play. Published 1918. Produced Birmingham Repertory Theatre, Oct. 12, 1918.

13. *Mary Stuart.* Play, prologue and 2 acts. Published 1921. Produced New York, Ritz Theatre, Mar. 21, 1921; London, Everyman Theatre, Sept. 25, 1922.

14. *Oliver Cromwell.* Play. Published 1921. Produced London, His Majesty's Theatre, May 29, 1923.

15. *Robert E. Lee.* Play. Published 1923. Produced London, Regent Theatre, June 20, 1923.

16. *Robert Burns.* Play. Published 1924.

17. *Bird in Hand.* Comedy. Published 1927. Produced Birmingham Repertory Theatre, Sept. 3, 1927.

18. *John Bull Calling.* Play. Published 1928. Produced London, Coliseum Theatre, Nov. 12, 1928.

19. *A Man's House.* Play. Published 1934. Produced Malvern Festival, July 23, 1931.

20. (Adaptation). *Napoleon: The Hundred Days.* Play. Published 1932. Produced London, New Theatre, Apr. 18, 1932. Based on *Campo di maggio,* by Giovacchino Forzano and Benito Mussolini.

21. *Midsummer Eve.* Radio play. Published 1932. Produced British Broadcasting Corporation, June 23, 1932.

22. *Laying the Devil.* Play. Published 1933. Produced Liverpool, Playhouse, May 2, 1933.

23. *Garibaldi.* Play. Published 1936.

EDITIONS

Collections.
Collected Plays, 2 vols., London, 1925.
Individual Plays.
Abraham Lincoln. Published in *Three Distinctive Plays about Abraham Lincoln,* ed. by W. Surre, New York, 1961.
Cophetua. Published in *Dramas by Present-day Writers,* ed. by R. W. Pence, New York, 1927.
Oliver Cromwell. Published in *Contemporary Plays,* ed. by T. H. Dickinson and J. R. Crawford, Boston, 1925.

CRITICISM

B. Matthews, *A History of the Birmingham Repertory Theatre,* London, 1924; A. W. Roeder, *John Drinkwater als Dramatiker,* 1927.

John Dryden
(1631 – 1700)

John Dryden, English dramatist, Poet Laureate, and man of letters, the eldest of fourteen children, was born in Aldwinkle, Northamptonshire, and baptized on August 14, 1631. He attended Westminster School as a King's scholar, then in 1650 entered Trinity College, Cambridge, on a scholarship. He graduated with a B.A. degree in 1654. The next few years of Dryden's life are obscure, but it is said that he spent most of this time in study, perhaps at Cambridge. Sometime before 1660 he settled in London.

Dryden's first published poem, an elegy on the death of a school companion, appeared in 1649. In 1659 he published *Heroic Stanzas,* in memory of Cromwell, and followed it in 1660 with *Astraea Redux,* a poem celebrating the restoration of Charles II. At about this time he became a friend of Sir Robert Howard, a wealthy supporter of the Theatre Royal, where, early in 1663, his first play, *The Wild Gallant,* was unsuccessfully acted. In December, 1663, Dryden married Howard's sister Lady Elizabeth Howard. A month later he achieved his first dramatic success with the production of *The Indian Queen,* written in collaboration with Howard. In 1665 he repeated the success with a sequel, *The Indian Emperor.*

When the London theatres were closed by the plague in 1666, Dryden and his wife retired to Charlton, in Wiltshire. It was here that he composed the poem *Annus Mirabilis;* his *Essay of Dramatic Poesy;* and the play *Secret Love,* which was produced in 1667. By this time the Drydens had returned to London, and there now followed a translation from Molière's *The Blunderer* (*L'étourdi*), entitled *Sir Martin Mar-All, or The Feign'd Innocence. See* MOLIÈRE.

The years following Dryden's appointment as writer to the Theatre Royal in 1667 were his most productive as a dramatist. He produced some fourteen plays, originals and adaptations, the most notable being *The Conquest of Granada by the Spaniards* (1670) and *All for Love* (1677). In 1668 he was appointed Poet Laureate, and in 1670 he was named Historiographer Royal.

By the 1680s, in the last years of the reign of Charles II, Dryden had become involved in the political unrest of the time and had given up writing for the stage. He was a Tory and a supporter of the Stuarts, and through satire he attacked his enemies and those of the King. In 1681 he published the poem *Absalom and Achitophel,* directed against the Earl of Shaftesbury. A year later, in another poem, *MacFlecknoe,* he made a devastating attack on Thomas Shadwell, who, as leader of the literary supporters of the Whig party, had chided Dryden for his political position. When James II, a Catholic, ascended the throne in 1685, Dryden became a convert to Roman Catholicism, a step that later cost him dearly. With James's replacement in 1688 by the Protestant monarchs William and Mary, he not only lost all his political offices but saw his old enemy Shadwell replace him as Poet Laureate. *See* SHADWELL, THOMAS.

Thus, in his old age, as in his youth, Dryden was forced to support himself by his writing. He turned once again to the theatre but found that his popularity had dwindled. In 1694, after the failure of *Love Triumphant,* he abandoned the stage. His remaining years were devoted to translating from the classics: Juvenal, Persius, Virgil (on whose works he

spent three years), Ovid, Chaucer, and Boccaccio. Dryden died in London on May 1, 1700, and was buried in Westminster Abbey, in Chaucer's grave. Twenty years later a monument was erected in his memory.

WORK

Dryden occupies a place in English drama not dissimilar to that held by Ben Jonson half a century earlier. Both were Poets Laureate, both enjoyed critical and popular success that in their later years developed into a sort of benevolent literary dictatorship, both were major influences on the drama of their time and the period immediately following, and both were overshadowed in their artistic achievements by other contemporary dramatists. *See* JONSON, BEN.

Much of Dryden's time and energy was given to the heroic drama, a form of serious play that had great early success and long continued to influence later tragedy, although it has little interest today. With this form Dryden sought to create something fresh, something larger than life, more thrilling and enthralling, with vehement passions and violent emotions, even though he tended to restrict these passions to "love" and "honor." At the same time, he attempted to express these emotions in a more disciplined and precise poetic form than that provided by the often-undisciplined post-Shakespearean blank verse. Thus he adopted the rhymed couplet, strict in its measure and shape. *See* HEROIC PLAY.

John Dryden. [New York Public Library Picture Collection]

He defended the use of this form in his *Essay of Dramatic Poesy* (1668), and it must be acknowledged that in *The Indian Emperor* (1665), *Tyrannic Love* (1669), and *Aureng-Zebe* (1675), English heroic drama reached its highest, though brief, success. By 1677 Dryden himself had come to realize the limitations of his "long-loved Mistress, rhyme" in drama, and in *All for Love* he deliberately returned to the blank-verse medium he had earlier rejected. His position in the theatre of his time is shown by the fact that as soon as he made this recantation, virtually all his fellow dramatists also abandoned rhymed couplets and adopted blank-verse dialogue.

Less important was Dryden's contribution to comedy. In prose dialogue he aimed at and achieved, though with less success than Etherege, a distillation of the easy, sophisticated "wit" in which the Whitehall courtiers delighted. Only one of his efforts in this genre is still revived: *Marriage à la Mode* (1672), which has two plots, a heroic plot dealing with royal characters who speak in rhymed couplets, and a comic plot introducing two young men and two ladies who speak in prose.

Dryden revealed his power of critical expression in the prefaces to his plays. These essays not only were written in a magnificently direct and effective prose style but were the first to establish dramatic criticism, indeed, literary criticism in general, in England.

Elizabeth White Hartley as Cleopatra in *All for Love.* [Theatre Collection, The New York Public Library at Lincoln Center, Astor, Lenox and Tilden Foundations]

Marriage à la Mode (1672).   Comedy with two plots. A heroic plot in rhymed couplets deals with Palmyra, a Princess whom her usurping royal father has never seen, and Leonidas, her childhood sweetheart, rightful heir to the throne. When Leonidas's true identity is revealed, he wins both Palmyra and his crown. A comic plot centers in the earthy intrigue between two couples. Rodophil and Doralice, after two years of marriage, have become indifferent to each other. Rodophil is enamored of Melanthe, who is engaged to his friend Palamede. Palamede, in turn, is enchanted by Doralice. After a series of comic complications, the two men agree not to violate the sanctity of each other's homes.

Aureng-Zebe (1675).   Heroic drama written in rhymed couplets. The aging Indian Emperor is defended against his sons' claims to the throne by Aureng-Zebe (Aurangzeb), his only loyal heir. Chief among Aureng-Zebe's opponents is his stepbrother Morat, whose mother Nourmahal is the Emperor's present wife. Aureng-Zebe, sought after by the passionate Nourmahal, soon learns that his promised bride Indamora is desired by both his own father and Morat. To rid himself of competition for Indamora, the Emperor takes away Aureng-Zebe's right to succession in favor of Morat. Finally Aureng-Zebe defeats his brothers, Morat is killed, and Nourmahal dies by poison. Reconciled, the Emperor restores his son's rights to both the throne and Indamora.

All for Love, or The World Well Lost (1677).   Blank-verse tragedy that tells the story of Antony and Cleopatra in Restoration "love and honor" terms. Ventidius, Antony's general, arrives and persuades his commander, who has been demoralized by his defeat at Actium and by Cleopatra's treachery, to quit the city, join his few remaining legions in Syria, and march against Octavius Caesar, who is nearby. Antony has agreed when, at the last moment, Cleopatra appears and convinces him not to leave her. After he leads his men against Caesar, winning a small victory, he is confronted by Octavia, his wife, who has been brought from Caesar's camp by Dolabella. Octavia pleads with her husband to return. She wins him over, and Antony then delegates Dolabella to tender his farewells to Cleopatra. In order to arouse Antony's jealousy, Cleopatra flirts with the susceptible Dolabella. Ventidius reports what has happened, and Antony's jealous outburst convinces Octavia that she has lost him for good. She then leaves. Antony confronts Cleopatra and Dolabella and refuses to believe their protestations of innocence, whereupon Cleopatra decides to feign suicide. When the Egyptian Fleet joins the Romans, Antony knows that the end is near. Then a servant brings word of Cleopatra's suicide, and Antony, believing him, falls on his sword. Seeing this, Ventidius kills himself. Cleopatra then arrives and assures the wounded Antony of her love. When he dies, she applies the asp that kills her.

PLAYS

All were first performed in London.

1. *The Wild Gallant.* Comedy. Published 1669. Produced Theatre Royal (Vere Street), February, 1663.

2. (With Sir Robert Howard). *The Indian Queen.* Heroic tragedy. Published 1665. Produced Theatre Royal (Bridges Street), January, 1664.

3. *The Rival Ladies.* Tragicomedy. Published 1664. Produced Theatre Royal (Bridges Street), ca. June, 1664.

4. *The Indian Emperor, or The Conquest of Mexico by the Spaniards.* Heroic tragedy. Published 1667. Produced Theatre Royal (Bridges Street), ca. April, 1665.

5. *Secret Love, or The Maiden Queen.* Tragicomedy, 5 acts. Published 1668. Produced Theatre Royal (Bridges Street), March, 1667.

6. *Sir Martin Mar-All, or The Feign'd Innocence.* Comedy. Published 1668. Produced Lincoln's Inn Fields Theatre, August, 1667. Adapted from Molière's *L'étourdi* after it had been translated by William Cavendish, Duke of Newcastle.

7. (Adaptation; with Sir William Davenant). *The Tempest, or The Enchanted Island.* Comedy. Pubished 1670. Produced Lincoln's Inn Fields Theatre, Nov. 7, 1667. Based on William Shakespeare's play.

8. *An Evening's Love, or The Mock Astrologer.* Comedy, 5 acts. Published 1671. Produced Theatre Royal (Bridges Street), June, 1668. Adapted from Thomas Corneille's *Le feint astrologue* (1648).

9. *Tyrannic Love, or The Royal Martyr.* Heroic tragedy. Published 1670. Produced Theatre Royal (Bridges Street), ca. June, 1669.

10. *The Conquest of Granada by the Spaniards, Part I.* Heroic tragedy. Published 1672. Produced Theatre Royal (Bridges Street), ca. December, 1670.

11. *The Conquest of Granada by the Spaniards, Part II.* Heroic tragedy. Published 1672. Produced Theatre Royal (Bridges Street), January, 1671.

12. *Marriage à la Mode.* Comedy. Published 1673. Produced Lincoln's Inn Fields Theatre, ca. April, 1672.

13. *The Assignation, or Love in a Nunnery.* Comedy. Published 1673. Produced Lincoln's Inn Fields Theatre, ca. November, 1672.

14. *Amboyna, or The Cruelties of the Dutch to the English Merchants.* Tragedy. Published 1673. Produced Lincoln's Inn Fields Theatre, ca. May, 1673.

15. *The Mistaken Husband.* Comedy. Published 1675. Produced Drury Lane Theatre, ca. September, 1675. Possibly Dryden's adaptation of an earlier play by Richard Brome (?).

16. *Aureng-Zebe.* Heroic tragedy. Published 1676. Produced Drury Lane Theatre, November, 1675.

17. *The State of Innocence and Fall of Man.* Dramatic opera. Published 1677. Unacted dramatic version of John Milton's *Paradise Lost* (1667, 1674).

18. *All for Love, or The World Well Lost.* Tragedy. Published 1678. Produced Drury Lane Theatre, December, 1677.

19. *The Kind Keeper, or Mr. Limberham.* Comedy. Published 1680. Produced Dorset Garden Theatre, March, 1678.

20. (With Nathaniel Lee). *Oedipus.* Tragedy. Published 1679. Produced Dorset Garden Theatre, ca. November, 1678.

21. *Troilus and Cressida, or Truth Found Too Late.* Tragedy. Published 1679. Produced Dorset Garden Theatre, ca. April, 1679.

22. *The Spanish Friar, or The Double Discovery.* Comedy. Published 1681. Produced Dorset Garden Theatre, March, 1680.

23. (With Lee). *The Duke of Guise.* Tragedy. Published 1683. Produced Drury Lane Theatre, November, 1682.

24. *Albion and Albanius.* Dramatic opera. Published 1685. Produced Dorset Garden Theatre, June, 1685. Music: Louis Grabu.

25. *Don Sebastian, King of Portugal.* Tragedy. Published 1690. Produced Drury Lane Theatre, ca. December, 1689.

26. (With Thomas Betterton?). *The Prophetess, or The History of Dioclesian.* Dramatic opera. Published 1690. Produced Dorset Garden Theatre, ca. June, 1690.

27. *Amphitryon, or The Two Socia's.* Comedy. Published 1690. Produced Drury Lane Theatre, October, 1690.

28. *King Arthur, or The British Worthy.* Dramatic opera. Published 1691. Produced Dorset Garden Theatre, ca. May, 1691. Music: Henry Purcell.

29. (With Thomas Southerne?). *Cleomenes, the Spartan Heroe.* Tragedy. Published 1692. Produced Drury Lane Theatre, April, 1692.

30. *Love Triumphant, or Nature Will Prevail.* Comedy. Published 1694. Produced Drury Lane Theatre, ca. January, 1694.

31. *The Secular Masque.* Masque. Published 1700. Produced Drury Lane Theatre, Apr. 29(?), 1700.

EDITIONS

Collections.

Prose Works, ed. by E. Malone, 3 vols., London, 1800; *The Works,* ed. by W. Scott, 18 vols., London, 1808, rev. by G. Saintsbury, Edinburgh, 1882–1892; *Poetical Works,* ed. by G. R. Noyes, Boston, 1908; *Essays,* ed. by W. P. Ker, Oxford, 1926; *Dramatic Works,* ed. by M. Summers, 6 vols., London, 1931–1932; *Prologues and Epilogues,* ed. by W. B. Gardner, New York, 1951; *Selected Works of John Dryden,* ed. by W. Frost, New York, 1953; *Dryden: Three Plays,* ed. by G. Saintsbury, New York, 1957; *John Dryden: 4 Comedies,* ed. by L. A. Beaurline and F. Bowers, Chicago, 1967; *John Dryden: 4 Tragedies,* ed. by L. A. Beaurline and F. Bowers, Chicago, 1967.

Individual Plays.

All for Love, or The World Well Lost. Published in *The Development of English Drama,* ed. by G. E. Bentley, New York, 1950.

Aureng-Zebe. Published in *Five Heroic Plays,* ed. by B. Dobrée, London, 1960.

The Conquest of Granada by the Spaniards, Part I. Published in *British Dramatists from Dryden to Sheridan,* ed. by G. H. Nettleton and A. E. Case, Boston, 1939.

The Indian Queen. Published in *Plays of the Restoration and Eighteenth Century,* ed. by D. MacMillan and H. M. Jones, New York, 1938.

The Secular Masque. Published in *The Norton Anthology of English Literature,* ed. by M. H. Abrams et al., New York, 1962.

The Spanish Friar, or The Double Discovery. Published in *Representative English Comedies,* ed. by C. M. Gayley, vol. 4, New York, 1903–1936.

CRITICISM

S. Johnson, *The Lives of the English Poets,* vol. 1, London, 1779; J. R. Lowell, *Among My Books,* New York, 1870; R. Garnett, *The Age of Dryden,* London, 1895; M. Sherwood, *Dryden's Dramatic Theory and Practice,* New York, 1898; M. D. Baumgarten, *On Dryden's Relation to Germany in the 18th Century,* New York, 1914; A. W. Verrall, *Lectures on Dryden,* ed. by M. de G. Verrall, Cambridge, England, 1914; A. Nicoll, *Dryden as an Adapter of Shakespeare,* London, 1922; B. J. Pendlebury, *Dryden's Heroic Plays,* London, 1923; A. Lubbock, *The Character of John Dryden,* London, 1925; T. S. Eliot, *John Dryden,* New York, 1932; N. B. Allen, *Sources of John Dryden's Comedies,* New York, 1935; T. W. Russell, *Vol-*

taire, *Dryden & Heroic Tragedy*, New York, 1946; A. Beljame, *Men of Letters and the English Public in the Eighteenth Century*, New York, 1948; S. H. Monk, *John Dryden: A List of Critical Studies Published from 1895 to 1948*, Minneapolis, 1950; D. N. Smith, *John Dryden*, Cambridge, England, 1950; F. L. Huntley, *On Dryden's Essay of Dramatic Poesy*, Ann Arbor, Mich., 1951; K. Young, *John Dryden*, London, 1954; L. I. Bredvold, *Intellectual Milieu of John Dryden*, Ann Arbor, Mich., 1956; B. Dobrée, *Dryden*, London and New York, 1956; M. Van Doren, *John Dryden: A Study of His Poetry*, Bloomington, Ind., 1960; C. E. Ward, *The Life of John Dryden*, Chapel Hill, N.C., 1961; U. Amarasinghe, *Dryden and Pope in the Early 19th Century*, New York, 1962; A. W. Hoffman, *John Dryden's Imagery*, Gainesville, Fla., 1962; E. M. Waith, *The Herculean Hero in Marlowe, Chapman, Shakespeare and Dryden*, New York, 1962; J. M. Aden, ed., *Critical Opinions of John Dryden*, Nashville, 1963; F. H. Moore, *The Nobler Pleasure: Dryden's Comedy in Theory and Practice*, Chapel Hill, N.C., 1963; A. C. Kirsch. *Dryden's Heroic Drama*, Princeton, N.J., 1964; J. M. Osborn, *John Dryden*, Gainesville, Fla., 1964; B. N. Schilling, *Dryden: A Collection of Critical Essays*, New York, 1964; G. R. Wasserman, *John Dryden*, New York, 1964; S. A. Zebouni, *Dryden: A Study in Heroic Characterization*, Baton Rouge, La., 1965; B. King, *Dryden's Major Plays*, New York, 1966; H. T. Swedenberg, Jr., ed., *Essential Articles for the Study of John Dryden*, Hamden, Conn., 1966; H. Macdonald, *John Dryden: A Bibliography*, Birmingham, Ala., 1967; P. Harth, *Contexts of Dryden's Thought*, Chicago, 1968; B. King, ed., *Twentieth Century Interpretations of All for Love*, New York, 1968; A. T. Barbeau, *The Intellectual Design of John Dryden's Heroic Plays*, New Haven, Conn., 1970.

DUBÉ, Marcel (1930–   ). French-Canadian playwright, author of some fifteen plays that present a mirror of everyday life in French Canada in a manner reminiscent of Chekhov, Tennessee Williams, and Eugene O'Neill. His first full-length play, *Zone* (1952), created for the Dramatic Arts Festival of the Province of Quebec, deals with the problem of French Canada. Among his other plays are *Room to Let* (*Chambre à louer*, 1955), *Le barrage* (1956), *A Simple Soldier* (*Un simple soldat*, 1958), *Florence* (1960), *The Beautiful Sundays* (*Les beaux dimanches*, 1965), and *It Is a Season* (*Il est un saison*, 1965). His *The Time of Lilacs* (*Le temps des lilas*) was a hit in 1958. Subsequently he wrote *The Wild Geese* (*Les oies sauvages*, 1966) and *At the Return of the White Geese* (*Au retour des oies blanches*, 1967).

DUFRESNY, Charles Rivière (b. Paris, ca. 1654; d. there, October 6, 1724). French comic dramatist who claimed to be the great-grandson of Henry IV. His reputation rests largely on the brilliant one-act comedy *The Contradictious Temper* (*L'esprit de contradiction*, 1700), although his *Double Widowhood* (*Le double veuvage*, 1702), an ironic comedy about a couple bound together by the mutual desire to outlive each other, is not far inferior. These two and thirteen other comedies were written for the Comédie-Française. The best of the others are *The Village Coquette, or The Assumed Portion* (*La coquette du village, ou Le lot supposé*, 1715), *The Norman Reconciliation* (*La réconciliation normande*, 1719), *The Retraction* (*Le dédit*, 1719), and *The Marriage Made and Broken, or The Hostess of Marseille* (*Le mariage fait et rompu, ou L'hôtesse de Marseille*, 1721). He also contributed eight farces to the Comédie-Italienne (two of them written with Louis Biancolelli). Four other comedies, including the lively *The Fair of Saint-Germain* (*La foire Saint-Germain*, 1695), were written with Regnard. *The Contradictious Temper* provided the plot for Carlo Goldoni's *The Spirit of Contradiction* (1758). *See* GOLDONI, CARLO; REGNARD, JEAN-FRANÇOIS.

The Contradictious Temper (*L'esprit de contradiction*, 1700). Comedy in one act dealing with the perverse Mme. Oronte, who devotes her life to discovering the desires of others so that she may oppose them. Her daughter Angélique is in love with a young officer named Valère. Knowing her mother's temper, Angélique, by a series of elaborate ruses, convinces Mme. Oronte that she detests Valère, whereupon the contradictious lady is duped into forcing a match between the two young lovers. Produced Paris, Comédie-Française, August 27, 1700.

DU GARD, Roger Martin. *See* MARTIN DU GARD, ROGER.

Alexandre Dumas fils
(1824 – 1895)

Alexandre Dumas *fils*, French novelist and dramatist, was born in Paris on July 28, 1824. He was the illegitimate son of Alexandre Dumas *père* and Marie-Catherine Labay. Legally recognized by his father in 1831, he was taken from his mother and sent to the first of a series of boarding schools where he was made miserable by taunts about his illegitimate birth.

Unlike his father and despite his personal difficulties, Dumas *fils* received a conventional education. Having inherited his father's vitality, however, he began to lead a wild life at an early age. By the time he was twenty-one, his debts amounted to 50,000 francs. In 1844 the elder Dumas was separated from his wife (whom his son hated), and father and son lived together amicably in Saint-Germain-en-Laye. There young Dumas met and fell in love with Marie Duplessis, a beautiful young courtesan who inspired the

Alexandre Dumas _fils_. [French Cultural Services]

novel _The Lady of the Camellias_ (_La dame aux camélias_), which was hastily written in 1848, a year after her death from tuberculosis. So successful was this novel that he was able to pay off some of his debts and provide handsomely for his mother. He wrote twelve other novels before 1852, the year he adapted _The Lady of the Camellias_ for the stage. Among them were _The Novel of a Woman_ (_Le roman d'une femme,_ 1848) and _Diane de Lys_ (1851).

After 1852 Dumas began to write didactic plays that showed a distaste for loose living. These include _Diane de Lys_ (1853), _The Demi-Monde_ (_Le demi-monde,_ 1855), _The Money Question_ (_La question d'argent,_ 1857), _The Natural Son_ (_Le fils naturel,_ 1858), and _A Prodigal Father_ (_Un père prodigue,_ 1859). At the same time he formed a liaison with the Russian princess Nadejda Naryschkine, who was already married. The relationship produced a daughter in 1860, but it was not until 1864 that he married his mistress. Another daughter was born in 1867, but the marriage was a failure, and when his wife died, Dumas married Henriette Régnier, who had been his mistress for eight years. The years between 1864 and 1867 saw no literary successes until _Madame Aubray's Ideas_ (_Les idées de Madame Aubray_) won public approval in 1867. The same year Dumas published _L'affaire Clémenceau,_ a semiautobiographical novel that is considered one of his best. In 1874 he was elected to the Académie Fran-

çaise, and at this point, finding himself well situated financially and socially, he began to express his growing interest in political and social problems in moralizing pamphlets. Several other failures on the stage were followed by the successful _Denise_ in 1885 and _Francillon_ in 1887. In 1894 he was admitted to the Légion d'Honneur. Dumas's last play, _The Return from Thebes_ (_Le retour de Thèbes_), was left unfinished at his death in Marly-le-Roi on November 27, 1895.

WORK

Realism had been waiting in the wings of the French theatre throughout the 1830s and 1840s. The bonds of classicism had been shed by the romantics; Scribe, Labiche, and Dumas _père_ had initiated a trend toward the drama of the future. And yet, with the possible exception of Balzac's _Mercadet_ (1851), there had been no serious realistic play until the younger Dumas's _Camille; The Lady of the Camellias_ took Paris by storm in 1852. The heroine over whom audiences wept was a courtesan, anathema by contemporary standards; the characters spoke in the rhythms and language of everyday speech; and the setting realistically portrayed a shadowy segment of Parisian society. Although sentimental, even melodramatic, the play was tightly constructed and proceeded logically to its

La dame aux camélias, with Edwige Feuillère in the title role. [French Cultural Services]

Scene from *La question d'argent.* [Courtesy of Centre Dramatique National Nord]

denouement. More than 100 years later, the play is still often given in Paris, and though its social conventions now seem exotic and the rhetoric sounds somewhat strained, the drama of Marguerite Gautier's love for Armand Duval is still capable of moving a modern audience. *See* REALISM.

In *The Demi-Monde* (1855), Dumas continued his exploration of the social scene by putting on stage another marginal segment of Parisian society, in which persons of dubious social status hover, waiting for the opportunity to claw their way back to respectability. In the play this demimonde is compared to a basket of beautiful peaches, each marked by an almost imperceptible wormhole. Dumas carefully constructed a tight plot that allows society and virtue to triumph when the heroine's self-seeking motives are exposed. The play is often compared with *Olympe's Marriage,* Augier's treatment of a similar theme. *See* AUGIER, ÉMILE.

His own unhappy childhood and the legal quarrels between his parents convinced Dumas that the disintegration of family life leads in turn to social decomposition. He inaugurated the modern thesis play (*pièce à thèse*) in which the *raisonneur,* or dramatist's spokesman, presents a point of view that challenges the social and moral preconceptions of the audience. The plays became frankly didactic. *The Money Question* (1857) deals with the ethics of the business community in a manner that was bold for the time. In the play a disreputable businessman who believes that "money is the only power that's never argued against" is undone by the honesty of those who surround him. *The Natural Son* (1858) concerns social attitudes toward illegitimate children, and knowing Parisian audiences were intrigued by the obvious use of autobiographical material. *The Woman's Friend* (*L'ami des femmes,* 1864) offers, in the figure of Ryons, a man peculiarly adept in feminine psychology and able to save a woman from adultery and reconcile her with her unfaithful but still beloved husband. _Madame Aubray's Ideas_ (1867) points up the discrepancy between professed Christian ethics and un-Christian behavior toward a woman "fallen" through no fault of her own. Both _A Honeymoon Call_ (_Une visite de noces,_ 1871) and _Princess George_ (_La princesse Georges,_ 1871) explore the consequences of marital infidelity.

In _The Wife of Claude_ (_La femme de Claude,_ 1873), Dumas mixed didacticism and symbolism. More than an adulterous wife, Césarine becomes that very "beast" that has attacked French society, while her husband represents all the traditional values. The same sort of symbolism is obvious in the later plays; in _The Foreigner_ (_L'étrangère,_ 1876), for example, evil is represented by disease. The ills besetting society were discussed by Dumas in prefaces to his published plays. He is often credited with legal reforms that attempted to deal with these problems.

Camille; The Lady of the Camellias (_La dame aux camélias,_ 1852).

Romantic tragedy about Marguerite Gautier, a beautiful young courtesan suffering from tuberculosis, who is loved by Armand Duval, a young man of good family. She returns his love, and they enjoy a few idyllic months together in the country. Their happiness ends abruptly, however, when M. Duval, Armand's father, visits Marguerite and entreats her to give up his son. Their romance, he asserts, will destroy Armand's career and social position and prevent the marriage of his young sister. Sacrificing herself for Armand and his family, Marguerite leaves her lover, pretending to be returning to a rich admirer for mercenary reasons. After following her to Paris, where he wounds his rival in a duel, Armand is compelled to quit France.

Now Marguerite's fortunes deteriorate rapidly. Seriously ill and deserted by friends and lovers, she is forced to pawn her possessions and move to a shabby flat. M. Duval writes to his son informing him of Marguerite's sacrifice and her misfortunes. Armand rushes to Marguerite's side, and she dies, happy, in his arms.

The English title of the play is the result of an erroneous christening of the heroine by an early translator. The play provided the basis for Verdi's opera _La Traviata._

The Demi-Monde (_Le demi-monde,_ 1855).

Drama in which Suzanne d'Ange, a calculating "baroness" on the outskirts of society (demimonde), tries to exchange her tarnished existence for a place in high society. Realizing that her surest escape route is through marriage, Suzanne fabricates a respectable identity for herself as an eligible widow. Her first matrimonial target is Olivier de Jalin,

Sketch of a performance of _Francillon._ Paris, Comédie-Française, 1887. [Goethe House]

who, when he discovers her past, refuses to marry her even though he loves her. Next she turns to Raymond de Nanjac, a young man recently arrived in Paris. But Raymond and Olivier become friends, and Olivier, considering it his duty, informs Raymond of Suzanne's past. His warning only serves to alienate Raymond and strengthen Suzanne's influence over him. Suzanne finally betrays her true character by agreeing to go off with Olivier after the latter pretends to have killed Raymond in a duel.

PLAYS

All were first performed in Paris.

1. _Le bijou de la reine_ (_The Queen's Jewel_). Comedy, 1 act; verse. Written 1845. Published 1880. Produced Théâtre de l'Hôtel Castellane, 1855; Théâtre du Gymnase, Feb. 15, 1874.

2. _Atala._ Lyric drama. Published 1848. Music: Pierre Varney.

3. _La dame aux camélias_* (_Camille; The Lady of the Camellias_). Play, 5 acts. Published 1852. Produced Théâtre du Vaudeville, Feb. 2, 1852. Based on Dumas's novel.

4. _Diane de Lys._ Comedy, 5 acts. Published 1852. Produced Théâtre du Gymnase-Dramatique, Nov. 15, 1853.

5. (With Armand Montjoye and Raimond Deslandes). _Eva._ Play with music. Published 1854. Produced Théâtre du Vaudeville, Nov. 3, 1854. Music: Jean-Baptiste-Édouard Montaubry.

6. _Le demi-monde_* (_The Demi-Monde_). Comedy, 5 acts. Published 1855. Produced Théâtre du Gymnase-Dramatique, Mar. 20, 1855.

7. _La question d'argent_* (_The Money Question_). Play. Published 1857. Produced Théâtre du Gymnase-Dramatique, Jan. 31, 1857.

8. (With Charles Pagesis, L. de Chambrait, and Crétet). _Comment la trouves-tu?_ (_What Do You Think of Her?_). Comedy-vaudeville, 1 act. Published 1857. Produced Théâtre du Vaudeville, Apr. 27, 1857.

9. _Le fils naturel_* (_The Natural Son_). Comedy, 5 acts. Published 1858. Produced Théâtre du Gymnase-Dramatique, Jan. 16, 1858.

10. (With Auguste Vivier). _Un mariage dans un chapeau_ (_Marriage in a Hat_). Buffoonery, 1 act. Published 1859. Produced Théâtre du Gymnase-Dramatique, Feb. 5, 1859.

11. _Un père prodigue_ (_A Prodigal Father_). Comedy, 5 acts. Published 1859. Produced Théâtre du Gymnase-Dramatique, Nov. 30, 1859.

12. *L'ami des femmes** (The Woman's Friend). Comedy, 5 acts. Published 1864. Produced Théâtre du Gymnase-Dramatique, Mar. 5, 1864.

13. (With Émile de Girardin). *Le supplice d'une femme* (*A Woman's Punishment*). Drama, 3 acts. Published 1865. Produced Comédie-Française. Apr. 20, 1865.

14. (With Anne-Adrien-Armand Durantin). *Héloïse Paranquet*. Play, 4 acts. Published 1866. Produced Théâtre du Gymnase-Dramatique, Jan. 20, 1866.

15. *Les idées de Madame Aubray* (*Madame Aubray's Ideas*). Comedy, 4 acts. Published 1867. Produced Théâtre du Gymnase-Dramatique, Mar. 16, 1867.

16. (With Alphonse François and Narcisse Fournier). *Le filleul de Pompignac* (*Pompignac's Godson*). Comedy, 4 acts. Published 1869. Produced Théâtre du Gymnase-Dramatique, May 7, 1869.

17. *Une visite de noces* (*A Honeymoon Call*). Comedy, 1 act. Published 1872. Produced Théâtre du Gymnase-Dramatique, Oct. 10, 1871.

18. *La princesse Georges** (*Princess George*). Play, 3 acts. Published 1872. Produced Théâtre du Gymnase-Dramatique, Dec. 2, 1871.

19. *La femme de Claude** (*The Wife of Claude*). Play, 3 acts. Published 1873. Produced Théâtre du Gymnase-Dramatique, Jan. 16, 1873.

20. *Monsieur Alphonse**. Play, 3 acts. Published 1874. Produced Théâtre du Gymnase-Dramatique, Nov. 26, 1873.

21. (With Pyotr Korvin-Krukovski). *Les Danicheff** (*The Danicheffs, or Married by Force*). Comedy, 4 acts. Published 1879. Produced Théâtre de l'Odéon, Jan. 8, 1876.

22. *L'étrangère** (*The Foreigner*). Comedy, 5 acts. Published 1877. Produced Comédie-Française, Feb. 14, 1876.

23. (With Gustave-Eugène Fould). *La comtesse Romani* (*Countess Romani*). Comedy, 3 acts. Published 1878. Produced Théâtre du Gymnase-Dramatique, Nov. 16, 1876.

24. *La princesse de Bagdad* (*The Princess of Baghdad*). Play, 5 acts. Published 1881. Produced Comédie-Française, Jan. 31, 1881.

25. *Denise**. Play, 4 acts. Published 1885. Produced Comédie-Française, Jan. 19, 1885.

26. *Francillon*. Play, 3 acts. Published 1887. Produced Comédie-Française, Jan. 17, 1887.

27. *Le retour de Thèbes* (*The Return from Thebes*). Fragment. Unfinished at Dumas's death.

EDITIONS

Collections.
Théâtre complet, 5 vols., Paris, 1868–1878; *Théâtre complet*, 7 vols., Paris, 1880–1892; *Théâtre complet: Théâtre des autres*, 2 vols., Paris, 1894–1895.

Individual Plays.
Camille. Published in *Nineteenth Century French Plays*, ed. by J. L. Borgerhoff, Century, New York, 1931; *Chief French Plays of the Nineteenth Century*, ed. by E. M. Grant, Harper, New York, 1934.

The Demi-Monde. Published in *The Chief European Dramatists*, ed. by B. Matthews, Houghton Mifflin, Boston, 1916; *World Drama*, ed. by B. H. Clark, vol. 2, Appleton, New York, 1933, 1956.

Madame Aubray's Ideas. Published in *Nineteenth Century French Plays*, ed. by J. L. Borgerhoff, Century, New York, 1931.

CRITICISM

French. C. M. Noel, *Les idées sociales dans le théâtre de Alexandre Dumas, fils*, Paris, 1912; E. Seillière, *La morale de Dumas, fils*, Paris, 1921; M. T. Bonney, *Les idées morales dans le théâtre de Alexandre Dumas, fils*, Quimper, 1921; J. Gros, *Alexandre Dumas et Marie Duplessis*, Paris, 1923; T. Linge *La conception de l'amour dans le drame de Dumas fils et d'Ibsen*, Paris, 1935; N. C. Arvin, *Alexandre Dumas fils*, Paris, 1939.

English. H. S. Schwartz, *Alexandre Dumas, fils, Dramatist*, New York, 1927; F. H. Gribble, *Dumas, Father and Son*, London, 1930; F. A. Taylor, *The Theatre of Alexandre Dumas fils*, Oxford, 1937; A. Maurois, *Three Musketeers: A Study of the Dumas Family*, tr. by G. Hopkins, London, 1957 (also published as *The Titans*, New York, 1957).

Alexandre Dumas pere
(1802 – 1870)

Alexandre Davy de la Pailleterie Dumas, French novelist and dramatist, was born on July 24, 1802, in Villers-Cotterêts, near Soissons. His father, the son of a marquis and a Haitian Negro slave, was a Napoleonic general who died in 1806, leaving his family little but the memory of his bravery. After a sketchy education, Dumas became a notary's clerk in Villers-Cotterêts. He went to Paris in 1823 and, because of his elegant handwriting, secured a position with the Duc d'Orléans (later King Louis Philippe). In time Dumas rounded out his education by omnivorous reading, especially of plays, which had interested him since adolescence.

Romantic by nature and in appearance and bursting with vitality, Dumas led a life as ebullient as that of his swashbuckling heroes. An illegitimate son called Alexandre Dumas *fils,* whose mother, Marie-Catherine Labay, was a dressmaker, was born in 1824. Dumas's first produced play, *The Chase and Love* (*La chasse et l'amour*), was written one year later. His third produced play, *Henry III and His Court* (*Henri III et sa cour*), performed at the Comédie-Française in 1829, was the first romantic prose drama to be staged in Paris and was immediately successful. During the 1830 Revolution, Dumas became a captain in the National Guard and a public idol, but his political activities made it expedient for him to flee France temporarily. In 1840 Dumas married his mistress Ida Ferrier, an actress, from whom he soon separated after having spent her entire dowry. Dumas wrote fifteen plays before 1843, the year he began his prodigious career as a novelist. The productive collaboration of Dumas and Auguste Maquet began in 1844 with *Les trois mousquetaires* (*The Three Musketeers*) and went on through many successful adventure novels. About the same time he built Monte-Cristo, his fantastic château on the outskirts of Paris. Nearby he established the Théâtre Historique, where a historical play, usually one of his own, was presented each evening. In 1851, having spent his funds too lavishly, he fled to Brussels to escape his creditors and began work on his *Mémoires.* Upon his return to Paris he founded a daily paper called *Le Mousquetaire,* but it lasted only until 1857. The following year he went to Russia, and in 1860 he went to Italy, where he joined Garibaldi's forces. He remained in Naples as keeper of the museums for four years. During this period his prodigious output included innumerable historical volumes and novels.

After his return to France his debts continued to mount. *Le d'Artagnan,* another review, fared no better than its predecessor, and in his last years Dumas was at the mercy of creditors and a series of tyrannical actresses. He died of a stroke in Puys, near Dieppe, on December 5, 1870. He had written 301 volumes in all.

WORK

Although Alexandre Dumas and Victor Hugo share the credit for introducing romanticism to the French stage, it was, strictly speaking, Dumas—self-educated, unknown, and untried—who, at the age of twenty-six, struck the first blow at the classical tradition with his *Henry III and His Court* (1829) a year before the appearance of Hugo's controversial *Hernani. See* HUGO, VICTOR.

Despite the fact that Hugo was already a well-known poet, many critics considered the more eclectic Dumas to be the better dramatist. He knew what the public wanted and, plunging enthusiastically into playwriting, relied on instinct to guide him in amalgamating romantic, melodramatic, and realistic elements into about 100 prose and verse dramas. He abandoned the classical unities; yet his plays have cohesion and logical construction. His characters speak a natural dialogue, and since he was less skillful at developing character than at formulating action, Dumas was fortunate in having some of the most gifted actors of his day perform in a number of his best plays. Dumas began with historical subjects because they lent themselves to romantic treatment, but he soon turned to his own experience and emotions as materials for drama. *See* UNITIES.

His most famous plays are *Henry III and His Court,* a spectacular prose drama involving assassination and other violence; *Antony* (1831), a contemporary drama of passion, jealousy, and death; and *The Tower of Nesle* (*La tour de Nesle,* 1832), a romantic thriller reconstructing medieval crimes on a grand scale. Other predominantly historical-romantic plays are *Christine, or Stockholm, Fontainebleau, and Rome* (*Christine, ou Stockholm, Fontainebleau et Rome,* 1830), a verse drama about the Swedish Queen; *Charles VII and His Chief Vassals* (*Charles VII chez ses grands vassaux,* 1831), a verse tragedy; *Napo-*

Alexandre Dumas *père.* [Giraudon]

leon Bonaparte, or Thirty Years in the History of France (*Napoléon Bonaparte, ou Trente ans dans l'histoire de France,* 1831); *Catherine Howard* (1834); and *Don Juan of Marana, or The Fall of an Angel* (*Don Juan de Marana, ou La chute d'un ange,* 1836). Plays with contemporary settings include *Richard Darlington* (1831), a domestic tragedy based on Sir Walter Scott's *The Surgeon's Daughter; Edmund Kean, or The Genius and the Libertine* (*Kean, ou Désordre et génie,* 1836), a comedy based on the life of the famous English actor (in 1953 it was adapted by Jean-Paul Sartre); and *The Lady of Belle Isle* (*Mademoiselle de Belle Isle,* 1839), a sparkling play that borders on a comedy of manners.

Henry III and His Court (*Henri III et sa cour,* 1829). Romantic historical drama set in the Renaissance court of Henry III. The Duc de Guise has formed the Holy League, an ostensibly anti-Protestant organization whose real aim is to overthrow the King and place De Guise himself in power. To retain her influence over her weak son, the Queen Mother, Catherine de' Medici, plots to destroy both De Guise and Saint-Mégrin, a loyal favorite of the King who is passionately in love with Catherine, Duchesse de Guise. Catherine is drugged and brought to a rendezvous with Saint-Mégrin; but when her husband unexpectedly appears on the scene, she is spirited away through a secret passage. She unfortunately leaves behind a handkerchief that is discovered by her already suspicious husband. On the very night De Guise hopes to make the King recognize the league and place him in charge with special powers, he brutally forces Catherine to write a note inviting Saint-Mégrin to visit her in secret.

While Catherine waits in anguish, knowing that if Saint-Mégrin comes he will be killed, the King, at the urging of his mother, tricks De Guise into surrendering leadership of the league to him. Because this devious policy is displeasing to Saint-Mégrin, who had hoped the King would take immediate action against the traitor, he provokes De Guise into a duel set for the next day. He then slips into Catherine's apartments, where he learns that the note was a trap meant to lure him to his death. After declaring her love, Catherine attempts to bolt the door against De Guise's men (by passing her arm through the ringbolts) while Saint-Mégrin escapes through the window. When De Guise finally breaks in, he drags his wife to the window to watch his confederates below strangle Saint-Mégrin with Catherine's own handkerchief.

This was the first romantic drama actually to be staged. For his sources Dumas drew on Louis-Pierre Anquetil's *Histoire de France* and Pierre de L'Estoile's *Mémoires-journaux*.

Antony (1831). Romantic tragedy and one of the first plays to deal with contemporary problems. Though the illegitimately born Antony loves Adèle and is loved in return, he suddenly disappears from Paris, leaving the way free for Adèle to marry Colonel d'Hervey. Three years later, unable to bear the torments of love, Antony returns. Aware that she still loves him, the virtuous Adèle attempts to flee to Strasbourg, where her husband is garrisoned. However, her horses bolt, and when Antony is wounded saving her life, she is forced to take him into her home. He reveals that he has always loved her and that his previous flight had been meant to save her from a marriage that would result in her social ostracism. After a series of wildly romantic episodes, the lovers are reconciled; but when Adèle learns that Colonel d'Hervey is about to return to Paris, she is consumed by guilt and fears the eventual effects of her lost reputation on her infant daughter. To save her honor, Antony stabs Adèle. When Colonel d'Hervey finds him near his wife's body, Antony announces: "She resisted me, and so I killed her."

The Tower of Nesle (*La tour de Nesle*, 1832). Written in collaboration with Frédéric Gaillardet, this romantic drama is set in Paris during the reign of Louis X. The action centers on Marguerite de Bourgogne, the Queen, who twenty years earlier gave birth to illegitimate male twins. After inducing her lover Léonet de Bournonville to kill her father, who wanted to put her in a convent, Marguerite gave orders for her infant sons to be drowned. As Queen, she now amuses herself by assignations at the infamous tower with handsome young men whom she later has murdered. When Philippe Daulnay is murdered on the Queen's orders, his brother Gaultier swears vengeance on his unknown murderers. However, he falls passionately in love with Marguerite, who is strangely and purely drawn to him. Since an officer named Buridan knows that Marguerite is responsible for Philippe's death, the Queen attempts to have him murdered; but Buridan reveals himself to be Léonet de Bournonville and manages to have himself named the King's Prime Minister. Only after Buridan has doomed Gaultier by sending him to the tower, whose occupants are to be arrested on the King's orders, does he learn that the young man is his son. He attempts to save him, but Gaultier, mistaken for Buridan, is killed on the Queen's orders. Marguerite learns that Philippe and Gaultier were her sons, and in the name of their dead children she and her former lover are reconciled. They are doomed to death, however, since the King has given orders for their arrest.

PLAYS

Unless otherwise noted, the plays were first performed in Paris.

1. *Ivanhoe.* Melodrama, 3 acts. Written 1822?

2. (With Adolphe de Leuven and P.-J. Rousseau). *La chasse et l'amour* (*The Chase and Love*). Vaudeville, 1 act. Written 1825. Published 1825. Produced Théâtre de l'Ambigu-Comique, Sept. 22, 1825.

3. *La noce et l'enterrement* (*The Wedding and the Burial*). Vaudeville, 3 scenes. Published 1826. Produced Théâtre de la Porte-Saint-Martin, Nov. 21, 1826.

4. (Adaptation). *Fiesque de Lavagna.* Historical drama, 5 acts. Written 1827. Based on Friedrich von Schiller's *Fiesko.*

5. *Henri III et sa cour** (*Henry III and His Court*). Historical drama, 5 acts. Published 1829. Produced Comédie-Française, Feb. 11, 1829.

6. *Christine, ou Stockholm, Fontainebleau et Rome* (*Christine, or Stockholm, Fontainebleau, and Rome*). Dramatic trilogy, 5 acts, verse. Published 1830. Produced Théâtre de l'Odéon, Mar. 30, 1830.

7. *Napoléon Bonaparte, ou Trente ans dans l'histoire de France* (*Napoleon Bonaparte, or Thirty Years in the History of France*). Drama, 6 acts. Published 1831. Produced Théâtre de l'Odéon, Jan. 10, 1831.

8. *Antony*.* Drama, 5 acts. Published 1831. Produced Théâtre de la Porte-Saint-Martin, May 3, 1831.

9. *Charles VII chez ses grands vassaux* (*Charles VII and His Chief Vassals*). Drama, 5 acts; verse. Published 1831. Produced Théâtre de l'Odéon, Oct. 20, 1831.

10. *Richard Darlington.* Drama, 3 acts. Published 1832.

Produced Théâtre de la Porte-Saint-Martin, Dec. 10, 1831.

11. (With Auguste Anicet-Bourgeois). *Teresa.* Drama, 5 acts. Published 1832. Produced Théâtre Royal de l'Opéra-Comique, Feb. 6, 1832.

12. *Le mari de la veuve (The Widow's Husband).* Comedy, 1 act. Published 1832. Produced Comédie-Française, Apr. 4, 1832.

13. (With Frédéric Gaillardet). *La tour de Nesle* (The Tower of Nesle).* Drama, 5 acts. Published 1832. Produced Théâtre de la Porte-Saint-Martin, May 29, 1832.

14. *Le fils de l'émigré (The Son of the Emigrant).* Drama, 4 acts. Published (selections) 1902. Produced Théâtre de la Porte-Saint-Martin, Aug. 28, 1832.

15. *Perinet Leclerc, ou Paris en 1418 (Perinet Leclerc, or Paris in 1418).* Drama, 5 acts. Published 1832. Produced Théâtre de la Porte-Saint-Martin, Sept. 3, 1832.

16. *Angèle.* Drama, 5 acts. Published 1834. Produced Théâtre de la Porte-Saint-Martin, Dec. 28, 1833.

17. *La vénitienne (The Venetian Woman).* Drama, 5 acts. Published 1834. Produced Théâtre de la Porte-Saint-Martin, Mar. 18, 1834.

18. *Catherine Howard*.* Drama, 5 acts. Published 1834. Produced Théâtre de la Porte-Saint-Martin, June 2, 1834.

19. (With others). *La tour de Babel (The Tower of Babel).* Episodic revue, 1 act. Published 1834. Produced Théâtre des Variétés, June 24, 1834.

20. (With E.-C.-H. Cordellier-Delanoue). *Cromwell et Charles I (Cromwell and Charles I).* Drama, 5 acts. Published 1835. Produced Théâtre de la Porte-Saint-Martin, May 21, 1835.

21. *L'écossais (The Scotsman).* Drama, 5 acts and epilogue. Written ca. 1835/36. Based on Sir Walter Scott's novel *Quentin Durward.*

22. (With M.-E.-G. Théaulon de Lambert and E. Rousseau). *Le Marquis de Brunoy (The Marquis of Brunoy).* Play, 5 acts. Published 1936. Produced Théâtre des Variétés, Mar. 14, 1836. Music: Masset.

23. *Don Juan de Marana, ou La chute d'un ange (Don Juan of Marana, or The Fall of an Angel).* Mystery, 5 acts, prose and verse. Published 1836. Produced Théâtre de la Porte-Saint-Martin, Apr. 30, 1836.

24. (With Théaulon de Lambert and Frédéric de Courcy?). *Kean, ou Désordre et génie* (Edmund Kean, or The Genius and the Libertine).* Comedy, 5 acts. Published 1836. Produced Théâtre des Variétés, Aug. 31, 1836.

25. (With Gérard de Nerval). *Piquillo.* Comic opera, 3 acts. Published 1837. Produced Opéra Comique, Oct. 31, 1837. Music: Hippolyte Monpou.

26. *Caligula.* Play, 5 acts and prologue; verse. Published 1838. Produced Comédie-Française, Dec. 26, 1837.

27. (With Hippolyte Romand). *Le bourgeois de Gand, ou Le secrétaire du Duc d'Albe. (The Man from Ghent, or The Duke of Alba's Secretary).* Drama, 5 acts. Published 1838. Produced Théâtre de l'Odéon, May 21, 1838.

28. *Paul Jones.* Drama, 5 acts. Published 1838. Produced Théâtre du Panthéon, Oct. 12, 1838.

29. (With Auguste Maquet). *Bathilde.* Drama, 3 acts. Published 1839. Produced Théâtre de la Renaissance, Jan. 14, 1839.

30. *Mademoiselle de Belle Isle* (The Lady of Belle Isle).* Comedy, 3 acts. Published 1839. Produced Comédie-Française, Apr. 2, 1839.

31. (With Nerval). *L'alchimiste (The Alchemist).* Drama, 5 acts; verse. Published 1839. Produced Théâtre de la Renaissance, Apr. 10, 1839.

32. (With Nerval). *Léo Burckart.* Drama, prologue and 5 acts. Published 1839. Produced Théâtre de la Porte-Saint-Martin, Apr. 16, 1839.

33. (With Charles Lafont). *Jarvis l'honnête homme, ou Le marchand de Londres (Jarvis the Gentleman, or The Merchant of London).* Drama, 2 acts. Published 1840. Produced Théâtre du Gymnase-Dramatique, June 3, 1840.

34. *Un mariage sous Louis XV* (A Marriage of Convenience: Period Louis XV).* Comedy, 5 acts. Published 1841. Produced Comédie-Française, June 1, 1841.

35. (With Eugène Bourgeois). *Jeannil le Breton, ou Le gérant responsable (Jeannil the Breton, or The Responsible Manager).* Drama, 5 acts. Published 1842. Produced Théâtre de la Porte-Saint-Martin, Nov. 27, 1841.

36. *Lorenzino.* Drama, 5 acts. Published 1842. Produced Comédie-Française, Feb. 24, 1842.

37. (With Lafont). *Le séducteur et le mari (The Seducer and the Husband).* Drama, 3 acts. Published 1842. Produced Théâtre des Délassements Comiques, Nov. 5, 1842.

38. (With Adolphe Dennery?). *Halifax.* Comedy, prologue and 3 acts. Published 1842. Produced Théâtre des Variétés, Dec. 2, 1842.

39. (With Leuven and Léon Lhérie). *Le mariage au tambour (Marriage to Drumbeats).* Comedy, 3 acts. Published 1843. Produced Théâtre des Variétés, Mar. 9, 1843.

40. *Les demoiselles de Saint-Cyr* (The Ladies of Saint-Cyr).* Comedy, 5 acts. Published 1843. Produced Comédie-Française, July 25, 1843.

41. (With Louis Lefèvre). *L'école des princes (The School of Princes).* Comedy, 5 acts; verse. Published 1843. Produced Théâtre de l'Odéon, Sept. 29, 1843.

42. (With Leuven and Lhérie). *Louise Bernard.* Drama, 5 acts. Published 1843. Produced Théâtre de la Porte-Saint-Martin, Nov. 18, 1843.

43. (With Leuven and Lhérie). *Le laird de Dumbicky (The Laird of Dumbicky).* Comedy, 5 acts. Published 1844. Produced Théâtre de l'Odéon, Dec. 30, 1843.

44. (With Leuven and Lhérie). *Le garde-forestier (The Forester).* Comedy, 2 acts; prose and verse. Published 1845. Produced Théâtre des Variétés, Mar. 15, 1845.

45. (With Leuven and Lhérie). *Un conte de fées (A Fairy Tale).* Comedy, 3 acts. Published 1845. Produced Théâtre des Variétés, Apr. 29, 1845.

46. (With Leuven and Louis-Émile Vanderburch). *Sylvandire.* Romance, 4 acts. Published 1845. Produced Théâtre du Palais-Royal, June 7, 1845.

47. (With Maquet). *Les mousquetaires (The Musketeers).* Drama, prologue and 5 acts. Published 1845. Produced Théâtre de l'Ambigu-Comique, Oct. 27, 1845. Based on Dumas's novel *Vingt ans après.*

48. *Une fille du régent (The Regent's Daughter).* Comedy, 5 acts. Published 1846. Produced Théâtre de l'Odéon, May 23, 1846.

49. (With Octave Feuillet and Paul Bocage). *Échec et mat (Check and Checkmate).* Comedy, 5 acts. Published 1846. Produced Théâtre de l'Odéon, May 23, 1846.

50. (With Maquet). *La Reine Margot (Queen Margot).* Drama, 5 acts. Published 1847. Produced Théâtre Historique, Feb. 20, 1847. Based on Dumas's novel.

51. (Adaptation). *Intrigue et amour (Love and Intrigue).* Drama, 5 acts. Published 1864. Produced Théâtre Historique, June 11, 1847. Based on Schiller's play.

52. (With Maquet). *Le chevalier de Maison-Rouge (The Knight of Maison-Rouge).* Drama, 5 acts. Published 1847. Produced Théâtre Historique, Aug. 3, 1847.

53. (Adaptation; with Paul Maurice). *Hamlet, prince de Danemark (Hamlet, Prince of Denmark).* Drama, 5 acts; verse. Published 1848. Produced Théâtre Historique, Dec. 15, 1847. Based on William Shakespeare's play.

54. (With Maquet). *Monte-Cristo, I.* Drama, 5 acts. Published 1848. Produced Théâtre Historique, Feb. 3, 1848.

55. (With Maquet). *Monte-Cristo, II.* Drama, 5 acts. Published 1848. Produced Théâtre Historique, Feb. 4, 1848.

56. (With Maquet). *Catalina.* Drama, 5 acts. Published 1848. Produced Théâtre Historique, Oct. 14, 1848.

57. (With Maquet). *La jeunesse des mousquetaires (The Youth of the Musketeers).* Drama, prologue, 5 acts, and epilogue. Published 1849. Produced Théâtre Historique, Feb. 17, 1849. Based on Dumas's novel *Les trois mousquetaires.*

58. (With Maquet). *Le chevalier d'Harmental* (*The Chevalier of Harmental*). Drama, prologue and 5 acts. Published 1849. Produced Théâtre Historique, July 26, 1849.

59. (With Maquet). *La guerre des femmes* (*The War of Women*). Drama, 5 acts. Published 1849. Produced Théâtre Historique, Oct. 1, 1849.

60. (With Eugène Grangé and Xavier de Montépin). *Le Connétable de Bourbon, ou L'Italie au seizième siècle* (*Constable Bourbon, or Italy in the Sixteenth Century*). Drama, 5 acts. Published 1849. Produced Théâtre de la Porte-Saint-Martin, Oct. 20, 1849.

61. (With Jules Lacroix). *Le testament de César* (*The Testament of Caesar*). Drama, 5 acts and epilogue; verse. Published 1849. Produced Comédie-Française, Nov. 10, 1849.

62. *Le comte Hermann* (*Count Hermann*). Drama, 5 acts and epilogue. Published 1849. Produced Théâtre Historique, Nov. 22, 1849.

63. (With Eugène Nus). *Le cachemire vert* (*The Green Cashmere*). Comedy, 1 act. Published 1850. Produced Théâtre du Gymnase, Dec. 15, 1849.

64. *Trois entr'actes pour "L'amour médecin"* (*Three Intermissions for "Love, the Doctor"*). Published 1864. Produced Comédie-Française, Jan. 15, 1850.

65. (With Maquet). *Urbain Grandier.* Drama, prologue and 5 acts. Published 1850. Produced Théâtre Historique, Mar. 30, 1850.

66. (Adaptation). *Le vingt-quatre février, ou L'auberge de Schwasbach* (*The Twenty-fourth of February, or The Tavern of Schwasbach*). Drama, 1 act. Published 1850. Produced Théâtre de la Gaîté, Mar. 30, 1850. Based on Zacharias Werner's play.

67. (With Maquet). *La chasse au chastre.* Fantasy, 3 acts. Published 1850. Produced Théâtre Historique, Aug. 3, 1850.

68. (With Grangé and Montépin). *Pauline.* Drama, 5 acts. Published 1850. Produced Théâtre Historique, June 1, 1850.

69. (With Grangé and Montépin). *Les chevaliers du Lansquenet* (*The Chevaliers of Lansquenet*). Drama, 5 acts. Published 1850. Produced 1850.

70. (With Grangé and Montépin). *Les frères corses* (*The Corsican Brothers*). Play. Published 1850. Produced Théâtre Historique, August, 1850. Based on Dumas's novel.

71. (With Maquet). *Le comte de Morcerf* (*The Count of Morcerf*). Drama, 5 acts. Published 1851. Produced Théâtre de l'Ambigu-Comique, Apr. 1, 1851.

72. *Romulus.* Comedy, 1 act. Published 1854. Produced Comedie-Française, Jan. 13, 1854.

73. *L'Orestie* (*The Oresteia*). Tragedy, 3 acts; verse. Published 1856. Produced Théâtre de la Porte-Saint-Martin, Jan. 5, 1856.

74. *L'envers d'une conspiration, ou Le fils de Donald le noir* (*Behind a Conspiracy, or The Son of Black Donald*). Comedy, 5 acts. Published 1860. Produced Théâtre du Vaudeville, Jan. 4, 1860.

75. (With Bernard Lopez). *La veillée allemande* (*The German Vigil*). Drama, 1 act. Published 1864. Produced Théâtre Belleville, Nov. 21, 1863.

76. *Madame de Chamblay.* Drama, 5 acts. Published 1869. Produced Salle Ventadour, June 4, 1868.

77. *Les blancs et les bleus* (*The Whites and the Blues*). Drama, 3 acts. Published 1874. Produced Théâtre du Châtelet, Mar. 10, 1869.

78. (With Maquet). *Villefort.* Play.

79. *La barrière de Clichy* (*The Clichy Gate*). Play.

80. (With Maquet). *Le vampire* (*The Vampire*). Play.

81. (With Maurice). *Benvenuto Cellini.* Play.

82. *La jeunesse de Louis XIV.* (*The Youth of Louis XIV*). Play.

83. *La jeunesse de Louis XV* (*The Youth of Louis XV*). Comedy, 5 acts.

84. (With Lhérie and Bocage). *Le marbrier* (*The Marble Polisher*). Play.

85. *La conscience* (*The Conscience*). Play.

86. (With Montépin). *La tour Saint-Jacques.* Play.

87. *Le verrou de la reine* (*The Queen's Bolt*). Play.

88. (With Charles Gabet). *Les compagnons de Jéhu* (*Jehu's Companions*). Play.

89. *L'invitation à la valse* (*The Invitation to the Waltz*). Play.

90. *Les forestiers* (*The Foresters*). Play.

91. *L'honneur est satisfait* (*Honor Is Satisfied*). Play.

92. (With Leuven). *Le roman d'Elvire* (*The Romance of Elvire*). Play.

93. *Le gentilhomme de la montagne* (*The Gentleman of the Mountain*). Play.

94. (With Maquet). *La dame de Monsoreau* (*The Lady From Monsoreau*). Play.

95. (With Maquet). *Le prisonnier de la Bastille: Fin des mousquetaires* (*The Prisoner of the Bastille: End of the Musketeers*). Drama, 5 acts.

96. (With Bocage). *Les Mohicans de Paris* (*The Mohicans of Paris*). Play.

97. (With Maurice). *Roméo et Juliette* (*Romeo and Juliet*). Play.

98. (With Amédée de Jallais). *Gabriel Lambert, où Gabriel le faussaire* (*Gabriel Lambert, or Gabriel the Forger*). Play.

99. *La femme sans amour* (*The Loveless Woman*). Comedy, 3 acts.

EDITIONS

Collections.
Théâtre complet, 15 vols., Paris, 1863–1874; *Théâtre complet,* 25 vols., Paris, 1873–1876.
Individual Plays.
Antony. Published in *Nineteenth Century French Plays,* ed. by J. L. Borgerhoff, Century, New York, 1931; *French Romantic Plays,* ed. by W. W. Comfort, Scribner, New York, 1933.
Henry III and His Court. Published in *Nineteenth Century French Plays,* ed. by J. L. Borgerhoff, Century, New York, 1931; *Chief French Plays of the Nineteenth Century,* ed. by E. M. Grant, Harper, New York, 1934.

CRITICISM

French. G. de Bellemare, *Les dernières années de Alexandre Dumas, 1864–1870,* Paris, 1883; C. Glinel, *Alexandre Dumas et son oeuvre,* Reims, 1884; H. Parigot, *Le drame d'Alexandre Dumas,* Paris, 1899; id., *Alexandre Dumas, père,* Paris, 1902; J. Lucas-Dubreton, *La vie d'Alexandre Dumas père,* Paris, 1928; M. Constantin-Weyer, *L'aventure vécue de Dumas père,* Geneva, 1944; S. Duriline, *Alexandre Dumas père en Russie,* Paris, 1947; R. Gaillard, *Alexandre Dumas,* Paris, 1953; H. Clouard, *Alexandre Dumas,* Paris, 1955.

English. P. Fitzgerald, *The Life and Adventures of Alexander Dumas,* 2 vols., London, 1873; A. F. Davidson, *Alexandre Dumas Père: His Life and Works,* London, 1902; J. Lucas-Dubreton, *The Fourth Musketeer: The Life of Alexandre Dumas,* tr. by M. C. Darnton, New York, 1928; H. S. Gorman, *The Incredible Marquis: Alexandre Dumas,* New York, 1929; H. A. Spurr, *The Life and Writings of Alexandre Dumas (1802–1870),* New York, 1902, London, 1929; F. H. Gribble, *Dumas, Father and Son,* London, 1930; G. R. Pearce, *Dumas père,* London, 1934; J. A. Thompson, *Alexandre Dumas père and Spanish Romantic Drama,* University, La., 1938; R. Todd, *The Laughing Mulatto: The Story of Alexandre Dumas,* London, 1940; R. Capes, *Punchinello: The Romantic Story of Alexandre Dumas,* Reading, England, 1947; A. C. Bell, *Alexandre Dumas: A Biography and Study,* London, 1950; A. Maurois, *Alexandre Dumas: A Great Life in Brief,* tr. by J. P. White, New York, 1955; id., *Three Musketeers,* tr. by G. Hopkins, London, 1957 (also published as *The Titans,* New York, 1957).

German. E. Döling, *Alexandre Dumas peres Subjektivismus in seinen Dramen aus der Zeit der Romantik,* Halle, 1931.

William Dunlap
(1766 — 1839)

William Dunlap, American artist, critic, theatrical producer, and dramatist, was born on February 19, 1766, in Perth Amboy, N.J., the son of a former soldier in the British Army. When his family moved to New York in 1777, he became interested in the theatre, although his principal ambition was to become a painter. In 1784 he went to London, where for three years he studied painting in a haphazard way. Returning to New York in 1787, he began to write plays, composing *The Modest Soldier, or Love in New York* (now lost), which was never performed. His second play, *The Father,* however, was performed in 1789 with great success. That same year Dunlap married Elizabeth Woolsey. For the next nine years he devoted himself to writing plays.

In 1796 he became manager of and a partner in the American Company. To provide the theatre with new material, Dunlap abandoned original composition for the expedient of translating from German and French writers. Despite his efforts, the theatre failed in 1805, and Dunlap went bankrupt. After this he wrote only a few plays and held a succession of transient jobs such as miniaturist, assistant theatre manager, portrait painter, magazine editor, military paymaster, and art teacher. In his last years he devoted himself to the National Academy of Design, which he had helped found; to painting; and to writing histories of New York State, American design, and the American theatre. After suffering a stroke, he died in New York on September 28, 1839.

WORK

Although Dunlap's dramatic and managerial skills were limited, he remains an important and versatile figure in the theatrical history of the United States. At a time when playwriting was dominated by amateurs, he was a professional who produced fifty-six plays, of which twenty-five are extant. Although none is a masterpiece, several of his plays are well written and have flashes of genuine artistry. As a manager, Dunlap was intelligent and considerate, and he staged his own plays. He also published two critical works of historical importance, *History of the American Theatre* (1832) and *History of the Rise and Progress of the Arts of Design in the United States* (1834). The first of these is thorough and judicious and contains criticism of the excesses of commercial theatre along with a plea for governmental support of the theatre.

Of Dunlap's original plays, the best are two verse tragedies in the new romantic style, *André* (1798) and *Leicester* (1794); and a comedy of manners, *The Father, or American Shandyism* (1789), revised as *The Father of an Only Child* (pub. 1806). *The Italian Father* (1799), is a reworking of Dekker's *The Honest Whore* (ca. 1604). Dunlap introduced Gothic drama to the United States with *Fontainville Abbey* (1795) and *Ribbemont, or The Feudal Baron* (1796). His numerous translations include many of the plays by the popular German dramatist August von Kotzebue. *See* DEKKER, THOMAS; KOTZEBUE, AUGUST VON.

Leicester (1794).   Verse tragedy set in England, in which Leicester, an English nobleman, is deceived by his bride Matilda with Henry Cecil, whom she has represented as her brother. When Leicester, who has been away from home, returns unexpectedly, Matilda urges Cecil to kill him. At first, Cecil's nobler instincts reject the idea, but his passion for Matilda prevails and he agrees. Believing he is killing Leicester as he lies asleep in bed, Cecil mistakenly slays his own brother, for the latter, having befriended Leicester, had been sleeping in Leicester's room. Undaunted, Matilda then devises a plan to poison her husband, but forewarned, Leicester thwarts the plan, whereupon Matilda commits suicide. Cecil then challenges Leicester to a duel and impales himself on Leicester's sword.

André (1798).   Tragedy based on the capture and execution of Major John André (1750–1780), a British officer and spy during the American Revolution. Having plotted with Benedict Arnold the betrayal of the garrison at West Point, N.Y., André is captured by the Americans. He manages, nevertheless, to win their admiration for his courage and refinement and causes General George Washington, who must determine André's fate, to decide between his sympathies and his duty. Despite the pleas of young Bland, the son of a prisoner of the British, and Honora, a young woman in love with André, Washington reluctantly does his duty and orders the execution of the spy.

PLAYS

All were first performed in New York.

1. *The Father, or American Shandyism.* Comedy, 5 acts. Published 1789. Produced John Street Theatre, Sept. 7, 1789. Early version of *The Father of an Only Child.*

2. *Darby's Return.* Comic sketch, 1 act. Published 1789. Produced John Street Theatre, Nov. 24, 1789.

3. *Leicester.* Tragedy, 5 acts; verse. Published 1806. Produced, John Street Theatre, Apr. 24, 1794, as *The Fatal Deception, or The Progress of Guilt.*

4. *Fontainville Abbey.* Tragedy, 5 acts; verse. Pub-

lished 1806. Produced John Street Theatre, Feb. 16, 1795.

5. *The Archers, or The Mountaineers of Switzerland.* Opera, 3 acts. Published 1796. Produced John Street Theatre, 1796. Music: Benjamin Carr.

6. *Ribbemont, or The Feudal Baron.* Tragedy, 5 acts. Produced 1796, as *The Mysterious Monk.*

7. *Tell Truth and Shame Devil.* Comedy, 2 acts. Published 1797. Produced John Street Theatre, Jan. 9, 1797. Adapted from A.-L.-B. Robineau's *Jérôme Pointu.*

8. *André.* Tragedy, 5 acts; verse. Published 1798. Produced Park Theatre, Mar. 30, 1798.

9. *Lovers' Vows.* Play, 5 acts. Published 1814. Produced Park Theatre, Mar. 11, 1799. Adapted from August von Kotzebue's *Das Kind der Liebe.*

10. *The Italian Father.* Comedy, 5 acts. Published 1810. Produced Park Theatre, Apr. 15, 1799. Based on Thomas Dekker's *The Honest Whore.*

11. *The False Shame, or The American Orphan in Germany.* Comedy, 4 acts. Published 1940. Produced Park Theatre, Dec. 11, 1799. Adapted from Kotzebue's *Falsche Scham.*

12. *The Wild Goose Chase.* Play, 4 acts. Published 1800. Produced Park Theatre, Jan. 24, 1800. Adapted from Kotzebue's *Der Wildfang.*

13. *The Virgin of the Sun.* Play, 5 acts. Published 1800. Produced Park Theatre, Mar. 12, 1800. Adapted from Kotzebue's *Die Sonnenjungfrau.*

14. *Pizarro in Peru, or The Death of Rolla.* Play, 5 acts. Published 1800. Produced Park Theatre, Mar. 26, 1800. Adapted from Kotzebue's *Die Spanier in Peru.*

15. *Fraternal Discord.* Drama, 5 acts. Published 1809. Produced Park Theatre, Oct. 22, 1800. Adapted from Kotzebue's *Die Versöhnung der Bruderzwist.*

16. *Abaellino, the Great Bandit.* Dramatic romance, 5 acts. Published 1802. Produced Park Theatre, Feb. 11, 1801. Adapted from Heinrich Zschokke's *Aböllino, der Grosse Bandit.*

17. *Peter the Great, or The Russian Mother.* Play, 5 acts. Published 1814. Produced Park Theatre, 1802. Adapted from Joseph Marius von Babo's *Die Strelizen.*

18. *The Voice of Nature.* Drama, 3 acts. Published 1803. Produced Park Theatre, Feb. 4, 1803. Adapted from L.-C. Caigniez's *Le jugement de Salomon.*

19. *The Good Neighbor.* Interlude, 1 act. Published 1814. Produced Feb. 28, 1803. Adapted from the German of August Wilhelm Iffland.

20. *The Glory of Columbia: Her Yeomanry!* Play, 5 acts. Published 1817. Produced Park Theatre, July 4, 1803. Adapted from *André.*

21. *The Wife of Two Husbands.* Drama, 5 acts. Published 1804. Produced Park Theatre, Apr. 4, 1804. Adapted from Guilbert de Pixérécourt's *La femme à deux maris.*

22. *The Father of an Only Child.* Play. Published 1806. Revision of *The Father, or American Shandyism.*

23. *Yankee Chronology, or Huzza for the Constitution!* Musical interlude, 1 act. Published 1812. Produced Park Theatre, Sept. 7, 1812.

24. *Thirty Years, or The Gambler's Fate.* Play, 3 days. Published 1940. Produced Bowery Theatre, Feb. 22, 1828. Adapted from *Trente ans, ou La vie d'un joueur,* by Prosper Goubaux and Victor Ducange.

25. *A Trip to Niagara, or Travellers in America.* Farce, 3 acts. Published 1830. Produced Bowery Theatre, Nov. 28, 1828.

Play Attributed to Dunlap.

Rinaldo Rinaldi, or The Great Banditti (pub. 1810).

EDITIONS

Dramatic Works, 2 vols., New York, 1806–1815; *False Shame and Thirty Years,* ed. by O. S. Coad, *America's Lost Plays,* vol. II, Princeton, N.J., 1940–1941.

André. Published in *Representative American Plays from 1767 to the Present Day,* ed. by A. H. Quinn, 7th ed., rev. and enl., New York, 1953.

CRITICISM

O. S. Coad, *William Dunlap: A Study of His Life and Works and of His Place in Contemporary Culture,* New York, 1917; R. H. Canary, *William Dunlap,* New York, 1970.

DUNNING, Philip (1891–1957). American actor and dramatist who with George Abbott wrote the successful gangster melodrama *Broadway* (1926). His other plays include *Night Hostess* (1928), a murder melodrama set in a nightclub; *The Understudy* (with Jack Donahue, 1927); *Lilly Turner* (with George Abbott, 1932); *Kill That Story* (with Harry Madden, 1934); *Page Miss Glory* (with Joseph Schrank, 1934); and *Remember the Day* (with Philo Higley, 1935). *See* ABBOTT, GEORGE.

Dorothy Hall and John Litel in Philip Dunning's *Lilly Turner.* New York, Morosco Theatre, 1932. [Theatre Collection, The New York Public Library at Lincoln Center, Astor, Lenox and Tilden Foundations]

DUNSANY, 18th Baron (b. London, July 24, 1878; d. Dublin, October 25, 1957). Lord Dunsany, Anglo-Irish critic, novelist, short-story writer, and dramatist, was born Edward John Moreton Drax Plunkett. He was unique among writers of the Irish renaissance in that his plays did not exploit Irish themes. A romantic, Dunsany preferred fantasy and ironic symbolism. In his first play, *The Glittering Gate* (1909), his characters force open the gates of heaven expecting to find riches but instead finding nothing. Many of his later plays have exotic settings and are peopled by mysterious beings subject to occult forces.

They include *King Argimenes and the Unknown Warrior* (1911), *The Gods of the Mountain* (1911), *The Golden Doom* (1912), *The Tents of the Arabs* (1917), *The Compromise of the King of the Golden Isles* (1920), and *The Amusements of Khan Kharuda* (1925). With Dunsany, even prosaic titles are apt to conceal the uncanny: *The Bureau de Change* (1937) is a place for bartering not goods but evils, one of the characters in *A Night at an Inn* (1916) is a stone idol, and in *If* (1921) time is reversed and telescoped.

Lord Dunsany's critical and autobiographical work includes *Patches of Sunlight* (1938) and the *Donellan Lectures* (1943), which he delivered at Trinity College, Dublin.

A Night at an Inn (1916). One-act melodrama in which four sailors, led by "the Toff," arrive at an English inn with a ruby that they have wrenched from the eye of Klesh, a pagan idol. The Toff and his confederates are celebrating their coup when the apparition of Klesh appears, seizes the ruby, replaces it in his forehead, and goes out. Then his voice is heard ordering each sailor to emerge from the inn to meet his doom. Produced New York, Neighborhood Playhouse, April 23, 1916.

If (1921). Fantasy in which a man is allowed to change his past life. John Beal receives a talisman that permits him to travel back in time and catch the train he missed ten years earlier. He meets a girl who tells him a story that causes him to go to the East, where he becomes a potentate. Eventually the smashing of the talisman breaks the spell, and he finds that only twenty-four hours have elapsed since his decision to reverse time. Produced London, Ambassadors Theatre, May 30, 1921.

DURAS, Marguerite (1914–). French journalist, author of novels, film scripts, and dramas. Born in Indochina, she moved to France in 1932 and studied law, political

Marguerite Duras.
[American
Heritage]

Marguerite Duras's *A Place Without Doors*, with (l. to r.) Alvin Epstein, Mildred Dunnock, and Richard A. Dysart. New Haven, Long Wharf Theatre, 1970. [Long Wharf Theatre, New Haven, Conn.]

science, and mathematics in Paris, taking a degree in law. Her activities as a member of the Resistance caused her to be deported to Germany during World War II. After the war she became a journalist for the *Observateur*. Her writings have been influenced by modern American literature, especially by the works of Hemingway and Steinbeck. Her novel *Dam Against the Pacific* (*Un barrage contre le Pacifique*, 1950), which is set in Indochina and deals with the fight against the overwhelming forces of nature, brought her considerable attention. However, it was the film script for *Hiroshima, mon amour*, directed by Alain Resnais in 1959, that made her world-famous.

Her plays include *The Viaducts of Seine-et-Oise* (*Les viaducs de la Seine-et-Oise*, 1960), in which an old couple murder their deaf-mute niece; an adaptation of the play *The Miracle Worker* (1959) by William Gibson, *Miracle in Alabama* (*Miracle en Alabama*, 1961), which she wrote with Gérard Jarlot; *The Beast in the Jungle* (*La bête dans la jungle*, 1962), a play about missed opportunities in love and life, written with James Lord and based on the short story of Henry James; *The Square* (*Le square;* abridged version, 1957; full version, 1965), in which a young servant girl, whose life consists of waiting for something meaningful to happen, and an elderly peddler, who lives completely in the present, strike up a conversation but fail to understand one another; *Days in the Trees* (*Des journées entières dans les arbres*, 1965), a play about futility and loneliness, exemplified by the relationship of an oppressive mother and her gigolo son; and *A Place Without Doors* (*L'amante anglaise*, 1968).

Friedrich Dürrenmatt
(1921 –   )

Friedrich Dürrenmatt, Swiss short-story writer, novelist, and dramatist, was born on January 5, 1921, in Konolfingen, the son of a Lutheran minister. Young Dürrenmatt grew up in an intellectually stimulating family circle that included relatives who had distinguished themselves in literature, journalism, and government. He gave early evidence of

Friedrich Dürrenmatt. [Photographer: Gertrude Fehr]

artistic talent, winning a prize for drawing at the age of twelve. In 1935 his family moved to Bern, where Dürrenmatt studied literature, theology, philosophy, and science at the university and began to go to the theatre regularly. Following one semester at the University of Zurich, during which he took courses in art and philosophy, he decided to make writing his profession.

In 1943 he completed his first play, *Comedy* (*Komödie*), which was neither published nor produced, but in the next few years he succeeded in publishing a number of plays, short stories, and articles while he continued to produce sketches, drawings, and paintings. After his marriage to Lotti Geissler, an actress from Ins, the couple moved to Ligerz, where Dürrenmatt supplemented his small income with drama criticism for the weekly magazine *Die Weltwoche*, sketches for nightclubs and radio plays, and mystery novels for serial publication. Friends helped him with loans and gifts until recognition came, in 1952, with the production of *The Marriage of Mr. Mississippi* (*Die Ehe des Herrn Mississippi*). At this time Dürrenmatt moved with his family to Neuchâtel, where he still lives. His continued interest in the visual arts is apparent in the grotesque symbolic illustrations with which a number of his plays are provided. In 1959 Dürrenmatt traveled to New York to receive the Drama Critics Circle award for *The Visit* (*Der Besuch der alten Dame*, 1956) and to Mannheim, Germany, for the Schiller Award.

In addition to *Frank the Fifth, Opera of a Private Bank* (*Frank der Fünfte, Oper einer Privatbank*, wr. 1959), which is reminiscent of Brecht's *The Threepenny Opera*, Dürrenmatt wrote three plays having Swiss settings but addressing themselves to universal problems. *The Visit* deals with the corrupting power of money, *The Physicists* (*Die Physiker*, wr. 1961) with the misdirection of scientific knowledge, and *The Meteor* (*Der Meteor*, 1966) with the conflicts inherent in artistic creativity. *See* BRECHT, BERTOLT.

WORK

With respect to both quantity and quality of work, Dürrenmatt is the most significant Swiss dramatist. He has explained his distinctively grotesque kind of comedy as "a way of expressing in a tangible manner, of making us perceive physically the paradoxical, the form of the unformed, the face of a world without a face." In his *Problems of the Theater* (*Theaterprobleme*, 1955), one of the most important postwar dramaturgical works, he expounds the theoretical foundations of his work. Acknowledging his indebtedness to Aristophanes, Nestroy, and Thornton Wilder, he states that only comedy can portray a world "about to fold like ours." For tragedy presupposes a community with a binding set of ethical rules, individual guilt, and responsibility—concepts that he contends are no longer applicable to our highly complex technological societies where "Creon's secretaries close Antigone's case."

While very much influenced by Brechtian techniques, Dürrenmatt denies that the world can be changed. This accounts for his pessimism. Yet he does not preach resignation; on the contrary: "The world, for me, stands as something monstrous, an enigma of calamity that has to be accepted but to which there must be no surrender." This conviction leads to the portrayal of man as a "courageous being" in spite of his awareness that individual heroism will have no social significance. Thus, accepting responsibility for his past, Alfred Ill assumes a heroic posture in *The Visit* (1956). His death, however, fails to right the course of the world: the play closes as the townspeople chant a song in praise of their god, money. In a similar manner, Romulus becomes great in *Romulus the Great* (*Romulus der grosse,* 1949) when he accepts his retirement, condemned to watch history take a course contrary to his wishes. In *The Physicists* (1962), realizing that knowledge is dangerous in a world ruled by power-hungry politicians, Möbius retreats to an insane asylum. Once again, however, personal sacrifice is ineffective, for an individual cannot affect the progress of science.

Dürrenmatt's first two produced plays, *It Is Written* (*Es steht geschrieben,* 1947) and *The Blind Man* (*Der Blinde,* 1948), both concern man's search for God, the former set during the Anabaptist movement in Münster, the latter during the Thirty Years' War. Spectacular stagecraft, rhetorical flights, sharp shifts in mood, and rapid scenic pace mark *It Is Written,* whereas *The Blind Man* is set simply on an almost bare stage. Both these early works show Dürrenmatt groping for his own dramatic idiom. His other plays of interest include *The Marriage of Mr. Mississippi* (1952), showing how men turn into automatons when pursuing an abstract ideal; *An Angel Comes to Babylon* (*Ein Engel kommt nach Babylon,* 1953), which deals with the impossibility of selfless love on earth and the ultimate triumph of the type of human being represented by Akki, the independent man; *Frank the Fifth* (1959), a satirical comedy with music; and *The Meteor* (1966), focusing on the conflicts inherent in artistic creativity.

Dürrenmatt has also written several radio plays. *Operation Wega* (*Das Unternehmen der Wega,* 1955) shows how men under conditions of extreme hardship on Venus have bridged

Ein Engel kommt nach Babylon. [German Information Center]

the gap between ideals and practice, for "if we don't help each other here, we perish." His prose work consists mainly of detective stories in which he constantly betrays the reader's expectations, thus forcing him to think anew. His preoccupation with detective stories mirrors his belief that art today can only be effective when created "where it is least suspected."

Romulus the Great (*Romulus der Grosse,* 1949). Comedy based on the historical Teutonic drive on Rome in A.D. 476. Romulus, last Emperor of the Western Roman Empire, busies himself with his chicken farm, ignoring his wife, ministers, and Zeno, ruler of the Eastern Roman Empire, who urges him to take action against the invading enemy. When Caesar Rupf, an affluent merchant, offers to help repel the invasion in exchange for Romulus's daughter, Romulus declines the proposition, confessing that he assumed his imperial post for the express purpose of hastening the dissolution of the corrupt Empire. After the Emperor's wife and daughter drown while attempting to escape the Teutons, Odoacer, the victor, arrives. He reveals himself to be, like Romulus, a chicken fancier bent on seeing his own nation liquidated, for he fears that Theodoric, his war-loving nephew and successor, would transform the Teutons into a savage horde of conquerors. As a makeshift to resolve their dilemma, Odoacer decides that he must govern the land while Romulus, who yearns for death to expiate his betrayal of Rome, lives out his years in pensioned retirement in a villa. Both leaders thus resign themselves to a compromise they realize is only temporary: as soon as Theodoric musters enough strength, he will surely rise to power, kill both of them, and pursue the fateful course of history.

The Marriage of Mr. Mississippi (*Die Ehe des Herrn Mississippi,* 1952). Comedy about justice in which Florestan Mississippi, a public prosecutor and a fanatical exponent of Mosaic law, has murdered his wife. He visits Anastasia, who confesses to having murdered her husband. After Mississippi has persuaded Anastasia to marry him as a gesture of grotesque retribution, the two dedicate themselves to presiding over a governmental system of "absolute justice" with Mississippi sentencing victims to death and Anastasia presiding over their execution. Five years of their bloody rule prove unpopular, and the Minister of Justice, Diego, is sent to ask for Mississippi's resignation. Saint-Claude, an old friend, also appears to urge Mississippi to exchange his views for those of Marxism. In each case the prosecutor refuses to reconsider his position.

Übelohe, Anastasia's former lover, who was

Der Besuch der alten Dame. [German Information Center]

forced to pursue evil ways for inadvertently helping her to murder her husband, returns to try to convince Anastasia that she must face the truth of their earlier affair and the related murder of her husband. She is unable to do so, however, and Übelohe departs after engaging in a discourse on truth and love with Mississippi. Anastasia attempts to poison her new lover Saint-Claude, who has fallen into disrepute with the Communists and who wants Anastasia to become a prostitute in order to support him. Mississippi drinks the poisoned coffee intended for Saint-Claude, and Anastasia dies after having drunk coffee poisoned by her husband. At the end, three Communists come to liquidate Saint-Claude.

An Angel Comes to Babylon (*Ein Engel kommt nach Babylon,* 1953). Symbolic comedy in which an angel sends Kurrubi, a virtuous young girl, to earth so that she may bestow selfless love upon Akki, a Babylonian begger and the world's lowliest man. On this same day, however, Nebuchadnezzar, the King of Babylon, embarrassed at having his welfare state blemished by the beggar's presence, has disguised himself in rags and challenges Akki to a begging contest with the understanding that if Akki loses, he must abandon his profession. In winning the contest, Akki makes Nebuchadnezzar the new titleholder among the lowly of the earth. When Kurrubi arrives, she mistakes the disguised King for the object of her mission and falls in love with him. Through certain technicalities of the begging contest, Nebuchadnezzar wins Kurrubi while Akki wins Nimrod, a dethroned King. Before he realizes that he loves her, Nebuchadnezzar trades Kurrubi for Nimrod. Enchanted by the girl, the Babylonians insist that she marry their King; but Kurrubi explains that as she was sent from heaven to love a beggar, she will be the King's wife only if he will resume his beggar's identity. Nebuchadnezzar is too proud to accept this; Kurrubi refuses to deny her divine origin in order to become his Queen. Bitter and enraged at having to renounce the girl for the sake of political power, Nebuchadnezzar vows to lead his nation into captivity and to build a tower (the tower of Babel) so high that his curses will reach his enemy in heaven. Akki flees with Kurrubi to the desert.

The Visit (*Der Besuch der Alten Dame,* 1956). Tragicomedy. When the millionairess Claire Zachanassian returns to Güllen, her impoverished hometown, the townspeople hope that her visit will result in financial benefits for all. However, it becomes clear that Claire has come for revenge rather than charity. Claire left Güllen as a girl after unjustly losing a paternity suit against her

The Visit, with Lynn Fontanne and Alfred Lunt (seated). New York, Lunt-Fontanne Theatre, 1958. [Walter Hampden Memorial Library at The Players, New York]

lover Alfred Ill, who rejected her in favor of a richer girl. She went to Hamburg, became the prostitute the court had declared her to be, and eventually amassed a fortune through a number of propitious marriages. She has now returned, with her seventh husband, to demand "justice"—Alfred Ill's life—in return for which she promises the town a million dollars. Although everyone expresses shock at her proposal, Ill grows nervous as he notices that the townspeople, including his own wife and son, are buying more and more luxuries on credit in anticipation of the million-dollar gift. The townspeople appeal to Claire for money without the murder clause only to discover that, having long owned all the town's factories, she has deliberately shut them down to ensure the acceptance of her barter. The citizens hold a town meeting at which they convince themselves that justice demands compliance with Claire's proposition. Ill is resigned to his fate and is strangled by the town athlete during festivities in honor of the town's new economic status. The doctor pronounces Ill dead of a heart attack; the newspapers publicize his death as the result of overwhelming joy for the future of Güllen.

Claire keeps her side of the bargain, and at her departure is cheered as Güllen's benefactress.

The Physicists (*Die Physiker,* 1962).   Comedy set in an asylum run by Fräulein von Zahnd where three voluntary patients, Möbius ("King Solomon"), Beutler ("Newton"), and Ernesti ("Einstein"), each of them physicists, are feigning insanity. Möbius has entered the asylum so that his formula unifying all scientific knowledge may be kept from a world that is morally unprepared for it; Beutler and Ernesti, actually agents of rival powers, have trailed Möbius there, each hoping to persuade him to join his side. Believing their positions in the asylum to be threatened, all three physicists murder their nurses, whereupon the remaining attendants are replaced by bodyguards.

Now the three inmates reveal their real motives to one another. At length, Möbius convinces his two pursuers that in order to protect mankind they must all remain secluded forever. This altruistic agreement produces a common sense of exaltation among them. Their serenity is destroyed, however, when Fräulein von Zahnd discloses that she,

Scene from *The Physicists*, with (l. to r.) Isa Thomas and Barbara Redmond. [Asolo State Theatre Company, Sarasota, Fla.]

under the influence of the historical King Solomon, has copied Möbius's documents and placed them at the disposal of a power seeking world domination. Realizing that they are held captive by someone madder than they themselves pretend to be, the physicists resign themselves to playing out their assumed roles of Solomon, Newton, and Einstein.

PLAYS

1. *Komödie* (*Comedy*). Play. Written 1943.
2. *Der Doppelgänger* (*The Double*). Radio play. Written 1946. Published 1960.
3. *Es steht geschrieben* (*It Is Written*). Tragedy. Written 1947. Published 1947. Produced Zurich, Schauspielhaus, Apr. 19, 1947. Early version of *Die Wiedertäufer*.
4. *Der Blinde* (*The Blind Man*). Parable play, or martyr drama. Written 1948. Published 1958, as *A Drama*. Produced Basel, Stadttheater, Jan. 10, 1948.
5. *Romulus der Grosse** (*Romulus the Great*). Comedy, 4 acts. Written, first version, 1949; second version, 1957. Published 1957. Produced Basel, Stadttheater, Apr. 25, 1949.
6. *Die Ehe des Herrn Mississippi** (*The Marriage of Mr. Mississippi*). Comedy, 2 parts. First version: Written 1951. Published 1952. Produced Munich, Kammerspiele, Mar. 26, 1952. Second version: Written 1957. Published 1957.
7. *Der Prozess um des Esels Schatten* (*The Trial about the Donkey's Shadow*). Radio play. Written 1951. Published 1958. Based on Christoph Martin Wieland's *Die Abderiten*.
8. *Nächtliches Gespräch* (*Nocturnal Conversation*). Radio play; later, stage drama, 1 act. Written 1951. Published 1962. Produced Munich, 1952, as *Nächtlicher Besuch* (*Nocturnal Visit*).

9. *Stranitzky und der Nationalheld* (*Stranitzky and the National Hero*). Radio play. Written 1952. Published 1953. Produced 1952.
10. *Ein Engel kommt nach Babylon** (*An Angel Comes to Babylon*). Symbolic comedy, 3 acts. First version: Written 1953. Published 1954. Produced Munich, Kammerspiele, Dec. 22, 1953; Zurich, 1953/54. Second version: Written 1957. Published 1957.
11. *Herkules und der Stall des Augias* (*Hercules and the Augean Stables*). Radio play, 1 act. Written 1954. Published 1959. Produced 1959. Rewritten as stage comedy, 1 act, 1963. Produced Zurich, Mar. 20, 1963.
12. *Das Unternehmen der Wega* (*Operation Wega*). Radio play. Written 1954. Published 1958. Produced 1955.
13. *Die Panne* (*The Breakdown*). Radio play. Written 1955. Published 1956.
14. *Abendstunde im Spätherbst* (*An Evening Hour in Late Autumn*). Radio play. Written 1956. Published 1959. Produced Berlin, Renaissancetheater, 1959.
15. *Der Besuch der alten Dame** (*The Visit*). Parable, or tragicomedy, 3 acts. Written 1956. Published 1957. Produced Zurich, Schauspielhaus, Jan. 29, 1956. Original title: *Komödie der Hochkonjunktur* (*Comedy of Business Prosperity*).
16. *Der Richter und sein Henker* (*The Judge and His Executioner*). Radio play. Written 1957.
17. *Herr Korbes empfängt* (*Mr. Korbes Receives*). Thriller comedy. Written 1957. Slightly altered version of *Abendstunde im Spätherbst*.
18. *Frank der Fünfte, Oper einer Privatbank* (*Frank the Fifth, Opera of a Private Bank*). Musical. Written 1959. Produced Zurich, Schauspielhaus, Mar. 19, 1959. Music: Paul Burkhard.
19. *Die Physiker** (*The Physicists*). Comedy, 2 acts. Written 1961. Published 1962. Produced Zurich, Feb. 21, 1962.
20. *Der Meteor* (*The Meteor*). Comedy, 2 acts. Written 1966. Produced Zurich, Jan. 20, 1966.
21. *Die Wiedertäufer* (*The Anabaptists*). Comedy, 2 parts. Published 1967. Produced Zurich, Schauspielhaus, Mar. 16, 1967. New version of *Es steht geschrieben*.
22. (Adaptation). *Play Strindberg*. Play. Written 1968. Produced Basel, Feb. 8, 1969. Based on August Strindberg's *The Dance of Death*.
23. (Adaptation). *König Johann* (*King John*). Play. Written 1968. Produced Basel, September, 1968. Based on William Shakespeare's *King John*.
24. *Portrait eines Planeten* (*Portrait of a Planet*). Play. Produced Düsseldorf, Schauspielhaus, Nov. 10, 1970.

EDITIONS

Komödien I, Zurich, 1957; *Gesammelte Hörspiele,* 1961; *Komödien II und frühe Stücke,* Zurich, 1964.

CRITICISM

H. Bänziger, *Frisch und Dürrenmatt,* Bern, 1962; *Der unbequeme Dürrenmatt,* ed. by W. Jäggi, Basel and Stuttgart, 1962; H. Mayer, *Dürrenmatt und Frisch,* Pfullingen, 1963; E. Brock-Sulzer, *Friedrich Dürrenmatt: Stationen seines Werkes,* Zurich, 1964; G. E. Wellwarth, *The Theater of Protest and Paradox,* New York, 1964; U. Jenny, *Friedrich Dürrenmatt,* Velber, 1965; M. B. Peppard, *Friedrich Dürrenmatt,* New York, 1969.

DU RYER, Pierre (b. Paris, 1606; d. there, November 6, 1658). French dramatist who, with Pierre Corneille and Jean Mairet, shares the credit for establishing the traditions of French classical tragedy. His most popular play, *Scaevola* (*Scévole,* 1644), is a well-constructed, forceful work but unfortunately one that is imitative of Corneille, though lacking in the logic and poetic power that pervade the works of that great dramatist. Nevertheless, Du Ryer's two Biblical tragedies, *Saul* (1640) and *Esther* (1642), are thought to have influenced the later work of Corneille and afterward that of Racine. Du Ryer's other tragedies, in particular, *Lucretia* (*Lucrèce*, 1638) and *Alcionée* (1637), contributed greatly to the structural cohesion and simplicity that mark French classical tragedy. Because he depended for his livelihood on his work as a translator and dramatist and because tragicomedies were the most popular and lucrative dramas of the period, Du Ryer cast most of his plays in this form. *Argenis* and *Argenis and Polyarchus* (*Argenis et Polyarque*), both produced in 1629, were originally one ten-act play about politics and patriotism. In *Arétaphile* (1628), Du Ryer dramatized questions of state; and in *Clarigène* (1638) we have a complicated story concerning a shipwreck and a case of mistaken identity. In addition, Du Ryer wrote *The Harvests of Suresne* (*Les vendanges de Suresne*, 1634), a comedy focusing on a conflict between provincial members of the bourgeoisie and the nobility. *See* CORNEILLE, PIERRE; TRAGICOMEDY.

Saul (*Saül*, 1640).   An attempt to use the tragic mode to revive medieval plays on Biblical themes. Convinced that God has abandoned him, Saul confides his fears to his children. His son Jonathan and his daughter Michal initially reject this notion, but they become distressed when word is received that Jerusalem has rebelled and that David has joined the Philistines. Conjured up by the Witch of Endor, the ghost of the prophet Samuel explains to Saul that God has condemned him and his sons to defeat and death because he murdered the innocent priests who aided David. Once Saul has accepted his fate, he recovers some of his former greatness of soul. He attempts to keep Jonathan away from the battle and encourages Michal to rejoin David. When the Philistines attack, Jonathan and Saul's other sons are killed. Himself wounded, Saul commits suicide to avoid capture.

Scaevola (*Scévole*, 1644).   This patriotic tragedy was Du Ryer's most successful play. Tarquin, former King of Rome who has been deposed and exiled for his crimes, has won to his cause Porsena, King of Etruria, whose army is now besieging Rome. Junia, daughter of Brutus, the man responsible for Tarquin's downfall, is captured and brought to the Etruscan camp. Here she spies Scaevola, her lover, who plans to save Rome by murdering Porsena. She persuades Scaevola to let her first appeal to Porsena, but the latter, instead of offering to lift the siege, proposes marriage. Junia rejects him, and Scaevola, still intent on Porsena's death, mistakenly murders a man he believes to be the Etruscan King. Arrested and threatened with torture, Scaevola defies the enemy by thrusting his right hand into the fire. Impressed by Scaevola's courage and alienated by Tarquin's churlishness, Porsena agrees to lift the siege. Scaevola is freed, and Junia becomes his bride.

DUTOURD, Jean (1920–   ). French journalist, essayist, novelist, and dramatist, who wrote *The Tree* (*L'arbre*, 1948).

Scene from Jean Dutourd's *L'arbre*. [Courtesy of Centre Dramatique National Nord]

DUVERNOIS, Henri, pseudonym of H. Simon Schwabacher (1875–1937). French novelist and dramatist whose plays focus on the life of the Parisian petty bourgeoisie and the atmosphere of Montmartre. He started his career as a journalist at the age of eighteen and soon turned to the sketchy one-act play form that seemed particularly suited to his dramatic temperament. His work is characterized by a roguish, mocking tone, a gay ambience, and a quick tempo; it reveals Duvernois as a keen observer and analyst of the human psyche. He collaborated with Maurice Donnay, Pierre Wolff, and Robert Dieudonné. Among his plays are some that were presented at the Grand-Guignol: *Alone* (*Seul*, 1922), *The Knight Canepin* (*Le chevalier Canepin*, one act, 1926), *The Professor* (*Le professeur*, 1928), and *The Operation* (*L'opération*, 1931). Other plays are *The Guitar and the Jazz Band* (*La guitare et le jazz-band*, with Dieudonné, 1924); *Before the Gate* (*Devant la porte*, 1928); *The Flight* (*La fugue*, 1929); *The Heart* (*Coeur*, 1930); *The Cadets* (*Les cadets*, 1932); *The Hedgehog* (*Le hérisson*, 1932); *Jeanne* (1932); and *The Absence* (*L'absence*, 1933). *See* DONNAY, MAURICE; GRAND GUIGNOL.